THE OFFICIAL RED

A GUIDE BOOK OF
UNITED STATES COINS

PROFESSIONAL EDITION

R.S. YEOMAN

SENIOR EDITOR
KENNETH BRESSETT

RESEARCH EDITOR
Q. DAVID BOWERS

VALUATIONS EDITOR
JEFF GARRETT

Sixth Edition

Fully Illustrated Catalog and
Retail Valuation List—Federal U.S. Coinage

A Guide Book of United States Coins™
THE OFFICIAL RED BOOK OF UNITED STATES COINS™
PROFESSIONAL EDITION

THE OFFICIAL RED BOOK and
THE OFFICIAL RED BOOK OF UNITED STATES COINS
are trademarks of Whitman Publishing, LLC.

www.whitman.com

ISBN: 0794842194
Printed in the United States of America.

© 2014 Whitman Publishing, LLC
3101 Clairmont Road • Suite G • Atlanta, GA 30329

WCG™   WHITMAN®   OCG™

Collect all the books in the Bowers Series. *A Guide Book of Morgan Silver Dollars • A Guide Book of Double Eagle Gold Coins • A Guide Book of United States Type Coins • A Guide Book of Modern United States Proof Coin Sets • A Guide Book of Shield and Liberty Head Nickels • A Guide Book of Flying Eagle and Indian Head Cents • A Guide Book of Washington and State Quarters • A Guide Book of Buffalo and Jefferson Nickels • A Guide Book of Lincoln Cents • A Guide Book of United States Commemorative Coins • A Guide Book of United States Tokens and Medals • A Guide Book of Gold Dollars • A Guide Book of Peace Dollars • A Guide Book of the Official Red Book of United States Coins • A Guide Book of Franklin and Kennedy Half Dollars • A Guide Book of Civil War Tokens • A Guide Book of Hard Times Tokens*

For a complete listing of numismatic reference books, supplies, and storage products, visit Whitman Publishing online at www.whitman.com

CONTENTS

Contents

CONTRIBUTORS TO THE SIXTH EDITION

Senior Editor: Kenneth Bressett. Research Editor: Q. David Bowers. Valuations Editor: Jeff Garrett.
Special Consultants: Philip Bressett and Ben Todd.

Special credit is due to the following for service and data in this book. Mark Albarian, The Harry W. Bass Jr. Foundation, Jack Beymer, Larry Briggs, Roger W. Burdette, Elizabeth Coggan, Stephen M. Cohen, *Coin World*, John W. Dannreuther, Tom DeLorey, Bill Fivaz, Kevin Flynn, Ira M. Goldberg, Kenneth M. Goldman, Heather Grant, Ash Harrison, Jesse Iskowitz, Matt Kleinsteuber, Denis W. Loring, Chris McCawley, Jim McGuigan, Charles Moore, Numismatic Guaranty Corporation of America (NGC), Dick Osburn, Professional Coin Grading Service (PCGS), Mark Salzberg, Gerald Scherer Jr., Rick Snow, J.T. Stanton, Anthony Swiatek, and Troy Thoreson.

Special photo credits are due to the following. Al Adams, Ira & Larry Goldberg Coins & Collectibles, Tom Mulvaney, Ken Potter, the Smithsonian Institution, Stack's Bowers Galleries, and the U.S. Mint.

Contributors to the regular edition of the Guide Book of United States Coins *include the following.*

Gary Adkins	Rusty Goe	Casey Noxon
John Albanese	Ira M. Goldberg	Paul Nugget
Mark Albarian	Lawrence Goldberg	Mike Orlando
Dominic Albert	Kenneth M. Goldman	John M. Pack
Buddy Alleva	James C. Gray	Joseph Parrella
Richard S. Appel	J.R. Grellman	Robert M. Paul
Richard M. August	Tom Hallenbeck	William P. Paul
Mitchell A. Battino	James Halperin	Ken Potter
Lee J. Bellisario	Ash Harrison	Joel Rettew Jr.
Stewart Blay	Steven Hayden	Joel Rettew Sr.
Mark Borckardt	Brian Hendelson	Robert Rhue
Q. David Bowers	Gene L. Henry	Greg Rohan
Kenneth Bressett	John W. Highfill	Len Roosmalen
Philip Bressett	Brian Hodge	Maurice Rosen
Larry Briggs	Charles Hoskins	P. Scott Rubin
Roger W. Burdette	Steve Ivy	Paul Rynearson
John Burns	James J. Jelinski	Mark Salzberg
H. Robert Campbell	Larry Johnson	Mary Sauvain
J.H. Cline	Robert W. Julian	Gerald R. Scherer Jr.
Elizabeth Coggan	Donald H. Kagin	Cherie Schoeps
Alan Cohen	Bradley S. Karoleff	Richard J. Schwary
Gary Cohen	Richard Kelly	Neil Shafer
James H. Cohen	Jim Koenings	Robert W. Shippee
Stephen M. Cohen	George F. Kolbe	Roger Siboni
Frank J. Colletti	John Kraljevich	James A. Simek
Columbus–America	David W. Lange	Craig Smith
Discovery Group	G.J. Lawson	Rick Snow
Steve Contursi	Richard A. Lecce	David M. Sundman
Adam Crum	Julian M. Leidman	Anthony J. Swiatek
Raymond Czahor	Stuart Levine	Anthony Terranova
Charles Davis	Kevin Lipton	Troy Thoreson
Tom DeLorey	Denis W. Loring	Ben Todd
Sheridan Downey	Andy Lustig	Jerry Treglia
Steven Ellsworth	Dwight N. Manley	Frank Van Valen
David Fanning	J.P. Martin	Mark R. Vitunic
John Feigenbaum	Syd Martin	Holland Wallace
George B. Fitzgerald	David McCarthy	Fred Weinberg
Bill Fivaz	Chris McCawley	Weimar White
Kevin Flynn	Robert T. McIntire	John Whitney
George Fuld	Harry Miller	Raymond Williams
Mike Fuljenz	Lee S. Minshull	Douglas Winter
Chuck Furjanic	Scott P. Mitchell	David Wnuck
Jeff Garrett	Michael C. Moline	John Wright
John Gervasoni	Paul Montgomery	Mark S. Yaffe
Dennis M. Gillio	Charles Morgan	
Ronald J. Gillio	Eric P. Newman	

INTRODUCTION

Numismatics, in its purest sense, is the study of items used as money. Today in the United States, as around the world, the term embraces the activities of a diverse community of hobbyists, historians, researchers, curators, and others who collect and study coins, tokens, paper money, and similar objects.

Since 1946 the *Guide Book of United States Coins* has served this community as the preeminent annual reference for coin specifications, mintages, values, photographs, and other information important to collectors and students. With more than 23 million copies in print since the first edition, the *Guide Book* (popularly known as "the Red Book") is well established as the most popular reference in numismatics—not to mention one of the best-selling nonfiction books in the history of American publishing. (In 1964 the 18th edition of the Red Book ranked no. 5 on the national sales lists, at 1.2 million copies—higher than Dale Carnegie's *How to Win Friends and Influence People* at no. 6, and John F. Kennedy's *Profiles in Courage* at no. 9.)

Building on this strong foundation, in 2009 Whitman Publishing launched the Professional Edition of the *Guide Book of United States Coins,* an expanded and enlarged volume intended to serve especially the intermediate to advanced coin collector, the professional coin dealer or auctioneer, the researcher, and the investor. Its combination of more photographs, detailed higher-grade valuations, listings of additional varieties and rare early Proof coins, certified-coin population data, auction records, and other resources provides a wealth of information on every coin type ever made by the U.S. Mint. The Professional Edition is not an exhaustive study of die varieties, though it does expand (with close-up photographs, valuations, and chart notes) on the regular edition's coverage of such coins. Rather, it is a handy single-source guide that educates its users in auction and certification trends, retail valuations, and similar aspects of the marketplace.

The Professional Edition is not a substitute for the regular-edition *Guide Book of United States Coins.* The regular edition includes information not found here, including grading instructions and valuations for lower-grade coins, an introductory overview of the history of U.S. coinage, stories of coins from treasures and hoards, and coverage of colonial and early American coins and tokens; private and territorial gold; Hard Times tokens; Civil War tokens; Confederate coins; Hawaiian, Puerto Rican, and Philippine coins; Alaskan tokens; misstrikes and errors; numismatic books; and other topics.

HOW TO USE THIS BOOK

The *Guide Book of United States Coins, Professional Edition,* covers all federal U.S. coin series, from copper half cents to gold double eagles, plus classic commemoratives (1892–1954), Proof and Mint sets, and bullion. Readers will find the following information:

Denomination introductions. Each coinage denomination is discussed first in an overview of its history, major design types and subtypes, and general collectability by type. (The trade dollar is treated as its own denomination, separate from other dollar coins.) A second essay gives the reader a more in-depth analysis of specializing in that denomination. *These sections encapsulate decades of numismatic research and market observation, and they should be read in conjunction with the charts, photographs, and other information that follow.*

Type-by-type studies. Within each denomination, each major coin type is laid out in chronological order. As in the regular-edition Red Book, the type's designer and its specifications (weight, composition, diameter, edge treatment, and production facilities) are given. Non-commemorative coinage designs are pictured either at actual size or enlarged (in the latter case, along with a notation on the scale of enlargement). Commemorative designs are shown reduced.

Each type section includes summary text on the type's history; aspects of its striking, sharpness, and related characteristics; and its market availability. Grading guidelines and advice are included for the grades covered in the coin type's data charts. For most series, the grades start at the high end of those covered by the regular-edition Red Book, and include more and higher Mint State levels. (Readers interested in detailed guidelines for lower circulated grades may consult *Grading Coins by Photographs: An Action Guide for the Collector and Investor,* which covers grades About Good through Mint State, as well as Proofs.)

The data charts include these elements:

Mintages. Mintage data is compiled from official Mint records whenever possible, and in other cases from more than 70 years of active numismatic research. In instances where the Mint's early records are in question or have been proven faulty, the official numbers are provided and further information is given in chart notes. For some early Proof coins for which no official mintage records exist, an estimated mintage, or the number of coins known in collections, is given. For modern issues (usually those minted within the past five years), the Mint has released production and/or sales numbers that are not yet officially finalized; these are given in italics.

Note that Mint reports are not always reliable for estimating the rarities of coins. In the early years of the Mint, dies of previous years often were used until they became worn or broken. Certain quantities reported, particularly for gold and silver coins, cover the number of pieces struck and make no indication of the quantity that actually reached circulation. Many issues were deposited in the Treasury as backing for paper currency and later were melted.

Gold coins struck before August 1, 1834, are rare today, because from 1821 onward (and at times before 1821) the gold in the coins was worth more than their face values, so they were struck as bullion and traded at a premium. Many were exported and melted for their precious-metal value.

Mintage figures shown for 1964 through 1966 are for coins bearing those dates. Some of them were struck in more than one year and at various mints, both with and without mintmarks. In recent years, mintage figures reported by the Mint have been revised several times and remain uncertain as to precise amounts.

Mintage figures shown in italics are estimates based on the most accurate information available. Numismatic research is constantly ongoing, and listed figures are sometimes revised, when new information becomes available.

Certified Populations. For each circulation-strike coin, a summary is provided of (1) the number of coins certified, (2) the average grade, on a 1–70 scale, of those coins graded, and (3) the percentage of coins certified in Mint State.

For early (generally pre-1916) Proof coins, certified populations are summarized as (1) the number of coins certified, and (2) the level of the finest Proof known.

For later Proofs, certified populations are summarized as (1) the number of coins certified, and (2) the average Proof level.

These summaries provide the collector and investor with working data useful in comparing coins offered for sale or bid.

Certified population data are provided courtesy of Numismatic Guaranty Corporation of America (NGC) and Professional Coin Grading Service (PCGS), two of the nation's leading professional third-party grading firms.

It should be noted that for most coins, especially rare dates and varieties, the number certified actually represents the quantity of *submissions,* rather than the number of individual coins submitted. For example, a particular 1916-D dime that is submitted for certification five times would be counted the same as five individual coins. Such resubmissions can sometimes result in numbers close to or higher than a coin's entire mintage.

Note, too, that the grade number assigned to a "slabbed" (graded and encapsulated) coin does not tell anything about the quality of that particular coin's planchet, the strength of its strike, whether it has been cleaned or dipped, or its overall eye appeal. Such factors are important to a coin's value. Two rare coins of the same date and variety, each with the same amount of surface wear and graded MS-63, will find different values in the marketplace if one is eye-pleasing and well struck, and the other is dull and poorly struck.

Valuations. Coin values shown in the Professional Edition are retail prices compiled from data and market observations provided by dealers, auctioneers, and other market observers, under the direction and analysis of Valuations Editor Jeff Garrett and Senior Editor Kenneth Bressett and their consultants. The values reflect typical auction and retail prices seen for *professionally certified* coins. The valuations of professionally certified coins, as listed in this book, often are higher than what collectors normally pay for non-certified ("raw") coins. Values of certified coins may vary widely, depending on the grading service.

The coin market is so active in some categories that values can easily change after publication. Values are shown as a guide and are not intended to serve as a price list for any dealer's stock.

A dash appearing in a valuations column indicates that coins in that grade exist even though there are no current retail or auction records for them. The dash does not necessarily mean that such coins are exceedingly rare. Italicized numbers indicate unsettled or speculative (estimated) values. A number of listings of rare coins lack valuations or dashes in certain grades, indicating that they are not available, or not believed to exist, in those grades.

For wholesale pricing, the *Handbook of United States Coins* (popularly called the Blue Book, and published since 1942), by R.S. Yeoman, contains average prices dealers nationwide will pay for U.S. coins. It is obtainable through most coin dealers, hobby shops, bookstores, and the Internet.

There is some overlap in the grades valued in the regular edition of the *Guide Book of United States Coins* and those valued in the Professional Edition. In some cases their values are different. This is because the regular edition and the Professional Edition are published some months apart, and the market can change in that time.

Auction Records. A recent auction record is provided for nearly every coin, some exceptions being coins that are too common to sell individually at auction. Each record indicates:

the price paid for the coin (including any fees)

the grade of the coin

the date (month and year) of the auction

This combination of data gives valuable market information for each coin. It also serves as a springboard for further research. Many auction firms have online archives of coins sold, or else their auction catalogs can be studied using the information provided.

ABBREVIATIONS USED IN THIS BOOK

%MS—Percentage of coins certified in Mint State

Avg—Average grade (on a 1–70 scale)

BN—Brown; descriptive of the coloration or toning on certain copper coins

Cam—Cameo

Cert—Certified population

DblDie—Doubled die

DCam—Deep Cameo

DMPL—Deep Mirror Prooflike

D/S—D Over S; a slash between words or letters represents an overdate or overmintmark

Dt—Date

Ex.—extremely

FB—Full Bands

FBL—Full Bell Lines

FH—Full Head

FS—Full Steps

Horiz—Horizontal

Inv—Inverted

Knbd—Knobbed-Top

Lg—Large

Ltrd—Lettered

Ltrs—Letters

Med—Medium

Mintmk—Mintmark

Obv—Obverse

QuintDie—Quintupled Die

RB—Red and brown; descriptive of the mixture of mint red and brown coloration or toning on a copper coin

RD—Red; descriptive of the mint red color on an untoned copper coin

Rev—Reverse

RPD—Repunched Date

RPM—Repunched Mintmark

Sm—Small

SMS—Special Mint Set

Sq—Square

TransRev—Transitional Reverse

TripDie—Tripled Die

UCam—Ultra Cameo

Var—Variety

INVESTING IN RARE COINS

As with the regular edition of the *Guide Book of United States Coins,* those who edit, contribute to, and publish the Professional Edition advocate the collecting of coins for pleasure and educational benefits. A secondary consideration is that of investment, the profits of which are usually realized over the long term based on careful purchases.

Use Common Sense

The rare-coin market combines some aspects of commodity trading with peculiarities seen more often among markets such as those for fine art, real estate, cut gemstones, and similar investments and collectibles. Armed with knowledge, an investor can have a very rewarding experience in rare coins. An uneducated investor can just as easily see substantial losses.

The regular edition of the *Guide Book of United States Coins* includes this bit of guidance, which bears repeating here: "The best advice given to anyone considering investing in rare coins is to use common sense." Any collector with common sense would think twice about buying a silver dollar at a flea market for less than its silver value. A common-sense collector who is offered a $5,000 coin from an "unsearched estate," or from a non-specialist who claims to know nothing of its provenance, would refuse it at $1,000—at least until a diligent examination was possible, and only with an iron-clad return policy and guarantee of authenticity. Profitable investment requires careful selection of qualified dealers (e.g., those professionally credentialed by groups such as the Professional Numismatists Guild and the International Association of Professional Numismatists), and educated evaluation of the coins offered for sale.

Learn About Grading

In the past, coin grading was very subjective, and grade descriptions were far from universal. One dealer's "Choice Extremely Fine" might have been another's "About Uncirculated," and adjectives such as *gem* and *brilliant* varied in meaning from collector to collector. Today grading is still a subjective art striving to be an exact science, but progress has been made. The hobby's guidelines have been clearly standardized in systems such as the Official American Numismatic Association Grading Standards for United States Coins, and explored further in illustrated books such as *Grading Coins by Photographs.* Today there are professional certification services such as NGC, PCGS, ICG, and ANACS that grade and authenticate coins, encapsulating them in sealed "slabs" with their grades noted. These are third-party firms, so called because they are neither buyer nor seller of the coins graded (which guarantees a professional level of impartiality).

Learn About What You're Buying

In addition to carefully vetting professional dealers, examining potential purchases for authenticity, and studying the art and science of grading, an investor can profit by *learning* about coins. Each coin type has a cultural history that provides useful collecting/investing knowledge. For example, Morgan dollars often were stored by the Treasury in the thousands (and millions), so a bag of 1,000 Mint State dollars is not unheard of. On the other hand, the purchaser of a seemingly original bag of Mint State Indian Head cents would likely be left holding a few pounds of counterfeit copper coins. Similarly, each coin type has a typical strike, surface quality, and related characteristics; knowledge of these features can help reveal fakes and lower-than-average-quality specimens. The investor who knows that a certain coin type is rarely encountered in a certain high grade is more alert to potential opportunities. Conversely, if a type is common in high grades, the savvy investor will pass on an average or below-average coin and wait for the sharpest, most attractive one he can find, knowing that time and the marketplace are on his side.

For these reasons, even if you consider yourself more *investor* than *collector,* it is recommended that you read every section of the Professional Edition that covers the coin series you're interested in. The data charts provide one level of information, the denomination introductions another, the type summaries and grading guides yet others; combined, they offer a well-rounded education that prices alone cannot provide.

Understand the General Market

Coin values rise when (1) the economic trend is inflationary and speculators turn to tangible assets as a hedge, or when the number of collectors increases, while coin supplies remain stationary or decrease through attrition or melting; (2) dealers replace their stocks of coins only from collectors or other dealers, who expect a profit over what they originally paid; (3) speculators attempt to influence the market through selective buying; or (4) bullion (gold and silver) prices rise.

Coin values decline when (1) changes in collecting habits or economic conditions alter demand for certain coins; (2) speculators sell in large quantities; (3) hoards or large holdings are suddenly released and cannot be quickly absorbed by the normal market; or (4) bullion (gold and silver) prices decline.

Learn From the Experts

A rich numismatic world is available to the investor and collector who seek to learn. News weeklies such as *Coin World* and *Numismatic News* cover the hobby and its markets from many angles, as do a variety of blogs and monthly magazines. Auction sale results, new U.S. Mint products, convention activities, market reports, and other information await the interested reader.

Web sites such as WhitmanCoinCollecting.com, NumisMaster.com, and CoinFacts.com gather and present information from authoritative sources.

Organizations such as the American Numismatic Association (ANA) and the American Numismatic Society (ANS), as well as dozens of specialized groups focused on particular coins or series, offer resources and connections to collectors worldwide.

Every major American city and many smaller cities have coin shops where experienced dealers can be consulted for advice and opinions.

Coin shows are another venue for learning from seasoned collectors and investors. The ANA mounts three popular shows annually, in different cities. Whitman Coin and Collectibles Expo (www.WhitmanExpo.com) hosts several shows yearly in Baltimore. Florida United Numismatists (FUN) organizes two shows in the winter and summer each year. All of these shows, and dozens of other local and regional conventions, offer opportunities to talk to other collectors and investors, meet market experts, listen to presentations, and examine hundreds of coins, tokens, and medals.

Books are another means of learning from the hobby's experts. Every collector and investor should have at least a basic numismatic library of standard references. In addition, nearly every specialty in American coins has one or more books devoted to greater in-depth exploration. Numismatic publishing has experienced a renaissance in recent years, making valuable knowledge more affordable and readily available than ever before. One book essential to the investor's understanding of the rare-coin market is a 672-page volume written by the "dean of American numismatics," Q. David Bowers. The *Expert's Guide to Collecting and Investing in Rare Coins* covers topics such as determining coin prices and values; focusing on rarity; quality and value for the smart buyer; coin market fads, trends, and cycles; making of the modern market for rare coins; predicting the rare coin market; techniques of smart buying and bidding; protecting your investment; and more.

In the long run, coin collectors—even those who seek mainly to profit financially from the hobby—are simply custodians of the relics they collect. Again, the regular edition of the *Guide Book of United States Coins* gives sound advice: "Those who treat rare coins with the consideration and respect they deserve will profit in many ways, not the least of which can be in the form of a sound financial return on one's investments of time and money."

AN OVERVIEW OF HALF CENTS

Building a type set of the six different major designs in the half cent series can be a challenging and rewarding pursuit. The first design, with Liberty Head facing left with pole and cap, minted only in 1793, is scarce in all grades and will be the most difficult to locate. However, hundreds exist of this American classic, and many are fairly attractive.

The second type, with a *large* Liberty Head facing right with pole and cap, made only in 1794, is scarce with good eye appeal. Most are dark and rough. The next type, the *small* Liberty Head facing right, with pole and cap, is scarce, but enough are on the market that a collector can find a specimen without difficulty.

The Draped Bust half cents, struck from 1800 to 1808, are easily available as a type, including in higher grades. The Classic Head (1809–1836) and Braided Hair (1840–1857) are plentiful as types.

For the earlier half cent types there is ample opportunity for connoisseurship, for quality often varies widely, and every coin is apt to have a different appearance and "personality," even within the same grade.

FOR THE COLLECTOR AND INVESTOR: HALF CENTS AS A SPECIALTY

Collecting half cents by dates and major varieties has been a popular niche specialty for a long time. Among the key issues in the series are the 1793; 1796 With Pole to Cap; 1796 Without Pole to Cap (the most famous of all the rarities); 1802, 2 Over 0 With Reverse of 1800 (a single leaf at each side of the wreath apex, rare but somewhat obscure); 1831; and the Proof-only issues of 1836, 1840 through 1848, Small Date, and 1852.

As there are so many Proof varieties, and each of these is rare as well as expensive, many collectors opt to acquire only the circulation strikes. However, the Proofs are not nearly as expensive as one might think, probably because with so many different dates and varieties needed to complete a collection the prospect is daunting to many buyers. Proofs of most dates are available in both original and restrike forms. Although this rule is not without exceptions, the original strikings of the 1840–1848 and 1849 Small Date half cents are usually described as having the Large Berries reverse, while restrikes are of the Small Berries reverse (within the Small Berries issues there are two dies—one with diagonal die striae below RICA and the other with doubling at the ribbon wreath). Assembling Proofs by reverse varieties is a somewhat arcane pursuit.

For an exhaustive study of die varieties of circulation strikes and Proofs, *Walter Breen's Encyclopedia of United States Half Cents, 1793–1857,* is definitive. Roger S. Cohen Jr.'s study, *American Half Cents, The "Little Half Sisters,"* gives detailed information on circulation strikes, but omits Proofs.

Die varieties are especially abundant among half cents of the first several types, 1793 to 1808. The year 1804 offers a panorama of dies, some of which have been studied as to *die states,* referring to the progression of use of a die as it develops wear, cracks, etc. Varieties of 1795 exist with and without the pole to the liberty cap, the without-pole being the result of a die being relapped (reground to dress the surface), during which process the pole was removed. On the other hand, the 1796 Without Pole half cent was the result of a die-engraving error—the diecutter forgot to add it. Some half cents of 1795 and 1797 were struck on planchets cut from copper tokens issued by the New York City firm of Talbot, Allum & Lee. Upon close inspection, some of the design details of the tokens can still be seen.

One curious and readily available variety of the 1828 half cent has 12 stars instead of the standard 13. However, in choice Mint State the 12-stars issue becomes a rarity, for, unlike the 13-stars issue, none were ever found in hoards.

The Early American Coppers Club is a special-interest group emphasizing copper half cents and large cents. Its journal, *Penny-Wise,* provides much research, social, and collecting news and information.

RECOMMENDED READING

Bowers, Q. David. *A Guide Book of Half Cents and Large Cents,* Atlanta, GA, 2015.
Breen, Walter. *Walter Breen's Encyclopedia of United States Half Cents 1793–1857,* South Gate, CA, 1983.
Cohen, Roger S., Jr. *American Half Cents—The "Little Half Sisters"* (2nd ed.), 1982.
Eckberg, William, Fagaly, Robert, Fuoss, Dennis, and Williams, Raymond. *Grading Guide for Early American Copper Coins,* Heath, OH, 2014.
Fivaz, Bill, and Stanton, J.T. *The Cherrypickers' Guide to Rare Die Varieties* (5th ed., vol. I), Atlanta, GA, 2009.
Manley, Ronald P. *The Half Cent Die State Book, 1793–1857,* United States, 1998.

LIBERTY CAP, HEAD FACING LEFT
(1793)

Designer probably Henry Voigt; weight 6.74 grams; composition, copper; approx. diameter 22 mm; edge: TWO HUNDRED FOR A DOLLAR.

Cohen-4, Breen-4.

History. Among U.S. coinage, the Liberty Cap, Head Facing Left, design belongs to the small class of one-year-only types. Its design was inspired by Augustin Dupré's Libertas Americana medal. The Liberty Cap dies often are credited to Joseph Wright, who also cut the dies for the related cent, but were more likely done by Henry Voigt.

Striking and Sharpness. Good-quality copper was used in these half cents, so they often are found light brown and on fairly smooth planchets. Unlike in later types, the borders on both sides are raised beads; certain of these beads can be weak, though this is not the norm. Some varieties are lightly defined at HALF CENT on the reverse, due to a combination of striking and shallow depth of letters in the die. This feature cannot be used in assigning a grade, as in lower grades (up to and including VG-8) these words may be completely missing.

Availability. Most half cents of 1793 are AG-3 to F-12. EF and AU examples are rare, and MS very rare (most being MS-60 to 63). Market grading is often liberal. Early American Coppers Club (EAC) "raw" grades often are lower than those of the certification services.

AG-3 (About Good). *Obverse:* The portrait is visible only in outline. LIBERTY is weak but usually fully discernible. 1793 is weak, and the bottoms of the digits may be worn away. *Reverse:* (Grading at AG-3 is usually done by the reverse.) Parts of the wreath are visible in outline form, and all but a few letters are gone.

G-4, 6 (Good). *Obverse:* The eye position can be discerned, though the portrait is worn smooth and is seen only in outline form. LIBERTY is complete. 1793 is complete, but may be weak. *Reverse:* (The reverse is key in assigning Good grades; it shows more evidence of wear than does the obverse.) Extensive wear is seen overall. From half to two-thirds of the letters in UNITED STATES OF AMERICA and the fraction numerals are worn away.

VG-8, 10 (Very Good). *Obverse:* Although the eye can be seen, the portrait is well worn. The hair tips at the right show separation. Border beads are worn away, and the border blends into the field in most if not all of the periphery. LIBERTY and 1793 are bold. *Reverse:* The wreath, bow, and lettering are seen in outline form, and some leaves and letters may be indistinct in parts. Border beads are worn away, and the border blends into the field in most if not all of the periphery.

F-12, 15 (Fine). *Obverse:* The hair details are mostly worn away, with about one-third visible, mainly at the edges. Border beads are weak or worn away in areas. *Reverse:* The wreath leaves are worn flat, but their edges are distinct. HALF CENT may be missing on variety B-1, C-1 (also true in lower grades). Border beads are weak or worn away in areas.

VF-20, 30 (Very Fine). *Obverse:* At VF-20, wear on the portrait has reduced the hair detail to indistinct or flat at the center; at VF-30 there is slightly more detail. The thin, more-or-less horizontal ribbon near the top of the hair is distinct. The border beads are blended together, with many blurred or missing. No luster is evident. *Reverse:* At VF-20 the leaf details are nearly completely worn away; at VF-30 there is slight detail in the leaves at VF-30. The border beads are blended together, with many indistinct. Some berries in the sprays may be worn away (though on strong strikes they can be evident in grades down to Good). No luster is evident. HALF CENT, while fully legible, may be weak on certain coins (such as B-1, C-1) in which this feature was shallowly cut into the dies.

EF-40, 45 (Extremely Fine). *Obverse:* Wear is seen on the portrait overall. The separation of the hair strands on the highest part is reduced or eliminated. The cheek is slightly flat on the highest part. Some leaves retain some detail, especially where they join the stems. At EF-40, luster is minimal or non-existent; at 45, luster may survive in traces in protected areas. *Reverse:* Wear is seen on the highest wreath and ribbon areas and the letters. Luster is minimal, but likely more noticeable than on the obverse, as the fields are protected by the designs and lettering.

AU-50, 53, 55, 58 (About Uncirculated). *Obverse:* (Grading at the AU level is done mainly by viewing the obverse.) Friction is seen on the higher parts, particularly on the rounded cheek and on the higher strands of the hair. Friction and scattered marks are in the field, ranging from extensive at AU-50 to minimal at AU-58. Luster may be seen in protected areas, minimal at AU-50, but sometimes extensive at AU-58. Border beads, if well struck, are separate and boldly defined. *Reverse:* Friction is seen on the higher wreath leaves and (not as easy to discern) on the letters. The fields, protected by the designs, show friction, but not as noticeably as on the obverse. At AU-55 and 58 little if any friction is seen. The reverse may have original luster, toned brown, minimal on lower About Uncirculated grades, sometimes extensive at AU-58. Border beads, if well struck, are separate and boldly defined.

MS-60 to 65 (Mint State). *Obverse:* In MS-60 and 61, some slight abrasions can be seen on the higher areas of the portrait. Luster in the field is incomplete, particularly in the center of the open areas. At MS-63, luster is complete, with no abrasions evident. In higher levels, the luster is deeper, and some original mint color may be seen. *Reverse:* In MS-60 and 61, some abrasions are seen on the higher areas of the leaves. Generally, luster is complete in all MS grades, as the open areas are protected by the lettering and wreath. Otherwise, same comments apply as for the obverse.

	Mintage	Cert	Avg	%MS	VG-8	F-12	VF-20	EF-40	AU-50	MS-60BN	MS-63BN	Recent Auction Record
1793	35,334	607	27.3	6	$5,750	$9,500	$14,000	$25,500	$40,000	$67,500	$95,000	$70,500, MS-62BN, April 2013

HALF CENTS, 1793–1857

LIBERTY CAP, HEAD FACING RIGHT
(1794–1797)

1794—Designer Robert Scot; weight 6.74 grams; composition copper; approx. diameter 23.5 mm; edge: TWO HUNDRED FOR A DOLLAR. 1795—Designer John Smith Gardner; weight 6.74 grams; composition copper; approx. diameter 23.5 mm; edge: TWO HUNDRED FOR A DOLLAR. 1795–1797 (thin planchet)—Weight 5.44 grams; composition copper; approx. diameter 23.5 mm; edge: plain (some 1797 are either lettered or gripped).

Cohen-4, Breen-6.

History. The design of the half cent changed in 1794 to a depiction, by Robert Scot, of Miss Liberty facing right. A smaller-headed portrait was used from 1795 on.

Striking and Sharpness. Half cents of 1794 usually are dark, with rough surfaces, and of low aesthetic quality. Most 1795s are on high-quality planchets, smooth and attractive, this being truer of the later plain-edge type than the early thick-planchet issue. Striking can be weak in areas. Often the dentils are incomplete on one or both sides. Many Small Head coins, particularly of 1795 to 1797, have very little detail on the hair, even in higher grades. Half cents of 1796 vary in quality; higher-grade pieces usually are attractive. Half cents of 1797 are usually seen in low grades and on poor planchets; striking varies widely, but is usually weak in areas. Dentils can be weak or can be prominent in various circulated grades, down to the lowest; on certain varieties of 1795 they are prominent even on well-worn coins.

Grades must be assigned carefully, and expertise is recommended—combining knowledge of a given die variety and its relief or sharpness in the die, with observations of actual circulation wear. Grades of certified coins can vary widely in their interpretations.

Availability. As a general type, this issue is scarce, but available. Most are in lower grades, but VF and EF coins appear in the market with regularity.

G-4, 6 (Good). *Obverse:* The portrait is worn smooth and is seen only in outline form, although the eye position can be discerned. LIBERTY and the date are complete, although the date may be weak. Dentils are gone on some, but not all, die varieties. *Reverse:* Extensive wear is seen overall. From half to two-thirds of the letters in UNITED STATES OF AMERICA, and the fraction numerals, are worn away. Certain shallow-relief dies may have letters missing.

VG-8, 10 (Very Good). *Obverse:* The portrait is well worn, although the eye can be seen, and the hair tips at the left show separation. Border dentils are worn away on some issues (not as much for 1795). The border blends into the field in most if not all of the periphery. LIBERTY and the date are bold. *Reverse:* The wreath, bow, and lettering are seen in outline form. Some leaves and letters may be indistinct in parts. Border dentils are worn away, and the border blends into the field in most if not all of the periphery. In certain die varieties and die states, especially of 1797, some letters may be very weak or missing.

F-12, 15 (Fine). *Obverse:* The hair details are mostly worn away, with about one-third visible, mainly at the edges. Border dentils are weak or worn away in areas. *Reverse:* The wreath leaves are worn flat, but their edges are distinct. Border dentils are weak or worn away in areas.

VF-20, 30 (Very Fine). *Obverse:* Wear on the portrait has reduced the hair detail to indistinct or flat at the center. The border dentils are blended together, with many indistinct. No luster is seen. *Reverse:* At VF-20 the leaf details are nearly completely worn away; at VF-30, there is slight detail. The border dentils are blended together, with many indistinct. No luster is seen. The sharpness of details depends on the die variety. Half cents of 1797 require special care in their study.

EF-40, 45 (Extremely Fine). *Obverse:* Wear is seen on the portrait overall, with reduction or elimination of some separation of hair strands on the highest part. This varies by die variety; some are better delineated than others. The cheek shows light wear. Luster is minimal or nonexistent at EF-40, and may survive in traces in protected areas (such as between the letters) at EF-45. *Reverse:* Wear is seen on the highest wreath and ribbon areas and the letters. Luster is minimal, but likely more noticeable than on the obverse, as the fields are protected by the designs and lettering. Sharpness varies depending on die variety; certain issues of 1794 and 1797 are lighter.

AU-50, 53, 55, 58 (About Uncirculated). *Obverse:* (Grading at AU is mainly done by viewing the obverse.) Friction is seen on the higher parts, particularly the center of the portrait. Friction and scattered marks are in the field, ranging from extensive at AU-50 to minimal at AU-58. Luster may be seen in protected areas, minimal at AU-50, but sometimes extensive on an AU-58 coin. Knowledge of the die variety is important; for certain shallow-relief dies (such as 1797) an About Uncirculated coin may appear to be in a lower grade. *Reverse:* Friction is seen on the higher wreath leaves and (not as easy to discern) on the letters. The fields, protected by the designs, show friction, but not as noticeably as on the obverse. At AU-55 and 58 little if any friction is seen. The reverse may have original luster, toned brown, minimal on lower AU grades, sometimes extensive on higher.

MS-60 to 70 (Mint State). *Obverse:* In MS-60 and 61, there are some traces of abrasion on the higher areas of the portrait. Luster in the field is incomplete, particularly in the center of the open areas. At MS-63, luster is complete, with no abrasions. At higher levels, the luster is deeper, and some original mint color may be seen. At MS-65 there are some scattered contact marks and possibly some traces of fingerprints or discoloration, but these should be minimal and not distracting. Above MS-65, a coin should approach perfection. *Reverse:* In the lower ranges some abrasions are seen on the higher areas of the leaves. Generally, luster is complete in all ranges, as the open areas are protected by the lettering and wreath. Otherwise, the same comments apply as for the obverse.

• 17

1794, Normal Head   **1794, High-Relief Head**

1795, With Pole   **1795, Punctuated Date**   **1795, No Pole**

1796, "Dr. Edwards" Copy

1797, 1 Above 1   **1797, Low Head**

	Mintage	Cert	Avg	%MS	VG-8	F-12	VF-20	EF-40	AU-50	MS-60BN	MS-63BN	Recent Auction Record
1794, All kinds	81,600											
1794, Normal Head		46	32.3	9	$825	$1,500	$2,500	$6,000	$14,000	$22,000	$45,000	$88,125, MS-63BN, April 2014
1794, High-Relief Head		21	37.9	14	825	1,600	3,000	6,200	14,500	25,000	47,500	$1,586, VF-20, October 2013
1795, All kinds	139,690											
1795, Lettered Edge, With Pole		175	32.9	8	800	1,500	2,750	6,000	12,000	17,000	24,000	$3,525, EF-40, September 2013
1795, Lettered Edge, Punctuated Date		27	27.3	7	800	1,500	3,000	6,500	12,000	25,000	45,000	$12,925, AU-55, August 2013
1795, Plain Edge, Punctuated Date		43	19.9	5	625	1,200	1,900	4,800	9,500	14,000	23,000	$1,501, VF-20, August 2011
1795, Plain Edge, No Pole (a)		268	25.8	3	625	1,200	1,900	4,800	9,500	14,000	23,000	$7,638, AU-55, June 2014
1796, With Pole (b)	1,390	62	29.8	21	27,500 (c)	37,500	60,000	85,000	110,000	200,000		$76,375, EF-40, August 2013
1796, No Pole	*	8	30.4	38	65,000 (d)	125,000	180,000	250,000	325,000	500,000		$382, VG-8, September 2013
1797, All kinds	127,840											
1797, 1 Above 1, Plain Edge		163	24.5	5	650	1,100	1,800	4,100	7,200	16,000		$7,931, AU, March 2014
1797, Plain Edge, Low Head		4	8.3	0	975	2,250	4,500	13,500	—	—	—	$1,495, VG-10, February 2012
1797, Plain Edge		206	23.3	4	700	1,250	3,000	6,000	8,100	16,000		$3,055, AU-50, April 2013
1797, Lettered Edge		13	12.9	0	2,900 (e)	6,000	15,000	30,000	60,000			$7,638, VG-10, November 2013
1797, Gripped Edge		3	6.3	0	65,000 (f)	150,000	—	—	—			$195,500, G-6, September 2011

* Included in number above. **a.** Many of this date/variety were struck on cut-down cents (coins that had been rejected for circulation by Mint workers), or on planchets cut from English-made Talbot, Allum & Lee tokens (see the *Whitman Encyclopedia of Colonial and Early American Coins*). **b.** The deceptive "Dr. Edwards" struck copy of this coin has a different head and larger letters, as pictured. **c.** Value in G-4 is $18,000. **d.** Value in G-4 is $35,000. **e.** Value in G-4 is $1,500. **f.** Value in G-4 is $30,000.

DRAPED BUST
(1800–1808)
Designer Robert Scot; weight 5.44 grams; composition copper; diameter 23.5 mm; plain edge.

Cohen-13, Breen-10.

History. By the turn of the century the Draped Bust design was already familiar to Americans, from its use on cents and silver coins. The motif was introduced to the half cent in 1800, and was used through 1808.

Striking and Sharpness. Striking varies. Weakness is often seen at the center of the obverse and on the wreath leaves on the reverse. Planchet quality is often porous and dark for 1802, 1803, 1807, and 1808 due to the copper stock used.

Availability. As a type, Draped Bust half cents are available in any grade desired, up to and including Mint State, the latter usually dated 1806 (occasionally 1800 and, less often, 1804). The year 1804 includes many different die varieties and die states. Apart from aspects of strike, cherrypicking for planchet quality is essential for 1802, 1803, 1807, and 1808.

G-4, 6 (Good). *Obverse:* The portrait is worn smooth and is seen only in outline form, although the eye position can be discerned. LIBERTY and the date are complete, although the date may be weak. The border blends into the field more extensively than in VG, but significant areas are still seen. *Reverse:* Extensive wear is seen overall. From half to two-thirds of the letters in UNITED STATES OF AMERICA and the fraction numerals are worn away.

VG-8, 10 (Very Good). *Obverse:* The portrait is well worn, although the eye can be seen, as can hints of hair detail (some at the left shows separation). Curls appear as mostly solid blobs. Border dentils are worn away on most varieties, and the rim, although usually present, begins to blend into the field. LIBERTY and the date are bold. *Reverse:* The wreath, bow, and lettering are seen in outline form. Some leaves and letters may be indistinct in parts. The border may blend into the field on some of the periphery.

F-12, 15 (Fine). *Obverse:* The hair details are mostly worn away, with about one-third visible, mainly at the edges. Border dentils are weak or worn away in areas. *Reverse:* The wreath leaves are worn flat, but their edges are distinct. HALF CENT may be missing on variety B-1, C-1 (also true of lower grades). Border dentils are weak or worn away in areas.

VF-20, 30 (Very Fine). *Obverse:* Wear on the portrait has reduced the hair detail to indistinct or flat at the center. The border dentils are blended together, with many indistinct. No luster is seen. *Reverse:* The leaf details have slight detail at VF-30, and are nearly completely worn away at VF-20. The border dentils are blended together, with many indistinct. No luster is seen.

EF-40, 45 (Extremely Fine). *Obverse:* Wear is seen on the portrait overall, with reduction or elimination of some separation of hair strands on the highest part. The cheek shows light wear. Luster may survive among the letters of LIBERTY at EF-45, and is minimal or nonexistent at EF-40. *Reverse:* Wear is seen on the highest wreath and ribbon areas, and the letters. Luster is minimal, but likely more noticeable than on the obverse, as the fields are protected by the designs and lettering.

AU-50, 53, 55, 58 (About Uncirculated). *Obverse:* Friction is seen on the higher parts, particularly the hair. Friction and scattered marks are in the field, minimal at AU-58 to extensive at AU-50. Luster may be seen in protected areas, more at AU-58, minimal at AU-50. At AU-58 the field may retain some luster, as well. The luster is lesser in area and in "depth" than on the reverse. *Reverse:* Friction is evident on the higher wreath leaves and (not as easy to discern) on the letters. The die variety should be checked. The fields, protected by the designs, show friction, but not as noticeably as on the obverse. At AU-55 and 58, little if any friction is seen. The reverse may have original luster, toned brown, often extensive at AU-58, and minimal at lower AU grades.

MS-60 to 70 (Mint State). *Obverse:* In MS-60 and 61, some slight abrasions can be seen on the higher areas of the portrait. Luster in the field is incomplete, particularly in the center of the open areas, which on this type are very extensive. At MS-63, luster should be nearly complete, and no abrasions evident. In higher levels, the luster is complete and deeper and some original mint color may be seen. MS-64 coins may have some slight discoloration or scattered contact marks. An MS-65 or higher coin has full, rich luster; no marks visible except under magnification; and a blend of brown toning or nicely mixed (not stained or blotchy) mint color and natural brown toning. *Reverse:* In lower MS grades some abrasions are seen on the higher areas of the leaves. Generally, luster is complete in MS, as the open areas are protected by the lettering and wreath. Sharpness of the leaves can vary by die variety. Otherwise, the same comments apply as for the obverse.

1st Reverse (Style of 1800) — 2nd Reverse (Style of 1803) — 1803, Regular — 1803, Widely Spaced 3 — 1804, Plain 4 — 1804, Crosslet 4

Stems to Wreath — Stemless Wreath — 1804, "Spiked Chin" — 1805, Medium 5 — 1805, Small 5 — 1805, Large 5

1806, Small 6 — 1806, Large 6 — 1808, 8 Over 7 — 1808, Normal Date

	Mintage	Cert	Avg	%MS	VF-20	EF-40	AU-50	MS-60BN	MS-63BN	MS-63RB	MS-65BN	Recent Auction Record
1800	202,908	384	45.7	29	$300	$700	$1,000	$2,100	$4,100	$6,750	$14,000	$4,113, VF-20, June 2013
1802, 2 Over 0, Reverse of 1800	*	11	14.5	0	65,000 (a)	100,000	—					$35,938, VG-8, April 2009
1802, 2 Over 0, Second Reverse	20,266	172	10.9	0	14,000 (b)	35,000	—					$4,406, F-12, February 2013
1803	*	356	34.7	9	325	950	1,500	3,200	7,000	9,000	20,000	$3,525, AU-53, January 2014
1803, Widely Spaced 3	92,000	15	36.7	13	325	950	1,500	3,500	7,250	9,100	21,000	$1,840, AU-55, April 2012
1804, All kinds	1,055,312											
1804, Plain 4, Stems to Wreath		51	36.2	2	475	1,300	2,200	4,000				$4,994, AU-58, October 2013
1804, Plain 4, Stemless Wreath		860	45.6	20	200	365	675	1,300	2,800	3,900	8,500	$19,975, MS-65BN, April 2013
1804, Crosslet 4, Stemless		143	52.3	34	200	365	675	1,300	2,800	4,000	9,000	$5,141, MS-64BN, September 2013

* Included in number below. **a.** Value in G-4 is $22,500; in VG-8, $35,000; in F-12, $50,000. **b.** Value in G-4 is $750; in VG-8, $1,800; in F-12, $4,500.

Chart continued on next page.

	Mintage	Cert	Avg	%MS	VF-20	EF-40	AU-50	MS-60BN	MS-63BN	MS-63RB	MS-65BN	Recent Auction Record
1804, Crosslet 4, Stems		398	42.2	14	$200	$375	$675	$1,300	$2,800	$3,750	$8,500	$2,820, MS-63BN, December 2013
1804, "Spiked Chin"		577	43.1	13	250	425	850	1,800	3,600	4,600	9,500	$3,173, MS-63BN, January 2014
1805, All kinds	814,464											
1805, Medium 5, Stemless		194	40.5	14	200	400	750	1,350	3,000	4,000	8,700	$4,113, MS-64BN, April 2014
1805, Small 5, Stems		44	14.7	0	8,000 (c)	16,000	35,000					$135, VF-20, April 2014
1805, Large 5, Stems		104	37.3	5	225	415	850	1,700	3,750			$441, EF-45, July 2014
1806, All kinds	356,000											
1806, Small 6, Stems		58	27.2	2	1,650	3,500	9,000	12,500				$5,464, AU, March 2014
1806, Small 6, Stemless		628	46.1	23	175	325	675	1,200	2,900	3,800	7,750	$4,700, AU-53, June 2013
1806, Large 6, Stems		226	53.7	48	175	325	675	1,200	2,900	3,800	7,750	$5,581, MS-63RB, June 2014
1807	476,000	435	39.9	8	200	500	1,000	2,000	3,750			$1,175, AU-58, February 2013
1808, All kinds	400,000											
1808, Normal Date		215	35.4	5	220	525	1,300	2,500	5,000			$823, AU-50, June 2014
1808, 8 Over 7		99	22.1	0	2,100	4,500	11,500					$2,585, EF-40, April 2013

c. Value in G-4 is $900; in VG-8, $1,650; in F-12, $4,500.

CLASSIC HEAD
(1809–1836)
Designer John Reich; weight 5.44 grams; composition copper; diameter 23.5 mm; plain edge.

History. The Classic Head design (by Mint engraver John Reich) made its first appearance on the half cent in 1809, a year after it was adopted for the one-cent coin. A very similar motif of Miss Liberty was used on the quarter eagles and half eagles of the 1830s.

Striking and Sharpness. Coins of 1809 to 1811 usually have areas of light or incomplete striking. Grading coins of the early years requires special care and expertise. Sometimes coins as high as MS appear "blurry" in areas, due to the dies and striking. Those of later years are often found well struck and are easier to grade. Areas to check include the dentils and rims on both sides, the star centers and hair detail on the obverse, and the leaf detail on the reverse.

Availability. As a type this issue is easily enough found, although 1811 is scarce and 1831 and 1836 are notable rarities. MS coins from old hoards exist for certain of the later dates, particularly 1828, 1833, and 1835, but often have spotting, and many seen in the marketplace are cleaned or recolored. Care is advised. Although 1809–1811 half cents are often seen with extensive wear, those of the 1820s and 1830s are not often seen less than VF, as they did not circulate extensively.

G-4, 6 (Good). *Obverse:* The portrait is worn smooth and is seen only in outline form. Much of LIBERTY on the headband is readable, but the letters are weak. The stars are bold in outline. Much of the rim can be discerned. *Reverse:* Extensive wear is seen overall. Lettering in UNITED STATES OF AMERICA ranges from weak but complete to having perhaps a third of the letters missing. HALF CENT is usually bold.

VG-8, 10 (Very Good). *Obverse:* The portrait is well worn, although the eye and ear can be seen, as can some hair detail. The border is well defined in most areas. *Reverse:* The wreath, bow, and lettering are seen in outline form, and some leaves and letters may be indistinct in parts. The border is well defined in most areas.

F-12, 15 (Fine). *Obverse:* The hair details are fewer than in VF, but many are still present. Stars have flat centers. *Reverse:* The wreath leaves are worn flat, but their edges are distinct.

VF-20, 30 (Very Fine). *Obverse:* Wear on the portrait has reduced the hair detail, but much can still be seen. *Reverse:* The wreath details, except for the edges of the leaves, are worn away at VF-20, and have slightly more detail at VF-30.

EF-40, 45 (Extremely Fine). *Obverse:* Wear is seen on the portrait overall, with reduction or elimination of some separation of hair strands. The cheek shows light wear. Luster may survive among the letters of LIBERTY at EF-45, but is minimal or nonexistent at EF-40. *Reverse:* Wear is seen on the highest wreath and ribbon areas and the letters. Luster is minimal, but likely more noticeable than on the obverse, as the fields are protected by the designs and lettering.

AU-50, 53, 55, 58 (About Uncirculated). *Obverse:* Friction is seen on the higher parts, particularly the cheek and hair (under magnification). Friction and scattered marks are in the field, from minimal at AU-58 to extensive at AU-50. Luster may be seen in protected areas, minimal at AU-50 with more at AU-58. At AU-58 the field may retain some luster as well. *Reverse:* Friction is seen on the higher wreath leaves and (not as easy to discern) on the letters. Half cents of 1809 to 1811 require special attention. The fields, protected by the designs, show friction, but not as noticeably as on the obverse. At AU-58 and 55, little if any friction is seen. The reverse may have original luster, toned brown, often extensive at AU-58, minimal on lower AU grades.

MS-60 to 70 (Mint State). *Obverse:* In MS-60 and 61, some slight abrasions can be seen on the portrait, most evident on the cheek, as the hair details are complex. Luster in the field is complete or nearly complete. At MS-63, luster should be complete, and no abrasions are evident. In higher levels, the luster is complete and deeper, and some original mint color may be seen. MS-64 coins may have some slight discoloration or scattered contact marks. An MS-65 or higher coin has full, rich luster, with no marks visible except under magnification, and has a nice blend of brown toning or nicely mixed (not stained or blotchy) mint color and natural brown toning. Coins dated 1809 to 1811 may exhibit significant weakness of details due to striking (and/or, in the case of most 1811s, porous planchet stock). *Reverse:* In the lower MS grades, some abrasions are seen on the higher areas of the leaves. Mint luster is complete in all MS grades, as the open areas are protected by the lettering and wreath. Sharpness of the leaves can vary by die variety. Otherwise, the same comments apply as for the obverse. Coins dated 1809 to 1811 may exhibit significant weakness of details due to striking (and/or, in the case of most 1811s, porous planchet stock).

1809, Small 0 Inside 0   1809, 9 Over Inverted 9   1809, Normal Date   1811, Wide Date   1811, Close Date

1828, 13 Stars   1828, 12 Stars

	Mintage	Cert	Avg	%MS	F-12	VF-20	EF-40	AU-50	MS-60BN	MS-63BN	MS-63RB	Recent Auction Record
1809, All kinds	1,154,572											
1809, Normal Date		574	46.9	28	$80	$100	$150	$300	$850	$1,500	$2,000	$1,880, MS-64BN, April 2013
1809, Small o Inside 0		26	36.4	4	110	160	450	900	1,400	2,500		$55, G-4, January 2013
1809, 9 Over Inverted 9 (a)		382	47.6	15	100	150	375	750	1,300	2,200	3,000	$8,225, MS, March 2014
1810	215,000	188	41.9	22	125	270	575	1,000	2,000	3,200	6,750	$2,800, MS-63BN, April 2014
1811, All kinds	63,140											
1811, Wide Date		6	22.7	0	1,650	2,750	6,500	8,500	12,500	17,000		$82,250, MS-63BN, April 2014
1811, Close Date		7	31.1	0	1,600	2,500	6,200	7,750	10,000	14,000		$26,450, AU-50, September 2011
1811, Reverse of 1802, Unofficial Restrike (extremely rare)		8	64.1	100			—	—	16,000	22,000	27,500	$23,000, MS-64BN, September 2008
1825	63,000	484	49.8	26	80	100	200	325	900	1,800	3,000	$2,027, MS-63BN, October 2013
1826	234,000	522	52.4	34	80	90	150	300	600	1,000	1,300	$1,528, MS-64BN, April 2013
1828, All kinds	606,000											
1828, 13 Stars		97	56.1	53	70	100	120	225	350	600	1,000	$3,055, MS-63RD, September 2013
1828, 12 Stars		392	49.5	23	75	120	250	425	1,300	1,850	3,500	$2,468, MS-63BN, February 2014
1829	487,000	550	54.0	47	70	100	140	220	400	700	1,100	$1,469, MS-63RB, August 2013

a. Traditionally called 9 Over Inverted 9, but recent research shows it not to have an inverted digit.

	Mintage	Cert	Avg	%MS	AU-50	MS-60BN	MS-63BN	MS-63RB	MS-65BN	MS-65RB	MS-65RD	Recent Auction Record
1831, Original (a)					$50,000	$80,000						
1832 (b)	51,000	684	54.5	38	200	325	$475	$875	$1,450	$4,000		$3,290, MS-64BN, March 2013
1833 (b)	103,000	1,077	58.5	62	200	325	450	750	1,250	3,500	$7,500	$10,575, MS-66RB, June 2014
1834 (b)	141,000	994	56.6	53	200	325	450	750	1,250	3,500	5,000	$999, MS-64BN, April 2013
1835 (b)	398,000	2,006	57.4	58	200	325	450	750	1,250	3,500	5,250	$3,525, MS-65RB, September 2013

a. Circulation strike. b. The figures given here are thought to be correct, although Mint records report these quantities for 1833 through 1836 rather than 1832 through 1835.

Proof Classic Head Half Cents

PF-60 to 70 (Proof). Proof half cents of 1831 and 1836 are rare; these dates were also restruck at the Mint around 1858 or 1859, and later. Carefully study any coin offered as a Proof; some prooflike circulation strikes (especially 1833) have been certified as Proofs. Blotchy and recolored Proofs are often seen. Probably fewer than 25 of the Proofs of this type are truly pristine and problem-free. *Obverse and Reverse:* Proofs that are extensively hairlined or have dull surfaces (common among many issues except for 1831 and 1836) are graded PF-60 to 62 or 63. This also applies to artificially toned and recolored coins. To qualify as PF-65 or higher, hairlines should be microscopic, and there should be no trace of friction. Surfaces should be prooflike or fully mirrored, without dullness.

| 1831, Original | 1831, Restrike | Reverse, 1831–1836 | Reverse, 1840–1857 |

	Mintage	Cert	Finest	PF-40	PF-50	PF-60BN	PF-63BN	PF-63RB	PF-65BN	PF-65RB	Recent Auction Record
1831, Original (a)	2,200	12	PF-65	$50,000	$60,000	$80,000	—				$57,281, PF-60BN, January 2014
1831, Restrike, Large Berries (Reverse of 1836)	25–35	26	PF-67	—	5,000	10,000	$15,000	$20,000	$23,000	$37,500	$47,000, PF-65RB, February 2014
1831, Restrike, Small Berries (Reverse of 1840–1857)	10–15	6	PF-66	—	7,000	14,000	21,500	32,500	40,000		$63,250, PF-66BN, July 2009
1832	10–15	5	PF-65	1,750	2,500	7,000	10,000	13,500	17,500	25,000	$44,063, PF-64BN, January 2014
1833	25–35	32	PF-66	1,500	2,000	5,000	6,000	8,500	10,500	13,000	$11,163, PF-65BN, March 2013
1834	25–35	27	PF-66	1,500	2,000	5,000	6,000	9,000	11,000	13,500	$18,800, PF-64RB, August 2013
1835	15–20	13	PF-65	1,500	2,000	5,000	6,000	8,500	10,500	13,000	$11,163, PF-64RB, January 2014
1836, Original	140–240	39	PF-66	1,750	2,500	6,000	8,000	10,000	12,500	15,000	$12,925, PF-64BN, April 2013
1836, Restrike (Reverse of 1840–1857)	8–15	5	PF-66	2,000	3,000	9,000	17,000	25,000	30,000	35,000	

a. Beware of altered date.

1837 "HALF CENT" TOKEN

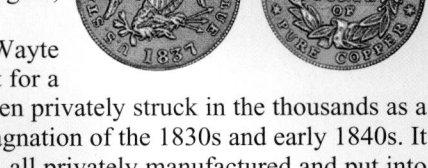

The last circulation-strike half cents of the Classic Head design were minted in 1835, and Proofs of the series were made in 1836 (see next section). No half cents of any format were minted in 1837, 1838, or 1839—it would be 1840 before the denomination started up again, with the Braided Hair type.

To help fill that gap for date-by-date collectors, in the 1930s Wayte Raymond included in his "National" brand of coin albums a slot for a half-cent–sized Hard Times token dated 1837. The token had been privately struck in the thousands as a supply of small change in the midst of the country's financial stagnation of the 1830s and early 1840s. It joined several hundred types of larger, cent-sized copper tokens, all privately manufactured and put into circulation by enterprising businesspeople, as substitutes for the federal government's half cents and large cents that were no longer circulating in any quantity.

Raymond's dignifying of the 1837 token brought about a new numismatic tradition. Half-cent collectors began to include the token—despite its not being official federal coinage—in their collections, and today the "Half Cent Worth of Pure Copper" is often found among their treasured coins.

BRAIDED HAIR
(1840–1857)

Designer Christian Gobrecht; weight 5.44 grams; composition copper; diameter 23 mm; plain edge.

History. The Braided Hair half cent debuted in 1840, a year after the same design was introduced on copper cents. There was scant commercial demand for this denomination, so only Proofs were struck from 1840 to 1848 and in 1852. (In 1849–1851 and 1853–1857 both Proofs and circulation strikes were made.) Ultimately the half cent was discontinued by the Act of February 21, 1857. After that point the coins were rapidly withdrawn from circulation, and by 1860 virtually all had disappeared from commerce.

Striking and Sharpness. Many if not most Braided Hair half cents are well struck, and nearly all are on good planchet stock. Check these points for sharpness: the dentils on both sides; the star centers and hair detail on the obverse; and the leaf detail on the reverse.

Availability. Because Braided Hair half cents were not struck for circulation until 1849 and they did not circulate after the 1850s, they never acquired extensive wear. Most coins grade EF-40 and finer. Lower grades are sometimes seen, but are not in demand.

VF-20, 30 (Very Fine). *Obverse:* Wear is more extensive than in EF. Some of the strands of hair are fused together. The center radials of the stars are worn nearly completely away. *Reverse:* The leaves show more extensive wear, with details visible at the edges, and only minimally and not on all leaves. The lettering shows smooth, even wear.

EF-40, 45 (Extremely Fine). *Obverse:* Wear is more extensive on the portrait than at AU, including the cheek, hair, and coronet. The star centers are worn down slightly. Traces of luster are minimal, if at all existent. *Reverse:* The centers of the leaves are well worn, with detail visible only near the edges of the leaves and nearby, with the higher parts worn flat. Letters show significant wear. Luster, if present, is minimal.

AU-50, 53, 55, 58 (About Uncirculated). *Obverse:* Wear is evident on the cheek, the hair above the forehead, and the tip of the coronet. Friction is evident in the field. In AU-50 wear is evident on the portrait; less so at 53, 55, and 58. Wear is seen on the stars, but is not as easy to discern as it is elsewhere. At AU-50 there is either no luster or only traces of luster close to the letters and devices. At AU-58, luster may be present except in the center of the fields. *Reverse:* Wear is most evident on the highest areas of the leaves and the ribbon bow. Luster is present in the fields. At AU-50 there is either no luster, or only traces of luster, close to the letters and devices. In higher AU grades wear is less, and luster increases.

MS-60 to 70 (Mint State). *Obverse:* In MS-60 and 61, some slight abrasion can be seen on the portrait, most evidently on the cheek. Also check the tip of the coronet. Luster in the field is complete, or nearly so. At MS-63, luster should be complete, and no abrasions evident. At higher levels, the luster is complete and deeper, and some original mint color may be seen. Mint frost on this type is usually deep, sometimes satiny, but hardly ever prooflike. MS-64 coins may have some slight discoloration or scattered contact marks. An MS-65 or higher coin has full, rich luster; no contact marks visible except under magnification; and a nice blend of brown toning or nicely mixed (not stained or blotchy) mint color and natural brown toning. *Reverse:* In the lower MS grades some abrasions are seen on the higher areas of the leaves. Mint luster is complete in all MS grades, as the open areas are protected by the lettering and wreath.

1849, Small Date (Proof Only)

1849, Large Date

	Mintage	Cert	Avg	%MS	EF-40	AU-50	MS-60BN	MS-63BN	MS-63RB	MS-65BN	MS-65RB	Recent Auction Record
1849, Large Date	39,864	238	59.1	67	$150	$240	$500	$700	$900	$2,100	$2,700	$1,058, MS-64BN, August 2013
1850	39,812	386	57.0	53	150	240	500	700	1,100	2,300	3,000	$1,880, MS-64BN, September 2013
1851	147,672	1,239	58.2	60	100	175	275	550	650	1,000	2,000 (a)	$1,998, MS-65RB, June 2014
1853	129,694	1,536	60.4	74	100	175	275	550	650	1,000	1,700	$89, EF-40, February 2012
1854	55,358	1,201	61.0	78	100	165	275	550	650	1,000	1,700	$1,293, MS-64RB, September 2013
1855	56,500	1,959	62.2	86	100	165	275	550	650	1,000	1,600	$5,288, MS-65RD, August 2013
1856	40,430	647	59.9	70	125	185	325	575	675	1,250	2,000	$4,113, MS-64RD, April 2014
1857	35,180	1,002	60.2	76	180	260	400	650	750	1,750	2,500	$1,763, MS-64RB, June 2014

a. Value in MS-65RD is $4,000.

Proof Braided Hair Half Cents

PF-60 to 70 (Proof). Only Proofs—not circulation strikes—were made for the half cent issues of 1840 to 1848, 1849 Small Date, and 1852. All were restruck at the Mint. Generally, the quality of these Proofs is very good, with excellent striking of details and nice planchet quality. Both originals and restrikes use the reverse of 1840–1857.

Originals have Large Berries in the wreath. This is the style used to strike half cents in the year indicated on the dies, for inclusion in Proof sets or for sale to numismatists. Until First Restrikes were made, circa 1856, Original die pairs for some dates were used to make a small number of restrikes. Some of these probably cannot be differentiated today from Original strikings.

First Restrike half cents have Small Berries, the NT of CENT is slightly doubled, and there is doubling of the wreath ribbon. This was the die used to strike Proof 1856 half cents for inclusion in sets of that year. Accordingly, it is sometimes called the Reverse of 1856.

Second Restrike half cents have Small Berries, and diagonal file marks over RICA of AMERICA. Likely, these were made from about the spring of 1859, or later, and continued in production in occasional batches for a decade or more. These are on planchets that are more or less within range of the normal weight of 84 grains.

Obverse and Reverse: PF-60 to 62 coins show a profusion of hairlines and a general dullness of the fields. Hairlines decrease until at PF-65 and 66 they show only under high magnification. At PF-67 no hairlines are seen, the fields are deeply mirrorlike, and there is no evidence of friction. Typical color for an undipped Proof ranges from light or iridescent brown to brown with some traces of mint color. Except for issues in the 1850s, Proofs are nearly always BN or, less often, RB. The rare Proofs of the 1840s are sometimes seen with light wear and can be classified using the AU and EF guidelines, except in place of "luster" read "Proof surface."

Proof Braided Hair Half Cent
Breen-1.

Large Berries   **Small Berries**

	Est Mintage	Cert	Finest	PF-60BN	PF-63BN	PF-63RB	PF-65BN	PF-65RB	Recent Auction Record
1840, Original	125–150	23	PF-66	$5,350	$6,500	$7,500	$9,250	$14,000	$7,475, PF-62BN, August 2006
1840, Restrike	21–25	16	PF-66	5,350	6,500	7,500	9,250	14,000	$25,850, PF-65RB, June 2014
1841, Original	150–250	53	PF-66	4,350	5,500	7,500	8,750	13,000	$21,150, PF-65BN, September 2013
1841, Restrike	15–19	16	PF-66	4,350	5,500	7,500	8,750	13,000	$8,625, PF-66BN, June 2008
1842, Original	120–180	11	PF-66	5,850	7,000	9,000	10,000	15,000	$15,275, PF-64BN, February 2014
1842, Restrike	35–45	22	PF-67	4,350	5,500	7,500	8,750	13,000	$20,700, PF-65RB, April 2010
1843, Original	125–200	27	PF-66	4,350	5,500	7,500	8,750	13,000	$73,438, PF-65RD, April 2014
1843, Restrike	37–44	19	PF-66	4,600	5,700	6,750	8,750	13,000	$9,988, PF-64BN, February 2014
1844, Original	120–180	20	PF-65	5,100	6,000	8,500	9,000	14,500	$4,888, PF-50, May 2008
1844, Restrike	21–26	14	PF-66	4,750	5,750	8,500	8,750	14,000	$1,777, PF, February 2014
1845, Original	110–170	11	PF-66	4,850	6,000	8,500	9,250	14,500	$23,500, PF-64BN, April 2013
1845, Restrike	20–24	20	PF-67	4,300	5,400	8,000	9,000	14,500	$9,200, PF-65BN, October 2011
1846, Original	125–200	19	PF-66	5,100	6,000	8,000	9,000	14,500	$21,150, PF-64BN, January 2014
1846, Restrike	19–24	19	PF-66	4,600	5,750	8,500	8,750	14,000	$23,630, PF-66BN, June 2014
1847, Original	200–300	20	PF-66	5,100	6,000	8,500	9,250	14,500	$5,288, PF-63BN, January 2014
1847, Restrike	33–44	35	PF-67	4,300	5,400	7,750	8,250	13,000	$15,275, PF-66BN, January 2014
1848, Original	150–225	14	PF-65	5,350	6,250	8,500	9,250	14,500	$10,350, PF-64RB, September 2003
1848, Restrike	40–47	32	PF-67	4,500	5,600	7,500	8,250	13,000	$6,169, PF-64BN, February 2014
1849, Original, Small Date	70–90	11	PF-65	4,400	5,500	7,500	10,000	25,000	$8,813, PF-64RB, April 2014
1849, Restrike, Small Date	30–36	17	PF-66	4,850	5,750	9,250	9,750	15,000	$7,344, PF-64BN, January 2014
1850	10–20	22	PF-66	5,000	7,000	10,000	13,000	17,000	$5,875, PF-63BN, January 2014
1851	10–20	1	PF-64	7,100	8,000	15,000	20,000	25,000	
1852, Original	225–325	2	PF-65	—					
1852, Restrike	110–140	79	PF-66	4,000	6,000	9,000	9,000	15,000	$6,463, PF, August 2013
1854	10–20	9	PF-65	3,650	4,500	7,500	7,200	11,500	$7,931, PF-65RB, February 2014
1855	40–60	42	PF-66	3,500	4,500	7,500	7,200	11,500	$5,750, PF-64BN, August 2011
1856	50–75	58	PF-66	3,500	4,500	7,500	7,200	11,500	$8,519, PF, February 2014
1857	75–100	88	PF-66	3,400	4,500	7,500	7,500	12,000	$14,100, PF-66RB, June 2014

AN OVERVIEW OF LARGE CENTS

Collecting one each of the major types of 1793–1857 copper cents can be a fascinating challenge. Early varieties were struck from hand-engraved dies, often on copper planchets of uncertain quality. It was not until 1836 that steam power was used to run coining presses at the Mint. All earlier issues were made by hand, by two men tugging on the weighted lever arm of a small screw-type press. As might be expected, this resulted in many variations in striking quality.

The first cents of 1793, the Chain varieties, are found with two major differences: AMERI. on the reverse, and the later version with AMERICA spelled out in full. These early issues have been highly desired from the beginning days of the numismatic hobby in America, and remain in the limelight today.

Wreath cents of 1793 occur with the edge displaying a vine and bars motif and also with lettering ONE HUNDRED FOR A DOLLAR. Liberty Cap cents of the 1793–1796 years have lettered edges (ONE HUNDRED FOR A DOLLAR) used in 1793, 1794, and part of 1795, and plain edges for most 1795 coins and all of 1796.

The Draped Bust type commenced partway through 1796 and was continued through 1807. This span includes the notably rare 1799, 9 Over 8 overdate and the 1799 as well as the somewhat rare 1804. Many interesting die varieties occur in this type, particularly with regard to errors on the reverse. The Classic Head cent, designed by John Reich, was introduced in 1808, and was continued through 1814. In 1815 no cents of this date were produced. Then in 1816 the Matron Head commenced, a new motif with a new reverse as well. With modifications this was continued through 1839, in which year the Braided Hair design by Christian Gobrecht made its appearance. Cents were made continually through January 1857 and then discontinued.

FOR THE COLLECTOR AND INVESTOR: LARGE CENTS AS A SPECIALTY

For the enjoyment of copper cents 1793–1857 it is possible to go *far* beyond a type set. Today, varieties of the 1793–1814 cents are generally collected by Sheldon numbers (S-1, S-2, etc.), given first in *Early American Cents* and, later, in its revision, *Penny Whimsy*. Building upon this foundation, *Walter Breen's Encyclopedia of Early United States Large Cents, 1793–1814,* gives more information on this date range than available in any other single source.

Among dates and major varieties in the early range of the series, the 1793 Chain AMERI., Chain AMERICA, Wreath, and Liberty Cap issues, the 1799 (far and away the rarest date in the series), and the 1804 are key issues, each a part of an extensive series of more than 300 die varieties through and including 1814.

The most popular way to collect large cents is by basic varieties, mainly dates, overdates, and major varieties. Sometimes, a particular date is selected as a specialty for collecting die varieties by Sheldon numbers.

Generally, grades from Good to VF are popular objectives for the early series from 1793 to 1814, and for some varieties no better coins exist. EF, AU, and Mint State coins are available and are more likely to be sought by collectors of basic dates and major varieties, rather than by specialists seeing long runs of Sheldon numbers. Type-set collectors are also important in the market for high-grade pieces, where sights can be set high as there are fewer varieties to obtain. Accordingly, as a type-set collector one may aspire to own an AU or Mint State cent of the 1796–1807 Draped Bust type. However, for a specialist in die varieties, who wants to acquire more than 100 different specimens from this date range, such high grades might not be feasible to acquire.

Collecting cents of the later dates by basic varieties is an interesting pursuit, and one that is quite attainable in such grades as EF, AU, or even MS-60, most dates after the 1820s being readily available for relatively inexpensive prices. Key issues among 1816–1857 cents include 1823, 3 Over 2; 1823; 1824, 4 Over 2; 1839, 9 Over 6; and a few others. Collecting Braided Hair cents toward the end of the series, 1839 to 1857, is least expensive of all, and most major varieties can be obtained in such grades as MS-60 to MS-63, with lustrous brown surfaces, for reasonable figures.

RECOMMENDED READING

Bowers, Q. David. *A Guide Book of Half Cents and Large Cents,* Atlanta, GA, 2015.
Breen, Walter. *Walter Breen's Encyclopedia of Early United States Cents, 1793–1814,* Wolfeboro, NH, 2001.
Eckberg, William, Fagaly, Robert, Fuoss, Dennis, and Williams, Raymond. *Grading Guide for Early American Copper Coins,* Heath, OH, 2014.
Fivaz, Bill, and Stanton, J.T. *The Cherrypickers' Guide to Rare Die Varieties* (5th ed., vol. I), Atlanta, GA, 2009.
Grellman, J.R. *Attribution Guide for United States Large Cents, 1840–1857* (3rd ed.), Bloomington, MN, 2002.
Newcomb, H.R. *United States Copper Cents, 1816–1857,* New York, 1944 (reprinted 1983).
Noyes, William C. *United States Large Cents, 1793–1794,* Ypsilanti, MI, 2006.
Noyes, William C. *United States Large Cents, 1793–1814,* Bloomington, MN, 1991.
Noyes, William C. *United States Large Cents, 1795–1797,* Ypsilanti, MI, 2007.
Noyes, William C. *United States Large Cents, 1816–1839,* Bloomington, MN, 1991.
Penny-Wise, official publication of Early American Coppers, Inc.
Sheldon, William H. *Penny Whimsy* (1793–1814), New York, 1958 (reprinted 1965, 1976).
Wright, John D. *The Cent Book, 1816–1839,* Bloomington, MN, 1992.

FLOWING HAIR, CHAIN REVERSE
(1793)

Designer Henry Voigt; weight 13.48 grams; composition copper; approx. diameter 26–27 mm; edge: bars and slender vine with leaves.

Sheldon-1.

AMERI. in Legend

AMERICA in Legend

Vine-and-Bars Edge

History. The first U.S. cents intended for circulation were struck at the Mint in Philadelphia from February 27 through March 12, 1793. These were of the Flowing Hair design, with a Chain reverse. Several varieties were struck, today attributed by Sheldon numbers. The first, or Sheldon-1, had AMERICA abbreviated as AMERI. A contemporary account noted that Miss Liberty appeared to be "in a fright," and that the chain motif on the reverse, 15 links intended to symbolize unity of the states in the Union, was an "ill omen" for a land of liberty; accordingly, the design was used for only a short time. The rims on both sides are raised, without dentils or beads.

Striking and Sharpness. The details of Miss Liberty's hair are often indistinct or missing, including on many higher-grade specimens. For all grades and varieties, the reverse is significantly sharper than the obverse. The portrait of Miss Liberty is shallow and is often weak, especially on the S-1 variety (which is often missing the date). Note that early copper coins of all kinds may exhibit "tooling" (engraving done outside the Mint in order to simulate details that were worn away or weakly struck to begin with). These old coppers also have sometimes been burnished, to smooth out areas of porosity. These alterations are considered to be damage, and they significantly decrease a coin's value.

Availability. Demand is higher than supply for all varieties, with fewer than 1,000 or so surviving today. Most are in lower grades, from Fair-2 to VG-8. Even heavily worn coins (still identifiable by the chain device) are highly collectible. VF and EF coins are few and far between, and AU and MS are very rare.

G-4, 6 (Good). *Obverse:* The portrait is worn smooth and is seen only in outline form, although the eye position can be discerned. LIBERTY may be weak. The date is weak, but the tops of the numerals can be discerned. *Reverse:* The chain is fully visible in outline form. Central lettering is mostly or completely readable, but light. Peripheral lettering is mostly worn away.

VG-8, 10 (Very Good). *Obverse:* The portrait is well worn, although Miss Liberty's eye remains bold. Hair detail is gone at the center, but is evident at the left edge of the portrait. LIBERTY is always readable, but may be faded or partly missing on shallow strikes. The date is well worn, with the bottom of the numerals missing. *Reverse:* The chain remains bold, and the center letters are all readable. Border letters may be weak or incomplete. The rim is smooth in most areas.

F-12, 15 (Fine). *Obverse:* The hair details are mostly worn away, with about one-third visible, that being on the left. The rim is distinct on most specimens. The bottoms of the date digits are weak or possibly worn away. *Reverse:* The chain is bold, as is the lettering within the chain. Lettering around the border shows extensive wear, but is complete. The rim may be flat in areas.

VF-20, 30 (Very Fine). *Obverse:* More wear is seen on the portrait than at EF, with perhaps half or slightly more of the hair detail showing, mostly near the left edge of the hair. The ear usually is visible (but might not be, depending on the sharpness of strike). The letters in LIBERTY show wear. The rim remains bold (more so than on the reverse). *Reverse:* The chain shows more wear than in EF, but is still bold. Other features show more wear and may be weak in areas. The rim may be weak in areas.

EF-40, 45 (Extremely Fine). *Obverse:* The center of the portrait is well worn, with the hair visible only in thick strands, although extensive detail remains in the hair tips at the left. No luster is seen. Contact marks are normal in the large expanse of open field. *Reverse:* The chain is bold and shows light wear. Other features show wear, as well—more extensive in appearance, as the relief is lower. The fields show some friction, but not as much as on the obverse.

AU-50, 53, 55, 58 (About Uncirculated). *Obverse:* Light wear is seen on the highest areas of the portrait. Little if any luster is seen in the large open fields at AU-50 and 53, with some seen at 55, and some more at 58. Scattered marks are normal and are most evident in the field. At higher levels, some vestiges of luster may be seen among the letters and numerals, and between the hair tips. *Reverse:* Light wear is most evident on the chain. The letters show wear, but not as extensive. Luster may be seen at AU-55 and 58, usually slightly more on the reverse than on the obverse. Generally, the reverse grades higher than the obverse.

MS-60 to 70 (Mint State). *Obverse:* In MS-60 and 61, some slight abrasions can be seen on the higher areas of the portrait. The large open field shows light contact marks and perhaps a few nicks. At MS-63 the luster should be complete, although some very light abrasions or contact marks may be on the portrait. At MS-64 or higher—nearly impossible for a Chain cent—there is no sign of abrasion anywhere. Mint color is not extensive on any known MS coin, but traces of red-orange are sometimes seen around the rim and devices on both sides. *Reverse:* In low MS grades some abrasions are seen on the chain links. There is some abrasion in the field. At MS-63, luster should be unbroken. Some abrasion and minor contact marks may be evident. In still higher grades, luster is deep and there is no sign of abrasion.

	Mintage	Cert	Avg	%MS	G-4	VG-8	F-12	VF-20	EF-40	AU-50	MS-60BN	Recent Auction Record
1793, Chain, All kinds	36,103											
1793, AMERI. in Legend		141	19.5	4	$11,000	$17,500	$28,000	$47,000	$85,000	$200,000	$300,000	$440,625, MS-63BN, June 2014
1793, AMERICA, Periods		80	22.1	3	8,000	15,000	19,000	37,500	60,000	120,000	225,000	$22,325, AU-50, September 2013
1793, AMERICA, No Periods		21	33.6	19	7,500	14,000	18,000	36,500	56,000	100,000	180,000	$998,750, MS-65BN, January 2013

FLOWING HAIR, WREATH REVERSE
(1793)

Designer Henry Voigt; weight 13.48 grams; composition copper; approx. diameter 26–28 mm; edge: vine and bars, or lettered ONE HUNDRED FOR A DOLLAR followed by either a single or a double leaf.

Sheldon-6.

Vine-and-Bars Edge

Lettered Edge (ONE HUNDRED
FOR A DOLLAR)

History. Between April 9 and July 17, 1793, the U.S. Mint struck and delivered 63,353 large copper cents. Most of these, and perhaps all, were of the Wreath type, although records do not specify when the design types were changed that year. The Wreath cent was named for the new reverse style. Both sides have raised beads at the border, similar to the style used on 1793 half cents.

Striking and Sharpness. These cents usually are fairly well struck, although high-grade pieces often exhibit some weakness on the highest hair tresses and on the leaf details. (On lower-grade pieces these areas are worn, so the point is moot.) Planchet quality varies widely, from smooth, glossy brown to dark and porous. The lettered-edge cents are often seen on defective planchets. Consult Sheldon's *Penny Whimsy (1793–1814)* and photographs to learn the characteristics of certain varieties. The borders have raised beads; on high-grade pieces these are usually very distinct, but they blend together on lower-grade coins and can sometimes be indistinct. The beads are not as prominent as those later used on the 1793 Liberty Cap cents.

Availability. At least several thousand examples exist of the different varieties of the type. Most are in lower grades, from AG-3 to VG-8, although Fine and VF pieces are encountered with regularity. Choice EF, AU, and finer coins see high demand. Some in MS have been billed as "specimen" or "presentation" coins, although this is supposition, as no records exist.

VG-8, 10 (Very Good). *Obverse:* The hair is well worn toward the face. Details at the left are mostly blended together in thick strands. The eye, nose, and lips often remain well defined. Border beads are completely gone, or just seen in traces, and part of the rim blends into the field. LIBERTY may be slightly weak. The 1793 date is fully visible, although there may be some lightness. Scattered marks are more common than on higher grades. *Reverse:* The wreath, bow, and lettering are seen in outline form, and some leaves and letters may be indistinct in parts. Most of the berries remain visible, but weak. Border beads are worn away, and the border blends into the field in most if not all of the periphery.

F-12, 15 (Fine). *Obverse:* The hair details are mostly worn away, with about one-third visible, mainly at the edges. Beads are weak or worn away in areas. Scat-

tered light scratches, noticeable contact marks, and the like are evident. Light porosity or granularity is common. *Reverse:* The wreath leaves are worn flat, but their edges are distinct. Border beads are weak or worn away in areas.

VF-20, 30 (Very Fine). *Obverse:* Wear on the hair is more extensive than at EF, and varies depending on the die variety and sharpness of strike. Two-thirds or so of the hair is visible. More beads are blended together, the extent of which depends on the striking and variety. Certain parts of the rim are smooth, with beads scarcely visible at all. No luster is seen. The date, LIBERTY, and hair ends are bold. *Reverse:* The leaf details are nearly completely worn away at VF-20, with slight detail at VF-30. The border beads are blended together, with many indistinct. Some berries in the sprays are light, but nearly all remain distinct. No luster is seen.

EF-40, 45 (Extremely Fine). *Obverse:* More extensive wear is seen on the high parts of the hair than at AU, creating mostly a solid mass (without detail of strands) of varying width in the area immediately to the left of the face. The cheek shows light wear. Luster is minimal or nonexistent at EF-40, and may survive in traces in protected areas (such as between the letters) at EF-45. *Reverse:* Wear is seen on the highest wreath and ribbon areas, and the letters. Luster is minimal, but likely more noticeable than on the obverse, as the fields are protected by the designs and lettering. Some of the beads blend together.

AU-50, 53, 55, 58 (About Uncirculated). *Obverse:* Friction is seen on the highest areas of the hair (which may also be lightly struck) and the cheek. Some scattered marks are normal in the field, ranging from more extensive at AU-50 to minimal at 58. *Reverse:* Friction is seen on the higher wreath leaves and (not as easy to discern) on the letters. The fields, protected by the designs (including sprays of berries at the center), show friction, but not as noticeably as on the obverse. At AU-55 and 58, little if any friction is seen. Border beads, if well struck, are separate and boldly defined.

MS-60 to 70 (Mint State). *Obverse:* On MS-60 and 61 coins there are some traces of abrasion on the higher areas of the portrait, most particularly the hair. This area can be lightly struck, so careful inspection is needed for evaluation, not as much in MS (as other features come into play), but in higher circulated grades. Luster in the field is incomplete at lower MS levels, but should be in generous quantity. At MS-63, luster should be complete, and no abrasion evident. At higher levels, the luster is deeper, and some original mint color may be seen. At MS-65 there might be some scattered contact marks and possibly bare traces of fingerprints or discoloration. Above MS-65, a coin should approach perfection. *Reverse:* In the lower MS grades some abrasion is seen on the higher areas of the leaves. Generally, luster is complete in all grades, as the open areas are protected by the lettering and wreath.

Regular Sprig   Strawberry Leaf

	Mintage	Cert	Avg	%MS	VG-8	F-12	VF-20	EF-40	AU-50	MS-60BN	MS-63BN	Recent Auction Record
1793, Wreath, All kinds	63,353											
1793, Vine/Bars Edge		680	27.1	8	$4,700	$7,000	$14,500	$26,000	$36,000	$55,000	$100,000	$558,125, MS-69BN, January 2013
1793, Lettered Edge		174	21.8	3	4,750	7,500	15,000	27,500	38,000	80,000	125,000	$18,800, F-15, January 2014
1793, Strawberry Leaf † (4 known)		4	7.0	0	450,000	950,000						$381,875, G-4, January 2014

† Ranked in the *100 Greatest U.S. Coins* (fourth edition).

LIBERTY CAP
(1793–1796)

1793–1795 (thick planchet)—Designer Joseph Wright; weight 13.48 grams; composition copper; approx. diameter 29 mm; edge: ONE HUNDRED FOR A DOLLAR followed by a single leaf. 1795–1796 (thin planchet)—Designer John Smith Gardner; weight 10.89 grams; composition copper; approx. diameter 29 mm; plain edge.

Lettered Edge (1793–1795)

Reeded Edge (1795)

History. The Liberty Cap design was created in the summer of 1793 by artist and engraver Joseph Wright, who is also believed by some to have designed the 1793 half cent. On the cent, Miss Liberty faces to the right, rather than to the left (as on the half cent). Liberty Cap cents of 1793 have raised beaded borders. Other issues have dentils. Cents of 1794 and some of 1795 are on thick planchets with the edge lettered ONE HUNDRED FOR A DOLLAR, while those made later in 1795, and in 1796, are on thinner planchets and have a plain edge.

Striking and Sharpness. The depth of relief and striking characteristics vary widely, depending on the variety. Points to check are the details of the hair on Miss Liberty, the leaf details on the wreath, and the dentils on both sides. Generally, the earlier, thick-planchet issues are better strikes than are the thin-planchet coins. Plain-edge 1795 cents often have low or shallow rims. To determine the difference between lightness caused by shallow dies and lightness caused by wear, study the characteristics of the die variety involved (see in particular the reverses of 1793, S-13, and 1793, S-12/S-15).

Availability. Cents of this type are readily available, although those of 1793 are rare and in great demand, and certain die varieties of the other dates are rare and can command high prices. Typical grades range from AG upward to Fine, VF, and, less often, EF. Attractive AU and MS coins are elusive, and when found are usually dated 1795, the thin planchet variety.

G-4, 6 (Good). *Obverse:* The portrait is worn smooth and is seen only in outline form, although the eye and nose can be discerned. LIBERTY and the date are complete, although the date may be weak. Dentils are gone on varieties struck with low or shallow rims. *Reverse:* Extensive wear is seen overall. From half to two-thirds of the letters in UNITED STATES OF AMERICA and the fraction numerals are worn away. Certain shallow-relief dies may have letters missing. Darkness, porosity, and marks are common.

VG-8, 10 (Very Good). *Obverse:* The hair is more worn than in Fine, with detail present only in the lower areas. Detail can differ, and widely, depending on the dies. Border dentils are worn away on some issues (not as much for 1793 and 1794 coins), and the border blends into the field in areas in which the rim was low to begin with, or in areas struck slightly off center. LIBERTY and the date are bold. *Reverse:* The wreath, bow, and lettering are seen in outline form, and some leaves and letters may be indistinct in parts. Border dentils are worn away, and the border blends into the field in most if not all of the periphery. In certain die varieties and die states, some letters may be very weak, or missing.

F-12, 15 (Fine). *Obverse:* The hair details are mostly worn away, with about one-third visible, mainly at the lower edges. Border dentils are weak or worn away in areas, depending on the height of the rim when the coin was struck. *Reverse:* The wreath leaves are worn flat, but their edges are distinct. Border dentils are weak or worn away in areas. In Fine and lower, planchet darkness and light porosity are common, as are scattered marks.

VF-20, 30 (Very Fine). *Obverse:* Wear on the portrait has reduced the hair detail to indistinct or flat at the center, and on most varieties the individual strands at the left edge are blended together. *Reverse:* The leaf details are nearly completely worn away at VF-20, and with slight detail at VF-30. Some border letters may be weak, and ditto for the central letters (on later varieties of this type). The border dentils are blended together with many indistinct. No luster is seen. The sharpness of details depends on the die variety.

EF-40, 45 (Extremely Fine). *Obverse:* For most varieties, the center of the coin shows wear or a small, flat area. Other hair details are strong. Luster is minimal or nonexistent at EF-40, and may survive in traces in protected areas (such as between the letters) at EF-45. *Reverse:* Wear is seen on the highest wreath and ribbon areas and the letters. Luster is minimal, but likely more noticeable than on the obverse, as the fields are protected by the designs and lettering. Sharpness varies depending on the die variety but is generally shallower than on the obverse, this being particularly true for many 1795 cents.

AU-50, 53, 55, 58 (About Uncirculated). *Obverse:* Very light wear is evident on the highest parts of the hair above and to the left of the ear. Friction is seen on the cheek and the liberty cap. Coins at this level are usually on smooth planchets and have nice eye appeal. Color is very important. Dark and porous coins are relegated to lower grades, even if AU-level sharpness is present. *Reverse:* (Grading at the AU level is mainly done by viewing the obverse, as many reverses are inherently shallow from lower-relief dies.) Very light wear is evident on the higher parts of the leaves and the ribbon, and, to a lesser extent, on the lettering. The reverse may have original luster, toned brown, varying from minimal (at lower AU grades) to extensive.

MS-60 to 70 (Mint State). *Obverse:* In MS-60 and 61 there are some traces of abrasion on the higher areas of the portrait. Luster is incomplete, particularly in the field. At MS-63, luster is complete, and no abrasion evident. At higher levels, the luster is deeper, and some original mint color may be seen on some examples. At MS-65 there may be some scattered contact marks and possibly some traces of fingerprints or discoloration, but these should be very minimal and not at all distracting. Generally, Liberty Cap cents of 1793 (in particular) and 1794 are harder to find with strong eye appeal than are those of 1795 and 1796. Mint State coins of 1795 often have satiny luster. Above MS-65, a coin should approach perfection, especially if dated 1795 or 1796. Certified MS cents can vary in their strictness of interpretation. *Reverse:* In the lower MS grades some abrasion is seen on the higher areas of the leaves. Generally, luster is complete in all grades, as the open areas are protected by the lettering and wreath. Often on this type the reverse is shallower than the obverse and has a lower rim.

Head of 1793 (1793–1794)
Head in high, rounded relief.

Head of 1794 (1794)
Well-defined hair; hook on lowest curl.

Head of 1795 (1794–1796)
Head in low relief; no hook on lowest curl.

1795, "Jefferson Head"

Beaded Border (1793)

Dentil Border (1794–1796)

1794, Normal Reverse

1794, Starred Reverse

	Mintage	Cert	Avg	%MS	VG-8	F-12	VF-20	EF-40	AU-50	MS-60BN	MS-63BN	Recent Auction Record
1793, Liberty Cap	11,056	113	17.9	1	$12,000	$17,500	$45,000	$80,000	$170,000			$282,000, AU-53, January 2013
1794, All kinds	918,521											
1794, Head of 1793		47	26.0	11	3,000	4,200	9,500	23,000	40,000	$90,000	$175,000	$881,250, MS-64BN, January 2013
1794, Head of 1794		864	33.1	8	550	800	1,800	4,000	6,100	13,000	26,000	$205,625, MS-66RB, April 2013
1794, Head in Low Relief					550	800	1,800	4,000	6,100	13,000	26,000	
1794, Exact Head of 1795 (a)		536	30.7	8	550	850	2,000	4,800	8,000	25,000	50,000	$235,000, MS-62, January 2014
1794, Starred Reverse †		35	13.4	0	20,000	42,000	83,000	175,000	625,000			$15,275, AG-3, October 2013
1794, No Fraction Bar		11	39.9	36	650	1,200	2,700	6,500	15,000	38,000	75,000	$381,875, MS-64BN, January 2014
1795, Lettered Edge	37,000	140	36.3	24	550	1,000	2,100	5,250	7,500	11,000	24,000	$79,313, MS-65BN, April 2013
1795, Plain Edge	501,500	561	29.7	11	425	650	1,350	3,000	6,000	8,200	20,000	$21,150, MS-63BN, April 2013
1795, Reeded Edge (9 known)		4	5.0	0	750,000 (b)	1,110,000						$646,250, VG-10, January 2014
1795, "Jefferson Head" (c)		12	14.0	0	34,000	55,000	125,000	250,000				$184,000, VF-25, March 2012
1795, "Jefferson Head," Lettered Edge (c) (3 known)		3	15.7	0	50,000	85,000	225,000					
1796, Liberty Cap	109,825	306	25.9	11	600	1,200	2,400	5,500	12,000	26,000		$141,000, MS-64RB, January 2014

† Ranked in the *100 Greatest U.S. Coins* (fourth edition). **a.** The 1794 coin with Head of 1795 has a hooked curl but is in low relief. **b.** Value in G-4 is $275,000. **c.** The "Jefferson Head" is not a regular Mint issue, but a design struck privately in an attempt to win a federal coinage contract.

DRAPED BUST
(1796–1807)
Designer Robert Scot; weight 10.89 grams; composition copper; approx. diameter 29 mm; plain edge.

History. The Draped Bust cent made its debut in 1796, following a coinage of Liberty Cap cents the same year. The motif, from a drawing by Gilbert Stuart, was first employed on certain silver dollars of 1795. (Its use on half cents did not take place until later, in 1800.) In 1798 Miss Liberty's head was slightly modified in design.

Striking and Sharpness. Most Draped Bust cents were struck on high-quality planchets. (This high planchet quality is less predictable for varieties of 1796, and almost never present for those of 1799 and 1800.) Detail sharpness differs by die variety. Weakness, when present, is usually on the hair behind the forehead, on the leaves in the upper part of the wreath, and among the dentils. However, a weak strike can show up in other areas as well. Many if not most Draped Bust cents are imperfectly centered, with the result that dentils can be bold on one side of a coin and light or even missing on the opposite side; this can occur on obverse as well as reverse. Typically this does not affect value. Certain Draped Bust cents of 1796 have semi-prooflike surfaces. Those of 1799 often have rough or porous surfaces and are found in lower grades.

Availability. As a type, Draped Bust cents are readily available, although the 1799, 9 Over 8, and 1799 are the keys to the series, and the 1804 is elusive. A different scenario evolves when considering engraving errors, repunched dates, and recut letters and numerals; many of these varieties are very difficult to locate. The eye appeal of these rarities usually is below par. Other years are generally available in high grades, VF and finer, well struck (except for some reverse leaves, in instances), on high-quality planchets, and with excellent eye appeal. Dark and porous coins are plentiful among coins graded below VF. True MS coins tend to be MS-60 to 63, when found.

VF-20, 30 (Very Fine). *Obverse:* Wear on the portrait has reduced the hair detail greater than at EF, especially to the left of the forehead. The rolling curls are solid or flat on their highest areas, as well as by the ribbon behind the hair. The border dentils are blended together, with many indistinct. No luster is seen. *Reverse:* The leaf details are nearly completely worn away at VF-20, and with slight detail at VF-30. The border dentils are blended together, with many indistinct. No luster is seen.

EF-40, 45 (Extremely Fine). *Obverse:* Wear is seen on the portrait overall, with reduction or elimination of some separation of hair strands on the highest part. By the standards of the Early American Coppers society, if the "spit curl" in front of Liberty's ear is missing, the coin is not EF. The cheek shows more wear than on higher grades, and the drapery covering the bosom is lightly worn on the higher areas. Often weakness in the separation of the drapery lines can be attributed to weakness in striking. Luster is minimal or nonexistent at EF-40, and may survive in among the letters of LIBERTY at EF-45. *Reverse:* Wear is seen on the highest wreath and ribbon areas, and on the letters. Luster is minimal, but likely more noticeable than on the obverse, as the fields are protected by the designs and lettering. Most or nearly all of the "ribbing" (veins) in the leaves is visible (striking plays a part, and some leaves may be weak even in higher grades).

AU-50, 53, 55, 58 (About Uncirculated). *Obverse:* Friction is seen on the higher parts, particularly the hair and the cheek. Friction and scattered marks are in the field, ranging from more extensive at AU-50 to minimal at 58. Luster may be seen in protected areas, minimal at AU-50, more visible at 58. At AU-58 the field may retain some luster as well. In many instances, the luster is smaller in area and lesser in "depth" than on the reverse of this type. *Reverse:* Friction is seen on the higher wreath leaves and (not as easy to discern) on the letters. The die variety should be checked. The fields, protected by the designs, show friction, but not as noticeably as on the obverse. At AU-55 and 58, little if any friction is seen. The reverse may have original luster, toned brown, minimal on lower AU grades, often extensive at AU-58.

MS-60 to 70 (Mint State). *Obverse:* In MS-60 and 61, some slight abrasion can be seen on the higher areas of the portrait, especially the cheek, and the hair behind the forehead. Luster in the field is incomplete, particularly in the center of the open areas, which on this type are very open, especially at the right. At MS-63, luster is nearly complete, and no abrasions evident. In higher levels, the luster is complete and deeper, and some original mint color should be seen. MS-64 coins may have some slight discoloration or

scattered contact marks. An MS-65 or higher coin has full, rich luster; no marks visible except under magnification; and a nice blend of brown toning or nicely mixed (not stained or blotchy) mint color and natural brown toning. *Reverse:* In the lower MS grades some abrasions are seen on the higher areas of the leaves. Generally, luster is complete in all MS grades, as the open areas are protected by the lettering and wreath. Sharpness of the leaves can vary by die variety. Otherwise, the same comments apply as for the obverse.

Reverse of 1794 (1794–1796)
Note double leaf at top right;
14–16 leaves on left, 16–18 leaves on right.
(Shown 1.5x actual size)

Reverse of 1795 (1795–1798)
Note single leaf at top right;
17–21 leaves on left, 16–20 leaves on right.
(Shown 1.5x actual size)

Reverse of 1797 (1796–1807)
Note double leaf at top right;
16 leaves on left, 19 leaves on right.
(Shown 1.5x actual size)

1796, LIHERTY Error

1797, Wreath With Stems

1797, Stemless Wreath

Style 1 Hair
Found on all coins of 1796 and 1797, many 1798 varieties, and 1800, 1800 Over 1798.
(Shown 1.5x actual size)

Style 2 Hair
Found on coins of 1798–1807.
Note the extra curl near shoulders.
(Shown 1.5x actual size)

1798, 8 Over 7

1799, 9 Over 8

1799, Normal Date

1800, 1800 Over 1798

1800, 80 Over 79

1800, Normal Date

1801, Normal Reverse

1801, Fraction 1/000

**1801, 3 Errors: 1/000,
One Stem, and IINITED**

1801, 1/100 Over 1/000

1802, Normal Reverse

1802, Fraction 1/000

1802, Stemless Wreath

1803, Small Date

1803, Large Date

*Note that Small Date varieties have a blunt 1 in the date,
and Large Date varieties have a pointed 1 and noticeably larger 3.*

1803, Small Fraction

1803, Large Fraction

1803, 1/100 Over 1/000

1803, Stemless Wreath

1804, Broken Dies
Sheldon-266c.

Unofficial 1804 "Restrike"
Breen-1761, Pollock-6050.

Small 1807, 7 Over 6, Blunt 1

Large 1807, 7 Over 6, Pointed 1

1807, Small Fraction

1807, Large Fraction

1807, "Comet" Variety
*Note the die break behind
Miss Liberty's head.*

	Mintage	Cert	Avg	%MS	VF-20	EF-40	AU-50	MS-60BN	MS-63BN	MS-63RB	MS-65BN	Recent Auction Record
1796, Draped Bust, All kinds	363,375											
1796, Reverse of 1794		59	22.9	5	$2,750	$6,250	$12,500	$18,000	$26,500	$46,000	$80,000	$11,750, AU-53, January 2014
1796, Reverse of 1795		108	27.6	12	2,750	6,500	13,000	19,500	30,000	50,000	80,000	$20,563, AU-58, January 2014
1796, Reverse of 1797		60	28.8	23	2,000	4,000	6,500	8,500	14,000	22,500	23,000	$28,200, MS-64BN, April 2013
1796, LIHERTY Error		32	26.1	13	4,800	12,000	30,000	60,000	85,000	110,000	125,000	$2,350, VF-20, August 2013
1796, Stemless Reverse *(3 known)*		1	2.0	0	(a)							
1797, All kinds	897,510											
1797, Gripped Edge, 1795-Style Reverse		52	24.6	6	1,000	3,500	7,750	26,000				$1,351, VG-8, March 2013
1797, Plain Edge, 1795-Style Reverse		22	33.0	23	1,200	4,000	8,250	26,500				$940, EF-40, June 2014
1797, 1797 Reverse, With Stems		435	36.0	24	975	2,100	3,600	5,750	11,750	16,500	21,500	$41,125, MS-65RB, January 2013
1797, 1797 Reverse, Stemless		40	29.5	10	2,250	6,750	26,000	60,000				$1,645, VF-25, January 2014
1798, All kinds	1,841,745											
1798, 8 Over 7		56	19.8	2	3,000	7,500	14,000					$14,688, AU-58, February 2013
1798, Reverse of 1796		31	24.7	6	2,000	6,750	9,500	20,000	35,000	—		$3,290, VF-20, September 2013
1798, Style 1 Hair		298	26.8	4	600	2,200	5,000	10,000	17,750	28,500		$11,750, MS-63BN, January 2014
1798, Style 2 Hair		508	29.3	2	575	1,950	3,500	8,350	16,500	27,500		$3,290, AU-55, February 2014
1799, 9 Over 8 (b)		68	13.6	3	30,000	80,000	210,000	475,000				$70,500, VF-25, January 2014
1799, Normal Date (b)		181	10.0	0	27,000	70,000	200,000	450,000				$99,875, EF-35, January 2013
1800, All kinds	2,822,175											
1800, 1800 Over 1798, Style 1 Hair		39	26.2	5	1,500	3,850	7,000	10,000	14,000	30,000		$2,585, G-6, January 2014

a. Value in AG-3 is $10,000; in G-4, $25,000. **b.** Included in "1798, All kinds" mintage.

	Mintage	Cert	Avg	%MS	VF-20	EF-40	AU-50	MS-60BN	MS-63BN	MS-63RB	MS-65BN	Recent Auction Record
1800, 80 Over 79, Style 2 Hair		132	25.6	6	$600	$2,200	$4,000	$8,000	$25,000	$40,000		$19,388, MS-62BN, June 2014
1800, Normal Date		246	29.3	10	550	1,900	3,000	6,250	11,500	17,500		$70,500, MS-65BN, January 2013
1801, All kinds	1,362,837											
1801, Normal Reverse		232	28.6	10	450	1,250	3,000	7,500	14,500	25,000		$14,100, F-15, January 2014
1801, 3 Errors: 1/000, One Stem, and IINITED		60	19.5	5	2,700	7,750	13,500	35,000	115,000			$3,525, EF-40, August 2013
1801, Fraction 1/000		68	24.8	6	650	2,200	4,500	12,500	28,000			$4,406, EF-40, January 2014
1801, 1/100 Over 1/000		22	30.4	18	1,000	2,500	6,250	15,000	27,500	57,500		$1,528, EF-45, January 2014
1802, All kinds	3,435,100											
1802, Normal Reverse		741	32.4	6	400	1,000	1,900	4,500	9,000	16,000	$27,500	$16,450, MS-64BN, January 2013
1802, Fraction 1/000		46	34.7	11	600	1,700	3,000	7,200	15,500	25,000	42,500	$11,163, AU-55, January 2014
1802, Stemless Wreath		85	31.8	7	500	1,400	2,750	6,300	13,500	22,500	38,500	$2,938, AU-55, October 2013
1803, All kinds	3,131,691											
1803, Small Date, Small Fraction		558	34.5	10	350	1,000	1,450	3,000	8,500	17,000	27,500	$55,813, MS-65BN, January 2014
1803, Small Date, Large Fraction		255	31.9	8	350	1,000	1,450	3,000	8,500	17,000	27,500	$18,800, MS-64BN, January 2014
1803, Large Date, Small Fraction		27	15.8	0	35,000	80,000						$15,275, VF-20, January 2014
1803, Large Date, Large Fraction		11	42.4	9	1,500	4,250	8,500					$353, VF-20, August 2013
1803, 1/100 Over 1/000		42	36.0	14	750	2,200	3,500	6,750	18,000	30,000	65,000	$2,820, EF-45, September 2013
1803, Stemless Wreath		25	42.0	20	750	2,000	2,750	6,000	17,000	30,000	65,000	$8,225, AU-58, January 2014
1804 (c)	96,500	253	15.5	1	7,500	16,000	47,000	130,000				$223,250, AU-55, January 2013
1804, Unofficial Restrike of 1860 (d)		120	59.8	83		1,000	1,100	1,200	1,450	2,000	1,700	$489, AU-55, August 2011
1805	941,116	285	37.2	11	475	1,200	2,500	5,250	15,000			$9,400, MS-62BN, April 2014
1806	348,000	169	34.7	11	600	2,000	3,000	8,500	28,000			$3,819, AU-50, February 2013
1807, All kinds	829,221											
1807, Small 1807, 7 Over 6, Blunt 1		21	19.5	0	21,000	46,000	150,000					$2,585, F-15, January 2014
1807, Large 1807, 7 Over 6, Pointed 1		161	28.9	11	500	1,200	2,300	5,850	23,500			$70,500, MS-65BN, April 2014
1807, Small Fraction		13	25.1	8	550	1,750	3,000	6,000	19,500			$1,763, AU-50, August 2013
1807, Large Fraction		93	30.2	11	450	1,100	2,300	4,600	16,500			$5,750, AU-58, August 2011
1807, "Comet" Variety		61	35.8	23	850	2,650	4,200	10,500	25,500	40,000		$27,600, MS-61BN, February 2012

c. All genuine 1804 cents have a crosslet 4 in the date and a large fraction. The 0 in the date is in line with the 0 in OF on the reverse. **d.** Discarded Mint dies were used, circa 1860, to create "restrikes" (actually novodels or fantasies) of the scarce 1804 cent for collectors. These combine two unrelated dies: an altered 1803 die was used for the obverse, and a die of the 1820 cent for the reverse. The resulting coins cannot be confused with genuine 1804 cents.

CLASSIC HEAD
(1808–1814)

Designer John Reich; weight 10.89 grams; composition copper; approx. diameter 29 mm; plain edge.

Sheldon-281.

History. The Classic Head design, by U.S. Mint assistant engraver John Reich, debuted in 1808. This cent type was minted through 1814. The quality of the coins' copper was poor during the War of 1812; the hostilities had ended the importation of high-quality planchets from England.

Striking and Sharpness. Striking sharpness varies, but often is poor. The cents of 1809 are notorious for having obverses much weaker than their reverses. Points to look for include sharpness of the dentils (which are often mushy, and in *most* instances incon-sistent), star centers (a key area), hair details, and leaf details. Classic Head cents often are dark and porous due to the copper stock used.

Availability. Examples are readily available in grades from well worn to VF and EF, although overall quality often leaves much to be desired. AU and MS coins are elusive. Grading numbers do not mean much, as a connoisseur might prefer a high-quality EF-45 to a poorly struck MS-63. Overall eye appeal of obverse and reverse is often sub-par, a characteristic of this type.

VF-20, 30 (Very Fine). *Obverse:* Wear on the portrait has reduced the hair detail, especially on the area to the right of the cheek and neck, but much can still be seen. *Reverse:* The wreath details, except for the edges of the leaves and certain of the tips (on leaves in lower relief), are worn away at VF-20, and with slightly more detail at VF-30.

EF-40, 45 (Extremely Fine). *Obverse:* Wear is seen on the portrait overall, but most hair detail still is present. The cheek shows light wear. Luster is minimal or nonexistent at EF-40, and may survive in among the letters of LIBERTY at EF-45. *Reverse:* Wear is seen on the highest wreath and ribbon areas and the letters. Leaf veins are visible except in the highest areas. Luster is minimal, but likely more noticeable than on the obverse, as the fields are protected by the designs and lettering.

AU-50, 53, 55, 58 (About Uncirculated). *Obverse:* Friction is seen on the higher parts, particularly the cheek. The hair will have friction and light wear, but will not be as obvious. Friction and scattered marks are in the field, ranging from more extensive at AU-50 to minimal at AU-58. Luster may be seen in protected areas, minimal at AU-50, but more visible at AU-58. At AU-58 the open field may retain some luster, as well. *Reverse:* Friction is seen on the higher wreath leaves and on the letters. Fields, protected by the designs, show some friction. At AU-55 and 58 little if any friction is seen. The reverse may have original luster, toned brown, minimal on lower AU grades, often extensive at AU-58.

MS-60 to 70 (Mint State). *Obverse:* In MS-60 and 61, some slight abrasions can be seen on the portrait, most evidently on the cheek, as the hair details are complex.

Luster in the field is complete or nearly complete; the field is not as open on this type as on the Draped Bust issues. At 63, luster should be complete, and no abrasion evident. In higher levels, the luster is complete and deeper, and some original mint color may be seen. MS-64 coins may have some slight discoloration or scattered contact marks. An MS-65 or higher coin has full, rich luster; no marks visible except under magnification; and a nice blend of brown toning or nicely mixed (not stained or blotchy) mint color and natural brown toning. Incomplete striking of some details, especially the obverse stars, is the rule. *Reverse:* In the lower MS grades, some abrasion is seen on the higher areas of the leaves. Mint luster is complete in all MS grades, as the open areas are protected by the lettering and wreath. Sharpness of the leaves can vary by die variety. Otherwise, the same comments apply as for the obverse.

| 1810, 10 Over 09 | 1810, Normal Date | 1812, Small Date | 1812, Large Date |

| 1811, Last 1 Over 0 | 1811, Normal Date | 1814, Plain 4 | 1814, Crosslet 4 |

	Mintage	Cert	Avg	%MS	VF-20	EF-40	AU-50	MS-60BN	MS-63BN	Recent Auction Record
1808	1,007,000	213	36.5	20	$750	$1,850	$3,250	$7,000	$14,500	$25,850, MS-64BN, January 2013
1809	222,867	154	29.9	9	1,400	4,000	7,200	11,500	22,500	$28,200, MS-63BN, January 2013
1810, All kinds	1,458,500									
1810, 10 Over 09		113	30.7	9	800	1,700	2,750	8,000	15,000	$10,575, AU-55, April 2013
1810, Normal Date		231	35.5	14	750	1,600	2,700	8,000	16,500	$32,900, MS-64BN, January 2014
1811, All kinds	218,025									
1811, Last 1 Over 0		59	28.0	5	1,750	5,250	10,000	25,000	55,000	$364, VF-20, August 2013
1811, Normal Date		175	33.3	14	1,000	2,200	5,500	10,000	20,000	$23,500, MS-64BN, January 2013
1812, All kinds	1,075,500									
1812, Small Date		249	34.3	7	750	1,600	2,500	5,250	11,000	$44,063, MS-65RB, June 2014
1812, Large Date		119	33.4	13	750	1,600	2,500	5,250	11,000	$3,819, AU-55, January 2014
1813	418,000	310	37.1	10	850	1,750	2,800	6,000	12,500	$211,500, MS-65BN, January 2013
1814, All kinds	357,830									
1814, Plain 4		204	34.6	15	750	1,600	2,400	5,000	10,000	$47,000, MS-65BN, April 2014
1814, Crosslet 4		307	38.1	15	750	1,600	2,400	5,000	10,500	$7,638, AU-58, March 2014

LIBERTY HEAD:
MATRON HEAD
(1816–1835)
AND
MATRON HEAD MODIFIED
(1835–1839)

Matron Head: Designer Robert Scot or John Birch; weight 10.89 grams; composition copper; approx. diameter 28–29 mm; plain edge.

Matron Head Modified: Designer Christian Gobrecht; weight 10.89 grams; composition copper; diameter 27.5 mm; plain edge.

Matron Head (1816–1835)
Newcomb-1.

Matron Head Modified (1835–1839)
Newcomb-5.

History. The term *Matron Head* describes cents of 1816 to 1835 (none were struck in 1815). Engraver Christian Gobrecht experimented with various "Matron Head Modified" portraits in the later 1830s.

Striking and Sharpness. Planchet quality is generally very good for Liberty Head cents. Color tends to be lighter on coins of the 1830s than on earlier dates. Striking can vary. Points to check include the obverse stars (in particular), the highest hair details, and the leaves on the reverse. Dentils can range from sharp to weak, and centering is often irregular. The reverse design is essentially the same as that used on the Classic Head of 1808 to 1814, and can be graded the same way. This motif stood up to circulation particularly well.

Availability. As a type, Liberty Head cents are easily available. The scarcest date by far is 1823 (and the related 1823, 3 Over 2 overdate). Cents of 1816 to 1820 (particularly 1818 and 1820) are readily available in MS. Other MS coins are generally scarce, although those of the 1830s are more readily available than those of the teens and 1820s. Circulated examples exist in approximate relationship to their mintages. Planchet quality and striking sharpness vary in all grades.

EF-40, 45 (Extremely Fine). *Obverse:* Wear is seen on the portrait overall, but most hair detail is still present, except in higher areas. The cheek shows light wear. Luster is minimal or nonexistent at EF-40, and may survive in among the letters of LIBERTY at EF-45. *Reverse:* Wear is seen on the highest wreath and ribbon areas, and on the letters. Leaf veins are visible except in the highest areas. Luster is minimal, but likely more noticeable than on the obverse, as the fields are protected by the designs and lettering.

AU-50, 53, 55, 58 (About Uncirculated). *Obverse:* Friction is seen on the higher parts, particularly the cheek. The hair has friction and light wear, usually most notable in the general area above BER (LIB-ERTY). Friction and scattered marks are in the field, ranging from extensive at AU-50 to minimal at 58. Luster may be seen in protected areas, minimal at AU-50, more visible at 58. At AU-58 the field may retain some luster as well. *Reverse:* Friction is seen on the higher wreath leaves and on the letters. Fields, protected by the designs, show friction. At AU-55 and 58 little if any friction is seen. The reverse may have original luster, toned brown, minimal on lower AU grades, often extensive at AU-58.

MS-60 to 70 (Mint State). *Obverse:* In MS-60 and 61, some slight abrasions can be seen on the portrait, most evidently on the cheek, which is very prominent. Check higher areas of the hair, particularly the top and back of Liberty's head, but do not confuse with lightness of strike. Luster in the field is complete or nearly complete. At MS-63, luster should be complete, and no abrasion is evident. In higher levels, the luster is complete and deeper, and some original mint color may be seen. MS-64 coins may have some minimal discoloration or scattered contact marks. An MS-65 or finer coin will have full, rich luster; no marks visible except under magnification; and a nice blend of brown toning or nicely mixed mint color and natural brown toning. *Reverse:* In lower MS some abrasion is seen on the higher areas of the leaves. Mint luster is complete in all MS grades, as the open areas are protected by the lettering and wreath. Sharpness of the leaves can vary by die variety. Otherwise, the same comments apply as for the obverse.

1817, 13 Stars

1817, 15 Stars

1819, 9 Over 8

1819, Large Date

1819, Small Date

1820, 20 Over 19
Note the 1 under the 2.

1820, Large Date
Note the plain-topped 2.

1820, Small Date
Note the curl-topped 2.

1823, 3 Over 2

Unofficial 1823 "Restrike"
Newcomb-3, Breen-1823, Pollock-6220.

1824, 4 Over 2

1826, 6 Over 5

**Date Size, Through 1828
(Large, Narrow Date)**

**Date Size, 1828 and Later
(Small, Wide Date)**

**Large Letters
(1808–1834)**
*Note the size and proximity
of individual letters.*

**Medium Letters
(1829–1837)**
*Note the isolation of the let-
ters, especially of STATES.*

**1834, Large 8, Large Stars,
Large Reverse Letters**
Newcomb-6.

**1834, Large 8, Large Stars,
Medium Reverse Letters**
Newcomb-5.

**1834, Large 8, Small Stars,
Medium Reverse Letters**
Newcomb-3.

**1834, Small 8, Large Stars,
Medium Reverse Letters**
Newcomb-1.

**1835, Large 8, Large Stars,
Matron Head**

**1835, Small 8, Small
Stars, Matron Head**

1835, Matron Head
Shown 1.5x actual size.

1835, Head of 1836
Shown 1.5x actual size.

**Medium Letters
(1829–1837)**

**Small Letters
(1837–1839)**

1837
Note the plain hair cords.

1837, Head of 1838
*Note the slim bust and
the beaded hair cords.*

1839, 1839 Over 1836
Note the closed 9 and the plain hair cords.

1839, Silly Head
Note the prominent lock of hair at the forehead.

1839, Booby Head
Note the shoulder tip. Also note the absence of a line under CENT.

	Mintage	Cert	Avg	%MS	EF-40	AU-50	MS-60BN	MS-63BN	MS-63RB	MS-65BN	MS-65RB	Recent Auction Record
1816	2,820,982	539	55.9	59	$190	$300	$500	$700	$1,200	$1,800	$3,200	$3,819, MS-65BN, April 2014
1817, All kinds	3,948,400											
1817, 13 Stars		581	54.3	55	140	225	450	600	900	1,550	2,700	$5,875, F-15, January 2014
1817, 15 Stars		102	47.2	13	600	900	2,800	3,600	8,000	21,000	40,000	$9,400, VF-20, January 2014
1818	3,167,000	1,394	59.0	75	135	225	450	600	925	1,600	2,800	$30,550, AU-55, January 2014
1819, All kinds	2,671,000											
1819, 9 Over 8		129	54.7	41	275	375	750	1,300	2,500	4,000		$2,115, MS-63BN, December 2013
1819, Large Date		218	54.8	50	150	300	475	700	1,250	2,000		$2,585, MS-64BN, January 2014
1819, Small Date		210	53.2	61	150	300	475	700	1,250	2,000		$11,750, MS-65RB, January 2013
1820, All kinds	4,407,550											
1820, 20 Over 19		108	46.4	31	335	550	1,000	1,600	2,750	4,500	10,500	$4,700, MS-64BN, January 2014
1820, Large Date		849	61.9	89	175	250	400	600	825	1,250	2,000	$16,450, MS-62BN, January 2014
1820, Small Date		76	53.8	62	250	450	900	1,200	2,000	2,800	4,200	$4,994, MS-64BN, January 2014
1821 (a)	389,000	250	34.3	8	1,300	2,300	7,750	11,000	27,000			$28,200, MS-63RB, January 2013
1822	2,072,339	344	46.9	29	425	700	1,200	1,800	3,000	4,900	12,000	$5,581, VG-8, January 2014

a. Wide and closely spaced AMER varieties are valued the same.

Chart continued on next page.

	Mintage	Cert	Avg	%MS	EF-40	AU-50	MS-60BN	MS-63BN	MS-63RB	MS-65BN	MS-65RB	Recent Auction Record
1823, 3 Over 2	(a)	149	24.5	3	$2,200	$4,500	$12,500	—				$11,163, AU-53, January 2014
1823, Normal Date	(a)	147	21.6	1	3,750	7,500	18,500	$30,000	$62,000	$115,000	$250,000	$3,584, EF-35, January 2014
1823, Unofficial Restrike (b)		89	63.7	98	550	925	1,250	1,500	1,600	1,750	2,200	$2,350, MS-64BN, December 2013
1824, All kinds	1,262,000											
1824, 4 Over 2		85	36.3	11	1,500	2,500	6,000	10,000	21,000	35,000		$32,900, MS-63BN, August 2013
1824, Normal Date		223	45.2	23	500	850	2,400	4,000	5,000	8,000		$23,500, MS-64RB, January 2013
1825	1,461,100	267	47.9	36	325	650	1,850	2,750	4,700	7,500		$6,463, MS-64BN, January 2014
1826, All kinds	1,517,425											
1826, 6 Over 5		36	47.1	25	975	1,500	2,800	5,300	7,500	19,000		$10,575, MS-62BN, January 2014
1826, Normal Date		379	52.0	38	250	450	900	1,500	2,650	3,100		$3,525, AU-58, January 2014
1827	2,357,732	351	48.5	32	225	425	775	1,400	2,500	3,250		$3,819, MS-65BN, January 2014
1828, All kinds	2,260,624											
1828, Large Narrow Date		223	46.2	27	210	400	1,250	1,750	2,800	4,250	10,000	$3,055, MS-61BN, January 2014
1828, Small Wide Date		39	49.3	33	275	650	1,950	3,500	5,500	20,000		$7,638, MS-64BN, February 2013
1829, All kinds	1,414,500											
1829, Large Letters		126	46.9	35	200	385	650	1,500	3,000	5,200	12,000	$8,519, MS-65BN, June 2014
1829, Medium Letters		35	36.5	14	800	2,500	6,500	10,500	13,000	17,000	25,000	$7,050, AU-58, January 2014
1830, All kinds	1,711,500											
1830, Large Letters		219	48.2	34	190	300	550	1,000	1,900	2,700	3,600	$11,750, AU-50, January 2014
1830, Medium Letters		20	37.1	10	2,000	4,100	14,000	25,000	30,000	32,000	56,000	$3,055, EF-40, June 2013
1831, All kinds	3,359,260											
1831, Large Letters		290	52.0	45	150	250	400	700	1,150	1,800	3,500	$5,875, MS-65RB, June 2014
1831, Medium Letters		83	49.7	40	200	350	750	1,600	2,750	2,300	3,700	$3,290, MS-62BN, January 2014
1832, All kinds	2,362,000											
1832, Large Letters		143	52.1	42	150	250	375	650	1,000	2,300	3,300	$3,525, MS-65BN, January 2014
1832, Medium Letters		57	53.7	42	200	550	900	1,200	2,250	2,900	4,500	$940, MS-62BN, July 2014
1833	2,739,000	442	53.4	46	150	250	375	750	1,500	2,600	3,700	$18,800, MS-67RB, January 2014
1834, All kinds	1,855,100											
1834, Lg 8, Stars, and Rev Ltrs		23	48.8	26	550	1,100	2,250	4,000	7,500	8,200		$2,820, AU-58, January 2014
1834, Lg 8 and Stars, Med Ltrs		17	44.8	24	3,400	6,500	10,000	12,000	17,000	22,000		$58,750, MS-65BN, January 2014
1834, Lg 8, Sm Stars, Med Ltrs		145	52.1	42	140	240	350	625	925	1,400	3,000	$1,528, MS-63BN, January 2014
1834, Sm 8, Lg Stars, Med Ltrs		158	52.2	42	140	240	350	625	925	1,400	3,000	$4,994, MS-66BN, January 2014
1835, All kinds	3,878,400											
1835, Large 8 and Stars		29	50.7	28	225	400	750	1,400	2,250	2,100	4,200	$16,450, MS-64BN, January 2013
1835, Small 8 and Stars		108	48.5	33	175	375	475	675	1,400	1,750	3,750	$3,819, MS-63BN, January 2014
1835, Head of 1836		209	53.2	44	125	250	350	550	900	1,300	2,000	$2,820, MS-64BN, January 2014
1836	2,111,000	346	54.9	51	125	250	350	550	900	1,300	2,000	$2,820, MS-64BN, January 2014
1837, All kinds	5,558,300											
1837, Plain Cord, Medium Letters		361	56.1	56	125	250	350	550	775	1,200	2,300	$3,525, MS-65RB, February 2013
1837, Plain Cord, Small Letters		71	51.0	39	125	250	375	600	825	1,500	2,600	$411, AU-58, February 2014
1837, Head of 1838		446	56.5	60	110	200	325	500	775	1,200	1,900	$2,233, MS-66BN, January 2014
1838	6,370,200	1,424	56.3	58	120	225	335	575	925	1,325	2,150	$5,288, MS-66BN, June 2014
1839, All kinds	3,128,661											
1839, 1839 Over 1836, Plain Cords		137	15.7	1	9,000	20,000	63,000	90,000	150,000	235,000		$5,581, EF-35, January 2014
1839, Head of 1838, Beaded Cords		180	55.4	51	115	225	325	550	1,000	1,450	2,000	$1,645, MS-64BN, September 2013
1839, Silly Head		201	54.2	53	200	400	850	1,200	2,200	2,700	3,800	$12,925, MS-67BN, January 2014
1839, Booby Head		372	55.0	55	150	300	675	1,100	2,150	2,350	3,200	$28,200, MS-65RD, April 2014

a. Included in "1824, All kinds" mintage. b. The unofficial 1823 "restrikes" (actually novodels or fantasies) were made at the same time (around 1860) and by the same people as those of 1804. The coins were made from a discarded obverse die of 1823 and an 1813 reverse die—both heavily rusted, producing surface lumps. Most examples have both dies cracked.

Proof Liberty Head, Matron Head, Large Cents

PF-60 to 70 (Proof). Proofs were made for cents from 1817 onward. Often, coins called "Proofs" are only partially mirrorlike, and sometimes the striking is casual, e.g., with weakness on certain of the stars. Complicating the situation: all but one of the same die pairs were also used to make circulation strikes. Many misattributions were made generations ago, some of which have been perpetuated. True Proofs with deeply mirrored surfaces are in the small minority. *Obverse and Reverse:* Proofs that are extensively hairlined or have dull surfaces, this being characteristic of many issues (exceptions, when found, are usu- ally dated in the 1830s), are graded PF-60 to 62 or 63. Artificially toned and recolored coins may be graded lower. To qualify as PF-65 or higher, hairlines should be microscopic, and there should be no trace of friction. Surfaces should be prooflike or, better, fully mirrored and without dullness.

Proof Liberty Head, Matron Head, Modified, Large Cent

	Est Mintage	Cert	Finest	PF-60BN	PF-63BN	PF-64BN	PF-65BN	Recent Auction Record
1817	2–3	3	PF-63	$29,000	$35,000	$45,000	*$75,000*	$48,300, PF-66, July 2005
1819, 9 Over 8	2–3	1	PF-64	24,000	30,000	40,000	*60,000*	$32,200, PF-64BN, June 2005
1820	8–15	6	PF-64	35,000	50,000	40,000	60,000	$46,000, PF-64, November 2008
1821	4–6	13	PF-66	20,000	25,000	35,000	55,000	$35,250, PF-62BN, August 2013
1822	4–6	9	PF-64	35,000	55,000	65,000		$25,300, PF-63, March 2004
1823	2–3	2	PF-65	50,000	65,000	95,000		
1823, 3 Over 2	5–8	7	PF-65	45,000	60,000	75,000		$47,000, PF-64BN, June 2014
1827	5–8	7	PF-64	17,500	20,000	25,000	40,000	$20,125, PF-64, March 2004
1828	2–3	2	PF-65					
1829	2–3	4	PF-64	16,500	20,000	27,000	45,000	$47,000, PF-64RB, January 2014
1829, Bronzed	10–15	10	PF-66	15,000	18,000	26,000	40,000	$41,125, PF-65BN, August 2013
1830	2–3	4	PF-65				185,000	$16,500, PF-64, November 1988
1831	10–20	18	PF-65	12,000	14,500	24,500	50,000	$30,550, PF-65BN, January 2014
1832	2–4	3	PF-64					
1833. 3 Over 2		n/a	n/a					
1834	6–8	12	PF-66	10,000	15,000	21,000	40,000	$52,875, PF-60BN, January 2014
1836	6–8	6	PF-66	10,000	15,000	21,000	40,000	$47,000, PF-63RB, June 2014
1837	8–12	6	PF-67	25,000	30,000			$27,025, PF-63BN, January 2014
1838	10–20	18	PF-66	10,500	14,000	20,000	38,000	$64,625, PF-64RD, January 2014

LIBERTY HEAD: BRAIDED HAIR
(1839–1857)

Designer Christian Gobrecht; weight 10.89 grams; composition copper; diameter 27.5 mm; plain edge.

History. Christian Gobrecht's Braided Hair design was introduced in 1839. It loosely following the design he had created for the 1838 gold eagle. On issues of 1839 through part of 1843, Miss Liberty's portrait is tilted forward, with the left tip of her neck truncation over the 8 of the date. For most issues of 1843 and all later dates her head is larger and aligned in a more vertical position, and the tip of her neck is over the first digit of the date. The reverse lettering was made larger beginning in 1844. The net result is that cents after 1843 are less delicate in appearance than are those of earlier dates. These coins were made in large quantities, except for their final year. They remained in circulation in the United States until the late 1850s, not long enough to be worn down to very low grades. (Some circulated in the eastern part of Canada through the 1860s, accounting for many of the more worn examples seen today.)

Striking and Sharpness. Sharpness can vary. On the obverse, the star centers can be weak, especially for dates in the 1850s, and, less often, there can be lightness on the front of the coronet and the hair. On the reverse the leaves can be light, but most are well struck. The dentils can be mushy and indistinct on either side, this being particularly true of dates in the early and mid-1850s. Flaky or laminated planchets can be a problem, again among coins of the 1850s, in which tiny pieces of metal fall away from the surface, leaving areas in the field that interrupt the luster on MS coins.

Availability. All dates of Braided Hair cents are readily available, with the 1857 somewhat less so (it was minted in January 1857 in low quantity; seemingly not all were released). The delicate-featured issues of 1839 to 1843 are becoming more difficult to find in EF or finer grades without surface problems. Cents dated in the 1850s are usually seen in VF or higher grades. Certain die varieties attributed by Newcomb numbers can be scarce or rare. For issues in the 1850s the differences can be microscopic, thus limiting their numismatic appeal and making them unattributable unless in high grades. Hoards were found of some dates, particularly 1850 to 1856, making MS coins of these years more readily available than would otherwise be the case. MS-64 RD or higher coins with *original* color range from scarce to very rare for dates prior to 1850, but those of the 1850s are seen regularly (except for 1857). Coins below VF-20 are not widely collected and, for many issues, are too worn to attribute by die variety.

EF-40, 45 (Extremely Fine). *Obverse:* Wear is more extensive on the portrait than at AU, including the cheek, the hair above the ear, and the coronet. The star centers are worn down slightly (if they were sharply struck to begin with). Traces of luster are minimal, if at all existent. *Reverse:* The centers of the leaves are well worn, with detail visible only near the edges of the leaves and nearby, with the higher parts worn flat. Letters show significant wear. Luster, if present, is minimal.

AU-50, 53, 55, 58 (About Uncirculated). *Obverse:* Wear is evident on the cheek, the hair above the ear, and the tip of the coronet. Friction is evident in the field. At AU-58, luster may be present except in the center of the fields. As grade goes up to AU-58, wear becomes less evident on the cheek. Wear is seen on the stars, but is not as easy to discern as it is elsewhere and, in any event, many stars are weakly struck. At AU-50 there will be either no luster or only traces of luster close to the letters and devices. *Reverse:* Wear is most evident on the highest areas of the leaves and the ribbon bow. Luster is present in the fields. As grade goes up from AU-50 to 58, wear increases and luster decreases. At AU-50 there is either no luster or just traces close to the letters and devices.

MS-60 to 70 (Mint State). *Obverse:* In MS-60 and 61, some slight abrasions can be seen on the portrait, most evidently on the cheek. Check the tip of the coronet and the hair above the ear, as well. Luster in the field is complete or nearly so. At MS-63, luster should be complete, and no abrasion evident. If there is weakness on the hair it is due to light striking, not to wear; this also applies for the stars. In higher levels, the luster is complete and deeper, and some original mint color may be seen. Mint frost on this type is usually deep, sometimes satiny, but hardly ever prooflike. MS-64 coins may have some slight discoloration or scattered contact marks. An MS-65 or higher coin will have full, rich luster; no marks visible except under magnification; and a nice blend of brown toning or nicely mixed (not stained or blotchy) mint color and natural brown toning. *Reverse:* In the lower MS grades some abrasion is seen on the higher areas of the leaves. Mint luster is complete in all MS grades, as the open areas are protected by the lettering and wreath. The quality of the luster is the best way to grade both sides of this type.

| 1840, Large Date | 1840, Small Date | 1840, Small Date Over Large 18 | 1842, Small Date | 1842, Large Date |

Small Letters (1839–1843)   **Large Letters (1843–1857)**

Head of 1840 ("Petite Head," 1839–1843)
Shown 1.5x actual size.

Head of 1844 ("Mature Head," 1843–1857)
Shown 1.5x actual size.

1844, 44 Over 81   **1847, 7 Over "Small 7"**   **1851, 51 Over 81**

These are not true overdates, but are three of the more spectacular of several date-punch blunders of the 1844–1854 period. The so-called overdates of 1844 and 1851 each have the date punched upside down, then corrected normally.

1846, Small Date
Note the squat date and the closed 6.

1846, Medium Date
Note the medium date height and the ball-top 6.

1846, Tall Date
Note the vertically stretched date and the open-mouthed 6.

1855, Upright 5's   1855, Slanting 5's   1855, Knob on Ear

1856, Upright 5   1856, Slanting 5   1857, Large Date   1857, Small Date

	Mintage	Cert	Avg	%MS	EF-40	AU-50	MS-60BN	MS-63BN	MS-63RB	MS-65BN	MS-65RB	Recent Auction Record
1839	(a)	131	54.3	52	$110	$265	$400	$650	$850	$2,250	$4,500 (b)	$17,625, MS-65RB, January 2014
1840, All kinds	2,462,700											
1840, Large Date		225	55.8	56	85	200	300	500	1,150	1,200	2,500	$14,100, MS-64RD, January 2013
1840, Small Date		114	51.8	42	85	200	300	500	1,150	1,200	2,500	$734, MS-64BN, January 2014
1840, Small Date Over Large 18		36	45.4	39	200	400	900	1,600	2,000	2,350	5,000	$16,100, MS-65RB, September 2011
1841, Small Date	1,597,367	220	55.5	52	125	250	450	950	1,200	1,650	3,000 (c)	$4,113, MS-66BN, June 2014
1842, All kinds	2,383,390											
1842, Small Date		77	49.9	39	90	220	375	650	1,300	2,200	4,000 (d)	$23,500, MS-64RD, January 2014
1842, Large Date		280	54.8	53	85	150	300	500	850	1,800	3,000 (e)	$3,672, MS-64RB, January 2014
1843, All kinds	2,425,342											
1843, Petite, Small Letters		295	55.8	58	85	160	300	450	875	1,750	2,750	$2,468, MS-64BN, January 2014
1843, Petite, Large Letters		65	55.3	57	210	320	825	1,500	1,850	2,300	4,000	$4,406, MS-64BN, January 2014
1843, Mature, Large Letters		60	53.9	53	150	275	550	900	1,500	2,100	3,500	$9,988, MS-64RB, January 2014
1844, Normal Date	2,398,752	46	60.2	65	85	160	300	500	950	1,500	2,600	$8,225, MS-65BN, January 2014
1844, 44 Over 81	*	82	43.2	22	250	550	1,200	2,750	4,000	5,500		$1,175, MS-60BN, January 2014
1845	3,894,804	495	55.8	59	75	135	225	375	800	1,200	2,500	$4,406, MS-64RB, January 2014
1846, All kinds	4,120,800											
1846, Small Date		457	55.1	60	75	135	225	350	750	1,200	2,000	$8,813, MS-67BN, January 2014
1846, Medium Date		53	53.2	51	85	150	250	400	900	1,350	2,700	$705, MS-61BN, March 2013
1846, Tall Date		61	51.9	49	150	225	500	950	1,400	1,800	3,500	$56, VF-30, September 2011
1847	6,183,669	738	56.8	58	75	135	225	350	600	950	1,900	$11,750, MS-65RD, January 2014
1847, 7 Over "Small 7"	*	59	51.6	44	175	420	1,000	1,350	1,800	2,750	4,300	$9,694, MS-65BN, January 2014
1848	6,415,799	1,133	56.0	58	75	130	225	350	600	925	1,850	$13,513, MS-64RD, June 2014
1849	4,178,500	658	55.8	55	85	150	250	450	1,000	1,200	2,450	$2,585, MS-66RB, January 2014
1850	4,426,844	1,676	60.7	80	60	125	180	230	350	650	1,200 (f)	$7,050, MS-66RD, January 2014
1851, Normal Date	9,889,707	1,365	58.2	68	60	125	180	230	350	650	1,200 (g)	$4,113, MS-66RB, January 2014
1851, 51 Over 81	*	164	57.1	62	200	250	500	1,000	1,300	2,400	3,750	$1,763, MS-65BN, June 2014
1852	5,063,094	2,150	60.4	76	60	125	180	230	350	635	1,150 (f)	$14,100, MS-66RD, January 2013
1853	6,641,131	3,384	60.1	75	60	125	180	230	350	635	1,150 (h)	$6,463, MS-66RD, August 2013
1854	4,236,156	1,764	58.6	66	60	125	180	230	350	650	1,200 (g)	$1,528, MS-65BN, January 2014
1855, All kinds	1,574,829											
1855, Upright 5's		1,168	60.7	77	60	125	180	230	350	635	1,150 (f)	$5,875, MS-66RD, April 2014
1855, Slanting 5's		179	59.2	71	65	130	200	275	650	1,250	2,000 (i)	$1,175, MS-64BN, April 2014
1855, Slanting 5's, Knob on Ear		215	53.6	34	110	225	360	525	1,250	2,150		$2,115, MS-65BN, April 2014
1856, All kinds	2,690,463											
1856, Upright 5		894	60.4	76	65	130	200	270	365	675	1,200 (h)	$8,225, MS-66RD, January 2013
1856, Slanting 5		620	57.1	60	65	130	200	270	365	675	1,200 (h)	$5,875, MS-66RB, January 2013
1857, All kinds	333,546											
1857, Large Date		975	57.5	58	200	300	400	750	1,000	1,200	2,200	$2,115, MS-65BN, April 2014
1857, Small Date		335	53.0	33	200	310	430	800	1,100	1,500	2,400	$5,288, MS-65RB, February 2014

* Included in number above. **a.** Included in "1839, All kinds" mintage on page 38. **b.** Value in MS-65RD is $7,000. **c.** Value in MS-65RD is $4,500. **d.** Value in MS-65RD is $7,500. **e.** Value in MS-65RD is $7,250. **f.** Value in MS-65RD is $3,400. **g.** Value in MS-65RD is $3,500. **h.** Value in MS-65RD is $3,300. **i.** Value in MS-65RD is $3,750.

Proof Liberty Head, Braided Hair, Large Cents

PF-60 to 70. Except for 1841, Proof Braided Hair cents before 1855 range from rare to very rare. Those from 1855 to 1857 are seen with some frequency. Most later Proofs are well struck and of nice quality, but there are exceptions. Most pieces from this era that have been attributed as Proofs actually are such, but beware of deeply toned "Proofs" that really are prooflike, or circulation strikes with polished fields, recolored. *Obverse and Reverse:* At PF-65 and 66 hairlines show only under high magnification, and at PF-67 none are seen. The fields usually are deeply mirrorlike on issues after 1843, sometimes less so on earlier dates. Striking should be sharp, including the stars (unlike the situation for many Proofs of the Matron Head type). There is no evidence of friction. In lower grades, hairlines are more numerous, with a profusion at PF-60 to 62, and there is also a general dullness of the fields. Typical color for an undipped coin ranges from light or iridescent brown to brown with some traces of mint color. Except for issues after 1854, Proofs are nearly always BN or, less often, RB.

Proof Liberty Head, Braided Hair, Large Cent

	Est Mintage	Cert	Finest	PF-60BN	PF-63BN	PF-64BN	PF-65BN	Recent Auction Record
1840	15–20	18	PF-65	$4,500	$7,000	$10,500	$20,000	$14,100, PF-63RB, January 2014
1841	30–50	52	PF-66	4,000	6,000	9,500	16,000	$21,150, PF-65RB, August 2013
1842	10–20	11	PF-66	4,500	7,000	11,000	20,000	$14,100, PF-64BN, January 2014
1843	10–20	17	PF-66	4,500	7,000	11,000	20,000	$25,850, PF-66RB, June 2014
1844	10–20	15	PF-65	6,000	13,000	20,000	30,000	$55,813, PF-65RD, January 2014
1845	8–12	10	PF-66	4,250	8,000	15,000	23,000	$16,450, PF-64BN, April 2013
1846	8–12	15	PF-66	4,250	8,000	15,000	23,000	$30,550, PF-65BN, June 2014
1847	8–12	9	PF-65	4,250	8,000	15,000	23,000	$31,050, PF-65RB, February 2011
1848	15–20	24	PF-66	5,000	10,000	15,000	23,000	$14,100, PF-64BN, August 2013
1849	6–10	16	PF-65	4,250	8,500	16,000	25,000	$23,500, PF-65RB, August 2013
1850	6–10	8	PF-66	5,000	10,000	17,000	28,000	$19,550, PF-64RB, February 2011
1852	4–6	4	PF-65	4,000	7,500	19,000	47,000	$47,150, PF-64BN, February 2011
1854	4–6	16	PF-66	4,750	8,500	10,000	14,000	$28,200, PF-65RB, June 2014
1855	15–20	33	PF-66	4,500	6,000	8,750	12,000	$8,050, PF-64RB August 2011
1856	40–60	18	PF-66	4,000	5,000	7,000	12,500	$25,850, PF-66RB, November 2013
1857, Large Date	100–150	36	PF-66	4,000	5,000	7,000	12,500	
1857, Small Date	15–20	75	PF-66	5,000	6,000	8,000	13,000	$52,875, PF-65RD, April 2014

Note: Numismatic anachronisms dated 1868 were struck in nickel and in copper, featuring the large cent design last used in 1857. These likely were quietly and unofficially sold by Mint employees to collectors. They are classified as Judd-610 and 611 in *United States Pattern Coins.*

THE PASSING OF THE LARGE CENT AND HALF CENT

By 1857 the U.S. Mint's costs for manufacturing and distributing its half cents and large cents had risen so high that Mint Director James Ross Snowden reported that the copper coins "barely paid expenses." Both denominations had become unpopular, and they rarely circulated outside the nation's larger cities. With this pressure, change was on the horizon. The Treasury Department had recent precedent to tinker with coinage sizes and compositions. For several years in the early 1850s the Mint had issued silver coins of reduced weight, as a way to discourage their melting and export (the coins' silver content was greater than their face values). On the heels of this coinage reform, new legislation in 1857 replaced the large copper cent with a smaller copper-nickel coin of the same value, and terminated the half cent outright.

The coinage legislation of 1857 brought important benefits to the United States. Under its terms, Spanish coins were redeemed for melting at the Mint and exchanged for the new, small cents. The old-fashioned reckoning of business transactions in Spanish reales and medios, British shillings, and other currencies was (officially, at least) abandoned, and the American decimal system was popularized. Citizens found the new small cent to be convenient, and it quickly became a favored and useful means of retail trade. Tens of millions would be minted before the decade closed.

The hobby of coin collecting experienced a boom when the large cent and half cent passed away. Casual observers set aside the obsolete coins as mementoes of a time gone by, while more experienced collectors sought to assemble one of each date. Over the ensuing decades the study and collecting of these old coppers has become more and more specialized while still attracting hobby newcomers. Their devoted enthusiasts appreciate the coins' historical connections and cultural significance.

AN OVERVIEW OF SMALL CENTS

On May 25, 1857, the new small-diameter Flying Eagle cent made its debut. Designed by Chief Engraver James B. Longacre, the obverse featured a flying eagle, copied after Christian Gobrecht's silver dollar of 1836. The reverse showed an agricultural wreath enclosing the denomination. Problems developed with striking the pieces up properly, and in 1859 a new motif, the Indian Head cent, was introduced. With several variations this design was continued through 1909. In that year the Lincoln Wheat Ears cent was introduced. The series was continued for many years, until 1959, when the Memorial Reverse type was introduced, continuing the same Lincoln portrait on the obverse. Then in 2009 several different reverses were introduced to commemorate the 200th anniversary of the birth of Lincoln and in 2010 a new reverse to symbolize Lincoln's preservation of the Union.

Forming a type set of small cents is done easily enough, although the first two issues, the 1857–1858 Flying Eagle cent and the 1859 Indian Head with laurel wreath reverse, can be expensive in higher grades. Striking quality is a consideration for all small cents from 1857 to the end of the Indian Head series in 1909, but enough exist that finding a needle-sharp piece is simply a matter of time. Lincoln cents are easy enough to find sharply struck, though some varieties are more difficult to find this way than others.

FOR THE COLLECTOR AND INVESTOR: SMALL CENTS AS A SPECIALTY

Flying Eagle and Indian Head cents often are collected together by specialists, who usually aspire to add the pattern 1856 Flying Eagle to the series. Proof Flying Eagle and Indian Head cents form a separate specialty and are widely collected. The Flying Eagle and Indian Cent Collectors Society welcomes aficionados of these series. Its journal, *Longacre's Ledger,* serves as a forum for new discoveries, market information, and the exchange of ideas.

One of the foundations of American numismatics is the collecting of Lincoln cents, 1909 to date. Collectors have a wide variety of folders, albums, and holders to choose from; these have a tradition dating back to the 1930s, when R.K. Post of Neenah, Wisconsin, launched his "penny boards" (made for him by Whitman Publishing Co., which later acquired the rights), and Wayte Raymond marketed a series of "National" album pages. Today, a search through pocket change might yield coins dating back to 1959, the first year of the Lincoln Memorial reverse, before which date even high-mintage issues are hardly ever seen. A generation ago it was possible to find cents from 1909 onward. However, key issues such as 1909-S V.D.B. (the most famous of all "popular rarities" in the U.S. series), 1914-D, 1924-D, 1926-S, 1931-S, and 1955 Doubled Die eluded most enthusiasts.

Lincoln cents can be collected casually, or a specialty can be made of them. A dedicated enthusiast may want to secure one each in a grade such as MS-65, also taking care that each is sharply struck. There are quite a few issues, including Denver and San Francisco varieties from about 1916 to the late 1920s, that are plentiful *except* if sharply struck (with full hair detail on the Lincoln portrait, no tiny marks on Lincoln's shoulder, and sharp details and a smooth field on the reverse). With the Mint's rollout of four new reverse designs in 2009, and another in 2010, the Lincoln cent promises to intrigue another generation of Americans and continue to bring new collectors to the hobby.

RECOMMENDED READING

Bowers, Q. David. *A Buyer's and Enthusiast's Guide to Flying Eagle and Indian Head Cents,* Wolfeboro, NH, 1996.

Bowers, Q. David. *A Guide Book of Lincoln Cents,* Atlanta, GA, 2008.

Fivaz, Bill, and Stanton, J.T. *The Cherrypickers' Guide to Rare Die Varieties* (5th ed., vol. I), Atlanta, GA, 2009.

Lange, David W. *The Complete Guide to Lincoln Cents,* Wolfeboro, NH, 1996.

Snow, Richard. *Flying Eagle and Indian Cent Attribution Guide 1856–1909* (2nd ed.), Tuscon, AZ, 2010.

Snow, Richard. *A Guide Book of Flying Eagle and Indian Head Cents* (2nd ed.), Atlanta, GA, 2009.

Steve, Larry, and Flynn, Kevin. *Flying Eagle and Indian Cent Die Varieties,* Jarretteville, MD, 1995.

Taylor, Sol. *The Standard Guide to the Lincoln Cent,* Anaheim, CA, 1999.

Wexler, John, and Flynn, Kevin. *The Authoritative Reference on Lincoln Cents,* Rancocas, NJ, 1996.

FLYING EAGLE
(1857–1858)

Designer James B. Longacre; weight 4.67 grams; composition .880 copper, .120 nickel; diameter 19 mm; plain edge. All coined at Philadelphia Mint.

Shown 1.5x actual size

History. Large copper cents became increasingly expensive to produce, and during the 1850s the U.S. Mint experimented with smaller versions. Finally a new design and format were chosen: the Flying Eagle cent, of smaller diameter and 4.67 grams' weight (compared to nearly 11). Many patterns were made of this design in 1856, and restrikes were extensive, with the result that many numismatists collect the 1856 cent along with the regular series. Distribution of the new cents for circulation commenced on May 25, 1857. Problems resulted from striking the design properly, and the motif was discontinued in 1858. The coins remained in circulation until the early 1900s, by which time any found in pocket change were well worn.

Striking and Sharpness. The heavy wreath on the reverse was opposite in the dies (while in the press) from the head and tail of the eagle on the obverse, and, accordingly, many Flying Eagle cents were weakly struck in these areas. Today, this lightness of strike is most visible at each end of the eagle and on the wreath, particularly the higher areas, and on the vertical separation at the middle of the ribbon knot. Striking weakness is most obvious (especially for novice collectors) on the eagle's tail feathers. Many Flying Eagle cents, however, are quite well struck.

Availability. As a type the Flying Eagle cent is easy to find, although some varieties, such as 1856 and 1858, 8 Over 7, range from scarce to rare. Most are seen in worn grades. In MS, many are in the marketplace, although dipping, cleaning, and recoloring (causing staining and spotting) have eliminated the majority from consideration by connoisseurs.

EF-40, 45 (Extremely Fine). *Obverse:* Wear is more extensive than at AU, especially on the eagle's breast and the top of the closest wing. Wear also shows on the other wing in the area below OF. Marks may be more extensive in the field. The wear is slightly greater at EF-40 than at EF-45, although in the marketplace these two grades are not clearly differentiated. *Reverse:* More wear shows on the higher areas of the wreath, but most detail still is present. There may be tinges of luster in protected areas, more likely at EF-45 than at 40.

AU-50, 53, 55, 58 (About Uncirculated). *Obverse:* At AU-50, light wear is seen on the breast of the eagle, the top edge of the closest wing, and, less so, on the head. As both the head and tail tip can be lightly struck, these are not reliable indicators of grade. Luster is present in traces among the letters. At higher AU levels the evidence of wear diminishes. An AU-58 coin has nearly full luster, but friction is seen in the fields, as are some marks. *Reverse:* At AU-50, light wear is seen on the ribbon bow and the highest areas of the leaves. Some luster is seen (more than on the obverse). Friction is evident, as are some marks, but these will not be as distracting as those on the obverse, as the heavy wreath and lettering are more protective of the reverse field. In higher grades, wear is less, and at AU-58 nearly full—or even completely full—luster is seen.

MS-60 to 70 (Mint State). *Obverse:* Contact marks, most obvious in the field, are evident at MS-60, diminishing at 61, 62, and higher. The eagle, the feathers of which usually hide marks, shows some evidence as well. At MS-65 or finer there is no trace of friction or rubbing. A few tiny nicks or marks may be seen, but none are obvious. Although in practice this is not always consistent, at MS-66 and higher there should be no staining or other problems, and the coin should have good eye appeal overall. *Reverse:* Check the higher parts of the wreath for slight abrasions at MS-60 to 62. Otherwise, the above guidelines apply.

1857, Reverse 25¢ Clash
FS-01-1857-901.

1857, Obverse $20 Clash
FS-01-1857-403.

1858, 8 Over 7
FS-01-1858-101.

1858, Large Letters

1858, Small Letters
Shown 2x actual size.

	Mintage	Cert	Avg	%MS	EF-40	AU-50	MS-60	MS-63	MS-64	MS-65	MS-66	Recent Auction Record
1856 † (a)	2,000	297	47.9	47	$13,500	$15,000	$18,000	$24,000	$33,000	$65,000	$150,000	$32,900, MS-64, April 2013
1857	17,450,000	6,120	57.4	72	150	215	380	900	1,500	4,200	12,000	$21,150, MS-66, June 2014
1857, Obverse 50¢ Clash (b)	*	89	42.3	39	230	450	800	1,250	2,000			$5,816, MS-65, October 2013
1857, Reverse 25¢ Clash (c)	*	50	46.4	40	230	450	850	2,750				$489, AU-55, March 2011
1857, Obverse $20 Clash (d)	*	25	23.7	0	2,400	6,000	15,000					$242, F-12, March 2011

* Included in number above. † Ranked in the *100 Greatest U.S. Coins* (third edition). **a.** Actually a pattern, but collected along with the regular issue since it shares the same design. See *United States Pattern Coins*, 10th edition. **b.** The obverse die was clashed with the obverse die of a Liberty Seated half dollar. This is most evident through AMERICA. **c.** The reverse die was clashed with the reverse die of a Liberty Seated quarter dollar. The outline of the eagle's head is evident above ONE. **d.** The obverse die was clashed with the obverse die of a Liberty Head double eagle.

	Mintage	Cert	Avg	%MS	EF-40	AU-50	MS-60	MS-63	MS-64	MS-65	MS-66	Recent Auction Record
1858, All kinds	24,600,000											
1858, Large Letters		2,946	55.5	67	$150	$215	$400	$950	$1,500	$4,200	$12,000	$17,625, MS-66, June 2013
1858, 8 Over 7 (e)		335	51.5	47	850	1,500	3,650	10,000	27,500	70,000		$70,500, MS-65, April 2013
1858, Small Letters		2,281	51.6	55	150	215	400	950	1,500	4,200	13,000	$16,450, MS-66, August 2013

e. The flag of the upper-right corner of a 7 can be seen above the second 8 in the date. There is a raised triangular dot in the field above the first 8. Late-die-state specimens are worth considerably less than the values listed, which are for early die states.

Proof Flying Eagle Cents

PF-60 to 70 (Proof). Proof 1856 Flying Eagle cents are the most plentiful of the available dates, surviving from perhaps 2,000 to 2,500 or more struck for sale to collectors beginning in 1859. Proofs of 1857 are very rare. Proofs of 1858 are rare, but significantly more readily available than those of 1857. A first-class Proof should have a fully and deeply mirrored field on both sides, except for those of 1856, which are usually a combination of mirrorlike and grainy in character. Note that some prooflike Mint State coins have wrongly been called Proofs. Quality is a challenge, and problem-free examples are in the minority. *Obverse and Reverse:* PF-65 coins have very few hairlines, and these are visible only under a strong magnifying glass. At PF-67 and higher there should be no evidence at all of hairlines or friction. PF-60 coins can be dull from repeated dipping and cleaning. (Proofs are without hairlines when struck; any hairlines on a Proof were caused by abrasive cleaning.) At PF-63 the mirrorlike fields should be attractive, with no rubbing, and with hairlines minimal (best seen when the coin is held at an angle to the light). PF-64 coins are even nicer.

Proof Flying Eagle Cent

	Est Mintage	Cert	Finest	PF-60	PF-63	PF-64	PF-65	PF-65Cam	Recent Auction Record
1856	1,500	1,105	PF-67	$16,000	$20,000	$25,000	$30,000	$45,000	$38,188, PF-65, January 2014
1857	100	95	PF-66	5,000	8,500	13,000	26,000	28,500	$34,075, PF, January 2013
1858, Large Letters	100	85	PF-67	5,000	8,500	13,000	26,000	28,500	$28,200, PF, January 2013
1858, Small Letters	200	93	PF-66	5,000	8,500	13,000	26,000	28,500	$32,900, PF-66, January 2014

INDIAN HEAD
(1859–1909)

Variety 1 (Copper-Nickel, Laurel Wreath Reverse, 1859): Designer James B. Longacre; weight 4.67 grams; composition .880 copper, .120 nickel; diameter 19 mm; plain edge. All coined at Philadelphia Mint.

Copper-Nickel, Laurel Wreath Reverse,
Without Shield (1859 Only)

Variety 2 (Copper-Nickel, Oak Wreath With Shield, 1860–1864): Designer James B. Longacre; weight 4.67 grams; composition .880 copper, .120 nickel; diameter 19 mm; plain edge. All coined at Philadelphia Mint.

Copper-Nickel, Oak Wreath Reverse,
With Shield (1860–1864)

Variety 3 (Bronze, 1864–1909): Designer James B. Longacre; weight 3.11 grams; composition .950 copper, .050 tin and zinc; diameter 19 mm; plain edge; mints: Philadelphia, San Francisco.

Bronze, Oak Wreath Reverse,
With Shield (1864–1909)

History. After nearly a dozen varieties of patterns were made in 1858, in 1859 the Indian Head was adopted as the new motif for the cent. The reverse of the 1859 coin illustrates an olive (or laurel) wreath. In 1860 this was changed to a wreath of oak and other leaves with a shield at the apex, a design continued through the end of the series in 1909. From 1859 through spring 1864 cents were struck in copper-nickel, the alloy used earlier for Flying Eagle cents. In 1864 a new bronze alloy was adopted.

Indian Head cents remained in circulation through the 1940s, but were rarely seen by the early 1950s. In the 1930s, when Whitman and other coin boards and folders became widely available for collectors, many key dates were picked out of circulation. The typical grade for the scarce issues of the 1870s was Good or so, and the 1908-S and 1909-S could be found in VF.

Striking and Sharpness. The strike on Indian Head cents can vary widely. On the obverse the points to check include the details at the tips of the feathers and the diamonds on the ribbon. The diamonds *cannot* be used as a grading marker, and the feather tips can be used only if you have familiarity with how sharp the coin was struck to begin with. In general, the reverse is usually sharper, but check the leaf and shield details. On many bronze cents beginning in the 1870s the bottom of N (ONE) and tops of EN (CENT) are light, as they were in the dies (not factored when grading). Check the dentils on both sides. Generally, copper-nickel cents of the early 1860s are candidates for light striking as are later issues in the bronze format, of the 1890s onward.

Availability. In worn grades Indian Head cents are available in proportion to their mintages, in combination with survival rates being higher for the later issues. The low-mintage 1909-S was saved in larger quantities than the higher-mintage 1877, as an example. MS coins survive as a matter of chance, with those of 1878 and before being much scarcer than those of 1879 and later, and some of the 1900s being readily available. Collectors who wanted single pieces often bought Proofs. Many if not most higher-grade MS coins have been dipped or recolored, unless they are a warm orange-red color with traces of natural brown. The search for quality among bronze cents is particularly challenging. Some tiny toning flecks are to be expected on many coins, and as long as they are microscopic they can often be ignored (except in grades on the far side of MS-65). A set of MS-65 coins in RB or RD can be formed quickly, but one with *original* color, sharp strike, and excellent eye appeal may take several years.

In the late 1930s, many 1878–1909 Proof Indian Head cents began to be released from several estate hoards. These had vivid violet and blue iridescent toning from being stored for decades in tissue paper. They are highly sought-after today.

EF-40, 45 (Extremely Fine). *Obverse:* Wear is more extensive than at AU, but all of LIBERTY is very clear. Wear is seen on the hair above and below the ear, on the central portion of the ribbon, and on the feather tips. Overall the coin is bold. Scattered marks are normal for this and lower grades, most often seen on the cheek and in the field. *Reverse:* The higher-relief parts of the leaves and ribbon bow show light wear, but details are sharp in lower areas. Some tiny lines in the vertical stripes in the shield may be blended. Scattered marks may be present, but on all grades they are usually fewer on the reverse than on the obverse.

AU-50, 53, 55, 58 (About Uncirculated). *Obverse:* At AU-50, wear is most noticeable on the hair above the ear, on the central portion of the ribbon, on the curl to the right of the ribbon, and near the feather tips, although the last is not a reliable indicator due to striking. Luster is present, but mostly in protected areas. At AU-53 and 55, wear is less. At AU-58 friction is evident, rather than actual wear. Luster, toned brown, is nearly complete at AU-58, but may be incomplete in the field. *Reverse:* At AU-50, light wear is seen on the ribbon and the higher-relief areas of the leaves, while the lower areas retain their detail. Some luster may be present in protected areas. At AU-53 and 55, wear is less and luster is more extensive. An AU-58 coin has nearly full luster and shows only light friction.

MS-60 to 70 (Mint State). *Obverse:* Contact marks, most obvious in the field, are evident at MS-60, diminishing at MS-61, 62, and higher. This abrasion is most noticeable on copper-nickel cents; on bronze issues, it blends in with the background. Liberty's cheek and the field show some evidence as well. Typical color is BN, occasionally RB at MS-63 and 64, unless dipped to be RD. At MS-65 or finer there is no trace of abrasion. A few tiny nicks or marks may be seen, but none are obvious. At MS-67 and finer the coin will approach perfection. Check so-called RD coins for originality. A theoretically perfect MS-70 will have no marks at all, even under a strong magnifier. Although in practice this is not always consistent, at MS-66 and higher there should be no staining or other problems, and the coin should have good eye appeal overall. *Reverse:* Check the high parts of the wreath for abrasion. Otherwise the above comments apply.

1860, Pointed Bust

1860, Rounded Bust

1863, Doubled-Die Reverse
FS-01-1863-801.

1864, No L

1864, With L

1865, Die Gouge in Headdress
FS-01-1865-1302.

1865, Doubled-Die Reverse
FS-01-1865-1801.

1869, 9 Over 9
FS-01-1869-301.

Shallow N

Bold N

1870, Doubled-Die
Reverse
FS-01-1870-801.

1873, Close 3

1873, Open 3

1873, Doubled LIBERTY
FS-01-1873-101.

1875, Dot
Reverse

1880, Doubled-Die
Obverse, Reverse Clash
FS-01-1880-101.

1882, Misplaced Date
FS-01-1882-401.

1886, Variety 1
*The last feather points
between the I and the C
in AMERICA.*

1886, Variety 2
*The last feather points
between the C and the A
in AMERICA.*

1887, Doubled-Die Obverse
FS-01-1887-101.

1891, Doubled-Die Obverse
FS-01-1891-101.

1888, Last 8 Over 7
FS-01-1888-301.

1894, Doubled Date
FS-01-1894-301.

COPPER-NICKEL COINAGE

	Mintage	Cert	Avg	%MS	EF-40	AU-50	MS-60	MS-63	MS-64	MS-65	MS-66	Recent Auction Record
1859	36,400,000	3,796	58.5	70	$110	$200	$285	$625	$1,250	$3,500	$6,200	$11,750, MS-66, April 2013
1860, Rounded Bust	20,566,000	2,266	61.0	81	70	110	185	250	425	1,200	3,000	$8,813, MS-66, January 2014
1860, Pointed Bust	*	404	59.4	73	100	165	300	575	1,500	3,500	10,000	$32,900, MS-67, February 2014
1861	10,100,000	2,105	60.7	79	110	175	225	325	525	1,100	3,000	$4,113, MS-66, February 2014
1862	28,075,000	3,375	62.1	87	50	75	110	200	375	1,000	3,000	$15,275, MS-67, February 2013
1863	49,840,000	4,464	61.4	84	50	75	110	200	375	1,000	3,000	$2,820, MS-66, August 2013
1863, Doubled-Die Reverse **(a)**	*	4	62.3	100	200	375	450	950	2,000	3,000		
1864, Copper-Nickel	13,740,000	2,664	61.4	83	100	150	200	325	550	1,600	7,500	$6,463, MS-66, April 2014

* Included in number above. **a.** Strong doubling is evident on the right leaves of the wreath, and, to a lesser degree, on the upper left leaves.

BRONZE COINAGE

	Mintage	Cert	Avg	%MS	AU-50	MS-60BN	MS-63BN	MS-64RB	MS-64RD	MS-65RB	MS-65RD	Recent Auction Record
1864, Bronze, All kinds	39,233,714											
1864, No L		2,507	61.9	88	$90	$115	$150	$235	$375	$400	$1,000	$7,050, VF-30, April 2013
1864, With L		2,695	53.2	54	375	425	600	1,000	2,000	1,800	5,000	$2,115, MS-65RB, May 2013
1865	35,429,286	1,990	62.1	88	65	90	150	250	550	600	1,750	$1,998, MS-65RD, March 2013
1865, Die Gouge in Headdress **(a)**	*	3	60.0	67	500	750	1,200					
1865, Doubled-Die Reverse	*	20	43.4	35	*1,100*	2,200	5,500					$1,175, AU-55, April 2013
1866	9,826,500	1,889	56.2	64	250	290	380	775	2,000	1,500	5,250	$3,290, MS-65RD, June 2014
1867	9,821,000	1,909	55.7	66	275	300	400	800	2,000	1,600	6,000	$6,463, MS-65RD, February 2014
1868	10,266,500	1,663	57.1	69	220	250	360	650	2,000	925	4,000	$29,375, MS-66RD, April 2014
1869	6,420,000	2,081	49.4	55	550	600	700	1,225	2,150	1,800	4,750	$3,290, MS-66RB, August 2013
1869, 9 Over 9	*	380	44.7	44	825	975	1,200	1,650	2,300	2,400		$7,344, MS-65RD, June 2014
1870, Shallow N **(b)**	5,275,000	1,775	51.7	57	500	550	900	1,000	1,500	1,600		$1,265, MS-64RB, March 2012
1870, Bold N **(b)**	*	*	*	*	450	500	850	900	1,200	1,300	4,200	$23,500, MS-66RD, May 2013
1870, Doubled-Die Reverse	*	18	63.1	89	750	850	1,000	1,300	2,500	2,500		$1,035, MS-64RB, January 2012
1871, Shallow N **(b)**	3,929,500	1,777	49.8	52	650	775	950	1,300	2,700	2,600		$2,585, MS-63RB, February 2013
1871, Bold N **(b)**	*	*	*	*	525	550	800	1,250	2,550	2,350	7,000	$44,063, MS-66RD, January 2014
1872, Shallow N **(b)**	4,042,000	2,245	45.9	43	700	950	1,250	2,150	5,500	4,500		$881, AU-55, April 2013
1872, Bold N **(b)**	*	*	*	*	650	785	1,150	1,750	5,250	4,000	17,000	$28,200, MS-65RD, June 2014

* Included in number above. **a.** Currently described as a die gouge in the *Cherrypickers' Guide to Rare Die Varieties*, fifth edition, volume I, the curved "gouge" is a mark from the Janvier reducing lathe. **b.** Cents dated 1869 and earlier have a shallow N in ONE. Those dated 1870, 1871, or 1872 have either shallow N or bold N. Those dated 1873 to 1876 all have the bold N. Circulation strikes of 1877 have the shallow N, while Proofs have the bold N.

Chart continued on next page.

	Mintage	Cert	Avg	%MS	AU-50	MS-60BN	MS-63BN	MS-64RB	MS-64RD	MS-65RB	MS-65RD	Recent Auction Record
1873, All kinds	11,676,500											
1873, Close 3		594	55.9	64	$235	$410	$550	$1,200	$2,400	$2,500	$10,000	$2,820, MS-65RB, December 2013
1873, Doubled LIBERTY		286	45.9	30	5,250	7,500	13,500	33,000		57,500		$7,638, MS-63BN, June 2013
1873, Open 3		1,148	57.0	67	190	250	325	500	2,000	1,275	7,500	$4,406, MS-65RD, April 2014
1874	14,187,500	1,686	58.9	73	150	225	250	385	1,050	725	3,500	$2,820, MS-65RD, April 2013
1875	13,528,000	1,565	58.6	75	160	235	260	410	1,100	900	3,750	$5,581, MS-65RD, December 2013
1875, Dot Reverse (a)	*	4	45.0	50			—					$700, AU-50BN, April 2012
1876	7,944,000	1,509	57.1	68	240	300	390	635	1,200	1,000	3,000	$1,880, MS-65RD, October 2013
1877 (b)	852,500	6,107	25.4	14	3,100	3,800	4,500	7,500	9,500	12,500	22,000	$14,100, MS-65RB, January 2014
1878	5,797,500	1,416	58.3	75	275	325	380	550	1,000	950	2,500	$1,645, MS-65RD, October 2013
1879	16,228,000	1,548	61.9	89	80	90	140	235	435	425	1,400	$2,233, MS-65RD, June 2014
1880	38,961,000	1,319	62.8	93	60	80	130	225	425	400	1,300	$5,288, MS-66RD, June 2014
1880, DblDie Obv, Rev Clash (c)	*	15	61.7	93	390	750	1,500	1,750	2,100	2,000	2,900	$2,070, MS-65BN, June 2009
1881	39,208,000	1,443	63.0	95	35	60	90	215	325	315	1,350	$1,880, MS-64BN, August 2013
1882	38,578,000	1,402	63.2	94	35	60	90	215	325	315	1,350	$3,525, EF-40, April 2013
1882, Misplaced Date (d)	*	9	59.8	78	450	875	1,700	3,000	4,000	6,000		$220, EF-45, February 2007
1883	45,591,500	1,439	63.1	94	35	60	90	215	325	315	1,350	$2,585, MS-66RD, February 2014
1884	23,257,800	1,267	63.1	94	40	75	120	260	450	450	1,650	$4,994, MS-66RD, June 2014
1885	11,761,594	1,211	62.3	88	80	110	200	335	550	650	2,100	$12,925, MS-66RD, April 2013
1886, All kinds	17,650,000											
1886, Variety 1		855	58.5	70	175	200	250	475	1,150	975	4,000	$8,813, MS-66RB, June 2013
1886, Variety 2		826	58.1	70	220	325	500	1,150	2,550	2,900	14,000	$9,400, MS-65RD, January 2013
1887	45,223,523	1,118	62.6	93	28	55	80	190	475	575	1,700	$8,813, MS-66RD, February 2013
1887, Doubled-Die Obverse	*	50	45.0	24	490	1,000	2,500	3,500	5,000	8,000		$881, MS-62BN, October 2013
1888	37,489,832	1,301	59.5	85	27	65	130	365	650	725	2,250	$11,750, MS-66RD, June 2014
1888, Last 8 Over 7	*	48	28.1	10	17,500	23,000	35,000					$23,500, AU-58, April 2013
1889	48,866,025	1,247	62.6	93	27	60	80	180	460	400	2,000	$4,113, MS-65RD, April 2014
1890	57,180,114	1,206	62.8	94	27	60	80	180	410	410	1,150	$4,113, MS-66RB, March 2014
1891	47,070,000	1,379	62.6	93	27	60	80	180	400	400	1,100	$1,528, MS-65RD, July 2014
1891, Doubled-Die Obverse	*	27	47.7	37	450	775	1,150	1,500	3,000			$138, VF-35, December 2011
1892	37,647,087	1,209	62.8	94	27	60	80	185	385	375	1,100	$8,813, MS-66RD, August 2013
1893	46,640,000	1,479	63.1	95	27	60	80	170	375	320	900	$6,463, MS-67RD, April 2013
1894	16,749,500	1,388	61.8	90	70	85	115	210	350	385	1,100	$3,290, MS-66RD, January 2014
1894, Doubled Date	*	194	47.6	54	385	675	1,200	2,200	4,800	4,000	9,000	$5,875, MS-64RD, January 2013
1895	38,341,574	1,593	63.2	95	25	40	65	140	260	200	800	$7,050, MS-66RD, January 2014
1896	39,055,431	1,188	63.1	96	25	40	65	140	260	220	925	$1,528, MS-65RD, July 2014
1897	50,464,392	1,461	61.3	90	25	40	65	125	260	200	925	$7,050, MS-66RD, January 2014
1898	49,821,284	1,660	62.8	94	25	40	65	115	230	195	575	$2,820, MS-66RD, April 2013
1899	53,598,000	2,949	63.5	96	25	40	65	115	210	195	460	$3,525, MS-66RD, January 2014
1900	66,831,502	1,890	63.1	94	20	38	60	100	185	170	460	$9,988, MS-67RD, December 2013
1901	79,609,158	2,922	63.3	96	20	38	60	100	185	170	440	$2,115, MS-67RB, November 2013
1902	87,374,704	2,738	63.0	95	20	38	60	100	185	170	485	$2,585, MS-66RD, December 2013
1903	85,092,703	2,718	63.0	95	20	38	60	100	185	170	440	$4,406, MS-67RD, July 2014
1904	61,326,198	2,398	63.2	95	20	38	60	100	185	170	460	$2,585, MS-66RD, June 2014
1905	80,717,011	2,662	62.9	94	20	38	60	100	185	170	490	$19,975, MS-67RD, April 2013
1906	96,020,530	3,049	62.5	92	20	38	60	100	185	170	440	$23,500, MS-67RD, June 2014
1907	108,137,143	3,409	62.4	92	20	38	60	100	185	170	440	$23,500, MS-67RD, December 2013
1908	32,326,367	2,886	63.2	95	20	38	60	100	185	170	440	$19,975, MS-67RD, February 2013
1908S	1,115,000	5,358	47.0	44	250	290	400	650	1,200	850	2,300	$3,290, MS-65RD, January 2014
1909	14,368,470	4,966	63.4	97	30	45	65	105	190	175	440	$3,819, MS-67RD, January 2014
1909S	309,000	6,500	40.9	33	900	1,050	1,200	1,500	2,200	2,500	5,250	$9,989, MS-66RD, June 2014

* Included in number above. **a.** In 1875, Mint officials suspected a longtime employee was stealing Indian Head cents. They secretly modified a reverse die by making a small gouge in the N in ONE, and then put the die into production one morning. Later that morning the suspect employee was called aside. He was asked to empty his pockets, revealing 33 of the marked cents. At first he insisted his son gave him this pocket change, but when confronted with the secretly marked die, he admitted his guilt. He tendered his resignation, disgraced, after more than 50 years of service to the Mint. The market value for this variety is not yet reliably established. **b.** Beware the numerous counterfeits and altered-date 1877 cents. The latter typically are altered from 1875- or 1879-dated cents. **c.** Doubling is visible on the obverse in higher grades, as a very close spread on LIBERTY. The primary diagnostic, though, is the misaligned die clash evident on the reverse, with obvious reeding running from the upper-right leaf tip, through the E of ONE, and down to the very top of the N of CENT. **d.** The bases of at least four 1s are evident within the beads of the necklace.

Proof Indian Head Cents

PF-60 to 70 (Proof). Proof Indian Head cents were made of all dates, 1859 to 1909. The 1864 bronze variety with a tiny L (for designer James B. Longacre) on the ribbon is a rarity, with only about two dozen known. Generally, Proofs are sharp strikes until the 1890s, when some can be weak. On bronze coins tiny carbon flecks are typical, but should be microscopic. The majority of Proofs have been dipped, and many bronze pieces have been retoned. Most undipped coins are either rich brown, or red and brown. Extra value can be found in BN and RB—investors typically don't buy them, instead preferring RD coins, most of which have actually been dipped.

Proofs are generally designated BN if the surfaces are mainly brown or iridescent, or have up to perhaps 30% original mint red-orange color. RB is designated if the surface is a mixture of red-orange and brown (best if blended together nicely, but often with patches of mint color among brown areas). RD designates a coin with original mint-red orange, always blending to slight natural brown toning unless the coin has been dipped. Likely, any RD coin with even a few hairlines has been cleaned (or at least mishandled) at one time; in most such cases, the RD is not original. Certification services take no notice of this. For this reason, a connoisseur will prefer a BN PF-63 coin with no hairlines to a PF-65 or 66 RD coin with some hairlines. The BN coin can always be dipped and cleaned (though this is not advised).

Proof copper-nickel Indian Head cents of 1859 to 1864 need no letters to indicate color. As a general rule, these survive in higher grades and with greater eye appeal, as they stayed "brilliant" and did not need dipping. Moreover, when such pieces were cleaned and acquired hairlines, they tended to be fewer than on a bronze coin, due to the very hard nature of the copper-nickel alloy.

Obverse and Reverse: PF-60 coins can be dull from repeated dipping and cleaning and are often toned iridescent colors. At PF-63 the mirrorlike fields should be attractive, and hairlines should be minimal; no rubbing is seen. PF-64 coins are even nicer. At PF-65 there are very few hairlines, visible only under strong magnification. At PF-67 or higher there should be no evidence of hairlines or friction; such a coin is fully original (not cleaned).

Proof Indian Head Cent

	Est Mintage	Cert	Finest	PF-63	PF-64	PF-65	PF-66	Recent Auction Record
1859	800	458	PF-67	$1,625	$3,000	$5,000	$8,750	$13,513, PF-66Cam, June 2014
1860, Rounded Bust	1,000	185	PF-68	1,000	2,200	3,500	7,500	$9,989, PF-66, April 2014
1861	1,000	216	PF-66	1,500	3,400	7,750	18,000	$24,675, PF-66, September 2013
1862	550	673	PF-68	900	1,300	2,500	4,300	$4,113, PF-66, June 2014
1863	460	303	PF-67	900	1,300	2,500	4,300	$12,925, PF, January 2013
1864, Copper-Nickel	370	407	PF-67	900	1,300	2,500	4,300	$12,925, PF-66DCam, July 2014

	Mintage	Cert	Finest	PF-63BN	PF-63RB	PF-64RB	PF-64RD	PF-65RD	PF-66RD	Recent Auction Record
1864, Bronze, No L	150+	275	PF-67	$650	$1,000	$1,750	$3,000	$9,000	$20,000	$17,625, PF-67RB, April 2013
1864, Bronze, With L	20+	20	PF-66	10,000	25,000	50,000	100,000			$141,000, PF-65RD, September 2013
1865	500+	313	PF-67	400	500	800	2,000	7,500	18,000	$12,925, PF-65RD, June 2014
1866	725+	350	PF-67	400	525	600	2,000	5,000	8,000	$21,150, PF-66Cam, June 2014
1867	625+	423	PF-67	400	525	600	1,850	5,000	8,000	$6,463, PF-66RD, March 2014
1868	600+	313	PF-67	375	415	550	1,600	5,000	15,000	$17,625, PF-66RD, June 2014
1869	600+	376	PF-67	380	550	650	1,300	3,000	7,500	$4,847, PF-66Cam, June 2014
1870, Shallow N	1,000+	416	PF-66	425	650	725	1,000	2,500		$1,380, PF-65RB, April 2012
1870, Bold N	*	*	n/a	325	385	525	925	1,900	3,800	$10,575, PF-66RD, January 2014
1871, Shallow N	960+	484	PF-66	500	750	875	1,200	2,350	8,000	$7,344, PF-65RD, January 2013
1871, Bold N	*	*	n/a	325	500	600	950	2,150	4,250	$2,350, PF-65RD, June 2014
1872, Bold N (a)	950+	552	PF-66	400	600	700	1,900	4,300	7,500	$12,925, PF, October 2013
1873, Close 3	1,100+	562	PF-66	265	325	550	775	2,050	8,300	$1,293, PF-65RB, April 2013
1874	700	393	PF-67	250	300	400	675	2,100	3,750	$1,175, PF-65RB, June 2013
1875	700	416	PF-67	250	300	500	1,600	4,000	11,500	$8,813, PF-65RD, June 2014
1876	1,150	482	PF-67	250	325	450	725	1,900	4,600	$15,275, PF-66Cam, January 2014
1877	900	709	PF-67	2,750	3,500	4,250	6,700	14,000	20,000	$14,100, PF-66RD, June 2013
1878	2,350	758	PF-67	235	285	450	575	1,500	2,900	$7,638, PF-66Cam, June 2014
1879	3,200	874	PF-68	150	215	325	450	1,200	2,300	$11,163, PF-67RD, July 2014
1880	3,955	971	PF-68	150	210	325	450	1,200	2,300	$8,813, PF-67RD, June 2014

* Included in number above. **a.** Proofs of 1872 were struck only with the bold N, not the shallow N.

Chart continued on next page.

	Mintage	Cert	Finest	PF-63BN	PF-63RB	PF-64RB	PF-64RD	PF-65RD	PF-66RD	Recent Auction Record
1881	3,575	920	PF-68	$150	$200	$325	$450	$1,200	$2,300	$1,880, PF-66RD, June 2013
1882	3,100	837	PF-67	150	200	325	500	1,000	2,200	$2,703, PF-65RD, January 2014
1883	6,609	1,291	PF-67	150	200	325	500	1,200	3,000	$2,938, PF-66RD, March 2013
1884	3,942	1,113	PF-68	150	200	325	450	1,200	2,300	$7,050, PF-67Cam, June 2013
1885	3,790	981	PF-68	150	200	325	450	1,200	2,300	$4,994, PF-68BN, September 2013
1886, All kinds	4,290									
1886, Variety 1		551	PF-67	150	200	325	575	1,800	3,100	$3,819, PF-66RD, June 2014
1886, Variety 2		197	PF-67	350	485	690				$1,116, PF-66BN, April 2013
1887	2,960	701	PF-67	150	200	300	1,000	3,500	9,000	$16,450, PF-66RD, June 2014
1888	4,582	623	PF-67	150	200	315	1,100	3,500	9,000	$2,585, PF, February 2013
1889	3,336	598	PF-67	150	200	315	500	1,750	3,750	$4,113, PF-66RD, February 2013
1890	2,740	559	PF-66	150	200	315	500	1,650	2,400	$1,293, PF-65RD, August 2013
1891	2,350	606	PF-67	150	200	315	575	1,375	3,800	$18,213, PF-65DCam, July 2014
1892	2,745	715	PF-67	150	200	315	450	1,200	2,300	$3,525, PF-67RD, November 2013
1893	2,195	575	PF-67	150	200	315	500	1,300	2,600	$499, PF-64RD, April 2013
1894	2,632	594	PF-67	150	200	315	465	1,200	2,450	$5,581, PF-66RD, September 2013
1895	2,062	589	PF-67	160	210	315	450	1,200	2,300	$9,988, PF-66Cam, June 2014
1896	1,862	450	PF-67	150	200	300	450	1,350	3,400	$5,875, PF-65Cam, June 2014
1897	1,938	554	PF-68	150	200	300	450	1,200	2,300	$10,575, PF, January 2013
1898	1,795	597	PF-67	150	200	300	450	1,200	2,300	$7,931, PF-66Cam, June 2014
1899	2,031	604	PF-67	150	200	300	450	1,200	2,300	$5,875, PF-67RD, June 2014
1900	2,262	585	PF-68	150	200	300	450	1,200	2,300	$5,581, PF-66RD, April 2013
1901	1,985	630	PF-68	150	200	300	450	1,200	2,300	$4,700, PF, March 2014
1902	2,018	681	PF-68	150	200	300	450	1,200	2,300	$7,344, PF-67RD, June 2014
1903	1,790	600	PF-68	150	200	300	450	1,200	2,300	$10,575, PF, January 2013
1904	1,817	538	PF-67	150	200	300	450	1,200	2,300	$4,994, PF-66Cam, June 2014
1905	2,152	584	PF-67	150	200	300	450	1,200	2,300	$8,225, PF, March 2014
1906	1,725	494	PF-67	150	200	300	450	1,200	2,300	$21,150, PF-67Cam, June 2014
1907	1,475	461	PF-67	150	200	300	450	1,250	2,400	$4,113, PF-66RD, April 2014
1908	1,620	608	PF-67	150	200	300	450	1,200	2,750	$1,175, PF-65RD, January 2014
1909	2,175	610	PF-67	150	200	300	450	1,300	2,500	$12,925, PF-67RD, June 2014

LINCOLN, WHEAT EARS REVERSE
(1909–1958)

Variety 1 (Bronze, 1909–1942): Designer Victor D. Brenner; weight 3.11 grams; composition .950 copper, .050 tin and zinc; diameter 19 mm; plain edge; mints: Philadelphia, Denver, San Francisco.

Variety 1, Bronze (1909–1942)

Variety 2 (Steel, 1943): Weight 2.70 grams; composition steel, coated with zinc; diameter 19 mm; plain edge.

Variety 2, Steel (1943)

Variety 1 Resumed (1944–1958): 1944–1946—Weight, 3.11 grams; composition .950 copper, .050 zinc; diameter 19 mm; plain edge. 1947–1958—Weight 3.11 grams; composition .950 copper, .050 tin and zinc; diameter 19 mm.

Variety 1 Resumed, Bronze (1944–1958)

History. The Lincoln cent, designed by Victor David Brenner, was first released on August 2, 1909. The earliest issues had Brenner's initials (V.D.B.) on the reverse; this was soon discontinued. In 1943, during World War II, zinc-coated steel was used for planchets, as copper was needed for the war effort. The Philadelphia, Denver, and San Francisco mints all produced these coins, but not in all years.

Striking and Sharpness. As a rule, Lincoln cents of 1909 through 1914 are fairly well struck. From 1915 through the end of the 1920s, many are weak, with Denver Mint coins particularly so. Issues of the 1930s onward are mostly well struck. With many different die pairs used over a long period of time, striking quality varies. On the obverse, check for details in Lincoln's hair and beard. Also check the lettering and the inner edge of the rim. *Tiny marks on the shoulder of Lincoln indicate a weak strike there;* this area cannot be used to determine *wear* on high-grade coins. (During striking, there was not enough die pressure to fill this, the deepest point of the obverse die; therefore, stray marks on the raw planchet remain evident in this spot.) On the reverse check the wheat stalks, letters, and inner rim. A weak strike will usually manifest itself on the O of ONE (the area directly opposite Lincoln's shoulder). Coins struck from overused or "tired" dies can have grainy or even slightly wavy fields on either side.

Availability. Cents of 1909 are easily found in MS; later dates are scarcer, although Philadelphia varieties were made in higher quantities and are more often seen. Beginning in the early 1930s, bank-wrapped rolls of Mint State cents were saved in large quantities (starting mainly in 1934, though the low-mintage 1931-S was also hoarded). Dates after this time all are plentiful, although some more so than others, and there are a number of scarce and rare varieties. The demand for scarcer Lincoln cents and higher-grade issues is intense, resulting in a strong market. Many Mint State coins before the 1930s have been dipped and recolored, this being particularly true of pieces listed as RD. Others are stained and blotchy. See the Indian Head cents commentary for similar situations.

AU-50, 53, 55, 58 (About Uncirculated). *Obverse:* Slight wear shows on Lincoln's cheekbone to the left of his nose, and also on his beard. At AU-55 or 58 there may be some hints of mint red-orange. Most coins in AU are BN, but often are not qualified by color. *Reverse:* Slight wear is evident on the stalks of wheat to the left and right. Otherwise, the same standards apply as for the obverse.

MS-60 to 70 (Mint State). *Obverse and Reverse:* At MS-65 and higher, the luster is rich on all areas, except perhaps the shoulder (which may be grainy and show original planchet surface). There is no rubbing, and no contact marks are visible except under magnification. Coins with full or nearly full mint orange-red color can be designated RD; those with full or nearly full brown-toned surfaces can be designated BN; and those with a substantial percentage of red-orange and of brown can be called RB. Ideally, MS-65 or finer coins should have good eye appeal, which in the RB category means nicely blended colors, not stained or blotched. Below MS-65, full RD coins become scarce, and at MS-60 to 62 are virtually non-existent, unless they have been dipped. Copper is a very active metal, and influences such as slight abrasions, contact marks, and so on that define the grade also affect the color. The official American Numismatic Association grading standards allow for "dull" and/or "spotted" coins at MS-60 and 61, as well as incomplete luster. In the marketplace, interpretations often vary widely. BN and RB coins at MS-60 and 61 tend to be more attractive than (dipped) RD coins.

Designer's initials, V.D.B.
(1909 Reverse Only)

No V.D.B. on Reverse
(1909–1958)

V.D.B. on Shoulder
(Starting 1918)

Mintmark
Location

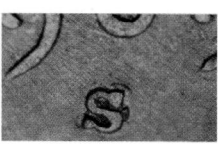
1909-S, S Over
Horizontal S
FS-01-1909S-1502.

1917, Doubled-Die
Obverse
FS-01-1917-101.

1922, No D
FS-01-1922-401.
Shown 1.5x actual size.

1922, Weak D

1934, Doubled-Die
Obverse
FS-01-1934-101.

1936, Doubled-Die Obverse
FS-01-1936-101.

1943-D, Boldly Doubled
Mintmark
FS-01-1943D-501.

1944-D, D Over S
FS-01-1944D-511.

1946-S, S Over D
FS-01-1946S-511.

1951-D, D Over S
FS-01-1951D-512.

1955, Doubled-Die Obverse	1955, Doubled-Die Obverse,	1956-D, D Above	1958, Doubled-Die Obverse
FS-01-1955-101.	Closeup of Date	Shadow D	FS-01-1958-101.
Shown 2x actual size.		FS-01-1956D-508.	

	Mintage	Cert	Avg	%MS	MS-63BN	MS-64BN	MS-64RB	MS-64RD	MS-65RB	MS-65RD	MS-66RD	Recent Auction Record
1909, V.D.B.	27,995,000	26,348	63.9	97	$30	$40.00	$65.00	$90	$95	$165	$280	$1,763, MS-67RD, June 2013
1909S, V.D.B. † (a)	484,000	19,572	47.7	46	2,000	2,200.00	2,500.00	3,350	3,650	5,500	13,000	$117,500, MS-67RD, February 2014
1909	72,702,618	4,339	63.9	97	20	27.00	45.00	70	70	140	375	$4,406, MS-67RD, April 2013
1909S	1,825,000	6,671	45.5	48	365	405.00	460.00	575	650	1,050	2,450	$10,281, MS-67RD, February 2013
1909S, S Over Horizontal S	*	1,290	53.1	70	370	420.00	480.00	600	725	1,250	2,500	$1,998, MS-66RD, January 2014
1910	146,801,218	2,667	63.8	95	25	50.00	55.00	70	140	230	775	$4,406, MS-67RD, June 2014
1910S	6,045,000	3,014	59.6	82	120	140.00	225.00	325	400	635	2,350	$15,275, MS-66RD, June 2014
1911	101,177,787	1,510	63.6	96	50	65.00	100.00	195	150	400	1,700	$7,050, MS-67RD, April 2014
1911D	12,672,000	1,805	59.9	79	125	195.00	345.00	480	650	1,400	6,650	$8,225, MS-66RD, April 2014
1911S	4,026,000	2,100	52.8	57	235	335.00	465.00	650	900	2,750	17,000	$2,820, MS-65RD, August 2013
1912	68,153,060	1,557	63.6	96	50	65.00	100.00	165	200	385	1,350	$18,800, MS-67RD, April 2013
1912D	10,411,000	1,360	59.7	78	240	275.00	335.00	800	700	1,850	10,750	$7,050, MS-65RD, February 2013
1912S	4,431,000	1,766	54.8	64	255	290.00	345.00	875	1,000	3,500		$4,406, MS-65RD, November 2013
1913	76,532,352	1,497	63.2	94	55	70.00	100.00	150	175	420	1,700	$19,975, MS-67RD, January 2013
1913D	15,804,000	1,332	59.8	79	175	225.00	375.00	550	700	2,200	6,750	$10,575, MS-66RD, January 2014
1913S	6,101,000	1,554	54.0	63	225	325.00	635.00	1,350	1,400	5,300	38,000	$4,406, MS-65RD, June 2014
1914	75,238,432	1,520	62.1	91	70	85.00	140.00	290	240	450	4,200	$28,200, MS-67RD, August 2013
1914D (b)	1,193,000	8,939	28.1	13	3,300	4,150.00	5,200.00	6,500	8,200	18,000	41,000	$18,800, MS-65RD, January 2014
1914S	4,137,000	1,677	50.1	45	460	575.00	1,050.00	1,950	2,400	8,200	51,000	$6,463, MS-65RD, September 2013
1915	29,092,120	1,523	62.0	89	105	130.00	160.00	275	265	900	1,700	$3,525, MS-66RD, January 2014
1915D	22,050,000	1,879	60.4	83	120	145.00	215.00	365	425	1,100	8,750	$7,638, MS-66RD, June 2013
1915S	4,833,000	1,358	50.5	51	235	385.00	1,150.00	1,750	2,700	5,000	25,750	$23,500, MS-66RD, September 2013
1916	131,833,677	2,284	63.9	97	35	42.50	57.00	75	95	300	625	$2,350, MS-67RD, March 2014
1916D	35,956,000	1,472	61.5	85	150	175.00	300.00	550	775	2,850	14,000	$17,625, MS-66RD, June 2014
1916S	22,510,000	1,528	58.6	74	175	235.00	550.00	1,650	1,550	7,500	20,000	$7,638, MS-65RD, August 2013
1917	196,429,785	1,714	62.2	93	32	35.00	42.50	90	140	425	1,300	$2,585, MS-66RD, January 2013
1917, Doubled-Die Obverse	*	219	30.0	18	5,750		8,350.00		14,000	19,500	29,500	$5,875, MS-63BN, August 2013
1917D	55,120,000	1,351	60.6	81	125	165.00	375.00	635	675	2,750	14,500	$2,350, MS-65RD, August 2013
1917S	32,620,000	1,099	60.5	81	160	225.00	575.00	1,600	1,275	13,000		$4,113, MS-65RD, December 2013
1918	288,104,634	1,514	63.3	94	27	30.00	40.00	140	175	330	1,500	$14,100, MS, March 2014
1918D	47,830,000	1,024	60.7	81	140	200.00	425.00	825	1,200	3,600		$25,850, MS-66RD, August 2013
1918S	34,680,000	1,157	60.4	77	185	325.00	500.00	2,000	1,400	9,500		$3,525, MS-64RD, February 2014
1919	392,021,000	2,013	63.8	96	28	32.00	45.00	100	120	200	435	$8,225, MS-68RD, April 2014
1919D	57,154,000	1,353	62.3	90	110	135.00	200.00	450	650	2,400	6,100	$1,763, MS-65RD, January 2014
1919S	139,760,000	1,502	60.1	80	115	250.00	410.00	1,600	1,100	5,500		$7,638, MS-65RD, April 2014
1920	310,165,000	2,087	63.5	96	28	34.00	42.50	65	95	220	750	$940, MS-66RD, January 2013
1920D	49,280,000	1,188	61.6	87	110	130.00	195.00	460	525	2,200		$22,325, MS-66RD, June 2014
1920S	46,220,000	1,161	59.7	75	185	300.00	385.00	2,000	2,100	12,000		$2,115, MS-64RD, February 2014
1921	39,157,000	1,450	63.5	95	80	82.50	90.00	130	190	345	1,550	$3,290, MS-66RD, January 2014
1921S	15,274,000	1,696	57.5	66	190	375.00	550.00	2,000	1,150	12,500		$1,880, MS-64RD, August 2013
1922D	7,160,000	2,816	48.5	55	165	190.00	275.00	530	465	2,000	9,000	$2,585, MS-65RD, August 2013
1922, No D (c)	*	7,538	25.1	2	27,000		47,500.00					$82,250, MS-65BN, April 2013
1922, Weak D (c)	*	1,259	19.0	4	750		5,000.00					$2,174, MS, April 2014

* Included in number above. † Ranked in the *100 Greatest U.S. Coins* (fourth edition). **a.** Many counterfeits exist—some die struck, some made by adding an "S" to a Philadelphia coin. **b.** Many counterfeits exist, including crude fakes, sophisticated die-struck forgeries, and altered 1944-D cents (the latter, unlike an authentic 1914-D cent, will have the designer's initials, V.D.B., on the shoulder). **c.** 1922 cents with a weak or completely missing mintmark were made from extremely worn dies that originally struck normal 1922-D cents. Three different die pairs were involved; two of them produced "Weak D" coins. One die pair (no. 2, identified by a "strong reverse") is acknowledged as having struck "No D" coins. Weak D cents are worth considerably less. Beware of fraudulently removed mintmark.

	Mintage	Cert	Avg	%MS	MS-63BN	MS-64BN	MS-64RB	MS-64RD	MS-65RB	MS-65RD	MS-66RD	Recent Auction Record
1923	74,723,000	1,317	63.8	97	$30.00	$40.00	$70.00	$130.00	$155	$360	$975	$4,700, MS-67RD, June 2013
1923S	8,700,000	1,090	57.1	64	390.00	500.00	1,500.00	3,000.00	3,600	17,000	31,500	$2,350, MS-65RB, June 2014
1924	75,178,000	1,147	63.6	95	50.00	60.00	77.50	120.00	110	375	1,900	$16,450, MS-67RD, April 2013
1924D	2,520,000	2,410	46.8	39	350.00	450.00	800.00	2,000.00	1,600	11,500		$9,400, MS-65RD, January 2014
1924S	11,696,000	1,315	56.6	64	225.00	325.00	740.00	3,700.00	2,100	9,500		$9,400, MS-64RD, January 2014
1925	139,949,000	2,275	64.4	98	20.00	26.00	50.00	65.00	75	135	320	$2,115, MS-67RD, September 2013
1925D	22,580,000	1,515	61.8	87	90.00	140.00	265.00	525.00	875	3,800	60,000	$4,113, MS-65RD, January 2014
1925S	26,380,000	1,248	57.7	68	200.00	250.00	675.00	4,850.00	3,400	14,000		$4,700, MS-65RB, February 2014
1926	157,088,000	3,137	64.7	99	18.00	24.00	35.00	50.00	65	110	260	$1,116, MS-67RD, January 2014
1926D	28,020,000	1,255	60.9	82	125.00	160.00	275.00	725.00	750	3,550		$4,700, MS-65RD, February 2013
1926S	4,550,000	1,834	54.8	51	325.00	1,050.00	2,100.00	11,500.00	4,900	90,000		$9,988, MS-65RB, October 2013
1927	144,440,000	1,937	63.9	96	20.00	25.00	37.50	80.00	40	135	425	$7,638, MS-67RD, February 2014
1927D	27,170,000	1,429	61.3	85	85.00	125.00	185.00	450.00	575	2,100		$2,233, MS-65RD, January 2014
1927S	14,276,000	1,177	60.2	82	140.00	190.00	375.00	1,450.00	2,000	7,750		$1,763, MS-64RD, June 2013
1928	134,116,000	2,089	64.3	97	13.00	19.00	33.00	67.50	70	120	365	$3,408, MS-67RD, April 2013
1928D	31,170,000	1,434	62.3	89	80.00	100.00	155.00	250.00	245	1,200	6,500	$1,410, MS-65RD, June 2014
1928S	17,266,000	1,045	59.8	79	100.00	160.00	300.00	750.00	875	4,850	26,500	$4,406, MS-65RD, September 2013
1929	185,262,000	2,330	64.5	98	14.00	22.00	33.00	42.50	45	105	275	$5,581, MS-67RD, April 2014
1929D	41,730,000	1,244	63.0	90	37.00	43.00	80.00	185.00	190	550	3,300	$4,113, MS-66RD, January 2014
1929S	50,148,000	1,837	63.0	92	29.00	37.50	60.00	110.00	185	475	3,300	$4,113, MS-66RD, March 2013
1930	157,415,000	5,923	65.1	99	10.00	13.00	16.00	20.00	22	43	105	$3,525, MS-67RD, February 2014
1930D	40,100,000	1,717	64.1	96	28.00	30.00	34.00	37.00	45	115	650	$1,645, MS-66RD, June 2014
1930S	24,286,000	3,026	64.6	99	12.00	14.00	19.00	38.00	29	90	375	$6,463, MS-66RD, April 2014
1931	19,396,000	2,370	64.4	98	35.00	39.00	42.00	65.00	90	125	425	$5,288, MS-67RD, August 2013
1931D	4,480,000	1,702	61.2	78	70.00	85.00	125.00	225.00	250	875	3,900	$4,113, MS-66RD, April 2013
1931S	866,000	8,740	57.4	69	195.00	210.00	240.00	300.00	315	550	1,600	$2,350, MS-66RD, January 2014
1932	9,062,000	2,274	64.8	98	28.00	31.00	34.00	45.00	48	115	265	$940, MS-66RD, September 2013
1932D	10,500,000	1,482	64.1	94	28.00	32.50	42.00	62.00	60	155	525	$8,519, MS-67RD, November 2013
1933	14,360,000	1,693	64.7	97	30.00	31.00	38.00	57.00	55	115	340	$3,557, MS-67RD, August 2013
1933D	6,200,000	2,588	64.4	97	25.00	26.00	28.00	80.00	85	135	415	$5,581, MS-67RD, February 2014
1934	219,080,000	4,322	65.6	99	7.00	10.00	11.00	16.00	16	37	60	$764, MS-67RD, December 2013
1934, Doubled-Die Obverse (d) *		11	62.1	82	250.00		350.00					$1,600, MS-64RB, October 2011
1934D	28,446,000	2,766	64.6	98	20.00	24.00	27.00	33.00	48	62	185	$11,163, MS-67RD, April 2014
1935	245,388,000	4,739	65.5	98	5.00	9.00	12.00	20.00	28	33	42	$1,293, MS-67RD, March 2014
1935D	47,000,000	2,881	65.5	99	6.00	11.00	14.00	21.00	35	39	54	$823, MS-67RD, February 2014
1935S	38,702,000	1,776	64.8	98	17.00	20.00	23.00	37.50	40	60	285	$3,055, MS-66RD, July 2014
1936	309,632,000	4,977	65.4	98	2.00	4.50	5.00	7.00	14	30	45	$705, MS-67RD, February 2014
1936, Doubled-Die Obverse (e) *		552	45.9	33	2,250.00							$259, AU-50, April 2014
1936D	40,620,000	3,085	65.7	99	2.00	5.00	6.00	9.00	16	21	60	$646, MS-67RD, August 2013
1936S	29,130,000	2,068	65.3	99	6.00	8.00	9.00	11.00	17	25	125	$4,259, MS-67RD, February 2014
1937	309,170,000	8,227	65.9	100	2.00	4.50	5.00	6.00	9	15	27	$2,233, MS-67RD, November 2013
1937D	50,430,000	5,484	65.9	99	6.00	8.50	9.00	9.50	12	17	33	$135, MS-67RD, January 2014
1937S	34,500,000	3,245	65.8	99	8.00	10.00	10.50	12.00	15	22	55	$1,998, MS-67RD, January 2014
1938	156,682,000	4,036	65.9	100	7.00	9.50	10.00	10.50	12	16	34	$2,820, MS-67RD, November 2013
1938D	20,010,000	4,224	65.9	99	7.00	10.00	10.50	11.00	13	17	35	$3,055, MS-67RD, January 2014
1938S	15,180,000	6,275	65.8	100	6.00	9.00	10.00	11.00	14	21	42	$2,115, MS-67RD, July 2014
1939	316,466,000	6,821	65.8	99	2.00	3.50	4.00	5.00	8	14	32	$705, MS-67RD, June 2013
1939D	15,160,000	3,855	65.9	99	4.00	7.00	8.00	10.50	13	18	37	$529, MS-67RD, April 2014
1939S	52,070,000	6,734	65.9	99	3.00	6.00	7.00	9.00	11	16	31	$3,966, MS-67RD, August 2013
1940	586,810,000	4,098	65.9	100	2.00	3.50	4.00	5.00	8	14	25	$3,819, MS-67RD, January 2014
1940D	81,390,000	4,066	66.0	100	2.00	5.50	6.00	7.00	9	15	26	$159, MS-67RD, January 2013
1940S	112,940,000	5,030	66.0	100	2.25	5.50	6.00	7.00	9	15	29	$306, MS-67RD, June 2013
1941	887,018,000	5,309	65.1	97	1.00	4.00	4.50	5.00	8	14	23	$4,994, MS-65RD, November 2013
1941D	128,700,000	3,072	66.1	99	2.00	6.50	7.00	10.00	11	15	30	$441, MS-67RD, August 2013
1941S	92,360,000	4,664	66.0	99	2.00	6.50	7.00	10.00	11	15	28	$1,880, MS-67RD, November 2013
1942	657,796,000	4,133	65.7	99	1.00	3.50	4.00	5.00	8	14	26	$14,100, AU-58, November 2013
1942D	206,698,000	5,324	65.9	99	1.00	3.50	4.00	5.00	8	14	29	$3,055, MS-67RD, November 2013
1942S	85,590,000	4,399	65.8	99	8.00	12.00	12.50	13.50	13	17	32	$3,290, MS-67RD, February 2014

* Included in number above. **d.** The remains of a secondary 3 and 4 are evident below the primary digits. **e.** FS-01-1936-101.

Chart continued on next page.

	Mintage	Cert	Avg	%MS	AU-50	MS-63	MS-65	MS-66	MS-67	MS-68	Recent Auction Record
1943	684,628,670	14,389	66.0	100	$0.50	$2.50	$8	$35	$90	$1,200	$88,125, 1, November 2013
1943, Bronze † (a)	*	14	56.6	43	160,000.00						$218,500, AU-58, January 2010
1943, Silver (a)	*	n/a	n/a	n/a	4,500.00						$4,313, AU-58, March 2010
1943D (a)	217,660,000	12,787	66.3	100	0.75	3.00	10	40	100	1,300	$2,820, MS-68, April 2013
1943D, Boldly Doubled Mintmark (b)	*	38	63.6	97	60.00	125.00	1,400	2,500	11,000		$1,116, MS-65, December 2013
1943S (a)	191,550,000	11,986	66.1	100	1.00	6.00	20	50	135	2,000	$141,000, EF-35, November 2013

* Included in number above. † Ranked in the *100 Greatest U.S. Coins* (fourth edition). **a.** In 1943 a handful of cents were accidentally struck on old bronze and silver planchets, instead of the intended steel planchets. Today about a dozen are known to exist. Numerous regular steel cents have been plated with copper as novelties or with intent to deceive; their true nature is easily revealed with a magnet. **b.** FS-01-1943D-501.

	Mintage	Cert	Avg	%MS	MS-63RB	MS-64RB	MS-64RD	MS-65RB	MS-65RD	MS-66RD	MS-67RD	Recent Auction Record
1944	1,435,400,000	5,724	65.7	99	$1.00	$2.00	$3	$5	$12	$25	$65	$30,550, AU-58, November 2013
1944D	430,578,000	5,816	65.3	97	0.85	1.00	2	4	14	26	85	$30,550, AU-53, November 2013
1944D, D Over S	*	638	54.7	54	450.00	500.00	1,000	700	2,500	9,200		$1,116, MS-64RD, January 2014
1944S	282,760,000	6,938	66.0	99	0.85	1.00	2	4	13	27	110	$141, MS-67RD, May 2014
1945	1,040,515,000	3,715	65.6	99	0.85	1.00	2	2	9	20		$3,819, MS-68RD, November 2013
1945D	266,268,000	5,189	65.9	100	0.85	1.00	2	2	10	27	140	$2,115, MS-67RD, June 2014
1945S	181,770,000	7,356	66.1	100	0.85	1.00	2	2	10	24	95	$7,050, AU-58, November 2013
1946	991,655,000	2,506	65.1	99	0.60	0.85	2	3	14	175		$7,168, MS-67RD, January 2014
1946D	315,690,000	3,199	65.9	99	0.60	0.85	2	2	10	23	300	$2,115, MS-67RD, March 2014
1946S	198,100,000	5,142	65.7	99	0.60	0.85	2	2	10	24	135	$940, MS-67RD, September 2013
1946S, S Over D	*	47	62.6	87	240.00		300		575			$1,998, MS-66RD, June 2014
1947	190,555,000	2,205	65.1	99	1.00	2.00	4	4	12	175		$4,113, MS-67RD, April 2013
1947D	194,750,000	2,936	65.7	99	0.60	0.85	2	2	10	29	650	$764, MS-67RD, February 2013
1947S	99,000,000	3,967	65.9	100	0.85	1.00	2	2	12	27	175	$1,704, MS-67RD, February 2014
1948	317,570,000	1,710	65.2	99	0.85	1.00	2	2	15	190		$7,168, MS-67RD, January 2014
1948D	172,637,500	2,432	65.7	100	0.60	0.85	2	2	11	32	900	$999, MS-67RD, August 2013
1948S	81,735,000	4,552	66.0	100	1.00	2.00	3	3	10	25	150	$306, MS-67RD, June 2013
1949	217,775,000	1,656	65.1	98	1.00	2.00	3	4	18	175		$4,406, MS, March 2014
1949D	153,132,500	1,742	65.4	99	1.00	2.00	3	3	14	42		$1,763, MS-67RD, June 2013
1949S	64,290,000	4,649	65.9	100	2.00	3.00	4	4	16	38	200	$3,173, MS-67RD, March 2014
1950	272,635,000	1,755	65.3	99	0.85	1.00	2	3	20	125	1,400	$3,055, MS-67RD, August 2013
1950D	334,950,000	2,337	65.6	99	0.60	0.85	2	3	17	34		$15,275, MS-67RD, November 2013
1950S	118,505,000	2,566	65.8	99	0.85	1.00	2	2	13	35		$1,293, MS-67RD, June 2013
1951	284,576,000	1,404	65.3	98	0.70	0.90	2	3	18	150		$5,288, MS-67RD, August 2013
1951D	625,355,000	2,891	65.5	98	0.60	0.85	2	2	10	24	750	$1,410, MS-67RD, June 2013
1951D, D Over S	*	125	60.7	78	100.00	125.00	150					$2,350, MS-67RD, April 2014
1951S	136,010,000	2,176	65.7	99	1.00	2.00	3	3	12	38	550	$823, MS-67RD, January 2014
1952	186,775,000	1,614	65.5	99	1.00	2.00	3	3	16	160	4,500	$4,994, MS-67RD, April 2014
1952D	746,130,000	3,275	65.5	98	0.75	0.90	2	2	10	24		$1,058, MS-67RD, December 2013
1952S	137,800,004	2,715	65.9	100	2.00	3.00	4	4	13	31	490	$999, MS-67RD, June 2013
1953	256,755,000	1,781	65.1	99	0.50	0.75	2	3	18	115		$14,100, MS-67RD, January 2014
1953D	700,515,000	2,970	65.4	98	0.50	0.75	1	1	11	29		$3,525, MS-67RD, August 2013
1953S	181,835,000	3,079	65.8	99	0.60	0.85	2	2	12	40	300	$3,055, MS-67RD, March 2014
1954	71,640,050	2,445	64.9	99	0.60	0.85	2	3	27	60		$23,500, MS-67RD, March 2014
1954D	251,552,500	3,305	65.6	98	0.50	0.75	1	1	10	55		$1,293, MS-67RD, June 2013
1954S	96,190,000	9,214	65.9	100	0.50	0.75	1	1	9	15		$1,880, MS-67RD, August 2013
1955	330,958,200	2,725	64.9	96	0.35	0.50	1	1	19	45		$3,819, MS-67RD, December 2013
1955, Doubled-Die Obverse †	*	6,562	58.8	48	3,500.00 (a)	5,300.00	*11,500*	*15,000*	*36,000*			$25,850, MS-64RD, January 2014
1955D	563,257,500	4,497	65.4	99	0.35	0.50	1	1	10	21		$7,050, MS-67RD, April 2013
1955S	44,610,000	14,525	65.9	100	0.85	2.00	3	3	9	18	145	$2,115, MS-67RD, February 2014
1956	420,745,000	3,317	65.5	99	0.35	0.50	1	2	13	50		$3,819, MS-67RD, August 2013
1956D	1,098,201,100	4,958	65.4	98	0.30	0.50	1	1	10	25	2,750	$1,175, MS-67RD, November 2013
1956D, D Above Shadow D (b)	*	150	63.0	87	35.00							$1,293, MS-67RD, February 2014
1957	282,540,000	3,071	65.5	99	0.30	0.50	1	2	15	42		$470, MS, December 2013
1957D	1,051,342,000	5,885	65.5	99	0.30	0.50	1	1	10	29		$2,115, MS-67RD, June 2013
1958	252,525,000	4,052	65.5	99	0.30	0.50	1	1	10	29	450	$1,528, MS-67RD, June 2013

* Included in number above. † Ranked in the *100 Greatest U.S. Coins* (fourth edition). **a.** Value in EF-45 is $2,000; in AU-50, $2,300; in AU-55, $2,500; in MS-60BN, $2,750; in MS-63BN, $3,000; in MS-64BN, $4,000; in MS-65BN, $5,500. Varieties exist with doubling that, while still strong, is weaker than that pictured; these command premiums, but are not nearly as valuable. Note that many counterfeit 1955 Doubled Die cents exist. On authentic pieces, there is a faint die scratch under the left horizontal bar of the T in CENT. **b.** The remains of a totally separated D mintmark are evident in the field below the primary D.

	Mintage	Cert	Avg	%MS	MS-63RB	MS-64RB	MS-64RD	MS-65RB	MS-65RD	MS-66RD	MS-67RD	Recent Auction Record
1958, DblDie Obv (3 known) (c)	**	3	64.3	100	—							
1958D	800,953,300	8,067	65.7	99	$0.30	$0.50	$1	$2	$9	$24		$1,939, MS-67RD, January 2014

** Included in regular 1958 mintage. **c.** No specimens have been reported being found in circulation, wheat cent bags, Uncirculated rolls, "or other means that would lead to credibility of a true accidental release from the mint" (*Cherrypickers' Guide to Rare Die Varieties*, fifth edition, volume l).

Proof Lincoln, Wheat Ears Reverse, Cents

PF-60 to 70 (Matte Proof). Matte Proof Lincoln cents of a new style were made from 1909 to 1916. These have minutely matte or pebbled surfaces caused by special treatment of the dies. The rims are square and sharp. Such pieces cannot easily be told from certain circulation strikes with similar borders. Expert verification is recommended. Certified holders usually list these simply as "Proof," not "Matte Proof." Most are brown, or brown with tinges of red. Nearly all full "red" coins have been dipped or recolored. Generally, Proofs below 63 are unattractive and are not desired by most collectors. *Obverse and Reverse:* At Matte PF-65 or higher there are no traces of abrasion or contact marks. Color will range from brown (BN)—the most common— to brown with significant tinges of mint red-orange (RB), or with much mint color (RD). Some tiny flecks are normal on coins certified as PF-65 but should be microscopic or absent above that. Coins in the PF-60 to 63 range are BN or sometimes RB—almost impossible to be RD unless dipped. Lower-grade Proofs usually have poor eye appeal.

PF-60 to 70 (Mirror Proof). Mirror-finish Proofs were made from 1936 to 1942 and again from 1950 to 1958. Proofs of this era are mostly from dies polished overall (including the portrait), although some later issues have frosted ("cameo") portraits. Quality can be a problem for the 1936 to 1942 issues. Check for carbon spots and recoloring. Proofs of later dates are easy to find. Generally, Proofs below 63 are unattractive and are not desired by most collectors. *Obverse and Reverse:* PF-65 and higher coins are usually RB (colors should be nicely blended) or RD, the latter with bright red-orange fading slightly to hints of brown. Some tiny flecks are normal on coins certified as PF-65 but should be microscopic or absent above that. PF-60 and 61 coins can be dull, stained, or spotted but still have some original mint color. Coins with fingerprints must be given a low numerical grade. Lower-grade Proofs usually have poor eye appeal.

**Matte Proof Lincoln,
Wheat Ears Reverse, Cent**

**Mirror Proof Lincoln,
Wheat Ears Reverse, Cent**

	Mintage	Cert	Avg	PF-63RB	PF-64RB	PF-65RB	PF-65RD	PF-66RB	PF-66RD	PF-67RD	Recent Auction Record
1909, V.D.B. (a)	1,194	169	64.6	$2,750	$5,000	$13,000					$55,813, PF-66RB, June 2014
1909	2,618	676	64.6	675	1,150	1,600	$2,700	$3,600	$6,750		$5,875, PF-66RD, April 2013
1910	4,118	618	64.4	600	1,100	1,500	2,550	3,400	5,750		$3,290, PF, January 2013
1911	1,725	556	64.4	600	1,050	1,500	3,400	3,200	10,500		$9,400, PF-66RD, June 2014
1912	2,172	590	64.2	600	1,050	1,600	6,250	4,500			$3,966, PF-66RB, February 2014
1913	2,983	767	64.4	600	1,050	1,550	2,450	3,100	4,750		$25,850, PF-67RD, January 2014
1914	1,365	482	64.7	600	1,100	1,550	2,450	3,100	5,000		$3,525, PF-66BN, June 2014
1915	1,150	388	64.5	650	1,250	1,900	3,500	3,600	7,000		$17,625, PF-65RD, January 2014
1916	1,050	275	64.6	1,250	2,500	4,750	12,000	9,750			$7,931, PF-64RB, June 2014
1936	5,569	1,990	64.0	200	485	1,000	2,800	4,500	7,000		$21,150, PF-66Cam, June 2013
1937	9,320	2,379	64.3	65	90	155	350	875	1,000		$21,150, PF-67Cam, September 2013
1938	14,734	2,674	64.5	60	80	140	200	425	900		$2,585, PF-66Cam, January 2014
1939	13,520	2,689	64.6	55	70	120	180	400	800		$2,820, PF-67RD, January 2014
1940	15,872	2,531	64.5	45	60	110	170	375	750		$7,931, PF-67RD, June 2013
1941	21,100	2,599	64.3	40	55	100	165	370	475		$28,200, PF-67RD, November 2013
1942	32,600	4,013	64.0	41	58	105	175	370	700		$2,115, PF-66Cam, June 2013
1950	51,386	2,572	65.1				70		90	$750	$5,141, PF-67DCam, January 2014
1951	57,500	2,330	65.3				65		85	225	$1,763, PF-67Cam, April 2013
1952	81,980	2,370	65.5				50		75	130	$1,528, PF-67Cam, April 2013
1953	128,800	3,079	65.8				30		40	100	$2,585, PF-67Cam, February 2014
1954	233,300	2,703	65.9				20		30	60	$2,820, PF-68Cam, April 2013
1955	378,200	3,346	66.4				18		30	50	$7,638, PF-68DCam, April 2013
1956	669,384	2,913	66.5				8		25	30	$7,638, PF-68DCam, June 2013
1957	1,247,952	3,305	66.3				8		25	30	$1,058, PF-68Cam, April 2013
1958	875,652	3,236	66.6				8		20	27	$1,293, PF-67DCam, June 2013

Note: No early references (pre-1960s), Mint records, or reliable market listings have been found to confirm the existence of true 1917 Proofs. "Examples seen have had nice matte-like surfaces, sometimes on just one side, but have lacked the vital combination of broad, flat rims on both sides and a mirror Proof edge (when viewed edge-on from the side)" *(A Guide Book of Lincoln Cents)*. The leading certification services do not recognize Proofs of this year. The editors of this book also do not believe that true Proofs of 1917 exist. **a.** Of the 1,194 coins reported struck, an estimated 400 to 600 were issued.

LINCOLN, MEMORIAL REVERSE
(1959–2008)

Copper Alloy (1959–1982): Designer Victor D. Brenner (obverse), Frank Gasparro (reverse); mints: Philadelphia, Denver, San Francisco. 1959–1962—Weight 3.11 grams; composition .950 copper, .050 tin and zinc; diameter 19 mm; plain edge. 1962–1982—Weight 3.11 grams; composition .950 copper, .050 zinc.

Copper Alloy (1959–1982)

Copper-Plated Zinc (1982 to date): Weight 2.5 grams; composition copper-plated zinc (core: .992 zinc, .008 copper, with a plating of pure copper; total content .975 zinc, .025 copper).

Copper-Plated Zinc (1982–2008)

History. In 1959 a new cent design, by Frank Gasparro, was introduced. In 1969, the dies were modified to strengthen the design, and Lincoln's head was made slightly smaller. In 1973, the dies were further modified, and the engraver's initials (FG) were enlarged. In 1974 the initials were reduced slightly. During 1982 the dies were modified again and the bust, lettering, and date were made slightly smaller. The Lincoln Memorial reverse was used until 2009, when a switch was made to four new reverse designs honoring the bicentennial of Abraham Lincoln's birth. Lincoln Memorial cents were struck at the Philadelphia, Denver, and San Francisco mints, with the latter in smaller numbers. Partway through 1982 the bronze alloy was discontinued in favor of copper-coated zinc.

Striking and Sharpness. Striking varies and can range from "sloppy" to needle sharp. On the obverse, check Lincoln's hair and beard (although the sharpness of this feature varied in the dies; for more information see *A Guide Book of Lincoln Cents* [Bowers, 2008]). Tiny marks on the shoulder of Lincoln indicate a weak strike there. On the reverse the sharpness can vary, including on the tiny statue of Lincoln and the shrubbery. On the reverse there can be light striking on the steps of the Memorial, and at IBU and M (E PLURIBUS UNUM). The quality of the fields can vary, as well. Some early copper-coated zinc cents, particularly of 1982 and 1983, can have planchet blisters or problems.

Availability. Coins in this series are plentiful for standard dates and mintmarks.

MS-60 to 70 (Mint State). *Obverse and reverse:* At MS-65 and higher, the luster is rich on all areas, except perhaps the shoulder (which may be grainy and show original planchet surface). There is no rubbing, and no contact marks are visible except under magnification. Coins with full or nearly full mint orange-red color can be designated RD; those with full or nearly full brown-toned surfaces can be designated BN; and those with a substantial percentage of red-orange and of brown can be called RB. Ideally, MS-65 or finer coins should have good eye appeal, which in the RB category means nicely blended colors, not stained or blotched. Below MS-65, full RD coins become scarce, and at MS-60 to 62 are virtually non-existent, unless they have been dipped. Copper is a very active metal, and influences such as slight abrasions, contact marks, and so on that define the grade also affect the color. The official American Numismatic Association grading standards allow for "dull" and/or "spotted" coins at MS-60 and 61, as well as incomplete luster. In the marketplace, interpretations often vary widely. BN and RB coins at MS-60 and 61 tend to be more attractive than (dipped) RD coins.

1960, Large Date

1960, Small Date

1960-D, D Over D, Large Over Small Date
FS-01-1960D-101.

1969-S, Doubled-Die Obverse
FS-01-1969S-101.

1970-S, Small Date (High 7)

1970-S, Large Date (Low 7)

1970-S, Doubled-Die Obverse
FS-01-1970S-101.

1972, Doubled-Die Obverse
FS-01-1972-101.

1980, Doubled-Die Obverse
FS-01-1980-101.

1982, Large Date　　　**1982, Small Date**　　　**1983, Doubled-Die Reverse**
FS-01-1983-801.　　　**1984, Doubled Ear**
FS-01-1984-101.

1992, Normal　　　**1992, Close AM**　　　**1995, Doubled-Die Obverse**
FS-01-1995-101.　　　**1997, Doubled Ear**
FS-01-1997-101.

1999, Normal　　　**1999, Wide AM**

	Mintage	Cert	Avg	%MS	MS-63RB	MS-65RD	MS-66RD	MS-67RD	Recent Auction Record
1959	609,715,000	2,202	65.3	100	$0.20	$0.40	$37	$550	$1,528, MS-67RD, April 2014
1959D	1,279,760,000	2,186	65.4	99	0.50	0.60	25	475	$646, MS-67RD, September 2013
1960, Large Date (a)	586,405,000	2,204	65.2	100	0.20	0.40	30		$3,819, MS-67RD, December 2013
1960, Small Date (a)	*	2,288	65.3	100	3.00	7.00	38		$3,349, MS-67RD, November 2013
1960D, Large Date (a,b)	1,580,884,000	1,776	64.9	98	0.20	0.40	29		$3,055, MS-67RD, September 2013
1960D, Small Date (a)	*	2,277	65.4	99	0.20	0.40	31	1,850	$1,880, MS-67RD, April 2013
1960, D Over D, Small Over Large Date	*	671	63.9	95	225.00	500.00	2,000		$1,998, MS-66RD, June 2013
1961	753,345,000	1,475	64.9	100	0.15	0.40	50		$176, MS-67RD, December 2013
1961D	1,753,266,700	1,985	64.9	99	0.15	0.40	70	100	$4,406, MS-67RD, June 2014
1962	606,045,000	1,632	65.2	100	0.15	0.40	50		$8,813, MS-67RD, February 2014
1962D	1,793,148,140	1,585	64.8	99	0.15	0.40	75	250	$4,994, MS-67RD, January 2014
1963	754,110,000	1,807	65.2	100	0.15	0.40	60		$3,173, MS-67RD, January 2014
1963D	1,774,020,400	1,460	64.5	99	0.15	0.40	90	425	$2,820, MS-67RD, September 2013
1964	2,648,575,000	1,305	65.0	99	0.15	0.40	65		$2,585, MS-61RD, April 2013
1964D	3,799,071,500	934	65.2	99	0.15	0.40	42		$2,820, MS-67RD, November 2013
1965 (c)	1,497,224,900	1,100	65.6	100	0.20	0.50	27		$7,638, MS-67RD, January 2014
1966 (c)	2,188,147,783	729	65.3	99	0.20	0.50	60		$382, MS-65RD, November 2013
1967 (c)	3,048,667,100	620	65.1	99	0.20	0.50	90		$2,350, MS-67RD, January 2014
1968	1,707,880,970	752	65.3	100	0.25	0.60	33		$1,293, MS-67RD, March 2013
1968D	2,886,269,600	1,332	65.0	98	0.15	0.40	27		$1,116, MS-67RD, April 2013
1968S	258,270,001	1,586	65.2	99	0.15	0.40	29		$529, MS-67RD, June 2013
1969	1,136,910,000	732	65.2	99	0.35	0.70	55		$3,819, MS-62RD, June 2014
1969D	4,002,832,200	1,064	64.9	98	0.15	0.40	28		$1,234, MS-64RD, January 2014
1969S	544,375,000	1,360	63.8	92	0.15	0.50	65		$4,406, MS-67RD, January 2014
1969S, DblDie Obverse ‡ (d)	*	46	57.5	33	75,000.00				$21,150, AU-55, June 2014

* Included in number above. ‡ Ranked in the *100 Greatest U.S. Modern Coins*. **a.** The alignment of the 1 and 9 in the date can be used for a quick determation of Large versus Small Date. *Large Date:* the top of the 1 is significantly lower than the top of the 9. *Small Date:* the tops of the 1 and 9 are at the same level. **b.** A variety once called 1960-D, Large Date, D Over Horizontal D has been disproved as such, and is now considered simply a triple-punched D. **c.** Values and auction records for Special Mint Set coins are listed with the Proofs for this type. **d.** Beware of specimens that exhibit only strike doubling, as opposed to a true doubled die; these are worth only face value. See appendix A of the *Cherrypickers' Guide to Rare Die Varieties*, fifth edition, volume I.

Chart continued on next page.

	Mintage	Cert	Avg	%MS	MS-63RB	MS-65RD	MS-66RD	MS-67RD	Recent Auction Record
1970	1,898,315,000	793	65.5	100	$0.30	$0.65	$25	$250	$4,406, MS-67RD, March 2014
1970D	2,891,438,900	721	65.1	100	0.15	0.40	70	1,000	$45, MS-66RD, June 2013
1970S, All kinds	690,560,004								
1970S, Sm Dt (High 7)		2,290	64.5	100	25.00	55.00	240		$499, MS-66RD, June 2013
1970S, Lg Dt (Low 7)		1,933	64.6	98	0.20	0.50	30		$1,410, MS-67RD, April 2013
1970S, Doubled-Die Obverse		55	62.5	80					$10,350, MS-64RD, December 2008
1971	1,919,490,000	1,061	64.9	96	0.25	0.60	25		$4,406, MS-67RD, June 2014
1971, Doubled-Die Obverse	*	n/a	n/a	n/a		50.00			$82, AU-58, December 2013
1971D	2,911,045,600	652	65.1	99	0.20	0.50	24	600	$329, MS-62BN, September 2013
1971S	525,133,459	845	65.1	99	0.20	0.75	50		$3,290, MS-67RD, June 2014
1972	2,933,255,000	1,216	65.0	97	0.15	0.40	32		$3,290, MS-67RD, December 2013
1972, Doubled-Die Obverse (e)	*	6,366	64.4	98	400.00	650.00	1,000	5,800	$12,925, MS-67RD, March 2014
1972D	2,665,071,400	691	65.1	98	0.15	0.40	28		$2,820, MS-67RD, June 2013
1972S	376,939,108	772	64.9	99	0.25	0.75	78	1,100	$1,410, MS-67RD, June 2013
1973	3,728,245,000	829	65.5	100	0.15	0.40	37	600	$470, MS-67RB, August 2013
1973D	3,549,576,588	889	65.2	100	0.15	0.40	37		$4,994, MS-67RD, February 2014
1973S	317,177,295	721	64.7	100	0.25	0.85	200		$558, MS-66RD, December 2013
1974	4,232,140,523	1,005	65.7	100	0.15	0.40	27	175	$382, MS-66RD, November 2013
1974D	4,235,098,000	971	65.7	100	0.15	0.40	23	100	$206, MS-67RD, July 2013
1974S	409,426,660	511	64.8	99	0.25	0.75	100	750	$1,998, MS-67RD, September 2013
1975	5,451,476,142	811	65.7	100	0.15	0.40	29	150	$6,463, MS-62RD, January 2014
1975D	4,505,275,300	690	65.5	100	0.15	0.40	28	350	$4,113, MS-67RD, March 2014
1976	4,674,292,426	761	65.8	100	0.15	0.40	27	55	$7,931, MS-68RD, January 2014
1976D	4,221,592,455	465	65.2	100	0.15	0.40	35	750	$529, MS-67RD, June 2013
1977	4,469,930,000	659	65.6	100	0.15	0.40	55	130	$113, MS-67RD, June 2013
1977D	4,194,062,300	410	65.0	100	0.15	0.40	85	675	$1,175, MS-67RD, June 2013
1978	5,558,605,000	423	65.2	98	0.15	0.40	80	625	$3,819, MS-67RD, September 2013
1978D	4,280,233,400	370	65.1	99	0.15	0.40	75	425	$259, MS-67RD, June 2013
1979	6,018,515,000	1,080	66.2	99	0.15	0.40	19	70	$23, MS-67RD, November 2009
1979D	4,139,357,254	527	65.2	99	0.15	0.40	60		$764, MS-67RD, June 2014
1980	7,414,705,000	555	65.5	99	0.15	0.40	27	125	$212, MS-67RD, June 2013
1980, Doubled-Die Obverse	*	255	61.8	80	225.00	350.00			$253, MS-65RD, September 2008
1980D (f)	5,140,098,660	632	65.4	100	0.15	0.40	40	400	$499, MS-67RD, March 2013
1981	7,491,750,000	576	65.3	99	0.15	0.40	35	125	$1,058, MS-66BN, September 2013
1981D	5,373,235,677	657	65.5	100	0.15	0.40	40	225	$823, MS-63RD, June 2013
1982, Large Date	10,712,525,000	1,074	65.6	99	0.20	0.50	25	55	$55, MS-67RD, October 2013
1982, Small Date	*	176	65.1	100	0.30	0.60	45		$92, MS-67RD, May 2014
1982D	6,012,979,368	702	65.8	99	0.15	0.40	23	35	$764, MS-68RD, June 2013
1982, Zinc, Large Date (g)		355	66.5	100	0.35	0.75	35	60	$646, MS-68RD, June 2013
1982, Zinc, Small Date (g)		437	66.5	100	0.50	0.85	37		$299, MS-66RD, December 2009
1982D, Zinc, Large Date (g)		268	66.4	100	0.20	0.50	25		$27, MS-66RD, April 2009
1982D, Zinc, Small Date (g)		288	66.3	100	0.15	0.40	15		$27, MS-66RD, April 2009
1983	7,752,355,000	760	65.5	98	0.15	0.40	18	45	$23,500, MS-62RB, December 2013
1983, Doubled-Die Reverse (h)	*	1,901	64.8	98	250.00	385.00	550	1,200	$1,763, MS-67RD, March 2014
1983D	6,467,199,428	638	66.4	100	0.15	0.40	15	31	$646, MS-68RD, March 2013
1984	8,151,079,000	698	66.0	99	0.15	0.40	15	35	$734, MS-64RD, September 2013
1984, Doubled Ear (i)	*				175.00	230.00	350	425	$1,528, MS-67RD, December 2013
1984D	5,569,238,906	591	66.1	99	0.15	0.40	15	35	$1,410, MS-68RD, June 2013
1985	5,648,489,887	972	66.4	100	0.15	0.40	15	35	$5,875, MS-68RD, February 2014
1985D	5,287,339,926	1,110	66.9	100	0.15	0.40	15	29	$44, MS-68RD, August 2009
1986	4,491,395,493	627	66.5	100	0.15	0.40	15	35	$881, MS-66BN, February 2014
1986D	4,442,866,698	999	66.8	100	0.15	0.40	15	35	$107, MS-68RD, June 2013
1987	4,682,466,931	930	66.6	100	0.15	0.40	14	29	$170, MS-68RD, June 2013
1987D	4,879,389,514	1,061	66.5	100	0.15	0.40	15	32	$529, MS-68RD, June 2013

* Included in number above. **e.** Several less dramatically doubled varieties exist; these command premiums over the normal coin but are worth considerably less than the variety pictured. Counterfeits of the 1972 doubled die are frequently encountered. **f.** A variety previously listed in the *Cherrypickers' Guide* as a 1980-D, D Over S, has since been delisted from that catalog. It should command no premium. **g.** Included in the mintage of the corresponding copper-alloy cent. **h.** All reverse lettering is strongly doubled, as are the designer's initials and portions of the Lincoln Memorial. **i.** Values are for coins certified as the Doubled Ear variety (FS-101). More than 1,500 certifications exist for all 1984 doubled-die varieties; this number certainly includes FS-101, but it is unknown how many.

	Mintage	Cert	Avg	%MS	MS-63RB	MS-65RD	MS-66RD	MS-67RD	Recent Auction Record
1988	6,092,810,000	588	66.2	99	$0.15	$0.40	$20	$40	$683, MS-68RD, June 2014
1988D	5,253,740,443	700	66.5	100	0.15	0.40	14	25	$683, MS-68RD, June 2014
1989	7,261,535,000	803	66.4	100	0.15	0.40	14	25	$4,113, MS-68RD, June 2013
1989D	5,345,467,111	867	66.4	100	0.15	0.40	14	31	$247, MS-68RD, June 2014
1990	6,851,765,000	577	66.4	100	0.15	0.40	19	36	$705, MS-62BN, February 2014
1990D	4,922,894,533	1,087	66.8	100	0.15	0.40	14	25	$118, MS-64RD, July 2014
1991	5,165,940,000	714	66.5	100	0.15	0.40	14	25	$585, MS-68RD, September 2013
1991D	4,158,446,076	1,088	66.9	100	0.15	0.40	14	25	$135, MS-68RD, June 2013
1992	4,648,905,000	1,274	66.9	100	0.15	0.40	14	25	$482, MS-68RD, February 2013
1992, Close AM ‡ (j)	*	9	58.4	33	—	—			
1992D	4,448,673,300	1,252	66.9	99	0.15	0.40	14	25	$58, MS-68RD, June 2013
1992D, Close AM ‡ (j)	*	18	59.6	44	—	—			
1993	5,684,705,000	993	66.8	100	0.15	0.40	14	25	$188, MS-65RD, July 2014
1993D	6,426,650,571	1,117	67.0	100	0.15	0.40	14	25	$40, MS-68RD, June 2013
1994	6,500,850,000	569	66.0	98	0.15	0.40	14	25	$881, MS-65RD, September 2013
1994D	7,131,765,000	727	66.8	100	0.15	0.40	15	27	$176, MS-68RD, March 2013
1995	6,411,440,000	933	66.4	100	0.15	0.40	15	30	$149, MS-68RD, June 2014
1995, DblDie Obverse ‡	*	28,501	67.0	100	35.00	50.00	90	220	$317, MS-68RD, May 2013
1995D	7,128,560,000	753	66.5	99	0.15	0.40	15	35	$1,880, MS-68RD, December 2013
1996	6,612,465,000	875	66.7	100	0.15	0.40	12	18	$188, MS-68RD, June 2013
1996, Wide AM (j)	*	n/a	n/a	n/a	—	—			
1996D	6,510,795,000	1,242	67.0	100	0.15	0.40	12	18	$3,525, MS-65RD, September 2013
1997	4,622,800,000	518	66.2	100	0.15	0.40	15	42	$1,998, MS-68RD, June 2013
1997, Doubled Ear	*	234	64.9	100	250.00	450.00			$153, MS-65RD, February 2014
1997D	4,576,555,000	637	66.6	100	0.15	0.40	14	30	$585, MS-68RD, September 2013
1998	5,032,155,000	830	66.2	100	0.15	0.40	12	18	$940, MS-67RD, April 2013
1998, Wide AM ‡ (j)	*	483	64.4	97	12.00	25.00	40		$72, MS-65RD, June 2014
1998D	5,225,353,500	535	66.6	100	0.15	0.40	17	57	$235, MS-68RD, June 2013
1999	5,237,600,000	1,234	66.2	100	0.15	0.40	13	30	$2,585, MS-63RD, January 2014
1999, Wide AM ‡ (j)	*	179	63.9	94		500.00			$764, MS-65RD, June 2014
1999D	6,360,065,000	1,100	67.3	100	0.15	0.40	12	25	$1,293, MS-69RD, June 2013
2000	5,503,200,000	1,696	66.3	100	0.15	0.40	12	25	$764, MS-66RD, April 2013
2000, Wide AM (j)	*	1,295	65.6	100	10.00	20.00	35	55	$18, MS-66RD, May 2009
2000D	8,774,220,000	910	67.0	100	0.15	0.40	12	25	$141, MS-62RD, April 2014
2001	4,959,600,000	1,065	67.5	100	0.15	0.40	11	18	$1,645, MS-63RD, April 2013
2001D	5,374,990,000	1,014	67.5	100	0.15	0.40	11	18	$441, MS-69RD, June 2013
2002	3,260,800,000	1,207	67.7	100	0.15	0.40	11	16	$123, MS-69RD, June 2014
2002D	4,028,055,000	1,288	67.6	100	0.15	0.40	12	19	$213, MS-69RD, June 2013
2003	3,300,000,000	1,970	67.8	100	0.15	0.40	11	16	$66, MS-69RD, June 2013
2003D	3,548,000,000	936	67.6	100	0.15	0.40	10	15	$141, MS-69RD, July 2013
2004	3,379,600,000	679	67.0	100	0.15	0.40	10	20	$353, MS-69RD, June 2013
2004D	3,456,400,000	689	66.7	100	0.15	0.40	10	18	$49, MS-68RD, June 2013
2005	3,935,600,000	489	66.9	100	0.15	0.40	10	20	$53, MS-69RD, June 2009
2005D	3,764,450,500	586	66.8	100	0.15	0.40	12	30	$42, MS-67RD, May 2009
2006	4,290,000,000	496	66.4	100	0.15	0.40	10	18	$23, MS-67RD, May 2009
2006D	3,944,000,000	526	66.4	100	0.15	0.40	13	20	$21, MS-67RD, May 2009
2007	3,762,400,000	442	66.3	100	0.15	0.40	16	22	$39, MS-67RD, May 2009
2007D	3,638,800,000	452	66.2	100	0.15	0.40	16	22	$646, MS-65RD, August 2013
2008	2,558,800,000	550	66.5	100	0.15	0.40	12	18	$21, MS-67RD, May 2009
2008D	2,849,600,000	543	66.3	100	0.15	0.40	15	30	$247, MS-68RD, March 2013

* Included in number above. ‡ Ranked in the *100 Greatest U.S. Modern Coins*. **j.** The reverse hub used for cents from 1974 to 1992 had the AM of AMERICA separated. A new reverse hub with the AM close together was used for all cents in 1993. At least one new reverse die of each type was used for 1992 P and D cents made for circulation but it is not known if this usage was deliberate or accidental. Proof coinage reverted to the wide AM design in 1994. In subsequent years a few dies from the circulation-strike hub were used for making Proof coins.

Proof Lincoln, Memorial Reverse, Cents

PF-60 to 70 (Proof). All Proof Lincoln Memorial cents are of the mirror format, usually with cameo or frosted contrast between the devices and the fields. High quality is common. Special Mint Set (SMS) coins were struck in lieu of Proofs from 1965 to 1967 and in some instances closely resemble Proofs. *Obverse and Reverse:* PF-65 and higher coins are usually RB (colors should be nicely blended) or RD, the latter with bright red-orange fading slightly to hints of brown. Some tiny flecks are normal on coins certified as PF-65 but should be microscopic or absent above that. PF-60 and 61 coins can be dull, stained, or spotted and still have some original mint color. Coins with fingerprints must be given a low numerical grade. Lower-grade Proofs usually have poor eye appeal. Generally, Proofs below PF-64 are not desired by most collectors.

Proof Lincoln, Memorial Reverse, Cent

| 1971-S, Proof, Doubled-Die Obverse | 1979-S, Filled S (Type 1) | 1979-S, Clear S (Type 2) | 1981-S, Rounded S (Type 1) | 1981-S, Flat S (Type 2) |

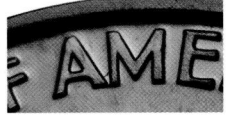

1990-S, No S, Proof
Shown 1.5x actual size.

1999-S, Normal   **1999-S, Close AM**

	Mintage	Cert	Avg	PF-65RD	PF-67RD	PF-67Cam	PF-68DC	Recent Auction Record
1959	1,149,291	3,046	66.6	$3.00	$22	$55	$865	$1,528, PF-68DCam, January 2014
1960, Large Date	1,691,602	2,834	66.8	2.00	26	45	375	$2,585, PF-69DCam, April 2013
1960, Small Date	*	2,689	66.6	22.00	37	75	2,300	$1,659, PF-68DCam, April 2013
1961	3,028,244	3,648	66.8	1.50	23	40	375	$3,055, PF-69DCam, June 2013
1962	3,218,019	4,335	67.0	1.50	10	15	100	$1,058, PF-69DCam, June 2014
1963	3,075,645	5,276	67.2	1.50	10	14	55	$499, PF-69DCam, February 2014
1964	3,950,762	8,790	67.7	1.50	10	11	23	$217, PF-69DCam, June 2014
1965, SMS ‡	2,360,000	2,115	65.8	11.00	55			$441, PF-65Cam, June 2013
1966, SMS ‡	2,261,583	2,665	66.5	10.00	25			$2,585, PF-67Cam, June 2014
1967, SMS ‡	1,863,344	2,719	66.6	11.00	42			$5,581, PF-68Cam, June 2014
1968S	3,041,506	1,827	67.1	1.00	12	16	50	$764, PF-69DCam, June 2014
1969S	2,934,631	2,041	67.1	1.00	12	13	33	$1,009, PF-69DCam, June 2014
1970S, All kinds	2,632,810							
1970S, Small Date (High 7)		1,051	66.4	40.00	65	150		$4,994, PF-69DCam, December 2013
1970S, Large Date (Low 7)		2,277	66.8	1.00	15	25	65	$1,058, PF-69DCam, December 2013
1971S	3,220,733	2,497	66.8	1.00	18	30	120	$764, PF-68RD, June 2014
1971S, Doubled-Die Obverse	*			650.00	800	1,000		
1972S	3,260,996	1,450	67.2	1.00	15	20	35	$499, PF-69DCam, June 2013
1973S	2,760,339	1,087	67.8	1.00	13	16	30	$61, PF-69DCam, May 2013
1974S	2,612,568	1,136	67.8	1.00	13	16	30	$45, PF-69DCam, May 2013
1975S	2,845,450	1,264	67.5	3.50	13	16	30	$109, PF-69DCam, August 2009

* Included in number above. ‡ Ranked in the *100 Greatest U.S. Modern Coins.*

	Mintage	Cert	Avg	PF-65RD	PF-67RD	PF-67Cam	PF-68DC	Recent Auction Record
1976S	4,149,730	1,586	67.5	$3.20	$13	$16	$30	$153, PF-69DCam, June 2013
1977S	3,251,152	1,749	68.4	2.50	13	16	30	$42, PF-69DCam, September 2009
1978S	3,127,781	2,063	68.4	2.50	13	16	30	$75, PF-69DCam, May 2009
1979S, Type 1	3,677,175	1,650	68.5	2.50	11	13	17	$920, PF-70DCam, January 2010
1979S, Type 2	*	2,279	68.0	6.00	17	20	30	$3,819, PF-70DCam, August 2013
1980S	3,554,806	2,723	68.7	2.50	10	11	15	$94, PF-70DCam, October 2009
1981S, Type 1	4,063,083	3,585	68.5	2.50	10	11	15	$4,113, PF-70DCam, August 2013
1981S, Type 2	*	1,671	67.5	18.00	28	38	55	$265, PF-69UCam, September 2009
1982S	3,857,479	1,989	68.6	2.50	10	11	15	$7,050, PF, October 2013
1983S	3,279,126	2,336	68.7	3.00	10	11	15	$115, PF-70DCam, October 2009
1984S	3,065,110	3,022	68.9	4.00	10	11	15	$544, PF-70DCam, June 2013
1985S	3,362,821	3,203	68.9	5.00	11	12	15	$881, PF-70DCam, June 2013
1986S	3,010,497	3,678	68.9	6.00	11	12	15	$558, PF-70DCam, June 2013
1987S	4,227,728	4,161	68.9	4.00	10	11	13	$353, PF-70DCam, June 2013
1988S	3,262,948	3,322	69.0	5.00	11	12	13	$115, PF-70DCam, May 2013
1989S	3,220,194	3,433	69.0	5.00	11	12	13	$86, PF-70DCam, August 2013
1990S	3,299,559	4,218	69.0	5.00	10	11	13	$529, PF-67RD, September 2013
1990, Proof, No S ‡	(a)	173	67.8	4,000.00	5,250	—		$19,975, PF-69DCam, January 2014
1991S	2,867,787	3,686	69.0	7.00	13	14	16	$84, PF-70DCam, May 2013
1992S	4,176,560	7,322	69.0	4.00	10	11	12	$66, PF-70DCam, May 2013
1993S	3,394,792	6,036	69.0	6.50	10	11	12	$55, PF-70DCam, May 2013
1994S	3,269,923	5,728	69.0	7.00	11	12	13	$66, PF-70DCam, May 2013
1995S	2,797,481	5,476	69.0	9.00	11	12	13	$115, PF, February 2014
1996S	2,525,265	5,060	69.0	4.50	9	10	12	$92, PF-70DCam, May 2013
1997S	2,796,678	4,817	69.0	10.00	12	13	14	$282, PF, February 2013
1998S	2,086,507	5,571	69.0	9.00	10	11	12	$115, PF-70DCam, December 2009
1998S, Close AM (b)	*	161	68.6	475.00	525	575	700	$7,475, PF-70DCam, April 2012
1999S	3,347,966	10,520	69.0	6.00	9	10	12	$62, PF-70DCam, January 2013
1999S, Close AM (b)	*	645	67.8	80.00	100	125	190	$212, PF-69DCam, May 2013
2000S	4,047,993	11,528	69.0	4.00	7	8	11	$55, PF-70DCam, May 2013
2001S	3,184,606	9,478	69.0	4.00	7	8	11	$64, PF-70DCam, May 2013
2002S	3,211,995	9,919	69.0	4.00	7	8	11	$79, PF-70DCam, June 2013
2003S	3,298,439	14,003	69.0	4.00	7	8	11	$60, PF-70DCam, May 2013
2004S	2,965,422	9,825	69.1	4.00	7	8	11	$59, PF-70DCam, May 2013
2005S	3,344,679	15,769	69.1	4.00	7	8	11	$51, PF-70DCam, May 2013
2006S	3,054,436	9,112	69.1	4.00	7	8	11	$58, PF-70DCam, May 2013
2007S	2,577,166	7,772	69.1	4.00	7	8	11	$59, PF-70DCam, May 2013
2008S	2,169,561	6,219	69.1	4.00	7	8	11	$60, PF-70DCam, May 2013

* Included in number above. ‡ Ranked in the *100 Greatest U.S. Modern Coins.* **a.** An estimated 100 to 250 Proofs of 1990 were struck without the S mintmark (apparently from a circulation-strike die, without a mintmark, which had been given a mirror finish). This error escaped the notice of at least 14 people during die preparation and coining. **b.** Varieties were made in the circulation-strike style, with the A and the M in AMERICA nearly touching each other. On normal Proofs the two letters have a wide space between them.

LINCOLN BICENTENNIAL
(2009)

Designers Victor D. Brenner (obverse), Richard Masters (Birth and Early Childhood reverse), Charles Vickers (Formative Years reverse), Joel Iskowitz (Professional Life reverse), and Susan Gamble (Presidency reverse); weight 2.5 grams; composition of regular-issue coins, copper-plated zinc (core: .992 zinc, .008 copper, with a plating of pure copper; total content .975 zinc, .025 copper). Composition of special coins included in collector sets, weight 3.1 grams; .950 copper, .005 tin and zinc; diameter 19 mm; plain edge; mints: Philadelphia, Denver, San Francisco.

Birth and Early Childhood   Formative Years

Professional Life   Presidency

History. The one-cent coins issued during 2009 pay unique tribute to President Abraham Lincoln, commemorating the bicentennial of his birth and the 100th anniversary of the first issuance of the Lincoln cent. Four different reverse designs were issued by the Mint, each representing a major aspect of Lincoln's life. The obverse retained the traditional profile portrait of previous years.

The reverse designs, released quarterly throughout 2009, are: Birth and Early Childhood (designer, Richard Masters; sculptor, Jim Licaretz); Formative Years (designer and sculptor, Charles Vickers); Professional Life (designer, Joel Iskowitz; sculptor, Don Everhart); and Presidency (designer, Susan Gamble; sculptor, Joseph Menna).

The coins issued for general circulation were made of the exact same copper-plated composition used in the cent since 1982. Special versions struck for inclusion in collector sets were made of the same alloy as the first Lincoln cents of 1909—95 parts copper and 5 parts tin and zinc—and with a Satin finish.

Several die varieties exist with minor doubling in the Formative Years reverse. Their values vary according to the severity of the doubling.

Striking and Sharpness. Striking is generally sharp. The quality of the fields can vary. Some 2009 cents, even from original rolls and bags, have surface marks that look like water spots.

Availability. Cents of this year were minted in large quantities. They are readily available in the numismatic marketplace, and are starting to be seen more frequently in circulation.

MS-60 to 70 (Mint State). *Obverse and reverse:* At MS-65 and higher, the luster is rich on all areas. There is no rubbing, and no contact marks are visible except under magnification. Coins with full or nearly full mint orange-red color can be designated RD; those with full or nearly full brown-toned surfaces can be designated BN; and those with a substantial percentage of red-orange and of brown can be called RB. Ideally, MS-65 or finer coins should have good eye appeal, which in the RB category means nicely blended colors, not stained or blotched. Below MS-65, full RD coins become scarce, and at MS-60 to 62 are virtually non-existent, unless they have been dipped. Regarding the special copper coins issued in collector sets: copper is a very active metal, and influences such as slight abrasions, contact marks, and so on that define the grade also affect the color.

2009, Formative Years, Seven Fingers
FS-01-2009-801. *Other varieties exist.*

2009, Formative Years, Seven Fingers
FS-01-2009-802. *Other varieties exist.*

2009, Formative Years, Doubled Pinky
FS-01-2009-805. *Other varieties exist.*

2009, Formative Years, Skeleton Finger
FS-01-2009-808. *Other varieties exist.*

	Mintage	Cert	Avg	%MS	MS-63RB	MS-65RD	MS-66RD	MS-67RD	MS-68RD	MS-69RD	Recent Auction Record
2009, Birth and Early Childhood	284,400,000	24,496	65.6	100	$0.15	$0.30	$12	$20			$4, MS-66RD, June 2013
2009, Birth and Early Childhood, copper, Satin finish	784,614	3,635	67.9	100	5.00	10.00	11	12	$15	$45	
2009D, Birth and Early Childhood	350,400,000	13,396	65.6	100	0.15	0.30	12	20			
2009D, Birth and Early Childhood, copper, Satin finish	784,614	3,631	67.8	100	5.00	10.00	11	12	17	95	

	Mintage	Cert	Avg	%MS	MS-63RB	MS-65RD	MS-66RD	MS-67RD	MS-68RD	MS-69RD	Recent Auction Record
2009, Formative Years (a)	376,000,000	35,858	65.7	100	$0.15	$0.30	$12	$20			$16, MS-66RD, March 2013
2009, Formative Years, copper, Satin finish	784,614	3,329	67.7	100	5.00	10.00	11	12	$15	$45	
2009D, Formative Years (a)	363,600,000	7,457	65.4	100	0.15	0.30	12	20			
2009D, Formative Years, copper, Satin finish	784,614	3,348	67.7	100	5.00	10.00	11	12	20	250	
2009, Professional Life	316,000,000	21,159	65.9	100	0.15	0.30	12	20			$4, MS-66RD, June 2013
2009, Professional Life, copper, Satin finish	784,614	3,838	67.8	100	5.00	10.00	11	12	15	45	
2009D, Professional Life	336,000,000	4,327	65.6	100	0.15	0.30	12	20			
2009D, Professional Life, copper, Satin finish	784,614	3,342	67.7	100	5.00	10.00	11	12	15	210	
2009, Presidency	129,600,000	8,658	65.7	100	0.15	0.30	12	20			$3, MS-65RD, August 2011
2009, Presidency, copper, Satin finish	784,614	3,396	67.8	100	5.00	10.00	11	12	15	45	
2009D, Presidency	198,000,000	3,069	65.5	100	0.15	0.30	12	20			
2009D, Presidency, copper, Satin finish	784,614	3,532	67.7	100	5.00	10.00	11	12	15	200	

a. Several varieties exist with minor die doubling. Their values vary and their market is not yet firmly established.

Proof Lincoln Bicentennial Cents

PF-60 to 70 (Proof). All Proof Lincoln Bicentennial cents are of the mirror format, usually with cameo or frosted contrast between the devices and the fields. High quality is common. *Obverse and Reverse:* PF-65 and higher coins are usually RB (colors should be nicely blended) or RD, the latter with bright red-orange fading slightly to hints of brown. Some tiny flecks are normal on coins certified as PF-65 but should be microscopic or absent above that. PF-60 and 61 coins can be dull, stained, or spotted and still have some original mint color. Coins with fingerprints must be given a low numerical grade. Lower-grade Proofs usually have poor eye appeal. Generally, Proofs below PF-64 are not desired by most collectors.

Proof Lincoln Bicentennial Cents

	Mintage	Cert	Avg	PF-65RD	PF-67RD	PF-67Cam	PF-68DC	Recent Auction Record
2009S, Birth and Early Childhood	2,995,615	18,568	69.1	$4	$7	$8	$11	$86, PF-70DCam, May 2013
2009S, Formative Years	2,995,615	18,717	69.1	4	7	8	11	$96, PF-70DCam, June 2013
2009S, Professional Life	2,995,615	18,553	69.1	4	7	8	11	$90, PF-70DCam, May 2013
2009S, Presidency	2,995,615	18,910	69.1	4	7	8	11	$66, PF-70DCam, June 2013

LINCOLN, SHIELD REVERSE (2010 TO DATE)

Designers Victor D. Brenner (obverse) and Lyndall Bass (reverse); weight 2.5 grams; composition copper-plated zinc (core: .992 zinc, .008 copper, with a plating of pure copper; total content .975 zinc, .025 copper); diameter 19 mm; plain edge; mints: Philadelphia, Denver, San Francisco.

History. Symbolically capping the life story told by the Lincoln Bicentennial cents of 2009, today's cents feature a reverse design "emblematic of President Lincoln's preservation of the United States as a single and united country." This is the seventh reverse used on the Lincoln type since 1909.

The shield motif was designed by U.S. Mint Artistic Infusion Program Associate Designer Lyndall Bass, and engraved by Mint Sculptor-Engraver Joseph Menna. It was unveiled during the launch ceremony for the fourth and final 2009 Bicentennial cent, held at the Ulysses S. Grant Memorial at the Capitol Building in Washington, DC, November 12, 2009.

In addition to a new reverse design, the Shield Reverse cents feature a modern update of Victor David Brenner's original portrait for the 1909 Lincoln cent.

Striking and Sharpness. Striking is generally sharp.

Availability. Cents of this design are minted in large quantities. They are readily available in the numismatic marketplace, and are starting to enter circulation through normal distribution channels.

MS-60 to 70 (Mint State). *Obverse and reverse:* At MS-65 and higher, the luster is rich on all areas. There is no rubbing, and no contact marks are visible except under magnification. Coins with full or nearly full mint orange-red color can be designated RD; those with full or nearly full brown-toned surfaces can be designated BN; and those with a substantial percentage of red-orange and of brown can be called RB. Ideally, MS-65 or finer coins should have good eye appeal, which in the RB category means nicely blended colors, not stained or blotched. Below MS-65, full RD coins become scarce, and at MS-60 to 62 are virtually non-existent, unless they have been dipped.

	Est Mintage	Cert	Avg	%MS	MS-63RB	MS-65RD	MS-66RD	MS-67RD	Recent Auction Record
2010	1,963,630,000	8,869	65.3	100	$0.15	$0.30	$10	$18	$50, MS-66RD, May 2014
2010D	2,047,200,000	3,177	65.4	100	0.15	0.30	10	18	$4,994, MS-67RD, April 2013
2011	2,402,400,000	873	66.3	100	0.15	0.30	10	18	$39, MS-67RD, June 2013
2011D	2,536,140,000	841	66.4	100	0.15	0.30	10	18	$23, MS-67RD, June 2013
2012	3,132,000,000	74	65.7	100	0.15	0.30	10	18	
2012D	2,883,200,000	42	66.0	100	0.15	0.30	10	18	
2013	3,750,400,000				0.15	0.30	10	18	
2013D	3,319,600,000				0.15	0.30	10	18	
2014					0.15	0.30	10	18	
2014D					0.15	0.30	10	18	

Proof Lincoln, Shield Reverse, Cents

PF-60 to 70 (Proof). All Proof Lincoln, Shield Reverse, cents are of the mirror format, usually with cameo or frosted contrast between the devices and the fields. High quality is common. *Obverse and Reverse:* PF-65 and higher coins are usually RB (colors should be nicely blended) or RD, the latter with bright red-orange fading slightly to hints of brown. Some tiny flecks are normal on coins certified as PF-65 but should be microscopic or absent above that. PF-60 and 61 coins can be dull, stained, or spotted and still have some original mint color. Coins with fingerprints must be given a low numerical grade. Lower-grade Proofs usually have poor eye appeal. Generally, Proofs below PF-64 are not desired by most collectors.

	Mintage	Cert	Avg	PF-65RD	PF-67RD	PF-67Cam	PF-68DC	Recent Auction Record
2010S	1,689,364	10,894	69.1	$5	$7	$8	$11	$118, PF, January 2014
2011S	1,673,010	7,808	69.1	5	7	8	11	$76, PF-70DCam, May 2014
2012S	1,237,415	103	69.2	5	7	8	11	$74, PF-70DCam, May 2013
2013S	1,237,976			5	7	8	11	
2014S				5	7	8	11	

AN OVERVIEW OF TWO-CENT PIECES

The two-cent piece was introduced in 1864. Made in bronze, it was designed by Chief Engraver James B. Longacre, and was the first circulating United States coin to bear the motto IN GOD WE TRUST. At the time, coins were scarce in circulation, and silver and gold issues were entirely absent. It was felt that the two-cent piece would prove to be very popular as a companion to the Indian Head cent. However, the introduction of the nickel three-cent piece in 1865 negated much of this advantage, the production of two-cent pieces declined, and by 1873, when the denomination was discontinued, their only coinage consisted of Proofs for collectors.

A full "type set" of the two-cent piece consists of but a single coin. Most available in Mint State are the issues of 1864 and 1865, often seen with original mint orange color fading to natural brown. Proofs are available for all years.

FOR THE COLLECTOR AND INVESTOR: TWO-CENT PIECES AS A SPECIALTY

Two-cent pieces can be collected advantageously by date and variety. A basic display consists of an 1864 Large Motto, 1864 Small Motto (rare), 1873 Close 3, and 1873 Open 3, the last two being available only in Proof format. Some specialists opt to include just one of the 1873 varieties.

Collectors should select both circulation strikes and Proofs with care, for the number of truly choice *original* (unprocessed, undipped, not retoned) coins is but a small percentage of the whole. As a type, though, the two-cent piece is readily available for collecting.

Several specialized studies of two-cent pieces have been published over a long span of years, the first of significance being "Two-Cent Pieces of the United States," by S.W. Freeman, published in *The Numismatist,* June 1954.

RECOMMENDED READING

Fivaz, Bill, and Stanton, J.T. *The Cherrypickers' Guide to Rare Die Varieties* (5th ed., vol. I), Atlanta, GA, 2009.
Flynn, Kevin. *Getting Your Two Cents Worth,* Rancocas, NJ, 1994.
Leone, Frank. *Longacre's Two Cent Piece Die Varieties and Errors,* College Point, NY, 1991.

Salmon P. Chase was secretary of the Treasury when the new coin was introduced. He personally supported the use of the motto IN GOD WE TRUST in its design.

The U.S. Mint's chief engraver, James Barton Longacre (seen here in an 1855 portrait), designed the two-cent piece while the American Civil War was raging.

TWO-CENT PIECES, 1864–1873

Designer James B. Longacre; weight 6.22 grams; composition .950 copper, .050 tin and zinc; diameter 23 mm; plain edge. All coined at Philadelphia Mint.

History. The two-cent piece, struck in bronze like the new Indian Head cents, made its debut under the Mint Act of April 22, 1864. Coins of all kinds were scarce in circulation at the time, due to hoarding. The outcome of the Civil War was uncertain, and Americans desired "hard money." Many millions of two-cent pieces were struck in 1864, after which the mintage declined, due to once-hoarded Indian Head cents becoming available again and to the new nickel three-cent coins being introduced in 1865. Continually decreasing quantities were made through 1872, and only Proofs were struck in the coin's final year, 1873.

Striking and Sharpness. Points to check for sharpness on the obverse include WE in the motto, the leaves, and the horizontal shield lines. On the reverse check the wreath details and the border letters. Check the dentils on both sides. Most coins are quite well struck.

Availability. Most MS coins are dated 1864 or 1865, after which the availability declines sharply, especially for the issue of 1872. Among 1864 coins most seen are of the Large Motto variety. Small Motto coins are elusive. Coins with much or nearly all *original* mint red-orange color are rare for the later years, with most in the marketplace being recolored.

AU-50, 53, 55, 58 (About Uncirculated). *Obverse:* WE shows light wear, this being the prime place to check. The arrowheads and leaves also show light wear. At AU-50, level wear is more noticeable. At 53 and 55, wear is less. At 58, friction is evident, rather than actual wear. Luster, toned brown, is nearly complete at 58, but may be incomplete in the field. *Reverse:* At AU-50, light wear is seen on the ribbon and the higher-relief areas of the leaves and grains, while the lower areas retain their detail. Some luster may be present in protected areas. At 53 and 55, wear is lesser and luster is more extensive. An AU-58 coin has nearly full luster and shows only light friction.

MS-60 to 70 (Mint State). *Obverse and Reverse:* At MS-65 and higher, the luster is rich on all areas. There is no rubbing, and no contact marks are visible except under magnification. Coins with full or nearly full mint orange-red color can be designated RD (the color on this is often more orange than red), those with full or nearly full brown-toned surfaces can be designated BN, and those with a substantial percentage of red-orange and of brown can be called RB. Ideally, MS-65 or finer coins have good eye appeal, which in the RB category means nicely blended colors, not stained or blotched, the latter problem mostly with dipped and irregularly retoned coins. Below

MS-65, full RD coins become scarce, although MS-64 RD coins can be attractive. These usually have more flecks and tiny spots, while the color remains bright. At MS-60 to 62, RD coins are virtually nonexistent, unless they have been dipped. The Official American Numismatic Association grading standards allow for "dull" and/or "spotted" coins at MS-60 and 61 as well as incomplete luster. MS-60 to 63 BN coins can be fairly attractive if not spotted or blotched, but those with hints of color usually lack eye appeal.

1864, Small Motto	**1864, Large Motto**	**1865, Plain 5**	**1865, Fancy 5**

1867, Doubled-Die Obverse
FS-02-1867-101.

1869, Doubled-Die Obverse
FS-02-1869-101.

	Mintage	Cert	Avg	%MS	MS-60BN	MS-63BN	MS-63RB	MS-64BN	MS-64RD	MS-65RB	MS-65RD	Recent Auction Record
1864, Small Motto (a)	*	1,156	52.2	63	$1,500	$1,750	$1,850	$2,000	$2,900	$3,750	$7,200	$22,325, MS-66RD, August 2013
1864, Large Motto (b)	19,822,500	6,847	61.6	88	110	175	185	200	700	600	1,700	$7,344, MS-67BN, January 2014
1865 (c)	13,640,000	4,562	61.7	88	110	175	185	200	700	600	1,700	$4,113, MS-66RD, March 2014
1866	3,177,000	1,003	60.8	84	120	175	185	220	750	650	2,450	$8,813, MS-66RD, February 2014
1867	2,938,750	1,094	60.5	84	130	190	200	235	1,000	650	3,250	$12,925, MS-66RD, April 2014
1867, Doubled-Die Obverse (d)	**	143	44.1	31	1,400	2,750	2,850	3,200	4,250			$22,325, MS-65RD, January 2014
1868	2,803,750	996	60.5	83	150	225	290	375	1,200	1,150	4,000	$9,400, MS-66RD, January 2014
1869	1,546,500	897	60.0	81	160	225	290	375	1,200	1,150	3,500	$15,275, MS-66RD, January 2014
1869, Doubled-Die Obverse	**	5	64.6	100	600	900	1,000	1,250	2,250			
1870	861,250	707	59.4	78	275	300	450	575	1,750	1,500	4,500	$11,163, MS-65RD, June 2014
1871	721,250	1,020	58.6	72	300	375	500	800	2,000	1,700	5,500	$28,200, MS-66RD, April 2013
1872	65,000	630	40.8	33	2,800	3,600	3,750	3,900	10,000	11,000	24,000	$39,950, MS-66RD, January 2014

* Included in number below. ** Included in number above. **a.** The Small Motto is distinguished by a wider D in GOD, and the first T in TRUST nearly touching the ribbon crease at left. **b.** The Large Motto is distinguished by a narrow D in GOD, and a 1 mm gap between the first T in TRUST and the ribbon crease. **c.** Varieties show the tip of the 5 either plain or fancy (curved). **d.** This variety is somewhat common in low-end circulated grades, but is considered rare in EF and AU, and very rare in MS.

Proof Two-Cent Pieces

PF-60 to 70 (Proof). The 1864 Small Motto Proof is a great rarity, with fewer than two dozen estimated to exist. Coins of 1873 were made only in Proof format, of the Close 3 and Open 3 styles. Proofs of most dates are easily enough acquired. Very few have original color. Do not overlook the many nice brown and red-and-brown pieces on the market (some investors acquire only "red" copper coins, leaving many great values among others). Refer to the comments under Proof Indian Head cents. *Obverse and Reverse:* PF-60 two-cent pieces can be dull from repeated dipping and cleaning and are often toned iridescent colors or have mottled surfaces. At PF-63, the mirrorlike fields should be attractive, and hairlines should be minimal, most easily seen when the coin is held at an angle to the light. No rubbing is seen. PF-64 coins are even nicer. PF-65 coins have very few hairlines, visible only under strong magnification. At any level and color, a Proof with hairlines likely has been cleaned. At PF-67 or higher there should be no evidence at all of hairlines or friction; such a coin is fully original (not cleaned). As a general rule, Proofs of 1873 are of very high quality but, unless dipped or cleaned, are nearly always toned light brown.

Proof Two-Cent Piece

	Est Mintage	Cert	Finest	PF-63BN	PF-64BN	PF-64RB	PF-65RB	Recent Auction Record
1864, Small Motto (20–30 known) †	*	22	PF-66	$18,500	$21,000	$30,000	$47,000	$105,750, PF-66RD, June 2014
1864, Large Motto	100+	263	PF-67	550	775	1,350	2,500	$14,100, PF-67RB, August 2013
1865	500+	357	PF-67	450	510	625	1,200	$15,275, PF-66RD, April 2013
1866	725+	384	PF-66	450	510	625	1,200	$11,163, PF-66RB, June 2013
1867	625+	444	PF-67	450	510	625	1,200	$3,525, PF-65RD, January 2014
1868	600+	430	PF-67	450	510	625	1,200	$16,450, PF-66Cam, June 2014
1869	600+	568	PF-67	450	510	625	1,250	$8,225, PF-66RD, June 2014
1870	1,000+	602	PF-67	450	550	650	1,275	$41,125, PF-67RD, February 2014
1871	960+	635	PF-67	450	550	650	1,275	$6,169, PF-66RD, February 2014
1872	950+	819	PF-67	900	925	975	1,300	$11,163, PF-66RD, April 2014
1873, Close 3	400	720	PF-67	3,200	3,500	3,750	4,300	$12,925, PF-66RB, November 2013
1873, Open 3 (Alleged Restrike)	200	290	PF-66	3,100	3,250	3,350	4,000	$11,750, PF-66RB, June 2014

* Included in number below. † Ranked in the *100 Greatest U.S. Coins* (fourth edition).

AN OVERVIEW OF THREE-CENT PIECES

SILVER THREE-CENT PIECES

The silver three-cent piece or *trime* is one of the more curious coins in American numismatics. The rising price of silver in 1850 created a situation in which silver coins cost more to produce than their face value. Mintages dropped sharply and older pieces disappeared from circulation. In 1851 a solution was provided by the three-cent piece. Instead of being made with 90% silver content, the quantity was set at 75%. Accordingly, the coins were worth less intrinsically, and there was no advantage in melting them. Large quantities were made through 1853. In that year, the standards for regular silver coins were changed, and other denominations reappeared on the marketplace, making the trime unnecessary. Mintages dropped beginning in 1854, until 1873, when production amounted to just 600 Proofs for collectors.

Of the three varieties of trimes, Variety 2 (1854–1858) is at once the scarcest and, by far, the most difficult to find with a sharp strike. In fact, not one in 50 Variety 2 coins is needle sharp. Curiously, when such pieces are found they are likely to be dated 1855, the lowest-mintage issue of the type. Trimes of the Variety 1 design (1851–1853) vary widely in striking, but can be found sharp. Variety 3 coins (1859–1873) often are sharp.

Mint State coins are readily found for Variety 1 and are usually in grades from MS-60 to 63 or so, although quite a few gems are around with attractive luster. Sharply struck gems are another matter and require some searching to find. Mint State Variety 2 trimes are all rare, and when seen are apt to be miserably struck and in lower grades. Variety 3 coins are readily found in Mint State, including in MS-65 and higher grades.

Proofs were made of all years, but not in quantity until 1858, when an estimated 210 were struck. For all dates after 1862, high-grade Proofs are much more readily available today than are Mint State coins. Circulated examples are available of all three varieties. While extensively worn coins of Variety 1 are available, most Variety 2 coins are Fine or better and most Variety 3 pieces are VF or better.

FOR THE COLLECTOR AND INVESTOR: SILVER THREE-CENT PIECES AS A SPECIALTY

Trimes cover a fairly long span of years and embrace several design types, but comprise no "impossible" rarities. Accordingly, it is realistic to collect one of each Philadelphia Mint coin from 1851 to 1873 plus the 1851-O. There are two overdates in the series, 1862, 2 Over 1 (which is distinct and occurs only in circulation strike format), and 1863, 3 Over 2 (only Proofs, and not boldly defined), which some specialists collect and others ignore. A curious variety of 1852 has the first digit of the date over an inverted 2.

Typically, a high-grade set includes Mint State examples of all issues 1851 through 1857 and Proofs after that date. As noted, Variety 2 trimes usually are very poorly struck, save the occasionally encountered sharp 1855. As an example, a specialist in the series who found an 1856 with needle-sharp details, at three times the regular market price, might be well advised to buy it. After 1862, Mint State coins are rare for most dates. The formation of a choice Mint State set 1851 through 1872 plus a Proof 1873 would be a formidable challenge.

A set of circulated coins can be gathered through and including 1862, after which such pieces become very rare. Most later dates will have to be acquired on a catch-as-catch-can basis, perhaps by acquiring impaired Proofs for certain of the years.

NICKEL THREE-CENT PIECES

Nickel three-cent pieces were introduced in 1865 to help fill the need for coins in circulation. At the time, silver and gold issues were hoarded, and were available only at a premium. The nickel three-cent piece joined the Indian Head cent and the new (as of 1864) two-cent piece. The coin proved to be very popular in its time, and millions were struck. In 1866 the nickel five-cent piece was introduced, after which time the demand for the nickel three-cent piece diminished somewhat. However, pieces were made in quantity until 1876. In that year silver coins again returned to circulation, and mintages for the nickel three-cent piece dropped sharply. Only Proofs were made in 1877 and 1878. In later years, mintages ranged from small to modest, except for 1881.

Mint State coins are readily available for the early years, although many if not most have weak striking in areas or are from clashed dies. Pristine, sharp Mint State coins on the market are mostly of later years, in the 1880s, where such pieces are the rule, not the exception.

FOR THE COLLECTOR AND INVESTOR: NICKEL THREE-CENT PIECES AS A SPECIALTY

Nickel three-cent coins are interesting to collect by date sequence from 1865 to 1889. Varieties are provided by the 1873, Close 3 and Open 3 and the 1887, 7 Over 6 overdate. A set of Mint State coins is considerably more difficult to form than a run of Proofs. A hand-selected set of well-struck coins MS-65 or finer could take several years to complete.

Among Proofs, the rarest year is 1865, probably followed by the "perfect date" (not overdate) 1887. Proofs of the 1860s and early 1870s are scarce in PF-65 with excellent strike and eye appeal. Proofs of the last decade of coinage are much more readily available and are usually choice.

SILVER THREE-CENT PIECES (TRIMES)
(1851–1873)

Variety 1 (1851–1853): Designer James B. Longacre; weight 0.80 gram; composition .750 silver, .250 copper; diameter 14 mm; plain edge; mints: Philadelphia, New Orleans.

Variety 1 (1851–1853)
Shown 2x actual size.

Variety 2 (1854–1858): Designer James B. Longacre; weight 0.75 gram; composition .900 silver, .100 copper; diameter 14 mm; plain edge. All coined at the Philadelphia Mint.

Variety 2 (1854–1858)
Shown 2x actual size.

Variety 3 (1859–1873): Designer James B. Longacre; weight 0.75 gram; composition .900 silver, .100 copper; diameter 14 mm; plain edge. All coined at the Philadelphia Mint.

Variety 3 (1859–1873)
Shown 2x actual size.

History. In 1850 Americans began hoarding their silver coins, as the flood of gold from California made silver disproportionately valuable. To provide a small coin for commerce, the Mint introduced the silver three-cent piece, or *trime*. These were .750 fine (as opposed to the standard .900 fineness), and contained less than 3¢ of metal, so there was no incentive to hoard or melt them. Three different designs were made, Variety 1 of which was struck from 1851 to 1853. These coins were popular in their time and circulated widely. These are distinguished from the other two designs by having no outline or frame around the obverse star. The Act of February 21, 1853, reduced the amount of silver in other denominations (from the half dime to the half dollar, but not the dollar), which discouraged people from hoarding them. The tiny trime lost the public's favor, and mintages decreased.

In 1854 the design was changed considerably, creating Variety 2, which was made through 1858. The alloy was modified to the standard for other issues and the weight was lightened. A raised border was added to the obverse star plus two line frames around it. On the reverse an olive branch was placed above the III and a bundle of arrows below it. This new motif proved to be very difficult to strike up properly.

In 1859 the design was modified again, creating Variety 3. Demand for the denomination continued to be small, and after 1862 very few were made for circulation, as silver coins were hoarded by the war-weary public and began to trade at a premium. Under the Coinage Act of 1873 the trime was discontinued, and

that year only Proofs were struck. Also in that year, nearly the entire production of non-Proof coins of 1863 to 1872 was melted.

Striking and Sharpness. On the Variety 1 obverse the tiny shield at the center of the star often lacks certain details. On the reverse check the details and strength of the III. On both sides check the rims. Needle-sharp coins are in the minority. Sharpness of strike has been nearly completely overlooked in the marketplace.

Trimes of Variety 2 are usually poorly struck, with some or all of these characteristics: obverse lettering weak in places; frames around the star of inconsistent strength or missing in certain areas; shield weak in places; reverse stars irregular and poorly formed; olive branch and arrows weak in areas; weak or irregular rims. Now and then a sharp 1855 is found.

Most Variety 3 trimes are sharply struck. Points to look for include full outlines around the star, full shield on the star, and full leaf details and sharp stars.

Availability. Circulated examples of the Variety 1 trimes are plentiful. MS coins are often seen, although the 1851-O is scarce in MS and high circulated grades. Most MS coins are lustrous and attractive, especially at 63 and above. Circulated Variety 2 coins are scarce in all grades, particularly so at MS-64 and higher. With a needle-sharp strike, MS-65 and higher are *rarities*. Among Variety 3 trimes, circulated coins of the years 1859 to 1862 are easy to find. All later dates range from scarce to rare in circulation-strike format. MS-63 and better coins 1865 and later are very rare.

EF-40, 45 (Extremely Fine). *Obverse:* More wear is seen than at AU, most noticeable on the ridges of the star arms, this in addition to more wear on the frames (Varieties 2 and 3). Luster is absent, or seen only in traces. *Reverse:* More wear is seen on the C ornament and III. On Variety 2 and Variety 3 more wear is seen on the leaves and arrows.

AU-50, 53, 55, 58 (About Uncirculated). *Obverse:* Light wear is most obvious on the star arms and shield on Variety 1, and on the points of the frames on Varieties 2 and 3. At AU-50, luster is evident, but only on part of the field. At 58 luster is nearly complete. *Reverse:* Light wear is seen on the C ornament and III. On Varieties 2 and 3, light wear is seen on the leaves and arrows.

MS-60 to 70 (Mint State). *Obverse and Reverse:* At MS-60, some abrasion and very minor contact marks are evident, most noticeably on the obverse star and the C ornament on the reverse. At MS-63, abrasion is hard to detect except under magnification. An MS-65 coin has no abrasion. Luster should be full and rich (not grainy). Coins above MS-65 have fewer marks as perfection is approached.

1852, 1 Over Inverted 2
FS-3S-1852-301.

1853, Repunched Date
FS-3S-1853-301.

1854, Repunched Date
FS-3S-1854-301.

1862, 2 Over 1
FS-3S-1862-301.

	Mintage	Cert	Avg	%MS	EF-40	AU-50	MS-60	MS-63	MS-64	MS-65	MS-66	Recent Auction Record
1851	5,447,400	2,353	62.6	91	$80	$150	$180	$275	$450	$950	$1,300	$4,700, MS-67, March 2013
18510	720,000	880	59.2	73	175	250	450	700	1,300	3,250	6,250	$12,925, MS-66, December 2013
1852, 1 Over Inverted 2 (a)	*	n/a	n/a	n/a	775	950	1,150	1,425	1,700	1,950		
1852	18,663,500	2,785	61.2	85	80	150	180	275	450	950	1,250	$5,875, MS-67, April 2013
1853	11,400,000	1,457	60.1	80	80	150	180	275	450	950	1,500	$7,638, MS-67, April 2014
1853, Repunched Date (b)	**	n/a	n/a	n/a	100	200	260	300	650	1,000		$170, MS-62, December 2011
1854	671,000	711	60.0	72	120	225	350	700	1,500	3,000	6,250	$64,625, MS-68, June 2014
1854, Repunched Date (c)	**	n/a	n/a	n/a	185	325	500	800	1,750	3,500		$219, AU-55, July 2005
1855	139,000	290	57.3	59	200	350	600	1,100	2,600	7,500	15,000	$9,400, MS-65, January 2014
1856	1,458,000	640	59.1	70	120	235	360	700	1,500	3,200	9,000	$4,553, MS-65, August 2013
1857	1,042,000	563	61.2	83	120	235	360	700	1,500	2,750	5,000	$11,750, MS-67, June 2014
1858	1,603,700	1,072	59.8	74	120	235	360	700	1,500	2,750	5,000	$4,700, MS-66, April 2013
1859	364,200	650	61.2	80	90	175	215	300	525	1,000	1,650	$2,703, MS-66, January 2014
1860	286,000	583	60.1	72	90	175	215	300	525	1,000	1,650	$4,406, MS-67, June 2014
1861	497,000	1,573	61.6	79	90	175	215	300	525	1,000	1,650	$4,113, MS-67, June 2013

* Included in number below. ** Included in number above. **a.** An inverted 2 is visible beneath the primary 1. "A secondary date punch was obviously punched into the die in an inverted orientation and then corrected after some effacing of the die" (*Cherrypickers' Guide to Rare Die Varieties,* fifth edition, volume I). **b.** Secondary digits are visible to the north of the primary 1 and 8. This repunched date can be detected on lower-grade coins. **c.** Secondary digits are visible to the west of the primary digits on the 8 and 5.

	Mintage	Cert	Avg	%MS	EF-40	AU-50	MS-60	MS-63	MS-64	MS-65	MS-66	Recent Auction Record
1862, 2 Over 1 (d)	*	674	63.5	91	$95	$190	$240	$350	$600	$1,200	$1,750	$8,225, MS-67, December 2013
1862	343,000	2,091	63.0	90	90	175	215	285	500	1,000	1,650	$3,819, MS-67, March 2013
1863	21,000	155	63.7	94	435	550	800	1,100	1,300	2,100	3,000	$23,500, MS-65, June 2014
1864	12,000	196	62.7	85	435	550	650	1,000	1,300	2,100	3,000	$5,288, MS-65, August 2013
1865	8,000	160	62.4	84	475	575	675	1,100	1,400	2,200	3,600	$9,400, MS-65, August 2013
1866	22,000	154	61.3	79	425	500	630	1,000	1,300	2,100	3,200	$23,500, MS-67, November 2013
1867	4,000	85	61.4	78	450	525	675	1,300	2,000	3,500	10,000	$16,450, MS-66, August 2013
1868	3,500	74	60.5	72	475	550	690	1,400	2,300	6,250	11,000	$3,525, MS-63, April 2013
1869	4,500	96	61.6	81	525	600	700	1,400	2,100	3,200	5,750	$15,863, MS-67, August 2013
1870	3,000	154	60.7	73	475	550	675	1,300	1,850	4,800	6,250	$30,550, MS-67, January 2014
1871	3,400	236	63.4	89	475	500	650	1,000	1,400	1,950	3,000	$4,994, MS-66, March 2013
1872	1,000	88	59.5	73	500	600	1,000	1,800	2,500	5,200	9,000	$9,400, MS-66, June 2014

* Included in number below. **d.** A secondary 1 is evident beneath the 2 of the date. "This overdate is believed to be due more to economy (the Mint having used a good die another year) than to error. Circulated examples are about as common as the regular-dated coin" (*Cherrypickers' Guide to Rare Die Varieties,* fifth edition, volume I).

Proof Silver Three-Cent Pieces

PF-60 to 70 (Proof). A few Proofs were made in the early 1850s and are great rarities today. After 1857, production increased. Most are needle sharp and have mirrored surfaces, although some of the late 1860s and early 1870s can have slightly grainy or satiny lustrous surfaces.

Striking quality varies. Lint marks and surface problems are not unusual. Careful examination is recommended. *Obverse and Reverse:* Proofs that are extensively cleaned and have many hairlines, or that are dull and grainy, are lower level, such as PF-60 to 62. These are difficult to verify

as Proofs. For a trime with medium hairlines and good reflectivity, a grade of PF-64 is assigned, and with relatively few hairlines, PF-65. PF-66 should have hairlines so delicate that magnification is needed to see them. Above that, a Proof should be free of such lines.

Proof Silver Three-Cent Piece
Shown 2x actual size.

	Mintage	Cert	Finest	PF-63	PF-64	PF-65	PF-65Cam	Recent Auction Record
1851 *(1–2 known)*		1	PF-66	—				
1852 *(1 known)*		n/a	n/a	—				
1854	25–35	25	PF-66	$13,000	$16,000	$35,000		$41,125, PF-65, June 2014
1855	30–40	38	PF-66	5,000	8,500	14,000		$9,775, PF-65, April 2012
1856	40–50	61	PF-67	4,300	6,500	17,000	$18,000	$21,738, PF-66, January 2014
1857	60–80	83	PF-67	3,750	5,000	12,000		$15,863, PF-66, June 2014
1858	210	202	PF-68	2,750	4,500	7,500	10,000	$16,450, PF-67, December 2013
1859	800	271	PF-67	750	1,100	2,000	3,000	$1,528, PF, August 2013
1860	1,000	198	PF-68	750	1,200	4,500		$9,694, PF, August 2013
1861	1,000	243	PF-68	750	1,000	2,000	5,000	$11,163, PF, August 2013
1862	550	361	PF-67	750	1,000	2,000	3,000	$14,100, PF-66Cam, June 2014
1863, So-Called 3 Over 2	*	n/a	n/a	1,800	3,600	6,250	7,500	$47,000, PF-66Cam, June 2014
1863	460	353	PF-68	750	1,000	1,500	2,000	$11,750, PF-68, June 2014
1864	470	376	PF-68	750	1,000	1,500	2,000	$10,281, PF-66Cam, April 2014
1865	500	347	PF-68	750	1,000	1,500	2,000	$15,416, PF, May 2013
1866	725	461	PF-68	750	1,000	1,500	2,000	$23,500, PF-67Cam, April 2013
1867	625	583	PF-68	750	1,000	1,500	2,000	$29,375, PF-67Cam, November 2013
1868	600	540	PF-67	750	1,000	1,500	2,000	$4,438, PF-67, September 2013
1869	600	429	PF-68	750	1,000	1,500	2,000	$15,275, PF-67Cam, August 2013
1869, So-Called 9 Over 8, Proof only	**	n/a	n/a	2,000	3,000	5,750	7,000	$16,450, PF-66Cam, August 2013
1870	1,000	543	PF-68	750	1,000	1,500	2,000	$21,738, PF-68Cam, April 2014
1871	960	549	PF-68	750	1,000	1,500	2,000	$12,339, PF-67, April 2013
1872	950	520	PF-68	750	1,000	1,500	2,000	$16,450, PF-66DCam, April 2014
1873, Close 3, Proof only	600	846	PF-68	2,000	2,500	2,800	3,500	$14,100, PF-67DCam, January 2014

* Included in number below. ** Included in number above.

NICKEL THREE-CENT PIECES (1865–1889)

Designer James B. Longacre; weight 1.94 grams; composition .750 copper, .250 nickel; diameter 17.9 mm; plain edge. All coined at Philadelphia Mint.

Shown 2x actual size.

History. The copper-nickel three-cent coin debuted in the final year of the Civil War, 1865. The American public was still hoarding silver coins (a situation that would continue until 1876), including the silver three-cent piece. The highest-denomination coin in circulation at the time was the recently introduced two-cent piece. After 1875, when silver coins circulated once again, the three-cent denomination became redundant and mintages dropped. The last pieces were coined in 1889.

Striking and Sharpness. On the obverse check the hair and other portrait details. On the reverse the tiny vertical lines in the Roman numeral III can be weak. Check the dentils on both sides of the coin. Among circulation strikes, clashed dies are common, particularly for the earlier high-mintage years. Generally, coins of the 1860s and 1870s have weakness in one area or another. Many if not most of the 1880s are well struck.

Availability. Circulated examples of dates from 1865 to the mid-1870s are readily available. MS coins, particularly from the 1860s, are easily found, but often have areas of weakness or lack aesthetic appeal. MS coins of the 1880s are readily found for most dates (except for 1883, 1884, 1885, and 1887), some of them probably sold as Proofs. Many Proofs of the era had slight to extensive mint luster.

EF-40, 45 (Extremely Fine). *Obverse:* More wear is seen on the cheek and the hair to the right of the face and neck than at AU. The hair to the right of the coronet beads shows light wear. *Reverse:* The wreath still shows most detail on the leaves. Some wear is seen on the vertical lines within III (but striking can also cause weakness). Overall the reverse appears to be very bold.

AU-50, 53, 55, 58 (About Uncirculated). *Obverse:* Light wear is seen on the portrait, most notably on the upper cheek and on the hair to the right of the face. Mint luster is present in the fields, ranging from partial at AU-50 to nearly complete at AU-58. All details are sharp, unless lightly struck. *Reverse:* Light wear is seen on the top and bottom horizontal edges of the III and the wreath. Luster is partial at AU-50, increasing to nearly full at AU-58. All details are sharp, unless lightly struck.

MS-60 to 70 (Mint State). *Obverse and Reverse:* Mint luster is complete in the obverse and reverse fields. Lower grades such as MS-60, 61, and 62 can show some evidence of abrasion. This is usually on the area of the hair to the right of the face (on the obverse), and on the highest parts of the wreath (on the reverse). Abrasion can appear as scattered contact marks elsewhere. At MS-63, these marks are few, and on MS-65 they are fewer yet. In grades above MS-65, marks can be seen only under magnification.

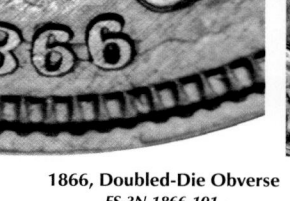

1866, Doubled-Die Obverse
FS-3N-1866-101.

	Mintage	Cert	Avg	%MS	EF-40	AU-50	MS-60	MS-63	MS-64	MS-65	MS-66	Recent Auction Record
1865	11,382,000	3,575	60.3	79	$40	$65	$120	$160	$235	$600	$1,200	$1,175, MS-66, February 2013
1866	4,801,000	1,412	60.7	83	40	65	120	160	235	600	1,500	$3,819, MS-66, September 2013
1866, Doubled-Die Obverse (a)	*	6	46.5	33	150	250	350	450	600	900		$250, MS-62, December 2007
1867	3,915,000	1,103	59.5	76	40	65	120	160	235	700	1,900	$1,410, MS-66, January 2014
1868	3,252,000	1,054	60.1	78	40	65	120	160	235	600	1,200	$1,116, MS-66, April 2014
1869	1,604,000	720	60.3	79	40	65	135	185	250	750	1,500	$823, MS-65, July 2014
1870	1,335,000	763	60.7	80	40	65	140	195	275	725	1,450	$3,525, MS-66, January 2014
1871	604,000	434	61.5	85	40	65	140	195	275	750	1,500	$2,585, MS-66, November 2013
1872	862,000	342	60.9	81	40	65	150	210	325	1,200	2,200	$2,115, MS-66, April 2013
1873, Close 3	390,000	298	60.7	81	40	65	150	210	400	1,400	2,750	$2,820, MS-66, April 2013
1873, Open 3	783,000	178	59.0	75	40	70	160	350	700	5,000		$10,575, MS-66, April 2013
1874	790,000	365	60.3	77	40	65	150	210	350	1,200	2,100	$2,585, MS-66, March 2013
1875	228,000	409	62.5	88	45	80	175	225	300	800	1,500	$1,645, MS-66, April 2013
1876	162,000	242	60.3	81	50	110	200	260	500	1,600	2,500	$6,463, MS-66, January 2014
1879	38,000	340	59.3	74	125	175	300	400	500	850	1,200	$4,113, MS-67, February 2014
1880	21,000	420	60.0	80	200	220	350	410	525	850	1,350	$3,290, MS-67, July 2014
1881	1,077,000	1,178	60.2	74	40	65	125	185	250	650	1,000	$999, MS-66, April 2014
1882	22,200	236	53.4	55	225	275	400	500	600	1,200	3,000	$593, MS-63, December 2013
1883	4,000	116	53.8	46	350	400	550	900	1,750	5,200	15,000	$25,850, MS-67, April 2013
1884	1,700	64	51.4	41	600	650	900	1,100	2,750	10,000	16,000	$4,700, AU-55, January 2014
1885	1,000	108	57.4	65	700	800	950	1,300	4,500	12,500	18,000	$22,325, MS-66, June 2014
1887	5,001	237	56.6	65	400	500	550	675	1,000	1,500	2,250	$2,350, MS-66, June 2013
1888	36,501	627	60.5	72	90	150	300	400	500	850	1,350	$2,115, MS-67, April 2013
1889	18,125	500	58.9	64	220	250	350	450	600	850	1,350	$2,585, MS-67, June 2014

* Included in number above. **a.** Moderate doubling is visible on AMERICA and on portions of the hair. "The dies clashed midway through the obverse's life. Mid- and late-die-state coins exhibit the clash marks and die cracks as progression occurs. This variety has proven extremely scarce" (*Cherrypickers' Guide to Rare Die Varieties,* fifth edition, volume I).

Proof Nickel Three-Cent Pieces

PF-60 to 70 (Proof). Proofs were struck of all dates and can be found easily enough in the marketplace. One of the rarest is 1865, the vast majority of which have a repunched date. Another is the 1887 (regular, not overdate) with a production of about 1,000 coins. Proofs of the years 1865 to 1876 can be difficult to find as true gems, while later Proofs nearly all are gems. Proofs from 1878 onward often have satiny or frosty fields, rather than mirrored surfaces, and resemble circulation strikes. *Obverse and Reverse:* PF-60, 61, and 62 coins show varying amounts of hairlines in the field, decreasing as the grade increases. Fields may be dull or cloudy on lower-level pieces. At PF-65, hairlines are visible only under magnification and are very light; the cheek of Miss Liberty does not show any friction or "album slide marks." Above PF-65, hairlines become fewer, and in ultra-high grades are nonexistent, this meaning that the coin has never been wiped or abrasively cleaned. Blotched, deeply toned, or recolored coins are sometimes seen from PF-60 through 65 or even 66 and should be avoided; these are seen less often than on contemporary Proof nickel *five-cent* pieces.

Proof Nickel Three-Cent Piece
Shown 2x actual size.

1887, 7 Over 6, Proof
FS-3N-1887-302.

	Mintage	Cert	Finest	PF-64	PF-65	PF-66	PF-66Cam	Recent Auction Record
1865	500+	463	PF-67	$2,500	$6,000	$8,000	$8,500	$11,750, PF, August 2013
1866	725+	599	PF-67	500	1,500	2,000	2,500	$17,625, PF, February 2013
1867	625+	573	PF-67	500	1,500	2,000	2,500	$6,463, PF-66DCam, July 2014
1868	600+	516	PF-67	500	1,500	2,000	2,700	$4,406, PF-66DCam, April 2013
1869	600+	691	PF-67	450	950	1,500	2,500	$9,173, PF-67DCam, January 2014
1870	1,000+	652	PF-67	450	950	1,500	3,000	$3,055, PF-66Cam, August 2013
1871	960+	696	PF-67	450	1,000	1,500	2,700	$1,528, PF-66Cam, December 2013
1872	950+	787	PF-67	425	950	1,400	2,700	$3,055, PF-67, June 2014
1873, Close 3	1,100+	952	PF-67	425	1,000	1,500	2,500	$7,050, PF-67, September 2013
1874	700+	684	PF-67	425	900	1,300	1,800	$8,519, PF-67, August 2013
1875	700+	573	PF-66	425	1,300	2,000	5,000	$8,225, PF-66Cam, February 2014
1876	1,150+	798	PF-67	425	900	1,300	2,500	$2,233, PF-66Cam, February 2013
1877, Proof only	900	971	PF-68	3,000	4,400	5,500	6,000	$11,163, PF-67Cam, January 2014
1878, Proof only	2,350	1,493	PF-68	1,000	1,100	1,450	1,600	$8,225, PF-68Cam, January 2014
1879	3,200	1,907	PF-68	525	700	850	1,000	$14,100, PF-67DCam, April 2013
1880	3,955	1,992	PF-68	525	700	850	1,000	$9,400, PF-67Cam, June 2014
1881	3,575	2,106	PF-68	525	700	850	1,000	$11,163, PF-67DCam, February 2014
1882	3,100	2,184	PF-68	525	700	850	1,000	$5,875, PF-68, January 2014
1883	6,609	3,247	PF-68	525	700	850	1,000	$2,820, PF, February 2013
1884	3,942	2,374	PF-68	600	700	850	1,000	$9,400, PF-68Cam, June 2014
1885	3,790	2,086	PF-68	600	700	850	1,000	$3,760, PF-67Cam, June 2014
1886, Proof only	4,290	2,225	PF-68	550	750	875	1,000	$1,998, PF-67Cam, June 2013
1887	2,960	322	PF-67	600	1,000	1,200	1,500	$2,115, PF-67, January 2014
1887, 7 Over 6 (a)	*	1,497	PF-68	625	900	1,100	1,400	$7,638, PF-67Cam, April 2014
1888	4,582	2,253	PF-68	425	700	850	1,000	$2,350, PF-66DCam, March 2014
1889	3,436	2,213	PF-68	525	700	850	1,000	$1,645, PF, March 2014

* Included in number above. **a.** Strong remnants of the underlying 6 are evident on either side of the lower portion of the 7, with the 1 and both 8's clearly repunched. This Proof overdate is relatively common; note that the regular date can be valued higher than the variety.

Five-cent pieces made of nickel were introduced in 1866, in an era in which the silver half dime as well as other silver denominations were not seen in circulation. More than a dozen designs and their variations have graced the "nickel" in the past 140-plus years.

While Shield nickels of both types are slightly scarce in upper Mint State levels, they are within the financial reach of most collectors. Proofs are available of each type, but the 1866–1867 With Rays and the 1913 Buffalo Variety 1 issues are rare.

The quality of strike presents a challenge across the various types of nickel five-cent pieces, most particularly with the 1866–1867 With Rays, for there are fewer possibilities from which to choose. Although 1913–1938 Variety 2 Buffalo nickels are often poorly struck, there are enough sharp ones that finding a choice example should present no great challenge for the collector.

FOR THE COLLECTOR AND INVESTOR: FIVE-CENT PIECES AS A SPECIALTY

Shield nickels of the 1866–1883 era are often collected by date sequence. A full set includes 1866 and 1867 With Rays plus 1867 to 1883 Without Rays. In addition, there is the 1879, 9 Over 8 overdate, which is found only in Proof format but is readily available (constituting perhaps a third or so of the Proof mintage of 3,200 for the 1879 year) and the 1883, 3 Over 2 (scarce, and available only as a circulation strike).

Circulation strikes are available of all Shield nickel dates, 1866 to 1883, except 1877 and 1878, which were made only in Proof format. A set of Proofs can be completed except for the 1867 With Rays, which is exceedingly rare in Proof, with an estimated population of fewer than two dozen coins. Most 1878 Proofs are frosty and appear not much different from Mint State, but as only Proofs were made this year, they are called Proofs.

In circulated grades, Shield nickels are available in proportion to their mintage figures. The dates 1879 to 1881 had high Proof mintages (in the context of Proof figures), but low circulation-strike mintages, and thus they are key dates in the latter format. In other words, a gem MS-65 1880 Shield nickel (16,000 coined, but few were saved, as collectors acquired Proofs instead) is exceedingly rare today. In the same year 3,955 Proofs were struck, all were preserved by collectors and dealers, and today the Proof 1880 is one of the most plentiful dates.

Liberty Head nickels of the 1883 Without CENTS (or "No CENTS") type are plentiful in Mint State and also in Proof. Later dates With CENTS, through 1912, are generally available in proportion to their mintages. The 1885 and 1886 are considered to be key dates. Proofs are readily collectible, although pristine high-quality specimens can be hard to find. The 1912-D and 1912-S are scarce. In 1913 an estimated five Liberty Head nickels were privately made, and today stand as famous rarities.

Among Buffalo nickels, 1913 to 1938, the different dates and mints can be collected easily enough in circulated grades, although certain issues such as 1913-S Variety 2, 1921-S, and 1926-S are on the scarce side. An overdate, 1918-D, 8 Over 7, is a rarity at all grade levels. Curious varieties are provided by the very rare 1916 Doubled Date, the scarce 1937-D, 3-Legged (the die was heavily polished, resulting in some loss of detail), and the fascinating and readily available 1938-D, D Over S overmintmark.

In choice or gem Mint State most branch-mint Buffalo nickels, 1914–1927, are fairly scarce, and some are quite rare. Most branch-mint coins of the 1920s are lightly struck in one area or another, with the 1926-D being particularly infamous in this regard. Sharply struck examples of such varieties are worth much more than lightly struck ones, although the grading services take no particular note of such differences. Matte Proofs of dates 1913 to 1916 were struck, and mirror-finish Proofs were made in 1936 and 1937. These exist today in proportion to their mintages.

Jefferson nickels from 1938 to date are readily collectible in Mint State and Proof format. Many otherwise common varieties can be very rare if sharply struck.

RECOMMENDED READING

Bowers, Q. David. *A Guide Book of Buffalo and Jefferson Nickels,* Atlanta, GA, 2007.
Bowers, Q. David. *A Guide Book of Shield and Liberty Head Nickels,* Atlanta, GA, 2006.
Fivaz, Bill, and Stanton, J.T. *The Cherrypickers' Guide to Rare Die Varieties* (5th ed., vol. I), Atlanta, GA, 2009.
Fletcher, Edward L., Jr. *The Shield Five Cent Series,* Ormond Beach, FL, 1994.
Lange, David W. *The Complete Guide to Buffalo Nickels,* Virginia Beach, VA, 2006.
Nagengast, Bernard. *The Jefferson Nickel Analyst* (2nd ed.), Sidney, Ohio, 1979.
Peters, Gloria, and Mahon, Cynthia. *The Complete Guide to Shield and Liberty Head Nickels,* Virginia Beach, VA, 1995.
Wescott, Michael. *The United States Nickel Five-Cent Piece,* Wolfeboro, NH, 1991.

SHIELD
(1866–1883)

Designer James B. Longacre; weight 5 grams; composition .750 copper, .250 nickel; diameter 20.5 mm; plain edge. All coined at Philadelphia Mint.

Variety 1, Rays Between Stars
(1866–1867)

Variety 2, Without Rays
(1867–1883)

History. The nickel five-cent piece was introduced in 1866. At the time, silver coins (except the trime) did not circulate in the East or Midwest. The new denomination proved popular, and "nickels" of the Shield type were made continuously from 1866 to 1883. All 1866 nickels have rays between the stars on the reverse, as do a minority of 1867 issues, after which this feature was dropped. In 1877 and 1878 only Proofs were made, with no circulation strikes. The design, by Chief Engraver James B. Longacre, is somewhat similar to the obverse of the two-cent piece. Some Shield nickels were still seen in circulation in the 1930s, by which time most had been worn nearly smooth.

Striking and Sharpness. Sharpness can be a problem for Shield nickels in the 1860s through 1876, much less so for later years. On the obverse the horizontal shield stripes, vertical stripes, and leaves should be checked. The horizontal stripes in particular can be blended together. On the reverse the star centers can be weak. Check all other areas as well. Die cracks are seen on *most* circulation-strike Shield nickels, and do not affect value.

Availability. Circulated coins generally are available in proportion to their mintage quantities (exceptions being the 1873 Open 3 and Close 3 varieties, which tend to be elusive in all grades despite their relatively high mintage). MS coins are similarly available, except that 1880 is a rarity. Those dated 1882 and 1883 are plentiful.

EF-40, 45 (Extremely Fine). *Obverse:* Nearly all shield border and leaf detail is visible. Light wear is seen on the shield stripes (but the horizontal stripes can be weakly struck). *Reverse:* More wear is seen on the numeral 5 than at AU. The radial lines in the stars (if sharply struck to begin with) show slight wear. The field shows more wear.

AU-50, 53, 55, 58 (About Uncirculated). *Obverse:* Light wear is seen on the outside edges of the leaves, the frame of the shield, and the horizontal stripes (although the stripes can also be weakly struck). Mint luster is present in the fields, ranging from partial at AU-50 to nearly complete at 58. All details are sharp, unless lightly struck. *Reverse:* Light wear is seen on the numeral 5, and friction is seen in the field, identifiable as a change of color (loss of luster). Luster is partial at AU-50, increasing to nearly full at 58. All details are sharp, unless lightly struck.

MS-60 to 70 (Mint State). *Obverse and Reverse:* At MS-60 some abrasion and very minor contact marks are evident, most noticeably on high points of the shield on the obverse and the field on the reverse. Sometimes light striking on the shield and stars can be mistaken for light wear, and marks on the numeral 5 on the reverse can be from the original planchet surface not struck up fully. At MS-63 abrasions are hard to detect except under magnification. An MS-65 coin has no abrasion. Luster should be full and rich (not grainy). Coins above MS-65 have no marks that can be seen by the naked eye. Higher-grade coins display deeper luster or virtually perfect prooflike surfaces, depending on the dies used.

1866, Repunched Date
Several varieties exist.

1873, Close 3	1873, Open 3	1873, Close 3, Doubled-Die Obverse	1883, 3 Over 2
		Several varieties exist. Pictured are FS-05-1873-101 (left) and FS-05-1873-102 (right).	*Several varieties exist, as well as pieces with a recut 3. Pictured are FS-05-1883-301 (left) and FS-05-1883-305 (right).*

	Mintage	Cert	Avg	%MS	EF-40	AU-50	MS-60	MS-63	MS-64	MS-65	MS-66	Recent Auction Record
1866, Rays	14,742,500	2,997	59.7	76	$160	$240	$275	$425	$750	$2,400	$5,000	$11,163, MS-66, October 2013
1866, Repunched Date **(a)**	*	38	46.9	34	260	375	575	950	2,000			$1,293, AU-50, March 2013
1867, Rays	2,019,000	1,071	58.6	69	190	285	375	500	850	3,750	8,500	$41,125, MS-67, October 2013
1867, No Rays	28,890,500	1,553	60.1	77	65	110	140	225	350	800	2,000	$7,638, MS, February 2014
1868	28,817,000	1,500	60.2	78	65	110	140	225	350	800	2,000	$7,638, MS, February 2014
1869	16,395,000	908	60.5	81	65	110	140	225	350	800	2,000	$11,750, MS-66, October 2013
1870	4,806,000	450	59.0	77	90	140	210	300	425	1,750	3,100	$4,994, MS-66, June 2014
1871	561,000	238	55.7	68	280	350	450	625	825	2,400	4,500	$5,875, MS-66, February 2014
1872	6,036,000	567	59.7	78	125	175	235	300	425	1,400	4,500	$25,850, MS-67, October 2013
1873, Close 3	436,050	128	60.4	81	140	200	325	585	950	2,750	5,500	$3,525, MS-65, October 2013
1873, Close 3, DblDie Obv **(b)**	*	16	52.1	50	425	675	900	1,500	2,000	3,500		$499, MS-62, June 2013
1873, Open 3	4,113,950	308	61.1	81	100	140	210	300	400	2,000	4,500	$10,575, MS-66, March 2013
1874	3,538,000	360	60.9	82	120	170	250	325	500	1,500	3,350	$11,163, MS, February 2014
1875	2,097,000	341	59.8	79	160	220	275	360	525	1,700	3,450	$4,406, MS-66, June 2014
1876	2,530,000	526	60.1	82	145	190	260	325	425	1,350	3,500	$5,875, MS-66, October 2013
1879	25,900	212	57.0	71	725	750	900	1,000	1,450	2,000	3,500	$7,638, MS-66, June 2013
1880	16,000	103	44.2	31	1,300	1,850	3,800	7,500	15,000	47,500	60,000	$193,875, MS, February 2014
1881	68,800	369	48.4	54	600	775	850	1,000	1,350	1,950	3,000	$8,519, MS-67, October 2013
1882	11,472,900	2,124	60.1	83	65	110	150	225	350	725	1,300	$8,519, AU-55, April 2014
1883	1,451,500	3,527	61.9	82	65	110	150	225	350	725	1,300	$3,525, MS-67, January 2014
1883, 3 Over 2 **(c)**	*	108	56.8	52	1,250	1,750	2,100	2,750	3,000	5,000	10,000	$15,275, MS-67, December 2013

* Included in number above. **a.** There are at least five similar, very strong repunched dates for 1866; the values shown are typical for each. **b.** There are several varieties of 1873, Close 3, Doubled-Die Obverse. The values shown are representative of the more avidly sought varieties; others command smaller premiums. **c.** Several varieties exist. For more information, see the *Cherrypickers' Guide to Rare Die Varieties,* fifth edition, volume I. "Beware of 1882 Shield nickels with a filled-in blobby 2, as these are very frequently offered as 1883, 3 Over 2. This is possibly the single most misunderstood coin in all U.S. coinage." (Howard Spindel, communication to Q. David Bowers, quoted in *A Guide Book of Shield and Liberty Head Nickels.*)

Proof Shield Nickels

PF-60 to 70 (Proof). Proof Shield nickels were struck of all dates 1866 to 1883, including both varieties of 1867. Fields range from deeply mirrorlike to somewhat grainy in character to mirror-surface, depending on a given year. Many of 1878, a date struck only in Proof format, have *lustrous* surfaces or prooflike surfaces combined with some luster, resembling a circulation strike. While most Proofs are sharp, some have weakness on the shield on the obverse and/or the star centers on the reverse. Lint marks or tiny recessed marks from scattered debris on the die faces are sometimes encountered, especially on issues of the 1870s, but not factored into the grade in commercial certification unless excessive. *Obverse and Reverse:* PF-60, 61, and 62 coins show varying amounts of hairlines in the reverse field in particular, decreasing as the grade increases. Fields may be dull or cloudy on lower-level pieces. At PF-65, hairlines are visible only under magnification and are very light and usually only on the reverse. Above PF-65, hairlines become fewer, and in ultra-high grades are nonexistent, this meaning that the coins have never been wiped or abrasively cleaned. At PF-65 or better, expect excellent aesthetic appeal.

Proof Shield Nickel
Shown 1.5x actual size.

	Mintage	Cert	Finest	PF-63	PF-64	PF-65	PF-66	PF-66Cam	Recent Auction Record
1866, Rays	600+	598	PF-67	$2,000	$2,750	$3,500	$5,500	$6,000	$41,125, PF, October 2013
1867, Rays †	25+	81	PF-67	37,500	46,000	75,000	95,000	110,000	$123,375, PF, October 2013
1867, Without Rays	600+	541	PF-67	475	1,400	2,500	4,500	5,000	$35,250, PF, October 2013
1867, Without Rays, Pattern Reverse (a)	21–30 known	1	PF-64	6,500	7,500	9,000			$1,495, PF-63, September 2009
1868	600+	456	PF-67	385	525	1,500	2,000	2,500	$9,400, PF-66DCam, August 2013
1869	600+	639	PF-67	385	525	900	1,400	2,000	$15,863, PF, October 2013
1870	1,000+	658	PF-67	385	525	900	1,400	2,500	$8,225, PF-67Cam, July 2014
1871	960+	678	PF-67	425	575	900	1,400	1,500	$17,038, PF, February 2014
1872	950+	716	PF-67	385	500	700	1,000	1,500	$8,519, PF, February 2014
1873, Close 3	1,100+	825	PF-67	385	500	700	1,000	2,000	$35,250, PF, February 2014
1874	700+	619	PF-67	385	525	800	1,100	1,500	$16,450, PF, February 2014
1875	700+	606	PF-67	425	600	1,500	2,000	2,200	$9,988, PF, February 2014
1876	1,150+	804	PF-68	385	525	900	1,100	1,300	$22,325, PF, February 2014
1877, Proof only	900	908	PF-67	3,400	3,700	4,800	5,000	6,200	$13,513, PF, February 2014
1878, Proof only	2,350	1,368	PF-67	2,000	2,250	2,750	3,500	3,750	$11,456, PF, February 2014
1879	3,200	983	PF-68	500	575	775	1,000	1,500	$7,931, PF, February 2014
1879, 9 Over 8 (b)	*	500	PF-69	725	800	850	1,100	1,500	$15,275, PF-67Cam, February 2014
1880	3,955	1,949	PF-68	500	575	700	900	1,100	$3,173, PF-67Cam, February 2013
1881	3,575	1,713	PF-68	500	575	700	900	1,100	$5,434, PF, February 2014
1882	3,100	1,848	PF-68	385	450	650	900	1,100	$27,025, PF, February 2014
1883	5,419	2,382	PF-68	385	450	650	900	1,100	$8,813, PF, February 2014

* Included in number above. † Ranked in the *100 Greatest U.S. Coins* (fourth edition). **a.** These were made from a pattern (Judd-573) reverse die that is slightly different than the regular Without Rays design. **b.** This variety is confirmed only with Proof finish, although Breen mentions two circulation strikes and further mentions that there are "at least two varieties" *(Walter Breen's Complete Encyclopedia of U.S. and Colonial Coins)*. In the *Guide Book of Shield and Liberty Head Nickels*, Bowers discusses research and theories from Breen, DeLorey, Spindel, and Julian, noting that the variety's overdate status is "not determined."

LIBERTY HEAD
(1883–1912)

Designer Charles E. Barber; weight 5 grams; composition .750 copper, .250 nickel; diameter 21.2 mm; plain edge; mints: Philadelphia, Denver, San Francisco.

Variety 1, Without CENTS
(1883 Only)

Variety 2, With CENTS
(1883–1912)

Mintmark is on the reverse, to the left of CENTS.

History. Liberty Head nickels were popular in their time, minted in large quantities most years, and remained in circulation through the 1940s, by which time most were worn down to grades such as AG-3 and G-4. Stray coins could still be found in the early 1950s. Serious numismatic interest in circulated examples began in the 1930s with the popularity of Whitman and other coin boards, folders, and albums. Many of the scarcer dates were picked from circulation at that time. The five known 1913 Liberty Head nickels were not an authorized Mint issue, and were never placed into circulation.

Striking and Sharpness. Many Liberty Head nickels have areas of light striking. On the obverse, this is often seen at the star centers, particularly near the top border. The hair above the forehead can be light as well, and always is thus on 1912-S (the obverse die on this San Francisco issue is slightly bulged). On the reverse, E PLURIBUS UNUM can vary in sharpness of strike. Weakness is often seen at the wreath bow and on the ear of corn to the left

(the kernels in the ear can range from indistinct to bold). Even Proofs can be weakly struck in areas. Mint luster can range from minutely pebbly or grainy (but still attractive) to a deep, rich frost. Some later Philadelphia coins show stress marks in the field, particularly the obverse, from the use of "tired" dies. This can be determined only by observation, as "slabbed" grades for MS coins do not indicate the quality of the luster or surfaces.

Availability. All issues from 1883 to 1912 are readily collectible, although the 1885 (in particular), 1886, and 1912-S are considered to be key dates. Most readily available are well-worn coins in AG-3 and G-4. As a class, VF, EF, and AU pieces are very scarce in relation to demand. MS coins are generally scarce in the 1880s, except for the 1883 Without CENTS, which is plentiful in all grades. MS pieces are less scarce in the 1890s and are easily found for most 20th-century years, save for 1909, 1912-D, and 1912-S, all of which are elusive.

EF-40, 45 (Extremely Fine). *Obverse:* Nearly all hair detail is visible, save for some lightness above the forehead. The stars show radial lines (except for those that may have been lightly struck). The appearance overall is bold. *Reverse:* The wreath shows most detail on the leaves. The dentils are bold inside the rim.

AU-50, 53, 55, 58 (About Uncirculated). *Obverse:* Light wear is seen on the portrait and on the hair under LIB. Mint luster is present in the fields, ranging from partial at AU-50 to nearly complete at 58. All details are sharp, unless lightly struck. *Reverse:* Light wear is seen on the V, the other letters, and the wreath. Luster is partial at AU-50, increasing to nearly full at 58. All details are sharp, unless lightly struck.

MS-60 to 70 (Mint State). *Obverse and Reverse:* Mint luster is complete in the obverse and reverse fields.

MS-60, 61, and 62 can show some evidence of abrasion, usually on the portrait on the obverse and highest parts of the wreath on the reverse, and scattered contact marks elsewhere. At MS-63 these marks are few, and at MS-65 they are fewer yet. In grades above MS-65, marks can only be seen under magnification.

1899, Repunched Date, Early Die State

1899, Repunched Date, Late Die State

FS-05-1899-301.

1900, Doubled-Die Reverse
FS-05-1900-801.

1913 Liberty Head Nickel
Shown 2x actual size.

	Mintage	Cert	Avg	%MS	EF-40	AU-50	MS-60	MS-63	MS-64	MS-65	MS-66	Recent Auction Record
1883, Without CENTS	5,474,300	13,787	63.2	93	$15	$18	$35	$50	$70	$225	$500	$5,288, MS-67, April 2013
1883, With CENTS	16,026,200	2,008	61.4	83	85	120	150	200	285	650	1,450	$9,694, MS-66, April 2014
1884	11,270,000	915	59.8	79	85	130	190	300	400	1,800	3,400	$8,225, MS-66, February 2014
1885	1,472,700	1,671	30.5	28	1,350	1,700	2,000	3,400	6,000	10,000	17,000	$22,325, MS-66, April 2013
1886	3,326,000	1,409	35.4	33	700	825	1,000	2,600	4,000	7,200	13,000	$5,875, MS-65, April 2013
1887	15,260,692	998	61.6	88	75	110	140	195	325	950	2,000	$11,163, MS-66, August 2013
1888	10,167,901	766	58.5	79	175	220	275	340	500	1,200	3,500	$7,638, MS-66, April 2013
1889	15,878,025	1,077	62.6	93	75	120	140	175	325	800	2,200	$3,819, MS-66, April 2013
1890	16,256,532	702	61.4	88	65	110	160	200	350	1,000	2,300	$9,988, MS-66, November 2013
1891	16,832,000	920	62.3	90	70	125	160	200	300	950	2,000	$2,585, MS-66, April 2013
1892	11,696,897	966	62.1	90	65	110	140	160	300	1,200	3,000	$7,050, MS-66, November 2013
1893	13,368,000	979	62.2	91	65	110	140	160	300	1,000	2,850	$9,694, MS-66, November 2013
1894	5,410,500	743	59.1	79	240	300	350	425	575	1,400	3,200	$4,700, MS-67, June 2014
1895	9,977,822	711	61.7	88	70	115	140	200	440	2,000	4,900	$5,288, MS-66, November 2013
1896	8,841,058	676	60.9	85	90	150	190	265	450	2,100	8,000	$19,975, MS, February 2014
1897	20,426,797	996	62.2	89	45	70	100	160	265	900	2,600	$4,113, MS-66, January 2014

Chart continued on next page.

	Mintage	Cert	Avg	%MS	EF-40	AU-50	MS-60	MS-63	MS-64	MS-65	MS-66	Recent Auction Record
1898	12,530,292	898	62.2	90	$45	$75	$150	$185	$290	$950	$2,000	$2,350, MS-66, March 2013
1899	26,027,000	1,581	62.3	92	30	60	90	140	200	600	1,000	$3,525, MS-66, January 2014
1899, Repunched Date (a)	*	n/a	n/a	n/a	85	150	190	240	550	800		$150, MS-63, April 2002
1900	27,253,733	1,628	62.8	93	30	65	90	140	200	525	1,000	$3,290, MS-66, January 2014
1900, Doubled-Die Reverse (b)	*	10	48.1	30	110	160	235	310	465	875		
1901	26,478,228	1,543	63.0	94	30	60	85	135	200	500	1,100	$28,200, MS-67, August 2013
1902	31,487,561	1,610	62.6	93	30	60	85	135	200	500	1,050	$28,200, MS-67, September 2013
1903	28,004,935	1,772	63.1	94	30	60	85	135	200	500	1,000	$2,233, MS-66, July 2014
1904	21,403,167	1,538	63.2	95	30	60	85	135	200	500	1,000	$4,113, MS-67, April 2013
1905	29,825,124	1,897	62.7	92	30	60	85	135	200	500	1,000	$7,050, MS-66, July 2014
1906	38,612,000	1,403	61.6	86	30	60	85	135	210	700	2,500	$4,113, MS-66, November 2013
1907	39,213,325	1,308	61.8	88	30	60	85	135	210	800	1,400	$1,528, MS-66, April 2013
1908	22,684,557	1,100	61.7	88	30	60	85	135	210	825	3,500	$3,525, MS-66, August 2013
1909	11,585,763	908	61.5	87	32	75	100	140	275	975	2,200	$2,115, MS-66, September 2013
1910	30,166,948	1,258	61.8	87	30	60	85	135	200	525	2,850	$8,225, MS-66, August 2013
1911	39,557,639	2,463	62.4	92	30	60	85	135	200	525	1,000	$2,350, MS-66, December 2013
1912	26,234,569	2,267	62.1	90	30	60	85	135	200	500	1,400	$1,528, MS-66, April 2013
1912D	8,474,000	1,564	60.6	87	85	175	300	400	550	1,900	5,000	$14,100, MS-67, June 2014
1912S	238,000	2,749	35.2	43	850	1,400	1,750	2,000	3,100	5,700	14,000	$30,550, MS, February 2014
1913 † (c) (5 known)		n/a	n/a	n/a				3,750,000				$3,172,500, PF-63, April 2013

* Included in number above. † Ranked in the *100 Greatest U.S. Coins* (fourth edition). **a.** "The loop of a 9, or possibly (but unlikely) an 8, is evident within the lower loop of the second 9. Some specialists believe this to be an 1899/8 overdate. However, we feel it is simply a repunched date, with the secondary 9 far to the south of the primary 9 at the last digit" (*Cherrypickers' Guide to Rare Die Varieties*, fifth edition, volume I). **b.** Doubling on this very popular variety is evident on all reverse design elements, including the V, with a stronger spread on the lower quadrant of the reverse. **c.** An estimated five 1913 Liberty Head nickels (four circulation-strike and one Proof) were struck under irregular circumstances at the Mint. Some researchers consider them all to be Proofs. They were dispersed and are now held in various public and private collections.

Proof Liberty Head Nickels

PF-60 to 70 (Proof). Proof Liberty Head nickels were struck of all dates 1883 to 1912, plus both varieties of 1883. The fields range from deeply mirrorlike to somewhat grainy character to mirror-surface, depending on a given year. While most Proofs are sharp, some have weakness at the star centers and/or the kernels on the ear of corn to the left of the ribbon bow. These weaknesses are overlooked by the certification services. Generally, later issues are more deeply mirrored than are earlier ones. Some years in the 1880s and

1890s can show graininess, a combination of mint luster and mirror quality. Lint marks or tiny recessed marks from scattered debris on the die faces are sometimes encountered, but not factored into third-party–certified grades unless excessive. *Obverse and Reverse:* PF-60, 61, and 62 coins show varying amounts of hairlines in the field, decreasing as the grade increases. Fields may be dull or cloudy on lower-level pieces. At PF-65, hairlines are visible only under magnification and are very light; the cheek of Miss Liberty does not

show any abrasion or "album slide marks." Above PF-65, hairlines become fewer, and in ultra-high grades are nonexistent, this meaning that the coins have never been wiped or abrasively cleaned. At PF-65 or finer, expect excellent aesthetic appeal. Blotched, deeply toned, or recolored coins can be found at most Proof levels from PF-60 through 65 or even 66, and should be avoided. Watch for artificially toned lower-grade Proofs colored to mask the true nature of the fields.

Proof Liberty Head Nickel
Shown 1.5x actual size.

	Mintage	Cert	Finest	PF-63	PF-64	PF-65	PF-66	PF-66Cam	Recent Auction Record
1883, Without CENTS	5,219	2,075	PF-67	$300	$450	$800	$1,200	$1,600	$16,450, PF-67DCam, June 2014
1883, With CENTS	6,783	1,448	PF-68	275	400	750	1,100	1,400	$10,575, PF-67Cam, June 2014
1884	3,942	1,595	PF-68	250	375	700	1,000	1,400	$15,275, PF-67DCam, November 2013
1885	3,790	1,731	PF-68	1,300	1,400	1,700	2,100	2,500	$7,344, PF-67, February 2014
1886	4,290	1,711	PF-67	650	675	1,000	1,200	2,350	$8,225, PF-67, June 2014
1887	2,960	1,209	PF-67	250	375	700	1,000	1,300	$7,050, PF-66Cam, March 2014

	Mintage	Cert	Finest	PF-63	PF-64	PF-65	PF-66	PF-66Cam	Recent Auction Record
1888	4,582	1,540	PF-67	$250	$375	$700	$1,000	$1,300	$6,463, PF-66Cam, July 2014
1889	3,336	1,283	PF-68	250	375	700	1,000	1,300	$6,463, PF-67, February 2014
1890	2,740	984	PF-68	250	375	700	1,000	1,300	$5,581, PF-66DCam, June 2013
1891	2,350	986	PF-68	250	375	700	1,000	1,300	$6,169, PF-66DCam, April 2014
1892	2,745	1,082	PF-68	250	375	700	1,000	1,300	$11,163, PF-66DCam, January 2014
1893	2,195	937	PF-68	250	375	700	1,000	1,300	$22,325, PF, February 2013
1894	2,632	965	PF-68	250	375	700	1,000	1,300	$9,988, PF-67Cam, April 2014
1895	2,062	922	PF-68	250	375	700	1,000	1,300	$5,875, PF-67, April 2014
1896	1,862	840	PF-67	250	375	700	1,000	1,300	$7,050, PF-66Cam, April 2014
1897	1,938	962	PF-69	250	375	700	1,000	1,300	$9,988, PF, August 2013
1898	1,795	875	PF-68	250	375	700	1,000	1,300	$5,006, PF-67Cam, June 2014
1899	2,031	911	PF-68	250	375	700	1,000	1,300	$2,585, PF-66Cam, April 2014
1900	2,262	980	PF-68	250	375	700	1,000	1,300	$2,585, PF-66Cam, November 2013
1901	1,985	1,012	PF-68	250	375	700	1,000	1,300	$4,700, PF-67Cam, July 2014
1902	2,018	940	PF-68	250	375	700	1,000	1,300	$7,050, PF-67Cam, June 2013
1903	1,790	1,070	PF-68	250	375	700	1,000	1,300	$19,975, PF-68Cam, January 2014
1904	1,817	943	PF-67	250	375	700	1,000	1,300	$4,113, PF-65Cam, August 2013
1905	2,152	918	PF-68	250	375	700	1,000	1,300	$4,994, PF-66Cam, April 2013
1906	1,725	871	PF-68	250	375	700	1,000	1,300	$4,113, PF-67Cam, April 2013
1907	1,475	793	PF-67	250	375	700	1,000	1,300	$7,344, PF-67Cam, March 2013
1908	1,620	875	PF-68	250	375	700	1,000	1,300	$5,581, PF-67Cam, April 2014
1909	4,763	2,520	PF-68	250	375	700	1,000	1,300	$5,875, PF-68Cam, March 2013
1910	2,405	1,297	PF-68	250	375	700	1,000	1,300	$4,994, PF-67, June 2013
1911	1,733	1,087	PF-68	250	375	700	1,000	1,300	$4,700, PF-66Cam, August 2013
1912	2,145	1,075	PF-68	250	375	700	1,000	1,300	$4,994, PF-67Cam, June 2014
1913 † (a) (5 known)		6	PF-66	3,172,500	3,750,000				$3,290,000, PF-64, January 2014

† Ranked in the *100 Greatest U.S. Coins* (fourth edition). **a.** An estimated five 1913 Liberty Head nickels (four circulation-strike and one Proof) were struck under irregular circumstances at the Mint. Some researchers consider them all to be Proofs. They were dispersed and are now held in various public and private collections.

INDIAN HEAD OR BUFFALO
(1913–1938)

Designer James Earle Fraser; weight 5 grams; composition .750 copper, .250 nickel; diameter 21.2 mm; plain edge; mints: Philadelphia, Denver, San Francisco.

Variety 1, FIVE CENTS
on Raised Ground (1913)

Mintmark position is below FIVE CENTS.

Variety 2, FIVE CENTS
in Recess (1913–1938)

Mintmark position is below FIVE CENTS.

History. The Indian Head nickel five-cent piece today is almost universally known as the "Buffalo" nickel, after the American bison on the reverse. The design made its debut in 1913. James Earle Fraser, a sculptor well known in the private sector, was its creator. The obverse features an authentic portrait of a Native American, modeled as a composite from life, with three subjects posing. Unlike any preceding coin made for circulation, the Buffalo nickel had little in the way of open, smooth field surfaces. Instead, most areas on the obverse and reverse were filled with design elements or, especially on the reverse, an irregular background, as on a bas-relief plaque.

Soon after the first coins were released, it was thought that the inscription FIVE CENTS, on a high area of the motif, would wear too quickly. The Mint modified the design to lower the ground under the bison, which had been arranged in the form of a mound (on what became known as Variety 1). The flat-ground design is called Variety 2.

Striking and Sharpness. Most circulation-strike Buffalo nickels are poorly struck in one or more areas, and for many Denver and San Francisco issues of the 1920s the striking is very poor. However, enough sharp strikes exist among common dates of the

1930s that one can be found with some patience. Certification services do not reflect the quality of strike on their labels, so examine carefully. The matter of striking sharpness on Buffalo nickels is an exceedingly important aspect for the connoisseur (who might prefer, for example, a sharply struck coin in AU-58 over a fully lustrous MS example with much shallower detail). Points to check on the obverse include the center of the coin, especially the area immediately above the tie on the braid. On the reverse check the fur on the head of the bison, and the fur "line" above the bison's shoulder on its back. On both sides, examine the overall striking of letters and other details.

Availability. Among circulated varieties of standard dates and mintmarks, availability is in proportion to their mintages. Among early issues the 1913-S, Variety 2, is the scarcest. The date wore away more quickly on the Variety 1 coins than on the modified design used from later 1913 through the end of the series. In the 1920s the 1926-S is the hardest to find. Collectors sought Buffalo nickels from circulation until the 1960s, after which most were gone. By that time the dates in the teens were apt to have their dates completely worn away, or be AG-3 or G-4. Among MS nickels, the issues of 1913 were saved in quantity as novelties, although 1913-S, Variety 2, is slightly scarce. Philadelphia Mint issues are readily available through the 1920s, while MS-63 and finer mintmarked issues from 1914 to 1927 can range from scarce to rare. From 1931 to 1938, all dates and mintmarks were saved in roll quantities, and all are plentiful today. Many Buffalo nickels in MS are very rare if with Full Details, this being especially true for mintmarked issues after 1913, into the early 1930s. Sharpness of strike is not noted on certification holders, but a connoisseur would probably rather own a Full Details coin in MS-65 than an MS-66 or higher with a flat strike.

EF-40, 45 (Extremely Fine). *Obverse:* More wear than at AU is seen on the cheek (in particular) and the rest of the face. The center of the coin above the braid is mostly smooth. Other details are sharp. *Reverse:* More wear is evident than at AU. The tip of the horn is well defined on better strikes. The shoulder, flank, and hip show more wear. The tip of the tail may be discernible, but is mostly worn away.

AU-50, 53, 55, 58 (About Uncirculated). *Obverse:* Light wear is seen on the highest area of the cheek, to the left of the nose, this being the most obvious checkpoint. Light wear is also seen on the highest-relief areas of the hair. Luster is less extensive, and wear more extensive, at AU-50 than at higher grades. An AU-58 coin will have only slight wear and will retain the majority of luster. *Reverse:* Light wear is seen on the shoulder and hip, these being the key checkpoints. Light wear is also seen on the flank of the bison and on the horn and top of the head. Luster is less extensive, and wear more extensive, at AU-50 than at higher grades. An AU-58 coin will have only slight wear and will retain the majority of luster.

MS-60 to 70 (Mint State). *Obverse and Reverse:* Mint luster is complete in the obverse and reverse fields, except in areas not fully struck up, in which graininess or marks from the original planchet surface can be seen. MS-60, 61, and 62 can show some evidence of abrasion, usually on the center of the obverse above the braid, and on the reverse at the highest parts of the bison. These two checkpoints are often areas of light striking, so abrasion must be differentiated from original planchet marks. At MS-63 evidences of abrasion are few, and at MS-65 they are fewer yet. In grades above MS-65, a Buffalo nickel should be mark-free.

1913, Variety 1, 3-1/2 Legged
FS-05-1913-901.

1914, 4 Over 3
FS-05-1914-101.

1916, Doubled-Die Obverse
FS-05-1916-101.

1916, Missing Designer's Initial
FS-05-1916-401.

1918, Doubled-Die Reverse
FS-05-1918-801.

1918-D, 8 Over 7
FS-05-1918D-101.

1935, Doubled-Die Reverse
FS-05-1935-501.

1936-D, 3-1/2 Legged
FS-05-1936D-901.

1937-D, 3-Legged
FS-05-1937D-901.

1938-D, D Over S
FS-05-1938D-511.

	Mintage	Cert	Avg	%MS	EF-40	AU-50	MS-60	MS-63	MS-64	MS-65	MS-66	Recent Auction Record
1913, Variety 1	30,992,000	17,199	64.3	97	$25	$35	$45	$60	$75	$170	$285	$22,325, MS-68, April 2014
1913, Variety 1, 3-1/2 Legged (a)	*	6	43.7	50	420	540	720	1,200	3,600	10,800	18,000	$10,350, MS-64, April 2009
1913D, Variety 1	5,337,000	4,872	63.2	91	42	60	75	80	115	300	550	$4,113, MS-67, June 2014
1913S, Variety 1	2,105,000	3,417	61.2	82	90	110	130	180	260	650	1,500	$8,813, MS-67, August 2013
1913, Variety 2	29,857,186	4,186	63.2	91	22	30	40	80	100	320	900	$4,994, MS-67, July 2014
1913D, Variety 2	4,156,000	2,445	53.3	60	235	260	300	400	575	1,150	2,000	$17,625, MS-67, August 2013
1913S, Variety 2	1,209,000	3,588	49.0	47	600	750	900	1,100	1,750	3,600	5,900	$28,200, MS-67, April 2014
1914	20,664,463	3,103	60.0	83	35	45	60	85	145	420	950	$7,638, MS-67, April 2014
1914, 4 Over 3 (b)	*	88	53.6	36	1,000	1,500	2,800	6,250	9,750	22,500		$8,338, MS-64, April 2012
1914D	3,912,000	2,532	53.4	59	325	400	450	550	650	1,300	2,250	$4,700, MS-66, July 2014
1914S	3,470,000	2,972	58.7	70	90	160	200	425	525	1,800	4,800	$7,638, MS-66, April 2014
1915	20,986,220	3,190	63.1	92	25	45	60	90	125	300	575	$5,581, MS-67, October 2013
1915D	7,569,000	2,058	58.0	63	130	160	270	350	475	1,700	3,800	$7,050, MS-66, April 2014
1915S	1,505,000	1,707	51.2	57	400	500	650	1,000	1,500	3,000	4,000	$4,113, MS-66, June 2014
1916	63,497,466	4,357	62.4	89	14	25	50	85	105	300	700	$4,994, MS-67, February 2014
1916, Doubled-Die Obverse (c)	*	231	33.6	7	18,500 (d)	32,000	60,000	140,000	240,000	335,000		$30,550, AU-55, January 2014
1916, Missing Initial (e)	*	5	15.8	20	200	280	375	600				$341, AU-55, February 2014
1916D	13,333,000	2,653	60.2	74	90	120	175	260	450	1,750	8,000	$24,675, MS-66, January 2014
1916S	11,860,000	1,926	59.8	73	90	125	190	275	465	1,800	3,500	$5,288, MS-66, April 2014
1917	51,424,019	2,214	62.6	89	16	35	60	150	210	485	725	$4,847, MS-67, June 2014
1917D	9,910,000	1,930	55.7	64	150	275	350	750	950	2,400	8,750	$11,163, MS-66, August 2013
1917S	4,193,000	1,397	52.4	56	200	375	450	1,200	1,900	3,750	7,750	$9,988, MS-66, April 2013
1918	32,086,314	1,462	62.0	88	32	50	125	325	500	1,275	2,500	$4,406, MS-66, January 2014
1918, Doubled-Die Reverse (f)	*	9	29.9	11	1,450 (g)	2,300	3,500	7,000				$170, VF-20, August 2013
1918D, 8 Over 7 † (h)	**	1,776	17.9	5	8,500	12,000	34,000	57,500	82,500	285,000		$258,500, MS-65, August 2013
1918D	8,362,000	1,469	52.0	58	225	350	450	1,050	1,450	3,600	7,400	$9,518, MS-66, March 2014
1918S	4,882,000	1,263	55.0	63	200	325	585	2,750	4,750	22,000	75,000	$22,325, MS-65, April 2014
1919	60,868,000	2,616	63.0	91	15	32	55	125	200	485	1,000	$13,513, MS-67, August 2013
1919D	8,006,000	1,335	51.6	50	260	350	600	1,500	2,500	6,500	12,750	$11,163, MS-66, June 2013
1919S	7,521,000	1,572	52.5	52	260	375	625	1,800	3,500	14,000	100,000	$89,300, MS-66, January 2013
1920	63,093,000	2,019	62.7	91	14	30	65	145	225	625	1,200	$10,575, MS-67, April 2013
1920D	9,418,000	1,382	53.9	62	275	325	585	1,400	1,850	5,000	69,000	$20,563, MS-65, April 2014
1920S	9,689,000	1,514	53.3	55	200	300	575	1,850	4,000	25,000	40,000	$16,450, MS-65, July 2014
1921	10,663,000	1,696	62.1	87	50	75	150	320	380	700	1,200	$9,988, MS-67, January 2014
1921S	1,557,000	2,255	34.5	26	950	1,200	1,600	2,100	2,700	7,250	23,000	$11,750, MS-66, September 2013
1923	35,715,000	2,176	63.2	92	13	35	65	160	185	575	1,000	$4,700, MS-66, February 2014
1923S	6,142,000	2,363	52.5	60	300	400	600	900	1,500	8,500	30,000	$67,563, MS-66, June 2013
1924	21,620,000	1,571	63.1	91	24	42	75	160	325	750	1,850	$28,200, MS-67, April 2013
1924D	5,258,000	1,604	51.9	60	235	325	390	765	1,250	3,850	25,000	$44,063, MS-66, June 2013
1924S	1,437,000	1,888	32.6	23	1,150	1,700	2,300	3,700	4,500	12,000	37,500	$18,800, MS-65, April 2014
1925	35,565,100	2,374	64.0	97	15	32	42	100	150	390	700	$8,813, MS-67, August 2013
1925D	4,450,000	1,669	55.9	71	185	265	400	750	1,400	4,750	22,000	$19,975, MS-66, January 2013
1925S	6,256,000	1,778	50.9	52	180	250	475	1,850	2,950	27,500	48,000	$28,200, MS-65, September 2013

* Included in number above. ** Included in number below. † Ranked in the *100 Greatest U.S. Coins* (fourth edition). **a.** The reverse die was heavily polished, possibly to remove clash marks, resulting in a die with most of the bison's front leg missing. **b.** The straight top bar of the underlying 3 is visible at the top of the 4. The start of the 3's diagonal is seen on the upper right, outside of the 4. On some coins, a hint of the curve of the lower portion of the 3 shows just above the crossbar of the 4. **c.** The date, chin, throat, feathers, and the tie on the braid are all doubled. "Beware of 1916 nickels with strike doubling on the date offered as this variety. . . . The true doubled die must look like the coin shown here" (*Cherrypickers' Guide to Rare Die Varieties*, fifth edition, volume I). **d.** Value in VF-20 is $11,000. **e.** The initial F, for Fraser—normally below the date—is clearly absent. Some dies exist with a partially missing or weak initial; these do not command the premium of the variety with a completely missing initial. **f.** Doubling is most obvious to the north on E PLURIBUS UNUM. Some coins show a die crack from the rim to the bison's rump, just below the tail. **g.** Value in VF-20 is $1,150. **h.** "Look for the small die crack immediately above the tie on the braid, leading slightly downward to the Indian's jaw. The beginning of this die break can usually be seen even on lower-grade coins" (*Cherrypickers' Guide to Rare Die Varieties*, fifth edition, volume I).

Chart continued on next page.

	Mintage	Cert	Avg	%MS	EF-40	AU-50	MS-60	MS-63	MS-64	MS-65	MS-66	Recent Auction Record
1926	44,693,000	3,737	64.2	98	$10	$20	$32	$75	$100	$190	$375	$4,406, MS-67, January 2014
1926D	5,638,000	1,901	57.1	77	185	300	350	500	1,700	4,600	9,200	$15,275, MS-66, April 2013
1926S	970,000	3,213	30.6	15	900	2,650	4,500	9,200	18,000	120,000		$105,750, MS-65, September 2013
1927	37,981,000	2,743	64.0	97	12	21	35	80	110	245	500	$1,998, MS-66, April 2013
1927D	5,730,000	1,742	59.6	84	80	135	180	310	675	7,000	22,000	$16,450, MS-65, August 2013
1927S	3,430,000	1,378	56.3	61	95	185	550	2,000	3,600	16,000	100,000	$14,100, MS-65, July 2014
1928	23,411,000	2,387	63.7	95	13	23	32	80	110	280	585	$2,585, MS-66, July 2014
1928D	6,436,000	3,745	63.4	98	45	50	60	110	125	600	3,000	$4,700, MS-66, February 2014
1928S	6,936,000	1,572	60.8	80	26	110	260	550	900	3,500	18,000	$19,975, MS-66, August 2013
1929	36,446,000	2,921	63.7	96	12	20	40	75	100	315	700	$23,500, MS-67, January 2014
1929D	8,370,000	1,784	62.8	94	32	45	60	130	325	1,175	2,200	$15,275, MS-66, February 2014
1929S	7,754,000	2,527	63.3	94	12	25	55	80	150	390	675	$11,750, MS-67, February 2014
1930	22,849,000	3,760	63.4	94	11	20	35	75	95	220	400	$3,819, MS-67, August 2013
1930S	5,435,000	1,986	62.7	92	14	35	65	120	200	385	900	$4,113, MS-66, February 2014
1931S	1,200,000	5,288	63.5	95	35	55	65	100	140	300	700	$38,188, MS-67, April 2014
1934	20,213,003	2,632	63.7	93	10	18	50	65	110	300	500	$8,521, MS-67, July 2014
1934D	7,480,000	3,069	63.3	96	20	45	80	125	260	550	2,000	$11,750, MS-66, June 2014
1935	58,264,000	4,232	61.9	90	3	10	22	45	60	120	230	$2,820, MS-67, June 2014
1935, Doubled-Die Reverse (i)	*	190	31.3	6	500	1,300	5,250	6,500	9,000	26,000		$4,994, MS-63, August 2013
1935D	12,092,000	3,243	63.4	97	18	42	75	85	125	400	875	$2,350, MS-66, June 2014
1935S	10,300,000	3,830	64.1	97	4	18	55	70	80	210	350	$4,994, MS-67, June 2014
1936	118,997,000	7,562	64.0	93	3	9	22	40	50	80	200	$3,819, MS-67, April 2014
1936D	24,814,000	5,858	63.3	95	4	12	38	45	55	100	300	$1,293, MS-67, September 2013
1936D, 3-1/2 Legged (j)	*	21	59.0	76	8,000 (k)	9,500	18,000					$3,290, AU-50, January 2014
1936S	14,930,000	4,587	64.2	96	4	12	38	45	55	95	250	$1,998, MS-67, April 2014
1937	79,480,000	17,345	65.1	98	3	9	22	40	45	60	100	$6,756, MS-68, January 2014
1937D	17,826,000	10,101	64.9	98	4	10	32	42	50	60	85	$3,819, MS-67, January 2014
1937D, 3-Legged (l)	*	11,721	47.9	21	1,200 (m)	1,450	2,500	5,500	10,000	40,000	65,000	$52,875, MS-66, February 2013
1937S	5,635,000	9,614	65.0	99	3	9	32	42	50	65	150	$8,813, MS-67, April 2013
1938D	7,020,000	83,102	65.6	100	5	8	22	36	40	60	130	$16,450, MS-68, June 2014
1938D, D Over D	*	4,620	65.5	100	20	25	45	50	55	75	150	$7,050, MS-68, October 2013
1938D, D Over S	*	5,657	65.2	99	20	32	55	80	120	160	375	$7,638, MS-67, August 2013

* Included in number above. **i.** Strong doubling is evident on FIVE CENTS, E PLURIBUS UNUM, and the eye, horn, and mane of the bison. This variety (FS-05-1935-801) is extremely rare above VF, and fewer than a dozen are known in MS. Do not mistake it for the more moderately doubled FS-05-1935-803, which commands much lower premiums. **j.** The right front leg has been partially polished off the die— similar to the 1937-D 3-Legged variety, but not as severe. (This variety is not from the same die as the 1937-D.) Fewer than 40 are known in all grades. Incorrectly listed by Breen as 1936-P. **k.** Value in VF-20 is $5,000. **l.** The reverse die was polished heavily, perhaps to remove clash marks, resulting in the shaft of the bison's right front leg missing. Beware altered specimens fraudulently passed as genuine. "Look for a line of raised dots from the middle of the bison's belly to the ground as one of the diagnostics on the genuine specimen" *(Cherrypickers' Guide to Rare Die Varieties)*. **m.** Value in VF-20 is $1,100. **n.** There are five different D Over S dies for this date. Varieties other than the one listed here (FS-05-1938D-511) command smaller premiums.

Proof Indian Head or Buffalo Nickels

PF-60 to 70 (Matte Proof). Matte Proofs were made from 1913 to 1916 and are rare. These have minutely granular or matte surfaces, are sharply struck with Full Details of the design on both sides, and have edges (as viewed edge-on) that are mirrored, a distinctive figure. These are easily confused with circulation strikes except for the features noted. Certified holders usually list these simply as "Proof," not "Matte Proof." Most Matte Proofs are in higher grades. *Obverse and Reverse:* Those Proofs with abrasion or contact marks can be graded PF-60 to 62; these are not widely desired. PF-64 can have some

abrasion. Tiny flecks are not common, but are sometimes seen. At the Matte PF-65 level or higher there will no traces of abrasion or flecks. Differences between higher-grade Proofs are highly subjective, and one certified at PF-65 can be similar to another at PF-67, and vice-versa.

PF-60 to 70 (Mirror Proof). Some early Proofs of 1936 have satiny rather than mirrorlike fields. Later Proofs of 1936 and all of 1937 have a mirror surface in the fields. The motifs of the 1936 and 1937 mirror Proofs are lightly polished in the die (not frosty or matte). Most mirror (also called

brilliant) Proofs are in higher grades. *Obverse and Reverse:* PF-60 to 62 coins can have abrasion or minor handling marks, but usually are assigned such grades because of staining or blotches resulting from poor cleaning. PF-63 and 64 can have minor abrasion and staining. Tiny flecks are sometimes seen, as are dark stripe lines from the glued seams in the cellophane envelopes used by the Mint. PF-65 and higher coins should be free of stains, flecks, and abrasion of any kind. Differences between higher-grade Proofs are highly subjective, and one certified PF-65 can be similar to another at PF-67, and vice-versa.

Matte Proof Indian Head or Buffalo Nickel (1913–1916)

Satin Proof Indian Head or Buffalo Nickel (1936)

Mirror Proof Indian Head or Buffalo Nickel (1936–1937)

	Mintage	Cert	Finest	PF-63	PF-64	PF-65	PF-66	PF-67	Recent Auction Record
1913, Variety 1	1,520	638	PF-68	$1,200	$1,800	$3,250	$4,300	$7,500	$9,988, PF-67, April 2014
1913, Variety 2	1,514	566	PF-68	1,000	1,600	2,250	3,000	5,500	$9,400, PF, October 2013
1914	1,275	892	PF-68	1,000	1,500	2,200	2,700	5,250	$9,400, PF-67, July 2014
1915	1,050	733	PF-69	1,000	1,600	2,250	2,750	5,250	$5,640, PF-67, October 2013
1916	600	409	PF-68	1,200	2,000	3,500	4,200	7,400	$10,869, PF-67, June 2014
1927, Presentation Strike (a)	unknown	5	PF-65		30,000	48,000	75,000		$43,125, SP-65, January 2012
1936, Both kinds	4,420								
1936, Satin Finish		1,476	PF-69	1,150	1,400	1,700	2,100	2,750	$16,450, PF-68, February 2013
1936, Brilliant Finish		1,426	PF-69	1,275	1,650	2,500	3,000	5,000	$12,925, PF-68, September 2013
1937	5,769	3,807	PF-69	1,250	1,500	1,750	2,200	3,000	$16,450, PF-68, January 2014

a. Some experts believe that certain 1927 nickels were carefully made circulation strikes; such pieces are sometimes certified as "Specimens" or "Presentation Strikes." Professional numismatic opinions vary. See Bowers, *A Guide Book of Buffalo and Jefferson Nickels.*

JEFFERSON (1938 TO DATE)

1938–2003: Designer Felix Schlag; weight 5 grams; composition (1938–1942, 1946 to date), .750 copper, .250 nickel, (1942–1945), .560 copper, .350 silver, .090 manganese, with net weight .05626 oz. pure silver; diameter 21.2 mm; plain edge; mints: Philadelphia, Denver, San Francisco.

2004: Designers Felix Schlag (obverse), Norman E. Nemeth (Peace Medal reverse), and Al Maletsky (Keelboat reverse).

2005: Designers Joe Fitzgerald (obverse), Jamie Franki (American Bison reverse), and Joe Fitzgerald (Ocean in View reverse).

2006 to date: Designers Jamie Franki (obverse) and Felix Schlag (reverse).

Monticello Reverse (1938–2003)

Wartime Silver Alloy (1942–1945)
Mintmark is above Monticello.

Peace Medal Reverse (2004)

Keelboat Reverse (2004)

Obverse (2005)

American Bison Reverse (2005)

Ocean in View Reverse (2005)

Obverse (2006 to Date)

Reverse (2006 to Date)

History. The Jefferson nickel, designed by Felix Schlag in a public competition, made its debut in 1938, and has been a numismatic favorite since. The obverse for many years featured a portrait of Thomas Jefferson after the famous bust by Jean Antoine Houdon, and the reverse a front view of Jefferson's home, Monticello.

From partway through 1942 to the end of 1945 a copper-silver-manganese alloy replaced the traditional 75% copper and 25% nickel composition. These silver-content coins bear a distinctive P, D, or S mintmark above the dome of Monticello.

Starting in 1966, Felix Schlag's initials, FS, were added below the presidential bust; this continued through 2004, when the obverse portrait changed. The coinage dies were remodeled to strengthen the design in 1971, 1972, 1977, and 1982. The mintmark position, originally on the reverse to the right of Monticello, was moved to the obverse starting in 1968.

In 2004 special designs commemorating the Westward Journey (Lewis and Clark expedition) were introduced; the program continued through 2005. In 2006 a new obverse portrait debuted, along with a return to Monticello on the reverse.

Striking and Sharpness. On the obverse, check for weakness on the portrait, especially in the lower jaw area. On the reverse, most circulation strikes have weak details on the six steps of Monticello, especially under the third pillar from the left, as this section on the reverse was opposite in the dies (in the press) from the high parts of the Jefferson portrait, and metal could not effectively flow in both directions at once. Planchet weight allowance was another cause, the dies being spaced slightly too far apart. Jefferson nickels can be classified as "Full Steps" (FS) if either five or six of Monticello's porch steps (with the top step counting as one) are clear. Notations of 5FS or 6FS can indicate the number of visible steps. It is easier to count the incuse lines than the raised steps. If there are four complete, unbroken lines, the coin qualifies as Full Steps (with five steps); five complete, unbroken lines indicate six full steps. There must be no nicks, cuts, or scratches interrupting the incuse lines. It is difficult to determine a full five-step count on the 1938 and some 1939 issues, as the steps are wavy and ill-defined; a great deal of subjectivity is common for these dates.

Even if the steps are mostly or fully defined, check other areas to determine if a coin has Full Details overall. Interestingly, nickels of the 1950s and 1960s are among the most weakly struck. The silver-content coins of the 1940s usually are well struck. Some nickels of the 1950s to 1970s discolored easily, perhaps due to some impurities in the alloy.

Availability. All basic dates and mintmarks were saved in roll quantities. Scarce issues in MS include 1939-D and 1942-D. The low-mintage 1950-D was a popular speculation, and most of the mintage went into numismatic hands, making MS coins common. Many different dates and mints are rare if with 5FS or 6FS; consult *A Guide Book of Buffalo and Jefferson Nickels* for details.

MS-60 to 70 (Mint State). *Obverse and Reverse:* Mint luster is complete in the obverse and reverse fields, except in areas not fully struck up, in which graininess or marks from the original planchet surface can be seen. This may include the jaw, the back of Jefferson's head, and the higher-relief central features of Monticello. MS-60, 61, and 62 can show some evidence of abrasion, usually on the same areas that display weak striking. At MS-63, evidences of abrasion are few, and at MS-65 fewer yet. In grades above MS-65, a Jefferson nickel should be mark-free.

Note: For modern issues of 2003 to date, check the higher parts of the obverse and reverse for abrasion and contact marks. Otherwise the same instructions apply.

Five Steps

Six Steps

1939, Doubled-Die Reverse
FS-05-1939-801.

1942-D, D Over Horizontal D
FS-05-1942D-501.

	Mintage	Cert	Avg	%MS	MS-64FS	MS-65	MS-65FS	MS-66	MS-66FS	MS-67	MS-67FS	Recent Auction Record
1938	19,496,000	2,698	65.1	98	$75	$16	$150	$55	$250	$200	$2,500	$3,290, MS-67FS, January 2014
1938D	5,376,000	5,026	65.9	100	50	14	125	40	225	150	1,600	$4,994, MS-67FS, January 2014
1938S	4,105,000	2,717	65.5	99	50	16	270	50	750	600	7,500	$4,259, MS-67FS, February 2014
1939	120,615,000	3,328	65.2	96	25	12	47	60	210	225	1,500	$5,288, MS-67FS, February 2014
1939, Doubled-Die Reverse (a)	*	596	54.8	52	600 (b)	1,000	2,400	2,200	5,750	4,500		$7,050, EF-40, August 2013
1939D	3,514,000	3,077	65.2	96	190	120	500	160	1,800	450		$2,115, MS-67, February 2014
1939S	6,630,000	2,002	64.9	96	175	70	400	130	1,750	450		$1,528, MS-67, November 2013
1940	176,485,000	2,316	65.4	98	25	15	45	30	125	250	500	$1,293, MS-67FS, June 2014
1940D	43,540,000	3,687	65.7	99	25	15	45	45	65	150	185	$229, MS-67FS, November 2013
1940S	39,690,000	1,548	65.2	99	40	12	70	40	280	350	3,000	$306, MS-66FS, March 2014
1941	203,265,000	1,844	65.4	99	30	12	65	35	200	250	1,500	$1,528, MS-68, September 2013
1941D	53,432,000	3,918	65.8	99	30	12	45	30	70	80	225	$1,410, MS-67FS, April 2014
1941S (c)	43,445,000	1,179	64.7	97	50	12	80	50	800	625	5,500	$2,585, MS-66FS, April 2014
1942	49,789,000	1,421	65.2	99	40	15	85	60	650	250	1,000	$940, MS-66FS, April 2014
1942D	13,938,000	2,928	64.5	95	45	60	80	75	175	380	600	$823, MS-67FS, March 2014
1942D, D Over Horizontal D (d)	*	83	47.8	23	17,500 (e)	10,000						$15,275, MS-66, April 2013

* Included in number above. **a.** Very strong doubling is evident to the east of the primary letters, most noticeably on MONTICELLO and FIVE CENTS. Lesser doubling is also visible on UNITED STATES OF AMERICA and the right side of the building. **b.** Value in MS-63 is $400. **c.** Large and small mintmark varieties exist. **d.** The initial D mintmark was punched into the die horizontally, then corrected. "This is the rarest of the major Jefferson nickel varieties in Mint State" (*Cherrypickers' Guide to Rare Die Varieties,* fifth edition, volume I). **e.** Value in MS-63 is $3,000.

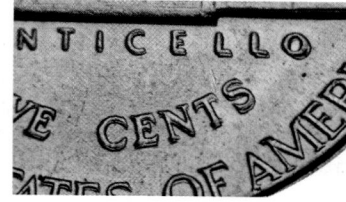

1943-P, 3 Over 2
FS-05-1943P-101.

1943-P, Doubled-Die Obverse
The "Doubled Eye" variety. FS-05-1943P-106.

1945-P, Doubled-Die Reverse
FS-05-1945P-803.

	Mintage	Cert	Avg	%MS	MS-64FS	MS-65	MS-65FS	MS-66	MS-66FS	MS-67	MS-67FS	Recent Auction Record
1942P, Silver	57,873,000	7,140	66.0	99	$30	$20	$75	$30	$150	$50	$1,000	$4,113, MS-68, June 2014
1942S	32,900,000	6,656	65.9	100	40	25	200	45	250	100	3,250	$3,525, MS-67FS, November 2013
1943P, 3 Over 2 (a)	*	265	56.4	68	500 (b)	700	1,100	1,350	2,750	2,850		$8,813, MS-67FS, March 2014
1943P	271,165,000	8,269	65.7	99	20	20	40	37	100	65	1,000	$9,400, MS-64, November 2013
1943P, Doubled-Die Obverse (c)	**	884	58.6	76	700 (d)	650	1,000	950	2,100	2,200	5,000	$1,998, MS-66FS, March 2014
1943D	15,294,000	14,438	66.0	100	20	20	45	35	60	55	300	$1,880, MS-67FS, February 2013
1943S	104,060,000	8,702	66.0	100	20	20	50	35	110	70	800	$4,113, AU-55, November 2013
1944P (e)	119,150,000	5,371	65.7	100	30	30	80	60	200	125	1,500	$9,400, MS-67FS, March 2014
1944D	32,309,000	9,804	66.0	100	20	25	35	35	60	70	200	$10,575, MS-68FS, February 2014
1944S	21,640,000	8,207	66.0	100	35	22	160	40	350	80	1,750	$1,998, MS-67FS, March 2014
1945P	119,408,100	5,681	65.7	100	50	20	125	35	300	750	4,000	$8,813, MS-67FS, April 2014
1945P, Doubled-Die Reverse (f)	**	410	63.6	95	1,000	800	7,000	3,600				$14,100, MS-66FS, March 2014
1945D	37,158,000	9,443	66.0	100	20	20	40	30	70	125	400	$4,847, MS-68, July 2014
1945S	58,939,000	9,469	65.9	100	60	20	200	35	750	150	1,600	$2,350, MS-64, November 2013
1946	161,116,000	750	64.8	100	60	15	200	90	1,400			$1,763, MS-67, December 2013
1946D	45,292,200	2,136	65.3	99	15	12	35	35	80	500	3,000	$4,113, MS-67FS, February 2014
1946S	13,560,000	2,026	65.3	100	40	11	125	32	525	125		$529, MS-66FS, April 2014
1947	95,000,000	1,068	65.0	100	20	12	65	55	400	135		$4,113, MS-67FS, June 2014
1947D	37,822,000	1,655	65.4	100	18	11	30	35	120	150	1,600	$1,586, MS-67FS, February 2014
1947S	24,720,000	1,148	65.0	99	20	12	50	35	500	750		$2,056, MS-66FS, June 2014

Note: Genuine specimens of some wartime dates were struck in nickel, in error. * Included in number below. ** Included in number above. **a.** "This popular variety was created when the die was first hubbed with a 1942-dated hub, then subsequently hubbed with a 1943-dated hub. The diagonal of the 2 is visible within the lower opening of the 3. Doubling is also visible on LIBERTY and IN GOD WE TRUST. . . . There is at least one 1943-P five-cent piece that has a faint, short die gouge extending upward from the lower ball of the 3; this is often mistaken for the overdate" (*Cherrypickers' Guide to Rare Die Varieties,* fifth edition, volume I). **b.** Value in MS-63 is $290. **c.** This variety is nicknamed the "Doubled Eye." Doubling is visible on the date, LIBERTY, the motto, and, most noticeably, Jefferson's eye. **d.** Value in MS-63 is $195. **e.** 1944 nickels without mintmarks are counterfeit. **f.** There are several collectible doubled-die reverses for this date. Values are for the variety pictured (FS-05-1945P-801), with a strongly doubled reverse. The doubling spread increases from left to right.

1949-D, D Over S
FS-05-1949D-501.

1954-S, S Over D
FS-05-1954S-501.

1955-D, D Over S
FS-05-1955D-501.

	Mintage	Cert	Avg	%MS	MS-64FS	MS-65	MS-65FS	MS-66	MS-66FS	MS-67	MS-67FS	Recent Auction Record
1948	89,348,000	655	64.8	99	$150	$10	$200	$75	$1,750			$147, MS-65FS, February 2013
1948D	44,734,000	1,876	65.4	100	20	10	30	45	90	$150		$2,115, MS-67FS, April 2013
1948S	11,300,000	2,095	65.4	100	25	9	45	40	280	175		$411, MS-66FS, June 2013
1949	60,652,000	668	65.0	99	400	12	1,750	35				$1,553, MS-65FS, February 2010
1949D	36,498,000	1,541	65.3	99	20	10	50	25	185	225		$411, MS-67, July 2014
1949D, D Over S (a)	*	367	63.7	96	750	500	1,800	1,200				$1,763, MS-65, April 2013
1949S	9,716,000	880	65.1	100	150	10	275	50	1,500			$15,275, MS-67FS, January 2014
1950	9,796,000	1,096	65.3	100	45	8	175	60	500			$4,994, MS-67FS, April 2014

* Included in number above. **a.** The top serif of the S is visible to the north of the D, with the upper left loop of the S visible to the west of the D. "This variety is quite rare in Mint State and highly sought after. Some may still be found in circulated grades. Some specimens have been located in original Mint sets" (*Cherrypickers' Guide to Rare Die Varieties,* fifth edition, volume I).

Chart continued on next page.

	Mintage	Cert	Avg	%MS	MS-64FS	MS-65	MS-65FS	MS-66	MS-66FS	MS-67	MS-67FS	Recent Auction Record
1950D	2,630,030	7,412	65.3	100	$35	$25.00	$60	$70	$150	$275	$3,000	$2,585, MS-67FS, January 2014
1951	28,552,000	655	65.0	100	90	15.00	425	80	2,000			$16,450, MS-67FS, February 2014
1951D	20,460,000	1,474	65.4	100	40	11.00	80	30	300	575		$2,820, MS-66FS, June 2013
1951S	7,776,000	1,278	65.3	100	55	12.00	200	55	1,000			$881, MS-66FS, February 2013
1952	63,988,000	479	65.0	100	150	9.00	950	175	2,000	400		$476, AU-55, April 2014
1952D	30,638,000	992	65.4	100	100	15.00	200	35	600	500		$15,275, MS-67FS, April 2014
1952S	20,572,000	1,168	65.2	100	100	12.00	300	35	2,500			$8,813, MS-66FS, April 2014
1953	46,644,000	598	65.1	100	1,600	8.00	3,000	80	4,000			$123, MS-66, June 2014
1953D	59,878,600	1,284	65.2	100	50	9.00	225	40	900	650		$329, MS-65FS, February 2013
1953S	19,210,900	1,387	64.8	100	1,800	10.00	5,000	100				$1,293, MS-64FS, June 2013
1954	47,684,050	811	64.7	100	75	15.00	375	25	2,000	250		$207, MS-65FS, February 2010
1954D	117,183,060	652	64.2	99	150	30.00	700	100		250		$3,055, MS-65FS, April 2014
1954S	29,384,000	1,513	64.6	99	2,000	15.00	4,000	165				$1,645, MS-64FS, October 2013
1954S, S Over D (b)	*	608	63.4	97	100	160.00	500	1,000				$558, MS-66, June 2014
1955	7,888,000	1,026	64.7	100	150	15.00	900	100				$382, MS-65FS, April 2014
1955D	74,464,100	1,470	64.3	99	500	20.00	4,500	150				$999, MS-64FS, February 2013
1955D, D Over S (c)	*	259	64.0	97	100	175.00	500	1,000				$2,820, MS-66, February 2013
1956	35,216,000	1,456	65.1	100	40	20.00	80	45	275		5,000	$588, MS-66FS, June 2014
1956D	67,222,940	1,035	65.2	100	185	20.00	675	35	3,000	500		$911, MS-65FS, February 2013
1957	38,408,000	897	64.7	100	40	15.00	125	80	2,600			$441, MS-66FS, April 2014
1957D	136,828,900	1,057	65.0	100	50	15.00	150	35	2,750			$208, MS-62, August 2013
1958	17,088,000	674	64.0	100	50	12.00	700					$764, MS-65, January 2014
1958D	168,249,120	1,261	65.1	99	20	12.00	50	50	100		3,500	$1,763, MS-67FS, December 2013
1959	27,248,000	1,326	64.6	99	25	10.00	80	125	1,000			$719, MS-66FS, October 2013
1959D	160,738,240	1,234	64.9	100	60	8.00	250	50	2,250			$1,293, MS-67FS, April 2014
1960	55,416,000	962	64.7	99	500	8.00	1,750	70				$1,495, MS-65FS, February 2010
1960D	192,582,180	999	64.8	99		10.00		100		500		$223, MS-66, February 2013
1961	73,640,100	861	64.9	100	900	20.00	2,500	60	3,500			$2,530, MS-65FS, February 2010
1961D	229,342,760	773	64.5	100	1,000	20.00	6,000	200		2,000		$11,163, MS-64FS, February 2013
1962	97,384,000	1,359	64.7	100	20	10.00	50	30	600	425		$21,150, MS-67FS, August 2013
1962D	280,195,720	970	64.1	99	275	30.00						$118, MS-63FS, June 2013
1963	175,776,000	1,108	64.9	100	75	10.00	150	40	1,200			$247, MS-66FS, March 2014
1963D	276,829,460	386	64.0	98	1,000	30.00	7,500					$7,475, MS-65FS, February 2010
1964	1,024,672,000	788	64.5	99	50	8.00	325	60	2,000			$1,058, MS-66FS, September 2013
1964D	1,787,297,160	1,050	64.6	98	110	5.00	750	55	4,000			$1,175, MS-65FS, April 2014
1965 (d)	136,131,380	713	65.2	99	10	5.00	50	25	250	200		$646, MS-66, August 2013
1966 (d)	156,208,283	373	64.7	99	10	5.00	50	25	250	200		$322, MS-65DCam, February 2010
1967 (d)	107,325,800	546	65.1	100	10	5.00	50	25	250	200		$132, MS-66, February 2013
1968D	91,227,880	927	65.3	100		4.00		35				$276, MS, January 2014
1968S	100,396,004	794	65.0	99	475	5.00	1,350	35	4,000	275		$588, MS-64, September 2013
1969D	202,807,500	523	65.2	99	10	4.00		115				$94, MS-66, February 2013
1969S	120,165,000	355	64.7	100		2.00		350				$306, AU-58, September 2013
1970D	515,485,380	501	64.9	100		10.00		180				$200, MS-63, August 2013
1970S	238,832,004	516	64.6	99	225	8.00	400	225	650			$999, MS-66FS, December 2013
1971	106,884,000	791	64.5	98	10	3.00	30	50	130			$127, MS-66FS, February 2010
1971D	316,144,800	1,510	65.3	100	10	3.00	20	30	60		875	$646, MS-67FS, August 2013
1972	202,036,000	414	64.7	99	10	3.00	40	60	300			$276, MS-66FS, March 2012
1972D	351,694,600	477	64.7	99	10	3.00	40	75	350			$823, MS-63, August 2013
1973	384,396,000	617	64.8	100	10	3.00	30	45	150	110		$103, MS-66FS, February 2013
1973D	261,405,000	685	65.0	99	10	3.00	25	30	60	90		$353, MS-65, February 2014
1974	601,752,000	355	64.6	100	40	3.00	175	35	900			$110, MS-65FS, March 2014
1974D	277,373,000	496	64.9	100	15	3.00	40	45	150		1,750	$200, MS-62, April 2013
1975	181,772,000	499	65.0	100	20	3.00	50	50	300			$259, MS-62, August 2013
1975D	401,875,300	515	65.0	100	15	3.00	60	55	300			$299, MS-66FS, February 2010

* Included in number above. **b.** The overall strength of the strike is the important factor in this overmintmark's value. **c.** There are 10 or more different D Over S varieties for 1955. Values shown are for the strongest (FS-05-1955D-501); others command smaller premiums. **d.** Values and auction records for Special Mint Set coins are listed with the Proofs for this type.

	Mintage	Cert	Avg	%MS	MS-64FS	MS-65	MS-65FS	MS-66	MS-66FS	MS-67	MS-67FS	Recent Auction Record
1976	367,124,000	294	64.2	99	$30	$3.00	$175	$37	$675		$3,600	$1,265, MS-66FS, February 2012
1976D	563,964,147	426	64.7	100	10	3.00	30	40	300			$235, MS-65, February 2014
1977	585,376,000	323	64.7	100	70	3.00	150	48	1,000			$329, MS-63, September 2013
1977D	297,313,422	396	64.6	99	10	3.00	35	40	275			$940, MS-68, August 2013
1978	391,308,000	363	64.7	99	35	3.00	175	55	900			$259, MS-64, September 2013
1978D	313,092,780	433	64.8	100	15	3.00	40	55	100			$104, MS-66FS, February 2010
1979	463,188,000	309	64.7	99	40	3.00	300	50	1,000			$499, MS-62, December 2013
1979D	325,867,672	331	64.7	99	10	4.00	30	37	150			$182, MS-66FS, February 2013
1980P	593,004,000	538	64.7	99	10	4.00	45	30	250			$646, MS-64, February 2013
1980D	502,323,448	485	64.6	100	10	3.00	20	60	250			$217, MS-66FS, February 2013
1981P	657,504,000	405	64.9	99	100	3.00	500	50	3,500			$188, MS-64, February 2014
1981D	364,801,843	568	64.7	100	10	3.00	30	35	180			$206, MS-66FS, June 2014
1982P	292,355,000	265	64.8	98	12	10.00	50	35	325			$881, MS-67, February 2014
1982D	373,726,544	350	64.8	98	25	6.00	55	30	400			$374, MS-66FS, February 2010
1983P	561,615,000	165	64.2	95	60	9.00	400	60	1,500			$558, MS-65, August 2013
1983D	536,726,276	202	64.7	98	15	4.00	175	35	875			$863, MS-66FS, June 2010
1984P	746,769,000	468	64.7	99	10	3.00	25	40	100			$66, MS-66FS, February 2013
1984D	517,675,146	382	64.7	99	10	3.00	30	65	275			$36, MS-65FS, February 2013
1985P	647,114,962	376	64.9	99	25	3.00	50	60	325			$259, MS-62, November 2013
1985D	459,747,446	332	64.9	100	10	3.00	40	40	225		2,000	$196, MS-66FS, June 2010
1986P	536,883,483	397	65.0	100	10	3.00	50	35	200			$99, MS-66FS, February 2013
1986D	361,819,140	335	64.7	100	10	3.00	35	50	275			$253, MS-66FS, February 2010
1987P	371,499,481	1,032	65.5	100	10	2.75	15	60	65		250	$329, MS-67FS, June 2014
1987D	410,590,604	789	65.1	100	10	3.50	20	30	150			$173, MS-67FS, April 2008
1988P	771,360,000	375	65.1	100	12	3.00	30	35	140			$329, MS-67, August 2013
1988D	663,771,652	461	64.8	99	10	3.00	35	32	125			$165, MS-67, June 2014
1989P	898,812,000	594	65.3	100	10	2.75	20	25	35		700	$18, AU-50, August 2013
1989D	570,842,474	380	64.6	99	12	2.75	40	35	180			$188, MS-66FS, February 2013
1990P	661,636,000	440	65.4	100	10	2.75	20	25	40			$24, MS-66FS, October 2009
1990D	663,938,503	461	64.5	100	9	2.75	30	45	200			$129, MS-67FS, June 2014
1991P	614,104,000	268	65.0	100	10	2.75	45	35	190			$90, MS-66FS, February 2013
1991D	436,496,678	360	64.8	100	10	2.75	25	35	160			$76, MS-66FS, February 2013
1992P	399,552,000	449	65.2	100	10	3.00	20	28	50		2,000	$88, MS-67FS, August 2013
1992D	450,565,113	384	64.8	99	10	2.75	30	30	160			$72, MS-66FS, February 2013
1993P	412,076,000	371	65.1	99	10	1.00	30	35	75			$68, MS-66FS, February 2013
1993D	406,084,135	571	65.2	100	10	1.00	20	20	40	$100	400	$374, MS-67FS, February 2010
1994P	722,160,000	494	66.1	100	10	2.50	25	25	100	35		$881, MS-63, April 2013
1994P, Special Unc ‡ (e)	167,703	2,636	68.7	100	75	75.00	125	125	150	250	500	$66, MS-69FS, March 2013
1994D	715,762,110	339	64.7	99	10	1.00	30	35	100	50		$92, MS-66FS, February 2013
1995P	774,156,000	445	65.3	99	20	1.00	40	20	90	25	250	$499, MS-65, August 2013
1995D	888,112,000	372	64.7	99	10	1.00	25	25	200	35	1,200	$940, MS-67FS, April 2014
1996P	829,332,000	519	65.4	100	18	1.00	20	25	30	35	350	$282, MS-63, July 2014
1996D	817,736,000	709	65.2	99	20	1.00	22	25	35	35	200	$161, MS-67FS, February 2010
1997P	470,972,000	276	65.1	99	10	2.00	45	25	175	50	350	$66, MS-66FS, August 2013
1997P, Special Unc ‡ (e)	25,000	1,080	68.9	100	100	225.00	300	300	375	450	800	$499, MS-70FS, June 2014
1997D	466,640,000	303	64.8	99	15	2.00	50	20	100	25	500	$33, MS-66FS, June 2014
1998P	688,272,000	318	64.6	100	8	1.00	35	45	125	110	400	$176, MS-65, July 2014
1998D	635,360,000	312	64.0	98	10	1.00	100	60	450	150		$90, MS-65FS, June 2014
1999P	1,212,000,000	679	65.0	98	10	1.00	10	25	75	35	250	$306, MS-63, September 2013
1999D	1,066,720,000	461	64.8	96	8	1.00	15	30	300	50		$100, MS-64, July 2014
2000P	846,240,000	438	65.2	100	10	1.00	12	18	35	25	500	$470, MS-67FS, August 2013
2000D	1,509,520,000	485	65.4	99	10	1.00	12	18	50	25	500	$94, MS-63, July 2014
2001P	675,704,000	721	66.0	100	8	1.00	10	12	20	25	40	$50, MS-67FS, June 2013
2001D	627,680,000	391	65.5	100	8	1.00	10	12	20	25	130	$138, MS-67FS, February 2010
2002P	539,280,000	552	65.5	100	8	1.00	10	12	20	30	75	$72, MS-67FS, June 2014
2002D	691,200,000	414	64.9	100	8	1.00	10	12	90			$74, MS-66FS, February 2013
2003P	441,840,000	838	65.6	100	8	1.00	10	12	20	22	50	$1,058, MS-68FS, November 2013
2003D	383,040,000	492	64.6	100	8	1.00	15	12	80			$86, MS-66FS, February 2013

‡ Ranked in the *100 Greatest U.S. Modern Coins*. e. Special "frosted" Uncirculated nickels were included in the 1993 Thomas Jefferson commemorative dollar packaging (sold in 1994) and in the 1997 Botanic Garden sets. They resemble Matte Proof coins.

Chart continued on next page.

	Mintage	Cert	Avg	%MS	MS-65FS	MS-66	MS-66FS	MS-67	MS-67FS	MS-68FS	MS-69FS	Recent Auction Record
2004P, Peace Medal	361,440,000	3,155	64.1	98		$8		$50				$200, MS-67, February 2013
2004D, Peace Medal	372,000,000	1,742	65.8	100		5		30				$374, MS-68, February 2010
2004P, Keelboat	366,720,000	980	65.9	100		5		20				$299, MS-68, February 2010
2004D, Keelboat	344,880,000	1,080	66.0	100		5		20				
2005P, American Bison	448,320,000	3,661	66.8	100		8		30				$28, MS-69, January 2010
2005D, American Bison	487,680,000	3,890	65.5	100		8		25				$388, MS-66, June 2014
2005P, Ocean in View	394,080,000	2,185	66.8	100		6		25				$19, MS-66, February 2010
2005D, Ocean in View	411,120,000	1,984	66.6	100		5		22				$15, MS-65, August 2009
2006P, Monticello	693,120,000	1,751	66.9	100	$4	3	$5	8	$10	$20	$30	$19, MS-64FS, January 2013
2006D, Monticello	809,280,000	1,955	66.9	100	5	4	6	9	22	30	50	$11, MS-67, July 2008
2007P	571,680,000	186	65.4	100	4	3	5	8	10	20	30	$11, MS-68FS, July 2008
2007D	626,160,000	129	64.9	100	5	4	6	9	22	30	50	$14, MS-68FS, July 2008
2008P	279,840,000	303	65.3	100	4	3	5	8	10	20	30	
2008D	345,600,000	184	64.7	100	5	4	6	9	22	30	50	
2009P	39,840,000	514	65.3	100	4	3	5	8	10	20	30	
2009D	46,800,000	290	65.2	100	5	4	6	9	22	30	50	
2010P	260,640,000	404	66.0	100	4	3	5	8	10	20	30	$15, MS-67FS, June 2013
2010D	229,920,000	430	66.1	100	5	4	6	9	22	30	50	
2011P	450,000,000	492	66.3	100	4	3	5	8	10	20	30	
2011D	540,240,000	558	66.4	100	5	4	6	9	22	30	50	
2012P	464,640,000	23	66.0	100	4	3	5	8	10	20	30	
2012D	558,960,000	n/a	n/a	n/a	5	4	6	9	20	27	40	
2013P	607,440,000				4	3	5	8	10	20	30	
2013D	615,600,000				5	4	6	9	20	27	40	
2014P					4	3	5	8	10	20	30	
2014D					5	4	6	9	20	27	40	

Proof Jefferson Nickels

PF-60 to 70 (Proof). All Proof Jefferson nickels have mirror fields. Striking is usually with Full Details, although there are scattered exceptions. Most survivors are PF-64 and finer. Most since the 1970s have frosted or cameo contrast on the higher features. Special Mint Set (SMS) coins were struck in lieu of Proofs from 1965 to 1967; these in some instances closely resemble Proofs. *Obverse and Reverse:* Those Proofs with abrasion or contact marks can be graded PF-60 to 62 or even 63; these are not widely desired by collectors. PF-64 can have some abrasion. Tiny flecks are sometimes seen on coins of 1938 to 1942, as are discolorations (even to the extent of black streaks); these flaws are from cellophane holders. Collectors should avoid such coins. Undipped Proofs of the early era often have a slight bluish or yellowish tint. At PF-65 or higher there are no traces of abrasion or flecks. Evaluation of differences between higher-grade Jefferson Proofs is highly subjective; one certified at PF-65 might be similar to another at PF-67, and vice-versa.

Proof Jefferson Nickel

Proof Jefferson Nickel, Silver

	Mintage	Cert	Avg	PF-65	PF-66	PF-67	Recent Auction Record
1938	19,365	3,443	65.3	$125	$175	$400	$1,880, PF-68, June 2013
1939	12,535	2,504	65.4	125	175	400	$11,163, PF-68, January 2014
1940	14,158	2,382	65.4	125	160	600	$12,925, PF-68, June 2013
1941	18,720	2,586	65.3	90	150	600	$18,800, PF-68, June 2013
1942	29,600	4,532	65.6	90	130	200	$11,750, PF-68, June 2013
1942P, Silver	27,600	7,181	65.3	180	250	275	$14,100, PF-67Cam, April 2014

	Mintage	Cert	Avg	PF-65	PF-66	PF-67	PF-68	Recent Auction Record
1950	51,386	2,562	65.9	$75	$85	$125	$550	$9,988, PF-68Cam, April 2014
1951	57,500	2,756	66.3	65	75	120	350	$4,700, PF-67DCam, April 2014
1952	81,980	2,896	66.5	45	60	75	175	$14,100, PF-68DCam, April 2013
1953	128,800	3,472	66.7	45	50	65	150	$15,275, PF-68DCam, April 2013

	Mintage	Cert	Avg	PF-65	PF-66	PF-67	PF-68	Recent Auction Record
1954	233,300	3,516	66.8	$22	$40	$55	$85	$5,875, PF-68DCam, March 2013
1955	378,200	4,400	67.1	18	30	45	75	$3,231, PF-69DCam, September 2013
1956	669,384	2,918	67.1	5	25	40	60	$5,581, PF-68DCam, June 2013
1957	1,247,952	2,776	66.9	4	12	20	50	$881, PF-68Cam, June 2013
1958	875,652	2,574	67.0	8	12	20	40	$7,050, PF-68DCam, April 2013
1959	1,149,291	2,441	66.9	3	10	20	35	$7,050, PF-69DCam, April 2013
1960	1,691,602	2,921	67.0	3	10	18	35	$6,463, PF-69DCam, March 2013
1961	3,028,144	3,408	66.9	3	10	18	25	$1,763, PF-69DCam, April 2013
1962	3,218,019	4,747	67.0	3	10	18	25	$823, PF-69Cam, September 2013
1963	3,075,645	5,744	67.2	3	10	18	25	$823, PF-69Cam, September 2013
1964	3,950,762	8,698	67.9	3	10	18	25	$194, PF-69DCam, March 2013
1965, SMS ‡	2,360,000	2,917	66.2	5 (a)	20	45		$5,288, PF-67DCam, July 2014
1966, SMS ‡	2,261,583	2,484	66.5	5 (b)	20	35		
1967, SMS ‡	1,863,344	2,886	66.5	5 (c)	20	30		$1,058, PF-69Cam, July 2014

‡ Ranked in the *100 Greatest U.S. Modern Coins.* **a.** Value in PF-64FS is $10; in PF-65FS, $55. **b.** Value in PF-64FS is $10; in PF-65FS, $65. **c.** Value in PF-64FS is $10; in PF-65FS, $60.

1979-S, Filled S (Type 1)	1979-S, Clear S (Type 2)	1981-S, Rounded S (Type 1)	1981-S, Flat S (Type 2)

	Mintage	Cert	Avg	PF-66	PF-67Cam	PF-68DC	PF-69DC	Recent Auction Record
1968S	3,041,506	2,230	67.7	$4	$16	$32	$115	$4,406, PF-65, August 2013
1969S	2,934,631	1,906	67.6	4	10	50	400	$1,116, PF-69DCam, June 2013
1970S	2,632,810	1,999	67.4	4	15	40	300	$499, PF-69DCam, September 2013
1971, No S ‡ (d)	1,655	234	67.3	1,250	1,500	2,750	8,000	$5,875, PF-69DCam, March 2013
1971S	3,220,733	2,115	67.4	8	20	35	600	$1,528, PF-69DCam, June 2013
1972S	3,260,996	1,666	67.6	8	20	35	120	$101, PF-69DCam, August 2013
1973S	2,760,339	3,133	68.7	7	15	25	30	$44, PF-69DCam, September 2009
1974S	2,612,568	3,885	68.7	8	12	18	20	$25, PF-69DCam, March 2008
1975S	2,845,450	4,648	68.8	8	12	18	20	$42, PF-68Cam, August 2013
1976S	4,149,730	6,080	68.8	8	12	18	20	$36, PF-70DCam, January 2010
1977S	3,251,152	5,707	68.8	7	12	18	20	$1,116, PF-70DCam, April 2013
1978S	3,127,781	5,998	68.9	7	12	18	20	$499, PF-70DCam, September 2013
1979S, Both kinds	3,677,175							
1979S, Type 1		5,364	68.9	7	12	18	22	$1,763, PF-70DCam, June 2013
1979S, Type 2		3,812	68.8	8	13	20	30	$646, PF-70DCam, June 2013
1980S	3,554,806	6,555	68.9	7	12	18	20	$1,528, PF-70DCam, June 2013
1981S, Type 1	4,063,083	7,304	68.9	7	12	18	20	$1,528, PF-70DCam, June 2013
1981S, Type 2	*	2,343	68.7	10	13	20	30	$3,525, PF-70DCam, April 2013
1982S	3,857,479	3,759	68.9	8	12	18	20	$1,322, PF, January 2014
1983S	3,279,126	3,866	68.9	8	12	18	20	$1,528, PF-70DCam, June 2013
1984S	3,065,110	3,660	68.9	10	12	18	20	$705, PF-70DCam, June 2013
1985S	3,362,821	3,586	68.9	8	12	18	20	$1,528, PF-70DCam, June 2013
1986S	3,010,497	3,988	68.9	9	13	19	20	$3,525, PF-70DCam, April 2013
1987S	4,227,728	3,778	68.9	8	12	18	20	$558, PF-70DCam, June 2013
1988S	3,262,948	2,962	68.9	9	13	19	25	$823, PF-70DCam, June 2013
1989S	3,220,194	3,309	69.0	8	12	18	20	$82, PF-70DCam, May 2013
1990S	3,299,559	4,266	69.0	8	12	18	20	$441, PF-69DCam, June 2014
1991S	2,867,787	3,541	69.0	10	12	18	20	$64, PF-70DCam, August 2013
1992S	4,176,560	6,861	69.0	8	12	18	20	$45, PF-70DCam, May 2013
1993S	3,394,792	6,016	69.0	8	12	18	20	$47, PF-70DCam, October 2009
1994S	3,269,923	5,640	69.0	8	12	18	20	$33, PF-70DCam, April 2013
1995S	2,797,481	5,031	69.0	10	13	19	20	$79, PF-70DCam, February 2010

* Included in the number above. ‡ Ranked in the *100 Greatest U.S. Modern Coins.* **d.** 1971 Proof nickels without the S mintmark were made in error after an assistant engraver forgot to punch a mintmark into a die. The U.S. Mint estimates that 1,655 such error coins were struck.

Chart continued on next page.

	Mintage	Cert	Avg	PF-66	PF-67Cam	PF-68DC	PF-69DC	Recent Auction Record
1996S	2,525,265	5,376	69.0	$8	$12	$15	$25	$56, PF-70DCam, February 2010
1997S	2,796,678	5,314	69.1	8	12	15	25	$36, PF-70DCam, December 2009
1998S	2,086,507	6,103	69.1	8	12	15	25	$47, PF-70DCam, November 2009
1999S	3,347,966	10,412	69.1	9	12	15	25	$42, PF-70DCam, September 2009
2000S	4,047,993	12,084	69.1	7	12	15	25	$17, PF-69DCam, March 2014
2001S	3,184,606	9,794	69.1	7	12	15	25	$17, PF-69DCam, March 2014
2002S	3,211,995	9,738	69.0	7	12	15	25	$15, PF-69DCam, February 2013
2003S	3,298,439	15,157	69.1	7	12	15	25	$15, PF-69DCam, March 2014

	Mintage	Cert	Avg	PF-67	PF-69DC	Recent Auction Record
2004S, Peace Medal	2,992,069	23,797	69.1	$12	$25	$15, PF-69DCam, March 2014
2004S, Keelboat	2,965,422	23,759	69.1	12	25	$31, PF-70DCam, November 2013
2005S, American Bison	3,344,679	32,358	69.1	14	30	$34, PF-70DCam, July 2013
2005S, Ocean in View	3,344,679	31,323	69.1	12	25	$21, PF-70DCam, November 2013
2006S, Monticello	3,054,436	12,339	69.2	12	25	$32, PF-70DCam, April 2013
2007S	2,577,166	8,727	69.2	12	30	$15, PF-69DCam, May 2013
2008S	2,169,561	6,473	69.3	12	30	$56, PF-70DCam, June 2009
2009S	2,179,867	8,276	69.3	12	30	$79, PF-70UCam, November 2009
2010S	1,689,364	6,052	69.2	12	30	$62, PF-70DCam, June 2013
2011S	1,453,276	8,361	69.2	12	30	$35, PF-70DCam, June 2013
2012S	1,237,415	99	69.2	12	30	
2013S	1,237,926			12	30	
2014S				12	30	

AN OVERVIEW OF HALF DISMES

Half dimes or five-cent silver coins were provided for in the Mint Act of April 2, 1792. The spelling was stated as *half disme.* The latter word (likely pronounced "deem," in the French mode) was used intermittently in government correspondence for years afterward, but on coins dated 1794 and beyond it appeared only as *dime.*

President George Washington, in his fourth annual message to the House of Representatives, November 6, 1792, referred to the half disme:

> In execution of the authority given by the Legislature, measures have been taken for engaging some artists from abroad to aid in the establishment of our Mint; others have been employed at home. Provision has been made of the requisite buildings, and these are now putting into proper condition for the purposes of the establishment.
>
> There has also been a small beginning in the coinage of half-dismes; the want of small coins in circulation calling the first attention to them. The regulation of foreign coins, in correspondence with the principles of our national Coinage, as being essential to their due operation, and to order in our money-concerns, will, I doubt not, be resumed and completed.

The 1792 half dismes are studied in *United States Pattern Coins* (the hobby's standard reference on pattern coins and experimental and trial pieces), and some numismatists have traditionally referred to them as patterns. It is true that they were struck at a private shop in Philadelphia while the official Mint buildings were still in planning. However, several factors point to their status as regular circulating coins. The half disme was authorized as a federal issue by congressional legislation. Its mintage was considerable—some 1,500 or so pieces—and, as noted by President Washington, the coins were meant to alleviate the national need for small change. Furthermore, nearly all surviving examples show signs of extensive wear.

The 1792 half dismes are not commonly collected, simply because they are not common coins; only 200 to 300 are estimated to still exist. However, their rarity, the romance of their connection to the nation's founding, and the mysteries and legends surrounding their creation (see next page) make them a perennial favorite among numismatists.

RECOMMENDED READING

Judd, J. Hewitt. *United States Pattern Coins* (10th ed., edited by Q. David Bowers), Atlanta, GA, 2009.
Logan, Russell, and McCloskey, John. *Federal Half Dimes, 1792–1837,* Manchester, MI, 1998.
Newlin, H.P. *The Early Half-Dimes of the United States,* Philadelphia, 1883 (reprinted 1933).
Valentine, D.W. *The United States Half Dimes,* New York, 1931 (reprinted 1975).

Legend has it that George and Martha Washington contributed the silver used to mint the first half dismes. (Portrait of Mrs. Washington by John Chester Buttre, after Gilbert Stuart.)

David Rittenhouse—scientist, inventor, mathematician, surveyor, and first director of the U.S. Mint—is said to have personally saved four of the 1792 half dismes.

HALF DISME
(1792)

Designer unknown (possibly Robert Birch); weight 1.35 grams; composition .8924 silver, .1076 copper; diameter 16.5 mm; reeded edge; minted at John Harper's shop, Philadelphia.

Shown 2x actual size.
Judd-7, Pollock-7, Logan-McCloskey-1.

History. Rumors and legends are par for the course with the 1792 half disme. Martha Washington is said to have posed for the portrait of Miss Liberty, despite the profile's dissimilarity to life images of the first lady. Longstanding numismatic tradition says that President George Washington had his own silver tableware taken to the mint factory to be melted down, with these little coins being the result. Whether these Washingtonian connections are true or not, other facts are certain: While the Philadelphia Mint was in the planning stage (its cornerstone would be laid on July 31, 1792), dies were being cut for the first federal coinage of that year. The designer may have been Robert Birch, a Mint engraver who created (or helped create) the dies for the half disme, the disme, and other coins. The half dismes were struck in a private facility owned by saw-maker John Harper, in mid-July. It is believed, from Thomas Jefferson's records, that 1,500 were made.

Most were placed into circulation. The coin's designs, with a unique head of Miss Liberty and an outstretched eagle, would not be revived when normal production of the half dime denomination started at the Mint's official facilities in 1795.

Striking and Sharpness. These coins usually are fairly well struck, but with some lightness on Miss Liberty's hair above her ear, and on the eagle's breast. Some examples have adjustment marks from the planchet being filed to adjust the weight prior to striking.

Availability. Most of the estimated 200 to 300 surviving coins show extensive wear. Some AU and MS coins exist, several in choice and gem state, perhaps from among the four examples that Mint Director David Rittenhouse is said to have reserved for himself.

AG-3 (About Good). *Obverse:* Extreme wear has reduced the portrait to a very shallow state. Around the border some letters are worn away completely, some partially. 1792 can be seen but is weak and may be partly missing. *Reverse:* Traces of the eagle remain and there are scattered letters and fragments of letters. Most of the coin is worn flat.

G-4, 6 (Good). *Obverse:* There is hardly any detail on the portrait, except that the eye can be seen, as well as some thick hair tips. The date is clear. Around the border the edges of the letters are worn away, and some are weak overall. *Reverse:* The eagle is only in outline form. The letters are very worn, with some missing.

VG-8, 10 (Very Good). *Obverse:* The head has less detail than in Fine and is essentially flat except at the neck. Some hair, in thick strands, can be seen. The letters show extensive wear, but are readable. *Reverse:* The eagle is mostly flat, and the letters are well worn, some of them incomplete at the borders. Detail overall is weaker than on the obverse.

F-12, 15 (Fine). *Obverse:* The portrait, above the neck, is essentially flat, but details of the eye, the

nose, and, to a lesser extent, the lips can be seen. The bust end and neck truncation are flat. Some hair detail can be seen to the right of the neck and behind the head, with individual strands blended into heavy groups. Both obverse and reverse at this grade and lower are apt to show marks, minor digs, and other evidence of handling. *Reverse:* Wear is more advanced than at VF, with significant reduction of the height of the lettering, and with some letters weak in areas, especially if the rim nearby is flat.

VF-20, 30 (Very Fine). *Obverse:* More wear is seen on the hair, including to the right of the forehead and face, where only a few strands may be seen. The hair tips at the right are well detailed. The bust end is flat on its high area. Letters all show light wear. *Reverse:* The eagle displays significant wear, with its central part flat and most of the detail missing from the right wing. The letters all show light wear.

EF-40, 45 (Extremely Fine). *Obverse:* The hair shows medium wear to the right of the face and on the bust end. The fields have no luster. Some luster may be seen among the hair strands and letters. *Reverse:* The eagle shows medium wear on its breast and the

right wing, less so on the left wing. HALF DISME shows wear. The fields have no luster. Some luster may be seen among the design elements and letters.

AU-50, 53, 55, 58 (About Uncirculated). *Obverse:* Light wear is seen on the cheek and on the hair (not as easily observable, as certain areas of the hair may be lightly struck). Luster ranges from light and mostly in protected areas at AU-50, to extensive at 58. Friction is evident in the field, less so in the higher ranges. *Reverse:* Light wear is seen on the eagle, but is less noticeable on the letters. Luster ranges from light and mostly in protected areas at AU-50, to extensive at 58. Friction is evident in the field, less in the higher ranges.

MS-60 to 70 (Mint State). *Obverse:* No wear is visible. Luster ranges from nearly full at MS-60 to frosty at 65 or higher. Toning often masks the surface, so careful inspection is required. *Reverse:* No wear is visible. The field around the eagle is lustrous, ranging from not completely full at MS-60 to deep and frosty at 65 and higher.

	Mintage	Cert	Avg	%MS	VG-8	F-12	VF-20	EF-40	AU-50	MS-60	MS-62	Recent Auction Record
1792 †	1,500	121	43.0	27	$35,000	$45,000	$75,000	$115,000	$180,000	$325,000	$400,000	$212,750, AU-58, March 2012

† Ranked in the *100 Greatest U.S. Coins* (fourth edition).

The first half dimes, dated 1794 and of the Flowing Hair type, were not actually struck until 1795. In that year additional half dimes with the 1795 date were made. In 1796 and 1797 the short-lived Draped Bust obverse combined with Small Eagle reverse was used, after which none were struck until 1801. From that year through 1805, excepting 1804, the Draped Bust obverse was used in combination with the Heraldic Eagle reverse. Then followed a long span of years without any coinage. In 1829 the laying of the cornerstone for the second Philadelphia Mint precipitated a new issue, the Capped Bust design, some examples of which were produced for the ceremony. Production was resumed for circulation, and half dimes of this motif were made through 1837. In that year the Liberty Seated motif, by Christian Gobrecht, was introduced, to be continued without interruption through 1873, although there were a number of design modifications and changes during that span.

Assembling a set of the different half-dime types is a challenge for the collector. The 1794 and 1795 Flowing Hair half dimes are fairly scarce at all levels and are quite rare in choice Mint State. Then come the Draped Bust obverse, Small Eagle reverse half dimes of 1796 and 1797. In the late 1960s, researcher Jim Ruddy found that of the various silver types (including the more famous 1796–1797 half dollars), half dimes of this type were the hardest to complete a photographic set of, from the lowest grades to the highest.

Draped Bust obverse, Heraldic Eagle reverse half dimes of the 1800–1805 years are scarce in all grades, more so than generally realized. In Mint State they are very rare, although on occasion some dated 1800 turn up (not often for the others). Finding a *sharply struck* example is next to impossible, and a collector may have to give up on this aspect and settle for one that has some weakness in areas.

Capped Bust half dimes and the several variations of Liberty Seated half dimes will pose no problem at all, and with some small amount of patience a collector will be able to find a sharply struck example in nearly any grade desired.

For the Collector and Investor: Half Dimes as a Specialty

Collecting half dimes early die varieties of 1794–1837, and/or by dates and mintmarks (beginning with the 1838-O), has captured the fancy of many numismatists over the years. As these coins are so small it is necessary to have a magnifying glass when studying the series—something the collector of silver dollars and double eagles does not need.

One of the earlier enthusiasts in the field was Philadelphia attorney and numismatist Harold P. Newlin, who in 1883 issued *A Classification of the Early Half Dimes of the United States.* Newlin's two favorite varieties were the 1792 half disme and the rare 1802, and after reading his enticing prose about the desirability of each, no doubt some collectors in 1883 put both coins on their "must have" lists.

Among early half dimes the rarest and most expensive is the 1802. In 1883, Newlin listed just 16 examples known to him. Although no one has compiled an up-to-date registry, it is likely that fewer than 30 exist. Most are well worn. Other early half dimes range from rare to very rare.

Capped Bust half dimes of the 1829–1837 years are all easily available as dates, but some of the die varieties are very rare. Today, most half dimes on the market are not attributed by varieties, making the search for such things rewarding when a rarity is found for the price of a regular coin.

In 1978 the numismatic world was startled to learn that Chicago dealer Edward Milas had located an 1870-S half dime, a variety not earlier known to exist and not listed in the annual Mint reports. Other than this coin, still unique today, the dates and mints in the Liberty Seated series 1837 to 1873-S are readily collectible by date and mint, with no great rarities. There are several very curious varieties within that span, the most interesting of which may be the 1858 Over Inverted Date. The date was first punched into the die upside down, the error noted, and then corrected.

Recommended Reading

Blythe, Al. *The Complete Guide to Liberty Seated Half Dimes,* Virginia Beach, VA, 1992.
Breen, Walter. *United States Half Dimes: A Supplement,* New York, 1958.
Fivaz, Bill, and Stanton, J.T. *The Cherrypickers' Guide to Rare Die Varieties* (5th ed., vol. II), Atlanta, GA, 2012.
Logan, Russell, and McCloskey, John. *Federal Half Dimes, 1792–1837,* Manchester, MI, 1998.
Newlin, Harold P. *The Early Half-Dimes of the United States,* Philadelphia, 1883 (reprinted 1933).
Valentine, D.W. *The United States Half Dimes,* New York, 1931 (reprinted 1975).

FLOWING HAIR
(1794–1795)

Designer unknown; engraver Robert Scot; weight 1.35 grams; composition .8924 silver, .1076 copper; approx. diameter 16.5 mm; reeded edge. All coined at Philadelphia Mint.

Shown 2x actual size.
Logan-McCloskey-3.

History. Half dimes dated 1794 and 1795, of the Flowing Hair type, were all struck in the calendar year 1795, although dies were ready by the end of 1794. The Flowing Hair motif was also used on half dollars and silver dollars of the same years, but not on other denominations.

Striking and Sharpness. Many Flowing Hair half dimes have problems of one sort or another, including adjustment marks from the planchet being filed, and/or light striking in some areas. On the obverse, check the hair and stars, and on the reverse the breast of the eagle. It may not be possible to find a *needle-sharp* example,

but with some extensive searching a fairly decent strike can be obtained. Sharp striking and excellent eye appeal add dramatically to the value.

Availability. Examples appear on the market with frequency, typically in lower circulated grades. Probably 250 to 500 could be classified as MS, most of these dated 1795. Some searching is needed to locate choice specimens in any grade. As a rule, half dimes are more readily available than are half dollars and dollars of the same design, and when found are usually more attractive and have fewer problems.

EF-40, 45 (Extremely Fine). *Obverse:* More wear is evident on the portrait, especially on the hair to the left of the face and neck; the cheek; and the tip of the neck truncation. Excellent detail remains in low-relief areas of the hair. The stars show wear, as do the date and letters. Luster, if present at all, is minimal and in protected areas. *Reverse:* The eagle, this being the focal point to check, shows more wear than at AU. Observe the coin in combination with knowledge of the die variety to determine its sharpness when it was first struck. Some were flat at the center at the time they were made. Additional wear is on the wreath and letters, but many details are present. Some luster may be seen in protected areas, and if present is slightly more abundant than on the obverse.

AU-50, 53, 55, 58 (About Uncirculated). *Obverse:* Light wear is seen on the hair area immediately to the left of the face and neck, on the cheek, and on the top of the neck truncation, more so at AU-50 than at 53 or 55. An AU-58 coin has minimal traces of wear. An AU-50 has luster in protected areas among the stars and letters, with little in the open fields or on the portrait. At AU-58, most luster is present in the fields, but is worn away on the highest parts of the motifs. *Reverse:* Light wear is seen on the eagle's body and right wing. At AU-50, detail is lost in most feathers in this area. However, striking can play a part, and some coins are weak to begin with. Light wear is seen on the wreath and lettering. Luster is the best key to actual wear. This ranges from perhaps 20% remaining in protected areas at AU-50 to nearly full mint bloom at 58.

MS-60 to 70 (Mint State). *Obverse:* At MS-60 some abrasion and contact marks are evident, most noticeably on the cheek and in the fields. Luster is present, but may be dull or lifeless, and interrupted in patches. At MS-63, contact marks are very few, and abrasion is hard to detect except under magnification. At MS-65 there is no abrasion, and contact marks are so minute as to require magnification. Luster should be full and rich. Coins graded above MS-65 are more theoretical than actual for this type—but they do exist, and are defined by having fewer marks as perfection is approached. *Reverse:* Comments apply as for the obverse, except that abrasion and contact marks are most noticeable on the eagle at the center. The field area is small and is protected by lettering and the wreath, and in any given grade shows fewer marks than on the obverse.

	Mintage	Cert	Avg	%MS	EF-40	AU-50	MS-60	MS-62	MS-63	MS-64	MS-65	Recent Auction Record
1794	*	301	45.5	31	$7,500	$11,000	$19,000	$27,500	$35,000	$42,500	$85,000	$4,313, VF-30, April 2012
1795	86,416	890	44.8	27	6,500	8,500	14,000	17,000	21,500	27,500	42,500	$94,000, MS-67, April 2013

* Included in number below.

DRAPED BUST, SMALL EAGLE REVERSE (1796–1797)

Designer probably Gilbert Stuart; engraver Robert Scot; weight 1.35 grams; composition .900 silver, .100 copper; approx. diameter 16.5 mm; reeded edge. All coined at Philadelphia Mint.

Shown 2x actual size.
Logan-McCloskey-2.

History. Although the Draped Bust obverse was used on various copper and silver coins circa 1795 to 1808, it was employed in combination with the *Small Eagle* reverse only on silver coins of 1795 to 1798—for the half dime series, only in 1796 and 1797.

Striking and Sharpness. Most 1796–1797 half dimes are weak in at least one area. Points to check for sharpness include the hair of Miss Liberty, the centers of the stars, the bust line, and, on the reverse, the center of the eagle. Check for planchet adjustment marks (these are infrequent). Dentils around the border are usu-

ally decent, but may vary in strength from one part of the border to another. Sharp striking and excellent eye appeal add to the value dramatically.

Availability. This type is fairly scarce in *any* grade; in MS-63 and finer, no more than a few dozen examples have been traced. As is true of other early silver types, beware of deeply toned or vividly iridescent-toned pieces whose true surface characters are flawed, but which are offered as MS; in truth some of these are barely better than EF.

EF-40, 45 (Extremely Fine). *Obverse:* More wear than at AU is evident on the upper hair area and the ribbon and on the drapery and bosom. Excellent detail remains in low-relief areas of the hair. The stars show wear, as do the date and letters. Luster, if present at all, is minimal and in protected areas. *Reverse:* The eagle (the focal point to check) shows more wear than at AU. On most examples, many feathers remain on the interior areas of the wings. Check the eagle, in combination with knowledge of the die variety, to determine the sharpness of the coin when it was first struck. Additional wear is evident on the wreath and letters, but many details are present. Some luster may be seen in protected areas and, if present, is slightly more abundant than on the obverse.

AU-50, 53, 55, 58 (About Uncirculated). *Obverse:* Light wear is seen on the hair area above the ear and

extending to the left of the forehead, on the ribbon, and on the bosom—more so at AU-50 than at 53 or 55. An AU-58 coin has minimal traces of wear. An AU-50 coin has luster in protected areas among the stars and letters, with little in the open fields or on the portrait. At AU-58, most luster is present in the fields, but is worn away on the highest parts of the motifs. *Reverse:* Light wear is seen on the eagle's body (this area might be lightly struck) and the edges of the wings. Light wear is seen on the wreath and lettering. Luster is the best key to judging actual wear. This ranges from perhaps 20% remaining in protected areas at AU-50 to nearly full mint bloom at AU-58.

MS-60 to 70 (Mint State). *Obverse:* At MS-60 some abrasion and contact marks are evident, most noticeably on the cheek, on the drapery, and in the right field. Lus-

ter is present, but may be dull or lifeless, and interrupted in patches. At MS-63, contact marks are very few, and abrasion is hard to detect except under magnification, although this type is sometimes graded liberally due to its rarity. An MS-65 coin has no abrasion, and contact marks are so minute as to require magnification. Luster should be full and rich. Coins graded above MS-65 are more theoretical than actual for this type—but they do exist, and are defined by having fewer marks as perfection is approached. *Reverse:* Comments apply as for the obverse, except that abrasion and marks are most noticeable on the eagle at the center, a situation complicated by the fact that this area was often flatly struck. Grading is best done by the obverse, then verified by the reverse. The field area is small and is protected by lettering and the wreath, and in any given grade shows fewer marks than on the obverse.

1796, 6 Over 5

1796, LIBERTY

1797, 15 Stars
Shown 2x actual size.

1797, 16 Stars
Shown 2x actual size.

1797, 13 Stars
Shown 2x actual size.

	Mintage	Cert	Avg	%MS	EF-40	AU-50	MS-60	MS-62	MS-63	MS-64	MS-65	Recent Auction Record
1796, 6 Over 5	10,230	31	55.4	58	$9,500	$15,000	$26,000	$35,000	$43,000	$65,000	$100,000	$31,725, MS-63, August 2013
1796, LIBERTY (a)	*	82	46.2	26	8,750	13,500	17,500	22,000	35,000	55,000	85,000	$17,625, MS-61, September 2013
1797, 15 Stars	44,527	210	35.4	9	8,750	12,500	16,000	19,000	25,000	40,000	85,000	$70,500, MS-64, June 2014
1797, 16 Stars	*	82	40.3	27	8,750	12,500	16,000	19,000	25,000	40,000	80,000	$54,344, MS-65, June 2014
1797, 13 Stars	*	31	32.9	3	13,500	25,000	40,000	50,000	65,000			$25,850, AU-55, February 2013

* Included in number above. **a.** A die imperfection makes the B in LIBERTY somewhat resemble a K.

DRAPED BUST, HERALDIC EAGLE REVERSE
(1800–1805)

Designer Robert Scot; weight 1.35 grams; composition .8924 silver, .1076 copper; approx. diameter 16.5 mm; reeded edge. All coined at Philadelphia Mint.

Shown 2x actual size.
Logan-McCloskey-1.

History. The combination of Draped Bust obverse / Heraldic Eagle reverse was used in the silver half dime series from 1800 to 1805. The obverse style, standardized with 13 stars, is the same as used in 1796 and 1797. During this span the rare 1802 was produced, and none were minted with the date 1804.

Striking and Sharpness. Most 1800–1805 half dimes are lightly struck in one area or another. The obverse stars usually show some weakness. On many coins the central details of Miss Liberty are not sharp. On the reverse the upper right of the shield and the adjacent part of the eagle's wing are often soft, and several or even most stars may be lightly defined (sharp stars show sharply peaked centers); high parts of the clouds are often weak. The area on the reverse opposite the bosom of Miss Liberty may be flat or weak, due to the metal having to flow in both directions when the coins were struck. (The area curving obliquely up and to the right of the eagle's head—exactly mirroring the curvature of the bust on the obverse—is especially prone to weakness of strike.) Dentils are likely to be weak or missing in areas. Many have Mint-caused planchet adjustment marks. In summary, *a sharply struck coin is a goal, not necessarily a reality*. Sharp striking and excellent eye appeal will add to the coin's value dramatically, this being particularly true for all issues from 1801 to 1805.

Availability. This is a challenging type to find with nice eye appeal. Many toned pieces are recolored. Some are porous or have other problems. The majority of pieces surviving today are dated 1800, and nearly all of the AU or finer coins are of this date.

VF-20, 30 (Very Fine). *Obverse:* The higher-relief areas of hair are well worn at VF-20, less so at 30. The drapery and bosom show extensive wear. The stars, being worn, appear larger than normal. *Reverse:* Wear is greater than at EF, including on the shield and wing feathers. Star centers are flat. Other areas have lost detail as well.

EF-40, 45 (Extremely Fine). *Obverse:* More wear than at AU is evident on the upper hair area and the ribbon, and on the drapery and bosom. Excellent detail remains in low-relief areas of the hair. The stars show wear, as do the date and letters. Luster, if present at all, is minimal and only in protected areas. *Reverse:* Wear is greater than at AU, overall. The neck lacks feather detail on its highest points. Feathers lose some detail near the edges of the wings, and some areas of the horizontal lines in the shield may be blended together. Some traces of luster may be seen, less so at EF-40 than at 45.

AU-50, 53, 55, 58 (About Uncirculated). *Obverse:* Light wear is seen on the hair area above the ear and extending to the left of the forehead, on the ribbon, and on the bosom, more so at AU-50 than at 53 or 55. An AU-58 coin has minimal traces of wear. Regarding luster: an AU-50 coin has luster in protected areas among the stars and letters, with little in the open fields or on the portrait. At AU-58, most luster is present in the fields, but is worn away on the highest parts of the motifs. *Reverse:* Comments as for MS coins, except that the eagle's neck, the tips and top of the wings, the clouds, and the tail show noticeable wear, as do other features. Luster ranges from perhaps 20% remaining in protected areas at AU-50 to nearly full mint bloom at 58. Often the reverse of this type retains much more luster than the obverse.

MS-60 to 70 (Mint State). *Obverse:* At MS-60 some abrasion and contact marks are evident, most noticeably on the cheek, on the drapery, and in the right field. Luster is present, but may be dull or lifeless, and interrupted in patches. At MS-63, contact marks are very few, and abrasion is hard to detect except under magnification, although this type is sometimes graded liberally due to its rarity. An MS-65 coin has no abrasion, and contact marks are so minute as to require magnification. Luster should be full and rich. Coins graded above MS-65 are more theoretical than actual for this type—but they do exist, and are defined by having fewer marks as perfection is approached. *Reverse:* Comments apply as for the obverse, except that abrasion and contact marks are most noticeable on the eagle's neck, the tips of the wing, and the tail. The field area is complex—with stars above the eagle, the arrows and olive branch, and other features, there is not much open space. Accordingly, marks will not be as noticeable as on the obverse.

1800, LIBEKTY

1803, Large 8

1803, Small 8

	Mintage	Cert	Avg	%MS	EF-40	AU-50	MS-60	MS-62	MS-63	MS-64	MS-65	Recent Auction Record
1800	24,000	423	41.5	19	$6,000	$8,500	$12,500	$15,000	$21,500	$25,000	$47,500	$25,300, MS-64, January 2012
1800, LIBEKTY (a)	16,000	97	42.4	29	6,200	8,500	13,000	16,000	22,000	25,500	50,000	$31,725, MS-64, April 2014
1801	27,760	77	32.8	13	6,500	10,000	16,000	20,000	27,500	37,500	65,000	$5,581, EF-40, February 2014
1802 †	3,060	13	33.2	0	250,000	350,000						$352,500, AU-50, June 2014
1803, Large 8	37,850	99	34.6	8	6,500	9,000	14,000	18,000	22,500	35,000	48,500	$7,050, AU-50, February 2014
1803, Small 8	*	16	36.4	13	7,000	10,000	20,000	26,000	35,000	50,000		$5,922, EF-35, April 2013
1805	15,600	83	28.6	1	9,000	20,000	45,000					$9,400, EF-45, August 2013

* Included in number above.   † Ranked in the *100 Greatest U.S. Coins* (fourth edition).   **a.** A defective die punch gives the R in LIBERTY the appearance of a K.

CAPPED BUST
(1829–1837)

Engraved by William Kneass, after a design by John Reich; weight 1.35 grams; composition .8924 silver, .1076 copper; approx. diameter 15.5 mm; reeded edge. Changed to 1.34 grams, .900 fine in 1837. All coined at Philadelphia Mint.

Shown 2x actual size.
Logan-McCloskey-7.

History. Half dimes of the Capped Bust design were first struck the morning of July 4, 1829, to include in the cornerstone time capsule of the new (second) Philadelphia Mint building and, presumably, to have some inexpensive coins on hand for distribution as souvenirs. Engraver John Reich's design was not new; it had been used on half dollars as early as 1807. It was logical to employ it on the new half dime, a coin that had not been made since 1805. The new half dimes proved popular and remained in circulation for many years.

Striking and Sharpness. Striking varies among Capped Bust half dimes, and most show lightness in one area or another. On the obverse, check the hair details to the left of the eye and the star centers. On the reverse, check the eagle's feathers and neck. The motto, which can be a problem on certain other coins of this design (notably half dollars), is usually bold on the half dimes. Dentils range from well defined to somewhat indistinct, and, in general, are sharper on the obverse than on the reverse.

Availability. Finding an example in any desired grade should not be a challenge. Finding one with Full Details will take more time. Connoisseurship is required at the MS level, due to over-graded and recolored coins.

AU-50, 53, 55, 58 (About Uncirculated). *Obverse:* Light wear is seen on the cap, the hair below LIBERTY, the hair near the clasp, and the drapery at the bosom. At AU-50 and 53, luster remains only in protected areas. At AU-58, the luster is extensive except in the open area of the field, especially to the right. *Reverse:* Wear is visible on the eagle's neck, the top of the wings, the claws, and the flat band above the eagle. At AU-50 and 53, there will still be significant luster, more than on the obverse. An AU-58 coin has nearly full luster.

MS-60 to 70 (Mint State). *Obverse:* At MS-60 some abrasion and contact marks are evident, most noticeably on the cheek, on the hair below the left part of LIBERTY, and on the area near the drapery clasp. Luster is present, but may be dull or lifeless, and interrupted in patches. At MS-63, contact marks are very few, and abrasion is hard to detect except under magnification. An MS-65 coin has no abrasion, and has contact marks so minute as to require magnification. Luster should be full and rich, usually more so on half dimes than larger coins of the Capped Bust type. Grades above MS-65 are seen now and again, and have fewer marks as perfection is approached. *Reverse:* Comments apply as for the obverse, except that abrasion and contact marks are most noticeable on the eagle's neck, the top of the wings, the claws, and the flat band that surrounds the incuse motto. The field is mainly protected by design elements and does not show abrasion as much as does the obverse.

1834, 3 Over Inverted 3
FS-H10-1834-301.

1835, Small Date

1835, Large Date

Small 5 C.

Large 5 C.

	Mintage	Cert	Avg	%MS	AU-50	MS-60	MS-62	MS-63	MS-64	MS-65	MS-66	Recent Auction Record
1829	1,230,000	1,267	57.1	59	$300	$400	$550	$925	$1,400	$3,000	$5,000	$11,750, AU-58, April 2013
1830	1,240,000	1,111	57.8	64	250	375	525	850	1,300	2,850	4,500	$9,400, MS-66, February 2014
1831	1,242,700	1,381	59.0	64	250	375	525	850	1,300	2,850	4,500	$7,050, MS-67, April 2014
1832	965,000	1,620	58.8	64	250	375	525	850	1,300	2,850	4,500	$14,100, MS-67, June 2014
1833	1,370,000	1,069	58.7	63	250	375	525	850	1,300	2,850	4,500	$21,150, MS-67, April 2014
1834	1,480,000	1,063	58.8	64	250	375	525	850	1,300	2,850	4,500	$7,050, MS-67, November 2013
1834, 3 Over Inverted 3	*	27	55.0	44	500	600	800	1,200	2,500	4,000	6,000	$1,645, AU-58, April 2013
1835, All kinds	2,760,000											
1835, Large Date and 5 C.		654	56.5	59	250	375	525	850	1,300	2,850	4,500	$8,813, MS-66, November 2013
1835, Large Date, Small 5 C.		21	58.3	52	250	375	525	850	1,300	2,850	4,500	$1,880, MS-64, March 2013
1835, Small Date, Large 5 C.		95	50.5	39	250	375	525	850	1,300	2,850	4,500	$7,638, MS-67, April 2013
1835, Small Date and 5 C.		184	53.7	48	250	375	525	850	1,300	2,850	4,500	$17,625, MS-67, March 2013
1836, Small 5 C.	1,900,000	124	51.0	36	250	375	525	850	1,300	2,850	4,500	$3,173, MS-66, August 2013
1836, Large 5 C.	*	302	55.9	56	250	375	525	850	1,300	2,850	4,500	$3,055, MS-64, February 2014
1836, 3 Over Inverted 3	*	34	54.8	53	475	675	825	1,200	2,000	4,000	7,500	$940, MS-63, June 2013
1837, Small 5 C.	871,000	78	55.1	50	500	1,000	1,500	2,200	4,500	10,000		$1,880, MS-63, June 2013
1837, Large 5 C.	*	203	52.3	40	250	400	650	850	1,550	3,500	7,000	$22,325, MS-66, November 2013

* Included in number above.

Proof Capped Bust Half Dimes

PF-60 to 70 (Proof). True Proofs have fully mirrored fields. Scrutinize deeply toned pieces (deep toning often masks the true nature of a coin, e.g., if it is not a true Proof, or if it has been cleaned or repaired). Some pieces attributed as "Proofs" are not. This advice applies across the entire Capped Bust silver series. *Obverse and Reverse:* Proofs that are extensively cleaned and have many hairlines, or that are dull and grainy, are lower level, such as PF-60 to 62. These are not of great interest to specialists unless they are of rare die varieties (such as 1829, LM-1 to 3). With medium hairlines, PF-64 may be assigned, and with relatively few hairlines, PF-65. PF-66 should have hairlines so delicate that magnification is needed to see them. Above that, a Proof should be free of such lines. Grading is highly subjective with early Proofs, and eye appeal also is a factor.

Proof Capped Bust Half Dime
Shown 2x actual size.
Logan-McCloskey-4.

	Est Mintage	Cert	Finest	PF-60	PF-63	PF-64	PF-65	Recent Auction Record
1829	20–30	24	PF-67	$4,500	$10,000	$21,000	$35,000	$36,719, PF-65Cam, January 2014
1830	10–15	4	PF-66	4,500	12,500	23,500	37,000	$49,938, PF-66, September 2013
1831	20–30	4	PF-67	4,500	12,500	24,000	38,000	$73,438, PF-67, January 2014
1832	5–10	2	PF-65	5,000	13,000	25,000	40,000	$19,550, PF-64, March 2004
1834	25–35	16	PF-66	4,500	10,000	20,000	35,000	$32,900, PF-66, November 2013
1835		n/a	n/a	5,000	13,000	25,000		
1836	5–10	3	PF-66	4,500	10,000	20,000	35,000	$47,000, PF-66, February 2014
1837 *(untraced)*	5–10	n/a	n/a					

LIBERTY SEATED, NO STARS ON OBVERSE (1837–1838)

Variety 1, No Stars on Obverse (1837–1838): Designer Christian Gobrecht; weight 1.34 grams; composition .900 silver, .100 copper; diameter 15.5 mm; reeded edge; mints: Philadelphia, New Orleans.

Variety 1 (1837–1838)
Shown 2x actual size.

History. The Liberty Seated design without obverse stars, known as Variety 1, was used in the half dime and dime series only at the Philadelphia Mint in 1837 and the New Orleans Mint in 1838 (1838-O). The motif, by Christian Gobrecht, follows the obverse inaugurated on the 1836 silver dollar. Miss Liberty has no drapery at her elbow.

Striking and Sharpness. Check the highest parts of the Liberty Seated figure (especially the head and horizontal shield stripes) and, on the reverse, the leaves. Check the dentils on both sides. These coins are very attractive, and the starless obverse gives them a cameo-like appearance.

Availability. The Philadelphia coins are easily available in all grades. The 1838-O is a rarity in true Mint State, often is overgraded, and typically has low eye appeal. Grades above MS-65 are seen with regularity, more often than the related No Stars dimes.

AU-50, 53, 55, 58 (About Uncirculated). *Obverse:* Light wear is seen on the thighs and knees, bosom, and head. At AU-50 and 53, luster is less than at 58, where the luster is extensive but incomplete. Friction is seen in the large open field. *Reverse:* Wear is noticeable on the leaves and ribbon. At AU-50 and 53, there still is significant luster, more than on the obverse, as the design elements protect the small field areas. An AU-58 coin has nearly full luster—more so than on the obverse.

MS-60 to 70 (Mint State). *Obverse:* At MS-60 some abrasion and contact marks are evident, most noticeably on the bosom, thighs, and knees. Luster is present, but may be dull or lifeless, and interrupted in patches in the large open field. At MS-63, contact marks are very few, and abrasion is hard to detect except under magnification. An MS-65 coin has no abrasion, and contact marks are so minute as to require magnification. Luster should be full and rich.

Reverse: Comments apply as for the obverse, except that abrasion and contact marks are most noticeable on the highest parts of the leaves and the ribbon. The field is mainly protected by design elements and does not show abrasion as much as does the open-field obverse on a given coin.

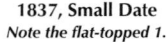

1837, Small Date
Note the flat-topped 1.

1837, Large Date
Note the pointed-top 1.

	Mintage	Cert	Avg	%MS	AU-50	MS-60	MS-62	MS-63	MS-64	MS-65	MS-66	Recent Auction Record
1837, Small Date	1,405,000	279	55.0	48	$500	$725	$900	$1,100	$1,500	$3,400	$5,000	$22,325, MS-67, June 2014
1837, Large Date	*	761	58.5	64	500	700	875	1,000	1,400	3,000	4,300	$19,975, MS-67, November 2013
18380, No Stars	70,000	97	40.2	27	1,250	2,400	5,000	8,500	17,500	32,000		$11,750, MS-64, February 2014

* Included in number above.

Proof Liberty Seated Half Dimes, Variety 1

PF-60 to 70 (Proof). It is likely that at least several dozen Proofs were made of the 1837 half dime. Today, attractive examples exist and are rare. Nearly all designated as Proofs are, indeed, Proofs. Seek an example with deep mirror surfaces. *Obverse and Reverse:* Proofs that are extensively cleaned and have many hairlines, or that are dull and grainy, are lower level, such as PF-60 to 62. These command little attention in the market. The 1837 half dime Proofs were often cleaned, resulting in coins that have lost much of their mirror surface. With medium hairlines and good reflectivity, PF-64 is assigned, and with relatively few hairlines, PF-65. In various grades hairlines are most easily seen in the obverse field. PF-66 should have hairlines so delicate that magnification is needed to see them. Above that, a Proof should be free of such lines.

Proof Liberty Seated Half Dime, Variety 1
Shown 2x actual size.

	Est Mintage	Cert	Finest	PF-60	PF-63	PF-64	PF-65	Recent Auction Record
1837	15–20	20	PF-67	$6,500	$14,000	$18,500	$37,500	$105,750, PF-67, June 2014

LIBERTY SEATED, STARS ON OBVERSE
(1838–1859)

Variety 2, Stars on Obverse (1838–1853): Designer Christian Gobrecht; weight 1.34 grams; composition .900 silver, .100 copper; diameter 15.5 mm; reeded edge; mints: Philadelphia, New Orleans.

Variety 2 (1838–1853)
Shown 2x actual size.

Variety 3, Arrows at Date, Reduced Weight (1853–1855): Designer Christian Gobrecht; weight 1.24 grams; composition .900 silver, .100 copper; diameter 15.5 mm; reeded edge; mints: Philadelphia, New Orleans.

Variety 3 (1853–1855)
Shown 2x actual size.

Variety 2 Resumed, With Weight Standard of Variety 3 (1856–1859): Designer Christian Gobrecht; weight 1.24 grams; composition .900 silver, .100 copper; diameter 15.5 mm; reeded edge; mints: Philadelphia, New Orleans.

Variety 2 Resumed, Weight Standard of Variety 3 (1856–1859)
Shown 2x actual size.

History. The Liberty Seated motif is essentially the same as before, but with 13 obverse stars added in 1838, and in 1840 a restyling (drapery added to the elbow) by Robert Ball Hughes. Arrows were added to the sides of the date starting in 1853, through 1855; these denoted the reduction of weight under the terms of the Act of February 21, 1853. The earlier design resumed in 1856. The reverse design stayed the same during these changes.

Striking and Sharpness. Strike quality varies widely among these half dimes. Most from 1838 to 1852 are sharper than later ones, but there are exceptions. (Coins with "mushy" details are especially common among the high-mintage dates of the mid- to late 1850s.) On the obverse, check the star centers, the head and center of Miss Liberty, and the dentils. On the reverse, check the wreath leaves and dentils.

Availability. These are easily available as a type, but with many scarce varieties. Such issues as 1849-O and 1846 are extreme rarities at the true MS level. Quality varies widely, and many MS coins are artificially toned.

EF-40, 45 (Extremely Fine). *Obverse:* Wear is seen on all areas, more so than at AU, especially on the knees, bosom, and head. Little or no luster is seen. *Reverse:* Wear is seen on all areas, more so than at AU, most noticeably at the leaves to each side of the wreath apex, and on the ribbon. Leaves retain details except on the higher areas.

AU-50, 53, 55, 58 (About Uncirculated). *Obverse:* Light wear is seen on the knees, bosom, and head. At AU-50 and 53, luster is less than at 58, where the lus-

ter is extensive but incomplete. *Reverse:* Wear is evident on the leaves (especially at the top of the wreath) and ribbon. At AU-50 and 53, there still is significant luster. An AU-58 coin has nearly full luster, more so than on the obverse, as the design elements protect the small field areas.

MS-60 to 70 (Mint State). *Obverse:* At MS-60 some abrasion and contact marks are evident, most noticeably on the bosom and knees. Luster is present, but may be dull or lifeless. At MS-63, contact marks are

very few, and abrasion is hard to detect except under magnification. An MS-65 coin has no abrasion, and contact marks are so minute as to require magnification. Luster should be full and rich. *Reverse:* Comments apply as for the obverse, except that in lower MS grades abrasion and contact marks are most noticeable on the highest parts of the leaves and the ribbon. At MS-65 or higher there are no marks visible to the unaided eye. The field is mainly protected by design elements and does not show abrasion as much as does the obverse on a given coin.

| No Drapery From Elbow (1837–1840) | Drapery From Elbow (Starting 1840) | 1838, Normal Stars
Shown 2x actual size. | 1838, Small Stars
Shown 2x actual size. |

| 1840-O, No Drapery,
Normal Reverse
Note four-leaf cluster next to DIME. | 1840-O, No Drapery,
Transitional Reverse
Note three-leaf cluster next to DIME. | 1848, Medium Date | 1848, Large Date |

| 1849, 9 Over 6
FS-H10-1849-302. | 1849, 9 Over 8
FS-H10-1849-301. | 1858, Repunched High Date
FS-H10-1858-301. | 1858, Over Inverted Date
FS-H10-1858-302. |

1860, Obverse of 1859, Reverse of 1860
Transitional pattern, with stars (Judd-247).

	Mintage	Cert	Avg	%MS	EF-40	AU-50	MS-60	MS-62	MS-63	MS-64	MS-65	Recent Auction Record
1838, No Drapery, Large Stars	2,225,000	1,150	60.6	74	$75	$175	$250	$310	$420	$775	$1,700	$30,550, MS-68, November 2013
1838, No Drapery, Small Stars	*	80	58.6	64	185	360	560	700	1,100	1,650	3,750	$3,408, MS-65, March 2013
1839, No Drapery	1,069,150	484	60.9	76	75	160	260	310	420	750	1,800	$4,700, MS-67, April 2013
18390, No Drapery	1,060,000	142	51.1	37	80	170	525	875	1,850	3,200	6,250	$2,820, MS-64, June 2014

* Included in number above.

Chart continued on next page.

	Mintage	Cert	Avg	%MS	EF-40	AU-50	MS-60	MS-62	MS-63	MS-64	MS-65	Recent Auction Record
1840, No Drapery	1,034,000	508	59.6	70	$75	$175	$260	$310	$420	$750	$2,000	$7,638, MS-67, June 2014
1840O, No Drapery	695,000	100	50.5	27	85	285	725	1,100	2,250	4,400	15,000	$18,213, MS-66, June 2014
1840O, No Drapery, Transitional Reverse (a)	100	2	27.5	0	800	1,250	1,600	2,500				$431, F-15, November 2011
1840, Drapery	310,085	123	59.2	72	210	360	460	600	825	1,150	2,700	$19,975, MS-67, June 2014
1840O, Drapery	240,000	65	45.1	11	425	1,250	3,100	4,500	8,200			$30,550, MS-63, June 2014
1841	1,150,000	277	60.7	79	75	160	210	275	325	575	1,300	$1,998, MS-66, June 2014
1841O	815,000	95	51.9	28	110	300	665	1,250	1,525	2,250	6,000	$881, AU-53, January 2014
1842	815,000	309	59.9	72	75	160	210	275	325	560	1,250	$1,293, MS-66, July 2014
1842O	350,000	76	46.5	29	525	825	1,275	1,700	2,250	6,000	12,500	$219, VF-30, December 2011
1843	1,165,000	388	59.5	67	75	160	210	275	325	560	1,400	$3,819, MS-67, June 2014
1844	430,000	305	61.1	79	75	160	210	275	325	560	1,400	$4,113, MS-67, February 2014
1844O	220,000	98	41.0	17	1,100	3,200	5,600	8,000	13,000	18,000	25,000	$1,386, EF-40, January 2012
1845	1,564,000	404	60.1	72	75	160	210	275	325	560	1,250	$1,528, MS-66, February 2013
1846	27,000	121	28.7	3	2,750	4,600	11,000	13,000	18,500			$23,501, MS-63, June 2014
1847	1,274,000	346	59.6	70	75	160	225	275	500	560	1,250	$7,050, MS-66, November 2013
1848, Medium Date	668,000	167	56.6	51	75	160	250	385	500	1,100	2,750	$3,055, MS-65, June 2013
1848, Large Date	*	77	56.1	51	130	285	575	1,000	1,600	2,000	3,500	$368, AU-55, December 2013
1848O	600,000	140	61.8	84	120	250	410	575	720	1,250	2,200	$12,338, MS-67, January 2014
1849, All kinds	1,309,000											
1849, 9 Over 6 (b)		76	57.1	61	125	225	500	700	1,200	1,450	2,250	$2,585, MS-65, June 2014
1849, 9 Over Widely Placed 6 (c)		79	57.7	67	175	260	620	800	1,400	2,000	2,750	$7,050, MS-67, June 2014
1849, Normal Date		89	55.2	52	75	160	235	300	520	850	1,600	$4,406, MS-67, June 2014
1849O	140,000	105	46.4	27	475	1,200	2,500	3,250	4,200	7,250	12,000	$7,638, MS-65, June 2014
1850	955,000	379	61.7	82	75	160	220	275	350	560	1,200	$920, MS-65, January 2012
1850O	690,000	119	55.0	45	120	310	750	950	1,650	2,600	4,000	$353, AU-55, April 2013
1851	781,000	252	60.4	77	75	160	210	265	325	560	1,200	$9,400, MS-68, April 2013
1851O	860,000	187	56.5	59	110	235	525	625	850	1,200	3,850	$2,644, MS-65, June 2013
1852	1,000,500	308	62.2	86	75	160	210	265	325	560	1,200	$7,050, MS-67, April 2013
1852O	260,000	110	49.3	33	260	525	865	1,300	2,000	4,750	8,250	$8,813, MS-66, June 2014
1853, No Arrows	135,000	231	58.5	71	260	500	750	800	1,200	1,500	2,500	$2,820, MS-66, October 2013
1853O, No Arrows	160,000	176	44.9	31	2,250	3,500	6,200	8,750	12,500	19,500		$3,819, AU-55, April 2013
1853, With Arrows	13,210,020	2,075	58.2	62	70	140	200	260	310	550	1,450	$6,463, MS-67, April 2013
1853O, With Arrows	2,200,000	80	55.8	51	75	160	275	500	925	1,500	3,400	$27,025, MS-67, April 2014
1854	5,740,000	1,023	59.0	69	65	140	230	275	325	550	1,500	$9,988, MS-67, August 2013
1854O	1,560,000	152	56.5	58	75	155	285	525	775	1,750	3,600	$3,290, MS-65, August 2013
1855	1,750,000	410	60.3	73	65	130	210	260	350	600	2,200	$9,400, MS-67, June 2014
1855O	600,000	141	60.3	70	175	200	575	750	1,100	1,900	4,200	$25,850, MS-68, June 2014
1856	4,880,000	732	59.7	74	65	130	185	220	320	550	1,200	$1,880, MS-66, January 2014
1856O	1,100,000	164	54.6	34	110	265	575	700	1,000	1,450	2,350	$1,058, MS-63, December 2013
1857	7,280,000	1,351	60.4	78	65	130	185	220	320	550	1,100	$115, AU-55, April 2012
1857O	1,380,000	386	57.9	61	70	200	375	375	500	725	1,600	$4,113, MS-67, April 2014
1858	3,500,000	1,218	60.9	79	65	130	185	220	320	550	1,100	$7,638, MS-66, August 2013
1858, Repunched High Date (d)	*	6	45.7	17	235	350	650	850	1,200	1,900	3,000	$65, VF-30, July 2011
1858, Over Inverted Date (e)	*	72	46.7	32	220	325	625	750	1,100	1,650	2,750	$7,638, MS-65, February 2014
1858O	1,660,000	442	60.3	75	80	155	265	325	450	600	1,450	$11,163, MS-67, June 2014
1859	340,000	416	61.3	80	80	130	220	225	425	575	1,250	$3,819, MS-67, August 2013
1859O	560,000	203	59.5	70	130	210	285	310	375	800	1,950	$2,585, MS-66, July 2014
1860, Obverse of 1859 (With Stars), Reverse of 1860 (f)	100	55	64.5	100	2,500	3,000	3,750	4,500	5,600			$5,750, MS-66, February 2012

* Included in number above. **a.** "This rare transitional variety exhibits large letters and open or split buds on the reverse die, along with a small O mintmark. The key diagnostic of the variety is three-leaf clusters on either side of the word DIME, while the common reverse has four-leaf clusters" (*Cherrypickers' Guide to Rare Die Varieties*, fifth edition, volume II). **b.** Fivaz and Stanton contend that this is actually a 9 Over 8 overdate (*Cherrypickers' Guide to Rare Die Varieties*, fifth edition, volume II). **c.** The 4 of the date is at least triple punched, with one secondary 4 south and one east of the primary 4. There is also a secondary numeral east of the lower portion of the 9. **d.** The date was first punched into the die very high, then corrected and punched into its normal location. The original high-date punch is clearly visible within the upper portions of the primary date. **e.** The date was first punched into the die in an inverted orientation, and then corrected. The bases of the secondary digits are evident above the primary digits. **f.** This transitional issue, made surreptitiously at the Mint for a private collector, has the new Liberty Seated die made in the old style of 1859, but with the date of 1860. The reverse is the regular die of 1860, with a cereal wreath. Classified as Judd-267 (*United States Pattern Coins*, tenth edition).

Proof Liberty Seated Half Dimes, Varieties 2 and 3

PF-60 to 70 (Proof). Proofs were first widely sold to collectors in 1858, in which year an estimated 210 silver sets were distributed. It is believed that 800 Proofs were struck of 1859, of which slightly more than 400 found buyers. Proofs were made of earlier dates, but in much smaller numbers. Excellent strike and deeply mirrored fields characterized nearly all. The quality of Proofs on the market varies widely, mainly due to cleaning and dipping. Patience and care are needed to find a choice example. *Obverse and Reverse:* Proofs that are extensively cleaned and have many hairlines, or that are dull and grainy, are lower level, such as PF-60 to 62. These are not widely desired, save for the rare (in any grade) date of 1846. With medium hairlines and good reflectivity, a grade of PF-64 is justified, and with relatively few hairlines, PF-65. In various grades hairlines are most easily seen in the obverse field. PF-66 should have hairlines so delicate that magnification is needed to see them. Above that, a Proof should be free of such lines.

Proof Liberty Seated Half Dime, Variety 2
Shown 2x actual size.

Proof Liberty Seated Half Dime, Variety 3
Shown 2x actual size.

	Est Mintage	Cert	Finest	PF-60	PF-63	PF-64	PF-65	Recent Auction Record
1838	4–5	2	PF-66	$10,000	$12,500	$30,000	$50,000	$182,125, PF-66, January 2014
1839	5–10	4	PF-65	10,000	12,500	22,000	37,500	$27,600, PF-65Cam, April 2008
1840, No Drapery	5–10	5	PF-66	10,000	12,500	22,000	37,500	$30,550, PF-64, April 2014
1840, Drapery	unknown	2	PF-65					
1841	10–20	6	PF-65	10,000	15,000	25,000	45,000	$46,000, PF-65, January 2008
1842	10–20	8	PF-68	8,000	12,000	15,000	26,000	$12,075, PF-64, January 2010
1843, 1843 Over 1843	10–20	1	PF-67	8,000	12,000	15,000	26,000	$55,813, PF-67, January 2014
1844	15–25	14	PF-67	8,000	12,000	15,000	26,000	$35,250, PF-67, February 2014
1845	10–15	8	PF-68	9,000	14,000	18,000	30,000	$64,625, PF-68, January 2014
1846	10–20	9	PF-67	8,000	12,000	15,000	26,000	$35,250, PF-66, June 2014
1847	8–12	8	PF-66	8,000	12,000	15,000	26,000	$36,719, PF-66Cam, April 2014
1848	6–8	3	PF-66	9,000	14,000	20,000	45,000	$63,250, PF-66, July 2008
1849	8–12	6	PF-66	8,000	12,000	15,000	26,000	$22,325, PF-65, June 2014
1850	8–12	3	PF-65	12,000	20,000	30,000	50,000	$57,500, PF-65, January 2008
1852	10–15	13	PF-66	8,000	12,000	21,000	30,000	$30,550, PF-65, January 2014
1853, Arrows (extremely rare)	3–5	1	PF-64	20,000	25,000	32,000		
1854, Arrows	15–25	22	PF-66	4,750	8,500	11,000	14,000	$9,694, PF-65, August 2013
1855, Arrows	15–25	28	PF-66	4,750	8,500	11,000	14,000	$21,150, PF-66, June 2014
1856	40–60	40	PF-67	2,500	4,500	6,000	9,000	$10,869, PF-65Cam, June 2013
1857	40–60	55	PF-67	2,200	3,000	3,400	5,500	$21,738, PF-67Cam, January 2014
1858	300	160	PF-67	850	1,400	2,250	4,500	$6,169, PF-66, June 2014
1859	800	427	PF-68	550	1,250	2,000	4,000	$12,925, PF-67, March 2013
1859, Transitional (a)	20	7	PF-66	20,000	35,000	45,000	55,000	$34,500, PF-63, August 2010

a. Classified as Judd-232 (*United States Pattern Coins*, tenth edition), this features the obverse design of 1859 and the reverse of 1860.

LIBERTY SEATED, LEGEND ON OBVERSE (1860–1873)

Variety 4, Legend on Obverse (1860–1873): Designer Christian Gobrecht; weight 1.24 grams; composition .900 silver, .100 copper; diameter 15.5 mm; reeded edge; mints: Philadelphia, New Orleans, San Francisco.

Variety 4 (1860–1873)
Shown 2x actual size.

History. In 1860 on the half dime the legend UNITED STATES OF AMERICA was moved to the obverse, in place of the stars. The reverse displayed a "cereal wreath" (as it was called in Mint records) enclosing the words HALF DIME.

Striking and Sharpness. Points to check include the head of Miss Liberty on the obverse, the wreath details on the reverse (particularly at the inside upper left, above H of HALF) and the dentils on both sides. Generally, MS coins have excellent luster, although some struck from relapped dies tend to be prooflike and with many striae. The word LIBERTY is not an infallible guide to grading at lower levels, as on some dies the shield was in lower relief, and the letters wore away less quickly. This guideline should be used in combination with other features.

Availability. These are easily available as a type, although some dates and varieties are rare. San Francisco coins, first made in 1863, are rare in MS for the first several years.

EF-40, 45 (Extremely Fine). *Obverse:* More wear than at AU is seen on all areas, especially the knees, bosom, and head. Little or no luster is seen. *Reverse:* More wear than at AU is seen on all areas, most noticeably at the high areas of the wreath and on the ribbon. Leaves retain excellent details except on the higher areas.

AU-50, 53, 55, 58 (About Uncirculated). *Obverse:* Light wear is seen on the knees, bosom, and head. At AU-50 and 53, luster is less evident than at 58, where the luster is extensive but incomplete. *Reverse:* Wear is observable on the leaves and ribbon. At AU-50 and 53 there still is significant luster, more so than on the obverse, as the design elements protect the small field areas. An AU-58 coin has nearly full luster.

MS-60 to 70 (Mint State). *Obverse:* At MS-60 some abrasion and contact marks are evident, most noticeably on the bosom and knees. Luster is present, but may be dull or lifeless. At MS-63, contact marks are very few, and abrasion is hard to detect except under magnification. An MS-65 coin has no abrasion, and contact marks are so minute as to require magnification. Luster should be full and rich, except for Philadelphia (but not San Francisco) half dimes of the early and mid-1860s. Most MS coins of 1861 to 1865, Philadelphia issues, have extensive die striae (from the dies being incompletely finished). Some low-mintage Philadelphia issues may be prooflike (and some may even be mislabeled as Proofs). Clashmarks are common in this era. *Reverse:* Comments apply as for the obverse, except that in lower MS grades abrasion and contact marks are most noticeable on the highest parts of the leaves and the ribbon, less so on HALF DIME. At MS-65 or higher there are no marks visible to the unaided eye. The field, mainly protected by design elements, does not show abrasion as much as does the obverse on a given coin.

1861, So-Called 1 Over 0
FS-H10-1861-301.

1872, Doubled-Die Obverse
FS-H10-1872-101.

Mintmark Below Bow
1860–1869, 1872–1873.

Mintmark Above Bow
1870–1872.

	Mintage	Cert	Avg	%MS	EF-40	AU-50	MS-60	MS-62	MS-63	MS-64	MS-65	Recent Auction Record
1860, Legend	798,000	939	62.7	88	$50	$85	$160	$190	$260	$385	$800	$8,225, MS-68, April 2013
18600	1,060,000	424	60.8	78	50	100	200	225	320	475	950	$1,234, MS-65, April 2014
1861	3,360,000	985	60.1	75	50	85	160	190	260	385	800	$5,875, MS-67, June 2014
1861, So-Called 1 Over 0	*	106	54.2	35	250	375	600	725	900	1,375	3,000	$11,750, MS-67, June 2014
1862	1,492,000	1,207	62.3	85	65	110	180	200	260	385	800	$11,163, MS-68, June 2014
1863	18,000	268	59.6	81	475	625	725	750	950	1,000	1,600	$4,406, MS-67, February 2013
1863S	100,000	160	58.1	65	160	320	750	825	1,000	1,600	3,000	$7,638, MS-65, August 2013
1864	48,000	103	56.3	75	925	1,100	1,200	1,275	1,350	1,650	2,450	$7,344, MS-67, June 2014
1864S	90,000	97	55.6	54	285	440	725	950	1,400	1,850	3,750	$7,931, MS-67, June 2014
1865	13,000	117	56.8	74	675	750	850	1,000	1,250	1,575	2,000	$1,116, MS-63, December 2013
1865S	120,000	100	54.6	41	175	550	950	1,275	2,100	3,300	4,750	$7,050, MS-65, June 2014
1866	10,000	124	58.3	77	650	700	825	900	1,200	1,350	2,500	$1,116, AU-50, December 2013

* Included in number above.

	Mintage	Cert	Avg	%MS	EF-40	AU-50	MS-60	MS-62	MS-63	MS-64	MS-65	Recent Auction Record
1866S	120,000	137	57.7	61	$160	$375	$475	$650	$950	$1,450	$3,500	$441, AU-55, November 2013
1867	8,000	173	61.1	86	850	925	1,100	1,200	1,400	1,500	2,000	$14,100, MS-67, June 2014
1867S	120,000	116	57.5	56	160	325	575	700	1,200	1,900	3,200	$8,225, MS-66, June 2014
1868	88,600	150	60.3	79	325	475	675	700	900	1,100	1,700	$4,406, MS-67, June 2014
1868S	280,000	235	60.7	70	45	130	320	400	600	1,000	2,200	$6,463, MS-66, November 2013
1869	208,000	193	61.7	85	45	160	260	300	400	875	1,100	$1,763, MS-66, February 2013
1869S	230,000	131	60.4	76	45	130	320	400	800	1,350	3,750	$1,763, MS-64, March 2014
1870	535,000	460	61.2	83	45	80	150	200	275	400	900	$10,575, MS-67, June 2014
1870S (unique) †		2	63.5	100					1,500,000			$661,250, MS-63, July 2004
1871	1,873,000	823	61.0	77	45	80	150	200	275	400	900	$1,998, MS-66, June 2013
1871S	161,000	240	60.4	66	80	180	310	345	500	700	2,200	$3,055, MS-66, November 2013
1872	2,947,000	717	60.5	74	45	80	150	200	275	400	900	$2,585, MS-66, February 2013
1872, Doubled-Die Obverse (a)	*	14	40.8	0	200	300	550	650	800			$89, EF-45, August 2011
1872S, All kinds	837,000											
1872S, Mintmark above bow		311	62.1	80	45	80	150	200	275	385	800	$3,055, MS-67, November 2013
1872S, Mintmark below bow		729	62.7	86	45	80	150	200	275	385	800	$1,763, MS-66, April 2013
1873 (Close 3 only)	712,000	241	60.7	76	45	80	150	200	275	385	900	$8,225, MS-67, June 2014
1873S (Close 3 only)	324,000	515	62.2	85	45	80	150	200	275	385	800	$5,875, MS-67, June 2014

* Included in number above. † Ranked in the *100 Greatest U.S. Coins* (fourth edition). **a.** "Doubling is evident on UNITED STATES OF AMERICA and on most elements of Miss Liberty. AMERICA is the strongest point" (*Cherrypickers' Guide to Rare Die Varieties*, fifth edition, volume II).

Proof Liberty Seated Half Dimes, Variety 4

PF-60 to 70 (Proof). Proof coins were made in fair quantities each year and are readily available today. Generally, they are well made, with deeply mirrored fields, although some of the late 1860s and early 1870s can have weak areas. Average quality in the marketplace is higher than for larger Liberty Seated denominations. *Obverse and Reverse:* Proofs that are extensively cleaned and have many hairlines, or that are dull and grainy, are lower level, such as PF-60 to 62. These are not widely desired in the marketplace. With medium hairlines and good reflectivity, PF-64 is appropriate, and with relatively few hairlines, PF-65. In various grades hairlines are most easily seen in the obverse field. PF-66 should have hairlines so delicate that magnification is needed to see them. Above that, a Proof should be free of such lines.

Proof Liberty Seated Half Dime, Variety 4
Shown 2x actual size.

	Mintage	Cert	Finest	PF-60	PF-63	PF-64	PF-65	PF-65Cam	Recent Auction Record
1860	1,000	218	PF-68	$350	$575	$800	$1,750	$2,000	$3,290, PF-66Cam, April 2014
1861	1,000	180	PF-67	350	575	800	1,750	2,000	$6,169, PF-67, June 2014
1862	550	368	PF-67	350	575	800	1,750	2,000	$44,063, PF-68Cam, November 2013
1863	460	401	PF-67	350	575	800	1,750	2,000	$3,290, PF-67, June 2014
1864	470	311	PF-68	350	575	800	1,750	2,000	$4,259, PF-67, June 2014
1865	500	349	PF-68	350	575	800	1,750	2,000	$9,400, PF-67Cam, March 2014
1866	725	354	PF-68	350	575	800	1,750	2,000	$5,875, PF-66Cam, August 2013
1867	625	440	PF-68	350	575	800	1,750	2,000	$8,813, PF-68, January 2014
1868	600	368	PF-67	350	575	800	1,750	2,000	$11,163, PF-67DCam, April 2014
1869	600	397	PF-68	350	575	800	1,750	2,000	$3,422, PF-67Cam, February 2014
1870	1,000	379	PF-68	350	575	800	1,750	2,000	$7,050, PF-68, June 2014
1871	960	391	PF-68	350	575	800	1,750	2,000	$403, PF-63, April 2012
1872	950	345	PF-68	350	575	800	1,750	2,000	$4,313, PF-67, December 2011
1873	600	501	PF-67	350	575	800	1,750	2,000	$11,163, PF-67DCam, January 2014

AN OVERVIEW OF DIMES

A collection of dimes ranging from 1796 to date includes many interesting issues. As a type, none are super-rare, but earlier types, combining low mintages with commonly weak striking, can be a challenge for the collector.

The 1796–1797 dime with Draped Bust obverse, Small Eagle reverse is the rarest of the dime types by far, with fewer than 50,000 pieces minted. These hail from an era in which there was no numismatic interest in saving such coins. Finding a choice example in whatever grade desired will require time and effort.

Then comes the Draped Bust obverse, Heraldic Eagle reverse type, made from 1798 through 1807 (except for 1799). Today these are available easily enough in circulated grades, but are elusive in Mint State. Nearly all are lightly struck—another challenge. Capped Bust dimes of the 1809–1828 years also require connoisseurship to locate a sharply struck specimen. For all of these early types some compromise with perfection is required.

Later Capped Bust dimes of 1828 to 1837 can be found well struck, as can be the later variations within the Liberty Seated type. Barber, Mercury, and Roosevelt dimes are easy to find in just about any grade desired.

Proofs are most readily available from the Liberty Seated era to the present and are sometimes included in type sets, usually answering the call for sharply struck pieces, as most (but not all) were made with care.

FOR THE COLLECTOR AND INVESTOR: DIMES AS A SPECIALTY

Dimes have been a very popular denomination to collect on a systematic basis. Generally, interest is separated into different eras. Those of the early years, the Draped Bust and Capped Bust issues, 1796 to 1837, are enthusiastically sought not only for dates and major varieties (as, for example, those listed in the charts to follow), but also by die varieties. Aficionados use the book *Early United States Dimes, 1796–1837*, whose listings are by JR numbers, for John Reich, the designer of the Capped Bust silver issues. The John Reich Collectors Society, publisher of the *John Reich Journal*, serves as a forum for the exchange of ideas and new information.

Among early varieties, the 1796, 1797 16 stars, and 1797 13 stars are each rare in all grades. Dimes with the Heraldic Eagle reverse, 1798–1807, are generally scarce, but not prohibitively rare, although Mint State coins are elusive. Among the reverse dies some were shared with contemporary quarter eagles of like design and diameter—feasible as there is no indication of denomination on them. Indeed, there was no mark of value on any dime until 1809.

Among Classic Head dimes of the 1809–1828 years, the 1822 is the key date and is especially rare in high grades. Among the modified Classic Head dimes of 1829–1837, all varieties listed in this book are available without difficulty. An example of how a newly discovered variety can be considered unique or exceedingly rare, and later be recognized as plentiful, is provided by the 1830, 30 Over 29 overdate, first publicized by Don Taxay in 1970 in *Scott's Comprehensive Catalogue of United States Coinage* (cover-dated 1971). The overdate was then considered one of a kind, but since then dozens more have been identified.

Liberty Seated dimes of the various types have been a popular specialty over a long period of time. There are no impossible rarities except for the unique 1873-CC Without Arrows, but certain other varieties are very hard to find, including the Carson City issues of the early 1870s.

Barber dimes can be collected by date and mint from 1892 to 1916, except for the 1894-S, of which only 24 are believed to have been struck, with only about 10 accounted for today. The other varieties range from common to scarce. Mercury dimes, 1916–1945, have an enthusiastic following. The key issues are 1916-D (in particular); 1921; 1921-D; 1942, 2 Over 1; and 1942-D, 2 Over 1. Roosevelt dimes from 1946 to date can easily be collected by date and mint and are very popular.

RECOMMENDED READING

Ahwash, Kamal M. *Encyclopedia of United States Liberty Seated Dimes, 1837–1891*, Kamal Press, 1977.

Davis, David; Logan, Russell; Lovejoy, Allen; McCloskey, John; and Subjack, William. *Early United States Dimes, 1796–1837*, Ypsilanti, MI, 1984.

Fivaz, Bill, and Stanton, J.T. *The Cherrypickers' Guide to Rare Die Varieties* (5th ed., vol. II), Atlanta, GA, 2012.

Flynn, Kevin. *The 1894-S Dime: A Mystery Unraveled*, Rancocas, NJ, 2005.

Flynn, Kevin. *The Authoritative Reference on Roosevelt Dimes*, Brooklyn, NY, 2001.

Greer, Brian. *The Complete Guide to Liberty Seated Dimes*, Virginia Beach, VA, 2005.

Lange, David W. *The Complete Guide to Mercury Dimes* (2nd ed.), Virginia Beach, VA, 2005.

Lawrence, David. *The Complete Guide to Barber Dimes*, Virginia Beach, VA, 1991.

DRAPED BUST, SMALL EAGLE REVERSE (1796–1797)

Designer probably Gilbert Stuart; engraver Robert Scot; weight 2.70 grams; composition .8924 silver, .1076 copper; approx. diameter 19 mm; reeded edge. All coined at Philadelphia Mint.

Shown 1.5x actual size.
John Reich–2.

History. Dimes were first minted for circulation in 1796. There are no records of publicity surrounding their debut. The coins featured the Draped Bust obverse, as used on cents and other silver coins, combined with the Small Eagle reverse. Some 1796 dimes exhibit prooflike surfaces, suggesting that they may have been "presentation pieces," but no records exist to confirm this possibility.

Striking and Sharpness. Most dimes of this type have weakness or problems in one area or another, usually more so on those dated 1797. Points to check for sharpness include the hair of Miss Liberty, the drapery lines on the bust, the centers of the stars, and, on the reverse, the breast and wing feathers of the eagle. Also check for adjustment marks. A sharply struck coin is a goal, not necessarily a reality. Sharp striking and excellent eye appeal add dramatically to the value.

Availability. This is the rarest and most expensive type in the dime series. Within any desired grade, examples should be selected with great care, as many have problems of one sort or another. MS coins are especially rare; when seen they are usually dated 1796. Dimes of 1797 are much rarer in all grades, and nearly impossible to find in MS-63 or finer.

F-12, 15 (Fine). *Obverse:* Wear is more extensive than at VF, particularly noticeable on the hair, face, and bosom, and the stars appear larger. About half the hair detail remains, most noticeably behind the neck and shoulder. The rim may be partially worn away and blend into the field. *Reverse:* Wear is more extensive than at VF. Feather details are diminished, with fewer than half remaining on the wings. The wreath and lettering are worn further, and the rim is usually weak in areas, although some dentils can be seen.

VF-20, 30 (Very Fine). *Obverse:* The higher-relief areas of hair are well worn at VF-20, less so at 30. The drapery and bosom show extensive wear. The stars are worn, making them appear larger than normal. *Reverse:* The body of the eagle shows few if any feathers, while the wings have about half of the feathers visible, depending on the strike. At VF-30 more than half of the feathers may show. The leaves lack most detail and are in outline form. Scattered, non-disfiguring marks are normal for this and lower grades. Any major defects should be noted separately.

EF-40, 45 (Extremely Fine). *Obverse:* More wear than at AU is evident on the upper hair area and the ribbon, and on the drapery and bosom. Excellent detail remains in low-relief areas of the hair. The stars show wear, as do the date and letters. Luster, if present at all, is minimal and in protected areas. *Reverse:* The eagle (the focal point to check) shows more wear than at AU. Many feathers remain on the interior areas of the wings. Additional wear is on the wreath and letters, but many details are present. Some luster may be seen in protected areas, and if present is slightly more abundant than on the obverse.

AU-50, 53, 55, 58 (About Uncirculated). *Obverse:* Light wear is seen on the hair area above the ear and extending to the left of the forehead, on the ribbon, and on the bosom, more so at AU-50 than at 53 or 55. An AU-58 coin has minimal traces of wear. Regarding luster: an AU-50 coin has luster in protected areas among the stars and letters, with little in the open fields or on the portrait. At AU-58, most luster is present in the fields, but is worn away on the highest parts of the motifs. *Reverse:* Light wear is seen on the eagle's body (note: the higher parts of this area might be lightly struck) and the edges of the wings. Light wear is seen on the wreath and lettering. Luster is the best key to actual wear. This ranges from perhaps 20% remaining in protected areas (at AU-50) to nearly full mint bloom (at AU-58).

MS-60 to 70 (Mint State). *Obverse:* At MS-60, some abrasion and contact marks are evident, most noticeably on the cheek, the drapery, and the right field. Luster is present, but may be dull or lifeless, and interrupted in patches. At MS-63, contact marks are very few, and abrasion is hard to detect except under magnification, although this type is sometimes graded liberally due to its rarity. An MS-65 coin has no abrasion, and contact marks are so minute as to require magnification. Luster should be full and rich. Coins graded above MS-65 are more theoretical than actual for this type—but they do exist, and are defined by having fewer marks as perfection is approached. *Reverse:* Comments apply as for the obverse, except that abrasion and marks are most noticeable on the eagle at the center, a situation complicated by the fact that this area was sometimes lightly struck. The field area is small and is protected by lettering and the wreath, and in any given grade shows fewer marks than on the obverse.

1797, 16 Stars

1797, 13 Stars

Shown 2x actual size.

	Mintage	Cert	Avg	%MS	VF-20	EF-40	AU-50	MS-60	MS-62	MS-63	MS-64	Recent Auction Record
1796	22,135	306	35.0	17	$7,000	$11,500	$16,500	$26,000	$32,500	$40,000	$55,000 **(a)**	$881,250, MS-67, June 2014
1797, All kinds	25,261											
1797, 16 Stars		72	33.7	13	7,500	12,000	18,000	35,000	40,000	47,500		$35,250, MS-62, April 2014
1797, 13 Stars		30	26.4	10	8,000	13,500	20,000	55,000	67,500	82,500		$38,188, AU-58, April 2014

a. Value in MS-65 is $85,000.

DRAPED BUST, HERALDIC EAGLE REVERSE (1798–1807)

Designer Robert Scot; weight 2.70 grams; composition .8924 silver, .1076 copper; approx. diameter 19 mm; reeded edge. All coined at Philadelphia Mint.

Shown 1.5x actual size.
John Reich–3.

History. Dimes of this style were minted each year from 1798 to 1807 (with the exception of 1799 and 1805). The designs follow those of other silver coins of the era.

Striking and Sharpness. Nearly all have one area or another of light striking. On the obverse, check the hair details and drapery lines, and the star centers. On the reverse, the upper right of the shield and the adjacent part of the eagle's wing often are soft, and several or even most stars may be lightly defined (sharp stars show sharply peaked centers); high parts of the clouds are often weak. Dentils are likely to be weak or missing in areas on either side. Expect to compromise on the strike; a sharply struck coin is a goal, not necessarily a reality. Certain reverse dies of this type were also used to coin quarter eagles. Sharp striking and excellent eye appeal dramatically add to a Draped Bust dime's value, this being particularly true for 1805 and 1807 (which are usually weakly struck, especially 1807), the dates most often seen in MS.

Availability. Although certain die varieties are rare, the basic years are available, with 1805 and 1807 being the most often seen. As a class, MS coins are rare. Again, when seen they are usually dated 1805 or 1807, and have areas of striking weakness. Coins of 1801 through 1804 are scarce in VF and higher grades, very scarce in AU and better.

F-12, 15 (Fine). *Obverse:* Wear is more extensive than at VF, particularly noticeable on the hair, face, and bosom. The stars are worn and appear larger than normal. About half the hair detail remains, most noticeably behind the neck and shoulder. The rim may be partially worn away and blend into the field. *Reverse:* Wear is more extensive than at VF, with the shield and wing feathers being points to observe. About half of the feathers are visible (depending on striking). E PLURIBUS UNUM may have a few letters worn away. The clouds all seem to be connected. The stars are weak. Parts of the border and lettering may be weak.

VF-20, 30 (Very Fine). *Obverse:* The higher-relief areas of hair are well worn at VF-20, less so at VF-30. The drapery and bosom show extensive wear. The stars are worn, making them appear larger than normal. *Reverse:* Wear is greater than at EF, including on the shield and wing feathers. The star centers are flat. Other areas have lost detail, as well. E PLURIBUS UNUM is complete (this incuse feature tended to wear away slowly).

EF-40, 45 (Extremely Fine). *Obverse:* More wear than at AU is evident on the upper hair area and the ribbon and on the drapery and bosom. Excellent detail remains in low-relief areas of the hair. The stars show wear, as do the date and letters. Luster, if present at all, is minimal and in protected areas. *Reverse:* The neck lacks feather detail on its highest points. Feathers have lost some detail near the edges of the wings, and some areas of the horizontal lines in the shield may be blended together, particularly at the right (an area that is also susceptible to weak striking). Some traces of luster may be seen, less so at EF-40 than at EF-45.

AU-50, 53, 55, 58 (About Uncirculated). *Obverse:* Light wear is seen on the hair area above the ear and extending to the left of the forehead, on the ribbon, and on the drapery at the shoulder, more so at AU-50 than at 53 or 55. An AU-58 coin has minimal traces of wear. Regarding luster: an AU-50 coin has luster in protected areas among the stars and letters, with little in the open fields or on the portrait. At AU-58, most luster is present in the fields, but is worn away on the highest parts of the motifs. *Reverse:* Comments apply as for the obverse, except that the eagle's neck, the tips and top of the wings, the clouds, and the tail now show noticeable wear, as do other features. As

always, a familiarity with a given die variety will help differentiate striking weakness from actual wear. Luster ranges from perhaps 20% remaining in protected areas (at AU-50) to nearly full mint bloom (at AU-58). Often the reverse of this type will retain much more luster than the obverse.

MS-60 to 70 (Mint State). *Obverse:* At MS-60 some abrasion and contact marks are evident, most noticeably on the cheek, the drapery at the shoulder, and the right field. Luster is present, but may be dull or lifeless, and interrupted in patches. At MS-63, contact marks are very few, and abrasion is hard to detect

except under magnification. An MS-65 coin has no abrasion, and contact marks are so minute as to require magnification. Luster should be full and rich. Coins graded above MS-65 are more theoretical than actual for this type—but they do exist, and are defined by having fewer marks as perfection is approached. *Reverse:* Comments apply as for the obverse, except that abrasion and marks are most noticeable on the eagle's neck, the tips of the wing, and the tail. The field area is complex, without much open space, given the stars above the eagle, the arrows and olive branch, and other features. Accordingly, marks are not as noticeable as on the obverse.

1798, 8 Over 7	1798, 8 Over 7, 16 Stars on Reverse	1798, 8 Over 7, 13 Stars on Reverse	1798, Large 8	1798, Small 8

Shown 2x actual size. *Shown 2x actual size.*

1804, 13 Stars on Reverse	1804, 14 Stars on Reverse	1805, 4 Berries	1805, 5 Berries

	Mintage	Cert	Avg	%MS	VF-20	EF-40	AU-50	MS-60	MS-62	MS-63	MS-64	Recent Auction Record
1798, All kinds	27,550											
1798, 8 Over 7, 16 Stars on Reverse		67	34.6	22	$2,500	$3,500	$5,250	$9,000	$15,000	$20,000		$88,125, MS-65, November 2013
1798, 8 Over 7, 13 Stars on Reverse		17	31.5	18	7,000	10,000	20,000	55,000				$58,750, MS-62, January 2014
1798, Large 8		90	35.9	18	2,500	3,750	4,600	8,000	15,000	20,000	$35,000 (a)	$70,500, MS-63, June 2014
1798, Small 8		n/a	n/a	n/a	3,500	5,500	12,500	25,000				$103,500, MS-64, January 2012
1800	21,760	67	32.9	9	3,000	4,000	8,000	22,500	35,000	42,000		$352,500, MS-66, June 2014
1801	34,640	55	23.7	4	3,750	6,000	11,000	30,000	35,000	48,500		$4,406, VF-25, February 2014
1802	10,975	61	27.1	10	5,000	10,000	17,500	35,000	65,000			$67,563, MS-62, September 2013
1803	33,040	63	25.0	2	3,200	6,000	11,500	48,000				$35,250, AU-53, August 2013
1804, All kinds	8,265											
1804, 13 Stars on Reverse		22	28.1	0	15,000	30,000	60,000					$48,175, EF-45, April 2013
1804, 14 Stars on Reverse		9	38.4	0	20,000	40,000	85,000					$367,188, MS-63, April 2013
1805, All kinds	120,780											
1805, 4 Berries		4	29.8	25	2,000	3,000	4,000	7,500	10,000	14,000	22,500 (b)	$49,938, MS-66, April 2014
1805, 5 Berries		434	33.3	23	2,200	3,400	4,500	9,000	12,500	20,000	30,000	$1,998, VF-20, June 2013
1807	165,000	347	38.4	25	2,000	2,750	3,800	6,500	9,000	12,500	20,000 (c)	$55,813, MS-65, June 2014

a. Value in MS-65 is $50,000. **b.** Value in MS-65 is $40,000. **c.** Value in MS-65 is $38,500.

CAPPED BUST, VARIETY 1, WIDE BORDER (1809–1828)

Designer John Reich; weight 2.70 grams; composition .8924 silver, .1076 copper; approx. diameter 18.8 mm; reeded edge. All coined at Philadelphia Mint.

Shown 1.5x actual size.
John Reich–1.

History. Dimes of this design were struck intermittently from 1809 to 1828. The design, by John Reich, closely follows that inaugurated with the Capped Bust half dollars of 1807.

Striking and Sharpness. Many if not most have areas of light striking. On the obverse, check the star centers, the hair details, and the drapery at the bosom. On the reverse, check the eagle, especially the area in and around the upper right of the shield. Dentils are sometimes weak, but are usually better defined on the reverse than on the obverse. The height of the rims on both sides can vary, and coins with a low rim or rims tend to show wear more quickly.

Availability. There are no extremely rare dates in this series, so all are available to collectors. In MS, most are scarce and some rare. Those exhibiting a strong strike, with Full Details, command a premium, especially the earlier dates.

EF-40, 45 (Extremely Fine). *Obverse:* Wear is more extensive than at AU, most noticeable on the higher areas of the hair. The cap shows more wear, as does the cheek. Stars still show their centers (unless lightly struck, and many are). Luster, if present, is in protected areas among the star points and close to the portrait. *Reverse:* The wings show wear on the higher areas of the feathers (particularly on the right wing), and some details are lost. Feathers in the neck are light. The eagle's claws show wear. Luster may be present in protected areas, even if there is little or none on the obverse.

AU-50, 53, 55, 58 (About Uncirculated). *Obverse:* Light wear is seen on the cap, the hair below LIB-ERTY, the hair near the clasp, and the drapery at the bosom. At AU-58, the luster is extensive except in the open area of the field, especially to the right. At AU-50 and 53, luster remains only in protected areas. As is true of all high grades, sharpness of strike can affect the perception of wear. *Reverse:* Wear is evident on the eagle's neck, the top of the wings, and the claws. At AU-50 and 53, there is significant luster, more than on the obverse. An AU-58 has nearly full luster.

MS-60 to 70 (Mint State). *Obverse:* At MS-60 some abrasion and contact marks are evident, most noticeably on the cheek and on the area near the drapery clasp. Luster is present, but may be dull or lifeless, and interrupted in patches. At MS-63, contact marks are very few, and abrasion is hard to detect except under magnification. An MS-65 coin has no abrasion, and contact marks are so minute as to require magnification. Luster should be full and rich. Grades above MS-65 have fewer marks as perfection is approached. *Reverse:* Comments apply as for the obverse, except that abrasion and contact marks are most noticeable on the eagle's neck, the top of the wings, the claws, and the flat band that surrounds the incuse motto. The field is mainly protected by design elements and does not show abrasion as much as does the obverse.

1811, 11 Over 09

1814, Small Date
Shown 2x actual size.

1814, Large Date

1814, STATESOFAMERICA
Shown 2x actual size.

1820, Large 0
Shown 2x actual size.

1820, Small 0

1820, STATESOFAMERICA
Shown 2x actual size.

1821, Large Date

1821, Small Date

Shown 2x actual size.

1823, 3 Over 2

Shown 2x actual size.

1823, 3 Over 2, Small E's

1823, 3 Over 2, Large E's

1824, 4 Over 2

1824 and 1827,
Flat Top 1

1824 and 1827,
Pointed Top 1

1828, Large Date,
Curl Base 2

1828, Small Date,
Square Base 2

The Small Date is of Variety 2 (see next section);
for comparison purposes, both are illustrated here.

	Mintage	Cert	Avg	%MS	EF-40	AU-50	MS-60	MS-62	MS-63	MS-64	MS-65	Recent Auction Record
1809	51,065	78	30.3	15	$1,800	$2,500	$4,500	$5,500	$7,200	$12,500	$22,500	$31,725, MS-64, June 2014
1811, 11 Over 09	65,180	74	35.7	22	1,700	2,200	4,000	4,500	6,500	10,000	32,500	$8,225, MS-64, February 2014
1814, All kinds	421,500											
1814, Small Date		31	42.0	29	725	1,200	2,500	3,500	5,000	7,500	15,000	$5,875, MS-64, January 2014
1814, Large Date		156	49.4	48	600	1,000	2,000	3,000	4,000	6,500	12,500	$14,100, MS-65, November 2013
1814, STATESOFAMERICA		20	23.6	0	900	1,500	3,000	3,800	5,000	7,000	13,000	$374, VG-10, February 2012
1820, All kinds	942,587											
1820, Large 0		184	47.5	42	500	675	1,400	2,000	2,750	5,000	12,500	$1,704, MS-62, December 2013
1820, Small 0		55	32.7	11	600	700	1,500	2,500	3,500	5,500	13,000	$1,293, MS, February 2014
1820, STATESOFAMERICA		24	40.9	29	750	1,250	3,000	3,500	5,000	6,500	15,000	$67,563, MS-66, June 2014
1821, All kinds	1,186,512											
1821, Small Date		65	42.6	20	525	850	1,750	2,200	3,500	5,500	14,000	$5,581, MS-64, March 2013
1821, Large Date		264	42.9	26	520	800	1,700	2,000	3,250	5,000	13,500	$19,975, MS-65, April 2014
1822	100,000	69	20.8	9	8,000	11,000	15,000	20,000	26,000	38,000		$70,500, MS-66, February 2013
1823, 3 Over 2, All kinds	440,000											
1823, 3 Over 2, Small E's		78	48.5	29	450	800	1,500	2,000	3,000	5,000	14,000	$8,813, MS-65, June 2014
1823, 3 Over 2, Large E's		58	40.2	28	450	800	1,500	2,000	3,000	5,000	15,000	$7,050, MS-65, April 2013
1824, 4 Over 2, Flat Top 1 in 10 C.	100,000	2	22.5	0	800	1,500	2,250	2,500	4,000	8,500	17,500	$6,169, MS, February 2014
1824, 4 Over 2, Pointed Top 1 in 10 C.	*	1	20.0	0	4,250							
1825	410,000	103	45.0	39	500	900	2,000	2,500	3,500	4,500	12,000	$4,700, MS-64, June 2013
1827, Flat Top 1 in 10 C.	1,215,000	1	35.0	0	1,800	3,000						
1827, Pointed Top 1 in 10 C.	*	22	35.5	9	450	700	1,500	2,000	3,000	4,500	13,500	$28,200, MS-66, June 2014
1828, Variety 1, Large Date, Curl Base 2	**	38	40.5	13	625	1,200	2,250	3,500	5,500	9,000	18,000	$4,113, AU-58, November 2013

* Included in number above. ** 1828, Variety 1 and Variety 2, have a combined mintage of 125,000.

Proof Capped Bust Dimes, Variety 1, Wide Border

PF-60 to 70 (Proof). Proof Capped Bust dimes of 1809 to 1828 were struck in small numbers, likely mostly as part of presentation sets. As is the case with any and all early Proofs, a collector should insist on a coin with deeply and fully (not partially) mirrored surfaces, well struck, and with good contrast. Carefully examine deeply toned pieces (deep toning can mask the true nature of a coin, e.g., if it is not a true Proof, or if it has been cleaned or repaired). More than a few pieces attributed as "Proofs" are not Proofs at all. *Obverse and Reverse:* Proofs of this type can have areas of light striking, such as at the star centers. Proofs that are extensively cleaned and have many hairlines, or that are dull and grainy, are lower level, such as PF-60 to 62. These are not of great interest to specialists unless they are of rare die varieties.

A PF-64 has fewer hairlines, but they are obvious, perhaps slightly distracting. A PF-65 should have fewer still and full mirrored surfaces (no trace of cloudiness or dullness). PF-66 should have hairlines so delicate that magnification is needed to see them. Above that, a Proof should be free of such lines. Grading is highly subjective with early Proofs, and eye appeal also is a major factor.

Proof Capped Bust Dime:
Variety 1, Wide Border
Shown 1.5x actual size.
John Reich–12.

	Est Mintage	Cert	Finest	PF-60	PF-63	PF-64	PF-65	Recent Auction Record
1820	2–5	n/a	n/a	$12,000	$20,000	$40,000	$65,000	$80,500, PF-66, February 2008
1821	5–8	1	PF-65	8,000	18,000	30,000	40,000	$55,200, PF-65, April 2005
1822 (extremely rare)	2–5	4	PF-66	15,000	25,000	50,000	70,000	$440,625, PF-66Cam, June 2014
1824, 4 Over 2	4–6	n/a	n/a	8,000	18,000	30,000	40,000	$42,550, PF-65, July 2005
1825	4–6	1	PF-66	8,000	18,000	30,000	40,000	$18,400, PF-63, June 2011
1827	10–15	n/a	n/a	8,000	18,000	30,000	40,000	$120,750, PF-67, February 2008

CAPPED BUST, VARIETY 2, MODIFIED DESIGN (1828–1837)

Designer John Reich; weight 2.70 grams; composition .8924 silver, .1076 copper; approx. diameter 18.5 mm; reeded edge. Changed to 2.67 grams, .900 fine in 1837. All coined at Philadelphia Mint.

Shown 1.5x actual size.
John Reich–7.

History. New equipment at the U.S. Mint was used to make the Small Date 1828 dimes, and those subsequent. The slightly modified design includes smaller dentils or beads in the border and other minor differences, and they are of uniform diameter. The 2 in the Small Date 1828 dime has a square (not curled) base.

Striking and Sharpness. Most dimes of this variety are fairly well struck, with fewer irregularities of strike than those of 1809 to 1828. On the obverse, check the hair and the brooch. The stars usually are sharp, but don't overlook them. On the reverse, check the details of the eagle. The dentils usually are sharp.

Availability. All dates are readily available, but certain die varieties range from rare to extremely rare. In MS the dates of the early 1830s to 1835 are the most readily available. Most have nice eye appeal.

EF-40, 45 (Extremely Fine). *Obverse:* The rims are more uniform than for the 1809–1828 type, striking is usually very sharp, and the wear occurs evenly on both sides. Wear is most noticeable on the higher areas of the hair. The cap shows wear, as does the cheek. Stars still show their centers. Luster, if present, is in protected areas among the star points and close to the portrait. *Reverse:* The wings show wear on the higher areas of the feathers (particularly on the right wing), and some details are lost. Feathers in the neck are light. The eagle's claws show wear. Luster may be present in protected areas.

AU-50, 53, 55, 58 (About Uncirculated). *Obverse:* The rims are more uniform than for the 1809–1828 type, striking is usually very sharp, and any abrasion occurs evenly on both sides. Light wear is seen on the cap, the hair below LIBERTY, the hair near the clasp, and the drapery at the bosom. At AU-50 and 53, luster remains only in protected areas. At AU-58, the luster is extensive except in the open area of the field, especially to the right. As is true of all high grades, sharpness of strike can affect the perception of wear. *Reverse:* Wear is evident on the eagle's neck, the top of the wings, and the claws. At AU-50 and 53, there still is significant luster. At AU-58, luster is nearly full.

MS-60 to 70 (Mint State). *Obverse:* The rims are more uniform than for the 1809–1828 type, striking is usually very sharp, and any abrasion occurs evenly on both sides. At MS-60, some abrasion and contact marks are evident, most noticeably on the cheek and on the area near the drapery clasp. Luster is present, but may be dull or lifeless, and interrupted in patches. At MS-63, contact marks are very few, and abrasion is hard to detect except under magnification. An MS-65 coin has no abrasion, and contact marks are so minute as to require magnification. Luster should be full and rich. Grades above MS-65 are seen now and again and are defined by having fewer marks as perfection is approached. *Reverse:* Abrasion and contact marks are most noticeable on the eagle's neck, the top of the wings, the claws, and the flat band that surrounds the incuse motto.

1828, Large Date, Curl Base 2   1828, Small Date, Square Base 2   1829, Curl Base 2

The Large Date is of Variety 1 (see previous section); for comparison purposes, both are illustrated here.

1829, Small 10 C.   1829, Medium 10 C.   1829, Large 10 C.
Shown 2x actual size.

1830, 30 Over 29   1830, Large 10 C.   1830, Small 10 C.

1833, Last 3 Normal   1833, Last 3 High

1834, Small 4   1834, Large 4

	Mintage	Cert	Avg	%MS	EF-40	AU-50	MS-60	MS-62	MS-63	MS-64	MS-65	Recent Auction Record
1828, Variety 2, Small Date, Square Base 2	*	89	44.9	34	$400	$750	$1,300	$1,650	$2,500	$4,000	$10,000	$2,820, MS-63, April 2013
1829, All kinds	770,000											$7,638, VG-8, June 2014
1829, Curl Base 2 (a)		23	9.1	0	(b)							$16,450, MS-66, November 2013
1829, Small 10 C.		274	50.6	45	375	475	1,200	1,750	2,200	3,750	8,000	$717, AU-55, August 2013
1829, Medium 10 C.		57	48.3	47	400	600	1,700	2,200	3,200	4,000	8,500	$259, F-12, November 2013
1829, Large 10 C.		24	46.4	29	425	750	2,000	2,800	4,000	6,000	12,000	$23,500, MS-66, June 2014
1830, All kinds	510,000											$35,250, MS-65, June 2014
1830, 30 Over 29 (c)		39	43.6	15	450	650	1,300	1,700	4,000	6,500	10,000	$1,331, MS-63, January 2012
1830, Large 10 C.		228	48.2	42	325	500	1,200	2,000	2,500	4,000	9,000	$8,225, MS-65, January 2014
1830, Small 10 C.		38	37.6	13	375	650	1,200	2,000	2,500	4,000	9,000	$3,819, MS-64, March 2013
1831	771,350	325	51.4	40	300	450	1,000	1,400	2,000	3,500	7,500	$18,800, MS-67, October 2013
1832	522,500	327	50.7	36	300	450	1,000	1,400	2,000	3,500	7,500	$17,625, MS-66, April 2013
1833, All kinds	485,000											
1833		366	48.4	31	300	450	1,000	1,400	2,000	3,500	7,500	$2,101, MS-63, October 2013
1833, Last 3 High		60	40.6	27	300	450	1,000	1,400	2,000	3,500	7,500	$28,200, MS-68, August 2013
1834, All kinds	635,000											$12,925, MS-66, March 2013
1834, Small 4		194	53.5	43	300	450	1,500	1,850	2,250	4,500	9,000	$44,063, MS-67, December 2013
1834, Large 4		219	43.7	22	300	450	1,000	1,400	2,000	3,500	7,500	$30,550, MS-66, November 2013
1835	1,410,000	594	45.8	28	300	450	1,000	1,400	2,000	3,500	7,500	
1836	1,190,000	279	46.7	31	300	450	1,000	1,400	2,000	3,500	7,500	
1837	359,500	168	45.9	30	300	450	1,000	1,400	2,000	3,500	7,500	

* 1828, Variety 1 and Variety 2, have a combined mintage of 125,000. **a.** Only one working die for the 1829 dime coinage featured a curled 2, rather than the normal square-based 2. Nearly all known specimens are in low grades. **b.** Value in F-12 is $15,000; in VF-20, $40,000. **c.** The tail of the 2 is evident to the right of the lower curve of the 3. The very top of the 9 is evident below the 0. Surface doubling from the initial 1829 punch is also evident on the 8. There are three of four known dies of this overdate; all are similar and command similar values. Today the variety is known to be more common than thought in the early 1970s, when it was first publicized.

Proof Capped Bust Dimes, Variety 2, Modified Design

PF-60 to 70 (Proof). Proofs were made of each year from 1828 to 1837, and are rare. Beware of so-called Proofs that have deeply toned surfaces or fields that show patches of mint frost. Use caution and take your time as you inspect coins for your collection. *Obverse and Reverse:* Generally, Proof dimes of this type are of better quality than the 1809–1828 type and have Full Details in almost all areas. Proofs that are extensively cleaned and have many hairlines, or that are dull and grainy, are lower level, such as PF-60 to 62. While every Capped Bust Proof deserves attention, those of lower levels are not of great interest to specialists unless they are of rare die varieties. With medium hairlines, an assigned grade of PF-64 may be in order, and with relatively few hairlines, PF-65. PF-66 should have hairlines so delicate that magnification is needed to see them. Above that, a Proof should be free of such lines.

Proof Capped Bust Dime:
Variety 2, Modified Design
Shown 1.5x actual size.
John Reich–4.

	Est Mintage	Cert	Finest	PF-60	PF-63	PF-64	PF-65	Recent Auction Record
1828	4–6	1	PF-65	$8,500	$15,000	$22,500	$32,500	$29,900, PF-65, February 2008
1829	6–10	3	PF-66	7,500	13,500	20,000	30,000	$37,375, PF-66, June 2002
1830 (a)	5–8	3	PF-65	7,500	13,500	20,000	30,000	$18,800, PF-63, April 2014
1831	15–25	14	PF-66	7,500	13,500	20,000	30,000	$27,025, PF-65, March 2013
1832 (extremely rare)	2–5	1	PF-64					
1833	5–10	2	PF-66	8,500	15,000	25,000	40,000	$13,800, PF-64, January 2009
1834	5–10	8	PF-67	7,500	13,500	20,000	30,000	$21,850, PF-65, August 2011
1835	5–10	11	PF-67	7,500	13,500	20,000	30,000	$41,125, PF-65Cam, April 2014
1836	2–5	n/a	n/a	8,500	15,000	25,000	37,500	$6,900, PF-66, September 1998
1837	2–5	n/a	n/a	8,500	15,000	25,000	40,000	$23,000, MS-64 Specimen, April 2010

a. Values are for JR-6. A very few Proof versions of the 1830, 30 Over 29 dime are known. A PF-60, JR-4, sold at auction in January 2012 for $5,750.

LIBERTY SEATED, VARIETY 1, NO STARS ON OBVERSE (1837–1838)

Designer Christian Gobrecht; weight 2.67 grams; composition .900 silver, .100 copper; diameter 17.9 mm; reeded edge; mints: Philadelphia, New Orleans.

Shown 1.5x actual size.

History. The first of the Liberty Seated designs, with no stars on the obverse, was inspired by Christian Gobrecht's silver dollar of 1836. The reverse features a different motif, with a wreath and inscription. This type was made only at the Philadelphia Mint in 1837 and at the New Orleans Mint in 1838.

Striking and Sharpness. Check the highest parts of the Liberty Seated figure (especially the head and horizontal shield stripes) and, on the reverse, the leaves. Check the dentils on both sides.

Availability. The 1837 is readily available in all grades, including MS-65 and higher. The 1838-O is usually seen with wear and is a rarity if truly MS-63 or above. Beware coins with deep or vivid iridescent toning, which often masks friction or evidence of wear. Coins with uniformly grainy etching on both sides have been processed and should be avoided.

AU-50, 53, 55, 58 (About Uncirculated). *Obverse:* Light wear is seen on the thighs and knees, bosom, and head. At AU-50 and 53, luster is less than at 58, where the luster is extensive but incomplete. Friction is seen in the large open field. *Reverse:* Wear is evident on the leaves and ribbon. At AU-50 and 53, there still is significant luster, more than on the obverse, as the design elements protect the small field areas. An AU-58 coin has nearly full luster, more so than on the obverse.

MS-60 to 70 (Mint State). *Obverse:* At MS-60, some abrasion and contact marks are evident, most noticeably on the bosom, thighs, and knees. Luster is present, but may be dull or lifeless, and interrupted in patches in the large open field. At MS-63, contact marks are very few, and abrasion is hard to detect except under magnification. An MS-65 coin has no abrasion, and contact marks are so minute as to require magnification. Luster should be full and rich.

Reverse: Comments apply as for the obverse, except that abrasion and contact marks are most noticeable on the highest parts of the leaves and the ribbon. The field is mainly protected by design elements and does not show abrasion as much as does the open-field obverse on a given coin.

1837, Large Date   1837, Small Date
Shown 2x actual size.

	Mintage	Cert	Avg	%MS	AU-50	MS-60	MS-62	MS-63	MS-64	MS-65	MS-66	Recent Auction Record
1837, All kinds	682,500											
1837, Large Date		404	50.5	41	$700	$1,100	$1,400	$1,800	$4,000	$7,750	$10,000	$44,063, MS-68, June 2014
1837, Small Date		103	49.6	43	725	1,200	1,500	2,000	4,500	8,500	15,000	$36,719, MS-67, November 2013
18380	406,034	222	39.4	17	1,200	3,000	4,200	6,750	11,000	18,000	26,000	$10,575, MS-64, November 2013

Proof Liberty Seated Dimes, Variety 1, No Stars on Obverse

PF-60 to 70 (Proof). Proofs of 1837 were struck in an unknown small quantity. The mintage appears to have been greater than that of the half dime of the same year. Examples have deep-mirror surfaces and are mostly quite attractive. Carefully examine deeply toned pieces to ensure the toning does not hide flaws. *Obverse and*

Reverse: Proofs that are extensively cleaned and have many hairlines, or that are dull and grainy, are lower level, such as PF-60 to 62. These command less attention in the marketplace than more visually appealing pieces. The dime Proofs of this year often were cleaned, resulting in coins that have lost much of their mirror surface.

With medium hairlines and good reflectivity, PF-64 is an appropriate designation, and with relatively few hairlines, PF-65. In various grades hairlines are most easily seen in the obverse field. PF-66 should have hairlines so delicate that magnification is needed to see them. Above that, a Proof should be free of such lines.

Proof Liberty Seated Dime:
Variety 1, No Stars on Obverse
Shown 1.5x actual size.

	Est Mintage	Cert	Finest	PF-60	PF-63	PF-64	PF-65	Recent Auction Record
1837	25–35	22	PF-66	$6,000	$12,000	$18,500	$32,500	$41,125, PF-65, June 2014

LIBERTY SEATED, VARIETIES 2 AND 3, STARS ON OBVERSE (1838–1860)

Designer Christian Gobrecht; weight 2.67 grams (reduced to 2.49 grams 1853–1860); composition .900 silver, .100 copper; diameter 17.9 mm; reeded edge; mints: Philadelphia, New Orleans, San Francisco.

Variety 2, Stars on Obverse
(1838–1853, 1856–1860)
Shown 1.5x actual size.

Variety 3, Stars on Obverse,
Arrows at Date (1853–1855)
Shown 1.5x actual size.

No Drapery From Elbow,
Tilted Shield (1838–1840)

Drapery From Elbow,
Upright Shield (1840–1891)

Shown 2x actual size.

History. Liberty Seated dimes of the Stars on Obverse varieties were first made without drapery at Miss Liberty's elbow. These early issues have the shield tilted sharply to the left. Drapery was added in 1840, and the shield reoriented, this being the style of the 1840s onward. Variety 3 coins (minted in part of 1853, and all of 1854 and 1855) have arrows at the date, signifying the reduction in weight brought on by the Coinage Act of February 21, 1853. The earlier design resumed in 1856 at the new weight standard. Liberty Seated dimes were made in large quantities, and circulated widely.

Striking and Sharpness. On the obverse, check the head of Miss Liberty, and the star centers. On the reverse, check the leaves. Check the dentils on both sides. Avoid coins struck from "tired" or overused dies, as evidenced by grainy rather than lustrous fields (on higher-grade coins).

Availability. These dimes are plentiful as a rule, although certain dates and varieties are rare. Most MS coins on the market are dated in the 1850s and are often found MS-63 to MS-65.

EF-40, 45 (Extremely Fine). *Obverse:* More wear than at AU is seen on all areas, especially the thighs and knees, bosom, and head. Little or no luster is seen. *Reverse:* Further wear than at AU is seen on all areas, most noticeably at the leaves to each side of the wreath apex and on the ribbon bow knot. Leaves retain details except on the higher areas.

AU-50, 53, 55, 58 (About Uncirculated). *Obverse:* Light wear is seen on the thighs and knees, bosom, and head. At AU-50 and 53, luster is less than at 58, where the luster is extensive but incomplete. *Reverse:* Wear is evident on the leaves (especially at the top of the wreath) and ribbon. At AU-50 and 53 there is significant luster. An AU-58 coin has nearly full luster, more so than on the obverse, as the design elements protect the small field areas.

MS-60 to 70 (Mint State). *Obverse:* At MS-60 some abrasion and contact marks are evident, most noticeably on the bosom and thighs and knees. Luster is present, but may be dull or lifeless. At MS-63, contact marks are very few, and abrasion is hard to detect except under magnification. An MS-65 coin has no abrasions, and contact marks are so minute as to require magnification. Luster should be full and rich. *Reverse:* Comments apply as for the obverse, except that abrasion and contact marks are most noticeable on the highest parts of the leaves and the ribbon. The field is mainly protected by design elements and does not show abrasion as much as does the open-field obverse on a given coin.

1838, Small Stars

1838, Large Stars

1838, So-Called Partial Drapery

1839-O, Repunched Mintmark

1841-O, Transitional Reverse, Small O

1841-O, Transitional Reverse, Large O

Regular Reverse Style of 1841-O

	Mintage	Cert	Avg	%MS	EF-40	AU-50	MS-60	MS-62	MS-63	MS-64	MS-65	Recent Auction Record
1838, All kinds	1,992,500											
1838, Small Stars		77	56.1	47	$175	$400	$700	$1,000	$1,350	$2,000	$4,000	$3,966, MS, March 2014
1838, Large Stars		318	56.3	60	135	250	375	650	850	1,100	3,000	$11,163, MS-67, August 2013
1838, Partial Drapery (a)		30	55.8	53	200	500	850	1,400	2,000			$345, AU-55, February 2012
1839	1,053,115	176	56.5	56	135	250	400	600	850	1,100	3,000	$14,100, MS-68, August 2013
1839O	1,291,600	95	43.3	22	135	275	450	750	1,400	2,400	6,000	$6,463, MS-64, June 2014
1839O, Repunched Mintmark	*	1	30.0	0	150	325	750	1,000	1,500			$13,800, MS-66 Plus, February 2012
1840, No Drapery	981,500	95	56.5	53	135	250	400	600	850	1,200	4,000	$11,163, MS-67, June 2014
1840O, No Drapery	1,175,000	70	45.7	19	230	800	2,500	3,750	6,000	13,500		$38,188, MS-65, June 2014
1840, Drapery	377,500	37	42.4	16	300	450	1,200	3,000	5,500	10,000		$38,188, MS-64, November 2013
1841 (b)	1,622,500	76	57.1	68	60	140	350	500	650	1,200	3,250	$4,700, MS-65, June 2013
1841O	2,007,500	93	42.3	17	85	225	900	1,200	1,800	2,750	5,000	$19,975, AU-58, April 2014
1841O, TransRev, Small O (c)	*	2	22.5	0								$940, G-6, June 2013
1841O, TransRev, Large O (c)	*	6	25.5	0								$2,611, F-12, January 2014

* Included in number above. **a.** The so-called "partial drapery" is not a design variation; rather, it is evidence of die clashing from the E in DIME on the reverse. **b.** Two examples are known of 1841, No Drapery, Small Stars, Upright Shield. One is a Proof (see next section) and the other is a circulation strike in VF. **c.** The 1841-O Transitional Reverse varieties were struck with a reverse die that was supposed to have been discontinued in 1840, but saw limited use into 1841. Note the closed buds (not open, as in the regular reverse die of 1841); also note that the second leaf from the left (in the group of four leaves to the left of the bow knot) reaches only halfway across the bottom of the U in UNITED.

Chart continued on next page.

	Mintage	Cert	Avg	%MS	EF-40	AU-50	MS-60	MS-62	MS-63	MS-64	MS-65	Recent Auction Record
1842	1,887,500	76	54.1	57	$50	$125	$400	$500	$650	$1,100	$3,500	$4,113, MS-65, April 2014
18420	2,020,000	90	40.5	13	265	1,300	2,500	4,000	5,500	7,500		$9,106, MS-65, October 2013
1843	1,370,000	75	55.1	53	50	125	400	600	800	1,250	3,500	$8,225, MS-66, June 2014
18430	150,000	60	26.2	3	1,900	6,500	18,000					$141,000, MS-62, June 2014
1844	72,500	215	25.1	4	1,200	1,800	4,000	6,000	12,000	20,000	32,500	$30,550, MS-65, October 2013
1845	1,755,000	104	56.5	57	50	125	400	600	800	1,250	3,500	$2,056, MS-65, April 2014
18450	230,000	69	31.1	3	550	1,200	3,500	5,500				$16,450, MS-62, August 2013
1846	31,300	96	27.2	2	2,400	8,500	15,000	20,000	38,000			$47,000, MS-63, June 2014
1847	245,000	57	48.7	28	125	350	950	1,500	2,500	4,500	9,500	$5,581, MS-63, February 2014
1848	451,500	54	53.6	50	85	150	550	600	850	1,500	6,500	$823, MS-63, February 2014
1849	839,000	52	53.6	46	60	125	300	500	900	1,750	4,500	$14,100, MS-66, June 2014
18490	300,000	83	41.3	12	300	750	2,500	3,500	6,000			$6,463, MS-64, June 2014
1850	1,931,500	133	54.2	55	60	125	300	500	700	1,200	5,500	$529, MS-63, January 2014
18500	510,000	38	47.1	18	175	375	1,200	2,000	2,600	4,500	6,500	$3,672, MS-63, October 2013
1851	1,026,500	51	56.6	55	60	125	350	550	850	1,400	5,000	$20,563, MS-67, June 2013
18510	400,000	34	41.1	12	175	450	2,000	3,000	3,750	6,500		$2,115, MS-60, February 2013
1852	1,535,500	115	58.6	75	60	125	300	500	700	1,200	3,250	$6,463, MS-67, June 2014
18520	430,000	54	44.5	26	250	350	1,600	2,000	2,750	4,000		$11,163, MS-65, June 2014
1853, No Arrows	95,000	113	48.6	54	625	725	900	1,100	1,500	2,500	3,500	$6,463, MS-67, November 2013
1853, With Arrows	12,078,010	751	57.5	62	50	175	300	450	675	1,100	2,600	$3,819, MS-66, November 2013
18530	1,100,000	55	44.7	18	275	500	1,750	2,450	3,250	5,000	8,500	$5,288, MS-64, August 2013
1854	4,470,000	217	55.1	60	50	175	300	450	675	1,100	2,600	$5,288, MS-67, June 2014
18540	1,770,000	85	52.2	55	85	200	400	650	1,100	1,500	3,600	$7,638, MS-65, August 2013
1855	2,075,000	82	57.0	66	60	185	325	500	900	1,400	3,400	$18,800, MS-67, June 2014
1856, All kinds	5,780,000											
1856, Large Date		37	51.0	24	60	160	400	550	850	2,000		$16,450, MS-65, August 2013
1856, Small Date		160	55.5	59	50	130	300	400	650	1,250	2,750	$10,575, MS-67, April 2014
18560	1,180,000	60	48.6	30	65	250	800	1,100	1,500	2,750	6,000	$1,469, MS-63, November 2013
1856S	70,000	52	37.1	15	1,250	1,700	3,800	6,500	15,000	20,000	45,000	$15,210, MS-63, September 2013
1857	5,580,000	250	58.4	66	50	130	300	450	700	1,000	2,500	$5,875, MS-66, January 2014
18570	1,540,000	158	57.1	58	70	200	425	500	750	1,100	2,750	$4,994, MS-66, November 2013
1858	1,540,000	133	55.2	59	50	130	300	450	700	1,000	2,500	$6,463, MS-67, June 2014
18580	290,000	51	49.7	31	135	300	600	800	1,000	2,500	6,000	$21,150, MS-66, June 2014
1858S	60,000	56	35.8	7	900	1,600	3,800	7,500	16,000	22,500		$88,125, MS-66, June 2014
1859	429,200	130	60.6	75	60	140	300	450	700	1,000	2,500	$8,225, MS-65, November 2013
18590	480,000	124	58.5	69	95	275	400	600	900	1,200	2,750	$6,756, MS-66, August 2013
1859S	60,000	50	32.1	6	1,500	4,000	11,000	17,000	26,000			$1,175, EF-45, January 2014
1860S	140,000	65	41.4	20	400	950	2,500	3,500	5,000	8,500	15,000	$1,998, MS-61, April 2014

Proof Liberty Seated Dimes, Varieties 2 and 3

PF-60 to 70 (Proof). Proofs were made of most years and are mostly available from 1854 onward, with 1858 and especially 1859 being those often seen. Most are well struck. *Obverse and Reverse:* Proofs that are extensively cleaned and have many hairlines, or that are dull and grainy, are lower level, such as PF-60 to 62. Generally, these are not widely desired, save for the scarce (in any grade) dates of 1844 and 1846. With medium hairlines and good reflectivity, an assigned grade of PF-64 is aappropriate, and with relatively few hairlines, PF-65. In various grades hairlines are most easily seen in the obverse field. PF-66 should have hairlines so delicate that magnification is needed to see them. Above that, a Proof should be free of such lines.

**Proof Liberty Seated Dime:
Variety 2, Stars on Obverse**

**Proof Liberty Seated Dime: Variety 3,
Stars on Obverse, Arrows at Date**

**Proof 1859 Pattern Dime:
Obverse of 1859, Reverse of 1860**

	Est Mintage	Cert	Finest	PF-60	PF-63	PF-64	PF-65	Recent Auction Record
1838 (a)	2–3	n/a	n/a					$161,000, PF-67Cam, January 2008
1839	4–5	3	PF-64	$7,000	$10,000	$25,000	$45,000	$36,719, PF-66, April 2013
18390	2–3	1	PF-63		25,000	45,000	75,000	$74,750, PF-65, October 2008
1840, No Drapery	4–5	1	PF-64	10,000	15,000	20,000	30,000	$27,600, PF-65Cam, August 2007
1841 (a)	2–3	n/a	n/a		65,000			$63,250, PF-63Cam, January 2008
1841, No Drapery	2–3	n/a	n/a		75,000			$305,500, PF-67, November 2013
1842	6–10	2	PF-65	10,000	15,000	25,000	40,000	$37,375, PF-65Cam, April 2008
1843	10–15	4	PF-64	5,000	10,000	17,000	25,000	$25,850, PF-66, June 2014
1844	4–8	3	PF-65	18,000	32,500	50,000	75,000	$103,500, PF-66, January 2008
1845	6–10	1	PF-61	7,500	12,500	25,000	35,000	$19,975, PF-65, April 2013
1846	8–12	10	PF-64	10,000	15,000	25,000	40,000	$31,725, PF-65, March 2013
1847	3–5	3	PF-66	8,000	13,000	25,000	40,000	$51,750, PF-66Cam, July 2008
1848	10–15	4	PF-65	5,000	10,000	16,000	25,000	$27,025, PF-66, February 2013
1849	4–6	2	PF-66	10,000	15,000	25,000	40,000	$35,250, PF-65, August 2013
1850	4–6	2	PF-66	10,000	15,000	25,000	40,000	$80,500, PF-67 Star, January 2008
1852	5–10	5	PF-66	5,000	10,000	16,000	25,000	$8,225, PF-62, January 2014
1853	5–10	2	PF-61	15,000	30,000	50,000	75,000	$52,875, PF-66, June 2014
1854	8–12	9	PF-65	8,000	15,000	25,000	40,000	$25,850, PF-65Cam, April 2013
1855	8–12	13	PF-65	8,000	15,000	25,000	40,000	$38,188, PF-67Cam, March 2013
1856	40–50	22	PF-66	2,500	4,500	8,500	15,000	$25,850, PF-67, June 2014
1857	45–60	35	PF-67	2,000	3,750	4,500	6,500	$8,813, PF-66, April 2013
1858	unknown	72	PF-66	1,000	2,000	2,500	4,500	$7,344, PF-66, September 2013
1859	unknown	193	PF-67	950	1,500	2,500	4,000	$22,325, PF-68DCam, September 2013
1859, Obverse of 1859, Reverse of 1860 (b)	unknown	n/a	n/a	10,000	18,500	20,000	25,000	$26,450, PF-65, March 2012

a. The 1838 and 1841 Proof dimes may be unique. b. In 1859 the Mint made a dime pattern, of which some 13 to 20 examples are known. These "coins without a country" do not bear the nation's identity (UNITED STATES OF AMERICA). They are transitional pieces, not made for circulation, but struck at the time that the dime's legend was being transferred from the reverse to the obverse (see Variety 4). For more information, consult *United States Pattern Coins*, 10th edition (Judd).

LIBERTY SEATED, VARIETIES 4 AND 5, LEGEND ON OBVERSE (1860–1891)

Designer Christian Gobrecht; weight 2.49 grams (increased to 2.50 grams 1873–1891); composition .900 silver, .100 copper; diameter 17.9 mm; reeded edge; mints: Philadelphia, New Orleans, San Francisco, Carson City.

Variety 4, Legend on Obverse
(1860–1873, 1875–1891)
Shown 1.5x actual size.

Variety 5, Legend on Obverse,
Arrows at Date (1873–1874)
Shown 1.5x actual size.

History. In 1860 the Liberty Seated design continued with UNITED STATES OF AMERICA replacing the stars on the obverse. A new reverse featured what the Mint called a "cereal wreath," encircling ONE DIME in two lines. In 1873 the dime was increased in weight to 2.50 grams (from 2.49); arrows at the date in 1873 and 1874 indicate this change, making Variety 5. Variety 4 (without the arrows) resumed from 1875 and continued to the end of the series in 1891.

Striking and Sharpness. Coins of these varieties usually are fairly well struck for the earlier years, somewhat erratic in the 1870s, and better from the 1880s to 1891. Many Civil War dimes of Philadelphia, 1861 to 1865, have parallel die striae from the dies not being finished (this being so for virtually all silver and gold issues of that period). Some dimes, especially dates from 1879 to 1881, are found prooflike. Points to check include the head of Miss Liberty on the obverse, the wreath details on the reverse, and the dentils on both sides. Issues of the Carson City Mint in the early 1870s, particularly 1873-CC With Arrows, are often seen with porous surfaces (a post-striking effect). Note: The word LIBERTY on the shield is not an infallible key to attributing lower grades. On some dies such as those of the early 1870s the shield was in low relief on the coins and wore away slowly, with the result that part or all of the word can be readable in grades below F-12.

Availability. While certain issues of the 1860s through 1881 range from scarce to very rare, those from 1882 to 1891 are for the most part very common, even in MS-63 and finer.

EF-40, 45 (Extremely Fine). *Obverse:* More wear than at AU is seen on all areas, especially the thighs and knees, bosom, and head. Little or no luster is seen. *Reverse:* Further wear than at AU is seen on all areas, most noticeably at on the high areas of the wreath and on the ribbon. The leaves retain excellent details except on the higher areas.

AU-50, 53, 55, 58 (About Uncirculated). *Obverse:* Light wear is seen on the thighs and knees, bosom, and head. At AU-50 and 53, luster is less than at AU-58, where the luster is extensive but incomplete. *Reverse:* Wear is evident on the leaves and ribbon. At AU-50 and 53, there still is significant luster. An AU-58 coin has nearly full luster, more so than on the obverse, as the design elements protect the small field areas.

MS-60 to 70 (Mint State). *Obverse:* At MS-60, some abrasion and contact marks are evident, most noticeably on the bosom and thighs and knees. Luster is present, but may be dull or lifeless. At MS-63, contact marks are very few, and abrasion is hard to detect except under magnification. An MS-65 coin has no abrasion, and contact marks are so minute as to require magnification. Luster should be full and rich, except for Philadelphia (but not San Francisco) dimes of the early and mid-1860s. Some low-mintage Philadelphia issues may be prooflike. Clashmarks are common. *Reverse:* Comments apply as for the obverse, except that in lower MS grades abrasion and contact marks are most noticeable on the highest parts of the leaves and the ribbon, less so on ONE DIME. At MS-65 or higher there are no marks visible to the unaided eye. The field is mainly protected by design elements and does not show abrasion as much as does the obverse on a given coin.

1861, Six Vertical Shield Lines

1872, Doubled-Die Reverse
FS-10-1872-801.

1873, Close 3

1873, Open 3

1873, With Arrows, Doubled-Die Obverse
FS-10-1873-2101.

1875-CC, Mintmark Above Bow

1875-CC, Mintmark Below Bow

1876-CC, Variety I Reverse

1876-CC, Variety II Reverse
FS-10-1876CC-301.

1891-O, O Over Horizontal O
FS-10-1891o-501.

1891-S, Repunched Mintmark
FS-10-1891S-501.

	Mintage	Cert	Avg	%MS	EF-40	AU-50	MS-60	MS-62	MS-63	MS-64	MS-65	Recent Auction Record
1860	606,000	125	61.6	85	$40	$100	$200	$300	$325	$425	$1,350	$3,055, MS-67, June 2013
18600	40,000	75	23.0	0	4,000	8,000	15,000					$5,581, EF-45, December 2013
1861 (a)	1,883,000	169	61.2	82	40	100	200	300	325	425	1,350	$1,763, MS-66, June 2014
1861S	172,500	38	40.4	18	450	1,000	2,100	3,500	5,500			$49,938, MS-66, June 2014
1862	847,000	143	62.0	87	40	100	185	225	350	500	1,500	$2,585, MS-66, April 2014
1862S	180,750	32	36.1	9	675	900	2,000	2,800	4,000	7,000		$646, VF-30, April 2014
1863	14,000	44	51.1	66	900	1,100	1,300	1,600	1,800	2,750	3,750	$6,463, MS-67, August 2013
1863S	157,500	48	42.0	23	350	700	1,500	2,000	4,500	9,000	26,000	$1,586, AU-58, February 2014

a. The dime's dies were modified slightly in 1861. The first (scarcer) variety has only five vertical lines in the top part of the shield.

	Mintage	Cert	Avg	%MS	EF-40	AU-50	MS-60	MS-62	MS-63	MS-64	MS-65	Recent Auction Record
1864	11,000	53	48.3	55	$875	$1,100	$1,200	$1,500	$1,750	$2,250	$4,000	$17,625, MS-66, June 2014
1864S	230,000	49	40.1	24	375	600	1,500	1,750	1,900	3,500	6,000	$25,850, MS-67, June 2014
1865	10,000	42	50.3	62	800	950	1,200	1,500	2,000	2,500	3,500	$9,988, MS-67, November 2013
1865S	175,000	44	34.1	9	750	2,200	6,750	7,500	12,000			$217, F, December 2013
1866	8,000	57	49.8	61	2,000	2,100	2,200	2,400	2,600	2,800	3,500	$12,925, MS-66, April 2013
1866S	135,000	42	41.3	24	350	600	1,150	2,100	4,500	6,500	17,500	$1,880, AU-53, February 2014
1867	6,000	50	55.9	78	1,100	1,300	1,500	2,000	2,500	3,250	4,000	$11,163, MS-68, June 2014
1867S	140,000	45	42.3	22	425	700	1,250	1,650	2,500	4,000	7,500	$8,225, MS-65, June 2014
1868	464,000	40	51.8	55	65	150	300	500	850	1,250	3,500	$24, F-12, November 2011
1868S	260,000	27	56.1	59	125	225	400	600	1,000	2,000	5,000	$212, AU-50, December 2013
1869	256,000	34	57.4	71	100	200	400	600	900	1,850	3,500	$4,553, MS, March 2014
1869S	450,000	52	54.5	63	150	250	400	550	800	1,500	3,400	$1,293, MS-62, April 2014
1870	470,500	63	59.6	75	50	100	200	300	450	950	1,850	$9,988, MS-66, June 2014
1870S	50,000	54	41.9	37	600	850	1,800	2,100	2,750	3,500	6,000	$22,325, MS-66, January 2014
1871	906,750	55	58.3	64	50	150	250	300	425	900	2,000	$2,233, MS-65, April 2013
1871CC	20,100	45	22.2	4	12,500	22,500	50,000					$27,025, AU-55, May 2013
1871S	320,000	39	47.5	38	225	300	550	750	1,200	2,500	7,000	$588, AU-58, July 2014
1872	2,395,500	69	55.0	64	40	90	175	225	300	750	1,350	$1,439, MS-65, March 2014
1872, DblDie Reverse *(rare)* (b)	*	7	43.0	29	250	350	750	1,000				$425, VF-20, May 2008
1872CC	35,480	62	23.4	2	7,500	18,500	50,000					$8,225, EF-45, March 2014
1872S	190,000	36	50.3	39	225	400	1,200	1,650	2,500	4,000	16,000	$7,638, MS-64, April 2013
1873, Close 3	1,506,800	42	58.8	69	40	90	150	200	250	650	1,500	$6,463, MS-67, June 2014
1873, Open 3	60,000	43	50.0	33	130	200	600	850	1,500	3,000	9,000	$9,400, MS-64, August 2013
1873CC *(unique)* † (c)	12,400	1	65.0	100					1,840,000			$891,250, MS-65, July 2004
1873, With Arrows	2,378,000	195	54.0	55	150	300	550	600	900	1,650	4,000	$23,500, AU-58, June 2014
1873, With Arrows, Doubled-Die Obverse (d)	*	3	31.7	0	1,000	1,500						$3,220, VF-25, October 2011
1873CC, With Arrows	18,791	72	18.8	1	17,000	37,000	50,000	55,000	65,000			$199,750, MS-65, June 2014
1873S	455,000	68	56.4	54	175	450	1,000	1,450	2,100	3,750	6,500	$24,675, MS-67, June 2014
1874	2,939,300	274	57.5	67	150	310	600	750	1,000	1,750	4,000	$67,563, MS-68, August 2013
1874CC	10,817	38	21.9	8	28,000	48,000	65,000					$41,125, AU-53, April 2014
1874S	240,000	51	57.5	63	225	500	900	1,200	2,000	4,000	8,500	$3,055, MS-64, April 2013
1875	10,350,000	372	61.0	80	35	80	150	200	250	450	1,000	$7,639, MS-67, September 2013
1875CC, All kinds	4,645,000											
1875CC, Above Bow		240	55.4	65	70	150	325	425	500	1,250	2,750	$3,525, MS-66, April 2014
1875CC, Below Bow		70	52.8	47	70	125	350	425	550	1,400	3,000	$4,994, MS-65, September 2013
1875S, All kinds	9,070,000											
1875S, Below Bow		165	60.4	83	35	85	160	200	250	450	1,200	$881, MS-65, June 2013
1875S, Above Bow		38	56.2	63	35	85	160	200	250	450	1,200	$1,998, MS-65, April 2014
1876	11,450,000	314	61.0	85	35	80	150	200	250	450	1,000	$2,589, MS-67, September 2013
1876CC	8,270,000	377	52.1	58	65	100	230	300	450	550	1,500	$14,100, MS-67, February 2013
1876CC, Variety II Reverse (e)	*	2	38.0	50	250	350	600	850	1,250			$3,738, MS-64, February 2012
1876S	10,420,000	101	58.2	70	35	80	150	200	250	450	1,750	$3,819, MS-66, April 2014
1877	7,310,000	110	58.8	81	35	80	150	200	250	450	925	$5,581, MS-67, November 2013
1877CC	7,700,000	399	54.6	66	65	100	230	300	400	600	1,350	$7,050, MS-67, April 2014
1877S	2,340,000	97	61.3	85	35	80	150	200	250	450	1,000	$2,820, MS-65, June 2013
1878	1,677,200	101	61.5	83	35	80	150	200	250	450	900	$8,225, MS-67, September 2013
1878CC	200,000	129	34.2	28	420	625	1,200	1,550	1,850	3,000	4,000	$13,513, MS-66, August 2013
1879	14,000	249	62.5	91	500	550	625	700	750	950	1,250	$4,113, MS-67, April 2013
1880	36,000	149	59.9	83	400	500	650	700	750	950	1,250	$4,113, MS-67, January 2014
1881	24,000	86	56.4	72	425	525	675	725	775	975	1,350	$4,994, MS-67, August 2013
1882	3,910,000	346	63.2	92	35	80	150	200	250	450	800	$3,672, MS-67, June 2014
1883	7,674,673	485	62.3	88	35	80	150	200	250	450	800	$9,400, MS-68, July 2014
1884	3,365,505	342	62.4	91	35	80	150	200	250	450	800	$7,344, MS-68, June 2013
1884S	564,969	72	53.9	49	100	300	750	950	1,200	1,850	5,000	$1,149, MS-64, June 2014
1885	2,532,497	304	62.1	85	35	80	150	200	250	450	800	$3,173, MS-67, June 2014

* Included in number above. † Ranked in the *100 Greatest U.S. Coins* (fourth edition). **b.** The first die hubbing was almost completely obliterated by the second, which was rotated about 170 degrees from the first. The key indicators of this variety are inside the opening of the D, and near the center arm of the E in ONE. **c.** Most of the mintage of 1873-CC (Without Arrows) was melted after the law of 1873, affecting the statuses and physical properties of U.S. coinage, was passed. **d.** Doubling is evident on the shield and on the banner across the shield. Although well known for decades, very few specimens of this variety have been reported. **e.** The scarce Variety II reverse exhibits a single point to the end of the left ribbon; the common Variety I reverse has a split at the ribbon's end.

Chart continued on next page.

	Mintage	Cert	Avg	%MS	EF-40	AU-50	MS-60	MS-62	MS-63	MS-64	MS-65	Recent Auction Record
1885S	43,690	72	33.3	13	$2,200	$4,000	$5,500	$6,500	$9,000	$16,000	$27,500	$49,938, MS-66, June 2014
1886	6,376,684	508	62.1	87	35	80	150	200	250	450	800	$1,116, MS-66, February 2013
1886S	206,524	53	57.2	66	135	200	600	850	1,200	2,000	4,500	$6,463, MS-66, June 2013
1887	11,283,229	524	62.0	87	35	80	150	200	250	450	800	$2,820, MS-65, February 2013
1887S	4,454,450	203	60.8	80	35	80	150	200	250	450	1,200	$805, MS-65, November 2013
1888	5,495,655	307	61.1	84	35	80	150	200	250	450	800	$9,988, MS-67, June 2014
1888S	1,720,000	58	57.8	64	35	100	250	450	650	1,000	2,750	$10,575, MS-66, June 2014
1889	7,380,000	378	61.3	81	35	80	150	200	250	450	800	$4,700, MS-67, January 2014
1889S	972,678	67	57.3	66	80	150	450	650	900	1,200	4,500	$4,113, MS-66, April 2014
1890	9,910,951	491	61.5	83	35	80	150	200	250	450	800	$4,113, MS-67, January 2014
1890S, Large S	1,423,076	97	57.3	65	85	150	350	550	700	1,000	1,750	$2,233, MS-65, August 2013
1890S, Small S (rare)	*	3	21.7	0	—	—	—					$1,208, MS-65, February 2006
1891	15,310,000	830	61.3	84	35	80	150	200	250	450	800	$3,819, MS-67, June 2014
1891O	4,540,000	231	57.9	71	50	100	175	225	375	600	1,350	$7,638, MS-67, August 2013
1891O, O Over Horizontal O (f)	*	4	40.0	0	225	—	—					$253, AU-58, May 2010
1891S	3,196,116	163	61.2	82	35	80	175	225	325	500	1,100	$7,638, MS-67, June 2014
1891S, Repunched Mintmark (g)	*	2	61.0	50	200	225	500					$5,750, MS-66, September 2010

* Included in number above. **f.** The primary O mintmark was punched over a previously punched horizontal O. **g.** The larger primary S mintmark (known as the medium S) was punched squarely over the smaller S, which is evident within both loops.

Proof Liberty Seated Dimes, Varieties 4 and 5

PF-60 to 70 (Proof). Proof Liberty Seated dimes of these varieties were made continuously from 1860 to 1891. They exist today in proportion to their mintages. Some of the 1860s and early 1870s can be carelessly struck, with areas of lightness and sometimes with lint marks. Those of the mid-1870s onward usually are sharply struck and without problems. *Obverse and Reverse:* Proofs that are extensively cleaned and have many hairlines, or that are dull and grainy, are lower level, such as PF-60 to 62. These are not widely sought in the marketplace, save for the rare (in any grade) dates of 1863 through 1867. With medium hairlines and good reflectivity, PF-64 is appropriate, and with relatively few hairlines, PF-65. At various levels, hairlines are most easily seen in the obverse field. PF-66 should have hairlines so delicate that magnification is needed to see them. Above that, a Proof should be free of such lines.

Proof Liberty Seated Dime:
Variety 4, Legend on Obverse
Shown 1.5x actual size.

Proof Liberty Seated Dime: Variety 5,
Legend on Obverse, Arrows at Date
Shown 1.5x actual size.

	Mintage	Cert	Finest	PF-60	PF-63	PF-64	PF-65	PF-65Cam	Recent Auction Record
1860	1,000	162	PF-67	$350	$750	$1,250	$1,850	$2,000	$8,225, PF-67Cam, December 2013
1861	1,000	102	PF-67	350	750	1,250	2,000	2,400	$2,943, PF-65Cam, July 2014
1862	550	139	PF-66	350	750	1,250	2,000	2,200	$2,351, PF-66Cam, February 2013
1863	460	147	PF-67	325	700	1,100	1,850	2,000	$15,863, PF-66DCam, April 2014
1864	470	155	PF-67	325	700	1,100	1,850	2,000	$5,581, PF-66Cam, September 2013
1865	500	120	PF-67	350	750	1,250	2,000	2,500	$4,700, PF-67, June 2014
1866	725	165	PF-67	325	700	1,100	1,850	2,000	$1,645, PF, May 2013
1867	625	163	PF-67	325	700	1,100	1,850	2,000	$2,585, PF-64DCam, June 2014
1868	600	188	PF-66	325	700	1,100	1,850	2,000	$7,050, PF-66Cam, September 2013
1869	600	169	PF-67	325	700	1,100	1,850	2,000	$1,528, PF-66, April 2013
1870	1,000	193	PF-67	325	700	1,100	1,850	2,000	$7,050, PF-67, January 2014
1871	960	153	PF-66	325	700	1,100	1,850	2,000	$14,100, PF-67Cam, September 2013
1872	950	185	PF-67	325	700	1,100	1,850	2,000	$3,290, PF-66Cam, March 2013
1873, Close 3	600	192	PF-67	325	700	1,100	1,850	2,000	$16,450, PF-68Cam, November 2013
1873, With Arrows	500	152	PF-66	750	1,500	2,500	5,500	7,000	$16,450, PF-67, November 2013
1874	700	227	PF-67	750	1,500	2,500	5,500	7,000	$27,025, PF-67, June 2014

	Mintage	Cert	Finest	PF-60	PF-63	PF-64	PF-65	PF-65Cam	Recent Auction Record
1875	700	171	PF-67	$300	$650	$1,000	$1,750	$1,900	$3,819, PF-66Cam, February 2014
1876	1,150	184	PF-66	300	650	1,000	1,750	1,900	$7,331, PF-67 Star, April 2012
1876CC	3–4	1	PF-66						$212,750, PF-66, August 2009
1877	510	158	PF-67	300	650	1,000	1,750	1,900	$9,400, PF-67, June 2014
1878	800	211	PF-66	300	650	1,000	1,750	1,900	$2,820, PF-66, September 2013
1879	1,100	357	PF-67	300	650	1,000	1,750	1,900	$4,406, PF-67, November 2013
1880	1,355	376	PF-67	300	650	1,000	1,750	1,900	$8,225, PF-68, April 2014
1881	975	301	PF-67	300	650	1,000	1,750	1,900	$6,463, PF-68Cam, April 2014
1882	1,100	316	PF-68	300	650	1,000	1,750	1,900	$7,638, PF-67Cam, March 2013
1883	1,039	312	PF-68	300	650	1,000	1,750	1,900	$8,225, PF-68, July 2014
1884	875	286	PF-68	300	650	1,000	1,750	1,900	$6,463, PF-68Cam, March 2013
1885	930	304	PF-68	300	650	1,000	1,750	1,900	$6,463, PF-68Cam, April 2013
1886	886	249	PF-67	300	650	1,000	1,750	1,900	$12,925, PF-68Cam, June 2014
1887	710	199	PF-67	300	650	1,000	1,750	1,900	$6,463, PF-67Cam, February 2014
1888	832	186	PF-67	300	650	1,000	1,750	1,900	$2,115, PF-66, February 2014
1889	711	174	PF-67	300	650	1,000	1,750	1,900	$8,519, PF-68, June 2014
1890	590	192	PF-67	300	650	1,000	1,750	1,900	$12,103, PF-68DCam, June 2014
1891	600	210	PF-67	300	650	1,000	1,750	1,900	$6,463, PF-67Cam, November 2013
18910 (extremely rare)	2–3	n/a	n/a						

BARBER OR LIBERTY HEAD
(1892–1916)

Designer Charles E. Barber; weight 2.50 grams; composition .900 silver, .100 copper (net weight: .07234 oz. pure silver); diameter 17.9 mm; reeded edge; mints: Philadelphia, Denver, New Orleans, San Francisco.

Shown 2x actual size.

History. This dime belongs to a suite of silver coins (including the quarter and half dollar) designed by U.S. Mint chief engraver Charles E. Barber. It features a large Liberty Head styled similarly to contemporary French coinage. The reverse of the dime continues the "cereal wreath" motif of the late Liberty Seated era.

Striking and Sharpness. Check the details of the hair on the obverse. The reverse usually is sharp. If weakness is seen, it is typically in the wreath details. The dentils usually are sharp on the obverse and reverse.

Availability. With the exception of the rare 1894-S, of which fewer than a dozen are known, all dates and mintmarks are collectible. Probably 90% or more of the survivors are in lower grades such as AG-3 and G-4. The word LIBERTY in the headband, a key to grading, tended to wear away quickly. Relatively few are in grades from Fine upward. MS coins are somewhat scarce, this being especially true of the branch-mint issues. MS-63 and finer Barber dimes usually are from the Philadelphia Mint or, if from a branch mint, are dated after 1905.

EF-40, 45 (Extremely Fine). *Obverse:* More wear than at AU is seen on the head. The hair above the forehead lacks most detail. LIBERTY shows wear but is strong. *Reverse:* More wear than at AU is seen on all areas, most noticeably at the wreath and ribbon. The leaves retain excellent details except on the higher areas.

AU-50, 53, 55, 58 (About Uncirculated). *Obverse:* Light wear is seen on the head, especially on the forward hair under LIBERTY. At AU-50 and 53, luster is less than at 58, where the luster is extensive but incomplete (especially on the higher parts and in the right field). *Reverse:* Wear is seen on the leaves and ribbon. At AU-50 and 53, there still is significant luster. An AU-58 coin will have nearly full luster, more so than on the obverse, as the design elements protect the small field areas.

MS-60 to 70 (Mint State). *Obverse:* At MS-60, some abrasion and contact marks are evident, most noticeably on the cheek and the obverse field to the right. Luster is present, but may be dull or lifeless. Many Barber coins, especially of the earlier dates, have been cleaned. At MS-63, contact marks are very few; abrasion still is evident, but less than at lower levels. An MS-65 coin may have minor abrasion on the cheek, but contact marks are so minute as to require magnification. Luster should be full and rich. *Reverse:* Comments apply as for the obverse, except that in lower MS grades abrasion and contact marks are most noticeable on the highest parts of the leaves and the ribbon, less so on ONE DIME. At MS-65 or higher, there are no marks visible to the unaided eye. The field is mainly protected by design elements and does not show abrasion as much as does the obverse on a given coin.

1893, 3 Over 2

1897, Repunched Date
FS-10-1897-301.

1905-O, Normal O

1905-O, Micro O

1912-S, Doubled-Die Obverse
FS-10-1912S-101.

	Mintage	Cert	Avg	%MS	EF-40	AU-50	MS-60	MS-62	MS-63	MS-64	MS-65	Recent Auction Record
1892	12,120,000	1,346	61.5	80	$30	$80	$135	$175	$240	$375	$650	$3,525, MS-67, June 2014
1892O	3,841,700	249	57.2	64	75	95	175	225	300	500	1,250	$4,994, MS-66, February 2013
1892S	990,710	188	47.1	46	280	330	425	600	775	1,500	4,000	$7,050, MS-65, June 2014
1893, 3 Over 2	*	35	61.6	69	200	300	700	1,200	1,800	3,000	5,250	$4,994, MS, March 2014
1893	3,339,940	287	60.6	77	45	80	150	200	250	375	950	$15,275, MS-67, August 2013
1893O	1,760,000	186	49.1	55	190	230	325	450	650	1,250	2,500	$2,115, MS-65, February 2013
1893S	2,491,401	162	54.3	60	90	150	290	425	700	1,500	3,250	$2,350, MS-65, July 2013
1894	1,330,000	260	50.0	47	180	220	325	400	500	700	1,200	$2,233, MS-66, June 2013
1894O	720,000	153	35.8	22	425	600	1,450	2,000	2,500	5,500	13,500	$10,575, MS-65, August 2013
1895	690,000	200	46.1	45	550	625	725	850	1,200	1,850	2,500	$5,500, MS-66, June 2014
1895O	440,000	408	21.9	9	2,400	3,400	6,000	7,000	10,000	15,000	22,500	$34,075, MS-65, January 2014
1895S	1,120,000	194	45.2	40	240	310	500	700	1,100	2,000	7,000	$15,863, MS-66, June 2014
1896	2,000,000	176	56.0	68	100	120	175	300	500	650	1,150	$1,058, MS-65, July 2014
1896O	610,000	142	33.8	25	450	650	1,000	1,600	2,400	4,500	8,500	$15,275, MS-66, January 2014
1896S	575,056	177	40.6	42	400	550	850	1,100	1,500	3,000	4,500	$9,400, MS-66, June 2014
1897	10,868,533	415	61.8	83	32	75	135	175	240	375	625	$3,055, MS-67, June 2014
1897, Repunched Date (a)	**	n/a	n/a	n/a	80	120	200					
1897O	666,000	179	41.5	41	475	600	900	1,300	1,700	2,500	4,500	$7,638, MS-64, September 2013
1897S	1,342,844	146	50.0	51	175	260	450	650	1,000	2,000	3,750	$1,880, MS-64, September 2013
1898	16,320,000	507	61.3	80	26	75	130	165	240	375	675	$2,233, MS-66, April 2014
1898O	2,130,000	127	45.9	41	190	280	450	650	1,200	1,750	3,250	$9,400, MS-66, June 2014
1898S	1,702,507	99	53.6	48	80	150	375	600	1,200	2,000	3,500	$10,281, MS-66, June 2014
1899	19,580,000	367	60.4	76	25	75	130	165	240	375	650	$188, MS-63, July 2013
1899O	2,650,000	110	47.7	39	140	225	400	600	1,150	2,500	4,000	$4,406, MS-65, November 2013
1899S	1,867,493	140	57.1	68	45	110	300	550	750	1,750	2,800	$5,875, MS-67, December 2013
1900	17,600,000	235	59.7	80	25	75	125	160	240	380	850	$6,463, MS-67, August 2013
1900O	2,010,000	142	42.2	32	220	360	650	775	1,150	2,750	5,250	$5,640, MS-66, September 2013
1900S	5,168,270	202	57.8	57	30	75	175	300	425	700	1,800	$1,116, MS-64, February 2013
1901	18,859,665	378	60.8	79	26	75	125	160	240	375	625	$1,763, MS-66, April 2013
1901O	5,620,000	127	52.5	44	75	180	450	650	950	2,500	3,800	$3,966, MS-66, April 2013
1901S	593,022	163	36.1	28	550	675	1,050	1,250	1,800	2,300	5,500	$6,463, MS-66, June 2013
1902	21,380,000	213	58.8	70	25	75	125	160	240	375	660	$1,116, MS-66, January 2014
1902O	4,500,000	99	54.8	48	65	150	400	650	1,000	1,500	4,000	$3,290, MS-65, June 2014
1902S	2,070,000	116	53.9	49	140	200	400	650	1,000	1,500	4,000	$2,820, MS-65, June 2014
1903	19,500,000	167	59.3	72	25	75	125	160	240	375	1,000	$1,175, MS-65, June 2014
1903O	8,180,000	180	55.4	45	55	110	275	400	550	1,000	4,500	$7,638, MS-66, April 2013
1903S	613,300	218	35.7	26	725	875	1,250	1,450	1,800	2,250	3,500	$3,525, MS-66, March 2013
1904	14,600,357	214	60.3	82	25	75	125	160	240	385	1,400	$2,938, MS-66, June 2014
1904S	800,000	184	42.6	33	325	475	800	1,000	1,500	3,000	4,500	$11,163, MS-66, June 2014
1905	14,551,623	217	60.0	77	25	75	125	160	240	375	660	$3,525, MS-66, January 2014
1905O	3,400,000	185	53.9	60	100	150	300	400	500	700	1,350	$1,792, MS-66, January 2014
1905O, Micro O	**	156	17.6	4	175	275	600	1,500	3,500			$4,113, MS-62, June 2014

* Included in number below. ** Included in number above. **a.** More than one repunched date exists for 1897. This listing is for FS-10-1897-301 (see the *Cherrypickers' Guide to Rare Die Varieties*, fifth edition, volume II), one of the most dramatic RPDs of the series. The secondary digits of the date are evident west of the primary digits.

	Mintage	Cert	Avg	%MS	EF-40	AU-50	MS-60	MS-62	MS-63	MS-64	MS-65	Recent Auction Record
1905S	6,855,199	223	59.1	65	$40	$95	$250	$285	$325	$600	$950	$646, MS-64, September 2013
1906	19,957,731	410	61.3	81	25	75	125	160	240	375	625	$1,175, MS-66, June 2014
1906D	4,060,000	141	60.4	76	35	80	175	300	400	850	1,500	$11,750, MS-67, April 2013
1906O	2,610,000	207	57.0	71	110	130	200	250	325	650	1,100	$14,100, MS-67, November 2013
1906S	3,136,640	113	61.1	80	45	110	275	325	550	850	1,250	$881, MS-65, July 2014
1907	22,220,000	438	60.7	81	25	75	125	160	240	375	625	$1,058, MS-66, June 2014
1907D	4,080,000	88	56.0	56	45	110	300	450	900	1,600	2,250	$8,519, MS-67, February 2013
1907O	5,058,000	168	57.3	73	70	110	200	250	375	450	1,200	$15,863, MS-67, November 2013
1907S	3,178,470	144	55.1	49	75	150	400	500	750	1,500	2,500	$5,288, MS-66, September 2013
1908	10,600,000	362	61.2	84	25	75	125	160	240	375	625	$705, MS-66, June 2014
1908D	7,490,000	167	57.1	68	28	75	130	175	300	750	1,000	$1,116, MS-65, November 2013
1908O	1,789,000	121	58.4	77	95	150	300	450	600	850	1,250	$7,638, MS-67, November 2013
1908S	3,220,000	145	59.2	67	45	170	350	500	800	1,250	1,600	$2,820, MS-66, June 2014
1909	10,240,000	343	60.9	83	25	75	125	160	240	375	625	$881, MS-66, July 2014
1909D	954,000	157	49.2	44	140	225	500	650	1,000	1,500	2,600	$3,525, MS-66, June 2014
1909O	2,287,000	140	56.2	65	70	150	250	375	575	1,100	1,500	$3,055, MS-66, June 2014
1909S	1,000,000	110	48.8	48	180	310	550	700	1,400	1,900	2,800	$2,350, MS-65, June 2014
1910	11,520,000	472	61.3	82	24	75	125	160	240	365	625	$5,170, MS-67, January 2014
1910D	3,490,000	106	58.9	75	48	95	220	300	450	650	1,500	$2,115, MS-66, June 2014
1910S	1,240,000	143	48.5	46	110	180	425	550	700	1,100	2,250	$7,344, MS-67, June 2014
1911	18,870,000	997	61.8	85	24	75	125	160	240	365	625	$3,525, MS-67, June 2013
1911D	11,209,000	294	60.1	79	24	75	125	160	240	365	625	$4,113, MS-67, July 2014
1911S	3,520,000	255	62.0	85	40	100	200	275	400	750	1,000	$1,175, MS-63, September 2013
1912	19,349,300	925	61.2	83	24	75	125	160	240	365	625	$1,410, MS-66, December 2013
1912D	11,760,000	351	59.0	69	24	75	125	160	240	365	625	$3,819, MS-66, November 2013
1912S	3,420,000	229	60.3	69	32	90	170	225	300	500	750	$1,293, MS-66, June 2013
1912S, DblDie Obverse (b)	*	n/a	n/a	n/a	100	180	425					
1913	19,760,000	836	61.0	82	24	75	125	160	240	365	625	$1,763, MS-66, April 2013
1913S	510,000	291	40.6	36	250	320	500	600	800	1,000	1,500	$4,113, MS-66, June 2014
1914	17,360,230	920	61.5	87	24	75	125	160	240	365	625	$911, MS-66, July 2014
1914D	11,908,000	505	59.0	70	24	75	125	160	240	365	625	$705, MS-65, July 2014
1914S	2,100,000	227	60.1	76	40	80	175	225	350	700	1,400	$1,880, MS-66, February 2013
1915	5,620,000	404	61.7	84	24	75	125	160	240	365	625	$1,028, MS-66, January 2014
1915S	960,000	196	54.4	63	70	140	275	325	475	675	1,400	$1,410, MS-65, February 2014
1916	18,490,000	1,308	61.0	82	24	75	125	160	240	365	625	$3,819, MS-67, June 2014
1916S	5,820,000	377	60.1	71	24	75	125	160	240	365	625	$3,525, MS-66, June 2014

* Included in number above. **b.** The doubling is most evident on UNITED.

Proof Barber Dimes

PF-60 to 70 (Proof). Proof Barber dimes survive in proportion to their mintages. PF-63 and 65 specimens are more easily found among dimes than among quarters and half dollars of this type. All were originally sold in silver-coin sets. The Proofs of 1892 to 1901 usually have cameo contrast between the designs and the mirror fields. Later Proofs vary in contrast. *Obverse and Reverse:* Proofs that are extensively cleaned and have many hairlines, or that are dull and grainy, are lower level, such as PF-60 to 62. These are not widely desired, save for the rare (in any grade) year of 1895, and even so most collectors would rather have a lustrous MS-60 than a dull PF-60. With medium hairlines and good reflectivity, PF-64 is assigned. Tiny horizontal lines on Miss Liberty's cheek, known as slide marks, from National and other album slides scuffing the relief of the cheek, are endemic among Barber silver coins. With noticeable marks of this type, the highest grade assignable is PF-64. With relatively few hairlines, a rating of PF-65 can be given. PF-66 should have hairlines so delicate that magnification is needed to see them. Above that, a Proof should be free of any hairlines or other problems.

Proof Barber Dime
Shown 1.5x actual size.

	Mintage	Cert	Finest	PF-60	PF-63	PF-64	PF-65	PF-65Cam	Recent Auction Record
1892	1,245	342	PF-68	$300	$600	$900	$1,750	$1,900	$17,625, PF-68Cam, April 2013
1893	792	225	PF-68	300	600	900	1,750	1,900	$8,225, PF-67Cam, January 2014
1894	972	375	PF-67	300	600	900	1,750	1,900	$5,699, PF-68, July 2013
1894S † (a)	24	5	PF-66		1,500,000				$1,552,500, PF-64, October 2007
1895	880	307	PF-67	300	600	900	1,750	1,900	$5,875, PF-68Cam, April 2013
1896	762	282	PF-67	300	600	900	1,750	1,900	$15,275, PF-68Cam, June 2014
1897	731	273	PF-68	300	600	900	1,750	1,900	$7,638, PF-68Cam, August 2013
1898	735	268	PF-68	300	600	900	1,750	1,900	$9,988, PF-68Cam, August 2013
1899	846	277	PF-68	300	600	900	1,750	1,900	$16,450, PF-68, June 2014
1900	912	247	PF-68	300	600	900	1,750	1,900	$7,050, PF-67Cam, August 2013
1901	813	229	PF-67	300	600	900	1,750	1,900	$2,585, PF-67, June 2014
1902	777	220	PF-67	300	600	900	1,750	1,900	$4,700, PF-67, February 2013
1903	755	221	PF-67	300	600	900	1,750	1,900	$14,100, PF-68, August 2013
1904	670	298	PF-68	300	600	900	1,750	1,900	$4,994, PF-67Cam, April 2013
1905	727	271	PF-67	300	600	900	1,750	1,900	$7,638, PF-68, June 2014
1906	675	213	PF-68	300	600	900	1,750	1,900	$3,525, PF, April 2013
1907	575	202	PF-68	300	600	900	1,750	1,900	$7,638, PF-68, December 2013
1908	545	183	PF-68	300	600	900	1,750	1,900	$8,225, PF-68, June 2014
1909	650	232	PF-68	300	600	900	1,750	1,900	$7,638, PF-68, December 2013
1910	551	189	PF-68	300	600	900	1,750	1,900	$4,994, PF-66DCam, August 2013
1911	543	215	PF-68	300	600	900	1,750	1,900	$19,975, PF-69, April 2013
1912	700	232	PF-67	300	600	900	1,750	1,900	$12,925, PF-67Cam, April 2013
1913	622	240	PF-67	300	600	900	1,750	1,900	$2,233, PF-66Cam, August 2013
1914	425	198	PF-68	300	600	900	1,750	1,900	$11,751, PF-68, June 2014
1915	450	159	PF-67	300	600	900	1,800	2,000	$4,406, PF-66Cam, June 2014

† Ranked in the *100 Greatest U.S. Coins* (fourth edition). **a.** The reason for the low mintage of the Proof 1894-S dime is unknown. Popular theories, among others, include a rounding out of the Mint's record books, or a special presentation to bankers visiting the San Francisco Mint. Fewer than a dozen examples are known to exist.

WINGED LIBERTY HEAD OR "MERCURY" (1916–1945)

Designer Adolph A. Weinman; weight 2.50 grams; composition .900 silver, .100 copper (net weight: .07234 oz. pure silver); diameter 17.9 mm; reeded edge; mints: Philadelphia, Denver, San Francisco.

Shown 2x actual size.

History. In 1916 a new dime, designed by sculptor Adolph A. Weinman (who also created the half dollar that debuted that year), replaced Charles Barber's Liberty Head type. Officially Weinman's design was known as the Winged Liberty Head, but numismatists commonly call the coin the *Mercury* dime, from Miss Liberty's wing-capped resemblance to the Roman god. The reverse depicts a fasces (symbolic of unity) and an olive branch. Production was continuous from 1916 to 1945, except for 1922, 1932, and 1933.

Striking and Sharpness. Many Mercury dimes exhibit areas of light striking, most notably in the center horizontal band across the fasces, less so in the lower horizontal band. The bands are composed of two parallel lines with a separation or "split" between. The term Full Bands, abbreviated FB, describes coins with both parallel lines in the center band distinctly separated. *In addition,* some dimes may display weak striking in other areas (not noted by certification services or others), including at areas of the obverse hair, rim, and date. Dimes of 1921 in particular can have FB but poorly struck dates.

Availability. Certain coins, such as 1916-D; 1921-P; 1921-D; 1942, 2 Over 1; and 1942-D, 2 Over 1, are elusive in any grade. Others are generally available in lower circulated grades, although some are scarce. In MS many of the issues before 1931 range from scarce to rare. If with FB and also sharply struck in other areas, some are rare. MS coins usually are very lustrous. In the marketplace certain scarce early issues such as 1916-D, 1921, and 1921-D are often graded slightly more liberally than are later varieties.

MS-60 to 70 (Mint State). *Obverse:* At MS-60, some abrasion and contact marks are evident on the highest part of the portrait, including the hair immediately to the right of the face and the upper left part of the wing. At MS-63, abrasion is slight at best, and slighter at 64. Album slide marks on the cheek, if present, should not exist at any grade above MS-64. An MS-65 coin should display no abrasion or contact marks except under magnification, and MS-66 and higher coins should have none at all. Luster should be full and rich. *Reverse:* Comments apply as for the obverse, except that the highest parts of the fasces, these being the horizontal bands, are the places to check. The field is mainly protected by design elements and does not show contact marks readily.

Full Bands

1928-S, Small Mintmark
FS-10-1928S-501.

1928-S, Large Mintmark

1929-S, Doubled-Die Obverse
FS-10-1929S-101.

	Mintage	Cert	Avg	%MS	MS-63	MS-64	MS-64FB	MS-65	MS-65FB	MS-66	MS-66FB	Recent Auction Record
1916	22,180,080	3,590	63.1	94	$48	$60	$70	$120	$175	$190	$425	$10,693, MS-68FB, February 2013
1916D † (a)	264,000	5,674	13.2	6	17,000	19,000	22,500	28,000	44,500	34,000	55,000	$152,750, MS-67FB, November 2013
1916S	10,450,000	1,375	60.2	86	65	90	170	215	700	400	1,300	$4,700, MS-67FB, November 2013
1917	55,230,000	1,139	62.8	86	60	80	100	170	400	360	850	$7,050, MS-67FB, November 2013
1917D	9,402,000	635	61.0	74	350	400	1,250	1,050	5,000	2,100	11,500	$7,638, MS-65FB, June 2014
1917S	27,330,000	896	62.2	83	180	265	425	500	1,000	750	1,800	$3,055, MS-67, July 2014
1918	26,680,000	583	62.4	86	125	160	350	425	1,200	1,150	2,000	$2,233, MS-66FB, January 2014
1918D	22,674,800	650	61.3	82	250	310	3,200	600	25,000	1,400	80,000	$88,125, MS-66FB, June 2014
1918S	19,300,000	509	61.9	83	275	450	2,500	725	6,750	1,950	11,500	$16,450, MS-66FB, August 2013
1919	35,740,000	705	63.0	88	150	180	275	375	725	1,200	1,700	$8,813, MS-67FB, March 2013
1919D	9,939,000	527	61.0	78	450	700	5,000	1,600	32,500	3,600	110,000	$5,288, MS-66, February 2014
1919S	8,850,000	366	59.7	67	450	700	6,200	1,200	14,000	1,475	67,500	$7,050, MS-64FB, December 2013
1920	59,030,000	1,089	63.3	92	75	100	150	260	500	540	900	$1,410, MS-66FB, August 2013
1920D	19,171,000	542	61.5	79	350	400	1,150	775	4,500	2,000	6,750	$44,063, MS-67FB, July 2014
1920S	13,820,000	406	60.6	72	325	465	2,300	1,450	6,500	2,850	15,500	$11,750, MS-66FB, February 2014
1921	1,230,000	1,264	30.2	24	2,200	2,300	2,850	3,500	4,200	4,400	7,200	$18,800, MS-67FB, June 2013
1921D	1,080,000	1,620	28.9	22	2,600	2,700	3,200	3,500	5,150	4,500	8,500	$9,400, MS-66FB, January 2014
1923 (b)	50,130,000	1,248	63.9	94	45	55	65	130	350	450	625	$4,406, MS-67FB, October 2013
1923S	6,440,000	462	59.5	69	400	575	2,150	1,250	5,800	2,400	18,500	$4,406, MS-65FB, August 2013
1924	24,010,000	730	63.5	94	100	125	160	210	500	450	975	$4,406, MS-67FB, March 2013
1924D	6,810,000	581	61.1	79	500	600	775	950	1,200	1,700	2,100	$1,116, MS-65FB, August 2013
1924S	7,120,000	469	59.6	70	525	600	2,900	1,250	15,000	3,200	60,000	$7,050, MS-65FB, June 2014
1925	25,610,000	565	63.4	91	85	130	225	225	875	550	1,600	$1,880, MS-67FB, August 2013
1925D	5,117,000	435	58.5	70	800	950	1,250	1,700	3,550	3,000	8,000	$10,575, MS-66FB, April 2014
1925S	5,850,000	451	60.6	77	500	700	1,375	1,400	3,100	2,600	7,000	$9,694, MS-66FB, April 2013
1926	32,160,000	945	63.4	91	65	100	145	250	400	475	900	$6,463, MS-67FB, August 2013
1926D	6,828,000	609	61.9	84	275	380	700	600	1,850	1,450	4,750	$5,875, MS-66FB, February 2013
1926S	1,520,000	571	48.2	40	1,500	1,875	3,600	2,850	6,000	4,600	14,000	$9,400, MS-67, August 2013
1927	28,080,000	864	63.7	93	60	100	140	150	385	310	800	$2,115, MS-67FB, June 2014
1927D	4,812,000	379	60.0	73	400	500	2,300	1,200	8,000	2,600	15,500	$8,813, MS-65FB, August 2013
1927S	4,770,000	349	60.3	75	550	700	2,300	1,400	7,500	2,350	17,750	$7,050, MS-65FB, June 2014
1928	19,480,000	887	63.9	95	55	70	100	130	350	350	600	$1,880, MS-67FB, August 2013
1928D	4,161,000	460	61.1	78	360	435	1,150	850	2,850	1,550	5,500	$4,259, MS-65FB, June 2014
1928S (c)	7,400,000	552	62.3	84	320	325	635	400	2,000	550	2,950	$4,406, MS-66FB, January 2014
1929	25,970,000	508	63.2	90	35	40	55	75	180	115	315	$6,463, MS-67FB, August 2013
1929D	5,034,000	2,617	64.4	99	36	42	70	75	225	130	460	$11,163, MS-68FB, July 2014
1929S	4,730,000	693	63.6	91	45	70	140	125	500	300	800	$5,288, MS-67FB, March 2013
1929S, DblDie Obverse (d)	*	7	54.0	29	150	175		200				$170, AU-58, December 2009
1930 (b)	6,770,000	829	63.7	92	50	55	145	125	450	225	910	$1,528, MS-66FB, August 2013
1930S	1,843,000	709	63.4	92	150	175	250	210	700	350	1,550	$11,163, MS-67FB, February 2013
1931	3,150,000	723	63.8	93	70	85	235	150	675	260	1,000	$12,338, MS-67FB, September 2013
1931D	1,260,000	1,171	63.6	94	140	165	190	280	400	380	600	$2,350, MS-67FB, August 2013
1931S	1,800,000	677	62.3	86	150	180	800	300	2,200	425	3,300	$28,200, MS-67FB, November 2013

* Included in number above. † Ranked in the *100 Greatest U.S. Coins* (fourth edition). **a.** Beware of altered or otherwise spurious mintmarks. **b.** Dimes dated 1923-D or 1930-D are counterfeit. **c.** Two mintmark styles exist: Large S (scarce) and Small S (common). About 80% of 1928-S dimes are of the Small S style. The scarcer Large S is worth about two to three times the values listed (which are for the Small S). **d.** Moderate doubling is evident on the date and IN GOD WE TRUST.

1936-S, Possible Overdate	1941-S, Small S	1941-S, Large S	1942, 2 Over 1
FS-10-1936S-110.		FS-10-1941S-511.	FS-10-1942-101.

1942-D, 2 Over 1	1943-S, Trumpet Tail Mintmark	1945-D, D Over Horizontal D
FS-10-1942D-101.	FS-10-1943S-511.	FS-10-1945D-506.

1945-S, S Over Horizontal S	1945-S, Normal S	1945-S, Micro S
FS-10-1945S-503.		FS-10-1945S-512.

	Mintage	Cert	Avg	%MS	MS-64FB	MS-65	MS-65FB	MS-66	MS-66FB	MS-67	MS-67FB	Recent Auction Record
1934	24,080,000	1,927	64.8	97	$40	$50	$140	$65	$220	$260	$370	$7,050, MS-68FB, February 2014
1934D	6,772,000	1,313	64.4	98	120	85	325	230	750	465	2,250	$4,406, MS-67FB, August 2013
1935	58,830,000	3,035	65.1	98	30	35	75	60	120	110	350	$7,638, MS-68FB, March 2013
1935D	10,477,000	946	64.1	94	180	90	525	325	800	500	2,900	$3,525, MS-67FB, June 2014
1935S	15,840,000	1,253	64.7	97	140	40	350	80	585	300	925	$3,819, MS-68, June 2014
1936	87,500,000	3,388	65.0	98	30	30	90	48	120	140	275	$5,289, MS-68FB, June 2014
1936D	16,132,000	1,291	64.5	96	120	55	275	80	350	325	700	$5,581, MS-68FB, August 2013
1936S	9,210,000	2,686	65.1	99	40	38	95	55	165	190	400	$1,763, MS-67FB, February 2013
1936S, Possible Overdate (a)	*	11	61.5	82	450	600						$1,500, MS-65FB, November 2011
1937	56,860,000	6,909	65.4	99	30	30	60	40	85	50	150	$2,820, MS-68FB, February 2013
1937D	14,146,000	1,995	65.0	98	38	45	100	85	180	120	300	$5,581, MS-68FB, August 2013
1937S	9,740,000	1,841	65.1	98	70	40	185	80	230	190	750	$1,998, MS-67FB, April 2014
1938	22,190,000	2,919	65.3	99	30	30	85	55	110	65	285	$6,463, MS-68FB, February 2013
1938D	5,537,000	3,285	65.2	99	32	35	65	75	120	235	265	$3,995, MS-68FB, August 2013
1938S	8,090,000	1,921	65.0	99	40	42	160	80	230	275	425	$3,819, MS-68FB, August 2013
1939	67,740,000	4,313	65.4	99	40	26	180	40	225	50	360	$10,281, MS-68FB, December 2013
1939D	24,394,000	6,395	65.4	99	30	32	55	60	85	110	175	$1,880, MS-68FB, November 2013
1939S	10,540,000	1,498	64.7	97	200	42	725	110	950	210	2,900	$3,819, MS-67FB, January 2014
1940	65,350,000	4,798	65.4	99	25	30	50	45	70	65	220	$9,988, MS-68FB, August 2013
1940D	21,198,000	3,565	65.3	99	26	35	50	50	65	80	180	$1,998, MS-68FB, August 2013
1940S	21,560,000	4,126	65.2	99	30	35	100	40	140	55	500	$6,463, MS-68FB, July 2014
1941	175,090,000	5,334	65.1	97	25	30	50	45	55	60	175	$5,288, MS-68FB, November 2013
1941D	45,634,000	6,359	65.2	99	25	25	50	32	55	60	175	$1,880, MS-68FB, November 2013
1941S	43,090,000	6,515	65.1	98	24	30	50	38	60	65	175	$8,225, MS-68FB, June 2013
1941S, Large S (b)	*	16	55.6	50		325						$120, MS-63, June 2010
1942, 42 Over 41 (c)	**	2,021	38.0	5	12,500 (d)	15,000	37,500	20,000	60,000	—	—	$8,225, MS-64, February 2014
1942	205,410,000	5,855	64.8	97	25	30	50	45	60	55	475	$5,288, MS-68FB, November 2013

* Included in number above. ** Included in number below. **a.** "The secondary image of a 2 is evident beneath the 3 of the date. Most evident is the flat portion of the base of the underlying 2. Remains of what is likely a secondary 9 are evident to the left of the primary 9. Many die polish marks are also evident throughout the surface of the obverse. No doubling is evident on other elements. . . . The length of time between the striking of the last 1929-dated coins and this 1936 coin would seem to eliminate the possibility of a 2 underlying the 3. However, examination has matched the shapes on the image under the 3 to that of the 2 on 1929-dated dimes. Stranger things have happened. Keep in mind that 1936 was during the Great Depression, when Mint personnel wanted to save money whenever possible." (*Cherrypickers' Guide to Rare Die Varieties,* fifth edition, volume II) **b.** This is the "Trumpet Tail" S mintmark, which is rare for this date. The upper serif points downward and the lower serif is rounded, like the bell of a trumpet. There are several dies known for the Large S dime, including one that is repunched. For more information, see the *Cherrypickers' Guide.* **c.** Doubling is evident in the 42 over 41 overdate, and slightly evident on IN GOD WE TRUST. Values for this variety fluctuate. **d.** Value in MS-64 is $7,200.

	Mintage	Cert	Avg	%MS	MS-64FB	MS-65	MS-65FB	MS-66	MS-66FB	MS-67	MS-67FB	Recent Auction Record
1942D, 42 Over 41 (e)	*	932	37.6	11	$11,500 (f)	$10,000	$32,000	$12,000	$38,000	—	—	$49,938, MS-66FB, June 2013
1942D	60,740,000	6,604	64.6	97	25	28	48	45	55	$75	$180	$2,115, MS-68FB, November 2013
1942S	49,300,000	3,089	64.9	97	30	30	150	50	225	125	650	$10,575, MS-68FB, January 2013
1943	191,710,000	6,370	65.2	98	24	27	55	35	60	45	300	$17,625, MS-68FB, November 2013
1943D	71,949,000	10,832	65.2	99	25	30	50	45	55	65	130	$3,055, MS-68FB, January 2014
1943S	60,400,000	4,790	65.2	99	25	30	70	40	80	55	175	$6,463, MS-68FB, January 2014
1943S, Trumpet Tail Mintmark (g)	**	20	59.7	75	500	450	750	500				$130, MS-62, December 2011
1944	231,410,000	7,116	65.2	99	24	25	80	45	165	50	850	$9,400, MS-67FB, January 2014
1944D	62,224,000	10,916	65.4	99	25	30	50	48	55	55	300	$3,290, MS-68FB, April 2013
1944S	49,490,000	7,633	65.3	99	25	30	55	50	75	60	180	$11,750, MS-68FB, November 2013
1945	159,130,000	5,809	65.0	98	5,250	28	10,000	45	18,000	50	32,000	$14,100, MS-65FB, November 2013
1945D	40,245,000	10,469	65.3	100	24	26	45	50	65	75	190	$9,988, MS-68FB, November 2013
1945D, D Over Horizontal D (h)	**	8	49.8	25	900	950						
1945S	41,920,000	6,634	65.3	99	28	30	125	40	165	60	640	$11,750, MS-68FB, November 2013
1945S, S Over Horizontal S (i)	**	6	46.3	17	900	950						
1945S, Micro S (j)	**	3,729	65.2	99	150	100	650	120	1,000	400	4,300	$7,638, MS-67FB, June 2014

* Included in number below. ** Included in number above. **e.** Doubling is evident in the 42 over 41 overdate, slightly evident on IN GOD WE TRUST, and as a D over D repunched mintmark (slanted west). Values for this variety fluctuate. **f.** Value in MS-64 is $7,200. **g.** This variety is considerably rarer than the 1941-S, Large S, which also features a Trumpet S mintmark. It is extremely rare in MS, and specimens with FB command a significant premium. The top serif of the S points downward, with the lower serif rounded, much like the bell of a trumpet. **h.** The first D mintmark was punched into the die horizontally and then corrected. **i.** The first S mintmark was punched into the die horizontally and then corrected. **j.** The S mintmark is significantly smaller than that of the normal S punch. This variety has the only mintmark punch of this type and size known to have been used during the 1940s. It was originally used for Philippine coins of 1907 through 1920.

Proof Winged Liberty Head (Mercury) Dimes

PF-60 to 70 (Proof). Proofs were minted from 1936 to 1942, and are available in proportion to their mintages. The dies were completely polished, including the portrait. *Obverse and Reverse:* Proofs that are extensively cleaned and have many hairlines, or that are dull and grainy, are lower level, such as PF-60 to 62. These are not widely desired in the marketplace, and represent coins that have been mistreated. With medium hairlines and good reflectivity, PF-63 or 64 is appropriate. Tiny horizontal lines on Miss Liberty's cheek, known as slide marks, from National and other album slides scuffing the relief of the cheek, are common; such coins should not be graded higher than PF-64, but sometimes are. With relatively few hairlines and no noticeable slide marks, a rating of PF-65 can be given. PF-66 should have hairlines so delicate that magnification is needed to see them. Above that, a Proof should be free of any hairlines or other problems.

**Proof Winged Liberty Head
(Mercury) Dime**
Shown 1.5x actual size.

	Mintage	Cert	Avg	PF-64	PF-65	PF-66	PF-67	Recent Auction Record
1936	4,130	1,418	64.6	$1,100	$1,400	$1,800	$5,000	$3,826, PF-67, April 2013
1937	5,756	1,818	65.1	600	800	1,150	1,400	$4,259, PF-68, June 2013
1938	8,728	2,439	65.0	325	500	750	1,100	$9,988, PF-68, June 2013
1939	9,321	2,620	65.5	300	400	600	750	$4,994, PF-68, June 2013
1940	11,827	2,948	65.2	225	300	550	625	$11,750, PF-69, January 2014
1941	16,557	3,967	65.0	210	275	525	600	$7,050, PF-68, June 2013
1942	22,329	5,391	65.2	210	275	525	600	$15,275, PF-69, November 2013

ROOSEVELT
(1946 TO DATE)

Silver (1946–1964, and some modern Proofs): Designer John R. Sinnock; weight 2.50 grams; composition .900 silver, .100 copper (net weight: .07234 oz. pure silver); diameter 17.9 mm; reeded edge; mints: Philadelphia, Denver, San Francisco.

Shown 2x actual size.

Clad (1965 to date): Designer John R. Sinnock; weight 2.27 grams; composition, outer layers of copper-nickel (.750 copper, .250 nickel) bonded to inner core of pure copper; diameter 17.9 mm; reeded edge; mints: Philadelphia, Denver, San Francisco, West Point.

Shown 2x actual size.

History. After President Franklin D. Roosevelt died in 1945, the Treasury rushed to create a coin in his honor. The ten-cent denomination was particularly appropriate, given the president's active support of the March of Dimes' fundraising efforts to cure polio. The obverse of the coin bears Roosevelt's profile portrait, while the reverse features a torch flanked by branches of olive and oak.

Striking and Sharpness. Little attention has been paid to the sharpness of these coins. The obverse portrait is such that lightness of strike on the higher points is difficult to detect. On the reverse,

check the leaves and the details of the torch. Some with complete separation on the lower two bands have been called Full Torch (FT), but interest seems to be minimal in today's marketplace.

Availability. All are common, although some are more common than others. MS coins in higher grades are usually very lustrous.

Note: Values of common-date silver coins have been based on the current bullion price of silver, $20 per ounce, and may vary with the prevailing spot price.

MS-60 to 70 (Mint State). *Obverse:* At MS-60, some abrasion and contact marks are evident on the cheek, the hair above the ear, and the neck. At MS-63, abrasion is slight at best, less so for MS-64. An MS-65 coin should display no abrasion or contact marks except under magnification, and MS-66 and higher coins should have none at all. Luster should be full and rich. *Reverse:* Comments apply as for the obverse, except that the highest parts of the torch, flame, and leaves are the places to check. On both sides the fields are protected by design elements and do not readily show contact marks.

1950-D, D Over S
FS-10-1950D-501.

1950-S, S Over D
FS-10-1950S-501.

1963, Doubled-Die Reverse
FS-10-1963-805.

1963-D, Doubled-Die Reverse
FS-10-1963D-801.

1964-D, Doubled-Die Reverse
FS-10-1964D-801. Other varieties exist.

	Mintage	Cert	Avg	%MS	MS-63	MS-65	MS-66	MS-67	MS-67FT	Recent Auction Record
1946	255,250,000	2,730	65.7	99	$4.25	$12	$28	$110	$850	$2,820, MS-68FB, June 2014
1946D	61,043,500	2,526	65.9	100	4.25	14	30	100	300	$3,525, MS-68FB, June 2014
1946S	27,900,000	2,407	65.9	100	4.50	20	32	90	245	$3,819, MS-68FB, February 2014
1947	121,520,000	1,228	65.8	100	6.00	12	24	55	1,000	$353, MS-67FB, April 2014
1947D	46,835,000	1,405	65.9	100	6.50	12	24	30	650	$1,763, MS-67FB, November 2013
1947S	34,840,000	2,397	65.9	99	6.00	12	30	110	500	$5,288, MS-68FB, November 2013
1948	74,950,000	1,107	65.6	100	4.25	12	30	85	500	$881, MS-67FB, April 2014
1948D	52,841,000	1,551	65.7	100	6.00	12	30	85	225	$141, MS-67FB, August 2013
1948S	35,520,000	1,636	66.0	100	5.50	12	32	100	225	$96, MS-67FB, June 2014
1949	30,940,000	1,095	65.6	99	27.00	38	65	125	825	$1,293, MS-67FB, February 2014
1949D	26,034,000	2,297	65.9	100	12.00	20	35	105	300	$4,113, MS-68FB, February 2013
1949S	13,510,000	1,938	65.6	99	45.00	55	75	190	2,000	$3,290, MS-67FB, June 2013
1950	50,130,114	1,132	65.9	100	13.00	16	35	135	600	$8,813, MS-68FB, April 2014
1950D	46,803,000	1,983	65.9	100	6.00	12	28	90	200	$1,410, MS-68FB, June 2014
1950D, D Over S (a)	*	1	65.0	100	400.00	650	825	1,100		
1950S	20,440,000	1,292	65.8	99	38.00	55	75	135	600	$1,763, MS-67FB, March 2014
1950S, S Over D (b)	*	n/a	n/a	n/a	250.00	375	750	1,000	1,675	$84, MS-65, June 2014
1951	103,880,102	1,383	65.8	99	4.25	10	30	110	450	$2,585, MS-67FB, February 2014
1951D	56,529,000	983	65.9	100	4.00	10	28	130	550	$3,525, MS-68FB, July 2014
1951S	31,630,000	1,512	66.0	100	14.00	25	45	110	450	$3,055, MS-68FB, April 2013
1952	99,040,093	1,189	65.6	99	4.25	10	30	85	1,000	$617, MS-67FB, August 2013
1952D	122,100,000	935	65.6	99	4.25	9	25	30	500	$2,115, MS-67FB, August 2013
1952S	44,419,500	1,306	65.9	99	8.00	12	35	75	750	$3,966, MS-69, January 2014
1953	53,490,120	818	65.7	100	4.00	8	15	90	225	$411, MS-67FB, June 2014
1953D	136,433,000	1,777	65.9	100	4.00	9	20	45	500	$411, MS-67FB, September 2013
1953S	39,180,000	3,338	66.0	100	4.00	9	25	65	875	$823, MS-67FB, April 2014
1954	114,010,203	1,227	65.8	100	4.00	8	20	32	1,000	$464, MS, February 2014
1954D	106,397,000	1,073	65.7	100	4.00	9	14	30	750	$141, MS-67, October 2013
1954S	22,860,000	2,112	65.8	100	4.00	9	16	40	750	$1,116, MS-67FB, August 2013
1955	12,450,181	1,660	65.8	100	4.00	8	16	25	1,000	$1,528, MS-67FB, September 2013
1955D	13,959,000	1,350	65.6	100	4.00	8	15	24	650	$88, MS-67, March 2014
1955S	18,510,000	2,069	65.7	100	4.00	8	15	60	2,300	$2,350, MS-67FB, August 2013
1956	108,640,000	1,826	65.9	100	3.00	6	14	45	1,000	$9,988, MS-68FB, December 2013
1956D	108,015,100	1,880	65.9	100	3.00	6	15	35	800	$217, MS-67FB, July 2013
1957	160,160,000	1,940	65.7	100	3.00	6	14	65	2,000	$1,998, MS-67FB, April 2014
1957D	113,354,330	1,401	65.9	100	3.00	6	14	20	2,000	$1,763, MS-67FB, February 2014
1958	31,910,000	1,820	65.9	100	3.00	7	15	55	2,000	$2,585, MS-67FB, June 2014
1958D	136,564,600	1,364	65.9	100	3.00	7	14	45	300	$2,115, MS-68FB, January 2014
1959	85,780,000	1,358	65.5	100	3.00	6	15	35	700	$1,528, MS-67FB, June 2014
1959D	164,919,790	1,351	65.8	100	3.00	6	14	25	150	$165, MS-67FB, October 2013
1960	70,390,000	1,064	65.6	100	3.00	6	14	25	800	$2,938, MS-67FB, June 2014
1960D	200,160,400	1,101	65.4	100	3.00	5	15	70	850	$2,233, MS-67FB, February 2014
1961	93,730,000	1,199	65.6	100	3.00	5	12	35	1,500	$1,880, MS-67FB, February 2014
1961D	209,146,550	1,158	65.5	100	3.00	5	12	25	700	$306, MS-67FB, October 2013
1962	72,450,000	1,518	65.5	100	3.00	5	12	40	500	$30, MS-66FB, March 2013
1962D	334,948,380	1,316	65.6	99	3.00	5	12	30	350	$294, MS-67FB, March 2014
1963	123,650,000	1,073	65.5	99	3.00	5	12	30	300	$5,581, MS-67FB, February 2014
1963, DblDie Reverse (c)	*	3	64.3	100	25.00	38	90			
1963D	421,476,530	1,301	65.6	99	3.00	5	12	30	2,000	$2,115, MS-67FB, September 2013
1963D, DblDie Reverse (d)	*	17	64.4	100	125.00	225	300			
1964 (e)	929,360,000	1,227	65.4	98	3.00	5	12	30	500	$1,058, MS-67FB, June 2014
1964D (e)	1,357,517,180	1,366	65.2	97	3.00	5	12	50	400	$1,439, MS, January 2014
1964D, DblDie Reverse (f)	*	57	60.9	68	100.00	160	235	450	—	$811, MS-65, April 2009

* Included in number above. **a.** The diagonal stroke of the initially punched S mintmark is visible within the opening of the primary D mintmark. The lower curve of the S is evident on the lower right curve of the D. **b.** The S mintmark is punched squarely over a previously punched D. CONECA lists this coin as an S Over Inverted S, indicating that the line enclosing the lower loop is that of the long upper serif on an inverted S. However, Fivaz and Stanton, in the *Cherrypickers' Guide to Rare Die Varieties*, fifth edition, volume II, "believe this to be an [overmintmark] (actually S/S/D) because the long upper serif of an S would not enclose the lower opening. In addition, the curve of the face of a D is clearly evident in the upper opening." **c.** Doubling is evident on UNITED, E PLURIBUS, the olive branch, and the stem. Lesser doubling is also visible on ONE DIME. **d.** Doubling is evident on all reverse lettering, with the most obvious doubling on AMERICA and on the top of the flame. Most MS specimens are MS-63 and lower. **e.** The 9 in the date has either a pointed tail or a straight tail. **f.** There are several varieties of 1964-D with a doubled-die reverse. The variety pictured and valued here is FS-10-1964D-801. For more information, see the *Cherrypickers' Guide to Rare Die Varieties*, fifth edition, volume II.

1967, Doubled-Die Obverse
FS-10-1967-101.

1970, Doubled-Die Reverse
FS-10-1970-801.

1982, No Mintmark, Strong Strike
FS-10-1982-501.

1982, No Mintmark, Weak Strike
FS-10-1982-502.

	Mintage	Cert	Avg	%MS	MS-65	MS-66	MS-67	MS-67FT	Recent Auction Record
1965 (a)	1,652,140,570	224	65.0	97	$2.50	$6	$25	$1,000	$3,819, MS-68FB, March 2013
1966 (a)	1,382,734,540	362	65.9	99	2.25	6	30	1,000	$2,820, MS-68FB, November 2013
1967 (a)	2,244,007,320	401	65.9	99	2.00	5	25	750	
1967, DblDie Obverse (b)	*	n/a	n/a	n/a	400.00	600	850		
1968	424,470,400	285	65.4	99	2.00	5	25	900	$1,116, MS-67FB, December 2013
1968D	480,748,280	978	66.1	100	2.00	5	20	125	$141, AU-58, November 2013
1969	145,790,000	111	64.5	97	3.00	6	30		$470, MS-67, April 2014
1969D	563,323,870	421	65.5	99	2.00	6	25	1,000	$17, MS-64, August 2013
1970	345,570,000	203	64.5	97	2.00	6	35		$55, MS-66, June 2014
1970, DblDie Reverse (c)	*	n/a	n/a	n/a	300.00	650	—		$56, MS-65, June 2009
1970D	754,942,100	328	65.2	99	2.00	5	35		$200, MS-61, January 2014
1971	162,690,000	241	64.9	99	2.50	6	40		$276, MS-66FB, January 2012
1971D	377,914,240	240	65.3	100	2.25	6	40	700	$109, MS-67FB, April 2012
1972	431,540,000	357	64.9	99	2.00	6	60		$99, MS-67, March 2004
1972D	330,290,000	300	65.4	100	2.00	6	40	800	$69, MS-66FB, September 2008
1973	315,670,000	291	65.0	100	2.00	5	70	1,200	$99, MS-67, March 2004
1973D	455,032,426	292	65.6	100	2.00	6	50	500	$27, MS-66FB, October 2008
1974	470,248,000	203	65.2	100	2.00	5	25		$52, MS-67, March 2004
1974D	571,083,000	231	65.6	100	2.00	5	25	1,000	$51, MS-67, October 2007
1975	585,673,900	185	65.0	99	2.00	5	25	1,000	$14, MS-66FB, September 2008
1975D	313,705,300	252	65.8	100	2.00	5	30	600	$270, MS-68, July 2014
1976	568,760,000	217	65.4	100	2.00	5	25	1,200	$1,035, MS-68, January 2012
1976D	695,222,774	199	65.6	99	2.00	5	45	1,200	$54, MS-67FB, October 2008
1977	796,930,000	198	65.4	99	2.00	5	25	1,200	$64, MS-66FB, October 2008
1977D	376,607,228	230	65.4	100	2.00	5	25	1,200	$64, MS-65FB, December 2007
1978	663,980,000	169	65.7	99	2.00	5	30	1,200	$17, MS-65, August 2008
1978D	282,847,540	195	65.7	100	2.00	5	25		$64, MS-66FB, October 2008
1979	315,440,000	109	65.6	100	2.00	5	30		$21, MS-66, December 2007
1979D	390,921,184	201	65.7	100	2.00	5	30		$28, MS-67, December 2004
1980P	735,170,000	185	65.6	99	2.00	5	25		$26, MS-67, March 2004
1980D	719,354,321	168	65.5	99	2.00	5	30		$13, MS-66, February 2008
1981P	676,650,000	448	65.8	100	2.00	5	40	70	$129, MS-65, January 2013
1981D	712,284,143	624	66.4	100	2.00	5	20	80	$38, MS-66FB, August 2009
1982, No Mintmark, Strong Strike ‡ (d)	*	2,114	64.6	97	225.00	300	650	1,800	$705, MS-67, June 2013
1982, No Mintmark, Weak Strike ‡ (d)	*	4	64.5	100	85.00	130	300		
1982P	519,475,000	232	64.8	94	7.50	18	50	1,000	$25, MS-66FB, October 2008
1982D	542,713,584	162	65.5	98	2.50	6	25	700	$1,410, MS-67FB, April 2014
1983P	647,025,000	128	65.2	99	6.50	15	30	250	$489, MS-68, April 2012

* Included in number below. ‡ Ranked in the *100 Greatest U.S. Modern Coins*. **a.** Values and auction records for Special Mint Set coins are listed with the Proofs for this type. **b.** This is a very rare doubled die. Its doubling is evident on IN GOD WE TRUST, the date, and the designer's initials. **c.** Doubling on this extremely rare variety is evident on all reverse lettering, especially on UNITED STATES OF AMERICA, with slightly weaker doubling on ONE DIME. **d.** The P mintmark was omitted from this working die. There are two versions of this variety: one with a strong strike, and one with a weak strike. The strong strike is far more valuable and in demand than the weak.

	Mintage	Cert	Avg	%MS	MS-65	MS-66	MS-67	MS-67FT	Recent Auction Record
1983D	730,129,224	146	64.8	93	$3.25	$8.50	$25	$200	$188, MS-68, December 2013
1984P	856,669,000	388	66.4	100	2.00	5.00	20	100	$11, MS-67FB, October 2008
1984D	704,803,976	310	66.0	100	2.25	5.00	20	150	$94, MS-67FB, May 2012
1985P	705,200,962	200	66.0	100	2.25	5.00	25	150	$13, MS-67FB, October 2008
1985D	587,979,970	347	66.5	100	2.25	5.00	30	100	$38, MS-66FB, August 2009
1986P	682,649,693	165	66.0	100	2.50	5.00	20	800	$150, MS-66FB, October 2008
1986D	473,326,970	170	66.2	100	2.50	5.00	20	700	$150, MS-66FB, September 2008
1987P	762,709,481	307	66.3	100	2.00	5.00	25	800	$31, MS-67, March 2008
1987D	653,203,402	322	66.4	100	2.00	5.00	20	200	$15, MS-65FB, October 2008
1988P	1,030,550,000	230	66.0	99	2.00	5.00	35	225	$103, MS-64, July 2014
1988D	962,385,489	221	66.1	99	2.00	5.00	40	100	$230, MS-68FB, April 2012
1989P	1,298,400,000	209	66.2	100	2.25	5.00	20	100	$45, MS-65, July 2014
1989D	896,535,597	324	66.4	99	2.00	6.00	20	75	$242, MS-68FB, April 2012
1990P	1,034,340,000	124	65.9	99	2.50	6.00	20	1,000	$27, MS-67, March 2004
1990D	839,995,824	142	66.1	99	2.00	4.00	25	1,100	$12, MS-67, March 2004
1991P	927,220,000	101	66.0	99	2.00	4.00	20	100	$27, MS-67, March 2004
1991D	601,241,114	91	65.4	98	2.00	4.00	20	200	$127, MS-67, May 2012
1992P	593,500,000	296	66.7	100	2.00	5.00	35	150	$322, MS-67FB, May 2010
1992D	616,273,932	164	66.0	99	2.00	4.00	30	200	$99, MS-67FB, April 2012
1993P	766,180,000	187	66.4	100	2.00	4.00	30	250	$53, MS-67FB, April 2012
1993D	750,110,166	98	65.4	98	2.00	4.00	25	500	$15, MS-66FB, October 2008
1994P	1,189,000,000	171	65.9	98	2.00	4.00	25	200	$76, MS-67FB, June 2014
1994D	1,303,268,110	101	65.5	98	2.00	4.00	25	300	$130, MS-64, July 2014
1995P	1,125,500,000	128	66.2	98	2.00	4.00	30	500	$21, MS-66FB, August 2009
1995D	1,274,890,000	137	66.1	99	2.25	5.00	35	425	$30, MS-67, August 2009
1996P	1,421,163,000	467	67.1	100	2.00	4.00	25	30	$14, MS-68, March 2009
1996D	1,400,300,000	373	66.8	100	2.00	4.00	20	75	$11, MS-67FB, October 2008
1996W ‡ (e)	1,457,000	4,630	66.5	100	20.00	30.00	50	100	$282, MS-68FB, April 2014
1997P	991,640,000	128	66.4	99	2.00	6.00	60	100	$21, MS-68, October 2008
1997D	979,810,000	126	66.4	99	2.00	6.00	65	100	$11, MS-65FB, October 2008
1998P	1,163,000,000	181	65.9	98	2.00	3.00	18	100	$11, MS-66FB, September 2008
1998D	1,172,250,000	113	65.9	100	2.00	3.00	15	100	$11, MS-65FB, November 2008
1999P	2,164,000,000	730	67.4	100	2.00	3.00	15	30	$3,055, MS-64, January 2014
1999D	1,397,750,000	361	67.2	99	2.00	3.00	15	40	$1,610, MS-69FB, April 2010
2000P	1,842,500,000	539	67.6	99	2.00	3.00	15	30	$823, MS-64, June 2013
2000D	1,818,700,000	527	67.4	99	2.00	3.00	15	30	$11, MS-68FB, September 2008
2001P	1,369,590,000	314	67.4	100	2.00	3.00	12	30	$21, MS-68, March 2009
2001D	1,412,800,000	627	67.7	100	2.00	3.00	12	30	$2,291, MS, December 2013
2002P	1,187,500,000	678	67.5	100	2.00	3.00	12	30	$11, MS-68FB, September 2008
2002D	1,379,500,000	451	67.3	100	2.00	3.00	12	30	$14, MS-68FB, October 2008
2003P	1,085,500,000	363	67.5	100	2.00	3.00	10	30	$11, MS-68FB, October 2008
2003D	986,500,000	342	67.2	100	2.00	3.00	10	30	$11, MS-68FB, September 2008
2004P	1,328,000,000	157	66.7	100	2.00	3.00	8	30	$104, MS-68FB, September 2008
2004D	1,159,500,000	192	67.0	99	2.00	3.00	8	35	$21, MS-68FB, October 2008
2005P	1,412,000,000	48	65.4	100	2.00	3.00	8	65	$17, MS-69 Satin, October 2008
2005D	1,423,500,000	78	65.8	95	2.00	3.00	8	80	$16, MS-69 Satin, September 2008
2006P	1,381,000,000	60	65.6	98	2.00	3.00	6	22	$16, MS-69FB Satin, September 2008
2006D	1,447,000,000	93	66.3	99	2.00	3.00	6	22	$19, MS-68FB Satin, December 2007
2007P	1,047,500,000	52	65.6	98	2.00	3.00	6	22	$223, MS-64, June 2013
2007D	1,042,000,000	90	66.3	100	2.00	3.00	6	22	$15, MS-69FB Satin, October 2008
2008P	391,000,000	47	65.4	100	2.00	3.00	5	22	
2008D	624,500,000	80	65.6	99	2.00	3.00	5	22	
2009P	96,500,000	225	65.6	100	2.00	3.00	5	22	
2009D	49,500,000	196	66.2	100	2.00	3.00	5	22	
2010P	557,000,000	182	66.7	100	2.00	3.00	4	20	
2010D	562,000,000	112	66.1	100	2.00	3.00	4	20	
2011P	748,000,000	303	66.4	100	2.00	3.00	4	20	
2011D	754,000,000	318	66.6	100	2.00	3.00	4	20	

‡ Ranked in the *100 Greatest U.S. Modern Coins*. **d.** The P mintmark was omitted from this working die. There are two versions of this variety: one with a strong strike, and one with a weak strike. The strong strike is far more valuable and in demand than the weak. **e.** Issued in Mint sets only, to mark the 50th anniversary of the design.

Chart continued on next page.

	Est Mintage	Cert	Avg	%MS	MS-65	MS-66	MS-67	MS-67FT	Recent Auction Record
2012P	808,000,000	n/a	n/a	n/a	$2	$3	$4	$20	
2012D	868,000,000	n/a	n/a	n/a	2	3	4	20	
2013P	1,086,500,000	n/a	n/a	n/a	2	3	4	20	
2013D	1,025,500,000	n/a	n/a	n/a	2	3	4	20	
2014P		n/a	n/a	n/a	2	3	4	20	
2014D		n/a	n/a	n/a	2	3	4	20	

Proof Roosevelt Dimes

PF-60 to 70 (Proof). Proofs have been made of the 1950 to 1964 years, and again from 1968 to date. Those of the 1970s onward usually have frosted or cameo contrast. Special Mint Set (SMS) coins, struck in lieu of Proofs from 1965 to 1967, in some instances closely resemble Proofs. The majority of Proofs made in recent decades are at high levels, MS-66 to 68 or higher. *Obverse and Reverse:* Proofs that are extensively cleaned and have many hairlines, or that are dull and grainy, are lower level, such as PF-60 to 62. These are coins that have been mistreated, and they are not widely sought in the marketplace. Only a few Proof Roosevelt dimes are in this category. With medium hairlines and good reflectivity, assigned grades of PF-63 or 64 are appropriate. PF-65 may have hairlines so delicate that magnification is needed to see them. Above that, a Proof should be free of any hairlines or other problems.

Proof Roosevelt Dime

1960, Proof, Doubled-Die Obverse
FS-10-1960-102. Various die states exist.

1963, Proof, Doubled-Die Reverse
FS-10-1963-802. Other varieties exist

1968-S, Proof, Doubled-Die Obverse

     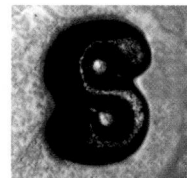

1968-S, Proof, No Mintmark *FS-10-1968S-102.*	1979-S, Filled S (Type 1)	1979-S, Clear S (Type 2)	1981-S, Rounded S (Type 1)	1981-S, Flat S (Type 2)

	Mintage	Cert	Avg	PF-65	PF-66	PF-66Cam	PF-67	PF-67Cam	PF-67DC	Recent Auction Record
1950	51,386	1,541	65.8	$50.00	$65	$250	$120			$18,800, PF-68DCam, March 2014
1951	57,500	1,658	66.1	50.00	65	225	100			$23,500, PF-68DCam, January 2014
1952	81,980	1,555	66.0	35.00	50	175	85			$1,116, PF-68Cam, April 2013
1953	128,800	1,514	66.0	38.00	55	160	80			$999, PF-68Cam, June 2013
1954	233,300	1,684	66.2	18.00	25	75	30			$9,400, PF-68DCam, April 2014
1955	378,200	1,651	66.5	15.00	20	70	25			$881, PF-68DCam, April 2013
1956	669,384	1,352	66.5	8.00	10	50	18			$646, PF-68DCam, June 2013
1957	1,247,952	1,691	66.7	5.00	8	70	25			$4,113, PF-69DCam, January 2014
1958	875,652	1,093	66.6	5.00	8	25	10			$2,585, PF-69DCam, April 2013
1959	1,149,291	1,225	66.7	5.00	8	25	10			$940, PF-68DCam, April 2014
1960	1,691,602	2,178	67.2	5.00	10	50	18			$499, PF-69DCam, November 2013
1960, Doubled-Die Obverse	*	96	65.6	150.00	250					$129, PF-67, June 2013

* Included in number above.

	Mintage	Cert	Avg	PF-65	PF-66	PF-66Cam	PF-67	PF-67Cam	PF-67DC	Recent Auction Record
1961	3,028,244	1,890	67.1	$5.00	$8	$30	$12			$2,115, PF, August 2013
1962	3,218,019	2,276	67.1	5.00	8	25	10			$329, PF, February 2013
1963	3,075,645	3,463	67.3	5.00	8	25	10			$147, PF-69DCam, May 2013
1963, DblDie Reverse (a)	*	180	66.1	150.00	250					$207, PF-67, February 2012
1964	3,950,762	4,161	67.8	5.00	8	25	10			$329, PF-70, June 2014
1965, SMS ‡	2,360,000	1,436	66.8	11.00	13	75	17	$170	—	$2,585, PF-68Cam, January 2014
1966, SMS ‡	2,261,583	1,518	67.0	11.00	13	45	20	90	—	$999, PF-69, April 2013
1967, SMS ‡	1,863,344	1,492	66.9	12.00	14	19	18	40	$1,500	$9,988, PF-68DCam, January 2014
1968S	3,041,506	1,058	68.0	2.00	4	5	6	15	30	$72, PF-69DCam, April 2013
1968S, DblDie Obverse (b)	*	27	66.1	350.00	500		750	—	—	$74, PF-67, March 2012
1968S, No Mintmark ‡ (c)	*	19	67.2	12,000.00	14,500		16,000	—	—	$30,550, PF-68Cam, April 2013
1969S	2,394,631	1,051	68.1	2.00	4	5	6	18	35	$74, PF-69DCam, May 2013
1970S	2,632,810	1,136	67.9	2.00	4	5	6	18	35	$57, PF-69DCam, April 2013
1970S, No Mintmark ‡ (c)	*	208	67.2	800.00	900	950	1,000	—	—	$1,528, PF-69Cam, June 2013
1971S	3,220,733	1,201	68.0	2.00	4	5	6	15	30	$306, PF-69DCam, June 2014
1972S	3,260,996	1,169	68.3	2.00	4	5	6	8	12	$24, PF-69DCam, August 2013
1973S	2,760,339	2,402	68.9	2.00	4	5	6	9	14	$7,050, PF-70DCam, January 2014
1974S	2,612,568	3,685	68.9	2.00	4	5	6	8	12	$1,293, PF-70DCam, April 2013
1975S	2,845,450	4,041	68.9	2.50	4	5	6	8	10	$611, PF-70DCam, January 2014
1975S, No Mintmark (c)	*	1	68.0	38,000.00	40,000	42,500	45,000	—	—	$349,600, PF-68, August 2011
1976S	4,149,730	5,245	69.0	2.75	4	5	6	8	10	$206, PF-70DCam, January 2014
1977S	3,251,152	4,614	69.0	2.50	4	5	6	8	9	$53, PF-70DCam, May 2013
1978S	3,127,781	5,566	69.0	2.50	4	5	6	8	9	$110, PF-70DCam, March 2013
1979S, Type 1	3,677,175	5,308	69.1	2.50	4	5	6	9	10	$74, PF-70DCam, January 2010
1979S, Type 2	*	3,774	69.0	5.00	6	7	8	10	15	$110, PF-70DCam, February 2013
1980S	3,554,806	5,652	69.0	2.50	4	5	6	8	9	$94, PF-70DCam, January 2013
1981S, Type 1	4,063,083	6,617	69.0	2.50	4	5	6	9	10	$31, PF-70DCam, January 2014
1981S, Type 2	*	1,423	68.9	5.50	6	7	8	12	18	$423, PF-70DCam, December 2013
1982S	3,857,479	3,060	69.0	2.50	4	5	6	8	9	$58, PF-70DCam, May 2013
1983S	3,279,126	3,233	69.1	3.00	4	5	6	8	10	$47, PF-70DCam, April 2013
1983S, No Mintmark (c) ‡	*	177	68.4	750.00	850	925	1,000	—	—	$6,463, PF-70DCam, March 2013
1984S	3,065,110	2,913	69.1	2.50	4	5	6	8	9	$106, PF-70DCam, March 2013
1985S	3,362,821	2,946	69.0	3.00	4	5	6	8	9	$16, PF-69DCam, August 2009
1986S	3,010,497	3,169	69.1	4.00	5	6	7	9	10	$48, PF-70DCam, April 2013
1987S	4,227,728	3,246	69.0	3.00	4	5	6	8	9	$15, PF-69DCam, August 2009
1988S	3,262,948	2,422	69.0	4.00	5	6	7	9	10	$60, PF-70DCam, May 2013
1989S	3,220,194	2,503	69.0	4.00	5	5	6	8	9	$15, PF-69DCam, August 2009
1990S	3,299,559	3,587	69.1	2.50	4	5	6	8	9	$56, PF-70DCam, December 2009
1991S	2,867,787	2,847	69.2	4.00	5	6	7	8	9	$31, PF-70DCam, June 2014
1992S	2,858,981	2,939	69.2	3.00	4	5	6	8	9	$53, PF-70DCam, December 2009
1992S, Silver	1,317,579	3,192	69.1	6.00	7	8	8	10	12	$59, PF-70DCam, February 2010
1993S	2,633,439	2,683	69.2	5.00	6	7	7	8	9	$62, PF-70DCam, December 2009
1993S, Silver	761,353	2,499	69.1	7.00	8	9	9	10	12	$94, PF-70DCam, February 2010
1994S	2,484,594	2,637	69.1	5.00	6	7	8	9	10	$59, PF-70DCam, October 2009
1994S, Silver	785,329	2,469	69.1	8.00	9	10	10	12	14	$96, PF-70DCam, May 2013
1995S	2,117,496	2,744	69.1	10.00	16	18	20	25	35	$84, PF-70DCam, December 2009
1995S, Silver	679,985	2,276	69.1	14.00	23	25	30	35	40	$100, PF-70DCam, May 2013
1996S	1,750,244	2,451	69.1	3.00	6	7	8	10	12	$42, PF-70DCam, February 2010
1996S, Silver	775,021	2,528	69.1	8.00	10	13	15	20	25	$88, PF-70DCam, May 2013
1997S	2,055,000	2,431	69.1	8.00	10	13	15	20	30	$69, PF-70DCam, December 2009
1997S, Silver	741,678	2,789	69.1	12.00	22	26	18	25	40	$46, PF-70DCam, May 2013
1998S	2,086,507	2,408	69.1	4.00	6	7	8	10	12	$17, PF-69DCam, August 2009
1998S, Silver	878,792	2,848	69.1	6.00	8	9	10	12	15	$79, PF-70DCam, February 2010
1999S	2,543,401	2,279	69.2	4.00	6	7	8	10	12	$67, PF-70DCam, January 2010
1999S, Silver	804,565	3,893	69.1	7.00	8	10	12	13	16	$76, PF-70DCam, May 2013
2000S	3,082,572	2,899	69.2	2.50	4	6	7	9	10	$59, PF-70DCam, December 2009
2000S, Silver	965,421	5,760	69.2	5.00	6	7	8	10	12	$28, PF-70DCam, April 2013
2001S	2,294,909	3,313	69.2	2.50	4	6	7	9	10	$50, PF-70DCam, December 2009

* Included in number above. ‡ Ranked in the *100 Greatest U.S. Modern Coins*. **a.** Several less-valuable 1963 Proof DDRs exist. Values shown are for FS-10-1963-802. **b.** There are several 1968-S Proof doubled-die obverse varieties. The one listed here is FS-10-1968S-102 (see the *Cherrypickers' Guide to Rare Die Varieties*, fifth edition, volume II). **c.** The S mintmark was inadvertently left off the coinage die; this defect was probably discovered before the end of the die's life.

	Mintage	Cert	Avg	PF-65	PF-66	PF-66Cam	PF-67	PF-67Cam	PF-67DC	Recent Auction Record
2001S, Silver	889,697	4,567	69.3	$5.00	$6	$7	$8	$10	$12	$36, PF-70UCam, February 2010
2002S	2,319,766	2,846	69.2	2.50	4	6	7	9	10	$44, PF-70DCam, December 2009
2002S, Silver	892,229	4,298	69.3	5.00	6	7	8	10	12	$42, PF-70DCam, March 2010
2003S	2,172,684	3,568	69.4	2.50	4	6	7	9	10	$52, PF-70DCam, March 2010
2003S, Silver	1,125,755	5,603	69.3	4.50	5	7	8	10	12	$38, PF-70DCam, March 2010
2004S	1,789,488	2,662	69.2	3.00	5	6	7	9	10	$69, PF-70DCam, October 2009
2004S, Silver	1,175,934	5,830	69.4	5.00	6	7	8	10	12	$40, PF-70DCam, November 2013
2005S	2,275,000	5,601	69.3	2.50	4	6	7	9	10	$40, PF-70DCam, December 2009
2005S, Silver	1,069,679	5,482	69.5	5.00	6	7	8	10	12	$40, PF-70DCam, November 2013
2006S	2,000,428	2,742	69.4	2.50	4	6	7	9	10	$69, PF-70UCam, October 2009
2006S, Silver	1,054,008	3,592	69.4	5.00	6	7	8	10	12	$56, PF-70UCam, February 2010
2007S	1,702,116	2,876	69.4	2.50	4	6	7	9	10	$40, PF-70DCam, December 2009
2007S, Silver	875,050	3,625	69.6	5.00	6	7	8	10	12	$26, PF-69DCam, February 2013
2008S	1,405,674	2,119	69.5	2.50	4	6	7	9	10	$56, PF-70DCam, October 2009
2008S, Silver	763,887	4,385	69.7	5.00	6	7	8	10	12	$36, PF-70UCam, March 2010
2009S	1,482,502	3,430	69.7	2.50	4	6	7	9	10	$23, PF-69DCam, February 2013
2009S, Silver	697,365	4,249	69.7	5.00	6	7	8	10	12	$40, PF-70UCam, March 2010
2010S	1,103,815	1,990	69.5	2.50	4	6	7	9	10	
2010S, Silver	585,401	4,056	69.7	5.00	6	7	8	10	12	
2011S	1,098,835	2,742	69.6	2.50	4	6	7	9	10	
2011S, Silver	574,175	5,034	69.7	5.00	6	7	8	10	12	
2012S	841,972	99	69.5	2.50	4	6	7	9	10	
2012S, Silver	395,443	n/a	n/a	5.00	6	7	8	10	12	
2013S	821,031			2.50	4	6	7	9	10	
2013S, Silver				5.00	6	7	8	10	12	
2014S				2.50	4	6	7	9	10	
2014S, Silver				5.00	6	7	8	10	12	

The twenty-cent piece, made in silver, proved to be the shortest-lived denomination in American coinage history. They were struck in quantity in their first year of issue, 1875, after which it was learned that the public confused them with quarter dollars. Mintages dropped sharply, and in 1877 and 1878 coinage was limited to just Proofs for collectors. Both sides of the twenty-cent piece were designed by Chief Engraver William Barber. The obverse is simply an adaptation of the Liberty Seated motif earlier used on other denominations. The reverse is new and depicts a perched eagle of the same general appearance as introduced by Barber on the 1873 silver trade dollar).

Only one twenty-cent piece is needed for inclusion in a type set. By far the most readily available in Mint State is the 1875-S, followed by the 1875-CC. These are often somewhat lightly struck on the reverse, particularly near the top of the eagle's wings. The 1875 and 1876 Philadelphia coins are occasionally encountered in Mint State and are usually well struck.

Proofs are readily available for all years, 1875 through 1878.

FOR THE COLLECTOR AND INVESTOR: TWENTY-CENT PIECES AS A SPECIALTY

A full date-and-mintmark set of twenty-cent pieces consists of the 1875, 1875-CC, 1875-S, 1876, 1876-CC, 1877, and 1878, the last two years being available only in Proof format. The great challenge in forming a set is the 1876-CC, of which 10,000 were minted, but, seemingly, all but about two dozen were melted. Those that do survive are typically encountered in Mint State and are widely heralded when they are offered at auction.

Civil War hero Ulysses S. Grant was president when the twenty-cent piece was introduced to American commerce.

LIBERTY SEATED
(1875–1878)

*Designer William Barber; weight 5 grams; composition
.900 silver, .100 copper; diameter 22 mm; plain edge;
mints: Philadelphia, Carson City, San Francisco.*

Shown 1.5x actual size.

History. The twenty-cent coin debuted in 1875 as a convenient denomination to make change in the West (at the time silver coins did not circulate in the East or Midwest). The coins sometimes were confused with quarter dollars, given their similar Liberty Seated design on the obverse, and their similar size. The quantity minted dropped considerably in 1876, and in 1877 and 1878 only Proofs were struck. Despite the brief time of their production, these coins were still seen in circulation through the early 1900s, by which time they were often casually used as quarters.

Striking and Sharpness. Areas of weakness are common. On the obverse, check the head of Miss Liberty and the stars. The word LIBERTY is *raised* on this coin, a curious departure from other Liberty Seated coins of the era, on which it is recessed or incuse (the Gobrecht silver dollars of 1836 and 1839 being exceptions). On the reverse, check the eagle's feathers, especially the top of the wing on the left, but other areas can be weak as well. Some 1875-S coins are highly prooflike.

Availability. Most often seen is the high-mintage 1875-S, although the 1875 and 1875-CC are encountered with frequency. The 1876 is quite scarce and when seen is usually in high grades and well struck. The 1876-CC is a rarity, and only about two dozen are known, nearly all of which are MS. The eye appeal of MS coins can vary widely. The number of letters in LIBERTY on certain coins graded from VG through VF can vary widely in the marketplace.

AU-50, 53, 55, 58 (About Uncirculated). *Obverse:* Light wear is seen on the thighs and knees, bosom, and head. At AU-50 and 53, some luster is evident. At AU-58, the luster is extensive but incomplete, especially in the right field. *Reverse:* Wear is evident on the eagle's breast (the prime focal point) and the top of the wings. At AU-50 and 53, there are traces of luster. An AU-58 coin has nearly full luster, more so than on the obverse, as the design elements protect the small field areas.

MS-60 to 70 (Mint State). *Obverse:* At MS-60, some abrasion and contact marks are evident, most noticeably on the bosom and thighs and knees. Luster is present, but may be dull or lifeless. At MS-63, contact marks are very few, and abrasion is hard to detect except under magnification. An MS-65 coin has no abrasion, and contact marks are sufficiently minute as to require magnification. Check the knees of Liberty and the right field. Luster should be full and rich.

Reverse: Comments apply as for the obverse, except that in lower MS grades abrasion and contact marks are most noticeable on the eagle's breast and the top of the wing to the left. At MS-65 or higher, there are no marks visible to the unaided eye. The field is mainly protected by design elements and does not show abrasion as much as does the obverse on a given coin.

	Mintage	Cert	Avg	%MS	AU-50	MS-60	MS-62	MS-63	MS-64	MS-65	MS-66	Recent Auction Record
1875	38,500	975	52.4	42	$710	$925	$1,300	$1,600	$2,500	$6,000	$12,500	$22,325, MS-67, June 2014
1875CC	133,290	1,813	42.1	32	1,800	2,300	3,200	4,500	5,750	12,500	40,000	$49,938, MS-66, June 2014
1875S (a)	1,155,000	5,491	52.6	52	400	650	1,000	1,400	2,100	5,500	11,000	$19,975, MS-67, June 2014
1876	14,400	927	56.0	56	650	950	1,200	1,500	2,500	6,000	15,000	$55,813, MS-67, June 2014
1876CC †	10,000	21	63.8	95	175,000	250,000	300,000	360,000	375,000	425,000	500,000	$564,000, MS-65, January 2013

† Ranked in the *100 Greatest U.S. Coins* (fourth edition). **a.** There are at least two misplaced-date die varieties of the 1875-S twenty-cent piece. These do not command a premium in the marketplace. A repunched mintmark is likewise common.

Proof Twenty-Cent Pieces

PF-20 to 70 (Proof). Proof coins were made of all years 1875 to 1878. Most often seen are those of 1875 and 1876. The 1877 and 1878 are Proof-only issues with no related circulation strikes. For some reason, high-quality Proofs of the last two years are very hard to find. Most have been cleaned or even lightly polished. Such coins are given "impaired Proof" designa-tions such as PF-20 or PF-40. Many Proofs in the marketplace have been convincingly retoned to mask problems. Proofs are usu-ally well struck, but more than just a few are somewhat flat on the hair details of Miss Liberty. *Obverse and Reverse:* Proofs that are extensively cleaned and have many hairlines, or that are dull and grainy, are lower level, such as PF-20 to 62. These are not widely desired. With medium hair-lines and good reflectivity, an assigned grade of PF-64 is indicated, and with rela-tively few hairlines, PF-65. In various grades hairlines are most easily seen in the obverse field. PF-66 should have hairlines so delicate that magnification is needed to see them. Above that, a Proof should be free of such lines.

Proof Twenty-Cent Piece
Shown 2x actual size.

	Mintage	Cert	Finest	PF-20	PF-40	PF-60	PF-63	PF-64	PF-65	Recent Auction Record
1875	1,200	577	PF-67			$1,500	$3,000	$5,000	$10,000	$28,200, PF-67, June 2014
1875S	*10–20*	5	PF-64			15,000	25,000	45,000	100,000	$103,500, PF-64, January 2009
1876	1,500	716	PF-68			1,500	3,000	5,000	10,000	$18,800, PF-66Cam, June 2013
1877	510	553	PF-67	$3,500	$4,000	4,500	6,000	8,000	12,500	$27,025, PF-66Cam, November 2013
1878	600	740	PF-67	2,500	2,800	4,250	5,250	7,500	12,000	$12,925, PF-65, April 2013

In 1796 the first silver quarters were struck at the Philadelphia Mint. The Draped Bust obverse in combination with the Small Eagle reverse was produced only in this year, after which no pieces of this denomination were produced until 1804. At that time the Draped Bust obverse was continued, but now with the Heraldic Eagle reverse. The coinage proved to be brief and lasted only through 1807, after which no quarters were struck until 1815. The new quarters dated 1815 were of the Capped Bust style, by John Reich. These were produced intermittently through 1838. In that year the Liberty Seated motif, by Christian Gobrecht, made its debut. Such pieces were produced continuously through 1891, with several modifications as to design and metallic content. The Liberty Head quarter, today called the Barber quarter after its designer, was introduced in 1892 and minted continuously through 1916. The obverse features the head of Miss Liberty, and the reverse a heraldic eagle. In late 1916 the Standing Liberty by Hermon A. MacNeil became the new design. This was produced through 1930, except for 1922. Some changes to both the obverse and reverse were made partway through 1917.

The Washington quarter dollar was struck in 1932 to observe the 200th anniversary of the birth of our first president. Pieces have been struck continuously since then, except for 1933, and with none dated 1975. In 1976 a special Bicentennial motif was introduced. Beginning in 1999 the statehood quarters were launched, issued at the rate of five per year, covering all 50 states, each coin having its own distinctive design. After this successful and popular program came quarter dollars with motifs celebrating the District of Columbia and U.S. territories. Others commemorating national parks have been slated for 2010 through 2021.

While there are no super-rarities among the different *types* of quarter dollars, the first one, the 1796 with Draped Bust obverse and Small Eagle reverse, is hard to find and expensive in all grades. The values are, of course, justified by the great demand for this single-year type.

The collector's greatest challenge in finding a decent strike is in the short-lived 1804–1807 type with Heraldic Eagle reverse. Sufficient quantities were made that examples from these years are not rarities but nearly all are weakly struck. Quarters of the 1815–1828 Capped Bust type, large planchet, are available easily enough in worn grades but are scarce to rare in Mint State. Some cherrypicking is needed to find a sharp strike.

Respite from the sharp-strike difficulty is at last found with the 1831–1838 type, Capped Bust, small diameter, and without E PLURIBUS UNUM. Most are quite nice. Also, for the first time Mint State coins are generally available with frequency in the marketplace, although those with good eye appeal are in the distinct minority.

The Liberty Seated quarters of the several types made from 1838 to 1891 are generally available in proportion to their mintages, with an allowance for the earlier dates being scarcer than the later ones—as they had a longer time to become worn or lost. Many quarters of earlier dates were melted circa 1850–1853, when the price of silver rose on international markets, and such coins were worth slightly more in melt-down value than face value.

Barber quarters, 1892–1916, present no difficulty for the collector, except that there is a challenge to find an example with sharp striking overall, including in the telltale area on the reverse at and near the eagle's leg to the right. MS-65 and better Barber quarters are scarcer than generally known (the same can be said for Barber half dollars). Proofs were sold to collectors and saved, and thus they are available in proportion to their mintages, with probably 70% to 80% surviving.

The Variety 1 Standing Liberty quarter is a rarity if dated 1916, for only 52,000 were struck, and not many were saved. The feasible alternative is the 1917 Variety 1, which is often seen in Mint State, sharply struck, and very beautiful. Standing Liberty quarters of the Variety 2 design, minted from partway through 1917 to 1930, often are weakly struck on the head of Miss Liberty and on the shield rivets, and sometimes other places as well. Searching is needed to locate a nice example.

Washington quarters present no difficulty for collectors. The State, D.C./Territorial, and National Parks reverses are appealing in their diversity and make a fascinating study in themselves.

FOR THE COLLECTOR AND INVESTOR: QUARTER DOLLARS AS A SPECIALTY

The formation of a specialized collection of quarter dollars from 1796 to date, by dates, mints, and major varieties, is a considerable challenge. As a class, quarters are considerably more difficult to acquire than are either dimes or half dollars. Relatively few numismatists have ever concentrated on the series

The 1796 is rare and popular both as a date and a type. The 1804, although elusive in worn grades, is of commanding importance if in AU or Mint State. The 1823, 3 Over 2 is a classic rarity and is nearly always encountered well worn. In the same decade the 1827 is famous. Although Mint records indicate that 4,000 circulation strikes were produced in calendar year 1827, they were probably struck from 1825-dated or earlier dies, as no unequivocal circulation strike has ever been located. There are, however, a dozen or so Proofs. Originals are distinguished by the 2 (in the 25 C. denomination) having a curved base, while restrikes, also very rare, have a square-base 2.

One of the unsolved mysteries in numismatics involves certain quarter dollars dated 1815 (the die variety known as Browning-1) and 1825, 5 Over 3 (Browning-2), which are often seen counterstamped, above the cap, with either an E or an L. Hundreds exist. As other quarter-dollar die varieties were made during this period, but only these two bear counterstamps, it may be that this was done either at the Mint or elsewhere before they were generally distributed.

Ard W. Browning's 1925 text, *The Early Quarters of the United States, 1796–1838,* remains the standard reference on the series, together with new information added here and there, including in issues of the *John Reich Journal,* the magazine of the John Reich Collectors Society.

The panorama of Liberty Seated quarters from 1838 to 1891 is highlighted by several rarities, notably the 1842 Small Date (known only in Proof format) and the 1873-CC Without Arrows (of which only five are known, at least three being Mint State). The others are generally available, but some can be almost impossible to find in Mint State, the 1849-O, certain early San Francisco issues, and Carson City coins of the early 1870s being well known in this regard. From the mid-1870s onward Mint State coins are generally available, including choice and gem pieces. Proofs from 1858 onward can be found in proportion to their mintages, with later dates often being seen with higher numerical designations than are earlier ones.

Barber quarters are collectible by date and mint, although the "big three" rarities, the 1896-S, 1901-S, and 1913-S, are expensive and hard to find.

Standing Liberty quarters, 1916–1930, represent a short-lived series, one easy enough to collect in grades up to MS-63, except for the rare 1918-S, 8 Over 7 overdate. Finding higher-grade coins that are sharply struck is another matter entirely, and over the years few sets of this nature have been assembled.

Washington quarters are all collectible, with no great rarities. However, in relation to the demand for them, certain early issues are elusive, the 1932-D being best known in this regard. Modern issues, including the Bicentennial, Statehood, D.C./Territorial, and National Parks coins, are at once plentiful, inexpensive, and interesting.

RECOMMENDED READING

Bowers, Q. David. *A Guide Book of Washington and State Quarters,* Atlanta, GA, 2006.

Bressett, Kenneth. *The Official Whitman Statehood Quarters Collector's Handbook,* New York, 2000.

Briggs, Larry. *The Comprehensive Encyclopedia of United States Seated Quarters,* Lima, Ohio, 1991.

Browning, Ard W. *The Early Quarter Dollars of the United States, 1796–1838,* New York, 1925 (reprinted 1992).

Cline, J.H. *Standing Liberty Quarters* (4th ed.), 2007.

Fivaz, Bill, and Stanton, J.T. *The Cherrypickers' Guide to Rare Die Varieties* (5th ed., vol. II), Atlanta, GA, 2012.

Haseltine, J.W. *Type Table of United States Dollars, Half Dollars and Quarter Dollars,* Philadelphia, 1881 (reprinted 1927, 1968).

Kelman, Keith N. *Standing Liberty Quarters,* 1976.

Lawrence, David. *The Complete Guide to Barber Quarters,* Virginia Beach, VA, 1989.

Tompkins, Steve M. *Early United States Quarters, 1796–1838,* Sequim, WA, 2010.

Four famous quarter dollar designers: Christian Gobrecht, Charles Barber, Hermon MacNeil, and John Flanagan.

DRAPED BUST, SMALL EAGLE REVERSE
(1796)

Designer probably Gilbert Stuart; engraver Robert Scot; weight 6.74 grams; composition .8924 silver, .1076 copper; approx. diameter 27.5 mm; reeded edge. All coined at Philadelphia.

Browning-2.

History. The U.S. Mint coined its first quarter dollar in 1796. Its design followed that of other silver U.S. coins. Only 6,146 were made, followed by a production hiatus until 1804, by which time a new reverse was used. Thus the 1796 was isolated as a single-year type.

Striking and Sharpness. On the obverse, check the hair details and the star centers. Most are well struck. On the reverse, most are well struck except for the head of the eagle, which can be shallow or flat, especially on the B-2 variety (there are two known die varieties for this year, B-1 being the rarer). Rarely is a Full Details coin encountered. The dentils are unusually bold and serve to frame the motifs. Check for planchet adjustment marks. Sharp striking (as on B-2) will add to the value. Most MS specimens have excellent eye appeal.

Availability. Examples are available in all grades from well worn to superb MS. Nearly all of the latter are highly prooflike, but there are some exceptions.

AU-50, 53, 55, 58 (About Uncirculated). *Obverse:* Light wear is seen on the hair area above the ear and extending to left of the forehead, on the ribbon, on the drapery at the shoulder, and on the high points of the bust line, more so at AU-50 than at 53 or 55. An AU-58 coin has minimal traces of wear. Concerning luster: An AU-50 coin has luster in protected areas among the stars and letters, with little in the open fields or on the portrait. At AU-58, most luster remains in the fields, but is worn away on the highest parts of the motifs. *Reverse:* Light wear is seen on the eagle's body (note: this area is nearly always lightly struck) and the edges of the wings. Light wear is seen on the wreath and lettering. Luster is the best key to actual wear. This ranges from perhaps 20% remaining in protected areas (at AU-50) to nearly full mint bloom (at AU-58).

MS-60 to 70 (Mint State). *Obverse:* At MS-60, some abrasion and contact marks are evident, most noticeably on the cheek, the drapery, and the right field. Luster is present, but may be dull or lifeless, and interrupted in patches. On prooflike coins the contact marks are more prominent. At MS-63, contact marks are very few, and abrasion is hard to detect except under magnification, although this type is sometimes graded liberally due to its rarity. An MS-65 coin has no abrasion, and contact marks are so minute as to require magnification. Luster should be full and rich. Grades above MS-65 have fewer marks as perfection is approached. *Reverse:* Comments apply as for the obverse, except that abrasion and contact marks are most noticeable on the eagle at the center, a situation complicated by the fact that this area is typically flatly struck (except on the B-2 variety). Grading is best done by the obverse, then verified by the reverse. The field area is small and is protected by lettering and the wreath and in any given grade shows fewer marks than on the obverse.

	Mintage	Cert	Avg	%MS	AU-55	AU-58	MS-60	MS-62	MS-63	MS-64	MS-65	Recent Auction Record
1796 †	6,146	491	28.3	13	$57,500	$62,500	$77,500	$90,000	$160,000	$190,000	$350,000	$1,527,500, MS-67, November 2013

† Ranked in the *100 Greatest U.S. Coins* (fourth edition).

DRAPED BUST, HERALDIC EAGLE REVERSE
(1804–1807)

Designer Robert Scot; weight 6.74 grams; composition .8924 silver, .1076 copper; approx. diameter 27.5 mm; reeded edge. All coined at Philadelphia.

Browning-4.

History. Early on, the U.S. Mint's production of silver coins in any given year depended on requests made by depositors of silver; they were not made for the Mint's own account. After 1796 no quarters were struck until 1804. When production started up again, the Draped Bust obverse was used, but with the new Heraldic Eagle reverse—similar to that on other silver (and gold) denominations of the time.

Striking and Sharpness. Virtually all examples are lightly struck in one area or another. On the obverse, check the hair details and the star centers. On the reverse, check the shield, stars, feathers, and other design elements. The dentils and rims on both sides often have problems. Quarters of 1807 are usually the lightest struck. Also check for planchet adjustment marks. Sharp striking

and excellent eye appeal add to a coin's value. This series often is misgraded due to lack of understanding of its strike anomalies.

Availability. All dates are collectible, with 1804 being scarcer than the others and a rarity in MS. Some die varieties are rare. High-grade coins with Full Details are very rare.

AU-50, 53, 55, 58 (About Uncirculated). *Obverse:* Light wear is seen on the hair area above the ear and extending to left of the forehead, on the ribbon, and on the drapery at the shoulder, more so at AU-50 than at 53 or 55. An AU-58 coin has minimal traces of wear. Concerning luster: An AU-50 coin has luster in protected areas among the stars and letters, with little in the open fields or on the portrait. At AU-58, most luster is present in the fields, but is worn away on the highest parts of the motifs. *Reverse:* The eagle's neck, the tips and top of the wings, the clouds, and the tail now show noticeable wear, as do other features. Luster ranges from perhaps

20% remaining in protected areas (at AU-50) to nearly full mint bloom (at AU-58). Often the reverse retains much more luster than the obverse, more so on quarter dollars than on other denominations of this design.

MS-60 to 70 (Mint State). *Obverse:* At MS-60, some abrasion and contact marks are evident, most noticeably on the cheek, the drapery, and the right field. Luster is present, but may be dull or lifeless, and interrupted in patches. At MS-63, contact marks are very few, and abrasion is hard to detect except under magnification. An MS-65 coin has no abrasion, and con-

tact marks are so minute as to require magnification. Luster should be full and rich. Coins graded above MS-65 are more theoretical than actual for this type—but they do exist, and are defined by having fewer marks as perfection is approached. Expect weakness in some areas. *Reverse:* Comments apply as for the obverse, except that abrasion and contact marks are most noticeable on the eagle's neck, the tips of the wing, and the tail. The field area is complex, without much open space, given the stars above the eagle, the arrows and olive branch, and other features; accordingly, marks are not as noticeable as on the obverse.

1806, 6 Over 5

	Mintage	Cert	Avg	%MS	AU-50	AU-55	MS-60	MS-62	MS-63	MS-64	MS-65	Recent Auction Record
1804	6,738	347	16.1	4	$50,000	$65,000	$85,000	$115,000	$170,000	$285,000	$350,000	$82,250, AU-55, November 2013
1805	121,394	752	23.5	4	5,250	6,500	10,000	15,000	21,000	36,000	87,500	$49,938, MS-64, November 2013
1806, All kinds	206,124											
1806, 6 Over 5		298	26.4	8	6,000	7,500	11,000	19,000	28,000	38,000	97,000	$152,750, MS-66, November 2013
1806		1,119	23.5	7	5,250	6,500	10,000	12,000	16,500	32,000	90,000	$94,000, MS-65, November 2013
1807	220,643	531	25.7	12	5,250	6,500	10,000	12,000	16,500	35,000	92,500	$411,250, MS-66, November 2013

CAPPED BUST, VARIETY 1, LARGE DIAMETER
(1815–1828)

Designer John Reich; weight 6.74 grams; composition .8924 silver, .1076 copper; approx. diameter 27 mm; reeded edge. All coined at Philadelphia.

Browning-1.

History. The Capped Bust design, by John Reich, was introduced on the half dollar of 1807 but was not used on the quarter until 1815.

Striking and Sharpness. Striking sharpness varies. On the obverse, check the hair of Miss Liberty, the broach clasp (a particular point of observation), and the star centers. On this type the stars are often well defined (in contrast with half dollars of the same design). On the reverse, check the neck of the eagle and its

wings, and the letters. Examine dentils on both sides. When weakness occurs it is usually in the center.

Availability. Most quarters of this type range from slightly scarce to rare, with the 1823, 3 Over 2, and the 1827 being famous rarities. Typical coins range from well worn to Fine and VF. AU and MS coins are elusive (and are usually dated before the 1820s), and gems are particularly rare.

AU-50, 53, 55, 58 (About Uncirculated). *Obverse:* Light wear is seen on the cap, the hair below LIB- ERTY, the curl on the neck, the hair near the clasp, and the drapery. At AU-50 and 53, luster remains only in protected areas. At AU-58, the luster is extensive except in the open area of the field, especially to the right. *Reverse:* Wear is evident on the eagle's neck, the top of the wings, the claws, and the flat band above the eagle. At AU-50 and 53, there still is significant luster, more than on the obverse; an AU-58 coin has

nearly full luster. Generally, light wear is most obvi- ous on the obverse.

MS-60 to 70 (Mint State). *Obverse:* At MS-60, some abrasion and contact marks are evident, most notice- ably on the cheek, the hair below LIBERTY, and the area near the drapery clasp. Luster is present, but may be dull or lifeless, and interrupted in patches. At MS-63, contact marks are very few, and abrasion is hard to detect except under magnification. An MS-65 coin has

no abrasion, and contact marks are so minute as to require magnification. Luster should be full and rich. Grades above MS-65 are seen now and again; they have fewer marks as perfection is approached. *Reverse:* Comments apply as for the obverse, except that abra- sion and contact marks are most noticeable on the eagle's neck, the top of the wings, the claws, and the flat band that surrounds the incuse motto. The field is mainly protected by design elements and does not show abrasion as much as does the obverse on a given coin.

	1818, 8 Over 5	1818, Normal Date	1819, Small 9	1819, Large 9
1820, Small 0	1820, Large 0	1822, 25 Over 50 C.	1823, 3 Over 2
1824, 4 Over 2	1825, 5 Over 2	1825, 5 Over 4	1828, 25 Over 50 C.

	Mintage	Cert	Avg	%MS	AU-50	AU-55	MS-60	MS-62	MS-63	MS-64	MS-65	Recent Auction Record
1815	89,235	297	37.4	29	$2,200	$2,700	$3,500	$4,500	$7,000	$12,000	$35,000	$282,000, MS-67, November 2013
1818, 8 Over 5	361,174	190	51.0	57	2,200	2,500	3,500	4,250	6,500	12,000	32,500	$176,250, MS-67, November 2013
1818, Normal Date	*	1,041	37.8	24	2,200	2,400	3,500	4,000	6,500	12,000	27,000	$67,563, MS-66, December 2013
1819, Small 9	144,000	182	30.1	11	2,200	2,500	3,500	4,500	7,500	14,000	32,500	$30,550, MS-64, November 2013
1819, Large 9	*	111	24.1	5	2,200	2,700	3,500	6,250	11,000	20,000	40,000	$23,501, MS-64, November 2013
1820, Small 0	127,444	110	36.9	12	2,200	2,400	3,500	4,500	6,500	16,000	45,000	$3,055, AU-55, February 2014
1820, Large 0	*	157	26.8	9	2,500	3,000	3,500	5,750	10,000	18,000	37,500	$41,125, MS-66, November 2013
1821	216,851	513	36.9	20	2,200	2,500	3,500	4,500	6,500	12,000	30,000	$30,550, MS-65, November 2013
1822	64,080	249	35.2	14	2,600	3,350	4,000	5,750	9,000	25,000		$25,850, MS-64, November 2013
1822, 25 Over 50 C.	*	31	29.1	19	24,000	28,000	40,000	55,000	75,000	100,000	150,000	$47,000, MS, February 2014
1823, 3 Over 2	17,800	25	29.5	8	100,000	125,000	—					$17,625, G-4, February 2014
1824, 4 Over 2	168,000	210	25.3	2	5,000	8,000	25,000	30,000	50,000	75,000	100,000	$35,250, MS-62, June 2014
1825, 5 Over 2	*	16	39.9	0	8,000	12,000	16,000	22,000	27,500	40,000		$3,290, VF-30, February 2014
1825, 5 Over 4	*	500	38.3	17	2,200	2,500	3,500	4,500	6,500	12,000	30,000	$1,495, EF-45, April 2012
1828	102,000	346	41.5	23	2,200	2,500	3,500	4,500	8,000	12,500	30,000	$49,938, MS-65, February 2013
1828, 25 Over 50 C.	*	64	27.7	9	4,000	8,500	13,000	16,000	22,000			$352,500, MS-67, November 2013

* Included in number above. *Note:* Although 4,000 1827 quarters were reported to have been made for circulation, their rarity today (only one worn piece is known, and it could be a circulated Proof) suggests that this quantity was for coins struck in calendar-year 1827 but bearing an earlier date, probably 1825.

Proof Capped Bust Quarters, Variety 1, Large Diameter

PF-60 to 70 (Proof). Proofs of some dates were struck for inclusion in sets and for numismatists. All authentic Proofs are rarities. Some deeply toned coins, and coins with patches of mint luster, have been described as Proofs, but most are not. *Obverse and Reverse:* Proofs that are extensively cleaned and have many hairlines, or that are dull and grainy, are lower level, such as PF-60 to 62. While any early Proof garners collector interest, lower levels are not of great interest to specialists unless they are of rare die varieties. With medium hairlines, an assigned grade of PF-64 may be in order, and with relatively few, PF-65. PF-66 should have hairlines so delicate that magnification is needed to see them. Above that, a Proof should be free of such lines. Grading is highly subjective with early Proofs, and eye appeal also is a factor.

Proof Capped Bust Quarter: Variety 1, Large Diameter
Shown 1.5x actual size.
Browning-4.

1827, Original
Curl-Base 2 in 25 C.
(Shown 1.5x actual size.)

1827, Restrike
Square-Base 2 in 25 C.
(Shown 1.5x actual size.)

	Est Mintage	Cert	Finest	PF-60	PF-63	PF-64	PF-65	Recent Auction Record
1820	6–10	5	PF-67		$45,000	$90,000	$130,000	$97,750, PF-64, May 2008
1821	6–10	5	PF-67		40,000	60,000	100,000	$51,750, PF-64, April 2009
1822	6–10	8	PF-68		40,000	60,000	100,000	$229,125, PF-65, January 2014
1823, 3 Over 2	2–4	1	PF-64		100,000	150,000		$396,563, PF-64, June 2014
1824, 4 Over 2	2–4	1	PF-63		50,000	75,000		
1825, 5 Over 4 Over 3	6–10	n/a	n/a		40,000	60,000		$4,313, PF-63, January 2010
1827, 7 Over 3, Original †	20–30	12	PF-66		135,000	200,000	300,000	$411,250, PF-64, June 2014
1827, 7 Over 3, Restrike	20–30	22	PF-66		50,000	80,000	115,000	$69,000, PF-66, July 2009
1828	8–12	17	PF-66	$15,000	40,000	60,000	100,000	$82,250, PF-65, June 2014

† Ranked in the *100 Greatest U.S. Coins* (fourth edition).

CAPPED BUST, VARIETY 2, REDUCED DIAMETER, MOTTO REMOVED (1831–1838)

Designer William Kneass; weight 6.74 grams; composition .8924 silver, .1076 copper; diameter 24.3 mm; reeded edge. Changed to 6.68 grams, .900 fine, in 1837. All coined at Philadelphia.

Browning-1.

History. Capped Bust, Reduced Diameter quarter dollars are similar in overall appearance to the preceding type, but with important differences. The diameter is smaller, E PLURIBUS UNUM no longer appears on the reverse, and the dentils are smaller and restyled.

Striking and Sharpness. Nearly all coins of this type are very well struck. Check all areas for sharpness. Some quarters of 1833 and 1834 are struck from rusted or otherwise imperfect dies and can be less attractive than coins from undamaged dies.

Availability. Examples are readily available of all dates, including many of the first year of issue. Mint frost ranges from satiny (usual) to deeply frosty.

AU-50, 53, 55, 58 (About Uncirculated). *Obverse:* Grading guidelines are the same as for the 1815–1828 type, except the rims are more uniform, striking is usually very sharp, and the wear occurs evenly on both sides. Light wear is seen on the cap, the hair below LIBERTY, the curl on the neck, the hair near the clasp, and the drapery. At AU-50 and 53, luster remains only in protected areas. At AU-58, the luster is extensive except in the open area of the field, especially to the right. *Reverse:* Wear is evident on the eagle's neck, the top of the wings, and the claws.

At AU-50 and 53, there still is significant luster, more than on the obverse. An AU-58 coin has nearly full luster.

MS-60 to 70 (Mint State). *Obverse:* Grading is similar to that of the 1815–1828 type, except the rims are more uniform, striking is usually very sharp, and the wear occurs evenly on both sides. At MS-60, some abrasion and contact marks are evident, most noticeably on the cheek, the hair below LIBERTY, and the area near the drapery clasp. Luster is present,

but may be dull or lifeless, and interrupted in patches. At MS-63, contact marks are very few, and abrasion is hard to detect except under magnification. An MS-65 coin has no abrasion, and contact marks are so minute as to require magnification. Luster should be full and rich. Grades above MS-65 are seen now and again, and have fewer marks as perfection is approached. *Reverse:* Comments apply as for the obverse, except that abrasion and contact marks are most noticeable on the eagle's neck, the top of the wings, and the claws.

1831, Small Letters	1831, Large Letters	1834, O Over F in OF
Browning-2.	Browning-6.	FS-25-1834-901.

Shown 1.5x actual size.

	Mintage	Cert	Avg	%MS	AU-55	MS-60	MS-62	MS-63	MS-64	MS-65	MS-66	Recent Auction Record
1831, Small Letters	398,000	548	49.5	32	$950	$1,300	$2,400	$4,500	$10,000	$27,500	$40,000	$117,500, MS-67, November 2013
1831, Large Letters	*	129	43.7	22	950	1,300	2,400	4,500	10,000	30,000	—	$32,900, MS-65, November 2013
1832	320,000	327	47.8	28	950	1,300	2,400	5,000	12,000	32,500	50,000	$18,800, MS-65, November 2013
1833	156,000	349	45.8	22	1,100	1,600	3,000	5,500	12,500	32,500	—	$76,375, MS-66, November 2013
1833, O Over F in OF **(a)**	*				1,200	1,700	3,250	6,000	14,000	34,000	—	
1834	286,000	1,019	46.5	23	950	1,300	2,400	4,500	8,500	24,000	40,000	$70,500, MS-67, April 2014
1834, O Over F in OF **(a)**	*	47	48.2	15	1,100	1,600	3,100	5,700	13,000	33,500	—	$7,050, MS-64, January 2014
1835	1,952,000	992	43.7	15	950	1,300	2,400	4,500	8,500	27,500	40,000	$58,750, MS-67, November 2013
1836	472,000	360	40.3	17	950	1,300	2,600	4,700	13,000	30,000	—	$99,875, MS-67, November 2013
1837	252,400	475	48.4	35	950	1,300	2,400	4,500	8,500	24,000	40,000	$76,375, MS-66, June 2014
1838	366,000	456	46.9	26	950	1,300	2,400	4,500	8,500	27,500	40,000	$25,850, MS-65, April 2013

* Included in number above. **a.** The OF is re-engraved with the letters connected at the top, and the first A in AMERICA is also re-engraved. Other identifying characteristics: there is no period after the C in the denomination; and the 5 and C are further apart than normal.

Proof Capped Bust Quarters, Variety 2, Reduced Diameter, Motto Removed

PF-60 to 70 (Proof). Proofs were struck for inclusion in sets and for sale or trade to numismatists. Most coins offered as Proofs are indeed of this format (as opposed to being high-grade circulation strikes misidentified as Proofs). Avoid any that show

patches of mint frost or that are darkly toned. *Obverse and Reverse:* Proofs that are extensively cleaned and have many hairlines, or that are dull and grainy, are lower level, such as PF-60 to 62. With medium hairlines, an assigned grade of PF-64 may

be in order and with relatively few hairlines, PF-65. A PF-66 coin has hairlines so delicate that magnification is needed to see them. Above that, a Proof should be free of such lines. Grading is highly subjective with early Proofs, and eye appeal also is a factor.

Proof Capped Bust Quarter: Variety 2,
Reduced Diameter, Motto Removed
Shown 1.5x actual size.

	Est Mintage	Cert	Finest	PF-60	PF-63	PF-64	PF-65	Recent Auction Record
1831, Large Letters	20–25	10	PF-66	$15,000	$22,500	$40,000	$75,000	$141,000, PF-66, January 2014
1833	10–15	6	PF-65	15,000	25,000	55,000	90,000	$46,000, PF-65Cam, April 2009
1834	20–25	16	PF-67	15,000	22,500	40,000	75,000	$235,000, PF-66, November 2013
1835	10–15	6	PF-65	15,000	25,000	50,000	90,000	$25,850, PF-63, August 2013
1836	8–12	3	PF-67	15,000	25,000	60,000	100,000	$97,750, PF-67, January 2006
1837	8–12	2	PF-67	15,000	25,000	60,000	90,000	$132,250, PF-67, August 2006
1838	8–12	4	PF-68	25,000	35,000	60,000	100,000	$48,875, PF-64, July 2011

LIBERTY SEATED
(1838–1891)

Variety 1, No Motto Above Eagle (1838–1853): Designer Christian Gobrecht; weight 6.68 grams; composition .900 silver, .100 copper; diameter 24.3 mm; reeded edge; mints: Philadelphia, New Orleans.

Variety 2, Arrows at Date, Rays Around Eagle (1853): Designer Christian Gobrecht; weight 6.22 grams; composition .900 silver, .100 copper; diameter 24.3 mm; reeded edge; mints: Philadelphia, New Orleans.

Variety 3, Arrows at Date, No Rays (1854–1855): Designer Christian Gobrecht; weight 6.22 grams; composition .900 silver, .100 copper; diameter 24.3 mm; reeded edge; mints: Philadelphia, New Orleans, San Francisco.

Variety 1 Resumed, With Weight Standard of Variety 2 (1856–1865): Designer Christian Gobrecht; weight 6.22 grams; composition .900 silver, .100 copper; diameter 24.3 mm; reeded edge; mints: Philadelphia, New Orleans, San Francisco.

Variety 4, Motto Above Eagle (1866–1873): Designer Christian Gobrecht; weight 6.22 grams; composition .900 silver, .100 copper; diameter 24.3 mm; reeded edge; mints: Philadelphia, San Francisco, Carson City.

Variety 5, Arrows at Date (1873–1874): Designer Christian Gobrecht; weight 6.25 grams; composition .900 silver, .100 copper; diameter 24.3 mm; reeded edge; mints: Philadelphia, San Francisco, Carson City.

Variety 4 Resumed, With Weight Standard of Variety 5 (1875–1891): Designer Christian Gobrecht; weight 6.25 grams; composition .900 silver, .100 copper; diameter 24.3 mm; reeded edge; mints: Philadelphia, New Orleans, San Francisco.

History. The long-running Liberty Seated quarter-dollar design was introduced in 1838. Early issues lack drapery at the elbow and have small lettering on the reverse. Drapery was added in 1840 and continued afterward. In 1853 a reduction in weight was indicated with the addition of arrows at the date and rays on the reverse side (in the field around the eagle). The rays were omitted after 1853, but the arrows were retained through 1855. The motto IN GOD WE TRUST was added to the reverse in 1866. Arrows were placed at the date in the years 1873 and 1874 to denote the change of weight from 6.22 to 6.25 grams. The new weight, without the arrows, continued through 1891.

Striking and Sharpness. On the obverse, check the head of Miss Liberty and the star centers. If these are sharp, then check the central part of the seated figure. On the reverse, check the eagle, particularly the area to the lower left of the shield. Check the dentils on both sides. Generally, the earliest issues are well struck, as are those of the 1880s onward. The word LIBERTY is not an infallible guide to grading at lower levels, as on some dies the shield was in lower relief, and the letters wore away less quickly. This guideline should be used in combination with other features.

Availability. Coins of this type are available in proportion to their mintages. MS coins can range from rare to exceedingly rare, as they were mostly ignored by numismatists until the series ended. Quality can vary widely, especially among branch-mint coins.

EF-40, 45 (Extremely Fine). *Obverse:* Further wear than at AU is seen on all areas, especially the thighs and knees, bosom, and head. Little or no luster is seen on most coins. *Reverse:* Further wear than at AU is evident on the eagle's neck, claws, and wings. Some feathers in the right wing may be blended together.

AU-50, 53, 55, 58 (About Uncirculated). *Obverse:* Light wear is seen on the thighs and knees, bosom, and head. There is some luster at AU-50 and 53. At AU-58, the luster is extensive, but incomplete, especially in the right field. *Reverse:* Wear is evident on the eagle's neck, claws, and top of the wings. At AU-50 and 53, there still are traces of luster. An AU-58 coin has nearly full luster, more so than on the obverse, as the design elements protect the small field areas.

MS-60 to 70 (Mint State). *Obverse:* At MS-60, some abrasion and contact marks are evident, most noticeably on the bosom and thighs and knees. Luster is present, but may be dull or lifeless. At MS-63, contact marks are very few, and abrasion is hard to detect except under magnification. An MS-65 coin has no abrasion, and contact marks are sufficiently minute as to require magnification. Check the knees of Liberty and the right field. Luster should be full and rich. Most MS coins of the 1861 to 1865 years, Philadelphia issues, have extensive die striae (from the dies not being completely finished). *Reverse:* Comments apply as for the obverse, except that in lower MS grades abrasion and contact marks are most noticeable on the eagle's neck, the claws, and the top of the wings (harder to see there, however). At MS-65 or higher there are no marks visible to the unaided eye. The field is mainly protected by design elements and does not show abrasion as much as does the obverse on a given coin.

No Drapery　　　　Drapery　　　　1840-O, Drapery, Normal O　　　1840-O, Drapery, Large O

Shown 1.5x actual size.　　　　　　　　　*Shown 1.5x actual size.*

1842, Small Date　　　　1842, Large Date　　　　1842-O, Small Date　　　　1842-O, Large Date

Philadelphia Small Date is Proof only.

1853, Repunched Date, No Arrows or Rays　　　　1853, 3 Over 4 (Arrows at Date, Rays Around Eagle)

FS-25-1853-301.　　　　　　　　　　　*FS-25-1853-1301.*

| 1854-O, Normal O | 1854-O, Huge O | 1854-O, Huge O (Detail) |

Shown 1.5x actual size.

	Mintage	Cert	Avg	%MS	AU-50	AU-55	MS-60	MS-62	MS-63	MS-64	MS-65	Recent Auction Record
1838, No Drapery	466,000	350	53.2	43	$750	$1,200	$2,000	$4,250	$6,750	$11,000	$35,000	$141,000, MS-66, November 2013
1839, No Drapery	491,146	270	50.1	27	750	1,150	1,850	3,500	5,500	11,000	45,000	$8,813, MS-64, July 2014
1840O, No Drapery	382,200	107	52.1	33	800	1,150	1,900	4,100	8,200	19,000	40,000	$329,000, MS-67, November 2013
1840, Drapery	188,127	77	51.8	34	300	400	950	2,500	4,500	10,000	25,000	$35,250, MS-66, November 2013
1840O, Drapery	43,000	204	42.8	21	500	900	1,300	2,500	3,900	7,500	25,000	$35,250, MS-64, April 2014
1840O, Drapery, Large O (a)	*	0	n/a	n/a	4,750	6,000	9,000					$3,220, MS-63, December 2010
1841	120,000	111	53.7	54	325	500	900	1,650	2,300	4,400	12,000	$41,125, MS-66, November 2013
1841O	452,000	224	50.7	45	320	500	800	1,500	1,900	3,650	14,000	$55,813, MS-67, June 2014
1842, Large Date (b)	88,000	90	47.2	30	650	1,000	1,750	2,200	4,500	9,000	15,000	$6,169, MS-64, August 2013
1842O, All kinds	769,000											
1842O, Small Date		65	20.5	3	7,500	9,000	18,000	25,000	75,000	95,000		$32,900, AU-58, December 2013
1842O, Large Date		115	44.7	34	600	850	1,750	2,800	4,800	9,000		$7,050, MS-64, April 2013
1843	645,600	160	56.4	52	175	220	450	900	1,250	3,000	8,000	$3,290, MS-64, November 2013
1843O	968,000	102	41.9	14	800	1,200	2,000	3,500	7,000	12,000	22,500	$3,819, AU-58, January 2014
1844	421,200	138	54.9	45	175	250	525	1,250	1,500	3,500	9,500	$17,625, MS-65, November 2013
1844O	740,000	112	48.6	29	360	550	1,400	2,000	3,500	5,000	10,000	$12,925, MS-65, June 2014
1845	922,000	206	55.3	49	160	250	550	1,000	1,400	2,350	5,900	$7,638, MS-65, November 2013
1846	510,000	128	54.4	36	180	280	600	1,100	1,500	4,000	12,000	$22,325, MS-66, January 2014
1847	734,000	133	54.4	42	160	250	575	850	1,200	3,000	9,000	$14,100, MS-65, November 2013
1847O	368,000	91	39.5	11	800	1,800	4,500	7,500	12,000	20,000		$12,925, MS-63, June 2014
1848	146,000	74	49.9	28	300	450	1,150	1,850	4,000	6,500	15,000	$21,150, MS-67, November 2013
1849	340,000	130	53.8	36	250	350	800	1,500	1,900	4,500	12,000	$10,575, MS-65, November 2013
1849O	**	92	29.2	7	7,750	9,500	17,000	18,500	21,000	25,000		$7,638, AU-53, February 2013
1850	190,800	84	51.0	37	240	400	1,000	1,750	2,800	5,250	11,000	$38,188, MS-67, June 2014
1850O	412,000	137	49.3	34	475	800	1,600	2,700	3,400	8,000	20,000	$11,163, MS-65, June 2014
1851	160,000	81	49.0	37	300	400	1,000	1,500	2,000	4,500	9,500	$25,850, MS-67, November 2013
1851O	88,000	82	27.9	11	3,000	4,500	8,000	15,000	32,500			$15,275, MS-62, July 2014
1852	177,060	113	52.4	52	300	375	675	1,000	1,500	3,750	7,000	$105,750, MS-68, November 2013
1852O	96,000	81	29.6	5	4,500	6,500	9,000	27,500	42,500			$1,998, VF-30, January 2014
1853, Repunched Date, No Arrows or Rays (c)	44,200	90	45.5	46	3,000	3,500	4,000	5,000	7,800	8,900	10,000	$38,188, MS-68, June 2014
1853, Variety 2	15,210,020	2,061	50.9	36	300	450	900	1,200	2,000	4,200	15,000	$67,563, MS-67, September 2013
1853, Variety 2, 3 Over 4 (d)	*	118	39.7	19	675	1,200	2,000	3,500	5,500	17,500		$12,925, MS-64, June 2014
1853O	1,332,000	182	44.2	13	1,100	1,600	3,250	6,000	11,000	22,500	30,000	$15,275, MS-64, June 2014
1854	12,380,000	1,056	53.2	39	225	300	500	900	1,100	2,500	8,000	$38,188, MS-67, November 2013
1854O	1,484,000	179	46.6	36	275	550	1,200	2,000	2,500	4,500	15,000	$353, AU-55, September 2013
1854O, Huge O (e)	*	105	20.8	0	12,000	15,000	18,000	20,000	24,000			$4,994, EF-45, February 2013
1855	2,857,000	267	55.0	43	225	300	575	1,025	1,450	4,000	12,000	$41,125, MS-67, November 2013
1855O	176,000	62	37.9	23	2,000	2,250	4,750	8,750	12,000	30,000		$1,528, EF-35, April 2013
1855S	396,400	69	41.9	22	1,100	2,000	3,000	5,500	8,500	17,000	35,000	$1,410, AU-55, August 2013

* Included in number above. ** Included in 1850-O mintage. **a.** The O mintmark punch is about 25% larger than normal. There are two known reverse dies for this variety, with one showing doubled denticles. **b.** The Large Date was used on the Philadelphia Mint's 1842 coins struck for circulation. The 1842 Small Date was made in Proof format only (see Proof listings). **c.** The secondary 5 and 3 are evident south of the primary digits. In the past, this variety was erroneously attributed as a 53 Over 2 overdate. This is the only die known for 1853 that lacks the arrows and rays. **d.** In addition to the 3 punched over a 4, there is also evidence of the repunched 8 and 5 (weaker images slightly north and west of the primary digits). The right arrow shaft is also doubled, north of the primary. "On well-worn or late-die-state specimens, the doubling of the arrow shaft may be the only evidence of the overdate. This is the only quarter dollar date known to be punched over the *following* year!" (*Cherrypickers' Guide to Rare Die Varieties*, fifth edition, volume II). **e.** The Huge O mintmark is very large, extremely thick on the left side, and irregular, suggesting that it was punched into the die by hand.

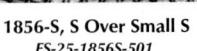

1856-S, S Over Small S
FS-25-1856S-501.

1857, Clashed Reverse Die
FS-25-1857-901.

1873, Close 3

1873, Open 3

1877-S, S Over Horizontal S
FS-25-1877S-501.

	Mintage	Cert	Avg	%MS	EF-40	AU-50	MS-60	MS-62	MS-63	MS-64	MS-65	Recent Auction Record
1856	7,264,000	444	55.0	56	$75	$175	$350	$450	$600	$1,350	$4,100	$10,575, MS-66, June 2014
1856O	968,000	138	45.7	21	80	250	1,100	1,800	2,500	5,000	12,000	$11,750, MS-65, June 2014
1856S, All kinds	286,000											
1856S		62	43.0	19	1,500	2,250	6,500	10,000	20,000	25,000	45,000	$18,800, MS-64, June 2014
1856S, S Over Small S (a)		19	12.8	0	2,500	6,000	—					$28,200, AU-58, June 2014
1857	9,644,000	814	57.3	63	75	175	350	450	600	1,100	3,500	$35,250, MS-68, November 2013
1857, Clashed Reverse Die (b)	*	8	50.0	38	500	750						
1857O	1,180,000	160	47.7	22	150	400	1,200	2,200	4,000	8,000		$1,439, MS-61, December 2013
1857S	82,000	88	45.0	19	600	1,200	4,000	6,000	8,750	14,500		$4,847, AU-58, March 2014
1858	7,368,000	724	56.4	59	75	175	350	450	600	1,100	3,700	$25,850, MS-67, November 2013
1858O	520,000	96	49.7	13	125	350	1,800	4,900	7,500	14,500	25,000	$705, AU-55, August 2013
1858S	121,000	63	34.6	2	2,000	5,250	15,000	—	—			$11,163, AU-58, March 2014
1859	1,343,200	240	55.3	48	80	175	400	800	1,100	2,000	5,750	$4,406, MS-65, June 2014
1859O	260,000	83	50.3	25	135	400	1,250	2,500	4,000	6,000	12,000	$25,263, MS-65, April 2013
1859S	80,000	66	28.0	0	4,200	17,500	55,000					$30,550, AU-58, June 2014
1860	804,400	206	57.1	49	80	175	400	700	975	1,550	5,500	$4,994, MS-65, February 2014
1860O	388,000	161	52.4	37	95	375	1,000	1,550	2,400	6,250	15,000	$4,994, MS-64, September 2013
1860S	56,000	60	20.6	2	12,500	22,500	50,000	65,000	—			$30,550, AU-55, March 2014
1861	4,853,600	1,075	58.3	61	80	175	350	475	750	1,300	4,000	$4,700, MS-66, August 2013
1861S	96,000	78	27.7	0	2,500	10,000	40,000					$3,173, EF-40, June 2013
1862	932,000	343	58.3	64	85	175	350	475	750	1,300	4,000	$25,850, MS-67, June 2014
1862S	67,000	107	42.1	27	800	1,800	3,800	4,750	9,000	14,500		$44,063, MS-64, June 2014
1863	191,600	136	56.2	66	240	375	625	850	1,100	1,550	4,400	$3,819, MS-65, February 2013
1864	93,600	138	52.4	58	275	425	625	850	1,700	2,550	5,500	$2,585, MS-64, June 2013
1864S	20,000	99	26.0	8	3,800	5,500	12,000	25,000	30,000	42,000		$28,200, MS-64, June 2014
1865	58,800	112	47.1	33	275	500	800	1,050	1,400	3,000	8,000	$41,125, MS-66, June 2014
1865S	41,000	89	41.7	30	1,000	1,500	3,000	5,000	6,000	8,000	15,000	$64,625, MS-66, February 2014
1866, Variety 4	16,800	84	51.1	58	1,600	1,850	2,200	2,400	2,600	3,750	6,250	$8,225, MS-65, January 2014
1866S	28,000	63	31.7	14	2,500	3,000	4,500	7,500	10,000	15,000	40,000	$18,800, MS-63, November 2013
1867	20,000	80	43.4	35	1,350	1,650	2,600	4,000	8,500	17,000		$14,100, MS-64, June 2014
1867S	48,000	56	29.1	14	4,500	8,400	18,000	25,000	35,000	50,000		$3,525, EF-40, September 2013
1868	29,400	90	50.3	47	525	625	1,200	1,400	2,200	5,000	9,000	$61,688, MS-66, June 2014
1868S	96,000	87	38.9	21	900	1,500	3,500	6,100	7,750	15,500	25,000	$17,625, MS-66, June 2014
1869	16,000	68	38.4	32	900	1,100	1,900	2,450	3,000	6,000	12,000	$1,175, EF-35, March 2013
1869S	76,000	91	34.1	13	1,000	1,600	4,000	5,500	6,500	10,000	15,000	$19,975, MS-64, August 2013
1870	86,400	87	49.9	34	275	450	800	1,100	2,200	4,500	8,750	$11,163, MS-66, January 2014
1870CC	8,340	69	21.9	1	35,000	52,500	75,000					$70,500, AU-53, January 2014
1871	118,200	85	53.1	53	225	350	600	900	1,500	4,400	8,000	$32,900, MS-67, June 2014
1871CC	10,890	43	22.0	5	28,000	47,500	68,000					$352,500, MS-65, June 2014

* Included in number above. **a.** A larger S mintmark was punched over a much smaller S mintmark, the latter probably intended for half-dime production. **b.** The reverse clashed with the reverse die of an 1857 Flying Eagle cent. Images of the cent reverse die are easily visible on either side of the eagle's neck, within the shield, and below the eagle's left wing.

	Mintage	Cert	Avg	%MS	EF-40	AU-50	MS-60	MS-62	MS-63	MS-64	MS-65	Recent Auction Record
1871S	30,900	69	42.7	41	$1,500	$4,500	$6,750	$8,000	$10,000	$15,000	$17,500	$30,550, MS-66, June 2014
1872	182,000	117	50.3	39	190	300	650	1,200	2,100	3,900	7,900	$8,550, MS-66, April 2013
1872CC	22,850	77	20.7	3	12,000	20,000	40,000	75,000				$17,625, AU-53, August 2013
1872S	83,000	44	36.8	27	6,000	8,000	15,000	20,000	25,000	35,000	55,000	$12,338, AU-55, January 2014
1873, Close 3	40,000	41	35.2	12	1,500	2,500	18,000	30,000	40,000			$9,988, AU-58, April 2014
1873, Open 3	172,000	79	51.4	54	200	300	500	750	1,100	2,000	5,500	$8,225, MS-65, November 2013
1873CC, Variety 4 † (6 known)	4,000	5	59.4	80	125,000				550,000			$431,250, MS-63, January 2009
1873, Variety 5	1,271,160	463	55.9	51	225	425	850	1,150	1,650	2,000	4,000	$1,188, MS-63, September 2013
1873CC	12,462	57	20.4	4	25,000	35,000	75,000	85,000	95,000	120,000		$9,988, VG-8, June 2014
1873S	156,000	109	45.9	27	350	750	2,000	3,500	6,000	9,500	20,000	$3,525, MS-64, November 2013
1874	471,200	198	57.1	57	200	450	900	1,200	1,550	2,200	4,700	$5,288, MS-65, January 2014
1874S	392,000	378	60.4	81	265	485	950	1,200	1,450	1,850	3,750	$23,501, MS-67, June 2014
1875	4,292,800	580	60.5	75	65	160	275	375	550	1,000	1,800	$1,880, MS-66, April 2013
1875CC	140,000	125	44.5	27	650	1,200	3,100	3,800	6,750	9,500	32,000	$2,820, AU-55, February 2014
1875S	680,000	172	56.0	60	200	300	600	1,100	1,400	2,000	3,750	$4,113, MS-65, August 2013
1876	17,816,000	1,050	59.0	71	65	160	275	400	550	1,000	1,850	$7,050, MS-67, June 2014
1876CC	4,944,000	642	49.5	47	120	250	600	1,000	1,300	2,000	4,500	$4,137, MS-66, April 2014
1876S	8,596,000	571	59.4	73	65	160	275	400	550	1,000	2,250	$1,293, MS-64, November 2013
1877	10,911,200	725	61.2	80	65	160	275	400	550	1,000	1,800	$14,100, MS-68, June 2014
1877CC (c)	4,192,000	990	55.2	67	120	220	475	700	900	1,750	2,500	$38,188, MS-67, June 2014
1877S	8,996,000	696	59.5	75	65	160	275	350	550	1,000	1,850	$10,810, MS-67, June 2014
1877S, S Over Horizontal S (d)	*	111	55.2	57	250	400	800	1,100	2,200	3,000	5,000	$23,500, MS-66, June 2014
1878	2,260,000	213	59.6	72	65	160	260	350	550	1,300	2,900	$529, MS-63, August 2013
1878CC	996,000	536	54.7	61	200	300	700	1,000	1,500	2,000	4,000	$18,800, MS-66, April 2013
1878S	140,000	66	48.2	41	700	1,300	2,250	3,250	4,000	10,000	21,500	$18,800, MS-65, March 2013
1879	13,600	435	61.9	88	325	400	575	700	800	1,150	2,400	$28,200, MS-68, August 2013
1880	13,600	338	60.8	87	325	400	575	700	800	1,150	2,400	$21,150, MS-68, April 2014
1881	12,000	223	58.5	80	375	425	625	750	850	1,300	2,500	$10,575, MS-66, April 2013
1882	15,200	182	59.2	81	325	425	625	750	900	1,350	2,300	$4,994, MS-67, January 2014
1883	14,400	181	57.5	76	325	425	625	750	900	1,500	2,400	$9,988, MS-67, June 2014
1884	8,000	211	56.5	75	550	600	700	825	900	1,350	2,050	$3,819, MS-66, December 2013
1885	13,600	209	58.5	75	325	400	675	950	1,100	1,700	2,750	$3,408, MS-66, November 2013
1886	5,000	116	59.3	81	675	750	1,000	1,200	1,400	2,000	3,200	$18,800, MS-67, June 2014
1887	10,000	225	60.6	85	475	525	750	1,000	1,100	1,350	2,050	$6,463, MS-67, September 2013
1888	10,001	298	62.7	91	500	650	700	850	1,000	1,250	2,050	$5,581, MS-67, January 2014
1888S	1,216,000	286	61.2	80	70	160	300	650	850	1,750	3,000	$9,988, MS-66, January 2014
1889	12,000	311	61.2	84	325	450	600	675	750	1,000	1,800	$5,434, MS-67, June 2014
1890	80,000	375	61.9	85	175	300	525	625	775	1,100	1,850	$8,813, MS-67, April 2014
1891	3,920,000	1,219	61.2	79	65	160	260	350	550	1,000	1,800	$6,527, MS-67, January 2014
1891O	68,000	108	31.1	17	2,250	3,200	4,400	5,400	8,500	17,500	27,000	$129,250, MS-66, August 2013
1891S	2,216,000	349	59.8	73	70	160	260	350	550	1,000	2,000	$705, MS-64, December 2013

* Included in number above. † Ranked in the *100 Greatest U.S. Coins* (fourth edition). **c.** The 1877-CC quarter with fine edge-reeding is scarcer than that with normally spaced reeding; in the marketplace, there is no price differential. **d.** This variety, known since the 1950s, was caused by an initial S mintmark being punched into the die horizontally, and then corrected with an upright S mintmark.

Proof Liberty Seated Quarters

PF-60 to 70 (Proof). Proofs of the earlier years are very rare. Beginning with 1856, they were made in larger numbers, and from 1859 onward the yearly production was in the multiple hundreds. Examples of the later era are readily available today. Some (1858 is an example) have lint marks, and others can have light striking (particularly in the 1870s and 1880s). Avoid "problem" coins and those with deep or artificial (and often colorful) toning. *Obverse and Reverse:* Proofs that are extensively cleaned and have many hairlines, or that are dull and grainy, are lower level, such as PF-60 to 62. With medium hairlines and good reflectivity, an assigned grade of PF-64 is appropriate and with relatively few hairlines, PF-65. In various grades hairlines are most easily seen in the obverse field. PF-66 should have hairlines so delicate that magnification is needed to see them. Above that, a Proof should be free of such lines.

**Proof Liberty Seated Quarter: Variety 1,
No Motto Above Eagle (1838–1853)**

1842, Small Date

Small Date is Proof only.

1842, Large Date

**Proof Liberty Seated Quarter: Variety 2,
Arrows at Date, Rays Around Eagle (1853)**

**Proof Liberty Seated Quarter: Variety 3,
Arrows at Date, No Rays (1854–1855)**

**Proof Liberty Seated Quarter: Variety 1 Resumed,
Weight Standard of Variety 3 (1856–1865)**

**Proof Liberty Seated Quarter: Variety 4,
Motto Above Eagle (1866–1873)**

**Proof Liberty Seated Quarter: Variety 5,
Arrows at Date (1873–1874)**

**Proof Liberty Seated Quarter: Variety 4 Resumed,
Weight Standard of Variety 5 (1875–1891)**

Coins designated Deep Cameo or Ultra Cameo bring a premium of 50% to 100% above listed values.

	Mintage	Cert	Finest	PF-60	PF-63	PF-64	PF-65	Recent Auction Record
1838	2–3	1	PF-63	*(extremely rare)*				
1839	2–3	1	PF-65	*(unique)*			$500,000	$411,250, PF-65, April 2013
1840, Drapery	5–8	3	PF-65			$75,000	125,000	$99,889, PF-65, August 2013
1841	3–5	4	PF-66	$65,000	$100,000	150,000	200,000	$235,000, PF-66, April 2013
1842, Small Date † (a)	3–5	2	PF-66		60,000	85,000	125,000	$258,500, PF-65, August 2013
1843	10–15	11	PF-66	12,500	20,000	38,000	50,000	$64,625, PF-66, April 2013
1844 (2 known)	3–5	1	PF-66					$276,000, PF-66, July 2009
1845	6–8	12	PF-66		30,000	45,000	75,000	$129,250, PF-66, August 2013
1846	15–20	18	PF-65	5,000	10,000	20,000	35,000	$25,850, PF-65, April 2013
1847	6–8	10	PF-66	5,000	10,000	20,000	35,000	$28,200, PF-65, November 2013
1848	5–8	6	PF-66	5,000	10,000	20,000	35,000	$55,813, PF-66, August 2013
1849	5–8	8	PF-66	5,000	10,000	18,000	30,000	$32,900, PF-65, January 2014
1850	5–8	4	PF-68					$258,500, PF-68, August 2013
1852	5–8	1	PF-65			75,000	125,000	$105,750, PF-65, April 2013
1853	10–15	9	PF-67	30,000	50,000	100,000	140,000	$141,000, PF-66Cam, August 2013
1854	20–30	23	PF-66	10,000	20,000	30,000	50,000	$30,550, PF-66, April 2013
1855	20–30	18	PF-66	8,500	17,500	27,500	45,000	$21,150, PF-65Cam, April 2013
1855S	1–2	1	PF-64	*(unique)*				$176,250, PF-64, August 2013
1856	40–50	54	PF-68	3,500	6,500	12,500	20,000	$24,675, PF-67Cam, April 2013
1857	40–50	68	PF-66	3,250	4,750	7,250	13,500	$15,275, PF-65Cam, June 2013
1858	300	125	PF-67	1,500	2,500	3,500	7,500	$44,063, PF-67, April 2013
1859	800	314	PF-67	1,050	2,150	2,900	5,750	$19,975, PF-67, November 2013
1860	1,000	266	PF-68	750	1,200	2,300	5,500	$44,063, PF-68, November 2013
1861	1,000	212	PF-67	750	1,200	2,300	5,150	$188,000, PF-68Cam, November 2013
1862	550	321	PF-67	750	1,200	2,300	5,150	$55,813, PF-68Cam, November 2013
1863	460	337	PF-67	750	1,200	2,300	5,150	$19,975, PF-67Cam, November 2013
1864	470	374	PF-68	750	1,200	2,350	5,150	$141,000, PF-68Cam, November 2013
1865	500	358	PF-68	750	1,200	2,350	5,150	$58,750, PF-68Cam, November 2013
1866, No Motto † (b)	1	n/a	n/a	*(unique)*				
1866, Variety 4	725	302	PF-68	500	1,000	1,500	2,850	$19,975, PF-68, November 2013
1867	625	361	PF-68	500	1,000	1,500	2,850	$8,225, PF-67Cam, November 2013
1868	600	328	PF-66	500	1,000	1,500	2,850	$47,000, PF-68Cam, November 2013

† Ranked in the *100 Greatest U.S. Coins* (fourth edition). **a.** For the Philadelphia Mint's quarters of 1842, the Small Date was used on Proofs only. The 1842 Large Date was made in circulation-strike format (see regular listings). **b.** The unique 1866 Proof quarter dollar without motto (as well as the half dollar and dollar of the same design) is not mentioned in the Mint director's report. "Not a pattern, but a muling created at a later date as a numismatic rarity" (*United States Pattern Coins*, 10th edition). Saul Teichman dates its creation to the 1870s. It is classified as Judd-536.

	Mintage	Cert	Finest	PF-60	PF-63	PF-64	PF-65	Recent Auction Record
1869	600	344	PF-67	$500	$1,000	$1,500	$2,850	$18,800, PF-67Cam, November 2013
1870	1,000	337	PF-67	500	975	1,400	2,600	$23,500, PF-67Cam, November 2013
1871	960	290	PF-68	500	975	1,400	2,600	$9,988, PF-67Cam, November 2013
1872	950	368	PF-68	500	950	1,350	2,400	$22,325, PF-68, August 2013
1873	600	352	PF-68	500	950	1,350	2,400	$44,063, PF-68Cam, November 2013
1873, Variety 5	540	515	PF-68	900	1,450	3,500	7,200	$52,875, PF-68Cam, November 2013
1874	700	275	PF-68	900	1,450	3,500	7,200	$22,325, PF-67, April 2014
1875	700	347	PF-68	500	950	1,350	2,400	$16,450, PF-67Cam, November 2013
1876	1,150	431	PF-68	500	950	1,350	2,400	$47,000, PF-68, November 2013
1877	510	287	PF-67	500	950	1,350	2,400	$22,325, PF-68Cam, November 2013
1878	800	385	PF-67	500	950	1,350	2,400	$25,850, PF-68, November 2013
1879	1,100	619	PF-67	500	950	1,350	2,400	$7,638, PF-67, November 2013
1880	1,355	763	PF-69	500	950	1,350	2,400	$28,200, PF-68, November 2013
1881	975	634	PF-68	500	950	1,350	2,400	$44,063, PF-68Cam, November 2013
1882	1,100	645	PF-68	500	950	1,350	2,400	$21,150, PF-68Cam, November 2013
1883	1,039	694	PF-69	500	950	1,350	2,400	$47,000, PF-69Cam, November 2013
1884	875	585	PF-69	500	950	1,350	2,400	$70,500, PF-69Cam, November 2013
1885	930	556	PF-68	500	950	1,350	2,400	$47,000, PF-68Cam, November 2013
1886	886	593	PF-68	500	950	1,350	2,400	$17,625, PF-67Cam, November 2013
1887	710	477	PF-68	500	950	1,350	2,400	$41,125, PF-68Cam, November 2013
1888	832	438	PF-68	500	950	1,350	2,400	$11,899, PF-68Cam, April 2013
1889	711	388	PF-68	500	950	1,350	2,400	$19,975, PF-68DCam, August 2013
1890	590	461	PF-68	500	950	1,350	2,400	$18,213, PF-68, June 2014
1891	600	479	PF-68	500	950	1,350	2,400	$16,450, PF-67Cam, November 2013

BARBER OR LIBERTY HEAD
(1892–1916)

Designer Charles E. Barber; weight 6.25 grams; composition .900 silver, .100 copper (net weight: .18084 oz. pure silver); diameter 24.3 mm; reeded edge; mints: Philadelphia, Denver, New Orleans, San Francisco.

History. The Liberty Head design was by Charles E. Barber, chief engraver of the U.S. Mint. Barber quarters feature the same obverse motif used on dimes and half dollars of the era, with the designer's initial, B, found at the truncation of the neck of Miss Liberty. The reverse depicts a heraldic eagle.

Striking and Sharpness. On the obverse, check the hair details and other features. On the reverse, the eagle's leg at the lower right and the arrows can be weak. Also check the upper right of the shield and the nearby wing. Once these coins entered circulation and acquired wear, the word LIBERTY on the headband tended to disappear quickly.

Availability. Barber quarters in Fine or better grade are scarce. Today, among circulation strikes, 90% or more in existence are G-4 or below. MS coins are available of all dates and mints, but some are very elusive. The 1896-S, 1901-S, and 1913-S are the key dates in all grades.

EF-40, 45 (Extremely Fine). *Obverse:* Further wear than at AU is seen on the head. The hair above the forehead lacks most detail. LIBERTY shows wear, but is strong. *Reverse:* Further wear than at AU is seen on the head and tail of the eagle and on the tips of the wings, most evident at the left and right extremes of the wings. At this level and below, sharpness of strike on the reverse is not important.

AU-50, 53, 55, 58 (About Uncirculated). *Obverse:* Light wear is seen on the head, especially on the forward hair under LIBERTY. There is some luster at AU-50 and 53. At AU-58, the luster is extensive but incomplete, especially on the higher parts and in the right field. *Reverse:* Wear is evident on the head and tail of the eagle and on the tips of the wings. At AU-50 and 53, there still is significant luster. An AU-58 coin (as determined by the obverse) can have the reverse appear to be full MS.

MS-60 to 70 (Mint State). *Obverse:* At MS-60, some abrasion and contact marks are evident, most noticeably on the cheek and the obverse field to the right. Luster is present, but may be dull or lifeless. Many Barber coins have been cleaned, especially of the earlier dates. At MS-63, contact marks are very few. Abrasion still is evident, but less than at lower levels. The cheek of Miss Liberty virtually showcases abrasion. An MS-65 coin may have minor abrasion, but contact marks are so minute as to require magnification. Luster should be full and rich. *Reverse:* Comments apply as for the obverse, except that in lower MS grades abrasion and contact marks are most noticeable on the head and tail of the eagle and on the tips of the wings. At MS-65 or higher, there are no marks visible to the unaided eye. The field is mainly protected by design elements, and often appears to grade a point or two higher than the obverse.

1892, Variety 1 Reverse **1892, Variety 2 Reverse**
Note position of wing tip relative to E in UNITED.

	Mintage	Cert	Avg	%MS	EF-40	AU-50	MS-60	MS-62	MS-63	MS-64	MS-65	Recent Auction Record
1892 (a)	8,236,000	3,268	61.1	74	$75	$130	$235	$310	$440	$625	$1,200	$12,925, MS-68, June 2014
1892O	2,460,000	864	59.5	66	95	160	300	400	475	650	1,550	$17,625, MS-68, June 2014
1892S	964,079	277	51.7	53	200	300	475	700	1,050	2,100	4,400	$35,250, MS-67, June 2014
1893	5,444,023	643	59.2	69	75	130	235	310	440	625	1,400	$22,325, MS-67, April 2013
1893O	3,396,000	418	58.3	63	110	170	275	400	500	800	1,800	$4,113, MS-66, August 2013
1893S	1,454,535	237	52.3	54	175	300	425	700	1,000	2,200	6,100	$3,819, MS, February 2014
1894	3,432,000	343	59.7	77	95	150	240	325	450	625	1,300	$1,645, MS-65, June 2014
1894O	2,852,000	263	56.7	63	130	230	325	550	725	1,200	2,000	$1,293, MS-64, February 2014
1894S	2,648,821	390	57.9	69	120	210	325	450	725	1,350	2,400	$2,468, MS-65, November 2013
1895	4,440,000	425	59.7	77	80	140	250	300	500	650	1,600	$8,813, MS-67, June 2014
1895O	2,816,000	245	55.1	63	140	230	400	600	900	1,400	2,600	$49,938, MS-68, June 2014
1895S	1,764,681	215	51.7	55	170	275	420	700	1,050	2,200	3,500	$12,925, MS-67, August 2013
1896	3,874,000	402	59.1	77	80	135	250	300	425	600	1,250	$999, MS-65, September 2013
1896O	1,484,000	250	44.0	36	550	800	1,000	1,300	2,000	4,000	6,500	$8,813, MS-65, August 2013
1896S	188,039	1,066	12.4	6	5,000	7,000	10,000	12,500	17,500	28,000	47,500	$47,000, MS-65, October 2013
1897	8,140,000	514	58.7	71	70	120	240	300	450	650	1,400	$16,450, MS-66, February 2013
1897O	1,414,800	233	43.7	39	385	600	850	1,300	1,800	2,350	3,300	$23,500, MS-67, October 2013
1897S	542,229	295	32.6	30	825	1,000	1,600	1,725	1,900	3,000	7,500	$15,275, MS-66, September 2013
1898	11,100,000	669	57.8	68	70	125	225	300	425	600	1,200	$15,275, MS-62, February 2014
1898O	1,868,000	203	47.9	42	300	390	625	1,000	1,500	3,250	8,750	$58,750, MS-68, June 2014
1898S	1,020,592	146	51.0	46	100	200	400	850	1,400	3,400	7,500	$18,800, MS-67, June 2014
1899	12,624,000	665	58.1	70	75	125	240	300	425	600	1,200	$2,820, MS-65, August 2013
1899O	2,644,000	242	55.6	61	120	260	400	600	800	1,250	2,500	$4,700, MS-65, August 2013
1899S	708,000	85	49.9	40	140	270	425	700	1,400	1,800	3,750	$4,406, MS-66, March 2014
1900	10,016,000	297	59.4	69	75	125	240	300	425	600	1,250	$3,409, MS-66, October 2013
1900O	3,416,000	367	57.2	74	150	310	525	700	850	1,300	3,500	$1,998, MS-64, October 2013
1900S	1,858,585	383	55.1	42	80	130	350	600	1,000	1,750	4,500	$6,463, MS-66, April 2014
1901	8,892,000	298	53.6	63	80	135	240	300	425	600	1,350	$15,275, MS-67, June 2014
1901O	1,612,000	356	49.5	57	550	750	950	1,300	1,850	3,150	5,000	$22,325, MS-67, June 2014
1901S	72,664	712	11.3	7	30,000	36,000	40,000	43,000	50,000	62,500	85,000	$258,500, MS-67, June 2014
1902	12,196,967	581	37.2	39	65	120	240	300	425	600	1,200	$1,351, MS-65, August 2013
1902O	4,748,000	395	54.3	58	140	225	475	800	1,300	1,900	3,900	$4,994, MS-66, September 2013
1902S	1,524,612	296	54.2	59	160	240	500	675	950	1,300	3,200	$19,975, MS-67, April 2013
1903	9,759,309	156	54.9	58	65	120	240	320	450	700	2,400	$5,875, MS-66, September 2013
1903O	3,500,000	237	54.5	59	120	275	425	750	1,200	2,100	4,400	$1,528, MS-63, February 2013
1903S	1,036,000	211	53.4	56	150	275	425	600	850	1,500	2,200	$4,259, MS-66, August 2013
1904	9,588,143	290	57.7	68	70	120	240	300	425	600	1,200	$7,344, MS-67, June 2014
1904O	2,456,000	289	54.5	55	240	450	800	1,050	1,300	1,800	2,500	$41,125, MS-67, June 2014
1905	4,967,523	288	57.8	62	70	120	240	320	440	600	1,300	$2,174, MS-66, August 2013
1905O	1,230,000	256	56.0	65	260	350	475	750	1,250	2,300	6,500	$5,288, MS-65, June 2013
1905S	1,884,000	177	55.4	64	105	225	350	600	1,000	1,400	3,500	$1,645, MS-64, August 2013
1906	3,655,760	338	61.1	80	70	120	240	300	425	600	1,200	$2,820, MS-66, June 2014
1906D	3,280,000	340	60.5	78	70	145	250	325	450	700	1,850	$1,175, MS-65, August 2013
1906O	2,056,000	282	60.9	82	100	200	300	400	550	800	1,350	$2,585, MS-66, June 2014
1907	7,132,000	547	60.4	75	65	120	240	300	425	600	1,200	$9,988, MS-68, June 2014
1907D	2,484,000	436	59.4	75	70	175	250	400	650	1,100	2,500	$7,050, MS-66, June 2014
1907O	4,560,000	314	59.2	73	70	135	275	340	500	750	1,850	$9,988, MS-68, June 2014
1907S	1,360,000	268	55.2	68	140	280	475	700	1,200	2,250	5,000	$15,275, MS-67, June 2014
1908	4,232,000	345	60.6	79	70	120	240	300	425	600	1,200	$1,645, MS-66, April 2013
1908D	5,788,000	515	58.0	67	70	120	240	300	425	600	1,275	$3,672, MS-66, August 2013
1908O	6,244,000	475	57.3	72	65	120	240	300	425	600	1,200	$3,819, MS-66, November 2013

a. There are two varieties of the 1892 reverse. Variety 1: the eagle's wing covers only half of the E in UNITED; Variety 2: the eagle's wing covers most of the E. Coins of Variety 1 are somewhat scarcer.

	Mintage	Cert	Avg	%MS	EF-40	AU-50	MS-60	MS-62	MS-63	MS-64	MS-65	Recent Auction Record
1908S	784,000	323	54.5	68	$325	$465	$750	$925	$1,200	$2,100	$4,500	$3,819, MS-65, August 2013
1909	9,268,000	653	59.2	75	65	120	240	300	425	600	1,200	$2,585, MS-66, April 2013
1909D	5,114,000	787	58.2	71	85	150	240	300	425	600	1,200	$2,585, MS-66, November 2013
1909O	712,000	409	43.3	47	1,000	1,800	3,000	3,250	4,000	4,800	7,750	$14,100, MS-65, August 2013
1909S	1,348,000	200	55.4	71	90	185	285	475	750	1,300	1,900	$3,055, MS-66, June 2014
1910	2,244,000	310	59.2	79	80	140	240	300	425	600	1,200	$4,700, MS-67, June 2014
1910D	1,500,000	288	58.5	75	125	240	350	600	900	1,150	1,600	$9,400, MS-67, June 2014
1911	3,720,000	461	59.7	77	70	125	240	300	425	600	1,150	$3,819, MS-66, September 2013
1911D	933,600	395	54.0	63	400	600	850	1,200	1,300	2,100	5,400	$4,994, MS-65, August 2013
1911S	988,000	251	55.7	67	165	280	375	550	750	1,000	1,400	$7,050, MS-67, April 2014
1912	4,400,000	692	60.8	80	70	120	240	300	425	600	1,150	$2,115, MS-66, January 2013
1912S	708,000	513	58.2	76	125	220	400	600	925	1,400	1,900	$1,116, MS-64, August 2013
1913	484,000	323	49.5	53	400	525	900	1,000	1,200	1,400	4,000	$5,581, MS-66, June 2014
1913D	1,450,800	316	56.8	67	85	175	275	325	450	600	1,150	$8,813, MS-67, June 2014
1913S	40,000	1,048	18.2	16	10,000	12,750	15,000	18,000	20,000	23,500	30,000	$70,500, MS-67, June 2014
1914	6,244,230	989	43.5	53	65	120	240	300	425	600	1,150	$2,585, MS-66, June 2013
1914D	3,046,000	957	59.1	75	65	120	240	300	425	600	1,150	$4,994, MS-67, November 2013
1914S	264,000	786	33.9	35	825	975	1,400	1,500	1,650	2,250	3,100	$7,931, MS-65, July 2014
1915	3,480,000	798	51.2	63	65	120	240	300	425	600	1,200	$6,169, MS-67, July 2013
1915D	3,694,000	1,161	60.6	80	70	120	240	300	425	600	1,150	$2,820, MS-67, November 2013
1915S	704,000	811	58.8	71	115	200	285	350	475	675	1,300	$6,463, MS-66, July 2014
1916	1,788,000	586	60.7	77	70	120	240	300	425	600	1,150	$7,638, MS-67, June 2014
1916D	6,540,800	4,794	55.3	68	70	120	240	300	425	600	1,150	$9,400, MS-68, November 2013

Proof Barber Quarters

PF-60 to 70 (Proof). Proofs exist in proportion to their mintages. Choicer examples tend to be of later dates. Most are sharply struck, although more than just a few are weak on the eagle's leg at the lower right and on certain parts of the arrows. The Proofs of 1892 to 1901 usually have cameo contrast between the designs and the mirror fields. *Obverse and*

Reverse: Proofs that are extensively cleaned and have many hairlines, or that are dull and grainy, are lower level, such as PF-60 to 62. With medium hairlines and good reflectivity, an assigned grade of PF-64 is appropriate. Tiny horizontal lines on Miss Liberty's cheek, known as slide marks, from National and other album slides scuffing the relief of the cheek, are

endemic on all Barber silver coins. With noticeable marks of this type, the highest grade assignable is PF-64. With relatively few hairlines, a rating of PF-65 can be given. PF-66 should have hairlines so delicate that magnification is needed to see them. Above that, a Proof should be free of any hairlines or other problems.

Proof Barber Quarter

Coins designated Deep Cameo or Ultra Cameo bring a premium of 50% to 100% above listed values.

	Mintage	Cert	Finest	PF-60	PF-63	PF-64	PF-65	PF-65Cam	Recent Auction Record
1892	1,245	780	PF-68	$450	$800	$1,175	$1,900	$2,300	$15,864, PF-68, February 2013
1893	792	584	PF-69	450	800	1,175	1,900	2,300	$29,375, PF, August 2013
1894	972	679	PF-69	450	800	1,175	1,900	2,300	$14,100, PF-68, September 2013
1895	880	555	PF-69	450	800	1,175	1,900	2,300	$22,325, PF-68Cam, November 2013
1896	762	591	PF-69	450	800	1,175	1,900	2,300	$23,500, PF-68Cam, November 2013
1897	731	530	PF-68	450	800	1,175	1,900	2,300	$8,813, PF-67, September 2013
1898	735	572	PF-69	450	800	1,175	1,900	2,300	$27,025, PF-69, June 2014
1899	846	444	PF-69	450	800	1,175	1,900	2,300	$14,100, PF-67DCam, January 2014
1900	912	515	PF-68	450	800	1,175	1,900	2,300	$14,100, PF-68Cam, April 2013
1901	813	467	PF-68	450	800	1,175	1,900	2,300	$8,813, PF-67Cam, November 2013
1902	777	436	PF-68	450	800	1,175	1,900	2,300	$11,163, PF-67, June 2013
1903	755	564	PF-69	450	800	1,175	1,900	2,300	$13,055, PF-68Cam, August 2013

Chart continued on next page.

	Mintage	Cert	Finest	PF-60	PF-63	PF-64	PF-65	PF-65Cam	Recent Auction Record
1904	670	505	PF-69	$450	$800	$1,175	$1,900	$2,300	$31,725, PF, October 2013
1905	727	944	PF-68	450	800	1,175	1,900	2,300	$5,581, PF-67, November 2013
1906	675	8	PF-67	450	800	1,175	1,900	2,300	$14,100, PF-68, November 2013
1907	575	505	PF-68	450	800	1,175	1,900	2,300	$11,750, PF-68Cam, November 2013
1908	545	389	PF-69	450	800	1,175	1,900	2,300	$7,344, PF-68, September 2013
1909	650	510	PF-68	450	800	1,175	1,900	2,300	$18,800, PF-68, November 2013
1910	551	507	PF-69	450	800	1,175	1,900	2,300	$15,275, PF-68Cam, November 2013
1911	543	485	PF-69	450	800	1,175	1,900	2,300	$17,038, PF-68Cam, November 2013
1912	700	454	PF-69	450	800	1,175	1,900	2,300	$14,100, PF-68, August 2013
1913	613	472	PF-69	450	850	1,200	1,900	2,500	$8,225, PF-67, February 2013
1914	380	392	PF-68	450	950	1,250	2,100	2,500	$14,100, PF-67Cam, April 2013
1915	450	335	PF-68	450	1,000	1,300	2,200	2,600	$19,975, PF-68, November 2013

STANDING LIBERTY, VARIETY 1, NO STARS BELOW EAGLE (1916–1917)

Designer Hermon A. MacNeil; weight 6.25 grams; composition .900 silver, .100 copper (net weight: .18084 oz. pure silver); diameter 24.3 mm; reeded edge; mints: Philadelphia, Denver, San Francisco.

Full Head Details, Variety 1

History. The Standing Liberty quarter dollar, designed by sculptor Hermon A. MacNeil (whose initial, M, is located above and to the right of the date), was greeted with wide acclaimed from its first appearance. All of 1916 and many of 1917 are of the Variety 1 design, with the right breast of Miss Liberty exposed on the obverse and with no stars below the eagle on the reverse. Variety 2 (see next section) has modified designs.

Striking and Sharpness. Many if not most 1916 quarters are somewhat lightly struck on the head and body of Miss Liberty. The 1917 Variety 1 quarters usually are quite well struck. When light striking is found, it is usually on the higher-relief parts of the head, the right knee (not as obvious), and the rivets on the left side of the shield. The 1917 Philadelphia Mint coins are usually sharper than the other varieties of this type. A misleading term, Full Head (FH), is widely used to describe quarters that have only *partial* head details. See further comments regarding Variety 2 coins, wherein the problem is more serious.

Availability. The 1916 quarter is the key to the series. Examples tend to be liberally graded in the real-life marketplace, especially in EF and AU, this in contrast to more careful grading for the less valuable 1917 issues. Circulated coins of 1916 and 1917 often have the date worn partly away, due to the high position of this feature in the design. On MS coins the luster is usually rich and attractive. No Proof coins of this type were officially issued, but specimen strikings dated 1917 are known to exist.

MS-60 to 70 (Mint State). *Obverse:* At MS-60 some abrasion and contact marks are evident on the higher areas, which also are the areas most likely to be weakly struck. This includes the rivets on the shield to the left and the central escutcheon on the shield, the head, and the right leg of Miss Liberty. The luster may be incomplete in those areas on weakly struck coins, even those certified above MS-65—the original planchet surface may be revealed, as it was not smoothed out by striking. Accordingly, grading is best done by evaluating abrasion and mint luster as it is observed. Luster may be dull or lifeless at MS-60 to 62 but should have deep frost at MS-63 or better, particularly in the lower-relief areas. At MS-65 or better, it should be full and rich. *Reverse:* Striking is usually quite good. Check the eagle's breast and the surface of the right wing. Luster may be dull or lifeless at MS-60 to 62 but should have deep frost at MS-63 or better, particularly in the lower-relief areas. At MS-65 or better, it should be full and rich.

	Mintage	Cert	Avg	%MS	MS-60	MS-63	MS-63FH	MS-64	MS-64FH	MS-65	MS-65FH	Recent Auction Record
1916 †	52,000	3,723	54.2	61	$15,000	$18,500	$19,500	$21,000	$22,500	$25,000	$35,000	$49,938, MS-66FH, June 2014
1917, Variety 1	8,740,000	11,637	61.8	84	250	350	400	425	600	750	1,200	$25,850, MS-67FH, August 2013
1917D, Variety 1	1,509,200	3,776	59.7	75	325	425	550	600	900	950	2,000	$4,994, MS-67FH, September 2013
1917S, Variety 1	1,952,000	2,517	60.3	73	350	475	700	700	1,150	1,200	3,200	$9,400, MS-67FH, September 2013

† Ranked in the *100 Greatest U.S. Coins* (fourth edition).

STANDING LIBERTY, VARIETY 2, STARS BELOW EAGLE (1917–1930)

Designer Hermon A. MacNeil; weight 6.25 grams; composition .900 silver, .100 copper (net weight: .18084 oz. pure silver); diameter 24.3 mm; reeded edge; mints: Philadelphia, Denver, San Francisco.

History. Variety 2 of the Standing Liberty design was introduced in 1917 and continued to the end of the series. Miss Liberty is clothed in a jacket of chainmail armor, and the reverse is slightly redesigned, with stars below the eagle. These changes came at the suggestion of the designer, Hermon A. MacNeil.

Striking and Sharpness. Most coins of this design have areas of light striking. On the obverse these are most notable on the head of Miss Liberty and on the shield, the latter often with the two lower-left rivets weak or missing and with the center emblem on the shield weak. The center of the standing figure can be weak as well, as can the upper-left area at and near the date. After 1924 the date was slightly recessed, eliminating that problem. On the reverse, check the eagle's breast. A misleading term, Full Head (FH), is widely used to describe quarters that have only *partial* head details;

such coins often actually have the two lower-left shield rivets poorly struck or not visible at all. Most third-party grading services define these criteria for "Full Head" designation (in order of importance): a full, unbroken hairline from Liberty's brow down to the jawline; all three leaves on the head showing; and a visible earhole.

Availability. The 1918-S, 8 Over 7, is recognized as the key issue, and the 1919-D, 1921, 1923-S, and 1927-S as quite scarce. MS coins are readily available for most issues, but Full Details coins can be *extreme* rarities. Circulated coins dated from 1917 through 1924 often have the date worn partly away, due to the high position of this feature in the design. On MS coins the luster usually is rich and attractive. No Proof coins of this type were officially issued, but specimen strikings of the first variety, dated 1917, are known to exist.

MS-60 to 70 (Mint State). *Obverse:* At MS-60, some abrasion and contact marks are evident on the higher areas, which are also the areas most likely to be weakly struck. This includes the lower left two rivets and the ornament at the center of the shield, the head, and the right leg of Miss Liberty. The luster may not be complete in those areas on weakly struck coins, even those certified above MS-65—the original planchet surface may be revealed as it was not smoothed out by striking. Accordingly, grading is best done by evaluating abrasion as it is observed, plus evaluation of the mint luster. This may be dull or lifeless at MS-60 to 62, but should have deep frost at MS-63 or better, particularly in the lower-relief areas. At MS-65 or better, it should be full and rich. *Reverse:* Striking is usually better, permitting observation of luster in all areas. Check the eagle's breast and the surface of the right wing. Luster may be dull or lifeless at MS-60 to 62, but should have deep frost at MS-63 or better, particularly in the lower-relief areas. At MS-65 or better, it should be full and rich.

Full Head (FH) Details, Variety 2
Note (1) the full unbroken hairline from brow to neck; (2) all three leaves clearly visible in Liberty's cap; and (3) a visible ear hole.

Pedestal Date (1917–1924)

Recessed Date (1925–1930)

1918-S, 8 Over 7

	Mintage	Cert	Avg	%MS	MS-60	MS-63	MS-63FH	MS-64	MS-64FH	MS-65	MS-65FH	Recent Auction Record
1917, Variety 2	13,880,000	3,003	61.5	79	$210	$275	$350	$350	$600	$600	$900	$7,638, MS-67FH, September 2013
1917D, Variety 2	6,224,400	1,733	60.4	71	260	350	600	500	1,000	1,300	3,000	$7,931, MS-66FH, June 2013
1917S, Variety 2	5,552,000	1,580	60.6	74	260	350	900	500	1,600	1,100	3,250	$45,825, MS-67FH, January 2013
1918	14,240,000	1,832	60.3	73	150	225	450	350	700	700	1,750	$58,750, MS-68FH, February 2013
1918D	7,380,000	1,825	58.3	66	275	400	1,000	650	2,200	1,300	4,000	$32,900, MS-67FH, May 2013
1918S	11,072,000	1,634	51.8	51	200	300	2,200	700	3,500	1,400	12,000	$35,250, MS-66FH, February 2013
1918S, 8 Over 7 † (a)	*	1,249	55.1	56	19,000	32,500	100,000	35,000	120,000	90,000	250,000	$188,000, MS-64FH, June 2014
1919	11,324,000	2,030	59.0	74	185	250	400	350	650	600	1,500	$36,719, MS-69, April 2013

* Included in number above. † Ranked in the *100 Greatest U.S. Coins* (fourth edition). **a.** This clear overdate was caused by the use of two differently dated hubs when the die was made. "Because of the boldness of the 7, this variety can be confirmed easily in low grades. . . . This variety is extremely rare in high grades. We recommend authentication because alterations do exist. Genuine specimens have a small die chip above the pedestal, just to the left of the lowest star on the right" (*Cherrypickers' Guide to Rare Die Varieties*, fifth edition, volume II).

Chart continued on next page.

	Mintage	Cert	Avg	%MS	MS-60	MS-63	MS-63FH	MS-64	MS-64FH	MS-65	MS-65FH	Recent Auction Record
1919D	1,944,000	1,011	50.1	38	$950	$1,600	$9,000	$2,200	$15,000	$3,000	$25,000	$42,594, MS-65FH, June 2014
1919S	1,836,000	2,138	59.0	68	900	1,500	9,000	2,400	15,000	4,000	30,000	$258,500, MS-67FH, April 2014
1920	27,860,000	2,340	61.1	80	160	230	400	350	750	600	1,500	$11,163, MS-67, February 2014
1920D	3,586,400	1,073	57.9	62	350	800	1,500	1,300	3,000	2,000	6,500	$16,450, MS-66FH, April 2013
1920S	6,380,000	1,679	49.4	50	270	750	5,000	1,300	8,000	2,200	24,000	$17,625, MS-65FH, June 2013
1921	1,916,000	2,642	58.3	73	1,600	2,200	3,000	3,000	4,000	3,750	5,500	$52,875, MS-67FH, November 2013
1923	9,716,000	2,522	55.2	65	170	240	450	350	1,800	600	4,000	$29,375, MS-67FH, February 2013
1923S	1,360,000	1,777	57.5	65	2,600	3,400	3,800	4,000	4,500	5,000	6,500	$21,150, MS-66FH, February 2013
1924	10,920,000	2,908	62.1	87	185	275	400	350	650	600	1,400	$16,450, MS-68, May 2013
1924D	3,112,000	2,076	62.2	86	325	375	1,000	425	2,000	600	4,500	$35,250, MS-67FH, February 2013
1924S	2,860,000	1,607	60.5	77	350	900	1,750	1,400	3,500	1,750	5,500	$12,925, MS-65FH, January 2014
1925	12,280,000	2,822	62.1	84	160	250	375	350	500	600	1,000	$12,925, MS-67FH, September 2013
1926	11,316,000	4,545	63.0	94	150	250	375	350	700	600	2,000	$27,025, MS-67FH, November 2013
1926D	1,716,000	2,580	62.2	90	180	250	6,000	350	10,000	550	24,000	$105,750, MS-67FH, April 2014
1926S	2,700,000	1,402	59.7	71	375	775	5,750	1,200	11,250	2,000	25,000	$48,175, MS-66FH, February 2013
1927	11,912,000	2,946	62.2	87	140	225	375	350	600	550	1,100	$15,275, MS-67FH, February 2013
1927D	976,000	2,663	43.9	47	270	310	650	400	1,100	600	3,000	$22,325, MS, February 2014
1927S	396,000	1,638	45.9	44	4,800	7,000	30,000	8,500	62,500	10,500	185,000	$94,000, MS-65FH, April 2014
1928	6,336,000	3,213	63.0	90	140	225	400	350	600	550	1,750	$5,875, MS-67FH, November 2013
1928D	1,627,600	2,868	63.1	90	150	235	1,400	350	2,800	550	5,000	$4,113, MS-67, February 2014
1928S (b)	2,644,000	2,731	62.2	83	140	235	360	350	575	550	900	$3,525, MS-67FH, April 2013
1929	11,140,000	3,969	62.4	85	140	225	350	325	500	525	900	$1,528, MS-66, November 2013
1929D	1,358,000	2,118	61.8	81	140	230	1,400	350	2,300	525	5,000	$7,050, MS-65FH, April 2013
1929S	1,764,000	1,908	63.1	90	140	225	350	325	500	525	850	$7,050, MS-67FH, April 2013
1930	5,632,000	8,245	62.4	84	140	225	350	325	500	525	850	$7,638, MS-67FH, November 2013
1930S	1,556,000	4,079	63.1	89	140	225	350	325	500	525	850	$3,819, MS-67FH, November 2013

b. Large and small mintmarks exist; their values are the same.

WASHINGTON, EAGLE REVERSE
(1932–1998)

Silver (1932–1964): Designer John Flanagan; weight 6.25 grams; composition .900 silver, .100 copper (net weight: .18084 oz. pure silver); diameter 24.3 mm; reeded edge; mints: Philadelphia, Denver, San Francisco.

Clad (1965–1998): Designer John Flanagan; weight 5.67 grams; composition outer layers of copper-nickel (.750 copper, .250 nickel) bonded to inner core of pure copper; diameter 24.3 mm; reeded edge.

Bicentennial variety: Designers John Flanagan and Jack L. Ahr; diameter 24.3 mm; reeded edge. Silver issue—Weight 5.75 grams; composition outer layers of .800 silver, .200 copper bonded to inner core of .209 silver, .791 copper (net weight.0739 oz. pure silver). Copper-nickel issue—Weight 5.67 grams; composition outer layers of .750 copper, .250 nickel bonded to inner core of pure copper.

Silver Proofs (1992–1998): Designer John Flanagan; weight 6.25 grams; composition .900 silver, .100 copper (net weight: .18084 oz. pure silver); diameter 24.3 mm; reeded edge; mint: San Francisco.

History. The Washington quarter, designed by New York sculptor John Flanagan, originally was intended to be a commemorative coin, but it ultimately was produced as a regular circulation issue. The obverse is from a bust by Jean Antoine Houdon. Flanagan's initials, JF, are at the base of Washington's neck. The reverse features a modernistic eagle. In October 1973, the Treasury announced an open contest for the selection of suitable designs for the Bicentennial reverses of the quarter, half dollar, and dollar, with $5,000 to be awarded to each winner. Twelve semifinalists were chosen, and from these the symbolic entry of Jack L. Ahr was selected for the quarter reverse. It features a military drummer facing left, with a victory torch encircled by 13 stars at the upper left. Except for the dual dating, "1776–1976," the obverse remained unchanged. Pieces with this dual dating were coined during 1975 and 1976. They were struck for general circulation and included in all the Mint's offerings of Proof and Uncirculated coin sets. (The grading instructions below are for the regular Eagle Reverse variety.)

Striking and Sharpness. The relief of both sides of the Washington quarter issues from 1932 to 1998 is shallow. Accordingly, any lightness of strike is not easily seen. Nearly all are well struck. On all quarters of 1932 and some of 1934, the motto IN GOD WE TRUST is light, as per the design. It was strengthened in 1934.

Availability. The 1932-D and S are key issues but not rarities. All others are readily available in high grades, but some are scarcer than others.

Note: Values of common-date silver coins have been based on the current bullion price of silver, $20 per ounce, and may vary with the prevailing spot price.

MS-60 to 70 (Mint State). *Obverse:* At MS-60, some abrasion and contact marks are evident on the hair above the ear and at the top of the head below E (LIBERTY). At MS-63, abrasion is slight, and less is evident at MS-64. An MS-65 coin should display no abrasion or contact marks except under magnification, and MS-66 and higher coins should have none at all. Luster should be full and rich. *Reverse:* Comments apply as for the obverse, except that the eagle's breast and legs are the places to check. On both sides the fields are protected by design elements and do not show contact marks readily.

1932, Doubled-Die Obverse
FS-25-1932-101.

  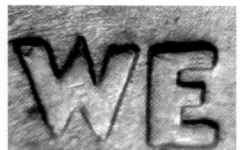

| | | **1934, Doubled-Die Obverse** *FS-25-1934-101.* | **1934, Light Motto** *FS-25-1934-401.* | **1934, Heavy Motto** *FS-25-1934-403.* |

	Mintage	Cert	Avg	%MS	MS-60	MS-62	MS-63	MS-64	MS-65	MS-66	MS-67	Recent Auction Record
1932	5,404,000	1,686	62.8	88	$25	$40	$60	$95	$410	$900	$20,000	$6,463, AU-50, November 2013
1932, DblDie Obverse (a)	*	4,728	46.4	37	350	400	500	600	800			$235, MS-62, December 2013
1932D	436,800	2,788	44.7	34	1,100	1,500	1,900	2,800	12,250	—		$12,338, MS-65, January 2014
1932S	408,000	8,982	51.3	49	450	750	850	1,350	4,800	20,000		$4,313, MS-65, April 2012
1934, All kinds	31,912,052											
1934, DblDie Obverse (b)		414	42.2	31	1,000	1,500	1,900	2,650	4,250	7,250		$3,055, MS-65, June 2013
1934, Light Motto (c)		800	63.7	91	60	80	135	265	385	725	3,500	$8,813, MS-67, January 2014
1934, Heavy Motto (d)		1,747	62.2	81	30	40	50	65	135	650	3,100	$6,463, MS-67, April 2014
1934D	3,527,200	1,147	61.6	81	250	280	340	500	850	1,800	11,000	$14,100, MS-67, June 2013
1935	32,484,000	4,253	64.6	96	22	30	35	50	135	200	550	$3,819, MS-67, January 2014
1935D	5,780,000	2,825	62.7	86	240	265	275	315	625	900	4,500	$4,700, MS-67, March 2014
1935S	5,660,000	3,042	63.0	87	100	120	135	160	300	575	3,300	$2,820, MS-67, August 2013

* Included in number above. **a.** The doubling is evident on the earlobe, the nostril, and the braid of hair. **b.** Very strong doubling is visible on the motto, LIBERTY, and the date. **c.** "Notice the considerable weakness in the letters of the motto. In addition, the center point of the W is pointed" (*Cherrypickers' Guide to Rare Die Varieties,* fifth edition, volume II). **d.** The motto has very thick letters, and the central apex of the W is pointed, rising slightly above the other letters.

1937, Doubled-Die Obverse

1942-D, Doubled-Die Obverse
FS-25-1942D-101.

1942-D, Doubled-Die Reverse
FS-25-1942D-801.

1943, Doubled-Die Obverse
FS-25-1943-103. Other varieties exist.

1943-S, Doubled-Die Obverse
FS-25-1943S-101.

1950-D, D Over S
FS-25-1950D-601.
Other varieties exist.

1950-S, S Over D
FS-25-1950S-601.

	Mintage	Cert	Avg	%MS	AU-50	MS-60	MS-63	MS-64	MS-65	MS-66	MS-67	Recent Auction Record
1936	41,300,000	3,853	64.5	96	$10	$25	$35	$50	$120	$200	$550	$2,350, MS-67, February 2014
1936D	5,374,000	2,775	61.3	80	250	525	800	900	1,100	1,900	8,200	$9,400, MS-67, June 2013
1936S	3,828,000	3,453	63.9	96	50	120	140	180	325	650	3,200	$3,525, MS-67, March 2013
1937	19,696,000	2,513	64.5	97	12	25	35	50	90	200	900	$5,875, MS-67, February 2014
1937, DblDie Obverse (a)	*	105	32.2	17	1,500	2,450	3,800	5,800	12,000	18,000		$1,778, MS-63, April 2013
1937D	7,189,600	2,927	64.3	97	30	70	90	110	150	400	2,750	$4,700, MS-67, January 2014
1937S	1,652,000	2,811	63.7	95	95	150	250	275	400	800	3,000	$5,581, MS-67, June 2013
1938	9,472,000	2,306	64.0	94	45	95	110	140	210	375	1,650	$3,819, MS-67, June 2014
1938S	2,832,000	3,187	64.3	97	55	105	140	170	230	375	1,800	$1,763, MS-67, June 2013
1939	33,540,000	4,247	65.2	98	12	15	25	40	60	100	350	$2,115, MS-67, August 2013
1939D	7,092,000	3,015	64.7	97	20	40	50	65	115	185	1,000	$546, MS-67, April 2012
1939S	2,628,000	2,518	64.2	95	60	95	135	185	310	500	2,800	$4,113, MS-67, February 2013
1940	35,704,000	2,634	65.1	97	9	17	35	45	60	120	425	$3,055, MS-67, April 2013
1940D	2,797,600	2,925	64.3	96	65	120	165	190	300	425	2,400	$5,288, MS-67, April 2014
1940S	8,244,000	3,154	65.0	98	16	21	32	45	65	120	1,000	$3,067, MS-67, August 2013
1941	79,032,000	4,309	65.1	98	8	10	14	25	45	80	425	$18,800, MS-68, November 2013
1941D	16,714,800	2,016	64.9	98	13	32	55	60	70	215	2,250	$3,525, MS-67, April 2013
1941S	16,080,000	2,468	64.5	96	11	28	55	60	70	190	1,600	$10,281, MS-68, January 2014
1942	102,096,000	2,101	64.4	94	7	9	10	20	35	200	1,800	$3,525, MS-67, November 2013
1942D	17,487,200	1,020	65.3	99	10	17	20	30	40	200	925	$3,819, MS-67, January 2014
1942D, DblDie Obverse (b)	*	1,687	62.7	91	750	1,800	4,000	4,850	6,000	10,500		$1,207, AU-55, April 2013
1942D, DblDie Reverse (c)	*	33	51.1	55	385	750	1,250	1,700	2,250	5,400		$823, MS-64, June 2014
1942S	19,384,000	2,690	64.0	93	20	70	115	140	175	375	1,350	$4,259, MS-67, April 2013
1943	99,700,000	3,700	65.1	97	7	9	10	15	40	100	500	$10,281, MS-68, November 2013
1943, DblDie Obverse (d)	*	58	52.1	48	500	1,600	3,500	4,600	5,500	8,000		$30, VF-20, March 2012
1943D	16,095,600	2,336	65.1	98	15	28	39	50	60	120	800	$12,925, MS-68, November 2013

* Included in number above. **a.** Very strong doubling is evident on the motto, LIBERTY, the date, and the end of the braid ribbons. "This variety is considered one of the most important in the series" (*Cherrypickers' Guide to Rare Die Varieties*, fifth edition, volume II). **b.** Doubling is evident, with a very strong spread, on LIBERTY, the date, and the motto. **c.** Doubling on this popular variety is most prominent on the eagle's beak, the arrows, and the branch above the mintmark. **d.** Doubling is very strong on the motto, LIBERTY, and the date.

	Mintage	Cert	Avg	%MS	AU-50	MS-60	MS-63	MS-64	MS-65	MS-66	MS-67	Recent Auction Record
1943S	21,700,000	2,746	64.9	97	$13	$26	$42	$50	$60	$120	$900	$6,463, MS-68, June 2014
1943S, DblDie Obverse (e)	*	273	50.9	56	350	500	1,000	1,200	2,600	6,250	8,250	$7,638, MS-66, November 2013
1944	104,956,000	3,831	65.2	98	7	9	10	15	32	60	500	$4,406, MS-62, November 2013
1944D	14,600,800	3,353	65.5	99	10	17	20	30	40	70	500	$2,820, MS-67, February 2013
1944S	12,560,000	3,747	65.5	99	10	14	20	30	35	60	525	$7,050, MS-68, November 2013
1945	74,372,000	2,574	65.0	98	7	9	10	15	38	150	1,300	$3,819, MS-68, January 2014
1945D	12,341,600	2,119	65.3	99	12	18	25	30	40	70	1,100	$1,645, MS-67, June 2014
1945S	17,004,001	3,025	65.3	99	7	9	13	20	35	60	900	$3,525, MS-67, April 2014
1946	53,436,000	1,985	65.0	98	7	9	10	15	40	100	1,500	$3,055, MS-67, June 2014
1946D	9,072,800	4,427	65.5	100	7	9	10	20	45	80	900	$881, MS-67, April 2013
1946S	4,204,000	9,342	65.4	100	7	9	10	20	40	60	400	$9,400, MS-68, April 2014
1947	22,556,000	2,776	65.4	99	7	11	19	25	42	80	550	$3,819, MS-67, March 2014
1947D	15,338,400	4,732	65.6	100	7	11	17	20	40	60	275	$2,350, MS-67, June 2013
1947S	5,532,000	8,209	65.6	100	7	9	15	20	32	55	275	$1,175, MS-67, August 2013
1948	35,196,000	4,238	65.4	99	7	9	10	20	35	60	425	$2,115, MS-67, April 2014
1948D	16,766,800	2,501	65.3	99	7	13	18	25	55	100	800	$1,880, MS-67, February 2014
1948S	15,960,000	4,516	65.3	99	7	9	13	20	45	70	600	$3,290, MS-67, September 2013
1949	9,312,000	2,498	65.1	99	14	35	47	55	70	115	800	$6,463, MS-67, January 2014
1949D	10,068,400	2,590	65.2	99	8	16	38	45	50	110	800	$3,831, MS-67, September 2013
1950	24,920,126	4,314	65.2	99	7	9	10	15	35	70	800	$2,949, MS-67, August 2013
1950D	21,075,600	2,893	64.1	94	7	9	10	15	35	70	800	$7,638, MS-68, November 2013
1950D, D Over S (f)	*	103	48.9	36	225	325	550	1,250	3,000	12,000	—	$29,375, MS-67, June 2013
1950S	10,284,004	2,904	64.9	97	8	12	16	20	45	60	825	$4,113, MS-67, January 2014
1950S, S Over D (g)	*	274	57.2	67	250	350	500	800	1,500	2,800	5,000	$16,450, MS-67, September 2013
1951	43,448,102	3,068	65.3	99	7	9	10	15	25	50	450	$808, MS, January 2014
1951D	35,354,800	2,830	65.2	100	7	9	10	15	35	60	1,500	$6,463, MS-67, February 2014
1951S	9,048,000	2,529	65.6	99	8	10	15	20	40	80	550	$2,938, MS-67, August 2013
1952	38,780,093	2,483	65.3	99	7	9	10	15	25	60	500	$499, MS, January 2014
1952D	49,795,200	1,862	65.0	99	7	9	10	15	40	100	3,500	$1,998, MS-67, June 2014
1952S	13,707,800	3,461	65.6	100	8	12	20	25	42	80	275	$11,750, MS-68, April 2013
1953	18,536,120	1,772	65.2	99	7	9	10	15	40	80	600	$1,410, MS-67, April 2013
1953D	56,112,400	1,599	65.0	98	7	9	10	15	35	100	1,500	$2,233, MS-67, June 2013
1953S	14,016,000	4,767	65.4	100	7	9	10	15	34	60	700	$3,055, MS-67, December 2013
1954	54,412,203	3,899	65.3	99	7	9	10	15	34	60	650	$867, MS, January 2014
1954D	42,305,500	2,177	65.1	100	7	9	10	15	35	60	2,250	$4,113, MS-67, July 2014
1954S	11,834,722	7,012	65.4	100	7	9	10	15	36	60	750	$4,113, MS-68, January 2014
1955	18,180,181	3,839	65.2	99	7	9	10	15	27	60	950	$823, MS-67, March 2013
1955D	3,182,400	3,682	64.5	99	7	9	10	15	60	400	2,000	$2,530, MS-66, April 2012
1956S	44,144,000	5,270	65.5	99	7	9	10	15	21	50	175	$153, MS-67, November 2013
1956D	32,334,500	2,021	65.1	99	7	9	10	15	27	60	2,150	$3,055, MS-67, August 2013
1957	46,532,000	4,140	65.5	99	7	9	10	15	27	50	175	$1,293, MS-68, January 2014
1957D	77,924,160	2,894	65.4	99	7	9	10	15	25	60	275	$1,528, MS-68, January 2014
1958	6,360,000	7,100	65.5	100	7	9	10	15	20	50	140	$217, MS-66, March 2014
1958D	78,124,900	3,802	65.5	99	7	9	10	15	25	50	335	$3,525, MS-67, August 2013
1959	24,384,000	3,335	65.2	99	7	9	10	15	25	50	850	$999, MS-65, August 2013
1959D	62,054,232	2,640	65.0	99	7	9	10	15	25	60	1,350	$8,225, MS-67, February 2013
1960	29,164,000	2,411	65.0	99	7	9	10	15	20	80	950	$2,820, MS-67, February 2014
1960D	63,000,324	2,145	65.0	99	7	9	10	15	20	50	1,900	$2,115, MS-67, April 2014
1961	37,036,000	2,417	65.0	99	7	9	10	12	15	60	2,400	$3,819, MS-67, April 2014
1961D	83,656,928	1,613	64.8	99	7	9	10	12	15	150	4,000	$8,225, MS-67, January 2014
1962	36,156,000	2,644	65.1	99	7	9	10	12	15	60	1,100	$2,585, MS-68, January 2014
1962D	127,554,756	1,581	64.7	99	7	9	10	12	15	120	2,000	$9,400, MS-67, July 2014
1963	74,316,000	3,410	64.9	98	7	9	10	12	15	60	1,500	$11,163, MS-67, February 2014
1963D	135,288,184	1,604	64.9	99	7	9	10	12	15	60	1,750	$15,863, MS-67, November 2013
1964	560,390,585	2,751	64.7	96	7	9	10	12	15	50	1,000	$3,819, MS-67, March 2013
1964D	704,135,528	3,433	64.4	94	7	9	10	12	15	50	650	$4,406, MS-67, April 2014

* Included in number above. **e.** Very strong doubling is visible on the motto, LIBERTY, the designer's initials, and the date. "Values for this variety are generally firm, but do change with market conditions and demand fluctuations" (*Cherrypickers' Guide*, fifth edition, volume II). **f.** The upper left curve of the underlying S is visible west and north of the D mintmark. Most Mint State specimens have brilliant surfaces. **g.** Most Mint State specimens have a frosty luster, rather than the brilliant surface seen on most of this year's Mint State D Over S coins.

1966, Doubled-Die Reverse
FS-25-1966-801.

1970-D, Doubled-Die Obverse
FS-25-1970D-101.

1989-D, Doubled Mintmark
FS-25-1989D-501.

	Mintage	Cert	Avg	%MS	MS-63	MS-65	MS-66	MS-67	Recent Auction Record
1965 (a)	1,819,717,540	704	64.3	90	$1.00	$9	$30	$175	$14,688, AU-58, June 2014
1966 (a)	821,101,500	445	65.4	97	1.00	7	30	120	$1,293, MS-62, April 2013
1966, DblDie Reverse (b)	*	5	47.2	20	900.00	1,400	2,250		$920, EF-45, April 2012
1967 (a)	1,524,031,848	525	65.4	96	1.00	6	35	180	$2,115, MS-65, September 2013
1968	220,731,500	544	65.6	99	1.25	8	25	100	$9,400, MS-68, September 2013
1968D	101,534,000	1,790	66.0	100	1.10	6	15	55	$123, MS-67, March 2013
1969	176,212,000	350	64.8	98	3.00	10	35	300	$135, MS-66, June 2014
1969D	114,372,000	856	65.7	99	2.50	10	25	75	$3,819, MS-68, November 2013
1970	136,420,000	493	65.3	100	1.00	10	40	100	$2,115, MS-67, November 2013
1970D	417,341,364	1,667	65.8	99	1.00	6	10	35	$2,926, MS-68, January 2014
1970D, DblDie Obverse (c)	*	5	58.8	40	300.00	375	500		$2,875, MS-65, January 2012
1971	109,284,000	364	64.5	98	1.00	6	50	150	$364, MS-66, June 2014
1971D	258,634,428	761	65.6	99	1.00	6	20	100	$4,113, MS-68, September 2013
1972	215,048,000	558	65.3	100	1.00	6	25	175	$588, MS-67, November 2013
1972D	311,067,732	1,319	66.0	100	1.00	6	18	30	$3,055, MS-68, January 2014
1973	346,924,000	530	65.2	100	1.00	6	25	175	$1,116, MS-67, September 2013
1973D	232,977,400	512	65.2	99	1.00	6	25	175	$1,410, MS-65, February 2014
1974	801,456,000	469	65.2	99	1.00	6	25	175	$382, MS-67, November 2013
1974D	353,160,300	491	65.5	100	1.00	7	25	75	$1,763, MS-64, September 2013
1776–1976, Copper-Nickel Clad ‡	809,784,016	995	65.1	97	1.25	6	15	50	$306, MS-62, February 2014
1776–1976D, Copper-Nickel Clad	860,118,839	1,431	65.3	97	1.25	6	15	60	$66, MS-67, March 2013
1776–1976S, Silver Clad	11,000,000	4,135	66.7	100	4.00	7	15	40	$118, MS-68, April 2014
1977	468,556,000	446	65.4	98	1.00	6	20	100	$282, MS-66, February 2013
1977D	256,524,978	302	65.1	99	1.00	6	25	125	$431, MS-67, February 2007
1978	521,452,000	435	65.5	99	1.00	6	20	100	$294, MS-63, June 2014
1978D	287,373,152	331	65.4	99	1.00	6	25	175	$331, MS-67, December 2007
1979	515,708,000	427	65.7	100	1.00	6	25	125	$411, MS-66, June 2014
1979D	489,789,780	401	65.5	100	1.00	6	25	125	$441, MS-67, September 2013
1980P	635,832,000	643	65.7	99	1.00	6	18	85	$382, MS-67, September 2013
1980D	518,327,487	369	65.2	100	1.00	6	20	175	$1,380, MS-67, February 2007
1981P	601,716,000	570	65.5	100	1.00	6	15	100	$176, MS-65, August 2013
1981D	575,722,833	461	65.4	100	1.00	6	15	150	$259, MS-67, September 2013
1982P	500,931,000	430	65.0	98	7.00	30	60	240	$16, MS-65, February 2014
1982D	480,042,788	430	64.9	97	5.00	18	60	200	$30, MS-66, March 2013
1983P ‡	673,535,000	604	64.6	97	30.00	65	200	400	$15,863, MS-65, January 2014
1983D	617,806,446	459	64.6	97	10.00	45	150	500	$1,058, MS-67, June 2014
1984P	676,545,000	461	65.1	99	2.00	10	20	125	$1,058, MS-67, September 2013
1984D	546,483,064	290	64.7	99	2.00	12	65	300	$764, MS-67, September 2013

* Included in number above. ‡ Ranked in the *100 Greatest U.S. Modern Coins*. **a.** Values and auction records for Special Mint Set coins are included with the Proofs for this type. **b.** Very strong doubling is visible on all reverse lettering. Note that this is not the 1966 Special Mint Set issue. **c.** This extremely rare variety (fewer than a half dozen known) shows very strong doubling on the date, IN GOD WE TRUST, and the ERTY of LIBERTY.

	Mintage	Cert	Avg	%MS	MS-63	MS-65	MS-66	MS-67	Recent Auction Record
1985P	775,818,962	401	65.2	99	$2.00	$15	$25	$100	$764, MS-65, June 2014
1985D	519,962,888	409	65.4	100	1.00	9	25	100	$66, MS-66, March 2013
1986P	551,199,333	398	64.9	99	2.50	12	30	125	$94, MS-66, March 2013
1986D	504,298,660	445	65.5	100	6.00	18	25	100	$104, MS-66, November 2007
1987P	582,499,481	366	65.0	99	1.00	9	40	200	$59, MS-66, December 2007
1987D	655,594,696	407	65.5	100	1.00	6	20	150	$431, MS-67, February 2007
1988P	562,052,000	349	64.9	99	1.25	15	30	175	$66, MS-66, March 2013
1988D	596,810,688	372	65.2	99	1.00	10	20	125	$66, MS-66, November 2007
1989P	512,868,000	320	64.7	98	1.00	12	30	150	$216, MS-66, August 2009
1989D	896,535,597	320	65.1	98	1.00	7	25	125	$70, MS-66, March 2013
1989D, RPM (c)	*	0	n/a	n/a					
1990P	613,792,000	296	65.4	99	1.00	10	20	100	$282, MS-64, June 2014
1990D	927,638,181	398	65.5	99	1.00	10	20	125	$646, MS-68, April 2014
1991P	570,968,000	281	65.4	100	1.00	12	30	100	$90, MS-66, November 2007
1991D	630,966,693	260	65.2	100	1.00	12	30	225	$66, MS-66, March 2013
1992P	384,764,000	346	65.1	99	1.50	16	35	225	$242, MS-66, February 2008
1992D	389,777,107	287	65.1	99	1.00	16	35	225	$1,763, MS-67, November 2013
1993P	639,276,000	387	65.6	98	1.00	7	20	85	$306, MS-64, June 2014
1993D	645,476,128	357	65.4	99	1.00	7	25	100	$40, MS-66, March 2013
1994P	825,600,000	309	65.2	99	1.00	10	25	100	$70, MS-66, March 2013
1994D	880,034,110	246	64.9	97	1.00	10	30	150	$212, MS-64, July 2014
1995P	1,004,336,000	304	65.8	98	1.25	14	20	65	$129, MS-67, March 2013
1995D	1,103,216,000	301	65.9	100	1.00	13	20	75	$219, MS-67, December 2007
1996P	925,040,000	825	66.4	100	1.00	10	18	30	$441, MS-68, March 2013
1996D	906,868,000	957	66.6	100	1.00	10	18	30	$447, MS-68, March 2013
1997P	595,740,000	272	65.8	100	1.00	11	18	40	$15, MS-60, January 2013
1997D	599,680,000	295	66.1	99	1.00	12	18	40	$66, MS-67, March 2013
1998P	896,268,000	442	66.1	99	1.00	7	18	40	$329, MS-68, June 2014
1998D	821,000,000	356	65.3	97	1.00	7	20	75	$32, MS-66, June 2014

* Included in number above. **c.** The secondary D mintmark is visible west of the primary D.

Proof Washington Quarters, Eagle Reverse

PF-60 to 70 (Proof). Dates available in Proof are 1936 to 1942 and 1950 to 1964 (from the Philadelphia Mint) and 1968 to 1998 (from San Francisco). Proof coins from 1937 through 1972 were made from special dies with high relief and minor detail differences. Certain later Proofs are available in clad metal as well as in silver.

Special Mint Set (SMS) coins were struck in lieu of Proofs from 1965 to 1967; these in some instances closely resemble Proofs. The majority of Proofs made in recent decades are in high levels, PF-66 to 68 or higher. *Obverse and Reverse:* Proofs that are extensively cleaned and have many hairlines, or that are dull and grainy, are

lower level, such as PF-60 to 62. Most low-level Proofs are of the 1936 to 1942 dates. With medium hairlines and good reflectivity, assigned grades of PF-63 or 64 are appropriate. PF-66 should have hairlines so delicate that magnification is needed to see them. Above that, a Proof should be free of any hairlines or other problems.

Proof Washington Quarter, Eagle Reverse

1952, Die Damage
"Superbird" variety. FS-25-1952-901.

	Mintage	Cert	Avg	PF-64	PF-65	PF-66	PF-67	Recent Auction Record
1936	3,837	2,070	64.2	$1,100	$1,450	$2,400	$9,500	$7,638, PF-67, June 2013
1937	5,542	2,355	64.9	370	475	650	1,200	$16,450, PF-68, June 2013
1938	8,045	2,967	64.9	200	275	375	900	$7,050, PF-68, June 2013
1939	8,795	2,924	65.2	175	235	275	675	$11,750, PF-68, June 2013
1940	11,246	3,429	65.2	120	175	225	440	$3,819, PF-68, November 2013
1941	15,287	4,161	65.1	100	140	175	440	$14,100, PF-68, June 2013
1942	21,123	5,530	65.1	100	135	150	400	$12,925, PF-68, June 2013
1950	51,386	3,270	65.6	60	70	100	150	$2,820, PF-67Cam, February 2014

Chart continued on next page.

	Mintage	Cert	Avg	PF-64	PF-65	PF-66	PF-67	Recent Auction Record
1951	57,500	3,006	65.7	$55	$65	$90	$125	$7,050, PF-68Cam, August 2013
1952	81,980	3,039	66.0	40	45	75	110	$8,225, PF-67DCam, January 2014
1952, Die Damage (a)	*	462	65.8	200	250	500		$3,525, PF-66DCam, April 2014
1953	128,800	4,707	66.4	40	45	60	80	$6,463, PF-68DCam, March 2013
1954	233,300	5,102	66.6	15	25	35	60	$7,050, PF-68DCam, December 2013
1955	378,200	4,817	66.8	15	25	35	50	$2,585, PF-68DCam, April 2013
1956	669,384	5,620	67.1	11	15	25	50	$3,819, PF-69DCam, January 2014
1957	1,247,952	4,425	66.8	11	15	25	45	$1,998, PF-68DCam, April 2013
1958	875,652	3,558	66.6	11	15	30	40	$1,175, PF-68DCam, September 2013
1959	1,149,291	3,795	66.9	11	12	25	35	$999, PF-68DCam, April 2014
1959, DblDie Obverse (b)	*	68	66.4	140	185	300		$150, PF-65, February 2012
1960	1,691,602	5,095	66.7	10	11	20	30	$2,174, PF-69DCam, April 2013
1961	3,028,244	7,081	67.0	10	11	20	30	$999, PF-69DCam, June 2013
1962	3,218,019	7,159	66.9	10	11	20	30	$823, PF-69DCam, April 2013
1963	3,075,645	9,343	67.3	10	11	20	30	$499, PF-69DCam, June 2013
1964	3,950,762	9,947	67.7	10	11	20	30	$940, PF-69DCam, June 2013

* Included in number above. **a.** "There is an unusual S-shaped mark on the breast of the eagle. The cause of this mark is unknown. The nickname for this well-known variety is, suitably, 'Superbird'!" (*Cherrypickers' Guide to Rare Die Varieties*, fifth edition, volume II). **b.** Dramatic doubling is evident on all obverse lettering, especially IN GOD WE TRUST. There are at least five different doubled-die obverses for this date; the one featured here is FS-25-1959-101.

1968-S, Doubled-Die Reverse
FS-25-1968S-801.

1979-S, Filled S (Type 1)   **1979-S, Clear S (Type 2)**   **1981-S, Rounded S (Type 1)**   **1981-S, Flat S (Type 2)**

1990-S, Doubled-Die Obverse
FS-25-1990S-101.

	Mintage	Cert	Avg	PF-65	PF-67Cam	PF-68Cam	PF-68DC	Recent Auction Record
1965, SMS ‡	2,360,000	2,923	66.4	$12	$375	$600	—	$505, MS-67Cam, January 2014
1966, SMS ‡	2,261,583	2,404	66.6	12	135	1,450	—	$1,293, MS-68Cam, June 2014
1967, SMS ‡	1,863,344	3,586	66.7	12	50	250	—	$188, MS-68Cam, August 2013
1968S	3,041,506	1,518	67.3	5	15	30	$150	$194, PF-64, May 2013
1968S, DblDie Reverse (a)	*	48	65.9	165				$196, PF-66, March 2012
1969S	2,934,631	1,895	67.8	5	15	20	100	$617, PF-69DCam, December 2013
1970S	2,632,810	1,888	67.8	5	15	25	125	$705, PF-69DCam, June 2013
1971S	3,220,733	1,659	67.6	5	15	25	300	$1,058, PF-69DCam, December 2013
1972S	3,260,996	1,449	67.9	5	10	20	30	$411, PF-65Cam, August 2013
1973S	2,760,339	2,354	68.6	5	10	16	20	$96, PF-67, March 2013
1974S	2,612,568	3,422	68.8	5	10	16	20	$7,015, PF-70DCam, April 2012
1776–1976S, Copper-Nickel Clad	7,059,099	14,376	68.8	5	10	16	20	$441, PF-70DCam, June 2013
1776–1976S, Silver Clad	4,000,000	18,503	68.8	8	12	16	25	$999, PF-70DCam, February 2013
1977S	3,251,152	5,851	68.9	5	10	16	20	$90, PF-70DCam, May 2013

* Included in number above. ‡ Ranked in the *100 Greatest U.S. Modern Coins*. **a.** Doubling is evident on all reverse lettering around the rim and the left tips.

	Mintage	Cert	Avg	PF-65	PF-67Cam	PF-68Cam	PF-68DC	Recent Auction Record
1978S	3,127,781	6,664	69.0	$5	$10	$16	$16	$80, PF-70DCam, May 2013
1979S, All kinds (b)	3,677,175							
1979S, Type 1 ("Filled" S)		6,461	68.9	5	10	16	16	$115, PF-70DCam, January 2010
1979S, Type 2 ("Clear" S)		3,382	68.9	6	12	20	25	$90, PF-70DCam, August 2013
1980S	3,554,806	7,242	68.9	5	10	16	16	$79, PF-70DCam, May 2013
1981S, All kinds (c)	4,063,083							
1981S, Type 1 ("Filled" S)		7,869	68.9	4	8	14	16	$70, PF-70DCam, May 2013
1981S, Type 2 ("Clear" S)		2,088	68.8	6	12	20	25	$705, PF-70DCam, April 2013
1982S	3,857,479	4,271	69.0	4	8	14	16	$103, PF-70DCam, May 2014
1983S	3,279,126	4,191	68.9	4	8	14	16	$90, PF-70DCam, August 2013
1984S	3,065,110	3,945	69.0	4	8	14	16	$80, PF-70DCam, May 2013
1985S	3,362,821	3,811	69.0	4	8	14	16	$86, PF-70DCam, May 2013
1986S	3,010,497	4,054	69.0	4	8	14	16	$39, PF-70DCam, August 2013
1987S	4,227,728	4,171	69.0	4	8	14	16	$112, PF, January 2014
1988S	3,262,948	3,214	69.0	4	8	14	16	$55, PF-70DCam, August 2013
1989S	3,220,194	3,353	69.0	4	8	14	16	$79, PF-70DCam, January 2010
1990S	3,299,559	4,350	69.0	4	8	14	16	$53, PF-68DCam, April 2013
1990S, DblDie Obverse ‡ (d)	*	15	67.8	225	700			$4,888, PF-70DCam, April 2012
1991S	2,867,787	3,767	69.1	4	8	14	16	$69, PF-70DCam, January 2010
1992S	2,858,981	3,692	69.1	4	8	14	16	$50, PF-70DCam, January 2010
1992S, Silver	1,317,579	4,289	69.0	9	12	18	22	$109, PF-70DCam, January 2010
1993S	2,633,439	3,721	69.1	4	8	14	16	$58, PF-70DCam, May 2013
1993S, Silver	761,353	3,255	69.0	9	12	18	22	$70, PF-70DCam, August 2013
1994S	2,484,594	3,287	69.1	4	8	14	16	$69, PF-70DCam, January 2010
1994S, Silver	785,329	3,169	69.0	9	14	20	25	$96, PF-70DCam, May 2013
1995S	2,117,496	3,158	69.1	8	10	16	20	$69, PF-70DCam, January 2010
1995S, Silver	679,985	3,102	69.0	9	14	20	25	$135, PF-70DCam, May 2013
1996S	1,750,244	3,279	69.1	5	8	14	18	$84, PF-70DCam, January 2010
1996S, Silver	775,021	3,239	69.0	9	14	20	25	$138, PF-70DCam, January 2010
1997S	2,055,000	2,987	69.1	5	8	14	18	$69, PF-70DCam, January 2010
1997S, Silver	741,678	3,531	69.1	9	14	20	25	$89, PF-70DCam, January 2010
1998S	2,086,507	2,956	69.1	6	8	14	18	$115, PF-70DCam, January 2010
1998S, Silver	878,792	3,749	69.1	9	12	18	22	$70, PF-70DCam, May 2013

* Included in number above. ‡ Ranked in the *100 Greatest U.S. Modern Coins*. **b.** The mintmark style was changed during 1979 Proof production, creating two distinctly different types. "The Type II is the rare variety, and is easily distinguished from the common Type I. The Type I has a very indistinct blob, whereas the Type II shows a well-defined S" (*Cherrypickers' Guide to Rare Die Varieties*, fifth edition, volume II). **c.** The mintmark style was changed during the 1981 Proof production, creating two distinct types. "The Type II is the rare variety, and is not easily distinguished from the common Type I. For most collectors, the easiest difference to discern on the Type II is the flatness on the top curve of the S, which is rounded on the Type I. Additionally, the surface of the Type II mintmark is frosted, and the openings in the loops slightly larger" (*Cherrypickers' Guide*). **d.** Very strong doubling is visible on the date and the mintmark, with slightly less dramatic doubling on IN GOD WE TRUST.

WASHINGTON, STATEHOOD, D.C., TERRITORIAL, AND AMERICA THE BEAUTIFUL (1999 TO DATE)

Clad: Designers John Flanagan and others; weight 5.67 grams; composition outer layers of copper-nickel (.750 copper, .250 nickel) bonded to inner core of pure copper; diameter 24.3 mm; reeded edge; mints: Philadelphia, Denver.

Silver Proofs: Designers John Flanagan and others; weight 6.25 grams; composition .900 silver, .100 copper (net weight: .18084 oz. pure silver); diameter 24.3 mm; reeded edge; mint: San Francisco.

History. In 1999 the U.S. Mint introduced a new program of statehood quarters. These were released at the rate of five new reverse designs each year, in combination with a restyled obverse, through 2008. The coins became very popular and are still widely collected with enthusiasm. In 2009 a similar program of quarter dollars was issued for Washington, D.C., and the five U.S. territories. A similar program for national parks and historic sites started in 2010 and will run through 2021. Circulation strikes are made at the Philadelphia and Denver mints, and special silver-content and Proof issues at San Francisco. Each coin combines a modified obverse depicting George Washington, without a date. The reverses are distinctive and bear the date of issue, the date of statehood (for the state quarters), and other design elements. Each state or district/territory selected its own design.

Some statehood quarters were accidentally made with "disoriented" dies and are valued higher than ordinary pieces. Normal United States coins have dies oriented in coin alignment, such that the reverse appears upside down when the coin is flipped from right to left. Values for the rotated-die quarters vary according to the amount of shifting. The most valuable are those that are shifted 180 degrees, so that both sides appear upright when the coin is turned over (called *medal alignment*).

Striking and Sharpness. These quarters can have light striking on the highest area of the obverse. On the reverse there can be weak areas, depending on the design, seemingly more often seen on Denver Mint coins. Some in the statehood quarter series were struck through grease, obliterating portions of both the obverse (usually) and reverse designs.

Availability. All modern quarters are readily available in high grades. Typical MS coins are MS-63 and 64 with light abrasion. MS-65 and higher coins are in the minority, but enough exist that finding them is no problem. Around MS-68 many issues are scarce, and higher grades are scarcer yet.

MS-60 to 70 (Mint State). *Obverse:* At MS-60, some abrasion and contact marks are evident on the highest-relief parts of the hair and the cheek. Abrasion is slight at MS-63, and slighter at MS-64. An MS-65 coin should display no abrasion or contact marks except under magnification, and MS-66 and higher coins should have none at all. Luster should be full. *Reverse:* Check the highest-relief areas of the design (these differ from coin to coin). Otherwise, comments are as for the obverse.

1999 Delaware	1999 Pennsylvania	1999 New Jersey
1999 Georgia	1999 Connecticut	2000 Massachusetts
2000 Maryland	2000 South Carolina	2000 New Hampshire
2000 Virginia	2001 New York	2001 North Carolina
2001 Rhode Island	2001 Vermont	2001 Kentucky
2002 Tennessee	2002 Ohio	2002 Louisiana
2002 Indiana	2002 Mississippi	2003 Illinois
2003 Alabama	2003 Maine	2003 Missouri

2003
Arkansas

2004
Michigan

2004
Florida

2004
Texas

2004
Iowa

2004
Wisconsin

2004-D, Wisconsin, Normal Reverse

2004-D, Wisconsin, Extra Leaf High
FS-25-2004D-5901.

2004-D, Wisconsin, Extra Leaf Low
FS-25-2004D-5902.

2005
California

2005
Minnesota

2005
Oregon

2005
Kansas

2005
West Virginia

2006
Nevada

2006
Nebraska

2006
Colorado

2006
North Dakota

2006
South Dakota

2007
Montana

2007
Washington

2007
Idaho

2007
Wyoming

2007
Utah

2008
Oklahoma

2008
New Mexico

2008
Arizona

2008
Alaska

2008
Hawaii

2009
District of Columbia

2009
Puerto Rico

2009
Guam

2009
American Samoa

2009
U.S. Virgin Islands

2009
Northern Mariana
Islands

2010
Hot Springs
National Park

2010
Yellowstone
National Park

2010
Yosemite
National Park

2010
Grand Canyon
National Park

2010
Mt. Hood
National Forest

2011
Gettysburg National
Military Park

2011
Glacier
National Park

2011
Olympic
National Park

2011
Vicksburg National
Military Park

2011
Chickasaw National
Recreation Area

2012
El Yunque
National Forest

2012
Chaco Culture National
Historical Park

2012
Acadia
National Park

2012
Hawai'i Volcanoes
National Park

2012
Denali National
Park and Preserve

2013
White Mountain
National Forest

2013
Perry's Victory
and International
Peace Memorial

2013
Great Basin
National Park

2013
Fort McHenry
National Monument
and Historic Shrine

2013
Mount Rushmore
National Memorial

2014
Great Smoky Mountains
National Park

2014
Shenandoah
National Park

2014
Arches
National Park

2014
Great Sand Dunes
National Park

2014
Everglades
National Park

	Mintage	Cert	Avg	%MS	MS-63	MS-65	MS-66	MS-67	Recent Auction Record
1999P, Delaware	373,400,000	3,982	65.7	99	$1.25	$3.00	$25	$55	$1,410, MS-66, April 2013
1999D, Delaware	401,424,000	3,277	65.6	99	1.25	3.00	25	55	$529, MS-64, April 2013
1999P, Pennsylvania	349,000,000	3,224	65.8	100	1.25	3.00	25	55	$129, MS-65, February 2013
1999D, Pennsylvania	358,332,000	2,539	65.6	99	1.25	3.00	25	55	$299, MS-68, April 2008
1999P, New Jersey	363,200,000	2,863	65.8	100	1.25	3.00	25	55	$14, MS-67, April 2008
1999D, New Jersey	299,028,000	3,134	65.7	100	1.25	3.00	25	55	$47, MS-67, August 2009
1999P, Georgia	451,188,000	2,982	65.5	99	1.25	3.00	25	55	$69, MS-65, February 2014
1999D, Georgia	488,744,000	3,423	65.5	100	1.25	3.00	25	55	$48, AU-58, May 2013
1999P, Connecticut	688,744,000	3,047	65.6	100	1.25	3.00	25	55	$441, MS-64, February 2014
1999D, Connecticut	657,880,000	4,724	65.6	100	1.25	3.00	25	55	$999, MS-64, February 2014
2000P, Massachusetts	628,600,000	3,734	66.5	100	1.00	2.00	15	40	$30, MS-68, August 2009
2000D, Massachusetts	535,184,000	2,593	66.1	100	1.00	2.00	15	40	$79, MS-60, January 2014
2000P, Maryland	678,200,000	2,611	66.2	100	1.00	2.00	15	40	$84, MS-63, February 2014
2000D, Maryland	556,532,000	2,792	66.1	100	1.00	2.00	15	40	$159, MS-64, November 2013
2000P, South Carolina	742,576,000	3,053	66.4	100	1.00	2.00	15	40	$141, MS-67, February 2013
2000D, South Carolina	566,208,000	3,437	66.4	100	1.00	2.00	15	40	$15, MS-67, March 2009
2000P, New Hampshire	673,040,000	2,332	66.0	99	1.00	2.00	15	40	$529, MS-66, November 2013
2000D, New Hampshire	495,976,000	1,996	66.0	100	1.00	2.00	15	40	$46, MS-62, May 2013
2000P, Virginia	943,000,000	2,642	66.3	100	1.00	2.00	15	40	$130, MS-63, April 2014
2000D, Virginia	651,616,000	2,149	66.1	100	1.00	2.00	15	40	$10, MS-66, June 2008
2001P, New York	655,400,000	3,303	66.7	100	1.00	2.00	15	40	$499, MS-65, June 2014
2001D, New York	619,640,000	2,348	65.9	100	1.00	2.00	15	40	$15, MS-66, August 2009
2001P, North Carolina	627,600,000	3,360	66.8	100	1.00	2.00	15	40	$558, MS-63, September 2013
2001D, North Carolina	427,876,000	1,929	66.2	100	1.00	2.00	15	40	$15, MS-66, August 2009

	Mintage	Cert	Avg	%MS	MS-63	MS-65	MS-66	MS-67	Recent Auction Record
2001P, Rhode Island	423,000,000	2,140	66.5	100	$1.00	$2.00	$15	$40	$86, MS-68, April 2008
2001D, Rhode Island	447,100,000	2,143	66.2	100	1.00	2.00	15	40	$59, MS-64, July 2014
2001P, Vermont	423,400,000	4,659	66.5	100	1.00	2.00	15	40	$45, MS-68, April 2008
2001D, Vermont	459,404,000	2,656	66.5	100	1.00	2.00	15	40	$15, MS-66, October 2009
2001P, Kentucky	353,000,000	2,965	66.8	100	1.25	1.50	16	40	$21, MS-61, August 2013
2001D, Kentucky	370,564,000	1,590	66.2	100	1.25	1.50	16	40	$460, MS-68, December 2007
2002P, Tennessee	361,600,000	3,102	67.2	100	1.75	3.00	18	40	$11, MS-66, January 2009
2002D, Tennessee	286,468,000	2,798	66.6	100	1.75	3.00	18	40	$18, MS-68, April 2008
2002P, Ohio	217,200,000	4,038	67.2	100	1.00	1.25	10	30	$15, MS-68, April 2008
2002D, Ohio	414,832,000	2,822	66.6	100	1.00	1.25	10	30	$15, MS-68, April 2008
2002P, Louisiana	362,000,000	3,187	67.3	100	1.00	1.25	10	30	$31, MS-68, April 2008
2002D, Louisiana	402,204,000	1,695	66.4	100	1.00	1.25	10	30	$25, MS-68, January 2009
2002P, Indiana	362,600,000	2,854	67.2	100	1.00	1.25	10	30	$15, MS-68, April 2008
2002D, Indiana	327,200,000	1,659	66.6	100	1.00	1.25	10	30	$18, MS-68, April 2008
2002P, Mississippi	290,000,000	2,424	66.9	100	1.00	1.25	10	30	$19, MS-68, April 2008
2002D, Mississippi	289,600,000	2,022	66.5	100	1.00	1.25	10	30	$48, MS-61, May 2013
2003P, Illinois	225,800,000	1,133	66.1	100	1.50	2.00	12	32	$11, MS-67, April 2008
2003D, Illinois	237,400,000	3,206	65.6	100	1.50	2.00	12	32	
2003P, Alabama	225,000,000	1,206	65.9	100	1.00	1.25	10	30	$59, MS-67, December 2007
2003D, Alabama	232,400,000	3,380	65.6	100	1.00	1.25	10	30	$13, MS-66, April 2006
2003P, Maine	217,400,000	907	66.1	100	1.00	1.25	10	30	$17, MS-67, April 2008
2003D, Maine	231,400,000	2,913	65.5	100	1.00	1.25	10	30	$1,093, MS-68, December 2007
2003P, Missouri	225,000,000	1,105	66.2	100	1.00	1.25	10	30	$57, MS-68, April 2008
2003D, Missouri	228,200,000	3,642	65.7	100	1.00	1.25	10	30	$57, MS-68, June 2014
2003P, Arkansas	228,000,000	1,046	66.2	100	1.00	1.25	10	30	$74, MS-60, May 2013
2003D, Arkansas	229,800,000	3,436	65.8	100	1.00	1.25	10	30	$80, MS-68, March 2013
2004P, Michigan	233,800,000	3,217	65.6	100	0.75	1.00	10	30	$21, MS-68, April 2008
2004D, Michigan	225,800,000	2,486	67.3	100	0.75	1.00	10	30	$16, MS-68, January 2009
2004P, Florida	240,200,000	2,982	65.5	100	0.75	1.00	10	30	$64, MS-68, April 2008
2004D, Florida	241,600,000	1,589	67.1	100	0.75	1.00	10	30	$15, MS-68, April 2008
2004P, Texas	278,800,000	3,199	65.5	100	0.75	1.00	10	30	$115, MS-68, December 2007
2004D, Texas	263,000,000	1,891	67.2	100	0.75	1.00	10	30	$19, MS-68, April 2008
2004P, Iowa	213,800,000	2,876	65.4	100	0.75	1.00	10	30	$25, MS-68, January 2009
2004D, Iowa	251,400,000	1,269	67.3	100	0.75	1.00	10	30	$15, MS-68, April 2008
2004P, Wisconsin	226,400,000	3,123	65.4	100	0.75	1.00	10	30	$31, MS-67, April 2008
2004D, Wisconsin	226,800,000	3,996	65.9	100	0.75	1.00	10	30	$33, MS-68, April 2008
2004D, Wisconsin, Extra Leaf High ‡ (a)	*	7,411	64.4	95	150.00	200.00	300	500	$705, MS-67, June 2014
2004D, Wisconsin, Extra Leaf Low ‡ (a)	*	10,113	64.5	96	130.00	165.00	275	450	$529, MS-67, June 2014
2005P, California	257,200,000	887	66.3	100	0.75	1.00	10	30	$2, MS-69 Satin, August 2009
2005D, California	263,200,000	908	67.1	100	0.75	1.00	10	30	$351, MS-68, December 2007
2005P, Minnesota	239,600,000	2,018	65.0	100	0.75	1.00	10	30	$306, MS-65, April 2014
2005D, Minnesota	248,400,000	691	66.3	100	0.75	1.00	10	30	$21, MS-69 Satin, December 2008
2005P, Oregon	316,200,000	511	65.9	100	0.75	1.00	10	30	$10, MS-67 Satin, July 2008
2005D, Oregon	404,000,000	565	66.4	100	0.75	1.00	10	30	$17, MS-69 Satin, September 2009
2005P, Kansas	263,400,000	747	65.7	99	0.75	1.00	10	30	$26, MS-69 Satin, March 2010
2005D, Kansas	300,000,000	817	66.5	100	0.75	1.00	10	30	$25, MS-69 Satin, January 2009
2005P, West Virginia	365,400,000	592	65.9	100	0.75	1.00	10	30	$10, MS-67 Satin, July 2008
2005D, West Virginia	356,200,000	562	66.5	99	0.75	1.00	10	30	$184, MS-68, April 2008
2006P, Nevada	277,000,000	680	66.3	100	0.75	1.00	10	30	$28, MS-68 Satin, August 2009
2006D, Nevada	312,800,000	999	66.5	100	0.75	1.00	10	30	$18, MS-69 Satin, August 2009
2006P, Nebraska	318,000,000	555	66.4	100	0.75	1.00	10	30	$40, MS-69 Satin, June 2008
2006D, Nebraska	273,000,000	764	66.6	100	0.75	1.00	10	30	$23, MS-69 Satin, December 2008
2006P, Colorado	274,800,000	578	66.5	100	0.75	1.00	10	30	$32, MS-69 Satin, August 2009
2006D, Colorado	294,200,000	784	66.5	100	0.75	1.00	10	30	$11, MS-69 Satin, January 2009
2006P, North Dakota	305,800,000	430	66.1	99	0.75	1.00	10	30	$148, MS-69 Satin, November 2007
2006D, North Dakota	359,000,000	690	66.4	100	0.75	1.00	10	30	$223, MS-65, January 2014
2006P, South Dakota	245,000,000	418	66.2	100	0.75	1.00	10	30	$25, MS-66, June 2013
2006D, South Dakota	265,800,000	526	66.4	100	0.75	1.00	10	30	$123, AU-58, July 2014
2007P, Montana	257,000,000	523	66.0	100	0.75	1.00	10	30	
2007D, Montana	256,240,000	648	65.8	100	0.75	1.00	10	30	

* Included in number above. ‡ Ranked in the *100 Greatest U.S. Modern Coins*. **a.** Some 2004-D Wisconsin quarters show one of two different die flaws on the reverse, in the shape of an extra leaf on the corn.

Chart continued on next page.

	Mintage	Cert	Avg	%MS	MS-63	MS-65	MS-66	MS-67	Recent Auction Record
2007P, Washington	265,200,000	542	66.5	100	$0.75	$1.00	$10	$30	
2007D, Washington	280,000,000	532	66.3	100	0.75	1.00	10	30	$24, MS-69 Satin, January 2009
2007P, Idaho	294,600,000	413	66.1	100	0.75	1.00	10	30	
2007D, Idaho	286,800,000	570	66.2	100	0.75	1.00	10	30	$1,175, MS-66, June 2014
2007P, Wyoming	243,600,000	259	66.0	100	0.75	1.00	10	30	
2007D, Wyoming	320,800,000	109	65.8	99	0.75	1.00	10	30	$48, AU-55, May 2013
2007P, Utah	255,000,000	306	66.2	100	0.75	1.00	10	30	
2007D, Utah	253,200,000	443	66.4	100	0.75	1.00	10	30	
2008P, Oklahoma	222,000,000	401	66.5	100	0.75	1.00	10	30	
2008D, Oklahoma	194,600,000	380	66.5	100	0.75	1.00	10	30	
2008P, New Mexico	244,200,000	315	66.3	100	0.75	1.00	10	30	
2008D, New Mexico	244,400,000	396	66.6	100	0.75	1.00	10	30	
2008P, Arizona	244,600,000	508	66.4	100	0.75	1.00	10	30	
2008D, Arizona	265,000,000	315	66.6	100	0.75	1.00	10	30	$1,152, MS-64, February 2013
2008P, Alaska	251,800,000	341	66.6	100	0.75	1.00	10	30	
2008D, Alaska	254,000,000	258	66.5	100	0.75	1.00	10	30	
2008P, Hawaii	254,000,000	472	66.3	100	0.75	1.00	10	30	
2008D, Hawaii	263,600,000	357	66.4	100	0.75	1.00	10	30	
2009P, District of Columbia	83,600,000	359	66.5	100	1.00	1.50	10	30	
2009D, District of Columbia	88,800,000	352	66.5	100	1.00	1.50	10	30	
2009P, Puerto Rico	53,200,000	470	66.1	100	1.00	1.50	10	30	
2009D, Puerto Rico	86,000,000	455	66.4	100	1.00	1.50	10	30	
2009P, Guam	45,000,000	338	66.6	100	1.00	1.50	10	30	
2009D, Guam	42,600,000	471	66.6	100	1.00	1.50	10	30	
2009P, American Samoa	42,600,000	384	66.7	100	1.00	1.50	10	30	
2009D, American Samoa	39,600,000	449	66.9	100	1.00	1.50	10	30	
2009P, U.S. Virgin Islands	41,000,000	299	66.8	100	1.00	1.50	12	32	
2009D, U.S. Virgin Islands	41,000,000	292	66.7	100	1.00	1.50	12	32	
2009P, Mariana Islands	35,200,000	292	66.7	100	1.00	1.50	10	30	
2009D, Mariana Islands	37,600,000	299	66.7	100	1.00	1.50	10	30	
2010P, Hot Springs National Park (AR)	35,600,000	971	66.1	100	0.50	1.00	10	30	
2010D, Hot Springs National Park (AR)	34,000,000	1,680	65.7	100	0.50	1.00	10	30	
2010P, Yellowstone National Park (WY)	33,600,000	575	65.8	100	0.50	1.00	10	30	
2010D, Yellowstone National Park (WY)	34,800,000	910	65.7	100	0.50	1.00	10	30	
2010P, Yosemite National Park (CA)	35,200,000	428	66.1	100	0.75	1.25	12	30	
2010D, Yosemite National Park (CA)	34,800,000	760	66.0	100	0.75	1.25	12	30	
2010P, Grand Canyon National Park (AZ)	34,800,000	648	66.4	100	0.50	1.00	10	30	
2010D, Grand Canyon National Park (AZ)	35,400,000	923	66.3	100	0.50	1.00	10	30	
2010P, Mt. Hood National Forest (OR)	34,400,000	303	66.1	100	0.50	1.00	10	30	
2010D, Mt. Hood National Forest (OR)	34,400,000	521	65.7	100	0.50	1.00	10	30	
2011P, Gettysburg National Military Park (PA)	30,800,000	1,083	66.3	100	0.75	1.25	12	30	
2011D, Gettysburg National Military Park (PA)	30,400,000	544	66.3	100	0.75	1.25	12	30	
2011P, Glacier National Park (MT)	30,400,000	638	66.7	100	0.50	1.00	10	30	
2011D, Glacier National Park (MT)	31,200,000	643	66.0	100	0.50	1.00	10	30	
2011P, Olympic National Park (WA)	30,400,000	639	66.6	100	0.50	1.00	10	30	
2011D, Olympic National Park (WA)	30,600,000	838	66.2	100	0.50	1.00	10	30	
2011P, Vicksburg National Military Park (MS)	30,800,000	555	66.5	100	0.50	1.00	10	30	
2011D, Vicksburg National Military Park (MS)	33,400,000	715	66.2	100	0.50	1.00	10	30	
2011P, Chickasaw National Recreation Area (OK)	73,800,000	688	66.7	100	0.50	1.00	10	30	
2011D, Chickasaw National Recreation Area (OK)	69,400,000	633	66.1	100	0.50	1.00	10	30	
2012P, El Yunque National Forest (PR)	25,800,000	397	66.0	100	0.50	1.00	10	30	
2012D, El Yunque National Forest (PR)	25,000,000	103	66.3	100	0.50	1.00	10	30	
2012S, El Yunque National Forest (PR) (b)	1,679,240	0	n/a	n/a	1.00	2.00	12	35	
2012P, Chaco Culture National Historical Park (NM)	22,000,000	0	n/a	n/a	0.50	1.00	10	30	
2012D, Chaco Culture National Historical Park (NM)	22,000,000	2	67.0	100	0.50	1.00	10	30	
2012S, Chaco Culture National Historical Park (NM) (b)	1,389,020	0	n/a	n/a	1.00	2.00	12	35	
2012P, Acadia National Park (ME)	24,800,000	0	n/a	n/a	0.50	1.00	10	30	
2012D, Acadia National Park (ME)	21,606,000	0	n/a	n/a	0.50	1.00	10	30	
2012S, Acadia National Park (ME) (b)	1,409,120	0	n/a	n/a	1.00	2.00	12	35	
2012P, Hawai'i Volcanoes National Park (HI)	46,200,000	0	n/a	n/a	0.50	1.00	10	30	

b. Not issued for circulation.

	Est Mintage	Cert	Avg	%MS	MS-63	MS-65	MS-66	MS-67	Recent Auction Record
2012D, Hawai'i Volcanoes National Park (HI)	78,600,000	0	n/a	n/a	$0.50	$1.00	$10	$30	
2012S, Hawai'i Volcanoes National Park (HI) (b)	1,407,520	0	n/a	n/a	1.00	2.00	12	35	
2012P, Denali National Park and Preserve (AK)	135,400,000	0	n/a	n/a	0.50	1.00	10	30	
2012D, Denali National Park and Preserve (AK)	166,600,000	0	n/a	n/a	0.50	1.00	10	30	
2012S, Denali National Park and Preserve (AK) (b)	1,401,920	0	n/a	n/a	1.00	2.00	12	35	
2013P, White Mountain National Forest (NH)	68,800,000	0	n/a	n/a	0.50	1.00	10	30	
2013D, White Mountain National Forest (NH)	107,600,000	0	n/a	n/a	0.50	1.00	10	30	
2013S, White Mountain National Forest (NH) (b)		0	n/a	n/a	1.00	2.00	12	35	
2013P, Perry's Victory and Int'l Peace Memorial (OH)	107,800,000	0	n/a	n/a	0.50	1.00	10	30	
2013D, Perry's Victory and Int'l Peace Memorial (OH)	131,600,000	0	n/a	n/a	0.50	1.00	10	30	
2013S, Perry's Victory and Int'l Peace Memorial (OH) (b)		0	n/a	n/a	1.00	2.00	12	35	
2013P, Great Basin National Park (NV)	122,400,000	0	n/a	n/a	0.50	1.00	10	30	
2013D, Great Basin National Park (NV)	141,400,000	0	n/a	n/a	0.50	1.00	10	30	
2013S, Great Basin National Park (NV) (b)		0	n/a	n/a	1.00	2.00	12	35	
2013P, Ft McHenry Nat'l Monument / Hist Shrine (MD)	120,000,000	0	n/a	n/a	0.50	1.00	10	30	
2013D, Ft McHenry Nat'l Monument / Hist Shrine (MD)	151,400,000	0	n/a	n/a	0.50	1.00	10	30	
2013S, Ft McHenry Nat'l Monument / Hist Shrine (MD) (b)		0	n/a	n/a	1.00	2.00	12	35	
2013P, Mount Rushmore National Memorial (SD)	231,800,000	0	n/a	n/a	0.50	1.00	10	30	
2013D, Mount Rushmore National Memorial (SD)	272,400,000	0	n/a	n/a	0.50	1.00	10	30	
2013S, Mount Rushmore National Memorial (SD) (b)		0	n/a	n/a	1.00	2.00	12	35	
2014P, Great Smoky Mountains National Park (TN)		0	n/a	n/a	0.50	1.00	10	30	
2014D, Great Smoky Mountains National Park (TN)		0	n/a	n/a	0.50	1.00	10	30	
2014S, Great Smoky Mountains National Park (TN) (b)		0	n/a	n/a	1.00	2.00	12	35	
2014P, Shenandoah National Park (VA)		0	n/a	n/a	0.50	1.00	10	30	
2014D, Shenandoah National Park (VA)		0	n/a	n/a	0.50	1.00	10	30	
2014S, Shenandoah National Park (VA) (b)		0	n/a	n/a	1.00	2.00	12	35	
2014P, Arches National Park (UT)		0	n/a	n/a	0.50	1.00	10	30	
2014D, Arches National Park (UT)		0	n/a	n/a	0.50	1.00	10	30	
2014S, Arches National Park (UT) (b)		0	n/a	n/a	1.00	2.00	12	35	
2014P, Great Sand Dunes National Park (CO)		0	n/a	n/a	0.50	1.00	10	30	
2014D, Great Sand Dunes National Park (CO)		0	n/a	n/a	0.50	1.00	10	30	
2014S, Great Sand Dunes National Park (CO) (b)		0	n/a	n/a	1.00	2.00	12	35	
2014P, Everglades National Park (FL)		0	n/a	n/a	0.50	1.00	10	30	
2014D, Everglades National Park (FL)		0	n/a	n/a	0.50	1.00	10	30	
2014S, Everglades National Park (FL) (b)		0	n/a	n/a	1.00	2.00	12	35	

b. Not issued for circulation.

Proof Washington, Statehood, D.C., Territorial, and America the Beautiful Quarters

PF-60 to 70 (Proof). Statehood and D.C./ territorial quarter Proofs were made in San Francisco. For certain later issues of Washington quarters as well as for all statehood and territorial issues, Proofs are available in clad metal as well as silver strikings. On some Proofs, over-polishing of dies has eliminated some details, as on part of the WC (for William Cousins) initials on certain 1999 Delaware pieces. *Obverse and Reverse:* Only a few have been cleaned, and most approach perfection and can be designated PF-68 to 70 (the latter only if no contact marks or other problems can be seen under magnification). A cleaned coin with extensive hairlines is not collectible for most numismatists and would be classified at a lower level such as PF-60 to 63. Those with lighter hairlines qualify for PF-64 or 65.

Proof Washington Quarter, Territorial

	Mintage	Cert	Avg	PF-66DC	PF-69DC	Recent Auction Record
1999S, Delaware	3,713,359	9,485	69.0	$8	$20	$259, PF-70DCam, June 2013
1999S, Delaware, Silver	804,565	15,940	69.0	35	50	$2,115, PF-70DCam, June 2013
1999S, Pennsylvania	3,713,359	9,368	69.1	8	20	$118, PF-70DCam, May 2013
1999S, Pennsylvania, Silver	804,565	15,710	69.0	35	50	$423, PF-70DCam, April 2013

Chart continued on next page.

	Mintage	Cert	Avg	PF-66DC	PF-69DC	Recent Auction Record
1999S, New Jersey	3,713,359	9,410	69.1	$8.00	$20	$182, PF-70DCam, May 2013
1999S, New Jersey, Silver	804,565	15,775	69.0	35.00	50	$253, PF-70DCam, June 2013
1999S, Georgia	3,713,359	9,484	69.1	8.00	20	$101, PF-70DCam, May 2013
1999S, Georgia, Silver	804,565	15,992	69.1	35.00	50	$159, PF-70DCam, May 2013
1999S, Connecticut	3,713,359	9,625	69.1	8.00	20	$85, PF-70DCam, May 2013
1999S, Connecticut, Silver	804,565	15,771	69.1	35.00	50	$113, PF-70DCam, May 2013
2000S, Massachusetts	4,020,172	9,440	69.1	4.00	15	$127, PF-70DCam, May 2009
2000S, Massachusetts, Silver	965,421	8,994	69.2	10.00	20	$150, PF-70DCam, August 2009
2000S, Maryland	4,020,172	9,270	69.1	4.00	15	$138, PF-70DCam, December 2009
2000S, Maryland, Silver	965,421	24,345	69.0	10.00	20	$144, PF-70DCam, October 2009
2000S, South Carolina	4,020,172	9,510	69.1	4.00	15	$94, PF-70DCam, August 2009
2000S, South Carolina, Silver	965,421	16,344	69.1	10.00	20	$100, PF-69DCam, February 2013
2000S, New Hampshire	4,020,172	9,417	69.1	4.00	15	$881, PF-69DCam, February 2013
2000S, New Hampshire, Silver	965,421	16,201	69.1	10.00	20	$144, PF-70DCam, November 2009
2000S, Virginia	4,020,172	9,366	69.1	4.00	15	$21, PF-70DCam, March 2014
2000S, Virginia, Silver	965,421	16,475	69.1	10.00	20	$20, PF-69DCam, March 2013
2001S, New York	3,094,140	7,276	69.1	8.00	15	$62, PF-70UCam, January 2010
2001S, New York, Silver	889,697	12,290	69.1	15.00	20	$66, PF-70DCam, April 2013
2001S, North Carolina	3,094,140	7,451	69.1	8.00	15	$55, PF-70DCam, June 2009
2001S, North Carolina, Silver	889,697	12,201	69.1	15.00	20	$76, PF-70DCam, May 2013
2001S, Rhode Island	3,094,140	6,877	69.1	8.00	15	$27, PF-70DCam, March 2014
2001S, Rhode Island, Silver	889,697	12,270	69.1	15.00	20	$58, PF-70DCam, May 2013
2001S, Vermont	3,094,140	7,152	69.1	8.00	15	$21, PF-70DCam, March 2014
2001S, Vermont, Silver	889,697	12,407	69.1	15.00	20	$66, PF-70DCam, May 2013
2001S, Kentucky	3,094,140	7,048	69.1	8.00	15	$130, PF-70DCam, December 2009
2001S, Kentucky, Silver	889,697	12,272	69.1	15.00	20	$66, PF-70DCam, May 2013
2002S, Tennessee	3,084,245	6,844	69.1	5.00	15	$89, PF-70DCam, October 2009
2002S, Tennessee, Silver	892,229	12,161	69.1	10.00	20	$23, PF-69DCam, February 2013
2002S, Ohio	3,084,245	6,768	69.1	5.00	15	$99, PF-70DCam, October 2009
2002S, Ohio, Silver	892,229	12,168	69.1	10.00	20	$35, PF-69DCam, January 2013
2002S, Louisiana	3,084,245	6,780	69.1	5.00	15	$56, PF-70UCam, February 2010
2002S, Louisiana, Silver	892,229	11,811	69.1	10.00	20	$150, PF-70DCam, December 2009
2002S, Indiana	3,084,245	6,849	69.1	5.00	15	$40, PF-70DCam, October 2009
2002S, Indiana, Silver	892,229	12,006	69.1	10.00	20	$19, PF-69DCam, January 2013
2002S, Mississippi	3,084,245	6,892	69.1	5.00	15	$26, PF-70DCam, March 2014
2002S, Mississippi, Silver	892,229	12,287	69.1	10.00	20	$19, PF-69DCam, January 2013
2003S, Illinois	3,408,516	9,510	69.2	5.00	15	$62, PF-70UCam, March 2010
2003S, Illinois, Silver	1,125,755	13,719	69.1	9.00	20	$16, PF-69DCam, January 2013
2003S, Alabama	3,408,516	9,599	69.2	5.00	15	$47, PF-70DCam, October 2009
2003S, Alabama, Silver	1,125,755	13,587	69.2	9.00	20	$23, PF-69DCam, February 2013
2003S, Maine	3,408,516	9,391	69.1	5.00	15	$36, PF-70UCam, March 2010
2003S, Maine, Silver	1,125,755	13,475	69.1	9.00	20	$45, PF-70UCam, March 2014
2003S, Missouri	3,408,516	5,488	69.3	5.00	15	$38, PF-70UCam, February 2010
2003S, Missouri, Silver	1,125,755	17,735	69.1	9.00	20	$17, PF-69DCam, May 2013
2003S, Arkansas	3,408,516	9,597	69.2	5.00	15	$44, PF-70UCam, February 2010
2003S, Arkansas, Silver	1,125,755	13,685	69.2	9.00	20	$104, PF-70UCam, March 2010
2004S, Michigan	2,740,684	6,957	69.2	5.00	15	$28, PF-70UCam, January 2010
2004S, Michigan, Silver	1,769,786	17,219	69.1	10.00	20	$18, PF-69DCam, January 2013
2004S, Florida	2,740,684	6,856	69.1	5.00	15	$36, PF-70UCam, December 2009
2004S, Florida, Silver	1,769,786	17,080	69.1	10.00	20	$24, PF-69DCam, February 2013
2004S, Texas	2,740,684	6,999	69.2	5.00	15	$21, PF-70DCam, March 2014
2004S, Texas, Silver	1,769,786	17,486	69.2	10.00	20	$69, PF-70DCam, October 2009
2004S, Iowa	2,740,684	7,044	69.2	5.00	15	$79, PF-70DCam, January 2010
2004S, Iowa, Silver	1,769,786	17,296	69.2	10.00	20	$17, PF-69DCam, February 2013
2004S, Wisconsin	2,740,684	7,006	69.2	5.00	15	$56, PF-70DCam, October 2009
2004S, Wisconsin, Silver	1,769,786	17,634	69.2	10.00	20	$56, PF-70DCam, January 2010
2005S, California	3,262,960	12,834	69.2	4.50	15	$16, PF-70DCam, March 2014
2005S, California, Silver	1,678,649	15,801	69.3	10.00	20	$15, PF-69DCam, January 2013
2005S, Minnesota	3,262,960	12,761	69.2	4.50	15	$40, PF-70UCam, March 2010
2005S, Minnesota, Silver	1,678,649	15,329	69.3	10.00	20	$33, PF-70DCam, March 2014

	Mintage	Cert	Avg	PF-66DC	PF-69DC	Recent Auction Record
2005S, Oregon	3,262,960	12,726	69.2	$4.50	$15	$59, PF-70DCam, October 2009
2005S, Oregon, Silver	1,678,649	15,392	69.3	10.00	20	$99, PF-70DCam, October 2009
2005S, Kansas	3,262,960	12,895	69.2	4.50	15	$44, PF-70UCam, February 2010
2005S, Kansas, Silver	1,678,649	15,607	69.2	10.00	20	$18, PF-69DCam, January 2013
2005S, West Virginia	3,262,960	12,828	69.2	4.50	15	$26, PF-70UCam, March 2010
2005S, West Virginia, Silver	1,678,649	15,586	69.3	10.00	20	$38, PF-70UCam, February 2010
2006S, Nevada	2,882,428	8,692	69.3	4.50	15	$15, PF-70DCam, May 2013
2006S, Nevada, Silver	1,585,008	13,361	69.3	9.00	20	$104, PF-70DCam, March 2010
2006S, Nebraska	2,882,428	8,644	69.3	4.50	15	$89, PF-70UCam, August 2009
2006S, Nebraska, Silver	1,585,008	13,155	69.4	9.00	20	$23, PF-70UCam, December 2008
2006S, Colorado	2,882,428	8,624	69.3	4.50	15	$29, PF-70DCam, November 2008
2006S, Colorado, Silver	1,585,008	13,307	69.4	9.00	20	$36, PF-70UCam, June 2009
2006S, North Dakota	2,882,428	8,670	69.3	4.50	15	$29, PF-70UCam, December 2008
2006S, North Dakota, Silver	1,585,008	13,196	69.3	9.00	20	$11, PF-70DCam, October 2008
2006S, South Dakota	2,882,428	8,708	69.3	4.50	15	$69, PF-70DCam, December 2009
2006S, South Dakota, Silver	1,585,008	13,272	69.4	9.00	20	$66, PF-70UCam, June 2009
2007S, Montana	2,374,778	5,690	69.3	4.50	15	$15, PF-69DCam, February 2013
2007S, Montana, Silver	1,313,481	11,867	69.3	9.00	20	$56, PF-70UCam, February 2010
2007S, Washington	2,374,778	5,626	69.3	4.50	15	$19, PF-70DCam, April 2013
2007S, Washington, Silver	1,313,481	11,816	69.3	9.00	20	$47, PF-70UCam, February 2010
2007S, Idaho	2,374,778	5,641	69.3	4.50	15	$53, PF-70DCam, October 2009
2007S, Idaho, Silver	1,313,481	11,857	69.3	9.00	20	$20, PF-69DCam, February 2013
2007S, Wyoming	2,374,778	5,531	69.2	4.50	15	$55, PF-70DCam, June 2014
2007S, Wyoming, Silver	1,313,481	11,630	69.2	9.00	20	$20, PF-69DCam, February 2013
2007S, Utah	2,374,778	5,597	69.3	4.50	15	$84, PF-70DCam, November 2009
2007S, Utah, Silver	1,313,481	11,807	69.3	9.00	20	$45, PF-70DCam, March 2014
2008S, Oklahoma	2,078,112	5,722	69.3	5.00	18	$30, PF-70UCam, March 2010
2008S, Oklahoma, Silver	1,192,908	11,943	69.3	10.00	22	$45, PF-70UCam, July 2008
2008S, New Mexico	2,078,112	5,762	69.3	5.00	18	$19, PF-70DCam, March 2014
2008S, New Mexico, Silver	1,192,908	11,754	69.3	10.00	22	$60, PF-70UCam, November 2008
2008S, Arizona	2,078,112	5,889	69.4	5.00	18	$53, PF-70UCam, March 2010
2008S, Arizona, Silver	1,192,908	12,155	69.4	10.00	22	$18, PF-69DCam, January 2013
2008S, Alaska	2,078,112	5,717	69.4	5.00	18	$40, PF-70UCam, March 2010
2008S, Alaska, Silver	1,192,908	12,053	69.4	10.00	22	$104, PF-70UCam, March 2010
2008S, Hawaii	2,078,112	5,711	69.3	10.00	25	$50, PF-70UCam, March 2010
2008S, Hawaii, Silver	1,192,908	12,048	69.3	10.00	22	$149, PF-70DCam, April 2013
2009S, District of Columbia	2,113,478	6,553	69.4	4.50	15	$15, PF-69DCam, November 2013
2009S, District of Columbia, Silver	996,548	8,699	69.6	9.00	20	
2009S, Puerto Rico	2,113,478	6,535	69.5	4.50	15	$38, PF-70DCam, February 2010
2009S, Puerto Rico, Silver	996,548	8,885	69.6	9.00	20	$104, PF-70UCam, March 2010
2009S, Guam	2,113,478	6,425	69.4	4.50	15	$15, PF-69DCam, March 2013
2009S, Guam, Silver	996,548	8,565	69.5	9.00	20	$18, PF-69DCam, January 2013
2009S, American Samoa	2,113,478	6,601	69.5	4.50	15	$16, PF-69DCam, November 2013
2009S, American Samoa, Silver	996,548	8,781	69.6	9.00	20	$62, PF-70UCam, January 2010
2009S, U.S. Virgin Islands	2,113,478	6,565	69.4	4.50	15	$104, PF-70DCam, March 2010
2009S, U.S. Virgin Islands, Silver	996,548	8,764	69.6	9.00	20	$60, PF-70UCam, March 2010
2009S, Northern Mariana Islands	2,113,478	6,572	69.5	4.50	15	$15, PF-69DCam, January 2013
2009S, Northern Mariana Islands, Silver	996,548	8,729	69.6	9.00	20	$17, PF-69DCam, November 2013
2010S, Hot Springs National Park (AR)	1,401,903	5,993	69.4	4.50	15	$15, PF-69DCam, January 2013
2010S, Hot Springs, National Park Silver (AR)	859,435	13,671	69.5	9.00	20	$21, PF-69DCam, February 2013
2010S, Yellowstone National Park (WY)	1,402,756	5,262	69.5	4.50	15	$16, PF-69DCam, March 2013
2010S, Yellowstone National Park, Silver (WY)	859,435	14,520	69.5	9.00	20	$21, PF-69DCam, February 2013
2010S, Yosemite National Park (CA)	1,400,215	5,923	69.4	4.50	15	$17, PF-69DCam, February 2013
2010S, Yosemite National Park, Silver (CA)	859,435	13,561	69.5	9.00	20	$18, PF-69DCam, March 2013
2010S, Grand Canyon National Park (AZ)	1,399,970	5,910	69.4	4.50	15	$19, PF-69DCam, February 2013
2010S, Grand Canyon National Park, Silver (AZ)	859,435	13,489	69.5	9.00	20	
2010S, Mt. Hood National Forest (OR)	1,397,101	5,880	69.3	4.50	15	$15, PF-69DCam, February 2013
2010S, Mt. Hood National Forest, Silver (OR)	859,435	13,556	69.5	9.00	20	
2011S, Gettysburg National Military Park (PA)	1,271,553	4,401	69.4	4.50	15	
2011S, Gettysburg National Military Park (PA), Silver	722,076	7,500	69.5	9.00	20	

Chart continued on next page.

	Est Mintage	Cert	Avg	PF-66DC	PF-69DC	Recent Auction Record
2011S, Glacier National Park (MT)	1,268,452	4,457	69.4	$4.50	$15	
2011S, Glacier National Park (MT), Silver	722,076	7,610	69.6	9.00	20	
2011S, Olympic National Park (WA)	1,267,361	4,458	69.5	4.50	15	
2011S, Olympic National Park (WA), Silver	722,076	7,470	69.5	9.00	20	
2011S, Vicksburg National Military Park (MS)	1,267,691	4,428	69.4	4.50	15	
2011S, Vicksburg National Military Park (MS), Silver	722,076	7,481	69.5	9.00	20	
2011S, Chickasaw National Recreation Area (OK)	1,266,010	4,432	69.4	4.50	15	
2011S, Chickasaw National Recreation Area (OK), Silver	722,076	7,449	69.5	9.00	20	
2012S, El Yunque National Forest (PR)	1,010,361	1,408	69.4	4.50	15	
2012S, El Yunque National Forest (PR), Silver	557,891	4,416	69.6	9.00	20	
2012S, Chaco Culture National Historical Park (NM)	960,049	1,372	69.4	4.50	15	
2012S, Chaco Culture National Historical Park (NM), Silver	557,891	4,382	69.5	9.00	20	
2012S, Acadia National Park (ME)	960,409	1,376	69.4	4.50	15	
2012S, Acadia National Park (ME), Silver	557,891	2,030	69.4	9.00	20	
2012S, Hawai'i Volcanoes National Park (HI)	961,272	3,766	69.6	4.50	15	
2012S, Hawai'i Volcanoes National Park (HI), Silver	557,891	4,429	69.6	9.00	20	
2012S, Denali National Park and Preserve (AK)	957,856	1,387	69.4	4.50	15	
2012S, Denali National Park and Preserve (AK), Silver	557,891	4,409	69.6	9.00	20	
2013S, White Mountain National Forest (NH)	950,080			4.50	15	
2013S, White Mountain National Forest (NH), Silver	579,409			9.00	20	
2013S, Perry's Victory and International Peace Memorial (OH)	913,563			4.50	15	
2013S, Perry's Victory and International Peace Memorial (OH), Silver	579,409			9.00	20	
2013S, Great Basin National Park (NV)	911,409			4.50	15	
2013S, Great Basin National Park (NV), Silver	579,409			9.00	20	
2013S, Fort McHenry Nat'l Monument and Historic Shrine (MD)	911,451			4.50	15	
2013S, Fort McHenry Nat'l Monument and Historic Shrine (MD), Silver	579,409			9.00	20	
2013S, Mount Rushmore National Memorial (SD)	920,695			4.50	15	
2013S, Mount Rushmore National Memorial (SD), Silver	579,409			9.00	20	
2014S, Great Smoky Mountains National Park (TN)				4.50	15	
2014S, Great Smoky Mountains National Park (TN), Silver				9.00	20	
2014S, Shenandoah National Park (VA)				4.50	15	
2014S, Shenandoah National Park (VA), Silver				9.00	20	
2014S, Arches National Park (UT)				4.50	15	
2014S, Arches National Park (UT), Silver				9.00	20	
2014S, Great Sand Dunes National Park (CO)				4.50	15	
2014S, Great Sand Dunes National Park (CO), Silver				9.00	20	
2014S, Everglades National Park (FL)				4.50	15	
2014S, Everglades National Park (FL), Silver				9.00	20	

AN OVERVIEW OF HALF DOLLARS

A collection of half dollars is one of the most satisfying in the American series. The panorama is extensive, and ranges from the early Flowing Hair issues of 1794 and 1795 down to the present day. The large size of such pieces makes them convenient to view and enjoy.

Among the types, the 1794–1795 Flowing Hair half dollar is readily available in circulated grades and rare in Mint State, but at any level is hard to find well struck and without adjustment marks. Most on the market are dated 1795. Careful selection is advised.

The next type, 1796–1797 with Draped Bust obverse and Small Eagle reverse, is the scarcest in the American silver series excepting the 1839 Gobrecht dollar. (However, the latter is available in Proof restrike form, yielding choice and gem examples, so it can be considered in a different category from the circulation-strike 1796–1797 half dollar type.) It might not be possible to be particular, but, finances permitting, a collector should take some time and endeavor to find a specimen sharply struck on both sides. Needle-sharp striking is more of a theory than a practicality, and some compromise may be necessary.

Half dollars of the 1801–1807 type, obverse as preceding but now with the Heraldic Eagle reverse, are plentiful enough in worn grades but somewhat scarce in Mint State. Striking is seldom needle sharp and ranges from average to very poor. However, there are enough coins in the marketplace that collectors can afford to take their time and select a sharp strike.

Capped Bust half dollars with lettered edge, 1807–1836, abound in just about any grade desired. Again, striking is a consideration, and some searching is needed. Generally, those in the late 1820s and the 1830s are better struck than are those of earlier dates, the earlier coins being scarcer and more expensive in any event.

The short-lived type of 1836–1837, Capped Bust with reeded edge, denomination spelled as 50 CENTS, is available easily enough through the high-mintage 1837, but most have problems with striking. Then comes the 1838–1839 type of the same obverse style, its reverse modified with a slightly different eagle and with the denomination as HALF DOL. Generally these are fairly well struck.

Liberty Seated half dollars of the several styles within the series, 1839–1891, admit of no great rarities for the type collector, save for the 1839 No Drapery in levels of MS-63 and finer. However, among the earlier types in particular, sharply struck pieces are in the minority. Curiously, the most readily available Mint State Liberty Seated half dollars also are the lowest mintage issues, the dates 1879 and later, as these were recognized as desirable at the time of issue, and were widely saved.

Barber half dollars were not popular in their time, and while Proofs exist in proportion to their production figures, Mint State coins are quite scarce. In fact, as a type, a Barber half dollar dated 1900 or later in Mint State is the scarcest of all silver issues of that century. Well-struck MS-63 and better Barber half dollars, with the upper-right corner of the shield and the leg at lower right showing full details, are significantly scarcer than generally realized.

Liberty Walking half dollars minted from 1916 to 1947 are plentiful in all grades. Again, some attention should be made to striking sharpness, at which time the search becomes more intense. Fortunately, there are countless thousands of MS-63 and finer coins of the 1940s on the market, giving collectors a wide choice. Then come Franklin half dollars, made only from 1948 to 1963, with representative coins easy enough to acquire in about any grade desired. Kennedy half dollars exist in several varieties, all of which are available without any problem. Among these and other modern coins care needs to be taken for value received versus price paid. Modern issues in, for example, MS-65 and 66, selected for quality, are for many collectors preferable to MS-69 or 70 coins offered at a much higher price.

For the Collector and Investor: Half Dollars as a Specialty

Many collectors over the years have pursued half dollars by date and variety. Except for the series of copper cents, half dollars are the most generally available coins over a nearly continuous span, making them possible to collect for reasonable cost. Also, enough die varieties exist that this can form another focus of interest and importance.

In general, the half dollars of the early era form a concentration in themselves. Die varieties can be attributed by Overton numbers, as listed by Al C. Overton in his immensely popular *Early Half Dollar Die Varieties 1794–1836*. To this, Glenn R. Peterson's book, *The Ultimate Guide to Attributing Bust Half Dollars*, is also useful. The John Reich Collectors Society publishes the *John Reich Journal* and serves as a forum for the exchange of information, updates and die varieties, and the like.

Among rarities in the early years, the 1796 and 1797 with Draped Bust obverse and Small Eagle reverse are perhaps the most famous, needed for variety collections as well as one example for a type set. Variety enthusiasts aspire to get two of 1796—one with 15 stars on the obverse and the other with 16 stars—plus the 1797.

Draped Bust half dollars from 1801 through 1807 have a number of rare die varieties (as listed by Overton), but the basic varieties are easy enough to find. The 1805, 5 Over 4 overdate is particularly popular, as there was no "perfect date" 1804, and this is the closest collectors can come to it.

A vast and interesting field in early American numismatics is that of the Capped Bust half dollar, 1807–1836, with a lettered edge. Several hundred different die combinations exist, and many collectors are active in their pursuit, using the Overton book as a road map. All the major varieties are readily collectible except the 1817, 7 Over 4 overdate, of which only about a half dozen exist. The 1815, 5 Over 2 is considered the key issue among the specific dates (rather than varieties of dates). The majority of these occur in VF grade, not often lower and not often higher either—an interesting situation. During the 1820s vast quantities of these were transferred among banks. While many if not most of the varieties listed herein can be obtained in Mint State, most collectors opt for VF or EF, these grades showing the necessary details but also permitting a budget to be stretched to include more varieties, rather than just a few high-grade pieces. Choice and gem examples can be found here and there, and are most plentiful among the later dates.

Among the Capped Bust half dollars of reduced size, 1836–1837, the 1836 is a key date, and fewer than 5,000 are believed to have been minted. The next type, 1838 and 1839, Capped Bust, reeded edge, with a modified eagle on the reverse, includes the famous 1838-O rarity, of which only 20 are said to have been struck (per a note published in 1894 in the catalog of the Friesner Collection). These have a prooflike surface. Interestingly, they were not struck until 1839. In the same year, 1839-O half dollars were also struck, to the extensive quantity of 178,976 pieces; they are unusual as the mintmark is on the obverse, an odd placement for the era.

The series of Liberty Seated half dollars is generally collected by varieties listed herein, although certain dedicated specialists will consult the *Complete Guide to Liberty Seated Half Dollars,* by Randy Wiley and Bill Bugert—a volume that delineates many interesting features, including the number of different reeds on the edges of certain coins.

Among Liberty Seated half dollars there is just one "impossible" rarity, that being the 1853-O without arrows at the date. Only three exist, and each shows extensive wear. Half dollars were first struck at the San Francisco Mint in 1855 and at the Carson City Mint in 1870. Generally, large quantities were minted of most dates and mintmark varieties of Liberty Seated half dollars, making them readily obtainable today. Except for the later dates, 1879–1891, Mint State pieces are generally scarce, gems especially so. Many specialists in half dollars belong to the Liberty Seated Collectors Club (LSCC) and receive its magazine, *The Gobrecht Journal.*

Proof Liberty Seated halves can be collected by date sequence from 1858 onward. Survivors exist in proportion to the mintage quantities. Generally, those before the mid-1870s often come cleaned or hairlined, and more care is needed in selecting choice specimens than is necessary for the later dates.

Barber half dollars were made continuously from 1892 through 1915, in such quantities that today there are no great rarities. However, a number of issues are quite scarce, even in well-worn grades, and in MS-63 and better many are difficult to find. These coins had little honor in the era in which they were issued, and few numismatists saved them. Proofs were made each year from 1892 to 1915 and can be obtained in proportion to their mintages. However, those of 1914 and 1915 are hard to find with choice, original surfaces—decades ago a collector hoarded these two dates and polished those in his possession.

Liberty Walking half dollars are popular to collect by date and mint. Scarce varieties include the 1917-S with obverse mintmark, the three issues of 1921, and the low mintage 1938-D, although the latter is not inordinately expensive. Uncirculated or Mint State pieces are most readily available for 1916 and 1917, and then especially so in the 1930s and 1940s. Striking can be a problem, particularly for issues of the mid-1920s and also the later varieties. For example, with a needle-sharp strike the 1923-S is an extreme rarity. Among later coins the 1940-S and 1941-S often are weakly struck.

Franklin half dollars minted from 1948 through 1963 have been very popular in recent decades. The complete series of dates and mintmarks is short and contains no scarce or rare pieces in grades such as MS-63 and MS-64. However, consider the element of sharp striking, usually defined as Full Bell Lines (FBL) on the reverse, and certain otherwise common dates become elusive. Proofs of most years can also be readily collected.

Kennedy half dollars are easily enough collected, and so many have been made by this time that nearly 200 dates and mintmarks extend from 1964 to present. The wise collector will select coins that have a meeting point between a high grade such as MS-65 or MS-66 (or equivalent Proofs) and a reasonable price.

RECOMMENDED READING

Fivaz, Bill, and Stanton, J.T. *The Cherrypickers' Guide to Rare Die Varieties* (5th ed., vol. II), Atlanta, GA, 2012.

Flynn, Kevin. *The Authoritative Reference on Barber Half Dollars,* Brooklyn, NY, 2005.

Fox, Bruce. *The Complete Guide to Walking Liberty Half Dollars,* Virginia Beach, VA, 1993.

Haseltine, J.W. *Type Table of United States Dollars, Half Dollars and Quarter Dollars,* Philadelphia, 1881 (reprinted 1927, 1968).

Lawrence, David. *The Complete Guide to Barber Halves,* Virginia Beach, VA, 1991.

Overton, Al C. *Early Half Dollar Die Varieties, 1794–1836,* Colorado Springs, CO, 1967 (3rd ed., 1990, edited by Donald Parsley).

Peterson, Glenn R. *The Ultimate Guide to Attributing Bust Half Dollars,* Rocky River, OH, 2000.

Tomaska, Rick. *A Guide Book of Franklin and Kennedy Half Dollars* (2nd ed.), Atlanta, GA, 2012.

Wiley, Randy, and Bugert, Bill. *The Complete Guide to Liberty Seated Half Dollars,* Virginia Beach, VA, 1993.

FLOWING HAIR
(1794–1795)

Designer Robert Scot; weight 13.48 grams; composition .8924 silver, .1076 copper; approx. diameter 32.5 mm; edge: FIFTY CENTS OR HALF A DOLLAR with decorations between the words.

Overton-105.

History. The Flowing Hair design inaugurated the half-dollar denomination. The same motif was used on half dimes and silver dollars of the same years. Early half dollars have been extensively collected by die varieties, of which many exist for most dates. Valuations given below are in each case for the most common variety; scarcer ones, as listed by Overton, generally command higher prices.

Striking and Sharpness. Many have problems of one sort or another, including adjustment marks from the planchet being filed and mushy dentils. On the obverse, check the hair details and the stars. On the reverse, check the breast of the eagle in particular. As with other silver coins of this design, it may not be possible to find a *needle-sharp* example, but with some extensive searching a fairly decent strike can be obtained. Sharp striking and excellent eye appeal add to the value dramatically. However, very few 1794 and 1795 halves are uniformly sharp on both sides.

Availability. Probably 3,500 to 6,000 exist. Most are dated 1795, the 1794 being considered a rare date. Typical grades are Good to Fine. EF and AU grades are elusive in regard to the total population. Probably 100 or so could be graded MS (nearly all of them 1795). Unlike half dollars of the 1796–1797 type, none of these are known to have been made with prooflike surfaces.

AU-50, 53, 55, 58 (About Uncirculated). *Obverse:* Light wear is seen on the hair area immediately to the left of the face and above the forehead, on the cheek, and, to a lesser extent, on the top of the neck truncation. An AU-58 coin has minimal traces of wear. Regarding luster: an AU-50 coin has luster in protected areas among the stars and letters, with little in the open fields or on the portrait. At AU-58, much luster is present in the fields but is worn away on the highest parts of the motifs. *Reverse:* Light wear is seen on the eagle's body and the upper part of both wings. On well-struck pieces the details of the wing features are excellent. At AU-50, detail is lost in some feathers in this area. However, striking can play a part, as some coins were weakly struck to begin with. Light wear is seen on the wreath and lettering, but is harder to discern. Luster is the best key to actual wear. This will range from perhaps 20% remaining in protected areas (at AU-50) to nearly full mint bloom (at AU-58).

MS-60 to 70 (Mint State). *Obverse:* At MS-60, some abrasion and contact marks are evident, most noticeably on the cheek and in the fields. Luster is present, but may be dull or lifeless, and interrupted in patches, perhaps as much from old cleaning as from contact the coin may have received. At MS-63, contact marks are very few, and abrasion is present, but not as noticeable. An MS-65 coin has no abrasion, and contact marks are very few. Luster should be full and rich. Higher grades are seldom seen in this type, but are defined in theory by having fewer marks as perfection is approached. *Reverse:* Comments apply as for the obverse, except that abrasion and contact marks are most noticeable on the eagle at the center. This area is often lightly struck, so in all grades do not mistake weak striking for actual wear. Knowledge of specific die varieties is helpful in this regard. The field area is small and is protected by lettering and the wreath, and in any given grade shows fewer marks than on the obverse.

1795, Normal Date

1795, Recut Date

1795, 2 Leaves Under Each Wing

1795, 3 Leaves Under Each Wing

	Mintage	Cert	Avg	%MS	AU-50	AU-55	AU-58	MS-60	MS-62	MS-63	MS-64	Recent Auction Record
1794	23,464	717	19.0	1	$75,000	$105,000	$125,000	$150,000	$250,000	$350,000	$450,000	$152,750, MS-61, June 2014
1795, All kinds (a)	299,680											
1795, Normal Date		2,548	21.0	3	19,000	21,000	27,000	42,000	63,000	95,000	250,000	$129,250, MS-62, November 2013
1795, Recut Date		48	19.3	0	20,500	25,000	30,000	45,000	65,000	100,000	250,000	$1,651, F-12, March 2014
1795, 3 Leaves Under Each Wing		51	19.9	2	40,000	42,000	45,000	65,000	80,000			$8,519, VF-Very Fine, March 2014

a. Varieties of 1795 are known with the final S in STATES over a D; with the A in STATES over an E; and with the Y in LIBERTY over a star. All are scarce. Some 1795 half dollars were weight-adjusted by insertion of a silver plug in the center of the blank planchet before the coin was struck.

DRAPED BUST,
SMALL EAGLE REVERSE
(1796–1797)

Designer Robert Scot; weight 13.48 grams; composition .8924 silver, .1076 copper; approx. diameter 32.5 mm; edge: FIFTY CENTS OR HALF A DOLLAR with decorations between words.

Overton-101.

History. Robert Scot's Draped Bust design is similar to that used on the half dime, dime, quarter, and silver dollar of this era.

Striking and Sharpness. On the obverse, check the hair details and the stars. On the reverse, first check the breast of the eagle, but examine other areas as well. Also check the dentils on both sides. Look especially for coins that do not have significant adjustment marks.

Coins of this denomination are on average better struck than are half dimes, dimes, quarters (which have reverse problems), and dollars.

Availability. Examples are rare in any grade. MS coins are particularly rare, and when seen are nearly always dated 1796. Some of these have partially prooflike surfaces. Any half dollar of this type has strong market demand.

AU-50, 53, 55, 58 (About Uncirculated). *Obverse:* Light wear is seen on the hair area above the ear and extending to the left of the forehead, on the ribbon, and on the drapery at the shoulder, more so at AU-50 than at 53 or 55. An AU-58 coin has minimal traces of wear. Regarding luster: an AU-50 coin has luster in protected areas among the stars and letters, with little in the open fields or on the portrait. At AU-58, most luster is present in the fields, but is worn away on the highest parts of the motifs. *Reverse:* Light wear is seen on the eagle's body and the edges of the wings. Light wear is seen on the wreath and lettering. Luster is the best key to actual wear; it ranges from perhaps

20% remaining in protected areas (at AU-50) to nearly full mint bloom (at AU-58).

MS-60 to 70 (Mint State). *Obverse:* At MS-60, some abrasion and contact marks are evident, most noticeably on the cheek, the drapery at the shoulder, and the right field. Also check the hair to the left of the forehead. Luster is present, but may be dull or lifeless, and interrupted in patches. At MS-63, contact marks are few, and abrasion is hard to detect, although this type is sometimes graded liberally due to its rarity. An MS-65 coin has no abrasion, and contact marks are so minute as to require magnification. Luster should be

full and rich. Coins graded above MS-65 are more theoretical than actual for this type, although some notable pieces have crossed the auction block. These are defined by having fewer marks as perfection is approached. *Reverse:* Comments apply as for the obverse, except that abrasion and contact marks are most noticeable on the eagle at the center, a situation that should be evaluated by considering the original striking (which can be quite sharp, but with many exceptions). The field area is small and is protected by lettering and the wreath, and in any given grade shows fewer marks than on the obverse.

1796, 15 Stars

1796, 16 Stars

Shown 1.25x actual size.

	Mintage	Cert	Avg	%MS	AU-50	AU-55	AU-58	MS-60	MS-62	MS-63	MS-64	Recent Auction Record
1796, 15 Stars †	3,918	71	30.8	11	$165,000	$175,000	$220,000	$290,000	$325,000	$375,000	$500,000	$340,750, MS, February 2014
1796, 16 Stars †	*	35	28.6	11	170,000	180,000	250,000	305,000	355,000	420,000	525,000	$470,000, MS-63, November 2013
1797, 15 Stars †	*	142	24.2	6	165,000	175,000	220,000	290,000	325,000	400,000	550,000	$282,000, MS-63, June 2014

* Included in number above. † Ranked in the *100 Greatest U.S. Coins* (fourth edition).

DRAPED BUST, HERALDIC EAGLE REVERSE (1801–1807)

Designer Robert Scot; weight 13.48 grams; composition .8924 silver, .1076 copper; approx. diameter 32.5 mm; edge: FIFTY CENTS OR HALF A DOLLAR with decorations between words.

Overton-101.

History. The half dollar's Draped Bust, Heraldic Eagle design is similar to that of other silver coins of the era.

Striking and Sharpness. Most have light striking in one area or another; on the obverse, check the hair details and, in particular, the star centers. On the reverse, check the stars above the eagle, the clouds, the details of the shield, and the eagle's wings. Check the dentils on both sides. Adjustment marks are sometimes seen, but not as often as on earlier half dollar types. Typically, the earlier years are better struck; many of 1806 and nearly all of 1807 are poorly struck. Sharp striking and excellent eye appeal add to the value dramatically, this being particularly true for 1805 to 1807, which are often weak (particularly 1807).

Availability. Earlier years are scarce in the marketplace, beginning with the elusive 1801 and including the 1802, after which they are more readily available. Some die varieties are scarce. Most MS coins are dated 1806 and 1807, but all are scarce. Finding sharply struck high-grade coins is almost impossible, a goal more than a reality.

EF-40, 45 (Extremely Fine). *Obverse:* More wear is evident on the upper hair area and the ribbon, and on the drapery and bosom than at AU. Excellent detail remains in low-relief areas of the hair. The stars show wear, as do the date and letters. Luster, if present at all, is minimal and in protected areas. *Reverse:* Wear is greater than at AU, overall. The neck lacks feather detail on its highest points. Feathers have lost some detail near the edges of the wings, and some areas of the horizontal lines in the shield may be blended together. Some traces of luster may be seen, less at EF-40 than at EF-45.

AU-50, 53, 55, 58 (About Uncirculated). *Obverse:* Light wear is seen on the hair area above the ear and extending to left of the forehead, on the ribbon, and on the bosom, more so at AU-50 than at 53 or 55. An AU-58 coin has minimal traces of wear. Regarding luster: an AU-50 coin has luster in protected areas among the stars and letters, with little in the open fields or on the portrait. At AU-58, most luster is present in the fields, but is worn away on the highest parts of the motifs. *Reverse:* Comments as preceding, except that the eagle's neck, the tips and top of the wings, the clouds, and the tail now show noticeable wear, as do other features. Luster ranges from perhaps 20% remaining in protected areas (at AU-50) to nearly full mint bloom (at AU-58). Often the reverse of this type retains much more luster than the obverse.

MS-60 to 70 (Mint State). *Obverse:* At MS-60, some abrasion and contact marks are evident, most noticeably on the cheek, the drapery at the shoulder, and the right field. Luster is present, but may be dull or lifeless, and interrupted in patches. At MS-63, contact marks are very few, and abrasion is hard to detect except under magnification. An MS-65 coin has no abrasion, and contact marks are so minute as to require magnification. Luster should be full and rich. Coins grading above MS-65 are more theoretical than actual for this type—but they do exist, and are defined by having fewer marks as perfection is approached. Later years usually have areas of flat striking. *Reverse:* Comments apply as for the obverse, except that abrasion and contact marks are most noticeable on the eagle's neck, the tips of the wing, and the tail. The field area is complex, without much open space, given the stars above the eagle, the arrows and olive branch, and other features. Accordingly, marks are not as noticeable as on the obverse.

1803, Small 3

1803, Large 3

1805, 5 Over 4

1805, Normal Date

1806, 6 Over 5

1806, 6 Over Inverted 6

1806, Stem Not Through Claw

1806, Stem Through Claw

1806, Knobbed-Top 6, Large Stars
With traces of overdate.

1806, Knobbed-Top 6, Small Stars

	Mintage	Cert	Avg	%MS	EF-40	AU-50	AU-55	MS-60	MS-62	MS-63	MS-64	Recent Auction Record
1801	30,289	363	26.9	1	$6,750	$16,000	$21,000	$45,000	$87,000	$160,000		$329,000, MS-64, November 2013
1802	29,890	272	30.8	1	7,750	17,000	25,000	60,000	90,000			$70,500, AU-58, August 2013
1803, All kinds	188,234											
1803, Small 3		110	34.9	3	2,600	6,000	10,000	21,000	43,500	65,000	$110,000	$49,938, MS-62, June 2014
1803, Large 3		1,032	30.9	1	2,050	5,000	7,000	16,000	30,000	40,000	80,000	$88,125, MS-63, August 2013
1805, All kinds	211,722											
1805, 5 Over 4		274	32.5	1	3,500	7,500	12,750	30,000	60,000	85,000		$152,750, MS-65, November 2013
1805, Normal Date		787	31.1	1	2,250	5,000	6,600	16,000	24,000	35,000	50,000	$42,594, MS-63, November 2013
1806, All kinds	839,576											
1806, 6 Over 5		409	31.7	2	2,200	5,000	6,500	12,000	18,000	26,000	37,500	$21,150, MS-61, November 2013
1806, 6 Over Inverted 6		169	27.2	1	3,750	7,000	12,500	27,500	30,000	38,000	67,500	$28,200, MS-61, November 2013
1806, Knbd 6, Lg Stars (Traces of Overdate)		150	27.8	0	2,000	5,000	7,000	10,000	15,000	21,500	32,500	$2,364, EF-40, August 2013
1806, Knbd 6, Sm Stars		125	29.6	1	2,000	5,000	7,000	11,000	16,000	25,000	40,000	$2,350, EF-45, January 2014
1806, Knbd 6, Stem Not Through Claw		4	31.3	0	200,000							$126,500, EF-40, January 2009
1806, Pointed 6, Stem Through Claw		1,282	33.1	5	1,750	4,500	5,250	8,500	11,000	16,000	28,000	$35,250, MS-64, November 2013
1806, Pointed 6, Stem Through Claw, E Over A in STATES		4	21.3	0	7,500	20,000						
1806, Pointed 6, Stem Not Through Claw		438	35.6	5	2,000	5,500	5,750	9,500	11,750	18,000	30,000	$12,925, MS-62, November 2013
1807	301,076	2,123	34.3	7	1,800	5,000	5,500	9,000	11,000	16,250	28,000	$70,500, MS-65, November 2013

CAPPED BUST, LETTERED EDGE (1807–1836)

Designer John Reich; weight 13.48 grams; composition .8924 silver, .1076 copper; approx. diameter 32.5 mm. 1807–1814—Edge: FIFTY CENTS OR HALF A DOLLAR. 1814–1831—Edge: Star added between DOLLAR and FIFTY. 1832–1836—Edge: Vertical lines added between words.

First Style (1807–1808)
Overton-104.

Remodeled Portrait and Eagle (1809–1836)
Overton-109.

History. The Capped Bust design was created by Mint assistant engraver John Reich; the motif was widely used, in several variations, on much of the era's coinage. Reich was the first artist to consistently include the denomination in his designs for U.S. gold and silver coins. The half dollar, minted continuously from 1807 to 1836, except 1816, was the largest silver coin of the realm at the time (silver dollars had not been struck since 1804).

Striking and Sharpness. On the obverse, check the hair and broach details. Stars are often flatly struck on Capped Bust half dollars, much more so than on other denominations. On the reverse, check the motto band and the eagle's head, and the wing to the left, as well as other areas (neck feathers, often lightly struck on other denominations of Capped Bust silver, are usually fairly sharp on half dollars). The E PLURIBUS UNUM band is often weak in the area left of its center; this does not normally occur on other Capped Bust silver coins. Inspect the dentils on both sides. Generally, later dates are better struck than are earlier ones. Many half dollars have semi-prooflike surfaces, or patches of mirrorlike character interspersed with luster. Others can have nearly full prooflike surfaces, with patches of luster being in the minority (and often in the left obverse field); some of these have been mischaracterized as "Proofs." Some issues from the early 1830s have little digs or "bite marks" on the portrait, possibly from some sort of a gadget used to eject them from the press. Unlike the Capped Bust half dime, dime, and quarter dollar, the half dollar is particularly subject to very wide variations in striking quality.

Availability. Examples of most dates and overdates are easily found in just about any grade desired, from Fine and VF to MS. (As the largest silver coin struck between 1803 and 1836, these half dollars spent much of their time in bags, transferred from bank to bank, rather than wearing down in circulation.) The later years are the most readily available and are also seen in higher average grades. Many die varieties range from scarce to rare.

AU-50, 53, 55, 58 (About Uncirculated). *Obverse:* Light wear is seen on the cheek, the hair below the left part of LIBERTY, the cap, and the front part of the bosom and drapery. Some of this apparent "wear" may be related to the original planchet surface (as noted under MS, below), but at the AU level the distinction is less important. At AU-50 and 53, luster remains only in protected areas. On a well-struck coin, at AU-58 the luster is extensive except in the open area of the field, especially to the right. *Reverse:* Wear is evident on the eagle's head, the top of the wings, the claws, and the flat band above the eagle. At AU-50 and 53, there still is significant luster, more than on the obverse. An AU-58 coin has nearly full luster.

MS-60 to 70 (Mint State). *Obverse:* At MS-60, some abrasion and contact marks are evident, most noticeably on the cheek, the hair below the left part of LIBERTY, the cap, and the front part of the bosom and drapery. These areas also coincide with the highest parts of the coin and are thus susceptible to lightness of strike. Complicating matters is that when an area is lightly struck, and the planchet is not forced into the deepest parts of the die, the original planchet surface (which may exhibit scuffing and nicks) is visible. A lightly struck coin can have virtually perfect luster in the fields, and yet appear to be "worn" on the higher parts, due to the lightness of strike. In practice, the original planchet surface will usually be considered as wear on the finished coin, which of course is not true. Such grades as high AU and low MS levels are often assigned to pieces that, if well struck, would be MS-64 and MS-65. If a coin has original planchet abrasions, but otherwise is a gem, those abrasions must be taken into consideration. Apart from this, on well-struck coins in lower MS grades, luster is present, but may be dull or lifeless, and interrupted in patches. At MS-63, on a well-struck coin, contact marks are very few, and abrasion is hard to detect except under magnification. A well-struck MS-65 coin has no abrasion, and contact marks are so minute as to require magnification. Luster should be full and rich. Grades above MS-65 are seen now and again and are defined by having fewer marks as perfection is approached. *Reverse:* Comments apply as for the obverse, except that nearly all coins with weak striking on the obverse (so as to reveal original planchet surface) do not show such original surface on the reverse, except perhaps on the motto ribbon. Accordingly, market grading is usually by the obverse only, even if the reverse seems to be in much better preservation. On well-struck coins, abrasion and contact marks are most noticeable on the eagle's head, the top of the wings, the claws, and the flat band that surrounds the incuse motto. The field is mainly protected by design elements and on a given coin does not show abrasion as much as does the obverse.

1807, Small Stars

1807, Large Stars

1807, Large Stars, 50 Over 20

1807, "Bearded" Liberty

1808, 8 Over 7

1809, xxxx Edge
Experimental edge has "xxxx" between the words.

1809, ||||| Edge
Experimental edge has "|||||" between the words.

1811, (18.11), 11 Over 10
The date is "punctuated" with a period.

1811, Small 8

1811, Large 8

1813, 50 C. Over UNI.

1812, 2 Over 1, Small 8

1812, 2 Over 1, Large 8

1812, Two Leaves Below Wing

1812, Single Leaf Below Wing

1814, 4 Over 3

1814, E Over A in STATES

1814, Two Leaves Below Wing

1814, Single Leaf Below Wing

1815, 5 Over 2

1817, 7 Over 3

1817, 7 Over 4

1817, Dated 181.7
The date is "punctuated" with a period between the second 1 and the 7.

1817, Two Leaves Below Wing

1817, Single Leaf Below Wing

1818, First 8 Small, Second 8 Over 7

1818, First 8 Large, Second 8 Over 7

1819, Small 9 Over 8

1819, Large 9 Over 8

1820, 20 Over 19, Square Base 2

1820, 20 Over 19, Curl Base 2

1820, Curl Base, No Knob 2, Small Date

1820, Square Base, Knob 2, Large Date

1820, Square Base, No Knob 2, Large Date

1820, Broken Serifs on E's
Compare with normal serifs on 1834 Large Letters reverse shown on page 187.

1822, 2 Over 1

1823, Normal Date

1823, Broken 3

1823, Patched 3

1823, Ugly 3

1824, Normal Date

1824, 4 Over 1

1824, 4 Over Various Dates
Probably 4 Over 2 Over 0.

1824, 4 Over 4
4 Over 4 varieties are easily mistaken for the scarcer 4 Over 1. Note the distance between the 2's and 4's in each.

1827, 7 Over 6

1827, Square Base 2

1827, Curl Base 2

1828, Curl Base, No Knob 2

1828, Curl Base, Knob 2

1828, Square Base 2, Large 8's

1828, Square Base 2, Small 8's

1828, Large Letters

1828, Small Letters

1829, 9 Over 7

1830, Small 0

1830, Large 0

1830, Large Letters

Experimental Edge of 1830
Raised segment lines angled to the right.

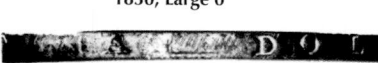
Experimental Edge of 1830–1831
Raised segment lines angled to the left.

Edge Adopted for Coinage, 1830–1836
Straight vertical lines.

1832, Large Letters Reverse
Note the prominent die crack.
Shown 1.5x actual size.

1834, Large Date

1834, Small Date

1834, Large Letters

1834, Small Letters

1836, Over 1336

	Mintage	Cert	Avg	%MS	AU-50	AU-55	MS-60	MS-62	MS-63	MS-64	MS-65	Recent Auction Record
1807, All kinds	750,500											
1807, Small Stars		124	36.0	4	$5,000	$6,000	$9,000	$11,500	$16,000	$27,500	$65,000	$28,200, MS-61, January 2014
1807, Large Stars		108	35.5	7	3,500	5,000	8,000	10,000	15,000	26,000	85,000	$152,750, MS-65, November 2013
1807, Large Stars, 50 Over 20		522	39.0	5	2,700	3,750	5,750	7,900	11,000	18,500	33,500	$28,200, MS-65, June 2014
1807, "Bearded" Liberty (a)		66	30.5	0	9,500	13,000	27,500	42,000	—			$8,225, VF-30, January 2014
1808, All kinds	1,368,600											
1808, 8 Over 7		392	40.9	10	1,500	2,000	4,200	6,000	10,000	17,500		$21,150, MS-65, November 2013
1808		1,089	43.1	13	1,000	1,200	3,000	5,000	6,000	8,500	19,000	$52,875, MS-66, November 2013
1809, All kinds	1,405,810											
1809, Normal Edge		1,146	43.5	11	900	1,500	3,000	4,000	5,500	7,000	19,000	$10,575, MS-63, November 2013
1809, xxxx Edge		135	41.5	7	1,000	2,750	5,000	6,500	7,000	9,250		$1,645, AU-50, April 2014
1809, lllll Edge		276	40.4	7	1,200	3,000	4,000	4,500	7,300	11,500	22,000	$38,188, MS-66, April 2014
1810	1,276,276	1,250	44.5	12	800	1,400	3,500	4,250	5,750	8,000	18,000	$64,625, MS-66, November 2013
1811, All kinds	1,203,644											
1811, (18.11), 11 Over 10		259	44.1	11	1,400	2,500	4,000	6,000	10,000	16,000		$6,463, AU-58, January 2014
1811, Small 8		629	46.8	18	700	1,200	2,500	3,000	4,500	5,750	17,000	$94,000, MS-67, June 2013
1811, Large 8		422	50.5	23	800	1,500	3,000	3,500	5,000	6,250	17,250	$5,581, MS-63, November 2013
1812, All kinds	1,628,059											
1812, 2 Over 1, Small 8		271	43.9	14	1,200	2,000	3,400	4,250	6,000	7,250	18,000	$22,325, MS-64, November 2013
1812, 2 Over 1, Large 8		47	34.7	0	24,000	30,000	40,000	75,000	—			$14,100, AU-58, August 2013
1812		1,779	47.9	24	700	950	2,200	2,900	3,600	5,500	14,000	$44,063, MS-65, November 2013
1812, Single Leaf Below Wing		2	47.5	0	7,000	12,000	17,000	22,000	30,000			
1813, All kinds	1,241,903											
1813		1,129	47.1	17	700	1,000	2,250	3,500	4,500	7,250	16,000	$141,000, MS-67, November 2013
1813, 50 C. Over UNI		181	46.7	17	1,400	2,600	3,500	4,500	6,000	15,000		$24,675, MS-64, June 2014
1814, All kinds	1,039,075											
1814, 4 Over 3		258	42.4	9	1,750	2,500	3,750	5,000	6,500	12,000	19,000	$22,325, MS-64, November 2013
1814, E Over A in STATES		109	40.5	6	1,500	2,500	4,000	5,000	6,000	13,000		$4,700, AU-55, January 2014
1814		1,063	48.5	24	800	1,300	2,500	3,500	4,500	6,000	14,000	$22,325, MS-65, November 2013
1814, Single Leaf Below Wing		29	38.8	7	1,750	2,250	3,200	4,500	6,000	12,000		$705, EF-40, November 2013
1815, 5 Over 2	47,150	510	39.7	6	8,500	13,000	17,500	22,000	32,000	55,000		$117,500, MS-64, November 2013
1817, All kinds	1,215,567											
1817, 7 Over 3		342	40.1	8	2,500	3,500	5,000	8,000	12,500	24,000	42,500	$28,200, MS-64, November 2013
1817, 7 Over 4 (8 known) †		9	23.2	0	350,000							$184,000, VF-20, August 2010
1817, Dated 181.7		91	42.2	8	1,750	2,500	3,500	5,000	7,500	12,000	22,000	$3,055, AU-58, August 2013
1817		1,063	44.7	14	700	1,100	2,000	3,000	4,000	7,000	15,500	$17,625, MS-65, January 2014
1817, Single Leaf Below Wing		22	39.4	5	1,000	1,650	2,750	3,600	4,500	10,000		$3,055, AU-55, April 2013
1818, All kinds	1,960,322											
1818, 8 Over 7, Small 8		211	44.4	9	950	1,900	2,900	4,000	6,500	10,000	18,500	$12,338, MS-63, November 2013
1818, 8 Over 7, Large 8		212	46.7	13	925	1,800	2,900	4,000	6,500	10,000	19,500	$7,344, MS-63, November 2013
1818		1,309	47.8	16	600	975	2,200	3,000	4,000	6,250	13,500	$9,988, MS-64, November 2013
1819, All kinds	2,208,000											
1819, Small 9 Over 8		268	44.7	12	750	1,200	1,750	2,500	3,500	6,750	16,000	$7,050, MS-63, November 2013
1819, Large 9 Over 8		335	45.4	9	750	1,400	2,000	3,000	3,600	7,000	16,500	$49,938, MS-65, November 2013
1819		873	46.3	16	450	700	1,500	2,050	3,000	5,500	14,500	$18,800, MS-64, April 2014
1820, All kinds	751,122											
1820, 20 Over 19, Square 2		158	44.9	12	1,150	2,000	2,650	4,600	7,000	11,000	22,000	$15,863, MS-63, January 2014
1820, 20 Over 19, Curl Base 2		158	45.2	8	1,100	1,800	2,350	4,150	6,000	9,000	18,500	$8,225, MS-63, January 2014
1820, Curl Base 2, Small Date		231	47.9	11	1,000	1,750	2,000	4,000	5,000	8,000	15,000	$10,575, MS-63, November 2013
1820, Sq Base Knob 2, Lg Dt		190	47.8	15	850	1,600	2,000	4,000	5,000	8,000	16,000	$18,800, MS-64, January 2014
1820, Sq Base No Knob 2, Lg Dt		197	45.4	7	850	1,600	2,000	4,000	5,000	8,000	16,000	$61,688, MS-65, June 2014
1820, Broken Serifs on E's		19	38.4	16	6,000	6,250	7,000	8,500	12,000	20,000	40,000	$4,888, VF-35, December 2011
1821	1,305,797	1,223	48.1	16	650	800	1,400	2,000	3,000	4,500	13,000	$15,275, MS-64, November 2013
1822, All kinds	1,559,573											
1822		1,396	49.8	26	450	800	1,200	1,900	2,850	4,250	14,000	$52,875, MS-66, November 2013
1822, 2 Over 1		215	49.3	23	800	1,150	1,600	2,750	3,750	8,000	16,000	$1,410, MS-60, November 2013
1823, All kinds	1,694,200											
1823, Broken 3		119	41.0	8	1,500	2,500	3,750	4,500	7,500	10,500	25,000	$23,500, MS-64, November 2013
1823, Patched 3		136	48.6	26	1,200	2,000	4,000	5,000	7,500	10,000	20,000	$11,750, MS-64, January 2014
1823, Ugly 3		80	45.4	11	1,000	2,500	4,500	5,250	7,500	10,000	18,000	$4,113, AU-55, January 2014
1823, Normal		1,573	49.8	24	500	800	1,250	1,750	2,500	3,500	13,500	$94,000, MS-67, November 2013

† Ranked in the *100 Greatest U.S. Coins* (fourth edition). **a.** Also called the Bearded Goddess variety; a die crack gives the illusion of long whiskers growing from Miss Liberty's chin.

	Mintage	Cert	Avg	%MS	AU-50	AU-55	MS-60	MS-62	MS-63	MS-64	MS-65	Recent Auction Record
1824, All kinds	3,504,954											
1824, 4 Over Various Dates		189	49.1	21	$750	$1,300	$1,700	$2,150	$3,100	$4,750	$12,000	$11,163, MS-64, June 2014
1824, 4 Over 1		210	47.9	29	750	1,300	1,700	2,150	3,100	4,750	15,000	$9,400, MS-64, November 2013
1824, 4 Over 4 (2 varieties)		284	47.6	19	700	1,200	1,500	2,000	2,950	4,750	12,000	$19,975, MS-65, November 2013
1824, Normal		1,865	48.7	22	600	850	1,150	1,400	2,000	3,450	14,000	$17,625, MS-65, April 2013
1825	2,943,166	2,239	51.5	25	450	700	1,150	1,400	2,000	3,450	12,000	$9,694, MS-66, August 2013
1826	4,004,180	3,235	51.7	27	400	525	1,150	1,400	2,000	3,450	9,500	$34,075, MS-66, November 2013
1827, All kinds	5,493,400											
1827, 7 Over 6		328	50.5	23	600	900	1,500	2,000	3,000	4,000	13,000	$18,800, MS-65, November 2013
1827, Square Base 2		2,566	49.8	19	500	700	1,200	1,475	2,100	3,600	10,000	$8,813, MS-64, June 2014
1827, Curl Base 2		172	47.9	10	500	800	1,500	2,000	2,500	4,000	10,000	$8,813, MS-64, January 2014
1828, All kinds	3,075,200											
1828, Curl Base No Knob 2		649	52.6	24	550	850	1,200	1,500	2,000	3,300	10,000	$15,275, MS-64, November 2013
1828, Curl Base Knob 2		117	49.5	17	700	950	1,300	2,000	2,500	4,500	12,000	$19,975, MS-65, April 2013
1828, Square Base 2, Large 8's		179	49.8	17	550	750	1,150	1,400	2,000	3,300	9,000	$32,900, MS-66, November 2013
1828, Square Base 2, Small 8's, Large Letters		808	49.4	16	525	700	1,150	1,400	2,000	3,300	9,000	$9,400, MS-64, November 2013
1828, Square Base 2, Small 8's and Letters		74	50.3	14	600	750	1,500	1,800	3,000	4,000	11,000	$30,550, MS-65, April 2014
1829, All kinds	3,712,156											
1829, 9 Over 7		453	49.5	22	600	750	1,500	2,300	3,500	6,000	18,000	$70,500, MS-66, November 2013
1829		2,536	49.4	20	400	500	1,000	1,300	2,000	3,050	10,000	$18,213, MS-64, November 2013
1829, Large Letters		41	50.2	22	400	550	1,200	1,400	2,500	3,450	10,500	$194, AU-50, September 2013
1830, All kinds	4,764,800											
1830, Small 0		2,076	49.1	18	375	550	1,000	1,400	2,100	3,350	10,000	$15,863, MS-65, August 2013
1830, Large 0		439	50.9	18	375	550	1,000	1,400	2,100	3,350	10,000	$41,125, MS-66, November 2013
1830, Large Letters		22	38.7	18	9,000	14,000	17,500	20,000	22,000			$2,990, VF-35, October 2011
1831	5,873,660	3,224	52.7	29	375	500	1,000	1,300	2,000	3,000	10,000	$11,750, MS-64, November 2013
1832, All kinds	4,797,000											
1832		3,923	51.3	20	375	500	1,000	1,300	2,000	3,000	10,000	$7,346, MS-65, November 2013
1832, Large Letters		214	49.0	10	375	500	1,000	1,300	2,000	3,000	10,000	$4,406, MS-64, November 2013
1833	5,206,000	2,815	51.6	23	375	500	1,000	1,300	2,000	3,000	10,000	$5,288, MS-64, November 20132012
1834, All kinds	6,412,004											
1834, Large Dt and Letters		1,129	52.4	25	375	500	1,000	1,300	2,000	3,100	9,000	$18,213, MS-65, January 2014
1834, Large Dt, Small Letters		692	49.6	17	375	500	1,000	1,300	2,000	3,100	9,000	$9,988, MS-65, August 2013
1834, Small Dt, Stars, Letters		1,316	48.7	15	375	500	1,000	1,300	2,000	3,100	9,000	$10,281, MS-65, August 2013
1835	5,352,006	1,703	50.1	20	375	500	1,000	1,300	2,000	3,100	9,000	$21,150, MS-65, November 2013
1836, All kinds	6,545,000											
1836		2,597	50.0	21	375	500	1,000	1,300	2,000	3,100	9,000	$19,975, MS-66, June 2014
1836 Over 1336		91	46.5	9	475	700	1,200	1,500	2,500	4,000	10,000	$5,581, MS-64, November 2013
1836, 50 Over 00		130	48.9	18	925	1,500	2,100	2,700	3,900	6,000		$1,645, AU-55, February 2013
1836, Beaded Border on Reverse (b)		66	46.5	15	525	675	1,300	1,600	2,400	3,500	9,500	$999, AU-58, November 2013

b. The same beaded-border reverse die was used for Proofs of 1833, 1834, and 1835 with the crushed edge lettering; all are very rare.

Proof Capped Bust, Lettered Edge, Half Dollars

PF-60 to 70 (Proof). Proofs were made in limited numbers, in most years from 1818 to 1836, for presentation purposes and for distribution to numismatists. True Proofs have deeply mirrored surfaces. Impostors are often seen, with deeply toned surfaces or with patches of mint luster. This situation is more prevalent with half dollars than with any other Capped Bust denomination. There are some crushed-lettered-edge ("CLE") Proofs of the 1833 to 1835 era that are especially beautiful and are more deeply mirrorlike than original issues. Some of these are restrikes (not necessarily an important consideration, but worth noting), believed to have been made at the Mint beginning in the spring of 1859. *Obverse and Reverse:* Proofs of this type have confused experts for a long time (as have large copper cents of the same era). Proofs that were extensively cleaned and therefore have many hairlines, or that are dull and grainy, are lower level, such as PF-60 to 62. While any early Proof half dollar will generate interest among collectors, lower levels are not of great interest to specialists unless they are of rare die varieties. With medium hairlines, an assigned grade of PF-64 may be in order and with relatively few, PF-65. PF-66 should have hairlines so delicate that magnification is needed to see them. Above that, a Proof should be free of such lines. Grading is highly subjective with early Proofs, with eye appeal being a major factor.

Proof Capped Bust, Lettered Edge, Half Dollar
Overton-103.

	Est Mintage	Cert	Finest	PF-63	PF-64	PF-65	Recent Auction Record
1818	3–5	4	PF-66	$50,000	$75,000	$105,000	$100,625, PF-65, April 2011
1820	3–5	1	PF-63	50,000	75,000	105,000	
1821	3–5	3	PF-65	50,000	75,000	105,000	
1822	3–5	4	PF-65	50,000	75,000	105,000	$55,813, PF-64, June 2014
1823	3–5	1	PF-63	50,000	75,000	105,000	$80,500, PF-63, April 2011
1825	3–5	3	PF-66	50,000	75,000	105,000	$32,200, PF-62, May 2008
1826	3–5	4	PF-65	50,000	75,000	105,000	$76,375, PF-65, September 2013
1827	5–8	7	PF-67	50,000	75,000	105,000	$21,150, PF-62, September 2013
1829	6–9	9	PF-66	40,000	65,000	95,000	$102,813, PF-64, January 2014
1830	3–5	2	PF-64	40,000	65,000	95,000	$41,400, PF-64, January 2005
1831	3–5	2	PF-65	40,000	65,000	95,000	$79,313, PF-65, April 2013
1832	6–9	9	PF-68	40,000	65,000	95,000	$29,900, PF-63, January 2008
1833	unverified	1	PF-63				
1833, Crushed Lettered Edge	3–5	3	PF-65	40,000	65,000	95,000	
1834	8–12	11	PF-67	40,000	65,000	95,000	$23,710, PF-63, November 2013
1834, Crushed Lettered Edge	3–5	2	PF-67	40,000	65,000	95,000	
1835	5–8	4	PF-64	40,000	65,000	95,000	$43,125, PF-64, August 2007
1835, Crushed Lettered Edge	3–5	2	PF-65	40,000	65,000	95,000	
1836, Lettered Edge	8–12	16	PF-67	40,000	65,000	95,000	$96,938, PF-66, November 2013
1836, 50 Over 00	3–5	2	PF-64	50,000	80,000	115,000	$81,937, PF-65, October 2006

CAPPED BUST, REEDED EDGE
(1836–1839)

Designer Christian Gobrecht; weight 13.36 grams; composition .900 silver, .100 copper; diameter 30 mm; reeded edge. All coined at Philadelphia.

Reverse 50 CENTS
(1836–1837)

Reverse HALF DOL.
(1838–1839)

History. This half dollar type features a slight restyling of John Reich's Capped Bust design. It is of smaller diameter than the preceding type, and made with a reeded edge. The reverse is of two variations: the 1836–1837, with 50 CENTS; and the 1838–1839, with HALF DOL.

Striking and Sharpness. The key points for observation are the stars on the obverse. On the reverse, check the border letters and the details of the eagle. The 1839-O nearly always shows die cracks, often extensive (these have no effect on desirability or market value).

Availability. The 1836 is rare. The 1838-O is a famous rarity, and the 1839-O is scarce. The others are easily available in nearly any grade desired, with 1837 being the most common.

AU-50, 53, 55, 58 (About Uncirculated). *Obverse and Reverse:* Grading guidelines are the same as for the 1807–1836 type, except on this type the rims are more uniform. On the 1836–1837 dates the reverse rim is generally lower than the obverse, causing the reverse to wear slightly more quickly. On the 1838– 1839 type (with slightly different lettering) the wear occurs evenly on both sides.

MS-60 to 70 (Mint State). *Obverse and Reverse:* Grading guidelines are the same as for the 1807–1836 type, except on this type the rims are more uniform. On the 1836–1837 dates the reverse rim is generally lower than the obverse, causing the reverse to wear slightly more quickly. On the 1838–1839 type (with slightly different lettering) the wear occurs evenly on both sides, and light striking showing areas of the original planchet on the obverse does not occur here.

1839, Regular Letters Reverse 1839, Small Letters Reverse
Shown 1.25x actual size.

	Mintage	Cert	Avg	%MS	AU-50	AU-55	MS-60	MS-62	MS-63	MS-64	MS-65	Recent Auction Record
1836	1,200+	484	43.6	12	$5,000	$6,000	$9,000	$12,000	$19,000	$32,500	$63,500	$52,875, MS-64, November 2013
1837	3,629,820	2,396	53.9	34	475	675	1,200	1,500	2,750	4,500	16,500	$23,500, MS-65, August 2013
1838	3,546,000	1,840	52.2	26	475	675	1,200	1,500	2,750	4,500	18,000	$14,100, MS-64, November 2013
1839	1,392,976	776	51.7	26	500	750	1,400	1,800	3,100	5,250	30,000	$38,188, MS-65, June 2014
1839, Small Letters Reverse (extremely rare)		8	39.6	13	65,000							$50,025, AU-50, January 2010
18390	116,000	554	45.6	14	2,100	2,500	3,500	5,000	6,500	15,000	42,500	$129,250, MS-66, June 2014

Proof Capped Bust, Reeded Edge, Half Dollars

PF-60 to 70 (Proof). Proofs of 1836 are occasionally encountered and are quite rare. Authentic Proofs of 1837 exist but for all practical purposes are unobtainable. Most 1838-O (a rarity) and a few 1839-O have been called branch-mint Proofs. *Obverse and Reverse:* Proofs in grades of PF-60 to 62 show extensive hairlines and cloudiness. At PF-63, hairlines are obvious, but the mirrored fields are attractive. PF-64 and 65 coins have fewer hairlines, but they still are obvious when the coin is slowly turned while held at an angle to the light. PF-66 coins require a magnifier to discern hairlines, and higher grades should have no hairlines.

Proof Capped Bust, Reeded Edge, Half Dollar

	Mintage	Cert	Finest	PF-60	PF-63	PF-64	PF-65	Recent Auction Record
1836, Reeded Edge	10–15	24	PF-65	$30,000	$45,000	$65,000	$90,000	$32,900, PF-63, April 2013
1837	4–6	2	PF-65	30,000	50,000	75,000	100,000	$32,200, PF-62, July 2008
1838	3–5	2	PF-66	30,000	50,000	75,000	100,000	$129,250, PF-64, April 2014
18380 † (a)	20	11	PF-64	500,000	750,000	950,000		$763,750, PF-64, January 2014
1839, Reeded Edge (unverified)	n/a	1	PF-40					
18390	5–10	5	PF-65	100,000	150,000	200,000	250,000	$92,000, PF-63, March 2012

† Ranked in the *100 Greatest U.S. Coins* (fourth edition). **a.** The 1838-O was the first branch-mint half dollar, though it was not mentioned in the Mint director's report. The New Orleans chief coiner stated that only 20 were struck.

LIBERTY SEATED
(1839–1891)

Variety 1, No Motto Above Eagle (1839–1853): Designer Christian Gobrecht; weight 13.36 grams; composition .900 silver, .100 copper; diameter 30.6 mm; reeded edge; mints: Philadelphia, New Orleans.

Variety 2, Arrows at Date, Rays Around Eagle (1853): Designer Christian Gobrecht; weight 12.44 grams; composition .900 silver, .100 copper; diameter 30.6 mm; reeded edge; mints: Philadelphia, New Orleans.

Variety 3, Arrows at Date, No Rays (1854–1855): Designer Christian Gobrecht; weight 12.44 grams; composition .900 silver, .100 copper; diameter 30.6 mm; reeded edge; mints: Philadelphia, New Orleans, San Francisco.

Variety 1 Resumed, With Weight Standard of Variety 2 (1856–1866): Designer Christian Gobrecht; weight 12.44 grams; composition .900 silver, .100 copper; diameter 30.6 mm; reeded edge; mints: Philadelphia, New Orleans, San Francisco.

Variety 4, Motto Above Eagle (1866–1873): Designer Christian Gobrecht; weight 12.44 grams; composition .900 silver, .100 copper; diameter 30.6 mm; reeded edge; mints: Philadelphia, San Francisco, Carson City.

Variety 5, Arrows at Date (1873–1874): Designer Christian Gobrecht; weight 12.50 grams; composition .900 silver, .100 copper; diameter 30.6 mm; reeded edge; mints: Philadelphia, San Francisco, Carson City.

Variety 4 Resumed, With Weight Standard of Variety 5 (1875–1891): Designer Christian Gobrecht; weight 12.50 grams; composition .900 silver, .100 copper; diameter 30.6 mm; reeded edge; mints: Philadelphia, San Francisco, Carson City.

Variety 1
(1839–1853)

Variety 2
(1853)

Variety 3
(1854–1855)

Variety 1, Weight Standard of Variety 2
(1856–1866)

Variety 4
(1866–1873)

Variety 5
(1873–1874)

Variety 4 Resumed, Weight Standard of Variety 5
(1875–1891)

History. Half dollars of the Liberty Seated type were struck every year from 1839 to 1891. The designs varied slightly over the years, but with the basic obverse and reverse motifs remaining the same (e.g., from 1842 to 1853 the coins bore a modified reverse with large letters in the legend, and in 1846 the date size was enlarged).

Large quantities were made until 1879, at which time there was a glut of silver coins in commerce. After that mintages were reduced.

Striking and Sharpness. On the obverse, first check the head of Miss Liberty and the star centers. On coins of the Arrows at Date subtype, especially 1855, the word LIBERTY tends to wear more quickly compared to earlier and later varieties. On the reverse, check the eagle at the lower left. Afterward, check all other features. Generally, the higher-mintage issues are the least well struck, and many New Orleans Mint coins can be lightly struck as well, particularly those in the 1850s. The luster on MS coins usually is very attractive. Resurfaced dies often are proof-like, some with the drapery polished away (as with 1877-S, in particular).

Above and beyond issues of strike, the Small Letters coins of 1839 to 1842 have narrower, lower rims that afforded less protection to the central devices of the reverse. In contrast, the No Motto, Large Letters coins have wider, higher rims that tended to better protect the central devices.

Many pre–Civil War dates, particularly of the 1840s, show evidence of extensive die polishing in the fields (especially evident in the open expanses of the obverse).

From grades of EF downward, sharpness of strike of stars and the head does not matter to connoisseurs.

Availability. Collecting these coins is a popular pursuit with many enthusiasts. Examples of the higher-mintage dates are readily available, with earlier years being much scarcer than later ones. Most often seen among MS coins are issues from the mid-1870s onward. Circulated coins from well worn through AU can be found of most dates and mintmarks; these are avidly sought.

AU-50, 53, 55, 58 (About Uncirculated). *Obverse:* Light wear is seen on the thighs and knees, bosom, and head. There is some luster at AU-50 and 53. At AU-58, the luster is extensive, but incomplete, especially in the right field. *Reverse:* Wear is evident on the eagle's neck, the claws, and the top of the wings. At AU-50 and 53, there are traces of luster. An AU-58 coin has nearly full luster, more so than on the obverse, as the design elements protect the small field areas.

MS-60 to 70 (Mint State). *Obverse:* At MS-60, some abrasion and contact marks are evident, most noticeably on the bosom and thighs and knees. Luster is present, but may be dull or lifeless. At MS-63, contact marks are very few, and abrasion is hard to detect except under magnification. An MS-65 coin has no abrasion, and contact marks are sufficiently minute as to require magnification. Check the knees of Liberty and the right field. Luster should be full and rich. Most MS coins of the 1861 to 1865 years, Philadelphia issues, have extensive die striae (from dies not being completely finished); note that these are raised (whereas cleaning hairlines are incuse). *Reverse:* Comments as preceding, except that in lower MS grades abrasion and contact marks are most noticeable on the eagle's head, neck, and claws, and the top of the wings (harder to see there, however). At MS-65 or higher there are no marks visible to the unaided eye. The field mainly is protected by design elements and on a given coin does not show abrasion as much as does the obverse.

No Drapery From Elbow (1839)

Drapery From Elbow (Starting 1839)

1842, Small Date

1842, Medium Date

1844-O, Doubled Date
FS-50-1844o-301.

Small Letters in Legend
(1839–1841)

1840 (Only), Medium Letters, Large Eagle
Shown 1.25x actual size.

Large Letters in Legend
(1842–1853)

1846, Medium Date

1846, Tall Date

1846-O, Medium Date

1846-O, Tall Date

1847, 7 Over 6
FS-50-1847-301.

1855, 1855 Over 854
FS-50-1855-301.

1861-O, Cracked Obverse Die
FS-50-1861o-401.

1873, Close 3

1873, Open 3

1877, 7 Over 6
FS-50-1877-301.

	Mintage	Cert	Avg	%MS	AU-50	AU-55	MS-60	MS-62	MS-63	MS-64	MS-65	Recent Auction Record
1839, No Drapery From Elbow	*	347	46.0	14	$2,800	$3,600	$6,500	$11,500	$30,000	$70,000	$160,000	$88,125, MS-65, June 2014
1839, Drapery From Elbow	1,972,400	291	52.1	31	350	450	850	1,600	2,300	3,750	18,000	$14,100, MS-65, June 2014
1840, Small Letters	1,435,008	398	52.8	35	300	400	650	875	1,300	2,600	6,000	$21,150, MS-65, August 2013
1840, Medium Letters (a)	**	93	41.2	14	1,600	2,500	3,750	6,000	7,750	13,500	23,500	$55,813, MS-65, April 2014
18400	855,100	188	46.0	19	400	500	900	2,200	3,500	12,000		$10,575, MS-64, August 2013
1841	310,000	129	53.7	30	450	700	1,400	1,900	2,800	4,750	9,000	$7,050, MS-64, November 2013
18410	401,000	213	50.3	30	400	600	950	2,200	3,500	5,500	19,000	$9,283, MS-65, January 2014
1842, Small Date, Small Letters	***	4	38.3	50	7,500	10,000	17,500					$99,875, MS-64, June 2014
18420, Small Date, Small Letters	203,000	85	34.2	1	8,000	10,750	18,500	31,000	39,000			$35,250, MS-62, January 2014
1842, Medium Date	2,012,764	266	51.4	24	325	500	875	1,375	2,100	2,650	7,000	$25,850, MS-66, June 2014
1842, Small Date, Large Letters	**	116	51.7	27	350	675	1,175	1,675	3,450	10,500	23,000	$21,150, MS-65, April 2014
18420, Medium Date, Large Letters	754,000	103	49.4	26	350	585	1,100	2,500	4,250	7,750	17,500	$28,200, MS-67, June 2014
1843	3,844,000	368	52.2	33	250	400	500	775	1,200	2,100	7,750	$44,063, MS-67, November 2013
18430	2,268,000	198	50.4	34	250	400	700	1,300	2,200	4,500	15,000	$3,819, MS-63, November 2013
1844	1,766,000	238	54.1	37	250	400	600	950	1,650	3,400	12,500	$5,141, MS-64, June 2014
18440	2,005,000	178	48.3	29	300	500	900	1,500	2,750	5,000	13,500	$3,055, MS-63, August 2013
18440, Doubled Date (b)	**	66	34.8	3	6,000	7,500	12,000	20,000				$6,463, AU-55, February 2013
1845	589,000	102	50.7	25	400	600	1,000	1,850	3,350	7,500	15,000	$16,450, MS-64, November 2013
18450	2,094,000	213	46.6	23	300	425	725	1,100	2,250	3,500	12,000	$8,813, MS-64, August 2013
18450, No Drapery (c)	**	49	47.0	18	500	600	1,400	3,000	4,800	11,000		$6,463, MS-64, June 2014
1846, All kinds	2,210,000											
1846, Medium Date		165	53.7	30	400	500	800	1,000	1,550	3,500	12,000	$16,450, MS-65, November 2013
1846, Tall Date		128	53.6	32	500	600	900	1,600	2,750	12,000		$47,000, MS-67, November 2013
1846, 6 Over Horizontal 6 (d)		81	46.0	17	1,500	2,250	3,800	7,000	11,000	15,000	25,000	$7,050, MS-62, June 2014
18460, Medium Date	2,304,000	162	43.9	17	300	500	1,050	1,650	3,400	4,500	12,000	$5,581, MS-62, April 2014
18460, Tall Date	**	62	35.6	6	2,500	4,000	7,500	10,000	12,000			$3,819, AU-58, January 2014
1847, 7 Over 6 (e)	*	20	38.9	15	16,000	25,000	30,000	47,500				$9,488, EF-45, October 2011
1847	1,156,000	192	53.5	30	250	400	500	900	1,350	2,600	7,000	$38,188, MS-62, November 2013
18470	2,584,000	147	49.5	30	300	450	800	1,600	2,750	7,500	18,500	$8,813, MS-64, August 2013
1848	580,000	131	54.1	43	500	750	1,000	1,375	1,750	2,800	7,600	$12,925, MS-65, June 2014
18480	3,180,000	163	51.4	27	285	375	875	1,700	2,200	3,700	12,000	$25,850, MS-66, June 2014
1849	1,252,000	199	54.5	35	400	500	975	1,550	2,450	3,750	18,000	$15,275, MS-65, November 2013
18490	2,310,000	138	52.3	28	300	525	850	1,600	2,500	5,150	13,500	$28,200, MS-65, August 2013
1850	227,000	172	53.1	37	1,000	1,200	1,800	2,650	4,000	6,750	19,500	$15,275, MS-65, November 2013
18500	2,456,000	229	56.2	55	300	450	650	950	1,375	3,000	9,000	$25,850, MS-66, August 2013
1851	200,750	130	54.7	51	1,500	1,800	2,500	3,000	4,000	6,000	13,500	$49,938, MS-66, June 2014
18510	402,000	103	54.6	47	350	450	800	1,400	2,000	4,250	12,000	$41,125, MS-66, June 2014
1852	77,130	145	56.6	53	1,400	1,900	2,300	2,750	3,100	4,500	10,000	$15,275, MS-65, August 2013

* Included in number below. ** Included in number above. *** Included in "1842, Medium Date" mintage. **a.** The 1840, Medium Letters, half dollars were struck at the New Orleans Mint from a reverse die of the previous style, without mintmark. **b.** This rare variety shows all four numerals protruding from the rock above the primary date. **c.** The drapery is missing because of excessive polishing of the die. **d.** This variety can be detected in low grades. **e.** Remains of an underlying 6 are visible below and between the primary 4 and 7. "The overdate might not be evident on later die states" (*Cherrypickers' Guide to Rare Die Varieties*, fifth edition, volume II).

	Mintage	Cert	Avg	%MS	AU-50	AU-55	MS-60	MS-62	MS-63	MS-64	MS-65	Recent Auction Record
1852O	144,000	118	43.9	12	$1,400	$2,300	$3,500	$6,250	$10,000	$19,500	$29,500	$15,275, MS-64, August 2013
1853O, Variety 1 (4 known) † (f)		3	27.0	0								$368,000, VF-35, October 2006
1853, Variety 2	3,532,708	2,000	52.4	35	550	700	1,450	2,000	3,500	5,000	22,000	$76,375, MS-66, April 2013
1853O, Variety 2	1,328,000	370	44.3	16	750	1,150	2,750	3,850	6,500	10,000	32,000	$7,344, MS-62, August 2013
1854	2,982,000	723	53.4	32	325	385	650	1,100	1,700	2,600	8,400	$5,288, MS-65, November 2013
1854O	5,240,000	1,170	52.9	37	325	385	650	1,100	1,700	2,600	8,400	$44,063, MS-67, June 2014
1855, All kinds	759,500											
1855, 1855 Over 854		94	48.3	23	675	1,100	2,250	2,600	4,500	6,500	19,000	$15,863, MS-65, August 2013
1855, Normal Date		248	54.1	40	325	385	750	1,100	1,750	2,700	11,000	$38,188, MS-66, November 2013
1855O	3,688,000	917	54.0	40	325	385	750	1,100	1,750	2,500	9,500	$14,100, MS-66, August 2013
1855S	129,950	120	31.6	4	7,600	10,500	24,000	35,000	—			$16,450, AU-58, March 2014
1856	938,000	210	54.3	44	225	350	500	865	1,100	2,150	5,750	$5,288, MS-65, August 2013
1856O	2,658,000	505	53.2	40	225	350	500	865	1,100	2,250	6,000	$7,638, MS-66, August 2013
1856S	211,000	94	43.7	7	1,275	2,300	4,250	8,000	13,000			$2,938, AU-55, November 2013
1857	1,988,000	360	53.2	37	250	325	500	825	1,100	2,000	4,800	$8,813, MS-66, June 2014
1857O	818,000	143	49.0	17	300	450	1,050	2,150	3,500	6,000	12,000	$9,400, MS-64, August 2013
1857S	158,000	91	43.0	10	1,350	2,300	4,850	12,000	18,000	23,000	35,000	$61,688, MS-66, June 2014
1858	4,225,700	913	53.7	35	225	350	450	775	1,100	1,950	5,100	$7,050, MS-65, August 2013
1858O	7,294,000	744	49.4	26	225	350	475	800	1,200	2,150	10,000	$15,275, MS-65, January 2013
1858S	476,000	151	47.6	19	450	600	1,100	2,500	4,000	7,900	12,000	$3,525, MS-63, August 2013
1859	747,200	291	54.0	37	250	325	500	825	1,100	2,000	5,250	$3,525, MS-64, January 2013
1859O	2,834,000	403	50.5	28	225	300	450	850	1,275	2,700	7,500	$12,925, MS-65, August 2013
1859S	566,000	151	53.8	40	350	500	1,050	2,100	3,000	6,000	14,500	$7,638, MS-65, February 2013
1860	302,700	179	56.0	47	275	375	600	875	1,100	2,250	5,400	$52,875, MS-67, June 2014
1860O	1,290,000	430	54.6	46	250	325	475	900	1,300	2,500	6,000	$12,925, MS-66, June 2014
1860S	472,000	150	52.3	33	300	500	1,000	2,500	3,500	6,500	15,000	$12,925, MS-64, August 2013
1861	2,887,400	805	57.2	54	235	410	525	775	1,100	2,250	5,250	$17,625, MS-66, August 2013
1861O (g)	2,532,633	508	53.7	47	275	350	500	1,000	1,500	2,500	5,500	$5,581, AU-55, September 2013
1861O, Cracked Obverse (h)	**	52	38.4	8	2,500	3,500	4,500	13,000	—			$11,750, AU-58, September 2013
1861S	939,500	165	51.7	38	300	500	775	1,800	2,350	4,500	13,500	$17,625, MS-65, November 2013
1862	253,000	175	56.4	57	400	600	800	950	1,300	2,500	6,000	$28,200, MS-67, April 2013
1862S	1,352,000	186	47.8	28	275	500	750	1,600	2,400	5,500	15,000	$11,163, MS-64, November 2013
1863	503,200	179	56.6	64	350	575	800	900	1,175	2,350	5,750	$23,500, MS-66, August 2013
1863S	916,000	232	52.4	38	265	450	700	1,150	1,975	4,200	14,000	$9,106, MS-65, June 2014
1864	379,100	190	54.8	59	550	650	1,000	1,250	1,600	2,500	8,000	$8,519, MS-65, August 2013
1864S	658,000	115	44.8	23	400	575	900	2,200	3,100	6,000	15,000	$3,819, MS-63, August 2013
1865	511,400	141	53.9	44	500	700	1,100	1,500	2,000	3,000	7,000	$22,325, MS-66, August 2013
1865S	675,000	132	47.9	34	500	800	1,200	1,800	2,900	7,000	75,000	$9,106, MS-62, August 2013
1866S, Variety 1	60,000	174	28.1	6	3,400	4,400	6,000	11,750	20,000	33,500	65,000	$164,500, MS-67, November 2013
1866, Variety 4	744,900	188	52.6	49	235	325	500	900	1,350	2,700	5,850	$28,200, MS-67, June 2014
1866S, Variety 4	994,000	116	48.9	33	275	450	675	1,375	2,250	5,250	13,000	$14,100, MS-66, June 2014
1867	449,300	116	53.4	42	300	500	700	1,500	2,000	4,000	8,000	$3,496, MS-64, August 2013
1867S	1,196,000	162	50.7	28	300	500	775	1,650	2,300	5,750	12,500	$9,106, MS-65, January 2014
1868	417,600	111	50.8	38	400	600	800	1,000	1,500	3,150	7,000	$4,113, MS-65, April 2013
1868S	1,160,000	122	51.6	23	275	450	800	1,400	1,800	3,750	9,500	$3,525, MS-64, August 2013
1869	795,300	260	53.5	40	250	375	525	865	1,300	2,100	5,600	$14,100, MS-65, June 2014
1869S	656,000	112	50.8	38	300	450	825	1,750	2,600	4,750	7,500	$18,800, MS-67, June 2014
1870	633,900	162	51.9	36	225	350	500	800	1,250	2,800	6,000	$25,850, MS-67, January 2014
1870CC	54,617	170	21.9	1	32,000	42,500	85,000	160,000	—			$88,125, MS-61, January 2014
1870S	1,004,000	91	45.8	20	450	500	1,200	2,200	3,750	6,500	15,000	$67,563, MS-65, January 2014
1871	1,203,600	271	55.1	45	250	325	500	775	1,150	2,300	5,350	$4,113, MS-65, August 2013
1871CC	153,950	157	30.0	3	5,000	7,500	15,000	35,000	55,000	90,000		$17,038, MS-61, January 2014
1871S	2,178,000	205	49.6	26	250	300	600	1,000	1,500	2,850	7,000	$6,463, MS-65, September 2013
1872	880,600	139	52.7	39	285	300	500	900	1,400	2,750	5,500	$21,150, MS-66, June 2014
1872CC	257,000	213	31.8	2	4,250	6,300	20,000	35,000	70,000	140,000		$57,281, MS-63, June 2014
1872S	580,000	100	48.9	30	400	600	1,300	2,500	3,000	6,000	13,000	$29,375, MS-67, June 2014
1873, Close 3, Variety 4	587,000	158	49.1	28	300	350	620	900	1,200	2,000	5,100	$1,645, MS-63, June 2013

** Included in number above. † Ranked in the *100 Greatest U.S. Coins* (fourth edition). **f.** Value in F-12 is $350,000; in VF-20, $500,000. **g.** The 1861-O mintage includes 330,000 half dollars struck by the United States government; 1,240,000 struck for the State of Louisiana after it seceded from the Union; and 962,633 struck after Louisiana joined the Confederate States of America. All of these coins were made from federal dies, rendering it impossible to distinguish one from another with but one exception. **h.** In 1861, the New Orleans Mint used a federal obverse die and a Confederate reverse die to strike a handful of Confederate half dollars. That particular obverse die was also paired with a regular federal reverse die to strike some 1861-O half dollars, which today are popular among collectors, especially in higher grades. Their identifying feature is a die crack running from the denticles to the right of the sixth star down to Miss Liberty's nose (and to her shoulder below her jaw).

Chart continued on next page.

	Mintage	Cert	Avg	%MS	AU-50	AU-55	MS-60	MS-62	MS-63	MS-64	MS-65	Recent Auction Record
1873, Open 3, Variety 4	214,200	49	28.8	10	$12,000	$16,000	$21,000	$35,000	$50,000			$6,463, EF-35, July 2014
1873CC, Variety 4	122,500	151	32.7	13	4,500	9,000	11,000	17,500	37,000	$45,000	$65,000	$14,100, MS-62, August 2013
1873S, Variety 4 (i)	5,000	n/a	n/a	n/a								
1873, Variety 5	1,815,200	532	53.7	45	425	525	950	1,350	1,950	3,400	17,500	$8,225, MS-64, July 2014
1873CC, Variety 5	214,560	286	36.7	12	3,750	5,000	7,500	12,500	20,000	30,000	52,000	$42,594, MS-65, March 2014
1873S, Variety 5	228,000	99	46.0	15	750	1,400	2,500	4,000	6,000	17,000	35,000	$18,800, MS-64, August 2013
1874	2,359,600	655	54.9	48	400	525	950	1,350	1,875	3,300	17,000	$30,550, MS-66, August 2013
1874CC	59,000	159	34.2	16	8,250	11,500	15,000	21,000	28,000	46,000	77,500	$32,900, MS-64, May 2013
1874S	394,000	114	51.8	37	700	975	1,700	2,500	3,500	5,450	25,000	$39,656, MS-66, November 2013
1875	6,026,800	642	56.7	58	200	250	475	600	800	1,350	4,000	$7,050, MS-66, June 2014
1875CC	1,008,000	314	49.0	42	375	600	900	1,900	2,400	4,000	8,500	$35,250, MS-66, June 2014
1875S	3,200,000	563	59.7	74	200	250	475	600	800	1,350	4,000	$22,325, MS-67, April 2013
1876	8,418,000	726	55.3	54	200	250	475	600	800	1,350	4,000	$7,344, MS, March 2014
1876CC	1,956,000	415	48.8	37	300	525	725	1,400	1,500	2,850	5,100	$15,275, MS-65, August 2013
1876S	4,528,000	400	57.6	61	200	250	475	600	800	1,350	4,000	$3,055, MS-65, August 2013
1877	8,304,000	599	55.7	60	200	250	475	600	800	1,350	4,000	$4,994, MS-66, August 2013
1877, 7 Over 6 (j)	**	6	57.0	67	1,350	2,000	3,000	6,000	12,000	25,000		$3,335, MS-62, August 2009
1877CC	1,420,000	457	53.3	63	350	500	800	1,200	2,000	2,600	5,000	$7,050, MS-66, August 2013
1877S	5,356,000	919	57.7	62	200	250	475	600	800	1,350	4,000	$12,338, MS-67, November 2013
1878	1,377,600	222	54.7	52	200	250	485	620	850	1,750	4,250	$21,150, MS-66, June 2014
1878CC	62,000	139	25.0	12	5,000	7,200	9,000	19,000	22,500	32,500	50,000	$64,625, MS-65, June 2014
1878S	12,000	40	39.6	48	70,000	75,000	80,000	100,000	160,000	145,000	195,000	$199,750, MS-64, June 2014
1879	4,800	617	61.8	87	675	700	850	950	1,150	1,650	4,000	$12,925, MS-67, June 2013
1880	8,400	229	58.4	78	675	700	850	950	1,150	1,650	4,000	$5,581, MS-66, July 2014
1881	10,000	249	56.0	71	675	700	850	950	1,150	1,800	4,250	$9,400, MS-67, June 2014
1882	4,400	172	57.1	75	675	700	850	950	1,150	1,800	4,250	$8,225, MS-67, August 2013
1883	8,000	226	55.1	65	675	700	850	1,000	1,225	1,650	4,000	$8,813, MS-66, August 2013
1884	4,400	225	60.6	83	850	1,000	1,100	1,300	1,500	1,800	4,000	$15,275, MS-67, June 2014
1885	5,200	176	55.8	72	850	900	950	1,000	1,300	1,750	4,250	$8,813, MS-67, February 2014
1886	5,000	213	57.8	77	900	1,000	1,100	1,300	1,500	1,800	4,250	$2,115, MS-64, August 2013
1887	5,000	239	58.1	74	875	950	1,000	1,200	1,400	1,850	4,250	$24,675, MS-67, June 2014
1888	12,001	282	56.8	71	650	675	800	950	1,150	1,750	4,000	$9,988, MS-67, April 2014
1889	12,000	260	56.9	72	650	675	800	950	1,150	1,650	4,000	$8,225, MS-66, June 2013
1890	12,000	206	59.3	79	650	675	800	950	1,150	1,650	4,000	$21,738, MS-68, June 2014
1891	200,000	381	58.1	70	225	275	450	625	775	1,350	4,000	$9,400, MS-66, January 2014

** Included in number above. **i.** The 1873-S, No Arrows, half dollar is unknown in any collection. **j.** The top portion of a 6 is visible on the upper surface of the last 7.

Proof Liberty Seated Half Dollars

PF-60 to 70 (Proof). Proofs were made in most years, with production beginning in a particularly significant way in 1858, when an estimated 210 silver sets were sold. Today, Proofs are readily available from 1858 through 1891. Quality often is lacking, with lint marks seen on some issues of the late 1850s and early 1860s. Light striking is occasionally seen on the star centers and the head of Miss Liberty; connois- seurs avoid these, but most buyers will not be aware. Slide marks (usually seen on the right knee) from coin albums can be a problem, more so on Liberty Seated half dollars than on smaller denominations of this design. *Obverse and Reverse:* Proofs that are extensively cleaned and have many hairlines, or that are dull and grainy, are lower level, such as PF-60 to 62. These are not widely desired, save for the low-mintage (in circulation-strike format) years from 1879 to 1891. With medium hairlines and good reflectivity, an assigned grade of PF-64 is appropriate, and with relatively few hairlines, PF-65. In various grades hairlines are most easily seen in the obverse field. PF-66 should have hairlines so delicate that magnification is needed to see them. Above that, a Proof should be free of such lines.

Proof Liberty Seated Half Dollar, Variety 1, No Motto Above Eagle (1839–1852, 1856–1866)

Proof Liberty Seated Half Dollar, Variety 2, Arrows at Date, Rays Around Eagle (1853)

Proof Liberty Seated Half Dollar, Variety 3, Arrows at Date, No Rays
(1854–1855)

Proof Liberty Seated Half Dollar, Variety 4, Motto Above Eagle
(1866–1873, 1875–1891)

Proof Liberty Seated Half Dollar, Variety 5, Arrows at Date
(1873–1874)

1866, No Motto, Irregular Issue
Judd-538.

	Mintage	Cert	Finest	PF-60	PF-63	PF-64	PF-65	Recent Auction Record
1839, No Drapery From Elbow	4–6	7	PF-65	$100,000	$135,000	$175,000	$250,000	$223,250, PF-64, November 2013
1839, With Drap From Elbow	unverified	1	PF-64		115,000	175,000	250,000	$184,000, PF-64, April 2008
1840, Small Letters	4–8	10	PF-65			75,000	100,000	$30,550, PF-63, November 2013
1841	4–8	7	PF-65	20,000	45,000	65,000	85,000	$30,550, PF-64, September 2013
1842, Small Date, Large Letters	4–8	7	PF-66	15,000	27,500	37,500	60,000	$44,063, PF-66, June 2014
1843	4–8	6	PF-66	15,000	27,500	37,500	60,000	$70,500, PF-65Cam, August 2013
1844	3–6	2	PF-66			80,000	125,000	$149,500, PF-66Cam, January 2008
1845	3–6	3	PF-66	15,000	30,000	42,500	67,500	$57,500, PF-64, May 2008
1846, Medium Letters	15–20	20	PF-65	11,000	21,000	32,500	50,000	$23,500, PF-63, January 2014
1847	15–20	20	PF-66	11,000	21,000	32,500	50,000	$12,338, PF-63, August 2013
1848	4–8	4	PF-66	13,000	27,500	37,500	60,000	$34,075, PF-64, June 2014
1849	4–8	7	PF-66	13,000	27,500	37,500	60,000	$70,500, PF-66, January 2014
1850	4–8	6	PF-66	13,000	27,500	37,500	60,000	$20,125, PF-64, July 2009
1852	3–6	3	PF-65		35,000	50,000	85,000	$74,750, PF-65, July 2008
1852O	2–3	1	PF-62		37,500	55,000		$24,150, PF-62, May 2001
1853, Arrows and Rays	5–10	9	PF-66		50,000	85,000	150,000	$184,000, PF-65, January 2012
1854, Arrows	15–20	26	PF-66	8,500	13,500	22,500	30,000	$70,500, PF-67, November 2013
1855, Arrows	15–20	16	PF-66	7,500	12,500	21,500	35,000	$41,125, PF-66Cam, June 2014
1855S	2–3	1	PF-65		150,000			$276,000, PF-65, August 2011
1855, 55 Over 54	1–2	n/a	n/a	10,000	22,000	35,000	60,000	$30,550, PF-64, June 2014
1856	20–30	40	PF-67	4,000	6,500	12,000	23,000	$17,625, PF-65, November 2013
1857	30–50	78	PF-67	3,000	4,500	8,250	27,500	$23,500, PF-66, June 2013
1858	300+	117	PF-68	1,400	2,250	3,800	8,000	$25,850, PF-67, June 2014
1859	800	293	PF-67	1,150	1,600	3,600	7,250	$18,213, PF-66Cam, November 2013
1860	1,000	279	PF-67	750	1,600	3,000	5,900	$38,188, PF, August 2013
1861	1,000	212	PF-67	750	1,600	3,000	5,900	$28,200, PF, August 2013
1862	550	372	PF-67	750	1,600	3,000	5,900	$23,500, PF-66, November 2013
1863	460	287	PF-69	750	1,600	3,000	5,900	$8,225, PF-65Cam, September 2013
1864	470	338	PF-68	750	1,600	3,000	5,900	$52,875, PF-66DCam, June 2014
1865	500	366	PF-68	750	1,600	3,000	5,900	$76,375, PF-66DCam, April 2013
1866, No Motto † (a)	1	1	PF-62		(unique)			
1866, With Motto	725	291	PF-68	700	1,500	1,900	3,900	$14,100, PF-66Cam, November 2013
1867	625	331	PF-67	700	1,500	2,000	4,000	$32,900, PF-67DCam, June 2014
1868	600	329	PF-68	700	1,500	1,900	3,900	$17,625, PF-66Cam, September 2013
1869	600	337	PF-68	700	1,500	1,900	3,900	$21,150, PF-67Cam, April 2013
1870	1,000	318	PF-67	700	1,350	1,900	3,800	$21,150, PF-67, June 2014
1871	960	313	PF-68	700	1,300	1,900	3,800	$8,930, PF-67Cam, February 2013
1872	950	320	PF-68	700	1,300	1,900	3,800	$8,813, PF-66DCam, April 2014
1873	600	373	PF-68	700	1,300	1,900	3,800	$12,925, PF-66, June 2014
1873, Arrows	500	310	PF-67	900	2,650	4,000	13,000	$35,250, PF-66, June 2014

† Ranked in the *100 Greatest U.S. Coins* (fourth edition). **a.** Classified as Judd-538 (*United States Pattern Coins*, 10th edition). This fantasy piece was deliberately struck for pharmacist and coin collector Robert Coulton Davis, likely around 1869 or in the early 1870s, along with the No Motto Proof quarter and dollar of the same date.

Chart continued on next page.

	Mintage	Cert	Finest	PF-60	PF-63	PF-64	PF-65	Recent Auction Record
1874	700	448	PF-68	$900	$2,650	$4,000	$13,000	$58,750, PF-67, April 2013
1875	700	303	PF-68	700	1,300	1,800	3,600	$8,813, PF, August 2013
1876	1,150	443	PF-67	700	1,300	1,800	3,600	$23,500, PF-67Cam, June 2014
1877	510	301	PF-66	700	1,300	1,800	3,600	$11,163, PF-66Cam, January 2014
1878	800	447	PF-68	700	1,300	1,800	3,600	$11,750, PF-67Cam, November 2013
1879	1,100	682	PF-68	700	1,300	1,800	3,600	$30,550, PF-68, June 2014
1880	1,355	784	PF-67	700	1,300	1,800	3,600	$8,813, PF-66Cam, January 2014
1881	975	648	PF-68	700	1,300	1,800	3,600	$8,813, PF-66Cam, November 2013
1882	1,100	667	PF-68	700	1,300	1,800	3,600	$15,275, PF-67Cam, November 2013
1883	1,039	685	PF-68	700	1,300	1,800	3,600	$12,925, PF-67Cam, April 2013
1884	875	480	PF-68	700	1,300	1,800	3,600	$9,988, PF-67Cam, November 2013
1885	930	592	PF-68	700	1,300	1,800	3,600	$12,925, PF-68, June 2014
1886	886	503	PF-68	700	1,300	1,800	3,600	$8,813, PF-67, July 2014
1887	710	407	PF-68	700	1,300	1,800	3,600	$29,375, PF-68DCam, November 2013
1888	832	423	PF-68	700	1,300	1,800	3,600	$14,688, PF, March 2014
1889	711	384	PF-67	700	1,300	1,800	3,600	$7,638, PF-66Cam, February 2013
1890	590	439	PF-68	700	1,300	1,800	3,600	$19,975, PF-67DCam, March 2013
1891	600	415	PF-68	700	1,300	1,800	3,600	$10,281, PF-66Cam, November 2013

BARBER OR LIBERTY HEAD
(1892–1915)

Designer Charles E. Barber; weight 12.50 grams; composition .900 silver, .100 copper; diameter 30.6 mm; reeded edge; mints: Philadelphia, Denver, New Orleans, San Francisco.

History. Charles E. Barber, chief engraver of the U.S. Mint, crafted the eponymous "Barber" or Liberty Head half dollars along with similarly designed dimes and quarters of the same era. Barber's initial, B, is at the truncation of Miss Liberty's neck. Production of the coins was continuous from 1892 to 1915, stopping a year before the Barber dime and quarter.

Striking and Sharpness. On the obverse, check the hair details and other features. On the reverse, the eagle's leg at the lower right and the arrows often are weak, and there can be weakness at the upper right of the shield and the nearby wing area. At EF and below, sharpness of strike on the reverse is not important.

Availability. Most examples seen in the marketplace are well worn. There are no rarities, although some are scarcer than others. Coins that are Fine or better are much scarcer—in particular the San Francisco Mint issues of 1901, 1904, and 1907. MS coins are available of all dates and mints, but some are very elusive.

AU-50, 53, 55, 58 (About Uncirculated). *Obverse:* Light wear is seen on the head, especially on the forward hair under LIBERTY. There is some luster at AU-50 and 53. At AU-58, the luster is extensive but incomplete, especially on the higher parts and in the right field. *Reverse:* Wear is seen on the head and tail of the eagle and on the tips of the wings. At AU-50 and 53, there is significant luster. An AU-58 coin (as determined by the obverse) can have the reverse appear to be full MS.

MS-60 to 70 (Mint State). *Obverse:* At MS-60, some abrasion and contact marks are evident, most noticeably on the cheek and the obverse field to the right. Luster is present, but may be dull or lifeless. Many Barber coins have been cleaned, especially of the earlier dates. At MS-63, contact marks are very few; abrasion still is evident but less than at lower levels. An MS-65 coin may have minor abrasion, but contact marks are so minute as to require magnification. Luster should be full and rich. *Reverse:* Comments apply as for the obverse, except that in lower MS grades abrasion and contact marks are most noticeable on the head and tail of the eagle and on the tips of the wings. At MS-65 or higher there are no marks visible to the unaided eye. The field is mainly protected by design elements, so the reverse often appears to grade a point or two higher than the obverse.

1892-O, Normal O

1892-O, Micro O
FS-50-1892o-501.

1909-S, Inverted Mintmark
FS-50-1909S-501.

1911-S, Repunched Mintmark
FS-50-1911S-501.

	Mintage	Cert	Avg	%MS	AU-50	AU-55	MS-60	MS-62	MS-63	MS-64	MS-65	Recent Auction Record
1892	934,000	2,041	59.3	71	$350	$425	$525	$725	$1,000	$1,400	$2,800	$21,150, MS-67, August 2013
18920	390,000	756	38.2	33	750	775	900	1,100	1,600	2,500	3,700	$108,688, MS-66, April 2013
18920, Micro 0 (a)	*	59	23.3	24	18,500	20,000	28,000	34,500	40,000	60,000	80,000	$36,014, MS-63, June 2014
1892S	1,029,028	598	35.0	29	700	800	975	1,500	2,250	2,700	4,500	$11,163, MS-66, June 2014
1893	1,826,000	584	55.0	53	325	350	550	850	1,200	2,000	4,300	$18,800, MS-67, August 2013
18930	1,389,000	449	51.3	53	425	525	700	1,000	1,500	2,250	8,500	$3,232, MS-64, June 2014
1893S	740,000	418	29.5	23	650	850	1,900	2,500	4,500	9,000	22,000	$11,750, MS-65, February 2013
1894	1,148,000	405	51.8	55	375	425	550	750	1,100	1,600	3,000	$16,450, MS-65, August 2013
18940	2,138,000	400	50.6	55	375	425	550	750	1,100	1,750	5,400	$6,169, MS-65, February 2013
1894S	4,048,690	494	48.1	45	375	475	600	1,000	1,500	2,750	8,500	$7,638, MS-65, August 2013
1895	1,834,338	432	52.7	50	400	475	575	800	1,000	1,600	3,200	$23,500, MS-66, April 2013
18950	1,766,000	301	44.7	39	385	500	625	1,000	1,300	2,500	6,000	$32,900, MS-67, June 2014
1895S	1,108,086	351	53.0	63	385	500	625	1,000	1,400	2,750	6,500	$25,850, MS-67, June 2014
1896	950,000	317	49.3	52	365	450	575	750	1,000	2,200	5,000	$17,625, MS-66, April 2013
18960	924,000	262	30.1	15	825	975	1,650	2,900	6,500	13,000	20,000	$17,625, MS-64, August 2013
1896S	1,140,948	367	32.2	27	825	975	1,550	2,500	3,700	5,500	9,500	$9,400, MS-65, February 2013
1897	2,480,000	474	53.4	52	375	475	575	750	1,000	1,200	3,250	$12,925, MS-66, April 2013
18970	632,000	516	21.5	15	1,300	1,450	2,000	3,100	4,000	5,750	8,000	$11,899, MS-66, April 2013
1897S	933,900	487	26.8	20	1,100	1,300	1,900	2,900	3,750	4,900	6,750	$6,463, MS-64, August 2013
1898	2,956,000	494	52.4	52	375	475	575	650	1,000	1,400	3,200	$18,800, MS-66, January 2014
18980	874,000	312	36.0	28	650	850	1,200	2,300	3,200	4,200	8,000	$15,863, MS-66, June 2014
1898S	2,358,550	292	41.5	23	450	650	925	2,500	3,600	7,000	9,000	$12,925, MS-66, August 2013
1899	5,538,000	729	51.6	47	375	475	575	700	1,000	1,300	3,400	$2,371, MS, February 2014
18990	1,724,000	329	42.9	39	400	500	685	975	1,600	3,500	7,500	$8,813, MS-66, February 2013
1899S	1,686,411	292	46.4	34	400	500	685	1,375	2,150	3,200	5,900	$6,463, MS-66, January 2014
1900	4,762,000	696	53.6	54	375	475	575	700	1,000	1,300	3,300	$6,756, MS-66, March 2013
19000	2,744,000	266	39.5	24	435	600	875	2,100	3,400	6,000	13,000	$11,163, MS-65, April 2013
1900S	2,560,322	311	47.8	28	375	500	650	1,500	2,400	4,000	8,100	$3,450, MS-64, August 2013
1901	4,268,000	660	51.5	42	375	450	550	800	1,000	1,300	3,700	$12,925, MS-66, June 2014
19010	1,124,000	203	37.8	31	475	625	1,350	3,000	4,850	9,000	13,500	$21,150, MS-66, June 2014
1901S	847,044	281	30.6	17	1,250	1,700	2,250	5,000	10,000	12,500	15,500	$30,550, MS-67, June 2014
1902	4,922,000	612	50.0	42	375	450	550	800	1,000	1,300	3,750	$3,055, MS-65, April 2014
19020	2,526,000	280	45.2	34	400	550	800	1,900	3,550	5,000	9,200	$4,113, MS-64, September 2013
1902S	1,460,670	192	45.5	38	400	550	800	1,500	2,800	4,800	7,750	$25,850, MS-67, April 2013
1903	2,278,000	278	49.1	43	375	450	550	1,000	1,500	3,100	7,200	$8,225, MS-65, May 2013
19030	2,100,000	368	50.6	49	400	500	675	1,175	1,600	3,200	8,200	$12,925, MS-66, August 2013
1903S	1,920,772	261	47.6	49	400	500	675	1,300	1,700	3,000	4,900	$3,290, MS-64, June 2014
1904	2,992,000	427	50.6	42	375	450	550	900	1,100	1,400	4,100	$15,275, MS-66, June 2014
19040	1,117,600	234	39.7	28	600	900	1,250	2,150	3,750	6,500	10,750	$25,850, MS-66, June 2014
1904S	553,038	448	23.8	10	2,300	4,800	9,500	16,000	19,500	23,500	39,000	$64,625, MS-66, August 2013
1905	662,000	292	48.0	44	375	450	600	1,100	1,600	3,200	5,500	$5,288, MS-66, January 2014
19050	505,000	344	47.1	54	450	550	750	1,200	1,750	2,250	4,200	$7,638, MS-66, November 2013
1905S	2,494,000	311	41.9	30	400	500	650	1,300	1,950	3,700	8,500	$9,694, MS-65, August 2013
1906	2,638,000	721	53.7	57	375	400	550	750	1,000	1,250	3,200	$4,406, MS-66, June 2014
1906D	4,028,000	618	49.9	45	375	400	550	750	1,000	1,250	3,200	$5,581, MS-66, November 2013
19060	2,446,000	299	43.7	35	400	500	625	1,000	1,400	2,750	5,500	$28,200, MS-67, June 2013
1906S	1,740,154	286	51.8	53	375	475	625	1,000	1,400	3,000	4,750	$6,463, MS-66, June 2013
1907	2,598,000	649	54.6	61	375	450	550	800	1,000	1,300	3,000	$19,975, MS-66, September 2013
1907D	3,856,000	689	50.7	48	375	450	550	800	1,000	1,300	3,000	$25,850, MS-67, April 2013
19070	3,946,600	586	51.2	51	375	450	550	800	1,000	1,300	3,000	$12,925, MS-67, June 2014
1907S	1,250,000	256	40.2	32	650	900	1,275	2,700	5,700	9,000	11,000	$38,188, MS-67, June 2014
1908	1,354,000	409	53.8	58	375	450	550	750	1,000	1,150	3,000	$4,553, MS-66, December 2013
1908D	3,280,000	714	51.2	50	375	450	550	750	1,000	1,150	2,800	$9,988, MS-66, November 2013
19080	5,360,000	734	48.3	49	375	450	550	750	1,000	1,150	2,800	$16,450, MS-67, January 2014
1908S	1,644,828	252	41.8	35	435	650	875	1,500	2,400	4,200	5,100	$7,050, MS-66, August 2013
1909	2,368,000	943	51.5	57	375	450	550	750	1,000	1,350	3,250	$5,875, MS-66, August 2013
19090	925,400	337	37.2	31	650	950	1,400	1,500	1,650	3,000	4,800	$4,994, MS-65, August 2013

* Included in number above. **a.** This variety "was created when an 0 mintmark punch for quarters was used in place of the regular, larger mintmark intended for use on half dollar dies. . . . Many examples show strong strike doubling on reverse" (*Cherrypickers' Guide to Rare Die Varieties,* fifth edition, volume II).

Chart continued on next page.

	Mintage	Cert	Avg	%MS	AU-50	AU-55	MS-60	MS-62	MS-63	MS-64	MS-65	Recent Auction Record
1909S	1,764,000	336	39.9	34	$375	$450	$600	$950	$1,300	$2,700	$4,100	$4,847, MS-66, August 2013
1909S, Inverted Mintmark (b)	*	8	35.1	25	425	500	675	1,150	1,550			$101, F-15, February 2014
1910	418,000	382	47.7	49	410	500	600	850	1,100	1,400	3,400	$11,163, MS-66, January 2014
1910S	1,948,000	328	42.6	34	375	475	650	1,500	2,000	3,000	5,750	$7,638, MS-66, June 2014
1911	1,406,000	731	55.1	63	375	400	550	625	1,000	1,300	2,900	$4,406, MS-66, February 2014
1911D	695,080	367	51.3	56	375	400	550	625	1,000	1,300	3,500	$2,350, MS-65, December 2013
1911S	1,272,000	280	39.6	33	385	450	650	1,050	1,500	2,650	5,200	$6,169, AU-58, November 2013
1911S, Repunched Mintmark (c)	*	3	61.3	67	475	550	750	1,200	1,600	3,150	5,400	$4,888, MS-65, December 2009
1912	1,550,000	814	53.0	60	375	400	550	625	1,000	1,300	2,900	$2,350, MS-65, June 2014
1912D	2,300,800	1,135	52.7	56	375	400	550	625	1,000	1,300	2,900	$9,400, MS-66, August 2013
1912S	1,370,000	529	44.6	44	425	475	600	850	1,150	2,200	4,100	$5,288, MS-66, June 2014
1913	188,000	1,153	17.6	10	825	975	1,350	1,500	2,000	3,000	4,500	$8,813, MS-66, June 2014
1913D	534,000	544	53.2	53	375	400	550	625	1,000	1,300	4,350	$12,925, MS-66, June 2014
1913S	604,000	347	44.4	46	400	475	635	1,000	1,375	2,450	3,900	$15,275, MS-66, June 2014
1914	124,230	1,199	21.4	17	900	1,000	1,400	1,700	2,100	3,000	7,500	$6,756, MS-65, August 2013
1914S	992,000	443	43.5	41	400	450	600	900	1,150	2,100	4,350	$11,750, MS-66, August 2013
1915	138,000	1,474	15.9	8	850	1,000	1,350	1,650	2,250	4,000	5,750	$7,050, MS-65, June 2013
1915D	1,170,400	1,269	54.5	59	375	400	550	650	1,000	1,200	3,200	$7,050, MS-66, November 2013
1915S	1,604,000	973	48.6	50	375	400	550	650	1,000	1,200	3,200	$8,225, MS-66, February 2013

* Included in number above. **b.** The S mintmark was punched into the die upside-down (with the top slightly wider than the base). **c.** The lower serif of the underlying mintmark is visible protruding from the primary serif.

Proof Barber Half Dollars

PF-60 to 70 (Proof). Proof Barber half dollars exist in proportion to their mintages. Choicer examples tend to be of later dates, similar to other Barber coins. Most are sharply struck, although many are weak on the eagle's leg at the lower right and on certain parts of the arrows and/or the upper right of the shield and the nearby wing. The Proofs of 1892 to 1901 usually have cameo contrast between the designs and the mirror fields. Those of 1914 and 1915 often have extensive hairlines or other problems. *Obverse and Reverse:* Proofs that are extensively cleaned and have many hairlines, or that are dull and grainy, are lower level, such as PF-60 to 62; these are not widely desired. With medium hairlines and good reflectivity, an assigned grade of PF-64 is appropriate. Tiny horizontal lines on Miss Liberty's cheek, known as slide marks, from National and other album slides scuffing the relief of the cheek, are endemic on all Barber silver coins. With noticeable marks of this type, the highest grade assignable is PF-64. With relatively few hairlines, a rating of PF-65 can be given. PF-66 should have hairlines so delicate that magnification is needed to see them. Above that, a Proof should be free of any hairlines or other problems.

Proof Barber Half Dollar

	Mintage	Cert	Finest	PF-60	PF-63	PF-64	PF-65	Recent Auction Record
1892	1,245	744	PF-68	$600	$1,200	$1,800	$3,450	$10,281, PF-67Cam, September 2013
1893	792	533	PF-68	600	1,200	1,800	3,450	$8,813, PF-67Cam, February 2014
1894	972	670	PF-68	600	1,200	1,800	3,450	$7,050, PF-67Cam, November 2013
1895	880	623	PF-69	600	1,200	1,800	3,450	$36,719, PF-68Cam, June 2014
1896	762	549	PF-68	600	1,200	1,800	3,450	$21,150, PF-68, February 2013
1897	731	590	PF-69	600	1,200	1,800	3,450	$27,025, PF-68DCam, November 2013
1898	735	578	PF-68	600	1,200	1,800	3,450	$18,800, PF-68Cam, June 2014
1899	846	461	PF-69	600	1,200	1,800	3,450	$18,800, PF-68Cam, November 2013
1900	912	565	PF-68	600	1,200	1,800	3,450	$22,325, PF-67DCam, January 2014
1901	813	557	PF-69	600	1,200	1,800	3,450	$23,500, PF-68, June 2014
1902	777	483	PF-68	600	1,200	1,800	3,450	$22,325, PF-67Cam, March 2013
1903	755	494	PF-68	600	1,200	1,800	3,450	$4,700, PF-67, September 2013
1904	670	517	PF-68	600	1,200	1,800	3,450	$7,050, PF-67, December 2013
1905	727	470	PF-68	600	1,200	1,800	3,450	$12,338, PF-67Cam, November 2013

	Mintage	Cert	Finest	PF-60	PF-63	PF-64	PF-65	Recent Auction Record
1906	675	500	PF-68	$600	$1,200	$1,800	$3,450	$5,581, PF-67, August 2013
1907	575	386	PF-68	600	1,200	1,800	3,450	$18,800, PF-68, June 2014
1908	545	380	PF-68	600	1,200	1,800	3,450	$5,002, PF-67, April 2013
1909	650	552	PF-68	600	1,200	1,800	3,450	$15,863, PF-68, December 2013
1910	551	442	PF-68	600	1,200	1,800	3,450	$14,100, PF-68, August 2013
1911	543	485	PF-69	600	1,200	1,800	3,450	$10,575, PF-67Cam, November 2013
1912	700	402	PF-68	600	1,200	1,800	3,450	$8,813, PF-67, April 2013
1913	627	441	PF-68	700	1,300	1,850	3,500	$9,400, PF-68, June 2014
1914	380	373	PF-68	800	1,450	1,900	3,600	$14,688, PF-67, August 2013
1915	450	346	PF-68	800	1,400	1,900	3,600	$22,325, PF-68, December 2013

LIBERTY WALKING
(1916–1947)

Designer Adolph A. Weinman; weight 12.50 grams; composition .900 silver, .100 copper (net weight: .36169 oz. pure silver); diameter 30.6 mm; reeded edge; mints: Philadelphia, Denver, San Francisco.

History. The Liberty Walking half dollar was designed by Adolph A. Weinman, the sculptor who also created the Mercury or Winged Liberty Head dime. His monogram appears under the tips of the eagle's wing feathers. Mintage was intermittent, with none struck in 1922, 1924, 1925, 1926, 1930, 1931, and 1932. On the 1916 coins and some of the 1917 coins, the mintmark is located on the obverse, below IN GOD WE TRUST. Other coins of 1917, and those through 1947, have the mintmark on the reverse, under the pine branch.

Striking and Sharpness. Most circulation-strike Liberty Walking half dollars are lightly struck. In this respect they are similar to Standing Liberty quarters of the same era. On the obverse, the key points to check are Miss Liberty's left hand, the higher parts and lines in the skirt, and her head; after that, check all other areas. *Very few* coins are sharply struck in these areas, and for some issues sharp strikes might not exist at all. On the reverse, check the breast of the eagle.

Availability. All dates and mintmarks are readily collectible, although some, such as 1917-S (obverse mintmark), 1919-D, the three issues of 1921, and 1938-D, are scarce. Earlier years are often seen with extensive wear. MS coins are most often seen of the three issues of 1916, the 1917, and from 1933 to 1947. Issues in the 1940s were saved in large quantities and are common. As noted, coins with Full Details can range from scarce to extremely rare for certain dates. Half dollars dated 1928-D are counterfeit.

Note: Values of common-date silver coins have been based on the current bullion price of silver, $20 per ounce, and may vary with the prevailing spot price.

AU-50, 53, 55, 58 (About Uncirculated). *Obverse:* Light wear is seen on the higher-relief areas of Miss Liberty, the vertical area from her head down to the date. There is some luster at AU-50 and 53. At AU-58, the luster in the field is extensive, but is interrupted by friction and light wear. *Reverse:* Wear is most evident on the eagle's breast immediately under the neck feathers, the left leg, and the top of the left wing. At AU-50 half or more of the luster is gone. Luster is nearly complete at AU-58.

MS-60 to 70 (Mint State). *Obverse:* At MS-60, some abrasion and contact marks are evident on the higher areas, which also are the areas most likely to be weakly struck. This includes Miss Liberty's left arm, her hand, and the areas of the skirt covering her left leg. The luster may not be complete in those areas on weakly struck coins (even those certified above MS-65)—the original planchet surface may be revealed, as it was not smoothed out by striking. Accordingly, grading is best done by evaluating abrasion as it is observed in the right field, plus evaluating the mint luster. Luster may be dull or lifeless at MS-60 to 62, but should have deep frost at MS-63 or better, particularly in the lower-relief areas. At MS-65 or better, it should be full and rich. Sometimes, to compensate for flat striking, certified coins with virtually flawless luster in the fields, evocative of an MS-65 or 66 grade, are called MS-63 or a lower grade. *Reverse:* Striking usually is better, permitting observation of luster in all areas except the eagle's body, which may be lightly struck. Luster may be dull or lifeless at MS-60 to 62, but should have deep frost at MS-63 or better, particularly in the lower-relief areas. At MS-65 or better, it should be full and rich.

Mintmark Location, 1916–1917

Mintmark Location, 1917–1947

	Mintage	Cert	Avg	%MS	AU-55	MS-60	MS-62	MS-63	MS-64	MS-65	MS-66	Recent Auction Record
1916	608,000	2,878	55.7	72	$290	$350	$415	$550	$850	$1,850	$3,100	$6,463, MS-67, October 2013
1916D, Obverse Mintmark	1,014,400	3,419	55.5	68	275	360	435	600	900	2,200	4,100	$15,275, MS-67, March 2013
1916S, Obverse Mintmark	508,000	1,986	41.9	46	925	1,200	1,500	2,100	3,000	6,000	13,000	$21,150, MS-66, June 2014
1917	12,292,000	4,426	61.8	83	85	150	175	210	440	1,100	2,000	$8,813, MS-67, October 2013
1917D, Obverse Mintmark	765,400	1,873	55.1	60	425	600	875	1,300	2,200	7,500	17,500	$12,925, MS-65, July 2014
1917D, Reverse Mintmark	1,940,000	1,166	54.6	52	600	950	1,500	2,200	3,450	16,000	29,000	$18,800, MS-65, August 2013
1917S, Obverse Mintmark	952,000	1,077	45.8	42	1,500	2,350	3,500	4,750	6,400	20,000	33,000	$30,550, MS-65, August 2013
1917S, Reverse Mintmark	5,554,000	1,716	57.8	66	250	425	1,175	2,000	3,000	14,000	30,000	$38,188, MS-66, September 2013
1918	6,634,000	1,632	57.6	66	325	625	775	975	1,300	3,400	9,000	$4,113, MS-65, August 2013
1918D	3,853,040	1,575	55.1	63	750	1,300	1,950	3,150	5,500	22,500	40,000	$30,550, MS-65, August 2013
1918S	10,282,000	1,842	57.1	65	310	525	1,225	2,100	3,200	16,000	45,000	$30,550, MS-65, August 2013
1919	962,000	1,115	47.0	49	1,035	1,350	2,550	3,500	4,200	6,800	10,000	$16,450, MS-66, November 2013
1919D	1,165,000	1,137	42.2	38	2,750	6,000	9,000	18,000	28,500	140,000	265,000	$52,875, MS-64, August 2013
1919S	1,552,000	1,061	40.6	33	2,250	3,250	5,500	8,750	11,000	18,000	26,000	$23,500, MS-65, August 2013
1920	6,372,000	1,767	59.7	75	225	325	525	700	1,200	4,400	11,500	$5,288, MS-65, October 2013
1920D	1,551,000	819	45.0	47	1,100	1,550	3,150	3,850	6,150	16,500	27,500	$17,625, MS-65, August 2013
1920S	4,624,000	1,040	51.6	54	675	875	2,100	3,000	4,150	14,000	26,500	$22,325, MS-65, August 2013
1921	246,000	2,068	25.8	23	3,150	5,000	7,000	7,750	10,000	20,000	32,500	$29,376, MS-65, April 2014
1921D	208,000	2,490	20.6	16	3,850	8,000	9,000	14,000	16,000	30,000	39,500	$32,900, MS-65, August 2013
1921S	548,000	2,180	21.0	10	10,000	16,000	25,000	29,000	48,000	110,000	200,000	$108,688, MS-65, August 2013
1923S	2,178,000	990	50.7	53	1,050	1,500	2,600	3,700	4,500	16,000	29,000	$47,000, MS-66, April 2014
1927S	2,392,000	1,426	56.6	70	575	950	1,500	2,050	3,400	9,000	23,000	$28,200, MS-66, October 2013
1928S (a,b)	1,940,000	1,075	54.1	63	575	950	1,575	2,750	4,200	10,000	22,500	$15,275, MS-66, October 2013
1929D	1,001,200	2,021	59.0	68	260	385	575	750	1,175	2,700	4,500	$10,575, MS-66, April 2014
1929S	1,902,000	1,649	58.6	72	280	410	690	900	1,350	2,850	4,800	$12,925, MS-66, June 2013

a. Large and small mintmark varieties exist. b. Half dollars dated 1928-D are counterfeit.

1936, Doubled-Die Obverse
FS-50-1936-101.

1945, Missing Designer's Initials
FS-50-1945-901.

1946, Doubled-Die Reverse
FS-50-1946-801.

	Mintage	Cert	Avg	%MS	AU-50	MS-60	MS-62	MS-63	MS-64	MS-65	MS-66	Recent Auction Record
1933S	1,786,000	2,292	58.7	64	$240	$635	$875	$1,200	$1,400	$3,200	$4,400	$12,925, MS-67, November 2013
1934	6,964,000	5,593	63.6	91	26	75	90	110	130	400	515	$6,756, MS-68, June 2014
1934D (a)	2,361,000	3,307	63.0	90	85	150	180	235	350	1,400	2,050	$3,290, MS-66, November 2013
1934S	3,652,000	2,193	60.2	72	90	325	525	800	1,150	3,700	4,950	$28,200, MS-67, April 2013
1935	9,162,000	5,614	63.7	93	25	45	60	80	95	275	450	$7,931, MS-67, November 2013
1935D	3,003,800	2,587	63.0	90	65	140	200	300	475	2,000	4,050	$7,638, MS-66, August 2013
1935S	3,854,000	2,191	61.4	82	95	250	350	465	650	2,800	3,450	$41,125, MS-67, March 2013
1936	12,614,000	8,456	64.0	95	25	45	60	75	90	210	325	$4,818, MS-68, May 2014
1936, DblDie Obverse (b)	*	20	63.3	95								$940, MS-65, December 2013
1936D	4,252,400	4,556	63.9	96	50	85	100	120	130	400	775	$7,638, MS-67, July 2014
1936S	3,884,000	3,185	63.4	94	60	130	160	200	260	750	1,025	$19,975, MS-67, April 2013
1937	9,522,000	7,292	63.9	94	25	40	55	70	85	215	325	$15,275, MS-68, June 2014
1937D	1,676,000	3,270	63.6	93	100	215	245	265	300	650	825	$6,169, MS-67, October 2013

* Included in number above. a. Large and small mintmark varieties exist. b. No examples have yet been discovered grading better than Fine. Value in VG-8 is $500; in F-12, $600. "Extremely strong doubling is evident on the date. Less doubling is evident on IN GOD WE TRUST, the skirt, and some other elements" (*Cherrypickers' Guide to Rare Die Varieties,* fifth edition, volume II). Several varieties exist; this one is FS-50-1936-101.

	Mintage	Cert	Avg	%MS	AU-50	MS-60	MS-62	MS-63	MS-64	MS-65	MS-66	Recent Auction Record
1937S	2,090,000	3,477	63.7	94	$60	$165	$185	$210	$255	$625	$900	$19,975, MS-67, June 2014
1938	4,110,000	5,385	64.0	94	45	70	115	160	180	300	450	$2,350, MS-67, June 2014
1938D	491,600	6,033	47.6	55	250	500	560	625	725	1,450	2,400	$19,975, MS-67, January 2014
1939	6,812,000	8,367	64.4	95	26	40	55	65	85	175	255	$9,400, MS-68, July 2014
1939D	4,267,800	7,269	64.4	97	25	43	65	75	95	160	325	$2,820, MS-67, January 2014
1939S	2,552,000	5,140	64.4	96	70	150	165	190	225	300	525	$6,463, MS-67, April 2013
1940	9,156,000	9,334	64.3	95	22	35	45	55	70	145	245	$6,463, MS-68, January 2014
1940S	4,550,000	7,257	63.9	97	35	45	60	80	115	325	900	$35,250, MS-67, April 2013
1941	24,192,000	23,668	64.2	94	22	35	45	55	75	150	235	$7,638, MS-68, April 2013
1941D	11,248,400	13,879	64.4	97	22	38	50	65	100	160	245	$12,925, MS-68, December 2013
1941S	8,098,000	13,843	63.4	92	26	75	95	120	225	850	1,700	$28,200, MS-67, April 2013
1942	47,818,000	33,428	63.9	93	22	40	45	60	70	150	230	$16,450, MS-68, November 2013
1942D	10,973,800	10,870	64.4	97	20	40	60	80	125	260	300	$4,994, MS-68, November 2013
1942S (a)	12,708,000	11,533	63.9	97	22	40	60	80	120	425	1,200	$47,000, MS-67, April 2013
1943	53,190,000	35,464	64.0	93	20	35	40	50	75	150	230	$11,750, MS-68, March 2013
1943D	11,346,000	12,144	64.6	97	24	48	65	75	95	220	275	$1,998, MS-67, April 2013
1943S	13,450,000	12,765	64.0	97	25	42	50	60	85	300	650	$5,141, MS-67, April 2014
1944	28,206,000	20,538	63.9	94	20	35	40	50	70	150	230	$9,106, MS-67, January 2014
1944D	9,769,000	15,154	64.6	98	20	40	50	60	80	160	230	$1,293, MS-67, January 2014
1944S	8,904,000	14,838	64.0	98	24	40	55	63	85	350	1,000	$14,100, MS-67, January 2014
1945	31,502,000	28,169	64.0	96	20	35	40	50	75	150	230	$8,225, MS-67, November 2013
1945, Missing Initials	*	12	56.1	58	100	150	190	250				$705, MS-64, January 2014
1945D	9,966,800	20,506	64.7	98	20	35	45	60	75	150	230	$16,450, MS-68, January 2014
1945S	10,156,000	17,245	64.2	99	24	38	45	55	80	160	425	$23,500, MS-67, March 2013
1946	12,118,000	16,270	64.0	96	20	37	45	50	75	160	325	$9,988, MS-67, March 2013
1946, Doubled-Die Reverse (c)	*	501	47.8	38	125	275	475	550	1,200	2,500	6,300	$7,050, MS-66, November 2013
1946D	2,151,000	29,980	64.7	100	32	47	55	60	75	150	230	$14,100, MS-67, June 2014
1946S	3,724,000	20,824	64.6	99	25	43	50	58	75	150	250	$7,638, MS-67, January 2014
1947	4,094,000	17,121	64.3	98	25	48	55	60	75	160	325	$15,275, MS-67, April 2013
1947D	3,900,600	19,177	64.5	99	30	45	55	60	70	150	280	$7,638, MS-67, August 2013

* Included in number above. **a.** Large and small mintmark varieties exist. **c.** Very strong doubling is visible on E PLURIBUS UNUM, the eagle's wing feathers and left wing, and the branch.

Proof Liberty Walking Half Dollars

PF-60 to 70 (Proof). Proofs were made beginning in 1936 and continuing through 1942. The entire die was polished (including the figure of Miss Liberty and the eagle), generating coins of low contrast. Proofs usually are fairly well struck. Most Proofs of 1941 are from over-polished dies, with the AW monogram of the designer no longer present. Striking sharpness can vary. A full head and complete left-hand details are points to check for. *Obverse and Reverse:* Proofs that are extensively cleaned and have many hairlines, or that are dull and grainy, are lower level, such as PF-60 to 62. With medium hairlines and good reflectivity, assigned grades of PF-63 or 64 are appropriate. Tiny horizontal lines on Miss Liberty's leg, known as slide marks, from National and other album slides scuffing the relief of the cheek, are common; coins with such marks should not be graded higher than PF-64, but sometimes are. With relatively few hairlines and no noticeable slide marks, a rating of PF-65 can be given. PF-66 should have hairlines so delicate that magnification is needed to see them. Above that, a Proof should be free of any hairlines or other problems.

Proof Liberty Walking Half Dollar

	Mintage	Cert	Avg	PF-64	PF-65	PF-66	PF-67	Recent Auction Record
1936	3,901	2,976	64.5	$2,600	$3,500	$5,000	$13,000	$18,800, PF-67, March 2013
1937	5,728	3,568	64.9	800	950	1,200	1,600	$21,150, PF, January 2013
1938	8,152	4,122	65.1	600	775	1,000	1,350	$10,575, PF-68, April 2014
1939	8,808	4,472	65.3	500	750	850	1,100	$6,169, PF-68, August 2013
1940	11,279	5,234	65.2	500	625	700	1,000	$3,525, PF-68, June 2013
1941 (a)	15,412	7,020	65.1	500	625	700	950	$18,213, PF-69, November 2013
1942	21,120	9,773	65.3	500	625	700	950	$9,399, PF, August 2013

a. The variety without the designer's initials was created by the over-polishng of dies.

FRANKLIN
(1948–1963)

Designer John R. Sinnock; weight 12.50 grams; composition .900 silver, .100 copper (net weight: .36169 oz. pure silver); diameter 30.6 mm; reeded edge; mints: Philadelphia, Denver, San Francisco.

History. U.S. Mint chief engraver John R. Sinnock developed a motif for a silver half dime in 1942; it was proposed but never adopted for regular coinage. In 1948 Sinnock's Franklin half dollar was introduced, its design an adaptation of his earlier half-dime motif. The Liberty Bell is similar to that used by Sinnock on the 1926 Sesquicentennial commemorative half dollar modeled from a sketch by John Frederick Lewis. The coin-collecting community paid little attention to the Franklin half dollar at the time, but today the coins are widely collected.

Striking and Sharpness. Given the indistinct details of the obverse, sharpness of strike usually is ignored. On the reverse, if the bottom lines of the Liberty Bell are complete the coin may be designated as Full Bell Lines (FBL).

Availability. All dates and mintmarks are easily available in grades from VF upward. Lower-level MS coins can be unattractive due to contact marks and abrasion, particularly noticeable on the obverse. High-quality gems are generally inexpensive, although varieties that are rare with FBL can be costly amid much competition in the marketplace. Most numismatists collect MS coins. Grades below EF are not widely desired.

Note: Values of common-date silver coins have been based on the current bullion price of silver, $20 per ounce, and may vary with the prevailing spot price.

MS-60 to 70 (Mint State). *Obverse:* At MS-60, some abrasion and contact marks are evident on the cheek, on the hair left of the ear, and the neck. At MS-63, abrasion is slight at best, less so for MS-64. An MS-65 coin should display no abrasion or contact marks except under magnification, and MS-66 and higher coins should have none at all. Luster should be full and rich. As details are shallow on this design, the amount and "depth" of luster is important to grading. *Reverse:* General comments apply as for the obverse. The points to check are the bell harness, the words PASS AND STOW on the upper area of the Liberty Bell, and the bottom of the bell.

1948, Doubled-Die Reverse
FS-50-1948-801.

1949-S, Repunched Mintmark
FS-50-1949S-501.

1951-S, Doubled-Die Reverse
FS-50-1951S-801.

Full Bell Lines

1955, Clashed Obverse Die
"Bugs Bunny" variety.
FS-50-1955-401.

1959, Doubled-Die Reverse
FS-50-1959-801.

	Mintage	Cert	Avg	%MS	MS-63	MS-64	MS-64FBL	MS-65	MS-65FBL	MS-66	MS-66FBL	Recent Auction Record
1948	3,006,814	10,036	64.2	98	$27	$35	$55	$80	$140	$300	$350	$4,994, MS-62, September 2013
1948, Doubled-Die Reverse (a)	*	35	63.5	94	75	125	150	200	300	550		
1948D	4,028,600	10,168	64.1	99	24	30	55	115	185	600	800	$2,820, MS-66FBL, January 2014
1949	5,614,000	6,200	63.3	90	70	75	85	120	155	350	550	$1,880, MS-66FBL, July 2014
1949D	4,120,600	6,788	63.5	95	75	90	115	500	750	2,500	10,000	$9,400, MS-66FBL, June 2013
1949S	3,744,000	7,595	63.8	94	95	115	250	140	500	225	750	$7,638, MS-67FBL, April 2014
1949S, Doubled Mintmark (b)	*	18	61.7	83	120	170	225	280	350	575		$223, MS-65, January 2014
1950	7,742,123	5,883	63.7	93	35	55	80	110	190	385	575	$12,925, MS-67FBL, June 2014
1950D	8,031,600	6,365	63.6	96	40	70	95	250	375	900	1,350	$16,450, MS-66FBL, September 2013
1951	16,802,102	6,079	63.9	96	24	35	85	70	235	225	775	$18,800, MS-67FBL, January 2014
1951D	9,475,200	4,720	63.8	96	45	70	100	150	250	650	1,000	$2,233, MS-66FBL, January 2014
1951S	13,696,000	6,534	64.2	97	35	50	175	70	400	275	1,100	$30,550, MS-67FBL, April 2013
1951S, Doubled-Die Reverse (c)	*	28	64.0	96	80	110	350	275	725	900		$188, MS-65, January 2014
1952	21,192,093	7,513	64.0	97	23	32	65	70	125	225	430	$6,345, MS-67FBL, December 2013
1952D	25,395,600	6,072	63.7	97	23	32	65	125	180	600	1,150	$1,880, MS-66FBL, January 2014
1952S	5,526,000	5,769	64.5	99	70	80	425	100	750	225	2,850	$14,100, MS-66FBL, February 2014
1953	2,668,120	5,351	64.0	98	27	40	150	100	635	450	2,750	$2,350, MS-66FBL, April 2013
1953D	20,900,400	7,728	63.9	98	23	38	55	110	175	550	725	$19,975, MS-67Cam, June 2014
1953S	4,148,000	11,568	64.7	100	35	48	10,000	70	25,500	350		$28,200, MS-65FBL, April 2014
1954	13,188,202	10,356	64.2	99	20	30	45	50	120	300	1,100	$2,644, MS-66FBL, January 2014
1954D	25,445,580	11,650	64.1	99	24	28	40	90	140	375	800	$5,288, MS-66FBL, February 2014
1954S	4,993,400	16,726	64.6	100	24	35	85	50	250	240	1,050	$4,994, MS-66FBL, February 2014
1955	2,498,181	16,286	64.1	100	30	40	50	55	115	150	425	$2,703, MS-66FBL, January 2014
1955, Clashed Obverse Die (d)	*	634	63.9	100	48	65	85	130	350	265	700	$423, MS-66FBL, February 2013
1956	4,032,000	16,210	64.5	100	25	28	38	42	100	80	275	$4,406, MS-67FBL, March 2014
1957	5,114,000	9,863	64.7	99	19	25	55	40	125	85	225	$2,115, MS-67FBL, June 2014
1957D	19,966,850	13,226	64.4	99	19	23	38	40	75	85	375	$6,463, MS-67FBL, June 2013
1958	4,042,000	13,164	64.7	100	19	24	55	45	125	80	350	$2,820, MS-67FBL, January 2014
1958D	23,962,412	14,410	64.5	99	18	19	33	45	70	75	475	$2,585, MS-67FBL, June 2013
1959	6,200,000	10,287	64.2	99	18	20	50	70	225	800	1,750	$4,994, MS-66FBL, January 2014
1959, Doubled-Die Reverse (e)	*	77	64.2	99	85	90	180	120	450	1,125		$431, MS-65FBL, March 2011
1959D	13,053,750	10,669	64.1	99	18	22	35	90	140	775	1,050	$1,998, MS-66FBL, July 2014
1960	6,024,000	11,377	64.1	100	18	19	40	100	225	550	2,000	$4,113, MS-66FBL, June 2013
1960D	18,215,812	10,317	64.0	99	18	28	45	200	450	900	4,250	$4,113, MS-63, September 2013
1961	8,290,000	8,285	64.1	99	18	25	160	75	900	600	5,000	$2,468, MS-65FBL, June 2014
1961D	20,276,442	8,229	64.0	99	18	25	60	110	450	1,000	3,000	$6,463, MS-66FBL, August 2013
1962	9,714,000	7,603	64.0	99	18	25	225	90	1,750	750	11,000	$3,819, MS-65FBL, March 2013
1962D	35,473,281	9,175	63.9	99	18	25	75	120	450	1,000	3,500	$6,463, MS-65, April 2014
1963	22,164,000	23,148	64.2	99	18	19	145	40	1,150	750	2,500	$28,200, MS-66FBL, July 2014
1963D	67,069,292	19,420	64.0	99	18	19	40	45	175	350	1,050	$7,344, MS-63, April 2014

* Included in number above. **a.** Doubling is visible on E PLURIBUS UNUM, UNITED, HALF DOLLAR, the dots, and the Liberty Bell's clapper. "There are several similar, yet lesser, DDRs for this date" (*Cherrypickers' Guide to Rare Die Varieties*, fifth edition, volume II). The variety listed and pictured is FS-50-1948-801. **b.** The secondary mintmark is visible south of the primary. CONECA lists two other repunched mintmarks for this date; the one illustrated and listed here is FS-50-1949S-501. **c.** Doubling is evident on the eagle's tail feathers and left wing, as well as on E PLURIBUS UNUM. This variety is FS-50-1951S-801. **d.** This variety, popularly known as the "Bugs Bunny," has evidence of clash marks that appear as two buckteeth on Benjamin Franklin. **e.** Strong doubling is evident on the eagle; doubling is also visible on E PLURIBUS UNUM, UNITED, and portions of the Liberty Bell.

Proof Franklin Half Dollars

PF-60 to 70 (Proof). Proofs were made from 1950 to 1963 and are available today in proportion to their mintages. Those with cameo-frosted devices are in the minority and often sell for strong premiums. Virtually all Proofs are well struck.

Only a few Proof Franklin half dollars are in the lower PF-60 to 62 range. *Obverse and Reverse:* Proofs that are extensively cleaned and have many hairlines, or that are dull and grainy, are lower level, such as PF-60 to 62. With medium hairlines

and good reflectivity, assigned grades of PF-63 or 64 are appropriate. PF-66 should have hairlines so delicate that magnification is needed to see them. Above that, a Proof should be free of any hairlines or other problems.

Proof Franklin Half Dollar

1957, Proof, Tripled-Die Reverse
FS-50-1957-801.

1961, Proof, Doubled-Die Reverse
FS-50-1961-801.

	Mintage	Cert	Avg	PF-64	PF-65	PF-65Cam	PF-65DC	PF-66	Recent Auction Record
1950	51,386	5,792	64.6	$425	$475	$1,200	$10,000	$575	$8,813, PF-67Cam, April 2013
1951	57,500	5,614	64.8	320	375	600	2,500	425	$7,050, PF-66DCam, April 2013
1952	81,980	6,058	65.0	180	230	375	4,500	265	$11,750, PF-68Cam, April 2014
1953	128,800	7,566	65.2	125	190	225	1,400	235	$10,575, PF-67DCam, August 2013
1954	233,300	9,345	65.9	65	85	110	425	100	$17,626, PF-68DCam, June 2013
1955	378,200	12,441	66.4	65	75	90	425	85	$5,288, PF-68DCam, February 2013
1956	669,384	20,711	66.8	35	45	55	100	70	$8,813, PF-68DCam, April 2013
1957	1,247,952	16,371	66.5	25	28	60	250	35	$3,408, PF-69Cam, April 2014
1957, Tripled-Die Reverse (a)	*	3	66.3	75	90	175	800	150	
1958	875,652	11,709	66.3	32	38	75	675	52	$4,994, PF-68DCam, March 2013
1959	1,149,291	12,606	66.2	18	22	60	2,000	38	$7,050, PF-67DCam, February 2013
1960	1,691,602	15,717	66.3	18	22	45	100	30	$17,625, PF-69DCam, April 2013
1960, Doubled-Die Obverse (b)	*	153	65.7	80	95	175	400	150	$160, PF-67, May 2012
1961	3,028,244	23,962	66.3	25	30	40	125	35	$2,938, PF-69Cam, April 2013
1961, Doubled-Die Reverse (c)	*	90	65.6	2,200	2,900	4,000		3,750	$2,350, PF-65, June 2014
1962	3,218,019	33,239	66.3	22	27	32	60	32	$7,050, PF-69DCam, September 2013
1962, Doubled-Die Obverse (d)	*	3	66.0	25	30	55	150	60	
1963	3,075,645	31,834	66.5	22	26	30	52	30	$7,638, PF-69DCam, January 2014

* Included in number above. **a.** A closely tripled image is evident on E PLURIBUS UNUM, portions of UNITED STATES OF AMERICA, and HALF DOLLAR. **b.** Doubling is visible on LIBERTY, TRUST, and the date. **c.** Other reverse doubled dies exist for this date. The variety pictured and listed here (FS-50-1961-801) is by far the most dramatic. Very strong doubling is evident on the reverse lettering. **d.** Doubling is visible on the 62 of the date and on WE TRUST.

KENNEDY
(1964 TO DATE)

Designers Gilroy Roberts and Frank Gasparro. 1964—Weight 12.50 grams; composition .900 silver, .100 copper (net weight: .36169 oz. pure silver); diameter 30.6 mm; reeded edge; mints: Philadelphia, Denver, San Francisco. 1965–1970—Weight 11.50 grams; composition, outer layers of .800 silver and .200 copper bonded to inner core of .209 silver, .791 copper (net weight .1479 oz. pure silver). 1971 to date—Weight 11.34 grams; composition, outer layers of copper-nickel (.750 copper, .250 nickel) bonded to inner core of pure copper; diameter 30.6 mm; reeded edge; mints: Philadelphia, Denver, San Francisco. Modern silver Proofs—Weight 12.50 grams; composition .900 silver, .100 copper (net weight: .36169 oz. pure silver); diameter 30.6 mm; reeded edge; mint: San Francisco.

Bicentennial variety: Designers Gilroy Roberts and Seth Huntington; diameter 30.6 mm; reeded edge. Silver clad—Weight 11.50 grams; composition outer layers of .800 silver, .200 copper bonded to inner core of .209 silver, .791 copper (net weight .14792 oz. pure silver). Copper-nickel clad—Weight 11.34 grams; composition outer layers of copper-nickel (.750 copper, .250 nickel) bonded to inner core of pure copper.

History. Kennedy half dollars, minted from 1964 to date, were struck in 90% silver the first year, then with 40% silver content through 1970, and in later years in copper-nickel (except for special silver issues made for collectors). The obverse, by Chief Engraver Gilroy Roberts, features a portrait of President John F. Kennedy, while the reverse, by Frank Gasparro, displays a modern version of a heraldic eagle. The 1976 Bicentennial coin shows Philadelphia's Independence Hall, a design by Seth G. Huntington, similar to that of the 1926 Sesquicentennial commemorative quarter eagle. The obverse was unchanged except for the dual dating 1776–1976. They were struck during 1975 and 1976 and were used for general circulation as well as being included in Proof and Uncirculated sets for 1975 and 1976.

Striking and Sharpness. Nearly all are well struck. Check the highest points of the hair on the obverse and the highest details on the reverse.

Availability. All issues are common in high circulated grades as well as MS.

Note: Values of common-date silver coins have been based on the current bullion price of silver, $20 per ounce, and may vary with the prevailing spot price.

MS-60 to 70 (Mint State). *Obverse:* At MS-60, some abrasion and contact marks are evident on the cheek, and on the hair to the right of the forehead and temple. Abrasion is slight at MS-63, and even slighter at MS-64. An MS-65 coin should display no abrasion or contact marks except under magnification, and MS-66 and higher coins should have none at all. Luster should be full and rich. *Reverse:* Comments apply as for the obverse, except that the highest parts of the eagle at the center are the key places to check.

1964, Doubled-Die Obverse
FS-50-1964-102.

1964-D, Doubled-Die Obverse
FS-50-1964D-101.

1964-D, Repunched Mintmark
FS-50-1964D-502.

1972, Doubled-Die Obverse
FS-50-1972-101.

1972-D, Missing Designer's Initials
FS-50-1972D-901.

1974-D, Doubled-Die Obverse
FS-50-1974D-101.

	Mintage	Cert	Avg	%MS	MS-63	MS-65	MS-66	MS-67	Recent Auction Record
1964	273,304,004	8,030	64.3	97	$16	$20	$40	$625	$4,406, MS-62, September 2013
1964, Doubled-Die Obverse (a)	*	29	63.9	93	35	65	250		$21, MS-65, July 2006

* Included in number above. **a.** There are several doubled-die obverses for the 1964 Kennedy half dollar. The one pictured and listed is FS-50-1964-102.

Chart continued on next page.

	Mintage	Cert	Avg	%MS	MS-63	MS-65	MS-66	MS-67	Recent Auction Record
1964D	156,205,446	3,806	64.0	95	$15	$20	$40	$800	$3,525, MS-64, February 2014
1964D, Doubled-Die Obverse (b)	*	43	62.4	74	45	70	150		$60, MS-66, November 2011
1964D, RPM (c)	*	16	62.7	81	45	65	125		$130, AU-55, June 2010
1965	65,879,366	980	64.2	95	6	17	150	650	$1,645, MS-63, September 2013
1966	108,984,932	838	63.5	90	6	25	170	400	$881, MS-63, February 2014
1967	295,046,978	1,136	63.4	88	6	22	95	750	$200, MS-64, September 2013
1968D	246,951,930	2,104	64.3	95	6	20	45	235	$2,585, MS-67, February 2014
1969D	129,881,800	1,490	64.2	95	6	30	225	1,100	$317, MS-66, July 2014
1970D ‡	2,150,000	4,446	64.5	100	20	42	215	775	$823, MS-63, August 2013
1971	155,164,000	557	64.4	95	3	15	45	200	$170, MS-66, May 2014
1971D	302,097,424	2,189	65.2	96	3	10	22	70	$1,880, MS-64, April 2013
1972	153,180,000	833	64.8	98	3	15	50	290	$36, MS-66, July 2014
1972, Doubled-Die Obverse (d)	*	12	55.7	17	140	165	225	450	$90, AU-50, March 2011
1972D	141,890,000	1,019	64.9	94	3	10	23	100	$5,288, MS-66, January 2014
1972D, Missing Initials	*	19	54.0	11	50	75	150	250	$380, EF-45, October 2009
1973	64,964,000	465	64.8	97	3	15	45	155	$22, MS-65, September 2008
1973D	83,171,400	839	65.0	96	3	11	20	170	$329, MS-67, July 2014
1974	201,596,000	488	64.5	95	3	20	35	145	$37, MS-66, March 2008
1974D	79,066,300	610	64.8	97	3	15	35	175	$65, MS-65, June 2014
1974D, DblDie Obverse ‡ (e)	*	828	63.4	92	40	100	200	450	$411, MS-66, July 2014
1976	234,308,000	755	63.9	94	3	15	50	125	$2,350, MS-62, February 2014
1976D	287,565,248	1,384	64.6	95	3	15	25	375	$2,585, MS-67, January 2014
1976S, Silver Clad	11,000,000	3,738	66.5	100	8	10	15	30	$217, MS-68, July 2014
1977	43,598,000	562	65.4	99	3	12	28	120	$764, MS-67, June 2014
1977D	31,449,106	373	64.9	97	3	15	22	85	$21, MS-66, August 2007
1978	14,350,000	535	65.2	99	3	12	20	150	$19, MS-66, July 2008
1978D	13,765,799	425	65.2	100	3	10	23	150	$18, MS-66, September 2008
1979	68,312,000	541	65.3	98	3	10	25	150	$999, AU-58, February 2014
1979D	15,815,422	479	65.4	100	3	12	25	160	$11, MS-66, September 2008
1980P	44,134,000	692	65.8	99	3	10	17	35	$153, MS-60, February 2013
1980D	33,456,449	299	64.8	98	3	15	55	175	$138, MS-66, September 2008
1981P	29,544,000	601	65.1	99	3	12	25	260	$1,410, MS-60, April 2013
1981D	27,839,533	346	64.5	97	3	18	40	350	$50, MS-66, June 2014
1982P	10,819,000	1,114	64.8	98	7	23	70	425	$382, MS-66, June 2014
1982D	13,140,102	467	65.4	99	7	18	40	325	$3,290, MS-67, November 2013
1983P	34,139,000	337	64.6	95	8	22	45	200	$147, MS-65, April 2014
1983D	32,472,244	321	65.0	98	7	15	30	330	$13, MS-66, October 2008
1984P	26,029,000	446	65.4	99	3	12	38	250	$98, MS-66, September 2008
1984D	26,262,158	367	65.1	99	3	17	40	350	$11, MS-66, September 2008
1985P	18,706,962	490	65.8	100	5	15	25	90	$123, MS-67, June 2014
1985D	19,814,034	648	65.9	99	5	12	15	45	$159, MS-67, July 2014
1986P	13,107,633	566	65.8	100	6	13	28	70	$282, MS-67, July 2014
1986D	15,336,145	716	66.0	100	5	11	20	45	$57, MS-67, July 2014
1987P ‡ (f)	2,890,758	714	65.6	100	5	15	30	100	$76, MS-67, June 2014
1987D ‡ (f)	2,890,758	991	65.9	100	5	12	23	50	$21, MS-67, October 2008
1988P	13,626,000	450	65.6	100	5	15	28	90	$282, MS-67, July 2014
1988D	12,000,096	761	66.1	100	4	12	25	40	$57, MS-67, July 2014
1989P	24,542,000	604	65.5	99	4	15	23	90	$259, MS-67, July 2014
1989D	23,000,216	711	65.8	99	3	11	18	60	$129, MS-67, July 2014
1990P	22,278,000	368	65.5	100	3	11	22	150	$76, MS-67, June 2014
1990D	20,096,242	400	65.5	100	3	16	32	200	$31, MS-66, October 2008
1991P	14,874,000	443	65.7	100	4	12	25	200	$217, MS-67, July 2014
1991D	15,054,678	471	65.6	99	4	15	30	300	$920, MS-67, September 2008
1992P	17,628,000	708	66.0	100	3	11	22	25	$11, MS-67, October 2008
1992D	17,000,106	653	66.1	100	3	10	18	30	$46, MS-67, July 2014
1993P	15,510,000	665	66.1	100	3	11	20	40	$58, MS-67, July 2014
1993D	15,000,006	912	66.0	100	3	10	22	60	$11, MS-66, October 2008
1994P	23,718,000	879	65.8	100	3	10	20	55	$10, MS-66, October 2008

* Included in number above. ‡ Ranked in the *100 Greatest U.S. Modern Coins*. **b.** Doubling on this variety is evident on the date, IN GOD WE TRUST, the designer's initials, and LI and TY of LIBERTY. "This is a very popular variety. It is extremely rare above MS-65" (*Cherrypickers' Guide to Rare Die Varieties,* fifth edition, volume II). There are other doubled-die obverses for 1964-D; the one pictured and listed is FS-50-1964D-101. **c.** There are several repunched mintmarks for 1964-D. The one listed is FS-50-1964D-502. **d.** Doubling is strongly evident on IN GOD WE TRUST and on the date. This variety is very rare above MS-65. **e.** Strong doubling is visible on IN GOD WE TRUST, the date, and LIBERTY. **f.** Not issued for circulation; included with Mint and Souvenir sets.

	Mintage	Cert	Avg	%MS	MS-63	MS-65	MS-66	MS-67	Recent Auction Record
1994D	23,828,110	418	65.9	100	$3	$10	$20	$75	$364, MS-67, July 2014
1995P	26,496,000	545	65.9	100	3	10	17	40	$55, MS-67, July 2014
1995D	26,288,000	509	66.0	100	3	10	20	50	$13, MS-67, October 2008
1996P	24,442,000	933	66.4	100	3	10	17	35	$247, MS-68, July 2014
1996D	24,744,000	927	66.2	100	3	10	17	35	$11, MS-67, October 2008
1997P	20,882,000	405	66.0	100	3	12	30	80	$60, MS-67, July 2014
1997D	19,876,000	465	65.8	100	3	13	30	90	$646, MS-68, June 2013
1998P	15,646,000	483	66.1	100	3	15	35	70	$76, MS-67, July 2014
1998D	15,064,000	467	65.8	100	3	11	20	70	$62, MS-67, July 2014
1999P	8,900,000	1,031	66.4	100	3	10	20	30	$2,115, MS-69, June 2013
1999D	10,682,000	855	66.3	100	3	10	16	23	$10, MS-66, October 2008
2000P	22,600,000	564	66.3	100	3	10	17	35	$48, MS-67, October 2008
2000D	19,466,000	537	65.8	100	3	10	20	40	$123, MS-67, July 2014
2001P	21,200,000	1,272	66.6	100	3	8	15	28	$99, MS-68, July 2014
2001D	19,504,000	1,272	66.2	100	3	8	13	28	$247, MS-68, July 2014
2002P (g)	3,100,000	891	66.5	100	3	8	15	30	$182, MS-68, June 2014
2002D (g)	2,500,000	791	66.1	100	3	9	20	40	$2,115, MS-69, June 2013
2003P (g)	2,500,000	731	66.0	100	3	9	20	30	$59, MS-67, July 2014
2003D (g)	2,500,000	685	65.9	100	3	8	16	25	$51, MS-67, July 2014
2004P (g)	2,900,000	475	66.0	100	3	8	17	30	$86, MS-67, July 2014
2004D (g)	2,900,000	969	66.5	100	3	8	16	25	$423, MS-68, July 2014
2005P (g,h)	3,800,000	2,816	66.8	100	4	18	25	75	$42, MS-66, July 2014
2005D (g,h)	3,500,000	2,610	66.5	100	4	15	23	40	$11, MS-66, October 2008
2006P (g,h)	2,400,000	1,791	66.7	100	2	9	22	26	$42, MS-69 Satin, January 2009
2006D (g,h)	2,000,000	1,720	66.7	100	2	7	15	28	$82, MS-67, July 2014
2007P (g,h)	2,400,000	897	66.6	100	2	6	11	17	$270, MS-68, July 2014
2007D (g,h)	2,400,000	611	66.5	100	2	6	15	30	$15, MS-69, January 2009
2008P (g,h)	1,700,000	581	66.5	100	2	8	20	40	$12, SP-67, April 2012
2008D (g,h)	1,700,000	228	66.0	100	2	8	20	45	$24, MS-66, June 2011
2009P (g,h)	1,900,000	518	66.4	100	2	6	12	25	$6, MS-66, November 2011
2009D (g,h)	1,900,000	386	66.4	100	2	6	12	30	$27, MS-66, February 2012
2010P (g,h)	1,800,000	878	66.5	100	2	6	12	25	$23, MS-67, July 2014
2010D (g,h)	1,700,000	713	66.7	100	2	6	12	30	$101, MS-67, July 2014
2011P (g)	1,750,000	919	66.7	100	2	6	12	25	$229, MS-68, July 2014
2011D (g)	1,700,000	759	66.5	100	2	6	12	25	$33, MS-67, January 2012
2012P (g)	1,800,000	n/a	n/a	n/a	2	6	12	25	
2012D (g)	1,700,000	n/a	n/a	n/a	2	6	12	25	
2013P (g)		n/a	n/a	n/a	2	6	12	25	
2013D (g)		n/a	n/a	n/a	2	6	12	25	
2014P (g)		n/a	n/a	n/a	2	6	12	25	
2014D (g)		n/a	n/a	n/a	2	6	12	25	

g. Not issued for circulation. Sold directly to the public in rolls and small bags. **h.** Mint sets issued from 2005 through 2010 have a special satin finish that is somewhat different from the finish on traditional Uncirculated coins.

Proof Kennedy Half Dollars

PF-60 to 70 (Proof). Proofs of 1964 were struck at the Philadelphia Mint. Those from 1968 to date have been made in San Francisco. All are easily obtained; most are PF-63 or finer. Most from the 1970s to date have cameo contrast. Special Mint Set (SMS) coins were struck in lieu of Proofs from 1965 to 1967; in some instances, these closely resemble Proofs. Silver Proofs have been struck in recent years for Silver Proof sets. In 1998, a special Matte Proof silver Kennedy half dollar was struck for inclusion in the Robert F. Kennedy commemorative coin set. *Obverse and Reverse:* Proofs that are extensively cleaned and have many hairlines, or that are dull and grainy, are lower level, such as PF-60 to 62. With medium hairlines and good reflectivity, assigned grades of PF-63 or 64 are appropriate. With relatively few hairlines a rating of PF-65 can be given. PF-66 should have hairlines so delicate that magnification is needed to see them. Above that, a Proof should be free of any hairlines or other problems.

Proof Kennedy Half Dollar

1964, Proof, Heavily Accented Hair
FS-50-1964-401.

1966, Special Mint Set, Doubled-Die Obverse
FS-50-1966-103.

1967, Special Mint Set, Quintupled-Die Obverse
FS-50-1967-101.

1979-S, Filled S (Type 1)

1979-S, Clear S (Type 2)

1981-S, Rounded S (Type 1)

1981-S, Flat S (Type 2)

1988-S, Doubled-Die Obverse
FS-50-1988S-101.

	Mintage	Cert	Avg	PF-65	PF-67Cam	PF-68DC	PF-69DC	Recent Auction Record
1964	3,950,762	28,205	67.3	$20	$45	$200	$1,600	$9,400, PF-70, December 2013
1964, Heavily Accented Hair ‡ (a)	*	9,829	66.4	45	180	4,900		$15,128, PF-68DCam, June 2013
1965, Special Mint Set ‡	2,360,000	7,546	66.2	11	175			$1,998, PF-66DCam, January 2014
1966, Special Mint Set ‡	2,261,583	7,973	66.5	11	80			$1,116, PF-68Cam, June 2013
1966, SMS, DblDie Obv (b)	*	476	66.4	85	325			$74, SP-67, April 2012
1967, Special Mint Set ‡	1,863,344	8,457	66.4	15	60			$893, PF-67DCam, June 2014
1967, SMS, QuintDie Obv (c)	*	27	65.5	135	500			$345, SP-66, February 2012
1968S	3,041,506	7,307	67.5	10	22	50	175	$229, PF-69DCam, July 2013
1969S	2,934,631	9,988	67.8	10	23	45	135	$224, PF-69DCam, January 2014
1970S	2,632,810	8,092	67.7	15	30	50	335	$329, PF-69DCam, June 2013
1971S	3,220,733	4,286	67.7	5	20	100	1,200	$1,821, PF-67, July 2013
1972S	3,260,996	3,035	68.0	5	16	25	60	$92, PF-69DCam, June 2014
1973S	2,760,339	6,441	68.8	4	16	25	50	$2,350, PF-70DCam, December 2011
1974S	2,612,568	7,258	68.8	5	9	18	20	$4,406, PF-70DCam, March 2014
1976S	7,059,099	22,196	68.8	5	13	18	20	$2,350, PF-70DCam, June 2013
1976S, Silver Clad (d)	4,000,000	15,496	68.7	12	15	25	35	$2,115, PF-70DCam, June 2013
1977S	3,251,152	8,229	68.9	5	9	15	20	$194, PF-70DCam, June 2014
1978S	3,127,781	8,610	68.9	4	12	18	20	$129, PF-70DCam, May 2014
1979S, All kinds (e)	3,677,175							
1979S, Type 1		8,947	68.9	4	11	14	20	$200, PF-70DCam, April 2012
1979S, Type 2		4,306	68.8	25	27	30	35	$588, PF-70DCam, February 2013
1980S	3,554,806	8,533	68.9	4	12	15	20	$129, PF-70DCam, August 2013
1981S, All kinds (f)	4,063,083							
1981S, Type 1		10,199	68.9	4	12	15	23	$259, PF-70DCam, June 2013
1981S, Type 2		2,571	68.6	25	29	33	55	$2,585, PF-70DCam, November 2013
1982S	3,857,479	1,072	68.8	5	12	15	20	$529, PF-70DCam, June 2013

* Included in number above. ‡ Ranked in the *100 Greatest U.S. Modern Coins*. **a.** This variety "is identifiable by the enhanced hairline in the central area of the hair, just below the part. However, the easiest way to identify the variety is the weak or broken lower left serif of the I (in LIBERTY)" (*Cherrypickers' Guide to Rare Die Varieties*, fifth edition, volume II). **b.** There are several doubled-die obverse varieties of the 1966 Special Mint Set half dollar. The one listed is FS-50-1966-103, with strong doubling evident on the profile, IN GOD WE TRUST, the eye, the hair, and the designer's initials. **c.** "A prominent quintupled (at least) spread is evident on RTY of LIBERTY, with strong multiple images on all obverse lettering and portions of the hair" (*Cherrypickers' Guide to Rare Die Varieties*, fifth edition, volume II). **d.** Mintage figures for 1976-S silver coins are approximate. Many were melted in 1982. **e.** The mintmark style of 1979-S Proof coins was changed during production, resulting in two distinct types. The scarcer, well-defined Type 2 is easily distinguished from the more common blob-like Type 1. **f.** The mintmark style of the 1981-S Proof coins was changed during production, creating two different types. The scarcer Type 2 is not easily distinguished from the common Type 1. Type 2 is flat on the top curve of the S, compared to Type 1, which has a more rounded top. The surface of Type 2 is frosted, and the openings in the loops are slightly larger.

	Mintage	Cert	Avg	PF-65	PF-67Cam	PF-68DC	PF-69DC	Recent Auction Record
1983S	3,279,126	9,704	69.0	$5	$12	$15	$20	$115, PF-70Cam, August 2013
1984S	3,065,110	4,884	68.9	6	12	15	20	$382, PF-70Cam, June 2013
1985S	3,362,821	5,048	69.0	5	12	15	20	$106, PF-70Cam, August 2013
1986S	3,010,497	5,265	69.0	6	12	15	20	$123, PF-70DCam, January 2013
1987S	4,227,728	5,632	69.0	5	12	15	20	$96, PF-70DCam, August 2013
1988S	3,262,948	4,588	69.0	5	12	15	20	$113, PF-70DCam, May 2013
1988S, Doubled-Die Obverse (g)	*	16	68.6	110	160			$260, PF-68UCam, February 2011
1989S	3,220,194	4,683	69.0	6	12	20	25	$123, PF-70DCam, May 2013
1990S	3,299,559	5,482	69.0	6	12	18	23	$82, PF-70DCam, May 2013
1991S	2,867,787	5,004	69.1	10	14	20	25	$68, PF-70DCam, July 2013
1992S	2,858,981	4,363	69.1	7	14	20	25	$35, PF-70DCam, May 2013
1992S, Silver	1,317,579	5,112	69.0	17	20	25	30	$92, PF-70DCam, July 2013
1993S	2,633,439	4,416	69.1	8	17	23	25	$31, PF-70DCam, May 2013
1993S, Silver	761,353	4,081	69.0	27	30	37	40	$99, PF-70DCam, May 2014
1994S	2,484,594	4,091	69.1	8	17	23	30	$45, PF-70DCam, May 2013
1994S, Silver	785,329	3,986	69.0	26	33	35	40	$206, PF-70DCam, February 2013
1995S	2,117,496	3,696	69.1	16	20	25	30	$66, PF-70DCam, August 2013
1995S, Silver ‡	679,985	3,959	69.0	38	40	45	50	$135, PF-70DCam, May 2014
1996S	1,750,244	3,639	69.0	10	15	22	25	$66, PF-70DCam, August 2013
1996S, Silver	775,021	3,804	69.0	30	35	40	45	$135, PF-70DCam, August 2013
1997S	2,055,000	3,497	69.1	12	20	25	30	$76, PF-70DCam, August 2013
1997S, Silver	741,678	4,294	69.0	30	40	50	55	$96, PF-70DCam, August 2013
1998S	2,086,507	3,474	69.1	10	17	23	25	$56, PF-70DCam, August 2013
1998S, Silver	878,792	4,267	69.1	18	25	35	40	$88, PF-70DCam, August 2013
1998S, Silver, Matte Finish ‡ (h)	62,000	3,925	69.0	125				$441, PF-70, April 2014
1999S	2,543,401	5,453	69.0	13	16	20	25	$90, PF-70DCam, May 2013
1999S, Silver	804,565	9,596	69.0	25	30	32	35	$147, PF-70DCam, August 2013
2000S	3,082,483	6,442	69.0	6	12	16	20	$58, PF-70DCam, May 2013
2000S, Silver	965,421	12,661	69.1	17	18	20	22	$78, PF-70DCam, May 2013
2001S	2,294,909	5,410	69.0	8	10	13	18	$76, PF-70DCam, May 2013
2001S, Silver	889,697	8,543	69.1	18	21	23	25	$90, PF-70DCam, May 2013
2002S	2,319,766	4,921	69.1	7	13	16	22	$60, PF-70DCam, May 2013
2002S, Silver	892,229	8,647	69.2	17	18	20	25	$61, PF-70DCam, May 2013
2003S	2,172,684	6,876	69.1	7	12	16	20	$35, PF-70DCam, May 2013
2003S, Silver	1,125,755	10,380	69.1	17	18	20	22	$82, PF-70DCam, May 2014
2004S	1,789,488	5,443	69.0	13	17	24	30	$66, PF-70DCam, August 2013
2004S, Silver	1,175,934	10,969	69.1	20	22	23	25	$69, PF-70DCam, January 2013
2005S	2,275,000	11,340	69.1	7	12	16	20	$66, PF-70DCam, August 2013
2005S, Silver	1,069,679	10,334	69.2	15	18	20	22	$74, PF-70DCam, January 2013
2006S	2,000,428	5,711	69.1	7	12	16	20	$46, PF-70DCam, August 2013
2006S, Silver	1,054,008	6,308	69.2	15	18	20	22	$76, PF-70DCam, August 2013
2007S	1,702,116	5,375	69.2	7	12	16	20	$64, PF-70DCam, January 2013
2007S, Silver	875,050	5,715	69.2	17	19	22	25	$86, PF-70DCam, August 2013
2008S	1,405,674	3,466	69.2	7	12	16	20	$71, PF-70DCam, November 2013
2008S, Silver	763,887	5,360	69.3	17	20	23	25	$66, PF-70DCam, August 2013
2009S	1,482,502	6,014	69.2	7	12	16	18	$31, PF-70DCam, May 2013
2009S, Silver	697,365	6,125	69.2	17	18	20	22	$41, PF-70DCam, May 2013
2010S	1,103,950	3,021	69.2	7	12	16	18	$48, PF-70DCam, August 2013
2010S, Silver	585,414	5,780	69.5	17	18	20	22	$48, PF-70DCam, May 2013
2011S	952,881	4,616	69.2	7	12	16	18	$21, PF-70UCam, March 2012
2011S, Silver	500,395	7,361	69.5	17	18	20	22	$36, PF-70DCam, April 2012
2012S		107	69.1	7	12	16	18	$51, PF-70DCam, May 2013
2012S, Silver		27	69.5	17	18	20	22	
2013S				7	12	16	18	
2013S, Silver				17	18	20	22	$147, PF-70DCam, May 2014
2014S				7	12	16	18	
2014S, Silver				17	18	20	22	

* Included in number above. ‡ Ranked in the *100 Greatest U.S. Modern Coins*. **g.** Clear doubling is visible on IN GOD WE TRUST, the date, and the mintmark. Some doubling is also evident on LIBERTY and the mintmark. **h.** Minted for inclusion in the Robert F. Kennedy commemorative set (along with an RFK commemorative dollar).

AN OVERVIEW OF SILVER AND RELATED DOLLARS

The silver dollar was authorized by Congress on April 2, 1792, and first coined in 1794. This denomination includes some of the most popular series in American numismatics. Starting in 1971, the U.S. Mint has released copper-nickel, clad, and other non-silver dollar coins, which are also included in this section.

The first silver dollar type, with Flowing Hair, is easy enough to obtain in grades from VF through low Mint State. Striking usually ranges from poor to barely acceptable, and adjustment marks (from an overweight planchet being filed down to correct weight) are often seen. Accordingly, careful examination is needed to find a good example.

The silver dollar with the Draped Bust obverse in combination with the Small Eagle reverse was made from 1795 through 1798, with most examples being dated 1796 or 1797. Today both the 1796 and 1797 exist in about the same numbers. Although mintage figures refer to the quantities produced in the given calendar year, these do not necessarily refer to the dates on the coins themselves. Silver dollars of this type are fairly scarce. Sharpness of strike presents a challenge to the collector, and usually there are weaknesses in details, particularly on the reverse eagle.

Next follows the 1798–1804 type with Draped Bust obverse and Heraldic Eagle reverse. Many such coins exist, again mostly in grades from VF through lower Mint State levels. Striking can be indifferent, but the population is such that collectors have more to choose from.

The Gobrecht silver dollars of 1836 (starless obverse, stars on reverse, plain edge) and 1839 (stars on obverse, starless reverse, reeded edge) present a special challenge in the formation of a type set. For quite a few years these were considered to be *patterns,* and thus anyone forming a type set of regular-issue U.S. coins did not have to notice them. However, in recent decades research by R.W. Julian (in particular), Walter Breen, and others, has revealed that the vast majority of 1836 and 1839 silver dollars originally produced went into circulation at face value. Accordingly, they were coins of the realm at the time, were freely spent, and are deserving of a place among regular coinage types.

The 1836 Gobrecht dollar is easy enough to find, although expensive. The original coinage amounted to 1,600, to which an unknown number of restrikes can be added. The main problem arises with the 1839, made only to the extent of 300 pieces. Those that exist nearly always have abundant signs of circulation. This is the rarest of all major United States design types, even outclassing the 1796–1797 half dollar and the 1808 quarter eagle.

In 1840 the regular Liberty Seated dollar made its appearance, with the reverse depicting a perched eagle holding an olive branch and arrows. This style was continued through 1873; however, in 1866 the motto IN GOD WE TRUST was added to the reverse. Generally, both of these types can be easily enough found in circulated grades from VF up, as well as low Mint State levels. MS-63 and higher pieces are in the minority, particularly of the 1840–1865 type.

Morgan silver dollars, made by the hundreds of millions from 1878 through 1921, are easily found, with the 1881-S being at once the most common of all varieties existing today in gem condition and also usually seen with sharp strike and nice appearance.

Peace silver dollars of 1921 through 1935 exist in large quantities. Some collectors select the first year of issue, 1921, as a separate type, as the design is in high relief. The 1921 is plentiful in Mint State, but rarely comes sharply struck at the obverse and reverse center. Later Peace dollars with shallow relief abound in MS-63 and finer grades, although strike quality can be a problem.

Among later dollars of the Eisenhower, Susan B. Anthony, Sacagawea, Native American, and Presidential types, large supplies are in the hands of dealers and collectors, and finding an excellent example is easy.

FOR THE COLLECTOR AND INVESTOR: SILVER AND RELATED DOLLARS AS A SPECIALTY

Generally, silver dollars of the 1794–1803 years are collected by dates and major types.

Although the 1794, of which an estimated 135 or so exist today, is famous and expensive, other varieties are eminently affordable in such decent grades as VF and EF. Beyond the listings herein, there is a rich panorama of die varieties, most extensively delineated in the 1993 two-volume study, *Silver Dollars and Trade Dollars of the United States: A Complete Encyclopedia.* This built upon earlier works, including J.W. Haseltine's *Type Table of United States Dollars, Half Dollars and Quarter Dollars,* and, especially, the long-term standard work by M.H. Bolender, *The United States Early Silver Dollars from 1794 to 1803.* In many instances among early dollars the number of aficionados desiring a particularly rare die combination may be even smaller than the population of specimens—with the result that not much premium has to be paid.

The 1804 silver dollar is a study in itself. These were first struck in 1834 from 1804-dated dies prepared at that time, as no originals were ever made. Later, probably circa 1859, a new reverse die was made up, ind combined with the earlier 1804 obverse (made in 1834). Those made in 1834 and around that time are today known as Class I dollars, whereas those made with a different reverse, beginning in 1859 and continuing perhaps through the 1870s, are known as Class III. An intermediate variety, from the Class III die combination but with a plain instead of lettered edge, is in the Smithsonian Institution's National Numismatic Collection and is known as Class II. All varieties combined comprise 15 different specimens. This has been called the "King of American Coins" for well over a century and has achieved great fame. Interested numismatists are directed to *The Fantastic 1804 Dollar, Tribute Edition* (2009).

After 1803 it is a long jump to 1836, when silver dollars (of the Gobrecht design) were again struck for circulation. In 1839 more Gobrecht dollars were struck, with the design modified. In addition to the listings in this book are a number of other die combinations, edge and metal varieties, etc., including pieces of the year 1838, most of which are pattern restrikes (studied in *United States Pattern Coins*). These are avidly desired and collected.

Forming a specialized collection of Liberty Seated dollars from 1840 through 1873 has been a pursuit of many collectors over the years. Generally, the Philadelphia Mint dates are available without difficulty, although the 1851 and 1852 are typically acquired as Proof restrikes—originals of both years being prohibitively rare. Most difficult to find in higher grades are coins of the branch mints, including the famous 1870-S, of which only 10 are known to exist and for which no mintage quantity figure was ever listed in official reports. Branch-mint pieces, beginning with the 1846-O, were placed into circulation and used extensively. Beginning in 1870, dollars of this type were struck at Carson City; these also are seen with evidence of circulation. The only exceptions to this are certain dollars of 1859-O and 1860-O which turned up in very "baggy" preservation among Treasury hoards, to the extent of several thousand pieces of both dates combined.

Morgan silver dollars from 1878 through 1921 are one of the most active and popular areas in American numismatics. Approximately 100 different major varieties can be collected, although certain unusual varieties (not basic dates and mintmarks) can be dropped or added as desired. The vast majority of Morgan dollars can be found in Mint State. When these coins were first minted there was little need for them in circulation, and hundreds of millions of coins piled up in Treasury and other vaults. Although many were melted in 1918, enough remained that untold millions exist today in the hands of the public.

Although varieties such as the 1881-S are common and are normally seen in high grades with sharp strike, others with high mintages, the 1886-O and 1896-O being examples, are quite rare in MS-63 and finer, and when seen usually have rather poor eye appeal. Accordingly, quite a bit of discernment is recommended for the savvy collector.

Peace silver dollars, minted from 1921 to 1935, include the High Relief style of 1921, and the shallow-relief motif of 1922 to 1935. A basic set of 24 different dates and mintmarks is easily enough obtained, including in Mint State. The most elusive is the 1934-S.

Eisenhower dollars from 1971 through 1978 are easily obtained in choice and gem Mint State, although some of the circulation strikes, especially the early years, tend to be bagmarked. There are many different varieties made especially for collectors, including Proofs and some in silver clad metals.

In 1979 the Susan B. Anthony dollar was introduced; it had an unpopular reception by the American public. The series was thus short lived, beginning in 1979 and ending in 1981, and comprising strikings from the Philadelphia, Denver, and San Francisco mints. Then, in 1999, the Mint struck more than 40 million additional Anthony dollars, expanding the series to include 1999-P and 1999-D coins.

Like the Anthony dollar, more recent issues of Sacagawea dollars, the related Native American dollars, and the ongoing Presidential dollar series are all readily collectible in high-end Mint State and Proof.

RECOMMENDED READING

Bolender, M.H. *The United States Early Silver Dollars From 1794 to 1803* (5th ed.), Iola, WI, 1987.

Bowers, Q. David. *The Encyclopedia of United States Silver Dollars, 1794–1804,* Irvine, CA, 2013.

Bowers, Q. David. *The Rare Silver Dollars Dated 1804,* Wolfeboro, NH, 1999.

Bowers, Q. David. *Silver Dollars and Trade Dollars of the United States: A Complete Encyclopedia,* Wolfeboro, NH, 1993.

Bowers, Q. David. *A Guide Book of Morgan Silver Dollars* (4th ed.), Atlanta, GA, 2012.

Burdette, Roger W. *A Guide Book of Peace Dollars* (2nd ed.), Atlanta, GA, 2012.

Fey, Michael S., and Oxman, Jeff. *The Top 100 Morgan Dollar Varieties,* Morris Planes, NJ, 1997.

Fivaz, Bill, and Stanton, J.T. *The Cherrypickers' Guide to Rare Die Varieties* (5th ed., vol. II), Atlanta, GA, 2012.

Haseltine, J.W. *Type Table of United States Dollars, Half Dollars and Quarter Dollars,* Philadelphia, 1881 (reprinted 1927, 1968).

Judd, J. Hewitt. *United States Pattern Coins* (10th ed., Q. David Bowers, editor), Atlanta, GA, 2009.

Logies, Martin A. *The Flowing Hair Silver Dollars of 1794,* 2004.

Newman, Eric P., and Bressett, Kenneth E. *The Fantastic 1804 Dollar, Tribute Edition,* Atlanta, GA, 2009.

Van Allen, Leroy C., and Mallis, A. George. *Comprehensive Catalogue and Encyclopedia of U.S. Morgan and Peace*

FLOWING HAIR
(1794–1795)

Engraver Robert Scot; weight 26.96 grams; composition .900 silver, .100 copper; approx. diameter 39–40 mm; edge: HUNDRED CENTS ONE DOLLAR OR UNIT with decorations between words.

Bowers-Borckardt-27, Bolender-5.

History. The first U.S. silver dollars were of the Flowing Hair design. In 1794 only 1,758 were released (slightly more were struck), and the next year nearly 100 times that amount. These coins were popular in their time and circulated for decades afterward. Many were used in international trade, particularly in the Caribbean.

Striking and Sharpness. On the obverse, check the hair details. It is essential to check the die variety, as certain varieties were struck with very little detail at the center. Accordingly, high-grade examples can appear to be well worn on the hair. Check the star centers, as well. On the reverse, check the breast and wings of the eagle. All 1794 dollars are lightly struck at the lower left of the obverse (often at portions of the date) and to a lesser extent the corresponding part of the reverse. Many coins of both dates have planchet adjustment marks, often heavy and sometimes even disfiguring; these are not noted by the certification services. Expect weakness in some areas on dollars of this type; a coin with Full Details on both sides is virtually unheard of. Sharp striking and excellent eye appeal add to the value dramatically. These coins are very difficult to find problem-free, even in MS.

Availability. The 1794 is rare in all grades, with an estimated 125 to 135 known, including a handful in MS. The 1795 is easily available, although some die varieties range from scarce to rare. Many if not most have been dipped at one time or another, and many have been retoned, often satisfactorily. The existence of *any* luster is an exception between EF-40 and AU-58. MS coins are quite scarce, especially at MS-63 or above.

Varieties listed are those most significant to collectors, but numerous minor variations may be found because each of the early dies was made individually. (Values of variations not listed in this guide depend on collector interest and demand.) Blanks were weighed before the dollars were struck and overweight pieces were filed to remove excess silver. Coins with old adjustment marks from this filing process may be worth less than values shown here. Some Flowing Hair dollars were weight-adjusted through insertion of a small (8 mm) silver plug in the center of the blank planchet before the coin was struck.

EF-40, 45 (Extremely Fine). *Obverse:* More wear than at AU is evident on the portrait, especially on the hair to the left of the face and neck (again, remember that some varieties were struck with flatness in this area), the cheek, and the tip of the neck truncation. Excellent detail remains in low-relief areas of the hair. The stars show wear, as do the date and letters. Luster, if present at all, is minimal and in protected areas. *Reverse:* The eagle (the focal point to check) shows more wear than at AU. Most or nearly all detail is well defined. These aspects should be reviewed in combination with knowledge of the die variety, to determine the sharpness of the coin when it was first struck. Most silver dollars of this type were flat at the highest area of the center at the time they were made, as this was opposite the highest point of the hair in the press when the coins were struck. Additional wear is on the wreath and letters, but many details are present. Some luster may be seen in protected areas, and if present is slightly more abundant than on the obverse.

AU-50, 53, 55, 58 (About Uncirculated). *Obverse:* Light wear is seen on the hair area immediately to the left of the face and neck (except that some varieties were flatly struck in this area to begin with), on the cheek, and on the top of the neck truncation, more so at AU-50 than at 53 or 55. An AU-58 coin has minimal traces of wear. An AU-50 coin has luster in protected areas among the stars and letters, with little luster in the open fields or on the portrait. Some certified coins have virtually no luster, but are considered to be of high quality in other aspects. At AU-58, most luster is partially present in the fields. On any high-grade dollar, luster is often a better key to grading than is the appearance of wear. *Reverse:* Light wear is seen on the eagle's body and the upper edges of the wings. At AU-50, detail is lost for some of the feathers in this area. However, striking can play a part, and some coins are weak to begin with. Light wear is seen on the wreath and lettering. Again, luster is the best key to actual wear. This ranges from perhaps 20% remaining in protected areas (at AU-50) to two-thirds or more (at AU-58). As a general rule, the reverse will have more luster than the obverse.

MS-60 to 70 (Mint State). *Obverse:* At MS-60, some abrasion and contact marks are evident, most noticeably on the cheek and in the fields. Luster is present, but may be dull or lifeless, and interrupted in patches. At MS-63, contact marks are very few, and abrasion is light and not obvious. An MS-65 coin has little or no abrasion, and contact marks are minute. Luster should be full and rich. Coins graded above MS-65 are more theoretical than actual for this type—but they do exist, and are defined by having fewer marks as perfection is approached. *Reverse:* Comments apply as for the obverse, except that abrasion and contact marks are most noticeable on the eagle, at the center, although most dollars of this type are lightly struck in the higher points of that area. The field area is small and is protected by lettering and the wreath, and in any given grade shows fewer marks than the obverse.

1795, Two Leaves Beneath
Each Wing

1795, Three Leaves Beneath
Each Wing

1795, Silver Plug
Bowers-Borckardt-15, Bolender-7.

	Mintage	Cert	Avg	%MS	AU-55	AU-58	MS-60	MS-62	MS-63	MS-64	MS-65	Recent Auction Record
1794 † (a)	1,758	121	30.7	7	$500,000	$600,000	$650,000	$825,000	$1,500,000	$2,000,000	$4,500,000	$305,500, EF-40, January 2014
1794, Silver Plug (b)	*	1	66.0	100								
1795, All kinds	160,295											
1795, Two Leaves		740	28.8	3	26,000	40,000	70,000	110,000	175,000	280,000	600,000	$25,850, AU-55, August 2013
1795, Three Leaves		1,566	28.8	2	24,500	37,500	65,000	100,000	160,000	265,000	550,000	$646,250, MS-65, November 2013
1795, Silver Plug		96	31.6	5	100,000	135,000	160,000	200,000				$99,875, AU-55, August 2013

* Included in number above. † Ranked in the *100 Greatest U.S. Coins* (fourth edition). **a.** Value in EF-40 is $250,000; in AU-50, $325,000. **b.** This unique piece, graded SP-66, shows evidence of adjustment marks, as well as traces of a silver plug that was added to bring the coin's weight up to specification.

DRAPED BUST, SMALL EAGLE REVERSE
(1795–1798)

Designer Robert Scot; weight 26.96 grams; composition .8924 silver, .1076 copper; approx. diameter 39–40 mm; edge: HUNDRED CENTS ONE DOLLAR OR UNIT with decorations between words.

Bowers-Borckardt-51, Bolender-14.

History. The Draped Bust silver dollar with the Small Eagle reverse, inaugurated in 1795, brought the first appearance of this popular obverse portrait—a depiction of Miss Liberty that later was used on other silver denominations as well as copper half cents and cents. The motif was continued into 1798.

Striking and Sharpness. On the obverse, check the highest areas of the hair, the bust line, and the centers of the stars. On the reverse, check the feathers on the eagle's breast and wings. Examine the dentils. Planchet adjustment marks are common and should be avoided. Studying die varieties can be helpful. For example, the Small Letters reverse, a long-lived die design used from 1795 to 1798, has shallow relief and is usually seen with a low rim, with the result that its grade is lower than that of the obverse. On some reverse dies the eagle has very little detail. Fairly sharp striking (not necessarily Full Details) and excellent eye appeal add to the value dramatically.

Availability. These silver dollars are readily available as a type, although certain varieties range from scarce to very rare. MS coins are elusive and when seen are usually of the 1795 date, sometimes with prooflike surfaces. Most coins have been dipped and/or retoned, some successfully. These coins acquired marks more readily than did lower denominations, and such are to be expected (but should be noted along with the grade, if distracting). Careful buying is needed to obtain coins with good eye appeal. Many AU examples are deeply toned and recolored.

The Smithsonian's National Numismatic Collection includes a unique Specimen 1794 dollar, plugged, and a unique Specimen 1797 10 Stars Left, 6 Stars Right dollar.

AU-50, 53, 55, 58 (About Uncirculated). *Obverse:* Light wear is seen on the hair area above the ear and extending to the left of the forehead, on the ribbon, and on the drapery at the shoulder, more so at AU-50 than at 53 or 55. An AU-58 coin has minimal traces of wear. Concerning luster: An AU-50 coin has luster in protected areas among the stars and letters, with little in the open fields or on the portrait. At AU-58, most luster is present in the fields, but is worn away on the highest parts of the motifs. *Reverse:* Light wear is seen on the eagle's body (note: this area might be lightly struck) and the edges of the wings. Light wear is seen on the wreath and lettering. Luster is the best key to actual wear; this ranges from per-

haps 20% remaining in protected areas (at AU-50) to nearly full mint bloom (at AU-58).

MS-60 to 70 (Mint State). *Obverse:* At MS-60, some abrasion and contact marks are evident, most noticeably on the cheek, the drapery at the shoulder, and the right field. Luster is present, but may be dull or lifeless, and interrupted in patches. At MS-63, contact marks are few, and abrasion is harder to detect. Many coins listed as MS are deeply toned, making it impossible to evaluate abrasion and even light wear; these are best avoided completely. An MS-65 coin has no abrasion, and contact marks are so minute as to require magnification. Luster should be full and rich.

Coins grading above MS-65 are more theoretical than actual for this type—but they do exist, and are defined by having fewer marks as perfection is approached. *Reverse:* Comments apply as for the obverse, except that abrasion and contact marks are most noticeable on the eagle at the center, a situation complicated by the fact that this area was often flatly struck, not only on the famous Small Letters dies used from 1795 to 1798, but on some others as well. Grading is best done by the obverse, then verified by the reverse. In MS the amount of luster is usually a good key to grading. The field area is small and is protected by lettering and the wreath, and in any given grade shows fewer marks than on the obverse.

1795, Off-Center Bust

1795, Centered Bust

Small Date

Large Date

Small Letters

Large Letters

1797, 10 Stars Left,
6 Right

1797, 9 Stars Left,
7 Right

1798, 15 Stars
on Obverse

1798, 13 Stars
on Obverse

	Mintage	Cert	Avg	%MS	AU-50	AU-55	AU-58	MS-60	MS-62	MS-63	MS-64	Recent Auction Record
1795, All kinds	42,738											
1795, Off-Center Bust (a)		324	35.5	3	$16,500	$22,500	$34,000	$60,000	$80,000	$150,000	$200,000	$910,625, MS-66, November 2013
1795, Centered Bust (b)		536	32.9	5	16,500	20,000	31,500	55,000	75,000	150,000	250,000	$17,625, AU-50, March 2013
1796, All kinds	79,920											
1796, Small Date, Small Letters (3 varieties)		365	29.8	0	15,000	22,000	32,500	62,500	87,500	150,000	350,000	$1,175,000, MS-65, April 2013
1796, Small Date, Large Letters		284	33.0	1	15,000	30,000	43,500	75,000	150,000	200,000		$352,500, MS-63, November 2013
1796, Large Date, Small Letters		203	34.3	3	15,000	25,500	40,000	62,500	90,000	160,000		$13,513, AU-50, August 2013
1797, All kinds	7,776											
1797, 10 Stars Left, 6 Right (c)		338	35.4	2	14,500	22,000	32,500	62,000	87,500	125,000	165,000	$440,625, MS-64, November 2013
1797, 9 Stars Left, 7 Right, Large Letters		543	30.7	1	15,300	25,000	43,000	63,000	92,500	135,000	165,000	$381,875, MS-64, November 2013
1797, 9 Stars Left, 7 Right, Small Letters		103	29.1	0	32,500	57,500	82,500	110,000				$164,500, MS-62, November 2013
1798, All kinds (d)	327,536											
1798, 15 Stars on Obverse		134	31.6	2	24,500	37,500	60,000	84,000	125,000	155,000		$258,500, MS-63, November 2013
1798, 13 Stars on Obverse		219	33.0	1	19,800	31,000	50,000	76,000	115,000			$129,250, AU-58, November 2013

a. Value in MS-65 is $500,000. **b.** Value in MS-65 is $450,000. **c.** Value in MS-65 is $250,000. **d.** The Mint struck 327,536 silver dollars in 1798, but did not record how many of each type (Small Eagle reverse and Heraldic Eagle reverse).

DRAPED BUST, HERALDIC EAGLE REVERSE (1798–1804)

Designer Robert Scot; weight 26.96 grams; composition .8924 silver, .1076 copper; approx. diameter 39–40 mm; edge: HUNDRED CENTS ONE DOLLAR OR UNIT with decorations between words.

Bowers-Borckardt-241, Bolender-6.

History. The design of the silver dollar closely follows that of other silver coins of the era. The two earliest reverse dies of 1798 have five vertical lines in the stripes in the shield. All dollar dies thereafter have four vertical lines. Production of the Draped Bust dollar continued through early 1804, but the last were from earlier-dated dies. Later, in 1834, new dies were made with the 1804 date, and still later, in 1859, additional 1804-dated dollars were struck. As a class these can be called *novodels,* rather than *restrikes,* as no originals were ever made. The 1804 dollars were produced in Proof format.

Striking and Sharpness. Very few coins have Full Details. On the obverse, check the highest points of the hair, the details of the drapery, and the centers of the stars. On the reverse, check the shield, the eagle, the stars above the eagle, and the clouds. Examine the dentils on both sides. Planchet adjustment marks are often seen, but they usually are lighter than on the earlier types. The relief of the dies and the height of the rims can vary, affecting sharpness. Sharp striking and excellent eye appeal add to the value dramatically. Top-grade MS coins, when found, usually are dated 1800.

Availability. This is the most readily available type among the early silver dollars. Most often seen are the dates 1798 and 1799. Many varieties are available in any grade desired, although MS-63 and 65 coins are elusive. Other die varieties are rare at any level. As with other early dollars, connoisseurship is needed to acquire quality coins. These coins usually have problems. To evaluate them for the market it is necessary to grade them, determine the quality of striking, and examine the characteristics of the surface. Nearly all have been dipped or cleaned.

AU-50, 53, 55, 58 (About Uncirculated). *Obverse:* Light wear is seen on the hair area above the ear and extending to the left of the forehead, on the ribbon, and on the drapery and bosom, more so at AU-50 than at 53 or 55. An AU-58 coin has minimal traces of wear. Concerning luster: An AU-50 coin has luster in protected areas among the stars and letters, with little in the open fields or on the portrait. At AU-58, much luster is present in the fields, but is worn away on the highest parts of the motifs. *Reverse:* Comments apply as for the obverse, except that the eagle's neck, the tips and top of the wings, the clouds, and the tail show noticeable wear, as do other features. Luster ranges from perhaps 20% remaining in protected areas (at AU-50) to nearly full mint bloom (at AU-58). Sometimes the reverse of this type retains much more luster than the obverse, depending on the height of the rim and the depth of the strike (particularly at the center).

MS-60 to 70 (Mint State). *Obverse:* At MS-60, some abrasion and contact marks are evident, most noticeably on the cheek, the drapery, and the right field. Luster is present, but may be dull or lifeless, and interrupted in patches. At MS-63, contact marks are very few, and abrasion is hard to detect except under magnification. Knowledge of the die variety is desirable, but on balance the portraits on this type are usually quite well struck. An MS-65 coin has no abrasion, and contact marks are so minute as to require magnification. Luster should be full and rich. Coins grading above MS-65 are more theoretical than actual for this type—but they do exist and are defined by having fewer marks as perfection is approached. *Reverse:* Comments apply as for the obverse, except that abrasion and contact marks are most noticeable on the eagle's neck, the tips of the wing, and the tail. The field area is complex, without much open space, given the stars above the eagle, the arrows and olive branch, and other features. Accordingly, marks will not be as noticeable as on the obverse.

1798, Knob 9

1798, Pointed 9

Five Vertical Lines
in Shield's Stripes

Four Vertical Lines
in Shield's Stripes

1798, Pointed 9,
Close Date

1798, Pointed 9,
Wide Date

1798, Pointed 9,
10 Arrows

1798, Pointed 9,
4 Berries

1799, 99 Over 98,
15-Star Reverse

1799, 99 Over 98,
13-Star Reverse

1799, Irregular Date

1799, 8 Stars Left,
5 Stars Right

1799, Irregular Date,
15-Star Reverse

1799, Irregular Date,
13-Star Reverse

1799, Normal Date

1800, Very Wide Date, Low 8

1800, "Dotted Date"

1800, Only 12 Arrows

1800, AMERICAI

1802, 2 Over 1, Narrow Date

1802, 2 Over 1, Wide Date

1802, Narrow Normal Date

1802, Wide Normal Date

1803, Small 3

1803, Large 3

	Mintage	Cert	Avg	%MS	AU-55	AU-58	MS-60	MS-62	MS-63	MS-64	MS-65	Recent Auction Record
1798, Knob 9, 5 Vertical Lines	*	52	39.3	6	$10,500	$16,000	$22,000	$33,000	$70,000	—	—	$10,063, AU-50, September 2011
1798, Knob 9, 4 Vertical Lines	*	24	43.3	8	12,500	19,000	—					$9,775, AU-50, September 2011
1798, Knob 9, 10 Arrows	*	106	32.6	1	12,500	19,000	—					$7,175, AU-53, September 2013
1798, Pointed 9, Close Date	*	181	39.3	3	11,500	16,000	22,000	33,000	70,000	$110,000	$165,000	$38,188, MS-62, April 2014
1798, Pointed 9, Wide Date	*	298	36.1	5	11,500	16,000	22,000	33,000	70,000	110,000	165,000	$9,988, AU-58, February 2013
1798, Pointed 9, 5 Vertical Lines	*	12	39.3	0	18,000	23,000	25,000	—	—	—	—	$8,225, AU-53, September 2013
1798, Pointed 9, 10 Arrows	*	62	36.4	3	11,500	16,000	23,500	33,000	80,000	—	—	$10,281, AU-55, August 2013
1798, Pointed 9, 4 Berries	*	29	33.2	0	10,500	15,000	21,500	32,500	67,500	110,000	165,000	$2,703, VF-30, July 2014
1799, All kinds	423,515											
1799, 99 Over 98, 15-Star Reverse (a)		267	38.3	6	8,500	14,500	23,000	35,500	57,000	115,000	—	$141,000, MS-64, November 2013
1799, 99 Over 98, 13-Star Reverse		205	33.2	4	8,400	14,000	22,400	34,000	56,500	110,000	—	$76,390, MS, February 2014
1799, Irregular Date, 15-Star Reverse		32	33.2	0	8,500	15,500	23,000	—	—	—	—	$3,055, EF-35, September 2013
1799, Irregular Date, 13-Star Reverse		70	36.2	6	8,200	14,000	22,000	34,000	56,500	105,000	190,000	$99,875, MS-64, August 2013
1799, Normal Date		451	37.6	4	8,200	14,000	22,400	34,000	56,500	105,000	190,000	$822,500, MS-67, November 2013
1799, 8 Stars Left, 5 Right		87	36.1	3	13,500	18,000	32,500	57,500	92,500	155,000	—	$41,125, MS-61, November 2013
1800, All kinds	220,920											
1800, Very Wide Date, Low 8		49	35.1	0	8,100	14,750	24,500	37,000	60,000	115,000	—	$11,750, AU-53, January 2014
1800, "Dotted Date" (b)		118	34.0	3	8,100	14,750	24,500	37,000	60,000	115,000	190,000	$9,988, AU-53, August 2013
1800, Only 12 Arrows		95	35.2	5	8,100	14,750	24,500	37,000	60,000	115,000	—	$6,463, AU-50, September 2013
1800, Normal Dies		196	38.4	2	8,100	14,000	24,000	34,000	56,500	105,000	190,000	$17,625, AU-55, August 2013
1800, AMERICAI (c)		156	35.4	4	8,100	17,500	26,500	48,500	—	—	—	$223,250, MS-65, November 2013
1801	54,454	731	34.7	2	8,350	19,500	29,500	49,000	82,500	155,000	250,000	$329,000, MS-65, November 2013
1802, All kinds	41,650											
1802, 2 Over 1, Narrow Date		325	31.9	2	9,100	17,500	30,000	46,000	68,500	115,000	—	$11,750, AU-58, February 2013
1802, 2 Over 1, Wide Date		52	34.7	6	11,100	19,000	32,000	48,500	71,000	120,000	—	$199,750, MS-64, November 2013
1802, Narrow Normal Date		95	42.6	12	8,100	14,250	23,500	37,500	68,500	105,000	240,000	$41,125, MS-61, November 2013
1802, Wide Normal Date		15	46.3	0	10,100	18,000	36,000	49,500	76,000	125,000	300,000	$10,869, AU-55, August 2013
1803, All kinds	85,634											
1803, Small 3		445	33.1	2	9,000	16,000	27,000	43,500	71,000	115,000	—	$117,500, MS-63, November 2013
1803, Large 3		334	33.3	2	9,000	16,000	27,000	43,500	71,000	115,000	—	$705,000, MS-65, November 2013

Note: The two earliest reverse dies of 1798 have five vertical lines in the stripes in the shield. All dollar dies thereafter have four vertical lines. * The Mint struck 327,536 silver dollars in 1798, but did not record how many of each type (Small Eagle reverse and Heraldic Eagle reverse). **a.** The engraver of the reverse die accidentally engraved 15 stars, instead of the 13 needed to represent the original Colonies. He attempted to cover the two extra stars under the leftmost and rightmost clouds, but their points stick out slightly. **b.** The "dotted" date is the result of die breaks. **c.** A reverse die flaw resulted in what appears to be a sans-serif letter I after AMERICA. "Perhaps from a punch or from a stray piece of metal during the die making process" (Bowers, *Silver Dollars & Trade Dollars of the United States*).

Proof Draped Bust, Heraldic Reverse, Dollars

PF-60 to 70 (Proof). There were no Proofs coined in the era this type was issued. Years afterward, in 1834, the U.S. Mint fabricated new dies with the 1804 date and struck an unknown number of Proofs, perhaps a dozen or so, for inclusion in presentation Proof sets for foreign dignitaries. Today these are called Class I 1804 dollars. Eight examples are known, one of which shows circulation. Circa 1858 the Mint prepared a new reverse die dated 1804 and struck an unknown number of examples for private sale to collectors and dealers—the Class III dollars. No records were kept. These were artificially worn to give them the appearance of original dollars struck in 1804.

Sometime between circa 1858 and the 1870s, the Mint prepared new obverse dies dated 1801, 1802, and 1803, and struck Proof dollars for secret sale to the numismatic market. Many if not most were distributed through J.W. Haseltine, a Philadelphia dealer who had close connections with Mint officials. Today these are known as "Proof restrikes." All are rare, the 1801 being particularly so.

Class I 1804 dollars typically show hairlines and light abrasion. Grading is usually very liberal, in view of the fame of this rarity (not that this is logical). Circulated examples of Class I and Class III 1804 dollars have been graded using pre-

fixes such as EF and AU. Proof restrikes of 1801 to 1803 generally survive in much higher grades, PF-64 or finer.

Detailed historical and technical information may be found in *The Fantastic 1804 Dollar, Tribute Edition* (Newman/Bressett, 2009).

Obverse and Reverse: For lower Proof levels, extensive abrasion is seen in the fields, or even evidence of circulation. Numbers assigned by grading services have been erratic. No rules are standardized, and grading has not been consistent.

Proof Draped Bust, Heraldic Eagle Reverse, Dollar (Restrike)
Bowers-Borckardt-302.

1804 Dollar   **1804, First Reverse**   **1804, Second Reverse**
Note the position of the words STATES OF in relation to the clouds.

	Est Mintage	Cert	Finest	PF-63	PF-64	PF-65	Recent Auction Record
1801, Restrike † **(a)**	*2 known*	n/a	n/a		$1,000,000	$1,500,000	
1802, Restrike † **(a)**	*4 known*	12	PF-65	$500,000	800,000	1,000,000	$920,000, PF-65Cam, April 2008
1803, Restrike † **(a)**	*3 known*	13	PF-66	500,000	800,000	1,000,000	$851,875, PF-66, January 2013
1804, First Reverse, Original, Class I	*8 known*	11	PF-68	4,000,000	4,500,000	6,000,000	$3,877,500, PF-62, August 2013
1804, Second Reverse, Restrike, Class III	*6 known*	5	PF-65				$2,300,000, PF-58, April 2009
1804, Second Reverse, Restrike, Plain Edge, Class II **(b)**	*1*						
1804, Electrotype of Unique Plain-Edge Specimen **(c)**	*4*						

Note: The 1804 dollars as a group are ranked among the *100 Greatest U.S. Coins.* † Ranked in the *100 Greatest U.S. Coins* (fourth edition). **a.** "The Proof silver dollars of 1801, 1802, and 1803 are all extremely rare, valuable, and desirable, although none of them were made anywhere near the dates on the coins, nor do they share any die characteristics with any real silver dollars made from 1801 to 1803" (*100 Greatest U.S. Coins,* fourth edition). **b.** The plain-edge restrike is in the Smithsonian's National Numismatic Collection. **c.** These electrotypes were made by the U.S. Mint.

GOBRECHT
(1836–1839)

1836, No Stars on Obverse, Stars on Reverse: Designer Christian Gobrecht; weight 26.96 grams; composition .8924 silver, .1076 copper; diameter 39–40 mm; plain edge.

No Stars on Obverse, Stars on Reverse

1838–1839, Stars on Obverse, No Stars on Reverse: Designer Christian Gobrecht; weight 26.73 grams; composition .900 silver, .100 copper; diameter 39–40 mm; reeded edge.

Stars on Obverse, No Stars on Reverse

History. Suspension of silver-dollar coinage was lifted in 1831, but it was not until 1835 that the Mint took steps to resume coinage. Late in that year Director R.M. Patterson ordered engraver Christian Gobrecht to prepare a pair of dies based on designs by Thomas Sully and Titian Peale. The first obverse die, dated 1836, bore the seated figure of Liberty on the obverse with the inscription C. GOBRECHT F. (the last letter for *Fecit,* Latin for "made it") in the field above the date. On the reverse was a large eagle flying left, surrounded by 26 stars and the legend UNITED STATES OF AMERICA • ONE DOLLAR •. It is unknown whether coins from these dies were struck at that time. A new obverse die was prepared with Gobrecht's name on the base of Miss Liberty, and in December 1836, 1,000 coins were struck for circulation. These coins weighed 416 grains, which was the standard enacted in 1792.

In January 1837 the standard weight of the dollar was lowered to 412-1/2 grains, and pieces were struck in March 1837 using the dies of 1836. The dies were oriented in medal fashion (top to top when the coin is rotated on its y axis) to distinguish them from those struck in December 1836. Dollars issued for circulation in 1836, 1837, and 1839 are found with different die alignments. The "original" issue of December 1836 has the normal coin orientation (reverse upright when coin is turned on the x axis), with the eagle flying upward.

From the late 1850s to the 1870s the Mint continued to strike Gobrecht dollars to satisfy collector demand. Mules, which had mismatched designs or edge devices, were made in that period and are very rare. Restrikes and mules are seldom seen in worn condition.

As a group, the Gobrecht dollars are ranked among the *100 Greatest U.S. Coins.*

Original 1836 die orientation using either "coin" or "medal" turn.

Die alignment of original issues dated 1838 and 1839.

Gobrecht dollars, both original issues and restrikes, were made in either coin-turn orientation ↑↓ (I and III), or medal-turn orientation ↑↑ (II and IV), and were struck in four basic die alignments.

- Die alignment I: ↑↓, head of Liberty opposite DO of DOLLAR, eagle flying upward.
- Die alignment II: ↑↑, head of Liberty opposite ES of STATES, eagle flying upward.

- Die alignment III: ↑↓, head of Liberty opposite N of ONE, eagle flying level.
- Die alignment IV: ↑↑, head of Liberty opposite F of OF, eagle flying level.

Rotated dies are common for original issue and restrike Gobrecht dollars. The 600 coins produced for circulation in March 1837 had dies that rotated from die alignment II to die alignment IV during the striking.

Striking and Sharpness. Striking is usually very good. Check the details on Miss Liberty's head and the higher parts of the eagle. Note that the word LIBERTY is raised.

Availability. 1836 Gobrecht dollars are available in grades from so-called Very Fine upward (the coins were struck as Proofs, and worn examples are properly designated as PF-30, PF-40, and so on; however, sometimes they are found graded as Fine, VF, and EF for levels below PF-50). Most in the marketplace range from PF-50 to 62. Most have contact marks. Truly pristine PF-65 and better examples are very elusive. The demand for these coins is intense. For the 1839, circulated grades typically are PF-50 or higher, often with damage. Pristine Proofs are available, but virtually all are restrikes.

Proof Gobrecht Dollars

PF-20, 25, 30, 35 (Impaired Proof, sometimes designated VF). *Obverse:* Many details of the gown are worn away, but the lower-relief areas above and to the right of the shield remain well defined. Hair detail is mostly or completely gone. LIBERTY is weak at the center. *Reverse:* Considerable wear is evident on the eagle, with only about 60% of the feathers visible.

PF-40 to 45 (Impaired Proof, sometimes designated EF). *Obverse:* Wear is seen on all areas, especially the thighs and knees, bosom, and head. The center of LIBERTY, which is in relief, is weak. *Reverse:* Wear is evident on the eagle, including the back edge of the closest wing, the top of the farthest wing, and the tail.

PF-50, 53, 55, 58 (Impaired Proof, sometimes designated AU). *Obverse:* Light wear is seen on the thighs and knees, bosom, and head. At PF-50 and 53, most if not all mirror surface is gone and there are scattered marks. At PF-58, the Proof surface is extensive, but the open fields show abrasion. *Reverse:* Wear is most evident on the eagle's breast and the top of the wings. Mirror surface ranges from none (at PF-50) to perhaps 60% complete (at PF-58).

PF-60 to 70 (Proof). *Obverse and Reverse:* Many Proofs have been extensively cleaned and have many hairlines and dull fields. This is more applicable to 1836 than to 1839. Grades are PF-60 to 61 or 62. With medium hairlines and good reflectivity, an assigned grade of PF-64 is appropriate, and with relatively few hairlines, PF-65. In various grades hairlines are most easily seen in the obverse field. PF-66 should have hairlines so delicate that magnification is needed to see them. Above that, a Proof should be free of such lines.

	Cert	PF-40	PF-50	PF-60	PF-62	PF-63	PF-64	PF-65	Recent Auction Record
1836. C. GOBRECHT F. on base. Judd-60. Plain edge, no stars on obverse, stars in field on reverse. Die alignment I, ↑↓. Circulation issue. 1,000 struck **(a)**	227	$15,500 **(b)**	$19,000	$25,000	$30,000	$45,000	$75,000	$150,000	$29,900, PF-62, April 2012
1836. As above. Plain edge. Judd-60. Die alignment II and die alignment IV, ↑↑. Circulation issue struck in 1837. 600 struck **(a)**	*	16,000 **(c)**	21,000	25,000	30,000	45,000	75,000	150,000	$16,100, PF-58, March 2012

* Included in number above. **a.** Originals. Although these are listed in Judd as patterns, they are considered circulation strikes. **b.** Value in PF-20 is $11,000. **c.** Value in PF-20 is $11,000.

	Cert	PF-40	PF-50	PF-60	PF-62	PF-63	PF-64	PF-65	Recent Auction Record
1838. Obverse stars added around border, reeded edge. Judd-84. Designer's name removed. Reverse eagle flying in plain field. Die alignment IV, ↑↑.	57			$70,000	$75,000	$85,000	$100,000	$150,000	$83,375, PF-64, July 2008
1839. As above. Reeded edge. Judd-104. Die alignment IV, ↑↑. Circulation issue. 300 struck	89	$17,500 (a)	$22,500	29,000	38,500	44,000	60,000	100,000	$18,975, PF-45, November 2011

a. Value in PF-20 is $15,000.

Restrike Gobrecht Dollar

	Cert	PF-40	PF-50	PF-60	PF-62	PF-63	PF-64	PF-65	Recent Auction Record
1836. Name below base; eagle in starry field; plain edge. Judd-58. Die alignment III, ↑↓, and die alignment IV, ↑↑. (a)	32 (b)	$17,500	$30,000	$70,000	$75,000	$80,000	$100,000	$125,000	$34,500, PF-63, April 2012
1836. Name on base; plain edge. Judd 60. Die alignment III, ↑↓. (30–40 known) (a)	*	15,000 (c)	20,000	23,500	26,000	35,000	55,000	90,000	$18,975, PF-61, September 2010
1836. C. GOBRECHT F. on base. Judd-61. Reeded edge. No stars on obverse, stars in field on reverse. Die alignment IV, ↑↑. (a)	2			(extremely rare)					$195,000, PF-63, May 2003
1838. Designer's name removed; reeded edge. Judd-84. Die alignment III, ↑↓, and die alignment IV, ↑↑. (a)	*	25,000	30,000	35,000	47,500	62,500	85,000	125,000	$83,375, PF-64, March 2012
1839. Designer's name removed; eagle in plain field; reeded edge. Judd-104. Die alignment III, ↑↓, and die alignment IV, ↑↑. (a)	*	20,000 (d)	25,000	37,500	42,500	50,000	65,000	100,000	$51,750, PF-64, April 2012

Note: Restrikes were produced from the late 1850s to the 1870s, and are not official Mint issues. They were all oriented in either die alignment III (coin turn) or die alignment IV (medal turn), with the eagle flying level. Almost all were struck from a cracked reverse die. For detailed analysis of these pieces, consult *United States Pattern Coins,* 10th edition. * Included in figure for first listing with this Judd number, as the grading services do not consistently distinguish between originals and restrikes. a. Restrikes. Listed in Judd as patterns. b. Many originals were certified as restrikes in years past. This figure includes some of these originals. c. Value in PF-20 is $12,500. d. Value in PF-20 is $17,500.

LIBERTY SEATED
(1840–1873)

No Motto (1840–1865): Designer Christian Gobrecht; weight 26.73 grams; composition .900 silver, .100 copper (net weight .77344 oz. pure silver); diameter 38.1 mm; reeded edge; mints: Philadelphia, New Orleans, San Francisco.

**No Motto
(1840–1865)**

With Motto IN GOD WE TRUST (1866–1873): Designer Christian Gobrecht; weight 26.73 grams; composition .900 silver, .100 copper (net weight .77344 oz. pure silver); diameter 38.1 mm; reeded edge; mints: Philadelphia, Carson City, San Francisco.

**With Motto IN GOD WE TRUST
(1866–1873)**

History. The Liberty Seated dollar was minted every year from 1840 to 1873, with an obverse design modified from that of the 1839 Gobrecht dollar. The flying eagle of the Gobrecht dollar was replaced with a perched eagle similar to that of contemporary quarter and half dollars. The dollars, minted in modest numbers, circulated in the United States through 1850. In that year the rising value of silver on the international markets brought the cost of minting each coin to more than $1. Production continued for the international, rather than domestic, market, through 1873, when the trade dollar took the Liberty Seated dollar's place.

Striking and Sharpness. On the obverse, check the head of Miss Liberty and the centers of the stars. On the reverse, check the feathers of the eagle. The dentils usually are sharp. Dollars of 1857 usually are weakly struck, but have semi-prooflike surfaces. The word LIBERTY is in a high-relief area on the coin, with the result that it wore away quickly. Therefore this feature cannot be used as the only guide to grading an obverse. From EF downward, strike sharpness in the stars and the head does not matter to connoisseurs.

Availability. All issues from 1840 to 1850 are available in proportion to their mintages. Those of 1851 to the late 1860s are either scarce or rare in circulated grades, and in MS they range from rare to extremely rare, despite generous mintages in some instances. The later-date coins were shipped to China and later melted. Coins of the 1870s are more readily available, although some are scarce to rare.

AU-50, 53, 55, 58 (About Uncirculated). *Obverse:* Light wear is seen on the thighs and knees, bosom, and head. There is some luster at AU-50 and 53. At AU-58, the luster is extensive but incomplete, especially in the right field. *Reverse:* Wear is visible on the eagle's neck, the claws, and the top of the wings. At AU-50 and 53, there are traces of luster. An AU-58 coin has nearly full luster.

MS-60 to 70 (Mint State). *Obverse:* At MS-60, some abrasion and contact marks are evident, most notice-ably on the bosom and thighs and knees. Luster is present, but may be dull or lifeless. At MS-63, contact marks are very few, and abrasion is minimal. An MS-65 coin has no abrasion in the fields (but may have a hint on the knees), and contact marks are trivial. Check the knees of Liberty and the right field. Luster should be full and rich on later issues, not necessarily so for dates in the 1840s. Most MS coins of 1861 to 1865, Philadelphia issues, have extensive die striae (from the die being incompletely finished). *Reverse:* Comments apply as for the obverse, except

that in lower MS grades, abrasion and marks are most noticeable on the eagle's head, the neck, the claws, and the top of the wings (harder to see there, however). At MS-65 or higher, there are no marks visible to the unaided eye. The field is mainly protected by design elements and does not show abrasion as much as does the obverse on a given coin.

1851, Original, High Date

1852, Original

1869, Repunched Date
FS-S1-1869-302. Other varieties exist.

	Mintage	Cert	Avg	%MS	AU-50	AU-58	MS-60	MS-62	MS-63	MS-64	MS-65	Recent Auction Record
1840	61,005	513	48.2	18	$1,150	$2,000	$3,800	$10,250	$19,000	$50,000	$110,000	$18,800, MS-63, June 2014
1841	173,000	494	49.8	18	900	1,300	2,650	4,500	7,000	15,000	90,000	$30,550, MS-64, February 2014
1842	184,618	1,016	48.3	15	800	1,250	2,400	3,750	5,750	13,000	90,000	$12,925, MS-64, August 2013
1843	165,100	829	47.7	11	800	1,250	2,400	4,900	8,750	20,000	100,000	$51,406, MS-64, June 2014
1844	20,000	346	49.7	15	1,500	2,250	5,000	8,000	16,000	30,000	100,000	$41,125, MS-64, June 2013
1845	24,500	364	47.2	9	1,500	3,500	9,000	16,000	30,000	80,000	150,000	$2,820, AU-58, March 2014
1846	110,600	913	49.4	14	900	1,325	2,500	3,900	6,500	13,000	90,000	$105,750, MS-65, November 2013
1846O	59,000	392	44.8	10	1,400	3,100	7,250	13,000	20,000	40,000	100,000	$17,625, MS-63, June 2014
1847	140,750	901	49.7	14	850	1,350	2,700	4,600	6,900	13,000	90,000	$4,406, MS-63, April 2014
1848	15,000	250	49.2	13	1,700	2,750	4,750	8,000	15,000	60,000	115,000	$5,288, AU-58, August 2013
1849	62,600	571	52.5	25	850	1,300	2,600	4,500	6,750	13,000	90,000	$11,163, MS-64, June 2014
1850	7,500	270	52.2	24	2,250	4,000	6,900	9,000	16,000	35,000	90,000	$14,688, MS-63, April 2014
1850O	40,000	283	42.9	9	3,200	7,500	13,500	18,000	25,000	45,000	120,000	$105,750, MS-64, August 2013
1851, Original, High Date † (a)	1,300	53	58.9	66	27,500	32,000	35,000	57,500	65,000	85,000	140,000	$70,500, AU-58, August 2013
1852, Original † (a)	1,100	53	57.3	49	27,500	30,000	33,000	47,500	60,000	75,000	140,000	$34,075, AU-58, June 2014
1853	46,110	329	55.1	43	1,350	2,350	3,200	5,250	7,250	13,000	85,000	$3,819, MS-61, August 2013
1854	33,140	139	53.9	32	5,500	6,850	8,100	11,000	13,000	20,000	95,000	$9,993, AU-55, March 2014
1855	26,000	162	51.1	25	4,750	6,600	7,500	15,000	25,000	50,000	90,000	$141,000, MS-64, June 2014
1856	63,500	169	50.7	22	2,250	3,300	4,250	8,000	15,000	25,000	85,000	$5,875, AU-55, June 2014
1857	94,000	198	56.1	51	1,900	2,350	3,250	5,900	9,250	22,000	85,000	$99,875, MS-66, January 2014
1859	255,700	199	52.4	33	1,225	1,700	2,500	3,800	6,000	16,000	85,000	$15,275, MS-64, June 2014
1859O	360,000	1,272	53.8	54	850	1,175	2,050	2,900	5,150	9,000	65,000	$41,125, MS-65, June 2014
1859S	20,000	325	43.7	11	3,350	5,000	13,000	16,500	29,000	50,000	130,000	$28,200, MS-63, June 2014
1860	217,600	274	55.6	50	850	1,200	2,100	3,200	5,100	9,750	75,000	$7,638, MS-64, July 2014
1860O	515,000	1,860	55.5	60	785	1,075	1,900	2,550	3,750	8,000	60,000	$10,575, MS-64, February 2013
1861	77,500	201	53.8	50	2,250	2,700	3,450	4,900	5,850	12,000	65,000	$12,338, MS-64, March 2014
1862	11,540	206	53.8	50	2,650	2,900	3,575	4,750	6,300	14,000	65,000	$31,725, MS-64, June 2014
1863	27,200	204	51.3	46	1,600	2,500	3,575	4,900	6,300	14,000	65,000	$17,625, MS-64, August 2013
1864	30,700	207	46.1	21	1,600	2,600	3,575	5,250	7,500	19,000	60,000	$3,525, AU-55, February 2013
1865 (b)	46,500	211	48.0	27	1,600	2,300	3,000	5,250	7,500	18,000	80,000	$25,850, MS-64, June 2014
1866	48,900	259	50.3	31	1,100	1,850	2,300	4,500	5,500	17,000	65,000	$1,880, MS-60, March 2014
1867	46,900	211	52.2	35	1,050	1,750	2,200	3,600	5,300	14,000	70,000	$1,645, AU-53, June 2014
1868	162,100	224	50.0	20	1,150	1,850	2,400	4,750	7,000	19,500	65,000	$30,550, MS-64, June 2014

† Ranked in the *100 Greatest U.S. Coins* (fourth edition). **a.** Silver dollars of 1851 and 1852 are found in three formats: originals struck for circulation, original Proofs, and Proof restrikes made years later. See the next section for a discussion of the Proofs. **b.** There is a common doubled-die reverse variety for 1865, which does not command a premium in today's market. "Doubling is evident only on the U of UNITED. . . . This is probably the most common variety for this date" (*Cherrypickers' Guide to Rare Die Varieties*, fifth edition, volume II).

Chart continued on next page.

	Mintage	Cert	Avg	%MS	AU-50	AU-58	MS-60	MS-62	MS-63	MS-64	MS-65	Recent Auction Record
1869	423,700	290	49.0	27	$1,050	$1,600	$2,300	$3,750	$5,250	$13,000	$65,000	$9,988, MS-64, June 2014
1869, Repunched Date (c)	*	1	62.0	100	1,100	1,800	2,750	4,500	7,000			$7,475, MS-64, April 2012
1870	415,000	421	50.3	31	950	1,250	2,100	2,900	4,750	8,750	55,000	$76,375, MS-65, January 2014
1870CC	11,758	580	39.4	6	7,000	11,750	26,000	32,500	40,000	100,000	—	$70,500, MS-62, January 2014
1870S † (d)	**	9	47.3	11	1,250,000	1,500,000	2,000,000	2,300,000	—	—	—	$763,750, EF-40, January 2014
1871	1,073,800	1,312	47.1	23	950	1,150	2,000	2,700	4,350	7,100	50,000	$57,281, MS-65, June 2014
1871CC	1,376	144	37.8	5	24,500	39,000	75,000	135,000	175,000	300,000	—	$82,250, MS-61, June 2014
1872	1,105,500	942	45.3	20	950	1,150	2,050	2,750	4,950	7,250	50,000	$58,750, MS-65, October 2013
1872CC	3,150	258	36.2	10	13,000	17,000	28,000	45,000	100,000	160,000	300,000	$44,063, MS-62, April 2014
1872S	9,000	276	41.3	7	3,500	6,900	12,000	18,500	37,500	150,000		$22,325, MS, March 2014
1873	293,000	344	52.4	41	975	1,350	2,100	3,000	4,850	8,250	60,000	$52,875, MS-65, July 2014
1873CC	2,300	100	37.0	7	41,500	52,500	115,000	150,000	190,000	300,000	500,000	$64,625, AU-55, March 2014
1873S (e)	700	n/a	n/a	n/a								

* Included in number above. ** The Mint shows no record of 1870-S dollars being struck, but about a dozen are known to exist. † Ranked in the *100 Greatest U.S. Coins* (fourth edition). **c.** There are several repunched dates known for 1869. The one listed is FS-S1-1869-302. The top flag of a secondary 1 is evident midway between the primary 1 and the 8. **d.** The 1870-S silver dollars may have been struck as mementos of the laying of the cornerstone of the San Francisco Mint (May 25, 1870). **e.** The 1873-S is unknown in any collection, public or private, despite Mint records indicating that 700 were struck. None has ever been seen.

Proof Liberty Seated Dollars

PF-60 to 70 (Proof). Proof Liberty Seated dollars were made for all dates. All of 1851 and 1853 are restrikes, as are most of 1852. In 1858 only Proofs were struck, to the extent of an estimated 210 pieces, with no related circulation strikes. Most early dates were restruck at the Mint, augmenting the supply of originals. Today, Proofs from 1858 to 1873 are readily available, but high-quality examples with superb eye appeal are in the minority. Most Proofs prior to 1860 survive only in grades below PF-65 if strict grading is applied. Nearly all Proofs are very well struck. *Obverse and Reverse:* Proofs that are extensively cleaned and have many hairlines, or that are dull and grainy, are lower level, such as PF-60 to 62. These are not widely desired, except for use as fillers for the dates (most circulation-strike dollars are rare after 1849 and before 1870). The rarities of 1851, 1852, and 1858 are in demand no matter what the grade. With medium hairlines and good reflectivity, an assigned grade of PF-64 is appropriate, and with relatively few hairlines, PF-65. In various grades hairlines are most easily seen in the obverse field. PF-66 should have hairlines so delicate that magnification is needed to see them. Above that, a Proof should be free of such lines.

1866, Proof, No Motto
Judd-540.

1851, Restrike
Date is centered.

1852, Restrike

Proof Liberty Seated Dollar

	Est Mintage	Cert	Finest	PF-60	PF-63	PF-64	PF-65	Recent Auction Record
1840	40–60	43	65	$16,000	$29,000	$40,000	$85,000	$85,188, PF-64Cam, April 2013
1841	10–15	5	64	25,000	70,000	175,000	250,000	$141,000, PF-64, April 2013
1842	10–15	10	65	17,500	39,000	75,000	125,000	$57,281, PF-65, August 2013
1843	10–15	12	64	17,000	35,000	52,500	110,000	$52,875, PF-64, August 2013
1844	10–15	14	66	15,000	35,000	52,500	110,000	$70,500, PF-65, April 2013
1845	10–15	20	67	14,000	30,000	47,500	100,000	$141,000, PF-67, August 2013
1846	10–15	23	66	14,000	30,000	47,500	105,000	$94,000, PF-66, April 2013
1847	10–15	23	65	16,000	26,000	32,500	65,000	$41,125, PF-65, April 2013
1848	10–15	16	67	16,000	31,000	45,000	90,000	$117,500, PF-67, August 2013
1849	10–15	13	67	19,000	34,000	57,500	115,000	$129,250, PF-67, April 2013
1850	20–30	30	66	16,500	28,000	33,500	65,000	$51,406, PF-66, August 2013
1851, Restrike (a)	35–50	46	66	21,000	31,000	38,500	80,000	$99,875, PF-65Cam, April 2014
1852, Original (a)	20–30	3	65	35,000	43,500	50,000	77,500	$57,500, PF-65Cam, January 2009
1852, Restrike (a)	20–30	26	65	17,500	30,000	39,000	75,000	$70,500, PF-65, June 2014
1853, Restrike (b)	15–20	13	66	21,000	37,000	57,500	110,000	$152,750, PF-66Cam, August 2013
1854	40–60	36	66	13,500	16,500	23,500	57,500	$49,938, PF-66, April 2013
1855	40–60	37	66	12,000	16,000	25,000	42,500	$45,531, PF-66, August 2013
1856	40–60	64	67	6,350	13,000	18,000	32,500	$27,025, PF-65, April 2013
1857	50–70	69	66	7,000	13,500	18,500	33,500	$38,188, PF, August 2013

a. Silver dollars of 1851 are found in two formats: originals struck for circulation and Proof restrikes made years later. Silver dollars of 1852 are found in these formats and also as original Proofs. "As part of [Mint Director] James Ross Snowden's restriking activities in 1859, Proof examples of certain rare silver dollars of earlier dates were made, including the 1851 and 1852. For the 1851 dollar, the original die (with four-date digit logotype slanting slightly upward and the date close to the base of Liberty) probably could not be located in 1859. In any event, a different die, not originally used in 1851, with the date horizontal and centered, was employed. Whether this die was created new in 1859 and given an 1851 date, or whether it was made in 1851 and not used at that time, is not known" (*United States Pattern Coins*, 10th edition). b. Made at the Mint from postdated dies circa 1862.

	Mintage	Cert	Finest	PF-60	PF-63	PF-64	PF-65	Recent Auction Record
1858 (a)	300	164	67	$10,000	$14,000	$19,000	$38,000	$41,125, PF-66, August 2013
1859	800	332	67	2,400	4,750	8,500	20,000	$82,250, PF-67, August 2013
1860	1,330	334	67	2,400	4,750	6,500	15,000	$64,625, PF-67, April 2013
1861	1,000	236	67	2,400	4,750	6,500	15,000	$76,375, PF-66, June 2014
1862	550	349	67	2,400	4,750	6,500	15,000	$52,875, PF-67Cam, January 2014
1863	460	346	69	2,400	4,750	7,500	18,000	$129,250, PF-69, April 2013
1864	470	356	68	2,400	4,750	6,500	15,000	$52,875, PF-68, April 2013
1865	500	404	68	2,400	4,750	6,500	15,000	$30,550, PF-67, February 2013
1866, No Motto † (b)	2 known	6	65				—	
1866, With Motto	725	519	69	2,100	3,800	5,750	14,000	$44,063, PF-67DCam, April 2013
1867	625	488	68	2,100	3,900	5,750	14,000	$23,500, PF-65DCam, April 2014
1868	600	468	68	2,100	3,800	5,750	14,000	$52,875, PF-67DCam, August 2013
1869	600	467	67	2,100	3,800	5,750	14,000	$30,550, PF-66, June 2013
1870	1,000	478	67	2,100	3,800	5,750	14,000	$44,063, PF-66, January 2014
1871	960	441	67	2,100	3,800	5,750	14,000	$52,875, PF-66, April 2014
1872	950	410	67	2,100	3,800	5,750	14,000	$32,900, PF-66Cam, April 2013
1873	600	430	68	2,100	3,800	5,750	14,000	$35,250, PF-66DCam, August 2013

† Ranked in the *100 Greatest U.S. Coins* (fourth edition). a. In 1858 only Proofs, not circulation strikes, were made. b. The 1866, No Motto, dollar is classified as Judd-540 (*United States Pattern Coins*). Two examples of this fantasy piece are known; at least one was deliberately struck for pharmacist and coin collector Robert Coulton Davis, likely around 1869 or in the early 1870s, along with the No Motto Proof quarter and half dollar of the same date. The three-coin set is on display at the American Numismatic Association's Edward C. Rochette Money Museum in Colorado Springs. "A second 1866 'No Motto' silver dollar resurfaced in the 1970s before entering a private Midwestern collection in the early 1980s. After not meeting its auction reserve price in September 2003, the coin was sold privately for nearly a million dollars some time later" (*100 Greatest U.S. Coins*, fourth edition).

TRADE DOLLARS (1873–1885)

The trade dollar was authorized and minted under the Coinage Act of 1873. It was intended not as a regular-circulation coin for domestic business, but as an international trade unit for commerce with Asia. Trade dollars are presented separately from other dollar coins, starting on page 250.

MORGAN
(1878–1921)

Designer George T. Morgan; weight 26.73 grams; composition .900 silver, .100 copper (net weight .77344 oz. pure silver); diameter 38.1 mm; reeded edge; mints: Philadelphia, New Orleans, Carson City, Denver, San Francisco.

History. The Morgan dollar, named for designer George T. Morgan, was struck every year from 1878 to 1904, and again in 1921. The coin's production benefited Western silver interests by creating an artificial federal demand for the metal, whose market value had dropped sharply by 1878. Hundreds of millions of the coins, stored in cloth bags of 1,000 each, piled up in government vaults. In the 1900s some were melted, but immense quantities were bought by collectors and investors; today they are the most widely collected of all coins of their era.

Striking and Sharpness. On coins of 1878 to 1900, check the hair above Miss Liberty's ear and, on the reverse, the breast feathers of the eagle. These are weak on many issues, particularly those of the New Orleans Mint. From 1900 to 1904 a new reverse hub was used, and breast feathers, while discernible, are not as sharp. In 1921 new dies were made in lower relief, with certain areas indistinct. Many Morgan dollars have partially or fully prooflike surfaces. These are designated as Prooflike (PL), Deep Prooflike (DPL), or Deep Mirror Prooflike (DMPL). Certification practices can be erratic, and some DMPL coins are not fully mirrored. All prooflike coins tend to emphasize contact marks, with the result that lower MS levels can be unattractive. *A Guide Book of Morgan Silver Dollars* (Bowers) and other references furnish information as to which dates and mintmarks are easily found with Full Details and which usually are weak, as well as the availability of the various levels of prooflike surface.

Availability. All dates and mints of Morgan dollars are available in grades from well worn to MS. Some issues such as certain Carson City coins are rare if worn and common in MS. Other issues such as the 1901 Philadelphia coins are common if worn and are rarities at MS-65. The 1889-CC and 1893-S, and the Proof 1895, are considered to be the key issues. Varieties listed herein are those most significant to collectors. Numerous other variations exist. Values are shown for the most common pieces. Values of varieties not listed in this guide depend on collector interest and demand.

Note: Values of common-date silver coins have been based on the current bullion price of silver, $20 per ounce, and may vary with the prevailing spot price.

MS-60 to 70 (Mint State). *Obverse:* At MS-60, some abrasion and contact marks are evident, most noticeably on the cheek and on the hair above the ear. The left field also shows such marks. Luster is present, but may be dull or lifeless. At MS-63, contact marks are extensive but not distracting. Abrasion still is evident, but less than at lower levels (the cheek of Miss Liberty showcases abrasion). An MS-65 coin may have minor abrasion, but contact marks are so minute as to require magnification. Luster should be full and rich. Coins with prooflike surfaces such as PL, DPL, and DMPL display abrasion and contact marks much more noticeably than coins with frosty surfaces; in grades below MS-64 many are unattractive. *Reverse:* Comments apply as for the obverse, except that in lower MS grades abrasion and contact marks are most noticeable on the eagle's breast. At MS-65 or higher there are no marks visible to the unaided eye. The field is mainly protected by design elements, so the reverse often appears to grade a point or two higher than the obverse.

First Reverse
Eight tail feathers.

Second Reverse
Parallel top arrow feather, concave breast.

Third Reverse
Slanted top arrow feather, convex breast.

1878, Doubled Tail Feathers
FS-S1-1878-032.

1878, 8 Feathers, Obverse Die Gouge
The "Wild Eye" variety. VAM 14-11. FS-S1-1878-014.

1878, 7 Over 8 Tail Feathers, Tripled Leaves
VAM 44. FS-S1-1878-044.

1880, 80 Over 79
VAM 6. FS-S1-1880-006.

1880-CC, 80 Over 79
VAM 4. FS-S1-1880CC-004.

1880-CC, 8 Over High 7
VAM 5. FS-S1-1880CC-005.

1880-CC, 8 Over Low 7
VAM 6. FS-S1-1880CC-006.

1880-O, 80 Over 79
VAM 4. FS-S1-1880o-004.

1880-O, Die Gouge
The "Hangnail" variety. VAM 49. FS-S1-1880o-048.

1881-O, Repunched Mintmark
VAM 5. FS-S1-1881o-005.

1882-O, O Over S
VAM 4. FS-S1-1882o-004.

1884, Large Dot
VAM 3. FS-S1-1884-003.

1884, Small Dot
VAM 4. FS-S1-1884-004.

1885, Die Chip
VAM 8. FS-S1-1885-008.

1886, Repunched Date
VAM 20. FS-S1-1886-020.

1887, 7 Over 6
VAM 2. FS-S1-1887-002.

1887-O, 7 Over 6
VAM 3. FS-S1-1887o-003.

1888-O, Obverse Die Break
The "Scarface" variety.
VAM 1b. FS-S1-1888o-001b.

1888-O, Doubled-Die Obverse
The "Hot Lips" variety.
VAM 4. FS-S1-1888o-002.

1889, Die Break
The "Bar Wing" variety.
VAM 22. FS-S1-1889-022.

1889-O, Clashed Die
VAM 1A. FS-S1-1889o-001a.

1890-CC, Die Gouge
The "Tailbar" variety.
VAM 4. FS-S1-1890CC-004.

1890-O, Die Gouges
The "Comet" variety.
VAM 10. FS-S1-1890o-010.

1891-O, Clashed Die
VAM 1A. FS-S1-1891o-001a.

1891-O, Pitted Reverse Die
VAM 1B. FS-S1-1891o-001b.

1899-O, Micro O
VAM 4, 6, 31, and 32. FS-S1-1899o-501.

1900-O, Obverse Die Crack
VAM 29A. FS-S1-1900o-029a.

1900-O, O Over CC
Various VAMs. FS-S1-1900o-501.

1901, Doubled-Die Reverse
The "Shifted Eagle" variety.
VAM 3. FS-S1-1901-003.

1903-S, Small S Mintmark
VAM 3. FS-S1-1903S-002.

	Mintage	Cert	Avg	%MS	MS-63	MS-64	MS-65	MS-66	MS-63 DMPL	MS-64 DMPL	MS-65 DMPL	Recent Auction Record
1878, 8 Feathers	749,500	22,284	61.8	93	$285	$475	$1,600	$9,000	$835	$4,850	$21,000	$9,400, MS-66, June 2013
1878, 8 Feathers, Obverse Die Gouge (a) *	16	56.0	56	24,000								$16,100, MS-62, August 2011
1878, 7 Feathers	9,759,300	n/a	n/a	n/a								
1878, 7 Over 8, Clear Doubled Feathers *	11,313	62.5	96	300	475	2,300	14,000	1,150	5,200	16,000	$16,450, MS-66DM, April 2014
1878, 7 Over 8, Tripled Leaves (b) *	64	49.3	17	23,000								$8,625, AU-55, January 2012
1878, 7 Feathers, 2nd Reverse *	25,098	61.8	92	150	250	1,050	5,500	400	2,200	11,000	$8,813, MS-65DM, April 2014
1878, 7 Feathers, 3rd Reverse *	10,004	61.7	91	210	500	2,100	—	1,000	5,500	23,000	$15,275, MS-66PL, August 2013
1878CC	2,212,000	43,235	61.4	92	475	600	1,850	6,250	1,600	2,800	10,000	$19,975, MS-66, December 2013
1878S	9,774,000	71,997	63.1	97	100	115	310	750	350	2,000	10,000	$9,988, MS-67, November 2013
1879	14,806,000	20,161	62.8	95	95	155	825	3,250	425	2,100	15,000	$19,975, MS-66DM, April 2014
1879CC, CC Over CC	756,000	3,769	51.8	62	6,300	9,900	40,000	60,000	13,500	42,000	60,000	$36,719, MS-65, April 2014
1879CC, Clear CC	*	7,001	51.5	66	7,500	11,000	30,000	80,000	12,000	25,000	47,500	$64,625, MS-66, April 2014
1879O	2,887,000	17,099	61.6	87	250	600	4,000	18,500	1,875	4,250	22,000	$19,975, MS-66, April 2014
1879S, 2nd Reverse	9,110,000	5,058	60.8	87	625	1,500	5,500	47,500	3,000	8,000	21,000	$8,225, MS-61, April 2013
1879S, 3rd Reverse	*	179,360	64.2	100	65	85	190	340	210	500	1,300	$12,338, MS-65PL, March 2014
1880	12,600,000	22,897	62.8	96	80	160	750	3,600	300	1,150	6,900	$14,100, MS-66, August 2013
1880, 80 Over 79 (c)	*	843	53.8	41	850							$969, AU-58, December 2013
1880CC, All kinds	591,000											
1880CC, 80 Over 79, 2nd Rev (d)		3,812	63.0	98	700	1,150	2,700	7,000	2,500	5,000	20,000	$10,575, MS-66, June 2013
1880CC, 8 Over 7, 2nd Rev		676	61.2	94	650	1,050	2,200	5,600	2,500	5,000	20,000	$8,813, MS, February 2014
1880CC, 8 Over High 7, 3rd Rev (e)		2,155	63.9	100	600	700	1,200	2,050	900	2,450	9,000	$22,325, MS-67, August 2013
1880CC, 8 Over Low 7, 3rd Rev (f)		387	63.5	100	640	750	1,275	4,250	1,400	2,700	9,000	$8,225, MS-66, January 2013
1880CC, 3rd Reverse		n/a	n/a	n/a	600	700	1,200	2,050	900	2,450	9,000	$12,925, MS-67, April 2013
1880O, All kinds	5,305,000											
1880O, 80 Over 79 (g)		725	59.9	68	625	2,500			3,000	8,000		$4,700, MS-64, January 2014
1880O		17,628	60.7	76	430	1,800	26,000	56,000	1,450	7,250	62,500	$41,125, MS-65, January 2014
1880O, Die Gouge (h)		351	53.7	30	—							$1,410, MS-64, December 2013
1880S, All kinds	8,900,000											
1880S, 80 Over 79		1,710	64.0	99	80	125	300	600	200	450	1,500	$1,528, MS-66DM, February 2013
1880S, 0 Over 9		2,626	64.2	100	80	125	300	600	200	450	1,500	$11,750, MS-68, April 2014
1880S		268,583	64.2	100	65	85	190	340	200	450	1,000	$9,400, MS-66, October 2013
1881	9,163,000	19,769	63.1	98	80	170	750	3,000	575	1,375	19,500	$15,275, MS-67, April 2014
1881CC	296,000	37,110	63.5	99	600	650	950	1,400	750	1,200	3,000	$28,200, MS-68, April 2014
1881O	5,708,000	29,491	62.6	95	75	190	1,400	14,500	325	900	18,000	$21,150, MS-66, January 2014
1881O, RPM (i)	*	n/a	n/a	n/a	250	—						$218, MS-64, March 2012
1881O, DblDie Obv (j)	*	65	55.4	20	—	—						$150, AU-50, September 2011
1881S	12,760,000	436,715	64.1	100	65	85	165	340	200	475	1,000	$12,925, MS-68, April 2014
1882	11,100,000	29,473	63.3	98	70	120	550	1,800	275	1,000	6,500	$11,750, MS-67, April 2014
1882CC	1,133,000	59,985	63.4	99	275	300	550	1,100	425	625	1,900	$7,638, MS-67, April 2013
1882O	6,090,000	31,607	62.9	97	85	135	1,500	8,000	275	1,300	5,200	$18,800, MS-67, April 2014
1882O, O Over S (k)	*	6,948	57.8	57	775	2,000	50,000	—	3,200	8,500	62,500	$4,994, MS-64, June 2013
1882S	9,250,000	140,225	64.2	100	70	85	200	340	275	950	3,800	$11,163, MS-68, April 2013
1883	12,290,000	40,797	63.7	99	75	110	220	500	250	450	1,600	$11,817, MS-68, April 2014
1883CC	1,204,000	80,857	63.6	99	250	275	525	850	400	525	1,300	$47,000, MS-68, August 2013
1883O	8,725,000	205,279	63.4	100	65	85	190	425	220	500	1,450	$5,288, MS-65, April 2014
1883S	6,250,000	9,290	56.5	46	2,500	6,000	45,000	85,000	20,000	75,000	125,000	$32,900, MS-65, April 2014
1884, All kinds	14,070,000											
1884					75	110	375	950	250	850	5,000	$17,038, MS-67, August 2013
1884, Large Dot (l)		151	53.2	39	250	—						$80, MS-62, May 2014
1884, Small Dot (l)		265	61.5	87	350	—						$259, MS-63, September 2013
1884CC	1,136,000	89,007	63.7	100	250	275	525	850	400	550	1,300	$16,450, MS-67DM, April 2014

* Included in number above. **a.** Two spikes protrude from the front of Liberty's eye. "Fewer than a dozen specimens are known of this Top 100 variety and any sale is a landmark event" (*Cherrypickers' Guide to Rare Die Varieties*, fifth edition, volume II). **b.** Called the "King of VAMs" (Van Allen / Mallis varieties), this variety shows three to five weak tail feathers under the seven primary feathers. On the obverse, tripling is evident on the cotton bolls and the leaves, and doubling on LIBERTY. Values are fluid for this popular variety. **c.** Several die varieties exist; values shown are for the most common. **d.** The top crossbar and diagonal stem of an underlying 79 are clearly seen within the 8. Extensive polishing marks are visible within the 0. **e.** An almost complete 7 is visible inside the last 8 of the date. The top edge of the 7 touches the top inside of the 8. **f.** A complete 7 is visible inside the last 8 of the date. The crossbar of the underlying 7 can be seen in the top loop and the diagonal of the 7 is visible in the lower loop. **g.** The crossbar of the underlying 7 is visible within the upper loop of the second 8. The 1 and the first 8 are slightly doubled to the right. **h.** On the reverse of the "Hangnail" variety, a die gouge runs from the bottom of the arrow feather, across the feathers, and out the eagle's rightmost tail feather. On the obverse, the top-left part of the second 8 has a spike. Value in AU-50 is $800. **i.** A diagonal image, the remains of one or two additional O mintmark punches, is visible within the primary O. **j.** Clear doubling is evident on the back outside of Liberty's ear. **k.** Several varieties exist. **l.** A raised dot, either Large or Small, is visible after the designer's initial and on the reverse ribbon. "These dots varieties are thought to have been used as some sort of identifier" (*Cherrypickers' Guide to Rare Die Varieties*, fifth edition, volume II).

Chart continued on next page.

	Mintage	Cert	Avg	%MS	MS-63	MS-64	MS-65	MS-66	MS-63 DMPL	MS-64 DMPL	MS-65 DMPL	Recent Auction Record
1884O	9,730,000	333,363	63.5	100	$65	$85	$190	$400	$200	$450	$1,000	$3,534, MS-66DM, June 2014
1884S	3,200,000	11,613	52.0	6	35,000	115,000	235,000	350,000	60,000	135,000	275,000	$88,125, MS-64, January 2014
1885	17,787,000	124,351	63.7	99	65	85	190	375	200	450	1,000	$21,150, MS-68, April 2013
1885, Die Chip (m)	*	89	61.7	87	550	—						
1885CC	228,000	37,147	63.6	99	825	875	1,100	2,200	900	1,300	2,400	$14,100, MS-67, March 2013
1885O	9,185,000	321,855	63.7	100	65	85	190	340	200	450	1,000	$9,988, MS-68, November 2013
1885S	1,497,000	13,612	61.7	90	315	675	1,800	7,000	2,000	5,000	45,000	$6,463, MS-66, April 2014
1886	19,963,000	208,422	63.8	100	65	85	190	375	200	475	1,300	$19,975, MS-68, July 2014
1886, RPD (n)	*	16	58.9	44	5,750	—						$3,819, MS-64, September 2013
1886O	10,710,000	8,752	56.6	39	3,500	11,000	185,000	480,000	20,000	70,000	300,000	$152,750, MS-65, January 2014
1886O, Clashed Die (o)	*	372	49.0	7	5,750	—						$3,055, MS-62, April 2014
1886S	750,000	9,417	61.0	84	500	850	3,250	9,500	2,300	8,500	27,000	$14,688, MS-67, April 2014
1887, 7 Over 6	**	2,585	62.7	96	500	750	1,800	10,500	2,300	4,750	26,000	$8,225, MS-66, April 2014
1887	20,290,000	287,155	63.7	100	65	85	190	375	200	450	1,000	$3,055, MS-67PL, February 2013
1887O, 7 Over 6	**	1,421	61.1	88	1,900	4,800	27,000	55,000				$5,581, MS-64, January 2014
1887O	11,550,000	18,057	62.2	95	150	400	2,750	45,000	575	1,700	13,500	$10,575, MS-65DMPL, April 2014
1887S	1,771,000	13,178	61.8	87	300	750	2,600	9,500	3,100	7,000	27,500	$30,550, MS-67, April 2014
1888	19,183,000	74,739	63.6	99	65	85	250	550	275	450	2,400	$8,813, MS-67, November 2013
1888O	12,150,000	40,136	63.0	98	75	115	625	2,700	225	500	4,500	$10,575, MS-67, April 2014
1888O, Obverse Die Break (p)	*	114	61.8	99		8,650						$14,688, MS-64, December 2013
1888O, DblDie Obverse (q)	*	1,568	31.7	1	30,000	—						$12,925, MS-60, February 2013
1888S	657,000	10,454	60.6	83	500	1,000	3,500	10,500	1,050	2,850	15,500	$7,638, MS-66, September 2013
1889	21,726,000	64,382	63.2	98	70	90	380	1,250	225	700	3,600	$14,100, MS-67, April 2013
1889, Die Break (r)	*	397	57.4	57	285		2,500					$99, MS-61, May 2012
1889CC	350,000	8,822	34.0	11	50,000	85,000	325,000	—	47,500	75,000	350,000	$881,250, MS-68, August 2013
1889O	11,875,000	9,616	60.9	88	400	1,000	7,500	20,000	1,350	6,500	17,500	$17,625, MS-66, January 2014
1889O, Clashed Die (s)	*	109	41.2	2	—	—						$764, AU-55, March 2014
1889S	700,000	13,020	61.8	86	375	675	2,200	6,000	1,700	5,500	37,500	$16,450, MS-66, April 2014
1890	16,802,000	27,254	62.8	96	95	175	2,050	12,500	330	2,500	20,000	$18,800, MS-66, June 2014
1890CC	2,309,041	17,882	58.4	83	900	1,500	5,000	23,000	1,300	2,800	13,750	$45,531, MS-66, February 2013
1890CC, Die Gouge (t)	*	1,056	49.3	56	2,950	—						$8,519, MS-64DM, April 2014
1890O	10,701,000	18,360	62.7	98	105	325	2,500	9,500	300	1,500	9,250	$11,750, MS-66, March 2013
1890O, Die Gouges (u)	*	175	60.5	86	260	—						$2,585, MS-65, July 2014
1890S	8,230,373	17,903	62.5	92	105	325	1,400	4,000	600	3,200	9,250	$8,225, MS-66, April 2014
1891	8,693,556	13,357	61.9	92	220	900	8,000	13,750	2,000	6,900	23,000	$14,688, MS-65DM, August 2013
1891CC	1,618,000	23,139	60.9	90	750	1,275	5,000	13,500	1,800	4,500	32,000	$11,163, MS-66, April 2014
1891O	7,954,529	9,155	61.8	94	400	825	7,500	—	2,750	7,250	36,500	$19,975, MS-66, April 2014
1891O, Clashed Die (v)	*	337	38.4	2	1,500	—						$382, AU-53, December 2013
1891O, Pitted Reverse Die (w)	*	32	48.4	0	—	—						
1891S	5,296,000	12,574	62.4	92	160	350	1,750	5,200	475	3,200	20,000	$7,638, MS-66, August 2013
1892	1,036,000	8,698	61.3	84	525	1,200	5,250	37,500	1,450	3,200	18,000	$8,813, MS-65, April 2013
1892CC	1,352,000	13,067	58.1	81	2,300	3,200	9,250	25,000	4,450	9,000	36,000	$31,725, MS-66, August 2013
1892O	2,744,000	10,421	61.6	90	425	1,050	7,500	42,500	9,500	20,000	50,000	$15,275, MS-65, January 2014
1892S	1,200,000	6,044	41.6	2	65,000	115,000	190,000	260,000	97,500	145,000	250,000	$70,500, MS-63, April 2014
1893	378,000	9,028	55.7	61	1,100	2,300	8,500	45,000	20,000	32,500	67,500	$8,225, MS-65, April 2014
1893CC	677,000	8,834	47.2	57	8,500	16,000	70,000	—	24,000	46,000	85,000	$141,000, MS-65BMCam, April 2013
1893O	300,000	5,595	45.8	29	6,500	17,000	200,000	—	25,000	105,000	275,000	$23,500, MS-64PL, January 2014
1893S † (x,y)	100,000	6,931	22.7	1	225,000	350,000	650,000	700,000	225,000	400,000	750,000	$329,000, MS-65, April 2014
1894 (y)	110,000	6,710	48.3	30	4,900	9,500	40,000	60,000	35,000	60,000	90,000	$39,656, MS-65, December 2013
1894O	1,723,000	7,711	50.9	27	4,750	11,500	65,000	—	17,000	29,000	65,000	$44,063, MS-65, August 2013

* Included in number above. ** Included in number below. † Ranked among the *100 Greatest U.S. Coins* (fourth edition). **m.** A large, raised die chip is evident below the second 8. **n.** Repunching is especially evident in the base of the 1, and the lower loop of the 6. **o.** Clashing of the E of LIBERTY is evident between the eagle's tail feathers and the bow on the wreath. **p.** A major die break runs from the rim between E and P, through the field, and all the way across Liberty's face and neck. This variety is nicknamed "Scarface." **q.** Doubling is visible on the lips (especially), nose, eye, chin, entire profile, and part of the hair. This variety is nicknamed "Hot Lips." Value in MS-60 is $25,000. **r.** A die break is visible on the top of the eagle's right wing. This variety is nicknamed the "Bar Wing." Different obverse die pairings exist. **s.** The E of LIBERTY is visible in the field below the eagle's tail feathers and slightly left of the bow. This variety is extremely rare in Mint State, and unknown above MS-61. Value in MS-60 is $2,250. **t.** A heavy die gouge extends from between the eagle's first tail feather and the lowest arrow feather to the leaves in the wreath below. "This is an extremely popular and highly marketable variety, especially in Mint State" *(Cherrypickers' Guide to Rare Die Varieties, fifth edition, volume II)*. This variety is nicknamed the "Tailbar." **u.** Die gouges are evident to the right of the date. This variety is nicknamed the "Comet." **v.** The evidence of a clashed die is visible below the eagle's tail feathers and slightly left of the bow, where the E in LIBERTY has been transferred from the obverse die. **w.** Pitting on the reverse is visible around the ONE and on the bottom of the wreath above and between ONE and DOLLAR. This variety is rare in circulated grades, and unknown in Mint State. **x.** "All 1893-S Morgan dollars were struck from a single die pairing. Genuine 1893-S silver dollars display a diagonal die scratch in the top of the T in LIBERTY. This diagnostic can be seen even on very low-grade examples" *(100 Greatest U.S. Coins, fourth edition)*. **y.** Beware of altered or otherwise fraudulent mintmarks.

	Mintage	Cert	Avg	%MS	MS-63	MS-64	MS-65	MS-66	MS-63 DMPL	MS-64 DMPL	MS-65 DMPL	Recent Auction Record
1894S	1,260,000	6,703	58.3	75	$1,200	$2,400	$7,000	$16,500	$6,000	$22,000	$35,000	$12,925, MS-66, January 2014
1895O	450,000	8,702	41.1	3	50,000	80,000	165,000	390,000	62,500	140,000	240,000	$82,250, MS-64, February 2013
1895S	400,000	5,215	42.8	38	6,250	11,000	26,000	95,000	11,000	19,500	40,000	$45,531, MS-66, April 2014
1896	9,976,000	68,662	63.5	98	65	90	250	525	200	450	1,200	$11,750, MS-67, September 2013
1896O	4,900,000	9,551	54.8	26	8,000	42,000	175,000	425,000	25,000	60,000	200,000	$94,000, MS-65, April 2013
1896S	5,000,000	3,714	52.3	58	3,750	5,750	17,500	74,000	26,000	57,500	100,000	$38,188, MS-66, April 2014
1897	2,822,000	27,382	63.4	97	75	100	350	1,050	220	500	3,700	$9,400, MS-66PL, June 2014
1897O	4,004,000	9,408	55.6	28	4,750	16,500	65,000	100,000	25,000	37,500	75,000	$38,188, MS-65, April 2014
1897S	5,825,000	16,309	63.0	95	150	200	650	1,500	280	1,100	3,000	$7,638, MS-66PL, March 2013
1898	5,884,000	33,644	63.5	98	65	90	270	700	220	450	1,300	$7,050, MS-67, September 2013
1898O	4,440,000	117,787	63.9	100	65	85	190	385	200	450	1,025	$9,400, MS-67, July 2014
1898S	4,102,000	6,912	60.8	80	475	650	2,400	6,000	1,250	3,250	13,750	$5,015, MS-66, August 2013
1899	330,000	19,406	62.2	92	300	400	925	2,050	650	1,200	2,300	$5,875, MS-66DM, April 2014
1899O	12,290,000	93,637	63.7	100	65	90	210	425	250	500	1,650	$17,625, MS-67, January 2014
1899O, Micro O (z)	*	1,003	38.1	5	1,000	—						$49,938, MS-64, January 2014
1899S	2,562,000	6,637	61.5	85	500	825	2,150	3,850	1,100	3,800	23,000	$4,994, MS-66, February 2014
1900	8,830,000	54,436	63.6	98	65	85	190	535	2,800	9,000	40,000	$9,400, MS-67, January 2014
1900O	12,590,000	71,634	63.7	99	65	85	190	450	500	1,100	5,750	$4,847, MS-67, August 2013
1900O, Obverse Die Break (aa)	*	174	29.2	3	—	—						$529, AU-55, April 2013
1900O, O Over CC (bb)	*	8,281	61.0	88	725	950	2,100	5,500	5,750	8,500	19,000	$15,275, MS-66, January 2014
1900S	3,540,000	8,214	61.8	86	400	650	1,800	3,800	6,250	19,000	35,000	$8,519, MS-66, August 2013
1901 (cc)	6,962,000	7,692	53.9	16	15,750	50,000	475,000	—	30,000	70,000		$58,750, MS-64, November 2013
1901, DblDie Reverse (dd)	*	312	41.6	1	—							$41,125, MS-62, August 2013
1901O	13,320,000	56,524	63.6	100	65	85	200	600	450	1,200	8,500	$7,075, MS-67, April 2014
1901S	2,284,000	5,325	60.2	80	850	1,200	3,500	12,500	11,000	21,000	30,000	$11,750, MS-66, April 2014
1902	7,994,000	11,819	63.4	96	135	180	475	1,000	7,500	13,000	20,000	$4,700, MS-67, November 2013
1902O	8,636,000	98,139	63.6	100	65	85	200	500	450	2,800	13,500	$12,925, MS-67, January 2014
1902S	1,530,000	7,234	60.3	82	650	875	2,800	8,000	3,600	8,000	14,000	$6,816, MS-65PL, April 2013
1903	4,652,000	22,573	63.5	96	90	120	320	575	2,400	7,500	22,500	$3,525, MS-67, June 2013
1903O	4,450,000	17,216	63.3	99	450	475	625	900	650	1,800	6,400	$5,141, MS-65DM, July 2014
1903S	1,241,000	4,237	38.4	21	6,500	8,000	11,000	15,500	10,000	15,000	38,000	$16,450, MS-66, April 2014
1903S, Small S (ee)	*	228	21.9	0	—	—						$6,756, AU-50, January 2014
1904	2,788,000	8,196	62.1	90	260	575	2,850	11,000	7,500	42,500	60,000	$11,163, MS-66, December 2013
1904O	3,720,000	213,263	63.7	100	65	85	190	400	200	450	1,150	$7,050, MS-67, February 2014
1904S	2,304,000	4,168	49.9	44	4,500	5,250	11,000	23,500	11,000	13,000	22,000	$30,550, MS-66PL, December 2013
1921	44,690,000	138,727	63.3	98	55	75	170	700	1,950	7,750	11,500	$15,863, MS-67, January 2014
1921D	20,345,000	26,932	62.7	91	65	120	375	1,250	2,100	7,500	12,000	$44,063, MS-67, April 2013
1921S	21,695,000	20,024	62.6	93	75	160	1,200	9,500	3,100	12,000	30,000	$14,100, MS-66, April 2013

* Included in number above. **z.** The O mintmark is smaller than normal; its punch was probably intended for a Barber half dollar. Five different dies are known, all scarce. **aa.** A die break is visible from the rim through the date to just below the lower point of the bust. This variety is very rare in Mint State. Value in AU-50 is $550. **bb.** An O mintmark was punched into the die over a previously punched CC mintmark. There are at least seven different dies involved; the one pictured is VAM 9. **cc.** Beware of a fraudulently removed mintmark intended to make a less valuable 1901-O or 1901-S appear to be a 1901 dollar. **dd.** Doubling is visible on the eagle's tail feathers, and also on IN GOD WE TRUST, as well as on the arrows, wreath, and bow. This variety is nicknamed the "Shifted Eagle." It is very rare in Mint State. Value in MS-60 is $5,000. **ee.** The S mintmark is smaller than normal, possibly intended to be punched into a Barber half dollar die.

Proof Morgan Dollars

PF-60 to 70 (Proof). Morgan dollar Proofs were struck in all years from 1878 to 1904. Those from 1878 to 1901 generally have cameo contrast, while those of 1902 to 1904 have the portrait lightly polished in the die. Some Proofs are lightly struck. Check the hair above Miss Liberty's ear (in particular), and the eagle's breast feathers on the reverse. In 1921 quite a few so-called Zerbe Proofs were made with fields that are slightly reflective but have many microscopic die-finish lines. A very small number of deeply mirrored 1921 coins were made, called Chapman Proofs. Some Zerbe Proofs have been miscertified as Chapman Proofs. *Obverse and Reverse:* Proofs that are extensively cleaned and have many hairlines, or that are dull and grainy, are lower level, such as PF-60 to 62. These are not widely desired, except for the solitary date of 1895. With medium hairlines and good reflectivity, an assigned grade of PF-64 is appropriate, and with relatively few hairlines, PF-65. In various grades hairlines are most easily seen in the obverse field. Horizontal slide marks on the cheek of Miss Liberty are common and are from abrasion from the clear slides on National and related coin albums. PF-66 may have hairlines so delicate that magnification is needed to see them. Above that, a Proof should be free of such lines, including slide marks.

Proof Morgan Dollar

	Mintage	Cert	Finest	PF-60	PF-63	PF-64	PF-65	Recent Auction Record
1878, 8 Tail Feathers	500	283	67	$1,400	$3,500	$4,300	$7,800	$38,188, PF-66Cam, December 2013
1878, 7 Tail Feathers	250	169	67	2,750	3,750	5,600	11,500	$32,900, PF-65Cam, January 2014
1878, Third Reverse (a)	*	15	64	16,500	60,000	115,000	200,000	$155,250, PF-64, November 2004
1879	1,100	653	68	1,300	3,000	4,300	6,100	$25,850, PF-68Cam, April 2013
1879O (b)	4–8	9	66			150,000	200,000	$176,250, PF-64, August 2013
1880	1,355	858	69	1,300	2,900	3,900	6,100	$36,719, PF-68Cam, August 2013
1881	984	556	69	1,300	2,900	3,900	6,100	$25,850, PF-68Cam, April 2013
1882	1,100	724	68	1,300	2,900	3,900	6,100	$24,675, PF-68Cam, August 2013
1883	1,039	558	68	1,300	2,900	3,900	6,100	$170,375, PF-65Cam, August 2013
1883O (c)	4–8	5	67			125,000	175,000	$270,250, PF-67Cam, April 2013
1884	875	446	69	1,300	2,900	3,900	6,100	$32,900, PF-68Cam, April 2013
1885	930	525	69	1,300	2,900	3,900	6,100	$25,850, PF-67, June 2014
1886	886	476	68	1,300	2,900	3,900	6,100	$28,200, PF-68Cam, April 2013
1887	710	477	68	1,300	2,900	3,900	6,100	$11,163, PF-67Cam, April 2013
1888	833	394	67	1,300	2,900	3,900	6,100	$24,675, PF-66Cam, April 2013
1889	811	401	68	1,300	2,900	3,900	6,100	$28,200, PF-67, July 2014
1890	590	454	69	1,300	2,900	3,900	6,100	$88,125, PF-69DCam, April 2013
1891	650	446	68	1,300	2,900	3,900	6,100	$35,250, PF-68Cam, August 2013
1892	1,245	740	68	1,300	2,900	3,900	6,100	$35,250, PF-68Cam, August 2013
1893	792	476	69	1,300	2,900	3,900	6,100	$55,813, PF-68Cam, April 2013
1893CC (d)	4–8	22	67			125,000	175,000	$149,500, PF-65, August 2011
1894	972	686	69	2,850	3,500	5,000	7,000	$44,063, PF-67Cam, April 2013
1895 † (e)	880	849	69	45,000	50,000	55,000	69,000	$117,500, PF-68Cam, April 2013
1895O (f)	2–3	5	66		*(extremely rare)*			$528,750, PF-66, June 2013
1896	762	565	69	1,300	2,900	3,900	6,100	$94,000, PF-69DCam, August 2013
1897	731	448	68	1,300	2,900	3,900	6,100	$35,250, PF-68, April 2014
1898	735	534	69	1,300	2,900	3,900	6,100	$28,200, PF-67DCam, February 2013
1899	846	494	69	1,300	2,900	3,900	6,100	$44,063, PF-67DCam, April 2013
1900	912	537	68	1,300	2,900	3,900	6,100	$27,025, PF-68Cam, August 2013
1901	813	562	68	1,600	3,250	4,100	6,500	$38,278, PF-68Cam, April 2013
1902	777	477	68	1,300	2,900	3,900	6,100	$23,649, PF-68, April 2013
1903	755	539	68	1,300	2,900	3,900	6,100	$32,900, PF-68Cam, August 2013
1904	650	626	68	1,300	2,900	3,900	6,100	$9,400, PF-67, August 2013
1921, Zerbe (g)	150–250	125	67	3,500	5,250	7,500	10,250	$35,250, PF-66, January 2014
1921S, Zerbe (g)	1–2	4	65			90,000	140,000	$117,500, PF-65, August 2013
1921, Chapman (h)	25–40	64	67	16,500	—	40,000	75,000	$61,688, PF-65, April 2013

* Included in number above. † Ranked among the *100 Greatest U.S. Coins* (fourth edition). **a.** The Second Reverse is sometimes known as "Concave Breast" or "Reverse of 1878." The Third Reverse is sometimes known as "Round Breast" or "Reverse of 1879." **b.** Some numismatists classify these as Deep Mirror Prooflike circulation strikes, rather than as Proofs. **c.** "A numismatic tradition exists, dating back well over a century, that 12 full Proofs were struck of the 1883-O Morgan dollar. And, they may have been, although the differentiation between a cameo DMPL and a 'branch mint Proof' would be difficult to explain" (*A Guide Book of Morgan Silver Dollars,* fourth edition). **d.** Some numismatists classify these as Deep Mirror Prooflike circulation strikes, rather than as Proofs. **e.** Mint records indicate that 12,000 1895 Morgan dollars were struck for circulation; however, none have ever been seen. In order to complete their collections, date-by-date collectors are forced to acquire one of the 880 Proofs struck that year, causing much competition for this, "The King of the Morgan Dollars." **f.** Some numismatists classify these as Deep Mirror Prooflike circulation strikes, rather than as Proofs. **g.** "Pieces called Zerbe Proofs are simply circulation strikes with a semi-prooflike character, not as nice as on the earlier-noted [mirrorlike] prooflike pieces, struck from dies that were slightly polished, but that retained countless minute striae and preparation lines. In the view of the writer [Bowers], Zerbe Proofs have no basis in numismatic fact or history, although opinions differ on the subject. It seems highly unlikely that these were produced as Proofs for collectors. If indeed they were furnished to Farran Zerbe, a leading numismatic entrepreneur of the era, it is likely that they were simply regular production pieces. Zerbe had a fine collection and certainly knew what a brilliant Proof should look like, and he never would have accepted such pieces as mirror Proofs" (*A Guide Book of Morgan Silver Dollars,* fourth edition). **h.** Breen stated that 12 Chapman Proofs were minted (*Walter Breen's Encyclopedia of U.S. and Colonial Proof Coins, 1792–1977*); Bowers estimates fewer than 30 (*A Guide Book of Morgan Silver Dollars,* fourth edition). These are sometimes called *Chapman Proofs* because Philadelphia coin dealer Henry Chapman advertised them for sale within a few months of their production.

PEACE
(1921–1935)

Designer Anthony de Francisci; weight 26.73 grams; composition .900 silver, .100 copper (net weight .77344 oz. pure silver); diameter 38.1 mm; reeded edge; mints: Philadelphia, Denver, San Francisco.

History. In 1921, following the Pittman Act of 1918, the U.S. Treasury struck millions more silver dollars of the Morgan type while a new Peace dollar was in development. Sculptor and medalist Anthony de Francisci created the Peace design, originally intended as a commemorative of the end of the hostilities of the Great War. The obverse features Miss Liberty, and the reverse an eagle perched before the rising sun. The designer's monogram is located in the field of the coin under the neck of Miss Liberty. Coins of 1921 were struck in high relief; this caused weakness at the centers, so the design was changed to low relief in 1922. The dollars were struck until 1928, then again in 1934 and 1935. Legislation dated August 3, 1964, authorized the coinage of 45 million silver dollars, and 316,076 dollars of the Peace design dated 1964 were struck at the Denver Mint in 1965. Plans for completing this coinage were subsequently abandoned and all of these coins were melted. None were preserved or released for circulation; details are found in *A Guide Book of Peace Dollars* (Burdette).

Striking and Sharpness. Peace dollars of 1921 are always lightly struck at the center of the obverse, with hair detail not showing in an area. The size of this flat spot can vary. For this and other Peace dollars, check the hair detail at the center and, on the reverse, the feathers on the eagle. Many coins are struck from overly used dies, giving a grainy appearance to the fields, particularly the obverse. On many Peace dollars tiny white "milk spots" are seen, left over from when they were struck; these are not as desirable in the marketplace as unspotted coins.

Availability. All dates and mintmarks are readily available. Although some are well worn, they are generally collected in EF and finer grades. MS coins are available for each, with the 1934-S considered to be the key date. San Francisco issues of the 1920s, except for 1926-S, are often heavily bagmarked. The appearance of luster varies from issue to issue and can be deeply frosty, or—in the instance of Philadelphia Mint coins of 1928, 1934, and 1935— satiny or "creamy."

Note: Values of common-date silver coins have been based on the current bullion price of silver, $20 per ounce, and may vary with the prevailing spot price.

AU-50, 53, 55, 58 (About Uncirculated). *Obverse:* Light wear is seen on the cheek and the highest-relief areas of the hair. The neck truncation edge also shows wear. Some luster exists at AU-50 to 55. At AU-58, the luster is extensive, but incomplete. *Reverse:* Wear is evident on the eagle's shoulder and back. Otherwise, comments apply as for the obverse.

MS-60 to 70 (Mint State). *Obverse:* At MS-60, some abrasion and contact marks are evident, most notice-ably on the cheek and on the hair to the right of the face and forehead. Luster is present, but may be dull or lifeless. At MS-63, contact marks are extensive but not distracting. Abrasion still is evident, but less than at lower levels. MS-64 coins are slightly finer. Some Peace dollars have whitish "milk spots" in the field; while these are not caused by handling, but seem to have been from liquid at the mint or in storage, coins with these spots are rarely graded higher than MS-63 or 64. An MS-65 coin may have minor abrasion, but contact marks are so minute as to require magnification. Luster should be full and rich on earlier issues, and either frosty or satiny on later issues, depending on the date and mint. *Reverse:* At MS-60 some abrasion and contact marks are evident, most noticeably on the eagle's shoulder and nearby. Otherwise, comments apply as for the obverse.

1921, Line Through L
VAM 3. FS-S1-1921-1003.

1922, Die Break in Field
VAM 1F. FS-S1-1922-001f.

1922, Die Break at Ear
The "Ear Ring" variety.
VAM 2A. FS-S1-1922-002a.

1922, Die Break in Hair
The 1922 "Extra Hair" variety.
VAM 2C. FS-S1-1922-002c.

1922, Die Break on Cheek
The "Scar Cheek" variety.
VAM 5A. FS-S1-1922-005a.

1922, Die Break at Nose
The "Moustache" variety.
VAM 12A. FS-S1-1922-012a.

1923, Die Break at Jaw
The "Whisker Jaw" variety.
VAM 1A. FS-S1-1923-001a.

1923, Die Break in Hair
The 1923 "Extra Hair" variety.
VAM 1B. FS-S1-1923-001b.

1923, Die Break on O in DOLLAR
The "Tail on O" variety.
VAM 1C. FS-S1-1923-001c.

1923, Die Break on Cheek
The "Whisker Cheek" variety.
VAM 1D. FS-S1-1923-001d.

1923, Doubled-Die Obverse
The "Double Tiara" variety.
VAM 2. FS-S3-1923-002.

1923-S, Pitted Reverse
VAM 1C. FS-S1-1923S-001c.

1924, Die Break on Wing
The "Broken Wing" variety.
VAM 5A. FS-S1-1924-005a.

1925, Missing Ray
VAM 5. FS-S1-1925-005.

1926-S, Reverse Dot
The "Extra Berry" variety.
VAM 4. FS-S1-1926S-004.

1934-D, Doubled-Die Obverse, Small D
VAM 4. FS-S1-1934D-004.

	Mintage	Cert	Avg	%MS	AU-50	MS-60	MS-62	MS-63	MS-64	MS-65	MS-66	Recent Auction Record
1921, High Relief	1,006,473	25,508	59.6	78	$150	$275	$375	$450	$900	$2,200	$7,000	$16,450, MS-66, November 2013
1921, High Relief, Line Through L (a)	*	106	61.5	81	225	315	400	500	950	2,500		$940, MS-63, June 2013
1922, High Relief (1 known)	35,401	1	55.0	0	—							
1922, Normal Relief	51,737,000	266,451	63.5	99	36	41	45	50	70	160	675	$17,625, MS-67, April 2013
1922, Die Break in Field (b)	*	124	55.0	23	400	800	1,750	2,500				$1,528, MS-64, December 2013
1922, Die Break at Ear (c)	*	103	57.6	49	290	650	1,400	2,300				$1,293, MS-63, December 2013
1922, Die Break in Hair (d)	*	378	56.8	44	90	180	300	385				$259, MS-64, February 2014
1922, Die Break on Cheek (e)	*	90	58.5	50	190	400	550					$940, MS-65, January 2014
1922, Die Break at Nose (f)	*	256	58.0	44	90	200	325	500				$120, AU-58, April 2012
1922D	15,063,000	14,812	63.0	94	37	42	50	80	150	625	2,350	$5,875, MS-66, November 2013
1922S	17,475,000	10,690	62.3	92	37	43	60	90	325	2,400	20,000	$11,750, MS-66, April 2014
1923	30,800,000	411,390	63.7	100	36	41	45	50	70	160	625	$7,638, MS-67, June 2014
1923, Die Break at Jaw (g)	*	342	61.0	75	80	125	175	265	550			$999, MS-66, December 2013
1923, Die Break in Hair (h)	*	361	62.3	88	125	200	300	400	600			$223, MS-64, February 2014
1923, Die Break on O (i)	*	124	58.6	62	275	650	1,150	1,800				$2,468, MS-65, April 2014
1923, Die Break on Cheek (j)	*	145	60.0	67	165	250	350	475	875			$259, MS-63, December 2013
1923, DblDie Obverse (k)	*	128	61.3	77	58	75	100	160	375			$223, MS-64, April 2014
1923D	6,811,000	7,339	62.4	90	36	58	85	150	400	1,300	4,750	$76,375, MS-67, June 2013
1923S	19,020,000	11,438	62.2	91	38	45	70	90	500	6,000	30,000	$14,100, MS-65, November 2013
1923S, Pitted Reverse (l)	*	76	57.0	47	125	250	—	450				$282, MS-63, December 2013
1924	11,811,000	65,259	63.7	99	37	41	45	50	70	160	650	$14,100, MS-67, September 2013
1924, Die Break on Wing (m)	*	115	60.8	67	130	200	375	475				$75, AU-50, March 2012
1924S	1,728,000	7,709	61.0	78	60	220	400	525	1,400	9,000	43,500	$7,638, MS-65, September 2013
1925	10,198,000	78,771	63.9	99	37	41	45	50	70	160	625	$9,106, MS-67, April 2014
1925, Missing Ray (n)	*	164	62.6	88	65	85	100	145	250	400		$129, MS-64, December 2013
1925S	1,610,000	10,920	62.1	90	45	100	180	280	1,100	27,500	—	$18,800, MS-65, August 2013
1926	1,939,000	16,468	63.2	96	37	52	100	110	140	600	2,100	$10,575, MS-66, April 2014
1926D	2,348,700	8,036	62.6	89	40	80	140	190	425	1,000	2,500	$4,994, MS-66, August 2013
1926S	6,980,000	11,447	62.5	90	38	57	75	120	325	1,100	4,850	$4,553, MS-66, June 2013
1926S, Reverse Dot (o)	*	107	56.4	47	55	90	140	200	360			$823, MS-65, December 2013
1927	848,000	10,607	62.2	89	50	85	120	200	625	2,900	23,000	$9,988, MS-65, February 2014
1927D	1,268,900	7,568	61.2	83	75	200	250	380	1,050	4,750	25,000	$9,988, MS-65, November 2013
1927S	866,000	8,101	61.7	87	75	200	265	600	1,300	9,750	45,000	$17,625, MS-65, April 2014
1928	360,649	13,230	60.2	74	400	500	600	900	1,300	4,500	25,000	$4,994, MS-65, September 2013
1928S	1,632,000	10,181	61.1	82	65	200	300	525	1,200	22,000	—	$17,625, MS-65, April 2013
1934	954,057	10,301	62.5	89	50	115	170	225	400	750	3,000	$11,163, MS-66, June 2014
1934D (p)	1,569,500	9,410	61.4	81	50	150	250	375	625	2,100	4,900	$22,325, MS-66, June 2013
1934D, DblDie Obv, Small D (q)	*	103	53.1	33	375	750	900	1,650				$881, MS-62, January 2014
1934S	1,011,000	7,212	51.7	42	500	2,000	2,800	4,000	5,250	9,000	27,500	$23,645, MS-66, April 2014
1935	1,576,000	12,910	62.7	91	50	85	90	125	275	800	2,500	$11,163, MS-66, April 2014
1935S (r)	1,964,000	7,235	61.9	85	88	275	325	500	675	1,500	4,250	$39,656, MS-65, April 2013
1964D (s)	316,076	n/a	n/a	n/a	(none known to exist)							

* Included in number above. **a.** A ray runs through the first L in DOLLAR, instead of behind it. **b.** A die break is visible in the field above DOLLAR. "This variety has turned out to be much rarer than previously thought, and is very scarce in grades above EF" (*Cherrypickers' Guide to Rare Die Varieties*, fifth edition, volume II). **c.** A major die break near Liberty's ear, dangling down to her neck, gives this variety its nickname, the "Ear Ring." Several die states are known. **d.** An irregular line of raised metal runs along the back of Liberty's hair. This is called the "Extra Hair" variety. Several die states are known. **e.** Liberty's cheek has a raised, almost triangular chunk of metal along a vertical die break. Also, the reverse is lightly tripled. This variety, called the "Scarface," is very scarce in Mint State. **f.** A die break is visible running from Liberty's nose along the top of her mouth. This is known as the "Moustache" variety. **g.** A die break bridges Liberty's cheek and jaw. This is the "Whisker Jaw" variety. **h.** A significant die break runs diagonally across the strands of Liberty's hair; die breaks may also be visible toward the back of her hair. This variety is nicknamed the 1923 "Extra Hair." **i.** A die break trails from the O of DOLLAR. This variety, called the "Tail on O," is very rare in any grade. **j.** A die break runs down Liberty's cheek toward the junction of the chin and neck. This is the "Whisker Cheek" variety. **k.** Doubling is most evident in the wide spread on the rays of Liberty's tiara, especially those under the BER of LIBERTY. This is the "Double Tiara" variety. **l.** "Pitting runs from the eagle's back tail-feathers, just to the right of the mintmark, upward to the N in ONE. . . . This is the most important Pitted Reverse variety in the Peace dollar series" (*Cherrypickers' Guide to Rare Die Varieties*). **m.** A dramatic die break runs down and across the entire width of the eagle's back. This is the "Broken Wing" variety. **n.** This variety is the result of a reverse die polished with too much gusto. The partially effaced remains of bold clash marks are evident, but the topmost internal ray is missing. **o.** A raised circular dot of metal is visible to the left of the bottom olive leaf. This is nicknamed the "Extra Berry" variety. **p.** Varieties exist with small and large mintmarks. **q.** The obverse shows strong doubling on most letters of IN GOD WE TRUST, the rays on the right, and especially on Liberty's profile. The mintmark is a small D, shaped much like that of the 1920s-era D punches. **r.** Varieties exist with either three or four rays below ONE. They are valued equally in the marketplace. **s.** The entire mintage of 1964-D Peace dollars was melted by government order. Deceptive reproductions exist.

Proof Peace Dollars

PF-60 to 70 (Proof). Some Sandblast Proofs were made in 1921 and a limited issue in 1922 in high relief. These are rare today. Seemingly, a few Satin Proofs were also made in 1921. Sandblast Proofs of 1922 have a peculiar whitish surface in most instances, sometimes interrupted by small dark flecks or spots. There are a number of impostors among certified "Proofs." *Obverse and Reverse:* Proofs of both types usually display very few handling marks or defects. To qualify as Satin PF-65 or Sandblast PF-65 or finer, contact marks must be microscopic.

Proof Peace Dollar

	Est Mintage	Cert	Avg	PF-60	PF-63	PF-64	PF-65	Recent Auction Record
1921, Satin Finish Proof	10–20	17	63.6	$15,000	$30,000	$50,000	$75,000	$32,200, PF-64, July 2009
1921, Matte Finish Proof	5–8	3	64.0			75,000	100,000	$99,875, PF-66, January 2014
1922, High Relief, Matte Proof	10–15	15	62.6			75,000	125,000	$329,000, PF-67, January 2014
1922, Low Relief, Matte Proof	3–6	3	65.3			100,000	150,000	$35,200, PF-65, November 1988
1922, Low Relief, Satin Proof	3–6	2	64.0			100,000	150,000	$44,850, PF-60, November 2009

EISENHOWER
(1971–1978)

Designer Frank Gasparro; diameter 38.1 mm; reeded edge; mints: Philadelphia, Denver, San Francisco. Silver issue: weight 24.59 grams; composition, 40% silver, 60% copper, consisting of outer layers of .800 silver, .200 copper bonded to inner core of .209 silver, .791 copper (net weight .3161 oz. pure silver). Copper-nickel issue: weight 22.68 grams; composition, outer layers of .750 copper, .250 nickel bonded to inner core of pure copper.

Bicentennial variety: Designers Frank Gasparro and Dennis R. Williams; diameter 38.1 mm; reeded edge; mints: Philadelphia, Denver, San Francisco. Silver issue: weight 24.59 grams; composition, outer layers of .800 silver, .200 copper bonded to inner core of .209 silver, .791 copper (net weight .3161 oz. pure silver). Copper-nickel issue: weight 22.68 grams; composition, outer layers of .750 copper, .250 nickel bonded to inner core of pure copper.

History. Honoring both President Dwight D. Eisenhower and the first landing of man on the moon, this design is the work of Chief Engraver Frank Gasparro, whose initials are on the truncation and below the eagle. The reverse is an adaptation of the official Apollo 11 insignia. Collectors' coins were struck in 40% silver composition, and the circulation issue (for some time a staple of the casino trade) in copper-nickel.

The dies for the Eisenhower dollar were modified several times by changing the relief, strengthening the design, and making Earth (above the eagle) more clearly defined.

Low-relief (Variety 1) dies, with flattened Earth and three islands off Florida, were used for all copper-nickel issues of 1971, Uncirculated silver coins of 1971, and most copper-nickel coins of 1972.

High-relief (Variety 2) dies, with round Earth and weak or indistinct islands, were used for all Proofs of 1971, all silver issues of 1972, and the reverse of some exceptional and scarce Philadelphia copper-nickel coins of 1972.

Improved high-relief reverse dies (Variety 3) were used for late 1972 Philadelphia copper-nickel coins and for all subsequent issues. Modified high-relief dies were also used on all issues beginning in 1973.

A few 1974-D and 1977-D dollars were made, in error, in silver clad composition.

A special reverse design was selected for the nation's Bicentennial. Nearly a thousand entries were submitted after the Treasury announced an open competition in October 1973. After the field was narrowed down to 12 semifinalists, the judges chose the rendition of the Liberty Bell superimposed on the moon to appear on the dollar coins. The obverse remained unchanged except for the dual date 1776–1976, which appeared on all dollars made during 1975 and 1976. These dual-dated coins were included in the various offerings of Proof and Uncirculated coins made by the Mint. They were also struck for general circulation. The lettering was modified early in 1975 to produce a more attractive design.

Striking and Sharpness. Striking generally is very good. On the obverse, check the high parts of the portrait, and on the reverse, the details of the eagle.

Availability. MS coins are common in the marketplace, although several early varieties are elusive at MS-65 or better. Lower grades are not widely collected.

Note: Values of common-date silver coins have been based on the current bullion price of silver, $20 per ounce, and may vary with the prevailing spot price.

MS-60 to 70 (Mint State). *Obverse:* At MS-60, some abrasion and contact marks are evident, most noticeably on the cheek, jaw, and temple. Luster is present, but may be dull or lifeless. At MS-63, contact marks are extensive but not distracting. Abrasion still is evident, but less than at lower levels. MS-64 coins are slightly finer. An MS-65 coin may have minor abrasion, but contact marks are so minute as to require magnification. Luster should be full and rich. *Reverse:* At MS-60, some abrasion and contact marks are evident, most noticeably on the eagle's breast, head, and talons. Otherwise, the same comments apply as for the obverse.

1971-S, Silver Clad, Repunched Mintmark

1971-S, Silver Clad, Polished Die
The "Peg Leg R" variety.

	Mintage	Cert	Avg	%MS	MS-63	MS-65	MS-66	Recent Auction Record
1971, Copper-Nickel Clad ‡	47,799,000	4,765	63.8	97	$6	$120	$1,000	$6,463, MS-64, February 2013
1971D, Copper-Nickel Clad, Variety I	68,587,424	7,173	64.5	98	5	50	130	$12,925, MS-64, May 2013
1971D, Copper-Nickel Clad, Variety II	*				5	50	130	
1971S, Silver Clad	6,868,530	8,075	65.3	100	13	20	40	$4,994, MS-67, January 2014
1971S, Silver Clad, Repunched Mintmark (a)	*	176	64.7	100		225	350	$96, MS-65, June 2013
1971S, Silver Clad, Polished Die (b)	*	n/a	n/a	n/a		125	250	$56, MS-64, January 2010
1972, Copper-Nickel Clad, All kinds	75,890,000							
1972, Copper-Nickel Clad, Variety I		3,073	63.8	98	5	140	7,000	$823, MS-65, August 2013
1972, Copper-Nickel Clad, Variety II ‡		1,890	62.1	83	80	1,300	8,500	$4,847, MS-65, January 2014
1972, Copper-Nickel Clad, Variety III		3,237	63.7	96	5	125	900	$4,700, MS-66, January 2014
1972D, Copper-Nickel Clad	92,548,511	4,487	64.3	97	5	30	150	$127, MS-66, March 2012
1972S, Silver Clad	2,193,056	13,667	66.6	100	13	15	20	$206, MS-68, January 2014
1973, Copper-Nickel Clad ‡	2,000,056	3,053	64.4	100	13	65	750	$999, MS-66, June 2013
1973D, Copper-Nickel Clad ‡	2,000,000	3,125	64.6	100	13	50	275	$12,925, MS-67, June 2013
1973S, Copper-Nickel Clad (c)	*							
1973S, Silver Clad	1,883,140	8,507	66.5	100	14	18	35	$282, MS-68, August 2013

* Included in number above. ‡ Ranked in the *100 Greatest U.S. Modern Coins.* Only issued in Mint sets. **a.** A secondary S is visible protruding northwest of the primary S. "This is one of fewer than a half dozen RPMs known for the entire series" (*Cherrypickers' Guide to Rare Die Varieties,* fifth edition, volume II). **b.** The left leg of the R in LIBERTY was overpolished. This is popularly known as the "Peg Leg R" variety. **c.** Two reported to exist.

Chart continued on next page.

	Mintage	Cert	Avg	%MS	MS-63	MS-65	MS-66	Recent Auction Record
1974, Copper-Nickel Clad	27,366,000	3,523	64.3	99	$6.00	$60	$550	$646, MS-66, June 2014
1974D, Copper-Nickel Clad	45,517,000	10,152	64.9	100	6.00	38	130	$14,100, MS-65, January 2014
1974S, Silver Clad	1,900,156	9,762	66.5	100	13.00	20	25	$259, MS-68, August 2013
1776–1976, Copper-Nickel Clad, Variety 1	4,019,000	2,885	64.0	100	8.00	160	1,250	$28,200, MS-64, January 2014
1776–1976, Copper-Nickel Clad, Variety 2	113,318,000	6,237	64.6	99	5.00	30	125	$823, MS-63, November 2013
1776–1976D, Copper-Nickel Clad, Variety 1	21,048,710	4,231	64.6	99	5.00	50	185	$5,581, MS-65, October 2013
1776–1976D, Copper-Nickel Clad, Variety 2	82,179,564	9,003	64.9	99	5.00	28	60	$2,938, MS-62, April 2013
1776–1976, Silver Clad, Variety 2		n/a	n/a	n/a				
1776–1976S, Silver Clad, Variety 1	11,000,000	n/a	n/a	n/a	17.00	20	30	$999, MS-68, July 2014
1977, Copper-Nickel Clad	12,596,000	5,162	64.9	100	6.00	35	135	$170, MS-66, March 2013
1977D, Copper-Nickel Clad	32,983,006	17,762	65.0	100	6.00	35	170	$4,700, MS-67, April 2013
1978, Copper-Nickel Clad	25,702,000	3,132	64.6	99	6.00	45	160	$44,063, MS-64, November 2013
1978D, Copper-Nickel Clad	33,012,890	7,051	64.9	100	5.50	40	125	$200, MS-66, July 2013

Proof Eisenhower Dollars

PF-60 to 70 (Proof). Proofs were made of the various issues (both copper-nickel clad and silver clad from 1971 to 1976; copper-nickel only in 1977 and 1978). All are readily available in today's marketplace. Nearly all are well struck and of high quality.

Obverse and Reverse: Proofs that are extensively cleaned and have many hairlines, or that are dull and grainy, are lower level, such as PF-60 to 62. There are not many of these in the marketplace. With medium hairlines and good reflectivity, assigned grades of PF-63 or 64 are appropriate. With relatively few hairlines a rating of PF-65 can be given. PF-66 may have hairlines so delicate that magnification is needed to see them. Above that, a Proof should be free of any hairlines or other problems.

Proof Eisenhower Dollar

Proof Eisenhower Dollar, Bicentennial

1971-S, Proof, Doubled-Die Obverse

1972-S, Proof, Silver Clad, Doubled-Die Obverse

1973-S, Proof, Silver Clad, Doubled-Die Obverse

	Mintage	Cert	Avg	PF-65	PF-67Cam	PF-67DC	PF-68DC	Recent Auction Record
1971S, Silver Clad	4,265,234	26,232	68.6	$14	$15	$20	$25	$4,700, PF-70DCam, June 2013
1971S, Silver Clad, DblDie Obv (a)	*	52	66.9	90	150			$1,528, PF-68Cam, April 2014
1972S, Silver Clad	1,811,631	20,266	68.7	14	15	20	25	$2,820, PF-70DCam, June 2013
1972S, Silver Clad, DblDie Obv (b)	*	20	67.2					$25, PF-67, March 2008
1973S, Copper-Nickel Clad	2,760,339	14,003	68.8	14	16	22	30	$56, PF-69DCam, January 2013
1973S, Silver Clad	1,013,646	16,811	68.6	35	37	40	50	$123, PF-67DCam, January 2014
1973S, Silver Clad, DblDie Obv (b)	*	18	67.7					

* Included in number above. **a.** Strong doubling is visible on IN GOD WE TRUST, the date, and LIBER of LIBERTY. There are at least two doubled-die obverses for this date (valued similarly); the one listed is FS-S1-1971S-103. "This obverse is also paired with a minor doubled-die reverse" (*Cherrypickers' Guide to Rare Die Varieties,* fifth edition, volume II). **b.** A medium spread of doubling is evident on IN GOD WE TRUST, LIBERTY, and slightly on the date.

	Mintage	Cert	Avg	PF-65	PF-67Cam	PF-67DC	PF-68DC	Recent Auction Record
1974S, Copper-Nickel Clad	2,612,568	12,970	68.8	$10	$15	$25	$30	$56, PF-69DCam, January 2013
1974S, Silver Clad	1,306,579	17,443	68.7	15	16	25	30	$529, PF-68Cam, June 2013
1776–1976S, Copper-Nickel Clad, Variety 1 ‡	2,845,450	13,209	68.7	12	15	20	30	$141, PF-69DCam, January 2013
1776–1976S, Copper-Nickel Clad, Variety 2	4,149,730	17,275	68.8	8	12	15	30	$56, PF-69DCam, January 2013
1776–1976, Silver Clad, Variety 2	n/a	n/a		—				$4,600, PF-70DCam, January 2012
1776–1976S, Silver Clad, Variety 1	4,000,000	23,887	68.7	19	20	25	35	$4,600, PF-70DCam, January 2012
1977S, Copper-Nickel Clad	3,251,152	15,615	68.8	10	15	20	25	$60, PF-69DCam, January 2013
1978S, Copper-Nickel Clad	3,127,781	16,556	68.8	10	15	20	25	$44, PF-69DCam, January 2013

‡ Ranked in the *100 Greatest U.S. Modern Coins.*

SUSAN B. ANTHONY
(1979–1999)

Designer Frank Gasparro; weight 8.1 grams; composition outer layers of copper-nickel (.750 copper, .250 nickel) bonded to inner core of pure copper; diameter 26.5 mm; reeded edge; mints: Philadelphia, Denver, San Francisco.

History. The Susan B. Anthony dollar was designed by Frank Gasparro, chief engraver of the U.S. Mint, following a congressional mandate. It features a portrait of the famous suffragette, along with an eagle-and-Moon motif reduced from the coin's larger predecessor, the Eisenhower dollar. Legislators hoped that these so-called mini-dollars would be an efficient substitute for paper dollars, which wear much more quickly in circulation. A large mintage in 1979 was followed by smaller quantities in 1980 and 1981, and then a hiatus of almost 20 years. A final coinage was struck in 1999.

Striking and Sharpness. Most are well struck, but check the highest areas of both sides.

Availability. Susan B. Anthony dollars are readily available in MS, although those of 1981 are scarcer. Circulated coins are not widely sought by collectors.

MS-60 to 70 (Mint State). *Obverse:* At MS-60, some abrasion and contact marks are evident, most noticeably on the cheek and upper center of the hair. Luster is present, but may be dull or lifeless. At MS-63, contact marks are extensive but not distracting. Abrasion still is evident, but less than at lower levels. MS-64 coins are slightly finer. An MS-65 coin may have minor abrasion, but contact marks are so minute as to require magnification. Luster should be full and rich. *Reverse:* At MS-60, some abrasion and contact marks are evident, most noticeably on the eagle's breast, head, and talons. Otherwise, the same comments apply as for the obverse.

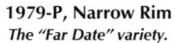

1979-P, Narrow Rim
The "Far Date" variety.

1979-P, Wide Rim
The "Near Date" variety.

	Mintage	Cert	Avg	%MS	MS-64	MS-65	MS-66	Recent Auction Record
1979P, Narrow Rim (a)	360,222,000	548	64.9	97	$6	$10	$20	$15,275, MS-67, January 2014
1979P, Wide Rim ‡ (a)	*	3,536	64.3	96	38	55	135	$4,406, MS-67, December 2013
1979D	288,015,744	1,982	65.1	98	7	12	25	$299, MS-67, July 2009
1979S	109,576,000	1,994	65.5	99	6	10	20	$3,819, MS-64, January 2014
1980P	27,610,000	2,306	65.7	100	5	10	15	$1,763, MS-68, June 2014

* Included in number above. ‡ Ranked in the *100 Greatest U.S. Modern Coins.* **a.** The obverse design was modified in 1979 to widen the border rim. Late issues of 1979-P and subsequent issues have the wide rim. The 1979-P Wide Rim dollar is nicknamed the "Near Date" because the numerals are closer to the rim.

Chart continued on next page.

	Mintage	Cert	Avg	%MS	MS-64	MS-65	MS-66	Recent Auction Record
1980D	41,628,708	2,097	65.6	100	$5	$10	$15	$264, MS-67, March 2014
1980S	20,422,000	1,709	65.1	100	10	15	25	$37, MS-66, July 2008
1981P (b)	3,000,000	2,011	65.1	100	12	20	55	$165, MS-67, June 2014
1981D (b)	3,250,000	2,180	65.5	100	10	15	25	$382, MS-67, June 2014
1981S ‡ (b)	3,492,000	1,722	64.3	100	20	35	250	$499, MS-66, December 2013
1999P (c)	29,592,000	2,335	65.9	100	5	10	15	$764, MS-64, January 2014
1999D (c)	11,776,000	2,547	66.4	100	5	10	15	$294, MS-68, June 2014

‡ Ranked in the *100 Greatest U.S. Modern Coins*. **b.** 1981-P, -D, and -S dollars were issued only in Mint Sets. **c.** Dies for the 1999 dollars were further modified to strengthen details on the reverse.

Proof Anthony Dollars

PF-60 to 70 (Proof). Proofs were made of all issues and are readily available in today's market. *Obverse and Reverse:* Proofs that are extensively cleaned and have many hairlines, or that are dull and grainy, are lower level, such as PF-60 to

62. This comment is more theoretical than practical, as nearly all Proofs have been well kept. With medium hairlines and good reflectivity, assigned grades of PF-63 or 64 are appropriate. With relatively few hairlines a rating of PF-65 can be given.

PF-66 may have hairlines so delicate that magnification is needed to see them. Above that, all the way to PF-70, a Proof should be free of any hairlines or other problems under strong magnification.

Proof Anthony Dollar

1979-S, Filled S
(Type 1)

1979-S, Clear S
(Type 2)

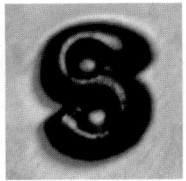

1981-S, Rounded S
(Type 1)

1981-S, Flat S
(Type 2)

1980-S, Repunched Mintmark
FS-C1-1980S-501.

	Mintage	Cert	Avg	PF-65	PF-68DC	PF-69DC	Recent Auction Record
1979S, Type 1 (a)	3,677,175	13,881	68.9	$7	$10	$20	$123, PF-70DCam, August 2013
1979S, Type 2 ‡ (a)	*	6,217	68.7	70	75	80	$441, PF-70DCam, March 2013
1980S	3,554,806	13,038	68.9	6	10	20	$90, PF-70DCam, August 2013
1980S, RPM (b)	n/a	n/a		—	—		
1981S, Type 1	4,063,083	15,263	68.9	6	10	20	$106, PF-70DCam, May 2013
1981S, Type 2 ‡	*	5,710	68.5	160	170	180	$764, PF-70DCam, February 2013
1999P (c)	750,000	13,010	69.1	20	28	33	$90, PF-70DCam, August 2013

* Included in number above. ‡ Ranked in the *100 Greatest U.S. Modern Coins*. **a.** The S mintmark punch was changed in 1979 to create a clearer mintmark. **b.** "The remnants of a previously punched S appear left of the primary S. . . . Very few specimens of this variety have surfaced to date" (*Cherrypickers' Guide to Rare Die Varieties*, fifth edition, volume II). **c.** The mintage reflects the total for the Proof coin dated 1999, which was sold through 2003.

SACAGAWEA
(2000–2008)

Designers: Glenna Goodacre (obverse), Thomas D. Rogers Sr. (reverse); weight 8.1 grams; composition, pure copper core with outer layers of manganese brass (.770 copper, .120 zinc, .070 manganese, and .040 nickel); diameter 26.5 mm; plain edge; mints: Philadelphia, Denver, San Francisco; 22-karat gold numismatic specimens dated 2000-W were struck at West Point in 1999.

History. The Sacagawea dollar was launched in 2000. The obverse shows a modern artist's conception of Sacagawea, the Shoshone Indian who assisted the Lewis and Clark expedition, and her infant son. (No known contemporary portraits of Sacagawea exist.) The reverse shows an eagle in flight.

Striking and Sharpness. Most are very well struck. Check the higher design points.

Availability. These coins are common in high grades, and are usually collected in MS and Proof.

MS-60 to 70 (Mint State). *Obverse:* At MS-60, some abrasion and contact marks are evident, most noticeably on the cheekbone and the drapery near the baby's head. Luster is present, but may be dull or lifeless. At MS-63, contact marks are extensive but not distracting. Abrasion still is evident, but less than at lower levels. MS-64 coins are slightly finer. An MS-65 coin may have minor abrasion, but contact marks are so minute as to require magnification. Luster should be full and rich. *Reverse:* At MS-60, some abrasion and contact marks are evident, most noticeably on the eagle's breast. Other-wise, the same comments apply as for the obverse.

2000-P, Reverse Die Aberrations
The "Speared Eagle" variety.

2000-P, Normal Feathers

2000-P, Boldly Detailed Tail Feathers

	Mintage	Cert	Avg	%MS	MS-64	MS-65	MS-66	Recent Auction Record
2000P	767,140,000	11,656	66.6	100	$3	$5	$12	$9,106, AU-58, June 2013
2000P, Reverse Die Aberrations (a)	*	117	64.1	91		775	1,500	$2,013, MS-67, January 2012
2000P, Goodacre Presentation Finish ‡ (b)	5,000	2,645	67.1	100		450	600	$5,288, MS-69, April 2013
2000P, Boldly Detailed Tail Feathers ‡ (c)	5,500	55	67.1	100		2,500	3,000	$5,060, MS-66 Plus, March 2012
2000D	518,916,000	11,167	66.3	100	4	8	15	$57, MS-68, March 2013
2001P	62,468,000	5,288	67.2	100	2	4	6	$4,406, MS-64, February 2013
2001D	70,939,500	2,474	66.2	100	2	4	6	$166, MS-68, March 2013
2002P (d)	3,865,610	3,183	67.1	100	2	4	10	$1,028, MS-69, March 2013
2002D (d)	3,732,000	2,167	66.5	100	2	4	8	$165, MS-68, March 2013
2003P (d)	3,080,000	2,970	67.0	100	3	5	8	$37, MS-68, July 2008
2003D (d)	3,080,000	2,680	66.2	100	3	5	8	$223, MS-68, March 2013
2004P (d)	2,660,000	2,269	66.9	100	2	4	8	$71, MS-68, July 2008
2004D (d)	2,660,000	2,307	66.8	100	2	4	8	$29, MS-68, March 2013
2005P (d)	2,520,000	5,364	66.8	100	7	10	20	$26, MS-69 Satin, August 2009
2005D (d)	2,520,000	5,288	66.5	100	7	10	20	$529, MS-68, March 2013
2006P (d)	4,900,000	3,091	66.5	100	2	4	8	$115, MS-69 Satin, July 2008
2006D (d)	2,800,000	2,965	66.4	100	2	4	8	$58, MS-67, June 2014
2007P (d)	3,640,000	3,510	66.8	100	3	5	8	$74, MS-68, March 2013
2007D (d)	3,920,000	2,589	66.2	100	3	5	8	$31, MS-69 Satin, May 2009
2008P (d)	1,820,000	2,213	66.7	100	3	5	8	$66, MS-68, March 2013
2008D (d)	1,820,000	2,324	66.6	100	3	5	8	$2,115, MS-68, May 2013

* Included in number above. ‡ Ranked in the *100 Greatest U.S. Modern Coins.* **a.** Two spike-like die aberrations appear through the breast of the eagle. This variety is nicknamed the "Speared Eagle." **b.** A group of 5,000 coins, dated 2000 and with a special finish, were presented to sculptor Glenna Goodacre in payment for the obverse design. **c.** The feathers of the eagle are finely enhanced. This is nicknamed the "Cheerios" variety, as the coins were included as a promotion in boxes of Cheerios cereal. **d.** Not issued for circulation.

Proof Sacagawea Dollars

PF-60 to 70 (Proof). Proofs have been made each year and are readily available. *Obverse and Reverse:* Proofs that are extensively cleaned and have many hairlines, or that are dull and grainy, are lower level, such as PF-60 to 62. This comment is more theoretical than practical, as nearly all Proofs have been well kept. With medium hairlines and good reflectivity, assigned grades of PF-63 or 64 are appropriate. With relatively few hairlines a rating of PF-65 can be given. PF-66 may have hairlines so delicate that magnification is needed to see them. Above that, all the way to PF-70, a Proof should be free of any hairlines or other problems under strong magnification.

Proof Sacagawea Dollar

	Mintage	Cert	Avg	PF-65	PF-69DC	Recent Auction Record
2000S	4,047,904	26,156	69.0	$12	$25	$82, PF-70DCam, April 2013
2001S	3,183,740	25,066	69.0	50	70	$72, PF-70DCam, May 2013
2002S	3,211,995	16,596	69.1	18	30	$41, PF-70DCam, November 2013
2003S	3,298,439	20,064	69.1	16	30	$16, PF-69DCam, January 2013
2004S	2,965,422	20,842	69.1	16	30	$46, PF-70DCam, January 2014
2005S	3,344,679	28,592	69.1	15	20	$46, PF-69DCam, March 2014
2006S	3,054,436	14,734	69.2	15	20	$17, PF-69DCam, January 2013
2007S	2,577,166	13,017	69.1	15	20	$15, PF-69DCam, January 2013
2008S	2,169,561	9,398	69.1	15	20	$63, PF-70DCam, March 2013

NATIVE AMERICAN (2009 TO DATE)

Designers: Glenna Goodacre (obverse), Norm Nemeth (2009 reverse), Thomas Cleveland (2010 reverse), Richard Masters (2011 reverse), Thomas Cleveland (2012 reverse); weight 8.1 grams; composition, pure copper core with outer layers of manganese brass (.770 copper, .120 zinc, .070 manganese, and .040 nickel); diameter 26.5 mm; lettered edge; mints: Philadelphia, Denver, San Francisco.

Common Obverse

Three Sisters (2009)

Great Law of Peace (2010)

Wampanoag Treaty (2011)

Trade Routes in the 17th Century (2012)

Treaty With the Delawares (2013)

Native Hospitality (2014)

History. Since 2009, the reverse of the golden dollar has featured an annually changing design that memorializes Native Americans and, in the words of the authorizing legislation, "the important contributions made by Indian tribes and individual Native Americans to the development [and history] of the United States." The coins are marked (incuse) on their edges with the year of minting, the mintmark, and the legend E PLURIBUS UNUM. The Native American $1 Coin Act also specified that at least 20% of the total mintage of dollar coins in any given year (including Presidential dollars) will be Native American dollars. Production of all dollar coins minted after 2011 is limited to numismatic sales; none issued for circulation.

Striking and Sharpness. Most examples are very well struck. Check the higher points of the design.

Availability. Native American dollars are common in high grades, and are usually collected in MS and Proof. Distribution for public circulation has been slow despite Mint efforts such as the $1 Coin Direct Ship program (intended "to make $1 coins readily available to the public, at no additional cost [including shipping], so they can be easily introduced into circulation—particularly by using them for retail transactions, vending, and mass transit").

MS-60 to 70 (Mint State). *Obverse and reverse:* At MS-60, some abrasion and contact marks are evident, most noticeably on the high points of the design, including, on the obverse, Sacagawea's cheekbone and the drapery near the baby's head. Luster is present, but may be dull or lifeless. At MS-63, contact marks are extensive but not distracting. Abrasion is still evident, but less than at lower levels. MS-64 coins are slightly finer. An MS-65 coin may have minor abrasion, but contact marks are so minute as to require magnification. Luster should be full and rich.

	Mintage	Cert	Avg	%MS	MS-64	MS-65	MS-66	Recent Auction Record
2009P, Three Sisters	39,200,000	3,067	66.5	100	$3	$5	$8	$441, MS-68, June 2014
2009D, Three Sisters	35,700,000	1,886	66.2	100	3	5	8	

	Est Mintage	Cert	Avg	%MS	MS-64	MS-65	MS-66	Recent Auction Record
2010P, Great Law	32,060,000	1,944	66.2	100	$3	$5	$8	
2010D, Great Law	48,720,000	1,442	66.1	100	3	5	8	
2011P, Wampanoag Treaty	29,400,000	973	66.7	100	3	5	8	
2011D, Wampanoag Treaty	48,160,000	968	66.8	100	3	5	8	
2012P, Trade Routes	2,800,000	n/a	n/a	n/a	3	5	8	
2012D, Trade Routes	3,080,000	n/a	n/a	n/a	3	5	8	
2013P, Treaty With the Delawares		n/a	n/a	n/a	3	5	8	
2013D, Treaty With the Delawares		n/a	n/a	n/a	3	5	8	
2014P, Native Hospitality		n/a	n/a	n/a	3	6	9	
2014D, Native Hospitality		n/a	n/a	n/a	3	6	9	

Proof Native American Dollars

PF-60 to 70 (Proof). Proofs have been made each year and are readily available. *Obverse and Reverse:* Proofs that are extensively cleaned and have many hairlines, or that are dull and grainy, are lower level, such as PF-60 to 62. This comment is more theoretical than practical, as nearly all Native American dollar Proofs have been well kept. With medium hairlines and good reflectivity, assigned grades of PF-63 or 64 are appropriate. With relatively few hairlines a rating of PF-65 can be given. PF-66 may have hairlines so delicate that magnification is needed to see them. Above thtat, all the way to PF-70, a Proof should be free of any hairlines or other problems under strong magnification.

Proof Native American Dollar

	Est Mintage	Cert	Avg	PF-65	PF-69DC	Recent Auction Record
2009S, Three Sisters	2,179,867	13,982	69.2	$10	$17	$17, PF-69DCam, January 2013
2010S, Great Law	1,689,364	8,747	69.2	10	17	$26, PF-69DCam, January 2013
2011S, Wampanoag Treaty	1,453,276	8,101	69.1	15	18	$17, PF-69DCam, January 2013
2012S, Trade Routes		n/a	n/a	15	18	
2013S, Treaty With the Delawares		n/a	n/a	15	18	
2014S, Native Hospitality		n/a	n/a	15	18	

PRESIDENTIAL
(2007–2016)

Various designers (obverse), Don Everhart (reverse); weight 8.1 grams; composition, pure copper core with outer layers of manganese brass (.770 copper, .120 zinc, .070 manganese, and .040 nickel; diameter 26.5 mm; plain edge; mints: Philadelphia, Denver, San Francisco.

Obverse Style, 2007–2008
No motto on obverse.

Obverse Style, 2009–2016
Motto beneath portrait.

Common Reverse

Date, Mintmark, and Mottos Incused on Edge
IN GOD WE TRUST moved to obverse in 2009.

History. Presidential dollars debuted in 2007 and are being issued at the rate of four designs per year, starting with George Washington and continuing in order of office. Each coin has a common reverse showing the Statue of Liberty. The motto IN GOD WE TRUST was moved from the edge to the obverse in 2009. After 2011, production will be for numismatic sales only.

Striking and Sharpness. These usually are well struck, but check the higher-relief parts of each side.

Availability. Presidential dollars are very common in MS. Most have from a few to many bagmarks, with true MS-65 and better coins in the minority.

MS-60 to 70 (Mint State). *Obverse:* At MS-60, some abrasion and contact marks are evident, most noticeably on the highest-relief areas of the portrait, the exact location varying with the president depicted. Luster is present, but may be dull or lifeless. At MS-63, contact marks are extensive but not distracting. Abrasion still is evident, but less than at lower levels. MS-64 coins are slightly finer. An MS-65 coin may have minor abrasion, but contact marks are so minute as to require magnification. Luster should be full and rich. *Reverse:* At MS-60, some abrasion and contact marks are evident, most noticeably on the cheek and arm. Otherwise, the same comments apply as for the obverse.

2007, Washington   2007, J. Adams   2007, Jefferson   2007, Madison

2008, Monroe   2008, J.Q. Adams   2008, Jackson   2008, Van Buren

2009, W.H. Harrison   2009, Tyler   2009, Polk   2009, Taylor

2010, Fillmore   2010, Pierce   2010, Buchanan   2010, Lincoln

2011, A. Johnson   2011, Grant   2011, Hayes   2011, Garfield

2012, Arthur   2012, Cleveland, First Term   2012, B. Harrison   2012, Cleveland, Second Term

2013, McKinley   2013, T. Roosevelt   2013, Taft   2013, Wilson

| 2014, Harding | 2014, Coolidge | 2014, Hoover | 2014, F.D. Roosevelt |

	Mintage	Cert	Avg	%MS	MS-64	MS-65	MS-66	Recent Auction Record
2007P, Washington	176,680,000	33,892	65.1	100	$2	$3	$6	$42, MS-68 Satin, April 2009
2007, Washington, Plain Edge ‡ (a)	*	63,064	64.8	100	40	50	100	$388, MS-67, June 2014
2007D, Washington	163,680,000	35,884	65.2	100	2	3	6	$17, MS-65, August 2009
2007P, J. Adams	112,420,000	36,511	64.7	100	2	3	6	$30, MS-65DCam, January 2013
2007D, J. Adams	112,140,000	17,022	65.1	100	2	3	6	$25, MS-69 Satin, May 2009
2007P, Jefferson	100,800,000	15,289	65.5	100	2	3	6	$65, MS-65, October 2009
2007D, Jefferson	102,810,000	17,293	65.7	100	2	3	6	$16, MS-65, August 2009
2007P, Madison	84,560,000	8,528	65.0	100	2	3	6	$16, MS-66, August 2009
2007D, Madison	87,780,000	10,096	66.0	100	2	3	6	$15, MS-66, August 2009
2008P, Monroe	64,260,000	6,661	66.0	100	2	3	6	$11, MS-67, July 2008
2008D, Monroe	60,230,000	6,439	66.0	100	2	3	6	$11, MS-67, July 2008
2008P, J.Q. Adams	57,540,000	6,015	66.0	100	2	3	6	
2008D, J.Q. Adams	57,720,000	5,388	66.0	100	2	3	6	
2008P, Jackson	61,180,000	4,959	66.0	100	2	3	6	
2008D, Jackson	61,070,000	3,913	65.0	100	2	3	6	
2008P, Van Buren	51,520,000	3,122	66.0	100	2	3	6	
2008D, Van Buren	50,960,000	3,034	66.0	100	2	3	6	
2009P, W.H. Harrison	43,260,000	3,362	66.0	100	2	3	6	
2009D, W.H. Harrison	55,160,000	2,737	66.0	100	2	3	6	
2009P, Tyler	43,540,000	2,376	66.0	100	2	3	6	
2009D, Tyler	43,540,000	2,042	65.0	100	2	3	6	
2009D, Tyler, 2010 Edge	*	945	66.0	100	—	—	—	$129, MS-66, February 2014
2009P, Polk	46,620,000	3,008	66.0	100	2	3	6	
2009D, Polk	41,720,000	2,473	66.0	100	2	3	6	
2009P, Taylor	41,580,000	2,434	66.2	100	2	3	6	
2009D, Taylor	36,680,000	2,154	66.0	100	2	3	6	
2010P, Fillmore	37,520,000	2,014	66.0	100	2	3	6	
2010D, Fillmore	36,960,000	1,820	66.0	100	2	3	6	
2010P, Pierce	38,220,000	2,043	66.0	100	2	3	6	
2010D, Pierce	38,360,000	1,850	66.2	100	2	3	6	
2010P, Buchanan	36,820,000	1,349	66.2	100	2	3	6	
2010D, Buchanan	36,540,000	1,444	66.3	100	2	3	6	
2010P, Lincoln	49,000,000	2,260	66.1	100	2	3	6	
2010D, Lincoln	48,020,000	1,923	66.5	100	2	3	6	
2011P, A. Johnson	35,560,000	1,312	66.2	100	2	3	6	
2011D, A. Johnson	37,100,000	1,180	66.4	100	2	3	6	
2011P, Grant	38,080,000	1,243	66.3	100	2	3	6	
2011D, Grant	37,940,000	1,158	66.4	100	2	3	6	
2011P, Hayes	37,660,000	1,080	66.3	100	2	3	6	
2011D, Hayes	36,820,000	1,157	66.6	100	2	3	6	
2011P, Garfield	37,100,000	995	66.3	100	2	3	6	
2011D, Garfield	37,100,000	936	66.5	100	2	3	6	
2012P, Arthur (b)	6,020,000	n/a	n/a	n/a	2	3	6	
2012D, Arthur (b)	4,060,000	n/a	n/a	n/a	2	3	6	
2012P, Cleveland, First Term (b)	5,460,000	n/a	n/a	n/a	2	3	6	
2012D, Cleveland, First Term (b)	4,060,000	n/a	n/a	n/a	2	3	6	
2012P, B. Harrison (b)	5,640,000	n/a	n/a	n/a	2	3	6	
2012D, B. Harrison (b)	4,200,000	n/a	n/a	n/a	2	3	6	
2012P, Cleveland, Second Term (b)	10,680,000	n/a	n/a	n/a	2	3	6	
2012D, Cleveland, Second Term (b)	3,920,000	n/a	n/a	n/a	2	3	6	

* Included in number above. ‡ Ranked in the *100 Greatest U.S. Modern Coins*. **a.** Some circulation-strike Washington dollars are known without the normal edge lettering (date, mintmark, IN GOD WE TRUST, and E PLURIBUS UNUM). **b.** Not issued for circulation.

Chart continued on next page.

	Mintage	Cert	Avg	%MS	MS-64	MS-65	MS-66	Recent Auction Record
2013P, McKinley (b)		n/a	n/a	n/a	$2	$3	$6	
2013D, McKinley (b)		n/a	n/a	n/a	2	3	6	
2013P, T. Roosevelt (b)		n/a	n/a	n/a	2	3	6	
2013D, T. Roosevelt (b)		n/a	n/a	n/a	2	3	6	
2013P, Taft (b)		n/a	n/a	n/a	2	3	6	
2013D, Taft (b)		n/a	n/a	n/a	2	3	6	
2013P, Wilson (b)		n/a	n/a	n/a	2	3	6	
2013D, Wilson (b)		n/a	n/a	n/a	2	3	6	
2014P, Harding (b)		n/a	n/a	n/a	2	3	6	
2014D, Harding (b)		n/a	n/a	n/a	2	3	6	
2014P, Coolidge (b)		n/a	n/a	n/a	2	3	6	
2014D, Coolidge (b)		n/a	n/a	n/a	2	3	6	
2014P, Hoover (b)		n/a	n/a	n/a	2	3	6	
2014D, Hoover (b)		n/a	n/a	n/a	2	3	6	
2014P, F.D. Roosevelt (b)		n/a	n/a	n/a	2	3	6	
2014D, F.D. Roosevelt (b)		n/a	n/a	n/a	2	3	6	

b. Not issued for circulation.

Proof Presidential Dollars

PF-60 to 70 (Proof). Proofs have been struck of each issue and are readily available. All have been well struck and are of exceptional quality. *Obverse and Reverse:* Proofs that are extensively cleaned and have many hairlines, or that are dull and grainy, are lower level, such as PF-60 to 62. (This comment is more theoretical than practical, as nearly all Proofs have been well kept.) With medium hairlines and good reflectivity, assigned grades of PF-63 or 64 are appropriate. With relatively few hairlines a rating of PF-65 can be given. PF-66 may have hairlines so delicate that magnification is needed to see them. Above that, all the way to PF-70, a Proof should be free of any hairlines or other problems under strong magnification.

Proof Presidential Dollar

	Mintage	Cert	Avg	PF-65	PF-69DC	Recent Auction Record
2007S, Washington	3,965,989	57,062	69.2	$10	$18	$36, PF-70DCam, December 2009
2007S, J. Adams	3,965,989	56,713	69.2	10	18	$26, PF-70DCam, December 2009
2007S, Jefferson	3,965,989	56,749	69.2	10	18	$646, PF-69DCam, July 2014
2007S, Madison	3,965,989	57,221	69.2	10	18	$30, PF-69DCam, February 2013
2008S, Monroe	3,083,940	30,720	69.2	10	16	$69, PF-70DCam, March 2010
2008S, J.Q. Adams	3,083,940	30,762	69.2	10	16	$69, PF-70DCam, March 2010
2008S, Jackson	3,083,940	30,638	69.2	10	16	$59, PF-70DCam, March 2010
2008S, Van Buren	3,083,940	30,790	69.3	10	16	$15, PF-69DCam, January 2013
2009S, W.H. Harrison	2,809,452	20,906	69.2	8	15	
2009S, Tyler	2,809,452	20,834	69.2	8	15	
2009S, Polk	2,809,452	20,863	69.2	8	15	$127, PF-70DCam, February 2010
2009S, Taylor	2,809,452	21,094	69.3	8	15	$47, PF-70DCam, March 2010
2010S, Fillmore	2,224,827	20,480	69.1	10	18	
2010S, Pierce	2,224,827	20,485	69.2	8	15	
2010S, Buchanan	2,224,827	20,356	69.1	8	15	
2010S, Lincoln	2,224,827	21,405	69.1	8	15	
2011S, A. Johnson	1,706,916	11,559	69.2	8	15	
2011S, Grant	1,706,916	11,657	69.2	8	15	
2011S, Hayes	1,706,916	11,634	69.2	8	15	
2011S, Garfield	1,706,916	11,612	69.2	8	15	
2012S, Arthur		n/a	n/a	9	16	
2012S, Cleveland, First Term		n/a	n/a	9	16	

Mintage	Cert	Avg	PF-65	PF-69DC	Recent Auction Record
2012S, B. Harrison	n/a	n/a	$9	$16	
2012S, Cleveland, Second Term	n/a	n/a	9	16	
2013S, McKinley	n/a	n/a	9	16	
2013S, T. Roosevelt	n/a	n/a	9	16	
2013S, Taft	n/a	n/a	9	16	
2013S, Wllson	n/a	n/a	9	16	
2014S, Harrding	n/a	n/a	9	16	
2014S, Coolidge	n/a	n/a	9	16	
2014S, Hoover	n/a	n/a	9	16	
2014S, F.D. Roosevelt	n/a	n/a	9	16	

AN OVERVIEW OF TRADE DOLLARS

A new denomination, the silver trade dollar, was authorized by the Coinage Act of 1873. This provided that a coin weighing 420 grains, 90% silver, be struck for use in the export trade. By comparison, contemporary Liberty Seated silver dollars weighed 412.5 grains. Produced in quantity from 1873 through 1878, the trade dollars were a great success, particularly in China, where merchants preferred silver to gold and would not accept paper money of any kind. Coinage would have continued except for the Bland-Allison Act of February 28, 1878, which authorized the government to buy millions of ounces of silver each year and resume the production of standard silver dollars (which had not been minted since 1873). The trade dollar was discontinued forthwith; however, Proof impressions were made for numismatists through 1883, plus a small quantity of Proofs distributed privately in 1884 and 1885, these last two being great rarities today.

Choosing a trade dollar for a type set is easy enough to do, the choices being a circulation strike, which requires some connoisseurship, or a Proof, most of which are sharply struck and attractive. Enough exist in both formats that collectors will easily find a nice example, except that MS-65 and better pieces are elusive.

FOR THE COLLECTOR AND INVESTOR: TRADE DOLLARS AS A SPECIALTY

There are two great rarities among trade dollars: the Proof-only 1884, of which just 10 are known, and the Proof-only 1885, of which only five are known. Neither was produced openly, and examples were sold for the private profit of Mint officials, going to John W. Haseltine, a Philadelphia dealer who was a favored outlet for such things. The existence of these coins was not generally known to numismatists until 1907–1908, when examples began to appear on the market. As to the mintage figures, the numbers 5 and 10 have no official origin, but are said to represent the number once held by Haseltine. Relatively few numismatists have been able to afford examples of these two dates.

Beyond the above, a complete collection of trade dollars of the 1873 to 1883 years can be formed with some effort. Proofs were made of each year during this span, and after 1878 *only* Proofs were made, at the Philadelphia Mint, with no branch-mint issues. These had greater appeal to collectors of an earlier era, and more were saved, with the result that Proofs of the otherwise common dates 1873–1877 are much harder to find today, especially in choice condition.

Circulation strikes were regularly produced from 1873 through 1878, with emphasis on the San Francisco and Carson City mints, these being closest to the Orient, where the coins were used in commerce. Some trade dollars (but not many) went into domestic circulation (they were legal tender until that status was repealed on July 22, 1876). Later, after 1876, they traded widely in the United States but were valued by their silver content, not their face value. In 1878 the 412.5-grain Morgan dollar was worth $1.00 in circulation, while the heavier 420-grain trade dollar was worth only its melt-down value of about $0.90.

Very few of the circulating issues were saved by numismatists, with the result today that assembling a collection in choice or gem Mint State can be a great challenge. The key issue, by far, is the 1878-CC, with the lowest mintage in the series—scarce in any and all grades. As trade dollars became numismatically popular in the United States, thousands were repatriated from China, often bearing Chinese characters called *chopmarks,* which were applied by bankers and merchants. More often than not the imported coins had been harshly cleaned in China, as the owners thought shiny coins were more desirable. However, many choice and undamaged pieces were imported as well. The pieces with chopmarks are collectible in their own right in view of their historical significance.

Collectors are warned that many modern counterfeit trade dollars lurk in the marketplace.

RECOMMENDED READING

Bowers, Q. David. *Silver Dollars and Trade Dollars of the United States: A Complete Encyclopedia,* Wolfeboro, NH, 1993.

Fivaz, Bill, and Stanton, J.T. *The Cherrypickers' Guide to Rare Die Varieties* (5th ed., vol. II), Atlanta, GA, 2012.

Willem, John M. *The United States Trade Dollar* (2nd ed.), Racine, WI, 1965.

TRADE DOLLAR
(1873–1885)

Designer William Barber; weight 27.22 grams; composition .900 silver, .100 copper (net weight .7874 oz. pure silver); diameter 38.1 mm; reeded edge; mints: Philadelphia, Carson City, San Francisco.

History. Trade dollars were minted under the Coinage Act of 1873. Containing 420 grains of .900 fine silver, they were heavier than the Liberty Seated dollar (of 412.5 grains). They were made for use in the China export trade and proved to be a great success. Some circulated in the United States, until they were demonetized by the Act of July 22, 1876. The Bland-Allison Act of 1878 provided for the new "Morgan" silver dollar, and trade dollars were discontinued, although Proofs continued to be made through 1885.

Modifications to the trade dollar design are distinguished as follows.

Reverse 1: Berry under eagle's left talon; arrowhead ends over 0. (Used on all coins from all mints in 1873 and 1874, and occasionally in 1875 and 1876.)

Reverse 2: Without extra berry under talon; arrowhead ends over 2. (Used occasionally at all mints from 1875 through 1876, and on all coins from all mints 1877 through 1885.)

Obverse 1: Ends of scroll point to left; extended hand has only three fingers. (Used on coins at all mints, 1873 through 1876.)

Obverse 2: Ends of scroll point downward; extended hand has four fingers. (Used in combination with Reverse 2 on one variety of 1876S, and on all coins at all mints from 1877 through 1885.)

Striking and Sharpness. Weakness is often seen. On the obverse, check Miss Liberty's head and the star centers first. On the reverse, check the feathers on the eagle, particularly on the legs. Luster can range from dull to deeply frosty. In EF and lower grades, strike sharpness on the stars and the head does not matter to connoisseurs.

Availability. Although the 1878-CC is a rarity, other dates and mintmarks are readily collected in grades from EF to MS. Lower grades are not often seen, for these coins did not circulate for a long time. Many used in China have counterstamps, called *chopmarks,* which are of interest to collectors. On an MS-63 or better coin a chopmark will decrease value, but on EF and AU coins they are eagerly sought. MS coins are mostly in the lower ranges, often with unsatisfactory surfaces. True gems are very scarce. *Note:* In recent years a flood of modern counterfeit trade dollars, many coming from China, has deluged the market.

EF-40, 45 (Extremely Fine). *Obverse:* More wear than at AU is seen on all areas, especially the head, the left breast, the left arm, the left leg, and the bale on which Miss Liberty is seated. Little or no luster is seen on most coins. *Reverse:* More wear than at AU is evident on the eagle's head, legs, claws, and wings, although on well-struck coins nearly all feather details on the wings are sharp.

AU-50, 53, 55, 58 (About Uncirculated). *Obverse:* Light wear is seen on the knees, bosom, and head. There is some luster at AU-50 to 55. At AU-58, the luster is extensive but incomplete. *Reverse:* Wear is visible on the eagle's head, the claws, and the top of the wings. There are traces of luster at AU-50 to 55. An AU-58 coin has nearly full luster.

MS-60 to 70 (Mint State). *Obverse:* At MS-60, some abrasion and contact marks are evident, most noticeably on the left breast, left arm, and left knee. Luster is present, but may be dull or lifeless. Many of these coins are light in color or even brilliant, having been repatriated from China, and have been cleaned to remove sediment and discoloration. At MS-63, contact marks are very few, and abrasion is minimal. An MS-65 coin has no abrasion in the fields (but may have a hint on the higher parts of the seated figure), and contact marks are trivial. Luster should be full and rich. *Reverse:* Comments apply as for the obverse, except that in lower MS grades abrasion and contact marks are most noticeable on the eagle's head, the claws, and the top of the wings. At MS-65 or higher there are no marks visible to the unaided eye. The field is mainly protected by design elements and does not show abrasion as much as does the obverse on a given coin.

Reverse 1
Arrowheads end over 0; berry under eagle's left talon.

Reverse 2
Arrowheads end over 2; no berry under talon.

Obverse 1
Hand has three fingers; scroll points left.

Obverse 2
Hand has four fingers; scroll points downward.

1874-CC, Chopmarked

Examples of chopmarks

1875-S, S Over CC
FS-T1-1875S-501.

1876-CC, Doubled-Die Reverse
FS-T1-1876CC-801.

1876-S, Doubled-Die Obverse
FS-T1-1876S-101.

1877, Doubled-Die Obverse
FS-T1-1877-101.

1877-S, Repunched Date
FS-T1-1877S-301.

1877-S, Doubled-Die Reverse
FS-T1-1877S-801.

1877-S, Doubled-Die Reverse
FS-T1-1877S-802.

1878-S, Doubled-Die Reverse
FS-T1-1878S-801.

	Mintage	Cert	Avg	%MS	EF-40	AU-50	MS-60	MS-62	MS-63	MS-64	MS-65	Recent Auction Record
1873	396,635	370	57.6	65	$250	$350	$1,050	$2,800	$3,300	$6,500	$18,000	$12,925, MS-65, April 2014
1873CC	124,500	335	50.5	22	975	1,700	10,000	18,000	22,500	55,000	110,000	$32,900, MS-63, June 2014
1873S	703,000	268	57.7	59	250	375	1,400	3,800	4,250	6,000	19,000	$28,200, MS-65, June 2014
1874	987,100	264	57.9	67	250	350	1,100	2,000	2,600	4,500	17,750	$5,288, MS-64, April 2013
1874CC	1,373,200	542	57.1	55	600	775	3,200	5,500	6,750	11,000	32,500	$8,813, MS-64, June 2014
1874S	2,549,000	726	58.4	63	245	325	1,100	2,200	2,600	4,500	17,500	$3,055, MS-64, November 2013
1875	218,200	217	54.5	54	575	875	2,450	4,500	4,650	9,000	18,500	$7,050, MS-64, November 2013
1875, Reverse 2	*	n/a	n/a	n/a	575	875	2,450	4,500	4,650	9,000	18,500	$4,888, MS-64, April 2012
1875CC, All kinds	1,573,700											
1875CC		708	54.4	47	500	750	2,450	4,750	5,000	12,000	35,000	$7,050, MS-64, March 2013
1875CC, Reverse 2		1	55.0	0	500	750	2,600	4,500	4,750	11,500	33,000	$1,610, AU-58, January 2012
1875S, All kinds	4,487,000											
1875S		2,111	60.2	75	245	325	1,000	1,800	2,000	3,250	11,000	$15,863, MS-65, November 2013
1875S, Reverse 2		1	55.0	0	250	335	1,025	1,850	2,350	3,600	11,500	$69,000, MS-67, January 2012
1875S, S Over CC (a)		133	57.1	46	975	1,550	4,350	9,000	12,500	25,000	53,000	$16,485, MS-63, August 2013
1876	455,000	856	59.9	75	250	335	1,050	2,000	2,400	3,200	12,000	$17,625, MS, February 2014
1876, Obverse 2, Reverse 2 (extremely rare)	*	n/a	n/a	n/a			—					
1876, Reverse 2	*	1	55.0	0	245	325	1,000	1,850	2,250	3,500	12,000	$2,760, MS-64, April 2012
1876CC, All kinds	509,000											
1876CC		261	52.9	31	625	1,250	5,750	18,000	24,500	35,000	80,000	$44,063, MS-64, April 2013
1876CC, Reverse 1		1	45.0	0	700	1,550	6,500	18,500	26,000	35,000	80,000	$3,220, MS-60, February 2006
1876CC, DblDie Reverse (b)		54	52.8	30	850	1,750	10,500	19,000	—			$2,350, MS-60, February 2014
1876S, All kinds	5,227,000											
1876S		1,580	57.9	58	245	325	1,000	1,800	2,000	3,250	16,500	$8,225, MS, March 2014
1876S, DblDie Obverse (c)		1	35.0	0	1,400	1,750	2,200					
1876S, Reverse 2		1	58.0	0	245	325	1,000	1,800	2,000	3,250	16,500	$1,506, MS-63, September 2011
1876S, Obverse 2, Reverse 2		n/a	n/a	n/a	250	375	1,300	2,000	2,650	3,700	17,500	$1,495, MS-60 CAC, August 2011
1877	3,039,200	1,035	53.1	48	245	325	1,025	2,000	2,100	4,000	20,000	$30,550, MS-66, November 2013
1877, DblDie Obverse (d)	*	8	56.8	50	300	400	1,250					
1877CC	534,000	293	54.3	48	675	825	2,700	10,000	11,500	22,000	60,000	$7,931, MS-62, September 2013
1877S	9,519,000	2,868	55.6	51	245	325	1,000	1,800	2,050	3,100	11,000	$25,850, MS-66, November 2013
1877S, Repunched Date (e)	*	3	51.7	0	300	425	1,300					$250, EF-45, May 2010
1877S, DblDie Reverse (f)	*	5	51.8	0	550	800	1,600					
1877S, DblDie Reverse (g)	*	11	53.4	36	300	400	1,200					$1,323, MS-62, April 2011
1878		n/a	n/a	n/a	1,500							
1878CC (h)	97,000	241	45.6	23	2,850	4,750	14,000	23,000	25,000	60,000	100,000	$25,850, MS-62, April 2013
1878S	4,162,000	1,868	53.7	44	245	325	1,000	1,800	2,200	3,250	12,000	$49,938, MS-67, April 2013
1878S, DblDie Reverse (i)	*	20	52.7	45	450	550	1,300					$1,000, MS-62, August 2011

* Included in number above. **a.** A weak C from the underlying CC mintmark is visible to the right of the S mintmark. **b.** Doubling is visible on the branches on the right, the eagle's talons, the right wing tip, and the eagle's beak; and is very strong on E PLURIBUS UNUM. Weaker doubling is seen on UNITED STATES OF AMERICA. "Considered by most to be the strongest reverse doubled die in the series, this variety is one of the highlights of the trade dollar varieties and is thought to be extremely rare in grades above AU" (*Cherrypickers' Guide to Rare Die Varieties*, fifth edition, volume II). **c.** Doubling is visible on Liberty's hand, chin, and left foot, and on the olive branch. "This DDO is easily the rarest doubled die in the series, and is considered extremely rare in grades above AU. Most known examples are cleaned. The variety is known as the king of the trade dollar varieties" (*Cherrypickers' Guide to Rare Die Varieties*, fifth edition, volume II). **d.** Doubling on this rare variety is evident on the wheat stalks, LIBERTY, IN GOD WE TRUST, and stars 11, 12, and 13. **e.** A secondary 7 protrudes prominently south from the last 7. **f.** Doubling is visible on E PLURIBUS UNUM, the ribbon, and UNITED STATES OF AMERICA. There are at least two different doubled-die reverses for 1877-S; this one is FS-T1-1877S-801. "Considered a highlight of the trade dollar varieties" (*Cherrypickers' Guide to Rare Die Varieties*, fifth edition, volume II). **g.** Minor doubling is visible on nearly all reverse lettering, especially on 420 GRAINS. This reverse doubled die is more common than the preceding; it is listed as FS-T1-1877S-802. **h.** On July 19, 1878, a quantity of 44,148 trade dollars was melted by the Mint. Many of these may have been 1878-CC. **i.** Strong doubling is visible on the entire lower left of the reverse, on the arrow points and shafts, and on 420 GRAINS; slight doubling is evident on the motto. Rare in AU and higher grades. There are at least two doubled-die reverses for this date; the one listed is FS-T1-1878S-801.

Proof Trade Dollars

PF-60 to 70 (Proof). Proofs were made for collectors from 1873 to 1883, in quantity to supply the demand. In addition, a few were secretly made in 1884 and 1885. Today most survivors are of high quality, although gems of the 1873 to 1877 years are much harder to find than are those of 1878 to 1883. Some Proofs are lightly struck on the head and the stars on the obverse and the leg feathers of the eagle on the reverse. *Obverse and Reverse:* Proofs that are extensively cleaned and have many hairlines, or that are dull and grainy, are lower level, such as PF-60 to 62. These are not widely desired. With medium hairlines and good reflectivity, an assigned grade of PF-64 is appropriate, and with relatively few hairlines, PF-65. In various grades hairlines are most easily seen in the obverse field. PF-66 may have hairlines so delicate that magnification is needed to see them. Above that, a Proof should be free of such lines.

Proof Trade Dollar

	Mintage	Cert	Finest	PF-60	PF-63	PF-64	PF-65	Recent Auction Record
1873	865	359	PF-67	$1,750	$3,300	$4,750	$10,000	$28,200, PF-66, June 2014
1874	700	444	PF-67	1,750	3,100	4,750	10,000	$7,726, PF-65, June 2013
1875	700	487	PF-67	1,750	3,300	4,600	10,500	$38,188, PF-67, April 2014
1876	1,150	573	PF-67	1,750	3,100	4,600	9,500	$10,575, PF-65, June 2014
1877	510	428	PF-67	1,750	3,250	4,600	9,500	$14,100, PF-65, December 2013
1878	900	640	PF-69	1,750	3,250	4,600	9,500	$36,719, PF, February 2014
1879	1,541	1,218	PF-68	1,750	3,200	4,600	9,500	$49,938, PF-67Cam, April 2013
1880	1,987	1,461	PF-68	1,750	3,200	4,600	9,500	$31,725, PF-67Cam, November 2013
1881	960	910	PF-68	1,750	3,200	4,600	9,500	$19,975, PF-66, April 2013
1882	1,097	1,042	PF-68	1,750	3,200	4,600	9,500	$30,550, PF, February 2013
1883	979	937	PF-69	1,750	3,200	4,600	9,500	$21,150, PF-67, August 2013
1884 † (a)	10	16	PF-67		500,000	550,000	650,000	$998,750, PF-65, January 2014
1885 † (a)	5	4	PF-63		2,000,000	*2,250,000*	*2,500,000*	$1,006,250, PF-62, November 2004

† Ranked in the *100 Greatest U.S. Coins* (fourth edition). **a.** Trade dollars of 1884 and 1885 were unknown to the numismatic community until 1907–1908. None are listed in the Mint director's report, and numismatists believe that they are not a part of the regular Mint issue.

AN OVERVIEW OF GOLD DOLLARS

Coinage of the gold dollar was authorized by the Act of March 3, 1849, after the start of the California Gold Rush.

Although a case could be made for designating the Small Head, Open Wreath gold dollar as a separate type, it is not generally collected as such. Instead, pieces dated from 1849 through 1854 are collectively designated as Type 1. Examples today are readily available in all grades, although truly choice and gem Mint State pieces are in the minority.

In contrast, the Type 2 design, produced at the Philadelphia Mint in part of 1854, and at the Philadelphia, Charlotte, Dahlonega, and New Orleans mints in 1855, and only at the San Francisco Mint in 1856, is a great challenge. Examples are scarcer in all grades than are those of Types 1 and 3. Choice and gem coins are especially rare. Striking is a great problem, and while some sharp pieces exist, probably 80% or more have areas of weakness, typically at the 85 (center two digits) of the date, but often on the headdress and elsewhere. Further, the borders are sometimes imperfect.

Type 3 gold dollars, made from 1856 through 1889, are easier to acquire in nearly any grade desired, including choice and gem Mint State, most of which are well struck and have excellent eye appeal. Among Type 3 gold dollars the dates from 1879 through 1889 inclusive are most often seen, as these were widely saved by coin dealers and collectors at the time and did not circulate to any appreciable extent. Some of these have very low mintage figures, making them very appealing to collectors.

FOR THE COLLECTOR AND INVESTOR: GOLD DOLLARS AS A SPECIALTY

Forming a specialized collection of gold dollars is a fascinating pursuit, one that has drawn the attention of many numismatists over the years. A complete run of date-and-mintmark issues from 1849 through 1889 includes no impossible rarities, although the 1875, with just 20 Proofs and 400 circulation strikes made, is the key date. While the dollars of 1879 through 1889 often have remarkably low mintages, they were saved in quantity, and certain of these dates are easily obtainable (although not necessarily inexpensive).

The branch-mint gold dollars of the early years present a special challenge. Among the Charlotte Mint varieties the 1849 comes with an Open Wreath (of which just five are presently known, with a rumor of a sixth) and with a Close Wreath, the latter being scarce but available. Later Charlotte gold dollars, extending through 1859, range from scarce to rare. The 1857-C is notorious for its poor striking.

Gold dollars were struck at the Dahlonega Mint from 1849 through 1861. In the latter year the facility was under the control of the Confederate States of America, and thus the 1861-D gold dollars, rare in any event, are even more desirable as true Confederate coins. The New Orleans Mint also produced gold dollars, which in general are better struck than those of the Charlotte and Dahlonega mints. From 1854 intermittently to 1860, and then in 1870, gold dollars were struck in San Francisco. These Western issues are usually sharply defined and range from scarce to rare. In particular, choice and gem Mint State pieces are elusive.

RECOMMENDED READING

Akers, David W. *Gold Dollars (and Other Gold Denominations),* Englewood, OH, 1975–1982.

Bowers, Q. David. *A Guide Book of Gold Dollars* (2nd ed.), Atlanta, GA, 2011.

Bowers, Q. David. *United States Gold Coins: An Illustrated History,* Wolfeboro, NH, 1982.

Breen, Walter. *Major Varieties of U.S. Gold Dollars (and Other Gold Denominations),* Chicago, 1964.

Fivaz, Bill. *United States Gold Counterfeit Detection Guide,* Atlanta, GA, 2005.

Fivaz, Bill, and Stanton, J.T. *The Cherrypickers' Guide to Rare Die Varieties* (5th ed., vol. II), Atlanta, GA, 2012.

Garrett, Jeff, and Guth, Ron. *Encyclopedia of U.S. Gold Coins, 1795–1933* (2nd ed.), Atlanta, GA, 2008.

LIBERTY HEAD
(1849–1854)

Designer James B. Longacre; weight 1.672 grams; composition .900 gold, .100 copper (net weight .04837 oz. pure gold); diameter 13 mm; reeded edge; mints: Philadelphia, Charlotte, Dahlonega, New Orleans, San Francisco.

Open Wreath Reverse   Close Wreath Reverse
Mintmark is below wreath. Coins shown 2x actual size.

History. U.S. Mint chief engraver James Barton Longacre designed the nation's gold dollars. This first type measured 13 mm in diameter, which proved to be inconvenient, and the two later types were enlarged to 15 mm.

Striking and Sharpness. As a rule, Philadelphia coins are sharper than those of the Charlotte and Dahlonega mints. On the obverse, check the highest areas of the hair below the coronet. On the reverse, check the wreath and the central two figures in the date. On both sides check the dentils, which can be mushy or indistinct (particularly on Charlotte and Dahlonega coins, which often have planchet roughness as well).

Availability. All dates and mintmarks are readily collectible, save for the 1849-C Open Wreath variety. MS coins often are found for the Philadelphia issues but can be elusive for the branch mints. Charlotte and Dahlonega coins often have striking problems. The few gold dollars of this type that are less than VF in grade usually are damaged or have problems.

AU-50, 53, 55, 58 (About Uncirculated). *Obverse:* Light wear on the hair below the coronet and the cheek is very noticeable at AU-50, and progressively less at higher levels to AU-58. Luster is minimal at AU-50 and scattered and incomplete at AU-58. Some tiny nicks and contact marks are to be expected and should be mentioned if they are distracting. *Reverse:* Light wear on the 1, the wreath, and the ribbon characterize an AU-50 coin, progressively less at higher levels to AU-58. Otherwise, the same comments apply as for the obverse.

MS-60 to 70 (Mint State). *Obverse:* At MS-60 to 62, there is abrasion on the hair below the coronet (an area that can be weakly struck, as well) and on the cheeks. Marks may be seen. At MS-63, there may be slight abrasion. Luster is irregular. At MS-64, abrasion is less. Luster is rich on most coins, less so on Charlotte and Dahlonega varieties. At MS-65 and above, luster is deep and frosty. At MS-66, and higher, no marks at all are visible without magnification. *Reverse:* On MS-60 to 62 coins, there is abrasion on the 1, the highest parts of the leaves, and the ribbon. Otherwise, the same comments apply as for the obverse.

1849, With L   1849, No L

	Mintage	Cert	Avg	%MS	AU-55	AU-58	MS-60	MS-62	MS-63	MS-64	MS-65	Recent Auction Record
1849, Open Wreath, So-Called Small Head, With L **(a)**	688,567	n/a	n/a	n/a	$300	$350	$900	$1,100	$1,550	$2,500	$5,000	$79,313, MS-63, April 2014
1849, Open Wreath, So-Called Small Head, No L **(a)**	*	678	61.9	85	400	475	1,100	1,350	2,000	2,750	5,750	$9,988, MS-65, April 2013
1849, Open Wreath, So-Called Large Head **(a)**	*	n/a	n/a	n/a	295	325	600	1,100	1,250	2,100	5,000	$1,495, MS-64, April 2012
1849, Close Wreath	*	620	61.5	81	295	325	600	1,100	1,250	2,100	5,000	$11,163, MS-66, February 2013
1849C, Open Wreath *(extremely rare)*	*	4	45.3	25	500,000	550,000	750,000	850,000	1,250,000			$218,500, EF-45, February 2010
1849C, Close Wreath	11,634	202	51.9	23	3,750	5,250	8,500	12,000	16,500	32,500		$10,281, MS-62, September 2013
1849D, Open Wreath	21,588	499	54.7	28	3,250	3,750	5,500	8,000	12,500	21,500	55,000	$22,325, MS-64, April 2013
1849O, Open Wreath	215,000	946	57.5	46	550	600	1,100	2,250	3,750	7,000	12,500	$5,581, MS-64, September 2013
1850	481,953	808	59.7	66	285	300	425	675	1,100	2,000	5,500	$4,700, MS-65, March 2013
1850C	6,966	159	52.7	22	4,250	6,250	8,500	14,000	32,500			$19,975, MS-63, January 2014
1850D	8,382	162	51.7	17	5,000	7,250	11,000	16,000	26,000	37,500		$3,204, AU-50, July 2014
1850O	14,000	242	56.6	36	1,350	2,000	3,200	5,250	7,000	14,500		$2,532, MS-61, April 2012

* Included in number above. **a.** It is now well known that the so-called Small Head and Large Head coins are from the same punch.

	Mintage	Cert	Avg	%MS	AU-55	AU-58	MS-60	MS-62	MS-63	MS-64	MS-65	Recent Auction Record
1851	3,317,671	6,427	60.7	77	$285	$300	$425	$650	$800	$1,000	$3,750	$9,400, MS-66, March 2013
1851C	41,267	696	54.9	27	2,250	2,550	3,200	4,750	6,250	12,500	25,000	$5,613, MS-63, March 2013
1851D	9,882	246	55.7	29	2,750	3,250	5,000	8,000	15,500	22,500	45,000	$11,163, MS-63, March 2013
1851O	290,000	1,136	58.3	48	425	450	850	1,400	2,250	5,500	9,500	$6,463, MS-65, January 2014
1852	2,045,351	5,687	60.8	76	285	300	425	650	800	1,000	3,750	$5,523, MS-65, July 2014
1852C	9,434	234	55.3	37	2,750	3,000	4,250	6,500	11,500	16,500	30,000	$15,863, MS-64, February 2013
1852D	6,360	167	53.6	20	3,600	4,850	8,750	14,500	27,500			$4,994, AU-55, July 2013
1852O	140,000	615	56.2	34	700	850	1,400	2,000	4,250	10,500	22,500	$2,820, MS-63, April 2013
1853	4,076,051	14,966	60.9	76	285	300	425	650	800	1,000	3,750	$152,750, MS-69, January 2014
1853C	11,515	203	54.6	33	2,600	3,500	4,750	7,500	13,500	26,000	40,000	$14,100, MS-64, January 2014
1853D	6,583	200	55.6	23	4,250	5,500	8,750	14,500	26,000	35,000	55,000	$17,625, MS-63, January 2014
1853O	290,000	1,715	59.2	56	425	450	825	1,300	2,150	5,000	11,000	$2,820, MS-64, April 2013
1854	855,502	5,360	61.1	78	285	300	425	650	800	1,000	3,750	$27,025, MS-67, January 2013
1854D	2,935	118	54.8	29	6,500	7,750	11,500	14,500	35,000			$64,625, MS-64, April 2013
1854S	14,632	235	57.6	39	1,150	1,350	2,500	3,500	5,750	13,500	30,000	$4,113, MS-62, July 2014

Proof Liberty Head Gold Dollars

PF-60 to 70 (Proof). A few Proofs were coined in the early years, and they are, for all practical purposes, unobtainable. Fewer than a dozen are known. *Obverse and*

Reverse: PF-60 to 62 coins have extensive hairlines and may have nicks and contact marks. At PF-63, hairlines are prominent, but the mirror surface is very reflective.

PF-64 coins have fewer hairlines. At PF-65, hairlines should be minimal and mostly seen only under magnification.

Proof Liberty Head Gold Dollar
Shown 2x actual size.

	Est Mintage	Cert	Finest	PF-60	PF-63	PF-64	PF-65	Recent Auction Record
1849, Open Wreath, Small Head, No L *(2–3 known)*	unknown	2	PF-63	*(extremely rare)*				
1850 *(2 known)*	unknown	1	PF-60	$140,000				
1854	unknown	n/a	n/a	*(unique, in the Bass Foundation Collection)*				

INDIAN PRINCESS HEAD, SMALL HEAD
(1854–1856)

Designer James B. Longacre; weight 1.672 grams; composition .900 gold, .100 copper (net weight .04837 oz. pure gold); diameter 15 mm; reeded edge; mints: Philadelphia, Charlotte, Dahlonega, New Orleans, San Francisco.

Mintmark is below wreath. Shown 2x actual size.

History. This style of gold dollar, with the diameter increased from 13 mm to 15 mm, was first made in 1854. The design proved difficult to strike, leading to its modification in 1856.

Striking and Sharpness. On the obverse, check the highest area of the hair below the coronet and the tips of the feathers. Check the letters. On the reverse, check the ribbon bow knot and in particular the two central digits of the dates. Examine the digits on both sides. Nearly all have problems. This type is often softly struck in the

centers, with weak hair detail and the numerals 85 in the date sometimes faint—this should not be confused with wear. The 1855-C and 1855-D coins are often poorly struck and on rough planchets.

Availability. All are collectible, but the Charlotte and Dahlonega coins are rare. With patience, Full Details coins are available of 1854, 1855, and 1856-S, but virtually impossible to find for the branch-mint issues of 1855. The few gold dollars of this type that are less than VF in grade usually are damaged or have problems.

AU-50, 53, 55, 58 (About Uncirculated). *Obverse:* Light wear on the hair below the coronet, the cheek, and the tips of the feather plumes is very noticeable at AU-50, progressively less at higher levels to AU-58. Luster is minimal at AU-50 and scattered and incomplete at AU-58. Some tiny nicks and contact marks are to be expected and should be mentioned if they are distracting. *Reverse:* Light wear on the 1, the wreath, and the ribbon knot characterize an AU-50 coin, pro-gressively less at higher levels to AU-58. Otherwise, the same comments apply as for the obverse.

MS-60 to 70 (Mint State). *Obverse:* At MS-60 to 62, there is abrasion on the hair below the band lettered LIBERTY (an area that can be weakly struck, as well), on the tips of the feather plumes, and through-out the field. Contact marks may also be seen. At MS-63, there should be only slight abrasions. Luster is irregular. At MS-64, abrasions and marks are less. Luster is rich on most coins, less so on Charlotte and Dahlonega issues. At MS-65 and above, luster is deep and frosty, with no marks at all visible without magnification at MS-66 and higher. *Reverse:* At MS-60 to 62, there may be abrasions on the 1, on the highest parts of the leaves, on the ribbon knot, and in the field. Otherwise, the same comments apply as for the obverse.

1854, Doubled-Die Obverse
FS-G1-1854-1101.

	Mintage	Cert	Avg	%MS	AU-55	AU-58	MS-60	MS-62	MS-63	MS-64	MS-65	Recent Auction Record
1854	783,943	8,723	56.7	31	$775	$950	$1,700	$2,950	$7,000	$12,000	$27,500	$49,938, MS-66, February 2013
1854, Doubled-Die Obverse (a)	*	9	56.4	11	1,100	1,350	2,350	4,150	10,000			$3,738, MS-62, December 2011
1855	758,269	8,308	56.6	33	775	950	1,700	2,950	7,000	12,000	27,500	$32,900, MS-65, October 2013
1855C	9,803	271	47.6	6	12,750	20,000	26,000	40,000				$22,913, MS, February 2014
1855D	1,811	92	51.2	12	27,500	32,500	50,000	65,000	95,000	135,000		$52,875, EF-45, July 2014
1855O	55,000	763	53.1	13	2,500	3,850	8,000	14,500	32,500	45,000		$38,188, MS-63, April 2013
1856S	24,600	369	53.1	14	3,250	4,750	8,000	16,000	34,500	50,000		$52,875, MS-64, February 2013

* Included in number above. **a.** Check for strong doubling on UNITED STATES OF AMERICA, the beads in the headdress, the feathers, and portions of LIBERTY.

Proof Indian Princess Head, Small Head, Gold Dollars

PF-60 to 70 (Proof). Proofs exist of the 1854 and 1855 issues, but were made in very small quantities. *Obverse and Reverse:* PF-60 to 62 coins have extensive hairlines and may have nicks and contact marks. At PF-63, hairlines are prominent, but the mirror surface is very reflective. PF-64 coins have fewer hairlines. At PF-65, hairlines should be minimal and mostly seen only under magnification. There should be no nicks or marks. PF-66 and higher coins have no marks or hairlines visible to the unaided eye.

Proof Indian Princess Head, Small Head, Gold Dollar
Shown 2x actual size.

	Est Mintage	Cert	Finest	PF-60	PF-63	PF-64	PF-65	Recent Auction Record
1854	4 known	5	PF-65	$100,000	$200,000	$300,000	$425,000	$218,500, PF-64DCam, March 2009
1855	unknown	11	PF-65	75,000	165,000	225,000	325,000	$397,800, PF, September 2013

INDIAN PRINCESS HEAD, LARGE HEAD
(1856–1889)

Designer James B. Longacre; weight 1.672 grams; composition .900 gold, .100 copper (net weight .04837 oz. pure gold); diameter 15 mm; reeded edge; mints: Philadelphia, Charlotte, Dahlonega, San Francisco.

Mintmark is below wreath. Shown 2x actual size.

History. The design of the Indian Princess Head was modified in 1856. The new portrait is larger and in shallower relief. After this change, most (but not all) gold dollars were struck with strong detail. Gold dollars of this type did not circulate extensively after 1861, except in the West. As they did not see heavy use, today most pieces are EF or better. MS coins are readily available, particularly of the dates 1879 through 1889 (during those years the coins were popular among investors and speculators, and many were saved).

Striking and Sharpness. These dollars usually are well struck, but many exceptions exist. Charlotte and Dahlonega coins are usually weak in areas and can have planchet problems. On all coins, check the hair details on the obverse. The word LIBERTY can be only partially present or missing completely, as the dies were made this way for some issues, particularly in the 1870s; this does not affect their desirability. On the reverse, check the ribbon knot and the two central date numerals. Check the dentils on both sides. Copper stains are sometimes seen on issues of the 1880s due to incomplete mixing of the alloy. Many coins of the 1860s onward have highly prooflike surfaces.

Availability. All are collectible, but many issues are scarce. Most MS-65 or finer coins are dated from 1879 to 1889. The few gold dollars of this type that are less than VF usually are damaged or have problems.

AU-50, 53, 55, 58 (About Uncirculated). *Obverse:* Light wear on the hair below the coronet, the cheek, and the tips of the feather plumes is very noticeable at AU-50, progressively less at higher levels to AU-58. Luster is minimal at AU-50 and scattered and incomplete at AU-58. Some tiny nicks and contact marks are to be expected and should be mentioned if they are distracting. *Reverse:* Light wear on the 1, the wreath, and the ribbon knot characterize an AU-50 coin, progressively less at higher levels to AU-58. Otherwise, the same comments apply as for the obverse.

MS-60 to 70 (Mint State). *Obverse:* At MS-60 to 62, there is abrasion on the hair below the band lettered LIBERTY (an area that can be weakly struck, as well), on the tips of the feather plumes, and throughout the field. Contact marks may also be seen. At MS-63, there should be only slight abrasions. Luster is irregular. At MS-64, abrasions and marks are less. Luster is rich on most coins, less so on Charlotte and Dahlonega issues. At MS-65 and above, luster is deep and frosty, with no marks at all visible without magnification at MS-66 and higher. *Reverse:* At MS-60 to 62, there may be abrasions on the 1, on the highest parts of the leaves, on the ribbon knot, and in the field. Otherwise, the same comments apply as for the obverse.

1862, Doubled-Die Obverse
FS-G1-1862-101.

	Mintage	Cert	Avg	%MS	AU-55	AU-58	MS-60	MS-62	MS-63	MS-64	MS-65	Recent Auction Record
1856, All kinds	1,762,936											
1856, Upright 5		404	58.9	50	$450	$475	$650	$875	$1,500	$2,150	$6,500	$2,585, MS-64, June 2013
1856, Slant 5		2,234	58.7	53	285	300	575	675	950	1,300	3,000	$5,581, MS-66, March 2014
1856D	1,460	79	53.8	14	11,000	16,500	28,500	43,500	80,000			$11,750, AU-58, September 2013
1857	774,789	1,765	59.6	61	285	300	575	675	900	1,200	2,850	$3,323, MS-65, March 2014
1857C	13,280	260	48.4	3	5,000	7,250	12,000	21,000				$16,450, MS-62, April 2013
1857D	3,533	184	53.5	14	4,850	6,500	10,000	16,000				$5,581, AU-58, April 2013
1857S	10,000	183	52.1	12	2,000	2,750	5,750	8,500	19,000	40,000		$2,350, AU-55, July 2014
1858	117,995	418	59.7	59	285	300	575	675	1,000	1,350	5,500	$7,638, MS-66, March 2013
1858D	3,477	215	54.3	27	4,850	6,500	8,750	13,000	19,500	37,500	60,000	$7,638, MS-61, December 2013
1858S	10,000	165	52.4	12	1,850	2,250	5,750	9,500	16,500	19,500	30,000	$8,813, MS-62, June 2014

Chart continued on next page.

	Mintage	Cert	Avg	%MS	AU-55	AU-58	MS-60	MS-62	MS-63	MS-64	MS-65	Recent Auction Record
1859	168,244	622	60.6	72	$285	$300	$575	$675	$900	$1,100	$2,500	$4,113, MS-66, October 2013
1859C	5,235	148	54.0	22	6,500	8,000	11,500	16,000	30,000			$10,575, MS-62, January 2014
1859D	4,952	226	54.9	25	4,750	6,750	8,750	12,000	22,500	35,000	60,000	$11,750, MS-62, June 2013
1859S	15,000	238	50.7	10	1,900	2,350	5,000	8,500	15,000	24,000		$6,169, MS-62, February 2013
1860	36,514	275	60.7	73	300	300	575	675	1,000	2,000	6,500	$1,998, MS-64, December 2013
1860D	1,566	131	53.1	17	9,750 (a)	12,500	18,500	27,500	50,000	75,000		$42,300, MS-64, February 2013
1860S	13,000	249	55.4	25	1,100	1,250	2,650	4,000	6,000	12,500	27,500	$9,929, MS-64, August 2013
1861	527,150	2,278	61.1	81	285	300	575	675	875	1,000	2,500	$3,525, MS-65, February 2013
1861D	1,250	80	56.5	36	57,500 (b)	60,000	72,500	85,000	115,000	135,000	185,000	$111,625, MS-63, June 2013
1862	1,361,355	4,935	61.5	83	285	300	575	675	825	1,100	2,500	$5,875, MS-67, July 2013
1862, Doubled-Die Obverse (c)	*	14	61.4	79	500	550	750	900	1,350			$675, MS-62, February 2011
1863	6,200	75	59.9	63	4,500	5,000	6,000	8,750	10,500	13,500	20,000	$8,813, MS-63, April 2013
1864	5,900	126	61.0	74	1,750	1,500	2,000	2,750	4,500	5,500	8,000	$58,750, MS-69, January 2014
1865	3,725	85	62.1	84	1,350	1,450	2,000	2,750	4,750	5,600	8,500	$18,213, MS-67, January 2014
1866	7,100	151	61.7	82	900	1,000	1,250	1,550	2,150	3,000	5,000	$29,375, MS-68, July 2014
1867	5,200	128	61.1	72	850	950	1,200	1,500	2,000	2,750	5,000	$10,281, MS-66, March 2014
1868	10,500	227	60.7	75	625	750	1,000	1,500	2,000	2,750	4,500	$21,150, MS-68, August 2013
1869	5,900	168	61.5	76	800	900	1,150	1,600	2,250	2,900	5,500	$7,638, MS-66, February 2014
1870	6,300	240	60.9	69	750	850	1,000	1,500	2,000	2,750	5,500	$22,325, MS-67, January 2014
1870S	3,000	113	59.8	62	1,750	2,000	2,750	4,000	8,000	12,500	25,000	$18,800, MS-65, April 2014
1871	3,900	307	61.2	77	675	750	900	1,100	1,900	2,250	4,000	$9,988, MS-66, April 2013
1872	3,500	68	60.7	72	700	850	1,000	1,250	2,250	3,000	5,000	$14,688, MS-68, February 2013
1873, Close 3	1,800	174	60.2	67	1,150	1,350	1,700	2,500	4,250	7,500	15,000	$7,638, MS-64, January 2014
1873, Open 3	123,300	3,650	61.6	88	285	300	525	675	800	950	2,250	$11,750, MS-67, April 2013
1874	198,800	6,626	62.1	91	285	300	525	675	800	950	2,250	$3,314, MS-67, April 2014
1875	400	88	60.7	70	6,500 (d)	7,500	8,500	10,000	17,500	25,000	40,000	$22,325, MS-64, April 2013
1876	3,200	264	61.3	78	600	650	750	1,000	1,350	1,500	3,500	$16,450, MS-66, April 2013
1877	3,900	323	61.8	80	600	650	800	1,000	1,400	1,550	3,500	$6,463, MS-65, December 2013
1878	3,000	278	61.7	83	500	575	775	900	1,200	1,450	3,250	$4,142, MS-65, February 2013
1879	3,000	452	63.3	91	325	350	650	800	1,150	1,300	2,750	$4,127, MS-66, August 2013
1880	1,600	665	65.3	99	325	350	575	700	1,000	1,150	2,350	$52,875, MS-69, January 2014
1881	7,620	798	64.8	97	325	350	575	700	1,000	1,150	2,350	$14,100, MS-68, April 2013
1882	5,000	437	64.1	95	325	350	575	700	1,000	1,150	2,350	$4,406, MS-67, April 2014
1883	10,800	1,081	64.1	96	325	350	575	700	1,000	1,150	2,350	$12,925, MS-67, October 2013
1884	5,230	449	63.2	94	325	350	575	700	1,000	1,150	2,350	$6,463, MS-67, January 2014
1885	11,156	824	63.3	93	325	350	575	700	1,000	1,150	2,350	$3,055, MS-67, January 2013
1886	5,000	642	63.0	95	325	350	575	700	1,000	1,150	1,800	$1,528, MS-65, June 2014
1887	7,500	1,039	63.5	97	285	325	575	675	825	1,000	1,750	$4,818, MS-65, August 2013
1888	15,501	1,594	63.8	98	285	325	575	675	800	975	1,500	$10,105, MS-68, February 2013
1889	28,950	4,175	64.1	98	285	325	575	675	800	975	1,500	$8,108, MS-68, August 2013

* Included in number above. **a.** Value in EF-40 is $4,250; in AU-50, $7,750. **b.** Value in EF-40 is $22,500; in AU-50, $32,500. **c.** Doubling, visible on the entire obverse, is most evident on the tops of the hair curls and the feathers. **d.** Value in EF-40 is $4,500; in AU-50, $5,750.

Proof Indian Princess Head, Large Head, Gold Dollars

PF-60 to 70 (Proof). Proofs were made of all years. Most range from rare to very rare, with some dates in the 1880s being exceptions. Some later dates have high Proof mintages, but likely many of these coins were sold to the jewelry trade (as the Mint was reluctant to release circulation strikes to this market sector). Such coins were incorporated into jewelry and no longer exist as collectible coins. *Obverse and Reverse:* PF-60 to 62 coins have extensive hairlines and may have nicks and contact marks. At PF-63, hairlines are prominent, but the mirror surface is very reflective. PF-64 coins have fewer hairlines. At PF-65, hairlines should be minimal and mostly seen only under magnification. There should be no nicks or marks. PF-66 and higher coins have no marks or hairlines visible to the unaided eye.

Proof Indian Princess Head, Large Head, Gold Dollar
Shown 2x actual size.

	Mintage	Cert	Finest	PF-60	PF-63	PF-64	PF-65	Recent Auction Record
1856, Slant 5	unknown	9	PF-67	$15,000	$30,000	$35,000	$65,000	$30,550, PF, January 2013
1857	unknown	11	PF-64	8,500	17,500	20,000	40,000	$16,100, PF-63Cam, June 2008
1858	unknown	30	PF-64	6,500	13,500	15,000	30,000	$79,313, PF, March 2014
1859	80	28	PF-64	5,500	12,000	10,000	17,500	$22,325, PF-64, August 2013
1860	154	43	PF-64	3,750	8,000	10,000	15,000	$27,600, PF-66, January 2012
1861	349	32	PF-65	3,750	8,000	8,500	13,500	$23,000, PF-66, January 2010
1862	35	34	PF-65	3,750	8,000	8,500	15,000	$7,475, PF-63UCam, April 2008
1863	50	33	PF-64	4,250	9,000	10,000	17,500	$58,750, PF, February 2013
1864	50	22	PF-64	4,250	9,000	10,000	15,000	$32,200, PF-66UCam, October 2011
1865	25	24	PF-65	4,750	9,000	11,500	16,500	$25,300, PF-66UCam, January 2012
1866	30	41	PF-65	4,750	9,000	11,500	16,500	$27,600, PF-67UCam, August 2007
1867	50	23	PF-63	3,750	7,500	10,000	15,000	$25,300, PF-65, August 2011
1868	25	17	PF-64	4,000	7,500	10,000	17,500	$29,900, PF-66UC Plus, August 2011
1869	25	19	PF-64	4,250	7,500	11,500	17,500	$19,975, PF-65Cam, April 2014
1870	35	20	PF-63	3,750	7,500	10,000	15,000	$17,625, PF-64, January 2014
1871	30	9	PF-65	3,750	8,000	10,000	15,000	$27,600, PF-65DCam, November 2011
1872	30	22	PF-64	4,250	8,000	11,500	17,500	$4,888, PF-61, March 2011
1873, Close 3	25	10	PF-64	7,750	15,000	22,500	32,500	$29,900, PF-65Cam, April 2012
1874	20	12	PF-64	5,250	12,000	15,000	24,500	$12,650, PF-64UC Plus, August 2010
1875	20	23	PF-64	12,500	18,500	30,000	40,000	$55,813, PF-66DCam, November 2013
1876	45	35	PF-64	3,750	7,000	11,000	15,000	$34,075, PF-66DCam, June 2013
1877	20	22	PF-65	4,250	8,000	11,000	15,000	$7,638, PF, February 2014
1878	20	21	PF-64	3,750	7,500	11,000	15,000	$19,550, PF-65DCam, January 2012
1879	30	24	PF-64	3,750	6,500	10,500	15,000	$8,225, PF, August 2013
1880	36	41	PF-64	3,750	5,500	10,500	12,000	$18,800, PF-65DCam, February 2013
1881	87	56	PF-64	3,750	5,000	8,500	12,500	$19,975, PF, March 2014
1882	125	93	PF-65	3,500	5,000	8,500	11,500	$15,275, PF, August 2013
1883	207	84	PF-65	3,250	5,000	8,000	11,500	$9,400, PF-65Cam, February 2013
1884	1,006	119	PF-65	3,250	5,000	6,500	10,500	$29,250, PF, September 2013
1885	1,105	197	PF-65	3,250	5,000	6,500	10,500	$28,200, PF, August 2013
1886	1,016	141	PF-64	3,250	5,000	6,500	10,500	$11,163, PF, October 2013
1887	1,043	165	PF-64	3,250	5,000	6,500	10,500	$10,575, PF-65DCam, September 2013
1888	1,079	222	PF-64	3,250	5,000	6,500	10,500	$18,800, PF-66DCam, April 2013
1889	1,779	103	PF-64	3,250	5,000	6,500	10,500	$12,925, PF-66Cam, April 2013

An Overview of
Gold Quarter Eagles

The quarter eagle, denominated at $2.50, was authorized by the Act of April 2, 1792.

Early types in the series range from rare to very rare. The first, the 1796 without stars on the obverse, Heraldic Eagle motif on the reverse, is a classic, one of the most desired of all pieces needed for a type set, and accordingly expensive. Most examples are in such grades as EF and AU.

Quarter eagles with stars on the obverse and with the Heraldic Eagle reverse were produced from 1796 intermittently through 1807. Today they exist in modest numbers, particularly in grades such as EF and AU, but on an absolute basis are fairly rare.

The stand-alone 1808 Capped Bust type, by John Reich, of which only 2,710 were minted, is the rarest single type coin in the entire American copper, nickel, silver, and gold series, possibly excepting the 1839 Gobrecht dollar (in a different category, as Proof restrikes were made). Examples of the 1808 can be found in various grades from VF through AU, and only rarely higher.

The next style of quarter eagle, from 1821 through 1827, is scarce, but when seen is usually in grades such as EF, AU, or even the low levels of Mint State. The same can be said for the modified quarter eagle of 1829 through early 1834.

Finally, with the advent of the Classic Head in late 1834, continuing through 1839, quarter eagles become more readily available. Specimens can be found in nearly any grade from VF into the lower levels of Mint State. Then come the Liberty Head quarter eagles, minted continuously from 1840 through 1907, in sufficient numbers and for such a long time that it is not difficult to obtain a specimen, with choice and gem Mint State coins being plentiful for the dates of the early 20th century.

The last quarter eagles are of the Indian Head type, minted from 1908 through 1929. These pieces are plentiful today, but grading can be difficult, as the highest part on the coin is the *field,* and this area was immediately subject to contact marks and wear. Although many opportunities exist in the marketplace, a collector should approach a purchase with care, seeking an example that has frosty, lustrous fields.

For the Collector and Investor: Gold Quarter Eagles as a Specialty

Collecting quarter eagles by dates, mintmarks, and major varieties is a very appealing pursuit. Although many are scarce and rare—this description applies to any variety from 1796 through early 1834—none are truly impossible to obtain. Among the Classic Head issues of 1834–1839, branch-mint coins are especially scarce in higher grades.

Liberty Head quarter eagles, produced continuously from 1840 through 1907, include a number of key issues, such as the famous 1854-S (usually seen in well-circulated grades), the Proof-only 1863 (of which only 30 were struck), and a number of elusive mintmarks. Of particular interest is the 1848 coin with CAL. counterstamped on the reverse, signifying that the coin was made from gold bullion brought in a special shipment from California.

Recommended Reading
Akers, David W. *Gold Dollars (and Other Gold Denominations),* Englewood, OH, 1975–1982.
Bowers, Q. David. *United States Gold Coins: An Illustrated History,* Wolfeboro, NH, 1982.
Breen, Walter. *Major Varieties of U.S. Gold Dollars (and Other Gold Denominations),* Chicago, 1964.
Dannreuther, John W., and Bass, Harry W. *Early U.S. Gold Coin Varieties,* Atlanta, GA, 2006.
Fivaz, Bill. *United States Gold Counterfeit Detection Guide,* Atlanta, GA, 2005.
Fivaz, Bill, and Stanton, J.T. *The Cherrypickers' Guide to Rare Die Varieties* (5th ed., vol. II), Atlanta, GA, 2012.
Garrett, Jeff, and Guth, Ron. *Encyclopedia of U.S. Gold Coins, 1795–1933* (2nd ed.), Atlanta, GA, 2008.

CAPPED BUST TO RIGHT
(1796–1807)

Designer Robert Scot; weight 4.37 grams; composition .9167 gold, .0833 silver and copper; approx. diameter 20 mm; reeded edge.

No Stars on Obverse (1796)

Stars on Obverse (1796–1807)
Bass-Dannreuther-1.

History. The first quarter eagles were struck intermittently during the late 1790s and early 1800s, with consistently small mintages. The earliest issues of 1796 lack obverse stars. They likely circulated domestically, rather than being exported in international trade.

Striking and Sharpness. Most have light striking in one area or another. On the obverse, check the hair details and the stars. On the reverse, check the shield, stars, and clouds. Examine the dentils on both sides. Planchet adjustment marks are seen on many coins and are not noted by the certification services. On high-grade coins the luster usually is very attractive. Certain reverse dies of this type were also used to make dimes.

Availability. Most in the marketplace are EF or AU. MS coins are elusive; when seen, they usually are of later dates.

VF-20, 30 (Very Fine). *Obverse:* The higher-relief areas of hair are well worn at VF-20, less so at VF-30. The stars are flat at their centers. *Reverse:* Wear is greater, including on the shield and wing feathers. The star centers are flat. Other areas have lost detail as well. E PLURIBUS UNUM is easy to read.

EF-40, 45 (Extremely Fine). *Obverse:* Wear is evident all over the portrait, with some loss of detail in the hair to the left of Miss Liberty's face. Excellent detail remains in low-relief areas of the hair, such as the front curl and the back of the head. The stars show wear, as do the date and letters. Luster, if present at all, is minimal and in protected areas. *Reverse:* Wear is greater than at AU. The neck lacks feather detail on its highest points. Feathers have lost some detail near the edges of the wings, and some areas of the horizontal lines in the shield may be blended together. Some traces of luster may be seen, less so at EF-40 than at EF-45. Overall, the reverse appears to be in a slightly higher grade than the obverse.

AU-50, 53, 55, 58 (About Uncirculated). *Obverse:* Light wear is seen on the cheek, the hair immediately to the left of the face, and the cap, more so at AU-50 than at 53 or 55. An AU-58 coin has minimal traces of wear. An AU-50 coin has luster in protected areas among the stars and letters, with little in the open fields or on the portrait. At AU-58 most luster is present in the fields, but is worn away on the highest parts of the motifs. The 1796 No Stars type has less luster in any given grade. *Reverse:* Abrasion and contact marks are most noticeable on the upper part of the eagle and the clouds. The eagle's neck, the tips and top of the wings, the clouds, and the tail show noticeable wear, as do other features. Luster ranges from perhaps 40% remaining in protected areas at AU-50 to nearly full mint bloom at AU-58. Often the reverse of this type retains much more luster than does the obverse.

MS-60 to 70 (Mint State). *Obverse:* At MS-60, some abrasion and contact marks are evident, most noticeably on the hair to the left of Miss Liberty's forehead and on the higher-relief areas of the cap. On the No Stars on Obverse quarter eagles, there is some abrasion in the field—more so than the Stars on Obverse coins, on which the field is more protected. Luster is present, but may be dull or lifeless, and interrupted in patches. At MS-63, contact marks are few, and abrasion is very light. An MS-65 coin has hardly any abrasion, and contact marks are so minute as to require magnification. Luster should be full and rich. Coins grading above MS-65 exist more in theory than in reality for this type—but they do exist, and are defined by having fewer marks as perfection is approached. *Reverse:* Comments apply as for the obverse, except that abrasion and contact marks are most noticeable on the upper part of the eagle and the clouds. The field area is complex; there is not much open space, with stars above the eagle, the arrows and olive branch, and other features. Accordingly, marks are not as noticeable as on the obverse.

| | | | 1798, Close Date | | 1798, Wide Date | | | 1804, 13-Star Reverse | | 1804, 14-Star Reverse | |

	Mintage	Cert	Avg	%MS	AU-50	AU-55	AU-58	MS-60	MS-62	MS-63	MS-64	Recent Auction Record
1796, No Stars on Obverse	963	94	53.4	21	$115,000	$135,000	$170,000	$225,000	$300,000	$500,000	$750,000 (a)	$94,000, VF-30, December 2013
1796, Stars on Obverse	432	42	55.7	36	95,000	120,000	165,000	185,000	260,000	375,000	600,000 (b)	$102,813, AU-58, March 2014
1797	427	26	48.3	15	72,500	95,000	100,000	137,500	185,000	235,000	375,000	$105,750, AU-53, April 2013
1798, All kinds	1,094											
1798, Close Date		2	54.0	0	30,000	43,500	55,000	67,500	85,000	125,000		$48,875, AU-58, September 2011
1798, Wide Date		20	52.8	35	30,000	43,500	55,000	67,500	85,000	125,000		$44,063, AU-50, June 2014
1802	3,035	145	53.4	29	17,500	20,000	23,500	32,500	50,000	65,000	125,000	$21,150, AU-58, March 2013
1804, 13-Star Reverse	*	7	50.9	0	300,000	450,000	600,000					$322,000, AU-58, July 2009
1804, 14-Star Reverse	3,327	131	52.9	19	18,000	21,000	23,500	32,500	55,000	100,000		$44,063, MS-62, April 2014
1805	1,781	101	53.2	22	18,000	21,000	23,500	32,500	55,000			$15,275, MS-60, March 2014

* Included in number below. **a.** Value in MS-65 is $1,600,000. **b.** Value in in MS-65 is $1,600,000.

Chart continued on next page.

	Mintage	Cert	Avg	%MS	AU-50	AU-55	AU-58	MS-60	MS-62	MS-63	MS-64	Recent Auction Record
1806, 6 Over 4, 8 Stars Left, 5 Right	1,136	54	51.8	22	$18,000	$21,000	$23,500	$32,500	$55,000	$100,000		$30,550, MS-61, June 2014
1806, 6 Over 5, 7 Stars Left, 6 Right	480	28	56.3	29	40,000	57,500	67,500	95,000	145,000	200,000		$67,563, AU, February 2014
1807	6,812	239	52.8	29	17,000	20,000	23,500	32,500	50,000	65,000	$115,000 (c)	$44,063, MS-62, March 2014

c. Value in MS-65 is $300,000.

CAPPED BUST TO LEFT, LARGE SIZE
(1808)

Designer John Reich; weight 4.37 grams; composition .9167 gold, .0833 silver and copper; approx. diameter 20 mm; reeded edge.

History. John Reich's Capped Bust was an adaptation of the design introduced in 1807 on the half dollar. On the quarter eagle it was used for a single year only, with fewer than 3,000 coins struck, making it the rarest of the major gold coin types.

Striking and Sharpness. All examples are lightly struck on one area or another, particularly the stars and rims. The rims are low and sometimes missing or nearly so (on the obverse), causing quarter eagles of this type to wear more quickly than otherwise might be the case.

Availability. Examples are rare in any grade. Typical grades are EF and AU. v coins are rare. Lower grades are rarely seen, as the coins did not circulate to any great extent. Gold coins of this era were not seen in circulation after 1821, so they did not get a chance to acquire significant wear.

VF-20, 30 (Very Fine). *Obverse:* Wear on the portrait has reduced the hair detail, especially to the right of the face and the top of the head, but much can still be seen. *Reverse:* Wear on the eagle is greater than at EF, and details of feathers near the shield and near the top of the wings are weak or missing. All other features show wear, but most are fairly sharp. Generally, Capped Bust gold coins at this grade level lack eye appeal.

EF-40, 45 (Extremely Fine). *Obverse:* More wear than at AU is seen on the portrait, the hair, the cap, and the drapery near the clasp. Luster is likely to be absent on the obverse due to the low rim. *Reverse:* Wear is extensive on the eagle, including the top of the wings, the head, the top of the shield, and the claws. Some traces of luster may be seen in protected areas, less so at EF-40 than at EF-45.

AU-50, 53, 55, 58 (About Uncirculated). *Obverse:* Light wear is seen on the cheek and higher-relief areas of the hair and cap. Friction and scattered marks are in the field, ranging from extensive at AU-50 to minimal at AU-58. The low rim affords little protection to the field of this coin, but the stars in relief help. Luster may be seen in protected areas, minimal at AU-50, but less so at AU-58. At AU-58 the field retains some luster as well. *Reverse:* Abrasion is most noticeable on the eagle's neck and highest area of the wings. The eagle's neck, the top of the wings, the leaves, and the arrowheads show noticeable wear, as do other features. Luster ranges from perhaps 40% remaining in protected areas at AU-50 to nearly full mint bloom at AU-58. Often the reverse of this type retains much more luster than does the obverse, as on this type the motto, eagle, and lettering protect the surrounding flat areas.

MS-60 to 70 (Mint State). *Obverse:* At MS-60, some abrasion and contact marks are seen on the cheek, on the hair below the LIBERTY inscription, and on the highest-relief folds of the cap. Luster is present, but may be dull or lifeless, and interrupted in patches. At MS-63, contact marks are few, and abrasion is very light. Abrasion is even less at MS-64. Quarter eagles of this type are almost, but not quite, non-existent in a combination of high grade and nice eye appeal. *Reverse:* Comments apply as for the obverse, except that abrasion is most noticeable on the eagle's neck and highest area of the wings.

	Mintage	Cert	Avg	%MS	AU-50	AU-55	AU-58	MS-60	MS-62	MS-63	MS-64	Recent Auction Record
1808	2,710	97	53.5	28	$90,000	$105,000	$120,000	$150,000	$275,000	$400,000	$650,000	$126,900, MS-60, January 2013

CAPPED HEAD TO LEFT
(1821–1834)

Designer John Reich; weight 4.37 grams; composition .9167 gold, .0833 silver and copper; approx. diameter 20 mm (1821–1827), approx. 18.2 mm (1829–1834); reeded edge.

Bass-Dannreuther-1.

History. Quarter eagles dated 1821 through 1827 have a larger diameter and larger letters, dates, and stars than those of 1829 to 1834. The same grading standards apply to both. Gold coins of this type did not circulate in commerce, because their face value was lower than their bullion value. Most wear was due to use as pocket pieces, or minor handling.

Striking and Sharpness. Most are well struck. On the obverse, check the hair details (which on the Large Diameter style can be light in areas) and the stars. On the reverse, check the eagle. On both sides inspect the dentils. Fields are often semi-prooflike on higher grades.

Availability. All are rare. Grades are from EF to MS, with choice examples in the latter category being scarce, and gems being very rare.

EF-40, 45 (Extremely Fine). *Obverse:* More wear than at AU is seen on the portrait, the hair, the cap, and the drapery near the clasp. Luster is likely to be absent on the obverse due to the low rim. *Reverse:* Wear is extensive on the eagle, including the top of the wings, the head, the top of the shield, and the claws. Some traces of luster may be seen in protected areas, less so at EF-40 than at EF-45.

AU-50, 53, 55, 58 (About Uncirculated). *Obverse:* Light wear is seen on the cheek and higher-relief areas of the hair and cap. Friction and scattered marks are in the field, ranging from extensive at AU-50 to minimal at AU-58. The low rim affords little protection to the field of this coin, but the stars in relief help. Luster may be seen in protected areas, minimal at AU-50, but less so at AU-58. At AU-58 the field retains some luster as well. *Reverse:* Abrasion is most noticeable on the eagle's neck and highest area of the wings. The eagle's neck, the top of the wings, the leaves, and the arrowheads show noticeable wear, as do other features. Luster ranges from perhaps 40% remaining in protected areas at AU-50 to nearly full mint bloom at AU-58. Often the reverse of this type retains much more luster than does the obverse, as on this type the motto, eagle, and lettering protect the surrounding flat areas.

MS-60 to 70 (Mint State). *Obverse:* At MS-60, some abrasion and contact marks are seen on the cheek, on the hair below the LIBERTY inscription, and on the highest-relief folds of the cap. Luster is present, but may be dull or lifeless, and interrupted in patches. At MS-63, contact marks are few, and abrasion is very light. Abrasion is even less at MS-64. Quarter eagles of this type are almost, but not quite, non-existent in a combination of high grade and nice eye appeal. *Reverse:* Comments apply as for the obverse, except that abrasion is most noticeable on the eagle's neck and highest area of the wings.

	Mintage	Cert	Avg	%MS	AU-55	AU-58	MS-60	MS-62	MS-63	MS-64	MS-65	Recent Auction Record
1821	6,448	37	57.7	51	$17,500	$23,500	$32,500	$45,000	$75,000	$125,000		$44,063, MS-62, March 2014
1824, 4 Over 1	2,600	48	55.4	38	18,750	25,000	32,500	45,000	80,000	135,000		$18,800, AU-58, August 2013
1825	4,434	98	56.7	50	17,500	23,500	32,500	42,500	60,000	90,000		$105,750, MS-64, March 2014
1826, 6 Over 6	760	22	53.4	14	32,500	40,000	62,500					$45,531, AU-55, September 2013
1827	2,800	50	59.0	62	19,500	32,500	35,000	42,500				$28,200, AU-55, February 2013
1829	3,403	97	58.5	56	17,000	18,500	24,000	27,500	35,000	50,000	$85,000	$41,125, MS-63, June 2013
1830	4,540	115	57.8	49	17,000	18,500	24,000	27,500	35,000	50,000	85,000	$29,375, MS-63, November 2013
1831	4,520	161	57.8	50	17,000	18,500	24,000	27,500	35,000	50,000	85,000	$18,800, AU-58, February 2013
1832	4,400	74	56.7	43	17,000	18,500	24,000	27,500	35,000	50,000	95,000	$21,150, MS-61, March 2014
1833	4,160	43	59.7	53	17,000	18,500	24,000	27,500	35,000	50,000	95,000	$41,125, MS-63, August 2013
1834, With Motto	4,000	18	56.0	33	40,000	45,000	60,000	80,000	125,000			$20,125, AU-55, September 1997

Proof Capped Head to Left Quarter Eagles

PF-60 to 70 (Proof). Proof Capped Head to Left quarter eagles were made on a limited basis for presentation and for distribution to numismatists. All examples are exceedingly rare today. They usually are encountered only when great collections are dispersed.

In the past, some prooflike examples have been auctioned or sold as actual Proofs. *Obverse and Reverse:* PF-60 to 62 coins have extensive hairlines and may have nicks and contact marks. At PF-63, hairlines are prominent, but the mirror surface is very reflective. PF-64 coins have fewer hairlines. At PF-65, hairlines should be minimal and mostly seen only under magnification. There should be no nicks or marks. PF-66 and higher coins should have no marks or hairlines visible to the unaided eye.

Proof Capped Head to Left Quarter Eagle
Shown 1.5x actual size.
Bass-Dannreuther-1.

	Est Mintage	Cert	Avg	PF-60	PF-63	PF-64	PF-65	Recent Auction Record
1821	3–5	7	64.4		$275,000	$450,000		$241,500, PF-64Cam, January 2007
1824, 4 Over 1	3–5	n/a	n/a	*(unique, in the Smithsonian's National Numismatic Collection)*				
1825 **(a)**	unknown	n/a	n/a					
1826, 6 Over 5 **(b)**	unknown	n/a	n/a					
1827 **(c)**	unknown	n/a	n/a					
1829	2–4	n/a	n/a	*(extremely rare; 2–3 known)*				
1830 **(d)**	unknown	n/a	n/a					
1831	6–10	5	64.4		100,000	150,000		$30,550, PF-60, September 2013
1832	2–4	n/a	n/a	*(unique, in the Bass Foundation Collection)*				
1833	2–4	3	66.3	*(extremely rare; 3–4 known)*				
1834, With Motto	4–8	n/a	n/a	*(extremely rare; 3–5 known)*				

a. The 1825 quarter eagle might not exist in Proof; see the *Encyclopedia of U.S. Gold Coins, 1795–1933*. **b.** Proofs have been reported, but none have been authenticated. **c.** Proof 1827 quarter eagles almost certainly were made, but none are known to exist. **d.** Examples identified as Proofs are extremely rare, many are impaired, and none have been certified.

CLASSIC HEAD,
NO MOTTO ON REVERSE
(1834–1839)

Designer William Kneass; weight 4.18 grams; composition .8992 gold, .1008 silver and copper (changed to .900 gold in 1837); diameter 18.2 mm; reeded edge; mints: Philadelphia, Charlotte, Dahlonega, New Orleans.

Breen-6151.

Mintmark is above date.

History. Gold quarter eagles had not circulated at face value in the United States since 1821, as the price of bullion necessitated more than $2.50 worth of gold to produce a single coin. Accordingly, they traded at their bullion value. The Act of June 28, 1834, provided lower weights for gold coins, after which the issues (of new designs to differentiate them from the old) circulated effectively. The Classic Head design by William Kneass is an adaptation of the head created by John Reich for the cent of 1808. The reverse illustrates a perched eagle. The motto E PLURIBUS UNUM, seen on earlier gold coins, no longer is present. These coins circulated widely until mid-1861 (for this reason, many show extensive wear). After that, they were hoarded because of public uncertainty during the Civil War.

Striking and Sharpness. Weakness is often seen on the higher areas of the hair curls. Also check the star centers. On the reverse, check the rims. The dentils usually are well struck.

Availability. Most coins range from VF to AU or lower ranges of MS. Most MS coins are of the first three years. MS-63 to 65 examples are rare. Good eye appeal can be elusive.

VF-20, 30 (Very Fine). *Obverse:* Wear on the portrait has reduced the hair detail, especially to the right of the face and the top of the head, but much can still be seen. *Reverse:* Wear is greater than at EF, including on the shield and wing feathers. Generally, Classic Head gold at this grade level lacks eye appeal.

EF-40, 45 (Extremely Fine). *Obverse:* Wear is seen on the portrait overall, with reduction or elimination of some separation of hair strands, especially in the area close to the face. The cheek shows light wear. Luster is minimal or nonexistent at EF-40, and may survive in among the letters of LIBERTY at EF-45. *Reverse:* Wear is greater than at AU. On most (but not all) coins the eagle's neck lacks some feather detail on its highest points. Feathers have lost some detail near the edges and tips of the wings. Some areas of the horizontal lines in the shield may be blended together. Some traces of luster may be seen, less so at EF-40 than at EF-45.

AU-50, 53, 55, 58 (About Uncirculated). *Obverse:* Friction is seen on the higher parts, particularly the cheek and hair (under magnification) of Miss Liberty. Friction and scattered marks are in the field, ranging from extensive at AU-50 to minimal at AU-58. Luster may be seen in protected areas, minimal at AU-50 but more visible at AU-58. On an AU-58 coin the field retains some luster as well. *Reverse:* Abrasion is most noticeable on the eagle's neck and the highest area of the wings. The eagle's neck, the top of the wings, the leaves, and the arrowheads now show noticeable wear, as do other features. Luster ranges from perhaps 40% remaining in protected areas at AU-50 to nearly full mint bloom at AU-58. Often the reverse of this type retains much more luster than does the obverse.

MS-60 to 70 (Mint State). *Obverse:* At MS-60, some abrasion and contact marks are seen on the portrait, most noticeably on the cheek, as the hair details are complex. Luster is present, but may be dull or lifeless, and interrupted in patches. Many low-level MS coins have grainy surfaces. At MS-63, contact marks are few, and abrasion is very light. Abrasion is even less at MS-64. An MS-65 coin has hardly any abrasion, and contact marks are minute. Luster should be full and rich and is often more intense on the obverse. Grades above MS-65 are defined by having fewer marks as perfection is approached. *Reverse:* Comments apply as for the obverse, except that abrasion is most noticeable on the eagle's neck and the highest area of the wings.

1836, Script 8   1836, Block 8

	Mintage	Cert	Avg	%MS	AU-55	AU-58	MS-60	MS-62	MS-63	MS-64	MS-65	Recent Auction Record
1834, No Motto	112,234	1,548	54.9	30	$1,650	$2,350	$3,500	$5,000	$10,000	$14,500	$45,000	$7,947, MS-63, March 2014
1835	131,402	450	53.1	28	1,650	2,350	3,800	5,000	10,000	15,000	50,000	$3,290, MS-60, March 2014
1836, All kinds	547,986											
1836, Script 8 (a)		962	50.4	23	1,650	2,750	3,750	5,500	10,500	14,500	45,000	$8,225, MS-63, June 2013
1836, Block 8		611	49.8	19	1,650	2,750	3,750	5,500	10,500	14,500	45,000	$7,344, MS-63, June 2013
1837	45,080	389	51.1	18	2,500	3,500	5,250	8,500	14,500	25,000	55,000	$11,750, MS-63, January 2014
1838	47,030	407	52.0	23	1,850	2,750	4,500	6,500	11,500	20,000	47,500	$5,288, MS-62, June 2013
1838C	7,880	139	50.9	13	11,750 (b)	16,000	26,500	37,500	50,000	75,000		$2,350, EF-40, January 2014
1839	27,021	149	48.8	7	2,900	5,500	6,500	12,500	19,500			$28,200, MS-61, August 2013
1839C	18,140	384	48.5	5	7,750	17,500	25,000	40,000	55,000			$10,575, AU-58, April 2013
1839D	13,674	256	44.6	10	10,000 (c)	18,500	28,500	42,500	50,000	80,000		$105,750, MS-64, January 2013
1839O	17,781	504	50.4	16	3,800	6,000	9,000	22,500	25,000	55,000		$12,925, AU-58, March 2014

Note: So-called 9 Over 8 varieties for Philadelphia, Charlotte, and Denver mints were made from defective punches. **a.** Also known as the "Head of 1835." **b.** Value in EF-40 is $4,000; in AU-50, $8,750. **c.** Value in EF-40 is $4,500; in AU-50, $8,500.

Proof Classic Head, No Motto, Quarter Eagles

PF-60 to 70 (Proof). Proof Classic Head, No Motto, quarter eagles were made in small quantities. Today probably only a couple dozen or so survive, most bearing the 1834 date. *Obverse and Reverse:* PF-60 to 62 coins have extensive hairlines and may have nicks and contact marks. At PF-63, hairlines are prominent, but the mirror surface is very reflective. PF-64 coins have fewer hairlines. At PF-65, hair-lines should be minimal and mostly seen only under magnification. There should be no nicks or marks. PF-66 and higher coins should have no marks or hairlines visible to the unaided eye.

Proof Classic Head, No Motto, Quarter Eagle
Shown 1.5x actual size.

	Est Mintage	Cert	Avg	PF-60	PF-63	PF-64	PF-65	Recent Auction Record
1834, No Motto	15–25	12	64.1	$35,000	$100,000	$150,000	$275,000	$138,000, PF-64Cam, January 2011
1835	5–8	2	65.0	35,000	100,000	150,000	300,000	
1836	5–8	14	65.0	35,000	115,000	200,000	300,000	$195,500, PF-64Cam, April 2012
1837	3–5 (a)	3	66.3	32,500	125,000	200,000	300,000	
1838	2–4	n/a	n/a	(unique, in the Bass Foundation Collection)				
1839	4–6 (b)	3	62.0	(extremely rare)				$136,679, PF-62, August 2006

a. Two Proofs of 1837 are known; one is in the Smithsonian's National Numismatic Collection. A third example has been rumored, but its existence is not verified. **b.** Three 1839 Proofs are reported to exist; only two are presently accounted for.

LIBERTY HEAD
(1840–1907)

Designer Christian Gobrecht; weight 4.18 grams; composition .900 gold, .100 copper (net weight .12094 oz. pure gold); diameter 18 mm; reeded edge; mints: Philadelphia, Charlotte, Dahlonega, New Orleans, San Francisco.

Mintmark is above denomination.

History. The Liberty Head quarter eagle debuted in 1840 and was a workhorse of American commerce for decades, being minted until 1907. Christian Gobrecht's design closely follows those used on half eagles and eagles of the same era.

In 1848, about 230 ounces of gold were sent to Secretary of War Marcy by Colonel R.B. Mason, military governor of California. The gold was turned over to the Mint and made into quarter eagles. The distinguishing mark CAL. was punched above the eagle on the reverse of these coins, while they were in the die. Several specimens with prooflike surfaces are known.

A modified reverse design (with smaller letters and arrowheads) was used on Philadelphia quarter eagles from 1859 through 1907. A few Philadelphia Mint pieces were made in 1859, 1860, and 1861 with the old Large Letters reverse design.

Striking and Sharpness. On the obverse, check the highest points of the hair, and the star centers. On the reverse, check the eagle's neck, and the area to the lower left of the shield and the lower part of the eagle. Examine the dentils on both sides. Branch-mint coins struck before the Civil War often are lightly struck in areas and have weak dentils. Often, a certified EF coin from the Dahlonega or Charlotte mints will not appear any sharper than a VF coin from Philadelphia. There are exceptions, and some C and D coins are sharp. The careful study of photographs is useful in acquainting you with the peculiarities of a given date or mint. Most quarter eagles from the 1880s to 1907 are sharp in all areas. Tiny copper staining spots can be a problem.

Availability. Early dates and mintmarks are generally scarce to rare in MS and very rare in MS-63 to 65 or finer, with only a few exceptions. Coins of Charlotte and Dahlonega (all of which are especially avidly collected) are usually EF or AU, or overgraded low MS. Rarities for the type include 1841, 1854-S, and 1875. Coins of the 1860s onward generally are seen with sharper striking and in higher average grades. Typically, San Francisco quarter eagles are in lower average grades than are those from the Philadelphia Mint, as Philadelphia coins did not circulate at par in the East and Midwest from late December 1861 until December 1878, and thus did not acquire as much wear. MS coins are readily available for the early-1900s years, and usually have outstanding eye appeal.

Note: Values of common-date gold coins have been based on the current bullion price of gold, $1,200 per ounce, and may vary with the prevailing spot price.

VF-20, 30 (Very Fine). *Obverse:* The higher-relief areas of hair are worn flat at VF-20, less so at VF-30. The hair to the right of the coronet is merged into heavy strands. The stars are flat at their centers. *Reverse:* Much of the eagle is flat, with less than 50% of the feather detail remaining. The vertical shield stripes, being deeply recessed, remain bold.

EF-40, 45 (Extremely Fine). *Obverse:* Wear is evident on all high areas of the portrait, including the hair to the right of the forehead, the tip of the coronet, and the hair bun. The stars show light wear at their centers. Luster, if present at all, is minimal and in protected areas such as between the star points. *Reverse:* Wear is greater than at AU. The neck of the eagle is nearly smooth, much detail is lost on the right wing, and there is flatness at the lower left of the shield, on the leaves, and on the arrowheads. Some traces of luster may be seen, less so at EF-40 than at EF-45. Overall, the reverse appears to be in a slightly higher grade than the obverse.

AU-50, 53, 55, 58 (About Uncirculated). *Obverse:* Light wear is seen on the face, the hair to the right of the face, and the highest area of the hair bun, more so at AU-50 than at 53 or 55. An AU-58 coin has minimal traces of wear. An AU-50 coin has luster in protected areas among the stars and letters, with little in the open fields or on the portrait. At AU-58, most luster is present in the fields, but is worn away on the highest parts of the motifs. *Reverse:* Abrasion and contact marks are most noticeable on the eagle's neck and to the lower left of the shield. The eagle shows wear in all of the higher areas, as well as the leaves and arrowheads. Luster ranges from perhaps 40% remaining in protected areas at AU-50 to nearly full mint bloom at AU-58. Often the reverse of this type retains more luster than the obverse.

MS-60 to 70 (Mint State). *Obverse:* At MS-60, some abrasion and contact marks are evident, most noticeably on the hair to the right of Miss Liberty's forehead, and on the jaw. Luster is present, but may be dull or lifeless, and interrupted in patches. At MS-63, contact marks are few, and abrasion is very light. An MS-65 coin has hardly any abrasion, and contact marks are so minute as to require magnification. Luster should be full and rich. Grades above MS-65 usually are found late in the series and are defined by having fewer marks as perfection is approached. *Reverse:* Comments apply as for the obverse, except that abrasion and contact marks are most noticeable on the eagle's neck and to the lower left of the shield.

1843-C, Small Date, Crosslet 4   1843-C, Large Date, Plain 4   1843-O, Small Date, Crosslet 4   1843-O, Large Date, Plain 4

	Mintage	Cert	Avg	%MS	EF-40	AU-50	AU-55	AU-58	MS-60	MS-62	MS-63	Recent Auction Record
1840	18,859	148	47.8	13	$850	$2,400	$3,000	$4,250	$6,000	$8,000	$11,000 (a)	$2,468, AU-58, April 2013
1840C	12,822	232	49.3	10	2,100	4,250	6,500	7,500	10,000	18,500	25,000	$7,638, AU, February 2014
1840D	3,532	83	44.0	4	8,000	12,000	18,000	25,000	35,000	75,000		$10,575, AU-53, March 2014
1840O	33,580	182	50.3	14	900	1,850	2,650	5,000	9,500	18,000	25,000	$14,100, MS-62, April 2014
1841 (b)	unknown	3	52.0	0	105,000	125,000	150,000	175,000	225,000			$105,800, EF-45, March 2012
1841C	10,281	173	47.3	4	2,250	3,250	5,500	8,500	14,000	25,000		$28,200, MS-62, March 2014
1841D	4,164	104	44.8	5	4,000	9,000	12,000	16,000	25,000	40,000	50,000	$7,638, AU-55, April 2013
1842	2,823	52	44.1	4	2,750	6,000	8,500	12,000	20,000	35,000		$15,275, MS-60, January 2014
1842C	6,729	129	42.5	5	3,250	7,500	9,500	13,000	22,500	35,000		$5,581, AU, February 2014
1842D	4,643	120	44.5	3	4,500	9,500	15,000	18,500	32,500	55,000		$9,694, AU-55, March 2014
1842O	19,800	236	45.9	11	1,400	2,500	4,250	7,000	11,500	15,000	27,500	$3,290, AU-55, February 2014
1843	100,546	245	53.2	13	450	800	900	1,250	2,500	4,500	6,750 (c)	$1,998, MS-61, January 2014
1843C, Small Date, Crosslet 4	2,988	102	48.3	11	5,250	7,500	10,000	14,000	24,000	50,000		$3,055, EF-40, April 2013
1843C, Large Date, Plain 4	23,076	348	44.9	8	2,000	3,000	4,500	5,750	8,000	13,000	20,000	$15,275, MS-63, March 2014
1843D, Small Date, Crosslet 4	36,209	500	46.6	7	2,000	3,000	4,500	6,000	9,000	18,000	27,500	$5,875, MS-61, January 2014
1843O, Small Date, Crosslet 4	288,002	752	50.6	17	400	550	775	1,100	2,000	3,250	8,000	$25,850, MS-65, February 2013
1843O, Large Date, Plain 4	76,000	177	51.8	13	750	1,750	2,750	4,250	6,250	12,500	20,000	$15,275, MS-62, February 2014
1844	6,784	88	49.6	8	775	2,000	3,250	4,500	8,500	13,500		$15,275, MS-61, January 2014
1844C	11,622	211	46.1	8	2,500	6,000	8,000	10,000	15,000	27,500	40,000	$14,100, MS-61, January 2014
1844D	17,332	294	49.6	12	2,500	3,000	4,000	5,000	7,500	14,000	25,000	$17,038, MS-63, April 2014
1845	91,051	359	53.6	27	385	500	650	850	1,250	2,250	5,000 (d)	$18,800, MS-65, January 2014
1845D	19,460	287	48.6	5	2,350	3,250	4,250	7,000	11,000	20,000	35,000	$35,250, MS-63, January 2014
1845O	4,000	97	45.9	3	2,600	6,000	8,500	11,500	22,500	30,000	50,000	$5,875, AU-50, January 2014
1846	21,598	188	52.9	15	550	1,000	1,600	2,500	5,000	15,000	22,500	$18,800, MS-63, April 2014
1846C	4,808	126	47.9	9	2,750	7,500	9,500	12,500	18,000	25,000	37,500	$15,275, MS-62, April 2014
1846D	19,303	319	48.5	6	2,400	3,250	4,500	6,500	9,000	13,500	28,500	$7,638, MS-61, June 2013
1846D, D Over D	*	21	50.4	5	2,750	3,750	6,500	9,000	15,000			$5,175, AU-55, November 2011
1846O	62,000	368	50.0	11	525	1,200	2,000	3,500	5,500	12,500	18,500	$4,700, MS-61, February 2013
1847	29,814	181	52.5	17	400	750	1,250	2,000	3,000	5,500	8,000	$1,175, AU-58, June 2013
1847C	23,226	426	50.5	14	2,350	3,000	4,000	5,000	6,000	8,000	14,000	$5,581, MS-61, January 2014
1847D	15,784	311	49.7	12	2,500	3,250	5,250	5,500	9,000	13,500	24,000	$9,404, MS, February 2014
1847O	124,000	432	47.7	10	475	1,000	1,750	2,750	4,000	9,500	15,000	$9,988, MS-62, January 2014

* Included in number above. **a.** Value in MS-64 is $20,000. **b.** Values are for circulated Proofs; existence of circulation strikes is unclear. **c.** Value in MS-64 is $13,500. **d.** Value in MS-64 is $8,500.

1848, CAL.
Above Eagle

1862, 2 Over 1

1873, Close 3

1873, Open 3

1891, Doubled-Die
Reverse
FS-G2.5-1891-801.

Old Reverse (Pre-1859)

Shown 1.5x actual size.

New Reverse

	Mintage	Cert	Avg	%MS	AU-55	AU-58	MS-60	MS-62	MS-63	MS-64	MS-65	Recent Auction Record
1848	6,500	120	51.5	21	$2,500	$3,500	$5,000	$8,500	$15,000	$25,000		$2,585, AU-50, February 2014
1848, CAL. Above Eagle	1,389	107	53.6	39	55,000	65,000	80,000	115,000	125,000	150,000	$200,000	$176,250, MS-64, January 2014
1848C	16,788	264	47.0	8	4,500	7,500	10,500	18,500	30,000			$15,275, MS-62, March 2014
1848D	13,771	290	52.0	14	4,250	6,000	8,000	14,000	28,500			$25,850, MS-63, April 2014
1849	23,294	199	52.8	17	1,250	1,850	2,500	4,500	8,000	14,000		$3,525, MS-62, March 2014
1849C	10,220	168	48.5	6	8,000	10,000	19,000	40,000	65,000			$15,275, MS-61, January 2014
1849D	10,945	239	49.9	5	6,000	8,500	15,000	25,000				$3,202, AU-53, October 2013

Chart continued on next page.

	Mintage	Cert	Avg	%MS	AU-55	AU-58	MS-60	MS-62	MS-63	MS-64	MS-65	Recent Auction Record
1850	252,923	583	55.2	27	$500	$650	$1,050	$2,000	$3,250	$7,500		$1,998, MS-62, June 2013
1850C	9,148	216	49.4	10	4,750	7,500	12,000	25,000	32,500			$12,925, MS-60, March 2014
1850D	12,148	262	49.5	7	5,500	8,500	13,500	27,500	47,500			$23,500, MS-62, April 2014
1850O	84,000	435	49.4	7	1,800	2,500	4,000	6,500	16,000			$4,700, MS-61, December 2013
1851	1,372,748	1,134	58.2	55	400	425	550	950	1,200	2,500	$5,500	$5,875, MS-65, April 2013
1851C	14,923	186	47.2	10	5,500	7,500	9,500	22,500	32,500			$28,200, MS-63, October 2013
1851D	11,264	162	46.7	5	5,500	7,000	10,750	17,500	35,000	50,000		$7,638, AU-58, December 2013
1851O	148,000	545	51.8	10	2,000	2,750	4,000	8,500	12,500	23,500		$4,406, MS-61, February 2013
1852	1,159,681	1,447	59.3	58	400	425	550	950	1,300	2,500	5,500	$1,763, MS-64, April 2014
1852C	9,772	176	48.7	8	5,750	9,000	12,750	25,000	32,500			$4,994, AU-55, March 2014
1852D	4,078	123	50.7	11	8,000	10,000	15,750	30,000	42,500	65,000		$8,813, AU-53, August 2013
1852O	140,000	643	51.0	6	1,250	2,500	4,750	8,500	11,000			$6,169, MS-62, August 2013
1853	1,404,668	2,113	59.1	58	385	425	550	1,100	1,200	2,500	5,500	$8,519, MS-65, March 2013
1853D	3,178	97	49.9	13	5,750	9,500	15,000	32,500	45,000			$25,850, MS-62, January 2014
1854	596,258	938	58.7	50	385	425	550	1,100	1,250	2,750	6,500	$8,225, MS-65, April 2013
1854C	7,295	175	50.5	14	6,500	7,500	12,500	22,500	37,500			$9,988, MS-61, June 2013
1854D	1,760	72	47.5	13	15,000	17,500	27,500	40,000	70,000			$15,275, AU-55, March 2014
1854O	153,000	693	52.4	9	800	900	1,500	4,500	9,000	15,000		$14,688, MS-63, April 2013
1854S	246	13	27.8	0	500,000 (a)							$282,000, EF-35, October 2013
1855	235,480	554	59.2	54	385	400	550	1,100	1,600	3,500	7,000	$3,290, MS-64, March 2013
1855C	3,677	134	51.8	16	10,000	13,500	22,500	30,000	42,500			$23,500, MS-62, January 2014
1855D	1,123	53	49.0	11	20,000	30,000	46,500					$25,850, AU-55, July 2014
1856	384,240	873	59.1	55	385	400	550	1,050	1,300	3,500	6,500	$951, MS-63, February 2013
1856C	7,913	133	47.9	11	6,500	8,500	11,500	20,000	25,000			$6,463, AU-58, April 2013
1856D	874	48	50.1	10	35,000	45,000	70,000					$55,813, AU-58, March 2014
1856O	21,100	202	51.4	8	2,100	3,000	7,000	20,000				$7,050, MS-61, August 2013
1856S	72,120	294	51.6	15	1,500	2,250	5,000	8,000	12,000	15,000	27,500	$2,703, AU-58, February 2014
1857	214,130	607	59.3	57	385	400	550	1,050	1,500	3,500	7,000	$4,994, MS-65, April 2013
1857D	2,364	121	54.9	22	5,500	8,500	12,000	22,000	30,000			$18,800, MS-62, April 2014
1857O	34,000	392	54.3	19	1,850	2,500	4,250	7,500	13,000	20,000		$6,463, MS-62, April 2014
1857S	69,200	277	49.9	11	2,000	3,000	6,000	8,500	15,000	25,000		$7,638, MS-62, January 2014
1858	47,377	288	57.3	36	550	800	1,200	1,850	3,000	6,000	12,000	$3,819, MS, February 2014
1858C	9,056	258	52.9	26	4,250	6,000	8,000	15,000	24,000			$11,163, MS-62, January 2014
1859, Old Reverse	39,364	164	57.0	30	1,200	1,600	3,000	5,500	8,000	13,500		$1,102, AU, February 2014
1859, New Reverse	*	113	56.4	34	700	950	1,200	2,000	3,200	7,500	11,000	$2,879, MS, January 2014
1859D	2,244	168	53.3	13	7,500	10,000	19,000	38,000				$7,050, AU, March 2014
1859S	15,200	147	47.3	10	3,250	4,000	7,000	10,000	16,000			$4,994, MS-61, April 2014
1860, Old Reverse	22,563	139	57.5	42	4,500	6,000	8,000	12,000	14,000			$6,463, MS-62, April 2013
1860, New Reverse	*	48	59.1	48	600	650	1,000	1,600	2,750			$1,763, MS-60, August 2013
1860C	7,469	201	48.6	6	6,500	10,000	15,000	26,000	37,500			$25,850, MS-63, January 2014
1860S	35,600	185	47.1	14	1,750	2,250	3,500	7,000	14,000			$6,756, MS-62, August 2013
1861, Old Reverse	1,283,788	143	57.7	43	2,350	3,000	4,000	7,500	9,000			$6,345, MS, January 2014
1861, New Reverse	*	2,144	59.3	56	385	400	600	1,300	1,800			$7,638, MS-65, March 2013
1861S	24,000	151	46.3	6	4,250	5,750	7,250	12,000				$5,875, AU-58, April 2013
1862, 2 Over 1	**	76	54.8	17	4,750	5,850	7,500	12,500				$9,400, MS-61, January 2014
1862	98,508	254	55.0	30	1,750	3,000	4,750	6,500	11,000	18,500		$9,400, MS-63, August 2013
1862S	8,000	112	45.3	4	5,000	8,500	16,500	24,000	35,000			$23,500, MS-62, January 2014
1863S	10,800	123	43.7	9	5,000	8,500	13,000	20,000	30,000			$3,290, EF-45, March 2013
1864	2,824	18	50.3	17	47,500	55,000	75,000					$48,469, AU-55, March 2014
1865	1,520	31	51.9	3	27,500	30,000	40,000	45,000	60,000			$15,891, AU-55, June 2013
1865S	23,376	149	44.8	7	2,000	2,750	4,500	7,500	11,000			$1,998, AU-53, March 2014
1866	3,080	61	48.6	13	8,000	10,000	12,500	20,000	25,000	35,000		$7,050, AU-58, February 2013
1866S	38,960	312	44.4	3	3,500	4,000	7,500	12,000	20,000			$16,450, MS-62, January 2014
1867	3,200	63	54.5	21	1,700	2,500	4,500	6,000	12,000	13,500	35,000	$1,645, AU-55, May 2013
1867S	28,000	264	47.0	8	1,700	2,250	3,850	5,000	12,000	15,000		$1,775, AU-58, August 2013
1868	3,600	238	55.6	16	800	1,100	2,000	3,850	7,500	12,000		$1,998, MS-61, December 2013
1868S	34,000	361	50.9	10	1,400	2,000	4,000	6,500	10,000	16,000		$15,275, MS-64, January 2014
1869	4,320	360	52.0	13	1,150	1,450	2,750	5,000	8,500			$9,360, MS-63, June 2014

* Included in number above. ** Included in number below. a. Value in VF-20 is $275,000; in EF-40, $400,000; in AU-50, $450,000.

	Mintage	Cert	Avg	%MS	AU-55	AU-58	MS-60	MS-62	MS-63	MS-64	MS-65	Recent Auction Record
1869S	29,500	203	51.7	8	$1,500	$2,000	$4,000	$6,000	$9,250	$13,000		$3,290, MS-61, May 2013
1870	4,520	242	51.8	12	1,250	1,500	3,250	5,500	8,000			$4,994, MS-61, January 2014
1870S	16,000	120	51.0	11	1,500	2,250	4,000	6,500	13,000	17,500		$8,225, MS-62, January 2014
1871	5,320	217	55.5	25	1,000	1,250	2,000	2,750	4,000	8,000		$6,463, MS-64, April 2014
1871S	22,000	301	52.1	14	1,000	1,250	2,000	3,000	4,350	9,000	$17,500	$911, AU-58, July 2014
1872	3,000	120	53.7	13	2,000	2,750	4,350	9,000	14,000	25,000		$2,596, AU-58, March 2014
1872S	18,000	301	48.7	7	1,350	2,000	4,000	6,000	10,500	15,000		$3,594, MS-61, April 2012
1873, Close 3	55,200	929	59.6	63	425	485	600	1,100	1,750	2,750	5,500	$16,450, MS-66, January 2014
1873, Open 3	122,800	975	60.2	72	385	425	585	700	800	1,250	4,500	$5,875, MS-65, February 2014
1873S	27,000	399	48.5	9	1,300	1,550	2,300	4,750	6,500	14,000		$11,163, MS-64, August 2013
1874	3,920	196	55.8	25	1,000	1,200	2,100	4,500	6,000	9,500	25,000	$3,525, MS-62, August 2013
1875	400	65	53.6	11	15,000	18,500	27,500	30,000	45,000			$25,850, MS-61, August 2013
1875S	11,600	272	51.9	14	1,100	2,000	3,500	5,000	7,250	12,000		$4,259, MS-62, September 2013
1876	4,176	204	52.5	13	1,750	2,250	3,000	4,000	6,500	12,000		$5,581, MS-62, March 2014
1876S	5,000	228	53.7	20	1,600	1,850	3,250	4,500	8,000			$8,225, MS-63, January 2014
1877	1,632	181	55.5	27	1,250	1,500	3,000	3,750	8,500	15,000		$4,406, MS-62, April 2014
1877S	35,400	582	58.0	41	400	425	650	1,500	2,350	4,000	9,000	$9,400, MS-65, December 2013
1878	286,240	3,487	60.7	72	385	415	500	700	900	1,300	2,500	$8,225, MS-66, June 2014
1878S	178,000	993	58.3	49	385	420	535	1,000	1,800	3,500	12,000	$3,525, MS-64, April 2013
1879	88,960	1,438	60.5	70	425	450	535	875	1,100	1,600	3,500	$3,290, MS-65, September 2013
1879S	43,500	309	51.5	9	1,000	1,200	1,750	3,500	4,800	7,500		$18,800, MS-64, January 2014
1880	2,960	217	57.9	47	800	1,100	1,500	2,000	3,750	6,000	12,500	$2,820, MS-62, October 2013
1881	640	130	55.7	25	6,000	7,500	10,000	14,000	20,000	30,000		$7,931, MS-60, June 2013
1882	4,000	303	59.3	52	700	800	925	1,500	2,750	4,000	9,000	$2,703, MS-63, January 2014
1883	1,920	135	56.9	30	1,000	1,300	1,750	2,350	6,500	6,750	9,000	$4,994, MS-61, June 2014
1884	1,950	188	59.1	53	800	900	1,500	1,900	3,000	3,500	5,000	$2,468, MS-62, June 2014
1885	800	110	58.0	42	3,000	3,250	4,750	5,750	8,000	12,500	20,000	$13,513, MS-63, March 2014
1886	4,000	257	58.4	45	600	800	1,000	1,750	3,000	7,000	12,000	$1,763, MS-62, March 2013
1887	6,160	343	59.6	62	500	600	800	1,250	2,750	4,500	15,000	$4,700, MS-64, April 2014
1888	16,001	723	61.7	87	375	385	550	850	1,375	1,475	5,500	$7,931, MS-63, March 2014
1889	17,600	669	61.1	82	375	385	525	825	1,350	1,425	5,500	$6,463, MS-65, July 2014
1890	8,720	409	60.3	65	400	415	600	900	1,350	2,750	9,000	$3,819, MS-64, June 2013
1891	10,960				385	400	550	800	1,450	1,850	6,000	$3,055, MS-64, April 2013
1891, Doubled-Die Reverse	*	515	60.4	70	450	550	750	1,100	1,750			
1892	2,440	243	60.7	74	525	575	900	1,100	2,250	4,000	8,000	$21,150, MS-67, November 2013
1893	30,000	1,532	62.1	87	375	385	550	800	1,300	1,475	2,250	$11,163, MS-67, March 2014
1894	4,000	408	61.6	82	475	500	750	1,000	1,650	1,875	6,000	$4,700, MS, February 2014
1895	6,000	462	62.2	90	375	385	600	725	1,100	1,350	3,750	$8,519, MS-66, March 2013
1896	19,070	1,276	62.5	92	375	385	500	700	950	1,100	2,500	$7,344, MS-67, March 2014
1897	29,768	1,892	62.6	93	375	385	500	575	825	900	2,000	$5,581, MS-67, September 2013
1898	24,000	1,410	62.9	94	375	385	500	575	775	850	2,000	$9,400, MS-67, April 2013
1899	27,200	1,481	62.7	95	375	385	500	575	700	800	1,400	$3,525, MS-66, June 2014
1900	67,000	3,493	62.9	94	375	385	500	575	700	800	1,400	$6,463, MS-67, November 2013
1901	91,100	4,052	62.8	95	375	385	500	575	700	800	1,400	$5,581, MS-67, November 2013
1902	133,540	6,339	62.9	95	375	385	500	575	700	800	1,400	$12,338, MS-68, February 2013
1903	201,060	11,063	62.9	95	375	385	500	575	700	800	1,400	$4,700, MS-67, August 2013
1904	160,790	8,082	62.9	94	375	385	500	575	700	800	1,400	$28,200, MS-68, January 2013
1905 (b)	217,800	11,478	63.0	95	375	385	500	575	700	800	1,400	$16,450, MS-68, June 2014
1906	176,330	9,856	62.9	95	375	385	500	575	700	800	1,400	$4,406, MS-67, February 2013
1907	336,294	17,202	63.0	96	375	385	500	575	700	800	1,400	$4,406, MS-67, June 2013

* Included in number above. **b.** Pieces dated 1905-S are counterfeit.

Proof Liberty Head Quarter Eagles

PF-60 to 70 (Proof). Proof Liberty Head quarter eagles exist in relation to their original mintages, with all issues prior to the 1890s being rare. Cameo contrast is the rule for Proofs prior to 1902. Beginning that year the portrait was polished in the die, although a few years later cameo-contrast coins were again made. *Obverse and Reverse:* PF-60 to 62 coins have extensive hairlines and may have nicks and contact marks. At PF-63, hairlines are prominent, but the mirror surface is very reflective. PF-64 coins have fewer hairlines. At PF-65, hairlines should be minimal and mostly seen only under magnification. There should be no nicks or marks. PF-66 and higher coins should have no marks or hairlines visible to the unaided eye.

GOLD QUARTER EAGLES, 1796–1929

Proof Liberty Head Quarter Eagle
Shown 1.5x actual size.

	Mintage	Cert	Avg	PF-60	PF-63	PF-64	PF-65	Recent Auction Record
1840	3–6	1	53.0	*(extremely rare; 3 known)*				
1841	15–20	13	50.4	$250,000				$164,500, PF-53, March 2014
1842	2–3	n/a	n/a	*(unique, in the Smithsonian's National Numismatic Collection)*				
1843	4–8	7	64.1	*(extremely rare; 5–6 known)*				
1844	3–6	1	66.0	*(extremely rare; 4–5 known)*				
1845	4–8	4	66.0	*(extremely rare; 4–5 known)*				
1846	4–8	2	64.5	*(extremely rare; 4–5 known)*				$106,375, PF-64Cam, January 2011
1847	2–3	n/a	n/a	*(unique, in the Smithsonian's National Numismatic Collection)*				
1848	3–6	2	63.0	*(extremely rare; 3–4 known)*				$96,600, PF-64, January 2008
1850	2–4	1	64.0	*(extremely rare; 1–2 known)*				$41,250, PF-62, June 1995
1854	2–4	n/a	n/a	*(unique, in the Bass Foundation Collection)*				
1856	6–8	3	65.0	$40,000	75,000	$85,000	$135,000	
1857	6–8	1	65.0	35,000	57,500	75,000	125,000	
1858	6–8	5	65.0	25,000	45,000	65,000	115,000	$82,250, PF, March 2014
1859 (a)	80	11	64.8	15,000	30,000	45,000	75,000	$80,500, PF-66, July 2005
1860 (b)	112	15	64.2	14,000	22,500	30,000	40,000	$11,550, PF-64Cam, October 1993
1861 (c)	90	8	64.8	12,000	20,000	27,500	40,000	$44,850, PF-65DCam, September 2005
1862	35	21	64.0	12,000	20,000	27,500	40,000	$46,000, PF-65UCam, February 2007
1863 (d)	30	22	63.9	50,000	75,000	95,000	125,000	$45,531, PF-58, April 2014
1864	50	31	64.9	12,000	25,000	27,500	45,000	$30,550, PF-64Cam, April 2014
1865	25	26	63.9	13,500	20,000	27,500	45,000	$48,875, PF-65UCam, January 2012
1866	30	20	64.1	10,000	17,500	20,000	32,500	$23,500, PF-64Cam, April 2014
1867	50	25	63.8	10,000	16,000	20,000	30,000	$99,875, PF, August 2013
1868	25	13	63.5	9,500	16,500	22,500	35,000	$43,700, PF-65Cam, January 2009
1869	25	30	64.2	6,500	14,000	18,000	30,000	$12,650, PF-63, October 2011
1870	35	10	62.7	6,500	14,000	18,000	30,000	$70,500, PF-66DCam, January 2014
1871	30	13	64.0	6,500	14,000	18,000	27,500	$17,250, PF-64UCam, January 2007
1872	30	21	63.8	6,500	14,000	18,000	27,500	$34,075, PF-65Cam, March 2013
1873, Close 3	25	21	62.7	7,500	14,000	18,000	30,000	$19,388, PF, August 2013
1874	20	15	63.4	7,500	15,000	25,000	45,000	$51,750, PF-66UCam, January 2011
1875	20	21	64.0	13,500	35,000	45,000	60,000	$94,000, PF, October 2013
1876	45	30	64.4	6,500	13,500	18,000	30,000	$39,950, PF, January 2013
1877	20	11	64.5	6,500	13,500	18,000	30,000	$8,050, PF-55, November 2011
1878	20	13	64.4	6,500	13,500	18,000	30,000	$50,313, PF-65DCam, April 2012
1879	30	19	64.6	6,000	13,000	18,000	30,000	$40,250, PF-67Cam, January 2011
1880	36	29	63.9	6,500	12,500	18,000	27,500	$3,244, PF-55, January 2011
1881	51	40	64.3	6,500	13,500	19,000	27,500	$34,075, PF-65DCam, August 2013
1882	67	40	64.8	4,500	9,500	14,000	22,500	$9,487, PF-64, May 2006
1883	82	58	63.3	4,500	9,500	14,000	22,500	$28,200, PF, March 2014
1884	73	50	63.6	4,500	9,500	14,000	22,500	$82,250, PF, August 2013
1885	87	42	64.1	5,000	9,000	14,000	27,500	$56,160, PF, September 2013
1886	88	57	63.8	4,500	9,500	13,500	22,500	$40,538, PF, August 2013
1887	122	52	63.6	4,500	9,500	13,500	22,500	$58,750, PF, August 2013
1888	97	68	64.0	4,500	8,500	13,500	22,500	$25,850, PF-65Cam, February 2013
1889	48	34	64.2	4,500	8,500	13,500	22,500	$28,750, PF-66Cam, April 2011
1890	93	78	64.2	4,500	8,500	13,500	20,000	$19,388, PF-65DCam, June 2014
1891	80	41	65.0	4,500	8,000	12,500	20,000	$30,550, PF, April 2013
1892	105	84	63.8	4,500	8,000	12,500	20,000	$111,625, PF, February 2013
1893	106	76	64.6	4,500	7,500	12,500	20,000	$19,975, PF, March 2014
1894	122	114	64.3	4,500	7,500	12,500	20,000	$44,063, PF, August 2013

a. Nearly all 1859 Proofs are of the Old Reverse style. **b.** All known 1860 Proofs are of the New Reverse style. **c.** All 1861 Proofs were struck in the New Reverse style. **d.** Only Proofs were struck in 1863.

	Mintage	Cert	Avg	PF-60	PF-63	PF-64	PF-65	Recent Auction Record
1895	119	122	64.7	$4,500	$7,500	$12,500	$20,000	$23,500, PF-66DCam, January 2014
1896	132	108	64.5	4,500	7,500	12,500	20,000	$21,150, PF, October 2013
1897	136	135	64.4	4,500	7,500	12,500	20,000	$27,025, PF, March 2014
1898	165	204	63.9	4,500	7,500	12,500	20,000	$45,678, PF, March 2014
1899	150	227	63.7	4,500	7,500	12,500	20,000	$36,425, PF, August 2013
1900	205	345	63.4	4,500	7,500	10,000	17,500	$111,625, PF, April 2013
1901	223	228	63.9	4,500	7,500	10,000	17,500	$42,300, PF, March 2014
1902	193	220	63.1	4,500	7,500	10,000	17,500	$8,813, PF-64, December 2013
1903	197	261	62.9	4,500	7,500	10,000	17,500	$22,325, PF, August 2013
1904	170	224	63.4	4,500	7,500	10,000	17,500	$15,393, PF, August 2013
1905	144	256	63.1	4,500	7,500	10,000	17,500	$8,225, PF-64, December 2013
1906	160	282	64.0	4,500	7,500	10,000	17,500	$44,063, PF, August 2013
1907	154	214	64.2	4,500	7,500	10,000	17,500	$32,900, PF-68, April 2013

INDIAN HEAD
(1908–1929)

Designer Bela Lyon Pratt; weight 4.18 grams; composition .900 gold, .100 copper (net weight .12094 oz. pure gold); diameter 18 mm; reeded edge; mints: Philadelphia, Denver.

Mintmark is on reverse, to left of arrows.

History. The Indian Head design—used on both the quarter eagle and the half eagle—is unusual in that the lettering and motifs are in sunken relief. (The design sometimes is erroneously described as *incuse*.) These coins circulated as money in the West, but not elsewhere. As the smallest gold denomination of the era, they were popular for use as souvenirs and gifts.

Striking and Sharpness. Striking varies. On many early issues the rims are flat, while on others, including most of the 1920s, they are slightly raised. Some have traces of a wire rim, usually on the reverse. Look for weakness on the high parts of the Indian's bonnet (particularly the garland of flowers) and in the feather details in the headdress. On the reverse, check the feathers on the highest area of the wing, the top of the shoulder. On some issues of the 1911-D, the D mintmark can be weak.

Availability. This design was not popular with collectors, and they saved relatively few of the coins. However, many coins were given as gifts and preserved in high quality. The survival of MS-63 and better coins is a matter of chance, especially for the issues dated from 1909 to 1915. The only scarce issue is 1911-D. Luster can range from deeply frosty to grainy. As the fields are the highest areas of the coin, luster diminished quickly as examples were circulated or jostled with others in bags. The Indian Head quarter eagle is one of the most challenging series for professional graders, and opinions can vary widely.

Note: Values of common-date gold coins have been based on the current bullion price of gold, $1,200 per ounce, and may vary with the prevailing spot price.

VF-20, 30 (Very Fine). *Obverse:* Many details of the ribbon above the forehead and the garland are worn away. Many feather vanes are blended together. The field is dull and has contact marks. *Reverse:* The neck and the upper part of the wing show extensive wear, other areas less so. The field is dull and has contact marks.

EF-40, 45 (Extremely Fine). *Obverse:* Light wear characterizes the portrait and headdress. Luster is gone. Marks and tiny scratches are to be expected, but not distracting. *Reverse:* Light wear is most evident on the eagle's head and wing, although other areas are lightly worn as well. Luster is gone. Marks and tiny scratches are to be expected, but not distracting.

AU-50, 53, 55, 58 (About Uncirculated). *Obverse:* Friction on the cheek is very noticeable at AU-50, progressively less at higher levels to AU-58. The headdress shows light wear, most evident on the ribbon above the forehead and on the garland. Luster is minimal at AU-50 and scattered and incomplete at AU-58. Nicks and contact marks are to be expected. *Reverse:* Friction on the wing and neck is very noticeable at AU-50, increasingly less at higher levels to AU-58. Otherwise, the same comments apply as for the obverse.

MS-60 to 70 (Mint State). *Obverse:* On MS-60 to 62 coins there is abrasion in the field, this representing the highest part of the coin. Abrasion is also evident on the headdress. Marks and, occasionally, a microscopic pin scratch may be seen. At MS-63, there may be some abrasion and some tiny marks. Luster is irregular. At MS-64, abrasion is less. Luster is rich. At MS-65 and above, luster is deep and frosty. No marks at all are visible without magnification at MS-66 and higher. *Reverse:* At MS-60 to 62, there is abrasion in the field, this representing the highest part of the coin. Abrasion is also evident on the eagle's wing. Otherwise, the same comments apply as for the obverse.

	Mintage	Cert	Avg	%MS	EF-40	AU-50	MS-60	MS-62	MS-63	MS-64	MS-65	Recent Auction Record
1908	564,821	14,596	61.6	84	$325	$350	$450	$575	$1,000	$1,600	$3,500	$13,806, MS, January 2014
1909	441,760	10,504	61.1	78	325	350	450	600	1,450	2,500	4,750	$14,981, MS-66, September 2013
1910	492,000	11,464	61.0	79	325	350	450	650	1,300	2,350	4,750	$17,625, MS-66, January 2014
1911	704,000	17,915	60.8	77	325	350	450	600	850	1,500	6,500	$7,638, MS-65, January 2014
1911D (a)	55,680	7,884	58.8	52	4,000	5,000	9,000	12,500	18,000	24,000	60,000	$176,250, MS-66, April 2013
1911D, Weak D	*	303	49.6	2	1,500	2,200	4,000					$2,645, AU-55, April 2012
1912	616,000	12,321	60.4	71	325	350	475	775	1,650	2,750	11,000	$15,275, MS-65, January 2014
1913	722,000	17,063	60.8	77	325	350	475	675	950	1,700	5,500	$28,200, MS-66, October 2013
1914	240,000	10,467	60.4	72	350	450	750	1,950	4,750	8,000	27,500	$32,900, MS-65, December 2013
1914D	448,000	15,627	60.9	77	325	350	475	775	1,500	3,500	30,000	$25,850, MS-65, August 2013
1915	606,000	16,384	61.0	78	325	350	450	600	1,000	1,500	6,500	$21,738, MS-66, January 2014
1925D	578,000	31,626	62.1	90	325	350	450	550	675	850	2,100	$7,990, MS-66, June 2014
1926	446,000	28,728	62.2	92	325	350	450	550	675	850	2,100	$8,813, MS-66, January 2014
1927	388,000	23,508	62.3	93	325	350	450	550	675	850	2,100	$11,750, MS-66, March 2013
1928	416,000	24,998	62.2	94	325	350	450	550	675	850	2,100	$10,575, MS-66, January 2014
1929	532,000	30,767	62.2	95	325	350	450	550	675	850	2,100	$30,550, MS-66, June 2014

* Included in number above. **a.** Beware of counterfeit and altered pieces.

Proof Indian Head Quarter Eagles

PF-60 to 70 (Proof). Sand Blast (also called Matte) Proofs were made in 1908 and 1911 to 1915, while Satin (also called Roman Finish) Proofs were made in 1909 and 1910. The Sand Blast issues usually are somewhat dull, while the Satin Proofs usually are of a light-yellow gold. In their time the Proofs of both styles, made for all gold series, were not popular with numismatists.

Today, they are in strong demand. As a class these are significantly more readily available than half eagles of the same date and style of finish. Most are in grades from PF-63 upward. At lower levels coins can show light contact marks. Some microscopic bright flecks may be caused by the sandblasting process and, although they do not represent handling, usually result in a

coin being assigned a slightly lower grade. *Obverse and Reverse:* At PF-60 to 63, there is light abrasion and some contact marks; the lower the grade, the higher the quantity. On Sand Blast Proofs these show up as visually unappealing bright spots. At PF-64 and higher levels, marks are fewer, with magnification needed to see any at PF-65. At PF-66, there should be none at all.

Proof Indian Head Quarter Eagle
Shown 1.5x actual size.

	Mintage	Cert	Finest	PF-60	PF-63	PF-64	PF-65	Recent Auction Record
1908, Sand Blast Finish	236	221	PF-65	$3,750	$9,000	$14,000	$25,000	$49,938, PF-68, April 2014
1909, Satin Finish	139	91	PF-64	4,000	9,000	15,000	27,500	$57,500, PF-67, January 2011
1910, Satin Finish	682	173	PF-65	4,000	9,000	15,000	27,500	$27,600, PF-64 Plus, September 2011
1910, Sand Blast Finish (a)	unknown	1	PF-66					
1911, Sand Blast Finish	191	175	PF-65	3,750	9,000	14,000	25,000	$27,025, PF-66, January 2014
1912, Sand Blast Finish	197	82	PF-65	3,750	10,000	14,000	25,000	$41,125, PF-66, September 2013
1913, Sand Blast Finish	165	94	PF-65	3,750	9,000	14,000	25,000	$31,050, PF-67, January 2012
1914, Sand Blast Finish	117	124	PF-64	3,750	10,000	14,000	25,000	$12,650, PF-64, April 2012
1915, Sand Blast Finish	100	75	PF-65	4,000	12,000	17,500	30,000	$41,688, PF-66, January 2012

a. Unique; part of a complete 1910 Sand Blast Finish Proof gold set. Others may exist, but have not yet been confirmed.

AN OVERVIEW OF THREE-DOLLAR GOLD PIECES

The three-dollar gold coin denomination was conceived in 1853 and first produced for circulation in 1854. Although there were high hopes for it at the outset, and mintages were generous, the value was redundant given the $2.50 quarter eagle then in circulation. Mintages declined, and although pieces were struck each year through 1889, very few actually circulated after the 1850s.

Although many different three-dollar dates are available at reasonable prices, most numismatists opt to acquire either a circulated or Mint State 1854 (significant as the first year of issue; also, in this year the word DOLLARS is in smaller letters than on later issues) or a Mint State coin from the low-mintage era of 1879–1889. Similar to the situation for gold dollars, although the mintages of these later pieces were low, they were popularly saved at the time, and many more exist than might otherwise be the case.

FOR THE COLLECTOR AND INVESTOR: THREE-DOLLAR GOLD PIECES AS A SPECIALTY

Collecting three-dollar pieces by date and mint would at first seem to be daunting, but it is less challenging than expected, outside of a handful of pieces. The 1870-S is unique (in the Harry W. Bass Jr. Collection on loan to the American Numismatic Association), the 1875 and 1876 were made only in Proof format to the extent of 20 and 45 pieces respectively, and the 1873 is quite rare. Beyond that, examples of coins in grades such as EF and AU (including some varieties with very low mintages) can be purchased for reasonable prices.

Choice examples can be elusive, this being particularly true of branch-mint issues of the 1854–1860 years. Generally, Mint State Philadelphia pieces are rare after 1855, but then come on the market with frequency for 1861 and later, with dates in the 1860s being scarcer than later issues. Coins of the years 1878 and 1879 were made in larger quantities, with the 1878 in particular being easy to find today, although examples usually are quite bagmarked. The low-mintage three-dollar pieces of 1879 through 1889 were popular at the time of issue, many were saved, and today Mint State pieces exist to a greater extent than would normally be the case.

RECOMMENDED READING

Akers, David W. *Gold Dollars (and Other Gold Denominations)*, Englewood, OH, 1975–1982.
Bowers, Q. David. *United States Gold Coins: An Illustrated History*, Wolfeboro, NH, 1982.
Bowers, Q. David, and Winter, Douglas. *United States $3 Gold Pieces 1854–1889*, Wolfeboro, NH, 2005.
Breen, Walter. *Major Varieties of U.S. Gold Dollars (and Other Gold Denominations)*, Chicago, 1964.
Fivaz, Bill. *United States Gold Counterfeit Detection Guide*, Atlanta, GA, 2005.
Fivaz, Bill, and Stanton, J.T. *The Cherrypickers' Guide to Rare Die Varieties* (5th ed., vol. II), Atlanta, GA, 2012.
Garrett, Jeff, and Guth, Ron. *Encyclopedia of U.S. Gold Coins, 1795–1933* (2nd ed.), Atlanta, GA, 2008.

Coincidence? A $3 gold piece would have conveniently paid for 100 3¢ postage stamps of the mid-1800s—perhaps a reason why Congress authorized the new coinage denomination, although facts are scarce.

INDIAN PRINCESS HEAD
(1854–1889)

Designer James B. Longacre; weight 5.015 grams; composition .900 gold, .100 copper (net weight .14512 oz. pure gold); diameter 20.5 mm; reeded edge; mints: Philadelphia, Dahlonega, New Orleans, San Francisco.

Mintmark is below wreath.

History. The three-dollar gold coin was designed by chief engraver James B. Longacre, and first struck in 1854. The quarter eagle and half eagle had already been in use for a long time, and the reason for the creation of this odd new denomination is uncertain, although some numismatists note it could have been used to buy a sheet of current 3¢ stamps or a group of 100 silver trimes. After a large initial mintage in 1854, the coins were struck in smaller annual quantities.

Striking and Sharpness. Points to observe on the obverse include the tips of the feathers in the headdress, and the hair details below the band inscribed LIBERTY. Focal points on the reverse are the wreath details (especially the vertical division in the ribbon knot), and the two central date numerals. Many of the later issues—particularly those of the early 1880s—are prooflike.

Availability. In circulated grades the issues of 1854 to 1860 survive in approximate proportion to their mintages. MS coins are plentiful for the first-year Philadelphia issue, 1854, but are scarce to rare for other years and all branch-mint issues. For the 1860s and 1870s most are in grades such as EF, AU, and low MS, except for 1874 and in particular 1878, easily found in MS. Dates from 1879 to 1889 have a higher survival ratio and are mostly in MS, often at MS-65.

VF-20, 30 (Very Fine). *Obverse:* Most hair detail is gone, except at the back of the lower curls. The feather plume ends are flat. *Reverse:* The wreath and other areas show more wear. Most detail is gone on the higher-relief leaves.

EF-40, 45 (Extremely Fine). *Obverse:* Medium wear is seen on the hair below the coronet and on the feather plume tips. Detail is partially gone on the hair. Luster is gone on most coins. *Reverse:* Light wear is seen overall, and the highest parts of the leaves are flat, but detail remains elsewhere. Luster is gone on most coins.

AU-50, 53, 55, 58 (About Uncirculated). *Obverse:* Light wear on the hair below the coronet, the cheek, and the tips of the feather plumes is very noticeable at AU-50, increasingly less at higher levels to AU-58. Luster is minimal at AU-50 and scattered and incomplete at AU-58. Some tiny nicks and contact marks are to be expected and should be mentioned if they are distracting. *Reverse:* Light wear on the 1, the wreath, and the ribbon knot characterize an AU-50 coin, increasingly less at higher levels to 58. Otherwise, the same comments apply as for the obverse.

MS-60 to 70 (Mint State). *Obverse:* On MS-60 to 62 coins there is abrasion on the hair below the band lettered LIBERTY (an area that can be weakly struck, as well) and on tips of the feather plumes. At MS-63, there may be slight abrasion. Luster can be irregular. At MS-64, abrasion is less. Luster is rich on most coins, less so on the 1854-D (which often is overgraded). At MS-65 and above, luster is deep and frosty, with no marks at all visible without magnification at MS-66 and higher. *Reverse:* On MS-60 to 62 coins there is abrasion on the 1, the highest parts of the leaves, and the ribbon knot. Otherwise, the same comments apply as for the obverse.

	Mintage	Cert	Avg	%MS	AU-55	AU-58	MS-60	MS-62	MS-63	MS-64	MS-65	Recent Auction Record
1854	138,618	6,575	55.3	25	$1,500	$2,100	$2,650	$4,500	$6,000	$8,000	$20,000	$19,975, MS-66, October 2013
1854D	1,120	221	47.9	6	45,000	57,500	80,000	175,000				$52,875, EF-35, March 2013
1854O	24,000	1,265	47.8	2	8,500	13,500	27,500	57,500	85,000			$25,850, AU-58, January 2014
1855	50,555	1,979	53.7	21	1,750	2,500	3,000	4,500	8,500	17,000	40,000	$15,275, MS-64, August 2013
1855S	6,600	298	40.8	2	12,000	18,000	25,000	55,000	95,000			$17,625, AU-58, November 2013
1856	26,010	1,226	55.1	24	1,850	2,250	3,250	6,000	8,500	15,000	35,000	$35,250, MS-65, January 2013
1856S (a)	34,500	912	44.1	3	4,000	7,500	12,000	18,000	30,000	48,000		$12,925, MS-61, March 2013
1857	20,891	941	54.1	21	1,900	2,500	3,500	7,000	9,500	17,000	35,000	$31,725, MS-65, March 2013
1857S	14,000	339	41.8	1	11,000	14,500	21,500	45,000				$6,463, AU-55, April 2013
1858	2,133	218	51.5	9	5,500	8,500	12,000	15,000	22,500	40,000		$7,931, AU-58, August 2013
1859	15,558	913	55.2	25	1,900	2,500	3,250	6,500	8,500	16,000	30,000	$38,188, MS-66, June 2013
1860 (b)	7,036	570	55.3	28	1,950	3,000	3,500	7,000	9,500	16,000	27,500	$114,563, MS-67, January 2014
1860S	7,000	265	41.2	3	11,500	16,000	27,500	50,000				$30,550, MS-61, August 2013
1861	5,959	458	54.1	26	3,500	4,500	6,500	11,000	11,500	22,000	35,000	$9,400, MS-62, November 2013
1862	5,750	358	54.7	25	3,500	4,500	6,500	11,000	12,500	21,500	40,000	$8,813, MS-62, April 2013

a. Collectors recognize three mintmark sizes: Large (very rare); Medium (common), and Small (rare). **b.** Of the already low 1860 Philadelphia mintage, 2,592 coins were melted at the Mint.

	Mintage	Cert	Avg	%MS	AU-55	AU-58	MS-60	MS-62	MS-63	MS-64	MS-65	Recent Auction Record
1863	5,000	382	54.7	25	$4,500	$5,500	$7,500	$11,000	$13,000	$20,000	$35,000	$211,500, MS-67, January 2014
1864	2,630	279	55.5	27	4,750	5,750	7,750	11,250	13,500	23,500	38,000	$32,900, MS-65, February 2013
1865	1,140	137	54.4	25	9,500	11,500	15,000	20,000	30,000	37,500	55,000	$70,500, MS-66, January 2014
1866	4,000	316	54.6	23	3,000	3,750	5,500	7,500	11,000	17,500	35,000	$13,513, MS-64, February 2013
1867	2,600	213	55.5	23	3,000	3,750	5,500	8,000	12,000	19,000	35,000	$141,000, MS-67, January 2014
1868 (c)	4,850	646	56.2	30	2,750	3,000	4,250	7,500	10,000	16,500	30,000	$8,879, MS-63, April 2013
1869 (c)	2,500	307	53.8	15	2,800	3,250	4,750	9,000	12,000	25,000	45,000	$7,050, MS-62, March 2013
1870	3,500	482	54.2	14	3,000	3,500	5,000	10,500	12,500	25,000		$14,688, MS-63, January 2014
1870S (d)		n/a	n/a	n/a			*(unique, in the Bass Foundation Collection)*					$687,500, EF-40, October 1982
1871	1,300	336	56.4	29	3,000	3,500	4,750	8,500	12,500	20,000	35,000	$8,813, MS-62, August 2013
1872	2,000	346	55.3	21	3,000	3,500	4,750	8,500	12,500	20,000		$7,344, MS-62, August 2013
1873, Close 3	(e)	116	55.7	16	18,500	22,500	32,500	37,500	55,000	75,000		$61,688, MS-63, January 2014
1874	41,800	4,716	56.5	32	1,500	1,650	2,500	3,500	5,500	7,500	15,000	$12,338, MS-65, September 2013
1877	1,468	82	55.6	22	20,000	22,500	28,500	35,000	50,000	70,000		$22,325, MS-61, August 2013
1878 (c)	82,304	10,783	59.7	62	1,500	1,650	2,350	3,250	4,750	7,000	10,000	$25,850, MS-66, January 2014
1879	3,000	854	61.1	73	2,750	3,000	3,750	6,000	8,000	10,000	20,000	$17,038, MS-65, August 2013
1880	1,000	326	62.5	89	3,850	4,200	5,500	7,500	11,000	15,000	25,000	$58,750, MS-66, January 2014
1881	500	198	57.2	32	8,500	9,500	12,000	15,000	18,500	25,000		$14,100, MS-61, August 2013
1882	1,500	539	58.9	55	3,000	3,400	4,250	6,750	10,000	15,000	28,000	$105,750, MS-67, January 2014
1883	900	319	58.9	57	3,500	4,000	5,500	7,500	10,000	14,000	28,000	$10,575, MS, March 2014
1884	1,000	142	61.6	80	4,000	4,250	5,500	7,500	10,000	14,000	28,000	$7,931, MS-62, August 2013
1885	801	293	59.4	57	4,500	4,750	6,000	9,000	15,000	22,500	35,000	$7,050, MS-62, January 2014
1886	1,000	314	57.2	36	3,750	4,250	5,000	7,500	10,500	14,000	35,000	$3,290, AU-58, January 2013
1887	6,000	480	61.2	75	2,250	2,500	3,500	4,750	10,500	12,500	24,000	$15,275, MS-65, January 2014
1888	5,000	1,213	61.3	76	1,850	2,250	3,000	4,500	7,000	8,000	13,500	$19,388, MS, March 2014
1889	2,300	681	60.4	67	1,650	2,000	2,900	4,000	6,000	7,500	13,500	$19,975, MS-66, April 2014

c. Varieties showing traces of possible overdating include 1868/7, 1869/8, and 1878/7. **d.** A second example of the 1870-S is rumored to exist in the cornerstone of the San Francisco Mint, but the cornerstone has never been located. **e.** The mintage of the 1873, Close 3, coins is unknown. Research suggests that only Proofs may have been struck (none for circulation), and those perhaps as late as 1879.

Proof Three-Dollar Gold Pieces

PF-60 to 70 (Proof). Three-dollar Proofs were struck of all years. All prior to the 1880s are very rare today, with issues of the 1850s exceedingly so. Coins of 1875 and 1876 were made only in Proof format, with no related circulation strikes. Most often seen in the marketplace are the higher-mintage Proofs of the 1880s. Some have patches of graininess or hints of non-Proof surface on the obverse, or an aura or "ghosting" near the portrait, an artifact of striking. *Obverse and Reverse:* PF-60 to 62 coins have extensive hairlines and may have nicks and contact marks. At PF-63, hairlines are prominent, but the mirror surface is very reflective. PF-64 coins have fewer hairlines. At PF-65, hairlines should be minimal and mostly seen only under magnification. There should be no nicks or marks. PF-66 and higher coins should have no marks or hairlines visible to the unaided eye.

Proof Three-Dollar Gold Piece
Shown 1.5x actual size.

	Est Mintage	Cert	Avg	PF-60	PF-63	PF-64	PF-65	Recent Auction Record
1854	15–20	14	62.6	$30,000	$95,000	$115,000	$175,000	$164,500, PF-64Cam, November 2013
1855	4–8	4	55.8	30,000	95,500	125,000	200,000	$75,900, PF-64Cam, November 2003
1855S	unknown	3	63.7			1,200,000		$1,322,500, PF-64Cam, August 2011
1856	8–10	5	63.0	19,500	45,000	60,000	100,000	$28,750, PF-62Cam, March 2011
1857	8–12	5	64.2	17,500	30,000	55,000	95,000	
1858	8–12	7	64.4	15,000	27,500	45,000	85,000	$85,188, PF-65Cam, April 2013

Chart continued on next page.

THREE-DOLLAR GOLD PIECES, 1854–1889

	Mintage	Cert	Avg	PF-60	PF-63	PF-64	PF-65	Recent Auction Record
1859	80	17	64.5	$8,500	$20,000	$40,000	$60,000	$59,925, PF-65DCam, April 2014
1860	119	23	64.3	8,000	16,000	30,000	55,000	$67,563, PF-66Cam, August 2013
1861	113	12	64.3	8,000	16,000	30,000	55,000	$37,375, PF-64Cam, January 2011
1862	35	18	64.4	8,000	16,000	30,000	55,000	$74,750, PF-66UCam, August 2009
1863	39	24	63.6	8,000	16,000	30,000	50,000	$80,500, PF-66UCam, March 2011
1864	50	46	63.1	8,000	16,000	30,000	47,500	$48,875, PF-64DCam, April 2012
1865	25	18	63.9	8,500	20,000	32,500	50,000	$46,000, PF-64Cam, March 2006
1865, Proof Restrike (a)	5	1	63.0		(extremely rare)			
1866	30	19	62.6	8,000	16,500	30,000	50,000	$46,000, PF-64DCam, April 2011
1867	50	22	62.8	8,000	16,500	30,000	50,000	$64,625, PF-66Cam, August 2013
1868	25	17	62.4	8,000	16,500	30,000	50,000	$57,500, PF-65Cam, January 2011
1869	25	11	64.7	8,000	16,500	30,000	50,000	$57,500, PF-65UCam, February 2009
1870	35	21	63.3	8,000	16,500	30,000	50,000	$55,813, PF-64Cam, January 2014
1871	30	18	62.6	8,000	16,500	30,000	55,000	$19,550, PF-63Cam, September 2007
1872	30	33	62.9	8,000	16,500	30,000	47,500	$18,800, PF, March 2014
1873, Open 3 (Original) (b)	25	26	63.7	25,000	32,500	50,000	70,000	$212,750, PF-65DCam, September 2008
1873, Close 3	*	4	63.5	25,000	37,500	52,500	75,000	$37,375, PF-61, January 2011
1874	20	29	63.3	12,500	28,000	40,000	60,000	$54,6250, PF-65Cam, January 2012
1875, Proof only	20	21	63.1	80,000	150,000	175,000	225,000	$218,500, PF-64, January 2012
1876, Proof only	45	79	63.3	25,000	45,000	50,000	75,000	$76,375, PF-65Cam, June 2013
1877	20	25	62.6	12,500	30,000	35,000	55,000	$64,400, PF-65DCam, November 2010
1878	20	19	64.1	12,500	27,500	35,000	55,000	$877, PF, June 2014
1879	30	24	64.2	10,000	17,000	32,500	42,500	$14,375, PF-63Cam, October 2011
1880	36	43	63.7	10,000	17,000	32,500	42,500	$51,113, PF, August 2013
1881	54	81	63.6	10,000	17,000	32,500	42,500	$32,200, PF-64Cam, January 2011
1882	76	77	63.0	7,500	13,500	20,000	35,000	$28,200, PF-64DCam, March 2014
1883	89	102	63.8	7,500	13,500	20,000	35,000	$38,188, PF-65Cam, April 2013
1884	106	104	63.4	7,500	13,500	20,000	35,000	$23,500, PF-64DCam, August 2013
1885	109	138	63.4	7,500	13,500	20,000	35,000	$76,050, PF, September 2013
1886	142	165	63.7	7,500	13,500	20,000	35,000	$38,188, PF-65DCam, April 2013
1887	160	161	63.7	7,500	13,500	20,000	35,000	$64,625, PF-67Cam, August 2013
1888	291	230	63.9	7,500	12,500	18,500	32,500	$38,188, PF-66Cam, November 2013
1889	129	144	63.6	7,500	12,500	18,500	35,000	$25,850, PF-65Cam, January 2014

* Included in number above. **a.** Sometime around 1873, the Mint restruck a small number of 1865 three-dollar pieces using an obverse die of 1872 and a newly created reverse with the date slanting up to the right (previously listed in *United States Pattern Coins* as Judd-440). Two examples are known in gold. Versions were also made in copper (Judd-441) for interested collectors. **b.** Mint records report 25 Proof coins (with no reference to the style, Open or Close, of the number 3 in the date). The actual mintage may be as high as 100 to 1,000 coins.

AN OVERVIEW OF
FOUR-DOLLAR GOLD PIECES

The four-dollar pattern gold coin, or Stella, is not widely collected, simply because of its rarity. For type-set purposes some numismatists opt to acquire a single example of the only issue readily available, Charles Barber's 1879 Flowing Hair, although these are expensive. However, the Coiled Hair style is a different type, much rarer, and a collector with the means might acquire an example of that design as well.

FOR THE COLLECTOR AND INVESTOR: FOUR-DOLLAR GOLD PIECES AS A SPECIALTY

Over the past century perhaps two dozen numismatists have put together complete sets of one of each gold striking of the 1879 and 1880 Flowing Hair and Coiled Hair Stella, this being made possible by collections being dispersed and sold to others, as it is unlikely that even as many as 20 complete sets could exist at one time.

RECOMMENDED READING

Akers, David W. *Gold Dollars (and Other Gold Denominations),* Englewood, OH, 1975–1982.
Bowers, Q. David. *United States Gold Coins: An Illustrated History,* Wolfeboro, NH, 1982.
Breen, Walter. *Major Varieties of U.S. Gold Dollars (and Other Gold Denominations),* Chicago, 1964.
Garrett, Jeff, and Guth, Ron. *Encyclopedia of U.S. Gold Coins, 1795–1933* (2nd ed.), Atlanta, GA, 2008.
Judd, J. Hewitt. *United States Pattern Coins* (10th ed., Q. David Bowers, editor), Atlanta, GA, 2009.

John A. Kasson—Iowa lawyer, politician, and diplomat—was influential in moving the $4 gold Stella from concept to coin.

FOUR-DOLLAR GOLD PIECES

Flowing Hair Obverse   **Coiled Hair Obverse**

STELLA, FLOWING HAIR AND COILED HAIR (1879–1880)

Designer Charles E. Barber (Flowing Hair), George T. Morgan (Coiled Hair); weight 7.0 grams; approx. composition .857 gold, .042 silver, .100 copper; diameter 22 mm; reeded edge.

Reverse
Shown 1.5x actual size.

History. The four-dollar gold Stellas of 1879 and 1880 are Proof-only patterns, not regular issues. However, as they have been listed in popular references for decades, collectors have adopted them into the regular gold series. The obverse inscription notes the coins' metallic content in proportions of gold, silver, and copper in the metric system, intended to facilitate their use in foreign countries, where the value could be quickly determined. The Stella was proposed by John A. Kasson (former chairman of the congressional Committee of Coinage, Weights, and Measures; in 1879 serving as envoy extraordinary and minister plenipotentiary to Austria-Hungary). Charles E. Barber designed the Flowing Hair type, and George T. Morgan the Coiled Hair. The only issue produced in quantity was the 1879 Flowing Hair. The others were made in secret and sold privately by Mint officers and employees. The Coiled Hair Stella was not generally known to the numismatic community until they were illustrated in *The Numismatist* in the early 20th century. Stellas are cataloged by their Judd numbers, assigned in the standard reference, *United States Pattern Coins*.

Striking and Sharpness. On nearly all examples the high parts of the hair are flat, often with striations. The other areas of the coin are typically well struck. Tiny planchet irregularities are common.

Availability. The 1879 Flowing Hair is often available on the market—usually in PF-61 to 64, although higher-condition examples come on the market with regularity (as do lightly handled and impaired coins). The 1880 Flowing Hair is typically found in PF-63 or higher. Both years of Coiled Hair Stellas are great rarities; typical grades are PF-63 to 65, with a flat strike on the head and with some tiny planchet flaws.

Proof Four-Dollar Gold Pieces

PF-60 to 70 (Proof). Striations are normally found on most pieces. *Obverse and Reverse:* PF-60 to 62 coins have extensive hairlines and may have nicks and contact marks. At PF-63, hairlines are prominent, but the mirror surface is very reflective. PF-64 coins have fewer hairlines. At PF-65, hairlines should be minimal and mostly seen only under magnification. There should be no nicks or marks. PF-66 and higher coins should have no marks or hairlines visible to the unaided eye.

	Est Mintage	Cert	Finest	PF-50	PF-60	PF-63	PF-64	PF-65	PF-66	PF-67	Recent Auction Record
1879, Flowing Hair	(425+)	526	PF-63	$85,000	$105,000	$150,000	$175,000	$215,000	$250,000	$375,000	$280,800, PF, September 2013
1879, Coiled Hair	(12–15 known)	24	PF-65		275,000	350,000	450,000	550,000	750,000	1,000,000	$1,041,300, PF, September 2013
1880, Flowing Hair	(17–20 known)	45	PF-65		150,000	225,000	275,000	350,000	450,000	600,000	$959,400, PF, September 2013
1880, Coiled Hair	(8–10 known)	19	PF-65		600,000	750,000	850,000	1,250,000	1,500,000	2,000,000	$2,574,000, PF, September 2013

Note: Many individual high-value rare coins are submitted for certification and grading multiple times over the years, which can inflate the number of certifications above the number of coins actually minted.

An Overview of Gold Half Eagles

The half eagle was the first gold coin actually struck for the United States. The five-dollar gold piece was authorized by the Act of April 2, 1792, and the first batch was minted in 1795.

Forming a type set of half eagles is a daunting but achievable challenge—if a collector has the finances and some determination. Examples of the first type, with Capped Bust to Right (conical cap obverse), and with an eagle on a palm branch on the reverse, readily come up on the market, usually of the date 1795. Typical grades range from EF to lower Mint State levels. Such pieces are scarce, and the demand for them is strong. The next type, the Heraldic Eagle motif, first struck in 1798, but also known from a 1795-dated die used later, was produced through 1807, and easily enough obtained today. Again, typical grades range from EF to Mint State. MS-63 and better coins are available, but are in the distinct minority.

The short-lived Capped Bust to Left style, 1807–1812, can be found in similar grades, although such pieces did not circulate as extensively, and AU and Mint State levels are the rule, with VF pieces scarce. Then follows the era of rarities. The Capped Head to Left, stars surrounding head, large diameter, 1813–1829 style is available courtesy of the first date of issue, 1813. This is the only date seen with some frequency. When available, examples tend to be choice. The later stretch of this series includes some formidable rarities, among which are the famous 1815 and the even rarer 1822, along with a whole string of other seldom-seen varieties in the 1820s. The same style, but of reduced diameter, 1829–1834, also is rare; examples of the 1830s turn up with some regularity, but these often lack eye appeal. For some reason, half eagles of the early 1830s are often heavily marked and abraded, which it not true at all for coins of the 1820s.

Classic Head half eagles, capless and without motto, first minted in August 1834, are easily enough obtained. They are usually of the first several dates, less frequently of 1837 or 1838. Grades range from VF upward, reflecting their extensive use in circulation. Mint State coins can be found on occasion and are scarce. Choice and gem pieces are rare.

With just a few exceptions, Liberty Head half eagles of the 1839–1866 type without motto are very plentiful in worn grades, including certain of the higher-mintage issues from the popular Charlotte and Dahlonega mints (permitting interesting varieties to be added to a type set). Mint State coins are scarce, and when seen are usually in lower levels such as MS-60 and MS-62. Gems of any date are rare. Then follow the Liberty Head pieces with the motto on the reverse, 1866 through 1908; the earlier years are mostly encountered in worn grades, the later ones are easy enough to find in Mint State. Proofs were made of all Liberty Head half eagle dates, and today they are generally collectible from about 1860 onward.

With two exceptions (1909-O and 1929), the Indian Head half eagles of 1908–1929 are common enough in worn grades as well as low Mint State levels, but true gems, accurately graded and with lustrous, frosty surfaces, are quite rare. The field is the highest area of the coin and thus is quite susceptible to scuffs and marks. Probably the most readily available dates in higher grades are 1908 and 1909, with the 1909-D being plentiful due to a hoard that came on the market a generation ago.

For the Collector and Investor: Gold Half Eagles as a Specialty

While in the annals of American numismatics dozens of old-time numismatists collected half eagles by date (or, less often, by date *and* mint), today rarities are so widely scattered and are so expensive that few collectors can rise to the challenge.

Early half eagles can be collected by dates and basic varieties, and also by die varieties. The year 1795 in particular is rich in the latter, and years ago several scholars described such varieties, beginning with J. Colvin Randall in the 1870s, continuing to William H. Woodin in the early 20th century, then Edgar H. Adams, Thomas Ollive Mabbott, and Walter Breen. In more recent times Robert Miller, Harry Bass, John Dannreuther, and others have added their research to the literature.

Among early half eagles there are two unique varieties: the 1797 with 16-star obverse, and 1797 with 15-star obverse, both with Heraldic Eagle reverse, likely struck in 1798. Of the later 1822, just three are known, two of which are at the Smithsonian Institution. Of all early half eagles the 1815 was far and away the most famous during the 19th century. (In the 1880s a publication on the Mint Collection stated that the two highlights there were the 1815 half eagle and the unique 1849 double eagle.) At the time the rarer 1822 had not been recognized for its elusive nature. Today an estimated 11 examples of the 1815 half eagles exist, mostly in higher circulated grades, including those in museums. The aforementioned 1822 is the rarity of rarities in the series, with just three known to exist, two

GOLD HALF EAGLES

of which are in the Smithsonian's National Numismatic Collection, with the third, the Eliasberg Collection coin, being a highlight of a private cabinet. There are only two known of the 1825, 5 Over 4 overdate, but it is not at all famous, probably because it is an overdate variety, not a single date on its own. Half eagles of 1826 through 1829 all are rare, with the 1829 being particularly well known. The latter date includes early pieces with regular diameter and later ones with the diameter reduced. Generally, all half eagles from 1815 through 1834 are scarce, some of them particularly so.

Classic Head half eagles of 1834–1838 include the scarce 1838-C and 1838-D, the first of the Charlotte and Dahlonega mints respectively; none are prohibitively rare. Generally, the higher-grade pieces are found toward the beginning of the Classic Head series, especially bearing the date 1834.

Liberty Head half eagles are readily available of most dates and mints from 1839 to 1908, save for the one great rarity, the 1854-S, of which just three are known (one is in the Smithsonian). There is a vast panorama of Charlotte and Dahlonega issues through 1861, most of which were made in fairly large quantities, as this was the highest denomination ever struck at each of these mints (larger-capacity presses were not on hand). Accordingly, they are highly collectible today. Some varieties are scarce, but none are out of reach. Typical grades range from VF to EF and AU, occasionally Mint State, though not often MS-63 or higher.

Among San Francisco half eagles most of the early issues are scarce, as such pieces circulated extensively and there was no thought to saving numismatic examples. However, there are not many specialists in the field, and for some varieties it can be said that collectors are harder to find than are the coins themselves, yielding the opportunity to purchase truly rare pieces for significantly less than would otherwise be the case. Carson City half eagles were minted beginning in 1870 and continuing intermittently through 1893. Most of the early issues range from scarce to rare, the 1870-CC being particularly well known in this regard. Proofs of the Liberty Head type are generally collectible from the 1860s onward, with most on the market being of the higher-mintage issues of the 1890s and 1900s.

Among Indian Head half eagles, 1908–1929, the 1909-O is the rarest of the early coins, and when seen is usually worn. A choice or gem Mint State 1909-O is an incredible rarity. However, enough worn 1909-O half eagles exist, including many brought from overseas hoards in recent decades, that a piece in VF or so grade presents no problem. Half eagles of 1929, of which just 662,000 were minted, were mostly melted, it seems. A couple hundred or so exist today, nearly all of which are Mint State, but nicked and with bagmarks, MS-60 to MS-62 or MS-63. Truly high-quality gems are exceedingly rare.

RECOMMENDED READING

Akers, David W. *Gold Dollars (and Other Gold Denominations),* Englewood, OH, 1975–1982.

Bowers, Q. David. *United States Gold Coins: An Illustrated History,* Wolfeboro, NH, 1982.

Breen, Walter. *Major Varieties of U.S. Gold Dollars (and Other Gold Denominations),* Chicago, 1964.

Dannreuther, John W., and Bass, Harry W. *Early U.S. Gold Coin Varieties,* Atlanta, GA, 2006.

Fivaz, Bill. *United States Gold Counterfeit Detection Guide,* Atlanta, GA, 2005.

Fivaz, Bill, and Stanton, J.T. *The Cherrypickers' Guide to Rare Die Varieties* (5th ed., vol. II), Atlanta, GA, 2012.

Garrett, Jeff, and Guth, Ron. *Encyclopedia of U.S. Gold Coins, 1795–1933* (2nd ed.), Atlanta, GA, 2008.

Miller, Robert W., Sr. *United States Half Eagle Gold Coins 1795–1834,* 1997.

CAPPED BUST TO RIGHT, SMALL EAGLE REVERSE (1795–1798)

Designer Robert Scot; weight 8.75 grams; composition .9167 gold, .0833 silver and copper; approx. diameter 25 mm; reeded edge.

Bass-Dannreuther-7.

History. Half eagles of this style, the first federal gold coins, were introduced in July 1795. The obverse features Miss Liberty wearing a conical cap, a design generally called Capped Bust to Right. The reverse depicts a "small" eagle perched on a palm branch. The same motif was used on contemporary $10 gold coins.

Striking and Sharpness. On the obverse, check the star centers and the hair details. On the reverse, check the feathers of the eagle, particularly on the breast. Examine the dentils on both sides. Adjustment marks often are visible, but are not noted by the grading services.

Availability. Typical grades range from EF to AU and low MS. MS-63 and better coins are rare; when seen, they usually are of the 1795 date (of which many different die varieties exist). Certain varieties are rare, most famously the 1798 with Small Eagle reverse.

EF-40, 45 (Extremely Fine). *Obverse:* Wear is evident all over the portrait, with some loss of detail in the hair to the left of Miss Liberty's face. Excellent detail remains in low-relief areas of the hair, such as the front curl and at the back of her head. The stars show wear, as do the date and letters. Luster, if present at all, is minimal and in protected areas. *Reverse:* Wear is greater than at AU. The breast, neck, and legs of the eagle lack nearly all feather detail. More wear is seen on the edges of the wing. Some traces of luster may be seen, less so at EF-40 than at EF-45.

AU-50, 53, 55, 58 (About Uncirculated). *Obverse:* Light wear is seen on the cheek, the hair immediately to the left of the face, and the cap, more so at AU-50 than at 53 or 55. An AU-58 coin has minimal traces of wear. An AU-50 coin has luster in protected areas among the stars and letters, with little in the open fields or on the portrait. At AU-58, most luster is present in the fields, but is worn away on the highest parts of the motifs. *Reverse:* The eagle shows light wear on the breast and head in particular, but also at the tip of the wing on the left and elsewhere. Luster ranges from perhaps 40% remaining in protected areas (at AU-50) to nearly full mint bloom (at AU-58).

MS-60 to 70 (Mint State). *Obverse:* At MS-60, some abrasion and contact marks are evident, most noticeably on the hair to the left of Miss Liberty's forehead and on the higher-relief areas of the cap. Luster is present, but may be dull or lifeless, and interrupted in patches. At MS-63, contact marks are few, and abrasion is very light. An MS-65 coin has hardly any abrasion, and contact marks are so minute as to require magnification. Luster should be full and rich. Grades above MS-65 for this type are more often theoretical than actual—but they do exist and are defined by having fewer marks as perfection is approached. *Reverse:* Comments apply as for the obverse, except that abrasion and contact marks are most noticeable on the breast and head of the eagle. The field area is mainly protected by the eagle, branch, and lettering.

1796, 6 Over 5

1797, 15-Star Obverse

1797, 16-Star Obverse

	Mintage	Cert	Avg	%MS	AU-50	AU-55	AU-58	MS-60	MS-62	MS-63	MS-64	Recent Auction Record
1795, Small Eagle	8,707	510	53.2	25	$40,000	$47,500	$55,000	$70,000	$97,500	$155,000	$275,000 (a)	$64,625, MS-61, February 2013
1795, Small Eagle, S Over D in States (b)	*	9	57.2	22	42,000	52,500	57,000	75,000				$345,000, MS-65PL, July 2009
1796, 6 Over 5	6,196	62	54.7	32	60,000	75,000	85,000	110,000	145,000	215,000	300,000	$67,563, AU-58, February 2014
1797, All kinds	3,609											
1797, 15-Star Obverse		8	55.9	13	100,000	150,000	175,000	275,000				$152,750, AU-53, January 2014
1797, 16-Star Obverse		19	54.7	11	80,000	135,000	165,000	275,000				$411,250, MS-61, August 2013
1798, Small Eagle (c) *(7 known)* unknown		4	48.8	0	850,000	1,000,000	—					

* Included in number above. **a.** Value in MS-65 is $525,000. **b.** The final S in STATES is punched over an erroneous D. **c.** The reverse of the 1798, Small Eagle, was from a 1795 die. The obverse has an arched die crack or flaw beneath the date. The finest known example is an AU-55 from the collection of King Farouk of Egypt.

CAPPED BUST TO RIGHT, HERALDIC EAGLE REVERSE
(1795–1807)

Designer Robert Scot; weight 8.75 grams; composition .9167 gold, .0833 silver and copper; approx. diameter 25 mm; reeded edge.

Bass-Dannreuther-13.

History. For this type, the obverse design is the same as that of the preceding. The reverse features a heraldic eagle, as used on other silver and gold coins of the era. Some half eagles of the Heraldic Eagle Reverse design are dated 1795, but these were actually struck in 1798, from a leftover obverse coinage die.

Striking and Sharpness. On the obverse, check the star centers and the hair details. On the reverse, check the upper part of the shield, the lower part of the eagle's neck, the eagle's wing, the stars above the eagle, and the clouds. Inspect the dentils on both sides. Adjustment marks can be a problem and are not identified by the grading services.

Availability. Although there are many rare die varieties, as a type this half eagle is plentiful. Typical grades are EF to lower MS. MS-63 and higher coins are seen with some frequency and usually are dated from 1802 to 1807. Sharply struck coins without adjustment marks are in the minority.

EF-40, 45 (Extremely Fine). *Obverse:* Wear is evident all over the portrait, with some loss of detail in the hair to the left of Miss Liberty's face. Excellent detail remains in low-relief areas of the hair, such as the front curl and at the back of her head. The stars show wear, as do the date and letters. Luster, if present at all, is minimal and in protected areas. *Reverse:* Wear is greater than at AU. The neck lacks feather detail on its highest points. Feathers have lost some detail near the edges of the wings, and some areas of the horizontal lines in the shield may be blended together. Some traces of luster may be seen, less so at EF-40 than at EF-45. Overall, the reverse appears to be in a slightly higher grade than the obverse.

AU-50, 53, 55, 58 (About Uncirculated). *Obverse:* Light wear is seen on the cheek, the hair immediately to the left of the face, and the cap, more so at AU-50 than at 53 or 55. An AU-58 coin has minimal traces of wear. An AU-50 coin has luster in protected areas among the stars and letters, with little in the open fields or on the portrait. At AU-58, most luster is present in the fields, but is worn away on the highest parts of the motifs. *Reverse:* The eagle's neck, the tips and top of the wings, the clouds, and the tail show noticeable wear, as do other features. Luster ranges from perhaps 40% remaining in protected areas (at AU-50) to nearly full mint bloom (at AU-58). Often the reverse of this type retains much more luster than the obverse.

MS-60 to 70 (Mint State). *Obverse:* At MS-60, some abrasion and contact marks are evident, most noticeably on the hair to the left of Miss Liberty's forehead and on the higher-relief areas of the cap. Luster is present, but may be dull or lifeless, and interrupted in patches. At MS-63, contact marks are few, and abrasion is very light. An MS-65 coin has hardly any abrasion, and contact marks are so minute as to require magnification. Luster should be full and rich. Grades above MS-65 are not often seen but are defined by having fewer marks as perfection is approached. *Reverse:* Comments apply as for the obverse, except that abrasion and contact marks are most noticeable on the upper part of the eagle and the clouds. The field area is complex, with not much open space, given the stars above the eagle, the arrows and olive branch, and other features. Accordingly, marks are not as noticeable as on the obverse.

1797, 7 Over 5

1797, 16-Star Obverse

1797, 15-Star Obverse

1798, Small 8

1798, Large 8

1798, 13-Star Reverse

1798, 14-Star Reverse

1799, Small Reverse Stars

1799, Large Reverse Stars

| 1800, Pointed 1 | 1800, Blunt 1 | 1800, 8 Arrows | 1800, 9 Arrows | 1802, 2 Over 1 FS-G5-1802/1-301. | 1803, 3 Over 2 |

| 1804, Small 8 | 1804, Small 8 Over Large 8 | 1806, Pointed-Top 6, Stars 8 and 5 | Closeup of Pointed-Top 6 | 1806, Round-Top 6, Stars 7 and 6 | Closeup of Round-Top 6 |

1807, Small Reverse Stars   1807, Large Reverse Stars

	Mintage	Cert	Avg	%MS	AU-50	AU-55	AU-58	MS-60	MS-62	MS-63	MS-64	Recent Auction Record
1795, Heraldic Eagle	(a)	42	59.3	64	$50,000	$60,000	$70,000	$90,000	$135,000	$185,000	$275,000	$15,275, AU-50, January 2014
1797, 7 Over 5	(a)	10	55.9	30	75,000	115,000	120,000	200,000				$126,500, AU-58, September 2005
1797, 16-Star Obverse	(a)	n/a	n/a	n/a	(unique, in the Smithsonian's National Numismatic Collection)							
1797, 15-Star Obverse	(a)	n/a	n/a	n/a	(unique, in the Smithsonian's National Numismatic Collection)							
1798, All kinds	24,867											
1798, Small 8		33	53.5	18	18,500	21,500	26,000	32,500	47,500	75,000		$18,800, AU-53, April 2014
1798, Large 8, 13-Star Reverse		181	50.2	15	16,000	23,000	30,000	50,000				$12,925, AU-50, January 2014
1798, Large 8, 14-Star Reverse		24	54.7	4	25,000	35,000	60,000	100,000				$25,850, AU, February 2014
1799, All kinds	7,451											
1799, Small Reverse Stars		61	57.3	46	14,000	18,000	22,000	27,500	37,500	65,000	100,000	$47,000, MS-62, February 2013
1799, Large Reverse Stars		43	55.3	37	14,000	18,000	22,000	27,500	37,500	65,000	100,000	$70,500, MS-63, January 2014
1800	37,628	590	54.6	33	10,000	12,000	13,500	15,000	18,000	33,500	75,000	$16,100, MS-62, April 2012
1800, Pointed 1 (b)	*	n/a	n/a	n/a	20,000	23,000	24,500	27,500				$21,150, MS-62, November 2013
1800, 9 Arrows (c)	*	n/a	n/a	n/a	16,500	20,000						
1802, 2 Over 1	53,176	549	56.2	35	10,000	12,000	13,500	15,000	18,500	32,500	50,000 (d)	$58,750, MS-64, January 2014
1803, 3 Over 2	33,506	695	55.7	37	10,000	12,000	13,500	15,000	18,500	32,500	50,000 (e)	$20,563, MS-62, October 2013
1804, All kinds	30,475											
1804, Small 8		212	57.0	44	10,000	11,500	15,000	15,500	22,000	32,500	60,000	$18,800, MS-62, January 2014
1804, Small 8 Over Large 8 (f)		123	58.8	49	10,000	12,500	18,000	19,500	25,000	42,500	75,000	$32,900, MS-63, January 2014
1805	33,183	443	58.5	60	10,000	11,500	12,500	15,000	19,000	32,500	57,000 (g)	$16,450, MS, February 2014
1806, Pointed-Top 6	9,676	141	57.9	50	10,000	12,000	13,500	16,500	20,000	36,500	60,000 (g)	$7,638, EF-45, August 2013
1806, Round-Top 6	54,417	619	56.7	50	10,000	11,500	12,500	15,500	19,000	32,500	50,000 (g)	$111,625, MS-65, March 2013
1807, All kinds	32,488											
1807, Small Reverse Stars		n/a	n/a	n/a	10,000	11,500	12,500	15,500	18,000	32,500	50,000	$44,563, MS-64, January 2012
1807, Large Reverse Stars		n/a	n/a	n/a	10,000	11,500	12,500	15,500	18,000	32,500	50,000	$21,850, MS-63, January 2012

* Included in number above. **a.** The 1795 and 1797 Heraldic Eagle half eagles are thought to have been struck in 1798 and included in that year's mintage figure of 24,867. **b.** 4 to 6 specimens are known. **c.** 18 to 25 specimens are known. **d.** Value in MS-65 is $135,000. **e.** Value in MS-65 is $125,000. **f.** Created when the engraver mistakenly used an 8 punch intended for $10 gold coins, then corrected the error by overpunching with a much smaller 8. **g.** Value in MS-65 is $120,000.

CAPPED BUST TO LEFT
(1807–1812)

Designer John Reich; weight 8.75 grams; composition .9167 gold, .0833 silver and copper; approx. diameter 25 mm; reeded edge.

Bass-Dannreuther-8.

History. This half eagle motif, designed by John Reich and stylistically related to his Capped Bust half dollar of 1807, was used for several years in the early 1800s. Quantities minted were high, and the coins saw wide circulation.

Striking and Sharpness. The striking usually is quite good and is significantly better than on earlier half eagle types. Adjustment marks are seen only occasionally. On the obverse, check the star centers and the hair details. On the reverse, check the eagle, particularity at the shield and the lower left. Examine the dentils on both sides.

Availability. After 1821 gold coins of this standard no longer circulated, as their bullion value exceeded their face value. Accordingly, they never sustained extensive wear, and nearly all examples are in EF or higher grades (coins used as pocket pieces or jewelry are exceptions). As a type this issue is readily available in grades up to MS-63, although MS-64 and 65 coins are seen on occasion. Most have excellent eye appeal.

VF-20, 30 (Very Fine). *Obverse:* Wear on the portrait has reduced the hair detail, especially to the right of the face and the top of the head, but much can still be seen. *Reverse:* Wear on the eagle is greater, and details of feathers near the shield and near the top of the wings are weak or missing. All other features show wear, but most are fairly sharp. Generally, Capped Bust gold coins at this grade level lack eye appeal.

EF-40, 45 (Extremely Fine). *Obverse:* More wear than at AU is seen on the portrait, the hair, the cap, and the drapery near the clasp. Luster is minimal or nonexistent at EF-40, and may be slight at EF-45. *Reverse:* Wear is more extensive than at AU on the eagle, including the top of the wings, the head, the top of the shield, and the claws. Some traces of luster may be seen, less so at EF-40 than at EF-45.

AU-50, 53, 55, 58 (About Uncirculated). *Obverse:* Light wear is seen on the cheek and the higher-relief areas of the hair and cap. Friction and scattered marks are in the field, ranging from extensive at AU-50 to minimal at AU-58. Luster may be seen in protected areas, minimal at AU-50 but more evident at AU-58. On an AU-58 coin the field retains some luster as well. *Reverse:* The eagle's neck, the top of the wings, the leaves, and the arrowheads show noticeable wear, as do other features. Luster ranges from perhaps 40% remaining in protected areas (at AU-50) to nearly full mint bloom (at AU-58). Often the reverse of this type retains much more luster than the obverse, as the motto, eagle, and lettering protect the surrounding flat areas.

MS-60 to 70 (Mint State). *Obverse:* At MS-60, some abrasion and contact marks are seen on the cheek, the hair below the LIBERTY inscription, and the highest-relief folds of the cap. Luster is present, but may be dull or lifeless, and interrupted in patches. At MS-63, contact marks are few, and abrasion is very light. At MS-64, abrasion is even less. An MS-65 coin has hardly any abrasion, and contact marks are minute. Luster should be full and rich and is often more intense on the obverse. Grades above MS-65 are defined by having fewer marks as perfection is approached. *Reverse:* Comments apply as for the obverse, except that abrasion is most noticeable on the eagle's neck and the highest area of the wings.

| 1808, 8 Over 7 | 1808, Normal Date | 1809, 9 Over 8 | 1810, Small Date | 1810, Large Date |

| Small 5 | Large 5 | Tall 5 |

	Mintage	Cert	Avg	%MS	AU-50	AU-55	AU-58	MS-60	MS-62	MS-63	MS-64		Recent Auction Record
1807	51,605	771	57.2	51	$8,000	$9,500	$11,000	$13,500	$15,500	$26,500	$35,500	(a)	$76,375, MS-65, April 2013
1808, All kinds	55,578												
1808, 8 Over 7		425	56.2	47	9,000	11,500	13,500	18,500	25,000	35,000	65,000		$19,388, MS-61, June 2014
1808		99	55.6	44	8,000	9,500	11,000	13,500	15,500	28,500	35,500	(b)	$25,850, MS-63, March 2013
1809, 9 Over 8	33,875	433	58.1	56	8,000	9,500	10,000	13,500	15,500	28,500	50,000		$51,406, MS-64, January 2014
1810, All kinds	100,287												
1810, Small Date, Small 5		11	54.5	27	90,000	110,000							$18,800, AU-50, January 2014
1810, Small Date, Tall 5		167	57.8	53	8,000	9,500	11,000	14,000	16,000	30,000	55,000		$12,925, MS-62, January 2014
1810, Large Date, Small 5		4	45.3	50	90,000	110,000	145,000	175,000					
1810, Large Date, Large 5		519	57.9	58	8,000	9,500	11,000	13,500	15,500	28,500	40,000	(c)	$32,900, MS-64, January 2014
1811, All kinds	99,581												
1811, Small 5		267	54.6	43	8,000	9,500	11,000	13,500	15,500	28,500	40,000	(c)	$64,625, MS-64, August 2013
1811, Tall 5		99	58.7	56	8,000	9,500	11,000	13,500	15,500	28,500	40,000	(c)	$76,375, MS-65, August 2013
1812	58,087	500	58.7	62	8,000	9,500	11,000	13,500	15,500	28,500	40,000		$61,688, MS-64, August 2013

a. Value in MS-65 is $100,000. b. Value in MS-65 is $127,500. c. Value in MS-65 is $100,000.

CAPPED HEAD TO LEFT
(1813–1834)

Designer John Reich (design modified by William Kneass in 1829); weight 8.75 grams; composition .9167 gold, .0833 silver and copper; diameter 25 mm (reduced to 23.8 mm in 1829); reeded edge.

Bass-Dannreuther-1.

History. Half eagles of this design are divided into issues of 1813 to 1829 (with a larger diameter), and issues of 1829 to 1834 (with a smaller diameter, and smaller letters, dates, and stars). Those dated 1813 to 1815 are in bold relief and sometimes collected as a separate variety.

Striking and Sharpness. On the obverse, check the star centers and the hair details (these details are usually less distinct on the 1829–1834 smaller-diameter coins). On the reverse, check the eagle. Most examples are well struck. Adjustment marks are not often encountered.

Availability. The 1813 and 1814, 4 Over 3, are seen with some frequency and constitute the main supply available for assembling type sets. Other dates range from very rare to extremely rare, with the 1822 topping the list (just three are known, two of which are in the Smithsonian Institution). As gold coins did not circulate after 1821, issues of 1813 to 1820 are usually seen in high-level AU or in MS, and those of the 1820s in MS. The half eagles of the early 1830s are exceptions; these usually show light wear and are much rarer in high-level MS.

EF-40, 45 (Extremely Fine). *Obverse:* More wear than at AU is seen on the portrait, the hair, the cap, and the drapery near the clasp. Luster is minimal or nonexistent at EF-40, and may be slight at EF-45. *Reverse:* Wear is more extensive than at AU on the eagle, including the top of the wings, the head, the top of the shield, and the claws. Some traces of luster may be seen, less so at EF-40 than at EF-45.

AU-50, 53, 55, 58 (About Uncirculated). *Obverse:* Light wear is seen on the cheek and the higher-relief areas of the hair and cap. Friction and scattered marks are in the field, ranging from extensive at AU-50 to

minimal at AU-58. Luster may be seen in protected areas, minimal at AU-50 but more evident at AU-58. On an AU-58 coin the field retains some luster as well. *Reverse:* The eagle's neck, the top of the wings, the leaves, and the arrowheads show noticeable wear, as do other features. Luster ranges from perhaps 40% remaining in protected areas (at AU-50) to nearly full mint bloom (at AU-58). Often the reverse of this type retains much more luster than the obverse, as the motto, eagle, and lettering protect the surrounding flat areas.

MS-60 to 70 (Mint State). *Obverse:* At MS-60, some abrasion and contact marks are seen on the cheek, the

hair below the LIBERTY inscription, and the highest-relief folds of the cap. Luster is present, but may be dull or lifeless, and interrupted in patches. At MS-63, contact marks are few, and abrasion is very light. At MS-64, abrasion is even less. An MS-65 coin has hardly any abrasion, and contact marks are minute. Luster should be full and rich and is often more intense on the obverse. Grades above MS-65 are defined by having fewer marks as perfection is approached. *Reverse:* Comments apply as for the obverse, except that abrasion is most noticeable on the eagle's neck and the highest area of the wings.

1820, Curved-Base 2

1820, Square-Base 2

1820, Small Letters

1820, Large Letters

1825, 5 Over Partial 4

1825, 5 Over 4

1828, 8 Over 7

1829, Large Date
Bass-Dannreuther-1.

1829, Small Date
Bass-Dannreuther-2.

Small 5D

Large 5D

1832, Curved-Base 2, 12-Star Obverse

1832, Curved-Base 2, 13-Star Obverse

1833, Large Date

1833, Small Date

1834, Plain 4

1834, Crosslet 4

	Mintage	Cert	Avg	%MS	AU-50	AU-55	AU-58	MS-60	MS-62	MS-63	MS-64	Recent Auction Record
1813	95,428	703	58.5	58	$10,000	$11,000	$12,500	$15,000	$17,500	$27,500	$40,000	$49,350, MS-64, January 2013
1814, 4 Over 3	15,454	114	59.2	65	10,000	12,000	13,500	16,500	25,000	35,000	55,000	$14,688, AU-58, January 2014
1815 (11 known)	635	7	59.7	57	250,000	300,000	350,000	450,000	550,000	750,000		$460,000, MS-64, January 2009
1818, All kinds	48,588											
1818		82	58.3	54	15,500	18,500	20,000	25,000	30,000	45,000	75,000 (b)	$15,863, AU-50, September 2013
1818, STATESOF one word		22	60.9	68	12,500	15,000	17,500	22,500	30,000	47,500	75,000	$23,500, MS-62, January 2014
1818, 5D Over 50		69	60.5	74	11,000	15,000	18,000	30,000	35,000	75,000	70,000 (c)	$135,125, MS-65, January 2014
1819, All kinds	51,723											
1819		3	53.7	67	70,000	85,000	90,000	130,000				
1819, 5D Over 50		14	57.9	43	65,000	80,000	85,000	125,000		200,000		$67,563, AU-55, January 2014
1820, All kinds	263,806											
1820, Curved-Base 2, Sm Ltrs		4	63.8	100	14,000	20,000	22,500	28,000	32,500	47,500	80,000	$172,500, MS-64, January 2012
1820, Curved-Base 2, Lg Ltrs		6	63.7	100	12,500	17,500	20,000	25,000	27,500	37,500	55,000	$19,975, MS-60, January 2014
1820, Square-Base 2		57	61.2	82	12,500	17,500	20,000	24,000	25,000	35,000	50,000	$31,725, MS-63, January 2014
1821	34,641	16	55.6	38	85,000	110,000	125,000	200,000	250,000	375,000		$141,000, AU-55, January 2014
1822 (3 known)	17,796	1	40.0	0		7,500,000						
1823	14,485	55	57.5	56	20,000	25,000	27,500	35,000	40,000	65,000	85,000	$82,250, MS-64, January 2014
1824	17,340	38	59.9	68	40,000	60,000	70,000	85,000	92,000	125,000	135,000 (d)	$199,750, MS-65, January 2014
1825, 5 Over Partial 4 (e)	29,060	20	59.5	65	37,500	47,500	55,000	67,500	85,000	100,000	125,000	$99,875, MS-61, January 2014
1825, 5 Over 4 (2 known)	*	2	56.5	50	675,000							$690,000, AU-50, July 2008
1826	18,069	18	62.1	83	30,000	40,000	45,000	55,000	65,000	85,000		$763,750, MS-66, January 2014
1827	24,913	28	62.3	89	40,000	50,000	55,000	65,000	75,000	115,000	150,000	$141,000, MS-64, January 2014
1828, 8 Over 7 (5 known)	**	10	60.6	60	100,000	150,000	200,000	250,000	350,000	450,000	650,000	$632,500, MS-64, January 2012
1828	28,029	5	61.6	80	75,000	100,000	125,000	175,000	200,000	300,000	450,000	$499,375, MS-64, April 2013
1829, Large Date	57,442	3	66.0	100				200,000	250,000	400,000		

* Included in number above. ** Included in number below. **a.** Value in MS-65 is $95,000. **b.** Value in MS-65 is $135,000. **c.** Value in MS-65 is $140,000. **d.** Value in MS-65 is $275,000. **e.** Sometimes called 1825, 5 Over 1.

	Mintage	Cert	Avg	%MS	EF-40	AU-50	AU-55	AU-58	MS-60	MS-62	MS-63	Recent Auction Record
1829, Small Date	*	8	62.3	100	$125,000	$165,000	$225,000	$250,000	$300,000	$350,000	$500,000	$431,250, MS-61, January 2012
1830, Small or Large 5 D. (a)	126,351	41	60.5	76	40,000	45,000	52,500	55,000	75,000	80,000	100,000	$73,438, MS-63, January 2014
1831, Small or Large 5 D. (b)	140,594	23	60.3	57	40,000	45,000	52,500	55,000	75,000	80,000	100,000	$82,250, MS-61, January 2014
1832, Curved-Base 2, 12 Stars												
(5 known)	**	3	61.3	67	350,000	450,000						
1832, Square-Base 2, 13 Stars	157,487	30	61.1	73	40,000	45,000	55,000	60,000	70,000	75,000	100,000 (c)	$176,250, MS-65, January 2014
1833, Large Date	193,630	19	57.1	58	40,000	45,000	52,500	55,000	67,500	75,000	100,000 (d)	$29,375, AU-50, April 2014
1833, Small Date (e)	***	9	62.7	89	40,000	45,000	52,500	55,000	70,000	100,000	125,000 (f)	$126,500, MS-63 PQ, May 2006
1834, All kinds	50,141											
1834, Plain 4		47	55.6	45	40,000	45,000	52,500	55,000	70,000	90,000	100,000	$143,750, MS-65, August 2011
1834, Crosslet 4		18	58.3	67	40,000	47,500	57,000	60,000	85,000	110,000	125,000	$45,531, AU-55, January 2014

* Included in "1829, Large Date" mintage. ** Included in number below. *** Included in number above. **a.** The 1830 Small 5 D. is slightly rarer than the Large 5 D. Certified population reports are unclear, and auction-lot catalogers typically do not differentiate between the two varieties. **b.** The 1831 Small 5 D. is estimated to be three to four times rarer than the Large 5 D. Both are extremely rare. **c.** Value in MS-64 is $135,000. **d.** Value in MS-64 is $130,000. **e.** The 1833 Small Date is slightly scarcer than the Large Date. **f.** Value in MS-64 is $150,000.

Proof Capped Head to Left Half Eagles

PF-60 to 70 (Proof). Proof coins were struck on a limited basis for inclusion in sets and for numismatists. All are exceedingly rare. Over the years some prooflike MS pieces have been classified as Proofs.

Obverse and Reverse: PF-60 to 62 coins have extensive hairlines and may have nicks and contact marks. At PF-63, hairlines are prominent, but the mirror surface is very reflective. PF-64 coins have fewer hairlines.

At PF-65, hairlines should be minimal and mostly seen only under magnification. There should be no nicks or marks. PF-66 and higher coins should have no marks or hairlines visible to the unaided eye.

Proof Capped Head to Left Eagle
Bass-Dannreuther-3.

	Est Mintage	Cert	Finest	PF-60	PF-63	PF-64	PF-65	Recent Auction Record
1820, Square-Base 2 (a)	2–3	n/a	n/a	(unique, in the Bass Foundation Collection)				
1821 (2–3 known) (b)	3–5	n/a	n/a	(extremely rare)				
1822 (3 known) (c)	unknown	n/a	n/a	(extremely rare)				
1823 (d)	unknown	n/a	n/a					
1824 (e)	unknown	n/a	n/a					
1825, 5 Over Partial 4 (f)	1–2	n/a	n/a	(unique, in the Smithsonian's National Numismatic Collection)				
1826	2–4	n/a	n/a	(unique, in the Smithsonian's National Numismatic Collection)				
1827 (g)	unknown	n/a	n/a					
1828	1–2	n/a	n/a	(unique, in the Smithsonian's National Numismatic Collection)				
1829, Large Date	2–4			(extremely rare)	$1,400,000			
1829, Small Date (2–3 known) (h)	2–4	1	PF-64	(extremely rare)				
1830 (2 known) (i)	2–4	1	PF-63	(extremely rare)				
1832, Square-Base 2, 13 Stars	2–3	1	PF-64	(extremely rare)				
1833 (4–5 known)	4–6	4	PF-62	(extremely rare)				$977,500, PF-67, January 2005

a. Some experts have questioned the Proof status of this unique piece; the surface of the coin is reflective, but it is not as convincing as other true Proofs of the type. Prior claims that as many as four Proofs exist of this date have not been substantiated. **b.** One is in the Bass Foundation Collection, and another is in the Smithsonian's National Numismatic Collection. **c.** The Proof status of the 1822 half eagles has been questioned. **d.** The only auction references for a Proof 1823 half eagle are from 1885 and 1962. Neither coin (assuming they are not the same specimen) has been examined by today's standards to confirm its Proof status. **e.** No 1824 Proof half eagles are known to exist, despite previous claims that the Smithsonian's Mint collection specimen (actually an MS-62 circulation strike) is a Proof. **f.** The Smithsonian's example is a PF-67 with a mirrored obverse and frosty reverse. A second example, reported to have resided in King Farouk's collection, has not been confirmed. **g.** Two purported 1827 Proofs have been revealed to be circulation strikes: the Smithsonian's example is an MS-64, and the Bass example is prooflike. **h.** One 1829 Proof is in the Bass Foundation Collection, and another of equal quality (PF-66) is in the Smithsonian's National Numismatic Collection. **i.** One 1830 Proof is in the Byron Reed collection at the Durham Museum, Omaha, Nebraska.

CLASSIC HEAD, NO MOTTO ON REVERSE (1834–1838)

Designer William Kneass; weight 8.36 grams; composition (1834–1836) .8992 gold, .1008 silver and copper (1837–1838) .900 gold; diameter 22.5 mm; reeded edge; mints: Philadelphia, Charlotte, Dahlonega.

Breen-6518.

Mintmark is above date.

History. U.S. Mint chief engraver William Kneass based the half eagle's Classic Head design on John Reich's cent of 1808. Minted under the Act of June 28, 1834, the coins' reduced size and weight encouraged circulation over melting or export, and they served American commerce until hoarding became extensive during the Civil War. Accordingly, many show extensive wear.

Striking and Sharpness. On the obverse, weakness is often seen on the higher areas of the hair curls. Also check the star centers. On the reverse, check the rims. The dentils are usually well struck.

Availability. Most coins range from VF to AU or lower grades of MS. Most MS coins are dated 1834. MS-63 and better examples are rare. Good eye appeal can be elusive.

AU-50, 53, 55, 58 (About Uncirculated). *Obverse:* Friction is seen on the higher parts, particularly the cheek and the hair (under magnification) of Miss Liberty. Friction and scattered marks are in the field, ranging from extensive at AU-50 to minimal at AU-58. Luster may be seen in protected areas, minimal at AU-50, more evident at AU-58. On an AU-58 coin the field retains some luster as well. *Reverse:* The eagle's neck, the top of the wings, the leaves, and the arrowheads show noticeable wear, as do other features. Luster ranges from perhaps 40% remaining in protected areas (at AU-50) to nearly full mint bloom (at AU-58). Often the reverse of this type retains much more luster than the obverse.

MS-60 to 70 (Mint State). *Obverse:* At MS-60, some abrasion and contact marks are seen on the portrait, most noticeably on the cheek, as the hair details are complex on this type. Luster is present, but may be dull or lifeless, and interrupted in patches. Many low-level MS coins have grainy surfaces. At MS-63, contact marks are few, and abrasion is very light. Abrasion is even less at MS-64. An MS-65 coin will have hardly any abrasion, and contact marks are minute. Luster should be full and rich and is often more intense on the obverse. Grades above MS-65 are defined by having fewer marks as perfection is approached. *Reverse:* Comments apply as for the obverse, except that abrasion is most noticeable in the field, on the eagle's neck, and on the highest area of the wings. Most MS coins in the marketplace are graded liberally, with slight abrasion on both sides of MS-65 coins.

1834, Plain 4   1834, Crosslet 4

	Mintage	Cert	Avg	%MS	AU-55	AU-58	MS-60	MS-62	MS-63	MS-64	MS-65	Recent Auction Record
1834, Plain 4 (a)	657,460	3,086	50.4	15	$1,900	$2,400	$4,500	$7,000	$10,500	$18,500	$55,000	$21,150, MS-64, April 2013
1834, Crosslet 4	*	172	45.7	10	9,500	15,000	23,500	27,500	55,000	100,000		$22,913, MS-62, April 2013
1835 (a)	371,534	1,055	50.0	13	1,900	2,400	4,500	7,000	11,500	25,000		$21,150, MS-64, March 2014
1836	553,147	1,775	48.9	13	1,900	2,400	4,500	7,000	11,500	25,000	70,000	$16,450, MS-63, February 2013
1837 (a)	207,121	607	50.4	15	2,100	2,600	4,750	9,000	17,000	35,000	95,000	$21,738, MS-63, October 2013
1838	286,588	990	50.5	15	2,050	2,550	4,500	7,000	11,500	25,000	65,000	$5,875, MS-62, March 2013
1838C	17,179	223	40.1	2	22,000	27,500	45,000	65,000	100,000			$10,575, EF-40, August 2013
1838D	20,583	292	46.4	7	17,500	25,000	35,000	50,000	85,000			$21,150, MS-60, January 2014

* Included in number above. **a.** Varieties have either a script 8 or block-style 8 in the date. (See illustrations of similar quarter eagles on page 267.)

Proof Classic Head, No Motto on Reverse Half Eagles

PF-60 to 70 (Proof). Proofs of the Classic Head type were made in small quantities, and today probably only a couple dozen or so survive, most bearing the 1834 date. *Obverse and Reverse:* PF-60 to 62 coins have extensive hairlines and may have nicks and contact marks. At PF-63, hairlines are prominent, but the mirror surface is very reflective. PF-64 coins have fewer hairlines. At PF-65, hairlines should be minimal and mostly seen only under magnification. There should be no nicks or marks. PF-66 and higher coins should have no marks or hairlines visible to the unaided eye.

Proof Classic Head, No Motto on Reverse Half Eagle
Breen-6501, McCloskey-3B.

	Est Mintage	Cert	Finest	PF-60	PF-63	PF-64	PF-65	Recent Auction Record
1834, Plain 4	8–12	8	PF-63	$35,000	$85,000	$135,000	$200,000	$109,250, PF-63Cam, January 2011
1835 *(3–4 known)*	4–6	2	PF-68	40,000	100,000	150,000	250,000	$690,000, PF-67, January 2005
1836 *(3–4 known)*	4–6	4	PF-66	*(extremely rare)*				
1837	4–6	n/a	n/a	*(unique; in the Smithsonian's National Numismatic Collection)*				
1838	2–3	1	PF-65	*(unique, in the Bass Foundation Collection)*				

LIBERTY HEAD
(1839–1908)

Designer Christian Gobrecht; weight 8.359 grams; composition .900 gold, .100 copper (net weight .24187 oz. pure gold); diameter (1839–1840) 22.5 mm, (1840–1866) 21.6 mm; reeded edge; mints: Philadelphia, Charlotte, Dahlonega, Denver, New Orleans, San Francisco, Carson City.

1839, mintmark is above date.

1840–1908, mintmark is below eagle.

History. Christian Gobrecht's Liberty Head half eagle design was introduced in 1839. The mintmark in that year was located on the obverse of branch-mint coins; for all later issues it was relocated to the reverse. The motto IN GOD WE TRUST was added to the reverse in 1866.

Striking and Sharpness. On the obverse, check the highest points of the hair and the star centers. On the reverse, check the eagle's neck, and the area to the lower left of the shield and the lower part of the eagle. Generally, the eagle on the $5 coins is better struck than on those of the $2.50 denomination. Examine the dentils on both sides. Branch-mint coins struck before the Civil War are often lightly struck in areas. San Francisco half eagles are in lower average grades than are those from the Philadelphia Mint, as Philadelphia coins did not circulate at par in the East and Midwest from late December 1861 until December 1878, and thus did not acquire as much wear. Most late 19th- and early 20th-century coins are sharp in all areas; for these issues, tiny copper staining spots can be a problem.

Availability. Early dates and mintmarks are generally scarce to rare in MS and very rare in MS-63 to MS-65, with only a few exceptions. Charlotte and Dahlonega coins are usually EF or AU, or overgraded as low MS, this situation paralleling that seen with quarter eagles. Rarities include 1854-S and several varieties in the 1860s and 1870s. Coins of the 1880s onward generally are seen in higher than average grades.

Note: Values of common-date gold coins have been based on the current bullion price of gold, $1,200 per ounce, and may vary with the prevailing spot price.

AU-50, 53, 55, 58 (About Uncirculated). *Obverse:* Light wear is seen on the face, the hair to the right of the face, and the highest area of the hair bun, more so at AU-50 than at 53 or 55. An AU-58 coin has minimal traces of wear. An AU-50 coin has luster in protected areas among the stars and letters, with little in the open fields or on the portrait. At AU-58, most luster is present in the fields, but is worn away on the highest parts of the motifs. Striking must be taken into consideration, for a lightly struck coin can be AU, but be weak in the central areas. *Reverse:* Abrasion and contact marks are most noticeable on the eagle's neck and to the lower left of the shield. The eagle shows wear in all of the higher areas, as well as the leaves and arrowheads. From 1866 to 1908 the motto IN GOD WE TRUST helped protect the field, with the result that luster is more extensive on this side in comparison to the obverse. Luster ranges from perhaps 50% remaining in protected areas (at AU-50) to nearly full mint bloom (at AU-58).

MS-60 to 70 (Mint State). *Obverse:* At MS-60, some abrasion and contact marks are evident, most notice- ably on the hair to the right of Miss Liberty's forehead and on the jaw. Luster is present, but may be dull or lifeless, and interrupted in patches. At MS-63, contact marks are few, and abrasion is very light. An MS-65 coin has only slight abrasion, and contact marks are so minute as to require magnification. Luster should be full and rich. Grades above MS-65 are defined by having fewer marks as perfection is approached. *Reverse:* Comments apply as for the obverse, except that abrasion and contact marks are most noticeable on the eagle's neck and to the lower left of the shield.

| Small Letters | Large Letters | Small Date | Large Date | 1846-D, High Second D Over D | 1847, Top of Extra 7 Very Low at Border FS-G5-1847-301. |

| 1848-D, D Over D | 1850-C, Normal C | 1850-C, Weak C | 1851-D, Normal D | 1851-D, Weak D | 1854, Doubled-Die Obverse FS-G5-1854-101. |

| 1854-C, Normal C | 1854-C, Weak C | 1854-D, Normal D | 1854-D, Weak D |

| 1873, Close 3 | 1873, Open 3 | 1881, Final 1 Over 0 | 1881, Recut 1881 Over 1881 | 1901-S, Final 1 Over 0 FS-G5-1901S-301. |

	Mintage	Cert	Avg	%MS	AU-55	AU-58	MS-60	MS-62	MS-63	MS-64	MS-65	Recent Auction Record
1839	118,143	385	48.5	14	$1,200	$1,800	$3,750	$13,500	$23,500	$35,000		$41,125, MS-64, January 2014
1839C	17,205	198	43.2	11	9,500	13,000	20,000	28,500	57,500			$23,500, MS-61, January 2014
1839D	18,939	232	42.9	5	10,000	14,000	23,500	40,000				$9,400, AU-53, September 2013
1840 (a)	137,382	498	49.7	8	1,650	2,300	3,250	4,500	10,000	23,000		$4,994, MS-61, March 2013
1840C	18,992	197	44.2	4	7,250	10,000	20,000	35,000	55,000	95,000		$28,200, MS-62, January 2014
1840D	22,896	148	46.9	13	7,500	10,500	14,250	26,000	42,500			$14,100, MS-61, December 2013
1840O (a)	40,120	254	48.8	11	2,500	4,000	9,000	16,000	32,500			$9,988, MS-61, April 2014
1841	15,833	155	52.8	23	1,650	2,500	4,500	6,500	10,250	17,500	$36,000	$1,763, AU-55, December 2013
1841C	21,467	181	46.4	7	6,500	9,500	12,500	25,000	40,000	80,000		$5,581, AU-58, January 2014
1841D	29,392	229	47.2	16	6,500	9,500	12,000	15,000	25,000	75,000		$9,988, MS-61, January 2014
1841O (b)	50											
1842, All kinds	27,578											
1842, Small Letters		40	52.8	20	4,000	7,000	11,000	15,000	22,000	35,000	65,000	$15,275, MS-62, January 2014
1842, Large Letters		53	45.8	2	6,500	8,000	12,500	16,000				$4,113, AU-55, April 2014
1842C, All kinds	27,432											
1842C, Small Date		67	43.8	9	32,500	55,000	70,000	125,000				$49,938, AU-58, January 2014
1842C, Large Date		223	47.4	8	4,750	7,500	14,000	18,500	30,000	47,500		$25,850, MS-63, September 2013

a. Scarce varieties of the 1840 coins have the fine edge-reeding and wide rims of the 1839 issues. This is referred to as the broad-mill variety. b. Official Mint records report 8,350 coins struck at the New Orleans Mint in 1841. However, most—if not all—were actually dated 1840. No 1841-O half eagle has ever appeared on the market.

	Mintage	Cert	Avg	%MS	AU-55	AU-58	MS-60	MS-62	MS-63	MS-64	MS-65	Recent Auction Record
1842D, All kinds	59,608											
1842D, Small Date		319	44.3	5	$5,000	$6,500	$10,500	$17,500	$30,000			$16,450, MS-62, April 2014
1842D, Large Date		95	40.2	3	18,500	25,000	37,500					$7,050, MS-60, January 2014
1842O	16,400	98	41.6	3	13,500	16,000	20,000	30,000				$7,638, AU-53, January 2014
1843	611,205	711	52.5	14	650	800	1,650	3,750	9,500	$17,500	$37,500	$8,813, MS-63, October 2013
1843C	44,277	281	42.7	9	6,000	8,000	9,500	15,000	26,000	55,000		$4,994, AU-55, August 2013
1843D	98,452	450	45.0	7	4,750	6,500	10,000	15,000	21,000	50,000		$19,975, MS-63, April 2013
1843O, Small Letters	19,075	95	46.0	8	4,500	6,250	17,500	26,000	35,000	50,000	65,000	$5,875, AU-58, November 2013
1843O, Large Letters	82,000	175	46.8	10	3,500	4,750	9,500	14,500	25,000	35,000		$19,975, MS-62, January 2014
1844	340,330	475	52.4	14	650	800	1,950	3,500	7,500	18,000	55,000	$14,100, MS-64, January 2014
1844C	23,631	170	43.5	8	7,000	12,000	13,000	25,000	30,000			$4,706, AU-53, March 2014
1844D	88,982	441	44.8	8	4,750	6,500	9,000	12,500	26,000	40,000		$11,163, MS, March 2014
1844O	364,600	959	49.6	9	1,350	2,200	4,000	6,000	12,500	23,500	45,000	$19,975, MS, February 2014
1845	417,099	517	52.5	16	650	850	2,000	4,500	8,000	16,000		$6,171, MS, March 2014
1845D	90,629	524	48.0	8	4,500	7,500	10,000	13,500	22,500	39,000	85,000	$4,700, AU-58, March 2013
1845O	41,000	225	48.9	9	4,750	7,750	9,750	12,500	22,500			$6,463, AU-58, December 2013
1846, All kinds	395,942											
1846, Large Date		325	51.9	14	900	1,250	2,500	3,500	12,500			$12,925, MS-64, April 2014
1846, Small Date		91	55.1	18	1,300	2,250	3,250	3,750	13,000	20,000		$1,528, AU-58, July 2014
1846C	12,995	137	47.3	9	6,500	10,000	13,500	30,000	50,000	85,000		$10,575, MS-60, January 2014
1846D, All kinds	80,294											
1846D (c)		211	45.1	5	4,750	7,000	12,000	17,500				$3,836, EF-45, January 2014
1846D, High Second D Over D		231	48.4	10	5,250	7,500	13,500	18,000	25,500			$21,150, MS-63, January 2014
1846O	58,000	211	48.6	6	4,500	7,250	10,500	15,000	25,000			$9,400, MS-61, January 2014
1847, All kinds	915,981											
1847		1,332	54.4	22	600	775	1,650	3,000	6,500	15,000		$12,925, MS-64, January 2014
1847, Top of Extra 7 Very Low at Border		12	57.7	33	1,100	1,450	2,150	4,500	8,500	13,000		$3,173, MS-62, October 2013
1847C	84,151	461	44.9	6	4,500	7,000	9,500	15,000	25,000	35,000	75,000	$4,406, AU-58, April 2014
1847D	64,405	306	46.6	9	4,500	6,500	8,750	12,000	16,000			$3,819, AU-55, February 2014
1847O	12,000	79	43.0	1	13,500	17,500	27,000					$14,100, AU-53, January 2014
1848	260,775	499	53.0	12	600	850	1,750	3,500	9,000	25,000		$1,058, MS-60, April 2013
1848C	64,472	328	44.1	3	6,750	9,500	15,000	25,000	42,500	67,500		$4,113, EF-45, October 2013
1848D	47,465	239	46.0	6	6,000	9,000	10,500	17,500	25,000			$4,113, AU-55, April 2014
1848D, D Over D	*	15	52.4	13	9,000	13,000	20,000	35,000				$29,900, MS-62, May 2008
1849	133,070	264	52.1	14	850	1,250	2,750	5,500	12,500	15,000		$5,288, MS-61, April 2013
1849C	64,823	395	47.6	11	4,500	7,500	10,000	14,000	23,500	40,000		$5,875, AU-58, December 2013
1849D	39,036	275	47.3	5	4,500	7,500	10,000	17,500	28,500			$5,288, AU-58, April 2013
1850	64,491	206	49.6	7	1,250	1,900	3,000	6,500	12,500	32,000	75,000	$1,028, AU-55, April 2014
1850C	63,591	323	47.5	11	4,500	8,000	9,500	14,000	17,000	38,000		$8,813, MS-61, February 2013
1850C, Weak C (d)	*	55	47.1	7	2,500	3,500						$4,600, MS-61, January 2012
1850D	43,984	256	46.0	3	5,250	8,000	21,000	50,000				$4,553, AU-55, February 2013
1851	377,505	564	54.4	20	600	800	2,500	4,500	9,000	23,000		$2,115, MS-61, June 2013
1851C	49,176	251	45.6	6	4,750	8,000	11,500	24,000	42,500	60,000		$30,550, MS-63, April 2013
1851D	62,710	241	45.9	5	5,500	8,000	12,000	18,000	26,000	45,000		$16,450, MS-62, January 2014
1851D, Weak D (d)	*	12	53.3	33	2,500	3,500						$2,185, AU-50, July 2009
1851O	41,000	213	45.5	4	5,500	8,000	9,500	16,000	20,500	60,000		$6,463, AU-58, June 2013
1852	573,901	1,032	54.6	23	600	775	1,650	3,000	8,000	15,000	27,500	$11,750, MS-64, April 2013
1852C	72,574	430	47.9	16	4,250	5,000	6,000	10,000	18,500	27,500		$28,200, MS-64, August 2013
1852D	91,584	469	46.5	6	5,000	6,500	9,500	16,000	21,000			$5,875, AU-58, February 2014
1853	305,770	744	53.9	20	600	775	1,700	3,500	8,000	15,000	60,000	$4,113, MS-63, September 2013
1853C	65,571	344	46.6	10	4,250	5,000	7,000	12,000	22,500	50,000		$6,463, MS-61, November 2013
1853D	89,678	635	50.0	10	4,500	5,000	6,500	10,500	16,500	55,000		$5,581, AU-58, February 2013
1854	160,675	566	54.4	26	900	1,400	2,000	3,500	8,250	15,000		$9,400, MS-64, June 2013
1854, Doubled-Die Obverse	*	22	53.8	23	1,350	1,850	2,500					$862, AU-50, August 2011
1854C	39,283	189	48.2	10	5,000	7,500	12,000	24,000	30,000			$35,250, MS-63, April 2014
1854C, Weak C (d)	*	53	48.6	11	3,000	4,000						$12,338, MS-63, January 2014

* Included in number above. **c.** The 1846-D half eagle with a normal mintmark actually is rarer than the variety with a boldly repunched D Over D mintmark. The latter is in greater demand, however, because of its dramatic visual appeal; hence its higher market values in some grades. **d.** Several branch-mint half eagles of the early 1850s can exhibit weak (sometimes very weak or almost invisible) mintmarks; such coins generally trade at deep discounts.

Chart continued on next page.

	Mintage	Cert	Avg	%MS	AU-55	AU-58	MS-60	MS-62	MS-63	MS-64	MS-65	Recent Auction Record
1854D	56,413	439	51.3	17	$4,500	$7,500	$8,750	$14,000	$23,500	$42,500	$75,000	$8,813, MS-62, June 2013
1854D, Weak D (d)	*	20	47.5	0	2,500	3,500						$1,998, AU-55, April 2014
1854O	46,000	266	50.2	8	2,250	3,000	6,750	14,000	22,500			$8,225, MS-61, August 2013
1854S (3 known)	268	1	58.0	0	4,000,000		—					
1855	117,098	360	53.4	14	600	825	1,750	3,500	7,500	16,000		$1,410, MS-61, August 2013
1855C	39,788	277	47.1	7	4,500	6,000	12,500	17,500	36,000	65,000		$9,694, MS-61, April 2013
1855D	22,432	180	46.1	5	5,000	8,000	13,500	18,000	38,000			$15,275, MS-61, January 2014
1855O	11,100	123	48.3	6	6,000	8,500	17,000					$10,575, AU-58, March 2014
1855S	61,000	218	47.2	2	4,500	6,000	12,500	22,000				$2,115, AU-53, July 2014
1856	197,990	587	53.1	12	600	825	2,000	3,750	10,500	17,000	42,500	$2,233, MS-61, December 2013
1856C	28,457	250	49.1	8	6,000	9,000	15,000	25,000	45,000			$17,625, MS-62, January 2014
1856D	19,786	214	49.2	19	5,750	7,750	10,000	15,000	30,000	50,000		$12,925, MS-62, January 2014
1856O	10,000	108	47.0	6	6,250	8,500	12,500	18,500				$10,575, MS-60, April 2014
1856S	105,100	262	46.7	5	2,000	3,500	6,000	13,000	23,500	38,000		$4,700, AU-58, January 2014
1857	98,188	463	54.9	18	600	775	1,750	4,000	8,000	16,000		$1,880, MS-61, February 2013
1857C	31,360	316	51.1	12	4,750	6,000	7,500	16,000	26,000			$22,325, MS-63, January 2014
1857D	17,046	217	49.0	10	4,750	7,500	10,000	16,500	28,500			$9,988, MS-61, January 2014
1857O	13,000	145	49.3	4	5,500	7,750	12,000	25,000	42,500			$41,125, MS-63, April 2014
1857S	87,000	224	47.2	7	2,500	4,000	10,500	14,000	20,000			$3,525, AU-58, June 2014
1858	15,136	133	51.7	17	1,250	1,750	3,000	5,000	10,500	14,000	35,000	$52,875, MS-66, April 2013
1858C	38,856	362	49.7	9	4,500	6,000	9,500	20,000	28,500			$9,400, MS-61, August 2013
1858D	15,362	238	50.0	8	5,000	5,750	10,500	20,000	32,500	45,000		$17,625, MS-61, June 2013
1858S	18,600	101	45.6	1	9,500	14,500	25,000					$7,050, AU-55, March 2014
1859	16,734	139	49.1	6	1,350	3,000	5,500	7,500	11,500			$4,700, AU-58, April 2013
1859C	31,847	269	48.4	7	4,750	7,500	11,750	23,000	32,500			$8,225, MS-61, January 2014
1859D	10,366	260	51.1	9	5,000	6,750	12,500	27,000	34,500			$19,975, MS-62, January 2014
1859S	13,220	68	43.9	6	8,500	13,500	23,500	30,000				$8,695, AU-58, October 2013
1860	19,763	165	51.2	5	1,350	2,250	3,250	7,500	13,500	24,000		$4,700, AU-58, January 2014
1860C	14,813	220	50.0	13	6,500	9,000	11,000	15,000	27,500	40,000		$20,124, MS-63, April 2013
1860D	14,635	328	52.1	12	6,750	9,500	13,500	22,500	40,000	75,000		$14,100, MS-62, March 2014
1860S	21,200	88	41.4	2	7,750	9,000	21,500	35,000				$19,975, AU-58, April 2014
1861	688,084	2,188	55.8	22	625	775	1,750	3,500	7,500	11,500	30,000	$32,900, MS-65, January 2014
1861C	6,879	190	49.4	5	16,000	20,000	30,000	45,000	100,000			$25,850, MS-61, January 2014
1861D	1,597	102	49.4	16	55,000	65,000	85,000	115,000	185,000			$99,875, MS-62, January 2014
1861S	18,000	80	38.7	0	9,000	14,000						$11,163, AU-53, March 2014
1862	4,430	68	49.1	3	3,750	6,500	15,000					$17,625, AU-55, April 2013
1862S	9,500	85	38.8	4	20,000	27,500	40,000					$15,275, AU-53, March 2014
1863	2,442	40	49.1	5	10,000	16,000	22,500					$30,550, AU-58, January 2014
1863S	17,000	115	42.0	1	13,500	20,000	28,500					$16,450, AU-55, March 2014
1864	4,170	93	50.2	6	6,500	10,000	14,000					$12,925, AU-55, January 2014
1864S	3,888	25	33.9	4	25,000	45,000						$79,313, EF-45, March 2014
1865	1,270	51	49.2	10	12,500	15,000	18,500					$18,800, AU-53, January 2014
1865S	27,612	133	42.8	5	7,500	13,000	17,500	27,500	40,000	60,000		$8,813, AU-55, March 2014
1866S, No Motto	9,000	115	30.5	0	15,000	21,000	30,000					$14,688, AU-58, March 2014
1866, Motto Above Eagle	6,700	82	50.4	11	4,500	7,500	13,000	25,000	45,000			$34,075, MS-63, February 2013
1866S, Motto Above Eagle	34,920	100	35.8	1	10,000	13,500						$4,994, AU-50, June 2013
1867	6,870	90	48.6	4	4,000	6,000	9,500					$8,813, MS-60, January 2014
1867S	29,000	150	37.0	0	13,000	20,000						$5,581, AU, March 2014
1868	5,700	129	51.7	2	4,750	7,500	10,000	22,500				$16,450, MS-61, April 2013
1868S	52,000	223	43.5	1	4,250	7,500	15,000					$23,500, MS-60, March 2014
1869	1,760	82	50.6	5	4,500	7,500	12,500	21,000	27,000	37,500		$9,400, AU-55, April 2014
1869S	31,000	205	38.8	2	7,000	10,000	20,000	25,000				$17,625, MS-61, July 2014
1870	4,000	107	49.6	2	4,750	7,500	13,500					$8,225, AU-55, January 2014
1870CC	7,675	1	58.0	0	60,000	75,000	115,000					$47,000, AU-53, January 2014
1870S	17,000	119	33.0	3	9,500	13,500	22,500					$7,696, AU-55, January 2014
1871	3,200	379	38.7	2	4,500	6,500	10,000					$15,275, MS-61, September 2013
1871CC	20,770	86	38.9	2	22,500	30,000	50,000	67,500	80,000			$48,469, MS-61, April 2013
1871S	25,000	204	44.6	2	5,500	8,000	11,500					$25,850, MS-61, March 2014
1872	1,660	55	53.2	16	4,250	6,000	10,500	14,000	17,500	22,500		$5,434, AU-58, April 2014

* Included in number above. **d.** Several branch-mint half eagles of the early 1850s can exhibit weak (sometimes very weak or almost invisible) mintmarks; such coins generally trade at deep discounts.

	Mintage	Cert	Avg	%MS	AU-55	AU-58	MS-60	MS-62	MS-63	MS-64	MS-65	Recent Auction Record
1872CC	16,980	156	34.0	0	$25,000	$35,000						$28,200, AU-58, March 2014
1872S	36,400	241	42.0	1	6,000	7,500	$12,000					$2,585, AU-53, February 2013
1873, Close 3	112,480	290	55.8	26	600	825	1,100	$2,500	$6,500	$10,000	$20,000	$5,875, MS-64, December 2013
1873, Open 3	112,505	633	55.8	31	500	525	700	1,350	4,000	6,500	12,500	$5,875, MS-64, September 2013
1873CC	7,416	101	30.7	3	30,000	42,500	65,000	115,000				$21,150, AU-50, January 2013
1873S	31,000	208	39.3	0	4,500	8,000	18,500					$3,173, AU-53, January 2014
1874	3,488	106	50.2	10	3,000	5,000	10,000	15,000	22,500			$4,700, AU-58, January 2014
1874CC	21,198	264	39.4	1	17,000	25,000	35,000	47,500				$21,150, AU-55, May 2013
1874S	16,000	159	39.9	0	6,000	9,000						$4,113, AU, March 2014
1875	200	11	50.4	0	200,000							$211,500, AU-55, April 2014
1875CC	11,828	189	36.3	1	18,000	22,500	45,000	67,500				$17,625, AU-58, January 2014
1875S	9,000	109	42.8	2	8,000	11,500	18,500	25,000				$3,055, AU-50, August 2013
1876	1,432	44	54.3	27	5,500	8,000	10,500	15,000	18,500	25,000	40,000	$19,975, MS-63, March 2013
1876CC	6,887	151	37.6	1	18,000	25,000	40,000					$21,150, AU-58, March 2014
1876S	4,000	52	36.4	2	8,500	13,000						$18,800, AU-58, March 2014
1877	1,132	79	53.9	20	4,500	6,500	12,500	17,500				$7,638, AU-58, April 2014
1877CC	8,680	197	38.6	1	13,500	20,000	40,000	75,000				$11,163, AU-53, July 2014
1877S	26,700	209	43.7	1	3,750	5,000	6,750	11,000		30,000		$1,116, AU-53, March 2014
1878	131,720	677	58.4	48	500	525	600	950	1,750	5,500	12,000	$8,813, MS-65, September 2013
1878CC	9,054	116	39.2	2	30,000	42,500						$47,000, AU-58, March 2014
1878S	144,700	714	56.6	32	500	575	900	1,500	4,000	7,000		$8,225, MS-64, September 2013
1879	301,920	992	58.9	55	450	475	600	700	2,000	4,750	10,000	$5,288, MS-64, August 2013
1879CC	17,281	318	42.9	3	7,500	10,000	22,500					$21,150, MS-60, March 2014
1879S	426,200	1,040	56.7	31	500	600	900	1,500	3,000	6,000	20,000	$5,581, MS-64, April 2014
1880	3,166,400	3,814	59.4	69	450	475	575	625	750	2,000	5,500	$4,700, MS-65, April 2014
1880CC	51,017	542	45.4	4	4,500	6,500	12,500	23,500				$11,750, MS-61, January 2014
1880S	1,348,900	3,072	60.6	80	450	475	575	625	750	1,750	6,000	$4,994, MS-65, February 2014
1881, Final 1 Over 0 (e)	*	201	57.5	51	675	775	1,350	2,000	5,000	10,000		$2,233, MS-63, January 2014
1881, Recut 1881 Over 1881	*	13	62.3	92	535	550	625	700	1,325			$1,528, MS-62, April 2014
1881	5,708,802	20,861	61.2	88	450	475	575	625	750	1,500	4,000	$6,463, MS-66, June 2013
1881CC	13,886	165	42.6	5	11,000	15,000	22,500	37,500	55,000			$32,900, MS-62, May 2013
1881S	969,000	2,860	61.1	85	450	475	575	625	750	1,500	5,000	$3,525, MS-65, November 2013
1882	2,514,520	10,288	61.3	89	450	475	575	625	750	1,500	4,500	$7,638, MS-66, August 2013
1882CC	82,817	886	50.4	5	3,000	4,750	10,000	18,000				$9,400, MS-61, April 2014
1882S	969,000	3,521	61.4	89	450	475	575	625	750	1,600	4,250	$7,344, MS-66, August 2013
1883	233,400	711	60.1	70	450	475	575	625	1,650	2,500	12,500	$17,625, MS-67, February 2013
1883CC	12,598	235	49.0	4	6,000	10,000	18,500	25,000				$16,450, AU-58, March 2014
1883S	83,200	439	57.4	51	450	475	800	1,500	3,250	7,000		$7,050, MS-64, August 2013
1884	191,030	608	58.5	51	450	475	750	1,300	3,000	3,000	9,000	$2,468, MS-64, February 2014
1884CC	16,402	292	48.8	3	6,000	9,000	20,000	27,500				$8,225, AU-58, January 2014
1884S	177,000	752	59.6	68	450	475	575	625	1,800	3,500	10,000	$3,466, MS-64, August 2013
1885	601,440	2,063	61.1	82	450	475	575	625	750	1,250	4,500	$1,528, MS-64, February 2014
1885S	1,211,500	6,427	61.9	92	450	475	575	625	750	1,250	4,000	$2,938, MS-65, January 2014
1886	388,360	964	59.3	60	450	475	575	625	750	1,250	7,000	$5,288, MS-65, June 2013
1886S	3,268,000	11,125	61.3	90	450	475	575	625	750	1,250	4,250	$3,525, MS-65, January 2014
1887S	1,912,000	4,799	60.9	87	450	475	575	625	750	1,500	5,000	$4,700, MS-65, June 2014
1888	18,201	355	59.3	70	450	550	575	1,000	2,250	3,500	7,500	$1,775, MS-63, January 2014
1888S	293,900	572	53.0	20	575	775	900	1,800	4,250			$2,350, MS-64, August 2013
1889	7,520	284	56.5	32	600	750	950	1,800	2,800	6,000		$4,406, MS-63, June 2014
1890	4,240	146	54.4	23	800	1,200	1,750	3,000	7,250	8,500	10,000	$5,581, MS-62, June 2014
1890CC	53,800	1,063	56.9	48	1,100	1,300	1,850	3,500	12,000	17,500	45,000	$5,875, MS-63, February 2013
1891	61,360	607	59.9	69	450	475	575	950	1,750	3,500	6,500	$4,700, MS-64, February 2013
1891CC	208,000	3,208	57.6	52	1,100	1,500	2,750	3,500	5,000	7,500	27,500	$4,406, MS-63, April 2013
1892	753,480	2,721	61.3	88	450	475	575	625	750	1,100	4,000	$3,672, MS-65, January 2014
1892CC	82,968	1,082	53.0	22	1,200	1,500	2,500	3,500	8,500	15,000	30,000	$20,563, MS-64, April 2013
1892O	10,000	81	57.6	49	1,500	2,000	2,750	5,500	11,000	16,000		$8,225, MS-62, December 2013
1892S	298,400	645	57.7	47	450	475	575	950	2,850	4,000	7,500	$2,350, MS-63, April 2013
1893	1,528,120	10,086	61.8	95	450	475	575	625	750	1,000	3,000	$12,338, MS-67, December 2013
1893CC	60,000	968	54.6	26	1,500	1,700	2,500	3,750	10,000	17,500	27,500	$7,050, MS-63, April 2014

* Included in number below. e. The last digit of the date is repunched over the remnants of a zero; this is easily visible with the naked eye, making the 1 Over 0 a popular variety.

Chart continued on next page.

	Mintage	Cert	Avg	%MS	AU-55	AU-58	MS-60	MS-62	MS-63	MS-64	MS-65	Recent Auction Record
1893O	110,000	715	58.1	47	$650	$925	$1,250	$2,200	$6,250	$10,000		$7,638, MS-64, January 2014
1893S	224,000	1,660	60.3	77	450	475	500	625	1,025	2,750	$8,500	$5,875, MS-65, April 2013
1894	957,880	4,199	61.6	94	450	475	500	625	675	1,000	3,000	$7,638, MS-66, April 2014
1894O	16,600	491	56.3	29	800	975	1,500	2,200	7,000			$3,525, MS-62, June 2014
1894S	55,900	323	51.7	12	900	1,200	2,500	3,500	8,500	16,000		$176,250, MS-69, January 2014
1895	1,345,855	10,153	61.5	92	450	475	500	625	685	1,000	3,250	$2,703, MS-65, August 2013
1895S	112,000	474	52.3	9	900	1,200	2,250	2,750	6,000	12,000	23,000	$1,645, MS-61, June 2013
1896	58,960	740	61.6	91	450	475	500	625	675	1,000	3,000	$1,880, MS-64, February 2014
1896S	155,400	627	53.5	22	700	925	1,250	2,500	6,000	8,500	20,000	$15,275, MS-65, December 2013
1897	867,800	5,450	61.4	89	450	475	500	575	675	1,000	3,000	$4,406, MS-65, February 2014
1897S	354,000	703	54.3	21	625	675	900	1,500	5,000	7,500		$1,645, MS-62, July 2014
1898	633,420	3,069	61.3	90	450	475	500	575	675	1,600	3,000	$1,528, MS-64, March 2013
1898S	1,397,400	1,042	58.9	66	450	475	500	575	1,100	2,750	7,500	$5,434, MS-65, June 2014
1899	1,710,630	17,188	62.3	96	450	475	500	575	675	850	3,000	$9,400, MS-67, September 2013
1899S	1,545,000	1,481	59.3	70	450	475	500	575	1,100	1,750	8,500	$4,700, MS, March 2014
1900	1,405,500	22,913	62.0	93	450	475	500	575	675	850	3,000	$5,875, MS-66, September 2013
1900S	329,000	1,113	60.9	78	450	475	500	575	1,100	1,650	9,500	$1,293, MS-64, March 2013
1901	615,900	8,096	61.7	90	450	475	500	575	675	850	3,000	$12,925, MS-67, August 2013
1901S, All kinds	3,648,000											
1901S, Final 1 Over 0		345	60.9	73	500	525	575	700	1,500	2,000	5,500	$1,763, MS-64, August 2013
1901S		12,059	61.9	90	450	475	500	575	675	850	3,000	$25,850, MS-67, August 2013
1902	172,400	2,166	61.8	92	450	475	500	575	675	850	3,000	$30,550, MS-67, July 2014
1902S	939,000	4,560	62.1	91	450	475	500	575	675	850	3,000	$23,500, MS-67, January 2014
1903	226,870	2,647	61.6	90	450	475	500	575	675	850	3,000	$3,819, MS-65, February 2014
1903S	1,855,000	7,465	62.0	92	450	475	500	575	675	850	3,000	$12,375, MS-67, September 2013
1904	392,000	6,093	61.7	90	450	475	500	575	675	850	3,000	$7,050, MS-66, March 2013
1904S	97,000	252	57.5	38	575	700	1,025	1,400	2,750	5,000	8,500	$4,113, MS-64, April 2013
1905	302,200	3,831	61.8	91	450	475	500	575	675	850	3,000	$12,338, MS-67, August 2013
1905S	880,700	1,379	57.1	34	490	525	675	1,025	1,950	3,000	8,000	$4,259, MS-64, March 2014
1906	348,735	4,262	61.8	90	450	475	500	575	675	850	3,000	$14,100, MS-67, November 2013
1906D	320,000	8	61.1	88	450	475	500	575	675	850	3,000	$2,938, MS-65, February 2013
1906S	598,000	4,585	62.0	92	450	475	525	750	1,100	1,750	4,750	$1,880, MS-64, September 2013
1907	626,100	14,564	61.9	93	450	475	500	575	675	850	2,500	$10,575, MS-67, June 2014
1907D	888,000	3	62.0	100	450	475	500	575	675	850	2,500	$2,938, MS-65, April 2014
1908	421,874	17,597	62.2	94	450	475	500	575	675	850	2,500	$51,406, MS-68, April 2014

Proof Liberty Head Half Eagles

PF-60 to 70 (Proof). Proof examples exist in relation to their original mintages, with all issues prior to the 1890s being rare. Cameo contrast is the rule for Proofs prior to 1902. Beginning that year the portrait was polished in the die, although a few years later cameo-contrast coins were again made. *Obverse and Reverse:* PF-60 to 62 coins have extensive hairlines and may have nicks and contact marks. At PF-63, hairlines are prominent, but the mirror surface is very reflective. PF-64 coins have fewer hairlines. At PF-65, hairlines should be minimal and mostly seen only under magnification. There should be no nicks or marks. PF-66 and higher coins should have no marks or hairlines visible to the unaided eye.

Proof Liberty Head Half Eagle

	Est Mintage	Cert	Finest	PF-60	PF-63	PF-64	PF-65	Recent Auction Record
1839 (2–3 known)	2–3	6	PF-63		(extremely rare)			$184,000, PF-61, January 2010
1840	2–3	n/a	n/a		(unique; in the Smithsonian's National Numismatic Collection)			
1841 (2 known) (a)	2–3	1	PF-63		(extremely rare)			
1842, Small Letters (b)	4–6	1	PF-64		(extremely rare)			$172,500, PF-64Cam Star, January 2009

a. One is in the Smithsonian's National Numismatic Collection; the other is ex Eliasberg Collection. b. One is in the Smithsonian's National Numismatic Collection; the other is ex Pittman Collection.

	Mintage	Cert	Finest	PF-60	PF-63	PF-64	PF-65	Recent Auction Record
1843 (4–5 known)	4–8	6	PF-63	(extremely rare)				$34,500, PF-58, August 2009
1843D (c)	unknown	1	PF-65				—	
1844 (2 known) (d)	3–5	1	PF-64	(extremely rare)				
18440 (e)	1	n/a	n/a	(unique)				
1845 (4–5 known)	5–8	6	PF-64	(extremely rare)				$149,500, PF-66UCam, August 2004
1846 (4–5 known) (f)	6–10	1	PF-64	(extremely rare)				$161,000, PF-64Cam, January 2011
1847	2–3	n/a	n/a	(unique; in the Smithsonian's National Numismatic Collection)				
1848 (2 known) (g)	3–5	1	PF-63	(extremely rare)				
1854 (h)	unknown	n/a	n/a					
1857 (2 known)	3–6	1	PF-65	(extremely rare)				$230,000, PF-65Cam, January 2007
1858 (4–5 known) (i)	4–6	5	PF-66	$30,000	—	$100,000	$150,000	$195,500, PF-66UCam Star, March 2006
1859	80	6	PF-63	22,500	$45,000	75,000	125,000	
1860	62	7	PF-64	20,000	37,500	65,000	100,000	$103,500, PF-66Cam Star, January 2012
1861	66	2	PF-65	18,500	35,000	55,000	87,500	
1862	35	13	PF-64	17,000	35,000	55,000	87,500	$92,000, PF-65UCam, August 2011
1863	30	19	PF-64	17,000	35,000	52,500	85,000	$69,000, PF-64DCam, November 2005
1864	50	21	PF-65	15,000	35,000	50,000	77,500	$103,500, PF-65UCam, October 2011
1865	25	23	PF-64	15,000	35,000	50,000	77,500	$86,250, PF-65UCam, April 2012
1866, Motto Above Eagle	30	13	PF-61	12,500	25,000	35,000	60,000	$80,500, PF-66UCam Star, August 2010
1867	50	14	PF-63	12,500	25,000	35,000	60,000	$74,750, PF-66Cam, December 2009
1868	25	10	PF-64	12,500	25,000	35,000	60,000	$69,000, PF-64DCam, June 2008
1869	25	14	PF-63	12,500	25,000	35,000	60,000	$69,000, PF-65Cam, April 2012
1870	35	4	PF-65	12,500	25,000	35,000	60,000	$82,250, PF-64, January 2014
1871	30	7	PF-61	12,500	25,000	35,000	60,000	$65,500, PF-65Cam, January 2008
1872	30	11	PF-63	12,500	22,500	35,000	60,000	$7,188, PF-55, March 2012
1873, Close 3	25	26	PF-64	12,500	22,500	35,000	60,000	$12,338, PF-58, January 2014
1874	20	6	PF-65	12,500	27,500	40,000	65,000	$54,625, PF-65Cam Star, August 2011
1875 (j)	20	14	PF-63	55,000	125,000	175,000	225,000	$176,250, PF-65Cam, January 2014
1876	45	27	PF-64	10,000	20,000	25,000	47,500	$48,469, PF-65Cam, February 2013
1877	20	8	PF-65	10,000	22,500	32,500	57,500	$51,750, PF-63, June 2005
1878	20	12	PF-64	10,000	22,500	32,500	57,500	$31,725, PF-63DCam, June 2014
1879	30	13	PF-64	10,000	22,500	30,000	55,000	$63,250, PF-65Cam, April 2012
1880	36	13	PF-64	8,500	17,500	30,000	52,500	$72,702, PF-67Cam, August 2006
1881	42	17	PF-65	7,500	16,500	25,000	40,000	$37,375, PF-65Cam, January 2011
1882	48	24	PF-64	7,500	15,500	25,000	40,000	$9,085, PF-63Cam, February 2010
1883	61	18	PF-59	7,500	15,500	25,000	40,000	$63,250, PF-66Cam, January 2012
1884	48	18	PF-64	7,500	15,500	25,000	40,000	$39,100, PF-66UCam, November 2010
1885	66	40	PF-64	7,500	15,500	25,000	40,000	$40,250, PF-65DCam, January 2012
1886	72	19	PF-64	7,500	15,500	25,000	40,000	$57,281, PF, March 2014
1887 (Proof only)	87	30	PF-62	40,000	65,000	80,000	115,000	$54,050, PF, August 2013
1888	95	52	PF-64	7,500	13,500	20,000	32,500	$34,500, PF-65DCam, October 2008
1889	45	25	PF-64	7,500	14,000	22,500	35,000	$29,900, PF-65Cam, January 2011
1890	88	49	PF-65	7,000	14,000	22,500	35,000	$24,675, PF-64DCam, January 2014
1891	53	42	PF-64	7,000	13,500	20,000	32,500	$19,550, PF-64DCam, January 2010
1892	92	36	PF-63	7,000	13,500	18,000	32,500	$6,325, PF-62Cam, December 2011
1893	77	50	PF-64	7,000	13,500	18,000	32,500	$70,500, PF, August 2013
1894	75	49	PF-64	6,500	13,500	18,500	32,500	$15,863, PF-64Cam, January 2014
1895	81	48	PF-65	6,000	12,500	18,000	30,000	$6,233, PF-60, February 2014
1896	103	53	PF-64	6,000	12,500	18,000	30,000	$37,375, PF-65DCam, January 2012
1897	83	43	PF-64	6,000	12,500	18,000	30,000	$9,988, PF-63, June 2014
1898	75	72	PF-64	6,000	12,500	18,000	30,000	$31,050, PF-65DCam, January 2012
1899	99	58	PF-64	6,000	12,500	18,000	30,000	$134,550, PF, September 2013
1900	230	126	PF-63	6,000	12,500	18,000	30,000	$35,250, PF-65DCam, September 2013

c. One example of the 1843-D half eagle, probably a presentation strike of some sort, has been certified by NGC as a Specimen (rated Specimen-65). **d.** One is in the Smithsonian's National Numismatic Collection; the other is ex Pittman Collection. **e.** First sold in 1890; pedigree is ex Seavy, Parmelee, Woodin, Newcomer, Farouk, Kosoff; current location unknown. **f.** Of the 20 or so Proof sets made in 1846, experts believe only 4 or 5 contained the year's gold coinage. **g.** One is in the Smithsonian's National Numismatic Collection; the other is ex Pittman Collection. **h.** A complete 1854 Proof set was presented to the sovereign German city of Bremen at the time of issue. The set disappeared almost 100 years later, during World War II. **i.** One example resides in the Smithsonian's National Numismatic Collection, another in the collection of the American Numismatic Society. In recent decades the collections of Eliasberg, Trompeter, and Bass have included examples. **j.** The mintages of only 200 circulation strikes and 20 Proofs for the year 1875 combine to make the Proof a high-demand coin; hence its strong market value.

Chart continued on next page.

	Mintage	Cert	Finest	PF-60	PF-63	PF-64	PF-65	Recent Auction Record
1901	140	95	PF-63	$6,000	$12,500	$18,000	$30,000	$7,762, PF-63, November 2011
1902	162	62	PF-62	6,000	12,500	18,000	30,000	$12,925, PF-64, April 2013
1903	154	117	PF-63	6,000	12,500	18,000	30,000	$66,975, PF, March 2014
1904	136	121	PF-63	6,000	12,500	18,000	30,000	$31,725, PF-66Cam, June 2013
1905	108	75	PF-62	6,000	12,500	18,000	30,000	$23,000, PF-65Cam, October 2010
1906	85	116	PF-63	6,000	12,500	18,000	30,000	$64,625, PF-66Cam, August 2013
1907	92	89	PF-64	6,000	12,500	18,000	30,000	$24,675, PF-65Cam, April 2014

INDIAN HEAD
(1908–1929)

Designer Bela Lyon Pratt; weight 8.359 grams; composition .900 gold, .100 copper (Net weight .24187 oz. pure gold); diameter 21.6 mm; reeded edge; mints: Philadelphia, Denver, New Orleans, San Francisco.

Mintmark is to left of arrows.

History. The Indian Head half eagle made its first appearance in 1908; it was minted continuously through 1916, and again in 1929. Its design elements are in sunken relief, like those of the similar quarter eagle; the mintmark is raised. On most examples the rims are flat, while on others they are slightly raised. These coins saw limited circulation in the West, and were rarely encountered elsewhere.

Striking and Sharpness. Striking varies. Look for weakness on the high parts of the Indian's bonnet and in the feather details in the headdress. On the reverse, check the feathers on the highest area of the wing.

Availability. These coins were not popular with numismatists of the time, who saved very few. Rare issues include the 1909-O, which usually is seen with evidence of circulation (often extensive) and the 1929, most of which are in MS. Luster can range from deeply frosty to grainy. Because the fields are the highest areas of the coin, luster diminished quickly as the coins were circulated or jostled with others in bags.

Note: Values of common-date gold coins have been based on the current bullion price of gold, $1,200 per ounce, and may vary with the prevailing spot price.

AU-50, 53, 55, 58 (About Uncirculated). *Obverse:* Friction on the cheek is very noticeable at AU-50, increasingly less at higher levels to AU-58. The headdress shows light wear, most evident on the ribbon above the forehead and on the garland. Luster is minimal at AU-50 and scattered and incomplete at AU-58. Nicks and contact marks are to be expected. *Reverse:* Friction on the wing and neck is very noticeable at AU-50, increasingly less noticeable at higher levels to 58. Otherwise, the same comments apply as for the obverse.

MS-60 to 70 (Mint State). *Obverse:* At MS-60 to 62, there is abrasion in the field, this representing the highest part of the coin. Abrasion is also evident on the headdress. Marks and, occasionally, a microscopic pin scratch may be seen. At MS-63, there may be some abrasion and some tiny marks. Luster is irregular. At MS-64, abrasion is less. Luster is rich. At MS-65 and above, luster is deep and frosty, with no marks at all visible without magnification at MS-66 and higher. *Reverse:* At MS-60 to 62 there is abrasion in the field, this representing the highest part of the coin. Abrasion is also evident on the eagle's wing. Otherwise, the same comments apply as for the obverse.

	Mintage	Cert	Avg	%MS	AU-55	AU-58	MS-60	MS-62	MS-63	MS-64	MS-65	Recent Auction Record
1908	577,845	12,162	61.3	83	$475	$500	$650	$700	$1,500	$3,500	$12,500	$35,250, MS-67, September 2013
1908D	148,000	5,750	62.2	95	475	500	650	700	1,750	3,500	35,000	$5,170, MS-64, May 2013
1908S	82,000	930	58.5	54	1,350	1,650	2,500	4,500	8,500	10,500	22,500	$47,000, MS-67, November 2013
1909	627,060	9,940	60.5	77	475	500	650	700	1,700	3,500	13,500	$11,163, MS, March 2014
1909D	3,423,560	58,639	61.5	86	475	500	650	700	1,450	2,500	12,000	$7,050, MS-64, March 2013
19090 (a)	34,200	1,472	53.9	13	15,000	24,000	32,500	50,000	85,000	155,000	400,000	$646,250, MS-66, January 2014
1909S	297,200	974	55.7	34	600	750	1,500	3,750	12,500	24,000	55,000	$30,550, MS-64, March 2014
1910	604,000	9,682	60.2	73	475	500	650	700	1,500	3,500	15,000	$7,050, MS-64, October 2013
1910D	193,600	1,987	60.0	75	475	500	650	700	3,750	7,500	35,000	$10,575, MS-64, February 2013
1910S	770,200	1,949	55.6	25	700	900	1,750	3,500	9,500	35,000	65,000	$11,163, MS-63, June 2013

a. Beware spurious "O" mintmark.

	Mintage	Cert	Avg	%MS	AU-55	AU-58	MS-60	MS-62	MS-63	MS-64	MS-65	Recent Auction Record
1911	915,000	16,007	60.3	72	$475	$500	$650	$700	$1,450	$3,500	$12,500	$23,500, MS-65, August 2013
1911D	72,500	1,807	54.9	18	2,500	3,500	10,000	17,500	45,000	65,000	225,000	$27,025, MS-62, August 2013
1911S	1,416,000	4,023	56.7	43	600	700	850	2,500	5,750	14,500	35,000	$32,900, MS-65, May 2013
1912	790,000	16,098	60.7	78	475	500	650	700	1,500	3,500	13,500	$10,575, MS-65, August 2013
1912S	392,000	1,942	55.4	20	700	950	2,500	5,000	15,000	30,000	150,000	$13,513, MS, March 2014
1913	915,901	18,160	60.7	78	475	500	650	700	15,000	3,500	12,500	$9,694, MS-65, February 2014
1913S	408,000	2,448	55.8	26	825	875	2,500	7,500	20,000	40,000	125,000	$35,250, MS-64, August 2013
1914	247,000	4,628	60.7	76	475	500	650	700	1,850	3,500	16,000	$21,150, MS-65, February 2013
1914D	247,000	4,086	60.4	71	475	500	650	700	2,250	5,000	24,000	$7,638, MS-64, April 2013
1914S	263,000	2,090	57.8	41	550	900	1,750	4,500	14,500	45,000	100,000	$12,925, MS, March 2014
1915 (b)	588,000	10,098	60.6	73	475	500	650	700	1,650	3,500	15,000	$16,450, MS, March 2014
1915S	164,000	1,695	56.0	26	750	1,050	2,500	5,500	17,000	45,000	120,000	$47,000, MS-64, December 2013
1916S	240,000	3,040	59.0	55	650	750	1,000	2,500	6,500	11,500	30,000	$18,800, MS-64, November 2013
1929	662,000	530	62.3	91	25,000	30,000	35,000	37,500	50,000	67,500	95,000	$70,500, MS-64, August 2013

b. Pieces dated 1915-D are counterfeit.

Proof Indian Head Half Eagles

PF-60 to 70 (Proof). Sand Blast (also called Matte) Proofs were made in 1908 and from 1911 to 1915, while Satin (also called Roman Finish) Proofs were made in 1909 and 1910. When seen, these are usually in higher Proof grades, PF-64 and above. As a class these are rarer than quarter eagles of the same date and style of finish. Most are in grades from PF-63 upward. At lower levels, coins can show light contact marks. Some microscopic bright flecks may be caused by the sand-blasting process and, although they do not represent handling, usually result in a coin being assigned a slightly lower grade. *Obverse and Reverse:* At PF-60 to 63, there is light abrasion and some contact marks (the lower the grade, the higher the quantity). On Sand Blast Proofs these show up as visually unappealing bright spots. At PF-64 and higher levels, marks are fewer, with magnification needed to see any at PF-65. At PF-66, there should be none at all.

Proof Indian Head Half Eagle
Shown 1.5x actual size.

	Mintage	Cert	Finest	PF-60	PF-63	PF-64	PF-65	Recent Auction Record
1908, Sand Blast Finish	167	147	PF-65	$6,000	$13,000	$18,000	$35,000	$152,750, PF, August 2013
1909, Satin Finish	78	1	PF-67	7,000	13,000	20,000	37,500	$99,875, PF-66, February 2013
1909, Sand Blast Finish *(unique)* **(a)** *unknown*		64	PF-65					
1910, Satin Finish	250	77	PF-65	7,000	13,000	20,000	37,500	$146,250, PF, September 2013
1910, Sand Blast Finish *(unique)* **(b)** *unknown*		1	PF-67					
1911, Sand Blast Finish	139	89	PF-65	6,000	13,000	18,000	35,000	$99,875, PF-67, April 2013
1912, Sand Blast Finish	144	66	PF-66	6,000	13,000	18,000	35,000	$58,750, PF-66, September 2013
1913, Sand Blast Finish	99	49	PF-66	6,000	13,000	18,000	35,000	$51,750, PF-67, July 2011
1914, Sand Blast Finish	125	58	PF-65	6,000	13,000	18,000	35,000	$93,600, PF, September 2013
1915, Sand Blast Finish	75	40	PF-65	6,250	15,000	25,000	45,000	$47,000, PF-66, June 2014

a. Certified by NGC as PF-67. **b.** Part of the unique complete 1910 Sand Blast Finish Proof gold set.

The ten-dollar gold coin, or *eagle,* was first produced in 1795.

The Capped Bust to Right with Small Eagle reverse is the rarest of the early ten-dollar coin types. However, when seen they tend to be in higher grades such as EF, AU, or low levels of Mint State. The Heraldic Eagle reverse issues from 1797 through 1804 are much more readily available and in slightly higher average grade.

The Liberty Head eagles without motto, minted from 1838 through 1865, are elusive in any Mint State grade, although VF and EF pieces are plentiful, and there are enough AU coins to easily satisfy collector demands. Some collectors have considered the 1838 and 1839, 9 Over 8, with the head of Miss Liberty tilted forward in relation to the date, to be a separate date. Eagles with IN GOD WE TRUST on the reverse, from 1866 to 1907, are plentiful in high grades, including choice and gem Mint State. Some of these were repatriated from overseas bank vaults beginning in the second half of the 20th century.

The Saint-Gaudens eagles of 1907 With Periods, existing in the Wire Rim or Rounded Rim varieties, can be collected as a separate type, or not. Most readily available is the Wire Rim style, of which somewhat over 400 probably exist today, nearly all in Mint State, often choice or gem. These coins were made as regular issues but soon became numismatic delicacies for Treasury officials to distribute as they saw fit. Some were to have gone to museums, but in reality most were secretly filtered out through favored coin dealers. Then comes the 1907–1908 style, without periods, easily available in EF, AU, and lower Mint State levels, although gems are elusive.

The final eagle type, the 1908–1933 style with IN GOD WE TRUST on the reverse, is readily obtained in grades from EF through MS-63. Higher-grade pieces are elusive, and when seen are often dated 1932, a year in which 4,463,000 were struck—more than any other coin in the history of the denomination.

FOR THE COLLECTOR AND INVESTOR: GOLD EAGLES AS A SPECIALTY

Collecting ten-dollar gold coins by varieties is unusual, as the series includes so many scarce and rare coins. However, unlike other denominations, none is in the "impossible" category, and with some patience a full set of significant varieties, as listed in this book, can be obtained.

The early issues with Small Eagle reverse from 1795 through 1797, and those with Heraldic Eagle reverse from 1797 through 1804, can be collected and studied by die varieties, with *United States Ten Dollar Gold Eagles 1795–1804,* by Anthony Teraskza, being one useful guide. *Early U.S. Gold Coin Varieties: A Study of Die States 1795–1834* (2006), by John W. Dannreuther and Harry W. Bass Jr., offers an abundance of information and enlarged photographs for study. In addition to the regular issues, a few 1804 *restrike* ten-dollar pieces exist from new 1804-dated dies created in 1834.

Liberty Head eagles from 1838 through 1866 (Without Motto) comprise many scarce dates and mintmarks. Years ago the 1858, of which only 2,521 were minted, was highly acclaimed as a landmark issue, but since then the publicity has faded. In any event, although certain date and mintmark varieties are rare, the number of numismatists collecting them by date sequence is very small, and thus opportunities exist to acquire very elusive pieces at a much smaller proportionate price than would be possible in, say, the gold dollar series. No full set of Mint State early eagles has ever been formed; probably none ever will be. EF and AU are typically the grades of choice, with Mint State pieces added where available.

Later Liberty Head eagles of the 1866–1907 style with motto include some low-mintage issues, but again these are not impossible. The most famous is the 1875 Philadelphia coin, of which just 100 circulation strikes were made. Although smaller numbers exist for Proof-only mintages, in terms of pieces made for commerce, the 1875 sets a record. The low-mintage 1879-O (1,500 made) and 1883-O (800) also have attracted much attention. Again, these pieces, while rare, are available to the specialist, as there is not a great deal of competition.

Among Indian Head eagles the 1907 With Periods style, Wire Rim, is famous, popular, and rare. Examples come on the market with regularity but are expensive due to the attention they attract. The Rounded Rim style is much rarer and when seen is usually in choice Mint State.

The regular without-periods 1907–1908 eagles are easy enough to obtain in Mint State, although gems are elusive. The varieties from 1908 through 1916 include no great rarities, although some are scarcer than others. Not many such pieces were saved at the time they were issued, and, accordingly, gems are elusive. However, grades such as AU and low Mint State will present no problem. Among later eagles, the 1920-S, 1930-S, and 1933 are rarities. In particular the 1920-S is difficult to find in choice and gem Mint State. The 1933 eagle is usually found in Mint State but is expensive due to the publicity given to it. Readily available at reasonable prices are the 1926 and 1932.

RECOMMENDED READING

Akers, David W. *Gold Dollars (and Other Gold Denominations),* Englewood, OH, 1975–1982.
Bowers, Q. David. *United States Gold Coins: An Illustrated History,* Wolfeboro, NH, 1982.
Breen, Walter. *Major Varieties of U.S. Gold Dollars (and Other Gold Denominations),* Chicago, 1964.
Dannreuther, John W., and Bass, Harry W. *Early U.S. Gold Coin Varieties,* Atlanta, GA, 2006.
Fivaz, Bill. *United States Gold Counterfeit Detection Guide,* Atlanta, GA, 2005.
Fivaz, Bill, and Stanton, J.T. *The Cherrypickers' Guide to Rare Die Varieties* (5th ed., vol. II), Atlanta, GA, 2012.
Garrett, Jeff, and Guth, Ron. *Encyclopedia of U. S. Gold Coins, 1795–1933* (2nd ed.), Atlanta, GA, 2008.
Teraskza, Anthony. *United States Ten Dollar Gold Eagles 1795–1804.*

CAPPED BUST TO RIGHT, SMALL EAGLE REVERSE
(1795–1797)

Designer Robert Scot; weight 17.50 grams; composition .9167 gold, .0833 silver and copper; approx. diameter 33 mm; reeded edge.

Bass-Dannreuther-1.

History. Eagles of this style, the first in the denomination, debuted in the autumn of 1795. The obverse features Miss Liberty dressed in a conical cap. The reverse shows a "small" eagle perched on a palm branch and holding a laurel in his beak. The same motif was used on contemporary gold half eagles.

Striking and Sharpness. On the obverse, check the star centers and the hair details. On the reverse, check the feathers of the eagle. In particular, the breast feathers often are weakly struck.

Examine the dentils on both sides. Planchet adjustment marks often are visible, but are not noted by the grading services.

Availability. Typical grades range from EF to AU and low MS. MS-63 and higher coins are rare, and when seen usually are of the 1795 or 1796 dates. Certain varieties are rare. Certain eagles of 1796 have prooflike surfaces and are particularly attractive if in high grades.

EF-40, 45 (Extremely Fine). *Obverse:* Wear is evident all over the portrait, with some loss of detail in the hair to the left of Miss Liberty's face. Excellent detail remains in low-relief areas of the hair, such as the front curl and at the back of her head. The stars show wear, as do the date and letters. Luster, if present at all, is minimal and in protected areas. *Reverse:* Wear is greater than at AU. The breast, neck, and legs of the eagle lack nearly all feather detail. More wear is seen on the edges of the wing. Some traces of luster may be seen, less so at EF-40 than at EF-45.

AU-50, 53, 55, 58 (About Uncirculated). *Obverse:* Light wear is seen on the cheek, the hair immediately to the left of the face, and the cap, more so at AU-50

than at 53 or 55. An AU-58 coin has minimal traces of wear. An AU-50 coin has luster in protected areas among the stars and letters, with little in the open fields or on the portrait. At AU-58, most luster is present in the fields, but is worn away on the highest parts of the motifs. *Reverse:* The eagle shows light wear on the breast and head in particular, but also at the tip of the wing on the left and elsewhere. Luster ranges from perhaps 40% remaining in protected areas (at AU-50) to nearly full mint bloom (at AU-58).

MS-60 to 70 (Mint State). *Obverse:* At MS-60, some abrasion and contact marks are evident, most noticeably on the hair to the left of Miss Liberty's forehead and on the higher-relief areas of the cap. Luster is

present, but may be dull or lifeless, and interrupted in patches. At MS-63, contact marks are few, and abrasion is very light. An MS-65 coin has hardly any abrasion, and contact marks are so minute as to require magnification. Luster should be full and rich. On prooflike coins in any MS grade, abrasion and surface marks are much more noticeable. Coins above MS-65 exist more in theory than in reality for this type—but they do exist, and are defined by having fewer marks as perfection is approached. *Reverse:* Comments apply as for the obverse, except that abrasion and contact marks are most noticeable on the breast and head of the eagle. The field area is mainly protected by the eagle, branch, and lettering.

1795, 13 Leaves   1795, 9 Leaves

	Mintage	Cert	Avg	%MS	EF-40	AU-50	AU-55	AU-58	MS-60	MS-62	MS-63	Recent Auction Record
1795, 13 Leaves Below Eagle	5,583	244	51.3	21	$47,500	$55,000	$70,000	$85,000	$100,000	$150,000	$300,000 (a)	$675,625, MS-65, August 2013
1795, 9 Leaves Below Eagle †	*	24	56.8	42	77,500	120,000	137,500	175,000	220,000	350,000	500,000	$47,000, EF-40, January 2014
1796	4,146	138	54.9	20	55,000	60,000	75,000	95,000	110,000	225,000	350,000	$164,500, MS-62, April 2014
1797, Small Eagle	3,615	50	54.1	20	75,000	115,000	130,000	160,000	215,000	325,000		$76,375, EF-45, February 2014

* Included in number above. † Ranked in the *100 Greatest U.S. Coins* (fourth edition). **a.** Value in MS-64 is $475,000.

CAPPED BUST TO RIGHT, HERALDIC EAGLE REVERSE (1797–1804)

Designer Robert Scot; weight 17.50 grams; composition .9167 gold, .0833 silver and copper; approx. diameter 33 mm; reeded edge.

Bass-Dannreuther-10.

History. Gold eagles of this type combine the previous obverse style with the Heraldic Eagle as used on other silver and gold coins of the era.

Striking and Sharpness. On the obverse, check the star centers and the hair details. On the reverse, check the upper part of the shield, the lower part of the eagle's neck, the eagle's wing, the stars above the eagle, and the clouds. Inspect the dentils on both sides. Planchet adjustment marks can be problematic; these are not identified by the grading services.

Availability. Eagles of 1797 appear in the market with some regularity. Those of 1798 are rare. Usually seen are the issues of 1799 through 1803. Typical grades range from EF to lower MS. MS-62 and higher coins are seen with some frequency and usually are dated 1799 and later. The 1804 is rare in true MS. Sharply struck coins without planchet adjustment marks are in the minority.

VF-20, 30 (Very Fine). *Obverse:* The higher-relief areas of hair are well worn at VF-20, less so at VF-30. *Reverse:* Wear is greater than at EF, including on the shield and wing feathers. The star centers are flat. Other areas have lost detail as well. E PLURIBUS UNUM may be faint in areas, but usually is sharp.

EF-40, 45 (Extremely Fine). *Obverse:* Wear is evident all over the portrait, with some loss of detail in the hair to the left of Miss Liberty's face. Excellent detail remains in low-relief areas of the hair, such as the front curl and at the back of her head. The stars show wear, as do the date and letters. Luster, if present at all, is minimal and in protected areas. *Reverse:* Wear is greater than at AU. The neck lacks some feather detail on its highest points. Feathers have lost some detail near the edges of the wings, and some areas of the horizontal lines in the shield may be blended together. Some traces of luster may be seen, less so at EF-40 than at EF-45. Overall, the reverse appears to be in a slightly higher grade than the obverse.

AU-50, 53, 55, 58 (About Uncirculated). *Obverse:* Light wear is seen on the cheek, the hair immediately to the left of the face, and the cap, more so at AU-50 than at 53 or 55. An AU-58 coin has minimal traces of wear. An AU-50 coin has luster in protected areas among the stars and letters, with little in the open fields or on the portrait. At AU-58, most luster is present in the fields, but is worn away on the highest parts of the motifs. *Reverse:* The eagle's neck, the tips and top of the wings, the clouds, and the tail show noticeable wear, as do other features. Luster ranges from perhaps 40% remaining in protected areas (at AU-50) to nearly full mint bloom (at AU-58). Often the reverse of this type retains much more luster than the obverse.

MS-60 to 70 (Mint State). *Obverse:* At MS-60, some abrasion and contact marks are evident, most noticeably on the hair to the left of Miss Liberty's forehead and on the higher-relief areas of the cap. Luster is present, but may be dull or lifeless, and interrupted in patches. At MS-63, contact marks are few, and abrasion is very light. An MS-65 coin has even less abrasion (most observable in the right field), and contact marks are so minute as to require magnification. Luster should be full and rich. Coins graded above MS-65 are more theoretical than actual for this type—but they do exist, and are defined by having fewer marks as perfection is approached. Gold eagles usually are graded with slightly less strictness than the smaller gold denominations of this design. *Reverse:* Comments apply as for the obverse, except that abrasion and contact marks are most noticeable on the upper part of the eagle and on the clouds. The field area is complex, without much open space, given the stars above the eagle, the arrows and olive branch, and other features. Accordingly, marks are not as noticeable as on the obverse.

1798, 8 Over 7,
9 Stars Left, 4 Right

1798, 8 Over 7,
7 Stars Left, 6 Right

1799, Small
Obverse Stars

1799, Large
Obverse Stars

1803, Small Reverse Stars

1803, Large Reverse Stars

	Mintage	Cert	Avg	%MS	AU-50	AU-55	AU-58	MS-60	MS-62	MS-63	MS-64	Recent Auction Record
1797, Large Eagle	10,940	346	54.0	26	$27,500	$37,500	$42,500	$52,500	$85,000	$125,000	$200,000	$117,500, MS-63, April 2014
1798, 8 Over 7, 9 Stars Left, 4 Right †	900	60	52.9	20	55,000	70,000	90,000	125,000	215,000	300,000		$176,250, MS-62, April 2014
1798, 8 Over 7, 7 Stars Left, 6 Right †	842	12	51.7	33	165,000	195,000	220,000	275,000	325,000			$161,000, AU-55, January 2005
1799, Small Obverse Stars	37,449	165	56.2	39	20,000	23,500	26,000	32,500	42,500	67,500	135,000	$24,675, AU-55, January 2014
1799, Large Obverse Stars	*	472	54.0	33	20,000	23,500	26,000	32,500	42,500	67,500	115,000	$17,625, EF-45, February 2013
1800	5,999	259	55.6	34	21,500	24,500	29,000	35,000	52,500	85,000	140,000	$117,500, MS-64, January 2014
1801	44,344	888	57.0	47	18,500	21,000	25,000	30,000	40,000	65,000	110,000	$88,125, MS-64, March 2013
1803, Small Reverse Stars	15,017	174	55.2	33	21,500	23,500	27,000	36,000	50,000	65,000	135,000	$28,200, MS-61, January 2014
1803, Large Reverse Stars (a)	*	79	59.1	54	21,500	23,500	27,000	36,000	50,000	65,000		$99,875, MS-64, January 2014
1804	3,757	87	56.8	45	50,000	65,000	70,000	85,000	100,000	165,000		$73,438, MS-61, January 2014

* Included in number above. † Ranked in the *100 Greatest U.S. Coins* (fourth edition). **a.** A variety without the tiny 14th star in the cloud is very rare; six or seven examples are known. It does not command a significant premium.

Proof Capped Bust to Right, Heraldic Eagle Reverse Eagles

PF-60 to 70 (Proof). There were no Proofs coined in the era in which this type was issued. Years later, in 1834, the Mint made up new dies with the 1804 date and struck an unknown number of Proofs, perhaps a dozen or so, for inclusion in presentation Proof sets for foreign dignitaries. A handful of these survive today. *Obverse and Reverse:* PF-60 to 62 coins have extensive hairlines and may have nicks and contact marks. At PF-63, hairlines are prominent, but the mirror surface is very reflective.

PF-64 coins have fewer hairlines. At PF-65, hairlines should be minimal and mostly seen only under magnification. There should be no nicks or marks.

Proof Capped Bust to Right,
Heraldic Eagle Reverse Eagle
Bass-Dannreuther-2.

	Est Mintage	Cert	Finest	PF-60	PF-63	PF-64	PF-65	Recent Auction Record
1804, Plain 4, Restrike † *(3–4 known)*	5–8	3	PF-65		$4,000,000	$4,500,000	$5,000,000	

† Ranked in the *100 Greatest U.S. Coins* (fourth edition).

LIBERTY HEAD
(1838–1907)

Designer Christian Gobrecht; weight 16.718 grams; composition .900 gold, .100 copper (net weight: .48375 oz. pure gold); diameter 27 mm; reeded edge; mints: Philadelphia, Carson City, Denver, New Orleans, San Francisco.

No Motto Above Eagle
(1838–1866)

Motto Above Eagle
(1866–1907)

History. Production of the gold eagle, suspended after 1804, started up again in 1838, with the Liberty Head design. Midway through 1839 the style was modified slightly, including in the letters and Miss Liberty's portrait. In 1866 the motto IN GOD WE TRUST was placed on a banner above the eagle's head.

Striking and Sharpness. On the obverse, check the highest points of the hair and the star centers. On the reverse, check the eagle's neck, and the area to the lower left of the shield and the lower part of the eagle. Examine the dentils on both sides. Branch-mint coins issued before the Civil War often are lightly struck in areas, and some Carson City coins of the early 1870s can have areas of lightness. Most late 19th-century and early 20th-century coins are sharp in all areas. Tiny copper staining spots can be a problem for those issues.

Availability. Early dates and mintmarks are generally scarce to rare in MS and very rare in MS-63 and better grades, with only a few exceptions. These were workhorse coins in commerce; VF and EF grades are the rule for dates through the 1870s, and for some dates the finest known grade can be AU. In MS, Liberty Head eagles as a type are rarer than either quarter eagles or half eagles. Some varieties are not known to exist at this level. Eagles of the 1880s onward generally are seen in higher average grades.

Note: Values of common-date gold coins have been based on the current bullion price of gold, $1,200 per ounce, and may vary with the prevailing spot price.

AU-50, 53, 55, 58 (About Uncirculated). *Obverse:* Light wear is seen on the face, the hair to the right of the face, and the highest area of the hair bun, more so at AU-50 than at 53 or 55. An AU-58 coin has minimal traces of wear. An AU-50 coin has luster in protected areas among the stars and letters, with little in the open fields or on the portrait. At AU-58 most luster is present in the fields, but is worn away on the highest parts of the motifs. *Reverse:* The eagle shows wear in all of the higher areas, as well as the leaves and arrowheads. Luster ranges from perhaps 40% remaining in protected areas (at AU-50) to nearly full mint bloom (at AU-58). Often the reverse of this type retains more luster than the obverse.

MS-60 to 70 (Mint State). *Obverse:* At MS-60, some abrasion and contact marks are evident, most noticeably on the hair to the right of Miss Liberty's forehead and on the jaw. Luster is present, but may be dull or lifeless, and interrupted in patches. At MS-63, contact marks are few, and abrasion is very light. An MS-65 coin has hardly any abrasion, and contact marks are so minute as to require magnification. Luster should be full and rich. For most dates, coins graded above MS-65 exist more in theory than in actuality—but they do exist, and are defined by having fewer marks as perfection is approached. *Reverse:* Comments apply as for the obverse, except that abrasion and contact marks are most noticeable on the eagle's neck and to the lower left of the shield.

1839, Large Letters
(Type of 1838)

1839, Small Letters
(Type of 1840)

| 1842, Small Date | 1842, Large Date | 1846-O, 6 Over 5 | 1850, Large Date | 1850, Small Date |

1853, 3 Over 2

1854-O, Large Date

1854-O, Small Date

1865-S, 865 Over
Inverted 186

1889-S, Repunched
Mintmark
FS-G10-1889S-501.

	Mintage	Cert	Avg	%MS	AU-55	AU-58	MS-60	MS-62	MS-63	MS-64	MS-65	Recent Auction Record
1838	7,200	114	45.9	5	$22,500	$35,000	$45,000	$75,000	$125,000			$47,000, AU-58, June 2013
1839, Large Letters (a)	25,801	274	48.2	11	10,500	16,000	35,000	45,000	85,000	$150,000	$350,000	$19,975, MS-60, January 2014
1839, Small Letters	12,447	66	44.5	3	20,000	30,000	45,000	60,000	135,000			$47,000, AU-58, February 2014
1840	47,338	254	47.0	3	2,750	5,500	12,000					$6,463, AU-58, January 2014
1841	63,131	338	47.5	6	2,500	4,250	8,500	17,500				$9,400, MS-61, February 2014
1841O	2,500	103	41.9	0	32,500	45,000						$25,850, AU-53, January 2014
1842, Small Date	18,623	133	49.7	5	3,500	7,500	16,000	25,000	40,000			$16,450, MS-61, July 2014
1842, Large Date	62,884	202	48.0	4	2,750	5,250	15,000	22,500	35,000	80,000	125,000	$2,233, MS-60, January 2014
1842O	27,400	360	46.1	2	8,500	14,000	27,500	45,000	75,000			$8,825, AU-55, March 2014
1843	75,462	280	46.7	1	3,500	5,500	14,000					$4,113, AU-58, January 2014
1843, Doubled Die	*	n/a	n/a	n/a								$748, EF-45, May 2008
1843O	175,162	616	47.7	2	3,250	5,500	12,500	30,000				$6,463, VF-30, July 2014
1844	6,361	66	48.3	3	7,500	10,000	15,000	22,500	50,000			$24,170, AU-55, January 2014
1844O	118,700	569	48.6	4	3,500	8,500	15,000	30,000				$7,931, AU-58, June 2013
1845	26,153	170	46.6	2	2,500	6,000	13,500	22,500				$4,994, AU-55, April 2013
1845O	47,500	384	47.9	4	5,000	8,500	15,000	32,500	50,000			$3,819, AU, March 2014
1846	20,095	157	45.5	4	7,500	12,000	20,000	45,000				$8,225, AU-55, January 2014
1846O, All kinds	81,780											
1846O		190	43.3	2	6,000	8,500	13,500	30,000				$2,820, AU-50, January 2014
1846O, 6 Over 5		66	44.0	2	7,500	10,000	25,000					$3,525, AU-50, January 2014
1847	862,258	1,457	50.6	6	1,150	1,500	3,500	7,500	21,500	45,000		$8,813, AU, March 2014
1847O	571,500	1,291	48.1	2	1,350	2,500	6,000	11,000	21,500	35,000		$1,998, AU-58, March 2013
1848	145,484	453	50.3	8	1,000	1,850	4,750	11,000	22,500	35,000		$4,994, MS-61, February 2013
1848O	35,850	331	47.5	5	6,750	9,500	15,000	22,000	35,000	50,000	85,000	$64,625, MS-63, January 2014
1849	653,618	1,229	49.3	6	1,000	1,750	3,250	8,000	13,500	30,000		$32,900, MS-64, August 2013
1849, Recut 1849 Over 849	*	13	53.8	8	1,250	2,100						$978, EF-40, May 2011
1849O	23,900	176	44.9	2	6,500	11,000	25,000					$5,875, AU-53, October 2013
1850, All kinds	291,451											
1850, Large Date		632	49.0	5	1,100	1,750	4,000	8,000	20,000			$4,406, MS-61, August 2013
1850, Small Date		219	47.5	5	3,000	4,500	8,000	17,500	30,000			$3,819, AU-58, January 2014
1850O	57,500	318	45.4	1	5,500	8,500	20,000					$4,994, AU-55, October 2013
1851	176,328	392	50.3	8	1,100	1,750	4,000	8,500	26,000			$3,819, MS-61, September 2013
1851O	263,000	1,363	49.1	2	2,750	3,750	6,500	10,000	27,500	47,500		$7,638, MS-61, February 2014
1852	263,106	863	51.2	6	1,200	1,500	5,000	9,500				$4,113, AU-55, June 2013
1852O	18,000	181	48.1	2	8,500	15,000	35,000					$18,800, AU, February 2014
1853, All kinds	201,253											
1853, 3 Over 2		218	50.5	1	3,250	7,500						$4,406, AU-58, January 2014
1853		951	52.5	7	1,000	1,500	4,000	7,500	17,000	30,000		$4,553, MS-61, September 2013
1853O	51,000	429	49.4	2	3,000	6,500	15,000					$15,275, AU-58, February 2014
1854	54,250	381	50.9	5	1,500	2,750	6,500	17,500	27,500			$3,290, AU-58, August 2013
1854O, Large Date (b)	52,500	349	49.7	1	3,250	4,500	10,500	25,000				$10,869, MS-60, August 2013
1854O, Small Date (c)	*	173	54.2	12	3,250	4,700	10,500					$1,821, AU-55, August 2013
1854S	123,826	724	48.6	1	3,000	5,500	12,500	22,500				$5,581, AU-58, April 2014
1855	121,701	751	52.9	10	1,200	2,000	4,750	8,000	17,500	35,000		$2,350, AU-58, March 2014
1855O	18,000	180	46.8	1	8,250	12,000	25,000					$17,625, AU-58, January 2014
1855S	9,000	91	43.7	0	8,750	16,500						$17,625, AU-58, March 2014
1856	60,490	508	52.8	10	1,000	1,500	4,000	7,500	15,000	30,000		$2,115, AU-58, April 2014
1856O	14,500	181	47.9	2	8,000	10,000	16,500					$4,406, AU-55, January 2014
1856S	68,000	441	49.7	2	2,500	4,000	9,000	19,500	25,000			$9,988, MS-61, April 2014
1857	16,606	228	48.6	3	3,750	5,500	12,000	25,000				$4,406, AU-58, April 2014
1857O	5,500	125	48.3	0	8,500	15,000						$8,225, AU-55, February 2014
1857S	26,000	138	47.2	6	4,250	6,000	11,500	14,000	25,000			$8,225, AU-58, July 2014
1858 (d)	2,521	73	47.1	7	17,500	25,000	40,000	85,000				$15,275, AU-53, February 2014
1858O	20,000	327	50.3	4	3,500	5,000	9,500	17,500	32,500			$5,288, AU-58, June 2013
1858S	11,800	101	46.7	0	12,000	22,500						$15,275, AU-58, April 2013
1859	16,013	251	48.9	5	2,250	4,000	9,500	25,000	40,000			$47,000, MS-62, April 2014
1859O	2,300	58	48.7	2	37,500	55,000						$28,200, AU-50, December 2013

* Included in number above. **a.** The Large Letters style is also known as the "Type of 1838," because of the distinct style of the 1838 Liberty Head motif. The Small Letters style (or "Type of 1840") was used on subsequent issues. **b.** The Large Date variety was made in error, when the diesinker used a date punch for a silver dollar on the much smaller $10 die. **c.** The Small Date variety is scarce in AU; only three or four MS examples are known, none finer than MS-60. **d.** Beware of fraudulently removed mintmark.

Chart continued on next page.

	Mintage	Cert	Avg	%MS	AU-55	AU-58	MS-60	MS-62	MS-63	MS-64	MS-65	Recent Auction Record
1859S	7,000	79	41.0	1	$20,000	$27,500	$50,000					$28,200, AU-50, February 2014
1860	15,055	238	50.1	8	2,700	3,000	7,500	$13,000	$25,000	$55,000		$70,500, MS-64, February 2013
1860O	11,100	235	49.9	2	5,000	6,500	15,000	35,000				$8,814, AU, March 2014
1860S	5,000	42	44.3	5	30,000	45,000	60,000					$28,200, AU-55, March 2014
1861	113,164	950	52.7	11	2,500	3,500	6,000	8,500	18,500	35,000		$25,850, MS-63, August 2013
1861S	15,500	141	47.1	1	13,500	20,000	45,000					$25,850, AU-58, March 2014
1862	10,960	183	49.7	7	5,000	6,500	16,500	25,000	35,000			$28,200, AU-58, March 2014
1862S	12,500	105	44.5	2	10,000	20,000	40,000					$5,581, EF-35, February 2014
1863	1,218	40	49.0	10	40,000	55,000	75,000					$49,938, AU-53, January 2014
1863S	10,000	67	44.5	4	20,000	35,000	45,000					$32,900, AU-53, February 2014
1864	3,530	41	49.0	15	22,500	27,500	37,500					$28,200, AU-55, January 2014
1864S	2,500	26	37.2	0	125,000							$146,875, AU-53, March 2014
1865	3,980	76	46.9	3	17,500	25,000	45,000			75,000		$18,800, AU-53, January 2014
1865S, All kinds	16,700											
1865S		49	37.2	2	27,500	35,000	60,000					$6,756, F-12, February 2013
1865S, 865 Over Inverted 186		69	38.9	3	20,000	25,000	37,500			150,000		$27,025, AU-53, March 2014
1866S, No Motto	8,500	68	41.4	1	20,000	27,500	55,000					$14,950, EF-45, August 2011
1866, With Motto	3,750	100	46.2	4	8,000	17,500	30,000					$14,100, AU-55, September 2013
1866S, With Motto	11,500	81	45.6	0	10,000	17,500						$15,275, AU-58, March 2014
1867	3,090	120	48.7	3	10,000	20,000	35,000					$30,550, AU-58, August 2013
1867S	9,000	69	41.6	0	14,500	25,000						$9,988, AU-53, June 2013
1868	10,630	277	48.0	1	3,500	6,000	17,500					$15,275, MS-60, June 2013
1868S	13,500	132	47.0	0	5,500	10,000						$18,213, AU-58, July 2014
1869	1,830	74	46.1	4	11,500	15,000	30,000	45,000				$14,100, AU-58, August 2013
1869S	6,430	81	47.0	4	10,000	20,000	30,000					$28,200, AU-58, March 2014
1870	3,990	142	47.0	1	6,000	11,000	18,500					$10,575, AU-55, January 2014
1870CC	5,908	81	39.2	0	150,000							$135,125, AU-55, March 2014
1870S	8,000	122	40.6	1	11,000	15,000	27,500					$12,925, AU-58, March 2014
1871	1,790	78	49.0	1	8,500	15,000	22,500					$15,275, AU-58, September 2013
1871CC	8,085	138	42.3	1	25,000	35,000	75,000					$18,213, AU-55, February 2014
1871S	16,500	152	42.8	0	7,500	12,500						$10,281, AU-58, March 2014
1872	1,620	51	47.5	10	12,000	17,500		30,000				$13,513, AU-55, February 2014
1872CC	4,600	109	41.3	0	40,000	55,000						$47,000, AU, February 2014
1872S	17,300	245	45.3	1	4,250	8,500	17,500					$7,050, AU-58, March 2014
1873	800	34	49.7	3	45,000	55,000	75,000					$55,813, AU-55, January 2014
1873CC	4,543	86	40.2	0	75,000	100,000						$58,750, AU-53, March 2014
1873S	12,000	146	41.7	1	7,000	12,000	20,000					$4,700, AU-53, March 2013
1874	53,140	672	53.8	17	875	925	1,650	3,500	7,500			$1,880, MS-61, June 2014
1874CC	16,767	381	41.4	1	17,500	32,500						$30,550, AU-58, May 2013
1874S	10,000	164	41.5	0	8,500	15,000						$12,338, AU-58, July 2014
1875	100	14	43.3	0	375,000							$211,500, AU-50, February 2014
1875CC	7,715	139	39.2	2	40,000	60,000	80,000	100,000	150,000			$8,225, EF-45, February 2014
1876	687	54	48.7	4	35,000	50,000	75,000					$70,500, AU-58, January 2014
1876CC	4,696	190	40.2	0	35,000	55,000						$14,100, AU-50, October 2013
1876S	5,000	110	42.3	0	10,000	20,000						$22,325, AU-55, October 2013
1877	797	65	51.2	3	15,000	20,000	30,000					$11,163, AU-55, January 2014
1877CC	3,332	87	39.5	0	40,000	65,000						$10,575, EF-45, April 2014
1877S	17,000	295	45.6	1	4,000	11,000	25,000					$22,325, MS-61, January 2014
1878	73,780	686	58.1	48	825	875	1,100	2,250	6,500	10,000		$7,638, MS-64, April 2013
1878CC	3,244	108	42.9	1	40,000	60,000	85,000					$28,200, AU-55, March 2014
1878S	26,100	382	46.0	2	2,500	4,000	11,500	15,000	25,000			$1,763, AU-55, October 2013
1879	384,740	1,493	58.4	52	825	875	1,000	1,500	4,000			$8,225, MS-64, August 2013
1879CC	1,762	76	42.3	1	40,000	55,000						$41,125, AU-50, March 2014
1879O	1,500	91	48.6	1	25,000	40,000	55,000					$88,125, MS-61, June 2014
1879S	224,000	739	56.0	27	825	875	1,150	2,350	7,500			$12,925, MS-64, November 2013
1880	1,644,840	2,990	59.5	75	825	875	950	1,000	2,000	4,500		$19,975, MS-65, August 2013
1880CC	11,190	335	48.9	5	5,000	8,000	17,500	27,500				$2,761, AU-53, August 2013
1880O	9,200	310	49.3	5	3,000	4,500	10,000	17,500				$4,113, EF-40, June 2014
1880S	506,250	1,564	59.9	74	825	875	950	1,000	2,500	8,500		$2,233, MS-63, August 2013

	Mintage	Cert	Avg	%MS	AU-55	AU-58	MS-60	MS-62	MS-63	MS-64	MS-65	Recent Auction Record
1881	3,877,220	16,568	60.7	90	$825	$850	$875	$925	$1,200	$2,500	$10,000	$2,820, MS-64, April 2013
1881CC	24,015	647	51.0	16	2,750	4,000	8,500	15,000				$12,925, MS-62, April 2013
1881O	8,350	267	49.4	6	3,000	5,000	10,000					$12,338, MS-60, January 2014
1881S	970,000	3,633	60.3	85	825	850	875	925	4,000			$999, MS-62, June 2013
1882	2,324,440	18,553	61.0	93	825	850	875	925	1,200	2,500		$3,290, MS-64, January 2014
1882CC	6,764	273	50.7	1	9,500	15,000	23,500	30,000				$25,850, MS-60, July 2014
1882O	10,820	323	50.3	8	2,500	4,000	7,500	20,000	45,000			$30,550, MS-62, January 2014
1882S	132,000	577	60.1	81	825	850	875	925	3,000	9,500		$14,100, MS-64, April 2014
1883	208,700	2,190	61.1	93	825	850	875	925	1,600	4,500		$1,880, MS-63, April 2013
1883CC	12,000	325	46.2	2	7,500	15,000	35,000					$64,625, MS-61, April 2013
1883O	800	45	48.7	2	75,000	100,000	125,000					$70,500, AU-55, February 2014
1883S	38,000	315	54.5	38	825	850	875	3,000	7,500			$11,163, MS-63, February 2013
1884	76,860	650	58.2	44	825	850	875	1,350	4,250	7,500		$823, AU-55, February 2014
1884CC	9,925	335	49.9	4	5,000	10,000	20,000	32,500	55,000			$17,625, AU-58, February 2014
1884S	124,250	890	58.8	62	825	850	875	1,500	4,500			$4,994, MS-63, July 2014
1885	253,462	1,052	60.1	76	825	850	875	925	3,500	6,000	20,000	$1,880, MS-63, October 2013
1885S	228,000	1,516	60.4	83	825	850	875	1,075	1,750	12,000		$4,406, MS-63, August 2013
1886	236,100	3,831	60.6	85	825	850	875	1,075	3,000	5,500		$2,820, MS-63, November 2013
1886S	826,000	2,089	60.5	83	825	850	875	925	1,400	4,500		$3,525, MS-64, April 2013
1887	53,600	1,505	59.9	81	825	850	875	2,000	4,500	8,000		$1,792, MS-62, September 2013
1887S	817,000	1,437	59.7	75	825	850	875	925	2,000	6,000		$8,813, MS-64, April 2013
1888	132,921	834	59.2	69	825	850	875	2,000	6,500			$2,350, MS-62, March 2013
1888O	21,335	2,044	60.5	85	1,000	1,100	1,250	1,750	7,500			$21,150, MS-64, August 2013
1888S	648,700	1,307	60.0	76	825	850	875	1,000	1,600	5,500		$1,528, MS-63, February 2013
1889	4,440	1,334	60.6	86	1,200	1,350	2,500	4,500	10,000			$4,259, MS-61, February 2014
1889S	425,400	1,498	60.4	79	825	850	875	1,000	1,650	4,000		$52,875, MS-65, November 2013
1889S, Repunched Mintmark	*	1	58.0	0	900	975	1,025	1,150	1,850			$1,035, MS-63, August 2006
1890	57,980	549	55.4	36	825	850	875	1,400	4,500	7,500	12,500	$4,113, MS-63, June 2013
1890CC	17,500	688	56.0	35	2,000	2,750	4,000	9,500	20,000			$18,800, MS-63, August 2013
1891	91,820	1,087	60.9	91	825	850	875	1,000	2,500	6,500		$7,344, MS-64, November 2013
1891CC	103,732	4,300	58.1	57	1,850	2,250	2,500	3,500	8,000	17,500		$15,275, MS-63, May 2013
1892	797,480	11,564	61.2	96	825	850	875	925	1,200	2,500	8,000	$6,756, MS-65, October 2013
1892CC	40,000	872	50.9	9	1,850	2,500	4,000	7,500	27,500	40,000		$6,463, MS-61, September 2013
1892O	28,688	1,261	59.8	75	900	975	1,150	2,200	6,000			$7,931, MS-63, February 2013
1892S	115,500	588	59.7	72	825	850	875	1,200	2,600	6,000		$3,055, MS-63, April 2014
1893	1,840,840	48,714	61.6	98	825	850	875	925	1,200	1,800	5,500	$2,234, MS-64, June 2013
1893CC	14,000	399	50.0	6	3,750	5,000	15,000	25,000				$18,800, MS-61, January 2014
1893O	17,000	885	59.8	73	975	1,000	1,200	1,600	5,000			$4,406, AU-58, September 2013
1893S	141,350	1,013	60.0	76	825	850	875	975	2,750	6,000		$2,233, MS-63, September 2013
1894	2,470,735	49,911	61.6	98	825	850	875	925	1,200	1,800	8,500	$7,931, MS-65, August 2013
1894O	107,500	1,207	56.9	37	975	1,000	1,200	2,000	6,000	12,500		$5,288, MS-63, January 2014
1894S	25,000	287	51.2	11	1,100	1,800	3,000	8,000	14,000			$9,988, MS-61, March 2014
1895	567,770	15,368	61.5	97	825	850	875	925	1,200	2,250	12,500	$11,163, MS-65, August 2013
1895O	98,000	1,139	58.6	53	975	1,000	1,200	1,600	6,000	20,000		$9,400, MS-63, February 2013
1895S	49,000	452	49.9	8	900	1,250	2,000	3,500	8,000	20,000		$1,105, AU-55, August 2013
1896	76,270	2,296	61.5	96	825	850	875	925	1,200	3,000	12,000	$2,585, MS-64, September 2013
1896S	123,750	756	53.5	19	875	925	1,750	2,750	8,000			$6,756, MS-63, December 2013
1897	1,000,090	13,663	61.4	95	825	850	875	925	1,200	1,500	7,500	$1,880, MS-64, June 2013
1897O	42,500	653	58.9	53	950	1,000	1,050	1,350	5,000	10,000	25,000	$6,169, MS-63, March 2013
1897S	234,750	612	56.0	33	825	850	875	1,300	4,500	9,000	25,000	$1,293, MS-62, March 2014
1898	812,130	5,659	61.1	91	825	850	875	925	1,200	2,500	6,500	$7,638, MS-65, April 2014
1898S	473,600	770	59.9	80	825	850	875	975	2,750	5,500	12,500	$3,290, MS-63, January 2014
1899	1,262,219	29,599	61.9	97	825	850	875	925	1,200	1,650	3,500	$4,113, MS-65, August 2013
1899O	37,047	422	59.0	53	950	1,000	1,250	1,500	6,000	13,500		$6,463, MS-63, March 2013
1899S	841,000	1,021	59.4	71	825	850	875	1,000	2,000	6,000	12,000	$49,938, MS-67, April 2014
1900	293,840	9,912	62.0	98	825	850	875	925	1,200	1,400	4,500	$3,231, MS-65, February 2014
1900S	81,000	495	55.0	34	825	850	875	1,250	5,500	12,500		$6,169, MS-63, September 2013
1901	1,718,740	36,803	62.2	96	825	850	875	925	1,200	1,400	3,500	$8,226, MS-66, April 2014

* Included in number above.

Chart continued on next page.

	Mintage	Cert	Avg	%MS	AU-55	AU-58	MS-60	MS-62	MS-63	MS-64	MS-65	Recent Auction Record
1901O	72,041	809	60.0	70	$925	$975	$1,250	$1,450	$3,000	$6,000	$15,000	$6,169, MS-64, June 2014
1901S	2,812,750	32,407	62.8	99	825	850	875	925	1,200	1,400	3,500	$7,638, MS, February 2014
1902	82,400	1,240	61.1	88	825	850	875	1,000	2,000	3,500	9,500	$7,344, MS-65, August 2013
1902S	469,500	5,064	62.7	99	825	850	875	925	1,200	1,400	4,000	$8,519, MS-66, February 2014
1903	125,830	1,762	61.4	90	825	850	875	925	1,200	3,250	8,500	$6,463, MS-65, January 2014
1903O	112,771	2,083	60.1	71	925	1,000	1,200	1,350	3,000	6,500	17,500	$5,288, MS-64, April 2014
1903S	538,000	1,856	62.3	92	825	850	875	925	1,200	1,400	3,750	$24,675, MS-67, April 2014
1904	161,930	2,089	61.1	88	825	850	875	925	1,500	3,250	8,500	$3,055, MS-64, September 2013
1904O	108,950	1,224	60.1	70	925	1,000	1,200	1,350	3,000	5,500	17,500	$7,344, MS-64, January 2014
1905	200,992	3,392	61.5	90	825	850	875	925	1,200	2,250	5,500	$31,725, MS-67, October 2013
1905S	369,250	898	56.3	26	825	850	875	2,000	5,000	8,500	20,000	$14,100, MS-64, August 2013
1906	165,420	2,265	61.0	86	825	850	875	1,000	1,750	3,500	9,500	$3,525, MS-64, January 2014
1906D	981,000	6,361	61.3	88	825	850	875	925	1,200	2,000	6,500	$14,100, MS-66, April 2014
1906O	86,895	642	60.1	70	925	1,000	1,100	1,250	4,500	6,500	16,500	$12,925, MS-64, December 2013
1906S	457,000	922	57.7	44	825	850	875	1,150	4,000	6,500	16,500	$12,368, MS-64, April 2014
1907	1,203,899	37,245	61.9	97	825	850	875	925	1,200	1,400	5,500	$4,700, MS-65, January 2014
1907D	1,030,000	1,073	61.3	88	825	850	875	925	1,200	3,500	13,500	$4,700, MS-64, June 2013
1907S	210,500	572	58.3	52	825	850	875	1,150	4,000	7,500	20,000	$9,988, MS-65, March 2014

Proof Liberty Head Eagles

PF-60 to 70 (Proof). Proof coins exist in relation to their original mintages, with all issues prior to the 1890s being very rare. Cameo contrast is the rule for Proofs prior to 1902. Beginning that year the portrait was polished in the die, although a few years later, cameo contrast coins were again made. *Obverse and Reverse:* PF-60 to 62 coins have extensive hairlines and may have nicks and contact marks. At PF-63, hairlines are prominent, but the mirror surface is very reflective. PF-64 coins have fewer hairlines. At PF-65, hairlines should be minimal and mostly seen only under magnification. There should be no nicks or marks. PF-66 and higher coins should have no marks or hairlines visible to the unaided eye.

Proof Liberty Head Eagle

	Est Mintage	Cert	Avg	PF-60	PF-63	PF-64	PF-65	Recent Auction Record
1838 † *(3 known)*	4–6	3	65.0		*(extremely rare)*			$550,000, ChPF, May 1998
1839, Large Letters *(3 known)*	4–6	2	64.0		*(extremely rare)*			$1,610,000, PF-67UCam, January 2007
1840 **(a)**	1–2	n/a	n/a		*(unique; in the Smithsonian's National Numismatic Collection)*			
1841 *(3 known)*	4–6	1	61.0		*(extremely rare)*			
1842, Small Date *(2 known)*	2	n/a	n/a		*(extremely rare)*			
1843 *(5 known)*	6–8	4	62.8		*(extremely rare)*			
1844 *(3–4 known)*	6–8	1	63.0		*(extremely rare)*			
1844O †	1	2	64.5					
1845 *(4–5 known)*	6–8	5	64.0		*(extremely rare)*			$120,750, PF-64, August 1999
1846 *(4 known)*	6–8	3	63.7		*(extremely rare)*			$161,000, PF-64Cam, January 2011
1847	1–2	n/a	n/a		*(unique; in the Smithsonian's National Numismatic Collection)*			
1848 *(2 known)*	3–5	1	64.0		*(extremely rare)*			
1853O **(b)**	1	1	61.0					

† Ranked in the *100 Greatest U.S. Coins* (fourth edition). **a.** It is possible that other 1840 Proof eagles were made, given that duplicates are known of the quarter eagle and half eagle denominations. **b.** Not a true Proof from a technical standpoint, this unique coin has in the past been called a *presentation piece* and a *branch-mint Proof.* "Although the piece does not have the same convincing texture as the 1844-O Proof eagle, it is clearly different from the regular-issue eagles found for the year and mint" (*Encyclopedia of U.S. Gold Coins, 1795–1933,* second edition).

	Mintage	Cert	Avg	PF-60	PF-63	PF-64	PF-65	Recent Auction Record
1854 (c)	unknown	1	55.0					
1855 (d)	unknown	n/a	n/a					
1856 (d)	unknown	n/a	n/a					
1857	2–3	1	66.0					$396,000, PF-66, May 1999
1858 (4–5 known)	4–6	3	64.0		(extremely rare)			
1859	80	4	64.3	$30,000	$75,000	$150,000	$200,000	
1860	50	9	63.8	15,000	50,000	80,000	135,000	$142,175, PF-64DCam, April 2014
1861	69	10	64.1	15,000	45,000	70,000	125,000	$129,250, PF-64Cam, March 2013
1862	35	23	64.0	15,000	42,500	70,000	125,000	$152,750, PF-65DCam, August 2013
1863	30	17	64.2	15,000	42,500	70,000	125,000	$299,000, PF-65DCam, August 2011
1864	50	26	63.6	15,000	42,500	70,000	125,000	$138,000, PF-64UCam, October 2011
1865	25	21	64.0	15,000	42,500	70,000	125,000	$528,750, PF, August 2013
1866	30	13	63.9	10,000	32,500	50,000	85,000	$66,125, PF-64UCam Plus Star, January 2012
1867	50	8	61.9	10,000	32,500	50,000	85,000	$71,875, PF-65Cam, January 2012
1868	25	11	63.7	10,000	32,500	50,000	85,000	$24,150, PF-62Cam, June 2005
1869	25	12	64.3	10,000	32,500	50,000	80,000	$161,000, PF-67UCam Star, February 2012
1870	35	6	64.5	10,000	32,500	50,000	80,000	$97,750, PF-65UCam, January 2010
1871	30	8	63.3	10,000	32,500	50,000	80,000	$76,375, PF-64DCam, August 2013
1872	30	17	64.4	10,000	32,500	50,000	80,000	$48,875, PF-64DCam, June 2012
1873, Close 3	25	15	62.8	12,000	37,500	55,000	85,000	$74,750, PF-65Cam Plus, February 2012
1874	20	3	63.7	12,000	32,500	55,000	85,000	$29,500, PF-64Cam, September 2006
1875	20	14	61.6	100,000	155,000	200,000	275,000	$164,500, PF-50, January 2014
1876	45	37	63.2	10,000	30,000	45,000	75,000	$100,625, PF-65Cam, April 2011
1877	20	5	64.4	10,000	32,500	45,000	75,000	$39,100, PF-64Cam, April 2002
1878	20	8	63.6	10,000	27,500	45,000	75,000	$25,300, PF-63, August 2011
1879	30	4	63.3	9,500	25,000	37,500	65,000	$52,875, PF-65Cam, February 2013
1880	36	15	64.3	8,500	22,500	35,000	60,000	$32,200, PF-64, October 1999
1881	40	9	63.6	8,500	22,500	32,500	55,000	$56,063, PF-65, October 2011
1882	40	14	62.5	8,500	20,000	32,500	55,000	$43,125, PF-65Cam, October 2009
1883	40	19	63.7	8,500	20,000	32,500	55,000	$8,813, PF-60, July 2014
1884	45	15	64.3	8,500	20,000	32,500	55,000	$37,375, PF-64DCam, March 2012
1885	65	22	63.8	7,500	20,000	32,500	52,500	$57,500, PF-66UCam, January 2012
1886	60	15	64.4	7,500	18,500	32,500	52,500	$39,656, PF-64DCam, April 2014
1887	80	25	64.4	7,500	18,500	32,500	52,500	$64,625, PF-65DCam, April 2014
1888	75	23	64.0	7,500	18,500	32,500	52,500	$17,250, PF-63DCam, February 2009
1889	45	9	64.2	7,500	18,000	32,500	52,500	$4,994, PF-60, April 2013
1890	63	43	63.8	7,000	16,500	25,000	47,500	$29,900, PF-64UCam, January 2012
1891	48	41	63.6	7,000	16,500	25,000	47,500	$54,625, PF-65Cam, February 2012
1892	72	36	62.4	7,000	16,500	25,000	47,500	$4,406, PF-55, January 2014
1893	55	27	63.1	7,000	16,500	25,000	47,500	$58,750, PF, March 2014
1894	43	19	63.9	7,000	16,500	25,000	47,500	$105,750, PF-65, January 2014
1895	56	45	64.0	7,000	16,000	25,000	47,500	$51,750, PF-65UCam, January 2012
1896	78	45	64.2	7,000	16,000	25,000	47,500	$89,125, PF-66DCam, April 2012
1897	69	29	62.5	7,000	16,000	25,000	47,500	$19,975, PF, August 2013
1898	67	57	64.5	7,000	16,000	25,000	47,500	$85,188, PF-66DCam, April 2013
1899	86	70	63.9	7,000	15,000	23,500	45,000	$56,400, PF, March 2014
1900	120	88	64.2	7,000	15,000	23,500	45,000	$1,880, PF, February 2014
1901	85	93	63.1	7,000	15,000	23,500	45,000	$48,875, PF-66Cam, January 2012
1902	113	62	63.2	7,000	15,000	23,500	45,000	$61,688, PF-67, February 2013
1903	96	93	63.7	7,000	15,000	23,500	45,000	$39,950, PF, October 2013
1904	108	75	62.1	7,000	15,000	23,500	45,000	$64,625, PF-66Cam, June 2013
1905	86	67	62.6	7,000	15,000	23,500	45,000	$76,050, PF, September 2013
1906	77	70	63.7	7,000	15,000	23,500	45,000	$41,125, PF, February 2013
1907	74	100	63.7	7,000	15,000	23,500	45,000	$33,638, PF-65Cam, March 2012

c. In July 1854 a set of Proof coins was given by the United States to the sovereign German city of Bremen. Various Proof 1854 gold dollars, quarter eagles, and three-dollar gold pieces have come to light, along with a single gold eagle, but the half eagle remains unconfirmed. d. No Proof 1855 or 1856 eagles have been confirmed, but Wayte Raymond claimed to have seen one of each some time prior to 1949.

INDIAN HEAD
(1907–1933)

Designer Augustus Saint-Gaudens; weight 16.718 grams; composition .900 gold, .100 copper (net weight: .48375 oz. pure gold); diameter 27 mm; edge: (1907–1911) 46 raised stars, (1912–1933) 48 raised stars; mints: Philadelphia, Denver, San Francisco.

Mintmark at tip of branch on 1908-D, and left of arrow points thereafter.

History. The Indian Head eagle, designed by sculptor Augustus Saint-Gaudens, was struck from 1907 to 1916, and again in intermittent issues through the 1920s and early 1930s. The motto IN GOD WE TRUST was added to the reverse in July 1908, and remained to the end of the series. These coins were widely used until 1918, in the American West and for export.

Striking and Sharpness. On the obverse, check the hair details and the vanes in the feathers. On the reverse, check the shoulder of the eagle. As well-struck coins are available for all varieties, avoid those that are weakly struck. Luster varies, but is often deeply frosty. On other coins, particularly from 1910 to 1916, it may be grainy.

Availability. The rolled (or round) rim and wire rim 1907 coins, the 1920-S, 1930-S, and the 1933 are the key rarities. Others are generally available. MS-63 and higher coins are generally scarce to rare for the mintmarked issues. This is a very popular series. Most in collectors' hands are coins that were exported in their time, then brought back to America after World War II.

Note: Values of common-date gold coins have been based on the current bullion price of gold, $1,200 per ounce, and may vary with the prevailing spot price.

AU-50, 53, 55, 58 (About Uncirculated). *Obverse:* Light wear is seen on the cheek, the hair to the right of the face, and the headdress, more so at AU-50 coin than at 53 or 55. An AU-58 coin has minimal traces of wear. An AU-50 coin has luster in protected areas among the stars and in the small field area to the right. At AU-58, most luster is present in the fields but is worn away on the highest parts of the Indian. *Reverse:* The eagle's left wing, left leg, neck, and leg show light wear. Luster ranges from perhaps 40% (at AU-50) to nearly full mint bloom (at AU-58).

MS-60 to 70 (Mint State). *Obverse:* At MS-60, some abrasion and contact marks are evident, most noticeably on the hair to the left of Miss Liberty's forehead and in the left field. Luster is present, but may be dull or lifeless, and interrupted in patches. At MS-63, contact marks are few, and abrasion is very light. An MS-65 coin has hardly any abrasion, and contact marks are minute. Luster should be full and rich. Grades above MS-65 are defined by having fewer marks as perfection is approached. *Reverse:* Comments apply as for the obverse, except that abrasion and contact marks are most noticeable on the front of the left wing and in the left field.

No Periods

Periods

**No Motto
(1907–1908)**

**With Motto
(1908–1933)**

	Mintage	Cert	Avg	%MS	AU-58	MS-60	MS-62	MS-63	MS-64	MS-65	MS-66	Recent Auction Record
1907, Wire Rim, Periods	500	479	63.4	95	$27,500	$30,000	$35,000	$45,000	$50,000	$70,000	$115,000	$211,500, MS-67, August 2013
1907, Rounded Rim, Periods												
Before and After												
•E•PLURIBUS•UNUM• † (a)	50	78	63.6	90	70,000	85,000	100,000	150,000	200,000	275,000	325,000	$470,000, MS-67, August 2013
1907, No Periods	239,406	11,559	61.4	81	875	1,150	2,000	3,500	5,750	9,500	14,000	$176,250, MS-68, August 2013
1908, No Motto	33,500	1,410	60.6	72	1,000	1,500	2,750	5,750	7,500	17,500	25,000	$105,750, MS-67, August 2013
1908D, No Motto	210,000	7,788	60.8	77	875	1,275	2,800	7,500	16,500	35,000	90,000	$82,250, MS-66, August 2013
1908, With Motto	341,370	1,551	59.3	52	875	1,100	1,500	2,500	4,500	11,500	15,000	$58,750, MS-68, August 2013
1908D, With Motto	836,500	1,325	59.1	58	875	1,150	2,750	7,750	15,000	26,000	40,000	$70,500, MS-67, August 2013
1908S	59,850	1,295	54.7	29	1,500	3,500	7,500	15,000	17,500	25,000	35,000	$182,125, MS-69, August 2013
1909	184,789	3,589	60.2	68	875	1,100	1,750	4,750	9,000	15,000	32,500	$28,200, MS-66, August 2013

† Ranked in the *100 Greatest U.S. Coins* (fourth edition). **a.** All but 50 of the 31,500 were melted at the mint.

	Mintage	Cert	Avg	%MS	AU-58	MS-60	MS-62	MS-63	MS-64	MS-65	MS-66	Recent Auction Record
1909D	121,540	2,000	59.5	61	$1,200	$1,500	$4,500	$7,500	$20,000	$32,500	$47,500	$105,750, MS-67, August 2013
1909S	292,350	1,352	57.2	40	875	1,250	4,250	8,000	10,000	17,500	27,500	$64,625, MS-67, August 2013
1910	318,500	9,834	61.4	85	875	1,000	1,100	1,550	2,750	9,500	16,000	$44,063, MS-67, August 2013
1910D	2,356,640	19,765	61.5	86	875	1,000	1,050	1,500	2,500	8,000	16,000	$52,875, MS-67, August 2013
1910S	811,000	2,925	56.5	34	875	1,200	3,750	10,500	17,500	50,000	85,000	$82,250, MS-66, August 2013
1911	505,500	16,188	61.3	83	875	1,000	1,050	1,500	2,500	7,500	15,000	$94,000, MS-68, August 2013
1911D	30,100	1,432	54.6	21	6,000	12,500	17,500	50,000	75,000	175,000		$67,563, MS-64, August 2013
1911S	51,000	594	57.2	37	1,200	1,750	6,000	12,500	14,000	20,000	45,000	$44,063, MS-66, August 2013
1912	405,000	11,024	61.2	83	875	1,000	1,100	1,500	3,000	11,000	18,000	$23,500, MS-66, August 2013
1912S	300,000	1,742	57.3	36	950	1,250	5,000	11,000	14,000	40,000	120,000	$64,625, MS-65, August 2013
1913	442,000	9,779	61.0	79	875	1,000	1,100	1,500	2,750	10,000	20,000	$25,850, MS-66, November 2013
1913S	66,000	1,421	54.7	17	2,750	10,000	14,000	40,000	57,500	100,000		$44,063, MS-64, August 2013
1914	151,000	3,871	61.1	80	875	1,000	1,050	2,500	4,500	11,000	22,000	$35,250, MS-67, August 2013
1914D	343,500	4,766	60.6	72	875	1,000	1,100	2,400	4,500	15,000	21,000	$30,550, MS-67, August 2013
1914S	208,000	1,653	58.9	50	875	1,250	3,750	10,000	15,000	30,000		$30,550, MS-65, August 2013
1915	351,000	7,128	60.9	76	875	1,000	1,150	2,200	3,500	10,000	20,000	$30,550, MS-67, August 2013
1915S	59,000	685	57.7	35	1,950	4,750	9,500	22,000	35,000	65,000	125,000	$99,875, MS-66, August 2013
1916S	138,500	1,550	59.4	56	975	1,250	2,900	8,000	12,500	25,000	50,000	$111,625, MS-67, August 2013
1920S	126,500	104	58.1	50	27,500	55,000	70,000	110,000	150,000	225,000	375,000	$199,750, MS-65, August 2013
1926	1,014,000	63,589	62.4	99	875	925	975	1,150	1,500	3,250	10,000	$9,400, MS-66, August 2013
1930S	96,000	169	63.5	94	20,000	35,000	40,000	55,000	65,000	75,000	95,000	$70,500, MS-64, March 2014
1932	4,463,000	95,401	62.8	99	875	925	975	1,150	1,500	3,250	12,500	$28,200, MS-67, August 2013
1933 † (b)	312,500	35	64.2	100	200,000	275,000	325,000	400,000	450,000	600,000		$367,188, MS-64, August 2013

† Ranked in the *100 Greatest U.S. Coins* (fourth edition). **b.** Nearly all were melted at the mint.

Proof Indian Head Eagles

PF-60 to 70 (Proof). Sand Blast (also called Matte) Proofs were made each year from 1907 through 1915. These have dull surfaces, much like fine-grained sandpaper. Satin (also called Roman Finish) Proofs were made in 1908, 1909, and 1910; they have satiny surfaces and are bright yellow. All are rare today. *Obverse and Reverse:* At PF-60 to 63, there is light abrasion and some contact marks (the lower the grade, the higher the quantity). On Sand Blast Proofs these show up as visually unappeal-ing bright spots. At PF-64 and higher levels, marks are fewer, with magnification needed to see any at PF-65. At PF-66, there should be none at all.

Proof Indian Head Eagle

	Mintage	Cert	Avg	PF-60	PF-63	PF-64	PF-65	Recent Auction Record
1907, Wire Rim, Periods, Plain Edge *(1–2 known)* **(a)** *unknown*		n/a	n/a					$359,375, PF-62, August 2010
1907, Rounded Rim, Periods, Satin Finish	*unknown*	2	67.0		(extremely rare)			$2,185,000, PF-67, January 2011
1907, Matte *(2–3 known)*	*unknown*	1	64.0		(extremely rare)			
1908, Matte	116	35	64.6	$7,500	$16,500	$25,000	$50,000	$69,000, PF-66, January 2012
1908, Satin Finish *(3–4 known)*	*	4	64.0		(extremely rare)			
1909, Satin Finish	74	83	64.6	8,000	17,500	25,000	55,000	$48,875, PF-65, July 2011
1909, Matte *(2–3 known)*	*	n/a	n/a		(extremely rare)			
1910, Satin Finish	204	n/a	n/a	8,000	17,500	30,000	65,000	$80,500, PF-67, January 2012
1910, Matte **(b)**	*	1	66.0					
1911	95	47	65.4	7,000	16,000	24,000	50,000	$152,750, PF-67, November 2013
1912	83	45	65.4	7,000	16,000	24,000	50,000	$99,875, PF, March 2014
1913	71	43	65.3	7,000	16,000	24,000	50,000	$63,250, PF-66, January 2012
1914	50	50	65.0	7,000	16,000	24,000	50,000	$96,938, PF, October 2013
1915	75	36	65.0	7,000	17,500	25,000	55,000	$94,000, PF, August 2013

* Included in number above. **a.** According to the *Encyclopedia of U.S. Gold Goins, 1795–1933*, the confirmed example of this rarity may be from the Capt. North set of 1907 and 1908 gold coins sold by Stack's in the 1970s. **b.** Part of the unique complete 1910 Matte Proof gold set.

The double eagle, or twenty-dollar coin—the largest denomination of all regular U.S. coinage issues—was authorized by the Act of March 3, 1849, in response to the huge amounts of gold coming from California.

Many gold collectors form a type set of the six major double eagle designs (with the 1861 Paquet added as a sub-type if desired). Double eagles are at once large and impressive to own. Thanks to overseas hoards repatriated since the 1950s, finding choice and gem Mint State examples is no problem at all for the later types.

The first double-eagle type, that of 1850–1866, is generally available in grades from VF up. Mint State pieces, while elusive, were greatly augmented by more than 5,000 pieces—including some gems— found in the discovery of the long-lost treasure ship SS *Central America*. The SS *Brother Jonathan*, lost at sea in 1865, was recovered and yielded hundreds of Mint State 1865-S double eagles, and some dated 1864 and a few earlier. The salvaged wreck of the SS *Republic*, lost in 1865 while on a voyage from New York City to New Orleans, has also yielded some very attractive Mint State double eagles of this first type.

The type from 1866 through 1876, with the motto IN GOD WE TRUST above the eagle and with the denomination expressed as TWENTY D., is the rarest in MS-63 and higher grades. Many EF and AU coins have been repatriated from overseas holdings, as have quite a few in such grades as MS-60 through MS-62. However, true gems are hardly ever seen.

Liberty Head double eagles of the 1877–1907 type with motto and with the denomination as TWENTY DOLLARS are exceedingly plentiful in just about any grade desired, with gems being available of certain issues of the early 20th century. While it is easy to obtain a gem of a common date, some collectors of type coins have opted to add a coin of special historical interest, such as a Carson City issue.

The famous MCMVII High Relief double eagle of 1907 was saved in quantity by the general public as well as by numismatists, and today it is likely that at least 5,000 to 6,000 exist, representing about half of the mintage. Most of these are in varying degrees of Mint State, with quite a few listed as MS-64 and MS-65. Lower grades such as VF and EF were often used for jewelry or polished, or have other problems. This particular design is a great favorite with collectors, and although the coins are not rarities, they are hardly inexpensive.

The so-called Arabic Numerals 1907–1908 Saint-Gaudens design is available in nearly any grade desired, with MS-60 through MS-63 or MS-64 pieces being plentiful and inexpensive. Double eagles of the final type, 1908–1933, are abundant in any grade desired, with choice and gem coins being plentiful.

FOR THE COLLECTOR AND INVESTOR: GOLD DOUBLE EAGLES AS A SPECIALTY

Collecting double eagles by date and mint is more popular than one might think. Offhand, it would seem that these high denominations, laden with a number of rare dates, would attract few enthusiasts. However, over a long period of years more people have specialized in double eagles than have specialized in five-dollar or ten-dollar pieces.

Two particularly notable collections of double eagles by date and mint, from the earliest times to the latest, were formed by Louis E. Eliasberg of Baltimore, and Jeff Browning of Dallas. Both have been dispersed across the auction block. The first was cataloged by Bowers and Ruddy in 1982, and the second was offered by Stack's and Sotheby's in 2001. In addition, dozens of other collections over the years have had large numbers of double eagles, some specializing in the Liberty Head type of 1850–1907, others only with the Saint-Gaudens type from 1907 onward, and others addressing the entire range.

Among rarities in the double eagle series are the 1854-O and 1856-O, each known only to the extent of a few dozen pieces; the 1861 Philadelphia Mint coins with Paquet reverse (two known); the Proof-only issues of 1883, 1884, and 1887; several other low-mintage varieties of this era; the famous Carson City issue of 1870-CC; and various issues from 1920 onward, including 1920-S, 1921, mintmarks after 1923, and all dates after 1928. Punctuating these rarities are a number of readily available pieces, including the very common Philadelphia issues from 1922 through 1928 inclusive.

RECOMMENDED READING

Akers, David W. *Gold Dollars (and Other Gold Denominations)*, Englewood, OH, 1975–1982.

Bowers, Q. David. *A Guide Book of Double Eagle Gold Coins*, Atlanta, GA, 2004.

Bowers, Q. David. *United States Gold Coins: An Illustrated History*, Wolfeboro, NH, 1982.

Bowers, Q. David. *U.S. Liberty Head $20 Double Eagles: The Gilded Age of Coinage*, Irvine, CA, 2014.

Fivaz, Bill. *United States Gold Counterfeit Detection Guide*, Atlanta, GA, 2005.

Fivaz, Bill, and Stanton, J.T. *The Cherrypickers' Guide to Rare Die Varieties* (5th ed., vol. II), Atlanta, GA, 2012.

Garrett, Jeff, and Guth, Ron. *Encyclopedia of U.S. Gold Coins, 1795–1933* (2nd ed.), Atlanta, GA, 2008.

Moran, Michael. *Striking Change: The Great Artistic Collaboration of Theodore Roosevelt and Augustus Saint-Gaudens*, Atlanta, GA, 2008.

LIBERTY HEAD
(1849–1907)

Designer James B. Longacre; weight 33.436 grams; composition .900 gold, .100 copper (net weight: .96750 oz. pure gold); diameter 34 mm; reeded edge; mints: Philadelphia, Carson City, Denver, New Orleans, San Francisco.

Mintmark is below eagle.

History. The $20 denomination was introduced to circulation in 1850 (a unique pattern that currently resides in the Smithsonian was minted in 1849). The large new coin was ideal for converting the flood of California Gold Rush bullion into federal legal tender. U.S. Mint chief engraver James B. Longacre designed the coin. In 1866 the motto IN GOD WE TRUST was added to the reverse. In 1877 the denomination on the reverse, formerly given as TWENTY D., was changed to TWENTY DOLLARS. The double eagle denomination proved to be very popular, especially for export. By 1933, more than 75% of the American gold used to strike coins from the early days onward had been used to make double eagles. Oddly, all the coins of 1850–1858 have the word LIBERTY misspelled as LLBERTY

Striking and Sharpness. On the obverse, check the star centers and the hair details. As made, the hair details are less distinct on many coins of 1859 (when a slight modification was made) through the 1890s, and knowledge of this is important. Later issues usually have exquisite detail. The reverse usually is well struck, but check the eagle and other features. The dentils are sharp on nearly all coins, but should be checked.

Availability. Basic dates and mintmarks are available in proportion to their mintages. The 1854-O, 1856-O, 1861 and 1861-S Paquet Reverse, 1866 No Motto, 1870-CC, 1879-O, and several Philadelphia Mint dates of the 1880s are key issues, but the vast majority of others are readily collectible. Among early coins, MS examples from about 1854 to 1857 are available, most notably the 1857-S and certain varieties of the 1860s. Most varieties of the 1880s onward, and particularly the 1890s and 1900s, are easily available in MS, due to the repatriation of millions of coins that had been exported.

Note: Values of common-date gold coins have been based on the current bullion price of gold, $1,200 per ounce, and may vary with the prevailing spot price.

AU-50, 53, 55, 58 (About Uncirculated). *Obverse:* Light wear is seen on the face, the hair to the right of the face, and the highest area of the hair behind the coronet, more so at AU-50 than at 53 or 55. An AU-58 coin has minimal traces of wear. An AU-50 coin has luster in protected areas among the stars and letters, with little in the open fields or on the portrait. At AU-58 most luster is present in the fields, but is worn away on the highest parts of the motifs. *Reverse:* The eagle and ornaments show wear in all of the higher areas. Luster ranges from perhaps 40% remaining in protected areas (at AU-50) to nearly full mint bloom (at AU-58). Often the reverse of this type retains more luster than the obverse.

MS-60 to 70 (Mint State). *Obverse:* At MS-60, some abrasion and contact marks are evident, most noticeably on the hair to the right of Miss Liberty's forehead and on the cheek. Luster is present, but may be dull or lifeless, and interrupted in patches. At MS-63, contact marks are few, and abrasion is light. An MS-65 coin has little abrasion, and contact marks are minute. Luster should be full and rich. Grades above MS-65 are defined by having fewer marks as perfection is approached. *Reverse:* Comments apply as for the obverse, except that abrasion and contact marks are most noticeable on eagle's neck, wingtips, and tail.

1853, So-called 3 Over 2
Note rust under LIBERTY.
FS-G20-1853-301.

1854, Small Date

1854, Large Date

1861-S, Normal Reverse

1861-S, Paquet Reverse
Note taller letters.

No Motto On Reverse

With Motto

1866, Doubled-Die Reverse
FS-G20-1866-801.

Open 3

Close 3

Value TWENTY D.
(1866–1876)

Value TWENTY DOLLARS
(1877–1907)

1888, Doubled-Die Reverse
FS-G20-1888-801.

	Mintage	Cert	Avg	%MS	AU-55	AU-58	MS-60	MS-62	MS-63	MS-64	MS-65	Recent Auction Record
1850	1,170,261	2,024	48.6	6	$8,500	$10,000	$12,000	$36,000	$50,000	$85,000	$175,000	$51,406, MS-63, April 2014
1850O	141,000	507	44.6	1	25,000	40,000	60,000					$111,625, MS-61, June 2014
1851	2,087,155	1,354	51.6	13	3,750	4,750	6,750	16,000	22,500	40,000		$23,500, MS-63, April 2014
1851O	315,000	1,064	47.7	3	12,500	17,500	27,500	55,000	100,000			$58,750, MS, February 2014
1852	2,053,026	2,129	51.4	8	3,500	4,500	6,500	12,500	18,000	45,000		$18,800, MS-63, January 2014
1852O	190,000	864	49.4	3	13,500	19,500	35,000	47,500	85,000			$1,763, VF-30, July 2014
1853, All kinds	1,261,326											
1853, So-Called 3 Over 2 (a)		308	52.7	6	12,000	18,500	40,000	65,000				$17,625, AU-58, April 2014
1853		1,683	50.6	5	3,750	5,500	8,500	18,000	30,000			$14,100, MS-62, August 2013
1853O	71,000	373	48.5	1	13,000	24,000	37,500					$64,625, MS-61, April 2014
1854, All kinds	757,899											
1854, Small Date		917	49.4	4	3,500	5,000	8,500	18,000	30,000			$8,225, MS-60, June 2013
1854, Large Date		148	53.4	7	15,000	23,500	37,500	55,000	65,000	100,000		$22,325, AU-58, March 2013
1854O † (b)	3,250	29	49.8	0	500,000	650,000						$440,625, AU-55, April 2014
1854S	141,468	320	52.8	31	11,500	18,500	22,500	28,500	35,000	65,000	85,000	$41,125, MS-62, March 2014
1855	364,666	571	51.0	6	4,500	5,500	11,500	22,500	65,000	125,000		$14,688, MS-61, January 2014
1855O	8,000	92	47.6	3	65,000	75,000	105,000					$141,000, MS-61, January 2014
1855S	879,675	1,647	51.2	7	4,500	5,500	9,000	13,500	22,500	35,000		$11,750, MS-61, April 2013
1856	329,878	480	50.7	10	4,500	5,500	10,000	20,000	30,000			$10,575, MS-60, July 2014
1856O † (c)	2,250	20	48.8	0	500,000	650,000						$381,875, EF-45, January 2014
1856S	1,189,750	2,526	53.5	15	3,500	4,250	6,500	10,000	15,000			$25,850, MS-64, April 2014
1857	439,375	751	51.8	13	4,000	5,500	6,750	13,000	27,500	45,000		$47,000, MS-63, August 2013
1857O	30,000	208	50.3	5	22,500	32,500	55,000	75,000	125,000			$176,250, MS-62PL, April 2014
1857S † (d)	970,500	7,053	60.3	68	3,500	4,250	6,000	7,500	10,000	12,000	16,500	$32,900, MS-66, August 2013
1858	211,714	662	51.0	8	4,250	5,250	8,500	25,000	37,500			$38,188, MS-62, August 2013
1858O	35,250	227	49.5	4	27,500	35,000	65,000					$38,188, AU-58, January 2014
1858S	846,710	1,204	50.2	3	4,000	5,500	11,000	15,000	45,000			$5,875, AU-58, January 2014
1859	43,597	203	51.0	5	13,000	16,000	32,000	45,000				$23,500, AU-58, February 2013
1859O	9,100	550	47.8	7	65,000	90,000	130,000					$54,344, AU-50, January 2014
1859S	636,445	713	50.8	3	4,500	6,000	10,500	25,000	52,500			$22,325, MS-61, April 2014
1860	577,670	1,367	52.4	10	3,500	4,500	7,500		21,500	40,000		$64,625, MS-64, April 2014
1860O	6,600	55	50.8	2	65,000	85,000						$55,813, AU-53, April 2014
1860S	544,950	1,062	49.4	4	4,500	6,000	11,000		30,000			$14,100, MS-61, January 2014
1861	2,976,453	4,282	53.8	17	3,500	4,250	6,500	10,000	18,500	25,000	50,000	$352,500, MS-67, August 2013
1861O	17,741	209	46.7	3	67,500	80,000	120,000	135,000				$146,875, MS-60, January 2014
1861S	768,000	1,228	49.3	3	5,000	6,250	13,500	22,000	42,500			$32,900, MS-62, January 2014
1861, Paquet Rev (Tall Letters) (2 known) † (e)	unknown	3	59.3	67			2,000,000					$1,610,000, MS-61, August 2006
1861S, Paquet Reverse (Tall Letters) † (f)	19,250	141	47.4	0	135,000	175,000	225,000					$223,250, AU-58, April 2014
1862	92,133	143	51.0	17	17,500	27,500	32,500	42,500	60,000	85,000		$31,725, AU-58, January 2014

† Ranked in the *100 Greatest U.S. Coins* (fourth edition). **a.** In addition to the clearly visible remnants of a numeral beneath the 3 in the date, this variety shows a rust spot underneath the R of LIBERTY. **b.** Probably fewer than 35 exist, most in VF and EF. **c.** Probably fewer than 25 exist, most in VF and EF. **d.** The treasure of the shipwrecked SS *Central America* included thousands of 1857-S double eagles in high grades. **e.** Once thought to be a pattern; now known to have been intended for circulation. **f.** About 100 are known, most in VF and EF.

	Mintage	Cert	Avg	%MS	AU-55	AU-58	MS-60	MS-62	MS-63	MS-64	MS-65	Recent Auction Record
1862S	854,173	1,392	49.3	4	$5,000	$8,000	$13,500	$25,000	$47,500			$34,075, MS-62, April 2014
1863	142,790	311	51.7	13	13,500	25,000	30,000	40,000	55,000			$30,550, AU-58, January 2014
1863S	966,570	1,554	51.4	11	3,750	5,500	8,500	18,500	32,000			$29,375, MS-63, April 2014
1864	204,235	463	51.9	11	8,500	12,500	18,500	45,000	65,000			$282,000, MS-65, April 2014
1864S	793,660	1,392	49.5	12	3,500	6,500	11,000	17,500	40,000			$41,125, MS-63, August 2013
1865	351,175	953	55.2	35	4,000	5,500	8,000	13,500	23,500	$27,000	$65,000	$88,125, MS-65, April 2013
1865S	1,042,500	2,011	54.9	46	3,500	4,250	6,750	10,000	13,500	16,500	27,500	$23,500, MS-64, March 2013
1866S	120,000	263	45.8	2	65,000	85,000	155,000	225,000				$88,125, AU-55, October 2013

	Mintage	Cert	Avg	%MS	AU-50	AU-55	AU-58	MS-60	MS-62	MS-63	MS-64	Recent Auction Record
1866	698,745	1,251	50.4	7	$2,500	$4,250	$6,500	$11,000	$32,500		$125,000	$176,250, MS-64DMPL, January 2014
1866, Doubled-Die Reverse	*	n/a	n/a	n/a	4,000	6,000	8,500					$12,650, MS-61, August 2010
1866S	842,250	704	49.6	3	3,500	8,000	13,000	20,000	45,000			$55,813, MS-62, September 2013
1867	251,015	697	56.7	45	1,850	2,750	3,850	6,000	13,500	$32,500		$28,200, MS-63, June 2014
1867S	920,750	1,450	49.7	2	2,000	4,000	8,500	18,000	30,000			$17,639, AU-58, March 2014
1868	98,575	316	51.5	6	3,500	6,500	10,000	22,500	40,000	75,000		$6,463, AU-55, March 2013
1868S	837,500	1,815	51.0	3	1,850	3,750	6,000	16,000	30,000			$17,038, MS-60, August 2013
1869	175,130	510	52.2	8	1,800	4,000	5,750	10,000	20,000	37,500	65,000	$108,688, MS-64, January 2014
1869S	686,750	1,816	51.3	6	1,775	4,000	4,500	10,000	25,000	42,500	75,000	$22,325, MS-62, December 2013
1870	155,150	417	53.3	18	2,500	5,500	7,000	17,500	25,000			$27,025, MS-61, August 2013
1870CC † (a)	3,789	63	40.8	0	350,000	500,000						$411,250, AU-53, March 2014
1870S	982,000	1,677	51.6	5	1,775	2,500	3,500	9,000	25,000	40,000		$28,200, MS-62, April 2013
1871	80,120	383	52.0	7	2,500	4,500	5,750	10,000	25,000	40,000	75,000	$5,875, AU-58, January 2014
1871CC	17,387	281	46.3	2	42,500	50,000	75,000	100,000				$52,875, AU-53, January 2014
1871S	928,000	1,946	53.3	9	1,775	2,250	2,850	5,750	12,000	27,500	50,000	$7,666, MS-61, August 2013
1872	251,850	1,326	53.0	12	1,775	2,200	2,850	6,500	16,000	35,000	75,000	$2,350, AU-55, July 2014
1872CC	26,900	403	49.8	3	10,000	18,500	27,500	50,000				$61,688, MS-61, January 2014
1872S	780,000	1,851	53.4	10	1,775	1,850	2,750	4,750	13,500	32,500		$4,994, MS-60, June 2014
1873, Close 3	1,709,825	494	53.9	13	1,775	2,000	2,500	4,500	10,000			$4,700, MS-61, March 2013
1873, Open 3	*	11,020	59.0	59	1,600	1,700	1,825	2,500	3,500	8,500	35,000	$41,125, MS-64, August 2013
1873CC, Close 3	22,410	624	51.0	4	12,500	20,000	30,000	47,500	85,000			$41,125, AU-58, March 2014
1873S, Close 3	1,040,600	1,908	54.8	19	1,675	1,750	1,950	2,650	8,000	27,500		$9,400, MS-62, September 2013
1873S, Open 3	*	979	54.1	12	1,775	2,750	3,500	11,000				$35,250, MS-62, September 2013
1874	366,780	1,459	57.0	31	1,600	1,700	1,900	3,000	12,500	20,000	55,000	$15,275, MS-62, June 2014
1874CC	115,085	2,120	47.7	1	5,000	8,000	12,500	23,500	35,000			$64,625, MS-62, April 2014
1874S	1,214,000	3,945	56.4	25	1,600	1,700	2,000	3,250	10,000	28,500		$28,200, MS-63, January 2014
1875	295,720	2,184	59.3	63	1,600	1,700	1,800	2,500	3,500	12,500	40,500	$8,813, MS-63, August 2013
1875CC	111,151	3,026	52.7	30	3,500	4,250	5,250	10,000	20,000	35,000	75,000	$38,188, MS-63, April 2014
1875S	1,230,000	5,055	56.8	31	1,600	1,700	1,800	2,750	3,750	20,250	40,500	$15,275, MS-63, April 2014
1876	583,860	3,524	58.0	41	1,600	1,700	1,800	2,750	3,750	15,000	38,000	$64,625, MS-64, September 2013
1876CC	138,441	3,493	51.0	13	4,000	5,500	7,000	10,000	22,000	45,000		$22,325, MS-62, April 2014
1876S	1,597,000	7,958	57.8	39	1,600	1,700	1,800	2,500	3,750	12,750	35,500	$28,200, MS-64, February 2013

* Included in number above. † Ranked in the *100 Greatest U.S. Coins* (fourth edition). **a.** An estimated 35 to 50 examples are believed to exist; most are in VF with extensive abrasions.

	Mintage	Cert	Avg	%MS	AU-55	AU-58	MS-60	MS-62	MS-63	MS-64	MS-65	Recent Auction Record
1877	397,650	1,706	58.6	62	$1,600	$1,775	$2,100	$4,000	$17,500	$25,000		$4,700, MS-62, March 2014
1877CC	42,565	1,389	47.6	3	9,500	15,000	22,000	60,000				$38,188, MS-61, March 2014
1877S	1,735,000	3,638	58.6	59	1,600	1,650	2,000	3,750	16,500	25,000	$30,000	$8,225, MS-62, April 2013
1878	543,625	2,602	59.5	66	1,600	1,650	2,000	3,000	15,000	25,000		$14,100, MS-63, April 2013
1878CC	13,180	564	45.7	2	18,500	28,500	35,000	65,000				$34,075, AU-58, April 2014
1878S	1,739,000	2,560	57.9	54	1,600	1,650	1,950	5,500	23,500	45,000		$11,163, MS-62, September 2013
1879	207,600	1,001	58.2	48	1,600	1,650	1,950	5,500	22,000			$19,975, MS-63, April 2013
1879CC	10,708	535	48.1	3	26,000	32,000	40,000	60,000				$24,205, AU-55, May 2013
1879O	2,325	140	47.1	7	60,000	80,000	120,000	150,000	175,000			$135,125, MS-60, January 2014
1879S	1,223,800	2,093	56.7	32	1,600	1,650	2,500	15,000	42,500			$14,723, MS-62, August 2013

Chart continued on next page.

	Mintage	Cert	Avg	%MS	AU-55	AU-58	MS-60	MS-62	MS-63	MS-64	MS-65	Recent Auction Record
1880	51,420	737	52.6	11	$1,750	$1,800	$4,000	$15,000	$37,500			$14,100, MS-61, April 2013
1880S	836,000	1,492	57.2	39	1,600	1,650	1,950	6,000	24,500	$35,000		$42,594, MS-63, March 2013
1881	2,199	45	50.8	11	60,000	80,000	100,000					$152,750, MS-61, April 2014
1881S	727,000	1,363	58.2	54	1,600	1,650	1,950	4,500	22,500			$7,638, MS-62, July 2014
1882	571	30	52.4	13	95,000	100,000	135,000	140,000	200,000			$94,000, AU-58, January 2014
1882CC	39,140	1,600	51.5	8	6,500	9,000	14,000	25,000				$24,675, MS-61, April 2013
1882S	1,125,000	2,518	58.7	60	1,600	1,650	2,000	4,000	18,500			$8,225, MS-62, September 2013
1883CC	59,962	2,001	50.7	8	5,500	7,000	10,000	20,000	40,000			$14,100, MS-61, April 2014
1883S	1,189,000	3,804	59.9	74	1,600	1,650	1,950	2,300	8,500	18,500		$8,225, MS-63, April 2013
1884CC	81,139	2,826	52.0	17	5,500	8,500	10,000	20,000	37,500			$35,838, MS-63, August 2013
1884S	916,000	4,720	60.5	81	1,600	1,650	1,900	2,350	6,500	15,000	$45,000	$6,463, MS-63, August 2013
1885	751	96	54.8	21	45,000	55,000	75,000	90,000	135,000			$58,750, AU-58, January 2014
1885CC	9,450	507	49.7	8	15,000	17,500	20,000	35,000	75,000			$25,850, AU-58, April 2014
1885S	683,500	4,190	60.8	86	1,600	1,650	1,900	2,300	5,500	14,000		$12,925, MS-64, April 2013
1886	1,000	50	52.2	10	75,000	95,000	125,000	145,000	195,000			$129,250, MS-60, January 2014
1887S	283,000	1,710	59.9	73	1,600	1,650	1,900	3,500	16,500	23,000		$5,434, MS-62, July 2014
1888	226,161	1,832	59.8	70	1,600	1,650	1,900	2,500	11,500	15,000	30,000	$4,700, MS-62, July 2014
1888, Doubled-Die Reverse	*	50	59.7	74	2,750	3,000	3,500					$3,819, MS-62, April 2013
1888S	859,600	4,578	60.7	84	1,600	1,650	1,900	2,500	5,250	11,000		$13,513, MS-64, April 2013
1889	44,070	948	60.2	79	1,600	1,650	1,950	3,500	17,500			$4,700, MS-62, April 2013
1889CC	30,945	1,392	52.0	14	6,000	9,500	12,000	25,000	35,000			$17,625, MS, February 2014
1889S	774,700	3,490	60.6	82	1,600	1,650	1,950	2,200	6,000	16,500		$15,275, MS-64, April 2013
1890	75,940	1,269	60.2	80	1,600	1,650	1,950	2,300	12,500	22,000	30,000	$9,988, MS-63, November 2013
1890CC	91,209	3,569	51.4	11	5,000	7,000	9,500	18,500	45,000			$41,125, MS-63, February 2013
1890S	802,750	3,036	59.9	72	1,600	1,650	1,900	2,000	7,000	15,000		$14,100, MS-64, April 2013
1891	1,390	76	54.2	13	35,000	45,000	65,000	100,000				$82,250, MS-61, January 2014
1891CC	5,000	384	52.4	14	22,500	32,500	40,000	65,000	85,000			$64,625, MS-62, January 2014
1891S	1,288,125	9,276	61.2	90	1,600	1,650	1,900	1,950	3,000	6,500		$5,581, MS-64, August 2013
1892	4,430	214	55.1	29	9,000	10,000	20,000	22,500	45,000	55,000	85,000	$30,550, MS-61, January 2014
1892CC	27,265	1,336	53.3	20	5,500	8,500	15,000	30,000	50,000			$38,188, MS-62, April 2014
1892S	930,150	7,219	61.1	89	1,600	1,650	1,700	1,750	4,000	7,500	28,500	$30,550, MS-65, August 2013
1893	344,280	9,210	61.5	96	1,600	1,650	1,700	1,750	3,000	4,600		$5,875, MS-64, August 2013
1893CC	18,402	1,316	56.9	47	6,500	10,000	12,000	20,000	42,500	65,000		$25,850, MS-62, April 2013
1893S	996,175	8,306	61.1	90	1,600	1,650	1,700	1,750	4,000	12,000		$12,925, MS-64, April 2013
1894	1,368,940	23,192	61.4	95	1,600	1,650	1,700	1,750	2,650	4,750	25,000	$4,700, MS-64, January 2014
1894S	1,048,550	9,095	61.2	91	1,600	1,650	1,700	1,750	3,000	5,000	22,000	$6,463, MS-64, August 2013
1895	1,114,605	33,111	61.6	96	1,600	1,650	1,700	1,750	2,500	3,500	17,000	$5,288, MS-64, July 2014
1895S	1,143,500	11,427	61.3	92	1,600	1,650	1,700	1,750	2,500	4,750	17,500	$5,141, MS-64, August 2013
1896	792,535	15,113	61.6	95	1,600	1,650	1,700	1,750	2,250	3,500	17,500	$5,288, MS-64, January 2014
1896S	1,403,925	14,308	61.3	92	1,600	1,650	1,700	1,750	2,500	4,850	25,000	$4,700, MS-64, April 2013
1897	1,383,175	27,190	61.6	96	1,600	1,650	1,700	1,750	2,500	3,500	16,000	$3,290, MS-64, July 2014
1897S	1,470,250	20,403	61.5	92	1,600	1,650	1,700	1,750	2,600	3,750	16,000	$5,875, MS-64, August 2013
1898	170,395	2,892	61.1	87	1,600	1,650	2,750	3,000	5,500	15,000		$14,100, MS-64, April 2013
1898S	2,575,175	36,143	61.7	94	1,600	1,650	1,700	1,750	2,750	3,750	8,500	$10,575, MS-65, September 2013
1899	1,669,300	34,662	61.9	97	1,600	1,650	1,700	1,750	2,100	2,500	8,000	$9,400, MS-65, August 2013
1899S	2,010,300	15,070	61.2	89	1,600	1,650	1,700	1,750	2,750	3,250	17,500	$4,406, MS-64, August 2013
1900	1,874,460	78,923	62.3	99	1,600	1,650	1,700	1,750	2,100	2,500	3,750	$6,463, MS-65, January 2014
1900S	2,459,500	12,140	61.1	90	1,600	1,650	1,700	1,750	2,750	5,500	24,000	$4,700, MS-64, April 2013
1901	111,430	9,723	63.0	99	1,600	1,650	1,700	1,750	2,100	2,500	3,750	$6,463, MS-65, April 2014
1901S	1,596,000	5,118	61.1	91	1,600	1,650	1,700	1,750	3,500	6,500	20,000	$16,450, MS-65, April 2013
1902	31,140	1,020	60.1	70	1,600	1,650	2,500	3,500	15,000	25,000		$12,925, MS-63, July 2014
1902S	1,753,625	7,601	61.1	92	1,600	1,650	1,700	1,750	3,500	10,000	23,000	$11,163, MS-64, April 2013
1903	287,270	21,360	62.9	99	1,600	1,650	1,700	1,750	2,100	2,500	3,750	$5,875, MS-65, November 2013
1903S	954,000	10,951	61.9	97	1,600	1,650	1,700	1,750	2,100	2,500	11,500	$12,925, MS-65, February 2013
1904	6,256,699	374,184	62.6	99	1,600	1,650	1,700	1,750	2,100	2,500	3,750	$10,575, MS-66, February 2013
1904S	5,134,175	41,597	62.4	98	1,600	1,650	1,700	1,750	2,100	2,500	4,750	$23,500, MS-66, April 2013
1905	58,919	1,376	59.5	65	1,600	1,650	2,500	5,750	15,000	32,500	60,000	$5,875, MS-62, April 2014
1905S	1,813,000	4,205	61.2	88	1,600	1,650	1,700	1,750	3,750	5,500	20,000	$21,752, MS-65, February 2014

* Included in number above.

	Mintage	Cert	Avg	%MS	AU-55	AU-58	MS-60	MS-62	MS-63	MS-64	MS-65	Recent Auction Record
1906	69,596	1,387	60.5	77	$1,700	$1,750	$1,800	$3,500	$8,500	$10,000	$30,000	$8,225, MS-63, July 2014
1906D	620,250	3,739	61.8	95	1,600	1,650	1,700	1,750	3,500	4,000	20,000	$6,169, MS, February 2014
1906S	2,065,750	8,394	61.6	95	1,600	1,650	1,700	1,750	2,400	4,000	20,000	$7,050, MS-64, February 2013
1907	1,451,786	49,165	61.9	99	1,600	1,650	1,700	1,750	2,100	2,500	7,500	$8,813, MS-65, June 2013
1907D	842,250	4,442	62.3	95	1,600	1,650	1,700	1,750	3,250	4,000	8,500	$21,150, MS-66, August 2013
1907S	2,165,800	6,255	61.8	94	1,600	1,650	1,700	1,750	3,000	4,250	22,500	$24,675, MS-65, July 2014

Proof Liberty Head Double Eagles

PF-60 to 70 (Proof). Proofs were struck in all years from 1858 to 1907, and a few were made before then. Those dated through the 1870s are all very rare today; those of the 1880s are less so; and those of the 1890s and 1900s are scarce. Many have been mishandled. Dates that are Proof only (and those that are very rare in circulation-strike form) are in demand even if impaired; these include 1883, 1884, 1885, 1886, and 1887. Proofs of 1902 onward, particularly 1903, have the portrait polished in the die and lack the cameo contrast of earlier dates. *Obverse and Reverse:* PF-60 to 62 coins have extensive hairlines and may have nicks and contact marks. At PF-63, hairlines are prominent, but the mirror surface is very reflective. PF-64 coins have fewer hairlines. At PF-65, hairlines should be relatively few. These large and heavy coins reveal hairlines more readily than do the lower denominations, mostly seen only under magnification. PF-66 and higher coins should have no marks or hairlines visible to the unaided eye.

Proof Liberty Head Double Eagle

	Mintage	Cert	Avg	PF-60	PF-63	PF-64	PF-65	Recent Auction Record
1849 (pattern) (a)	1	n/a	n/a	(unique; in the Smithsonian's National Numismatic Collection)				
1850 (b)	1–2	n/a	n/a					
1854S † (c)	unknown	n/a	n/a	(unique; in the Smithsonian's National Numismatic Collection)				
1856O (d)	unknown	2	63.0					$1,437,500, SP-63, May 2009
1858 (3–4 known)	unknown	n/a	n/a	(extremely rare)				
1859 (7–8 known)	80	5	63.0	$75,000	$150,000	$275,000	$400,000	$210,600, PF, June 2014
1860 (<10 known)	59	15	62.1	45,000	100,000	185,000	350,000	$230,000, PF-64Cam, April 2011
1861 (5–6 known)	66	4	64.8	40,000	95,000	185,000	325,000	$483,000, PF-67UCam, August 2006
1862 (about 12 known)	35	10	64.0	40,000	85,000	150,000	300,000	$381,875, PF-65Cam, April 2014
1863 (about 12 known)	30	16	64.0	40,000	85,000	150,000	300,000	$345,150, PF, September 2013
1864 (12–15 known)	50	16	64.3	40,000	85,000	150,000	300,000	$199,750, PF-64Cam, April 2014
1865 (<10 known)	25	11	64.5	40,000	85,000	150,000	300,000	$440,625, PF-66DCam, April 2014
1866, With Motto (about 15 known)	30	12	64.3	25,000	57,500	125,000	200,000	$126,500, PF-64, May 2007
1867 (10–12 known)	50	7	63.9	25,000	57,500	125,000	200,000	$138,000, PF-64DCam, April 2012

† Ranked in the *100 Greatest U.S. Coins* (fourth edition). **a.** An unknown quantity of 1849 double eagles was struck as patterns; all but two were melted. One (current location unknown) was sent to Treasury secretary W.M. Meredith; the other was placed in the Mint collection, and transferred with that collection to the Smithsonian in 1923. **b.** Although no examples currently are known, it is likely that a small number of Proof 1850 double eagles were struck. For the years 1851 to 1857, no Proofs are known. **c.** This unique coin, perhaps more accurately described as a *presentation strike* than a *Proof*, was sent to the Mint collection by superintendent Lewis A. Birdsall. It may have been the first coin struck for the year, set aside to recognize the opening of the San Francisco Mint. **d.** Fewer than 25 1856-O double eagles exist; of them, this prooflike presentation strike is unique.

Chart continued on next page.

	Mintage	Cert	Avg	PF-60	PF-63	PF-64	PF-65	Recent Auction Record
1868 *(about 12 known)*	25	12	64.2	$35,000	$65,000	$125,000	$200,000	$149,500, PF-64DCam Plus, August 2011
1869 *(about 12 known)*	25	12	64.8	35,000	65,000	125,000	200,000	$106,375, PF-64DCam, February 2009
1870 *(about 12 known)*	35	9	64.3	35,000	65,000	125,000	200,000	$503,100, PF, September 2013
1871 *(<10 known)*	30	9	63.3	35,000	65,000	125,000	200,000	$26,450, PF-62Cam, August 2004
1872 *(<12 known)*	30	12	63.8	35,000	65,000	125,000	200,000	$71,875, PF-63DCam, July 2009
1873, Close 3 *(10–12 known)*	25	12	63.3	35,000	65,000	125,000	200,000	$230,000, PF-65UCam, April 2011
1874 *(<10 known)*	20	12	63.1	35,000	75,000	135,000	225,000	$218,500, PF-64UCam Star, January 2012
1875 *(10–12 known)*	20	11	63.2	50,000	100,000	150,000	250,000	$94,300, PF-63Cam, August 2009
1876 *(about 15 known)*	45	22	63.4	20,000	55,000	75,000	115,000	$152,750, PF-64DCam, February 2013
1877 *(10–12 known)*	20	12	63.7	20,000	40,000	75,000	125,000	$21,150, PF-58, February 2013
1878 *(<10 known)*	20	13	64.1	20,000	40,000	65,000	115,000	$69,000, PF-64Cam, April 2011
1879 *(10–12 known)*	30	8	63.9	20,000	40,000	65,000	115,000	$57,500, PF-64, July 2009
1880 *(10–12 known)*	36	8	64.4	20,000	40,000	65,000	115,000	$235,000, PF, March 2014
1881 *(<20 known)*	61	21	63.9	20,000	40,000	75,000	115,000	$172,500, PF-65Cam, January 2011
1882 *(12–15 known)*	59	17	63.7	20,000	40,000	75,000	115,000	$161,000, PF-64Cam, January 2011
1883, Proof only *(about 20 known)*	92	23	64.3	45,000	115,000	150,000	200,000	$282,000, PF-65DCam, January 2014
1884, Proof only *(about 20 known)*	71	17	62.6	45,000	110,000	150,000	200,000	$246,750, PF-66Cam, April 2014
1885 *(15–20 known)*	77	19	64.3	27,500	40,000	85,000	120,000	$241,500, PF-67Cam, April 2012
1886 *(20–25 known)*	106	32	64.2	20,000	42,500	75,000	115,000	$19,975, PF-60, January 2014
1887, Proof only *(<30 known)*	121	29	63.3	32,500	67,500	85,000	125,000	$258,500, PF-66, January 2014
1888 *(20–30 known)*	105	37	63.5	20,000	27,500	45,000	85,000	$126,500, PF-65DCam, April 2012
1889 *(10–12 known)*	41	17	62.7	20,000	27,500	45,000	85,000	$352,500, PF-65, January 2014
1890 *(about 15 known)*	55	19	65.1	20,000	27,500	45,000	85,000	$92,000, PF-65UCam, August 2011
1891 *(20–25 known)*	52	48	62.4	20,000	27,500	45,000	85,000	$655,200, PF, September 2013
1892 *(about 25 known)*	93	35	63.8	20,000	27,500	45,000	85,000	$188,000, PF-66DCam, January 2014
1893 *(15–20 known)*	59	12	60.3	20,000	27,500	45,000	85,000	$15,525, PF-60Cam, August 2011
1894 *(15–20 known)*	50	27	62.9	20,000	27,500	45,000	85,000	$54,625, PF-64Cam, January 2005
1895	51	33	63.2	20,000	27,500	45,000	85,000	$94,875, PF-65UCam, April 2012
1896 *(45–50 known)*	128	69	63.9	20,000	27,500	45,000	85,000	$97,750, PF-65DCam, April 2012
1897 *(20–25 known)*	86	42	63.7	20,000	27,500	45,000	85,000	$30,550, PF-62Cam, April 2013
1898 *(35–40 known)*	75	78	63.3	20,000	27,500	45,000	85,000	$117,500, PF-65Cam, April 2013
1899 *(<30 known)*	84	52	63.7	20,000	27,500	45,000	85,000	$76,375, PF, March 2014
1900 *(about 50 known)*	124	81	63.5	20,000	27,500	45,000	85,000	$88,125, PF, March 2014
1901 *(40–50 known)*	96	81	62.5	20,000	27,500	45,000	85,000	$68,150, PF, February 2013
1902 *(<50 known)*	114	59	62.2	20,000	27,500	45,000	85,000	$9,400, PF-50, January 2014
1903 *(40–50 known)*	158	75	62.3	20,000	27,500	45,000	85,000	$63,450, PF, March 2014
1904 *(about 50 known)*	98	108	63.2	20,000	27,500	45,000	85,000	$146,875, PF-67Cam, August 2013
1905 *(30–40 known)*	92	54	62.1	20,000	27,500	45,000	85,000	$10,005, PF-58, January 2012
1906 *(45–50 known)*	94	96	62.8	20,000	27,500	45,000	85,000	$85,188, PF, August 2013
1906D *(2 known)* **(e)**	6	1	66.0		*(extremely rare)*			
1907 *(40–50 known)*	78	101	63.5	20,000	27,500	45,000	85,000	$40,250, PF-64Cam, January 2012
1907D **(f)**	*unknown*	1	62.0					$71,875, PF-62, January 2004

e. Six 1906-D presentation strikes were made to commemorate the first coinage of double eagles at the Denver Mint. The coins were well documented at the time; however, at present only two are accounted for. **f.** Believed to have once been part of the King Farouk collection; cleaned.

SAINT-GAUDENS, HIGH RELIEF AND ULTRA HIGH RELIEF, MCMVII (1907)

Designer Augustus Saint-Gaudens; weight 33.436 grams; composition .900 gold, .100 copper (net weight: .96750 oz. pure gold); diameter 34 mm; edge: E PLURIBUS UNUM with words divided by stars (one specimen of the high-relief variety with plain edge is known); mint: Philadelphia.

History. Created by famous artist Augustus Saint-Gaudens under a commission arranged by President Theodore Roosevelt, this double eagle was first made (in pattern form) with sculptured-effect ultra high relief on both sides and the date in Roman numerals. The story of its production is well known and has been described in several books, notably *Renaissance of American Coinage, 1905–1908* (Burdette, 2006) and *Striking Change: The Great Artistic Collaboration of Theodore Roosevelt and August Saint-Gaudens* (Moran, 2008). After the Ultra High Relief patterns of 1907, a modified High Relief version was developed to facilitate production. Each coin required three blows of the press to strike up properly. They were made on a medal press in December 1907 and January 1908, to the extent of fewer than 13,000 pieces. In the meantime, production was under way for low-relief coins, easier to mint in quantities sufficient for commerce—these dated 1907 rather than MCMVII. Today, the MCMVII double eagle is a favorite, and when surveys are taken of beautiful and popular designs (as in *100 Greatest U.S. Coins,* by Garrett and Guth), it usually ranks at the top.

Striking and Sharpness. The striking usually is good. Check the left knee of the standing figure, which sometimes shows lightness of strike and, most often, shows flatness or wear (sometimes concealed by post-Mint etching or clever tooling). Check the Capitol at the lower left. On the reverse, check the high points at the top of the eagle. The surface on all is a delicate matte texture, grainy rather than deeply frosty. Under examination the fields show myriad tiny raised curlicues and other die-finish marks. There is no record of any being made as *Proofs,* nor is there any early numismatic record of any being sold as Proofs. Walter Breen in the 1960s made up some "guidelines" for Proofs, which some graders have adopted. Some homemade "Proofs" have been made by pickling or sandblasting the surface of regular coins—caveat emptor.

Availability. Half or more of the original mintage still exist today, as many were saved, and these grade mostly from AU-50 to MS-62. Circulated examples have often been cleaned, polished, or used in jewelry. Higher-grade coins are seen with some frequency, up to MS-65. Overgrading is common.

MS-60 to 70 (Mint State). *Obverse:* At MS-60, some abrasion and contact marks are seen on Liberty's chest. The left knee is flat on lower MS coins and all circulated coins. Scattered marks and abrasion are in the field. Satiny luster is present, but may be dull or lifeless, and interrupted in patches. Many coins at this level have been cleaned. At MS-63, contact marks are fewer, and abrasion is light, but the knee still has a flat spot. An MS-65 coin has little abrasion and few marks. Grades above MS-65 are defined by having fewer marks as perfection is approached. *Reverse:* Comments apply as for the obverse, except that abrasion and contact marks are most noticeable on the side of the eagle's body and the top of the left wing.

	Mintage	Cert	Avg	%MS	MS-60	MS-62	MS-63	MS-64	MS-65	MS-66	MS-67	Recent Auction Record
1907, High Relief, MCMVII, Wire Rim † (a)	12,367	5,240	61.5	84	$15,000	$22,000	$25,000	$30,000	$50,000	$70,000	$125,000	$217,375, MS-67, April 2013
1907, Same, Flat Rim †	*	1,159	62.1	85	15,000	22,000	25,000	32,500	52,500	75,000	140,000	$573,300, PF-69, September 2013

* Included in number above. † Ranked in the *100 Greatest U.S. Coins* (fourth edition). **a.** The Wire Rim and Flat Rim varieties were the result of different collars used in the minting process. The Flat Rim is considered slightly scarcer, but this has not led to large value differentials, as both varieties are very popular among collectors.

Proof Saint-Gaudens High Relief and Ultra High Relief Double Eagles

PF-60 to 70 (Proof). For all practical purposes the Ultra High Relief design of 1907 was unsuitable for production for circulation purposes. Between 16 and 22 Proof examples were struck. Among High Relief coins, NGC recognizes coins with certain characteristics as Proofs, while PCGS does not certify any High Relief examples as such. *Obverse and Reverse:* PF-60 to 62 coins have extensive hairlines and may have nicks and contact marks. At PF-63, hairlines are prominent, but the mirror surface is very reflective. PF-64 coins have fewer hairlines. At PF-65, hairlines should be relatively few. These large and heavy coins reveal hairlines more readily than do the lower denominations, mostly seen only under magnification. PF-66 and higher coins should have no marks or hairlines visible to the unaided eye.

Proof Saint-Gaudens MCMVII
Ultra High Relief Pattern Double Eagle

	Est Mintage	Cert	Avg	PF-60	PF-63	PF-64	PF-65	PF-67	Recent Auction Record
1907, High Relief, MCMVII, Wire or Flat Rim	unknown	246	64.0	$25,000	$32,500	$40,000	$75,500		$32,900, PF-64, February 2013
1907, Ultra High Relief, Plain Edge	*	2	63.0						
1907, Ultra High Relief, Inverted Edge	*	2	68.0						
1907, Ultra High Relief, Lettered Edge †	16–22	11	67.7					$2,500,000	$1,840,000, PF-68, January 2007

* Included in number below. † Ranked in the *100 Greatest U.S. Coins* (fourth edition).

SAINT-GAUDENS, FLAT RELIEF, ARABIC NUMERALS
(1907–1933)

Designer Augustus Saint-Gaudens; weight 33.436 grams; composition .900 gold, .100 copper (net weight: .96750 oz. pure gold); diameter 34 mm; edge: E PLURIBUS UNUM with words divided by stars; mints: Philadelphia, Denver, San Francisco.

History. In autumn 1907 chief engraver Charles E. Barber modified Augustus Saint-Gaudens's design by lowering the relief and using Arabic (not roman) numerals. Coins of this type were struck in large quantities from 1907 to 1916 and again from 1920 to 1933. In July 1908 the motto IN GOD WE TRUST was added to the reverse. The vast majority of these coins were exported. Since World War II millions have been repatriated, supplying most of those in numismatic hands today. Coins dated 1907 to 1911 have 46 stars on the obverse; coins of 1912 to 1933 have 48 stars.

Striking and Sharpness. The details are often light on the obverse. Check the bosom of Miss Liberty, the covering of which tends to be weak on 1907 and, especially, 1908 No Motto coins. Check the Capitol building and its immediate area at the lower left. The reverse usually is well struck, but check the feathers on the eagle and the top of the wings.

Availability. Most dates and mintmarks range from very common to slightly scarce, punctuated with scarce to very rare issues such as 1908-S, 1920-S, 1921, mintmarks from 1924 to 1927, and all issues of 1929 to 1933.

From their initial mintages, most of the double eagles of the 1920s were returned to the Mint and melted in the 1930s. Some, however, were unofficially saved by Treasury employees. Estimates of the quantities saved range from a few dozen to several hundred thousand, depending on the date; this explains the high values for coins that, judged only by their initial mintages, should otherwise be more common.

Probably a million or more MS coins exist of certain dates, most notably 1908 No Motto, 1924, 1925, 1926, and 1928 (especially common). Quality varies, as many have contact marks. Philadelphia Mint coins from 1922 onward usually are seen with excellent eye appeal. Common varieties are not usually collected in grades below MS.

Note: Values of common-date gold coins have been based on the current bullion price of gold, $1,200 per ounce, and may vary with the prevailing spot price.

AU-50, 53, 55, 58 (About Uncirculated). *Obverse:* Light wear is seen on the chest, the left knee, the midriff, and across the field, more so at AU-50 than at 53 or 55. An AU-58 coin has minimal traces of wear. An AU-50 coin has luster in protected areas among the rays, with little in the open field above. At AU-58, most luster is present. *Reverse:* The side of the eagle below the front of the wing, the top of the wing, and the field show light wear. Luster ranges from perhaps 40% (at AU-50) to nearly full mint bloom (at AU-58).

MS-60 to 70 (Mint State). *Obverse:* At MS-60, some abrasion and contact marks are seen on Liberty's chest and left knee, and scattered marks and abrasion are in the field. Luster is present, but may be dull or lifeless, and interrupted in patches. At MS-63, contact marks are fewer, and abrasion is light. An MS-65 coin has little abrasion and few marks, although quality among certified coins can vary. On a conservatively graded coin the luster should be full and rich. Grades above MS-65 are defined by having fewer marks as perfection is approached. Generally, Mint State coins of 1922 onward are choicer and more attractive than the earlier issues. *Reverse:* Comments apply as for the obverse, except that abrasion and contact marks are most noticeable on the eagle's left wing.

No Motto

With Motto

1909, 9 Over 8

1922, Doubled-Die Reverse

1925, Doubled-Die Reverse

1933 Saint-Gaudens Double Eagle

	Mintage	Cert	Avg	%MS	AU-58	MS-60	MS-62	MS-63	MS-64	MS-65	MS-66	Recent Auction Record
1907, Arabic Numerals	361,667	23,798	63.0	97	$1,600	$1,850	$1,875	$2,100	$2,500	$4,000	$7,500	$47,000, MS-67, April 2013
1908, No Motto	4,271,551	244,582	63.4	99	1,600	1,750	1,775	1,875	1,950	2,350	3,250	$76,375, MS-69, August 2013
1908D, No Motto	663,750	8,723	62.5	96	1,600	1,750	1,800	2,050	2,500	9,500	25,000	$8,284, MS, February 2014

	Mintage	Cert	Avg	%MS	AU-50	AU-55	MS-60	MS-62	MS-63	MS-64	MS-65	Recent Auction Record
1908, With Motto	156,258	4,125	62.2	93	$1,750	$1,800	$1,875	$1,900	$2,500	$5,000	$19,500	$10,575, MS-65, August 2013
1908D, With Motto	349,500	4,982	62.6	92	1,600	1,625	1,675	1,700	2,000	2,500	5,000	$22,325, MS-66, June 2013
1908S	22,000	915	55.5	34	6,000	7,000	12,500	17,500	24,500	27,500	50,000	$22,325, MS-63, February 2014
1909, All kinds	161,282											
1909, 9 Over 8 (a)		3,596	59.4	62	1,900	1,950	2,250	3,500	6,750	20,000	42,000	$67,563, MS-65, February 2014
1909		3,386	61.1	81	1,600	1,625	1,700	2,000	3,500	8,500	40,000	$70,500, MS-66, September 2013
1909D	52,500	1,171	59.8	64	1,900	1,950	3,250	5,000	8,000	13,500	40,000	$11,457, MS-64, March 2013
1909S	2,774,925	11,598	62.6	95	1,600	1,625	1,675	1,700	2,000	2,100	4,500	$7,344, MS-65, March 2013
1910	482,000	14,224	62.3	96	1,600	1,625	1,675	1,700	2,100	2,300	9,500	$9,106, MS-65, January 2014
1910D	429,000	12,740	63.0	96	1,600	1,625	1,675	1,700	1,800	1,900	3,000	$10,575, MS-66, March 2013
1910S	2,128,250	8,592	61.8	88	1,600	1,625	1,675	1,700	2,000	2,250	7,000	$9,694, MS-65, February 2014

a. This is one of the few Saint-Gaudens double eagle die varieties that commands a premium over the regular coin.

Chart continued on next page.

	Mintage	Cert	Avg	%MS	AU-50	AU-55	MS-60	MS-62	MS-63	MS-64	MS-65	Recent Auction Record
1911	197,250	5,082	61.8	87	$1,600	$1,625	$1,700	$1,750	$2,250	$3,750	$15,000	$42,300, MS-66, January 2013
1911D	846,500	22,307	63.4	97	1,600	1,625	1,675	1,700	1,850	2,000	2,500	$17,550, MS-67, September 2013
1911S	775,750	9,728	62.8	96	1,600	1,625	1,675	1,700	1,850	2,000	4,000	$18,214, MS-66, March 2013
1912	149,750	5,825	61.7	89	1,600	1,625	1,675	1,700	2,300	5,500	22,000	$19,975, MS-65, March 2013
1913	168,780	5,109	61.5	87	1,600	1,625	1,725	1,900	2,750	7,500	45,000	$48,469, MS-65, February 2014
1913D	393,500	7,916	62.6	94	1,600	1,625	1,675	1,700	1,850	2,100	5,500	$16,450, MS, February 2014
1913S	34,000	2,899	61.9	88	1,800	2,000	2,350	3,000	5,000	6,500	35,000	$8,225, MS-64, June 2013
1914	95,250	3,676	62.2	91	1,600	1,625	1,675	1,800	3,500	5,500	17,500	$7,638, MS-64, February 2014
1914D	453,000	12,851	63.1	96	1,600	1,625	1,675	1,700	1,850	1,900	3,250	$8,225, MS-66, June 2014
1914S	1,498,000	38,618	63.0	98	1,600	1,625	1,675	1,700	1,850	1,900	2,400	$9,694, MS-66, March 2013
1915	152,000	4,139	61.8	87	1,600	1,625	1,700	1,800	1,850	4,750	25,000	$51,406, MS-65, April 2013
1915S	567,500	28,391	63.3	99	1,600	1,625	1,675	1,700	1,850	1,900	2,400	$6,756, MS-66, January 2014
1916S	796,000	8,738	63.5	97	1,600	1,625	1,675	1,700	1,850	1,900	3,000	$9,988, MS-66, January 2014
1920	228,250	11,835	62.2	98	1,600	1,625	1,675	1,700	1,850	4,250	55,000	$9,988, MS-64, December 2013
1920S	558,000	169	60.0	65	25,000	32,500	50,000	75,000	85,000	165,000	300,000	$55,813, MS-61, February 2014
1921	528,500	158	58.9	51	55,000	65,000	100,000	125,000	175,000	375,000	700,000	$164,500, MS-63, January 2014
1922	1,375,500	87,399	62.6	98	1,600	1,625	1,675	1,700	1,850	1,900	4,000	$11,163, MS-65, April 2014
1922, Doubled-Die Reverse	*	9	63.1	100	2,000	2,200	2,500	2,750	3,500			$2,115, MS-64, December 2013
1922S	2,658,000	2,046	62.5	94	2,000	2,150	2,650	3,000	5,000	9,000	40,000	$28,200, MS, March 2014
1923	566,000	48,685	62.5	99	1,600	1,625	1,675	1,700	1,850	1,900	4,000	$9,401, MS-65, January 2014
1923D	1,702,250	13,986	64.3	100	1,600	1,625	1,675	1,700	1,850	1,900	2,350	$19,975, MS-67, January 2014
1924	4,323,500	553,918	63.4	100	1,600	1,625	1,675	1,700	1,800	1,850	2,250	$19,388, MS-67, January 2014
1924D	3,049,500	1,080	62.0	86	2,650	3,250	4,500	5,500	8,750	14,000	75,000	$70,500, MS-65, September 2013
1924S	2,927,500	944	62.2	90	2,650	3,250	4,500	5,500	10,000	16,500	65,000	$47,000, MS-65, January 2014
1925	2,831,750	94,438	63.2	99	1,600	1,625	1,675	1,700	1,800	1,850	2,250	$13,055, MS-66, January 2014
1925, Doubled-Die Reverse (b)	*	29	64.0	100	2,000	2,500	2,750	3,000	3,500			$3,055, MS-65, December 2013
1925D	2,938,500	684	62.6	95	3,750	4,250	5,500	7,500	11,000	20,000	75,000	$19,975, MS-64, January 2014
1925S	3,776,500	819	59.0	55	3,750	5,250	9,500	12,000	16,500	35,000	100,000	$16,450, MS-63, July 2014
1926	816,750	45,344	63.4	98	1,600	1,625	1,675	1,700	1,800	1,850	2,250	$6,522, MS-66, November 2013
1926D	481,000	284	61.4	86	14,000	15,500	17,500	32,500	40,000	55,000	150,000	$47,000, MS-64, March 2014
1926S	2,041,500	1,351	63.0	96	2,750	2,950	3,500	4,000	5,500	7,500	32,500	$38,188, MS-65, February 2014
1927	2,946,750	270,939	63.5	99	1,600	1,625	1,675	1,700	1,800	1,850	2,250	$17,625, MS-67, April 2013
1927D †	180,000	14	65.1	93	475,000	550,000	750,000	850,000	1,300,000	1,400,000	1,600,000	$1,997,500, MS-66, January 2014
1927S	3,107,000	247	60.6	70	14,000	16,000	26,000	37,500	47,500	67,500	110,000	$105,750, MS-65, March 2014
1928	8,816,000	94,139	63.4	99	1,600	1,625	1,675	1,700	1,800	1,850	2,250	$21,150, MS-67, June 2014
1929	1,779,750	304	63.3	96	13,500	15,500	20,000	30,000	35,000	45,000	75,000	$49,938, MS-63, March 2014
1930S	74,000	63	62.9	95	42,000	45,000	65,000	75,000	90,000	140,000	175,000	$176,382, MS-65, March 2014
1931	2,938,250	113	64.2	99	20,000	25,000	34,000	47,500	65,000	75,000	80,000	$76,375, MS-65, March 2014
1931D	106,500	135	63.3	98	20,000	25,000	34,000	47,500	65,000	90,000	100,000	$99,875, MS-64, January 2014
1932	1,101,750	142	64.2	100	20,000	25,000	34,000	47,500	65,000	80,000	95,000	$108,688, MS-66, March 2014
1933 *(13 known)* † (c)	445,500	n/a	n/a	n/a				*(extremely rare)*				$7,590,000, Gem BU, July 2002

* Included in number above. † Ranked in the *100 Greatest U.S. Coins* (fourth edition). **b.** Doubling is evident on the eagle's feathers, the rays, and IN GOD WE TRUST. **c.** All but a few 1933 double eagles were to have been melted at the mint. Today 13 examples are known to have survived. Only one, previously in the King Farouk collection, has ever been sold at auction.

Proof Saint-Gaudens, Flat Relief, Arabic Numerals, Double Eagles

PF-60 to 70 (Proof). Sand Blast (also called Matte) Proofs were made in 1908 and from 1911 to 1915. These have dull surfaces, much like fine-grained sandpaper. Satin (also called Roman Finish) Proofs were made in 1909 and 1910. They have satiny surfaces and are bright yellow. All are rare today. *Obverse and Reverse:* At PF-60 to 63, there is light abrasion and some contact marks (the lower the grade, the higher the quantity). On Sand Blast Proofs these show up as visually unappealing bright spots. At PF-64 and higher levels, marks are fewer, with magnification needed to see any at PF-65. At PF-66, there should be none at all.

Proof Saint-Gaudens, Flat Relief, Arabic Numerals,
Double Eagle

	Mintage	Cert	Avg	PF-60	PF-63	PR-64	PF-65	Recent Auction Record
1907 *(2–3 known)*	*unknown*	6	67.3	*(extremely rare)*				$920,000, PF-68 Sm Ed Lt, November 2005
1908, With Motto, Sand Blast Finish	101	109	64.4	$15,000	$27,500	$42,500	$75,000	$57,500, PF-66 Plus, June 2012
1908, With Motto, Satin Finish *(3–4 known)*	*unknown*	6	64.5	*(extremely rare)*				$152,750, PF, August 2013
1909	67	46	64.9	15,000	28,500	45,000	80,000	$184,860, PF, September 2013
1910, Satin Finish	167	70	65.0	15,000	30,000	45,000	80,000	$56,063, PF-65, June 2012
1910, Sand Blast Finish **(a)**	*unknown*	1	66.0					
1911	100	67	65.6	15,000	27,500	45,000	75,000	$157,950, PF, September 2013
1912	74	76	65.4	15,000	27,500	45,000	75,000	$211,500, PF-67, August 2013
1913	58	74	65.0	15,000	27,500	45,000	75,000	$79,313, PF, August 2013
1914	70	45	64.4	15,000	27,500	45,000	75,000	$60,375, PF-66, June 2012
1915	50	56	64.5	17,500	30,000	50,000	85,000	$63,250, PF-66, August 2011
1921 *(2 known)* † **(b)**	*unknown*	1	64.0	*(extremely rare)*				

† Ranked in the *100 Greatest U.S. Coins* (fourth edition). **a.** Part of the unique complete 1910 Sand Blast Finish Proof gold set. **b.** Prior to the first public auction of a 1921 presentation-strike double eagle (a lightly cleaned specimen) in summer 2000, this variety was unknown to the numismatic community at large. That example reportedly was struck in 1921 to celebrate the birth of Joseph Baker, nephew of U.S. Mint director Raymond T. Baker. In 2006 a second example (this one with original, uncleaned surfaces) was discovered and subsequently auctioned.

AN OVERVIEW OF CLASSIC COMMEMORATIVES

CLASSIC COMMEMORATIVES, 1892–1954

Commemorative coins have been popular since the time of ancient Greece and Rome. In the beginning they recorded and honored important events, and passed along the news of the day. Today commemorative coins, which are highly esteemed by collectors, have been issued by many modern nations—none of which has surpassed the United States when it comes to these impressive mementoes.

The unique position occupied by commemoratives in the United States coinage is largely due to the fact that, with few exceptions, all commemorative coins have real historical significance. The progress and advance of people in the New World are presented in an interesting and instructive manner on our commemorative coins. Such a record of history artistically presented on U.S. gold, silver, and other memorial issues appeals strongly to the collector who favors the romantic, story-telling side of numismatics. It is the historical features of our commemoratives, in fact, that create interest among many people who would otherwise have little interest in coins, and would not otherwise consider themselves collectors.

Concepts for commemorative issues are reviewed by two committees of Congress: the Committee on Banking, Housing, and Urban Affairs; and the Committee on Banking and Financial Services of the House; as well as by the Citizens Coinage Advisory Committee. Congress is guided to a great extent by the reports of these committees when considering bills authorizing commemorative coins.

These special coins are usually issued either to commemorate events or to help pay for monuments, programs, or celebrations that commemorate historical persons, places, or things. Pre-1982 commemorative coins were offered in most instances by a commission in charge of the event to be commemorated, and sold at a premium over face value.

Commemorative coins are popularly collected either by major types or in sets with mintmark varieties. The pieces covered here in the *Guide Book of United States Coins, Professional Edition,* are those of the "classic" era of U.S. commemoratives, 1892 to 1954. All commemoratives are of the standard weight and fineness of their regular-issue 20th-century gold and silver counterparts, and all are legal tender.

A note about mintages and distribution numbers. Unless otherwise stated, the coinage figures given in each "Distribution" column represent the total released mintage: the total mintage (including assay coins), minus the quantity of unsold coins. In many cases, larger quantities were minted but not all were sold. Unsold coins usually were returned to the mint and melted, although sometimes quantities were placed in circulation at face value. A limited number of Proof strikings or presentation pieces were made for some of the classic commemorative issues.

A note about price performance. It has mostly been in recent years that the general public has learned about commemorative coins. They have long been popular with coin collectors who enjoy the artistry and history associated with them, as well as the profit to be made from owning these rare pieces. Very few of them ever reached circulation because they were all originally sold above face value, and because they are all so rare. Most of the early issues were of the half dollar denomination, and were often made in quantities of fewer than 20,000 pieces. This is minuscule when compared to the regular half dollar coins that are made by the millions each year, and still rarely seen in circulation.

At the beginning of 1988, prices of classic commemoratives in MS-65 condition had risen so high that most collectors had to content themselves with pieces in lower grades. Investors continued to apply pressure to the high-quality pieces, driving prices even higher, while the collector community went after coins in grades from AU to MS-63. For several months the pressure from both influences caused prices to rise very rapidly (for all issues and grades) without even taking the price-adjustment breather that usually goes along with such activity.

By 1990, prices dropped to the point that several of the commemoratives began to look like bargains once again. Many of the MS-65 pieces held firm at price levels above the $3,000 mark, but others were still available at under $500 even for coins of similar mintage. Coins in MS-63 or MS-64 were priced at but a fraction of the MS-65 prices, which would seem to make them reasonably priced because the demand for these pieces is universal, and not keyed simply to grade, rarity, or speculator pressure.

Historically, the entire series of commemorative coins has frequently undergone a roller-coaster cycle of price adjustments. These cycles have usually been of short duration, lasting from months to years, with prices always recovering and eventually exceeding previous levels.

RECOMMENDED READING

Bowers, Q. David. *A Guide Book of United States Commemorative Coins,* Atlanta, GA, 2008.

Bullowa, David M. *The Commemorative Coinage of the United States, 1892–1938,* New York, 1938.

Fivaz, Bill, and Stanton, J.T. *The Cherrypickers' Guide to Rare Die Varieties* (5th ed., vol. II), Atlanta, GA, 2012.

Flynn, Kevin. *The Authoritative Reference on Commemorative Coins, 1892–1954,* Roswell, GA, 2008.

Mosher, Stuart. *The Commemorative Coinage of the United States, 1892–1938,* New York, 1940.

Slabaugh, Arlie. *United States Commemorative Coinage,* Racine, WI, 1975.

Swiatek, Anthony. *Encyclopedia of the Commemorative Coins of the United States,* Chicago, IL, 2012.

Swiatek, Anthony, and Breen, Walter. *The Encyclopedia of United States Silver and Gold Commemorative Coins, 1892–1954,* New York, 1981.

Taxay, Don. *An Illustrated History of U.S. Commemorative Coinage,* New York, 1967.

ALPHABETICAL REFERENCE TO DATES
FOR CLASSIC COMMEMORATIVES

Alabama Centennial, 1921

Albany, NY, Charter, 1936

American Independence, 1926

Antietam, Battle of, 1937

Arkansas Centennial, 1935–1939

Booker T. Washington. *See* Washington, Booker T.

Boone, Daniel, 1934–1938

Bridgeport, CT, Centennial, 1936

California Diamond Jubilee, 1925

California Pacific International Exposition, 1935–1936

Carver, George Washington, 1951–1954

Cincinnati Music Center, 1936

Cleveland / Great Lakes Exposition, 1936

Columbia, SC, Sesquicentennial, 1936

Columbian Exposition. *See* World's Columbian Exposition.

Connecticut Tercentenary, 1935

Delaware Tercentenary, 1936

Elgin, IL, Centennial, 1936

Fort Vancouver Centennial, 1925

Gettysburg, Battle of, 1936

Grant Memorial, 1922

Hawaiian Sesquicentennial, 1928

Hudson, NY, Sesquicentennial, 1935

Huguenot-Walloon Tercentenary, 1924

Illinois Centennial, 1918

Iowa Centennial, 1946

Isabella Quarter Dollar, 1893

Lafayette Dollar, 1900

Lewis and Clark Exposition, 1904–1905

Lexington-Concord Sesquicentennial, 1925

Long Island Tercentenary, 1936

Louisiana Purchase Exposition, 1903

Lynchburg, VA, Sesquicentennial, 1936

Maine Centennial, 1920

Maryland Tercentenary, 1934

McKinley Memorial, 1916–1917

Missouri Centennial, 1921

Monroe Doctrine Centennial, 1923

New Rochelle, NY, 250th Anniversary, 1938

Norfolk, VA, Bicentennial, 1936

Old Spanish Trail, 1935

Oregon Trail Memorial, 1926–1939

Panama-Pacific Exposition, 1915

Pilgrim Tercentenary, 1920–1921

Providence, RI, Tercentenary, 1936

Roanoke Island, NC, 350th Anniversary, 1937

Robinson–Arkansas Centennial, 1936

San Francisco–Oakland Bay Bridge, 1936

Spanish Trail, Old, 1935

Stone Mountain Memorial, 1925

Texas Centennial, 1934–1938

Vermont Sesquicentennial, 1927

Washington, Booker T., 1946–1951; 1951–1954

Wisconsin Territorial Centennial, 1936

World's Columbian Exposition, 1892–1893

York County, ME, Tercentenary, 1936

WORLD'S COLUMBIAN EXPOSITION HALF DOLLAR (1892–1893)

Designers Charles E. Barber (obv), George T. Morgan (rev); weight 12.50 grams; composition .900 silver, .100 copper; diameter 30.6 mm; reeded edge; mint: Philadelphia.

Designs. *Obverse:* Charles Barber's conception of Christopher Columbus, derived from a plaster model by Olin Levi Warner, taken from the explorer's portrait on an 1892 Spanish medal. The medal's portrait was inspired by a statue by Jeronimo Suñel, which itself was from an imagined likeness by Charles Legrand. *Reverse:* A sailing ship atop two globes representing the Old World and the New World. The vessel is from a plaster model by Olin Levi Warner, taken from a model made in Spain of Columbus's flagship, the *Santa Maria.*

Mintage and Melting Data. 1892: *Maximum authorized—* 5,000,000 (also includes coins dated 1893). *Number minted* (including an unknown number of assay coins)—950,000. Approximately 100 Proofs were struck. *Net distribution*—950,000. 1893: *Number minted* (including 2,105 assay coins)—4,052,105. *Number melted*—2,501,700. *Net distribution*—1,550,405.

Original Cost and Issuer. Sale price $1. Issued by the Exposition.

Key to Collecting. Both dates are common in all grades through MS-65, and are often available in MS-66 and higher. The typical high-grade coin is lustrous and frosty; some have attractive, original light-blue or iridescent toning. Well-worn examples are very common, as the Treasury Department eventually released large quantities into circulation at face value. Striking usually is good. Some coins can be weak at the center—on the higher areas of the portrait and, on the reverse, in the details of the ship's sails. Most have bagmarks from handling and distribution. High-grade 1892 coins typically are better struck than those of 1893. Approximately 100 brilliant Proofs were struck for each date; they vary widely in quality and eye appeal.

First Points of Wear. *Obverse:* The eyebrow, the cheek, and the hair at the back of the forehead. (The hair area sometimes is flatly struck.) *Reverse:* The top of the rear sail, and the right side of the Eastern Hemisphere.

	Distribution	Cert	Avg	%MS	MS-60	MS-62	MS-63	MS-64	MS-65	MS-66	Recent Auction Record
1892	950,000	11,152	63.0	93	$30	$45	$85	$140	$475	$1,100	$35,250, MS-67, August 2013
1893	1,550,405	11,647	62.1	86	30	38	80	120	450	1,000	$9,988, MS-67, August 2013

Note: Various repunched dates exist for both dates; these command little or no premium in the marketplace. For more information, see the *Cherrypickers' Guide to Rare Die Varieties,* fourth edition, volume II.

	Est Mintage	Cert	Finest	PF-60	PF-63	PF-64	PF-65	PF-66	Recent Auction Record
1892, Proof	100	83	PF-68	$2,750	$5,750	$7,000	$13,000	$20,000	$8,225, PF-65, November 2013
1893, Proof	3–5	2	PF-64						$5,830, PF-64, September 1993

WORLD'S COLUMBIAN EXPOSITION ISABELLA QUARTER (1893)

Designer Charles E. Barber; weight 6.25 grams; composition .900 silver, .100 copper; diameter 24.3 mm; reeded edge; mint: Philadelphia.

Designs. *Obverse:* Crowned profile portrait of Spain's Queen Isabella, who sponsored Christopher Columbus's voyages to the New World. *Reverse:* A lady kneeling with a distaff and spindle, symbolic of the industry of American women.

Mintage and Melting Data. Authorized on March 3, 1893. *Maximum authorized*—40,000. *Number minted* (including 23 assay coins)—40,023. *Number melted*—15,809. *Net distribution*— 24,214.

Original Cost and Issuer. Sale price $1. Sold by the Board of Lady Managers, World's Columbian Exposition.

Key to Collecting. Most examples in the marketplace are in Mint State, including many choice and gem pieces. Most are well struck and show full details, with richly lustrous fields. Connoisseurs avoid darkly toned, stained, and recolored coins. Many lower-grade Mint State examples have marks on Isabella's cheek and on the higher parts of the reverse design. The left obverse field often has bagmarks. The certification services have classified some coins with mirrored fields as Proofs, although no official records exist for the production of such.

First Points of Wear. *Obverse:* Isabella's cheekbone, and the center of the lower part of the crown. *Reverse:* The strand of wool at the lower left thigh.

	Distribution	Cert	Avg	%MS	MS-60	MS-62	MS-63	MS-64	MS-65	MS-66	Recent Auction Record
1893	24,214	8,004	62.3	87	$500	$550	$600	$800	$2,600	$5,500	$64,625, MS-68, November 2013

	Est Mintage	Cert	Finest	PF-60	PF-63	PF-64	PF-65	PF-66	Recent Auction Record
1893, Proof	100–105	42	PF-66	$2,500	$4,750	$7,750	$13,000	$18,000	$15,275, PF-66, January 2014

LAFAYETTE DOLLAR (1900)

Designer Charles E. Barber; weight 26.73 grams; composition .900 silver, .100 copper; diameter 38.1 mm; reeded edge; mint: Philadelphia.

Designs. *Obverse:* Conjoined portraits of the marquis de Lafayette and George Washington. *Reverse:* Side view of the equestrian statue erected by the youth of the United States in honor of Lafayette. This view was based on an early model of the statue; the final version that was erected in Paris is slightly different.

Mintage and Melting Data. Authorized March 3, 1899. *Maximum authorized*—50,000. *Number minted* (including 26 assay coins)—50,026. *Number melted*—14,000. *Net distribution*—36,026.

Original Cost and Issuer. Sale price $2. Sold by the Lafayette Memorial Commission through the American Trust & Savings Bank of Chicago.

Key to Collecting. Most surviving examples show evidence of circulation or other mishandling. The typical grade is AU. In Mint State, most are MS-60 to 63, and many are dull or unattractive, having been dipped or cleaned multiple times. Many have marks and dings. Properly graded MS-64 coins are very scarce, and MS-65 or higher gems are very rare, especially if with good eye appeal. Several die varieties exist and are collected by specialists.

Varieties. *Obverse varieties:* (1) Small point on the bust of Washington. The tip of Lafayette's bust is over the top of the L in DOL-LAR. The AT in STATES is cut high. (2) The left foot of the final A in AMERICA is recut, and the A in STATES is high. The second S in STATES is repunched (this is diagnostic). (3) The AT in STATES is recut and the final S is low. The letter F in OF and in LAFAYETTE is broken from the lower tip of the crossbar and to the right base extension, and AMERICA is spaced A ME RI C A. The period after OF is close to the A of AMERICA. The tip of Lafayette's vest falls to the right of the top of the first L in DOL-LAR. (4) The C in AMERICA is repunched at the inside top (this is diagnostic). The CA in AMERICA is spaced differently from the obverses previously described. *Reverse varieties:* (A) There are 14 long leaves and a long stem. The tip of the lowest leaf is over the 1 in 1900. (B) There are 14 shorter leaves and a short stem. The tip of the lowest leaf is over the space between the 1 and 9 in 1900. (C) There are 14 medium leaves and a short, bent stem. The tip of the lowest leaf is over the 9 in 1900. (D) There are 15 long leaves and a short, bent stem. The tip of the lowest leaf is over the 9 in 1900. (E) The tip of the lowest leaf is over the space to the left of the 1 in 1900.

First Points of Wear. *Obverse:* Washington's cheekbone, and Lafayette's lower hair curl. *Reverse:* The fringe of Lafayette's epaulet, and the horse's blinder and left rear leg bone.

	Distribution	Cert	Avg	%MS	MS-60	MS-62	MS-63	MS-64	MS-65	MS-66	Recent Auction Record
1900	36,026	5,516	61.6	84	$875	$1,100	$1,800	$3,000	$10,000	$19,000	$36,719, MS-67, April 2014

LOUISIANA PURCHASE EXPOSITION GOLD DOLLAR (1903)

Designer Charles E. Barber (assisted by George T. Morgan); weight 1.672 grams; composition .900 gold, .100 copper; diameter 15 mm; reeded edge; mint: Philadelphia.

Designs, Jefferson. *Obverse:* Bewigged profile portrait of Thomas Jefferson, inspired by an early 19th-century medal by John Reich, after Houdon's bust. *Reverse:* Inscription and branch.

Designs, McKinley. *Obverse:* Bareheaded profile portrait of William McKinley, derived from his presidential medal (also designed by Barber). *Reverse:* Inscriptions and branch.

Mintage and Melting Data. Authorized June 28, 1902. *Maximum authorized*—250,000 (total for both varieties). *Number minted* (including 258 assay coins comprising *both* varieties)—250,258 (125,000 of each variety). *Number melted*—215,250 (total for both varieties; no account was kept of the portraits; 250 assay coins were melted). *Net distribution*—35,000; estimated at 17,500 of each variety.

Original Cost and Issuer. Sale price $3. Louisiana Purchase Exposition Company, St. Louis, Missouri (sales through Farran Zerbe). Some were sold as mounted in spoons, brooches, and stick pins; 100 certified Proofs of each design were made, mounted in an opening in a rectangular piece of imprinted cardboard.

Key to Collecting. Market demand is strong, from collectors and investors alike, as most surviving examples are in choice or gem Mint State, with strong eye appeal. Most specimens are very lustrous and frosty. An occasional coin is prooflike. Avoid any with copper stains (from improper mixing of the gold/copper alloy). Proofs enter the market rarely and garner much publicity.

First Points of Wear. *Obverse:* Portrait's cheekbone (usually more evident on the McKinley variety) and sideburn. *Reverse:* Date and denomination.

	Distribution	Cert	Avg	%MS	MS-60	MS-62	MS-63	MS-64	MS-65	MS-66	Recent Auction Record
1903, Jefferson	17,500	5,341	63.9	95	$675	$750	$850	$1,250	$1,700	$2,150	$6,463, MS-67, April 2013
1903, McKinley	17,500	5,056	63.8	95	650	725	775	1,050	1,675	2,000	$12,925, MS-68, October 2013

Continued on next page.

	Mintage	Cert	Finest	PF-60	PF-63	PF-64	PF-65	PF-66	Recent Auction Record
1903, Jefferson, Proof **(a)**	100	64	PF-67						$37,375, PF-67UCam Star, January 2012
1903, McKinley, Proof **(b)**	100	72	PF-68						$14,950, PF-65Cam, April 2012

a. The first 100 Jefferson gold dollars were struck in brilliant Proof format. True Proofs exhibit deeply mirrored fields and are sharply struck. Many also have frosted devices, giving them a cameo appearance. "Although many of the coins seen today have been certified and lack original packaging, they were originally housed in cardboard holders certifying each coin as having been one of the first 100 impressions from the dies. The original holders are quite interesting, with the coin covered by a small piece of wax paper and a piece of string sealed by dark red wax. The coins are difficult to see behind the wax paper, and the author has seen holders with a circulation-strike example substituted for the Proof piece. Caution should be used when purchasing an example of this extreme rarity" (*Encyclopedia of U.S. Gold Coins, 1795–1933,* second edition). **b.** Like the Jefferson issue, the first 100 McKinley gold dollars were struck as Proofs, and packaged as such. "Prooflike circulation strikes are quite common for the issue, and true Proofs can be distinguished by deeply mirrored surfaces and cameo devices. Certification is highly recommended" (*Encyclopedia of U.S. Gold Coins, 1795–1933,* second edition).

LEWIS AND CLARK EXPOSITION GOLD DOLLAR (1904–1905)

Designer Charles E. Barber; weight 1.672 grams; composition .900 gold, .100 copper; diameter 15 mm; reeded edge; mint: Philadelphia.

Designs. *Obverse:* Bareheaded profile portrait of Meriwether Lewis. *Reverse:* Bareheaded profile portrait of William Clark. These portraits were inspired by works of Charles Willson Peale.

Mintage and Melting Data. 1904: Authorized on April 13, 1904. *Maximum authorized*—250,000 (total for 1904- and 1905-dated coins). *Number minted* (including 28 assay coins)—25,028. *Number melted*—15,003. *Net distribution*—10,025. 1905: *Number minted* (including 41 assay coins)—35,041. *Number melted*—25,000. *Net distribution*—10,041.

Original Cost and Issuer. Sales price $2 (some at $2.50); many were probably discounted further. Lewis and Clark Centennial and American Pacific Exposition and Oriental Fair Company, Portland, Oregon (sales through Farran Zerbe and others).

Key to Collecting. Most surviving examples show evidence of handling. Some exhibit die problems (a rough raised area of irregularity at the dentils). Most range from AU-50 to 58, with an occasional MS-60 to 63. MS-64 coins are scarce, and MS-65 rare. Pristine examples are very rare. Most MS coins have areas of prooflike finish; some are deeply lustrous and frosty. The 1905-dated issue is noticeably scarcer than the 1904.

First Points of Wear. *Obverse:* Lewis's temple. *Reverse:* Clark's temple.

	Distribution	Cert	Avg	%MS	MS-60	MS-62	MS-63	MS-64	MS-65	MS-66	Recent Auction Record
1904	10,025	3,096	63.2	93	$1,000	$1,100	$1,575	$2,750	$7,500	$10,000	$16,450, MS-67, June 2013
1905	10,041	3,307	62.8	91	1,300	1,500	1,800	3,000	8,500	15,000	$25,850, MS-66, June 2013

	Est Mintage	Cert	Finest	PF-60	PF-63	PF-64	PF-65	PF-66	Recent Auction Record
1904, Proof	2–3	4	PF-64						

PANAMA-PACIFIC EXPOSITION HALF DOLLAR (1915)

Designers Charles E. Barber (obv), George T. Morgan (assisting Barber on rev); weight 12.50 grams; composition .900 silver, .100 copper; diameter 30.6 mm; reeded edge; mint: Philadelphia.

Designs. *Obverse:* Columbia scattering flowers, alongside a child holding a cornucopia, representing the bounty of the American West; the Golden Gate in the background. *Reverse:* A spread-winged eagle perched on a shield, with branches of oak and olive.

Mintage and Melting Data. Authorized by the Act of January 16, 1915. *Maximum authorized*—200,000. *Number minted* (including 30 assay coins)—60,030. *Number melted*—32,896, including 30 assay coins (29,876 were melted on September 7, 1916 and the balance on October 30, 1916). *Distribution*—27,134.

Original Cost and Issuer. Sale price $1. Coin and Medal Department (Farran Zerbe), Panama-Pacific International Exposition, San Francisco, California. (Combination offers included a set of four coins, including the buyer's choice of one $50, in a leather case, for $100; and a set of five coins in a copper frame for $200.)

Key to Collecting. The half dollar does not have the typical deep mint frost associated with earlier silver issues. Most are satiny in appearance with the high parts in particular having a microscopically grainy finish. Many pieces have an inner line around the perimeter near the rim, a die characteristic. On the reverse of all known coins, the eagle's breast feathers are indistinct, which sometimes gives MS coins the appearance of having light wear. Most surviving coins grade from AU-50 to MS-63.

First Points of Wear. *Obverse:* Columbia's left shoulder. *Reverse:* The eagle's breast.

	Distribution	Cert	Avg	%MS	MS-60	MS-62	MS-63	MS-64	MS-65	MS-66	Recent Auction Record
1915S	27,134	5,603	63.2	92	$515	$625	$725	$1,100	$2,200	$3,500	$11,750, MS-67, November 2013

PANAMA-PACIFIC EXPOSITION GOLD DOLLAR (1915)

Designer Charles Keck; weight 1.672 grams; composition .900 gold, .100 copper; diameter 15 mm; reeded edge; mint: Philadelphia.

Designs. *Obverse:* Capped profile portrait of a Panama Canal laborer. *Reverse:* Two dolphins, symbolizing the Atlantic and Pacific oceans, and legends.

Mintage and Melting Data. Authorized by the Act of January 16, 1915. *Maximum authorized*—25,000. *Number minted* (including 34 assay coins)—25,034. *Number melted*—10,034, including 34 assay coins (melted at the San Francisco Mint on October 30, 1916). *Net distribution*—15,000.

Original Cost and Issuer. Sale price $2 (and a few at $2.25). Coin and Medal Department (Farran Zerbe), Panama-Pacific International Exposition, San Francisco, California. (Combination offers included, among others, a set of four coins, with the buyer's choice of one fifty-dollar coin, in a leather case, for $100; and a set of five coins in a copper frame for $200.)

Key to Collecting. Most examples are in Mint State. Many exhibit deep mint frost. Friction is common, especially on the obverse.

First Points of Wear. *Obverse:* The peak of the laborer's cap. *Reverse:* The heads of the dolphins, and the denomination.

	Distribution	Cert	Avg	%MS	MS-60	MS-62	MS-63	MS-64	MS-65	MS-66	Recent Auction Record
1915S	15,000	9,283	63.6	93	$635	$660	$700	$975	$1,250	$1,850	$8,813, MS-67, July 2014

PANAMA-PACIFIC EXPOSITION QUARTER EAGLE (1915)

Designer Charles E. Barber (obv), George T. Morgan (rev); weight 4.18 grams; composition .900 gold, .100 copper; diameter 18 mm; reeded edge; mint: Philadelphia.

Designs. *Obverse:* Columbia seated on a hippocampus, holding a caduceus, symbolic of Medicine's triumph over yellow fever in Panama during the canal's construction. *Reverse:* An eagle, standing on a plaque inscribed E PLURIBUS UNUM, with raised wings.

Mintage and Melting Data. Authorized by the Act of January 16, 1915. *Maximum authorized*—10,000. *Number minted* (including 17 assay coins)—10,017. *Number melted*—3,268, including 17 assay coins (melted at the San Francisco Mint on October 30, 1916). *Distribution*—6,749.

Original Cost and Issuer. Sale price $4. Coin and Medal Department (Farran Zerbe), Panama-Pacific International Exposition, San Francisco, California. (Combination offers included, among others, a set of four coins, with the buyer's choice of one fifty-dollar coin, in a leather case, for $100; and a set of five coins in a copper frame for $200.)

Key to Collecting. Most grade from AU-55 to MS-63. MS-64 coins are elusive, and MS-65 rare. Most MS pieces show a satiny, sometimes grainy luster.

First Points of Wear. *Obverse:* Columbia's head, breast, and knee. *Reverse:* The torch band and the eagle's leg.

	Distribution	Cert	Avg	%MS	MS-60	MS-62	MS-63	MS-64	MS-65	MS-66	Recent Auction Record
1915S	6,749	4,212	64.1	96	$1,850	$2,750	$3,800	$5,000	$6,000	$7,000	$21,150, MS-67, February 2013

	Est Mintage	Cert	Finest	PF-60	PF-63	PF-64	PF-65	PF-66	Recent Auction Record
1915S, Proof **(a)**	*unique*	n/a	n/a						

a. This unique Satin Finish Proof resides in the National Numismatic Collection of the Smithsonian Institution.

PANAMA-PACIFIC EXPOSITION FIFTY-DOLLAR GOLD PIECE (1915)

Designer Robert Aitken; weight 83.59 grams; composition .900 gold, .100 copper; diameter 44 mm; reeded edge; mint: Philadelphia.

Designs. Round—*Obverse:* Helmeted profile portrait of Minerva, with shield and armor. *Reverse:* An owl, symbolic of wisdom, vigilant on a pine branch, with pinecones. Octagonal: *Obverse and reverse:* Same as the round coin, but with dolphins in the eight angled exergues on obverse and reverse.

Mintage and Melting Data. Authorized by the Act of January 16, 1915. Round: *Maximum authorized*—1,500. *Number minted* (including 10 assay coins)—1,510. *Number melted*—1,027. *Distribution*—483. Octagonal: *Maximum authorized*—1,500. *Number minted* (including 9 assay coins)—1,509. *Number melted*—864. *Distribution*—645.

Original Cost and Issuer. Round and octagonal: Sale price, each, $100. Coin and Medal Department (Farran Zerbe), Panama-Pacific International Exposition, San Francisco, California. Com-

bination offers included a set of four coins (buyer's choice of one fifty-dollar coin) in a leather case for $100, and a set of five coins in a copper frame for $200, this issued after the Exposition closed.

Key to Collecting. Because such small quantities were issued, these hefty gold commemoratives today are rare in any grade. The round coins trade hands slightly less frequently than the octagonal. Typical grades are MS-63 or 64 for coins kept in an original box or frame over the years, or AU-58 to MS-63 if removed. Coins that have been cleaned or lightly polished exhibit a multitude of tiny hairlines; such pieces are avoided by connoisseurs.

First Points of Wear. *Obverse:* Minerva's cheek. *Reverse:* The owl's upper breast.

	Distribution	Cert	Avg	%MS	MS-60	MS-62	MS-63	MS-64	MS-65	MS-66	Recent Auction Record
1915S, Round	483	732	62.7	92	$60,000	$67,500	$85,000	$110,000	$150,000	$200,000	$146,875, MS-66, February 2013
1915S, Octagonal	645	922	62.6	91	60,000	65,000	80,000	100,000	140,000	200,000	$282,000, MS-67, April 2014

MCKINLEY MEMORIAL GOLD DOLLAR (1916–1917)

Designers Charles E. Barber (obv) and George T. Morgan (rev); weight 1.672 grams; composition .900 gold, .100 copper; diameter 15 mm; reeded edge; mint: Philadelphia.

Designs. *Obverse:* Bareheaded profile portrait of William McKinley. *Reverse:* Artist's rendition of the proposed McKinley Birthplace Memorial intended to be erected in Niles, Ohio.

Mintage and Melting Data. Authorized February 23, 1916. *Maximum authorized*—100,000 (total for both years). 1916: *Number minted* (including 26 assay coins)—20,026 *Number melted*—5,000 (estimated). *Distribution*—15,000 (estimated). 1917: *Number minted* (including 14 assay coins)—10,014. *Number melted*—5,000 (estimated). *Distribution*—5,000 (estimated).

Original Cost and Issuer. Sale price $3. National McKinley Birthplace Memorial Association, Youngstown, Ohio.

Key to Collecting. The obverse of the 1916 issue often displays friction while its reverse can appear as choice Mint State. Proof-like fields are common. Some are highly prooflike on both sides. The 1917 issue is much harder to find than the 1916; examples usually are in higher grades with rich luster on both sides, and often exhibit a pale yellow color.

First Points of Wear. *Obverse:* McKinley's temple area, and the hair above his ear. *Reverse:* The pillar above the second 1 in the date; and the bottom of the flagpole.

	Distribution	Cert	Avg	%MS	MS-60	MS-62	MS-63	MS-64	MS-65	MS-66	Recent Auction Record
1916	15,000	6,887	63.8	96	$550	$625	$675	$925	$1,450	$1,850	$4,259, MS-67, November 2013
1917	5,000	4,077	63.8	95	700	750	875	1,250	1,850	3,250	$5,288, MS-67, February 2013

	Est Mintage	Cert	Finest	PF-60	PF-63	PF-64	PF-65	PF-66	Recent Auction Record
1916, Proof	3–6	4	PF-64						$37,375, PF-63, January 2012

ILLINOIS CENTENNIAL HALF DOLLAR (1918)

Designers George T. Morgan (obv) and John R. Sinnock (rev); weight 12.50 grams; composition .900 silver, .100 copper; diameter 30.6 mm; reeded edge; mint: Philadelphia.

Designs. *Obverse:* Bareheaded, beardless profile portrait of Abraham Lincoln, facing right. *Reverse:* A fierce eagle atop a crag, clutching a shield and carrying a banner; from the Illinois state seal.

Mintage Data. Authorized on June 1, 1918. *Maximum authorized*—100,000. *Number minted*—100,000 plus 58 for assay.

Original Cost and Issuer. Sale price $1. The Illinois Centennial Commission, through various outlets.

Key to Collecting. Examples were struck with deep, frosty finishes, giving Mint State pieces an unusually attractive appear-

ance. The obverse typically shows contact marks or friction on Lincoln's cheek and on other high parts of his portrait. The field typically shows contact marks. The reverse usually grades from one to three points higher than the obverse, due to the protective nature of its complicated design. Most examples are lustrous and frosty, although a few are seen with partially prooflike fields.

First Points of Wear. *Obverse:* The hair above Lincoln's ear. *Reverse:* The eagle's breast. (Note that the breast was sometimes flatly struck; look for differences in texture or color of the metal.)

	Distribution	Cert	Avg	%MS	MS-60	MS-62	MS-63	MS-64	MS-65	MS-66	Recent Auction Record
1918	100,058	9,853	63.9	98	$150	$160	$170	$225	$535	$800	$7,050, MS-67, January 2013

MAINE CENTENNIAL HALF DOLLAR (1920)

Designer Anthony de Francisci; weight 12.50 grams; composition .900 silver, .100 copper; diameter 30.6 mm; reeded edge; mint: Philadelphia.

Designs. *Obverse:* Arms of the state of Maine, with the Latin word DIRIGO ("I Direct"). *Reverse:* The centennial inscription enclosed by a wreath.

Mintage Data. Authorized on May 10, 1920. *Maximum authorized*—100,000. *Number minted*—50,028, including 28 for the U.S. Assay Commission.

Original Cost and Issuer. Sale price $1. Maine Centennial Commission.

Key to Collecting. Relatively few Maine half dollars were sold to the hobby community; the majority of coins distributed

saw careless handling by the general public. Most examples show friction or handling marks on the center of the shield on the obverse. The fields were not completely finished in the dies and always show tiny raised lines or die finishing marks; at first glance these may appear to be hairlines or scratches, but they have no effect on the grade. Appealing examples in higher Mint State levels are much more elusive than the high mintage might suggest.

First Points of Wear. *Obverse:* The left hand of the scythe holder; the right hand of the anchor holder. (Note that the moose and the pine tree are weakly struck.) *Reverse:* The bow knot.

	Distribution	Cert	Avg	%MS	MS-60	MS-62	MS-63	MS-64	MS-65	MS-66	Recent Auction Record
1920	50,028	6,209	64.0	98	$165	$175	$200	$250	$460	$685	$7,050, MS-67, August 2013

PILGRIM TERCENTENARY (1920–1921)

Designer Cyrus E. Dallin; weight 12.50 grams; composition .900 silver, .100 copper; diameter 30.6 mm; reeded edge; mint: Philadelphia.

Designs. *Obverse:* Artist's conception of a partial standing portrait of Governor William Bradford holding a book. *Reverse:* The *Mayflower* in full sail.

Mintage and Melting Data. Authorized May 12, 1920. *Maximum authorized*—300,000. 1920: *Number minted* (including 112

assay coins)—200,112. *Number melted*—48,000. *Net distribution*—152,112. 1921: *Number minted* (including 53 assay coins)—100,053. *Number melted*—80,000. *Net distribution*—20,053.

Original Cost and Issuer. Sale price $1. Pilgrim Tercentenary Commission.

Continued on next page.

Key to Collecting. The 1920 issue is common, and the 1921 slightly scarce. Coins grading MS-64 and higher usually have excellent eye appeal, though many exceptions exist. Most coins have scattered contact marks, particularly on the obverse. Nearly all 1921 coins are this way. Many coins (particularly coins which are early impressions from the dies) show tiny raised lines in the obverse field, representing die finish marks; these are not to be confused with hairlines or other evidences of friction (which are recessed).

First Points of Wear. *Obverse:* Cheekbone, hair over ear, and the high areas of Governor Bradford's hat. *Reverse:* The ship's rigging and stern, the crow's nest, and the rim.

	Distribution	Cert	Avg	%MS	MS-60	MS-62	MS-63	MS-64	MS-65	MS-66	Recent Auction Record
1920	152,112	9,679	63.6	97	$110	$120	$125	$155	$350	$850	$7,344, MS-67, February 2014
1921, With Added Date	20,053	4,592	64.1	99	210	220	235	275	425	900	$4,113, MS-67, August 2013

MISSOURI CENTENNIAL HALF DOLLAR (1921)

Designer Robert Aitken; weight 12.50 grams; composition .900 silver, .100 copper; diameter 30.6 mm; reeded edge; mint: Philadelphia.

Designs. *Obverse:* Coonskin-capped profile portrait of a frontiersman. One variety has 2★4 in the field; the other is plain. *Reverse:* Standing figures of a frontiersman and an Indian looking westward, against a starry field; SEDALIA (the location of the Missouri centennial exposition) incused below.

Mintage and Melting Data. Authorized on March 4, 1921. *Maximum authorized*—250,000 (combined for both types). *Number minted*—50,028 in all. *Number melted*—29,600. *Net distribution*—20,428 (estimated), with 9,400 for 1921 2★4 and 11,400 for 1921 Plain. The 28 remaining were for the U.S. Assay Commission.

Original Cost and Issuer. Sale price $1. Missouri Centennial Committee, through the Sedalia Trust Company.

Key to Collecting. Most grade from AU-55 to MS-63; have friction and contact marks on the higher areas of the design; and are lightly struck at the center of the portrait of Boone on the obverse, and at the torsos of the two figures on the reverse. MS-65 and higher coins with sharply struck centers are rarities.

First Points of Wear. *Obverse:* The hair in back of the ear. *Reverse:* The frontiersman's arm and shoulder.

	Distribution	Cert	Avg	%MS	MS-60	MS-62	MS-63	MS-64	MS-65	MS-66	Recent Auction Record
1921, "2★4" in Field	9,400	3,314	63.5	96	$750	$800	$1,100	$1,300	$3,700	$10,000	$7,638, MS-66, August 2013
1921, Plain	11,400	3,953	63.0	93	600	750	850	1,200	3,500	9,000	$12,925, MS-66, August 2013

	Est Mintage	Cert	Finest	PF-60	PF-63	PF-64	PF-65	PF-66	Recent Auction Record
1921, "2★4," Matte Proof	1–2	1	PF-66						

ALABAMA CENTENNIAL HALF DOLLAR (1921)

Designer Laura Gardin Fraser; weight 12.50 grams; composition .900 silver, .100 copper; diameter 30.6 mm; reeded edge; mint: Philadelphia.

Designs. *Obverse:* Conjoined bareheaded profile portraits of William Wyatt Bibb, the first governor of Alabama, and T.E. Kilby, governor at the time of the centennial. *Reverse:* A dynamic eagle perched on a shield, clutching arrows and holding a banner; from the Alabama state seal.

Mintage and Melting Data. Authorized on May 10, 1920. *Maximum authorized*—100,000. *Number minted*—70,044 (including 44 for assay). *Number melted*—5,000. *Net distribution*—2X2: estimated as 30,000. Plain: estimated as 35,000.

Original Cost and Issuer. Sale price $1. Alabama Centennial Commission.

Key to Collecting. Most of these coins were sold to citizens of Alabama, and of those, few were acquired by numismatists.

Many are in circulated grades (typical being EF or AU), with most surviving pieces grading MS-63 or less. Those grading MS-65 or finer are rare. Nearly all show friction or contact marks on Governor Kilby's cheek on the obverse, and many are flatly struck on the eagle's left leg and talons on the reverse. These coins were produced carelessly, and many lack sharpness and luster (sharply struck examples are very rare). Nicks and marks from the original planchets are often found on the areas of light striking. The eagle's upper leg is often lightly struck, particularly on the plain variety. The 2X2 coins usually are better struck than the plain variety.

First Points of Wear. *Obverse:* Kirby's forehead and the area to the left of his earlobe. *Reverse:* The eagle's lower neck and the top of its wings.

	Distribution	Cert	Avg	%MS	MS-60	MS-62	MS-63	MS-64	MS-65	MS-66	Recent Auction Record
1921, Plain	*35,000*	4,030	62.9	91	$230	$275	$450	$570	$1,300	$2,850	$25,850, MS-67, August 2013
1921, "2X2" in Field	*30,000*	3,627	63.3	94	325	350	525	675	1,400	3,100	$3,525, MS-66, April 2013

GRANT MEMORIAL HALF DOLLAR (1922)

Designer Laura Gardin Fraser; weight 12.50 grams; composition .900 silver, .100 copper; diameter 30.6 mm; reeded edge; mint: Philadelphia.

Designs. *Obverse:* Bareheaded profile portrait of Ulysses S. Grant in a military coat. One variety has a star above GRANT. *Reverse:* View of the house Grant was born in (Point Pleasant, Ohio), amidst a wooded setting.

Mintage and Melting Data. Authorized on February 2, 1922. *Maximum authorized*—250,000. No Star: *Number minted* (including 55 assay coins)—95,055. *Number melted*—27,650. *Net distribution*—67,405. With Star: *Number minted* (including 6 assay coins)—5,006. *Number melted*—750. *Net distribution*—4,256.

Original Cost and Issuer. Sale price $1.50, later reduced to 75¢. U.S. Grant Centenary Memorial Commission (mail orders were serviced by Hugh L. Nichols, chairman, Batavia, Ohio).

Key to Collecting. The surface shows numerous raised die-finishing lines and other mint preparation marks (even on MS pieces). Most specimens are lightly struck on the center of the obverse. These factors combined make it very difficult to differentiate minute gradations among MS coins. A few are prooflike. The No Star variety is common, with typical grades ranging from MS-60 to 63 (MS-65 and higher coins are seen with some frequency, but are much scarcer). The With Star variety in MS is one of the very rarest pieces of U.S. commemoratives, because of the low mintage and the fact that few coins were sold to preservation-minded collectors.

First Points of Wear. *Obverse:* Grant's cheekbone. (Worn dies caused flatness in the hair above his ear.) *Reverse:* The leaves of the tree under the U in TRUST. (The coin often is weakly struck in the branches above the house.)

	Distribution	Cert	Avg	%MS	MS-60	MS-62	MS-63	MS-64	MS-65	MS-66	Recent Auction Record
1922, Star in Obverse Field	4,256	2,472	63.3	96	$1,300	$1,400	$1,900	$2,750	$7,000	$14,000	$21,150, MS-67, January 2014
1922, No Star in Field	67,405	7,345	63.5	96	125	135	175	275	750	1,150	$9,400, MS-66, April 2013

GRANT MEMORIAL GOLD DOLLAR (1922)

Designer Laura Gardin Fraser; weight 1.672 grams; composition .900 gold, .100 copper; diameter 15 mm; reeded edge; mint: Philadelphia.

Designs. *Obverse:* Bareheaded profile portrait of Ulysses S. Grant in a military coat. One variety has a star above GRANT. *Reverse:* View of the house Grant was born in (Point Pleasant, Ohio), amidst a wooded setting.

Mintage Data. Authorized on February 2, 1922. No Star: *Number minted and distributed*—5,000. With Star: *Number minted and distributed*—5,016. Assay coins: 16.

Original Cost and Issuer. Sale price $3 for either variety. U.S. Grant Centenary Memorial Commission (mail orders were serviced by Hugh L. Nichols, chairman, Batavia, Ohio).

Key to Collecting. Almost all known specimens are MS-63 to 65 or better. MS-66 and 67 examples are easy to find. Some lower-grade coins show friction on Grant's cheek and hair. Some specimens have dull surfaces; these are avoided by connoisseurs.

First Points of Wear. *Obverse:* Grant's cheekbone and hair. *Reverse:* The leaves of the tree under the U in TRUST.

	Distribution	Cert	Avg	%MS	MS-60	MS-62	MS-63	MS-64	MS-65	MS-66	Recent Auction Record
1922, With Star	5,016	3,449	64.8	99	$1,600	$1,675	$1,750	$2,100	$2,500	$2,850	$12,338, MS-67, April 2013
1922, No Star	5,016	3,195	64.3	97	1,600	1,725	1,750	2,150	2,600	3,000	$9,988, MS-67, June 2014

MONROE DOCTRINE CENTENNIAL HALF DOLLAR (1923)

Designer Chester Beach; weight 12.50 grams; composition .900 silver, .100 copper; diameter 30.6 mm; reeded edge; mint: Philadelphia.

Designs. *Obverse:* Conjoined bareheaded profile portraits of presidents James Monroe and John Quincy Adams. *Reverse:* Stylized depiction of the continents of North and South America as female figures in the outlines of the two land masses.

Mintage Data. Authorized on January 24, 1923. *Maximum authorized*—300,000. *Number minted* (including 77 assay coins)—274,077. *Net distribution*—274,077.

Original Cost and Issuer. Sale price $1. Los Angeles Clearing House, representing backers of the First Annual American Historical Revue and Motion Picture Industry Exposition.

Key to Collecting. Most examples show friction or wear. MS coins are common. Evaluating the numerical grade of MS-60 to 63 coins is difficult because of the design's weak definition. Low-magnification inspection usually shows nicks and graininess at the highest point of the obverse center; these flaws are from the original planchets. Many examples of this coin have been doctored and artificially toned in attempts to earn higher grades upon certification; these are avoided by connoisseurs.

First Points of Wear. *Obverse:* Adams's cheekbone. *Reverse:* The upper figure, underneath CT in DOCTRINE.

	Distribution	Cert	Avg	%MS	MS-60	MS-62	MS-63	MS-64	MS-65	MS-66	Recent Auction Record
1923S	274,077	7,248	63.0	95	$75	$100	$150	$300	$1,800	$5,900	$11,750, MS-66, December 2013

HUGUENOT-WALLOON TERCENTENARY HALF DOLLAR (1924)

Designer George T. Morgan (with model modifications by James Earle Fraser); weight 12.50 grams; composition .900 silver, .100 copper; diameter 30.6 mm; reeded edge; mint: Philadelphia.

Designs. *Obverse:* Hat-clad profile portraits representing Admiral Gaspard de Coligny and William the Silent, first stadtholder of the Netherlands. *Reverse:* The ship *Nieuw Nederland* in full sail.

Mintage Data. Authorized February 26, 1923. *Maximum authorized*—300,000. *Number minted* (including 80 assay coins)—142,080. *Net distribution*—142,080.

Original Cost and Issuer. Sale price $1. Huguenot-Walloon New Netherland Commission, Inc., and designated outlets.

Key to Collecting. This coin is readily available on the market, with most examples in MS-60 to 63. Those grading MS-64 and 65 are also found quite often; MS-66 coins are scarcer. Relatively few worn pieces exist. Friction and contact marks are sometimes seen on the cheek of Admiral Coligny on the obverse, and on the masts and ship's rigging on the reverse. Many coins have been cleaned or repeatedly dipped. Connoisseurs avoid deeply toned or stained coins, even those certified with high numerical grades. MS coins usually have satiny (rather than deeply lustrous or frosty) surfaces, and may have a gray appearance. High in the reverse field of most coins is a "bright" spot interrupting the luster, from a touch of polish in the die.

First Points of Wear. *Obverse:* Coligny's cheekbone. *Reverse:* The rim near the F in FOUNDING and over RY in TERCENTENARY; the lower part of the highest sail; the center of the ship's stern.

	Distribution	Cert	Avg	%MS	MS-60	MS-62	MS-63	MS-64	MS-65	MS-66	Recent Auction Record
1924	142,080	6,976	64.0	98	$160	$165	$175	$200	$400	$800	$2,820, MS-67, June 2013

LEXINGTON-CONCORD SESQUICENTENNIAL HALF DOLLAR (1925)

Designer Chester Beach; weight 12.50 grams; composition .900 silver, .100 copper; diameter 30.6 mm; reeded edge; mint: Philadelphia.

Designs. *Obverse:* A view of the *Minute Man* statue, by Daniel Chester French, located in Concord, Massachusetts. *Reverse:* Lexington's Old Belfry, whose tolling bell roused the Minute Men to action in 1775.

Mintage and Melting Data. Authorized January 14, 1925. *Maximum authorized*—300,000. *Number minted* (including 99 assay coins)—162,099. *Number melted*—86. *Net distribution*—162,013.

Original Cost and Issuer. Sale price $1. U.S. Lexington-Concord Sesquicentennial Commission, through local banks.

Key to Collecting. Examples are easily found in all grades, with most being in high AU or low MS grades, although eye appeal can vary widely. MS-65 coins are scarce in comparison to those in MS-60 through 64. Some specimens are deeply frosty and lustrous, whereas others have partially prooflike fields.

First Points of Wear. *Obverse:* The thighs of the Minuteman. *Reverse:* The top edge of the belfry.

	Distribution	Cert	Avg	%MS	MS-60	MS-62	MS-63	MS-64	MS-65	MS-66	Recent Auction Record
1925	162,013	8,531	63.6	97	$120	$130	$150	$175	$500	$1,000	$11,880, MS-67, November 2013

STONE MOUNTAIN MEMORIAL HALF DOLLAR (1925)

Designer Gutzon Borglum; weight 12.50 grams; composition .900 silver, .100 copper; diameter 30.6 mm; reeded edge; mint: Philadelphia..

Designs. *Obverse:* Equestrian portraits of Civil War generals Robert E. Lee and Thomas "Stonewall" Jackson. *Reverse:* An eagle perched on a cliff with wings in mid-spread.

Mintage and Melting Data. *Maximum authorized*—5,000,000. *Number minted (including 4,709 assay coins)*—2,314,709. *Number melted*—1,000,000. *Net distribution*—1,314,709.

Original Cost and Issuer. Sale price $1. Sold by the Stone Mountain Confederate Monumental Association through many outlets, including promotions involving pieces counterstamped with abbreviations for Southern states.

Key to Collecting. This is the most plentiful commemorative from the 1920s. Examples are easily found in grades ranging from lightly worn through gem Mint State (many with outstanding eye appeal). Circulated coins are also found, as well as those that were counterstamped for special fundraising sales. The typical coin has very lustrous and frosty surfaces, although the reverse field may be somewhat satiny.

First Points of Wear. *Obverse:* Lee's elbow and leg. *Reverse:* The eagle's breast.

	Distribution	Cert	Avg	%MS	MS-60	MS-62	MS-63	MS-64	MS-65	MS-66	Recent Auction Record
1925	1,314,709	16,826	63.8	96	$75	$80	$85	$150	$275	$335	$2,820, MS-66, June 2013

CALIFORNIA DIAMOND JUBILEE HALF DOLLAR (1925)

Designer Jo Mora; weight 12.50 grams; composition .900 silver, .100 copper; diameter 30.6 mm; reeded edge; mint: Philadelphia.

Designs. *Obverse:* A rustic miner, squatting to pan for gold. *Reverse:* A grizzly bear, as taken from the state flag.

Mintage and Melting Data. Authorized February 24, 1925, part of the act also providing for the 1925 Fort Vancouver and 1927 Vermont half dollars. *Maximum authorized*—300,000. *Number minted (including 200 assay coins)*—150,200. *Number melted*—63,606. *Net distribution*—86,594.

Original Cost and Issuer. Sale price $1. Sold by the San Francisco Citizens' Committee through the San Francisco Clearing House Association and the Los Angeles Clearing House.

Key to Collecting. This coin's design is such that even a small amount of handling produces friction on the shoulder and high parts of the bear, in particular. As a result, most grade in the AU-55 to MS-62 range, and higher-level MS examples are rare. This issue exists in two finishes: frosty/lustrous, and the rarer "chrome-like" or prooflike. The frosty-finish pieces display some lack of die definition of the details. The prooflike pieces have heavily brushed and highly polished dies. Many specimens certified in high grades are toned, sometimes deeply, which can mask evidence of friction. Coins with no traces of friction are rarities.

First Points of Wear. *Obverse:* The folds of the miner's shirt sleeve. *Reverse:* The shoulder of the bear.

	Distribution	Cert	Avg	%MS	MS-60	MS-62	MS-63	MS-64	MS-65	MS-66	Recent Auction Record
1925S	86,594	8,650	63.6	95	$225	$275	$300	$450	$925	$1,300	$4,700, MS-67, February 2013

	Est Mintage	Cert	Finest	PF-60	PF-63	PF-64	PF-65	PF-66	Recent Auction Record
1925S, Matte Proof	1–2	1	PF-65						

FORT VANCOUVER CENTENNIAL HALF DOLLAR (1925)

Designer Laura Gardin Fraser; weight 12.50 grams; composition .900 silver, .100 copper; diameter 30.6 mm; reeded edge; mint: Philadelphia.

Designs. *Obverse:* Bareheaded profile portrait of Dr. John McLoughlin, who built Fort Vancouver (Washington) on the Columbia River in 1825. *Reverse:* A pioneer in buckskin with a musket in his hands, with Fort Vancouver in the background.

Mintage and Melting Data. Authorized February 24, 1925. *Maximum authorized*—300,000. *Number minted* (including 28 assay coins)—50,028. *Number melted*—35,034. *Net distribution*—14,994.

Original Cost and Issuer. Sale price $1. The Fort Vancouver Centennial Corporation, Vancouver, Washington.

Key to Collecting. This coin's design is such that even a small amount of handling produced friction on the higher spots. As a result, higher-level MS examples are rare.

First Points of Wear. *Obverse:* McLaughlin's temple area. *Reverse:* The pioneer's right knee.

	Distribution	Cert	Avg	%MS	MS-60	MS-62	MS-63	MS-64	MS-65	MS-66	Recent Auction Record
1925	14,994	5,184	63.9	97	$400	$420	$450	$500	$1,000	$1,300	$8,225, MS-67, September 2013

	Est Mintage	Cert	Finest	PF-60	PF-63	PF-64	PF-65	PF-66	Recent Auction Record
1925, Matte Proof	2–3	1	PF-66						

SESQUICENTENNIAL OF AMERICAN INDEPENDENCE HALF DOLLAR (1926)

Designer John R. Sinnock; weight 12.50 grams; composition .900 silver, .100 copper; diameter 30.6 mm; reeded edge; mint: Philadelphia.

Designs. *Obverse:* Conjoined profile portraits of bewigged George Washington and bareheaded Calvin Coolidge. *Reverse:* The Liberty Bell.

Mintage and Melting Data. Authorized on March 23, 1925. *Maximum authorized*—1,000,000. *Number minted* (including 528 assay coins)—1,000,528. *Number melted*—859,408. *Net distribution*—141,120.

Original Cost and Issuer. Sale price $1. National Sesquicentennial Exhibition Association.

Key to Collecting. Accurate grading can be problematic for this coin. Many examples certified at high grades have mottled or deeply toned surfaces that obfuscate examination, and others have been recolored. Most have graininess—marks from the original planchet—on the highest part of the portrait.

First Points of Wear. *Obverse:* Washington's cheekbone. *Reverse:* The area below the lower inscription on the Liberty Bell.

	Distribution	Cert	Avg	%MS	MS-60	MS-62	MS-63	MS-64	MS-65	MS-66	Recent Auction Record
1926	141,120	8,669	63.1	96	$120	$125	$140	$375	$2,500	$26,000	$19,975, MS-66, April 2014

SESQUICENTENNIAL OF AMERICAN INDEPENDENCE QUARTER EAGLE (1926)

Designer John R. Sinnock; weight 4.18 grams; composition .900 gold, .100 copper; diameter 18 mm; reeded edge; mint: Philadelphia.

Designs. *Obverse:* Miss Liberty standing, holding in one hand a scroll representing the Declaration of Independence and in the other, the Torch of Freedom. *Reverse:* A front view of Independence Hall in Philadelphia.

Mintage and Melting Data. Authorized on March 23, 1925. *Maximum authorized*—200,000. *Number minted* (including 226 assay coins)—200,226. *Number melted*—154,207. *Net distribution*—46,019.

Original Cost and Issuer. Sale price $4. National Sesquicentennial Exhibition Association.

Key to Collecting. Nearly all examples show evidence of handling and contact from careless production at the Mint, and from later indifference by their buyers. Most coins range from AU-55 to MS-62 in grade, and have scattered marks in the fields. MS-65 examples are rare. Well-struck coins are seldom seen. Some pieces show copper stains; connoisseurs avoid these.

First Points of Wear. *Obverse:* The bottom of the scroll held by Liberty. *Reverse:* The area below the top of the tower; and the central portion above the roof.

	Distribution	Cert	Avg	%MS	MS-60	MS-62	MS-63	MS-64	MS-65	MS-66	Recent Auction Record
1926	46,019	18,463	63.1	93	$475	$525	$775	$1,250	$3,400	$14,000	$9,400, MS-66, April 2013

	Est Mintage	Cert	Finest	PF-60	PF-63	PF-64	PF-65	PF-66	Recent Auction Record
1926, Matte Proof (a)	*unique*	n/a	n/a						

a. "The coin is unique and displays a matte surface similar to the Proof gold coins of 1908 to 1915. The coin was reportedly from the estate of the designer, John R. Sinnock, who is best known for his Roosevelt dime and Franklin half dollar designs. The piece was in the possession of coin dealer David Bullowa in the 1950s. Another example is rumored by Breen, but the whereabouts or existence of the coin is unknown" (*Encyclopedia of U.S. Gold Coins, 1795–1933*, second edition).

OREGON TRAIL MEMORIAL HALF DOLLAR (1926–1939)

Designers James Earle Fraser and Laura Gardin Fraser; weight 12.50 grams; composition .900 silver, .100 copper; diameter 30.6 mm; reeded edge; mint: Philadelphia.

Designs. *Obverse:* A pioneer family in a Conestoga wagon, heading west into the sunset. *Reverse:* A standing Indian with a bow, arm outstretched, and a map of the United States in the background.

Mintage and Melting Data. *Maximum authorized*—6,000,000 (for the entire series from 1926 onward). 1926: *Number minted* (including 30 assay coins)—48,030. *Number melted*—75 (defective coins). *Net distribution*—47,955. 1926-S: *Number minted* (including 55 assay coins)—100,055. *Number melted*—17,000. *Net distribution*—83,055. 1928: *Number minted* (including 28 assay coins)—50,028. *Number melted*—44,000. *Net distribution*—6,028. 1933-D: *Number minted* (including unrecorded number of assay coins)—5,250. *Number melted*—242 (probably defective coins). *Net distribution*—5,008. 1934-D: *Number minted* (including 6 assay coins)—7,006. *Net distribution*—7,006. 1936: *Number minted* (including 6 assay coins)—10,006. *Net distribution*—10,006. 1936-S: *Number minted* (including 6 assay coins)—5,006. *Net distribution*—5,006. 1937-D: *Number minted* (including 8 assay coins)—12,008. *Net distribution*—12,008. 1938 P-D-S: *Number minted* (including 6, 5, and 6 assay coins)—6,006, 6,005, 6,006. *Net distribution*—6,006, 6,005, 6,006. 1939 P-D-S: *Number minted* (including 4, 4, and 5 assay coins)—3,004, 3,004, 3,005. *Net distribution*—3,004, 3,004, 3,005.

Original Cost and Issuer. Sale price $1 (with various increases). Oregon Trail Memorial Association, Inc., sold through Scott Stamp & Coin Co., Inc., some sold through Whitman Centennial, Inc., Walla Walla, Washington. 1937 onward distributed by the Oregon Trail Memorial Association, Inc.

Key to Collecting. Although most of the later issues have low mintages, they are not rare in the marketplace, because the majority were originally sold to coin collectors and dealers. As a result, most surviving coins are in MS. The quality of the surface finish varies, with earlier issues tending to be frosty and lustrous and later issues (particularly those dated 1938 and 1939) having somewhat grainy or satiny fields. Grading requires care. Look for friction or contact marks on the high points of the Indian and the Conestoga wagon, but, more importantly, check both surfaces carefully for scattered cuts and marks. All three mints had difficulty in striking up the rims properly, causing many rejections. Those deemed acceptable and shipped out usually had full rims, but it is best to check when buying.

First Points of Wear. *Obverse:* The hip of the ox, and high points of the wagon (note that the top rear of the wagon was weakly struck in some years). *Reverse:* The Indian's left thumb and fingers (note that some pieces show flatness on the thumb and first finger, due to a weak strike).

	Distribution	Cert	Avg	%MS	MS-60	MS-62	MS-63	MS-64	MS-65	MS-66	Recent Auction Record
1926	47,955	4,957	64.2	98	$170	$175	$180	$200	$320	$450	$5,288, MS-67, August 2013
1926S	83,055	6,372	64.3	98	170	175	180	200	320	435	$7,638, MS-68, November 2013
1928 (same as 1926)	6,028	2,992	65.0	100	230	250	300	275	380	500	$4,113, MS-67, September 2013
1933D	5,008	2,856	64.9	100	380	390	400	425	500	575	$5,581, MS-67, June 2013
1934D	7,006	3,574	64.7	100	215	220	235	270	350	625	$1,645, MS-67, March 2013
1936	10,006	3,866	65.0	100	210	215	220	240	330	435	$9,400, MS-68, September 2013
1936S	5,006	2,636	65.2	100	210	230	240	250	375	500	$10,575, MS-68, January 2013
1937D	12,008	5,530	65.6	100	215	225	250	275	375	435	$863, MS-67 Plus, Star, June 2012
1938 (same as 1926)	6,006	3,045	65.1	100							$10,575, MS-68, January 2014
1938D	6,005	3,364	65.5	100							$7,931, MS-68, April 2013
1938S	6,006	3,091	65.2	100							$35,250, MS-68, January 2013
Set of 1938 P-D-S					500	550	600	650	900	1,350	$2,070, MS-67, February 2012

Chart continued on next page.

	Distribution	Cert	Avg	%MS	MS-60	MS-62	MS-63	MS-64	MS-65	MS-66	Recent Auction Record
1939	3,004	1,846	65.2	100							$8,225, MS-68, June 2013
1939D	3,004	1,957	65.4	100							$805, MS-67, June 2012
1939S	3,005	1,848	65.2	100							$5,875, MS-68, February 2013
Set of 1939 P-D-S					$1,600	$1,625	$1,700	$1,800	$2,000	$2,850	$5,175, MS-67, January 2012

	Est Mintage	Cert	Finest	PF-60	PF-63	PF-64	PF-65	PF-66	Recent Auction Record
1926, Matte Proof	1–2	1	PF-65						

VERMONT SESQUICENTENNIAL HALF DOLLAR (1927)

Designer Charles Keck; weight 12.50 grams; composition .900 silver, .100 copper; diameter 30.6 mm; reeded edge; mint: Philadelphia.

Designs. *Obverse:* Profile portrait of a bewigged Ira Allen. *Reverse:* A catamount walking left.

Mintage and Melting Data. Authorized by the Act of February 24, 1925. *Maximum authorized*—40,000. *Number minted* (including 34 assay coins)—40,034. *Number melted*—11,892. *Net distribution*—28,142.

Original Cost and Issuer. Sale price $1. Vermont Sesquicentennial Commission (Bennington Battle Monument and Historical Association).

Key to Collecting. The Vermont half dollar was struck with the highest relief of any commemorative issue. Despite the depth of the work in the dies, nearly all specimens were struck up properly and show excellent detail. Unfortunately, the height of the obverse portrait encourages evidence of contact at the central points, and nearly all coins show some friction on Allen's cheek. Most are in grades of MS-62 to 64 and are deeply lustrous and frosty. Cleaned examples are often seen—and are avoided by connoisseurs.

First Points of Wear. *Obverse:* Allen's cheek, and the hair above his ear and in the temple area. *Reverse:* The catamount's upper shoulder.

	Distribution	Cert	Avg	%MS	MS-60	MS-62	MS-63	MS-64	MS-65	MS-66	Recent Auction Record
1927	28,142	7,003	63.8	98	$310	$325	$375	$375	$800	$1,000	$8,225, MS-67, August 2013

HAWAIIAN SESQUICENTENNIAL HALF DOLLAR (1928)

Designer Juliette M. Fraser; weight 12.50 grams; composition .900 silver, .100 copper; diameter 30.6 mm; reeded edge; mint: Philadelphia.

Designs. *Obverse:* Portrait of Captain James Cook. *Reverse:* A Hawaiian chieftain standing with arm outstretched and holding a spear.

Mintage and Melting Data. Authorized March 7, 1928. *Maximum authorized*—10,000. *Number minted* (including 8 assay coins and 50 Sandblast Proofs)—10,008. *Net distribution*—10,008.

Original Cost and Issuer. Sale price $2. Captain Cook Sesquicentennial Commission, through the Bank of Hawaii, Ltd.

Key to Collecting. This is the scarcest of U.S. commemorative coins. It is elusive in all grades, and highly prized. Most are

AU-55 to MS-62 or slightly finer; those grading MS-65 or above are especially difficult to find. Most examples show contact or friction on the higher design areas. Some coins have a somewhat satiny surface, whereas others are lustrous and frosty. Many undipped pieces have a yellowish tint. Beware of coins which have been repeatedly dipped or cleaned. Problem-free examples are rarer even than the low mintage would suggest. Fake "Sandblast Proofs" exist; these are coins dipped in acid.

First Points of Wear. *Obverse:* Cook's cheekbone. *Reverse:* The chieftain's legs; his fingers and the hand holding the spear.

	Distribution	Cert	Avg	%MS	MS-60	MS-62	MS-63	MS-64	MS-65	MS-66	Recent Auction Record
1928	10,008	4,181	63.5	97	$2,500	$2,700	$3,250	$3,500	$5,500	$10,750	$25,850, MS-66, February 2013

	Est Mintage	Cert	Finest	PF-60	PF-63	PF-64	PF-65	PF-66	Recent Auction Record
1928, Proof (a)	50	34	PF-66	$12,000	$15,000	$20,000	$25,000	$100,000	$21,850, PF-63, October 2006

a. Sandblast Proof presentation pieces. "Of the production figure, 50 were Sandblast Proofs, made by a special process which imparted a dull, grainy finish to the pieces, similar to that used on certain Mint medals of the era as well as on gold Proof coins circa 1908–1915" *(Guide Book of United States Commemorative Coins).*

MARYLAND TERCENTENARY HALF DOLLAR (1934)
Designer Hans Schuler; weight 12.50 grams; composition .900 silver, .100 copper;
diameter 30.6 mm; reeded edge; mint: Philadelphia.

Designs. *Obverse:* Three-quarters portrait of Cecil Calvert, Lord Baltimore. *Reverse:* The state seal and motto of Maryland.

Mintage and Melting Data. Authorized May 9, 1934. *Maximum authorized*—25,000. *Number minted* (including 15 assay coins)—25,015. *Net distribution*—25,015.

Original Cost and Issuer. Sale price $1. Maryland Tercentenary Commission, through various outlets.

Key to Collecting. The coin's field has an unusual "rippled" appearance, similar to a sculptured plaque, so nicks and other marks that would be visible on a coin with flat fields are not as readily noticed. Most examples grade MS-62 to 64. Finer pieces, strictly graded, are elusive. This issue was not handled with care at the time of mintage and distribution, and nearly all show scattered contact marks. Some exist struck from a reverse die broken from the right side of the shield to a point opposite the upper right of the 4 in the date 1634.

First Points of Wear. *Obverse:* Lord Baltimore's nose (the nose usually appears flatly struck; also check the reverse for wear). *Reverse:* The top of the coronet on top of the shield, and the tops of the draperies.

	Distribution	Cert	Avg	%MS	MS-60	MS-62	MS-63	MS-64	MS-65	MS-66	Recent Auction Record
1934	25,015	7,840	64.5	100	$165	$175	$190	$210	$385	$550	$64,625, MS-62, November 2013

	Est Mintage	Cert	Finest	PF-60	PF-63	PF-64	PF-65	PF-66	Recent Auction Record
1934, Matte Proof	2–4	2	PF-64						

TEXAS INDEPENDENCE CENTENNIAL HALF DOLLAR (1934–1938)
Designer Pompeo Coppini; weight 12.50 grams; composition .900 silver, .100 copper;
diameter 30.6 mm; reeded edge; mint: Philadelphia.

Designs. *Obverse:* A perched eagle with a large five-pointed star in the background. *Reverse:* The goddess Victory kneeling, with medallions and portraits of General Sam Houston and Stephen Austin, founders of the republic and state of Texas, along with other Texan icons.

Mintage and Melting Data. Authorized June 15, 1933. *Maximum authorized*—1,500,000 (maximum total for all coins in the series 1934 onward). 1934: *Number minted* (including 113 assay coins)—205,113. *Number melted*—143,650. *Net distribution*—61,463. 1935-P-D-S: *Number minted* (including 8, 7, and 8 assay coins)—10,008; 10,007; 10,008. *Number melted*—12 Philadelphia (probably defective coins). *Net distribution*—9,996; 10,007; 10,008. 1936-P-D-S: *Number minted* (including 8, 7, and 8 assay coins)—10,008; 10,007; 10,008. *Number melted*—12 Philadelphia (probably defective coins). *Net distribution*—9,996; 10,007; 10,008. 1937-P-D-S: *Number minted* (including 5, 6, and 7 assay coins)—8,005; 8,006;8,007. *Number melted*—1,434; 1,401; 1,370.

Net distribution—6,571; 6,605; 6,637. 1938-P-D-S: *Number minted* (including 5, 5, and 6 assay coins)—5,005; 5,005; 5,006. *Number melted*—1,225; 1,230; 1,192. *Net distribution*—3,780; 3,775; 3,814.

Original Cost and Issuer. 1934: Sale price $1. American Legion Texas Centennial Committee, Austin, Texas. 1935: Sale price $1.50 each; $4.50 per set of three. Issuer as preceding. 1936: Sale price $1.50 each; $4.50 per set of three. Texas Memorial Museum Centennial Coin Campaign. 1937: Sale price $1.50 each; $4.50 per set of three. Issuer as preceding. 1938: Sale price $2 each; $6 per set of three. Issuer as preceding.

Key to Collecting. The typical example grades MS-64 or 65. Early issues are very lustrous and frosty; those produced toward the end of the series are more satiny.

First Points of Wear. *Obverse:* The eagle's upper breast and upper leg. *Reverse:* The forehead and knee of Victory.

	Distribution	Cert	Avg	%MS	MS-60	MS-62	MS-63	MS-64	MS-65	MS-66	Recent Auction Record
1934	61,463	5,809	64.3	98	$155	$160	$165	$190	$300	$425	$2,820, MS-67, August 2013
1935 (same as 1934)	9,996	3,822	65.4	100							$11,163, MS-68, September 2013
1935D	10,007	3,873	65.3	100							$9,988, MS-68, September 2013
1935S	10,008	3,269	65.0	100							$27,025, MS-68, January 2014
Set of 1935 P-D-S					450	460	475	600	900	1,400	$871, MS-66/66/66, December 2011

Chart continued on next page.

	Distribution	Cert	Avg	%MS	MS-60	MS-62	MS-63	MS-64	MS-65	MS-66	Recent Auction Record
1936 (same as 1934)	8,911	3,577	65.2	100							$4,406, MS-68, September 2013
1936D	9,039	3,981	65.5	100							$5,875, MS-68, September 2013
1936S	9,055	3,249	65.1	100							$2,820, MS-67, February 2013
Set of 1936 P-D-S					$450	$460	$475	$600	$900	$1,400	$863, MS-66/66/66, December 2011
1937 (same as 1934)	6,571	2,770	65.0	100							$2,350, MS-67, August 2013
1937D	6,605	2,964	65.2	100							$19,975, MS-68, September 2013
1937S	6,637	2,784	65.1	100							$2,585, MS-67, August 2013
Set of 1937 P-D-S					450	460	475	600	900	1,400	$625, MS-66/66/66, April 2012
1938 (same as 1934)	3,780	1,925	64.8	100							$4,406, MS-67, February 2013
1938D	3,775	2,032	65.1	100							$32,900, MS-68, August 2013
1938S	3,814	1,988	65.1	100							$3,525, MS-67, January 2014
Set of 1938 P-D-S					650	700	750	875	1,350	3,000	$604, MS-64/65/64, June 2012

DANIEL BOONE BICENTENNIAL HALF DOLLAR (1934–1938)

Designer Augustus Lukeman; weight 12.50 grams; composition .900 silver, .100 copper; diameter 30.6 mm; reeded edge; mint: Philadelphia.

Designs. *Obverse:* Artist's conception of Daniel Boone in a profile portrait. *Reverse:* Standing figures of Boone and Blackfish, war chief of the Chillicothe band of the Shawnee tribe. (In 1935 the date 1934 was added to the reverse design.)

Mintage and Melting Data. Authorized May 26, 1934 and, with "1934" added to modify the design, on August 26, 1935. *Maximum authorized*—600,000 (for total of all issues 1934 and onward). 1934: *Number minted* (including 7 assay coins)—10,007. *Net distribution*—10,007. 1935-P-D-S: *Number minted* (including 10, 5, and 5 assay coins): 10,010; 5,005; 5,005. Net distribution: 10,010; 5,005; 5,005. 1935 "small 1934" P-D-S: *Number minted* (including 8 assay coins)—10,008; 2,003; 2,004. *Net distribution*—10,008. 1936-P-D-S: *Number minted* (including 12, 5, and 6 assay coins) —12,012; 5,005; 5,006. *Net distribution*—12,012; 5,005; 5,006. 1937-P-D-S: *Number minted* (including 10, 6, and 6 assay coins) —15,010; 7,506; 5,006. Number melted: 5,200; 5,000; 2,500. *Net distribution*—9,810; 2,506; 2,506. 1938-P-D-S: *Number minted* (including 5, 5, and 6 assay coins)—5,005; 5,005; 5,006. Number melted: 2,905; 2,905; 2,906. *Net distribution*—2,100, 2,100, 2,100.

Original Cost and Issuer. 1934: Sale price $1.60. 1935: Sale price $1.10 for the Philadelphia issue; $1.60 each for the Denver and San Francisco coins. 1935, With 1934: Sale price $1.10 (raised to $1.60 on December 21, 1935); Denver and San Fran-cisco $3.70 per pair. 1936: Sale price $1.10 Philadelphia; $1.60 each Denver and San Francisco. 1937: Sale price, Philadelphia, $1.60 singly; later as a pair with a Denver coin for $7.25 (Denver coins were not offered singly); P-D-S sets $12.40; San Francisco coins singly $5.15. 1938 P-D-S: Sale price $6.50 per set of three. Daniel Boone Bicentennial Commission (and its division, the Pioneer National Monument Association), Phoenix Hotel, Lexington, Kentucky (C. Frank Dunn, "sole distributor").

Key to Collecting. Most collectors desire just a single coin to represent the type, but there are enough specialists who want one of each date and mintmark to ensure a ready market whenever the scarcer sets come up for sale. Most surviving coins are in MS, with MS-64 to 66 pieces readily available for most issues. Early issues in the series are characterized by deep frosty mint luster, whereas issues toward the end of the run, particularly 1937 and 1938, often are seen with a satin finish and relatively little luster (because of the methods of die preparation and striking). The 1937-S is very often seen with prooflike surfaces, and the 1938-S occasionally so. In general, the Boone commemoratives were handled carefully at the time of minting and distribution, but scattered marks are often visible.

First Points of Wear. *Obverse:* The hair behind Boone's ear. *Reverse:* The left shoulder of the Indian.

	Distribution	Cert	Avg	%MS	MS-60	MS-62	MS-63	MS-64	MS-65	MS-66	Recent Auction Record
1934	10,007	2,448	64.6	100	$135	$140	$150	$170	$275	$400	$334, MS-66, June 2012
1935	10,010	2,708	64.5	100							$3,055, MS-67, January 2014
1935D	5,005	1,600	64.4	100							$3,290, MS-67, November 2013
1935S	5,005	1,827	64.8	100							$2,585, MS-67, April 2013
Set of 1935 P-D-S					410	425	450	475	850	1,500	$380, MS-64/64/64, December 2011
1935, With Small 1934	10,008	3,010	64.7	100							$2,233, MS-67, July 2014
1935D, Same type	2,003	1,160	65.1	100							$1,116, MS-67, June 2013
1935S, Same type	2,004	1,109	64.7	100							$7,050, MS-67, January 2014
Set of 1935 P-D-S, With Added Date					850	935	975	1,100	2,000	3,750	$925, MS-65/63/64, May 2012

	Distribution	Cert	Avg	%MS	MS-60	MS-62	MS-63	MS-64	MS-65	MS-66	Recent Auction Record
1936	12,012	3,501	64.6	100							$25,850, MS-68, April 2013
1936D	5,005	2,117	64.8	100							$294, MS-66, June 2013
1936S	5,006	2,066	64.9	100							$4,553, MS-68, November 2013
Set of 1936 P-D-S					$410	$425	$450	$475	$850	$1,500	$920, MS-66/66/66 Plus, November 2011
1937	9,810	3,347	64.8	100							$3,290, MS-67, November 2013
1937D	2,506	1,290	64.9	100							$3,290, MS-67, March 2013
1937S	2,506	1,313	64.9	100							$1,175, MS-66, February 2013
Set of 1937 P-D-S					820	875	900	1,000	1,300	1,800	$564, MS-66/65/64, November 2011
1938	2,100	1,137	64.8	100							$9,635, MS-67, August 2013
1938D	2,100	1,197	65.0	100							$1,645, MS-67, April 2013
1938S	2,100	1,140	64.8	100							$1,410, MS-67, April 2013
Set of 1938 P-D-S					1,000	1,150	1,200	1,250	1,600	3,000	$4,312, MS-66/66/65, September 2011

CONNECTICUT TERCENTENARY HALF DOLLAR (1935)

Designer Henry Kreiss; weight 12.50 grams; composition .900 silver, .100 copper; diameter 30.6 mm; reeded edge; mint: Philadelphia.

Designs. *Obverse:* A modernistic eagle, standing. *Reverse:* The Charter Oak.

Mintage Data. Authorized June 21, 1934. *Maximum authorized*—25,000. *Number minted* (including 18 assay coins)— 25,018. *Net distribution*—25,018.

Original Cost and Issuer. Sale price $1. Connecticut Tercentenary Commission.

Key to Collecting. Most examples survive in upper AU and lower MS grades. Higher-grade coins such as MS-65 are elusive. Friction and/or marks are often obvious on the broad expanse of wing on the obverse, and, in particular, at the ground or baseline of the oak tree on the reverse. Examples that are otherwise lustrous, frosty, and very attractive, often have friction on the wing.

First Points of Wear. *Obverse:* The top of the eagle's wing. *Reverse:* The ground above ON and TI in CONNECTICUT.

	Distribution	Cert	Avg	%MS	MS-60	MS-62	MS-63	MS-64	MS-65	MS-66	Recent Auction Record
1935	25,018	7,634	64.3	99	$250	$270	$285	$300	$500	$800	$7,638, MS-67, February 2014

	Est Mintage	Cert	Finest	PF-60	PF-63	PF-64	PF-65	PF-66	Recent Auction Record
1935, Matte Proof	1–2	1	PF-65						

ARKANSAS CENTENNIAL HALF DOLLAR (1935–1939)

Designer Edward E. Burr; weight 12.50 grams; composition .900 silver, .100 copper; diameter 30.6 mm; reeded edge; mint: Philadelphia.

Designs. *Obverse:* An eagle with outstretched wings, stars, and other elements of the Arkansas state seal. *Reverse:* Portraits of an Arkansas youth of 1936 and an Indian chief of 1836.

Mintage and Melting Data. Authorized May 14, 1934. *Maximum authorized*—500,000 (maximum total for all issues 1935 onward). 1935-P-D-S: *Number minted* (including 5, 5, and 6 assay coins)— 13,012; 5,505; 5,506. *Net distribution*—13,012; 5,505; 5,506. 1935-P-D-S: *Number minted* (including 10, 10, and 12 assay coins)—10,010; 10,010; 10,012. *Number melted*—350; 350; 350. *Net distribution*—9,660; 9,660; 9,662. 1937-P-D-S: *Number minted* (including 5, 5, and 6 assay coins)—5,505; 5,505; 5,506. *Net distribution*—5,505; 5,505; 5,506. 1938-P-D-S: *Number minted* (including 6, 5, and 6 assay coins)—6,006; 6,005; 6,006. *Number melted*—2,850; 2,850; 2,850. *Net distribution*—3,156; 3,155;

3,156. 1939-P-D-S: *Number minted* (including 4, 4, and 5 assay coins)—2,104; 2,104; 2,105. *Net distribution*—2,104; 2,104; 2,105.

Original Cost and Issuer. 1935: Sale price $1 per coin; however, few Denver and San Francisco coins were sold at this price as B. Max Mehl bought nearly the entire mintage and soon raised the "issue price" to $2.75 each. 1936: Sale price $1 per coin; then on February 1, 1936, $1.50 per coin; then $4.50 per set of three; then $6.75 per set of three; price for unsold sets was raised to $10 on March 1, 1940. 1937: $8.75 per set of three. 1938: $8.75 post-paid per set of three; $10 after July 1, 1938; $12 on and after March 1, 1940. 1939: $10 per set of three. Issuers: 1935, 1936, 1938, 1939: Arkansas Centennial Commission throughout. 1935: B. Max Mehl bought quantities and retailed them at higher prices. 1937: Stack's of New York City.

Continued on next page.

Key to Collecting. The coin sets were produced with a satiny, almost "greasy" finish; even freshly minted coins appeared as if they had been dipped or repeatedly cleaned. Issues of 1937 to 1939 are usually more satisfactory but still are not deeply lustrous. The prominence of the girl's portrait on the center of the obverse renders that part of the coin prone to receiving bagmarks, scuffs, and other evidence of handling. As a result, relatively few pieces have great eye appeal. The obverse area where the ribbon crosses the eagle's breast is often very weak. Some examples are lightly struck on the eagle just behind its head.

First Points of Wear. *Obverse:* The eagle's head and the top of the left wing. *Reverse:* The band of the girl's cap, behind her eye.

	Distribution	Cert	Avg	%MS	MS-60	MS-62	MS-63	MS-64	MS-65	MS-66	Recent Auction Record
Single type coin					$100	$110	$115	$170	$235	$800	
1935	13,012	2,708	64.3	100							$288, MS-66, June 2012
1935D	5,505	2,084	64.6	100							$1,410, MS-67, February 2013
1935S	5,506	2,059	64.5	100							$37,600, MS-64, November 2013
Set of 1935 P-D-S					290	320	335	400	700	2,400	$322, MS-64/64/64 Plus, April 2012
1936	9,660	2,153	64.1	100							$4,994, MS-67, June 2013
1936D	9,660	2,380	64.3	100							$4,406, MS-67, February 2014
1936S	9,662	2,207	64.3	100							$4,406, MS-67, March 2014
Set of 1936 P-D-S					290	320	335	400	750	2,700	$300, MS-64/64/65, December 2011
1937	5,505	1,739	64.2	100							$3,525, MS-67, January 2014
1937D	5,505	1,875	64.4	100							$4,113, MS-67, January 2014
1937S	5,506	1,559	64.1	100							$3,525, MS-66, April 2014
Set of 1937 P-D-S					290	320	365	400	900	5,250	$600, MS-65/65/65, January 2012
1938	3,156	1,261	64.2	100							$9,400, MS-66, November 2013
1938D	3,155	1,336	64.4	100							$2,820, MS-67, April 2014
1938S	3,156	1,207	64.1	100							$1,293, MS-66, April 2013
Set of 1938 P-D-S					500	525	550	675	1,800	5,550	$2,900, MS-66/66/66, April 2012
1939	2,104	1,027	64.0	100							$3,055, MS-66, December 2013
1939D	2,104	1,108	64.3	100							$4,700, MS-66, September 2013
1939S	2,105	1,159	64.4	100							$7,050, MS-67, June 2013
Set of 1939 P-D-S					1,000	1,100	1,200	1,500	2,700	8,850	$1,610, MS-65/65/65, February 2012

	Est Mintage	Cert	Finest	PF-60	PF-63	PF-64	PF-65	PF-66	Recent Auction Record
1938, set of P-D-S, Matte Proof	1–2	n/a	n/a						

ARKANSAS CENTENNIAL—ROBINSON HALF DOLLAR (1936)

Designers Henry Kreiss (obv) and Edward E. Burr (rev); weight 12.50 grams; composition .900 silver, .100 copper; diameter 30.6 mm; reeded edge; mint: Philadelphia.

Designs. *Obverse:* An eagle with outstretched wings, stars, and other elements of the Arkansas state seal. *Reverse:* Bareheaded profile portrait of Senator Joseph T. Robinson.

Mintage and Melting Data. Authorized June 26, 1936. *Maximum authorized*—50,000 (minimum 25,000). *Number minted* (including 15 assay coins)—25,265. *Net distribution*—25,265.

Original Cost and Issuer. Sale price $1.85. Stack's of New York City.

Key to Collecting. Most known coins are in MS, as most or all were originally sold to collectors and coin dealers. Examples are plentiful in the marketplace, usually grading MS-62 to 64. The coins were not handled with care during production, so many have contact marks on Robinson's portrait and elsewhere. Some examples are lightly struck on the eagle, just behind the head.

First Points of Wear. *Obverse:* The eagle's head and the top of the left wing. *Reverse:* Robinson's cheekbone.

	Distribution	Cert	Avg	%MS	MS-60	MS-62	MS-63	MS-64	MS-65	MS-66	Recent Auction Record
1936	25,265	6,871	64.2	100	$175	$185	$200	$225	$275	$650	$2,233, MS-67, April 2014

HUDSON, NEW YORK, SESQUICENTENNIAL HALF DOLLAR (1935)

Designer Chester Beach; weight 12.50 grams; composition .900 silver, .100 copper; diameter 30.6 mm; reeded edge; mint: Philadelphia.

Designs. *Obverse:* The ship *Half Moon,* captained by Henry Hudson, in full sail. *Reverse:* The ocean god Neptune seated backward on a whale (derived from the seal of the city of Hudson); in the background, a mermaid blowing a shell.

Mintage Data. Approved May 2, 1935. *Maximum authorized—* 10,000. *Number minted* (including 8 assay coins)—10,008. *Net distribution*—10,008.

Original Cost and Issuer. Sale price $1. Hudson Sesquicentennial Committee, through the First National Bank & Trust Company of Hudson.

Key to Collecting. Examples are readily available in the marketplace. Note that deep or artificial toning, which can make close inspection impossible, has led some certified coins to certified grades that are higher than they should be. True gems are very rare. These coins were struck at high speed and with little care to preserve their quality; by the time they were originally distributed most pieces showed nicks, contact marks, and other evidence of handling. Most are lustrous and frosty (except on the central devices), and grade in the lower MS levels. MS-62 to 64 are typical. Carefully graded MS-65 coins are scarce, and anything higher is very rare.

First Points of Wear. *Obverse:* The center of the lower middle sail. *Reverse:* The motto on the ribbon, and the figure of Neptune (both of which may also be lightly struck).

	Distribution	Cert	Avg	%MS	MS-60	MS-62	MS-63	MS-64	MS-65	MS-66	Recent Auction Record
1935	10,008	4,846	64.0	98	$800	$875	$975	$1,100	$1,750	$2,500	$15,275, MS-67, November 2013

CALIFORNIA PACIFIC INTERNATIONAL EXPOSITION HALF DOLLAR (1935–1936)

Designer Robert Aitken; weight 12.50 grams; composition .900 silver, .100 copper; diameter 30.6 mm; reeded edge; mint: Philadelphia.

Designs. *Obverse:* Minerva seated, holding a spear and shield, with a grizzly bear to her right (from California's state seal). *Reverse:* The Chapel of St. Francis and the California Tower, at the California Pacific International Exposition in San Diego.

Mintage and Melting Data. 1935-S: Authorized May 3, 1935. *Maximum authorized*—250,000. *Number minted* (including 132 assay coins)—250,132. *Number melted*—180,000. *Net distribution*—70,132. 1936-D: Authorized May 6, 1936 (special authorization for recoinage of melted 1935-S half dollars). *Maximum authorized*—180,000. *Number minted* (including 92 assay coins)—180,092. *Number melted*—150,000. *Net distribution*—30,092.

Original Cost and Issuer. 1935-S: Sale price $1 (increased to $3 in 1937; dropped to $2 in 1938). 1936-D: Sale price $1.50 (increased to $3 in 1937; reduced to $1 in 1938). California Pacific International Exposition Company.

Key to Collecting. Both the 1935-S and 1936-D issues were coined with deeply frosty and lustrous surfaces. The eye appeal usually is excellent. The design made these coins susceptible to bagmarks, and most survivors, even in higher MS grades, show evidence of handling. Minerva, in particular, usually displays some graininess or contact marks, even on coins given high numerical grades. Most coins are deeply lustrous and frosty. On the 1935 San Francisco coins the S mintmark usually is flat, and on the Denver coins the California Tower is often lightly struck at the top.

First Points of Wear. *Obverse:* The bosom and knees of Minerva. *Reverse:* The top right edge of the tower. (The 1936-D was flatly struck in this area; examine the texture of the surface to determine if actual wear exists.)

	Distribution	Cert	Avg	%MS	MS-60	MS-62	MS-63	MS-64	MS-65	MS-66	Recent Auction Record
1935S	70,132	15,224	64.8	100	$110	$115	$120	$130	$160	$200	$4,994, MS-67, January 2014
1936D	30,092	9,577	64.8	100	130	135	140	150	200	250	$4,113, MS-67, August 2013

OLD SPANISH TRAIL HALF DOLLAR (1935)

Designer L.W. Hoffecker; weight 12.50 grams; composition .900 silver, .100 copper; diameter 30.6 mm; reeded edge; mint: Philadelphia.

Designs. *Obverse:* The head of a steer. *Reverse:* A map of the Southeastern states and a yucca tree.

Mintage Data. Authorized June 5, 1935. *Maximum authorized—* 10,000. *Number minted—*10,008.

Original Cost and Issuer. Sale price $2. L.W. Hoffecker, trading as the El Paso Museum Coin Committee.

Key to Collecting. These coins were handled with care during their production and shipping—still, most show scattered contact marks. The typical grade is MS-65 and higher. The fields are usually somewhat satiny and gray, not deeply lustrous and frosty.

First Points of Wear. *Obverse:* The top of the cow's head. *Reverse:* The lettering at the top.

	Distribution	Cert	Avg	%MS	MS-60	MS-62	MS-63	MS-64	MS-65	MS-66	Recent Auction Record
1935	10,008	5,016	64.8	100	$1,300	$1,375	$1,475	$1,650	$1,750	$2,000	$5,288, MS-67, February 2013

PROVIDENCE, RHODE ISLAND, TERCENTENARY HALF DOLLAR (1936)

Designers Arthur G. Carey and John H. Benson; weight 12.50 grams; composition .900 silver, .100 copper; diameter 30.6 mm; reeded edge; mint: Philadelphia.

Designs. *Obverse:* Roger Williams, the founder of Rhode Island, being welcomed by an Indian. *Reverse:* Elements from the Rhode Island state seal, including the anchor of Hope and a shield.

Mintage and Melting Data. Authorized May 2, 1935. *Maximum authorized—50,000. 1936-P-D-S: Number minted and distribution—*20,013; 15,010; 15,011. Assay coins: 13; 10; 11.

Original Cost and Issuer. Sale price $1. Rhode Island and Providence Plantations Tercentenary Committee, Inc.

Key to Collecting. These coins are readily available singly and in sets, with typical grades being MS-63 to 65. Contact marks are common. Higher-level coins, such as MS-66 and 67, are not hard to find, but are elusive in comparison to the lesser-condition pieces. The 1936 (in particular) and 1936-S are sometimes found with prooflike surfaces. Most specimens have a combination of satiny/frosty surface. Many are light gray in color.

First Points of Wear. *Obverse:* The prow of the canoe, and the Indian's right shoulder. *Reverse:* The center of the anchor, and surrounding areas.

	Distribution	Cert	Avg	%MS	MS-60	MS-62	MS-63	MS-64	MS-65	MS-66	Recent Auction Record
Single type coin					$110	$115	$120	$135	$225	$475	
1936	20,013	5,506	64.6	100							$1,880, MS-67, April 2013
1936D	15,010	4,377	64.6	100							$1,175, MS-67, February 2013
1936S	15,011	3,685	64.4	100							$1,645, MS-67, September 2013
Set of 1936 P-D-S					330	345	350	410	775	1,500	$2,185, MS-66, January 2012

CLEVELAND CENTENNIAL / GREAT LAKES EXPOSITION HALF DOLLAR (1936)

Designer Brenda Putnam; weight 12.50 grams; composition .900 silver, .100 copper; diameter 30.6 mm; reeded edge; mint: Philadelphia.

Designs. *Obverse:* Bewigged profile portrait of Moses Cleaveland. *Reverse:* A map of the Great Lakes region with nine stars marking various cities, and a compass point at the city of Cleveland.

Mintage Data. Authorized May 5, 1936. *Minimum authorized—* 25,000, *Maximum authorized—50,000. Number minted* (including 30 assay coins)—50,030. *Net distribution—*50,030.

Original Cost and Issuer. Sale price: one coin for $1.65; two for $1.60 each; three for $1.58 each; five for $1.56 each; ten for $1.55 each; twenty for $1.54 each; fifty for $1.53 each; one hundred for $1.52 each. Cleveland Centennial Commemorative Coin Association (Thomas G. Melish, Cleveland).

Key to Collecting. The Cleveland half dollar is the most readily available issue from 1936—a bumper-crop year for U.S. commemoratives. Nearly all coins are in Mint State, typically from MS-63 to 65, and most are very lustrous and frosty. This issue was not handled with care at the Mint, and scattered contact marks are typically found on both obverse and reverse.

First Points of Wear. *Obverse:* The hair behind Cleaveland's ear. *Reverse:* The top of the compass, and the land (non-lake) areas of the map.

	Distribution	Cert	Avg	%MS	MS-60	MS-62	MS-63	MS-64	MS-65	MS-66	Recent Auction Record
1936	50,030	11,783	64.3	100	$130	$135	$140	$150	$200	$390	$4,700, MS-67, February 2014

WISCONSIN TERRITORIAL CENTENNIAL HALF DOLLAR (1936)

Designer David Parsons; weight 12.50 grams; composition .900 silver, .100 copper; diameter 30.6 mm; reeded edge; mint: Philadelphia.

Designs. *Obverse:* A badger on a log, from the state emblem; and arrows representing the Black Hawk War of the 1830s. *Reverse:* A miner's arm holding a pickaxe over a mound of lead ore, derived from Wisconsin's territorial seal.

Mintage Data. Authorized May 15, 1936. *Minimum authorized*—25,000 (unlimited maximum). *Number minted* (including 15 assay coins)—25,015. *Net distribution*—25,015.

Original Cost and Issuer. Sale price $1.50 plus 7¢ postage for the first coin, 2¢ postage for each additional coin (later sold for $1.25 each in lots of 10 coins, and still later sold for $3 per coin).

Wisconsin Centennial Coin Committee (also known as the Coinage Committee of the Wisconsin Centennial Commission). Unsold remainders were distributed, into the 1950s, by the State Historical Society.

Key to Collecting. Examples are readily available in the marketplace. Most grade MS-62 to 64—although higher grades are not rare—and are very lustrous and frosty, except for the higher areas of the design (which often have a slightly polished appearance).

First Points of Wear. *Obverse:* The flank and shoulder of the badger. *Reverse:* The miner's hand.

	Distribution	Cert	Avg	%MS	MS-60	MS-62	MS-63	MS-64	MS-65	MS-66	Recent Auction Record
1936	25,015	9,507	65.1	100	$265	$275	$280	$300	$370	$425	$5,288, MS-68, August 2013

CINCINNATI MUSIC CENTER HALF DOLLAR (1936)

Designer Constance Ortmayer; weight 12.50 grams; composition .900 silver, .100 copper; diameter 30.6 mm; reeded edge; mint: Philadelphia.

Designs. *Obverse:* Bareheaded profile portrait of Stephen Foster, "America's Troubadour." *Reverse:* A woman playing a lyre, personifying Music.

Mintage Data. Authorized March 31, 1936. *Maximum authorized*—15,000. 1936-P-D-S: *Number minted* (including 5, 5, and 6 assay coins)—5,005; 5,005; 5,006. *Net distribution*—5,005; 5,005; 5,006.

Original Cost and Issuer. Sale price $7.75 per set of three (actually $7.50 plus 25¢ for the display container with cellophane slide front). Cincinnati Musical Center Commemorative Coin Association, Ohio (Thomas G. Melish).

Key to Collecting. Nearly all sets of these coins were bought by collectors and investors, thus most still exist in Mint State, primarily MS-63 to 65. Conservatively graded MS-65 and finer specimens are rare. Most coins were carelessly handled at the mints, and nearly all show scattered contact marks. This issue has a somewhat satiny or "greasy" surface, instead of fields with deep luster and frost. Denver Mint coins are typically found in slightly higher grades than their Philadelphia and San Francisco Mint companions.

First Points of Wear. *Obverse:* The hair at Foster's temple. *Reverse:* The left breast, and the skirt, of the female figure.

	Distribution	Cert	Avg	%MS	MS-60	MS-62	MS-63	MS-64	MS-65	MS-66	Recent Auction Record
Single type coin					$310	$315	$340	$365	$700	$1,800	
1936	5,005	2,213	64.3	100							$7,931, MS-67, February 2014
1936D	5,005	2,944	64.7	100							$4,259, MS-67, June 2013
1936S	5,006	2,174	64.0	100							$14,100, MS-67, January 2014
Set of 1936 P-D-S					925	940	1,000	1,200	2,175	5,000	$4,198, MS-66, February 2012

LONG ISLAND TERCENTENARY HALF DOLLAR (1936)

Designer Howard K. Weinman; weight 12.50 grams; composition .900 silver, .100 copper; diameter 30.6 mm; reeded edge; mint: Philadelphia.

Designs. *Obverse:* Conjoined profile portraits of a Dutch settler and an Algonquin Indian. *Reverse:* A Dutch vessel with full-blown sails.

Mintage and Melting Data. Authorized April 13, 1936. *Maximum authorized*—100,000. *Number minted* (including 53 assay coins)—100,053. *Number melted*—18,227. *Net distribution*—81,826.

Original Cost and Issuer. Sale price $1. Long Island Tercentenary Committee, through various banks and other outlets.

Key to Collecting. These are among the most plentiful survivors from the commemorative issues of the 1930s, and examples grading MS-64 to 66 are readily obtainable. The coins were minted and handled carelessly, and at the time of distribution most showed nicks, bagmarks, and other evidence of contact; these grade from AU-50 to MS-60. Most coins have, as struck, a satiny or slightly "greasy" luster and are not deeply frosty.

First Points of Wear. *Obverse:* The hair and the cheekbone of the Dutch settler. *Reverse:* The center of the lower middle sail.

	Distribution	Cert	Avg	%MS	MS-60	MS-62	MS-63	MS-64	MS-65	MS-66	Recent Auction Record
1936	81,826	9,813	64.0	99	$100	$110	$125	$130	$350	$800	$32,900, MS-67, April 2013

YORK COUNTY, MAINE, TERCENTENARY HALF DOLLAR (1936)

Designer Walter H. Rich; weight 12.50 grams; composition .900 silver, .100 copper; diameter 30.6 mm; reeded edge; mint: Philadelphia.

Designs. *Obverse:* Brown's Garrison, on the Saco River (site of a town settled in 1636). *Reverse:* An adaptation of the seal of York County.

Mintage Data. *Maximum authorized*—30,000. *Number minted* (including 15 assay coins)—25,015.

Original Cost and Issuer. Sale price $1.50 ($1.65 postpaid by mail to out-of-state buyers). York County Tercentenary Commemorative Coin Commission, York National Bank, Saco, Maine.

Key to Collecting. This issue was well handled at the Mint and in distribution, so most examples are in higher grades and are relatively free of marks. On the reverse, the top of the shield is a key point. Some coins have been brushed and have a myriad of fine hairlines; these can be detected by examining the coin at various angles to the light. MS-64 and 65 coins are readily found in the marketplace.

First Points of Wear. *Obverse:* The mounted sentry near the corner of the fort; the stockade; and the rim of the coin. *Reverse:* The pine tree in the shield; the top-right area of the shield; and the rim.

	Distribution	Cert	Avg	%MS	MS-60	MS-62	MS-63	MS-64	MS-65	MS-66	Recent Auction Record
1936	25,015	8,743	65.2	100	$200	$210	$225	$250	$300	$350	$2,585, MS-67, February 2013

BRIDGEPORT, CONNECTICUT, CENTENNIAL HALF DOLLAR (1936)

Designer Henry Kreiss; weight 12.50 grams; composition .900 silver, .100 copper; diameter 30.6 mm; reeded edge; mint: Philadelphia.

Designs. *Obverse:* Bareheaded profile portrait of P.T. Barnum, Bridgeport's most famous citizen. *Reverse:* An art deco eagle, standing.

Mintage Data. Authorized May 15, 1936. *Minimum authorized*—25,000 (unlimited maximum). *Number minted* (including 15 assay coins)—25,015. *Net distribution*—25,015.

Original Cost and Issuer. Sale price $2. Bridgeport Centennial, Inc., through the First National Bank and Trust Co. and other banks.

Key to Collecting. These coins are readily available in the marketplace. Most grade from MS-62 to 64. Many have been cleaned or lightly polished, but pristine MS-65 pieces are readily available. Obvious friction rub and/or marks are often seen. Some coins were struck from dies with lightly polished fields and have a prooflike or partially prooflike appearance in those areas.

First Points of Wear. *Obverse:* Barnum's cheek. *Reverse:* The eagle's wing.

	Distribution	Cert	Avg	%MS	MS-60	MS-62	MS-63	MS-64	MS-65	MS-66	Recent Auction Record
1936	25,015	7,656	64.5	100	$150	$155	$200	$225	$350	$435	$3,819, MS-67, March 2013

LYNCHBURG, VIRGINIA, SESQUICENTENNIAL HALF DOLLAR (1936)

Designer Charles Keck; weight 12.50 grams; composition .900 silver, .100 copper;
diameter 30.6 mm; reeded edge; mint: Philadelphia.

Designs. *Obverse:* Bareheaded profile portrait of Senator Carter Glass, a native of Lynchburg and former secretary of the Treasury. *Reverse:* A figure of Miss Liberty standing before the old Lynchburg courthouse.

Mintage Data. Authorized May 28, 1936. *Maximum authorized*—20,000. *Number minted* (including 13 assay coins)—20,013. *Net distribution*—20,013.

Original Cost and Issuer. Sale price $1. Lynchburg Sesqui-Centennial Association.

Key to Collecting. Most of these half dollars are in higher grades; MS-65 and 66 examples are readily available in the marketplace. Some show graininess (from striking) on the high areas of the obverse portrait and on the bosom and skirt of Miss Liberty, or show evidences of handling or contact in the same areas. Surfaces are often somewhat satiny, instead of deeply lustrous and frosty. Often the reverse field is semi-prooflike. This issue must have been handled with particular care at the Mint.

First Points of Wear. *Obverse:* The hair above Glass's ear. *Reverse:* The hair of Miss Liberty, the folds of her gown, and her bosom.

	Distribution	Cert	Avg	%MS	MS-60	MS-62	MS-63	MS-64	MS-65	MS-66	Recent Auction Record
1936	20,013	6,253	64.6	100	$275	$280	$300	$320	$375	$510	$11,750, MS-67, January 2013

ELGIN, ILLINOIS, CENTENNIAL HALF DOLLAR (1936)

Designer Trygve Rovelstad; weight 12.50 grams; composition .900 silver, .100 copper;
diameter 30.6 mm; reeded edge; mint: Philadelphia.

Designs. *Obverse:* The fur-capped profile of a bearded pioneer (a closeup view of the statue depicted on the reverse). *Reverse:* The *Pioneer Memorial* statuary group, whose creation was financed by the sale of these coins.

Mintage and Melting Data. Authorized June 16, 1936. *Maximum authorized*—25,000. *Number minted* (including 15 assay coins)—25,015. *Number melted*—5,000. *Net distribution*—20,015.

Original Cost and Issuer. Sale price $1.50. Elgin Centennial Monumental Committee, El Paso, Texas (L.W. Hoffecker in charge); banks in and near Elgin, including the First National Bank of Elgin, the Elgin National Bank, and the Union National Bank.

Key to Collecting. Elgin half dollars are fairly plentiful in today's marketplace. They seem to have been handled with particular care at the time of minting, as most have fewer bagmarks than many other commemoratives of the same era. Typical coins grade MS-64 to 66. The surfaces often have a matte-like appearance (seemingly a combination of a lustrous circulation strike and a Matte Proof) quite different from other commemorative issues of 1936. Some coins are fairly frosty. On many a bright spot is evident on the reverse below the A of AMERICA, the result of an inadvertent polishing on a small area of the die. Chief Engraver John Sinnock made a few Matte Proofs, perhaps as many as 10, by pickling coins in acid at the Mint.

First Points of Wear. *Obverse:* The cheek of the pioneer. *Reverse:* The rifleman's left shoulder. (Note that a lack of detailed facial features is the result of striking, not wear, and that the infant is always weakly struck.)

	Distribution	Cert	Avg	%MS	MS-60	MS-62	MS-63	MS-64	MS-65	MS-66	Recent Auction Record
1936	20,015	8,759	64.8	100	$240	$245	$250	$275	$300	$475	$49,938, MS-68, January 2014

ALBANY, NEW YORK, CHARTER HALF DOLLAR (1936)

Designer Gertrude K. Lathrop; weight 12.50 grams; composition .900 silver, .100 copper; diameter 30.6 mm; reeded edge; mint: Philadelphia.

Designs. *Obverse:* A plump beaver gnawing on a maple branch—fauna and flora evocative of Albany and New York State, respectively. *Reverse:* A scene with Albany's first mayor, Peter Schuyler, and his secretary, Robert Livingston, accepting the city's charter in 1686 from Governor Thomas Dongan of New York.

Mintage and Melting Data. Authorized on June 16, 1936. *Maximum authorized*—25,000. *Number minted* (including 13 assay coins)—25,013. *Number melted*—7,342. *Net distribution*—17,671.

Original Cost and Issuer. Sale price $1. Albany Dongan Charter Coin Committee.

Key to Collecting. This issue was fairly carefully handled during production and distribution, and most examples are relatively free of marks in the fields. Most specimens are lustrous and frosty, although the frost has satiny aspects. Albany half dollars are readily available on the market. The typical example grades from MS-63 to 65 and has at least minor friction and marks.

First Points of Wear. *Obverse:* The hip of the beaver (nearly all coins show at least minor evidence of contact here). *Reverse:* The sleeve of Dongan (the figure at left).

	Distribution	Cert	Avg	%MS	MS-60	MS-62	MS-63	MS-64	MS-65	MS-66	Recent Auction Record
1936	17,671	7,330	64.6	100	$340	$350	$360	$400	$450	$535	$6,815, MS-68, April 2013

SAN FRANCISCO–OAKLAND BAY BRIDGE OPENING HALF DOLLAR (1936)

Designer Jacques Schnier; weight 12.50 grams; composition .900 silver, .100 copper; diameter 30.6 mm; reeded edge; mint: Philadelphia.

Designs. *Obverse:* A stylized grizzly bear standing on all fours and facing the viewer. *Reverse:* A fading-to-the-horizon view of the San Francisco–Oakland Bay Bridge and part of San Francisco.

Mintage and Melting Data. Authorized June 26, 1936. *Maximum authorized*—200,000. *Number minted* (including 55 assay coins)—100,055. *Number melted*—28,631. *Net distribution*—71,424.

Original Cost and Issuer. Sale price $1.50. Coin Committee of the San Francisco-Oakland Bay Bridge Celebration.

Key to Collecting. These coins are readily available in today's marketplace, with most grading MS-62 to 64, typically with contact marks on the grizzly bear. The reverse design, being complex with many protective devices, normally appears free of marks, unless viewed at an angle under a strong light. The grade of the reverse for a given coin often is a point or two higher than that of the obverse. The fields of this coin often have a "greasy" appearance, rather than being deeply lustrous and frosty.

First Points of Wear. *Obverse:* The bear's body, in particular the left shoulder. *Reverse:* The clouds.

	Distribution	Cert	Avg	%MS	MS-60	MS-62	MS-63	MS-64	MS-65	MS-66	Recent Auction Record
1936S	71,424	8,923	64.4	99	$175	$190	$210	$250	$350	$475	$7,638, MS-68, January 2014

COLUMBIA, SOUTH CAROLINA, SESQUICENTENNIAL HALF DOLLAR (1936)

Designer A. Wolfe Davidson; weight 12.50 grams; composition .900 silver, .100 copper; diameter 30.6 mm; reeded edge; mint: Philadelphia.

Designs. *Obverse:* Justice, with sword and scales, standing before the state capitol of 1786 and the capitol of 1936. *Reverse:* A palmetto tree, the state emblem, with stars encircling.

Mintage Data. Authorized March 18, 1936. *Maximum authorized*—25,000. 1936-P-D-S: *Number minted and distribution*—9,007; 8,009; 8,007.

Original Cost and Issuer. Sale price $6.45 per set of three (single coins $2.15 each). Columbia Sesqui-Centennial Commission.

Key to Collecting. These coins were widely distributed at the time of issue, and examples are readily obtainable today. Most grade from MS-63 to 65. They were treated carefully in their minting and distribution, so most coins exhibit lustrous surfaces with very few handling marks. Nearly all, however, show friction on the bosom of Justice and, to a lesser extent, on the high areas of the palmetto tree foliage on the reverse.

First Points of Wear. *Obverse:* The right breast of Justice. *Reverse:* The top of the palmetto tree.

	Distribution	Cert	Avg	%MS	MS-60	MS-62	MS-63	MS-64	MS-65	MS-66	Recent Auction Record
Single type coin					$265	$275	$300	$320	$335	$375	
1936	9,007	3,553	64.9	100							$15,275, MS-68, August 2013
1936D	8,009	3,526	65.3	100							$4,818, MS-68, September 2013
1936S	8,007	3,454	65.1	100							$2,820, MS-68, September 2013
Set of 1936 P-D-S					800	810	900	950	1,000	1,125	$690, MS-65/66/65, February 2012

DELAWARE TERCENTENARY HALF DOLLAR (1936)

Designer Carl L. Schmitz; weight 12.50 grams; composition .900 silver, .100 copper; diameter 30.6 mm; reeded edge; mint: Philadelphia.

Designs. *Obverse:* Old Swedes Church, the oldest Protestant church in the United States still used for worship. *Reverse:* The ship *Kalmar Nyckel.*

Mintage and Melting Data. Authorized May 15, 1936. *Minimum authorized*—25,000 (unlimited maximum). *Number minted (including 15 assay coins)*—25,015. *Number melted*—4,022. *Net distribution*—20,993.

Original Cost and Issuer. Sale price $1.75. Delaware Swedish Tercentenary Commission, through the Equitable Trust Company of Wilmington.

Key to Collecting. Most examples in today's marketplace grade MS-64 or 65, though they typically exhibit numerous original planchet nicks and marks. Most coins are very lustrous and frosty.

First Points of Wear. *Obverse:* The roof above the church entrance. (Note that the triangular section at the top of the entrance is weakly struck, giving an appearance of wear.) *Reverse:* The center of the lower middle sail (also often shows graininess and nicks from the original planchet).

	Distribution	Cert	Avg	%MS	MS-60	MS-62	MS-63	MS-64	MS-65	MS-66	Recent Auction Record
1936	20,993	6,980	64.6	100	$275	$285	$300	$325	$385	$600	$12,925, MS-67, January 2013

BATTLE OF GETTYSBURG ANNIVERSARY HALF DOLLAR (1936)

Designer Frank Vittor; weight 12.50 grams; composition .900 silver, .100 copper; diameter 30.6 mm; reeded edge; mint: Philadelphia.

Designs. *Obverse:* Uniformed profile portraits of a Union soldier and a Confederate soldier. *Reverse:* Union and Confederate shields separated by a fasces.

Mintage and Melting Data. Authorized June 16, 1936. *Maximum authorized*—50,000. *Number minted (including 28 assay coins)*—50,028. *Number melted*—23,100. *Net distribution*—26,928.

Original Cost and Issuer. Sale price $1.65. The Pennsylvania State Commission, Hotel Gettysburg, Gettysburg. The price was later raised to $2.65 for coins offered by the American Legion, Department of Pennsylvania.

Key to Collecting. Examples are fairly plentiful in the marketplace. The typical coin grades from MS-63 to 65, is deeply frosty and lustrous, and shows scattered contact marks, which are most evident on the cheeks of the soldiers on the obverse and, on the reverse, on the two shields (particularly at the top of the Union shield on the left side of the coin).

First Points of Wear. *Obverse:* The cheekbones of each soldier. *Reverse:* The three ribbons on the fasces, and the top of the Union shield.

	Distribution	Cert	Avg	%MS	MS-60	MS-62	MS-63	MS-64	MS-65	MS-66	Recent Auction Record
1936	26,928	8,191	64.4	99	$475	$480	$500	$550	$900	$1,200	$633, MS-65, June 2012

NORFOLK, VIRGINIA, BICENTENNIAL HALF DOLLAR (1936)

Designers William M. and Marjorie E. Simpson; weight 12.50 grams; composition .900 silver, .100 copper; diameter 30.6 mm; reeded edge; mint: Philadelphia.

Designs. *Obverse:* The seal of the city of Norfolk, with a three-masted ship at center. *Reverse:* The city's royal mace, presented by Lieutenant Governor Dinwiddie in 1753.

Mintage and Melting Data. Authorized June 28, 1937. *Maximum authorized*—25,000. *Number minted* (including 13 assay coins)—25,013. *Number melted*—8,077. *Net distribution*—16,936.

Original Cost and Issuer. Sale price $1.50 locally ($1.65 by mail for the first coin, $1.55 for each additional). Norfolk Advertising Board, Norfolk Association of Commerce.

Key to Collecting. Examples are fairly plentiful in today's marketplace, with most in high MS grades. The cluttered nature of the design had a positive effect: all of the lettering served to protect the fields and devices from nicks and marks, with the result that MS-65 and 66 coins are plentiful.

First Points of Wear. *Obverse:* The sails of the ship, especially the lower rear sail. *Reverse:* The area below the crown on the royal mace.

	Distribution	Cert	Avg	%MS	MS-60	MS-62	MS-63	MS-64	MS-65	MS-66	Recent Auction Record
1936	16,936	7,265	65.7	100	$410	$425	$450	$480	$560	$625	$5,288, MS-68, August 2013

ROANOKE ISLAND, NORTH CAROLINA, 350TH ANNIVERSARY HALF DOLLAR (1937)

Designer William M. Simpson; weight 12.50 grams; composition .900 silver, .100 copper; diameter 30.6 mm; reeded edge; mint: Philadelphia.

Designs. *Obverse:* Profile portrait of Sir Walter Raleigh in plumed hat and fancy collar. *Reverse:* Ellinor Dare and her baby, Virginia, the first white child born in the Americas to English parents.

Mintage and Melting Data. *Minimum authorized*—25,000 (unlimited maximum). *Number minted* (including 30 assay coins)—50,030. *Number melted*—21,000. *Net distribution*—29,030.

Original Cost and Issuer. Sale price $1.65. Roanoke Colony Memorial Association of Manteo.

Key to Collecting. Most of these coins were handled with care during their minting, and today are in high grades. MS-65 pieces are plentiful. Most coins are lustrous and frosty. Partially prooflike pieces are occasionally seen (sometimes offered as "presentation pieces" or "prooflike presentation pieces").

First Points of Wear. *Obverse:* Raleigh's cheek and the brim of his hat. *Reverse:* The head of Ellinor Dare.

	Distribution	Cert	Avg	%MS	MS-60	MS-62	MS-63	MS-64	MS-65	MS-66	Recent Auction Record
1937	29,030	9,373	64.9	100	$250	$265	$275	$300	$325	$375	$4,259, MS-68, January 2014

BATTLE OF ANTIETAM ANNIVERSARY HALF DOLLAR (1937)

Designer William M. Simpson; weight 12.50 grams; composition .900 silver, .100 copper; diameter 30.6 mm; reeded edge; mint: Philadelphia.

Designs. *Obverse:* Uniformed profile portraits of generals Robert E. Lee and George B. McClellan, opponent commanders during the Battle of Antietam. *Reverse:* Burnside Bridge, an important tactical objective of the battle.

Mintage and Melting Data. Authorized June 24, 1937. *Maximum authorized*—50,000. *Number minted* (including 28 assay coins)—50,028. *Number melted*—32,000. *Net distribution*—18,028.

Original Cost and Issuer. Sale price $1.65. Washington County Historical Society, Hagerstown, Maryland.

Key to Collecting. Antietam half dollars were handled with care during production. More often seen are scattered small marks, particularly on the upper part of the obverse. Most examples are very lustrous and frosty. MS-65 and finer coins are plentiful in the marketplace.

First Points of Wear. *Obverse:* Lee's cheekbone. *Reverse:* The leaves of the trees; the bridge; and the rim of the coin.

	Distribution	Cert	Avg	%MS	MS-60	MS-62	MS-63	MS-64	MS-65	MS-66	Recent Auction Record
1937	18,028	7,027	64.9	100	$700	$710	$725	$750	$800	$900	$8,225, MS-68, January 2014

NEW ROCHELLE, NEW YORK, 250TH ANNIVERSARY HALF DOLLAR (1938)

Designer Gertrude K. Lathrop; weight 12.50 grams; composition .900 silver, .100 copper; diameter 30.6 mm; reeded edge; mint: Philadelphia.

Designs. *Obverse:* John Pell, who sold the French Huguenots the land for New Rochelle, and a fatted calf, an annual provision of the sale. *Reverse:* A fleur-de-lis, adapted from the seal of the city.

Mintage and Melting Data. Authorized May 5, 1936. *Maximum authorized*—25,000. *Number minted (including 15 assay coins)*—25,015. *Number melted*—9,749. *Net distribution*—15,266.

Original Cost and Issuer. Sale price $2. New Rochelle Commemorative Coin Committee, through the First National Bank of New Rochelle, New Rochelle, New York.

Key to Collecting. These half dollars received better-than-average care and handling during the minting and distribution process. The typical coin grades MS-64 or higher. Some examples show very light handling marks, but most are relatively problem-free. Some show areas of graininess or light striking on the high spots of the calf on the obverse, and on the highest area of the iris on the reverse. The majority of pieces have lustrous, frosty surfaces, and a few are prooflike (the latter are sometimes offered as "presentation pieces").

First Points of Wear. *Obverse:* The hip of the calf. *Reverse:* The bulbous part of the fleur-de-lis. (Note that on the central petal the midrib is flatly struck.)

	Distribution	Cert	Avg	%MS	MS-60	MS-62	MS-63	MS-64	MS-65	MS-66	Recent Auction Record
1938	15,266	6,518	64.9	100	$390	$400	$415	$450	$575	$700	$10,281, MS-66, March 2013

	Est Mintage	Cert	Finest	PF-60	PF-63	PF-64	PF-65	PF-66	Recent Auction Record
1938, Proof	1–2	11	PF-68						

Note: Certification figures include 10 coins graded SP-64 to SP-68. The single Proof coin is graded PF-61.

IOWA CENTENNIAL HALF DOLLAR (1946)

Designer Adam Pietz; weight 12.50 grams; composition .900 silver, .100 copper; diameter 30.6 mm; reeded edge; mint: Philadelphia.

Designs. *Obverse:* The Old Stone Capitol building at Iowa City. *Reverse:* An eagle with wings spreading, adapted from the Iowa state seal.

Mintage Data. Authorized August 7, 1946. *Maximum authorized*—100,000. *Number minted (including 57 assay coins)*—100,057.

Original Cost and Issuer. Sale price $2.50 to in-state buyers, $3 to those out of state. Iowa Centennial Committee, Des Moines, Iowa.

Key to Collecting. Most specimens are in varying degrees of Mint State, and are lustrous and frosty. MS-63 to 66 are typical grades. The nature of the design, without open field areas, is such that a slight amount of friction and contact is usually not noticeable.

First Points of Wear. *Obverse:* The clouds above the Capitol, and the shafts of the building near the upper-left and upper-right windows. *Reverse:* The back of the eagle's head and neck. (Note that the head sometimes is flatly struck.)

	Distribution	Cert	Avg	%MS	MS-60	MS-62	MS-63	MS-64	MS-65	MS-66	Recent Auction Record
1946	100,057	14,538	65.2	100	$125	$130	$135	$140	$150	$185	$9,400, MS-68, January 2013

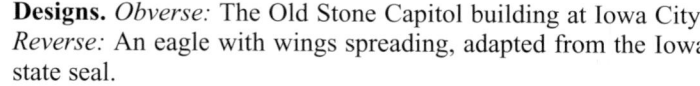

BOOKER T. WASHINGTON MEMORIAL HALF DOLLAR (1946–1951)

Designer Isaac S. Hathaway; weight 12.50 grams; composition .900 silver, .100 copper; diameter 30.6 mm; reeded edge; mint: Philadelphia.

Designs. *Obverse:* Bareheaded three-quarters profile portrait of Booker T. Washington. *Reverse:* The Hall of Fame at New York University and a slave cabin.

Mintage and Melting Data. Signed into law by President Harry S Truman on August 7, 1946. *Maximum authorized*—5,000,000, with dates not specified. 1946-P-D-S: *Number minted* (including 546, 113, and 279 assay coins)—1,000,546; 200,113; 500,279. *Net distribution*—700,546 (estimated); 50,000 (estimated); 500,279 (estimated). 1947-P-D-S: *Number minted* (including 17 assay coins each mint)—100,017; 100,017; 100,017. *Net distribution*—6,000 (estimated); 6,000 (estimated); 6,000 (estimated). 1948-P-D-S: *Number minted* (including 5 assay coins each mint): 20,005; 20,005; 20,005. *Net distribution*—8,005; 8,005; 8,005. 1949-P-D-S: *Number minted* (including 4 assay coins each mint)—12,004; 12,004; 12,004. *Net distribution*—6,004; 6,004; 6,004. 1950-P-D-S: *Number minted* (including 4, 4, and 91 assay coins)—12,004; 12,004; 512,091. *Net distribution*—6,004; 6,004; 62,091 (estimated). 1951-P-D-S: *Number minted* (including 82, 4, and 4 assay coins)—510,082; 12,004; 12,004. *Net distribution*—210,082 (estimated); 7,004; 7,004.

Original Cost and Issuer. 1946: Sale price $1 per coin for Philadelphia and San Francisco, $1.50 for Denver, plus 10¢ postage per coin. Booker T. Washington Birthplace Memorial Commission, Inc., Rocky Mount, Virginia (Dr. S.J. Phillips in charge), Stack's of New York City, Bebee Stamp & Coin Company (a.k.a. Bebee's). Later issues: Costs and distributors varied.

Key to Collecting. Of all commemorative half dollar issues produced up to this point, the Booker T. Washington half dollars were made with the least amount of care during the coining process at the mints. At the time of release, nearly all were poorly struck on the obverse and were marked with abrasions and nicks. Many have graininess and marks on Washington's cheek, from the original planchet surface that did not strike up fully. Many coins grade from MS-60 to (liberally graded) 65. Some have natural or artificial toning that masks the true condition and facilitates gem certification. Prooflike coins are sometimes seen, including for 1947-S (in particular), 1948-S, 1949, and 1951-S. These are not at all mirrorlike, but still have surfaces different from the normal mint frost.

First Points of Wear. *Obverse:* Washington's cheekbone. *Reverse:* The center lettering (FROM SLAVE CABIN, etc.).

	Distribution	Cert	Avg	%MS	MS-60	MS-62	MS-63	MS-64	MS-65	MS-66	Recent Auction Record
Single type coin					$20	$21	$25	$35	$60	$150	
1946	700,546	5,909	64.5	99							$2,585, MS-67, February 2014
1946D	50,000	3,466	64.7	100							$104, MS-66, June 2012
1946S	500,279	5,170	64.7	100							$3,525, MS-68, August 2013
Set of 1946 P-D-S					65	70	80	100	175	600	$110, MS-65, May 2012
1947	6,000	2,005	64.8	100							$646, MS-66, June 2014
1947D	6,000	1,425	64.8	100							$8,813, MS-67, February 2014
1947S	6,000	1,912	65.0	100							$3,525, MS-67, August 2013
Set of 1947 P-D-S					125	130	150	195	310	2,050	$196, MS-65/65/65, January 2012
1948	8,005	1,933	65.0	100							$2,350, MS-67, April 2014
1948D	8,005	1,974	65.0	100							$4,406, MS-67, February 2013
1948S	8,005	2,092	65.1	100							$2,820, MS-67, February 2013
Set of 1948 P-D-S					180	200	235	255	325	1,200	$220, MS-66/65/65, June 2012
1949	6,004	2,027	65.0	100							$3,055, MS-67, March 2013
1949D	6,004	1,969	65.0	100							$4,406, MS-67, February 2014
1949S	6,004	2,130	65.3	100							$1,011, MS-67, March 2013
Set of 1949 P-D-S					240	250	265	295	350	800	$320, MS-65/66/66, May 2012
1950	6,004	1,461	65.0	100							$705, MS-66, April 2014
1950D	6,004	1,491	64.9	100							$7,374, MS-67, February 2013
1950S	62,091	2,975	65.0	100							$3,525, MS-67, April 2014
Set of 1950 P-D-S					150	160	170	190	250	1,500	$725, MS-66/66/66, April 2012
1951	210,082	2,787	64.6	100							$3,202, MS-67, November 2013
1951D	7,004	1,577	65.1	100							$3,819, MS-67, August 2013
1951S	7,004	1,780	65.4	100							$1,880, MS-67, August 2013
Set of 1951 P-D-S					150	165	180	200	230	1,100	$475, MS-66/66/66, May 2012

CARVER/WASHINGTON COMMEMORATIVE HALF DOLLAR (1951–1954)

Designer Isaac S. Hathaway; weight 12.50 grams; composition .900 silver, .100 copper; diameter 30.6 mm; reeded edge; mint: Philadelphia.

Designs. *Obverse:* Conjoined bareheaded profile portraits of George Washington Carver and Booker T. Washington. *Reverse:* A map of the United States, with legends.

Mintage Data. Signed into law by President Harry S Truman on September 21, 1951. *Maximum authorized*—3,415,631 (total for all issues 1951 onward; consisting of 1,581,631 undistributed Booker T. Washington coins which could be converted into Carver-Washington coins, plus the unused 1,834,000 earlier authorization for Booker T. Washington coins). The following include author's estimates: 1951-P-D-S: *Number minted* (including 18, 4, and 4 assay coins)—110,018; 10,004; 10,004. *Net distribution*—20,018 (estimated); 10,004 (estimated); 10,004 (estimated). 1952-P-D-S: *Number minted* (including 292, 6, and 6 assay coins)—2,006,292; 8,006; 8,006. *Net distribution*—1,106,292 (estimated); 8,006 (estimated); 8,006 (estimated). 1953-P-D-S: *Number minted* (including 3, 3, and 20 assay coins)—8,003; 8,003; 108,020. *Net distribution*—8,003 (estimated); 8,003 (estimated); 88,020 (estimated). 1954-P-D-S: *Number minted* (including 6, 6, and 24 assay coins)—12,006; 12,006; 122,024. *Net distribution*—12,006 (estimated); 12,006 (estimated); 42,024 (estimated).

Original Cost and Issuer. 1951-P-D-S: $10 per set. 1952-P-D-S: $10 per set; many Philadelphia coins were sold at or near face value through banks. 1953-P-D-S: $10 per set; some 1953-S coins were distributed at or near face value (Bebee's prices $9 until January 15, 1952, $10 after that date). 1954-P-D-S: Official sale price: $10 per set; some 1954-S coins were paid out at face value (Bebee's prices for sets $9 until January 20, 1954, $12 after that date). Issued mainly by the Carver-Washington Coin Commission acting for the Booker T. Washington Birthplace Memorial Foundation (Booker Washington Birthplace, Virginia) and the George Washington Carver National Monument Foundation (Diamond, Missouri). Also, for some issues, these dealers: Stack's, Bebee Stamp & Coin Company, Sol Kaplan, and R. Green.

Key to Collecting. Nearly all coins of this issue were handled casually at the mints and also during the distribution process. Most were not fully struck up, with the result that under magnification many tiny nicks and marks can be seen on the higher parts, originating from planchet marks that were not obliterated during the striking process. Many MS examples are available on the market.

First Points of Wear. *Obverse:* Carver's cheekbone. (Note that some pieces were struck poorly in this area; check the reverse also for wear.) *Reverse:* The lettering U.S.A. on the map.

	Distribution	Cert	Avg	%MS	MS-60	MS-62	MS-63	MS-64	MS-65	MS-66	Recent Auction Record
Single type coin					$21	$23	$25	$40	$75	$320	
1951	20,018	1,901	64.0	99							$8,225, MS-67, February 2014
1951D	10,004	1,617	64.5	100							$3,290, MS-66, January 2013
1951S	10,004	2,017	64.9	100							$8,813, MS-67, March 2013
Set of 1951 P-D-S					135	145	200	215	550	3,750	$140, MS-64/64/64, June 2012
1952	1,106,292	7,383	64.3	99							$150, MS-66, June 2012
1952D	8,006	1,331	64.4	100							$940, MS-66, May 2013
1952S	8,006	1,775	64.8	100							$1,410, MS-66, June 2013
Set of 1952 P-D-S					140	150	180	190	385	1,650	$230, MS-65/65/65, March 2012
1953	8,003	1,501	64.5	100							$10,281, MS-67, September 2013
1953D	8,003	1,294	64.3	100							$14,100, MS-67, September 2013
1953S	88,020	2,707	64.6	100							$403, MS-66, June 2012
Set of 1953 P-D-S					140	150	210	230	540	1,650	$300, MS-65/65/65, May 2012
1954	12,006	1,913	64.4	100							$9,988, MS-67, August 2013
1954D	12,006	1,724	64.3	100							$1,880, MS-66, January 2013
1954S	42,024	2,619	64.4	100							$207, MS-66, June 2012
Set of 1954 P-D-S					135	145	180	190	390	1,650	$316, MS-65/65/65, March 2012

AN OVERVIEW OF PROOF AND MINT SETS

PROOF COINS AND SETS

A Proof is a specimen coin struck for presentation, souvenir, exhibition, or numismatic purposes. Before 1968, Proofs were made only at the Philadelphia Mint, except in a few rare instances in which presentation pieces were struck at branch mints. Today Proofs are made at the San Francisco and West Point mints.

The term Proof refers not to the condition of a coin, but to its method of manufacture. Regular-production coins (struck for circulation) in Mint State have coruscating, frosty luster; soft details; and minor imperfections. A Proof coin can usually be distinguished by its sharpness of detail, high wire edge, and extremely brilliant, mirrorlike surface. All Proofs are originally sold by the Mint at a premium.

Very few Proof coins were made prior to 1856. Because of their rarity and infrequent sales, they are not all listed in the regular edition of the *Guide Book of United States Coins*. However, here, in the Professional Edition, you will find them listed individually within their respective denominations.

Frosted Proofs were issued prior to 1936 and starting again in the late 1970s. These have a brilliant, mirrorlike field with contrasting dull or frosted design.

Matte Proofs have a granular, "sandblast" surface instead of the mirror finish. Matte Proof cents, nickels, and gold coins were issued from 1908 to 1916; a few 1921 and 1922 silver dollars and a 1998-S half dollar were also struck in this manner.

Brilliant Proofs have been issued from 1936 to date. These have a uniformly brilliant, mirrorlike surface and sharp, high-relief details.

"Prooflike" coins are occasionally seen. These are examples from dies that have been lightly polished, often inadvertently during the removal of lines, contact marks, and other marks in the fields. In other instances, such as with certain New Orleans gold coins of the 1850s, the dies were polished in the machine shop of the mint. They are not true Proofs, but may have most of the characteristics of a Proof coin and generally command a premium. Collectors should beware of coins that have been buffed to look like Proofs; magnification will reveal polishing lines and lack of detail.

After a lapse of some 20 years, Proof coins were struck at the Philadelphia Mint from 1936 to 1942, inclusive. During these years the Mint offered Proof coins to collectors for individual sale, rather than in officially packaged sets, as such.

In 1942, when the composition of the five-cent piece was changed, there were two types of this denomination available to collectors. The striking of Proof coins was temporarily suspended from 1943 through 1949, and again from 1965 through 1967; during the latter period, Special Mint Sets were struck (see page 358). Proof sets were resumed in 1968.

Sets from 1936 through 1972 include the cent, nickel, dime, quarter, and half dollar; from 1973 through 1981 the dollar was also included, and again from 2000 on. Regular Proof sets issued from 1982 to 1998 contain the cent through the half dollar. Specially packaged Prestige sets containing commemorative coins were sold from 1983 through 1997 at an additional premium. From 1999 to 2009, sets contain five different Statehood or Territorial quarters, and from 2010 to 2021, different National Parks quarters. In 1999 Proof dollars were sold separately. Four-piece Presidential dollar sets have been issued since 2007.

From time to time the Mint issues special Proof sets. One recent example is the four-piece 2009-S Lincoln Bicentennial set, which included each of the special cent designs issued that year, but coined in 95% copper (the Lincoln cent's original 1909 alloy).

HOW MODERN PROOF COINS ARE MADE

Selected dies are inspected for perfection and are highly polished and cleaned. They are again wiped clean or polished after every 15 to 25 impressions and are replaced frequently to avoid imperfections from worn dies. Coinage blanks are polished and cleaned to ensure high quality in striking. They are then hand fed into the coinage press one at a time, each blank receiving two or more blows from the dies to bring up sharp, high-relief details. The coinage operation is done at slow speed with extra pressure. Finished Proofs are individually inspected and are handed with gloves or tongs. They also receive a final inspection by packers before being sonically sealed in special plastic cases.

MINT SETS

Official Uncirculated Mint sets are specially packaged by the government for sale to collectors. They contain Uncirculated specimens of each year's coins for every denomination issued from each mint. Before 2005, the coins were the same as those normally intended for circulation and were not minted with any special consideration for quality. From 2005 to 2010, however, Mint sets were made with a satin finish rather than the traditional Uncirculated luster. As in the past, coins struck only as Proofs are not included.

Uncirculated Mint sets sold by the Treasury from 1947 through 1958 contained two examples of each regular-issue coin. These were packaged in cardboard holders that did not protect the coins from tarnish. Nicely preserved early sets generally command a 10 to 20% premium above average values. No official Uncirculated Mint sets were produced in 1950, 1982, or 1983.

Since 1959, sets have been sealed in protective plastic envelopes. In 1965, 1966, and 1967, Special Mint Sets (see next section) of higher-than-normal quality were made to substitute for Proof sets, which were not being made during that period. Similar experimental coins dated 1964 also exist.

Privately assembled Mint sets, and Souvenir sets produced for sale at the Philadelphia or Denver mints for special occasions, are valued according to the individual pieces they contain. Only the official, government-packaged full sets are included in the following list.

From time to time the Mint issues special Mint sets. One recent example is the 1996-P-D Mint set, which also included a 1996-W dime (released only in those sets).

SPECIAL MINT SETS

In mid-1964 the Treasury department announced that the Mint would not offer Proof sets or Mint sets the following year. This was prompted by a nationwide shortage of circulating coins, which was wrongly blamed on coin collectors.

In 1966 the San Francisco Assay Office began striking coins dated 1965, for inclusion in so-called United States Special Mint Sets. These were issued in pliofilm packaging similar to that of recent Proof sets. The coins in early 1965 Special Mint Sets are semi-brilliant or satiny (distinctive, but not equal in quality to Proofs); the coins in later 1965 sets feature very brilliant fields (but again not reaching Proof brilliance).

The San Francisco Assay Office started striking 1966-dated coins in August of that year, and its Special Mint Sets were packaged in rigid, sonically sealed plastic holders. The coins were struck once on unpolished planchets, unlike Proof coins (which are struck at least twice on polished planchets). Also unlike Proofs, the SMS coins were allowed to come into contact with each other during their production, which accounts for minor contact marks and abrasions. To achieve a brilliant finish, Mint technicians overpolished the coinage dies. The result was a tradeoff: most of the coins have prooflike brilliance, but many are missing polished-off design details, such as Frank Gasparro's initials on the half dollar.

All 1967-dated coinage was struck in that calendar year. Nearly all SMS coins of 1967 have fully brilliant, prooflike finishes. This brilliance was achieved without overpolishing the dies, resulting in coins that approach the quality of true Proofs. Sales of the 1967 sets were lackluster, however. The popularity of coin collecting had dropped from its peak in 1964. Also, collectors and speculators did not anticipate much secondary-market profit from the sets, which had an issue price of $4.00, compared to $2.10 for a 1964 Proof set. As a result, fewer collectors bought multiples of the 1967 sets, and today they are generally worth more than those of 1965 and 1966.

Similar SMS coins dated 1964 exist as single pieces and in sets. Like the 1965 through 1967 SMS coins, they have a semi-brilliant or satiny finish but are not equal in quality to Proofs. They are referred to as SP (Special Strike) coins and command much higher prices than their regular SMS counterparts.

RECOMMENDED READING

Lange, David W. *A Guide Book of Modern United States Proof Coin Sets* (2nd ed.), Atlanta, GA, 2010.

1936 Proof Set
*Liberty Walking half dollar, Washington quarter dollar, Mercury or Winged Liberty dime,
Buffalo nickel, and Lincoln cent with Wheat Ears reverse.*

1938 Proof Set
Buffalo nickel replaced with the new Jefferson nickel.

1950 Proof Set
*There was a seven-year hiatus (1943–1949) before Proof sets were issued again after World War II. By 1950 the Liberty Walking half dollar
had been replaced by the Franklin half dollar (introduced 1948), and the Mercury dime by the Roosevelt dime (introduced 1946).*

1955 Proof Set
*Issued in traditional individual envelopes, or in the new pliofilm package (pictured),
with a Philadelphia Mint embossed paper seal with a metallic finish.*

MODERN PROOF SETS (1936 TO DATE)

	Mintage	Issue Price
1936	(3,837)	$1.89
1937	(5,542)	1.89
1938	(8,045)	1.89
1939	(8,795)	1.89
1940	(11,246)	1.89
1941	(15,287)	1.89
1942, Both nickels	(21,120)	1.89
1942, One nickel	*	1.89
1950	(51,386)	2.10
1951	(57,500)	2.10
1952	(81,980)	2.10
1953	(128,800)	2.10
1954	(233,300)	2.10
1955, Box pack	(378,200)	2.10
1955, Flat pack	*	2.10
1956	(669,384)	2.10
1957	(1,247,952)	2.10
1958	(875,652)	2.10
1959	(1,149,291)	2.10
1960, With Large Date cent	(1,691,602)	2.10
1960, With Small Date cent	*	2.10
1961	(3,028,244)	2.10
1962	(3,218,019)	2.10
1963	(3,075,645)	2.10
1964	(3,950,762)	2.10
1968S	(3,041,506)	5.00
1968S, With No S dime	*	5.00
1969S	(2,934,631)	5.00
1970S	(2,632,810)	5.00
1970S, With Small Date cent	*	5.00
1970S, With No S dime (estimated mintage: 2,200)	*	5.00
1971S	(3,220,733)	5.00
1971S, With No S nickel (estimated mintage: 1,655)	*	5.00
1972S	(3,260,996)	5.00
1973S	(2,760,339)	7.00
1974S	(2,612,568)	7.00
1975S, With 1976 quarter, half, and dollar	(2,845,450)	7.00
1975S, With No S dime	*	7.00
1976S	(4,149,730)	7.00
1976S, Silver clad, 3-piece set	(3,998,621)	15.00
1977S	(3,251,152)	9.00
1978S	(3,127,781)	9.00
1979S, Type 1	(3,677,175)	9.00
1979S, Type 2	*	9.00
1980S	(3,554,806)	10.00
1981S, Type 1	(4,063,083)	11.00
1981S, Type 2 (all six coins in set)	*	11.00
1982S	(3,857,479)	11.00
1983S	(3,138,765)	11.00
1983S, With No S dime	*	11.00
1983S, Prestige set (Olympic dollar)	(140,361)	59.00
1984S	(2,748,430)	11.00
1984S, Prestige set (Olympic dollar)	(316,680)	59.00
1985S	(3,362,821)	11.00

	Mintage	Issue Price
1986S	(2,411,180)	$1.00
1986S, Prestige set (Statue of Liberty half, dollar)	(599,317)	48.50
1987S	(3,792,233)	11.00
1987S, Prestige set (Constitution dollar)	(435,495)	45.00
1988S	(3,031,287)	11.00
1988S, Prestige set (Olympic dollar)	(231,661)	45.00
1989S	(3,009,107)	11.00
1989S, Prestige set (Congressional half, dollar)	(211,807)	45.00
1990S	(2,793,433)	11.00
1990S, With No S cent	(3,555)	11.00
1990S, With No S cent (Prestige set)	*	45.00
1990S, Prestige set (Eisenhower dollar)	(506,126)	45.00
1991S	(2,610,833)	11.00
1991S, Prestige set (Mt. Rushmore half, dollar)	(256,954)	59.00
1992S	(2,675,618)	11.00
1992S, Prestige set (Olympic half, dollar)	(183,293)	56.00
1992S, Silver	(1,009,586)	11.00
1992S, Silver Premier set	(308,055)	37.00
1993S	(2,409,394)	12.50
1993S, Prestige set (Bill of Rights half, dollar)	(224,045)	57.00
1993S, Silver	(570,213)	21.00
1993S, Silver Premier set	(191,140)	37.50
1994S	(2,308,701)	12.50
1994S, Prestige set (World Cup half, dollar)	(175,893)	57.00
1994S, Silver	(636,009)	21.00
1994S, Silver Premier set	(149,320)	37.50
1995S	(2,010,384)	12.50
1995S, Prestige set (Civil War half, dollar)	(107,112)	57.00
1995S, Silver	(549,878)	21.00
1995S, Silver Premier set	(130,107)	37.50
1996S	(1,695,244)	12.50
1996S, Prestige set (Olympic half, dollar)	(55,000)	57.00
1996S, Silver	(623,655)	21.00
1996S, Silver Premier set	(151,366)	37.50
1997S	(1,975,000)	12.50
1997S, Prestige set (Botanic dollar)	(80,000)	57.00
1997S, Silver	(605,473)	21.00
1997S, Silver Premier set	(136,205)	37.50
1998S	(2,086,507)	12.50
1998S, Silver	(638,134)	21.00
1998S, Silver Premier set	(240,658)	37.50
1999S, 9-piece set	(2,543,401)	19.95
1999S, 5-piece quarter set	(1,169,958)	13.95
1999S, Silver 9-piece set	(804,565)	31.95
2000S, 10-piece set	(3,082,572)	19.95
2000S, 5-piece quarter set	(937,600)	13.95
2000S, Silver 10-piece set	(965,421)	31.95
2001S, 10-piece set	(2,294,909)	19.95
2001S, 5-piece quarter set	(799,231)	13.95

	Mintage	Issue Price
2001S, Silver 10-piece set	(889,697)	$31.95
2002S, 10-piece set	(2,319,766)	19.95
2002S, 5-piece quarter set	(764,479)	13.95
2002S, Silver 10-piece set	(892,229)	31.95
2003S, 10-piece set	(2,172,684)	19.95
2003S, 5-piece quarter set	(1,235,832)	13.95
2003S, Silver 10-piece set	(1,125,755)	31.95
2004S, 11-piece set	(1,789,488)	22.95
2004S, 5-piece quarter set	(951,196)	15.95
2004S, Silver 11-piece set	(1,175,934)	37.95
2004S, Silver 5-piece quarter set	(593,852)	23.95
2005S, 11-piece set	(2,275,000)	22.95
2005S, 5-piece quarter set	(987,960)	15.95
2005S, Silver 11-piece set	(1,069,679)	37.95
2005S, Silver 5-piece quarter set	(608,970)	23.95
2006S, 10-piece set	(2,000,428)	22.95
2006S, 5-piece quarter set	(882,000)	15.95
2006S, Silver 10-piece set	(1,054,008)	37.95
2006S, Silver 5-piece quarter set	(531,000)	23.95
2007S, 14-piece set	(1,702,116)	26.95
2007S, 5-piece quarter set	(672,662)	13.95
2007S, 4-piece Presidential set	(1,285,972)	14.95
2007S, Silver 14-piece set	(875,050)	44.95
2007S, Silver 5-piece quarter set	(672,662)	25.95
2008S, 14-piece set	(1,405,674)	26.95
2008S, 5-piece quarter set	(672,438)	13.95
2008S, 4-piece Presidential set	(869,202)	14.95
2008S, Silver 14-piece set	(763,887)	44.95
2008S, Silver 5-piece quarter set	(429,021)	25.95
2009S, 18-piece set	(1,482,502)	29.95
2009S, 6-piece quarter set	(630,976)	14.95
2009S, 4-piece Presidential set	(629,585)	14.95
2009S, Silver 18-piece set	(697,365)	52.95
2009S, Silver 6-piece quarter set	(299,183)	29.95
2009S, 4-piece Lincoln Bicentennial set		7.95
2010S, 14-piece set	(1,103,815)	31.95
2010S, 5-piece quarter set	(276,296)	14.95
2010S, 4-piece Presidential set	(535,397)	15.95
2010S, Silver 14-piece set	(585,401)	56.95
2010S, Silver 5-piece quarter set	(274,034)	32.95
2011S, 14-piece set	(1,098,835)	31.95
2011S, 5-piece quarter set	(152,032)	14.95
2011S, 4-piece Presidential set	(299,835)	19.95
2011S, Silver 14-piece set	(574,175)	67.95
2011S, Silver 5-piece quarter set	(147,901)	39.95
2012S, 14-piece set	(794,002)	31.95
2012S, 5-piece quarter set	(148,498)	14.95
2012S, 4-piece Presidential set	(249,265)	18.95
2012S, Silver 14-piece set	(395,443)	67.95
2012S, Silver 8-piece Limited Edition set		149.95
2012S, Silver 5-piece quarter set	(162,448)	41.95
2013S, 14-piece set	(775,795)	41.95
2013S, 5-piece quarter set	(122,123)	14.95
2013S, 4-piece Presidential set	(256,725)	18.95
2013S, Silver 14-piece set	(416,895)	53.95
2013S, Silver 8-piece Limited Edition set		139.95
2013S, Silver 5-piece quarter set	(128,067)	31.95

* Included in number above.

UNCIRCULATED MINT SETS (1947 TO DATE)

	Mintage	Issue Price	Face Value
1947 P-D-S	5,000	$4.87	$4.46
1948 P-D-S	6,000	4.92	4.46
1949 P-D-S	5,000	5.45	4.96
1951 P-D-S	8,654	6.75	5.46
1952 P-D-S	11,499	6.14	5.46
1953 P-D-S	15,538	6.14	5.46
1954 P-D-S	25,599	6.19	5.46
1955 P-D-S	49,656	3.57	2.86
1956 P-D	45,475	3.34	2.64
1957 P-D	34,324	4.40	3.64
1958 P-D	50,314	4.43	3.64
1959 P-D	187,000	2.40	1.82
1960 P-D	260,485	2.40	1.82
1961 P-D	223,704	2.40	1.82
1962 P-D	385,285	2.40	1.82
1963 P-D	606,612	2.40	1.82
1964 P-D	1,008,108	2.40	1.82
1968 P-D-S	2,105,128	2.50	1.33
1969 P-D-S	1,817,392	2.50	1.33
1970 P-D-S, With Large Date cent	2,038,134	2.50	1.33
1970 P-D-S, Small Date cent	*	2.50	1.33

	Mintage	Issue Price	Face Value
1971 P-D-S (no Ike dollar)	2,193,396	$3.50	$1.83
1972 P-D-S (no Ike dollar)	2,750,000	3.50	1.83
1973 P-D-S	1,767,691	6.00	3.83
1974 P-D-S	1,975,981	6.00	3.83
1975 P-D, With 1976 quarter, half, dollar	1,921,488	6.00	3.82
1976, Silver clad, 3-piece set	4,908,319	9.00	1.75
1976 P-D	1,892,513	6.00	3.82
1977 P-D	2,006,869	7.00	3.82
1978 P-D	2,162,609	7.00	3.82
1979 P-D (a)	2,526,000	8.00	3.82
1980 P-D-S	2,815,066	9.00	4.82
1981 P-D-S	2,908,145	11.00	4.82
1984 P-D	1,832,857	7.00	1.82
1985 P-D	1,710,571	7.00	1.82
1986 P-D	1,153,536	7.00	1.82
1987 P-D	2,890,758	7.00	1.82
1988 P-D	1,646,204	7.00	1.82
1989 P-D	1,987,915	7.00	1.82
1990 P-D	1,809,184	7.00	1.82
1991 P-D	1,352,101	7.00	1.82
1992 P-D	1,500,143	7.00	1.82

	Mintage	Issue Price	Face Value
1993 P-D	1,297,431	$8.00	$1.82
1994 P-D	1,234,813	8.00	1.82
1995 P-D	1,038,787	8.00	1.82
1996 P-D, Plus			
1996W dime	1,457,949	8.00	1.92
1997 P-D	950,473	8.00	1.82
1998 P-D	1,187,325	8.00	1.82
1999 P-D (18 pieces) (b)	1,243,867	14.95	3.82
2000 P-D (20 pieces)	1,490,160	14.95	5.82
2001 P-D (20 pieces)	1,116,915	14.95	5.82
2002 P-D (20 pieces)	1,139,388	14.95	5.82
2003 P-D (20 pieces)	1,001,532	14.95	5.82
2004 P-D (22 pieces)	842,507	16.95	5.92
2005 P-D (22 pieces)	1,160,000	16.95	5.92
2006 P-D (20 pieces)	847,361	16.95	5.82
2007 P-D (28 pieces)	895,628	22.95	13.82
2008 P-D (28 pieces)	745,464	22.95	13.82
2009 P-D (36 pieces)	784,614	27.95	14.38
2010 P-D (28 pieces)	583,897	31.95	13.82
2011 P-D (28 pieces)	(533,529)	31.95	13.82
2012 P-D (28 pieces)	(392,224)	27.95	13.82
2013 P-D (28 pieces)	(349,940)	27.95	13.82

a. S-mint dollar not included. b. Dollar not included.

SPECIAL MINT SETS (1964 AND 1965–1967)

See page 355 for details on 1964 SMS coins. Values for these coins are approximately $13,000 for each denomination.

	Mintage	Issue Price	Face Value
1965	2,360,000	$4	$0.91
1966	2,261,583	$4	$0.91
1967	1,863,344	$4	$0.91

Popular Die Varieties From Proof and Mint Sets

As noted in the *Cherrypickers' Guide to Rare Die Varieties,* "Beginning with those modern Mint sets from 1947, and Proof sets from 1950, there are many years of one or the other that are absent of a significant variety. Not all of the known varieties are signifi- cant." The following are some popular die varieties from Proof and Mint sets; for more information and additional examples, consult the *Cherrypickers' Guide.*

PROOF SETS

1951	5¢	doubled-die obverse
1952	25¢	"Superbird" variety
1953	5¢	doubled-die obverse
1955	5¢	tripled-die reverse
1957	5¢	quadrupled-die obverse
1960	1¢	doubled-die obverse (a)
1960	10¢	doubled-die reverse
1960	25¢	doubled-die reverse
1961	50¢	doubled-die reverse
1963	10¢	doubled-die reverse
1968-S	10¢	doubled-die obverse
1968-S	10¢	doubled-die reverse
1968-S	25¢	doubled-die reverse
1968-S	50¢	doubled-die obverse
1969-S	25¢	repunched mintmark
1970-S	10¢	No S
1971-S	5¢	No S
1975-S	10¢	No S
1983-S	10¢	No S
1990-S	1¢	No S

MINT SETS

1949	5¢	D/S—over mintmark (a)
1954	25¢	doubled-die reverse (b)
1960	5¢	(P)—doubled-die obverse (c)
1960	25¢	(P)—doubled-die obverse (c)
1961	50¢	D/D—repunched mintmark
1963	10¢	(P)—doubled-die obverse
1963	25¢	(P)—doubled-die obverse
1963	25¢	(P)—doubled-die reverse
1963	50¢	(P)—doubled-die obverse
1963	50¢	(P)—doubled-die reverse
1968	10¢	(P)—doubled-die obverse
1968	25¢	D—doubled-die reverse
1969	5¢	D/D—repunched mintmark
1969	10¢	D/D—repunched mintmark
1969	25¢	D/D—repunched mintmark
1969	50¢	D—doubled-die reverse
1970	1¢	D/D—repunched mintmark
1970	1¢	D—doubled-die obverse
1970	10¢	D—doubled-die reverse
1970	25¢	D—doubled-die reverse

1970	50¢	D—doubled-die reverse (d)
1971	5¢	D/D—repunched mintmark
1971	10¢	D/D—repunched mintmark
1971	10¢	D—doubled-die reverse
1971	50¢	D—doubled-die obverse
1971	50¢	D—doubled-die reverse
1972	1¢	(P)—doubled-die obverse
1972	5¢	D—doubled-die reverse
1972	50¢	D—doubled-die reverse
1973	50¢	(P)—doubled-die obverse
1973	50¢	D—doubled-die obverse
1974	50¢	D—doubled-die obverse
1981	5¢	D—doubled-die reverse
1984	50¢	D/D—repunched mintmark
1987	5¢	D/D—repunched mintmark
1987	10¢	D/D—repunched mintmark
1989	5¢	D—doubled-die reverse
1989	10¢	P—doubled-die reverse
1989	50¢	D/D—repunched mintmark
1991	5¢	D—doubled-die obverse

a. Check for both Large Over Small Date, and Small Over Large Date, varieties.

a. Although known, most have already been removed from their Mint-packaged sets.
b. Small Date. c. Found in sets labeled as Small Date. d. Small Date.

AN OVERVIEW OF
U.S. MINT BULLION COINS

The United States' bullion-coin program was launched in 1986. Since then, American Eagle and other U.S. silver, gold, and platinum coins have provided investors with convenient vehicles to add physical bullion to their investment portfolios.

In addition to regular investment-grade strikes, the U.S. Mint offers its bullion coins in various collectible formats. Proofs are created in a specialized minting process: a polished coin blank is manually fed into a press fitted with special dies; the blank is struck multiple times "so the softly frosted yet detailed images seem to float above a mirror-like field" (per Mint literature); a white-gloved inspector scrutinizes the coin; and it is then sealed in a protective plastic capsule and mounted in a satin-lined velvet presentation case along with a certificate of authenticity. Members of the public can purchase Proofs directly from the Mint, at fixed prices.

From 2006 to 2011, Burnished (called Uncirculated by the Mint) coins were also sold directly to the public. These coins have the same design as other bullion coins of that year, but are distinguished from regular bullion strikes by a W mintmark (for West Point), and by their distinctive finish (the result of burnished coin blanks). Their blanks were individually fed by hand into specially adapted coining presses. After striking, each Burnished specimen was carefully inspected, encapsulated in plastic, and packaged in a satin-lined velvet presentation case, along with a certificate of authenticity.

Regular bullion-strike coins are bought in bulk by Mint-authorized purchasers (wholesalers, brokerage companies, precious-metal firms, coin dealers, and participating banks). These authorized purchasers in turn sell them to secondary retailers, who then make them available to the general public. Authorized purchasers are required to meet financial and professional criteria, attested to by an internationally accepted accounting firm. They must be an experienced and established market-maker in bullion coins; provide a liquid two-way market for the coins; be audited annually; have an established and broad retail-customer base for distribution; and have a tangible net worth of $5 million (for American Silver Eagles) or $50 million (for gold and platinum American Eagles). Authorized purchasers of gold must have sold more than 100,000 ounces of gold bullion coins over any 12-month period since 1990. For gold and platinum, the initial order must be for at least 1,000 ounces, with reorders in increments of 500 ounces. For American Eagles, an authorized purchaser's cost is based on the market value of the bullion, plus a premium to cover minting, distribution, and other overhead expenses. For ASEs, the premium is $1.50 per coin. For gold, the premiums are 3% (for the one-ounce coin), 5% (1/2 ounce), 7% (1/4 ounce), and 9% (1/10 ounce). For platinum: 4% (for the one-ounce coin), 6% (1/2 ounce), 10% (1/4 ounce), and 15% (1/10 ounce).

Note that the U.S. Mint does not release bullion mintage data on a regular basis; the numbers given herein reflect the most recently available official data.

The listed values of uncertified, average Mint State coins have been based on current bullion prices of silver ($20 per ounce), gold ($1,200 per ounce), and platinum ($1,400 per ounce).

AMERICAN SILVER EAGLES
(1986 TO DATE)

Designers Adolph A. Weinman (obverse) and John Mercanti (reverse); weight 31.101 grams; composition .9993 silver, .0007 copper (net weight 1 oz. pure silver); diameter 40.6 mm; reeded edge; mints: Philadelphia, San Francisco, West Point.

Mintmark location.

History. The American Silver Eagle (face value $1, actual silver weight one ounce) is a legal-tender bullion coin with weight, content, and purity guaranteed by the federal government. It is the only silver coin allowed in individual retirement accounts (IRAs).The obverse design features Adolph A. Weinman's Liberty Walking, as used on the circulating half dollar of 1916 to 1947. Weinman's initials appear on the hem of Miss Liberty's gown. The reverse design, by John Mercanti, is a rendition of a heraldic eagle.

From 1986 to 1999 all American Silver Eagles were struck at the Philadelphia and San Francisco mints (with the exception of the 1995 West Point Proof). In 2000 they were struck at both Philadelphia (Proofs) and the U.S. Mint's West Point facility (bullion strikes). Since 2001, West Point has been their sole producer (with one exception), making regular bullion strikes (without mintmarks) and Proof and "Burnished" specimens (with

mintmarks). (The exception is the 2006 Reverse Proof, which was struck in Philadelphia.)

In addition to the individual coins listed below, American Silver Eagles were issued in two 2006 "20th Anniversary" sets (see page 366) and in several of the bullion coin sets (see pages 361 and 366).

Striking and Sharpness. Striking is generally sharp. The key elements to check on the obverse are Miss Liberty's left hand, the higher parts and lines of her skirt, and her head. On the reverse, the eagle's breast is a main focal point.

Availability. The American Silver Eagle is one of the most popular silver-investment vehicles in the world. Between the bullion coins and various collectible formats, more than 220 million have been sold since 1986. The coins are readily available in the numismatic marketplace and from some banks, investment firms, and other non-numismatic channels.

MS-60 to 70 (Mint State). *Obverse and reverse:* At MS-60, some abrasion and contact marks are evident on the higher design areas (Miss Liberty's left arm, her hand, and the areas of the skirt covering her left leg). Luster may be dull or lifeless at MS-60 to 62, but there should be deep frost at MS-63 and better, particularly in the lower-relief areas. At MS-65 and above, the luster should be full and rich. These guidelines are more academic than practical, as American Silver Eagles are not intended for circulation, and nearly all are in high Mint State grades.

Regular Finish

Burnished Finish

Reverse Lettering Style of 1986–2007
Note the lack of spur or stem at bottom right of U.

Reverse Lettering Style of 2008 to Date
Note the spur at bottom right of U.

	Mintage	Unc.	MS-69	MS-70		Mintage	Unc.	MS-69	MS-70		Mintage	Unc.	MS-69	MS-70
1986 ‡ (a)	5,393,005	$43	$50	$800	1989 (a)	5,203,327	$37	$43	$1,500	1992 (a)	5,540,068	$38	$45	$1,600
1987 (a)	11,442,335	36	42	1,850	1990 (a)	5,840,210	36	42	1,500	1993 (a)	6,763,762	38	45	2,900
1988 (a)	5,004,646	38	45	2,500	1991 (a)	7,191,066	36	42	—	1994 (a)	4,227,319	43	50	4,000

Note: For more information, consult American Silver Eagles: A Guide to the U.S. Bullion Coin Program, 2nd edition (Mercanti and Standish). Values in the Unc. column are for uncertified, average Mint State coins. ‡ Ranked in the 100 Greatest U.S. Modern Coins. a. Minted at Philadelphia, without mintmark.

	Mintage	Unc.	MS-69	MS-70
1995 (a)	4,672,051	$40	$48	$1,000
1996 ‡ (a)	3,603,386	70	85	—
1997 (a)	4,295,004	43	50	900
1998 (a)	4,847,549	41	48	1,100
1999 (a)	7,408,640	38	44	—
2000 (b)	9,239,132	32	38	3,200
2001 (b)	9,001,711	32	38	800
2002 (b)	10,539,026	32	38	250
2003 (b)	8,495,008	32	38	200
2004 (b)	8,882,754	32	38	200
2005 (b)	8,891,025	32	38	160

	Mintage	Unc.	MS-69	MS-70
2006 (b)	10,676,522	$31	$37	$160
2006W, Burnished (c)	468,020	79	85	245
2007 (b)	9,028,036	31	38	95
2007W, Burnished	621,333	42	48	75
2008 (b)	20,583,000	31	38	95
2008W, Burnished	533,757	70	75	90
2008W, Burnished, Rev of 2007 ‡ (d)	47,000	500	550	1,000
2009 (b)	30,459,000	30	36	95
2010 (b)	34,764,500	30	36	85
2011 (b,e)	40,020,000	30	36	95

	Est Mintage	Unc.	MS-69	MS-70
2011W, Burnished	310,000	$50	$55	$80
2011S, Burnished	100,000	275	300	450
2012 (b,e)	33,742,500	31	36	80
2012W, Burnished	230,872	65	70	100
2013 (b,e)	42,675,000	28	34	80
2013W, Burnished	178,941	50	56	95
2013W, Enhanced Uncirculated	281,310	110	125	150
2014 (b,e)		28	34	80
2014W, Burnished		45	55	80

Note: For more information, consult *American Silver Eagles: A Guide to the U.S. Bullion Coin Program*, 2nd edition (Mercanti and Standish). Values in the Unc. column are for uncertified, average Mint State coins. ‡ Ranked in the *100 Greatest U.S. Modern Coins*. **a.** Minted at Philadelphia, without mintmark. **b.** Minted at West Point, without mintmark. **c.** In celebration of the 20th anniversary of the Bullion Coinage Program, in 2006 the W mintmark was used on bullion coins produced in sets at West Point. **d.** Reverse dies of 2007 and earlier have a plain U in UNITED. Modified dies of 2008 and later have a small spur at the bottom right of the U. **e.** Minted at San Francisco, without mintmark.

AMERICAN EAGLE SILVER BULLION COIN SETS

	Uncert.	69	70
2006 20th Anniversary Three-Coin Set. Silver dollars, Uncirculated, Proof, Reverse Proof	$440	$475	$770
2006W 20th Anniversary 1-oz. Gold- and Silver-Dollar Set. Uncirculated	1,775	1,850	2,150
2011 25th Anniversary Five-Coin Set	725	800	1,400
2012S 75th Anniversary of San Francisco Mint Two-Coin Set. Proof, Reverse Proof	190	225	380
2013W 75h Anniversary of West Point Depository Two-Coin Set. Reverse Proof, Enhanced Uncirculated	200	230	275

Note: Values in the Uncert. column are for uncertified sets of average quality. The $50 Silver Eagle of 1997 is also included in the 1997 Impressions of Liberty set, listed on page 366.

Proof American Silver Eagles

PF-60 to 70 (Proof). Proofs that are extensively cleaned and have many hairlines are lower level, such as PF-60 to 62. Those with fewer hairlines or flaws are deemed PF-63 to 65. (These exist more in theory than actuality, as nearly all Proof ASEs have been maintained in their original high condition by collectors and inves- tors.) Given the quality of modern U.S. Mint products, even PF-66 and 67 are unusually low levels for ASE Proofs.

2006-P, Reverse Proof

	Mintage	PF	PF-69	PF-70
1986S	1,446,778	$70	$85	$550
1987S	904,732	70	85	900
1988S	557,370	70	85	550
1989S	617,694	70	85	325
1990S	695,510	70	85	275
1991S	511,925	70	85	600
1992S	498,654	70	85	450
1993P	405,913	125	140	3,000
1994P ‡	372,168	180	195	2,400
1995P	438,511	85	100	460
1995W ‡	30,125	3,750	4,700	—
1996P	500,000	80	95	400

	Mintage	PF	PF-69	PF-70
1997P	435,368	$80	$95	$450
1998P	450,000	70	85	250
1999P	549,769	70	85	400
2000P	600,000	70	85	375
2001W	746,398	70	85	150
2002W	647,342	70	85	150
2003W	747,831	70	85	120
2004W	801,602	70	85	110
2005W	816,663	70	85	110
2006W	1,092,477	70	85	110
2006P, Reverse Proof ‡ (a,b)	248,875	290	305	425

	Mintage	PF	PF-69	PF-70
2007W	821,759	$70	$85	$100
2008W	700,979	70	85	125
2010W (c)	860,000	70	85	100
2011W	849,861	70	85	105
2011P, Reverse Proof (b)	100,000	290	315	700
2012W	832,779	70	85	115
2012S	60,203	80	95	150
2012S, Reverse Proof	224,998	110	125	230
2013W	918,680	65	80	95
2013W, Reverse Proof		90	105	125
2013W, Enhanced Finish		110	125	150
2014W		65	80	95

Note: Values in the PF column are for uncertified Proof coins of average quality. ‡ Ranked in the *100 Greatest U.S. Modern Coins*. **a.** The 2006-P Reverse Proof coins were issued to mark the 20th anniversary of the Bullion Coinage Program. **b.** Reverse Proofs have brilliant devices, and their background fields are frosted (rather than the typical Proof format of frosted devices and mirror-like backgrounds). **c.** The U.S. Mint did not strike any Proof American Silver Eagles in 2009.

AMERICA THE BEAUTIFUL SILVER BULLION COINS (2010–2021)

Designers various; weight 155.517 grams; composition .999 silver, .001 copper (net weight 5 oz. pure silver); diameter 76.2 mm; lettered edge; mint: Philadelphia.

Actual size: 76.2 mm

History. In conjunction with the National Park quarter dollars, the U.S. Mint issues silver-bullion coins based on each of the "America the Beautiful" program's circulation-strike coins. The coinage dies are cut on a CNC milling machine, bypassing a hubbing operation, which results in finer details than seen on the smaller quarter dollars. The bullion coins are made of .999 fine silver, have a diameter of three inches, weigh five ounces, and carry a face value of 25 cents. The fineness and weight are incused on each coin's edge. The Mint's German-made Gräbener press strikes 22 coins per minute, with two strikes per coin at 450 to 500 metric tons of pressure. In December 2010 the Mint announced it would produce Uncirculated and Proof versions for collectors.

Striking and Sharpness. Striking is generally sharp.

Availability. The National Park silver bullion coins are distributed through commercial channels similar to those for the Mint's American Silver Eagle coins. Production of the 2010 coins was delayed (finally starting September 21) as the Mint worked out the technical details of striking such a large product. Production and distribution are expected to be smooth, and the Mint anticipates striking up to 500,000 of the coins annually, divided equally between each year's issues, through the program's duration.

MS-65 to 70 (Mint State). *Obverse and reverse:* At MS-65, some abrasion and contact marks are evident on the higher design areas. Luster may be dull or lifeless at MS-65 to 66, but there should be deep frost at MS-67 and better, particularly in the lower-relief areas. At MS-68 and above, the luster should be full and rich. These guidelines are more academic than practical, as these coins are not intended for circulation, and nearly all are in high Mint State grades.

25¢ 5-OUNCE AMERICA THE BEAUTIFUL SILVER BULLION COINS

	Est Mintage	Unc.	MS-69	MS-70		Est Mintage	Unc.	MS-69	MS-70
2010, Hot Springs National Park	26,788	$135	$195	$330	2012, Hawai'i Volcanoes National Park	14,863	$210	$275	$350
2010, Yellowstone National Park	26,711	135	195	330	2012, Denali National Park and Preserve	15,225	210	275	350
2010, Yosemite National Park	26,716	135	195	330	2013, White Mountain National Forest	20,530	125	175	320
2010, Grand Canyon National Park	25,967	135	195	330	2013, Perry's Victory and Int'l Peace Memorial	17,707	125	175	320
2010, Mt. Hood National Forest	26,637	135	195	330	2013, Great Basin National Park	17,792	125	175	320
2011, Gettysburg National Military Park	24,625	145	200	340	2013, Ft. McHenry Nat'l Mon & Historic Shrine	19,802	125	175	320
2011, Glacier National Park	20,805	145	200	340	2013, Mount Rushmore National Monument	23,547	125	175	320
2011, Olympic National Park	18,345	145	200	340	2014, Great Smoky Mountains National Park		125	175	320
2011, Vicksburg National Military Park	18,528	145	200	340	2014, Shenandoah National Park		125	175	320
2011, Chickasaw National Recreational Area	16,746	145	200	340	2014, Arches National Park		125	175	320
2012, El Yunque National Forest	17,314	210	275	350	2014, Great Sand Dunes National Park		125	175	320
2012, Chaco Culture National Historical Park	17,146	210	275	350	2014, Everglades National Park		125	175	320
2012, Acadia National Park	14,978	210	275	350					

Note: Values in the Unc. column are for uncertified, average Mint State coins.

Specimen America the Beautiful Silver Bullion Coins

SP-68 to 70 (Specimen). *Obverse and reverse:* These pieces should be nearly perfect and with full luster, in their original Mint packaging. Any with imperfections due to careless handling or environmental damage are valued lower.

The U.S. Mint produces the America the Beautiful™ 5-ounce silver coins in bullion and numismatic versions. The bullion version, which lacks the P mintmark, has a brilliant Uncirculated finish and is sold only through dealers. The numismatic version, with the mintmark, has a matte or burnished finish. These coins are designated "Specimens" (SP) by most collectors and grading services. They are sold directly to the public by the Mint.

	Est Mintage	SP	SP-69	SP-70		Est Mintage	SP	SP-69	SP-70
2010, Hot Springs National Park	33,000	$250	$285	$475	2010, Yosemite National Park	33,000	$250	$285	$475
2010, Yellowstone National Park	33,000	250	285	475	2010, Grand Canyon National Park	33,000	250	285	475

	Est Mintage	SP	SP-69	SP-70
2010, Mt. Hood National Forest	33,000	$250	$285	$475
2011, Gettysburg National Military Park	126,700	180	215	400
2011, Glacier National Park	126,700	240	265	400
2011, Olympic National Park	95,600	250	275	425
2011, Vicksburg National Military Park	41,200	280	315	450
2011, Chickasaw National Recreational Area	31,400	300	325	450
2012, El Yunque National Forest	21,900	300	325	450
2012, Chaco Culture National Historical Park	20,000	300	325	450
2012, Acadia National Park	25,400	320	345	450
2012, Hawai'i Volcanoes National Park	20,000	650	700	1,050
2012, Denali National Park and Preserve	20,000	290	315	550

	Mintage	SP	SP-69	SP-70
2013, White Mountain National Forest		$195	$220	$325
2013, Perry's Victory and Int'l Peace Memorial		195	220	325
2013, Great Basin National Park		195	220	325
2013, Ft. McHenry Nat'l Mon & Historic Shrine		195	220	325
2013, Mount Rushmore National Monument		195	220	325
2014, Great Smoky Mountains National Park		155	185	225
2014, Shenandoah National Park		155	185	225
2014, Arches National Park		155	185	225
2014, Great Sand Dunes National Park		155	185	225
2014, Everglades National Park		155	185	225

AMERICAN EAGLE GOLD BULLION COINS (1986 TO DATE)

Designers Augustus Saint-Gaudens (obverse) and Miley Busiek (reverse); composition .9167 gold, .03 silver, .0533 copper; reeded edge; mints: Philadelphia, West Point. Weights and diameters: $5 1/10 oz., 3.393 grams, 16.5 mm; $10 1/4 oz., 8.483 grams, 22 mm; $25 1/2 oz., 16.966 grams, 27 mm; $50 1 oz., 33.931 grams, 32.7 mm.

Design common to all denominations.   *Mintmark location.*

History. American Eagle gold bullion coins are made in four denominations: $5 (1/10 ounce pure gold), $10 (1/4 ounce), $25 (1/2 ounce), and $50 (1 ounce). Each shares the same obverse and reverse designs: a modified rendition of Augustus Saint-Gaudens's famous Liberty (as depicted on the double eagle of 1907 to 1933), and a "family of eagles" motif by sculptor Miley Tucker-Frost (nee Busiek). From 1986 to 1991 the obverse bore a Roman numeral date, similar to the first Saint-Gaudens double eagles of 1907; this was changed to Arabic dating in 1992. The coins are legal tender—with weight, content, and purity guaranteed by the federal government—and are produced from gold mined in the United States. Investors can include them in their individual retirement accounts.

"American Eagles use the durable 22-karat standard established for gold circulating coinage over 350 years ago," notes the U.S. Mint. "They contain their stated amount of pure gold, plus small amounts of alloy. This creates harder coins that resist scratching and marring, which can diminish resale value."

Since the Bullion Coin Program started in 1986, these gold pieces have been struck in Philadelphia and West Point, in various formats similar to those of the American Silver Eagles—regular bullion strikes, Burnished, Proof, and Reverse Proof. Unlike their silver counterparts, none of the American Eagle gold coins have been struck at San Francisco.

In addition to the individual coins listed below, American Eagle gold bullion coins have been issued in various sets (see page 366).

Striking and Sharpness. Striking is generally sharp. The key elements to check on the obverse are Liberty's chest and left knee, and the open fields.

Availability. American Eagles are the most popular gold-coin investment vehicle in the United States. The coins are readily available in the numismatic marketplace as well as from participating banks, investment firms, and other non-numismatic channels.

MS-60 to 70 (Mint State). *Obverse and reverse:* At MS-60, some abrasion and contact marks are evident on the higher design areas (in particular, Miss Liberty's chest and left knee) and the open fields. Luster may be dull or lifeless at MS-60 to 62, but there should be deep frost at MS-63 and better, particularly in the lower-relief areas. At MS-65 and above, the luster should be full and rich. Contact marks and abrasion are less and less evident at higher grades. These guidelines are more academic than practical, as these coins are not intended for circulation, and nearly all are in high Mint State grades.

Regular Finish

$5 1/10-OUNCE AMERICAN EAGLE GOLD BULLION COINS

	Mintage	Unc.	MS-69	MS-70
$5 MCMLXXXVI (1986)	912,609	$180	$195	$800
$5 MCMLXXXVII (1987)	580,266	180	195	800
$5 MCMLXXXVIII (1988)	159,500	210	240	4,000
$5 MCMLXXXIX (1989)	264,790	180	195	3,000
$5 MCMXC (1990)	210,210	185	200	4,000
$5 MCMXCI (1991)	165,200	225	240	1,200
$5 1992	209,300	170	185	1,500
$5 1993	210,709	170	185	1,500
$5 1994	206,380	170	185	400
$5 1995	223,025	170	185	975
$5 1996	401,964	170	180	500
$5 1997	528,266	170	180	450
$5 1998	1,344,520	$155	$175	$300
$5 1999	2,750,338	155	175	275
$5 1999W, Unc made from unpolished Proof dies ‡ (a)	14,500	800	900	3,000
$5 2000	569,153	155	175	275
$5 2001	269,147	170	185	245
$5 2002	230,027	190	205	220
$5 2003	245,029	180	195	220
$5 2004	250,016	160	175	220
$5 2005	300,043	155	175	220
$5 2006	285,006	155	175	210
$5 2006W, Burnished	20,643	$190	$215	$270
$5 2007	190,010	180	195	225
$5 2007W, Burnished	22,501	210	225	270
$5 2008	305,000	155	175	235
$5 2008W, Burnished	12,657	325	345	425
$5 2009	270,000	165	190	210
$5 2010	435,000	155	175	210
$5 2011	350,000	155	175	210
$5 2012		155	175	210
$5 2013		155	175	210
$5 2014		155	175	210

Note: Values in the Unc. column are for uncertified, average Mint State coins. ‡ Ranked in the *100 Greatest U.S. Modern Coins*. **a.** Unpolished Proof dies were used to mint some 1999 $5 gold coins, resulting in a regular bullion-strike issue bearing a W mintmark (usually reserved for Proofs). A similar error exists in the $10 (1/4-ounce) series. The mintage listed is an estimate. Other estimates range from 6,000 to 30,000 pieces.

$10 1/4-OUNCE AMERICAN EAGLE GOLD BULLION COINS

	Mintage	Unc.	MS-69	MS-70
$10 MCMLXXXVI (1986)	726,031	$525	$550	$1,500
$10 MCMLXXXVII (1987)	269,255	525	550	2,000
$10 MCMLXXXVIII (1988)	49,000	650	675	3,000
$10 MCMLXXXIX (1989)	81,789	650	675	1,500
$10 MCMXC (1990)	41,000	750	775	4,000
$10 MCMXCI (1991)	36,100	750	775	2,250
$10 1992	59,546	575	600	2,000
$10 1993	71,864	575	600	2,250
$10 1994	72,650	575	600	2,050
$10 1995	83,752	575	600	2,000
$10 1996	60,318	575	600	2,100
$10 1997	108,805	375	400	2,000
$10 1998	309,829	$375	$400	$2,200
$10 1999	564,232	375	400	3,000
$10 1999W, Unc. made from unpolished Proof dies ‡ (a)	10,000	1,500	1,550	8,750
$10 2000	128,964	375	400	900
$10 2001	71,280	575	600	650
$10 2002	62,027	575	600	650
$10 2003	74,029	375	400	500
$10 2004	72,014	375	400	500
$10 2005	72,015	375	400	500
$10 2006	60,004	375	400	500
$10 2006W, Burnished	15,188	$575	$600	$700
$10 2007	34,004	600	625	725
$10 2007W, Burnished	12,766	600	625	750
$10 2008	70,000	375	400	500
$10 2008W, Burnished	8,883	1,350	1,400	1,500
$10 2009	110,000	370	395	475
$10 2010	86,000	375	400	500
$10 2011	80,000	370	395	450
$10 2012		370	395	450
$10 2013		370	395	425
$10 2014		370	395	425

Note: Values in the Unc. column are for uncertified, average Mint State coins. ‡ Ranked in the *100 Greatest U.S. Modern Coins*. **a.** Unpolished Proof dies were used to mint some 1999 $10 gold coins, resulting in a regular bullion-strike issue bearing a W mintmark (usually reserved for Proofs). A similar error exists in the $5 (1/10-ounce) series. The mintage listed is an estimate. Other estimates range from 6,000 to 30,000 pieces.

$25 1/2-OUNCE AMERICAN EAGLE GOLD BULLION COINS

	Mintage	Unc.	MS-69	MS-70
$25 MCMLXXXVI (1986)	599,566	$850	$900	$1,150
$25 MCMLXXXVII (1987)	131,255	1,100	1,250	2,000
$25 MCMLXXXVIII (1988)	45,000	1,700	1,900	5,000
$25 MCMLXXXIX (1989)	44,829	1,800	2,000	4,000
$25 MCMXC (1990)	31,000	2,000	2,300	5,000
$25 MCMXCI (1991) ‡	24,100	3,200	3,400	5,000
$25 1992	54,404	1,300	1,500	3,800
$25 1993	73,324	900	1,100	3,500
$25 1994	62,400	900	1,100	3,000
$25 1995	53,474	1,400	1,600	4,500
$25 1996	39,287	1,400	1,600	4,000
$25 1997	79,605	$850	$950	$2,800
$25 1998	169,029	750	800	1,250
$25 1999	263,013	750	800	3,000
$25 2000	79,287	850	950	1,200
$25 2001	48,047	1,300	1,400	1,700
$25 2002	70,027	850	950	1,000
$25 2003	79,029	800	850	900
$25 2004	98,040	770	795	900
$25 2005	80,023	770	795	900
$25 2006	66,005	770	790	900
$25 2006W, Burnished	15,164	1,300	1,350	1,600
$25 2007	47,002	$850	$900	$1,000
$25 2007W, Burnished	11,455	1,250	1,300	1,700
$25 2008	61,000	770	790	870
$25 2008W, Burnished	15,682	1,300	1,350	1,600
$25 2009	110,000	770	790	870
$25 2010	81,000	800	820	950
$25 2011	70,000	770	790	870
$25 2012		770	790	870
$25 2013		770	790	870
$25 2014		750	775	870

Note: Values in the Unc. column are for uncertified, average Mint State coins. ‡ Ranked in the *100 Greatest U.S. Modern Coins*.

$50 1-OUNCE AMERICAN EAGLE GOLD BULLION COINS

	Mintage	Unc.	MS-69	MS-70
$50 MCMLXXXVI (1986)	1,362,650	$1,375	$1,425	$5,500
$50 MCMLXXXVII (1987)	1,045,500	1,375	1,425	5,000
$50 MCMLXXXVIII (1988)	465,000	1,400	1,450	11,000
$50 MCMLXXXIX (1989)	415,790	1,400	1,450	—
$50 MCMXC (1990)	373,210	1,400	1,450	5,500
$50 MCMXCI (1991)	243,100	1,400	1,450	5,500
$50 1992	275,000	1,375	1,425	2,100
$50 1993	480,192	1,375	1,425	2,600
$50 1994	221,633	1,375	1,425	6,500
$50 1995	200,636	1,375	1,425	—
$50 1996	189,148	1,375	1,425	—
$50 1997	664,508	1,375	1,400	5,000
$50 1998	1,468,530	$1,375	$1,400	$2,300
$50 1999	1,505,026	1,375	1,400	2,300
$50 2000	433,319	1,375	1,400	2,500
$50 2001	143,605	1,375	1,400	3,000
$50 2002	222,029	1,375	1,400	2,800
$50 2003	416,032	1,375	1,400	2,500
$50 2004	417,019	1,375	1,400	2,500
$50 2005	356,555	1,375	1,400	2,000
$50 2006	237,510	1,375	1,565	1,700
$50 2006W, Burnished	45,053	1,700	1,750	1,900
$50 2007	140,016	1,375	1,400	1,950
$50 2007W, Burnished	18,066	1,750	1,800	2,050
$50 2008	710,000	$1,375	$1,400	$1,950
$50 2008W, Burnished	11,908	1,900	1,950	2,300
$50 2009	1,493,000	1,375	1,400	1,750
$50 2010	1,125,000	1,375	1,400	1,550
$50 2011	857,000	1,375	1,400	1,550
$50 2011W, Burnished	8,729	2,150	2,200	2,600
$50 2012		1,375	1,400	1,550
$50 2012W, Burnished	5,829	2,450	2,550	3,100
$50 2013		1,375	1,400	1,600
$50 2013W, Burnished	7,293	1,600	1,700	2,200
$50 2014		1,375	1,400	1,500
$50 2014W, Burnished		1,550	1,575	1,750

Note: Values in the Unc. column are for uncertified, average Mint State coins.

Proof American Eagle Gold Bullion Coins

PF-60 to 70 (Proof). Proofs that are extensively cleaned and have many hairlines are lower level, such as PF-60 to 62. Those with fewer hairlines or flaws are deemed PF-63 to 65. (These exist more in theory than actuality, as nearly all Proof American Eagle gold bullion coins have been maintained in their original high condition by collectors and investors.) Given the quality of modern U.S. Mint products, even PF-66 and 67 are unusually low levels for these Proofs.

$5 1/10-OUNCE PROOF AMERICAN EAGLE GOLD BULLION COINS

	Mintage	PF	PF-69	PF-70		Mintage	PF	PF-69	PF-70		Mintage	PF	PF-69	PF-70
$5 MCMLXXXVIII (1988)P	143,881	$190	$205	$350	$5 1997W	34,977	$200	$215	$750	$5 2006W	47,277	$190	$205	$275
$5 MCMLXXXIX (1989)P	84,647	195	210	375	$5 1998W	39,395	190	205	500	$5 2007W	58,553	190	205	275
$5 MCMXC (1990)P	99,349	195	210	375	$5 1999W	48,428	190	205	450	$5 2008W	28,116	190	205	300
$5 MCMXCI (1991)P	70,334	195	210	400	$5 2000W	49,971	190	205	450	$5 2010W	54,285	200	215	300
$5 1992P	64,874	190	205	450	$5 2001W	37,530	200	215	500	$5 2011W	42,697	190	205	300
$5 1993P	58,649	195	210	475	$5 2002W	40,864	190	205	500	$5 2012W	20,740	190	205	275
$5 1994W	62,849	190	205	450	$5 2003W	40,027	190	205	500	$5 2013W	21,879	190	205	235
$5 1995W	62,667	190	205	450	$5 2004W	35,131	210	225	550	$5 2014W		180	195	225
$5 1996W	57,047	190	205	500	$5 2005W	49,265	205	220	400					

Note: Values in the PF column are for uncertified Proof coins of average quality, in their complete original U.S. Mint packaging.

$10 1/4-OUNCE PROOF AMERICAN EAGLE GOLD BULLION COINS

	Mintage	PF	PF-69	PF-70		Mintage	PF	PF-69	PF-70		Mintage	PF	PF-69	PF-70
$10 MCMLXXXVIII (1988)P	98,028	$425	$455	$700	$10 1997W	29,805	$425	$455	$900	$10 2006W	36,127	$425	$455	$550
$10 MCMLXXXIX (1989)P	54,170	480	500	850	$10 1998W	29,503	425	465	900	$10 2007W	46,189	425	460	600
$10 MCMXC (1990)P	62,674	470	500	600	$10 1999W	34,417	425	465	750	$10 2008W	18,877	500	525	700
$10 MCMXCI (1991)P	50,839	480	500	700	$10 2000W	36,036	425	465	750	$10 2010W	44,507	425	455	525
$10 1992P	46,269	495	520	750	$10 2001W	25,613	425	455	750	$10 2011W	28,782	425	455	525
$10 1993P	46,464	495	520	750	$10 2002W	29,242	425	455	575	$10 2012W	13,375	425	465	550
$10 1994W	48,172	425	455	700	$10 2003W	30,292	425	455	575	$10 2013W	12,624	425	455	525
$10 1995W	47,526	425	475	700	$10 2004W	28,839	425	455	600	$10 2014W		425	455	525
$10 1996W	38,219	425	455	900	$10 2005W	37,207	425	455	550					

Note: Values in the PF column are for uncertified Proof coins of average quality, in their complete original U.S. Mint packaging.

$25 1/2-OUNCE PROOF AMERICAN EAGLE GOLD BULLION COINS

	Mintage	PF	PF-69	PF-70		Mintage	PF	PF-69	PF-70		Mintage	PF	PF-69	PF-70
$25 MCMLXXXVII (1987)P	143,398	$830	$850	$2,000	$25 1996W	35,058	$850	$925	$1,200	$25 2005W	34,311	$830	$850	$1,100
$25 MCMLXXXVIII (1988)P	76,528	900	925	1,600	$25 1997W	26,344	850	925	1,200	$25 2006W	34,322	830	850	950
$25 MCMLXXXIX (1989)P	44,798	950	1,000	3,000	$25 1998W	25,374	850	925	1,200	$25 2007W	44,025	830	850	950
$25 MCMXC (1990)P	51,636	950	1,000	—	$25 1999W	30,427	900	950	1,400	$25 2008W	22,602	1,000	1,050	1,200
$25 MCMXCI (1991)P	53,125	950	1,000	1,300	$25 2000W	32,028	850	900	1,100	$25 2010W	44,527	830	850	950
$25 1992P	40,976	850	950	1,400	$25 2001W	23,240	850	925	1,200	$25 2011W	26,781	830	850	950
$25 1993P	43,819	1,000	1,050	—	$25 2002W	26,646	830	850	1,200	$25 2012W	12,809	830	850	950
$25 1994W	44,584	850	950	1,250	$25 2003W	28,270	830	850	1,200	$25 2013W	12,570	830	850	950
$25 1995W	45,388	850	925	1,200	$25 2004W	27,330	830	850	1,600	$25 2014W		820	845	950

Note: Values in the PF column are for uncertified Proof coins of average quality, in their complete original U.S. Mint packaging.

$50 1-OUNCE PROOF AMERICAN EAGLE GOLD BULLION COINS

	Mintage	PF	PF-69	PF-70		Mintage	PF	PF-69	PF-70		Mintage	PF	PF-69	PF-70
$50 MCMLXXXVI (1986)W	446,290	$1,750	$1,800	$2,350	$50 MCMXC (1990)W	62,401	$1,750	$1,800	$2,200	$50 1994W	46,674	$1,700	$1,750	$2,500
$50 MCMLXXXVII (1987)W	147,498	1,750	1,800	2,200	$50 MCMXCI (1991)W	50,411	1,750	1,800	3,000	$50 1995W	46,368	1,700	1,750	2,500
$50 MCMLXXXVIII (1988)W	87,133	1,750	1,800	2,200	$50 1992W	44,826	1,700	1,750	3,000	$50 1996W	36,153	1,700	1,750	2,500
$50 MCMLXXXIX (1989)W	54,570	1,750	1,800	2,250	$50 1993W	34,369	1,800	1,850	3,500	$50 1997W	32,999	1,700	1,750	2,500

Note: Values in the PF column are for uncertified Proof coins of average quality, in their complete original U.S. Mint packaging.

	Mintage	PF	PF-69	PF-70
$50 1998W	25,886	$1,800	$1,850	$4,000
$50 1999W	31,427	1,700	1,750	3,000
$50 2000W	33,007	1,700	1,750	2,500
$50 2001W ‡	24,555	1,850	1,900	5,000
$50 2002W	27,499	1,700	1,750	2,200
$50 2003W	28,344	1,700	1,750	2,200

	Mintage	PF	PF-69	PF-70
$50 2004W	28,215	$1,700	$1,750	$2,200
$50 2005W	35,246	1,700	1,750	2,150
$50 2006W	47,092	1,700	1,750	2,100
$50 2006W, Rev Proof ‡ (a)	9,996	2,500	2,750	3,650
$50 2007W	51,810	1,650	1,700	2,100
$50 2008W	30,237	1,700	1,750	2,500

	Mintage	PF	PF-69	PF-70
$50 2010W	59,480	$1,700	$1,750	$2,100
$50 2011W	48,306	1,650	1,700	2,100
$50 2012W	23,630	1,650	1,700	2,100
$50 2013W	24,753	1,650	1,700	2,100
$50 2014W		1,650	1,700	2,100

Note: Values in the PF column are for uncertified Proof coins of average quality, in their complete original U.S. Mint packaging. ‡ Ranked in the *100 Greatest U.S. Modern Coins.* **a.** The 2006-W Reverse Proof coins were issued to mark the 20th anniversary of the Bullion Coinage Program. They have brilliant devices, and their background fields are frosted (rather than the typical Proof format of frosted devices and mirror-like backgrounds).

AMERICAN EAGLE BULLION COIN SETS

	PF	PF-69	PF-70
1987 Gold Set. $50, $25	$2,600	$2,650	$4,200
1988 Gold Set. $50, $25, $10, $5	3,250	3,400	4,850
1989 Gold Set. $50, $25, $10, $5	3,350	3,500	6,400
1990 Gold Set. $50, $25, $10, $5	3,350	3,500	—
1991 Gold Set. $50, $25, $10, $5	3,350	3,500	5,400
1992 Gold Set. $50, $25, $10, $5	3,200	3,400	5,600
1993 Gold Set. $50, $25, $10, $5	3,450	3,600	—
1993 Bicentennial Gold Set. $25, $10, $5, Silver Eagle, and medal (a)	1,600	1,850	—
1994 Gold Set. $50, $25, $10, $5	3,150	3,350	4,900
1995 Gold Set. $50, $25, $10, $5	3,150	3,350	4,850

	PF	PF-69	PF-70
1995 Anniversary Gold Set. $50, $25, $10, $5, and Silver Eagle (b)	$7,000	$8,000	—
1996 Gold Set. $50, $25, $10, $5	3,150	3,350	$5,100
1997 Gold Set. $50, $25, $10, $5	3,150	3,350	5,350
1997 Impressions of Liberty Set. $100 platinum, $50 gold, Silver Eagle (c)	3,625	3,735	6,935
1998 Gold Set. $50, $25, $10, $5	3,250	3,450	6,500
1999 Gold Set. $50, $25, $10, $5	3,200	3,350	5,500
2000 Gold Set. $50, $25, $10, $5	3,165	3,300	4,800
2001 Gold Set. $50, $25, $10, $5	3,300	3,500	7,450

	PF	PF-69	PF-70
2002 Gold Set. $50, $25, $10, $5	$3,150	$3,250	$4,475
2003 Gold Set. $50, $25, $10, $5	3,150	3,250	4,475
2004 Gold Set. $50, $25, $10, $5	3,150	3,250	4,950
2005 Gold Set. $50, $25, $10, $5	3,150	3,250	4,200
2006 Gold Set. $50, $25, $10, $5	3,150	3,250	3,750
2007 Gold Set. $50, $25, $10, $5	3,100	3,200	3,900
2008 Gold Set. $50, $25, $10, $5	3,350	3,500	4,700
2010 Gold Set. $50, $25, $10, $5 (d)	3,150	3,250	3,850
2011 Gold Set. $50, $25, $10, $5	3,100	3,225	3,850
2012 Gold Set. $50, $25, $10, $5	3,100	3,225	3,850
2013 Gold Set. $50, $25, $10, $5	3,100	3,200	3,800
2014 Gold Set. $50, $25, $10, $5	3,100	3,200	3,800

Note: Values in the PF column are for uncertified Proof coins of average quality, in their complete original U.S. Mint packaging. **a.** The 1993 set was issued to commemorate the bicentennial of the first coins struck by the U.S. Mint in Philadelphia. **b.** The 1995 set marked the 10th anniversary of the passage of the Liberty Coin Act, which authorized the nation's new bullion coinage program. **c.** The Impressions of Liberty set was issued in the first year that platinum coins were added to the Mint's bullion offerings. **d.** The U.S. Mint did not issue a 2009 gold set.

2006 20TH-ANNIVERSARY BULLION COIN SETS

	Uncert.	69	70
2006W $50 Gold Set. Uncirculated, Proof, and Reverse Proof	$5,900	$6,250	$7,650
2006W 1-oz. Gold- and Silver-Dollar Set. Uncirculated	1,775	1,850	2,150

Note: Values in the Uncert column are for uncertified sets of average quality.

AMERICAN BUFFALO .9999 FINE GOLD BULLION COINS (2006 TO DATE)

Designer James Earle Fraser; composition .9999 gold; reeded edge; mint: West Point. Weights and diameters: $5 1/10 oz., 3.393 grams, 16.5 mm; $10 1/4 oz., 8.483 grams, 22 mm; $25 1/2 oz., 16.966 grams, 27 mm; $50 1 oz., 31.108 grams, 32.7 mm.

Design common to all denominations.

History. American Buffalo gold bullion coins, authorized by Congress in 2005 and produced since 2006, are the first 24-karat (.9999 fine) gold coins made by the U.S. Mint. They are coined, by mandate, of gold derived from newly mined sources in America. They feature an adaptation of James Earle Fraser's iconic Indian Head / Buffalo design, first used on circulating five-cent pieces of 1913 to 1938.

Only 1-ounce ($50 face value) coins were struck in the American Buffalo program's first two years, 2006 and 2007. For 2008, the Mint expanded the coinage to include fractional pieces of 1/2 ounce ($25), 1/4 ounce ($10), and 1/10-ounce ($5), in various finishes, individually and in sets.

The coins are legal tender, with weight, content, and purity guaranteed by the federal government. Investors can include them in some individual retirement accounts. Proofs and Burnished (*Uncirculated,* in the Mint's wording) pieces undergo special production processes, similar to the American Eagle gold-bullion coinage, and can be purchased directly from the Mint. As with other products in the Mint's bullion program, regular bullion-strike pieces are distributed through a network of authorized distributors.

All American Buffalo gold bullion coins (Proofs, Burnished, and regular bullion pieces) are struck at the U.S. Mint's West Point facility.

Striking and Sharpness. Striking is generally sharp.

Availability. American Buffalo .9999 fine gold bullion coins are a popular way to buy and sell 24-karat gold. The coins are readily available in the numismatic marketplace as well as from participating banks, investment firms, and other non-numismatic channels.

MS-60 to 70 (Mint State). *Obverse and reverse:* At MS-60, some abrasion and contact marks are evident on the higher design areas and the open areas of the design. Luster may be dull or lifeless at MS-60 to 62, but there should be deep frost at MS-63 and better, particularly in the lower-relief areas. At MS-65 and above, the luster should be full and rich. Contact marks and abrasion are less and less evident at higher grades. These guidelines are more academic than practical, as these coins are not intended for circulation, and nearly all are in high Mint State grades, as struck.

Regular Finish   Burnished Finish

	Mintage	Unc.	MS-69	MS-70
$5 2008W, Burnished	17,429	$500	$525	$600
$10 2008W, Burnished ‡	9,949	1,300	1,350	1,450
$25 2008W, Burnished	16,908	1,300	1,350	1,650
$50 2006	337,012	1,375	1,400	1,650
$50 2007	136,503	1,375	1,400	1,650

	Mintage	Unc.	MS-69	MS-70
$50 2008	189,500	$1,375	$1,400	$1,650
$50 2008W, Burnished	9,074	2,900	2,950	3,500
$50 2009	200,000	1,375	1,400	1,550
$50 2010	209,000	1,375	1,400	1,550
$50 2011	174,500	1,375	1,400	1,500

	Est Mintage	Unc.	MS-69	MS-70
$50 2012	132,000	$1,375	$1,400	$1,500
$50 2013		1,375	1,400	1,500
$50 2014		1,375	1,400	1,500

Note: Values in the Unc. column are for uncertified, average Mint State coins. ‡ Ranked in the *100 Greatest U.S. Modern Coins*.

Proof American Buffalo .9999 Fine Gold Bullion Coins

PF-60 to 70 (Proof). Proofs that are extensively cleaned and have many hairlines are lower level, such as PF-60 to 62. Those with fewer hairlines or flaws are deemed PF-63 to 65. (These exist more in theory than actuality, as nearly all Proof American Buffalo gold coins have been maintained in their original high condition by collectors and investors.) Given the quality of modern U.S. Mint products, even PF-66 and 67 are unusually low levels for these Proofs.

	Mintage	PF	PF-69	PF-70
$5 2008W	18,884	$600	$625	$700
$10 2008W	13,125	1,500	1,550	1,650
$25 2008W	12,169	1,600	1,650	1,800
$50 2006W	246,267	1,450	1,500	1,850
$50 2007W	58,998	1,450	1,500	1,850

	Mintage	PF	PF-69	PF-70
$50 2008W ‡	18,863	$3,550	$3,600	$3,900
$50 2009W	49,306	1,450	1,500	1,850
$50 2010W	49,263	1,450	1,500	1,850
$50 2011W	28,693	1,450	1,500	1,850
$50 2012W	19,765	1,450	1,500	1,850

	Est Mintage	PF	PF-69	PF-70
$50 2013W	18,594	$1,450	$1,500	$1,850
$50 2013W, Rev Proof	47,836	1,700	1,750	2,000
$50 2014W		1,690	1,740	1,850

Note: Values in the PF column are for uncertified Proof coins of average quality, in their complete original U.S. Mint packaging. ‡ Ranked in the *100 Greatest U.S. Modern Coins*.

AMERICAN BUFFALO .9999 FINE GOLD BULLION COIN SETS

	MS-69	MS-70	PF-69	PF-70
2008W Four-coin set ($5, $10, $25, $50)			$7,400	$8,700
2008W Four-coin set ($5, $10, $25, $50), Burnished	$6,000	$7,000		
2008W Double Prosperity set (Unc. $25 Buffalo gold and $25 American Eagle coins)	2,700	3,200		

FIRST SPOUSE $10 GOLD BULLION COINS (2007 TO DATE)

Weight 8.483 grams; composition .9999 gold; diameter 26.5 mm; reeded edge; mint: West Point. Designers: Martha Washington—Joseph Menna (obv), Susan Gamble (rev); Abigail Adams— Joseph Menna (obv), Thomas Cleveland (rev); Thomas Jefferson's Liberty—Robert Scot / Phebe Hemphill (obv), Charles Vickers (rev); Dolley Madison—Don Everhart (obv), Joel Iskowitz (rev); Elizabeth Monroe—Joel Iskowitz (obv), Donna Weaver (rev); Louisa Adams— Susan Gamble (obv), Donna Weaver (rev); Andrew Jackson's Liberty—John Reich (obv), Justin Kunz (rev); Martin Van Buren's Liberty—Christian Gobrecht (obv), Thomas Cleveland (rev); Anna Harrison—Donna Weaver (obv), Thomas Cleveland (rev); Letitia Tyler—Phebe Hemphill (obv), Susan Gamble (rev); Julia Tyler—Joel Iskowitz; Sarah Polk—Phebe Hemphill; Margaret Taylor—Phebe Hemphill (obv), Mary Beth Zeitz (rev); Abigail Fillmore—Phebe Hemphill(obv), Susan Gamble (rev); Jane Pierce—Donna Weaver; James Buchanan's Liberty—Christian Gobrecht (obv), David Westwood (rev); Mary Todd Lincoln—Phebe Hemphill (obv), Joel Iskowitz); Alice Paul—Susan Gamble (obv), Phebe Hemphill (rev); Frances Cleveland, Variety 1—Joel Iskowitz (obv), Barbara Fox (rev); Caroline Harrison—Frank Morris (obv), Donna Weaver (rev); Frances Cleveland, Variety 2—Barbara Fox (obv), Joseph Menna (rev).

Martha Washington
The first coin in the series.

History. The U.S. Mint's First Spouse bullion coins are struck in .9999 fine (24-karat) gold. Each weighs one-half ounce and bears a face value of $10. The coins honor the nation's first spouses on the same schedule as the Mint's Presidential dollars program. Each features a portrait on the obverse, and on the reverse a unique design symbolic of the spouse's life and work. In cases where a president held office widowed or unmarried, the coin bears "an obverse image emblematic of Liberty as depicted on a circulating coin of that era and a reverse image emblematic of themes of that president's life." All First Spouse gold bullion coins (Proofs and regular bullion pieces) are struck at the U.S. Mint's West Point facility.

Note that the Mint does not release bullion mintage data on a regular basis; the numbers given herein reflect the most recently available official data.

Striking and Sharpness. Striking is generally sharp.

Availability. These coins are readily available in the numismatic marketplace. They can be purchased by the public, in both bullion-strike and Proof formats, directly from the U.S. Mint.

MS-60 to 70 (Mint State). *Obverse and reverse:* At MS-60, some abrasion and contact marks are evident on the higher design areas and the open areas of the design. Luster may be dull or lifeless at MS-60 to 62, but there should be deep frost at MS-63 and better, particularly in the lower-relief areas. At MS-65 and above, the luster should be full and rich. Contact marks and abrasion are less and less evident at higher grades. These guidelines are more academic than practical, as these coins are not intended for circulation, and nearly all are in high Mint State grades, as struck.

	Mintage	Unc.	MS-69	MS-70
$10 2007W, M. Washington	17,661	$775	$790	$850
$10 2007W, A. Adams	17,142	775	790	850
$10 2007W, Jefferson's Liberty	19,823	775	790	850
$10 2007W, D. Madison	11,813	775	790	850
$10 2008W, E. Monroe	4,519	900	950	1,100
$10 2008W, L. Adams	4,223	950	1,000	1,250
$10 2008W, Jackson's Liberty ‡	4,281	1,300	1,350	1,550
$10 2008W, Van Buren's Liberty	3,443	1,250	1,300	1,500
$10 2009W, A. Harrison	2,993	1,200	1,250	1,450
$10 2009W, L. Tyler	2,381	1,300	1,350	1,550
$10 2009W, J. Tyler	2,188	1,300	1,350	1,550

	Mintage	Unc.	MS-69	MS-70
$10 2009W, S. Polk	1,893	$1,100	$1,150	$1,400
$10 2009W, M. Taylor		900	950	1,100
$10 2010W, A. Fillmore	3,482	1,050	1,100	1,350
$10 2010W, J. Pierce	3,338	900	950	1,100
$10 2010W, Buchanan's Liberty	5,162	900	950	1,100
$10 2010W, M. Lincoln	3,695	850	900	1,050
$10 2011W, E. Johnson	2,915	850	900	1,050
$10 2011W, J. Grant	2,952	900	950	1,150
$10 2011W, L. Hayes	2,263	1,300	1,350	1,500
$10 2011W, L. Garfield	2,498	1,600	1,650	1,900
$10 2012W, A. Paul	2,798	800	850	950
$10 2012W, F. Cleveland, Variety 1	2,454	800	850	950

	Mintage	Unc.	MS-69	MS-70
$10 2012W, C. Harrison	2,436	$800	$850	$950
$10 2012W, F. Cleveland, Variety 2	2,425	800	850	950
$10 2013W, I. McKinley	1,508	820	850	900
$10 2013W, E. Roosevelt	1,347	820	850	900
$10 2013W, H. Taft	1,326	820	850	900
$10 2013W, Ellen Wilson	1,248	820	850	900
$10 2013W, Edith Wilson	1,173	820	850	900
$10 2014W, F. Harding		820	850	900
$10 2014W, G. Coolidge		820	850	900
$10 2014W, L. Hoover		820	850	900
$10 2014W, E. Roosevelt		820	850	900

Note: Values in the Unc. column are for uncertified, average Mint State coins. ‡ Ranked in the *100 Greatest U.S. Modern Coins.*

Proof First Spouse Gold Bullion Coins

PF-60 to 70 (Proof). Proofs that are extensively cleaned and have many hairlines are lower level, such as PF-60 to 62. Those with fewer hairlines or flaws are deemed PF-63 to 65. (These exist more in theory than actuality, as nearly all Proof First Spouse gold coins have been maintained in their original high condition by collectors and investors.) Given the quality of modern U.S. Mint products, even PF-66 and 67 are unusually low levels for these Proofs.

	Mintage	PF	PF-69	PF-70
$10 2007W, M. Washington	19,169	$700	$725	$800
$10 2007W, A. Adams	17,149	700	725	800
$10 2007W, Jefferson's Liberty	19,815	700	725	800
$10 2007W, D. Madison	17,661	700	725	800
$10 2008W, E. Monroe	7,933	900	950	1,200
$10 2008W, L. Adams	7,454	1,100	1,150	1,400
$10 2008W, Jackson's Liberty	7,454	1,100	1,150	1,400
$10 2008W, Van Buren's Liberty	6,187	1,350	1,400	1,650
$10 2009W, A. Harrison	5,801	1,000	1,050	1,250
$10 2009W, L. Tyler	4,341	1,300	1,350	1,550
$10 2009W, J. Tyler	3,878	1,400	1,450	1,650

	Mintage	PF	PF-69	PF-70
$10 2009W, S. Polk	3,512	$950	$1,000	$1,250
$10 2009W, M. Taylor		1,250	1,300	1,550
$10 2010W, A. Fillmore	6,130	950	1,000	1,200
$10 2010W, J. Pierce	4,775	1,000	1,050	1,350
$10 2010W, Buchanan's Liberty	7,110	900	950	1,200
$10 2010W, M. Lincoln	6,861	950	1,000	1,200
$10 2011W, E. Johnson	3,907	900	950	1,150
$10 2011W, J. Grant	3,969	950	1,000	1,200
$10 2011W, L. Hayes	3,885	950	1,000	1,200
$10 2011W, L. Garfield	3,652	950	1,000	1,200
$10 2012W, A. Paul	3,506	800	850	950
$10 2012W, F. Cleveland, Variety 1	3,158	800	850	950

	Mintage	PF	PF-69	PF-70
$10 2012W, C. Harrison	3,046	$800	$850	$950
$10 2012W, F. Cleveland, Variety 2	3,104	800	850	950
$10 2013W, I. McKinley	2,194	840	870	920
$10 2013W, E. Roosevelt	2,116	840	870	920
$10 2013W, H. Taft	1,933	840	870	920
$10 2013W, E. Wilson	1,922	840	870	920
$10 2013W, E. Wilson	1,733	840	870	920
$10 2014W, F. Harding		840	870	920
$10 2014W, G. Coolidge		840	870	920
$10 2014W, L. Hoover		840	870	920
$10 2014W, E. Roosevelt		840	870	920

Note: Values in the PF column are for uncertified Proof coins of average quality, in their complete original U.S. Mint packaging.

MMIX ULTRA HIGH RELIEF GOLD COIN
(2009)

Designer Augustus Saint-Gaudens; weight 31.101 grams; composition .9999 gold (actual gold weight 1 oz.); diameter 27 mm; lettered edge; mint: Philadelphia.

MMIX Ultra High Relief Gold Coin
Photographed at an angle to show the edge (lettered E PLURIBUS UNUM), the thickness (4 mm), and the depth of relief.

History. In 2009 the U.S. Mint produced a modern collector's version of the first Saint-Gaudens double eagle. When the original debuted in 1907, the Mint had been unable to strike large quantities for circulation—the ultra high relief design was artistic, but difficult to coin. (It was modified later in 1907 to a lower relief suitable for commercial production.) Just over 100 years later, the 2009 version was a showcase coin: a tangible demonstration of the Mint's 21st-century ability to combine artistry and technology to make an outstanding numismatic treasure.

Like its predecessor, the new coin was dated in Roman numerals (with 2009 as MMIX). The Mint digitally mapped Saint-Gaudens's original plasters and used the results in the die-making process. The date was changed, and four additional stars were inserted, to represent the nation's current 50 states. Augustus Saint-Gaudens's striding Liberty occupied the obverse. On the reverse was his flying eagle, with the addition of IN GOD WE TRUST, a motto not used in the original design. The 2009 version was made in a smaller diameter (27 mm instead of 34) and composed of 24-karat (.9999 fine) gold, thus making it easier to strike and stay true to the ultra high relief design.

As with other bullion products of the U.S. Mint, the coins are legal tender and their weight, content, and purity are guaranteed by the federal government. They were packaged in a fancy mahogany box and sold directly to the public, instead of through a network of distributors.

Note that the Mint does not release bullion mintage data on a regular basis; the number given here reflects the most recently available official data.

Striking and Sharpness. Striking is sharp.

Availability. The coins are available in the numismatic marketplace for a premium above their gold bullion value.

MS-60 to 70 (Mint State). *Obverse and reverse:* At MS-60, some abrasion and contact marks are evident on the higher design areas and the open areas of the design. Luster may be dull or lifeless at MS-60 to 62, but there should be deep frost at MS-63 and better, particularly in the lower-relief areas. At MS-65 and above, the luster should be full and rich. Contact marks and abrasion are less and less evident at higher grades. These guidelines are more academic than practical, as these coins are not intended for circulation, and presumably all are in high Mint State grades, as struck.

	Mintage	Unc.	MS-69	MS-70
MMIX Ultra High Relief $20 Gold Coin ‡	114,427	$2,500	$2,750	$3,400

Note: Values in the Unc. column are for uncertified, average Mint State coins. ‡ Ranked in the 100 Greatest U.S. Modern Coins.

AMERICAN EAGLE PLATINUM BULLION COINS
(1997 TO DATE)

Designers John M. Mercanti (obverse), Thomas D. Rogers Sr. (original reverse) (see image captions for other reverse designers); composition .9995 platinum; reeded edge; mints: Philadelphia, West Point. Weights and diameters: $10 1/10 oz., 16.5 mm; $25 1/4 oz., 22 mm; $50 1/2 oz., 27 mm; $100 1 oz., 32.7 mm.

Common obverse and original reverse design.

History. Platinum American Eagles (face values of $10 to $100) are legal-tender bullion coins with weight, content, and purity guaranteed by the federal government. They were added to the U.S. Mint's program of silver and gold bullion coinage in 1997.

In their debut year, Proofs had the same reverse design as regular bullion strikes. Since then, the regular strikes have continued with the 1997 reverse, while the Proofs have featured new reverse designs each year. From 1998 through 2002, these special Proof designs comprised a "Vistas of Liberty" subset, with eagles flying through various American scenes. Since 2003, they have featured patriotic allegories and symbolism. From 2006 to 2008 the reverse designs honored "The Foundations of Democracy"—the nation's legislative branch (2006), executive branch (2007), and judicial branch (2008). In 2009 the Mint introduced a new six-year program of reverse designs, exploring the core concepts of American democracy as embodied in the preamble to the Constitution. The first design is *To Form a More Perfect Union* (2009), featuring four faces representing the nation's diversity, with the hair and clothing interweaving symbolically. The tiny eagle privy mark is from an original coin punch from the Philadelphia Mint's archives. This design is followed by *To Establish Justice* (2010), *To Insure Domestic Tranquility* (2011), *To Provide for the Common Defence* (2012), *To Promote the General Welfare* (2013), and *To Secure the Blessings of Liberty to Ourselves and our Posterity* (2014). The themes for the reverse designs are inspired by narratives prepared by the chief justice of the United States.

The Philadelphia Mint strikes regular bullion issues, which are sold to the public by a network of Mint-authorized precious-metal firms, coin dealers, banks, and brokerages. The West Point facility strikes Burnished pieces (called *Uncirculated* by the Mint), which are sold directly to collectors. Proofs are also struck at West Point and, like the Burnished coins, are sold by the Mint to

the public, without middlemen. Similar to their gold-bullion cousins, the platinum Proofs and Burnished coins bear a W mintmark and are specially packaged in plastic capsules and fancy presentation cases.

In addition to the individual coins listed below, platinum American Eagles were issued in the 1997 "Impressions of Liberty" bullion coin set (see page 366); in 2007 "10th Anniversary" sets; and in annual platinum-coin sets.

Striking and Sharpness. Striking is generally sharp.

Availability. The platinum American Eagle is one of the most popular platinum-investment vehicles in the world. The coins are readily available in the numismatic marketplace and through some banks, investment firms, and other non-numismatic channels.

MS-60 to 70 (Mint State). *Obverse and reverse:* At MS-60, some abrasion and contact marks are evident on the higher design areas. Luster may be dull or life- | less at MS-60 to 62, but there should be deep frost at MS-63 and better, particularly in the lower-relief areas. At MS-65 and above, the luster should be full and rich. | These guidelines are more academic than practical, as platinum American Eagles are not intended for circulation, and nearly all are in high Mint State grades.

Regular Finish

$10 1/10-OUNCE AMERICAN EAGLE PLATINUM BULLION COINS

	Mintage	Unc.	MS-69	MS-70		Mintage	Unc.	MS-69	MS-70		Mintage	Unc.	MS-69	MS-70
$10 1997	70,250	$175	$200	$1,250	$10 2002	23,005	$175	$200	$300	$10 2006W, Burnished	3,544	$375	$400	$450
$10 1998	39,525	175	200	1,450	$10 2003	22,007	175	200	300	$10 2007	13,003	250	280	325
$10 1999	55,955	175	200	800	$10 2004	15,010	175	200	300	$10 2007W, Burnished	5,556	220	260	300
$10 2000	34,027	175	200	400	$10 2005	14,013	175	200	300	$10 2008	17,000	175	205	300
$10 2001	52,017	175	200	325	$10 2006	11,001	175	200	300	$10 2008W, Burnished	3,706	300	325	375

Note: Values in the Unc. column are for uncertified, average Mint State coins.

$25 1/4-OUNCE AMERICAN EAGLE PLATINUM BULLION COINS

	Mintage	Unc.	MS-69	MS-70		Mintage	Unc.	MS-69	MS-70		Mintage	Unc.	MS-69	MS-70
$25 1997	27,100	$415	$440	$2,200	$25 2002	27,405	$415	$440	$575	$25 2006W, Burnished	2,676	$600	$625	$850
$25 1998	38,887	415	440	1,200	$25 2003	25,207	415	440	550	$25 2007	8,402	415	440	550
$25 1999	39,734	415	440	2,750	$25 2004	18,010	415	440	550	$25 2007W, Burnished	3,690	425	450	550
$25 2000	20,054	415	440	800	$25 2005	12,013	415	440	550	$25 2008	22,800	415	440	575
$25 2001	21,815	415	440	2,300	$25 2006	12,001	415	440	550	$25 2008W, Burnished	2,481	750	775	950

Note: Values in the Unc. column are for uncertified, average Mint State coins.

$50 1/2-OUNCE AMERICAN EAGLE PLATINUM BULLION COINS

	Mintage	Unc.	MS-69	MS-70		Mintage	Unc.	MS-69	MS-70		Mintage	Unc.	MS-69	MS-70
$50 1997	20,500	$800	$825	$2,250	$50 2002	24,005	$800	$825	$1,700	$50 2006W, Burnished	2,577	$1,050	$1,100	$1,300
$50 1998	32,415	800	825	3,500	$50 2003	17,409	800	825	1,100	$50 2007	7,001	800	825	950
$50 1999	32,309	800	825	3,500	$50 2004	13,236	800	825	1,100	$50 2007W, Burnished	3,635	850	875	1,000
$50 2000	18,892	800	825	4,000	$50 2005	9,013	800	825	1,100	$50 2008	14,000	800	825	1,000
$50 2001	12,815	800	825	3,750	$50 2006	9,602	800	825	950	$50 2008W, Burnished ‡	2,253	1,300	1,325	2,400

Note: Values in the Unc. column are for uncertified, average Mint State coins. ‡ Ranked in the *100 Greatest U.S. Modern Coins.*

$100 1-OUNCE AMERICAN EAGLE PLATINUM BULLION COINS

	Mintage	Unc.	MS-69	MS-70		Mintage	Unc.	MS-69	MS-70		Mintage	Unc.	MS-69	MS-70
$100 1997	56,000	$1,650	$1,700	$9,000	$100 2003	8,007	$1,650	$1,700	$3,750	$100 2007W, Burnished	4,177	$1,900	$1,950	$2,150
$100 1998	133,002	1,650	1,700	9,000	$100 2004	7,009	1,650	1,700	2,500	$100 2008	21,800	1,700	1,750	1,950
$100 1999	56,707	1,650	1,700	10,000	$100 2005	6,310	1,650	1,700	2,500	$100 2008W, Burnished	2,876	2,050	2,100	2,900
$100 2000	10,003	1,650	1,700	10,000	$100 2006	6,000	1,650	1,700	2,200	$100 2014		1,600	1,650	1,800
$100 2001	14,070	1,650	1,700	10,000	$100 2006W, Burnished ‡	3,068	1,950	2,000	2,200					
$100 2002	11,502	1,650	1,700	7,000	$100 2007	7,202	1,650	1,700	2,100					

Note: Values in the Unc. column are for uncertified, average Mint State coins.

AMERICAN EAGLE PLATINUM BULLION COIN SETS

	Unc.	MS-69	MS-70		Unc.	MS-69	MS-70		Unc.	MS-69	MS-70
1997 Platinum Set. $100, $50, $25, $10	$3,000	$3,150	$14,700	2003 Platinum Set. $100, $50, $25, $10	$3,000	$3,150	$5,700	2006W Platinum Burnished Set.			
1998 Platinum Set. $100, $50, $25, $10	3,000	3,150	15,150	2004 Platinum Set. $100, $50, $25, $10	3,000	3,150	4,450	$100, $50, $25, $10	$4,000	$4,100	$4,800
1999 Platinum Set. $100, $50, $25, $10	3,000	3,150	17,050	2005 Platinum Set. $100, $50, $25, $10	3,000	3,150	4,450	2007W Platinum Burnished Set.			
2000 Platinum Set. $100, $50, $25, $10	3,000	3,150	15,200	2006 Platinum Set. $100, $50, $25, $10	2,900	3,025	4,000	$100, $50, $25, $10	3,400	3,550	4,000
2001 Platinum Set. $100, $50, $25, $10	3,000	3,150	16,375	2007 Platinum Set. $100, $50, $25, $10	3,100	3,250	4,000	2008W Platinum Burnished Set.			
2002 Platinum Set. $100, $50, $25, $10	3,000	3,150	9,575	2008 Platinum Set. $100, $50, $25, $10	3,100	3,225	3,775	$100, $50, $25, $10	4,400	4,550	6,500

Note: Values in the Unc. column are for uncertified Mint State coins of average quality, in their complete original U.S. Mint packaging.

Proof American Eagle Platinum Bullion Coins

PF-60 to 70 (Proof). Proofs that are extensively cleaned and have many hairlines are lower level, such as PF-60 to 62. Those with fewer hairlines or flaws are deemed PF-63 to 65. (These exist more in theory than actuality, as nearly all Proof American Eagle platinum bullion coins have been maintained in their original high condition by collectors and investors.) Given the quality of modern U.S. Mint products, even PF-66 and 67 are unusually low levels for these Proofs.

Common Proof Obverse

Proof Reverse, 1998: Eagle Over New England. Vistas of Liberty series. Designer: John Mercanti.

Proof Reverse, 1999: Eagle Above Southeastern Wetlands. Vistas of Liberty series. Designer: John Mercanti.

Proof Reverse, 2000: Eagle Above America's Heartland. Vistas of Liberty series. Designer: Alfred Maletsky.

Proof Reverse, 2001: Eagle Above America's Southwest. Vistas of Liberty series. Designer: Thomas D. Rogers Sr.

Proof Reverse, 2002: Eagle Fishing in America's Northwest. Vistas of Liberty series. Designer: Alfred Maletsky.

Proof Reverse, 2003. Designer: Alfred Maletsky.

Proof Reverse, 2004. Designer: Donna Weaver.

Proof Reverse, 2005. Designer: Donna Weaver.

Proof Reverse, 2006: "Legislative Branch." Designer: Joel Iskowitz.

Proof Reverse, 2007: "Executive Branch." Designer: Thomas Cleveland.

Proof Reverse, 2008: "Judicial Branch." Designer: Joel Iskowitz.

Proof Reverse, 2009: "To Form a More Perfect Union." Designer: Susan Gamble.

Proof Reverse, 2010: "To Establish Justice." Designer: Donna Weaver.

Proof Reverse, 2011: "To Insure Domestic Tranquility." Designer: Joel Iskowitz.

Proof Reverse, 2012: "To Provide for the Common Defence." Designer: Barbara Fox.

$10 1/10-OUNCE PROOF AMERICAN EAGLE PLATINUM BULLION COINS

	Mintage	PF	PF-69	PF-70
$10 1997W	36,993	$200	$225	$350
$10 1998W	19,847	200	225	650
$10 1999W	19,133	200	225	400
$10 2000W	15,651	200	225	400

	Mintage	PF	PF-69	PF-70
$10 2001W	12,174	$200	$225	$425
$10 2002W	12,365	200	225	400
$10 2003W	9,534	250	275	450
$10 2004W	7,161	435	460	650

	Mintage	PF	PF-69	PF-70
$10 2005W	8,104	$275	$300	$400
$10 2006W	10,205	200	225	350
$10 2007W	8,176	200	225	400
$10 2008W	5,138	425	450	550

Note: Values in the PF column are for uncertified Proof coins of average quality, in their complete original U.S. Mint packaging.

$25 1/4-OUNCE PROOF AMERICAN EAGLE PLATINUM BULLION COINS

	Mintage	PF	PF-69	PF-70
$25 1997W	18,628	$440	$475	$740
$25 1998W	14,873	440	475	700
$25 1999W	13,507	440	475	700
$25 2000W	11,995	440	475	700
$25 2001W	8,847	440	475	750

	Mintage	PF	PF-69	PF-70
$25 2002W	9,282	$440	$475	$750
$25 2003W	7,044	440	475	750
$25 2004W	5,193	965	1,000	1,600
$25 2005W	6,592	565	600	1,100
$25 2006W	7,813	440	475	750

	Mintage	PF	PF-69	PF-70
$25 2007W	6,017	$440	$475	$750
$25 2007W, Frosted FREEDOM	21			
$25 2008W	4,153	750	785	1,000

Note: Values in the PF column are for uncertified Proof coins of average quality, in their complete original U.S. Mint packaging.

$50 1/2-OUNCE PROOF AMERICAN EAGLE PLATINUM BULLION COINS

	Mintage	PF	PF-69	PF-70
$50 1997W	15,431	$875	$915	$1,200
$50 1998W	13,836	875	915	1,200
$50 1999W	11,103	875	915	1,350
$50 2000W	11,049	875	915	1,350
$50 2001W	8,254	875	915	1,400

	Mintage	PF	PF-69	PF-70
$50 2002W	8,772	$875	$915	$1,400
$50 2003W	7,131	875	915	1,400
$50 2004W	5,063	1,500	1,550	1,850
$50 2005W	5,942	1,100	1,150	1,450
$50 2006W	7,649	875	915	1,300

	Mintage	PF	PF-69	PF-70
$50 2007W	25,519	$875	$915	$1,200
$50 2007W, Rev Proof	19,583	900	930	1,200
$50 2007W, Frosted FREEDOM	21			
$50 2008W ‡	4,020	1,325	1,375	1,675

Note: Values in the PF column are for uncertified Proof coins of average quality, in their complete original U.S. Mint packaging. ‡ Ranked in the *100 Greatest U.S. Modern Coins.*

$100 1-OUNCE PROOF AMERICAN EAGLE PLATINUM BULLION COINS

	Mintage	PF	PF-69	PF-70
$100 1997W	20,851	$1,850	$1,900	$3,500
$100 1998W	14,912	1,850	1,900	3,500
$100 1999W	12,363	1,850	1,900	4,150
$100 2000W	12,453	1,850	1,900	4,150
$100 2001W	8,969	1,850	1,900	4,600
$100 2002W	9,834	1,850	1,900	4,600
$100 2003W	8,246	1,850	1,900	4,600

	Mintage	PF	PF-69	PF-70
$100 2004W	6,007	$2,050	$2,100	$4,000
$100 2005W	6,602	2,150	2,200	3,300
$100 2006W	9,152	1,850	1,900	2,700
$100 2007W	8,363	1,850	1,900	2,700
$100 2007W, Frosted FREEDOM	12	—		
$100 2008W	4,769	2,775	2,825	3,200

	Mintage	PF	PF-69	PF-70
$100 2009W ‡	7,945	$2,100	$2,150	$2,750
$100 2010W	9,871	1,950	2,000	2,400
$100 2011W	14,835	1,900	1,950	2,400
$100 2012W	10,084	1,850	1,900	2,200
$100 2013W	5,310	1,900	1,950	2,200
$100 2014W		1,800	1,850	2,200

Note: Values in the PF column are for uncertified Proof coins of average quality, in their complete original U.S. Mint packaging. ‡ Ranked in the *100 Greatest U.S. Modern Coins.*

PROOF AMERICAN EAGLE PLATINUM BULLION COIN SETS

	PF	PF-69	PF-70
1997W Platinum Set. $100, $50, $25, $10	$3,350	$3,500	$5,800
1998W Platinum Set. $100, $50, $25, $10	3,350	3,500	6,000
1999W Platinum Set. $100, $50, $25, $10	3,350	3,500	6,500
2000W Platinum Set. $100, $50, $25, $10	3,350	3,500	6,500

	PF	PF-69	PF-70
2001W Platinum Set. $100, $50, $25, $10	$3,350	$3,500	$7,100
2002W Platinum Set. $100, $50, $25, $10	3,350	3,500	7,100
2003W Platinum Set. $100, $50, $25, $10	3,400	3,600	7,200
2004W Platinum Set. $100, $50, $25, $10	5,000	5,200	8,000

	PF	PF-69	PF-70
2005W Platinum Set. $100, $50, $25, $10	$4,000	$4,300	$6,250
2006W Platinum Set. $100, $50, $25, $10	3,350	3,500	5,100
2007W Platinum Set. $100, $50, $25, $10	3,350	3,500	5,100
2008W Platinum Set. $100, $50, $25, $10	4,850	5,400	6,400

Note: Values in the PF column are for uncertified Proof coins of average quality, in their complete original U.S. Mint packaging.

2007 10TH-ANNIVERSARY PLATINUM PROOF COIN SETS

	Est Mintage	PF	PF-69	PF-70
2007W Two-Coin Set (a)	19,583	$1,775	$1,845	$2,400

Note: The $100 Platinum Eagle of 1997 is also included in the 1997 Impressions of Liberty Set, listed on page 366. a. This two-coin set, housed in a mahogany-finish hardwood box, includes one half-ounce Proof (with the standard cameo-finish background and frosted design elements) and one half-ounce Reverse Proof (with frosted background fields and mirrored raised elements) dated 2007-W.

APPENDIX A:
GREAT COLLECTORS AND COLLECTIONS OF THE PAST
by Ron Guth and Jeff Garrett

Appleton, William Sumner—William Sumner Appleton was an active buyer in the latter half of the 19th century, purchasing J.J. Mickley's 1804 silver dollar, Mickley's entire gold coin collection, and virtually all of Lorin G. Parmelee's collection. He authored several works, including one on Washington-related coins and medals.

Bass, Harry W.—Harry W. Bass Jr. did what most collectors can only dream of—he built a nearly complete collection of United States gold coins, with an emphasis on superb quality. A true numismatist in the classic sense, Bass collected by die variety, both major and minor. The bulk of his collection was sold over a series of four auctions from 1999 to 2000, but the core collection of gold types and three-dollar gold pieces (including the unique 1870-S) is now on display at the Money Museum of the American Numismatic Association in Colorado Springs, Colorado.

Boyd, Frederick C.C.—F.C.C. Boyd was active as a coin dealer and collector during the first half of the 20th century. He acquired many great rarities, including an 1894-S dime, an 1876-CC twenty-cent piece, a 1927-D double eagle, and many others; for a short time, he owned an 1804 silver dollar. His silver and gold coins were sold at auction in 1946, with the silver portion billed as "The World's Greatest Collection." His U.S. colonial coins were sold via the John J. Ford collection in 2003–2007.

Brand, Virgil M.—Virgil Brand was a Chicago brewer, and used his fortune to amass one of the largest coin collections of all time. Active from 1879 until his death in 1926, Brand was not averse to buying multiple items of great rarities (he owned six of the ten 1884 trade dollars, 30 four-dollar gold Stellas, five 1792 silver-center cents, etc., but only one 1804 silver dollar). At his death, his collection contained more than 350,000 coins, which required several decades to disperse completely.

Browning, Jeff—Jeff Browning was the name behind the Dallas Bank Collection of gold coins, sold at auction in 2001. Collecting during the 1960s and 1970s, Browning acquired a complete set of Liberty Head double eagles, a complete set of four-dollar Stellas, and a 1907 Ultra High Relief double eagle.

Carter, Amon, Sr. and Jr.—Amon Carter Sr. was a Texas oilman and cofounder of American Airlines. In the 1930s, he was introduced to coins by B. Max Mehl and went on a two-decade buying binge that netted him fabulous rarities such as an 1804 silver dollar, an 1884 trade dollar, an 1885 trade dollar, an 1822 half eagle, and many other rarities. Upon his death, Carter's collection passed to his son, who developed his own reputation as a top-ranked collector of United States currency.

Dunham, William F.—William Dunham was a Chicago druggist who was an active collector in the first half of the 20th century. His collection included one of the finest known 1802 half dimes, an 1804 silver dollar, and an 1822 half eagle. Following Dunham's death, Texas coin dealer B. Max Mehl purchased the collection intact. Mehl's 1941 Mail Bid Sale of the Dunham collection, offered in a lavish catalog, was a deception, as many of the best coins had already been sold privately!

Eckfeldt, Adam—A Mint employee for many years, Adam Eckfeldt was instrumental in building the Mint Cabinet that is now part of the National Numismatic Collection at the Smithsonian Institution. Beginning with the Mint's inception in 1792, Eckfeldt set aside coins each year with an eye to someday establishing a conservatory of coins. His dream was realized in 1838, when Mint Director Robert Maskell Patterson established a national collection at the Philadelphia Mint. Thanks to Adam Eckfeldt's foresight, collectors of today can enjoy many rarities that might otherwise have been lost forever.

Eliasberg, Louis E., Sr.—Louis Eliasberg is famous in numismatic circles for having assembled the only complete collection of federally issued United States coins. In 1942, Eliasberg purchased John Clapp's comprehensive collection intact, reducing his want list to a mere handful of coins. In 1950 Eliasberg achieved his goal of completion with the purchase of the unique 1873-CC No Arrows dime. His gold coins were sold at auction in 1982 and the balance of the collection was sold at auction in 1996 and 1997. The combined sales reached a total of $44 million.

Ellsworth, Colonel James W.—James Ellsworth's collection, begun during the late 1800s and continued through 1923, included many important rarities, such as a 1787 Brasher doubloon and two (!) 1804 silver dollars. Unlike most collectors, Ellsworth sold his collection during his lifetime, sharing many of the most significant coins with another famous collector, John Work Garrett.

King Farouk of Egypt—Farouk was a flamboyant king who used the Egyptian treasury to build a fabulous collection of U.S. and world coins. Farouk was deposed in 1952 and the sale of his collection in 1954 was one of the great numismatic events of history. The 1933 double eagle he once held reappeared in 2002, selling for a record price of $7.59 million!

Garrett, John Work—In 1919, John Work Garrett acquired a collection, built by his father and brother, that was already one of the most celebrated in America. While not as complete as Louis Eliasberg's U.S. coin collection, Garrett's included U.S. colonial and pre-federal issues, plus rarities from around the world. The sale of his U.S. coins (from 1979 through 1981) realized more than $25 million, setting a modern record for a single coin collection. In adjusted dollars, it would still be the most valuable collection today.

Green, Colonel Edward Howland Robinson—Colonel E.H.R. Green was a prolific collector, thanks to the fortune left him by his mother, Hetty Green (the "Witch of Wall Street"). He once owned all five of the 1913 Liberty Head nickels, an 1804 silver dollar, several 1838-O half dollars, and more than two hundred 1796 Draped Bust quarter dollars. In 1939, his coin collection was appraised at over $1.2 million, a staggering figure at the time.

Lilly, Josiah K.—Josiah K. Lilly amassed a huge collection of U.S. and world gold coins during the 1950s and 1960s. After his death, the Smithsonian Institution accepted the donation of the collection in exchange for a $5 million estate tax credit (worth roughly $50 million today). The U.S. section was virtually complete and included such rarities as the 1787 Brasher half doubloon, an 1822 half eagle, and a 1907 Ultra High Relief twenty-dollar gold piece. His collection was formerly exhibited in a special room in the National Museum of American History.

Mickley, Joseph J.—Joseph Mickley was one of the pioneer collectors of American coins, beginning a quest for a cent of his birth year (1799) in the early 1800s. Legend had Mickley visiting the U.S. Mint in 1827 to purchase four of the rare quarter dollars of that date; however, that tale has been debunked in recent years. Mickley is best known for the restrikes that he made of certain U.S. coins (1811 half cent, 1804 large cent, and 1823 large cent) using dies that the Mint had sold years earlier as scrap metal. Most of Mickley's dies were bought back by the U.S. government when they appeared in an auction of Mickley's estate in 1878.

Mitchelson, John C.—In December 1911, Joseph Mitchelson donated his collection of more than 10,000 U.S. and world coins to the Connecticut State Library in Hartford, where the bulk of the collection remains to this day. Provisions were made for the addition of new U.S. coins as they were minted in subsequent years. Highlights of the collection include a 1907 Ultra High Relief double eagle, a 1737 Higley copper, and many other fabulous rarities, few of which have been seen by the general public. In 1995, selected duplicates from the Connecticut State Library's collection were sold at auction, including a 1927-D double eagle.

Newcomer, Waldo—Waldo Newcomer began collecting in the 1890s and quickly built one of the largest and most complete collections of American colonial and federal coins. His collection of U.S. gold coins was said to be complete except for one half eagle and one double eagle. Newcomer also owned examples of such great rarities as two 1787 Brasher doubloons, an 1802 half dime, an 1838-O half dollar, an 1853 half dollar (without rays and arrowheads), and an 1804 silver dollar. Newcomer's coins were sold at auction over nearly a decade, from 1932 to 1941.

Norweb, Emery May Holden—Over the course of decades in the late 1800s, and throughout the 20th century, the Norweb family built an extensive collection of rare colonials and superb-quality U.S. coins. Mrs. Norweb acquired the love of numismatics at her father's feet and continued adding coins after his death. Highlights of the collection included a 1787 Brasher doubloon, a 1792 pattern quarter dollar, a 1913 nickel, an 1815 half eagle, and the finest known 1861 Paquet Reverse double eagle. The Norweb collection realized $20 million at auction in 1987 and 1988, despite the previous gifting-away of the Brasher doubloon and the 1913 nickel!

Parmelee, Lorin G.—Lorin Parmelee, a Boston bean-baker, started collecting coins in the 1850s, when U.S. colonial copper coins and large cents still circulated at face value. As his taste and fortunes advanced, he began purchasing coins at auction, then began buying entire collections, taking what he wanted and selling off the duplicates. The remainders, from the Charles Bushnell collection (purchased by Parmelee in 1880) alone, represented one of the finest coin auctions of the 19th century. In its time, Parmelee's collection was generally perceived to be the finest and most complete collection of coins ever assembled. Included were great rarities such as the 1796 and 1797 half dollars, an 1804 silver dollar, and a set of 1783 Nova Constellatio pattern coins in silver.

Pittman, John Jay—Unlike most of the collectors in this section, John Jay Pittman had limited resources with which to buy rare coins. However, through shrewd purchases, Pittman amassed a collection that realized more than $30 million when it was sold between 1997 and 1998. Some of his best purchases were made at the 1954 sale of King Farouk's coin collection.

Reed, Byron—A real estate operator in Omaha, Nebraska, Byron Reed built a fine collection of American coins, books, and autographs. Reed worked on his collection from the 1880s until his death in 1891. Reed bequeathed his coins and library to the city of Omaha, along with a plot of land for a building that would eventually house both collections. In 1996, selections from his coin collection were sold at auction to raise money for the city. However, the majority of Reed's collection, including his 1804 silver dollar and rare U.S. patterns, remains largely intact, with many of the coins now on display at the Western Heritage Museum in Omaha.

Sheldon, William H.—William Sheldon collected large cents by die variety, and in 1949 he wrote *Early American Cents* (renamed *Penny Whimsy* in 1958), the standard reference book on the 1793 through 1814 cent varieties. The 70-point grading system used by numismatists today was developed by Sheldon.

Snowden, James Ross—James Snowden served as director of the Mint from 1853 to 1861, and was a serious numismatist as well. He built the cabinet of Washington coins, tokens, and medals that went on display at the Philadelphia Mint in 1860. Snowden acquired many of the items in the display by trading restrikes of rare United States coins.

Stickney, Matthew Adams—Matthew Stickney was a contemporary of Joseph J. Mickley and thus among the first truly serious collectors of American coins. Stickney acquired many of his best coins directly from the Mint: some through trades and some through an annual purchase of Proof coins beginning in 1845. Other rarities came from his special relationship with a New York bullion firm, which sent him gold rarities for their intrinsic metal value. Around 1843, Stickney traded a gold 1785 Immune Columbia colonial coin for one of the Mint's 1804 silver dollars! Other highlights from his collection include the unique 1776 New Hampshire cent and a 1776 Massachusetts "Janus Head" copper.

Trompeter, Ed—Ed Trompeter built a collection of Proof U.S. gold coins, complete for the period from 1858 through 1915 (save for the 1858 double eagle), plus extra rarities such as an 1855 Proof gold dollar, a complete set of four-dollar gold Stellas, a quintuple "Stella," a 1907 Ultra High Relief double eagle, and more. Trompeter's Proof gold dollars through three-dollar gold pieces were sold at auction in 1992; his Proof half eagles through double eagles were sold privately for more than $15 million in 1998. The Trompeter pedigree is one of the most desirable of modern times.

Wilkison, John—John Wilkison built the finest collection of U.S. gold pattern coins ever assembled outside the Mint. His collection included unique rarities such as the 1907 Indian Head double eagle and the complete set of gold 1872 "Amazonian" one-through twenty-dollar patterns. The collection formed the basis for David Akers's 1975 book *United States Gold Patterns,* a modern numismatist's "wish book."

Woodin, William H.—William Woodin once owned the unique 1870-S three-dollar piece. In 1909, he acquired the two known gold 1877 fifty-dollar half unions, prompting an outrage that the government had allowed them to be released. Shortly thereafter, Woodin traded them for a "trunkful" of patterns that served as the basis for the first book on U.S. pattern coins. The half unions are now in the Smithsonian Institution, and Woodin's patterns represent the majority of the pieces that appear on the market today.

APPENDIX B:
COIN CLEANING, CONSERVATION, AND PRESERVATION

There is a common misconception among collectors that because coins are durable enough to circulate for decades, they are also resistant to most types of mishandling. In fact, the metal surfaces of coins record their history of treatment exceptionally well—for better or worse. On the positive side, for example, the patina of a coin can reveal if it resided in an old collection, because some types of storage albums impart distinctive toning patterns that develop gradually over many years.

This 1881-S Morgan dollar shows toning from its contact with the environment—the bag it was transported in, the other coins it touched, the very air that surrounded it. "A relatively common date with a not-so-common display of toning" is how it was described at auction. Many collectors find such natural displays of color attractive. Others might be tempted to dip such a coin to make it brilliant and white. "Coin doctors" try to imitate such toning through artificial means like baking and chemical applications. (shown actual size)

Old fingerprints add some mystery to these Braided Hair large cents—could they be Abraham Lincoln's?—but they detract from the coins' value. (shown 1.5x actual size)

Unfortunately, an examination of a coin's surface just as readily reveals if it has been mistreated. A coin can have dark stains, thick residues, or fingerprints—undesirable consequences of mishandling that negatively affect value. As a further detriment, many coins suffer even more severe and irreversible damage as a result of amateur efforts to save them or improve their appearance. Once a coin exhibits hairlines, impaired luster, or changes in color, or develops corrosion from inadequate neutralization, its surface will always bear evidence.

In today's marketplace, for example, most old copper, nickel, silver, and gold Proof coins are less than superb gem grade—that is, less than Proof-66. The vast majority has tiny hairlines visible under magnification, and Proofs in the 60 to 63 range are apt to have many. When they left the mint, the coins had no hairlines at all. How did the hairlines happen? From improper cleaning. Similarly, most brilliant silver coins dated before 1900 are "white" because they've been cleaned (certain Treasury-hoard Morgan dollars being exceptions); perhaps 90 percent of all pre-federal

(colonial) coins and tokens have been cleaned; and all high-grade ancient coins have been cleaned at one point or another.

This appendix explains the philosophy about coin cleaning that was prevalent from the mid-1800s until just a generation or two ago. It discusses old methods of cleaning that are discouraged today because of the harm they do to coins. It looks at modern methods of professional conservation. And it offers advice on how to clean coins yourself, in the rare instances that this is advisable.

WHY COINS CHANGE IN APPEARANCE

Coins are most often produced in copper, nickel, silver, or gold. All of these metals are derived from ores that are smelted from a mineral state (which is relatively stable) to a crystalline solid or a metal state (which is somewhat unstable). Virtually all coinage metals are a mixture of more than one elemental metal. These alloys are mixed in order to attain desired coinage characteristics such as color, intrinsic value, and durability.

A coin's survival and state of preservation are influenced by its environment. The interaction of both organic and synthetic elements with the coin's metallic composition can alter its surface in a variety of ways. Coins produced during the last couple of centuries commonly have debris particles, residues, and other potentially corrosive elements on their surfaces. Such particles often are found stuck in the recesses of design features. Over time, they can develop severe spots of active corrosion.

Other harmful surface conditions result from handling and storage. Even the most careful handling enables contaminants on your fingers to be transferred to your coins. Oils and salts are continuously secreted through the skin and will be transferred to the coin, along with many other potentially harmful substances that adhered to the skin through contact with other items. To avoid putting very noticeable and often irremovable fingerprints on the fields of a coin, collectors emphasize handling coins by their edges—but even this allows residues to transfer. Sometimes this is seen on early copper coins, where the obverse and reverse display an attractive brown color while the rim has a slightly lighter and pink coloration from contact with fingertips. In more extreme examples, the obverse and reverse may appear to be in Very Good condition, while small green spots of corrosion are visible on the edge and rim.

EARLY ATTITUDES TOWARD CLEANING

The numismatic hobby in America commenced on a large scale in 1857 and 1858, when the discontinuation of the large copper cent prompted many people to try to find as many dates as possible. Since that boom more than 150 years ago, there has been the philosophy that "brilliant is best."

An improperly cleaned Capped Bust half dollar. (shown 1.25x actual size)

Accordingly, a silver coin (in particular) with natural toning (perhaps brown, perhaps golden, perhaps iridescent, perhaps somewhat spotted) was a candidate to be brightened by using acid, silver polish, or some other substance. This did the trick, and the result was a brilliant coin. However, nature and chemistry being what they are, the typical coin retoned over a period of time, as it was subjected to various influences such as dampness, warmth, fumes with sulfur (from home heating, industrial residue in the air, etc.), and careless handling. The coin would be sent back to the polish and chemicals, and again it would be bright.

While today this sounds unusual, perhaps even improbable, the scenario was very much the case generations ago. In August 1903, *The Numismatist* included this comment from Farran Zerbe, who had just viewed the Mint Collection in Philadelphia:

> I found many of the silver Proof coins of late years partially covered with a white coating. On inquiry I learned that an over zealous attendant during the last vacation months when the numismatic room was closed took it on himself to clean the tarnished coins, purchase some metal polish at a department store, and proceeded with his cleaning operation. Later a coating of white appeared on the coins, which was now slowly disappearing.
>
> I expressed my displeasure at this improper treatment of Proof coins, and the custodian explained, "That is nothing. I have been here eight years and they have been cleaned three or four times in my time."

Zerbe speculated that should this cleaning continue, in the future one would have nothing left except plain planchets and badly worn coins!

In 1921, one of America's leading collectors, J. Sanford Saltus, was in a hotel room, using potassium cyanide—a lethal liquid—to clean silver coins. He was found dead shortly afterward. The presence of a glass of ginger ale on the table suggested he mistook one for the other. Even so, for many years the advice to use cyanide to clean coins continued.

In the 1950s James F. Kelly, a leading Dayton, Ohio, dealer, suggested that potassium cyanide, if very carefully used, would remove signs of friction from the higher parts of silver coins that were graded About Uncirculated, giving them an appearance of full Mint State.

In the meantime, in *The Numismatist, The Numismatic Scrapbook Magazine,* and elsewhere, products were offered to brighten coins. In one instance, a compound plus a wire brush was said to be very effective on copper coins.

During this era, American dealers found that coins that were toned, even very attractively, met with very few buyers. The operative term of the day was "BU," for Brilliant Uncirculated. A Morgan silver dollar, a commemorative half dollar, or some other coin, if toned, would be rejected by buyers nine times out of ten.

Dipping in a jewelry- or silver-cleaning liquid was very popular. Baking soda might be applied to the surface of a coin and rubbed vigorously to remove stubborn stains. The latter process imparted tiny hairlines. Coins toned, and then were cleaned again, creating more hairlines.

Collectors got into the game also when they found that a bright coin would sell readily, but a toned coin wouldn't. Again, this mostly applied to silver. Gold, an inert metal, but with 10% copper as alloy, tended to tone very slowly, and relatively few gold coins were dipped or brightened. Copper coins were a different story. Dip used for silver coins would instantly brighten a Lincoln or Indian Head cent that had some brown toning. (For a while it would look as good as new, so to speak. However, the dipping had its own problems.) Sometimes gentle heat, such as from a lightbulb, was applied to add toning. If all went well, and the copper cent was kept in a plastic holder, it might remain attractive. On the other hand, if there was the slightest residue of leftover dip, or other contaminants, the result eventually would be staining and blotching, making the coin less attractive than it was to begin with.

The leading grading services have been trapped a number of times on this, by certifying copper coins as "RD" (red) in gem (65 and higher) categories, only to find that a later buyer ended up with a coin that had developed spots. Accordingly, guarantees concerning the stability of copper coins have been revised. The grading services make no comment as to whether a coin has been cleaned or not.

The secret that is not a secret is that any Proof coin on the market today that has hairlines in the field—and virtually all of them do that are graded below Proof-66, as well as many that are graded higher—have been cleaned at one time by using friction. When the coins were minted the hairlines weren't there. Curiously, this fact is very difficult to find in print, and most collectors are not aware of it. Many readers of the *Professional Edition* will learn this information about coins for the first time. In a broader view, in other areas of collecting and connoisseurship (such as antiquities, Old Masters paintings, and historical documents), cleaning, good and bad, is often discussed. Not so in numismatics.

CHANGING PHILOSOPHIES

The mindset for "brilliant is best" began to change—although slowly—in the 1960s and 1970s. New Netherlands Coin Company, a leading New York City dealer at the time, offered many coins at auction, suggesting that attractive toning was an asset, and often describing it in detail. Lester Merkin, another leading dealer, did likewise.

John J. Ford Jr., the co-owner of New Netherlands, gave this commentary in the 1950s in an issue of the firm's magazine, *Numisma:*

> There are as many "expert" ways to clean coins as there are coin dealers. We suggest you read Dr. Sheldon's comments in his book [*Early American Cents,* 1949, the standard reference on large copper cents of the 1793–1814 years; succeeded by *Penny Whimsy,* 1958], and talk to older, experienced collectors. Well toned coins, strictly Uncirculated or Proof and without blemishes, are valued more highly by us than the usually found "cleaned" silver examples. It is almost inevitable that a really old silver coin which has so-called brilliance must have been meticulously cleaned so as to seem so. The aluminum pan with baking soda in solution, often used for cleaning silverware, is good for ordinary dull tarnish and is probably the commonest method, as well as one of the safest. . . .
>
> For my money, "expert cleaning" leaves the coin looking as if it *had not been touched.* In this light, we suggest coins with an even and attractively colored toning be left alone, as it will for a long time protect them against less desirable tarnish.
>
> Abrasives of any sort are dangerous. Jeweler's rouge is to be avoided; it is simply iron oxide (rust) ground to fine powder, and its action is simply scouring. . . .
>
> Proofs are no different from other coins, except they show the results of sloppy cleaning more easily. We do not retouch 99% of the material we handle, except for an occasional brushing, or the judicious use of a little mineral oil. To sum it up, it is much better to leave "improving" to the other fellow, as well as the "expert" designation in this field of endeavor.

THE GARRETT COLLECTION

In 1979 came the first of four auction offerings of the Garrett Collection, put on the market by The Johns Hopkins University. This cabinet had been gathered, beginning in the 1870s, by T. Harrison Garrett, an heir to the Baltimore and Ohio Railroad fortune. After his untimely death in a boating accident in 1888, the collection remained dormant and later passed to his son, John Work Garrett. The latter was an ardent numismatist who picked up the traces from his father, and made significant additions to his collection. The thought of cleaning or brightening a coin did not enter his mind. In 1942 Garrett died, and the collection was willed to the university. Then, in the 1970s, it was deaccessioned, as it had been stored in a subterranean bank vault for years, not accessible for scholarship or anything else. The funds from its sale were needed elsewhere. The firm of Bowers and Ruddy cataloged and described each coin, nearly all of which were attractively toned, reflecting the connoisseurship of the past owners. The prices realized amazed the hobby, with many pieces bringing double or triple current values, or even more. From that point forward, attractive toning was in style, and the practice of dipping and brightening of coins lessened.

COIN STORAGE

In an effort to minimize the handling of coins, manufacturers have created a wide variety of storage devices for hobbyists. Over the years hundreds of different products, ranging from flips and envelopes to books and boxes, have been sold to help collectors store and manage their collections. The earliest versions were not without problems. Many holders contained sulfur, polyvinyl chloride (PVC), and a variety of other potential contaminants. In recent decades, manufacturers have become better informed and more responsible, and we have seen the development of much safer storage products. Nevertheless, not all collectors and dealers seek out these coin-friendly products, and many hobbyists have not removed their coins from the old and potentially hazardous holders.

Coins from improper holders are seen every day in the marketplace. PVC contamination is one of the more commonly seen problems resulting from bad coin holders. In many cases PVC "goo" has corroded into the surfaces of the coin.

Even if coin-friendly holders are used, the surrounding environment can still adversely affect a coin's condition by facilitating corrosion or tarnish. An attractive pattern of colors on a coin is called *toning.* When unattractive, this same condition is called *tarnish* or *spots.* And when very dark it often is called *environmental damage.* Tarnish is a form of oxidation and is primarily caused by hydrogen sulfide and carbonyl sulfide. Tarnish can result from direct contact with reactive elements, or through vapors.

Some common tarnish-causing elements are wool, silk, felt, dyed fabrics, paper, cardboard, wood, and wood products, to name just a few. In short, traces of tarnish-causing elements can be found all around the house and office, and even in the clothes we wear. While people are not able to smell sulfur until it reaches unhealthy levels, coins are many times more sensitive. Add fluctuations in temperature and humidity, and the speed and effect of the tarnish-causing materials is increased.

Coins displaying the effects of these hazards are prevalent in the marketplace. Their appearance may vary considerably, but it is generally unappealing and can worsen over time. The difficulty most dealers and collectors experience when attempting to conserve their coins is that they lack the technical expertise, appropriate materials, and, more importantly, experience and training. The results of amateur attempts to address these problems are also easy to find in the many improperly cleaned or "problem" coins that display hairlines, scratches, impaired luster, or unnatural color.

During all of this time, knowledgeable dealers carefully conserved gold, silver, and copper by removing "vault grime," dirt, grease, and other distractions through the use of inert chemicals, without friction. In many instances acetone—a powerful solvent (which must be used carefully and with ventilation)—helped. Ammonia was useful as well (but tended to give copper coins an iridescent color), and the use of plain soap and water could be advantageous. Meanwhile, as some coins were being conserved, some others (in the distinct minority) were being artificially toned to increase their marketability, and still others were being dipped.

THE *PHOTOGRADE* COMMENTARY AND ADVICE

Photograde, written by James F. Ruddy and published in 1970, contained this advice (excerpted):

> Many products for cleaning coins are available on the market, and in some instances the representation is made that the use of such products will enhance a coin's value. At one time a "kit" was offered, consisting of a brass wire brush in combination with a cleaning solution. The statement was made that by using the kit an "ugly" old copper coin could be transformed to a brilliant, and thus desirable piece. Left unstated was the fact that most experienced collectors of copper coins would not have touched the resultant coin with a 10-foot pole!
>
> Although many other examples and quotations could be given concerning the harm done by cleaning coins, human nature being what it is, you may be tempted to try your hand at the cleaning process. If you do, consider the subject carefully. Probably for every one coin "improved" by cleaning, 10 or more have had their values lessened.
>
> Cleaning, when necessary, should be done only with nickel, silver, and gold coins in top grades. To clean such pieces in grades less than About Uncirculated will produce an unnatural appearance that is not acceptable to most collectors. The cleaning of copper and bronze coins in any condition should be avoided unless it is necessary to remove an unsightly carbon spot or fingerprint. In all instances, practice cleaning methods with low-value coins, so if you ruin them, they can simply be spent!
>
> To clean a high-grade nickel, silver, or gold coin, use only a clear liquid "dip," not a paste, powder, or polish. Pour some dip, full strength, into a pliable plastic dish. Completely immerse the coin in the liquid. Do not leave the coin in the liquid longer than a few seconds. Immediately rinse the coin thoroughly under running cold water. Pat (do not rub) the coin dry with a soft absorbent cloth; a terry cloth towel is ideal. Holding the coin in your fingers and using a cotton swab may result in uneven cleaning. For copper coins, if you must experiment with them, use a mixture of half "dip" and half cold water.
>
> In lieu of rinsing the coin for a long period of time under running cold water, the "dip" can be neutralized somewhat by immersing the coin, after dipping, in water in which a generous amount of baking soda has been dissolved. Swish the coin around in the water, remove it, and then hold it under running cold water. After drying the coin with a soft absorbent cloth, be sure there is no moisture adhering to the surfaces. It is a good idea to allow the coin to remain exposed to the open atmosphere for an hour or more before encasing it in an airtight holder. Trace amounts of "dip" adhering to a coin's surface will eventually tarnish or corrode the coin.
>
> The "dip" acts on the coin's surface by removing the tarnish and, at the same time, minute parts of the coin's metal. If a silver coin is dipped repeatedly, it will take on a dull, gray appearance. Under magnification, the mirror surface of a Proof coin will be seen to be finely etched, resulting in a cloudy surface which cannot be corrected.
>
> In the cleaning of a coin, never use any substance which requires friction. To be avoided are jeweler's rouge, silver-cleaning paste, baking soda, salt, or any similar substances. These substances clean coins by forcibly removing metal from the surface. The result will be a coin showing many hairlines. The application of a cleaning paste to a Proof coin can reduce its value to a tiny fraction of what would have been otherwise.
>
> It is sometimes desirable on circulated coins, Uncirculated coins, and Proofs as well, to remove a light film of dirt, grease, or PVC residue (the latter from storing coins in plastic holders which over a period of time exude a substance which forms a greenish coating on coins). Residues from tape, spots of glue, and other substances are sometimes found on coin surfaces and need to be removed. A commercial solvent, acetone (a chemical available at drug stores), usually will do the trick. Acetone is highly flammable and gives off fumes which should not be inhaled. Use acetone only in an open area, well ventilated, and away from spark or flame. Do not treat acetone casually.
>
> The removal of dirt, grit, and other verdigris, which sometimes accumulates on the surface of a coin, particularly one which has been in circulation for many years, can be done by using an ultrasonic cleaning machine in combination with a solution which does not change the surface coloration. Jewelers commonly use such devices to clean dirty rings, bracelets, and the like.
>
> Cleaning with acetone or by ultrasonic methods is different from dipping, for the latter methods simply remove dirt or residue without affecting the toning or coloration of a coin. In general, dipping and cleaning to change the color of a coin's surface is undesirable; removing dirt and residue is desirable.

CLEANING COPPER AND BRONZE COINS

Having given you ample warning, but with the realization that on occasion cleaning can be desirable, we now discuss cleaning of various coins.

The "dipping" or chemical cleaning of copper and bronze coins is to be avoided. The only exceptions, and such exceptions are rare, are coins which have unsightly fingerprints, blotches, or areas of oxidation. Cleaning by dipping, following the procedure outlined earlier, will result in the surface becoming bright yellow or orange, an unnatural hue quite unlike a normal uncleaned coin. As such, a piece then becomes a candidate for judicious retoning. Under no circumstances should a *worn* copper or bronze coin be dipped or chemically cleaned, for the result will be a bright and unnatural color. Worn copper coins in their natural state are toned varying shades from black to light brown; this natural toning is destroyed by dipping.

Dirt, green PVC goo, grease, and other substances adhering to the surface of a coin can be removed by acetone (be sure to use it in a well-ventilated area, away from flame), or in some instances simply by the application of soap and water. A bath in a cleaning solution (but not a solution which will remove toning) in a jeweler's ultrasonic cleaner may likewise be desirable. None of these methods will remove toning or change the basic surface color.

After dirt has been removed from the surface of a copper coin, it can be given a glossy surface by brushing it carefully with a No. 4 jeweler's camelhair brush (a method employed by many collectors of early half cents and large cents), or by gentle rubbing with a soft cloth lightly treated with mineral oil.

CLEANING NICKEL COINS

What we call "nickel" coins are primarily copper. For example, nickel three-cent pieces minted from 1865 to 1889 and nickel five-cent pieces produced beginning in 1866 are composed of three parts copper and one part nickel.

If a nickel coin displays unsightly toning blotches, oxidation areas, or fingerprints, the surface can sometimes be made brilliant by immersing in a liquid "dip."

Graded as having Very Good details, but corroded and at some point improperly cleaned, this key-date 1885 Liberty Head nickel sold in 2009 for about half of what an original, uncleaned VG-8 specimen would bring. (shown 2x actual size)

Nickel coins are more chemically active than silver or gold, so it becomes even more critical to neutralize the "dip" by immersing the coins in cold running water for a long period of time, and then drying each piece thoroughly. Failure to do this will result in the coin acquiring unsightly brown blotches within a matter of weeks. If a nickel coin is dipped more than two or three times, it

A key-date 1914-D Lincoln cent, before and after professional conservation. The unattractive toning has been lightened, and environmental damage from polyvinyl chloride (PVC) removed. (shown 3x actual size)

will become cloudy and soon will have a "cleaned" appearance. As is true with copper and bronze coins, the typical nickel coin is best left uncleaned.

Grease, PVC goo, and dirt on nickel coins can be removed by the judicious application of acetone (again we mention that this substance must be used carefully, in a well-ventilated area and away from flame), by ultrasonic cleaning, or by soap and water. Done correctly, none of these processes is harmful to the coin, and such treatment is recommended in indicated cases.

CLEANING SILVER COINS

Think twice, and then think again, before immersing any silver coin in "dip," for it is often the case that attractively toned coins are worth more than brilliant ones. Dipping of silver coins is recommended only to remove unsightly or blotchy spotting, fingerprints, or oxidation. In these instances, use silver "dip" following the methods outlined earlier. If a silver coin has a very deep surface tarnish—deep gray or even coal black—the removal of this tarnish or toning will usually result in a cloudy, etched surface. Cleaning a heavily toned silver coin usually has unfavorable results.

In 2008 this improperly cleaned 1871-CC Liberty Seated dollar sold for about half of what an original specimen in the same grade (Fine-15) would have brought. "Dipped long ago then improperly rinsed afterward," noted its auction description, "leaving deep brown and umber stains behind—anyone who remembers the dipping craze of the late '70s will know exactly the hue of the stains we write about." (shown actual size)

In instances in which a silver coin has surface dirt, PVC goo, or other residue, the judicious application of the dangerous substance acetone (note the safety precautions mentioned earlier), or the use of a jeweler's ultrasonic bath, or the application of soap and water, can have favorable results and is recommended.

CLEANING GOLD COINS

Of all metals used in U.S. coinage—copper, nickel, steel, zinc, silver, gold, and others—gold is the most inert. In general, gold coins retain their brilliance for many decades, even centuries. As most U.S. gold coins consist of nine parts gold and one part copper, the copper alloy will cause a light toning over a period of time, so that early pieces often obtain a warm rosy or golden appearance. This is desirable and should not be changed.

The use of a "dip" on gold coins will make the surface brilliant—sometimes brassy—in appearance, which for very early pieces is not desirable. Dipping rarely removes copper-colored spots or staining occasionally seen on gold coins (the result of an imperfect alloy mixture). For such copper stains, professional conservators use a heat treatment that is quite efficient but should not be attempted by others.

Surface film, dirt, and grease can be removed from gold coins with acetone (note the safety precautions mentioned earlier), a jeweler's ultrasonic bath, or soap and water. Ammonia, carefully applied to a gold coin's surface, can remove a film which sometimes is seen on higher-grade pieces, including Proofs. In all instances, avoid rubbing or the use of friction as this will generate undesirable hairlines.

THE IMPORTANCE OF CONSERVATION

Professional numismatic conservation has grown out of the need to rescue coins from detrimental surface problems and to preserve our numismatic heritage, while also providing hobbyists with a safe alternative to cleaning coins on their own. While professional conservation may be relatively new to numismatics, other cultural and historical artifacts have been routinely conserved for a very long time. Conservation is a very specialized field, and conservators usually focus on one type of artifact or conservation method. This specialization is necessary because they must possess tremendous knowledge of the item they are conserving. They must be experts in evaluating the composition, production, and condition of the item in order to be able to master the complexities of treating it to produce successful and consistent results. This specialization, along with extensive hands-on experience, can lead the conservator to sound judgments during evaluation and subsequent conservation. There are professional conservation services that specialize in numismatics.

EXPERT PROFESSIONAL CONSERVATION OF COINS

Today, in the early 21st century, careful conservation by experts continues. The greatest American numismatic treasure ever found included gold coins recovered in the 1980s from the SS *Central America* (lost at sea off the coast of North Carolina on February 12, 1857). These were brought up from a depth of 7,200 feet. Many pieces had become encrusted with stains, iron that had been dissolved from the ship's mechanisms, coral, and other substances. Highly skilled scientists who assisted in the recovery of the ship set up a conservation laboratory to carefully dissolve these substances. They used separate baths, but no friction or acids. Their work revealed double eagles, for example, which were as brilliant and lustrous as the day they were made, without any hairlines or problems. In spite of wide recognition in the press, the conservators would not reveal their methods. This was for good reason, as improper use and experimenting could certainly result in damage.

About the same time, recovered gold coins from the SS *Brother Jonathan* (lost at sea on July 30, 1865), were carefully conserved by a laboratory in California. Then, in 2002, the wreck of the SS *Republic* (lost at sea October 18, 1865) was found. Many of the

An 1896 gold quarter eagle, before and after professional conservation. In its stained and dirty state, such a coin might be sold for its bullion content alone. Professionally conserved to an eye-pleasing Mint State, its value increases to 10 times that amount. (shown 3x actual size)

recovered coins were conserved with great success. Shipwreck-recovered coins in silver (a chemically active metal) often were etched or corroded by the seawater. Even with the coral and other substances removed, they still showed the effects of immersion. Marketing terms such as *saltwater effect* were devised, and added to the holders of such coins.

ATTITUDES IN TODAY'S MARKETPLACE

In the numismatic marketplace the words "cleaned" and "dipped" are rarely heard. "Conserved" is acceptable, due to the great publicity given to the SS *Central America* and later discoveries, and advances made in professional numismatic conservation.

Artificial toning or re-toning is not mentioned either, although it is widely practiced. Various methods have been used including frying coins in a pan, subjecting them to iodine fumes, gently heating them, placing them in old cardboard holders or fast-food napkins (which contain residual sulfur), and adding rainbow toning through various chemical interactions. Such artificially induced toning may be "pretty" at first, but the tarnish can alter and become ugly over time.

One of the more dramatic situations involves the coins of the late King Farouk of Egypt. For many years, especially in the period from the late 1930s until he was deposed by a military junta in 1952, the king amassed a great collection of copper, silver, and gold coins. All of his silver and copper coins were cleaned with friction, using silver polish. They were then lac-

quered. The sale of Farouk's collection took place in Cairo in early 1954, and the coins were dispersed, with many American coins returning to the United States. Included were vast holdings of rare, sometimes unique, patterns. Dealers and collectors removed the lacquer, and in some instances endeavored to retone the coins, but without much success. The auction of certain pattern coins in the Harry W. Bass Jr. Collection in 1999 contained a number of Farouk pieces that had not been touched—with the copper being bright orange. After being sold, certain of these went to coin conservators and were given attractive brown finishes, of a mahogany or chestnut color. The leading certification services encapsulated them with sometimes high Proof grades, with no mention that they had been cleaned. The coins had been improved in appearance, and most people would agree that they are more attractive and more desirable now than before. However, if a detailed explanation were given about retoning them, they might not be marketable.

Similarly, if just about any brilliant 19th-century Proof coin were described as, for example, "Proof-63, brilliant, once cleaned and now with hairlines," it would not be readily saleable. Accordingly, such aspects are rarely mentioned. However, they exist, and the detailed discussion of them here is simply to make you aware of the different processes and possibilities.

Picking up on the commentary in *Photograde*, good advice today is to *not* clean any coin you have. Possible exceptions include the careful use of soap and water, or (for nickel, silver, and gold coins) acetone. Cleaning can improve a coin, but it also can damage it, and over a long period of years more have been harmed than have been benefited. Besides, a dipped or cleaned coin is apt to retone. If the coin is valuable, a professional numismatic con-servation service should be consulted as to costs and advisability. Alternatively, a trained, skilled dealer might be able to help.

A coin not "improved" today can always, if advisable, be treated at a later date.

HOW NUMISMATIC CONSERVATION WORKS

In professional numismatic conservation, before any procedure is undertaken, a careful and thorough evaluation of the coin is made. During this detailed analysis, the evaluator assesses the condition of the coin's underlying surfaces, identifies the surface problems, and determines what, if any, treatment will be most beneficial in removing or reducing the contamination and stabilizing the coin to limit further deterioration. The coin's method of manufacture, age, composition, and grade are especially important, because they influence which procedure will be most effective in producing results of the highest standards.

Since the evaluation process is every bit as important as the procedure undertaken, the evaluator has to have seen hundreds of thousands of coins. He must understand their production and the subtleties of their luster patterns, color, and originality.

Unlike with other conservation specialties, the third-party-certified grading system used in numismatics makes the job of the evaluator very difficult. When reviewing a certified coin the evaluator must determine if it will maintain its current grade after conservation. Even though the procedure only removes foreign material from the coin, these materials might conceal minor marks that affect the grade once the coin's true surfaces are visible again. This is a very important consideration, especially when only very slight differences in luster brilliance can mean the difference between a coin grading MS-68 or MS-67.

Having the most experienced evaluators and foremost conservation experts working in unison ensures results of the highest caliber, while reducing the risk of a coin not maintaining its current grade. In many cases, when all of the elements work well together, coins can and do increase in grade, as their original surfaces become visible and unimpeded by residues.

After the specimen has been evaluated and a procedure is prescribed, the coin is conserved in a laboratory setting specifically designed and equipped to ensure consistency and quality of results. Through the systematic application of chemicals and solvents, the conservator is able to reduce or remove the detrimental surface conditions while protecting the integrity of the coin's surfaces. In some cases, several different treatments may be used to address several different contaminants. In addition to removing foreign materials, the procedure also neutralizes the coin's surface, ensuring longer-term stability.

Professional conservators use inert solvents. A coin is introduced into a liquid that will dissolve surface contaminants and suspend them in solution. The coin can be removed from the solution and then rinsed and stabilized for reevaluation and assessment. Oftentimes proper conservation will involve a multi-step process, and very dilute solvents are used under precise temperature to control the rate of reaction. Because these treatments are prescribed and performed by experienced numismatists, it's possible to halt or arrest the conservation process as soon as a desired result has been achieved.

The most important difference between numismatic conservation and many other conservation specialties is in regard to the restoration of the object. In other fields it is acceptable to strip down the item and its outermost original surfaces and then restore it by rebuilding its surfaces before applying preservative materials. For obvious reasons this is not acceptable in numismatic conservation, where the principle goal is to remove detrimental foreign materials and protect the originality of the specimen's surface. No materials are ever added to a coin's surface during professional numismatic conservation.

RECOMMENDED READING

White, Weimar W. *Coin Chemistry, Including Preservation and Cleaning* (3rd ed.), Victor, NY, 2012.

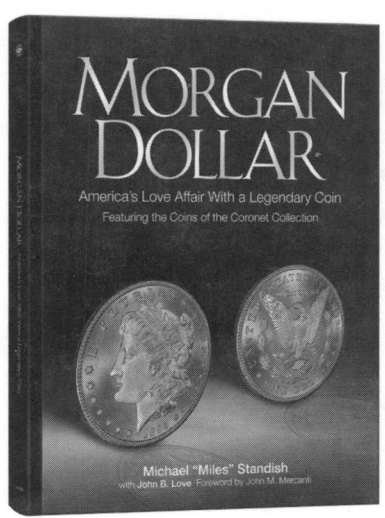

Historian William Rice has picked up the torch where researchers like Aubrey Mayhew and the great Edward C. Rochette left off, shining new light on U.S. and world coins, medals, tokens, challenge coins, and other collectibles that celebrate the life of President John F. Kennedy. Richly illustrated and cataloged with hundreds of images, *The Kennedy World in Medallic Art* is a must-have for every collector and American history buff. *320 pages, hardcover, full color.*

$19.95 postpaid
(free shipping with this special offer).

To order, call 1-800-546-2995 and mention code P6.
Order online at www.Whitman.com, and use code P6.
Or mail this card, with your payment, to:
Customer Service • 4001 Helton Dr. • Florence, AL 35630-9802

PLEASE PRINT

Name _____

Address _____

City _____ State ____ Zip _____

Email _____

Phone _____

❑ Check enclosed

❑ Credit card: _____

❑ VISA ❑ MasterCard ❑ American Express ❑ Discover

Offer expires 9/30/15. Code **P6**.

Coins and Collectors:
Golden Anniversary Edition

Q. David Bowers weaves his storytelling magic in this brand-new, full-color update of a hobby classic. You'll meet famous coin designers, unscrupulous Treasury officials, brilliant scholars, Confederate raiders, burlesque dancers, globe-trotting magicians, and dueling numismatists. *Coins and Collectors* includes interviews, stories, and images never before seen in print. *416 pages. Hardcover. 8.5 x 11 inches.*

$29.95 with FREE shipping and handling.

To order, call 1-800-546-2995. Mention code P6.
Order online at www.Whitman.com, and use code P6.
Email: customerservice@Whitman.com
Or mail this card, with your payment, to:
Customer Service, 4001 Helton Drive, Florence AL 35630-9802

PLEASE PRINT

Name _____

Address _____

City _____ State ____ Zip _____

Email _____

Phone _____

❑ Check enclosed

❑ Credit card: _____

❑ VISA ❑ MasterCard ❑ American Express ❑ Discover

Offer expires 9/30/15. Code **P6**.

Morgan Dollar: America's Love Affair With a Legendary Coin—Michael "Miles" Standish, vice president and senior grader of PCGS, presents an engaging history and coin-by-coin study of the famous Morgan silver dollar. Featuring the recollections of longtime dollar dealer John Love, beautiful high-resolution photographs of the #1-ranked Coronet Collection, certified-coin populations, retail prices in multiple grades, and other valuable contents for collectors, investors, and history buffs alike. 160 pages, hardcover, full color, 8.5 x 11 inches. **$29.95—with free shipping.**

To order, call 1-800-546-2995, and mention code P6.
Order online at www.Whitman.com; use code P6.
Or mail this card, with your payment, to:
Customer Service, 4001 Helton Drive, Florence AL 35630-9802

PLEASE PRINT

Name _____

Address _____

City _____ State ____ Zip _____

Email _____

Phone _____

❑ Check enclosed

❑ Credit card: _____

❑ VISA ❑ MasterCard ❑ American Express ❑ Discover

Offer expires 9/30/15. Code **P6**.

If you're a coin collector, you want your heirs to make smart, confident decisions—and avoid expensive mistakes when it comes time to sell. Keep a copy of this book with your collection for the benefit of your loved ones. *Cash In Your Coins: Selling the Rare Coins You've Inherited* is for everyone who's built a collection of coins, or inherited one. **Updated and expanded second edition:** 304 pages, full color, $9.95. **Free shipping when you use code P6.**

To order, call 1-800-546-2995; mention code P6.
Order online at www.Whitman.com, and use code P6.
Email: customerservice@Whitman.com
Or mail this card, with your payment, to:
Customer Service, 4001 Helton Drive, Florence AL 35630-9802

PLEASE PRINT

Name _____

Address _____

City _____ State ____ Zip _____

Email _____

Phone _____

❑ Check enclosed

❑ Credit card: _____

❑ VISA ❑ MasterCard ❑ American Express ❑ Discover

Offer expires 9/30/15. Code **P6**.